SCRABBLE®

The Official
SCRABBLE®
Players
Dictionary

Third Edition

REDWOOD
EDITIONS

THE OFFICIAL SCRABBLE DICTIONARY THIRD EDITION

Published in Australia and New Zealand in 2000
by Redwood Editions
a division of
Hinkler Book Distributors Pty. Ltd.
17-23 Redwood Drive Dingley, Victoria 3172

First Printed 2001
Reprinted 2002 (three times)

ISBN 1 86515 3826

Printed & bound in Australia

2011. Oh dear... here we go again.
New Year... Old Score. Lizzy Lou is beating
Crawford Cake again!   2 - 0.

Oh no... 6th Jan ... final Score 4 - 0
    Poor old Crawford Cake ... And the
Lion Won Mastermind too. Deary me!!
    6 - 0!

P₃REFACE

This is the third edition of the enormously popular Official SCRABBLE®
Players Dictionary, and it includes more than 1,000 words not included in
the previous edition. This dictionary has been prepared especially for
lovers of SCRABBLE® Brand crossword games and is endorsed by the
National SCRABBLE® Association for recreational and school use.

It is important to remember that The Official SCRABBLE® Players
Dictionary was edited solely with this limited purpose in mind. It is not
intended to serve as a general dictionary of English; thus, such important
features of general dictionaries as definitions of multiple senses,
pronunciation respellings, etymologies, and usage labels are omitted.

It is the intention of the makers of SCRABBLE® Brand crossword
games that they be enjoyed by children and adults alike. With this
consideration in mind, words likely to offend players of the game have
been omitted from this edition. The words omitted are those that would
qualify for a warning usage note on the basis of standards applied in
other Merriam-Webster dictionaries.

The detailed organization and special features of the dictionary are
explained in the Introduction which follows. It should be read with care by
all who use the dictionary. Now that this new updated work is available,
we are confident that it will afford satisfaction and enjoyment to
SCRABBLE® Brand crossword game players everywhere.

MAIN ENTRIES

• Main entries are listed in boldface type and are set flush with the left-hand margin of each column. Except for an occasional cross-reference (such as **MISSPOKEN** past participle of misspeak) main entries contain from two to eight letters since words within this range are considered to be most useful to SCRABBLE® crossword game players. Words that are not permissible in SCRABBLE® crossword games have not been included in this dictionary. Thus, proper names, words requiring hyphens or apostrophes, words considered foreign, and abbreviations have been omitted. Because dictionaries have different standards for selecting entries, several desk dictionaries were consulted in preparing the list of main entries for this book. Obsolete, archaic, slang, and nonstandard words are included since they are permitted by the rules of the game. All variant forms of a main entry are shown at their own alphabetical places and defined in terms of the principal form. Words that exceed eight letters in length and are not inflected forms of words entered in this dictionary should be looked up in a desk dictionary. The National SCRABBLE® Association recommends Merriam-Webster's Collegiate Dictionary, Tenth Edition, as a source of additional words.

RUN-ON ENTRIES

• A main entry may be followed by one or more derivatives in boldface type with a different part-of-speech label. These are run-on entries. Run-on entries are not defined since their meanings are readily derivable from the meaning of the root word.

FENDER *n* pl. -S a metal guard over the wheel of a motor vehicle **FENDERED** *adj*

HAMULUS *n* pl. -LI a small hook **HAMULAR, HAMULATE, HAMULOSE, HAMULOUS** *adj*

No entry has been run on at another if it would fall alphabetically more than three places from the entry. When you do not find a word at its own place, it is always wise to check several entries above and below to see if it is run on.

CROSS-REFERENCES

• A cross-reference is a main entry that is an inflected form (such as the plural form of a noun, the past tense form of a verb, or the comparative form of an adjective) of another word. An inflected form is entered as a main entry if it undergoes a spelling change in addition to or instead of suffixation *and* if it falls alphabetically more than three places away from the root word.

For example, in the entries reproduced below **DICING** is a main entry because it involves a spelling change (the final -*e* of *dice* is dropped) besides the addition of the -ING ending and because it falls more than three places from the entry **DICE**. On the other hand, *dices* is not a main entry because it involves no spelling change beyond the addition of the ending -S. The word *diced,* although involving a spelling change (the final -*e* of *dice* is dropped), is not a main entry because it does not fall more than three places from **DICE**. **DICIER** and **DICIEST** are main entries because they involve a spelling change (the -*e*- is dropped and the final -*y* is changed to -*i*) besides the addition of the -ER, -EST endings and they fall more than three places from the entry **DICEY**.

DICE	*v* DICED, DICING, DICES to cut into small cubes
DICENTRA	*n* pl. -S a perennial herb
DICER	*n* pl. -S a device that dices food
DICEY	*adj* DICIER, DICIEST dangerous
DICHASIA	*n/pl* flower clusters
DICHOTIC	*adj* affecting the two ears differently
DICHROIC	*adj* having two colors
DICIER	comparative of dicey
DICIEST	superlative of dicey
DICING	present participle of dice

This policy is intended to make the word desired as easy to find as possible without wasting space. Nevertheless, many inflected forms will appear only at the main entry.

You should always look at several entries above and below the expected place if you do not find the desired word as a main entry.

Cross-reference entries for present tense third person singular forms of verbs use the abbreviation "sing."

PARTS OF SPEECH ● An italic label indicating a part of speech follows each main entry except cross-references (such as **DICIER, DICIEST, DICING**), for which the label is given at the root word. The eight traditional parts of speech are indicated as follows:

n	noun	*pron*	pronoun
v	verb	*prep*	preposition
adj	adjective	*conj*	conjunction
adv	adverb	*interj*	interjection

The label *n/pl* is given to two kinds of nouns. One is the plural noun that has no singular form.

KINETICS *n/pl* a branch of science dealing with motion

The other is the plural noun of which the singular is not entered in this dictionary. Singular forms are omitted if they contain more than eight letters.

NUCLEOLI *n/pl* nucleoles

Nucleolus, the singular form, has nine letters and is not entered.

When a word can be used as more than one part of speech, each part of speech is entered separately if the inflected forms are not spelled alike. For example, both the adjective *pale* and the verb *pale* are entered because the inflected forms vary.

PALE   *adj* PALER, PALEST lacking intensity of color
PALE   *v* PALED, PALING, PALES to make or
                become pale

On the other hand, the verb *leg* is entered while the noun *leg* is not because the inflected form *legs* at the verb is spelled the same as the plural form of the noun. In a dictionary for SCRABBLE® crossword game players, entry of the noun is therefore redundant. Homographs (words spelled alike) which may be used as the same part of speech are treated in the same way. For example, *gin* is entered as a verb twice because the inflected forms are spelled differently.

GIN   *v* GINNED, GINNING, GINS to remove seeds
                from cotton
GIN   *v* GAN, GUNNEN, GINNING, GINS to begin

If both sets of inflected forms were spelled alike, only one *gin* would be entered in this dictionary. In this way the dictionary includes as many different spellings as possible yet avoids wasting space with repeated entry of words spelled in the same way. The SCRABBLE® crossword game player, after all, needs only one entry to justify a play.

INFLECTED FORMS ● Inflected forms include the past tense, past participle, present participle, and present tense third person singular of verbs, the plural of nouns, and the comparative and superlative of adjectives and adverbs. They are shown in capital letters immediately following the part-of-speech label. Irregular inflected forms are listed as main entries when they fall four or more alphabetical places away from the root word (see **Cross-References** above). All inflected forms are allowable for play in SCRABBLE® crossword games.

The principal parts of the majority of verbs are shown as -ED, -ING, -S (or -ES when applicable). This indicates that the past tense and past participle are formed simply by adding -*ed* to the entry word, that the present participle is formed simply by adding -*ing* to the entry word, and that the present third person singular is formed simply by adding -*s* (or -*es*) to the entry word.

NEATEN   *v* -ED, -ING, -S to make neat

When inflection of an entry word involves any spelling change in addition to the suffixal ending (such as the dropping of a final -*e*, the doubling of a final consonant, or the changing of a final -*y* to -*i*-) or when the inflection is irregular, the inflected forms given indicate such changes.

MOVE   *v* MOVED, MOVING, MOVES to change from
                one position to another
SUP   *v* SUPPED, SUPPING, SUPS to eat supper

PLY	v PLIED, PLYING, PLIES to supply with or offer repeatedly PLYINGLY adv
EAT	v ATE or ET, EATEN, EATING, EATS to consume food

For verbs of more than one syllable either the last syllable or the last two syllables are shown.

MUMBLE	v -BLED, -BLING, -BLES to speak unclearly
BENEFIT	v -FITED, -FITING, -FITS or -FITTED, -FITTING, -FITS to be helpful or useful to

The plurals of nouns are preceded by the abbreviation "pl." Most plurals are shown as -S (or -ES when applicable) to indicate that the plural is formed simply by adding the given suffix to the entry word.

ACID	n pl. -S a type of chemical compound

When pluralizing a noun involves any spelling change in addition to the suffixal ending (such as the changing of a final -y to -i- or a final -f to -v-) or when the plural is irregular, the plural form shown indicates such change.

CITY	n pl. CITIES a large town
BEEF	n pl. BEEFS or BEEVES a steer or cow fattened for food
ORNIS	n pl. ORNITHES avifauna

In such cases involving polysyllabic nouns at least the last syllable is shown.

EULOGY	n pl. -GIES a formal expression of high praise

For the sake of clarity, two groups of nouns that are confusing to many, those ending in -o and those ending in -y, are always indicated in this dictionary by showing at least the last syllable, even though no spelling change is involved.

MUNGO	n pl. -GOS a low-quality wool
NAY	n pl. NAYS a negative vote

Variant plurals are shown wherever they add another word permissible in SCRABBLE® crossword games.

CELLO	n pl. -LOS or -LI a stringed musical instrument

Plurals which have the same form as the singular are shown only when they are the only plural for that entry. This is done to show that for the entry in question it is not permissible to add -s (or -es) to the singular to create a plural.

TAKA	n pl. TAKA a monetary unit of Bangladesh
VEG	n pl. VEG a vegetable

Otherwise, they are omitted and only the plural with the inflection is shown.

DEER	n pl. -S a ruminant mammal

The comparative and superlative forms of adjectives and adverbs are shown, when applicable, immediately following the part-of-speech label. Any spelling changes are indicated in the forms shown.

JUST   *adj* JUSTER, JUSTEST acting in conformity
            with what is morally good
FAR   *adv* FARTHER, FARTHEST or FURTHER,
            FURTHEST at or to a great distance
LACEY *adj* LACIER, LACIEST lacy

Not all adjectives or adverbs can be inflected, and only those inflected forms shown are acceptable. None of the adjectives and adverbs listed as run-on entries in this dictionary have inflected forms.

DEFINITIONS   ●   In most cases, only one very brief definition

is given for each main entry since definitions do not play a significant role in the SCRABBLE® crossword game. This definition serves only to orient the player in a general way to a single meaning of the word. It is not intended to have all the precision and detail of a definition in a good general dictionary.

When a word consisting of eight letters or less appears in a definition but is not an entry in this dictionary, it is glossed in parentheses. For example, at the entry for the verb *hand,* the noun "hand" is used in the definition and is glossed because the noun *hand* is not a separate entry.

HAND   *v* -ED, -ING, -S to present with the hand (the
            end of the forearm)

A main entry that is a variant form of another entry is defined in terms of the most common form, which is entered and defined at its own alphabetical place.

MATZA   *n* pl. -S matzo
MATZAH *n* pl. -S matzo
MATZO   *n* pl. -ZOS, -ZOT, or -ZOTH an unleavened
             bread

SCRABBLE® crossword game players in Canada will be pleased to learn that variant forms such as *honour, centre,* and *cheque,* which are often omitted from general dictionaries, have also been included in this book.

LISTS OF UNDEFINED WORDS   ●   Lists of undefined

words appear after the entries of the prefixes **RE-** and **UN-**. These words are not defined because they are self-explanatory: their meanings are simply the sum of a meaning of the prefix combined with a meaning of the root word. All of their inflected forms are given, however.

A₁

AA *n* pl. -S rough, cindery lava

AAH *v* -ED, -ING, -S to exclaim in amazement, joy, or surprise

AAL *n* pl. -S an East Indian shrub

AALII *n* pl. -S a tropical tree

AARDVARK *n* pl. -S an African mammal

AARDWOLF *n* pl. -WOLVES an African mammal

AARGH *interj* — used to express disgust

AARRGH *interj* aargh

AARRGHH *interj* aargh

AASVOGEL *n* pl. -S a vulture

AB *n* pl. -S an abdominal muscle

ABA *n* pl. -S a sleeveless garment worn by Arabs

ABACA *n* pl. -S a Philippine plant

ABACK *adv* toward the back

ABACUS *n* pl. -CI or -CUSES a calculating device

ABAFT *adv* toward the stern

ABAKA *n* pl. -S abaca

ABALONE *n* pl. -S an edible shellfish

ABAMP *n* pl. -S abampere

ABAMPERE *n* pl. -S a unit of electric current

ABANDON *v* -ED, -ING, -S to leave or give up completely

ABAPICAL *adj* directed away from the apex

ABASE *v* ABASED, ABASING, ABASES to lower in rank, prestige, or esteem **ABASEDLY** *adv*

ABASER *n* pl. -S one that abases

ABASH *v* -ED, -ING, -ES to make ashamed or embarrassed

ABASIA *n* pl. -S a defect in muscular coordination in walking

ABASING present participle of abase

ABATE *v* ABATED, ABATING, ABATES to reduce in degree or intensity **ABATABLE** *adj*

ABATER *n* pl. -S one that abates

ABATIS *n* pl. -TISES a barrier made of felled trees

ABATOR *n* pl. -S one that unlawfully seizes an inheritance

ABATTIS *n* pl. -TISES abatis

ABATTOIR *n* pl. -S a slaughterhouse

ABAXIAL *adj* situated away from the axis

ABAXILE *adj* abaxial

ABBA *n* pl. -S father — used as a title of honor

ABBACY *n* pl. -CIES the office of an abbot

ABBATIAL *adj* pertaining to an abbot

ABBE *n* pl. -S an abbot

ABBESS *n* pl. -ES the female superior of a convent of nuns

ABBEY *n* pl. -BEYS a monastery or convent

ABBOT *n* pl. -S the superior of a monastery

ABBOTCY *n* pl. -CIES abbacy

ABDICATE *v* -CATED, -CATING, -CATES to give up formally

ABDOMEN *n* pl. -MENS or -MINA the body cavity containing the viscera

ABDUCE *v* -DUCED, -DUCING, -DUCES to abduct

ABDUCENS *n* pl. -CENTES a cranial nerve

ABDUCENT *adj* serving to abduct

ABDUCING present participle of abduce

ABDUCT *v* -ED, -ING, -S to draw away from the original position

ABDUCTOR *n* pl. -ES or -S an abducent muscle

ABEAM *adv* at right angles to the keel of a ship

ABED *adv* in bed

ABELE *n* pl. -S a Eurasian tree

ABELIA *n* pl. -S an Asian or Mexican shrub

ABELIAN *adj* being a commutative group in mathematics

ABELMOSK *n* pl. -S a tropical herb

ABERRANT *n* pl. -S a deviant

ABET *v* ABETTED, ABETTING, ABETS to encourage and support

ABETMENT *n* pl. -S the act of abetting

ABETTAL *n* pl. -S abetment

ABETTED past tense of abet

ABETTER *n* pl. -S abettor

ABETTING present participle of abet

ABETTOR *n* pl. -S one that abets

ABEYANCE *n* pl. -S temporary inactivity

ABEYANCY *n* pl. -CIES abeyance

ABEYANT *adj* marked by abeyance

ABFARAD *n* pl. -S a unit of capacitance

ABHENRY *n* pl. -RIES or -RYS a unit of inductance

ABHOR *v* -HORRED, -HORRING, -HORS to loathe

ABHORRER *n* pl. -S one that abhors

ABIDANCE *n* pl. -S the act of abiding

ABIDE *v* ABODE or ABIDED, ABIDING, ABIDES to accept without objection

ABIDER *n* pl. -S one that abides

ABIGAIL *n* pl. -S a lady's maid

ABILITY *n* pl. -TIES the quality of being able to do something

ABIOSIS *n* pl. -OSES absence of life **ABIOTIC** *adj*

ABJECT *adj* sunk to a low condition **ABJECTLY** *adv*

ABJURE *v* -JURED, -JURING, -JURES to renounce under oath

ABJURER *n* pl. -S one that abjures

ABLATE *v* -LATED, -LATING, -LATES to remove by cutting

ABLATION *n* pl. -S surgical removal of a bodily part

ABLATIVE *n* pl. -S a grammatical case

ABLAUT *n* pl. -S a patterned change in root vowels of verb forms

ABLAZE *adj* being on fire

ABLE *adj* ABLER, ABLEST having sufficient power, skill, or resources

ABLE *n* pl. -S a communications code word for the letter A

ABLEGATE *n* pl. -S a papal envoy

ABLER comparative of able

ABLEST superlative of able

ABLINGS *adv* ablins

ABLINS *adv* perhaps

ABLOOM *adj* blooming

ABLUENT *n* pl. -S a cleansing agent

ABLUSH *adj* blushing

ABLUTED *adj* washed clean

ABLUTION *n* pl. -S a washing

ABLY *adv* in an able manner

ABMHO *n* pl. -MHOS a unit of electrical conductance

ABNEGATE *v* -GATED, -GATING, -GATES to deny to oneself

ABNORMAL *n* pl. -S a mentally deficient person

ABOARD *adv* into, in, or on a ship, train, or airplane

ABODE *v* ABODED, ABODING, ABODES to forebode

ABOHM *n* pl. -S a unit of electrical resistance

ABOIDEAU *n* pl. -DEAUS or -DEAUX a type of dike

ABOIL *adj* boiling

ABOITEAU *n* pl. -TEAUS or -TEAUX aboideau

ABOLISH *v* -ED, -ING, -ES to do away with

ABOLLA *n* pl. -LAE a cloak worn in ancient Rome

ABOMA *n* pl. -S a South American snake

ABOMASAL *adj* pertaining to the abomasum

ABOMASUM *n* pl. -SA the fourth stomach of a ruminant

ABOMASUS *n* pl. -MASI abomasum

ABOON *adv* above

ABORAL *adj* situated away from the mouth **ABORALLY** *adv*

ABORNING *adv* while being born

ABORT *v* -ED, -ING, -S to bring forth a fetus prematurely

ABORTER *n* pl. -S one that aborts

ABORTION *n* pl. -S induced expulsion of a nonviable fetus

ABORTIVE *adj* failing to succeed

ABOUGHT past tense of aby and abye

ABOULIA *n* pl. -S abulia **ABOULIC** *adj*

ABOUND *v* -ED, -ING, -S to have a large number or amount

ABOUT *adv* approximately

ABOVE *n* pl. -S something that is above (in a higher place)

ABRACHIA *n* pl. -S a lack of arms

ABRADANT *n* pl. -S an abrasive

ABRADE *v* ABRADED, ABRADING, ABRADES to wear away by friction

ABRADER *n* pl. -S a tool for abrading

ABRASION *n* pl. -S the act of abrading

ABRASIVE *n* pl. -S an abrading substance

ABREACT *v* -ED, -ING, -S to release repressed emotions by reliving the original traumatic experience

ABREAST *adv* side by side

ABRI *n* pl. -S a bomb shelter

ABRIDGE *v* ABRIDGED, ABRIDGING, ABRIDGES to reduce the length of

ABRIDGER *n* pl. -S one that abridges

ABROACH *adj* astir

ABROAD *adv* out of one's own country

ABROGATE *v* -GATED, -GATING, -GATES to abolish by authoritative action

ABROSIA *n* pl. -S a fasting from food

ABRUPT *adj* -RUPTER, -RUPTEST rudely brief **ABRUPTLY** *adv*

ABSCESS *v* -ED, -ING, -ES to form an abscess (a localized collection of pus surrounded by inflamed tissue)

ABSCISE *v* -SCISED, -SCISING, -SCISES to cut off

ABSCISIN *n* pl. -S a regulatory substance found in plants

ABSCISSA *n* pl. -SAS or -SAE a particular geometric coordinate

ABSCOND *v* -ED, -ING, -S to depart suddenly and secretly

ABSEIL *v* -ED, -ING, -S to rappel

ABSENCE *n* pl. -S the state of being away

ABSENT *v* -ED, -ING, -S to take or keep away

ABSENTEE *n* pl. -S one that is not present

ABSENTER *n* pl. -S one that absents himself

ABSENTLY *adv* in an inattentive manner

ABSINTH *n* pl. -S absinthe

ABSINTHE *n* pl. -S a bitter liqueur

ABSOLUTE *adj* -LUTER, -LUTEST free from restriction

ABSOLUTE *n* pl. -S something that is absolute

ABSOLVE *v* -SOLVED, -SOLVING, -SOLVES to free from the consequences of an action

ABSOLVER *n* pl. -S one that absolves

ABSONANT *adj* unreasonable

ABSORB *v* -ED, -ING, -S to take up or in

ABSORBER *n* pl. -S one that absorbs

ABSTAIN *v* -ED, -ING, -S to refrain voluntarily

ABSTERGE *v* -STERGED, -STERGING, -STERGES to cleanse by wiping

ABSTRACT *adj* -STRACTER, -STRACTEST difficult to understand

ABSTRACT *v* -ED, -ING, -S to take away

ABSTRICT *v* -ED, -ING, -S to form by cutting off

ABSTRUSE *adj* -STRUSER, -STRUSEST difficult to understand

ABSURD *adj* -SURDER, -SURDEST ridiculously incongruous or unreasonable **ABSURDLY** *adv*

ABSURD *n* pl. -S the condition in which man exists in an irrational and meaningless universe

ABUBBLE *adj* bubbling

ABULIA *n* pl. -S loss of will power **ABULIC** *adj*

ABUNDANT *adj* present in great quantity

ABUSE *v* ABUSED, ABUSING, ABUSES to use wrongly or improperly **ABUSABLE** *adj*

ABUSER *n* pl. -S one that abuses

ABUSIVE *adj* characterized by wrong or improper use

ABUT *v* ABUTTED, ABUTTING, ABUTS to touch along a border

ABUTILON *n* pl. -S a flowering plant

ABUTMENT *n* pl. -S something that abuts

ABUTTAL *n* pl. -S an abutment

ABUTTED past tense of abut

ABUTTER *n* pl. -S one that abuts

ABUTTING present participle of abut

ABUZZ *adj* buzzing

ABVOLT *n* pl. -S a unit of electromotive force

ABWATT *n* pl. -S a unit of power

ABY *v* ABOUGHT, ABYING, ABYS to pay the penalty for

ABYE *v* ABOUGHT, ABYING, ABYES to aby

ABYSM *n* pl. -S an abyss

ABYSMAL *adj* immeasurably deep

ABYSS *n* pl. -ES a bottomless chasm **ABYSSAL** *adj*

ACACIA *n* pl. -S a flowering tree or shrub

ACADEME *n* pl. -S a place of instruction

ACADEMIA *n* pl. -S scholastic life or environment

ACADEMIC *n* pl. -S a college student or teacher

ACADEMY *n* pl. -MIES a secondary school

ACAJOU *n* pl. -S a tropical tree

ACALEPH *n* pl. -LEPHAE or -LEPHS a jellyfish

ACALEPHE *n* pl. -S acaleph

ACANTHUS *n* pl. -THI or -THUSES a prickly herb

ACAPNIA *n* pl. -S a lack of carbon dioxide in blood and tissues

ACARI pl. of acarus

ACARID *n* pl. -S a type of arachnid

ACARIDAN *n* pl. -S acarid

ACARINE *n* pl. -S acarid

ACAROID *adj* resembling an acarid

ACARPOUS *adj* not producing fruit

ACARUS *n* pl. -RI a mite

ACAUDAL *adj* having no tail

ACAUDATE *adj* acaudal

ACAULINE *adj* having no stem

ACAULOSE *adj* acauline

ACAULOUS *adj* acauline

ACCEDE *v* -CEDED, -CEDING, -CEDES to consent

ACCEDER *n* pl. -S one that accedes

ACCENT *v* -ED, -ING, -S to pronounce with prominence

ACCENTOR *n* pl. -S a songbird

ACCEPT *v* -ED, -ING, -S to receive willingly

ACCEPTEE *n* pl. -S one that is accepted

ACCEPTER *n* pl. -S one that accepts

ACCEPTOR *n* pl. -S accepter

ACCESS *v* -ED, -ING, -ES to get at

ACCIDENT *n* pl. -S an unexpected or unintentional occurrence

ACCIDIA *n* pl. -S acedia

ACCIDIE *n* pl. -S acedia

ACCLAIM *v* -ED, -ING, -S to shout approval of

ACCOLADE *n* pl. -S an expression of praise

ACCORD *v* -ED, -ING, -S to bring into agreement

ACCORDER *n* pl. -S one that accords

ACCOST *v* -ED, -ING, -S to approach and speak to first

ACCOUNT *v* -ED, -ING, -S to give an explanation

ACCOUTER *v* -ED, -ING, -S to equip

ACCOUTRE *v* -TRED, -TRING, -TRES to accouter

ACCREDIT *v* -ED, -ING, -S to give official authorization to

ACCRETE *v* -CRETED, -CRETING, -CRETES to grow together

ACCRUAL *n* pl. -S the act of accruing

ACCRUE *v* -CRUED, -CRUING, -CRUES to come as an increase or addition

ACCURACY *n* pl. -CIES the quality of being accurate

ACCURATE *adj* free from error

ACCURSED *adj* damnable

ACCURST *adj* accursed

ACCUSAL *n* pl. -S the act of accusing

ACCUSANT *n* pl. -S an accuser

ACCUSE *v* -CUSED, -CUSING, -CUSES to make an assertion against

ACCUSER *n* pl. -S one that accuses

ACCUSTOM *v* -ED, -ING, -S to make familiar

ACE *v* ACED, ACING, ACES to score a point against in a single stroke

ACEDIA *n* pl. -S apathy

ACELDAMA *n* pl. -S a place of bloodshed

ACENTRIC *adj* having no center

ACEQUIA *n* pl. -S an irrigation ditch or canal

ACERATE *adj* acerose

ACERATED *adj* acerose

ACERB *adj* ACERBER, ACERBEST sour

ACERBATE *v* -BATED, -BATING, -BATES to make sour

ACERBIC *adj* acerb

ACERBITY *n* pl. -TIES sourness

ACEROLA *n* pl. -S a West Indian shrub

ACEROSE *adj* needle-shaped

ACEROUS *adj* acerose

ACERVATE *adj* growing in compact clusters

ACERVULI *n/pl* spore-producing organs of certain fungi

ACESCENT *n* pl. -S something that is slightly sour

ACETA pl. of acetum

ACETAL *n* pl. -S a flammable liquid

ACETAMID *n* pl. -S an amide of acetic acid

ACETATE n pl. -S a salt of acetic acid **ACETATED** adj

ACETIC adj pertaining to vinegar

ACETIFY v -FIED, -FYING, -FIES to convert into vinegar

ACETIN n pl. -S a chemical compound

ACETONE n pl. -S a flammable liquid **ACETONIC** adj

ACETOSE adj acetous

ACETOUS adj tasting like vinegar

ACETOXYL n pl. -S a univalent radical

ACETUM n pl. -TA vinegar

ACETYL n pl. -S a univalent radical **ACETYLIC** adj

ACHE v ACHED, ACHING, ACHES to suffer a dull, continuous pain

ACHENE n pl. -S a type of fruit **ACHENIAL** adj

ACHIER comparative of achy

ACHIEST superlative of achy

ACHIEVE v ACHIEVED, ACHIEVING, ACHIEVES to carry out successfully

ACHIEVER n pl. -S one that achieves

ACHILLEA n pl. -S yarrow

ACHINESS n pl. -ES the state of being achy

ACHING present participle of ache

ACHINGLY adv in an aching manner

ACHIOTE n pl. -S a yellowish red dye

ACHOLIA n pl. -S a lack of bile

ACHOO interj ahchoo

ACHROMAT n pl. -S a type of lens

ACHROMIC adj having no color

ACHY adj ACHIER, ACHIEST aching

ACICULA n pl. -LAE or -LAS a needlelike part or process **ACICULAR** adj

ACICULUM n pl. -LA or -LUMS a bristlelike part

ACID n pl. -S a type of chemical compound

ACIDEMIA n pl. -S a condition of increased acidity of the blood

ACIDHEAD n pl. -S one who uses LSD

ACIDIC adj sour

ACIDIFY v -FIED, -FYING, -FIES to convert into an acid

ACIDITY n pl. -TIES sourness

ACIDLY adv sourly

ACIDNESS n pl. -ES acidity

ACIDOSIS n pl. -DOSES an abnormal condition of the blood **ACIDOTIC** adj

ACIDURIA n pl. -S a condition of having excessive amounts of acid in the urine

ACIDY adj sour

ACIERATE v -ATED, -ATING, -ATES to turn into steel

ACIFORM adj needle-shaped

ACING present participle of ace

ACINUS n pl. -NI a small, saclike division of a gland **ACINAR, ACINIC, ACINOSE, ACINOUS** adj

ACKEE n pl. -S akee

ACLINIC adj having no inclination

ACME n pl. -S the highest point **ACMATIC, ACMIC** adj

ACNE n pl. -S a skin disease **ACNED** adj

ACNODE n pl. -S an element of a mathematical set that is isolated from the other elements

ACOCK adj cocked

ACOLD adj cold

ACOLYTE n pl. -S an assistant

ACONITE n pl. -S a poisonous herb **ACONITIC** adj

ACONITUM n pl. -S aconite

ACORN n pl. -S the fruit of the oak tree

ACOUSTIC n pl. -S a hearing aid

ACQUAINT v -ED, -ING, -S to cause to know

ACQUEST n pl. -S something acquired

ACQUIRE v -QUIRED, -QUIRING, -QUIRES to come into possession of

ACQUIRER n pl. -S one that acquires

ACQUIT v -QUITTED, -QUITTING, -QUITS to free or clear from a charge of fault or crime

ACRASIA n pl. -S a lack of self-control

ACRASIN n pl. -S a substance secreted by the cells of a slime mold

ACRE n pl. -S a unit of area

ACREAGE n pl. -S area in acres

ACRED adj owning many acres

ACRID adj -RIDER, -RIDEST sharp and harsh to the taste or smell

ACRIDINE n pl. -S a chemical compound

ACRIDITY n pl. -TIES the state of being acrid

ACRIDLY adv in an acrid manner

ACRIMONY n pl. -NIES sharpness or bitterness of speech or temper

ACROBAT n pl. -S one skilled in feats of agility and balance

ACRODONT n pl. -S an animal having rootless teeth
ACROGEN n pl. -S a plant growing at the apex only
ACROLECT n pl. -S a high form of a language
ACROLEIN n pl. -S a flammable liquid
ACROLITH n pl. -S a type of statue
ACROMION n pl. -MIA the outward end of the shoulder blade **ACROMIAL** adj
ACRONIC adj occurring at sunset
ACRONYM n pl. -S a word formed from the initials of a compound term or series of words
ACROSOME n pl. -S a thin sac at the head of a sperm.
ACROSS prep from one side of to the other
ACROSTIC n pl. -S a poem in which certain letters taken in order form a word or phrase
ACROTISM n pl. -S weakness of the pulse **ACROTIC** adj
ACRYLATE n pl. -S an acrylic
ACRYLIC n pl. -S a type of resin
ACT v -ED, -ING, -S to do something
ACTA n/pl recorded proceedings
ACTABLE adj suitable for performance on the stage
ACTIN n pl. -S a protein in muscle tissue
ACTINAL adj having tentacles
ACTING n pl. -S the occupation of an actor
ACTINIA n pl. -IAE or -IAS a marine animal
ACTINIAN n pl. -S actinia
ACTINIC adj pertaining to actinism
ACTINIDE n pl. -S any of a series of radioactive elements
ACTINISM n pl. -S the property of radiant energy that effects chemical changes
ACTINIUM n pl. -S a radioactive element
ACTINOID n pl. -S an actinide
ACTINON n pl. -S an isotope of radon
ACTION n pl. -S the process of acting
ACTIVATE v -VATED, -VATING, -VATES to set in motion
ACTIVE n pl. -S a participating member of an organization
ACTIVELY adv with activity

ACTIVISM n pl. -S a doctrine that emphasizes direct and decisive action
ACTIVIST n pl. -S an advocate of activism
ACTIVITY n pl. -TIES brisk action or movement
ACTIVIZE v -IZED, -IZING, -IZES to activate
ACTOR n pl. -S a theatrical performer **ACTORISH** adj
ACTRESS n pl. -ES a female actor **ACTRESSY** adj
ACTUAL adj existing in fact **ACTUALLY** adv
ACTUARY n pl. -ARIES a statistician who computes insurance risks and premiums
ACTUATE v -ATED, -ATING, -ATES to set into action or motion
ACTUATOR n pl. -S one that actuates
ACUATE adj sharp
ACUITY n pl. -ITIES sharpness
ACULEATE adj having a sting
ACULEUS n pl. -LEI a sharp-pointed part
ACUMEN n pl. -S mental keenness
ACUTANCE n pl. -S a measure of photographic clarity
ACUTE adj ACUTER, ACUTEST marked by sharpness or severity **ACUTELY** adv
ACUTE n pl. -S a type of accent mark
ACYCLIC adj not cyclic
ACYL n pl. -S a univalent radical
ACYLATE v -ATED, -ATING, -ATES to introduce acyl into
ACYLOIN n pl. -S a type of chemical compound
AD n pl. -S an advertisement
ADAGE n pl. -S a traditional saying expressing a common observation **ADAGIAL** adj
ADAGIO n pl. -GIOS a musical composition or movement played in a slow tempo
ADAMANCE n pl. -S adamancy
ADAMANCY n pl. -CIES unyielding hardness
ADAMANT n pl. -S an extremely hard substance
ADAMSITE n pl. -S a lung-irritating gas
ADAPT v -ED, -ING, -S to make suitable
ADAPTER n pl. -S one that adapts
ADAPTION n pl. -S the act of adapting **ADAPTIVE** adj

ADAPTOR *n* pl. -S adapter

ADAXIAL *adj* situated on the same side as

ADD *v* -ED, -ING, -S to combine or join so as to bring about an increase **ADDABLE** *adj*

ADDAX *n* pl. -ES a large antelope

ADDEDLY *adv* additionally

ADDEND *n* pl. -S a number to be added to another

ADDENDUM *n* pl. -DA something added or to be added

ADDER *n* pl. -S a venomous snake

ADDIBLE *adj* capable of being added

ADDICT *v* -ED, -ING, -S to devote or surrender to something habitually or compulsively

ADDITION *n* pl. -S something added

ADDITIVE *n* pl. -S a substance added to another to impart desirable qualities

ADDITORY *adj* making an addition

ADDLE *v* -DLED, -DLING, -DLES to confuse

ADDRESS *v* -DRESSED or -DREST, -DRESSING, -DRESSES to speak to

ADDUCE *v* -DUCED, -DUCING, -DUCES to bring forward as evidence

ADDUCENT *adj* serving to adduct

ADDUCER *n* pl. -S one that adduces

ADDUCING present participle of adduce

ADDUCT *v* -ED, -ING, -S to draw toward the main axis

ADDUCTOR *n* pl. -S an adducent muscle

ADEEM *v* -ED, -ING, -S to take away

ADENINE *n* pl. -S an alkaloid

ADENITIS *n* pl. -TISES inflammation of a lymph node

ADENOID *n* pl. -S an enlarged lymphoid growth behind the pharynx

ADENOMA *n* pl. -MAS or -MATA a tumor of glandular origin

ADENOSIS *n* pl. -NOSES abnormal growth of glandular tissue

ADENYL *n* pl. -S a univalent radical

ADEPT *adj* ADEPTER, ADEPTEST highly skilled **ADEPTLY** *adv*

ADEPT *n* pl. -S an adept person

ADEQUACY *n* pl. -CIES the state of being adequate

ADEQUATE *adj* sufficient for a specific requirement

ADHERE *v* -HERED, -HERING, -HERES to become or remain attached or close to something

ADHEREND *n* pl. -S the surface to which an adhesive adheres

ADHERENT *n* pl. -S a supporter

ADHERER *n* pl. -S one that adheres

ADHERING present participle of adhere

ADHESION *n* pl. -S the act of adhering

ADHESIVE *n* pl. -S a substance that causes adhesion

ADHIBIT *v* -ED, -ING, -S to take or let in

ADIEU *n* pl. ADIEUS or ADIEUX a farewell

ADIOS *interj* — used to express farewell

ADIPOSE *n* pl. -S animal fat **ADIPIC** *adj*

ADIPOSIS *n* pl. -POSES obesity

ADIPOUS *adj* pertaining to adipose

ADIT *n* pl. -S an entrance

ADJACENT *adj* next to

ADJOIN *v* -ED, -ING, -S to lie next to

ADJOINT *n* pl. -S a type of mathematical matrix

ADJOURN *v* -ED, -ING, -S to suspend until a later time

ADJUDGE *v* -JUDGED, -JUDGING, -JUDGES to determine judicially

ADJUNCT *n* pl. -S something attached in a subordinate position

ADJURE *v* -JURED, -JURING, -JURES to command solemnly

ADJURER *n* pl. -S one that adjures

ADJUROR *n* pl. -S adjurer

ADJUST *v* -ED, -ING, -S to bring to a more satisfactory state

ADJUSTER *n* pl. -S one that adjusts

ADJUSTOR *n* pl. -S adjuster

ADJUTANT *n* pl. -S an assistant

ADJUVANT *n* pl. -S an assistant

ADMAN *n* pl. -MEN a man employed in the advertising business

ADMASS *adj* pertaining to a society strongly influenced by advertising

ADMIRAL *n* pl. -S a high-ranking naval officer

ADMIRE *v* -MIRED, -MIRING, -MIRES to regard with wonder, pleasure, and approval

ADMIRER *n* pl. -S one that admires

ADMIT *v* -MITTED, -MITTING, -MITS to allow to enter

ADMITTER *n* pl. -S one that admits

ADMIX   *v* -MIXED or -MIXT, -MIXING, -MIXES to mix

ADMONISH   *v* -ED, -ING, -ES to reprove mildly or kindly

ADNATE   *adj* joined to another part or organ

ADNATION   *n* pl. -S the state of being adnate

ADNEXA   *n/pl* conjoined anatomical parts **ADNEXAL** *adj*

ADNOUN   *n* pl. -S an adjective when used as a noun

ADO   *n* pl. ADOS bustling excitement

ADOBE   *n* pl. -S an unburnt, sun-dried brick

ADOBO   *n* pl. -BOS a Philippine dish of fish or meat

ADONIS   *n* pl. -ISES a handsome young man

ADOPT   *v* -ED, -ING, -S to take into one's family by legal means

ADOPTEE   *n* pl. -S one that is adopted

ADOPTER   *n* pl. -S one that adopts

ADOPTION   *n* pl. -S the act of adopting **ADOPTIVE** *adj*

ADORABLE   *adj* worthy of being adored **ADORABLY** *adv*

ADORE   *v* ADORED, ADORING, ADORES to love deeply

ADORER   *n* pl. -S one that adores

ADORN   *v* -ED, -ING, -S to add something to for the purpose of making more attractive

ADORNER   *n* pl. -S one that adorns

ADOWN   *adv* downward

ADOZE   *adj* dozing

ADRENAL   *n* pl. -S an endocrine gland

ADRIFT   *adj* drifting

ADROIT   *adj* ADROITER, ADROITEST skillful **ADROITLY** *adv*

ADSCRIPT   *n* pl. -S a distinguishing symbol written after another character

ADSORB   *v* -ED, -ING, -S to gather on a surface in a condensed layer

ADSORBER   *n* pl. -S one that absorbs

ADULARIA   *n* pl. -S a mineral

ADULATE   *v* -LATED, -LATING, -LATES to praise excessively

ADULATOR   *n* pl. -S one that adulates

ADULT   *n* pl. -S a fully developed individual

ADULTERY   *n* pl. -TERIES voluntary sexual intercourse between a married person and someone other than his or her spouse

ADULTLY   *adv* in a manner typical of an adult

ADUMBRAL   *adj* shadowy

ADUNC   *adj* bent inward

ADUNCATE   *adj* adunc

ADUNCOUS   *adj* adunc

ADUST   *adj* scorched

ADVANCE   *v* -VANCED, -VANCING, -VANCES to move or cause to move ahead

ADVANCER   *n* pl. -S one that advances

ADVECT   *v* -ED, -ING, -S to convey or transport by the flow of a fluid

ADVENT   *n* pl. -S arrival

ADVERB   *n* pl. -S a word used to modify the meaning of a verb, adjective, or other adverb

ADVERSE   *adj* acting in opposition

ADVERT   *v* -ED, -ING, -S to call attention

ADVICE   *n* pl. -S recommendation regarding a decision or course of conduct

ADVISE   *v* -VISED, -VISING, -VISES to give advice to

ADVISEE   *n* pl. -S one that is advised

ADVISER   *n* pl. -S one that advises

ADVISING   present participle of advise

ADVISOR   *n* pl. -S adviser

ADVISORY   *n* pl. -RIES a report giving information

ADVOCACY   *n* pl. -CIES the act of advocating

ADVOCATE   *v* -CATED, -CATING, -CATES to speak in favor of

ADVOWSON   *n* pl. -S the right of presenting a nominee to a vacant church office

ADYNAMIA   *n* pl. -S lack of physical strength **ADYNAMIC** *adj*

ADYTUM   *n* pl. -TA an inner sanctuary in an ancient temple

ADZ   *n* pl. -ES a cutting tool

ADZE   *n* pl. -S adz

AE   *adj* one

AECIA   pl. of aecium

AECIAL   *adj* pertaining to an aecium

AECIDIAL   *adj* pertaining to an aecium

AECIDIUM   *n* pl. -IA an aecium

AECIUM   *n* pl. -IA a spore-producing organ of certain fungi

AEDES *n* pl. AEDES any of a genus of mosquitoes

AEDILE *n* pl. -S a magistrate of ancient Rome

AEDINE *adj* pertaining to an aedes

AEGIS *n* pl. -GISES protection

AENEOUS *adj* having a greenish gold color

AENEUS *adj* aeneous

AEOLIAN *adj* eolian

AEON *n* pl. -S eon

AEONIAN *adj* eonian

AEONIC *adj* eonian

AEQUORIN *n* pl. -S a protein secreted by jellyfish

AERATE *v* -ATED, -ATING, -ATES to supply with air

AERATION *n* pl. -S the act of aerating

AERATOR *n* pl. -S one that aerates

AERIAL *n* pl. -S an antenna

AERIALLY *adv* in a manner pertaining to the air

AERIE *n* pl. -S a bird's nest built high on a mountain or cliff **AERIED** *adj*

AERIER comparative of aery

AERIES pl. of aery

AERIEST superlative of aery

AERIFORM *adj* having the form of air

AERIFY *v* -FIED, -FYING, -FIES to aerate

AERILY *adv* in an aery manner

AERO *adj* pertaining to aircraft

AEROBE *n* pl. -S an organism that requires oxygen to live **AEROBIC** *adj*

AEROBICS *n/pl* exercises for conditioning the heart and lungs by increasing oxygen consumption

AEROBIUM *n* pl. -BIA aerobe

AERODUCT *n* pl. -S a type of jet engine

AERODYNE *n* pl. -S an aircraft that is heavier than air

AEROFOIL *n* pl. -S airfoil

AEROGEL *n* pl. -S a highly porous solid

AEROGRAM *n* pl. -S an airmail letter

AEROLITE *n* pl. -S a meteorite containing more stone than iron

AEROLITH *n* pl. -S aerolite

AEROLOGY *n* pl. -GIES the study of the atmosphere

AERONAUT *n* pl. -S one who operates an airship

AERONOMY *n* pl. -MIES the study of the upper atmosphere

AEROSAT *n* pl. -S a satellite for use in air-traffic control

AEROSOL *n* pl. -S a gaseous suspension of fine solid or liquid particles

AEROSTAT *n* pl. -S an aircraft that is lighter than air

AERUGO *n* pl. -GOS a green film that forms on copper

AERY *adj* AERIER, AERIEST airy

AERY *n* pl. AERIES aerie

AESTHETE *n* pl. -S esthete

AESTIVAL *adj* estival

AETHER *n* pl. -S the upper region of the atmosphere **AETHERIC** *adj*

AFAR *n* pl. -S a great distance

AFEARD *adj* afraid

AFEARED *adj* afeard

AFEBRILE *adj* having no fever

AFF *adv* off

AFFABLE *adj* easy to talk to **AFFABLY** *adv*

AFFAIR *n* pl. -S anything done or to be done

AFFAIRE *n* pl. -S a brief amorous relationship

AFFECT *v* -ED, -ING, -S to give a false appearance of

AFFECTER *n* pl. -S one that affects

AFFERENT *n* pl. -S a nerve that conveys impulses toward a nerve center

AFFIANCE *v* -ANCED, -ANCING, -ANCES to betroth

AFFIANT *n* pl. -S one who makes a written declaration under oath

AFFICHE *n* pl. -S a poster

AFFINAL *adj* related by marriage

AFFINE *n* pl. -S a relative by marriage

AFFINED *adj* closely related

AFFINELY *adv* in the manner of a type of mathematical mapping

AFFINITY *n* pl. -TIES a natural attraction or inclination

AFFIRM *v* -ED, -ING, -S to state positively

AFFIRMER *n* pl. -S one that affirms

AFFIX *v* -ED, -ING, -ES to attach

AFFIXAL *adj* pertaining to a prefix or suffix

AFFIXER *n* pl. -S one that affixes

AFFIXIAL *adj* affixal

AFFLATUS *n* pl. -ES a creative inspiration

AFFLICT *v* -ED, -ING, -S to distress with mental or physical pain

AFFLUENT *n* pl. -S a stream that flows into another

AFFLUX *n* pl. -ES a flowing toward a point

AFFORD *v* -ED, -ING, -S to have sufficient means for

AFFOREST *v* -ED, -ING, -S to convert into forest

AFFRAY *v* -ED, -ING, -S to frighten

AFFRAYER *n* pl. -S one that affrays

AFFRIGHT *v* -ED, -ING, -S to frighten

AFFRONT *v* -ED, -ING, -S to insult openly

AFFUSION *n* pl. -S an act of pouring a liquid on

AFGHAN *n* pl. -S a woolen blanket or shawl

AFGHANI *n* pl. -S a monetary unit of Afghanistan

AFIELD *adv* in the field

AFIRE *adj* being on fire

AFLAME *adj* flaming

AFLOAT *adj* floating

AFLUTTER *adj* nervously excited

AFOOT *adv* on foot

AFORE *adv* before

AFOUL *adj* entangled

AFRAID *adj* filled with apprehension

AFREET *n* pl. -S an evil spirit in Arabic mythology

AFRESH *adv* anew

AFRIT *n* pl. -S afreet

AFT *adv* toward the stern

AFTER *prep* behind in place or order

AFTERS *n/pl* dessert

AFTERTAX *adj* remaining after payment of taxes

AFTMOST *adj* nearest the stern

AFTOSA *n* pl. -S a disease of hoofed mammals

AG *adj* pertaining to agriculture

AGA *n* pl. -S a high-ranking Turkish military officer

AGAIN *adv* once more

AGAINST *prep* in opposition to

AGALLOCH *n* pl. -S the fragrant wood of a tropical tree

AGALWOOD *n* pl. -S agalloch

AGAMA *n* pl. -S a tropical lizard

AGAMETE *n* pl. -S an asexual reproductive cell

AGAMIC *adj* asexual

AGAMOUS *adj* agamic

AGAPE *n* pl. -PAE or -PAI the love of God for mankind **AGAPEIC** *adj*

AGAR *n* pl. -S a viscous substance obtained from certain seaweeds

AGARIC *n* pl. -S any of a family of fungi

AGAROSE *n* pl. -S a sugar obtained from agar

AGATE *n* pl. -S a variety of quartz **AGATOID** *adj*

AGATIZE *v* -IZED, -IZING, -IZES to cause to resemble agate

AGAVE *n* pl. -S a tropical plant

AGAZE *adj* gazing

AGE *v* AGED, AGING or AGEING, AGES to grow old

AGEDLY *adv* oldly

AGEDNESS *n* pl. -ES oldness

AGEE *adv* to one side

AGEING *n* pl. -S aging

AGEISM *n* pl. -S discrimination based on age

AGEIST *n* pl. -S an advocate of ageism

AGELESS *adj* never growing old

AGELONG *adj* lasting for a long time

AGENCY *n* pl. -CIES an organization that does business for others

AGENDA *n* pl. -S a list of things to be done

AGENDUM *n* pl. -S an item on an agenda

AGENE *n* pl. -S a chemical compound used in bleaching flour

AGENESIA *n* pl. -S agenesis

AGENESIS *n* pl. AGENESES absence or imperfect development of a bodily part **AGENETIC** *adj*

AGENIZE *v* -NIZED, -NIZING, -NIZES to treat with agene

AGENT *n* pl. -S one who is authorized to act for another **AGENTIAL** *adj*

AGENTING *n* pl. -S the business or activities of an agent

AGENTIVE *n* pl. -S a word part that denotes the doer of an action

AGENTRY *n* pl. -RIES the office or duties of an agent

AGER *n* pl. -S one that ages

AGERATUM *n* pl. -S a flowering plant

AGGADIC *adj* haggadic

AGGER *n* pl. -S a mound of earth used as a fortification

AGGIE *n* pl. -S a type of playing marble

AGGRADE *v* -GRADED, -GRADING, -GRADES to fill with detrital material

AGGRESS *v* -ED, -ING, -ES to commit the first act of hostility

AGGRIEVE *v* -GRIEVED, -GRIEVING, -GRIEVES to distress

AGGRO   *n* pl. -GROS a rivalry or grievance

AGHA   *n* pl. -S aga

AGHAST   *adj* shocked by something horrible

AGILE   *adj* able to move quickly and easily **AGILELY** *adv*

AGILITY   *n* pl. -TIES the quality of being agile

AGIN   *prep* against

AGING   *n* pl. -S the process of growing old

AGINNER   *n* pl. -S one that is against change

AGIO   *n* pl. AGIOS a premium paid for the exchange of one currency for another

AGIOTAGE   *n* pl. -S the business of a broker

AGISM   *n* pl. -S ageism

AGIST   *v* -ED, -ING, -S to feed and take care of for a fee, as livestock

AGITATE   *v* -TATED, -TATING, -TATES to move with a violent, irregular action **AGITABLE** *adj*

AGITATO   *adj* fast and stirring — used as a musical direction

AGITATOR   *n* pl. -S one that agitates

AGITPROP   *n* pl. -S pro-Communist propaganda

AGLARE   *adj* glaring

AGLEAM   *adj* gleaming

AGLEE   *adv* agley

AGLET   *n* pl. -S a metal sheath at the end of a lace

AGLEY   *adv* awry

AGLIMMER   *adj* glimmering

AGLITTER   *adj* glittering

AGLOW   *adj* glowing

AGLY   *adv* agley

AGLYCON   *n* pl. -S a type of chemical compound

AGLYCONE   *n* pl. -S aglycon

AGMA   *n* pl. -S eng

AGMINATE   *adj* clustered together

AGNAIL   *n* pl. -S a piece of loose skin at the base of a fingernail

AGNATE   *n* pl. -S a relative on the father's side **AGNATIC** *adj*

AGNATION   *n* pl. -S the relationship of agnates

AGNIZE   *v* -NIZED, -NIZING, -NIZES to acknowledge

AGNOMEN   *n* pl. -MINA or -MENS an additional name given to an ancient Roman

AGNOSIA   *n* pl. -S loss of ability to recognize familiar objects

AGNOSTIC   *n* pl. -S one who disclaims any knowledge of God

AGO   *adv* in the past

AGOG   *adv* in a state of eager curiosity

AGON   *n* pl. -S or -ES the dramatic conflict between the main characters in a Greek play

AGONAL   *adj* pertaining to agony

AGONE   *adv* ago

AGONES   a pl. of agon

AGONIC   *adj* not forming an angle

AGONIES   pl. of agony

AGONISE   *v* -NISED, -NISING, -NISES to agonize

AGONIST   *n* pl. -S one that is engaged in a struggle

AGONIZE   *v* -NIZED, -NIZING, -NIZES to suffer extreme pain

AGONY   *n* pl. -NIES extreme pain

AGORA   *n* pl. -RAS or -RAE a marketplace in ancient Greece

AGORA   *n* pl. AGOROT or AGOROTH a monetary unit of Israel

AGOUTI   *n* pl. -S or -ES a burrowing rodent

AGOUTY   *n* pl. -TIES agouti

AGRAFE   *n* pl. -S agraffe

AGRAFFE   *n* pl. -S an ornamental clasp

AGRAPHA   *n/pl* the sayings of Jesus not found in the Bible

AGRAPHIA   *n* pl. -S a mental disorder marked by inability to write **AGRAPHIC** *adj*

AGRARIAN   *n* pl. -S one who favors equal distribution of land

AGRAVIC   *adj* pertaining to a condition of no gravitation

AGREE   *v* AGREED, AGREEING, AGREES to have the same opinion

AGRESTAL   *adj* growing wild

AGRESTIC   *adj* rural

AGRIA   *n* pl. -S severe pustular eruption

AGRIMONY   *n* pl. -NIES a perennial herb

AGROLOGY   *n* pl. -GIES the science of soils in relation to crops

AGRONOMY   *n* pl. -MIES the application of scientific principles to the cultivation of land

AGROUND *adv* on the ground

AGRYPNIA *n* pl. -S insomnia

AGUE *n* pl. -S a malarial fever AGUELIKE, AGUISH *adj* AGUISHLY *adv*

AGUEWEED *n* pl. -S a flowering plant

AH *interj* — used to express delight, relief, or contempt

AHA *interj* — used to express surprise, triumph, or derision

AHCHOO *interj* — used to represent the sound of a sneeze

AHEAD *adv* at or to the front

AHEM *interj* — used to attract attention

AHIMSA *n* pl. -S the Hindu principle of nonviolence

AHOLD *n* pl. -S a hold or grasp of something

AHORSE *adv* on a horse

AHOY *interj* — used in hailing a ship or person

AHULL *adj* abandoned and flooded, as a ship

AI *n* pl. -S a three-toed sloth

AIBLINS *adv* ablins

AID *v* -ED, -ING, -S to help

AIDE *n* pl. -S an assistant

AIDER *n* pl. -S one that aids

AIDFUL *adj* helpful

AIDLESS *adj* helpless

AIDMAN *n* pl. -MEN a corpsman

AIGLET *n* pl. -S aglet

AIGRET *n* pl. -S aigrette

AIGRETTE *n* pl. -S a tuft of feathers worn as a head ornament

AIGUILLE *n* pl. -S a sharp, pointed mountain peak

AIKIDO *n* pl. -DOS a Japanese art of self-defense

AIL *v* -ED, -ING, -S to cause pain or discomfort to

AILERON *n* pl. -S a movable control surface on an airplane wing

AILMENT *n* pl. -S a physical or mental disorder

AIM *v* -ED, -ING, -S to direct toward a specified object or goal

AIMER *n* pl. -S one that aims

AIMFUL *adj* full of purpose AIMFULLY *adv*

AIMLESS *adj* lacking direction or purpose

AIN *n* pl. -S ayin

AINSELL *n* pl. -S own self

AIOLI *n* pl. -S garlic mayonnaise

AIR *v* -ED, -ING, -S to expose to the air (the mixture of gases that surrounds the earth)

AIR *adv* AIRER, AIREST early

AIRBOAT *n* pl. -S a boat used in swampy areas

AIRBORNE *adj* flying

AIRBOUND *adj* stopped up by air

AIRBRUSH *v* -ED, -ING, -ES to apply in a fine spray by compressed air, as paint

AIRBURST *n* pl. -S an explosion in the air

AIRBUS *n* pl. -BUSES or -BUSSES a passenger airplane

AIRCHECK *n* pl. -S a recording made from a radio broadcast

AIRCOACH *n* pl. -ES the cheaper class of accommodations in commercial aircraft

AIRCRAFT *n* pl. AIRCRAFT any machine or device capable of flying

AIRCREW *n* pl. -S the crew of an aircraft

AIRDATE *n* pl. -S the scheduled date of a broadcast

AIRDROME *n* pl. -S an airport

AIRDROP *v* -DROPPED, -DROPPING, -DROPS to drop from an aircraft

AIRER *n* pl. -S a frame on which to dry clothes

AIRFARE *n* pl. -S payment for travel by airplane

AIRFIELD *n* pl. -S an airport

AIRFLOW *n* pl. -S a flow of air

AIRFOIL *n* pl. -S a part of an aircraft designed to provide lift or control

AIRFRAME *n* pl. -S the framework and external covering of an airplane

AIRGLOW *n* pl. -S a glow in the upper atmosphere

AIRHEAD *n* pl. -S a stupid person

AIRHOLE *n* pl. -S a hole to let air in or out

AIRIER comparative of airy

AIRIEST superlative of airy

AIRILY *adv* in an airy manner

AIRINESS *n* pl. -ES the state of being airy

AIRING *n* pl. -S an exposure to the air

AIRLESS *adj* having no air

AIRLIFT *v* -ED, -ING, -S to transport by airplane

AIRLIKE *adj* resembling air

AIRLINE *n* pl. -S an air transportation system

AIRLINER *n* pl. -S a large passenger aircraft

AIRMAIL *v* -ED, -ING, -S to send mail by airplane

AIRMAN *n* pl. -MEN an aviator

AIRN *n* pl. -S iron

AIRPARK *n* pl. -S a small airport

AIRPLANE *n* pl. -S a winged aircraft propelled by jet engines or propellers

AIRPLAY *n* pl. -PLAYS the playing of a record on a radio program

AIRPORT *n* pl. -S a tract of land maintained for the landing and takeoff of aircraft

AIRPOST *n* pl. -S a system of conveying mail by airplane

AIRPOWER *n* pl. -S the military strength of a nation's air force

AIRPROOF *v* -ED, -ING, -S to make impermeable to air

AIRSCAPE *n* pl. -S a view of the earth from an aircraft or a high position

AIRSCREW *n* pl. -S an airplane propeller

AIRSHED *n* pl. -S the air supply of a given region

AIRSHIP *n* pl. -S a lighter-than-air aircraft having propulsion and steering systems

AIRSICK *adj* nauseated from flying in an airplane

AIRSPACE *n* pl. -S the portion of the atmosphere above a particular land area

AIRSPEED *n* pl. -S the speed of an aircraft with relation to the air

AIRSTRIP *n* pl. -S a runway

AIRT *v* -ED, -ING, -S to guide

AIRTH *v* -ED, -ING, -S to airt

AIRTIGHT *adj* not allowing air to escape or enter

AIRTIME *n* pl. -S the time when a broadcast begins

AIRWARD *adv* toward the sky

AIRWAVE *n* pl. -S the medium of radio and television transmission

AIRWAY *n* pl. -WAYS a passageway in which air circulates

AIRWISE *adj* skillful in aviation

AIRWOMAN *n* pl. -WOMEN a female aviator

AIRY *adj* AIRIER, AIRIEST having the nature of air

AISLE *n* pl. -S a passageway between sections of seats

AISLED *adj*

AISLEWAY *n* pl. -WAYS an aisle

AIT *n* pl. -S a small island

AITCH *n* pl. -ES the letter H

AIVER *n* pl. -S a draft horse

AJAR *adj* partly open

AJEE *adv* agee

AJIVA *n* pl. -S inanimate matter

AJOWAN *n* pl. -S the fruit of an Egyptian plant

AJUGA *n* pl. -S a flowering plant

AKEE *n* pl. -S a tropical tree

AKELA *n* pl. -S a leader of a cub scout pack

AKENE *n* pl. -S achene

AKIMBO *adj* having hands on hips and elbows bent outward

AKIN *adj* related by blood

AKVAVIT *n* pl. -S aquavit

AL *n* pl. -S an East Indian tree

ALA *n* pl. ALAE a wing or winglike part

ALACK *interj* — used to express sorrow or regret

ALACRITY *n* pl. -TIES cheerful promptness

ALAE pl. of ala

ALAMEDA *n* pl. -S a shaded walkway

ALAMO *n* pl. -MOS a softwood tree

ALAMODE *n* pl. -S a silk fabric

ALAN *n* pl. -S a large hunting dog

ALAND *n* pl. -S alan

ALANE *adj* alone

ALANG *adv* along

ALANIN *n* pl. -S alanine

ALANINE *n* pl. -S an amino acid

ALANT *n* pl. -S alan

ALANYL *n* pl. -S a univalent radical

ALAR *adj* pertaining to wings

ALARM *v* -ED, -ING, -S to frighten by a sudden revelation of danger

ALARMISM *n* pl. -S the practice of alarming others needlessly

ALARMIST *n* pl. -S one who alarms others needlessly

ALARUM *v* -ED, -ING, -S to alarm

ALARY *adj* alar

ALAS *interj* — used to express sorrow or regret

ALASKA *n* pl. -S a heavy fabric

ALASTOR *n* pl. -S an avenging deity in Greek tragedy

ALATE *n* pl. -S a winged insect

ALATED *adj* having wings

ALATION *n* pl. -S the state of having wings

ALB *n* pl. -S a long-sleeved vestment

ALBA *n* pl. -S the white substance of the brain

ALBACORE *n* pl. -S a marine food fish

ALBATA *n* pl. -S an alloy of copper, nickel, and zinc

ALBEDO *n* pl. -DOS or -DOES the ratio of the light reflected by a planet to that received by it

ALBEIT *conj* although

ALBICORE *n* pl. -S albacore

ALBINAL *adj* albinic

ALBINIC *adj* pertaining to albinism

ALBINISM *n* pl. -S the condition of being an albino

ALBINO *n* pl. -NOS an organism lacking normal pigmentation

ALBITE *n* pl. -S a mineral **ALBITIC** *adj*

ALBIZIA *n* pl. -S a tropical tree

ALBIZZIA *n* pl. -S albizia

ALBUM *n* pl. -S a book for preserving photographs or stamps

ALBUMEN *n* pl. -S the white of an egg

ALBUMIN *n* pl. -S a simple protein

ALBUMOSE *n* pl. -S a proteose

ALBURNUM *n* pl. -S sapwood

ALCADE *n* pl. -S alcalde

ALCAHEST *n* pl. -S alkahest

ALCAIC *n* pl. -S a type of verse form

ALCAIDE *n* pl. -S the commander of a Spanish fortress

ALCALDE *n* pl. -S the mayor of a Spanish town

ALCAYDE *n* pl. -S alcaide

ALCAZAR *n* pl. -S a Spanish fortress or palace

ALCHEMY *n* pl. -MIES a medieval form of chemistry **ALCHEMIC** *adj*

ALCHYMY *n* pl. -MIES alchemy

ALCID *n* pl. -S a diving seabird

ALCIDINE *adj* pertaining to a family of seabirds

ALCOHOL *n* pl. -S a flammable liquid

ALCOVE *n* pl. -S a recessed section of a room **ALCOVED** *adj*

ALDEHYDE *n* pl. -S a type of chemical compound

ALDER *n* pl. -S a shrub or small tree

ALDERFLY *n* pl. -FLIES a winged insect

ALDERMAN *n* pl. -MEN a member of a municipal legislative body

ALDOL *n* pl. -S a chemical compound

ALDOLASE *n* pl. -S an enzyme

ALDOSE *n* pl. -S a type of sugar

ALDRIN *n* pl. -S an insecticide

ALE *n* pl. -S an alcoholic beverage

ALEATORY *adj* pertaining to luck

ALEC *n* pl. -S a herring

ALEE *adv* toward the side of a vessel sheltered from the wind

ALEF *n* pl. -S aleph

ALEGAR *n* pl. -S sour ale

ALEHOUSE *n* pl. -S a tavern where ale is sold

ALEMBIC *n* pl. -S an apparatus formerly used in distilling

ALENCON *n* pl. -S a needlepoint lace

ALEPH *n* pl. -S a Hebrew letter

ALERT *adj* ALERTER, ALERTEST ready for sudden action **ALERTLY** *adv*

ALERT *v* -ED, -ING, -S to warn

ALEURON *n* pl. -S aleurone

ALEURONE *n* pl. -S protein matter found in the seeds of certain plants

ALEVIN *n* pl. -S a young fish

ALEWIFE *n* pl. -WIVES a marine fish

ALEXIA *n* pl. -S a cerebral disorder marked by the loss of the ability to read

ALEXIN *n* pl. -S a substance in the blood that aids in the destruction of bacteria

ALEXINE *n* pl. -S alexin

ALFA *n* pl. -S a communications code word for the letter A

ALFAKI *n* pl. -S alfaqui

ALFALFA *n* pl. -S a plant cultivated for use as hay and forage

ALFAQUI *n* pl. -S a teacher of Muslim law

ALFAQUIN *n* pl. -S alfaqui

ALFORJA *n* pl. -S a leather bag

ALFRESCO *adv* outdoors

ALGA *n* pl. -GAE or -GAS any of a group of primitive aquatic plants **ALGAL** *adj*

ALGAROBA *n* pl. -S the mesquite

ALGEBRA *n* pl. -S a branch of mathematics

ALGERINE *n* pl. -S a woolen fabric

ALGICIDE *n* pl. -S a substance used to kill algae

ALGID *adj* cold

ALGIDITY *n* pl. -TIES coldness

ALGIN *n* pl. -S a viscous substance obtained from certain algae

ALGINATE *n* pl. -S a chemical salt

ALGOID *adj* resembling algae

ALGOLOGY *n* pl. -GIES the study of algae

ALGOR *n* pl. -S coldness

ALGORISM *n* pl. -S the Arabic system of arithmetic notation

ALGUM *n* pl. -S almug

ALIAS *n* pl. -ES an assumed name

ALIBI *v* -BIED, -BIING, -BIES or -BIS to make excuses for oneself

ALIBLE *adj* nourishing

ALIDAD *n* pl. -S alidade

ALIDADE *n* pl. -S a device used in angular measurement

ALIEN *v* -ED, -ING, -S to transfer to another, as property

ALIENAGE *n* pl. -S the state of being foreign

ALIENATE *v* -ATED, -ATING, -ATES to make indifferent or unfriendly

ALIENEE *n* pl. -S one to whom property is transferred

ALIENER *n* pl. -S alienor

ALIENISM *n* pl. -S alienage

ALIENIST *n* pl. -S a physician who treats mental disorders

ALIENLY *adv* in a foreign manner

ALIENOR *n* pl. -S one that transfers property

ALIF *n* pl. -S an Arabic letter

ALIFORM *adj* shaped like a wing

ALIGHT *v* ALIGHTED or ALIT, ALIGHTING, ALIGHTS to come down from something

ALIGN *v* -ED, -ING, -S to arrange in a straight line

ALIGNER *n* pl. -S one that aligns

ALIKE *adj* having close resemblance

ALIMENT *v* -ED, -ING, -S to nourish

ALIMONY *n* pl. -NIES an allowance paid to a woman by her divorced husband

ALINE *v* ALINED, ALINING, ALINES to align

ALINER *n* pl. -S aligner

ALIPED *n* pl. -S an animal having a membrane connecting the toes

ALIQUANT *adj* not dividing evenly into another number

ALIQUOT *n* pl. -S a number that divides evenly into another

ALIST *adj* leaning to one side

ALIT a past tense of alight

ALIUNDE *adv* from a source extrinsic to the matter at hand

ALIVE *adj* having life

ALIYA *n* pl. -S aliyah

ALIYAH *n* pl. -YAHS or -YOS or -YOT the immigration of Jews to Israel

ALIZARIN *n* pl. -S a red dye

ALKAHEST *n* pl. -S the hypothetical universal solvent sought by alchemists

ALKALI *n* pl. -LIES or -LIS a type of chemical compound ALKALIC *adj*

ALKALIFY *v* -FIED, -FYING, -FIES to alkalize

ALKALIN *adj* alkaline

ALKALINE *adj* containing an alkali

ALKALISE *v* -LISED, -LISING, -LISES to alkalize

ALKALIZE *v* -LIZED, -LIZING, -LIZES to convert into an alkali

ALKALOID *n* pl. -S a type of chemical compound

ALKANE *n* pl. -S a type of chemical compound

ALKANET *n* pl. -S a European plant

ALKENE *n* pl. -S a type of chemical compound

ALKIES pl. of alky

ALKINE *n* pl. -S alkyne

ALKOXIDE *n* pl. -S a type of chemical salt

ALKOXY *adj* containing a univalent radical composed of alkyl united with oxygen

ALKY *n* pl. -KIES one who is habitually drunk

ALKYD *n* pl. -S a synthetic resin

ALKYL *n* pl. -S a univalent radical ALKYLIC *adj*

ALKYLATE *v* -ATED, -ATING, -ATES to combine with alkyl

ALKYNE *n* pl. -S a type of chemical compound

ALL *n* pl. -S everything that one has

ALLANITE *n* pl. -S a mineral

ALLAY *v* -ED, -ING, -S to reduce in intensity or severity

ALLAYER *n* pl. -S one that allays

ALLEE *n* pl. -S a tree-lined walkway

ALLEGE *v* -LEGED, -LEGING, -LEGES to assert without proof or before proving

ALLEGER *n* pl. -S one that alleges

ALLEGORY *n* pl. -RIES a story presenting a moral principle

ALLEGRO *n* pl. -GROS a musical passage played in rapid tempo

ALLELE   n pl. -S any of several forms of a gene **ALLELIC** adj

ALLELISM   n pl. -S the state of possessing alleles

ALLELUIA   n pl. -S a song of praise to God

ALLERGEN   n pl. -S a substance capable of inducing an allergy

ALLERGIC   adj pertaining to allergy

ALLERGIN   n pl. -S allergen

ALLERGY   n pl. -GIES a state of hypersensitive reaction to certain things

ALLEY   n pl. -LEYS a narrow passageway

ALLEYWAY   n pl. -WAYS an alley

ALLHEAL   n pl. -S a medicinal herb

ALLIABLE   adj capable of being allied

ALLIANCE   n pl. -S an association formed to further the common interests of its members

ALLICIN   n pl. -S a liquid compound

ALLIED   past tense of ally

ALLIES   present 3d person sing. of ally

ALLIUM   n pl. -S a bulbous herb

ALLOBAR   n pl. -S a change in barometric pressure

ALLOCATE   v -CATED, -CATING, -CATES to set apart for a particular purpose

ALLOD   n pl. -S allodium

ALLODIUM   n pl. -DIA land held in absolute ownership **ALLODIAL** adj

ALLOGAMY   n pl. -MIES fertilization of a flower by pollen from another

ALLONGE   n pl. -S an addition to a document

ALLONYM   n pl. -S the name of one person assumed by another

ALLOPATH   n pl. -S one who treats diseases by producing effects incompatible with those of the disease

ALLOT   v -LOTTED, -LOTTING, -LOTS to give as a share or portion

ALLOTTEE   n pl. -S one to whom something is allotted

ALLOTTER   n pl. -S one that allots

ALLOTTING   present participle of allot

ALLOTYPE   n pl. -S a type of antibody

ALLOTYPY   n pl. -TYPIES the condition of being an allotype

ALLOVER   n pl. -S a fabric having a pattern extending over the entire surface

ALLOW   v -ED, -ING, -S to put no obstacle in the way of

ALLOXAN   n pl. -S a chemical compound

ALLOY   v -ED, -ING, -S to combine to form an alloy (a homogenous mixture of metals)

ALLSEED   n pl. -S a plant having many seeds

ALLSPICE   n pl. -S a tropical tree

ALLUDE   v -LUDED, -LUDING, -LUDES to make an indirect reference

ALLURE   v -LURED, -LURING, -LURES to attract with something desirable

ALLURER   n pl. -S one that allures

ALLUSION   n pl. -S the act of alluding **ALLUSIVE** adj

ALLUVIA   a pl. of alluvium

ALLUVIAL   n pl. -S soil composed of alluvium

ALLUVION   n pl. -S alluvium

ALLUVIUM   n pl. -VIA or -VIUMS detrital material deposited by running water

ALLY   v -LIED, -LYING, -LIES to unite in a formal relationship

ALLYL   n pl. -S a univalent radical **ALLYLIC** adj

ALMA   n pl. -S almah

ALMAGEST   n pl. -S a medieval treatise on astrology or alchemy

ALMAH   n pl. -S an Egyptian girl who sings and dances professionally

ALMANAC   n pl. -S an annual publication containing general information

ALME   n pl. -S almah

ALMEH   n pl. -S almah

ALMEMAR   n pl. -S a bema

ALMIGHTY   adj having absolute power over all

ALMNER   n pl. -S almoner

ALMOND   n pl. -S the edible nut of a small tree

ALMONER   n pl. -S one that distributes alms

ALMONRY   n pl. -RIES a place where alms are distributed

ALMOST   adv very nearly

ALMS   n pl. ALMS money or goods given to the poor

ALMSMAN   n pl. -MEN one who receives alms

ALMUCE   *n* pl. -S a hooded cape

ALMUD   *n* pl. -S a Spanish unit of capacity

ALMUDE   *n* pl. -S almud

ALMUG   *n* pl. -S a precious wood mentioned in the Bible

ALNICO   *n* pl. -COES a magnetic alloy

ALODIUM   *n* pl. -DIA allodium **ALODIAL** *adj*

ALOE   *n* pl. -S an African plant **ALOETIC** *adj*

ALOFT   *adv* in or into the air

ALOGICAL   *adj* being outside the bounds of that to which logic can apply

ALOHA   *n* pl. -S love — used as a greeting or farewell

ALOIN   *n* pl. -S a laxative

ALONE   *adj* apart from others

ALONG   *adv* onward

ALOOF   *adj* distant in interest or feeling **ALOOFLY** *adv*

ALOPECIA   *n* pl. -S baldness **ALOPECIC** *adj*

ALOUD   *adv* audibly

ALOW   *adv* in or to a lower position

ALP   *n* pl. -S a high mountain

ALPACA   *n* pl. -S a ruminant mammal

ALPHA   *n* pl. -S a Greek letter

ALPHABET   *v* -ED, -ING, -S to arrange in the customary order of the letters of a language

ALPHORN   *n* pl. -S a wooden horn used by Swiss herdsmen

ALPHOSIS   *n* pl. -SISES lack of skin pigmentation

ALPHYL   *n* pl. -S a univalent radical

ALPINE   *n* pl. -S a plant native to high mountain regions

ALPINELY   *adv* in a lofty manner

ALPINISM   *n* pl. -S mountain climbing

ALPINIST   *n* pl. -S a mountain climber

ALREADY   *adv* by this time

ALRIGHT   *adj* satisfactory

ALSIKE   *n* pl. -S a European clover

ALSO   *adv* in addition

ALT   *n* pl. -S a high-pitched musical note

ALTAR   *n* pl. -S a raised structure used in worship

ALTER   *v* -ED, -ING, -S to make different

ALTERANT   *n* pl. -S something that alters

ALTERER   *n* pl. -S one that alters

ALTHAEA   *n* pl. -S althea

ALTHEA   *n* pl. -S a flowering plant

ALTHO   *conj* although

ALTHORN   *n* pl. -S a brass wind instrument

ALTHOUGH   *conj* despite the fact that

ALTITUDE   *n* pl. -S the vertical elevation of an object above a given level

ALTO   *n* pl. -TOS a low female singing voice

ALTOIST   *n* pl. -S one who plays the alto saxophone

ALTRUISM   *n* pl. -S selfless devotion to the welfare of others

ALTRUIST   *n* pl. -S one that practices altruism

ALUDEL   *n* pl. -S a pear-shaped vessel

ALULA   *n* pl. -LAE a tuft of feathers on the first digit of a bird's wing **ALULAR** *adj*

ALUM   *n* pl. -S a chemical compound

ALUMIN   *n* pl. -S alumina

ALUMINA   *n* pl. -S an oxide of aluminum

ALUMINE   *n* pl. -S alumina

ALUMINUM   *n* pl. -S a metallic element **ALUMINIC** *adj*

ALUMNA   *n* pl. -NAE a female graduate

ALUMNUS   *n* pl. -NI a male graduate

ALUMROOT   *n* pl. -S a flowering plant

ALUNITE   *n* pl. -S a mineral

ALVEOLAR   *n* pl. -S a sound produced with the tongue touching a place just behind the front teeth

ALVEOLUS   *n* pl. -LI a small anatomical cavity

ALVINE   *adj* pertaining to the abdomen and lower intestines

ALWAY   *adv* always

ALWAYS   *adv* at all times

ALYSSUM   *n* pl. -S a flowering plant

AM   present 1st person sing. of be

AMA   *n* pl. -S amah

AMADAVAT   *n* pl. -S an Asian songbird

AMADOU   *n* pl. -S a substance prepared from fungi for use as tinder

AMAH   *n* pl. -S an Oriental nurse

AMAIN   *adv* with full strength

AMALGAM   *n* pl. -S an alloy of mercury with another metal

AMANDINE   *adj* prepared with almonds

AMANITA   *n* pl. -S any of a genus of poisonous fungi

AMANITIN   *n* pl. -S a chemical compound

AMARANTH   *n* pl. -S a flowering plant

AMARELLE   *n* pl. -S a variety of sour cherry

AMARETTI   *n/pl* macaroons made with bitter almonds

AMARETTO *n* pl. -TOS a kind of liqueur

AMARNA *adj* pertaining to a certain historical period of ancient Egypt

AMASS *v* -ED, -ING, -ES to gather

AMASSER *n* pl. -S one that amasses

AMATEUR *n* pl. -S one that engages in an activity for pleasure

AMATIVE *adj* amorous

AMATOL *n* pl. -S a powerful explosive

AMATORY *adj* pertaining to sexual love

AMAZE *v* AMAZED, AMAZING, AMAZES to overwhelm with surprise or wonder AMAZEDLY *adv*

AMAZON *n* pl. -S a tall, powerful woman

AMBAGE *n* pl. -S a winding path

AMBARI *n* pl. -S ambary

AMBARY *n* pl. -RIES an East Indian plant

AMBEER *n* pl. -S tobacco juice

AMBER *n* pl. -S a fossil resin

AMBERINA *n* pl. -S a type of glassware

AMBEROID *n* pl. -S ambroid

AMBERY *n* pl. -BERIES ambry

AMBIANCE *n* pl. -S ambience

AMBIENCE *n* pl. -S the character, mood, or atmosphere of a place or situation

AMBIENT *n* pl. -S ambience

AMBIT *n* pl. -S the external boundary of something

AMBITION *v* -ED, -ING, -S to seek with eagerness

AMBIVERT *n* pl. -S a person whose personality type is intermediate between introvert and extravert

AMBLE *v* -BLED, -BLING, -BLES to saunter

AMBLER *n* pl. -S one that ambles

AMBO *n* pl. AMBOS or AMBONES a pulpit in an early Christian church

AMBOINA *n* pl. -S amboyna

AMBOYNA *n* pl. -S the mottled wood of an Indonesian tree

AMBRIES pl. of ambry

AMBROID *n* pl. -S a synthetic amber

AMBROSIA *n* pl. -S the food of the Greek and Roman gods

AMBRY *n* pl. -BRIES a recess in a church wall for sacred vessels

AMBSACE *n* pl. -S bad luck

AMBULANT *adj* ambulating

AMBULATE *v* -LATED, -LATING, -LATES to move or walk about

AMBUSH *v* -ED, -ING, -ES to attack from a concealed place

AMBUSHER *n* pl. -S one that ambushes

AMEBA *n* pl. -BAS or -BAE amoeba AMEBAN, AMEBIC, AMEBOID *adj*

AMEBEAN *adj* alternately responding

AMEER *n* pl. -S amir

AMEERATE *n* pl. -S amirate

AMELCORN *n* pl. -S a variety of wheat

AMEN *n* pl. -S a word used at the end of a prayer to express agreement

AMENABLE *adj* capable of being persuaded AMENABLY *adv*

AMEND *v* -ED, -ING, -S to improve

AMENDER *n* pl. -S one that amends

AMENITY *n* pl. -TIES the quality of being pleasant or agreeable

AMENT *n* pl. -S a mentally deficient person

AMENTIA *n* pl. -S mental deficiency

AMERCE *v* AMERCED, AMERCING, AMERCES to punish by imposing an arbitrary fine

AMERCER *n* pl. -S one that amerces

AMESACE *n* pl. -S ambsace

AMETHYST *n* pl. -S a variety of quartz

AMI *n* pl. -S a friend

AMIA *n* pl. -S a freshwater fish

AMIABLE *adj* having a pleasant disposition AMIABLY *adv*

AMIANTUS *n* pl. -ES a variety of asbestos

AMICABLE *adj* friendly AMICABLY *adv*

AMICE *n* pl. -S a vestment worn about the neck and shoulders

AMICUS *n* pl. AMICI one not party to a lawsuit but permitted by the court to advise it

AMID *n* pl. -S amide

AMIDASE *n* pl. -S an enzyme

AMIDE *n* pl. -S a type of chemical compound AMIDIC *adj*

AMIDIN *n* pl. -S the soluble matter of starch

AMIDINE *n* pl. -S a type of chemical compound

AMIDO *adj* containing an amide united with an acid radical

AMIDOGEN *n* pl. -S a univalent chemical radical

AMIDOL *n* pl. -S a chemical compound

AMIDONE *n* pl. -S a chemical compound

AMIDSHIP *adv* toward the middle of a ship

AMIDST *prep* in the midst of

AMIE *n* pl. -S a female friend

AMIGA *n* pl. -S a female friend

AMIGO *n* pl. -GOS a friend

AMIN *n* pl. -S amine

AMINE *n* pl. -S a type of chemical compound **AMINIC** *adj*

AMINITY *n* pl. -TIES the state of being an amine

AMINO *adj* containing an amine united with a nonacid radical

AMIR *n* pl. -S a Muslim prince or governor

AMIRATE *n* pl. -S the rank of an amir

AMISS *adj* being out of proper order

AMITIES pl. of amity

AMITOSIS *n* pl. -TOSES a type of cell division **AMITOTIC** *adj*

AMITROLE *n* pl. -S an herbicide

AMITY *n* pl. -TIES friendship

AMMETER *n* pl. -S an instrument for measuring amperage

AMMINE *n* pl. -S a type of chemical compound

AMMINO *adj* pertaining to an ammine

AMMO *n* pl. -MOS ammunition

AMMOCETE *n* pl. -S the larva of a lamprey

AMMONAL *n* pl. -S a powerful explosive

AMMONIA *n* pl. -S a pungent gas

AMMONIAC *n* pl. -S a gum resin

AMMONIC *adj* pertaining to ammonia

AMMONIFY *v* -FIED, -FYING, -FIES to treat with ammonia

AMMONITE *n* pl. -S the coiled shell of an extinct mollusk

AMMONIUM *n* pl. -S a univalent chemical radical

AMMONO *adj* containing ammonia

AMMONOID *n* pl. -S ammonite

AMNESIA *n* pl. -S loss of memory

AMNESIAC *n* pl. -S one suffering from amnesia

AMNESIC *n* pl. -S amnesiac

AMNESTIC *adj* pertaining to amnesia

AMNESTY *v* -TIED, -TYING, -TIES to pardon

AMNION *n* pl. -NIONS or -NIA a membranous sac enclosing an embryo **AMNIC, AMNIONIC, AMNIOTIC** *adj*

AMNIOTE *n* pl. -S a vertebrate that develops an amnion during the embryonic stage

AMOEBA *n* pl. -BAS or -BAE a unicellular microscopic organism **AMOEBAN, AMOEBIC, AMOEBOID** *adj*

AMOEBEAN *adj* amebean

AMOK *n* pl. -S a murderous frenzy

AMOLE *n* pl. -S a plant root used as a substitute for soap

AMONG *prep* in the midst of

AMONGST *prep* among

AMORAL *adj* lacking a sense of right and wrong **AMORALLY** *adv*

AMORETTO *n* pl. -TI or -TOS a cupid

AMORINO *n* pl. -NI an amoretto

AMORIST *n* pl. -S a lover

AMOROSO *adv* tenderly — used as a musical direction

AMOROUS *adj* pertaining to love

AMORT *adj* being without life

AMORTISE *v* -TISED, -TISING, -TISES to amortize

AMORTIZE *v* -TIZED, -TIZING, -TIZES to liquidate gradually, as a debt

AMOSITE *n* pl. -S a type of asbestos

AMOTION *n* pl. -S the removal of a corporate officer from his office

AMOUNT *v* -ED, -ING, -S to combine to yield a sum

AMOUR *n* pl. -S a love affair

AMP *n* pl. -S ampere

AMPERAGE *n* pl. -S the strength of an electric current expressed in amperes

AMPERE *n* pl. -S a unit of electric current strength

AMPHIBIA *n/pl* organisms adapted for life both on land and in water

AMPHIOXI *n/pl* lancelets

AMPHIPOD *n* pl. -S a small crustacean

AMPHORA *n* pl. -RAE or -RAS a narrow-necked jar used in ancient Greece **AMPHORAL** *adj*

AMPLE *adj* -PLER, -PLEST abundant **AMPLY** *adv*

AMPLEXUS *n* pl. -ES the mating embrace of frogs

AMPLIFY *v* -FIED, -FYING, -FIES to make larger or more powerful

AMPOULE *n* pl. -S ampule

AMPUL *n* pl. -S ampule

AMPULE *n* pl. -S a small glass vial

AMPULLA *n* pl. -LAE a globular bottle used in ancient Rome **AMPULLAR** *adj*

AMPUTATE *v* -TATED, -TATING, -TATES to cut off by surgical means

AMPUTEE *n* pl. -S one that has had a limb amputated

AMREETA *n* pl. -S amrita

AMRITA   *n* pl. -S a beverage that bestows immortality in Hindu mythology

AMTRAC   *n* pl. -S a military vehicle equipped to move on land and water

AMTRACK   *n* pl. -S amtrac

AMU   *n* pl. -S a unit of mass

AMUCK   *n* pl. -S amok

AMULET   *n* pl. -S an object worn to protect against evil or injury

AMUSE   *v* AMUSED, AMUSING, AMUSES to occupy pleasingly **AMUSABLE** *adj* **AMUSEDLY** *adv*

AMUSER   *n* pl. -S one that amuses

AMUSIA   *n* pl. -S the inability to recognize musical sounds

AMUSIVE   *adj* amusing

AMYGDALA   *n* pl. -LAE an almond-shaped anatomical part

AMYGDALE   *n* pl. -S amygdule

AMYGDULE   *n* pl. -S a small gas bubble in lava

AMYL   *n* pl. -S a univalent radical

AMYLASE   *n* pl. -S an enzyme

AMYLENE   *n* pl. -S a flammable liquid

AMYLIC   *adj* pertaining to amyl

AMYLOGEN   *n* pl. -S amylose

AMYLOID   *n* pl. -S a hard protein deposit resulting from degeneration of tissue

AMYLOSE   *n* pl. -S the relatively soluble component of starch

AMYLUM   *n* pl. -S starch

AN   *indefinite article* — used before words beginning with a vowel sound

ANA   *n* pl. -S a collection of miscellaneous information about a particular subject

ANABAENA   *n* pl. -S a freshwater alga

ANABAS   *n* pl. -ES a freshwater fish

ANABASIS   *n* pl. -ASES a military advance

ANABATIC   *adj* pertaining to rising wind currents

ANABLEPS   *n* pl. -ES a freshwater fish

ANABOLIC   *adj* pertaining to a process by which food is built up into protoplasm

ANACONDA   *n* pl. -S a large snake

ANADEM   *n* pl. -S a wreath for the head

ANAEMIA   *n* pl. -S anemia **ANAEMIC** *adj*

ANAEROBE   *n* pl. -S an organism that does not require oxygen to live

ANAGLYPH   *n* pl. -S a type of carved ornament

ANAGOGE   *n* pl. -S a spiritual interpretation of words **ANAGOGIC** *adj*

ANAGOGY   *n* pl. -GIES anagoge

ANAGRAM   *v* -GRAMMED, -GRAMMING, -GRAMS to transpose the letters of a word or phrase to form a new one

ANAL   *adj* pertaining to the anus

ANALCIME   *n* pl. -S analcite

ANALCITE   *n* pl. -S a mineral

ANALECTA   *n/pl* analects

ANALECTS   *n/pl* selections from a literary work or group of works

ANALEMMA   *n* pl. -MAS or -MATA a type of graduated scale

ANALGIA   *n* pl. -S inability to feel pain

ANALITY   *n* pl. -TIES a type of psychological state

ANALLY   *adv* at or through the anus

ANALOG   *n* pl. -S analogue

ANALOGIC   *adj* pertaining to an analogy

ANALOGUE   *n* pl. -S something that bears an analogy to something else

ANALOGY   *n* pl. -GIES resemblance in some respects between things otherwise unlike

ANALYSE   *v* -LYSED, -LYSING, -LYSES to analyze

ANALYSER   *n* pl. -S analyzer

ANALYSIS   *n* pl. -YSES the separation of a whole into its parts

ANALYST   *n* pl. -S one that analyzes

ANALYTIC   *adj* pertaining to analysis

ANALYZE   *v* -LYZED, -LYZING, -LYZES to subject to analysis

ANALYZER   *n* pl. -S one that analyzes

ANANKE   *n* pl. -S a compelling necessity in ancient Greek religion

ANAPAEST   *n* pl. -S anapest

ANAPEST   *n* pl. -S a type of metrical foot

ANAPHASE   *n* pl. -S a stage of mitosis

ANAPHOR   *n* pl. -S a word or phrase that takes reference from a preceding word or phrase

ANAPHORA   *n* pl. -S the repetition of a word or phrase at the beginning of several successive verses or sentences

ANARCH   *n* pl. -S an advocate of anarchy

ANARCHY   *n* pl. -CHIES absence of government **ANARCHIC** *adj*

ANASARCA n pl. -S a form of dropsy
ANATASE n pl. -S a mineral
ANATHEMA n pl. -MAS or -MATA a formal ecclesiastical ban or curse
ANATOMY n pl. -MIES the structure of an organism **ANATOMIC** adj
ANATOXIN n pl. -S a toxoid
ANATTO n pl. -TOS annatto
ANCESTOR v -ED, -ING, -S to be an ancestor (a person from whom one is descended) of
ANCESTRY n pl. -TRIES a line or body of ancestors
ANCHOR v -ED, -ING, -S to secure by means of an anchor (a device for holding a floating vessel in place)
ANCHORET n pl. -S a recluse
ANCHOVY n pl. -VIES a small food fish
ANCHUSA n pl. -S a hairy-stemmed plant
ANCHUSIN n pl. -S a red dye
ANCIENT adj -CIENTER, -CIENTEST of or pertaining to time long past
ANCIENT n pl. -S one who lived in ancient times
ANCILLA n pl. -LAE or -LAS a helper
ANCON n pl. -ES the elbow **ANCONAL, ANCONEAL, ANCONOID** adj
ANCONE n pl. -S ancon
ANCRESS n pl. -ES a female recluse
AND n pl. -S an added condition or stipulation
ANDANTE n pl. -S a moderately slow musical passage
ANDESITE n pl. -S a volcanic rock
ANDESYTE n pl. -S andesite
ANDIRON n pl. -S a metal support for holding wood in a fireplace
ANDROGEN n pl. -S a male sex hormone
ANDROID n pl. -S a synthetic man
ANE n pl. -S one
ANEAR v -ED, -ING, -S to approach
ANECDOTE n pl. -DOTES or -DOTA a brief story
ANECHOIC adj neither having nor producing echoes
ANELE v ANELED, ANELING, ANELES to anoint
ANEMIA n pl. -S a disorder of the blood **ANEMIC** adj
ANEMONE n pl. -S a flowering plant
ANEMOSIS n pl. -MOSES separation of rings of growth in timber due to wind
ANENST prep anent

ANENT prep in regard to
ANERGIA n pl. -S anergy
ANERGY n pl. -GIES lack of energy **ANERGIC** adj
ANEROID n pl. -S a type of barometer
ANESTRUS n pl. -TRI a period of sexual dormancy
ANETHOL n pl. -S anethole
ANETHOLE n pl. -S a chemical compound
ANEURIN n pl. -S thiamine
ANEURISM n pl. -S aneurysm
ANEURYSM n pl. -S an abnormal blood-filled dilation of a blood vessel
ANEW adv once more
ANGA n pl. -S any of the eight practices of yoga
ANGAKOK n pl. -S an Eskimo medicine man
ANGARIA n pl. -S angary
ANGARY n pl. -RIES the right of a warring state to seize neutral property
ANGEL v -ED, -ING, -S to support financially
ANGELIC adj pertaining to an angel (a winged celestial being)
ANGELICA n pl. -S an aromatic herb
ANGELUS n pl. -ES a Roman Catholic prayer
ANGER v -ED, -ING, -S to make angry
ANGERLY adv in an angry manner
ANGINA n pl. -S a disease marked by spasmodic attacks of intense pain **ANGINAL, ANGINOSE, ANGINOUS** adj
ANGIOMA n pl. -MAS or -MATA a tumor composed of blood or lymph vessels
ANGLE v -GLED, -GLING, -GLES to fish with a hook and line
ANGLEPOD n pl. -S a flowering plant
ANGLER n pl. -S one that angles
ANGLICE adv in readily understood English
ANGLING n pl. -S the sport of fishing
ANGORA n pl. -S the long, silky hair of a domestic goat
ANGRY adj -GRIER, -GRIEST feeling strong displeasure or hostility **ANGRILY** adv
ANGST n pl. -S a feeling of anxiety or dread
ANGSTROM n pl. -S a unit of length
ANGUINE adj resembling a snake
ANGUISH v -ED, -ING, -ES to suffer extreme pain

ANGULAR *adj* having sharp corners

ANGULATE *v* -LATED, -LATING, -LATES to make angular

ANGULOSE *adj* angular

ANGULOUS *adj* angular

ANHINGA *n* pl. -S an aquatic bird

ANI *n* pl. -S a tropical American bird

ANIL *n* pl. -S a West Indian shrub

ANILE *adj* resembling an old woman

ANILIN *n* pl. -S aniline

ANILINE *n* pl. -S a chemical compound

ANILITY *n* pl. -TIES the state of being anile

ANIMA *n* pl. -S the soul

ANIMAL *n* pl. -S a living organism typically capable of voluntary motion and sensation ANIMALIC *adj*

ANIMALLY *adv* physically

ANIMATE *v* -MATED, -MATING, -MATES to give life to

ANIMATER *n* pl. -S animator

ANIMATO *adv* in a lively manner — used as a musical direction

ANIMATOR *n* pl. -S one that animates

ANIME *n* pl. -S a resin obtained from a tropical tree

ANIMI *n* pl. -S anime

ANIMISM *n* pl. -S the belief that souls may exist apart from bodies

ANIMIST *n* pl. -S an adherent of animism

ANIMUS *n* pl. -ES a feeling of hostility

ANION *n* pl. -S a negatively charged ion ANIONIC *adj*

ANISE *n* pl. -S a North African plant

ANISEED *n* pl. -S the seed of the anise used as a flavoring

ANISETTE *n* pl. -S a liqueur flavored with aniseed

ANISIC *adj* pertaining to an anise

ANISOLE *n* pl. -S a chemical compound

ANKERITE *n* pl. -S a mineral

ANKH *n* pl. -S an Egyptian symbol of enduring life

ANKLE *v* -KLED, -KLING, -KLES to walk

ANKLET *n* pl. -S an ornament for the ankle

ANKUS *n* pl. -ES an elephant goad

ANKUSH *n* pl. -ES ankus

ANKYLOSE *v* -LOSED, -LOSING, -LOSES to unite or grow together, as the bones of a joint

ANLACE *n* pl. -S a medieval dagger

ANLAGE *n* pl. -GEN or -GES the initial cell structure from which an embryonic organ develops

ANLAS *n* pl. -ES anlace

ANNA *n* pl. -S a former coin of India and Pakistan

ANNAL *n* pl. -S a record of a single year

ANNALIST *n* pl. -S a historian

ANNATES *n/pl* the first year's revenue of a bishop paid to the pope

ANNATTO *n* pl. -TOS a yellowish-red dye

ANNEAL *v* -ED, -ING, -S to toughen

ANNEALER *n* pl. -S one that anneals

ANNELID *n* pl. -S any of a phylum of segmented worms

ANNEX *v* -ED, -ING, -ES to add or attach

ANNEXE *n* pl. -S something added or attached

ANNOTATE *v* -TATED, -TATING, -TATES to furnish with critical or explanatory notes

ANNOUNCE *v* -NOUNCED, -NOUNCING, -NOUNCES to make known publicly

ANNOY *v* -ED, -ING, -S to be troublesome to

ANNOYER *n* pl. -S one that annoys

ANNUAL *n* pl. -S a publication issued once a year

ANNUALLY *adv* once a year

ANNUITY *n* pl. -TIES an allowance or income paid at regular intervals

ANNUL *v* -NULLED, -NULLING, -NULS to make or declare void or invalid

ANNULAR *adj* shaped like a ring

ANNULATE *adj* composed of or furnished with rings

ANNULET *n* pl. -S a small ring

ANNULI *a* pl. of annulus

ANNULLED past tense of annul

ANNULLING present participle of annul

ANNULUS *n* pl. -LI or -LUSES a ring or ringlike part ANNULOSE *adj*

ANOA *n* pl. -S a wild ox

ANODE *n* pl. -S a positively charged electrode ANODAL, ANODIC *adj* ANODALLY *adv*

ANODIZE *v* -IZED, -IZING, -IZES to coat with a protective film by chemical means

ANODYNE *n* pl. -S a medicine that relieves pain ANODYNIC *adj*

ANOINT   v -ED, -ING, -S to apply oil to as a sacred rite

ANOINTER   n pl. -S one that anoints

ANOLE   n pl. -S a tropical lizard

ANOLYTE   n pl. -S the part of an electricity-conducting solution nearest the anode

ANOMALY   n pl. -LIES a deviation from the common rule, type, or form

ANOMIE   n pl. -S a collapse of the social structures governing a given society **ANOMIC** adj

ANOMY   n pl. -MIES anomie

ANON   adv at another time

ANONYM   n pl. -S a false or assumed name

ANOOPSIA   n pl. -S a visual defect

ANOPIA   n pl. -S anoopsia

ANOPSIA   n pl. -S anoopsia

ANORAK   n pl. -S a parka

ANORETIC   n pl. -S anorexic

ANOREXIA   n pl. -S loss of appetite

ANOREXIC   n pl. -S one affected with anorexia

ANOREXY   n pl. -OREXIES anorexia

ANORTHIC   adj denoting a certain type of crystal system

ANOSMIA   n pl. -S loss of the sense of smell **ANOSMIC** adj

ANOTHER   adj one more

ANOVULAR   adj not involving ovulation

ANOXEMIA   n pl. -S a disorder of the blood **ANOXEMIC** adj

ANOXIA   n pl. -S absence of oxygen **ANOXIC** adj

ANSA   n pl. -SAE the projecting part of Saturn's rings

ANSATE   adj having a handle

ANSATED   adj ansate

ANSERINE   n pl. -S a chemical compound

ANSEROUS   adj silly

ANSWER   v -ED, -ING, -S to say, write, or act in return

ANSWERER   n pl. -S one that answers

ANT   n pl. -S a small insect

ANTA   n pl. -TAE or -TAS a pilaster formed at the termination of a wall

ANTACID   n pl. -S a substance that neutralizes acid

ANTALGIC   n pl. -S an anodyne

ANTBEAR   n pl. -S an aardvark

ANTE   v ANTED or ANTEED, ANTEING, ANTES to put a fixed stake into the pot before the cards are dealt in poker

ANTEATER   n pl. -S any of several mammals that feed on ants

ANTECEDE   v -CEDED, -CEDING, -CEDES to precede

ANTED   a past tense of ante

ANTEDATE   v -DATED, -DATING, -DATES to be of an earlier date than

ANTEFIX   n pl. -FIXES or -FIXA an upright ornament at the eaves of a tiled roof

ANTELOPE   n pl. -S a ruminant mammal

ANTENNA   n pl. -NAE or -NAS a metallic device for sending or receiving radio waves **ANTENNAL** adj

ANTEPAST   n pl. -S an appetizer

ANTERIOR   adj situated in or toward the front

ANTEROOM   n pl. -S a waiting room

ANTETYPE   n pl. -S an earlier form

ANTEVERT   v -ED, -ING, -S to displace by tipping forward

ANTHELIA   n/pl halolike areas seen in the sky opposite the sun

ANTHELIX   n pl. -LICES or -LIXES the inner curved ridge on the cartilage of the external ear

ANTHEM   v -ED, -ING, -S to praise in a song

ANTHEMIA   n/pl decorative floral patterns used in Greek art

ANTHER   n pl. -S the pollen-bearing part of a stamen **ANTHERAL** adj

ANTHERID   n pl. -S a male reproductive organ of certain plants

ANTHESIS   n pl. -THESES the full bloom of a flower

ANTHILL   n pl. -S a mound formed by ants in building their nest

ANTHODIA   n/pl flower heads of certain plants

ANTHOID   adj resembling a flower

ANTHRAX   n pl. -THRACES an infectious disease

ANTI   n pl. -S one that is opposed

ANTIAIR   adj directed against attacking aircraft

ANTIAR   n pl. -S an arrow poison

ANTIARIN   n pl. -S antiar

ANTIATOM   n pl. -S an atom comprised of antiparticles

ANTIBIAS   adj opposed to bias

ANTIBODY   n pl. -BODIES a body protein that produces immunity against certain microorganisms or toxins

ANTIBOSS   adj opposed to bosses

ANTIBUG *adj* effective against bugs

ANTIC *v* -TICKED, -TICKING, -TICS to act in a clownish manner

ANTICAR *adj* opposed to cars

ANTICITY *adj* opposed to cities

ANTICK *v* -ED, -ING, -S to antic

ANTICLY *adv* in a clownish manner

ANTICOLD *adj* effective against the common cold

ANTICULT *adj* opposed to cults

ANTIDORA *n/pl* holy breads

ANTIDOTE *v* -DOTED, -DOTING, -DOTES to counteract the effects of a poison with a remedy

ANTIDRUG *adj* opposed to illicit drugs

ANTIFAT *adj* preventing the formation of fat

ANTIFLU *adj* combating the flu

ANTIFOAM *adj* reducing or preventing foam

ANTIFUR *adj* opposed to the wearing of animal furs

ANTIGAY *adj* opposed to homosexuals

ANTIGEN *n* pl. -S a substance that stimulates the production of antibodies

ANTIGENE *n* pl. -S antigen

ANTIGUN *adj* opposed to guns

ANTIHERO *n* pl. -ROES a protagonist who is notably lacking in heroic qualities

ANTIJAM *adj* blocking interfering signals

ANTIKING *n* pl. -S a usurping king

ANTILEAK *adj* preventing leaks

ANTILEFT *adj* opposed to leftism

ANTILIFE *adj* opposed to life

ANTILOCK *adj* designed to prevent the wheels of a vehicle from locking

ANTILOG *n* pl. -S the number corresponding to a given logarithm

ANTILOGY *n* pl. -GIES a contradiction in terms or ideas

ANTIMALE *adj* opposed to men

ANTIMAN *adj* antimale

ANTIMASK *n* pl. -S a comic performance between the acts of a masque

ANTIMERE *n* pl. -S a part of an organism symmetrical with a part on the opposite side of the main axis

ANTIMONY *n* pl. -NIES a metallic element

ANTING *n* pl. -S the deliberate placing, by certain birds, of living ants among the feathers

ANTINODE *n* pl. -S a region between adjacent nodes

ANTINOMY *n* pl. -MIES a contradiction between two seemingly valid principles

ANTINUKE *adj* opposing the use of nuclear power plants or nuclear weapons

ANTIPHON *n* pl. -S a psalm or hymn sung responsively

ANTIPILL *adj* opposing the use of contraceptive pills

ANTIPODE *n* pl. -S an exact opposite

ANTIPOLE *n* pl. -S the opposite pole

ANTIPOPE *n* pl. -S one claiming to be pope in opposition to the one chosen by church law

ANTIPORN *adj* opposed to pornography

ANTIPOT *adj* opposing the use of pot (marijuana)

ANTIPYIC *n* pl. -S a medicine that prevents the formation of pus

ANTIQUE *v* -TIQUED, -TIQUING, -TIQUES to give an appearance of age to

ANTIQUER *n* pl. -S one that antiques

ANTIRAPE *adj* concerned with preventing rape

ANTIRED *adj* opposed to communism

ANTIRIOT *adj* designed to prevent or end riots

ANTIROCK *adj* opposed to rock music

ANTIROLL *adj* designed to reduce roll

ANTIRUST *n* pl. -S something that prevents rust

ANTISAG *adj* designed to prevent sagging

ANTISERA *n/pl* serums that contain antibodies

ANTISEX *adj* opposed to sexual activity

ANTISHIP *adj* designed for use against ships

ANTISKID *adj* designed to prevent skidding

ANTISLIP *adj* designed to prevent slipping

ANTISMOG *adj* designed to reduce pollutants that cause smog

ANTISMUT *adj* opposed to pornography

ANTISNOB *adj* opposed to snobbery

ANTISTAT *adj* designed to prevent the buildup of static electricity

ANTITANK *adj* designed to combat tanks

ANTITAX *adj* opposing taxes

ANTITYPE *n* pl. -S an opposite type

ANTIWAR *adj* opposing war

ANTIWEAR *adj* designed to reduce the effects of long or hard use

ANTIWEED *adj* concerned with the destruction of weeds

ANTLER *n* pl. -S the horn of an animal of the deer family **ANTLERED** *adj*

ANTLIKE *adj* resembling an ant

ANTLION *n* pl. -S a predatory insect

ANTONYM *n* pl. -S a word opposite in meaning to another

ANTONYMY *n* pl. -MIES the state of being an antonym

ANTRA a pl. of antrum

ANTRAL *adj* pertaining to an antrum

ANTRE *n* pl. -S a cave

ANTRORSE *adj* directed forward or upward

ANTRUM *n* pl. -TRA or -TRUMS a cavity in a bone

ANTSY *adj* -SIER, -SIEST fidgety

ANURAL *adj* anurous

ANURAN *n* pl. -S a frog or toad

ANURESIS *n* pl. -RESES inability to urinate **ANURETIC** *adj*

ANURIA *n* pl. -S absence of urine **ANURIC** *adj*

ANUROUS *adj* having no tail

ANUS *n* pl. -ES the excretory opening at the end of the alimentary canal

ANVIL *v* -VILED, -VILING, -VILS or -VILLED, -VILLING, -VILS to shape on an anvil (a heavy iron block)

ANVILTOP *n* pl. -S an anvil-shaped cloud mass

ANXIETY *n* pl. -ETIES painful or apprehensive uneasiness of mind

ANXIOUS *adj* full of anxiety

ANY *adj* one, no matter which

ANYBODY *n* pl. -BODIES a person of some importance

ANYHOW *adv* in any way

ANYMORE *adv* at the present time

ANYONE *pron* any person

ANYPLACE *adv* in any place

ANYTHING *n* pl. -S a thing of any kind

ANYTIME *adv* at any time

ANYWAY *adv* in any way

ANYWAYS *adv* anyway

ANYWHERE *n* pl. -S any place

ANYWISE *adv* in any way

AORIST *n* pl. -S a verb tense **AORISTIC** *adj*

AORTA *n* pl. -TAS or -TAE a main artery **AORTAL, AORTIC** *adj*

AOUDAD *n* pl. -S a wild sheep

APACE *adv* swiftly

APACHE *n* pl. -S a Parisian gangster

APAGOGE *n* pl. -S establishment of a thesis by showing its contrary to be absurd **APAGOGIC** *adj*

APANAGE *n* pl. -S appanage

APAREJO *n* pl. -JOS a type of saddle

APART *adv* not together

APATETIC *adj* having coloration serving as natural camouflage

APATHY *n* pl. -THIES lack of emotion

APATITE *n* pl. -S a mineral

APE *v* APED, APING, APES to mimic

APEAK *adv* in a vertical position

APEEK *adv* apeak

APELIKE *adj* resembling an ape (a large, tailless primate)

APER *n* pl. -S one that apes

APERCU *n* pl. -S a brief summary

APERIENT *n* pl. -S a mild laxative

APERITIF *n* pl. -S an alcoholic drink taken before a meal

APERTURE *n* pl. -S an opening

APERY *n* pl. -ERIES the act of aping

APETALY *n* pl. -ALIES the state of having no petals

APEX *n* pl. APEXES or APICES the highest point

APHAGIA *n* pl. -S inability to swallow

APHANITE *n* pl. -S an igneous rock

APHASIA *n* pl. -S loss of the ability to use words

APHASIAC *n* pl. -S one suffering from aphasia

APHASIC *n* pl. -S aphasiac

APHELION *n* pl. -ELIA or -ELIONS the point in a planetary orbit farthest from the sun **APHELIAN** *adj*

APHESIS *n* pl. -ESES the loss of an unstressed vowel from the beginning of a word **APHETIC** *adj*

APHID *n* pl. -S any of a family of small, soft-bodied insects

APHIDIAN *n* pl. -S an aphid

APHIS *n* pl. APHIDES an aphid

APHOLATE *n* pl. -S a chemical used to control houseflies

APHONIA *n* pl. -S loss of voice

APHONIC *n* pl. -S one affected with aphonia

APHORISE v -RISED, -RISING, -RISES to aphorize

APHORISM n pl. -S a brief statement of a truth or principle

APHORIST n pl. -S one that aphorizes

APHORIZE v -RIZED, -RIZING, -RIZES to write or speak in aphorisms

APHOTIC adj lacking light

APHTHA n pl. -THAE a small blister in the mouth or stomach **APHTHOUS** adj

APHYLLY n pl. -LIES the state of being leafless

APIAN adj pertaining to bees

APIARIAN n pl. -S an apiarist

APIARIST n pl. -S a person who raises bees

APIARY n pl. -ARIES a place where bees are kept

APICAL n pl. -S a sound articulated with the apex (tip) of the tongue

APICALLY adv at or toward the apex

APICES a pl. of apex

APICULUS n pl. -LI a sharp point at the end of a leaf

APIECE adv for each one

APIMANIA n pl. -S an excessive interest in bees

APING present participle of ape

APIOLOGY n pl. -GIES the study of bees

APISH adj slavishly or foolishly imitative **APISHLY** adv

APLASIA n pl. -S defective development of an organ or part

APLASTIC adj not plastic

APLENTY adj being in sufficient quantity

APLITE n pl. -S a fine-grained rock **APLITIC** adj

APLOMB n pl. -S self-confidence

APNEA n pl. -S temporary cessation of respiration **APNEAL, APNEIC** adj

APNOEA n pl. -S apnea **APNOEAL, APNOEIC** adj

APOAPSIS n pl. -APSIDES the high point in an orbit

APOCARP n pl. -S a fruit having separated carpels

APOCARPY n pl. -PIES the state of being an apocarp

APOCOPE n pl. -S an omission of the last sound of a word **APOCOPIC** adj

APOCRINE adj pertaining to a type of gland

APOD n pl. -S an apodal animal

APODAL adj having no feet or footlike appendages

APODOSIS n pl. -OSES the main clause of a conditional sentence

APODOUS adj apodal

APOGAMY n pl. -MIES a form of plant reproduction **APOGAMIC** adj

APOGEE n pl. -S the point in the orbit of a body which is farthest from the earth **APOGEAL, APOGEAN, APOGEIC** adj

APOLLO n pl. -LOS a handsome young man

APOLOG n pl. -S apologue

APOLOGAL adj pertaining to an apologue

APOLOGIA n pl. -GIAS or -GIAE a formal justification or defense

APOLOGUE n pl. -S an allegory

APOLOGY n pl. -GIES an expression of regret for some error or offense

APOLUNE n pl. -S the point in the orbit of a body which is farthest from the moon

APOMICT n pl. -S an organism produced by apomixis

APOMIXIS n pl. -MIXES a type of reproductive process

APOPHONY n pl. -NIES ablaut

APOPHYGE n pl. -S a concave curve in a column

APOPLEXY n pl. -PLEXIES a sudden loss of sensation and muscular control

APORT adv on or toward the left side of a ship

APOSPORY n pl. -RIES a type of reproduction without spore formation

APOSTACY n pl. -CIES apostasy

APOSTASY n pl. -SIES an abandonment of one's faith or principles

APOSTATE n pl. -S one who commits apostasy

APOSTIL n pl. -S a marginal note

APOSTLE n pl. -S a disciple sent forth by Christ to preach the gospel

APOTHECE n pl. -S a spore-producing organ of certain fungi

APOTHEGM n pl. -S a maxim

APOTHEM n pl. -S the perpendicular from the center to any side of a regular polygon

APPAL v -PALLED, -PALLING, -PALS to appall

APPALL *v* -ED, -ING, -S to fill with horror or dismay

APPANAGE *n* pl. -S land or revenue granted to a member of a royal family

APPARAT *n* pl. -S a political organization

APPAREL *v* -ELED, -ELING, -ELS or -ELLED, -ELLING, -ELS to provide with outer garments

APPARENT *adj* easily seen

APPEAL *v* -ED, -ING, -S to make an earnest request

APPEALER *n* pl. -S one that appeals

APPEAR *v* -ED, -ING, -S to come into view

APPEASE *v* -PEASED, -PEASING, -PEASES to bring to a state of peace or contentment

APPEASER *n* pl. -S one that appeases

APPEL *n* pl. -S a feint in fencing

APPELLEE *n* pl. -S the defendant in a type of judicial proceeding

APPELLOR *n* pl. -S a confessed criminal who accuses an accomplice

APPEND *v* -ED, -ING, -S to add as a supplement

APPENDIX *n* pl. -DIXES or -DICES a collection of supplementary material at the end of a book

APPESTAT *n* pl. -S the mechanism in the central nervous system that regulates appetite

APPETENT *adj* marked by strong desire

APPETITE *n* pl. -S a desire for food or drink

APPLAUD *v* -ED, -ING, -S to express approval by clapping the hands

APPLAUSE *n* pl. -S the sound made by persons applauding

APPLE *n* pl. -S an edible fruit

APPLIED past tense of apply

APPLIER *n* pl. -S one that applies

APPLIQUE *v* -QUED, -QUEING, -QUES to apply as a decoration to a larger surface

APPLY *v* -PLIED, -PLYING, -PLIES to bring into contact with something

APPOINT *v* -ED, -ING, -S to name or assign to a position or office

APPOSE *v* -POSED, -POSING, -POSES to place side by side

APPOSER *n* pl. -S one that apposes

APPOSITE *adj* relevant

APPRAISE *v* -PRAISED, -PRAISING, -PRAISES to set a value on

APPRISE *v* -PRISED, -PRISING, -PRISES to notify

APPRISER *n* pl. -S one that apprises

APPRIZE *v* -PRIZED, -PRIZING, -PRIZES to appraise

APPRIZER *n* pl. -S one that apprizes

APPROACH *v* -ED, -ING, -ES to come near or nearer to

APPROVAL *n* pl. -S the act of approving

APPROVE *v* -PROVED, -PROVING, -PROVES to regard favorably

APPROVER *n* pl. -S one that approves

APPULSE *n* pl. -S the approach of one moving body toward another

APRAXIA *n* pl. -S loss of the ability to perform coordinated movements **APRACTIC, APRAXIC** *adj*

APRES *prep* after

APRICOT *n* pl. -S an edible fruit

APRON *v* -ED, -ING, -S to provide with an apron (a garment worn to protect one's clothing)

APROPOS *adj* relevant

APROTIC *adj* being a type of solvent

APSE *n* pl. -S a domed, semicircular projection of a building **APSIDAL** *adj*

APSIS *n* pl. -SIDES an apse

APT *adj* APTER, APTEST suitable

APTERAL *adj* apterous

APTERIUM *n* pl. -RIA a bare area of skin between feathers

APTEROUS *adj* having no wings

APTERYX *n* pl. -ES the kiwi

APTITUDE *n* pl. -S an ability

APTLY *adv* in an apt manner

APTNESS *n* pl. -ES the quality of being apt

APYRASE *n* pl. -S an enzyme

APYRETIC *adj* having no fever

AQUA *n* pl. AQUAE or AQUAS water

AQUACADE *n* pl. -S a swimming and diving exhibition

AQUANAUT *n* pl. -S a scuba diver trained to live in underwater installations

AQUARIA a pl. of aquarium

AQUARIAL *adj* pertaining to an aquarium

AQUARIAN *n* pl. -S a member of the old sects that used water rather than wine in religious ceremonies

AQUARIST *n* pl. -S one who keeps an aquarium

AQUARIUM *n* pl. -IUMS or -IA a water-filled enclosure in which aquatic animals are kept

AQUATIC *n* pl. -S an organism living or growing in or near water

AQUATINT *v* -ED, -ING, -S to etch, using a certain process

AQUATONE *n* pl. -S a type of printing process

AQUAVIT *n* pl. -S a Scandinavian liquor

AQUEDUCT *n* pl. -S a water conduit

AQUEOUS *adj* pertaining to water

AQUIFER *n* pl. -S a water-bearing rock formation

AQUILINE *adj* curving like an eagle's beak

AQUIVER *adj* quivering

AR *n* pl. -S the letter R

ARABESK *n* pl. -S a design of intertwined floral figures

ARABIC *adj* derived from gum arabic

ARABICA *n* pl. -S an evergreen shrub that produces coffee beans

ARABIZE *v* -IZED, -IZING, -IZES to cause to acquire Arabic customs

ARABLE *n* pl. -S land suitable for cultivation

ARACEOUS *adj* belonging to the arum family of plants

ARACHNID *n* pl. -S any of a class of segmented invertebrate animals

ARAK *n* pl. -S arrack

ARAMID *n* pl. -S a type of chemical compound

ARANEID *n* pl. -S a spider

ARAPAIMA *n* pl. -S a large food fish

ARAROBA *n* pl. -S a Brazilian tree

ARB *n* pl. -S a type of stock trader

ARBALEST *n* pl. -S a type of crossbow

ARBALIST *n* pl. -S arbalest

ARBELEST *n* pl. -S arbalest

ARBITER *n* pl. -S one chosen or appointed to judge a disputed issue **ARBITRAL** *adj*

ARBOR *n* pl. -S a shady garden shelter

ARBOR *n* pl. -ES a tree

ARBOREAL *adj* living in trees

ARBORED *adj* having trees

ARBORETA *n/pl* places for the study and exhibition of trees

ARBORIST *n* pl. -S a tree specialist

ARBORIZE *v* -IZED, -IZING, -IZES to form many branches

ARBOROUS *adj* pertaining to trees

ARBOUR *n* pl. -S a shady garden shelter **ARBOURED** *adj*

ARBUSCLE *n* pl. -S a dwarf tree

ARBUTE *n* pl. -S an evergreen tree **ARBUTEAN** *adj*

ARBUTUS *n* pl. -ES an evergreen tree

ARC *v* ARCED, ARCING, ARCS or ARCKED, ARCKING, ARCS to move in a curved course

ARCADE *v* -CADED, -CADING, -CADES to provide with an arcade (a series of arches)

ARCADIA *n* pl. -S a region of simple pleasure and quiet

ARCADIAN *n* pl. -S one who lives in an arcadia

ARCADING *n* pl. -S an arcade

ARCANE *adj* mysterious

ARCANUM *n* pl. -NA or -NUMS a mystery

ARCATURE *n* pl. -S a small arcade

ARCH *v* -ED, -ING, -ES to bend like an arch (a curved structure spanning an opening)

ARCHAIC *adj* pertaining to an earlier time

ARCHAISE *v* -ISED, -ISING, -ISES to archaize

ARCHAISM *n* pl. -S an archaic word, idiom, or expression

ARCHAIST *n* pl. -S one that archaizes

ARCHAIZE *v* -IZED, -IZING, -IZES to use archaisms

ARCHDUKE *n* pl. -S an Austrian prince

ARCHER *n* pl. -S one that shoots with a bow and arrow

ARCHERY *n* pl. -CHERIES the sport of shooting with a bow and arrow

ARCHIL *n* pl. -S orchil

ARCHINE *n* pl. -S a Russian unit of linear measure

ARCHING *n* pl. -S a series of arches

ARCHIVE *v* -CHIVED, -CHIVING, -CHIVES to file in an archive (a place where records are kept) **ARCHIVAL** *adj*

ARCHLY *adv* slyly

ARCHNESS *n* pl. -ES slyness

ARCHON *n* pl. -S a magistrate of ancient Athens

ARCHWAY *n* pl. -WAYS a passageway under an arch

ARCIFORM *adj* having the form of an arch

ARCKED a past tense of arc

ARCKING a present participle of arc

ARCO *adv* with the bow — used as a direction to players of stringed instruments

ARCSINE *n* pl. -S the inverse function to the sine

ARCTIC *n* pl. -S a warm, waterproof overshoe

ARCUATE *adj* curved like a bow

ARCUATED *adj* arcuate

ARCUS *n* pl. -ES an arch-shaped cloud

ARDEB *n* pl. -S an Egyptian unit of capacity

ARDENCY *n* pl. -CIES ardor

ARDENT *adj* characterized by intense emotion **ARDENTLY** *adv*

ARDOR *n* pl. -S intensity of emotion

ARDOUR *n* pl. -S ardor

ARDUOUS *adj* involving great labor or hardship

ARE *n* pl. -S a unit of surface measure

AREA *n* pl. AREAE a section of the cerebral cortex having a specific function

AREA *n* pl. -S a particular extent of space or surface **AREAL** *adj* **AREALLY** *adv*

AREAWAY *n* pl. -WAYS a sunken area leading to a basement entrance

ARECA *n* pl. -S a tropical tree

AREIC *adj* pertaining to a region of the earth contributing little surface drainage

ARENA *n* pl. -S an enclosed area for contests

ARENITE *n* pl. -S rock made up chiefly of sand grains

ARENOSE *adj* sandy

ARENOUS *adj* arenose

AREOLA *n* pl. -LAE or -LAS a small space in a network of leaf veins **AREOLAR, AREOLATE** *adj*

AREOLE *n* pl. -S areola

AREOLOGY *n* pl. -GIES the study of the planet Mars

ARETE *n* pl. -S a sharp mountain ridge

ARETHUSA *n* pl. -S a flowering plant

ARF *n* pl. -S a barking sound

ARGAL *n* pl. -S argol

ARGALA *n* pl. -S a type of stork

ARGALI *n* pl. -S a wild sheep

ARGENT *n* pl. -S silver **ARGENTAL, ARGENTIC** *adj*

ARGENTUM *n* pl. -S silver

ARGIL *n* pl. -S a white clay

ARGINASE *n* pl. -S an enzyme

ARGININE *n* pl. -S an amino acid

ARGLE *v* -GLED, -GLING, -GLES to argue

ARGOL *n* pl. -S a crust deposited in wine casks during aging

ARGON *n* pl. -S a gaseous element

ARGONAUT *n* pl. -S a marine mollusk

ARGOSY *n* pl. -SIES a large merchant ship

ARGOT *n* pl. -S a specialized vocabulary **ARGOTIC** *adj*

ARGUABLE *adj* capable of being argued about **ARGUABLY** *adv*

ARGUE *v* -GUED, -GUING, -GUES to present reasons for or against

ARGUER *n* pl. -S one that argues

ARGUFIER *n* pl. -S one that argufies

ARGUFY *v* -FIED, -FYING, -FIES to argue stubbornly

ARGUING present participle of argue

ARGUMENT *n* pl. -S a discussion involving differing points of view

ARGUS *n* pl. -ES an East Indian pheasant

ARGYLE *n* pl. -S a knitting pattern

ARGYLL *n* pl. -S argyle

ARHAT *n* pl. -S a Buddhist who has attained nirvana

ARIA *n* pl. -S an elaborate melody for a single voice

ARID *adj* -IDER, -IDEST extremely dry **ARIDLY** *adv*

ARIDITY *n* pl. -TIES the state of being arid

ARIDNESS *n* pl. -ES aridity

ARIEL *n* pl. -S an African gazelle

ARIETTA *n* pl. -S a short aria

ARIETTE *n* pl. -S arietta

ARIGHT *adv* rightly; correctly

ARIL *n* pl. -S an outer covering of certain seeds **ARILED, ARILLATE, ARILLOID** *adj*

ARILLODE *n* pl. -S a type of aril

ARIOSE *adj* characterized by melody

ARIOSO *n* pl. -SOS or -SI a musical passage resembling an aria

ARISE *v* AROSE, ARISEN, ARISING, ARISES to get up

ARISTA *n* pl. -TAE or -TAS a bristlelike structure or appendage **ARISTATE** *adj*

ARISTO   n pl. -TOS an aristocrat
ARK   n pl. -S a large boat
ARKOSE   n pl. -S a type of sandstone
            ARKOSIC adj
ARLES   n/pl money paid to bind a
            bargain
ARM   v -ED, -ING, -S to supply with
            weapons
ARMADA   n pl. -S a fleet of warships
ARMAGNAC   n pl. -S a French brandy
ARMAMENT   n pl. -S a military force
            equipped for war
ARMATURE   v -TURED, -TURING, -TURES
            to furnish with armor
ARMBAND   n pl. -S a band worn around
            an arm (an upper appendage
            of the human body)
ARMCHAIR   n pl. -S a chair with armrests
ARMER   n pl. -S one that arms
ARMET   n pl. -S a medieval helmet
ARMFUL   n pl. ARMFULS or ARMSFUL
            as much as the arm can hold
ARMHOLE   n pl. -S an opening for the arm
            in a garment
ARMIES   pl. of army
ARMIGER   n pl. -S one who carries the
            armor of a knight
ARMIGERO   n pl. -GEROS armiger
ARMILLA   n pl. -LAE or -LAS a thin
            membrane around the stem of
            certain fungi
ARMING   n pl. -S the act of one that
            arms
ARMLESS   adj having no arms
ARMLET   n pl. -S an armband
ARMLIKE   adj resembling an arm
ARMLOAD   n pl. -S an armful
ARMLOCK   n pl. -S a hold in wrestling
ARMOIRE   n pl. -S a large, ornate cabinet
ARMONICA   n pl. -S a type of musical
            instrument
ARMOR   v -ED, -ING, -S to furnish with
            armor (a defensive covering)
ARMORER   n pl. -S one that makes or
            repairs armor
ARMORIAL   n pl. -S a treatise on heraldry
ARMORY   n pl. -MORIES a place where
            weapons are stored
ARMOUR   v -ED, -ING, -S to armor
ARMOURER   n pl. -S armorer
ARMOURY   n pl. -MOURIES armory
ARMPIT   n pl. -S the hollow under the
            arm at the shoulder
ARMREST   n pl. -S a support for the arm
ARMSFUL   a pl. of armful
ARMURE   n pl. -S a woven fabric

ARMY   n pl. -MIES a large body of
            men trained and armed for war
ARMYWORM   n pl. -S a destructive moth
            larva
ARNATTO   n pl. -TOS annatto
ARNICA   n pl. -S a perennial herb
ARNOTTO   n pl. -TOS a tropical tree
AROID   n pl. -S a flowering plant
AROINT   v -ED, -ING, -S to drive away
AROMA   n pl. -S a pleasant odor
AROMATIC   n pl. -S a fragrant plant or
            substance
AROSE   past tense of arise
AROUND   prep on all sides of
AROUSAL   n pl. -S the act of arousing
AROUSE   v AROUSED, AROUSING,
            AROUSES to stimulate
AROUSER   n pl. -S one that arouses
AROYNT   v -ED, -ING, -S to aroint
ARPEGGIO   n pl. -GIOS a technique of
            playing a musical chord
ARPEN   n pl. -S arpent
ARPENT   n pl. -S an old French unit of
            area
ARQUEBUS   n pl. -ES an early portable
            firearm
ARRACK   n pl. -S an Oriental liquor
ARRAIGN   v -ED, -ING, -S to call before
            a court of law to answer an
            indictment
ARRANGE   v -RANGED, -RANGING,
            -RANGES to put in definite or
            proper order
ARRANGER   n pl. -S one that arranges
ARRANT   adj outright ARRANTLY adv
ARRAS   n pl. ARRAS a tapestry
            ARRASED adj
ARRAY   v -ED, -ING, -S to place in
            proper or desired order
ARRAYAL   n pl. -S the act of arraying
ARRAYER   n pl. -S one that arrays
ARREAR   n pl. -S an unpaid and
            overdue debt
ARREST   v -ED, -ING, -S to seize and
            hold by legal authority
ARRESTEE   n pl. -S one that is arrested
ARRESTER   n pl. -S one that arrests
ARRESTOR   n pl. -S arrester
ARRHIZAL   adj rootless
ARRIS   n pl. -RISES a ridge formed
            by the meeting of two surfaces
ARRIVAL   n pl. -S the act of arriving
ARRIVE   v -RIVED, -RIVING, -RIVES to
            reach a destination
ARRIVER   n pl. -S one that arrives

ARROBA   *n* pl. -S a Spanish unit of weight

ARROGANT   *adj* overly convinced of one's own worth or importance

ARROGATE   *v* -GATED, -GATING, -GATES to claim or take without right

ARROW   *v* -ED, -ING, -S to indicate the proper position of with an arrow (a linear figure with a wedge-shaped end)

ARROWY   *adj* moving swiftly

ARROYO   *n* pl. -ROYOS a brook or creek

ARSENAL   *n* pl. -S a collection or supply of weapons

ARSENATE   *n* pl. -S a chemical salt

ARSENIC   *n* pl. -S a metallic element

ARSENIDE   *n* pl. -S an arsenic compound

ARSENITE   *n* pl. -S a chemical salt

ARSENO   *adj* containing a certain bivalent chemical radical

ARSENOUS   *adj* pertaining to arsenic

ARSES   pl. of arsis

ARSHIN   *n* pl. -S archine

ARSINE   *n* pl. -S a poisonous gas

ARSINO   *adj* containing a certain univalent chemical radical

ARSIS   *n* pl. ARSES the unaccented part of a musical measure

ARSON   *n* pl. -S the malicious or fraudulent burning of property ARSONOUS *adj*

ARSONIST   *n* pl. -S one that commits arson

ART   *n* pl. -S an esthetically pleasing and meaningful arrangement of elements

ARTAL   a pl. of rotl

ARTEFACT   *n* pl. -S artifact

ARTEL   *n* pl. -S a collective farm in Russia

ARTERIAL   *n* pl. -S a type of highway

ARTERY   *n* pl. -TERIES a vessel that carries blood away from the heart

ARTFUL   *adj* crafty ARTFULLY *adv*

ARTICLE   *v* -CLED, -CLING, -CLES to charge with specific offenses

ARTIER   comparative of arty

ARTIEST   superlative of arty

ARTIFACT   *n* pl. -S an object made by man

ARTIFICE   *n* pl. -S a clever stratagem

ARTILY   *adv* in an arty manner

ARTINESS   *n* pl. -ES the quality of being arty

ARTISAN   *n* pl. -S a trained or skilled workman

ARTIST   *n* pl. -S one who practices one of the fine arts

ARTISTE   *n* pl. -S a skilled public performer

ARTISTIC   *adj* characteristic of art

ARTISTRY   *n* pl. -RIES artistic quality or workmanship

ARTLESS   *adj* lacking cunning or guile

ARTSY   *adj* -SIER, -SIEST arty

ARTWORK   *n* pl. -S illustrative or decorative work in printed matter

ARTY   *adj* ARTIER, ARTIEST showily or pretentiously artistic

ARUGOLA   *n* pl. -S arugula

ARUGULA   *n* pl. -S a European annual herb

ARUM   *n* pl. -S a flowering plant

ARUSPEX   *n* pl. -PICES haruspex

ARVAL   *adj* pertaining to plowed land

ARVO   *n* pl. -VOS afternoon

ARYL   *n* pl. -S a univalent radical

ARYTHMIA   *n* pl. -S an irregularity in the rhythm of the heartbeat ARYTHMIC *adj*

AS   *adv* to the same degree

ASANA   *n* pl. -S a posture in yoga

ASARUM   *n* pl. -S a perennial herb

ASBESTOS   *n* pl. -ES a mineral ASBESTIC *adj*

ASBESTUS   *n* pl. -ES asbestos

ASCARID   *n* pl. -S a parasitic worm

ASCARIS   *n* pl. -RIDES ascarid

ASCEND   *v* -ED, -ING, -S to go or move upward

ASCENDER   *n* pl. -S one that ascends

ASCENT   *n* pl. -S the act of ascending

ASCESIS   *n* pl. -CESES the conduct of an ascetic

ASCETIC   *n* pl. -S one who practices extreme self-denial for religious reasons

ASCI   pl. of ascus

ASCIDIAN   *n* pl. -S a small marine animal

ASCIDIUM   *n* pl. -DIA a flask-shaped plant appendage

ASCITES   *n* pl. ASCITES accumulation of serous fluid in the abdomen ASCITIC *adj*

ASCOCARP   *n* pl. -S a spore-producing organ of certain fungi

ASCORBIC   *adj* relieving scurvy

ASCOT   *n* pl. -S a broad neck scarf

ASCRIBE   *v* -CRIBED, -CRIBING, -CRIBES to attribute to a specified cause, source, or origin

ASCUS   *n* pl. ASCI a spore sac in certain fungi

ASDIC   *n* pl. -S sonar

ASEA   *adv* at sea

ASEPSIS   *n* pl. -SEPSES the condition of being aseptic

ASEPTIC   *adj* free from germs

ASEXUAL   *adj* occurring or performed without sexual action

ASH   *v* -ED, -ING, -ES to convert into ash (the residue of a substance that has been burned)

ASHAMED   *adj* feeling shame, guilt, or disgrace

ASHCAN   *n* pl. -S a metal receptacle for garbage

ASHEN   *adj* consisting of ashes

ASHFALL   *n* pl. -S a deposit of volcanic ash

ASHIER   comparative of ashy

ASHIEST   superlative of ashy

ASHINESS   *n* pl. -ES the condition of being ashy

ASHLAR   *v* -ED, -ING, -S to build with squared stones

ASHLER   *v* -ED, -ING, -S to ashlar

ASHLESS   *adj* having no ashes

ASHMAN   *n* pl. -MEN one who collects and removes ashes

ASHORE   *adv* toward or on the shore

ASHPLANT   *n* pl. -S a walking stick

ASHRAM   *n* pl. -S a secluded dwelling of a Hindu sage

ASHTRAY   *n* pl. -TRAYS a receptacle for tobacco ashes

ASHY   *adj* ASHIER, ASHIEST covered with ashes

ASIDE   *n* pl. -S a comment by an actor intended to be heard by the audience but not the other actors

ASININE   *adj* obstinately stupid or silly

ASK   *v* -ED, -ING, -S to put a question to

ASKANCE   *adv* with a side glance

ASKANT   *adv* askance

ASKER   *n* pl. -S one that asks

ASKESIS   *n* pl. ASKESES ascesis

ASKEW   *adv* to one side

ASKING   *n* pl. -S the act of one who asks

ASKOS   *n* pl. ASKOI an oil jar used in ancient Greece

ASLANT   *adj* slanting

ASLEEP   *adj* sleeping

ASLOPE   *adj* sloping

ASOCIAL   *adj* avoiding the company of others

ASP   *n* pl. -S a venomous snake

ASPARKLE   *adj* sparkling

ASPECT   *n* pl. -S appearance of something to the eye or mind

ASPEN   *n* pl. -S any of several poplars

ASPER   *n* pl. -S a Turkish money of account

ASPERATE   *v* -ATED, -ATING, -ATES to make uneven

ASPERGES   *n* pl. ASPERGES a Roman Catholic rite

ASPERITY   *n* pl. -TIES acrimony

ASPERSE   *v* -PERSED, -PERSING, -PERSES to spread false charges against

ASPERSER   *n* pl. -S one that asperses

ASPERSOR   *n* pl. -S asperser

ASPHALT   *v* -ED, -ING, -S to coat with asphalt (a substance used for paving and roofing)

ASPHERIC   *adj* varying slightly from an exactly spherical shape

ASPHODEL   *n* pl. -S a flowering plant

ASPHYXIA   *n* pl. -S unconsciousness caused by lack of oxygen

ASPHYXY   *n* pl. -PHYXIES asphyxia

ASPIC   *n* pl. -S the asp

ASPIRANT   *n* pl. -S one that aspires

ASPIRATA   *n* pl. -TAE a type of plosive

ASPIRATE   *v* -RATED, -RATING, -RATES to pronounce with an initial release of breath

ASPIRE   *v* -PIRED, -PIRING, -PIRES to have an earnest desire or ambition

ASPIRER   *n* pl. -S an aspirant

ASPIRIN   *n* pl. -S a pain reliever

ASPIRING   present participle of aspire

ASPIS   *n* pl. -PISES aspic

ASPISH   *adj* resembling an asp

ASQUINT   *adv* with a sidelong glance

ASRAMA   *n* pl. -S ashram

ASS   *n* pl. -ES a hoofed mammal

ASSAGAI   *v* -GAIED, -GAIING, -GAIS to pierce with a light spear

ASSAI   *n* pl. -S a tropical tree

ASSAIL   *v* -ED, -ING, -S to attack

ASSAILER   *n* pl. -S one that assails

ASSASSIN   *n* pl. -S a murderer

ASSAULT   v -ED, -ING, -S to attack

ASSAY   v -ED, -ING, -S to attempt

ASSAYER   n pl. -S one that assays

ASSEGAI   v -GAIED, -GAIING, -GAIS to assagai

ASSEMBLE   v -BLED, -BLING, -BLES to come or bring together

ASSEMBLY   n pl. -BLIES the act of assembling

ASSENT   v -ED, -ING, -S to express agreement

ASSENTER   n pl. -S one that assents

ASSENTOR   n pl. -S assenter

ASSERT   v -ED, -ING, -S to state positively

ASSERTER   n pl. -S one that asserts

ASSERTOR   n pl. -S asserter

ASSESS   v -ED, -ING, -ES to estimate the value of for taxation

ASSESSOR   n pl. -S one that assesses

ASSET   n pl. -S a useful quality or thing

ASSIGN   v -ED, -ING, -S to set apart for a particular purpose

ASSIGNAT   n pl. -S one of the notes issued as currency by the French revolutionary government

ASSIGNEE   n pl. -S one to whom property or right is legally transferred

ASSIGNER   n pl. -S one that assigns

ASSIGNOR   n pl. -S one who legally transfers property or right

ASSIST   v -ED, -ING, -S to give aid or support to

ASSISTER   n pl. -S one that assists

ASSISTOR   n pl. -S assister

ASSIZE   n pl. -S a session of a legislative or judicial body

ASSLIKE   adj resembling an ass

ASSOIL   v -ED, -ING, -S to pardon

ASSONANT   n pl. -S a word or syllable that resembles another in sound

ASSORT   v -ED, -ING, -S to distribute into groups according to kind or class

ASSORTER   n pl. -S one that assorts

ASSUAGE   v -SUAGED, -SUAGING, -SUAGES to make less severe

ASSUME   v -SUMED, -SUMING, -SUMES to take on

ASSUMER   n pl. -S one that assumes

ASSURE   v -SURED, -SURING, -SURES to insure

ASSURED   n pl. -S an insured person

ASSURER   n pl. -S one that assures

ASSURING   present participle of assure

ASSUROR   n pl. -S assurer

ASSWAGE   v -SWAGED, -SWAGING, -SWAGES to assuage

ASTASIA   n pl. -S inability to stand resulting from muscular incoordination

ASTATIC   adj unstable

ASTATINE   n pl. -S a radioactive element

ASTER   n pl. -S a flowering plant

ASTERIA   n pl. -S a gemstone cut to exhibit asterism

ASTERISK   v -ED, -ING, -S to mark with an asterisk (a star-shaped printing mark)

ASTERISM   n pl. -S a property of certain minerals of showing a starlike luminous figure

ASTERN   adv at or toward the rear of a ship

ASTERNAL   adj not connected to the sternum

ASTEROID   n pl. -S a type of celestial body

ASTHENIA   n pl. -S lack of strength

ASTHENIC   n pl. -S a slender, lightly muscled person

ASTHENY   n pl. -NIES asthenia

ASTHMA   n pl. -S a respiratory disease

ASTIGMIA   n pl. -S a visual defect

ASTILBE   n pl. -S an Asian perennial

ASTIR   adj moving about

ASTOMOUS   adj having no stomata

ASTONISH   v -ED, -ING, -ES to fill with sudden wonder or surprise

ASTONY   v -TONIED, -TONYING, -TONIES to astonish

ASTOUND   v -ED, -ING, -S to amaze

ASTRAGAL   n pl. -S a convex molding

ASTRAL   n pl. -S a type of oil lamp

ASTRALLY   adv in a stellar manner

ASTRAY   adv off the right course

ASTRICT   v -ED, -ING, -S to restrict

ASTRIDE   adv with one leg on each side

ASTRINGE   v -TRINGED, -TRINGING, -TRINGES to bind or draw together

ASTUTE   adj shrewd **ASTUTELY** adv

ASTYLAR   adj having no columns

ASUNDER   adv into pieces

ASWARM   adj swarming

ASWIRL   adj swirling

ASWOON   adj swooning

ASYLUM   n pl. -LUMS or -LA an institution for the care of the mentally ill

ASYNDETA	*n/pl* omissions of certain conjunctions
AT	*prep* in the position of
ATABAL	*n* pl. -S a type of drum
ATACTIC	*adj* showing no regularity of structure
ATAGHAN	*n* pl. -S yataghan
ATALAYA	*n* pl. -S a watchtower
ATAMAN	*n* pl. -S a hetman
ATAMASCO	*n* pl. -COS a flowering plant
ATAP	*n* pl. -S the nipa palm tree
ATARAXIA	*n* pl. -S peace of mind
ATARAXIC	*n* pl. -S a tranquilizing drug
ATARAXY	*n* pl. -RAXIES ataraxia
ATAVIC	*adj* pertaining to a remote ancestor
ATAVISM	*n* pl. -S the reappearance of a genetic characteristic after several generations of absence
ATAVIST	*n* pl. -S an individual displaying atavism
ATAXIA	*n* pl. -S loss of muscular coordination
ATAXIC	*n* pl. -S one suffering from ataxia
ATAXY	*n* pl. ATAXIES ataxia
ATE	*n* pl. -S blind impulse or reckless ambition that drives one to ruin
ATECHNIC	*adj* lacking technical knowledge
ATELIC	*adj* pertaining to a type of verb form
ATELIER	*n* pl. -S a workshop or studio
ATEMOYA	*n* pl. -S a fruit of a hybrid tropical tree
ATHANASY	*n* pl. -SIES immortality
ATHEISM	*n* pl. -S the belief that there is no God
ATHEIST	*ʀ* pl. -S a believer in atheism
ATHELING	*n* pl. -S an Anglo-Saxon prince or nobleman
ATHENEUM	*n* pl. -S a literary institution
ATHEROMA	*n* pl. -MAS or -MATA a disease of the arteries
ATHETOID	*adj* affected with a type of nervous disorder
ATHIRST	*adj* having a strong desire
ATHLETE	*n* pl. -S one skilled in feats of physical strength and agility **ATHLETIC** *adj*
ATHODYD	*n* pl. -S a type of jet engine
ATHWART	*adv* from side to side
ATILT	*adj* being in a tilted position
ATINGLE	*adj* tingling
ATLAS	*n* pl. ATLANTES or ATLASES a male figure used as a supporting column
ATLATL	*n* pl. -S a device for throwing a spear or dart
ATMA	*n* pl. -S atman
ATMAN	*n* pl. -S the individual soul in Hinduism
ATOLL	*n* pl. -S a ring-shaped coral island
ATOM	*n* pl. -S the smallest unit of an element **ATOMIC, ATOMICAL** *adj*
ATOMICS	*n/pl* the science dealing with atoms
ATOMIES	pl. of atomy
ATOMISE	*v* -ISED, -ISING, -ISES to atomize
ATOMISM	*n* pl. -S the theory that the universe is composed of simple, indivisible, minute particles
ATOMIST	*n* pl. -S an adherent of atomism
ATOMIZE	*v* -IZED, -IZING, -IZES to reduce to a fine spray
ATOMIZER	*n* pl. -S a device for atomizing liquids
ATOMY	*n* pl. -MIES a tiny particle
ATONAL	*adj* lacking tonality **ATONALLY** *adv*
ATONE	*v* ATONED, ATONING, ATONES to make amends or reparation **ATONABLE** *adj*
ATONER	*n* pl. -S one that atones
ATONIC	*n* pl. -S an unaccented syllable or word
ATONING	present participle of atone
ATONY	*n* pl. -NIES muscular weakness
ATOP	*adj* being on or at the top
ATOPY	*n* pl. -PIES a type of allergy **ATOPIC** *adj*
ATRAZINE	*n* pl. -S an herbicide
ATREMBLE	*adj* trembling
ATRESIA	*n* pl. -S absence or closure of a natural bodily passage
ATRIA	a pl. of atrium
ATRIAL	*adj* pertaining to an atrium
ATRIP	*adj* aweigh
ATRIUM	*n* pl. ATRIA or ATRIUMS the main room of an ancient Roman house
ATROCITY	*n* pl. -TIES a heinous act

ATROPHIA *n* pl. -S a wasting away of the body or any of its parts **ATROPHIC** *adj*

ATROPHY *v* -PHIED, -PHYING, -PHIES to waste away

ATROPIN *n* pl. -S atropine

ATROPINE *n* pl. -S a poisonous alkaloid

ATROPISM *n* pl. -S atropine poisoning

ATT *n* pl. ATT a monetary unit of Laos

ATTABOY *interj* —used to express encouragement or approval

ATTACH *v* -ED, -ING, -ES to connect as an associated part

ATTACHE *n* pl. -S a diplomatic official

ATTACHER *n* pl. -S one that attaches

ATTACK *v* -ED, -ING, -S to set upon violently

ATTACKER *n* pl. -S one that attacks

ATTAIN *v* -ED, -ING, -S to gain or achieve by mental or physical effort

ATTAINER *n* pl. -S one that attains

ATTAINT *v* -ED, -ING, -S to disgrace

ATTAR *n* pl. -S a fragrant oil

ATTEMPER *v* -ED, -ING, -S to modify the temperature of

ATTEMPT *v* -ED, -ING, -S to make an effort to do or accomplish

ATTEND *v* -ED, -ING, -S to be present at

ATTENDEE *n* pl. -S an attender

ATTENDER *n* pl. -S one that attends

ATTENT *adj* heedful

ATTEST *v* -ED, -ING, -S to affirm to be true or genuine

ATTESTER *n* pl. -S one that attests

ATTESTOR *n* pl. -S attester

ATTIC *n* pl. -S a story or room directly below the roof of a house

ATTICISM *n* pl. -S a concise and elegant expression

ATTICIST *n* pl. -S one who uses atticisms

ATTIRE *v* -TIRED, -TIRING, -TIRES to clothe

ATTITUDE *n* pl. -S a state of mind with regard to some matter

ATTORN *v* -ED, -ING, -S to acknowledge a new owner as one's landlord

ATTORNEY *n* pl. -NEYS a lawyer

ATTRACT *v* -ED, -ING, -S to cause to approach or adhere

ATTRITE *adj* attrited

ATTRITED *adj* worn down by rubbing

ATTUNE *v* -TUNED, -TUNING, -TUNES to bring into harmony

ATWAIN *adv* in two

ATWEEN *prep* between

ATWITTER *adj* twittering

ATYPIC *adj* atypical

ATYPICAL *adj* not typical

AUBADE *n* pl. -S a morning song

AUBERGE *n* pl. -S an inn

AUBRETIA *n* pl. -S aubrieta

AUBRIETA *n* pl. -S a flowering plant

AUBURN *n* pl. -S a reddish brown color

AUCTION *v* -ED, -ING, -S to sell publicly to the highest bidder

AUCUBA *n* pl. -S a shrub of the dogwood family

AUDACITY *n* pl. -TIES boldness

AUDAD *n* pl. -S aoudad

AUDIAL *adj* aural

AUDIBLE *n* pl. -S a type of play in football

AUDIBLY *adv* in a way so as to be heard

AUDIENCE *n* pl. -S a group of listeners or spectators

AUDIENT *n* pl. -S one that hears

AUDILE *n* pl. -S one whose mental imagery is chiefly auditory

AUDING *n* pl. -S the process of hearing, recognizing, and interpreting a spoken language

AUDIO *n* pl. -DIOS sound reception or transmission

AUDIT *v* -ED, -ING, -S to examine with intent to verify

AUDITION *v* -ED, -ING, -S to give a trial performance

AUDITIVE *n* pl. -S an auditory

AUDITOR *n* pl. -S one that audits

AUDITORY *n* pl. -RIES a group of listeners

AUGEND *n* pl. -S a number to which another is to be added

AUGER *n* pl. -S a tool for boring

AUGHT *n* pl. -S a zero

AUGITE *n* pl. -S a mineral **AUGITIC** *adj*

AUGMENT *v* -ED, -ING, -S to increase

AUGUR *v* -ED, -ING, -S to foretell from omens

AUGURAL *adj* pertaining to augury

AUGURER *n* pl. -S one that augurs

AUGURY *n* pl. -RIES the practice of auguring

AUGUST	adj -GUSTER, -GUSTEST inspiring reverence or admiration **AUGUSTLY** adv	**AUSTRAL**	n pl. -ES or -S a former monetary unit of Argentina
AUK	n pl. -S a diving seabird	**AUSUBO**	n pl. -BOS a tropical tree
AUKLET	n pl. -S a small auk	**AUTACOID**	n pl. -S a hormone
AULD	adj AULDER, AULDEST old	**AUTARCHY**	n pl. -CHIES absolute rule or power
AULIC	adj pertaining to a royal court	**AUTARKY**	n pl. -KIES national economic self-sufficiency **AUTARKIC** adj
AUNT	n pl. -S the sister of one's father or mother	**AUTECISM**	n pl. -S the development of the entire life cycle of a parasitic fungus on a single host
AUNTHOOD	n pl. -S the state of being an aunt		
AUNTIE	n pl. -S aunt		
AUNTIES	pl. of aunty	**AUTEUR**	n pl. -S the creator of a film
AUNTLIKE	adj resembling an aunt	**AUTHOR**	v -ED, -ING, -S to write
AUNTLY	adj -LIER, -LIEST of or suggesting an aunt	**AUTISM**	n pl. -S extreme withdrawal into fantasy **AUTISTIC** adj
AUNTY	n pl. AUNTIES aunt	**AUTO**	v -ED, -ING, -S to ride in an automobile
AURA	n pl. -RAS or -RAE an invisible emanation		
AURAL	adj pertaining to the sense of hearing **AURALLY** adv	**AUTOBAHN**	n pl. -BAHNS or -BAHNEN a German superhighway
AURAR	pl. of eyrir	**AUTOBUS**	n pl. -BUSES or -BUSSES a bus
AURATE	adj having ears		
AURATED	adj aurate	**AUTOCADE**	n pl. -S a procession of automobiles
AUREATE	adj golden		
AUREI	pl. of aureus	**AUTOCOID**	n pl. -S autacoid
AUREOLA	n pl. -LAS or -LAE a halo	**AUTOCRAT**	n pl. -S an absolute ruler
AUREOLE	v -OLED, -OLING, -OLES to surround with a halo	**AUTODYNE**	n pl. -S a type of electrical circuit
AURES	pl. of auris	**AUTOGAMY**	n pl. -MIES fertilization of a flower by its own pollen
AUREUS	n pl. -REI a gold coin of ancient Rome	**AUTOGENY**	n pl. -NIES the production of living organisms from inanimate matter
AURIC	adj pertaining to gold		
AURICLE	n pl. -S an ear or ear-shaped part **AURICLED** adj	**AUTOGIRO**	n pl. -ROS a type of airplane
AURICULA	n pl. -LAS or -LAE an auricle	**AUTOGYRO**	n pl. -ROS autogiro
AURIFORM	adj ear-shaped	**AUTOLYSE**	v -LYSED, -LYSING, -LYSES to autolyze
AURIS	n pl. AURES the ear		
AURIST	n pl. -S a specialist in diseases of the ear	**AUTOLYZE**	v -LYZED, -LYZING, -LYZES to break down tissue by the action of self-contained enzymes
AUROCHS	n pl. -ES an extinct European ox		
AURORA	n pl. -RAS or -RAE the rising light of the morning **AURORAL, AUROREAN** adj	**AUTOMAN**	n pl. -MEN an automobile maker
		AUTOMATA	n/pl robots
AUROUS	adj pertaining to gold	**AUTOMATE**	v -MATED, -MATING, -MATES to convert to a system of automatic control
AURUM	n pl. -S gold		
AUSFORM	v -ED, -ING, -S to subject steel to a strengthening process		
		AUTOMEN	n pl. of automan
		AUTONOMY	n pl. -MIES the state of being self-governing
AUSPEX	n pl. -PICES a soothsayer of ancient Rome	**AUTOPSIC**	adj pertaining to an autopsy
AUSPICE	n pl. -S a favorable omen	**AUTOPSY**	v -SIED, -SYING, -SIES to examine a dead body to determine the cause of death
AUSTERE	adj -TERER, -TEREST grave in disposition or appearance		
		AUTOSOME	n pl. -S a type of chromosome

AUTOTOMY   *n* pl. -MIES the shedding of a damaged body part

AUTOTYPE   *n* pl. -S a type of photographic process

AUTOTYPY   *n* pl. -TYPIES autotype

AUTUMN   *n* pl. -S a season of the year **AUTUMNAL** *adj*

AUTUNITE   *n* pl. -S a mineral

AUXESIS   *n* pl. AUXESES an increase in cell size without cell division

AUXETIC   *n* pl. -S a substance that promotes auxesis

AUXIN   *n* pl. -S a substance used to regulate plant growth **AUXINIC** *adj*

AVA   *adv* at all

AVADAVAT   *n* pl. -S a small songbird

AVAIL   *v* -ED, -ING, -S to be of use or advantage to

AVANT   *adj* culturally or stylistically new

AVARICE   *n* pl. -S greed

AVAST   *interj* — used as a command to stop

AVATAR   *n* pl. -S the incarnation of a Hindu deity

AVAUNT   *interj* — used as an order of dismissal

AVE   *n* pl. -S an expression of greeting or farewell

AVELLAN   *adj* having the four arms shaped like filberts — used of a heraldic cross

AVELLANE   *adj* avellan

AVENGE   *v* AVENGED, AVENGING, AVENGES to exact retribution for

AVENGER   *n* pl. -S one that avenges

AVENS   *n* pl. -ES a perennial herb

AVENTAIL   *n* pl. -S ventail

AVENUE   *n* pl. -S a wide street

AVER   *v* AVERRED, AVERRING, AVERS to declare positively

AVERAGE   *v* -AGED, -AGING, -AGES to calculate the arithmetic mean of

AVERMENT   *n* pl. -S the act of averring

AVERRED   past tense of aver

AVERRING   present participle of aver

AVERSE   *adj* opposed; reluctant **AVERSELY** *adv*

AVERSION   *n* pl. -S a feeling of repugnance **AVERSIVE** *adj*

AVERT   *v* -ED, -ING, -S to turn away

AVGAS   *n* pl. -GASES or -GASSES gasoline for airplanes

AVIAN   *n* pl. -S a bird

AVIANIZE   *v* -IZED, -IZING, -IZES to make less severe by repeated culture in a chick embryo, as a virus

AVIARIST   *n* pl. -S the keeper of an aviary

AVIARY   *n* pl. -ARIES a large enclosure for live birds

AVIATE   *v* -ATED, -ATING, -ATES to fly an aircraft

AVIATION   *n* pl. -S the act of aviating

AVIATOR   *n* pl. -S one that aviates

AVIATRIX   *n* pl. -TRICES or -TRIXES a female aviator

AVICULAR   *adj* pertaining to birds

AVID   *adj* eager

AVIDIN   *n* pl. -S a protein found in egg white

AVIDITY   *n* pl. -TIES the state of being avid

AVIDLY   *adv* in an avid manner

AVIDNESS   *n* pl. -ES avidity

AVIFAUNA   *n* pl. -NAS or -NAE the bird life of a particular region

AVIGATOR   *n* pl. -S one that navigates aircraft

AVION   *n* pl. -S an airplane

AVIONICS   *n/pl* the science of electronics applied to aviation **AVIONIC** *adj*

AVISO   *n* pl. -SOS advice

AVO   *n* pl. AVOS a monetary unit of Macao

AVOCADO   *n* pl. -DOS or -DOES the edible fruit of a tropical tree

AVOCET   *n* pl. -S a shore bird

AVODIRE   *n* pl. -S an African tree

AVOID   *v* -ED, -ING, -S to keep away from

AVOIDER   *n* pl. -S one that avoids

AVOSET   *n* pl. -S avocet

AVOUCH   *v* -ED, -ING, -ES to affirm

AVOUCHER   *n* pl. -S one that avouches

AVOW   *v* -ED, -ING, -S to declare openly **AVOWABLE** *adj* **AVOWABLY, AVOWEDLY** *adv*

AVOWAL   *n* pl. -S an open declaration

AVOWER   *n* pl. -S one that avows

AVULSE   *v* AVULSED, AVULSING, AVULSES to tear off forcibly

AVULSION   *n* pl. -S the act of avulsing

AW   *interj* — used to express protest, disgust, or disbelief

AWA   *adv* away

AWAIT   v -ED, -ING, -S to wait for
AWAITER   n pl. -S one that awaits
AWAKE   v AWAKED or AWOKE, AWOKEN, AWAKING, AWAKES to wake up
AWAKEN   v -ED, -ING, -S to awake
AWAKENER   n pl. -S one that awakens
AWAKING   present participle of awake
AWARD   v -ED, -ING, -S to grant as due or merited
AWARDEE   n pl. -S one that is awarded something
AWARDER   n pl. -S one that awards
AWARE   adj having perception or knowledge
AWASH   adj covered with water
AWAY   adv from a certain place
AWAYNESS   n pl. -ES the state of being distant
AWE   v AWED, AWING or AWEING, AWES to inspire with awe (reverential fear)
AWEARY   adj weary
AWEATHER   adv toward the windward side of a vessel
AWED   past tense of awe
AWEE   adv awhile
AWEIGH   adj hanging just clear of the bottom — used of an anchor
AWELESS   adj lacking awe
AWESOME   adj inspiring awe
AWFUL   adj -FULLER, -FULLEST extremely bad or unpleasant AWFULLY adv
AWHILE   adv for a short time
AWHIRL   adj whirling
AWING   a present participle of awe
AWKWARD   adj -WARDER, -WARDEST lacking skill, dexterity, or grace
AWL   n pl. -S a pointed tool for making small holes
AWLESS   adj aweless
AWLWORT   n pl -S an aquatic plant
AWMOUS   n pl. AWMOUS alms
AWN   n pl. -S a bristlelike appendage of certain grasses AWNED, AWNLESS, AWNY adj
AWNING   n pl. -S a rooflike canvas cover AWNINGED adj
AWOKE   a past tense of awake
AWOKEN   a past participle of awake
AWOL   n pl. -S one who is absent without leave
AWRY   adv with a turn or twist to one side

AX   v -ED, -ING, -ES to work on with an ax (a type of cutting tool)
AXAL   adj axial
AXE   v AXED, AXING, AXES to ax
AXEL   n pl. -S a jump in figure skating
AXEMAN   n pl. -MEN axman
AXENIC   adj free from germs
AXES   pl. of axis
AXIAL   adj pertaining to or forming an axis AXIALLY adv
AXIALITY   n pl. -TIES the state of being axial
AXIL   n pl. -S the angle between the upper side of a leaf and its supporting stem
AXILE   adj axial
AXILLA   n pl. -LAE or -LAS the armpit
AXILLAR   n pl. -S a feather on the undersurface of a bird's wing
AXILLARY   n pl. -LARIES an axillar
AXING   present participle of axe
AXIOLOGY   n pl. -GIES the study of values and value judgments
AXIOM   n pl. -S a self-evident truth
AXION   n pl. -S a hypothetical subatomic particle
AXIS   n pl. AXES a straight line about which a body rotates AXISED adj
AXIS   n pl. AXISES an Asian deer
AXITE   n pl. -S a fiber of an axon
AXLE   n pl. -S a shaft upon which a wheel revolves AXLED adj
AXLETREE   n pl. -S a type of axle
AXLIKE   adj resembling an ax
AXMAN   n pl. -MEN one who wields an ax
AXOLOTL   n pl. -S a salamander of Mexico and western United States
AXON   n pl. -S the central process of a neuron AXONAL, AXONIC adj
AXONE   n pl. -S axon
AXONEMAL   adj pertaining to an axoneme
AXONEME   n pl. -S a part of a cilium
AXOPLASM   n pl. -S the protoplasm of an axon
AXSEED   n pl. -S a European herb
AY   n pl. AYS aye
AYAH   n pl. -S a native maid or nurse in India
AYE   n pl. -S an affirmative vote
AYIN   n pl. -S a Hebrew letter

AYURVEDA *n* pl. -S a Hindu system of medicine
AZALEA *n* pl. -S a flowering shrub
AZAN *n* pl. -S a Muslim call to prayer
AZIDE *n* pl. -S a type of chemical compound **AZIDO** *adj*
AZIMUTH *n* pl. -S an angle of horizontal deviation
AZINE *n* pl. -S a type of chemical compound
AZLON *n* pl. -S a textile fiber
AZO *adj* containing nitrogen
AZOIC *adj* pertaining to geologic time before the appearance of life
AZOLE *n* pl. -S a type of chemical compound
AZON *n* pl. -S a radio-controlled aerial bomb
AZONAL *adj* pertaining to a type of a soil group

AZONIC *adj* not restricted to any particular zone
AZOTE *n* pl. -S nitrogen **AZOTED** *adj*
AZOTEMIA *n* pl. -S an excess of nitrogenous substances in the blood **AZOTEMIC** *adj*
AZOTH *n* pl. -S mercury
AZOTIC *adj* pertaining to azote
AZOTISE *v* -TISED, -TISING, -TISES to azotize
AZOTIZE *v* -TIZED, -TIZING, -TIZES to treat with nitrogen
AZOTURIA *n* pl. -S an excess of nitrogenous substances in the urine
AZURE *n* pl. -S a blue color
AZURITE *n* pl. -S a mineral
AZYGOS *n* pl. -ES an azygous anatomical part
AZYGOUS *adj* not being one of a pair

BA   *n* pl. -S the eternal soul, in Egyptian mythology

BAA   *v* -ED, -ING, -S to bleat

BAAL   *n* pl. -S or -IM a false god

BAALISM   *n* pl. -S the worship of a baal

BAAS   *n* pl. -ES master; boss

BAASKAAP   *n* pl. -S the policy of domination by white people in South Africa

BABA   *n* pl. -S a rum cake

BABASSU   *n* pl. -S a palm tree

BABBITT   *v* -ED, -ING, -S to line with babbitt (an alloy of tin, copper, and antimony)

BABBLE   *v* -BLED, -BLING, -BLES to talk idly or excessively

BABBLER   *n* pl. -S one that babbles

BABBLING   *n* pl. -S idle talk

BABE   *n* pl. -S a baby

BABEL   *n* pl. -S confusion

BABESIA   *n* pl. -S a parasitic protozoan

BABICHE   *n* pl. -S rawhide thongs

BABIED   past tense of baby

BABIES   present 3d person sing. of baby

BABIRUSA   *n* pl. -S a wild pig

BABKA   *n* pl. -S a coffee cake

BABOO   *n* pl. -BOOS a Hindu gentleman

BABOOL   *n* pl. -S babul

BABOON   *n* pl. -S a large ape

BABU   *n* pl. -S baboo

BABUL   *n* pl. -S a North African tree

BABUSHKA   *n* pl. -S a woman's scarf

BABY   *v* -BIED, -BYING, -BIES to coddle

BABYHOOD   *n* pl. -S the state of being a baby (an infant)

BABYISH   *adj* resembling a baby

BACALAO   *n* pl. -LAOS codfish

BACCA   *n* pl. -CAE a berry

BACCARA   *n* pl. -S baccarat

BACCARAT   *n* pl. -S a card game

BACCATE   *adj* pulpy like a berry

BACCATED   *adj* baccate

BACCHANT   *n* pl. -S or -ES a carouser

BACCHIC   *adj* riotous

BACCHIUS   *n* pl. -CHII a type of metrical foot

BACH   *v* -ED, -ING, -ES to live as a bachelor

BACHELOR   *n* pl. -S an unmarried man

BACILLAR   *adj* rod-shaped

BACILLUS   *n* pl. -LI any of a class of rod-shaped bacteria

BACK   *v* -ED, -ING, -S to support

BACKACHE   *n* pl. -S a pain in the back

BACKBEAT   *n* pl. -S a type of rhythm in music

BACKBEND   *n* pl. -S an acrobatic feat

BACKBITE   *v* -BIT, -BITTEN, -BITING, -BITES to slander

BACKBONE   *n* pl. -S the spine

BACKCAST   *n* pl. -S a backward movement in casting a fishing line

BACKCHAT   *n* pl. -S repartee

BACKDATE   *v* -DATED, -DATING, -DATES to predate

BACKDOOR   *adj* secretive

BACKDROP   *n* pl. -S a stage setting

BACKER   *n* pl. -S a supporter

BACKFILL   *v* -ED, -ING, -S to refill

BACKFIRE   *v* -FIRED, -FIRING, -FIRES to result in undesirable consequences

BACKFIT   *v* -FITTED, -FITTING, -FITS to retrofit

BACKFLOW *n* pl. -S a flowing back toward a source

BACKHAND *v* -ED, -ING, -S to strike with the back of the hand

BACKHAUL *v* -ED, -ING, -S to return after delivering a load

BACKHOE *n* pl. -S an excavating machine

BACKING *n* pl. -S support

BACKLAND *n* pl. -S a region remote from cities

BACKLASH *v* -ED, -ING, -ES to cause a reaction

BACKLESS *adj* having no back

BACKLIST *v* -ED, -ING, -S to include in a publisher's list of older book titles

BACKLIT *adj* illuminated from behind

BACKLOG *v* -LOGGED, -LOGGING, -LOGS to accumulate

BACKMOST *adj* hindmost

BACKOUT *n* pl. -S a reversal of launching procedures

BACKPACK *v* -ED, -ING, -S to hike with a pack on one's back

BACKREST *n* pl. -S a back support

BACKROOM *adj* made or operating inconspicuously

BACKRUSH *n* pl. -ES the seaward return of water from a wave

BACKSAW *n* pl. -S a type of saw

BACKSEAT *n* pl. -S a rear seat

BACKSET *n* pl. -S a setback

BACKSIDE *n* pl. -S the hind part

BACKSLAP *v* -SLAPPED, -SLAPPING, -SLAPS to show much approval

BACKSLID past tense of backslide (to revert to sin)

BACKSPIN *n* pl. -S a backward rotation

BACKSTAY *n* pl. -STAYS a support for a mast

BACKSTOP *v* -STOPPED, -STOPPING, -STOPS to bolster

BACKUP *n* pl. -S a substitute

BACKWARD *adv* toward the back

BACKWASH *v* -ED, -ING, -ES to spray water backward

BACKWOOD *adj* uncouth

BACKWRAP *n* pl. -S a wraparound garment that fastens in the back

BACKYARD *n* pl. -S an area at the rear of a house

BACON *n* pl. -S a side of a pig cured and smoked

BACTERIA *n/pl* microscopic organisms

BACTERIN *n* pl. -S a vaccine prepared from dead bacteria

BACULINE *adj* pertaining to a rod

BACULUM *n* pl. -LA or -LUMS a bone in the penis of many mammals

BAD *adj* BADDER, BADDEST very good

BAD *adj* WORSE, WORST not good in any way

BAD *n* pl. -S something that is bad

BADDIE *n* pl. -S a bad person

BADDY *n* pl. -DIES baddie

BADE past tense of bid

BADGE *v* BADGED, BADGING, BADGES to supply with an insignia

BADGER *v* -ED, -ING, -S to harass

BADGERLY *adj* bothersome

BADGING present participle of badge

BADINAGE *v* -NAGED, -NAGING, -NAGES to banter

BADLAND *n* pl. -S a barren, hilly area

BADLY *adv* in a bad manner

BADMAN *n* pl. -MEN an outlaw

BADMOUTH *v* -ED, -ING, -S to criticize

BADNESS *n* pl. -ES the state of being bad

BAFF *v* -ED, -ING, -S to strike under a golf ball

BAFFIES pl. of baffy

BAFFLE *v* -FLED, -FLING, -FLES to confuse

BAFFLER *n* pl. -S one that baffles

BAFFY *n* pl. -FIES a wooden golf club

BAG *v* BAGGED, BAGGING, BAGS to put into a bag (a flexible container)

BAGASS *n* pl. -ES bagasse

BAGASSE *n* pl. -S crushed sugarcane

BAGEL *n* pl. -S a ring-shaped roll

BAGFUL *n* pl. BAGFULS or BAGSFUL as much as a bag can hold

BAGGAGE *n* pl. -S luggage

BAGGED past tense of bag

BAGGER *n* pl. -S one that bags

BAGGIE *n* pl. -S the stomach

BAGGING *n* pl. -S material for making bags

BAGGY *adj* -GIER, -GIEST loose-fitting **BAGGILY** *adv*

BAGHOUSE *n* pl. -S a facility for removing particulates from exhaust gases

BAGMAN *n* pl. -MEN a traveling salesman

BAGNIO *n* pl. -NIOS a brothel

BAGPIPE	*n* pl. -S a wind instrument
BAGPIPER	*n* pl. -S one that plays bagpipes
BAGSFUL	a pl. of bagful
BAGUET	*n* pl. -S baguette
BAGUETTE	*n* pl. -S a rectangular gem
BAGWIG	*n* pl. -S a type of wig
BAGWORM	*n* pl. -S the larva of certain moths
BAH	*interj* — an exclamation of disgust
BAHADUR	*n* pl. -S a Hindu title of respect
BAHT	*n* pl. -S a monetary unit of Thailand
BAIDARKA	*n* pl. -S bidarka
BAIL	*v* -ED, -ING, -S to transfer property temporarily **BAILABLE** *adj*
BAILEE	*n* pl. -S a person to whom property is bailed
BAILER	*n* pl. -S bailor
BAILEY	*n* pl. -LEYS an outer castle wall
BAILIE	*n* pl. -S a Scottish magistrate
BAILIFF	*n* pl. -S a court officer
BAILMENT	*n* pl. -S the act of bailing
BAILOR	*n* pl. -S a person who bails property to another
BAILOUT	*n* pl. -S the act of parachuting from an aircraft
BAILSMAN	*n* pl. -MEN one who provides security for another
BAIRN	*n* pl. -S a child **BAIRNISH** *adj*
BAIRNLY	*adj* -LIER, -LIEST childish
BAIT	*v* -ED, -ING, -S to lure
BAITER	*n* pl. -S one that baits
BAITH	*adj* both
BAIZA	*n* pl. -S a monetary unit of Oman
BAIZE	*n* pl. -S a green, woolen fabric
BAKE	*v* BAKED, BAKING, BAKES to prepare food in an oven
BAKEMEAT	*n* pl. -S a pastry
BAKER	*n* pl. -S one that bakes
BAKERY	*n* pl. -ERIES a place where baked goods are sold
BAKESHOP	*n* pl. -S a bakery
BAKING	*n* pl. -S a quantity baked
BAKLAVA	*n* pl. -S a Turkish pastry
BAKLAWA	*n* pl. -S baklava
BAKSHISH	*v* -ED, -ING, -ES to give a tip
BAL	*n* pl. -S a balmoral
BALANCE	*v* -ANCED, -ANCING, -ANCES to weigh
BALANCER	*n* pl. -S one that balances
BALAS	*n* pl. -ES a red variety of spinel
BALATA	*n* pl. -S a tropical tree
BALBOA	*n* pl. -S a monetary unit of Panama
BALCONY	*n* pl. -NIES an elevated platform
BALD	*adj* BALDER, BALDEST lacking hair
BALD	*v* -ED, -ING, -S to become bald
BALDHEAD	*n* pl. -S a bald person
BALDIES	pl. of baldy
BALDISH	*adj* somewhat bald
BALDLY	*adv* in a plain and blunt manner
BALDNESS	*n* pl. -ES the state of being bald
BALDPATE	*n* pl. -S a baldhead
BALDRIC	*n* pl. -S a shoulder belt
BALDRICK	*n* pl. -S baldric
BALDY	*n* pl. BALDIES a bald person
BALE	*v* BALED, BALING, BALES to form into tightly compressed bundles
BALEEN	*n* pl. -S whalebone
BALEFIRE	*n* pl. -S a bonfire
BALEFUL	*adj* menacing
BALER	*n* pl. -S one that bales
BALING	present participle of bale
BALISAUR	*n* pl. -S a long-tailed badger
BALK	*v* -ED, -ING, -S to stop short and refuse to proceed
BALKER	*n* pl. -S one that balks
BALKLINE	*n* pl. -S the starting line in track events
BALKY	*adj* BALKIER, BALKIEST stubborn **BALKILY** *adv*
BALL	*v* -ED, -ING, -S to form into a ball (a spherical object)
BALLAD	*n* pl. -S a narrative poem or song **BALLADIC** *adj*
BALLADE	*n* pl. -S a type of poem
BALLADRY	*n* pl. -RIES ballad poetry
BALLAST	*v* -ED, -ING, -S to stabilize
BALLER	*n* pl. -S one that balls
BALLET	*n* pl. -S a classical dance form **BALLETIC** *adj*
BALLGAME	*n* pl. -S a game played with a ball
BALLHAWK	*n* pl. -S a very good defensive ballplayer
BALLIES	pl. of bally
BALLISTA	*n* pl. -TAE an ancient weapon
BALLON	*n* pl. -S lightness of movement
BALLONET	*n* pl. -S a small balloon

BALLONNE *n* pl. -S a ballet jump

BALLOON *v* -ED, -ING, -S to swell out

BALLOT *v* -ED, -ING, -S to vote

BALLOTER *n* pl. -S one that ballots

BALLPARK *n* pl. -S a facility in which ballgames are played

BALLROOM *n* pl. -S a large room for dancing

BALLUTE *n* pl. -S a small inflatable parachute

BALLY *n* pl. -LIES a noisy uproar

BALLYHOO *v* -ED, -ING, -S to promote by uproar

BALLYRAG *v* -RAGGED, -RAGGING, -RAGS to bullyrag

BALM *n* pl. -S a fragrant resin BALMLIKE *adj*

BALMORAL *n* pl. -S a type of shoe

BALMY *adj* BALMIER, BALMIEST mild BALMILY *adv*

BALNEAL *adj* pertaining to baths

BALONEY *n* pl. -NEYS bologna

BALSA *n* pl. -S a tropical tree

BALSAM *v* -ED, -ING, -S to anoint with balsam (an aromatic, resinous substance)

BALSAMIC *adj* containing balsam

BALUSTER *n* pl. -S a railing support

BAM *v* BAMMED, BAMMING, BAMS to strike with a dull resounding noise

BAMBINO *n* pl. -NOS or -NI a baby

BAMBOO *n* pl. -BOOS a tropical grass

BAN *v* BANNED, BANNING, BANS to prohibit

BAN *n* pl. BANI a monetary unit of Romania

BANAL *adj* ordinary BANALLY *adv*

BANALITY *n* pl. -TIES something banal

BANALIZE *v* -IZED, -IZING, -IZES to make banal

BANANA *n* pl. -S an edible fruit

BANAUSIC *adj* practical

BANCO *n* pl. -COS a bet in certain gambling games

BAND *v* -ED, -ING, -S to decorate with flexible strips of material

BANDAGE *v* -DAGED, -DAGING, -DAGES to cover a wound with a strip of cloth

BANDAGER *n* pl. -S one that bandages

BANDANA *n* pl. -S bandanna

BANDANNA *n* pl. -S a large, colored handkerchief

BANDBOX *n* pl. -ES a lightweight box

BANDEAU *n* pl. -DEAUX or -DEAUS a headband

BANDER *n* pl. -S one that bands

BANDEROL *n* pl. -S a streamer

BANDIED past tense of bandy

BANDIES present 3d person sing. of bandy

BANDIT *n* pl. -DITS or -DITTI a robber

BANDITRY *n* pl. -TRIES robbery by bandits

BANDOG *n* pl. -S a watchdog

BANDORA *n* pl. -S bandore

BANDORE *n* pl. -S an ancient lute

BANDSMAN *n* pl. -MEN a member of a musical band

BANDY *v* -DIED, -DYING, -DIES to throw to and fro

BANE *v* BANED, BANING, BANES to kill with poison

BANEFUL *adj* poisonous

BANG *v* -ED, -ING, -S to hit sharply

BANGER *n* pl. -S a sausage

BANGKOK *n* pl. -S a straw hat

BANGLE *n* pl. -S a bracelet

BANGTAIL *n* pl. -S a racehorse

BANI pl. of ban

BANIAN *n* pl. -S a Hindu merchant

BANING present participle of bane

BANISH *v* -ED, -ING, -ES to expel

BANISHER *n* pl. -S one that banishes

BANISTER *n* pl. -S a handrail

BANJAX *v* -ED, -ING, -ES to damage or ruin

BANJO *n* pl. -JOS or -JOES a musical instrument

BANJOIST *n* pl. -S one who plays the banjo

BANK *v* -ED, -ING, -S to keep money in a bank (an institution dealing in money matters) BANKABLE *adj*

BANKBOOK *n* pl. -S a depositor's book

BANKCARD *n* pl. -S a credit card issued by a bank

BANKER *n* pl. -S one who works in a bank BANKERLY *adj*

BANKING *n* pl. -S the business of a bank

BANKNOTE *n* pl. -S a promissory note

BANKROLL *v* -ED, -ING, -S to supply the capital for

BANKRUPT *v* -ED, -ING, -S to impoverish

BANKSIA *n* pl. -S an Australian plant

BANKSIDE *n* pl. -S the slope of a river bank

BANNED past tense of ban

BANNER *n* pl. -S a flag

BANNERET *n* pl. -S a small banner
BANNEROL *n* pl. -S a banderol
BANNET *n* pl. -S a bonnet
BANNING present participle of ban
BANNOCK *n* pl. -S a type of cake
BANNS *n/pl* a marriage notice
BANQUET *v* -ED, -ING, -S to feast
BANSHEE *n* pl. -S a female spirit
BANSHIE *n* pl. -S banshee
BANTAM *n* pl. -S a small fowl
BANTENG *n* pl. -S a wild ox
BANTER *v* -ED, -ING, -S to exchange
mildly teasing remarks
BANTERER *n* pl. -S one that banters
BANTLING *n* pl. -S a very young child
BANTY *n* pl. -TIES a bantam
BANYAN *n* pl. -S an East Indian tree
BANZAI *n* pl. -S a Japanese battle cry
BAOBAB *n* pl. -S a tropical tree
BAP *n* pl. -S a small bun or roll
BAPTISE *v* -TISED, -TISING, -TISES to
baptize
BAPTISIA *n* pl. -S a flowering plant
BAPTISM *n* pl. -S a Christian ceremony
BAPTIST *n* pl. -S one who baptizes
BAPTIZE *v* -TIZED, -TIZING, -TIZES to
administer baptism to
BAPTIZER *n* pl. -S a baptist
BAR *v* BARRED, BARRING, BARS
to exclude
BARATHEA *n* pl. -S a silk fabric
BARB *v* -ED, -ING, -S to furnish with
a barb (a sharp projection)
BARBAL *adj* pertaining to the beard
BARBARIC *adj* uncivilized
BARBASCO *n* pl. -COS or -COES a
tropical tree
BARBATE *adj* bearded
BARBE *n* pl. -S a medieval cloth
headdress
BARBECUE *v* -CUED, -CUING, -CUES to
cook over live coals or an open
fire
BARBEL *n* pl. -S an organ of a fish
BARBELL *n* pl. -S an exercise apparatus
BARBEQUE *v* -QUED, -QUING, -QUES
barbecue
BARBER *v* -ED, -ING, -S to cut hair
BARBERRY *n* pl. -RIES a shrub
BARBET *n* pl. -S a tropical bird
BARBETTE *n* pl. -S a platform
BARBICAN *n* pl. -S an outer fortification
BARBICEL *n* pl. -S a part of a feather
BARBITAL *n* pl. -S a sedative
BARBLESS *adj* having no barbs
BARBULE *n* pl. -S a small barb

BARBUT *n* pl. -S a type of helmet
BARBWIRE *n* pl. -S barbed wire
BARCHAN *n* pl. -S a type of sand dune
BARD *v* -ED, -ING, -S to armor a
horse
BARDE *v* BARDED, BARDING,
BARDES to bard
BARDIC *adj* poetic
BARE *adj* BARER, BAREST naked
BARE *v* BARED, BARING, BARES
to expose
BAREBACK *adv* without a saddle
BAREBOAT *n* pl. -S a pleasure boat rented
without personnel
BAREFIT *adj* barefoot
BAREFOOT *adj* being without shoes
BAREGE *n* pl. -S a sheer fabric
BAREHEAD *adv* without a hat
BARELY *adv* scarcely
BARENESS *n* pl. -ES the state of being
bare
BARER comparative of bare
BARESARK *n* pl. -S an ancient warrior
BAREST superlative of bare
BARF *v* -ED, -ING, -S to vomit
BARFLY *n* pl. -FLIES a drinker who
frequents bars
BARGAIN *v* -ED, -ING, -S to discuss
terms for selling or buying
BARGE *v* BARGED, BARGING,
BARGES to move by barge (a
long, large boat)
BARGEE *n* pl. -S a bargeman
BARGELLO *n* pl. -LOS a needlepoint stitch
that makes a zigzag pattern
BARGEMAN *n* pl. -MEN the master or a
crew member of a barge
BARGHEST *n* pl. -S a goblin
BARGING present participle of barge
BARGUEST *n* pl. -S barghest
BARHOP *v* -HOPPED, -HOPPING,
-HOPS to visit a number of
bars during an evening
BARIC *adj* pertaining to barium
BARILLA *n* pl. -S a chemical compound
BARING present participle of bare
BARITE *n* pl. -S a mineral
BARITONE *n* pl. -S a male singing voice
BARIUM *n* pl. -S a metallic element
BARK *v* -ED, -ING, -S to cry like a
dog
BARKEEP *n* pl. -S a bartender
BARKER *n* pl. -S one that barks
BARKLESS *adj* having no bark; unable to
bark

BARKY	*adj* BARKIER, BARKIEST covered with bark (tough outer covering of a root or stem)
BARLEDUC	*n pl.* -S a fruit jam
BARLESS	*adj* having no restraints
BARLEY	*n pl.* -LEYS a cereal grass
BARLOW	*n pl.* -S a jackknife
BARM	*n pl.* -S the foam on malt liquors
BARMAID	*n pl.* -S a female bartender
BARMAN	*n pl.* -MEN a male bartender
BARMIE	*adj* barmy
BARMY	*adj* BARMIER, BARMIEST full of barm; frothy
BARN	*n pl.* -S a large storage building
BARNACLE	*n pl.* -S a shellfish
BARNLIKE	*adj* resembling a barn
BARNY	*adj* BARNIER, BARNIEST resembling a barn in size, shape, or smell
BARNYARD	*n pl.* -S a yard near a barn
BAROGRAM	*n pl.* -S a barometric reading
BARON	*n pl.* -S a lower member of nobility
BARONAGE	*n pl.* -S the rank of a baron
BARONESS	*n pl.* -ES the wife of a baron
BARONET	*n pl.* -S the holder of a rank below that of a baron
BARONG	*n pl.* -S a broad knife
BARONIAL	*adj* pertaining to a baron
BARONNE	*n pl.* -S a baroness
BARONY	*n pl.* -ONIES the domain of a baron
BAROQUE	*n pl.* -S an ornate object
BAROUCHE	*n pl.* -S a type of carriage
BARQUE	*n pl.* -S a sailing vessel
BARRABLE	*adj* capable of being barred
BARRACK	*v* -ED, -ING, -S to shout boisterously
BARRAGE	*v* -RAGED, -RAGING, -RAGES to subject to a massive attack
BARRANCA	*n pl.* -S a steep ravine
BARRANCO	*n pl.* -COS barranca
BARRATER	*n pl.* -S barrator
BARRATOR	*n pl.* -S one who commits barratry
BARRATRY	*n pl.* -TRIES fraud committed by a master or crew of a ship
BARRE	*v* BARRED, BARRING, BARRES to play a type of guitar chord
BARRED	past tense of bar

BARREL	*v* -RELED, -RELING, -RELS or -RELLED, -RELLING, -RELS to move fast
BARREN	*adj* -RENER, -RENEST unproductive **BARRENLY** *adv*
BARREN	*n pl.* -S a tract of barren land
BARRET	*n pl.* -S a flat cap
BARRETOR	*n pl.* -S barrator
BARRETRY	*n pl.* -TRIES barratry
BARRETTE	*n pl.* -S a hair clip
BARRIER	*n pl.* -S an obstacle
BARRING	present participle of bar and barre
BARRIO	*n pl.* -RIOS a district
BARROOM	*n pl.* -S a room where liquor is sold
BARROW	*n pl.* -S a type of cart
BARSTOOL	*n pl.* -S a stool in a barroom
BARTEND	*v* -ED, -ING, -S to tend a barroom
BARTER	*v* -ED, -ING, -S to trade
BARTERER	*n pl.* -S one that barters
BARTISAN	*n pl.* -S bartizan
BARTIZAN	*n pl.* -S a small turret
BARWARE	*n pl.* -S barroom equipment
BARYE	*n pl.* -S a unit of pressure
BARYON	*n pl.* -S a type of subatomic particle **BARYONIC** *adj*
BARYTA	*n pl.* -S a compound of barium **BARYTIC** *adj*
BARYTE	*n pl.* -S barite
BARYTONE	*n pl.* -S baritone
BASAL	*adj* pertaining to the foundation **BASALLY** *adv*
BASALT	*n pl.* -S a volcanic rock **BASALTIC** *adj*
BASALTES	*n pl.* BASALTES unglazed stoneware
BASCULE	*n pl.* -S a type of seesaw
BASE	*adj* BASER, BASEST morally low
BASE	*v* BASED, BASING, BASES to found
BASEBALL	*n pl.* -S a type of ball
BASEBORN	*adj* of low birth
BASED	past tense of base
BASELESS	*adj* having no foundation
BASELINE	*n pl.* -S a line at either end of a court in certain sports
BASELY	*adv* in a base manner
BASEMAN	*n pl.* -MEN a certain player in baseball
BASEMENT	*n pl.* -S the part of a building below ground level
BASENESS	*n pl.* -ES the state of being base

BASENJI *n* pl. -S a barkless dog
BASER comparative of base
BASES pl. of basis
BASEST superlative of base
BASH *v* -ED, -ING, -ES to smash
BASHAW *n* pl. -S a pasha
BASHER *n* pl. -S one that bashes
BASHFUL *adj* shy; timid
BASHLYK *n* pl. -S a cloth hood
BASIC *n* pl. -S a fundamental
BASICITY *n* pl. -TIES the state of being alkaline
BASIDIUM *n* pl. -IA a structure on a fungus **BASIDIAL** *adj*
BASIFIER *n* pl. -S one that basifies
BASIFY *v* -FIED, -FYING, -FIES to alkalize
BASIL *n* pl. -S an aromatic herb
BASILAR *adj* basal
BASILARY *adj* basilar
BASILIC *adj* pertaining to a basilica
BASILICA *n* pl. -CAS or -CAE an ancient Roman building
BASILISK *n* pl. -S a fabled serpent
BASIN *n* pl. -S a large bowl **BASINAL, BASINED** *adj*
BASINET *n* pl. -S a medieval helmet
BASINFUL *n* pl. -S as much as a basin can hold
BASING present participle of base
BASION *n* pl. -S a part of the skull
BASIS *n* pl. BASES the foundation of something
BASK *v* -ED, -ING, -S to lie in a pleasant warmth
BASKET *n* pl. -S a wooden container
BASKETRY *n* pl. -RIES basket weaving
BASOPHIL *n* pl. -S a type of cell
BASQUE *n* pl. -S a bodice
BASS *n* pl. -ES an edible fish
BASSET *v* -SETED, -SETING, -SETS or -SETTED, -SETTING, -SETS to outcrop
BASSI a pl. of basso
BASSINET *n* pl. -S a basket used as a baby's crib
BASSIST *n* pl. -S a person who plays a double bass
BASSLY *adv* in a low-pitched manner
BASSNESS *n* pl. -ES the state of being low in pitch
BASSO *n* pl. -SOS or -SI a low-pitched singer
BASSOON *n* pl. -S a low-pitched instrument
BASSWOOD *n* pl. -S a linden tree

BASSY *adj* low in pitch
BAST *n* pl. -S a woody fiber
BASTARD *n* pl. -S an illegitimate child
BASTARDY *n* pl. -TARDIES the state of being a bastard
BASTE *v* BASTED, BASTING, BASTES to sew loosely together
BASTER *n* pl. -S one that bastes
BASTILE *n* pl. -S bastille
BASTILLE *n* pl. -S a prison
BASTING *n* pl. -S the thread used by a baster
BASTION *n* pl. -S a fortified place
BAT *v* BATTED, BATTING, BATS to hit a baseball
BATBOY *n* pl. -BOYS a boy who minds baseball equipment
BATCH *v* -ED, -ING, -ES to bring together
BATCHER *n* pl. -S one that batches
BATE *v* BATED, BATING, BATES to reduce the force of
BATEAU *n* pl. -TEAUX a flat-bottomed boat
BATFISH *n* pl. -ES a batlike fish
BATFOWL *v* -ED, -ING, -S to catch birds at night
BATH *n* pl. -S a washing
BATHE *v* BATHED, BATHING, BATHES to wash
BATHER *n* pl. -S one that bathes
BATHETIC *adj* trite
BATHING present participle of bathe
BATHLESS *adj* not having had a bath
BATHMAT *n* pl. -S a mat used in a bathroom
BATHOS *n* pl. -ES triteness
BATHROBE *n* pl. -S a housecoat
BATHROOM *n* pl. -S a room in which to bathe
BATHTUB *n* pl. -S a tub in which to bathe
BATHYAL *adj* pertaining to deep water
BATIK *n* pl. -S a dyeing process
BATING present participle of bate
BATISTE *n* pl. -S a sheer fabric
BATLIKE *adj* resembling a bat (a flying mammal)
BATMAN *n* pl. -MEN an orderly
BATON *n* pl. -S a short rod
BATSMAN *n* pl. -MEN one who bats
BATT *n* pl. -S a sheet of cotton
BATTALIA *n* pl. -S a military unit
BATTEAU *n* pl. -TEAUX bateau
BATTED past tense of bat

BATTEN v -ED, -ING, -S to fasten with strips of wood

BATTENER n pl. -S one that battens

BATTER v -ED, -ING, -S to beat repeatedly

BATTERIE n pl. -S a ballet movement

BATTERY n pl. -TERIES a device for generating an electric current

BATTIER comparative of batty

BATTIEST superlative of batty

BATTIK n pl. -S batik

BATTING n pl. -S a batt

BATTLE v -TLED, -TLING, -TLES to fight

BATTLER n pl. -S one that battles

BATTU adj pertaining to a ballet movement

BATTUE n pl. -S a type of hunt

BATTY adj -TIER, -TIEST crazy

BATWING adj shaped like a bat's wing

BAUBEE n pl. -S bawbee

BAUBLE n pl. -S a cheap trinket

BAUD n pl. -S a unit of data transmission speed

BAUDEKIN n pl. -S a brocaded fabric

BAUDRONS n pl. -ES a cat

BAUHINIA n pl. -S a small tropical tree

BAULK v -ED, -ING, -S to balk

BAULKY adj BAULKIER, BAULKIEST balky

BAUSOND adj having white marks

BAUXITE n pl. -S an ore of aluminum BAUXITIC adj

BAWBEE n pl. -S a Scottish coin

BAWCOCK n pl. -S a fine fellow

BAWD n pl. -S a madam

BAWDIER comparative of bawdy

BAWDIES pl. of bawdy

BAWDIEST superlative of bawdy

BAWDILY adv in a bawdy manner

BAWDRIC n pl. -S baldric

BAWDRY n pl. -RIES obscenity

BAWDY adj BAWDIER, BAWDIEST obscene

BAWDY n pl. BAWDIES obscene language

BAWL v -ED, -ING, -S to cry loudly

BAWLER n pl. -S one that bawls

BAWSUNT adj bausond

BAWTIE n pl. -S a dog

BAWTY n pl. -TIES bawtie

BAY v -ED, -ING, -S to howl

BAYADEER n pl. -S bayadere

BAYADERE n pl. -S a dancing girl

BAYAMO n pl. -MOS a strong wind

BAYARD n pl. -S a horse

BAYBERRY n pl. -RIES a berry tree

BAYMAN n pl. -MEN a person who fishes on a bay

BAYONET v -NETED, -NETING, -NETS or -NETTED, -NETTING, -NETS to stab with a dagger-like weapon

BAYOU n pl. -S a marshy body of water

BAYWOOD n pl. -S a coarse mahogany

BAZAAR n pl. -S a marketplace

BAZAR n pl. -S bazaar

BAZOO n pl. -ZOOS the mouth

BAZOOKA n pl. -S a small rocket launcher

BDELLIUM n pl. -S a gum resin

BE v present sing. 1st person AM, 2d ARE or ART, 3d IS, past sing. 1st and 3d persons WAS, 2d WERE or WAST or WERT, past participle BEEN, present participle BEING to have actuality

BEACH v -ED, -ING, -ES to drive ashore

BEACHBOY n pl. -BOYS a male beach attendant

BEACHY adj BEACHIER, BEACHIEST sandy or pebbly

BEACON v -ED, -ING, -S to warn or guide

BEAD v -ED, -ING, -S to adorn with beads (round pieces of glass)

BEADIER comparative of beady

BEADIEST superlative of beady

BEADILY adv in a beady manner

BEADING n pl. -S beaded material

BEADLE n pl. -S a parish official

BEADLIKE adj beady

BEADMAN n pl. -MEN beadsman

BEADROLL n pl. -S a list of names

BEADSMAN n pl. -MEN one who prays for another

BEADWORK n pl. -S beading

BEADY adj BEADIER, BEADIEST resembling beads

BEAGLE n pl. -S a small hound

BEAK n pl. -S a bird's bill BEAKED, BEAKLESS, BEAKLIKE adj

BEAKER n pl. -S a large cup

BEAKY adj BEAKIER, BEAKIEST resembling a beak

BEAM v -ED, -ING, -S to emit in beams (rays of light)

BEAMIER comparative of beamy

BEAMIEST superlative of beamy

BEAMILY *adv* in a beamy manner
BEAMISH *adj* cheerful
BEAMLESS *adj* having no beam
BEAMLIKE *adj* resembling a beam
BEAMY *adj* BEAMIER, BEAMIEST beaming
BEAN *v* -ED, -ING, -S to hit on the head
BEANBAG *n* pl. -S a small cloth bag
BEANBALL *n* pl. -S a baseball thrown at the head
BEANERY *n* pl. -ERIES a cheap restaurant
BEANIE *n* pl. -S a small cap
BEANLIKE *adj* resembling a bean
BEANO *n* pl. BEANOS a form of bingo
BEANPOLE *n* pl. -S a thin pole
BEAR *v* BORE, BORNE or BORN, BEARING, BEARS to endure **BEARABLE** *adj* **BEARABLY** *adv*
BEARCAT *n* pl. -S a small mammal
BEARD *v* -ED, -ING, -S to oppose boldly
BEARER *n* pl. -S one that bears
BEARHUG *n* pl. -S a rough tight embrace
BEARING *n* pl. -S demeanor
BEARISH *adj* resembling a bear (a large mammal)
BEARLIKE *adj* bearish
BEARSKIN *n* pl. -S the skin of a bear
BEARWOOD *n* pl. -S a small tree of the buckthorn family
BEAST *n* pl. -S an animal
BEASTIE *n* pl. -S a tiny animal
BEASTLY *adj* -LIER, -LIEST resembling a beast
BEAT *v* BEAT, BEATEN, BEATING, BEATS to strike repeatedly **BEATABLE** *adj*
BEATER *n* pl. -S one that beats
BEATIFIC *adj* blissful
BEATIFY *v* -FIED, -FYING, -FIES to make happy
BEATING *n* pl. -S a defeat
BEATLESS *adj* having no rhythm
BEATNIK *n* pl. -S a nonconformist
BEAU *n* pl. BEAUX or BEAUS a boyfriend **BEAUISH** *adj*
BEAUCOUP *adj* many or much
BEAUT *n* pl. -S something beautiful
BEAUTIFY *v* -FIED, -FYING, -FIES to make beautiful
BEAUTY *n* pl. -TIES one that is lovely
BEAUX a pl. of beau
BEAVER *v* -ED, -ING, -S to work hard

BEBEERU *n* pl. -S a tropical tree
BEBLOOD *v* -ED, -ING, -S to cover with blood
BEBOP *n* pl. -S a type of jazz
BEBOPPER *n* pl. -S one that likes bebop
BECALM *v* -ED, -ING, -S to make calm
BECAME past tense of become
BECAP *v* -CAPPED, -CAPPING, -CAPS to put a cap on
BECARPET *v* -ED, -ING, -S to cover with a carpet
BECAUSE *conj* for the reason that
BECHALK *v* -ED, -ING, -S to cover with chalk
BECHAMEL *n* pl. -S a white sauce
BECHANCE *v* -CHANCED, -CHANCING, -CHANCES to befall
BECHARM *v* -ED, -ING, -S to hold under a spell
BECK *v* -ED, -ING, -S to beckon
BECKET *n* pl. -S a securing rope
BECKON *v* -ED, -ING, -S to signal by sign or gesture
BECKONER *n* pl. -S one that beckons
BECLAMOR *v* -ED, -ING, -S to clamor loudly
BECLASP *v* -ED, -ING, -S to embrace
BECLOAK *v* -ED, -ING, -S to place a cloak on
BECLOG *v* -CLOGGED, -CLOGGING, -CLOGS to clog thoroughly
BECLOTHE *v* -CLOTHED, -CLOTHING, -CLOTHES to clothe
BECLOUD *v* -ED, -ING, -S to make cloudy
BECLOWN *v* -ED, -ING, -S to cause to appear ridiculous
BECOME *v* -CAME, -COMING, -COMES to come to be
BECOMING *n* pl. -S a process of change
BECOWARD *v* -ED, -ING, -S to accuse of cowardice
BECRAWL *v* -ED, -ING, -S to crawl over
BECRIME *v* -CRIMED, -CRIMING, -CRIMES to make guilty of a crime
BECROWD *v* -ED, -ING, -S to crowd closely
BECRUST *v* -ED, -ING, -S to cover with a crust
BECUDGEL *v* -GELLED, -GELLING, -GELS or -GELED, -GELING, -GELS to cudgel thoroughly
BECURSE *v* -CURSED or -CURST, -CURSING, -CURSES to curse severely

BED   v BEDDED, BEDDING, BEDS to provide with a bed (a piece of furniture used for sleeping)

BEDABBLE   v -BLED, -BLING, -BLES to soil

BEDAMN   v -ED, -ING, -S to swear at

BEDARKEN   v -ED, -ING, -S to darken

BEDAUB   v -ED, -ING, -S to besmear

BEDAZZLE   v -ZLED, -ZLING, -ZLES to confuse

BEDBUG   n pl. -S a bloodsucking insect

BEDCHAIR   n pl. -S a chair near a bed

BEDCOVER   n pl. -S a cover for a bed

BEDDABLE   adj suitable for taking to bed

BEDDED   past tense of bed

BEDDER   n pl. -S one that makes up beds

BEDDING   n pl. -S material for making up a bed

BEDEAFEN   v -ED, -ING, -S to deafen

BEDECK   v -ED, -ING, -S to clothe with finery

BEDEL   n pl. -S an English university officer

BEDELL   n pl. -S bedel

BEDEMAN   n pl. -MEN beadsman

BEDESMAN   n pl. -MEN beadsman

BEDEVIL   v -ILED, -ILING, -ILS or -ILLED, -ILLING, -ILS to harass

BEDEW   v -ED, -ING, -S to wet with dew

BEDFAST   adj confined to bed

BEDFRAME   n pl. -S the frame of a bed

BEDGOWN   n pl. -S a dressing gown

BEDIAPER   v -ED, -ING, -S to ornament with a kind of design

BEDIGHT   v -ED, -ING, -S to bedeck

BEDIM   v -DIMMED, -DIMMING, -DIMS to make dim

BEDIMPLE   v -PLED, -PLING, -PLES to dimple

BEDIRTY   v -DIRTIED, -DIRTYING, -DIRTIES to make dirty

BEDIZEN   v -ED, -ING, -S to dress gaudily

BEDLAM   n pl. -S confusion

BEDLAMP   n pl. -S a lamp near a bed

BEDLESS   adj having no bed

BEDLIKE   adj resembling a bed

BEDMAKER   n pl. -S one that makes beds

BEDMATE   n pl. -S a bed companion

BEDOTTED   adj covered with dots

BEDOUIN   n pl. -S a nomadic Arab

BEDPAN   n pl. -S a toilet pan

BEDPLATE   n pl. -S a frame support

BEDPOST   n pl. -S a post of a bed

BEDQUILT   n pl. -S a quilt for a bed

BEDRAIL   n pl. -S a board at the side of a bed

BEDRAPE   v -DRAPED, -DRAPING, -DRAPES to drape

BEDRENCH   v -ED, -ING, -ES to drench thoroughly

BEDRID   adj bedfast

BEDRIVEL   v -ELLED, -ELLING, -ELS or -ELED, -ELING, -ELS to cover with saliva

BEDROCK   n pl. -S the rock under soil

BEDROLL   n pl. -S a portable roll of bedding

BEDROOM   n pl. -S a room for sleeping

BEDRUG   v -DRUGGED, -DRUGGING, -DRUGS to make sleepy

BEDSHEET   n pl. -S a sheet for a bed

BEDSIDE   n pl. -S the side of a bed

BEDSONIA   n pl. -S a virus

BEDSORE   n pl. -S a type of sore

BEDSTAND   n pl. -S a table next to a bed

BEDSTEAD   n pl. -S a support for a bed

BEDSTRAW   n pl. -S a woody herb

BEDTICK   n pl. -S the cloth case of a mattress

BEDTIME   n pl. -S a time for going to bed

BEDU   n pl. BEDU a bedouin

BEDUIN   n pl. -S bedouin

BEDUMB   v -ED, -ING, -S to render speechless

BEDUNCE   v -DUNCED, -DUNCING, -DUNCES to make a dunce of

BEDWARD   adv toward bed

BEDWARDS   adv bedward

BEDWARF   v -ED, -ING, -S to cause to appear small by comparison

BEE   n pl. -S a winged insect

BEEBEE   n pl. -S a pellet

BEEBREAD   n pl. -S a pollen mixture

BEECH   n pl. -ES a type of tree **BEECHEN** adj

BEECHNUT   n pl. -S the nut of a beech

BEECHY   adj BEECHIER, BEECHIEST abounding in beeches

BEEF   n pl. BEEFS or BEEVES a steer or cow fattened for food

BEEF   v -ED, -ING, -S to add bulk to

BEEFALO   n pl. -LOS or -LOES the offspring of an American buffalo and domestic cattle

BEEFCAKE   n pl. -S pictures of male physiques

BEEFIER   comparative of beefy

BEEFIEST   superlative of beefy

BEEFILY	adv in a beefy manner
BEEFLESS	adj being without beef
BEEFWOOD	n pl. -S a hardwood tree
BEEFY	adj BEEFIER, BEEFIEST brawny
BEEHIVE	n pl. -S a hive for bees
BEELIKE	adj resembling a bee
BEELINE	n pl. -S a direct route
BEEN	past participle of be
BEEP	v -ED, -ING, -S to honk a horn
BEEPER	n pl. -S a signaling device
BEER	n pl. -S an alcoholic beverage
BEERY	adj BEERIER, BEERIEST affected by beer
BEESWAX	n pl. -ES a type of wax
BEESWING	n pl. -S a crust that forms on old wines
BEET	n pl. -S a garden plant
BEETLE	v -TLED, -TLING, -TLES to jut out
BEETLER	n pl. -S one that operates a cloth-finishing machine
BEETROOT	n pl. -S the root of the beet
BEEVES	a pl. of beef
BEEYARD	n pl. -S an apiary
BEEZER	n pl. -S the nose
BEFALL	v -FELL, -FALLEN, -FALLING, -FALLS to happen to
BEFINGER	v -ED, -ING, -S to touch all over
BEFIT	v -FITTED, -FITTING, -FITS to be suitable to
BEFLAG	v -FLAGGED, -FLAGGING, -FLAGS to deck with flags
BEFLEA	v -ED, -ING, -S to infest with fleas
BEFLECK	v -ED, -ING, -S to fleck
BEFLOWER	v -ED, -ING, -S to cover with flowers
BEFOG	v -FOGGED, -FOGGING, -FOGS to envelop in fog
BEFOOL	v -ED, -ING, -S to deceive
BEFORE	adv previously
BEFOUL	v -ED, -ING, -S to foul
BEFOULER	n pl. -S one that befouls
BEFRET	v -FRETTED, -FRETTING, -FRETS to gnaw
BEFRIEND	v -ED, -ING, -S to act as a friend to
BEFRINGE	v -FRINGED, -FRINGING, -FRINGES to border with a fringe
BEFUDDLE	v -DLED, -DLING, -DLES to confuse
BEG	v BEGGED, BEGGING, BEGS to plead
BEGALL	v -ED, -ING, -S to make sore by rubbing
BEGAN	past tense of begin
BEGAZE	v -GAZED, -GAZING, -GAZES to gaze at
BEGET	v -GOT or -GAT, -GOTTEN, -GETTING, -GETS to cause to exist
BEGETTER	n pl. -S one that begets
BEGGAR	v -ED, -ING, -S to impoverish
BEGGARLY	adj very poor
BEGGARY	n pl. -GARIES extreme poverty
BEGGED	past tense of beg
BEGGING	present participle of beg
BEGIN	v -GAN, -GUN, -GINNING, -GINS to start
BEGINNER	n pl. -S one that begins
BEGIRD	v -GIRT or -GIRDED, -GIRDING, -GIRDS to surround
BEGIRDLE	v -DLED, -DLING, -DLES to surround
BEGLAD	v -GLADDED, -GLADDING, -GLADS to gladden
BEGLAMOR	v -ED, -ING, -S to dazzle with glamor
BEGLOOM	v -ED, -ING, -S to make gloomy
BEGONE	interj — used as an order of dismissal
BEGONIA	n pl. -S a tropical herb
BEGORAH	interj begorra
BEGORRA	interj — used as a mild oath
BEGORRAH	interj begorra
BEGOT	a past tense of beget
BEGOTTEN	past participle of beget
BEGRIM	v -GRIMMED, -GRIMMING, -GRIMS to begrime
BEGRIME	v -GRIMED, -GRIMING, -GRIMES to dirty
BEGROAN	v -ED, -ING, -S to groan at
BEGRUDGE	v -GRUDGED, -GRUDGING, -GRUDGES to concede reluctantly
BEGUILE	v -GUILED, -GUILING, -GUILES to deceive
BEGUILER	n pl. -S one that beguiles
BEGUINE	n pl. -S a lively dance
BEGULF	v -ED, -ING, -S to engulf
BEGUM	n pl. -S a Muslim lady of high rank
BEGUN	past participle of begin
BEHALF	n pl. -HALVES interest, support, or benefit

BEHAVE v -HAVED, -HAVING, -HAVES to act properly

BEHAVER n pl. -S one that behaves

BEHAVIOR n pl. -S demeanor

BEHEAD v -ED, -ING, -S to cut off the head of

BEHELD past tense of behold

BEHEMOTH n pl. -S a large beast

BEHEST n pl. -S a command

BEHIND n pl. -S the buttocks

BEHOLD v -HELD, -HOLDING, -HOLDS to view

BEHOLDEN adj indebted

BEHOLDER n pl. -S one that beholds

BEHOOF n pl. -HOOVES use, advantage, or benefit

BEHOOVE v -HOOVED, -HOOVING, -HOOVES to be proper for

BEHOVE v -HOVED, -HOVING, -HOVES to behoove

BEHOWL v -ED, -ING, -S to howl at

BEIGE n pl. -S a tan color

BEIGNET n pl. -S a type of fritter or doughnut

BEIGY adj of the color beige

BEING n pl. -S something that exists

BEJABERS interj bejesus

BEJEEZUS interj bejesus

BEJESUS interj — used as a mild oath

BEJEWEL v -ELED, -ELING, -ELS or -ELLED, -ELLING, -ELS to adorn with jewels

BEJUMBLE v -BLED, -BLING, -BLES to jumble

BEKISS v -ED, -ING, -ES to cover with kisses

BEKNIGHT v -ED, -ING, -S to raise to knighthood

BEKNOT v -KNOTTED, -KNOTTING, -KNOTS to tie in knots

BEL n pl. -S a unit of power

BELABOR v -ED, -ING, -S to discuss for an absurd amount of time

BELABOUR v -ED, -ING, -S to belabor

BELACED adj adorned with lace

BELADY v -DIED, -DYING, -DIES to apply the title of lady to

BELATED adj late or too late

BELAUD v -ED, -ING, -S to praise

BELAY v -ED, -ING, -S to fasten a rope

BELCH v -ED, -ING, -ES to expel gas through the mouth

BELCHER n pl. -S one that belches

BELDAM n pl. -S an old woman

BELDAME n pl. -S beldam

BELEAP v -LEAPT or -LEAPED, -LEAPING, -LEAPS to leap upon

BELFRY n pl. -FRIES a bell tower **BELFRIED** adj

BELGA n pl. -S a former Belgian monetary unit

BELIE v -LIED, -LYING, -LIES to misrepresent

BELIEF n pl. -S acceptance of the truth or actuality of something

BELIER n pl. -S one that belies

BELIEVE v -LIEVED, -LIEVING, -LIEVES to accept as true or real

BELIEVER n pl. -S one that believes

BELIKE adv perhaps

BELIQUOR v -ED, -ING, -S to soak with liquor

BELITTLE v -TLED, -TLING, -TLES to disparage

BELIVE adv in due time

BELL v -ED, -ING, -S to provide with a bell (a ringing device)

BELLBIRD n pl. -S a tropical bird

BELLBOY n pl. -BOYS a hotel's errand boy

BELLE n pl. -S an attractive woman

BELLEEK n pl. -S a very thin translucent porcelain

BELLHOP n pl. -S a bellboy

BELLIED past tense of belly

BELLIES present 3d person sing. of belly

BELLMAN n pl. -MEN a town crier

BELLOW v -ED, -ING, -S to shout in a deep voice

BELLOWER n pl. -S one that bellows

BELLPULL n pl. -S a cord pulled to ring a bell

BELLWORT n pl. -S a flowering plant

BELLY v -LIED, -LYING, -LIES to swell out

BELLYFUL n pl. -S an excessive amount

BELONG v -ED, -ING, -S to be a member of

BELOVED n pl. -S one who is loved

BELOW n pl. -S something that is beneath

BELT v -ED, -ING, -S to fasten with a belt (a strap or band worn around the waist)

BELTER n pl. -S one that belts

BELTING n pl. -S material for belts

BELTLESS adj having no belt

BELTLINE n pl. -S the waistline

BELTWAY *n* pl. -WAYS a highway around an urban area

BELUGA *n* pl. -S a white sturgeon

BELYING present participle of belie

BEMA *n* pl. -MATA or -MAS a platform in a synagogue

BEMADAM *v* -ED, -ING, -S to call by the title of madam

BEMADDEN *v* -ED, -ING, -S to madden

BEMATA a pl. of bema

BEMEAN *v* -ED, -ING, -S to debase

BEMINGLE *v* -GLED, -GLING, -GLES to mix together

BEMIRE *v* -MIRED, -MIRING, -MIRES to soil with mud

BEMIST *v* -ED, -ING, -S to envelop in a mist

BEMIX *v* -MIXED or -MIXT, -MIXING, -MIXES to mix thoroughly

BEMOAN *v* -ED, -ING, -S to lament

BEMOCK *v* -ED, -ING, -S to mock

BEMUDDLE *v* -DLED, -DLING, -DLES to confuse completely

BEMURMUR *v* -ED, -ING, -S to murmur at

BEMUSE *v* -MUSED, -MUSING, -MUSES to confuse

BEMUZZLE *v* -ZLED, -ZLING, -ZLES to muzzle

BEN *n* pl. -S an inner room

BENAME *v* -NAMED, -NEMPT or -NEMPTED, -NAMING, -NAMES to name

BENCH *v* -ED, -ING, -ES to take a player out of a game

BENCHER *n* pl. -S a magistrate

BEND *v* BENT or BENDED, BENDING, BENDS to curve **BENDABLE** *adj*

BENDAY *v* -ED, -ING, -S to reproduce using a certain process

BENDEE *n* pl. -S bendy

BENDER *n* pl. -S one that bends

BENDWAYS *adv* bendwise

BENDWISE *adv* diagonally

BENDY *n* pl. -DYS okra

BENE *n* pl. -S benne

BENEATH *prep* under

BENEDICK *n* pl. -S benedict

BENEDICT *n* pl. -S a newly married man

BENEFIC *adj* kindly

BENEFICE *v* -FICED, -FICING, -FICES to endow with land

BENEFIT *v* -FITED, -FITING, -FITS or -FITTED, -FITTING, -FITS to be helpful or useful to

BENEMPT a past participle of bename

BENEMPTED a past participle of bename

BENIGN *adj* kind **BENIGNLY** *adv*

BENISON *n* pl. -S a blessing

BENJAMIN *n* pl. -S benzoin

BENNE *n* pl. -S the sesame plant

BENNET *n* pl. -S a perennial herb

BENNI *n* pl. -S benne

BENNY *n* pl. -NIES an amphetamine tablet

BENOMYL *n* pl. -S a chemical compound

BENT *n* pl. -S an inclination

BENTHAL *adj* benthic

BENTHIC *adj* pertaining to oceanic depths

BENTHOS *n* pl. -ES benthic sea life

BENTWOOD *n* pl. -S wood bent for use in furniture

BENUMB *v* -ED, -ING, -S to make numb

BENZAL *adj* pertaining to a certain chemical group

BENZENE *n* pl. -S a volatile liquid

BENZIDIN *n* pl. -S a hydrocarbon

BENZIN *n* pl. -S benzine

BENZINE *n* pl. -S a volatile liquid

BENZOATE *n* pl. -S a chemical salt

BENZOIN *n* pl. -S a gum resin **BENZOIC** *adj*

BENZOL *n* pl. -S a benzene

BENZOLE *n* pl. -S benzol

BENZOYL *n* pl. -S a univalent chemical radical

BENZYL *n* pl. -S a univalent chemical radical **BENZYLIC** *adj*

BEPAINT *v* -ED, -ING, -S to tinge

BEPIMPLE *v* -PLED, -PLING, -PLES to cover with pimples

BEQUEATH *v* -ED, -ING, -S to grant by testament

BEQUEST *n* pl. -S a legacy

BERAKE *v* -RAKED, -RAKING, -RAKES to rake all over

BERASCAL *v* -ED, -ING, -S to accuse of being a rascal

BERATE *v* -RATED, -RATING, -RATES to scold severely

BERBERIN *n* pl. -S a medicinal alkaloid

BERBERIS *n* pl. -ES a barberry

BERCEUSE *n* pl. -S a lullaby

BERDACHE *n* pl. -S an American Indian male transvestite

BEREAVE *v* -REAVED or -REFT, -REAVING, -REAVES to deprive

BEREAVER *n* pl. -S one that bereaves

BERET *n* pl. -S a soft, flat cap

BERETTA *n* pl. -S biretta

BERG	*n* pl. -S an iceberg
BERGAMOT	*n* pl. -S a citrus tree
BERGERE	*n* pl. -S an upholstered armchair
BERHYME	*v* -RHYMED, -RHYMING, -RHYMES to compose in rhyme
BERIBERI	*n* pl. -S a thiamine deficiency disease
BERIME	*v* -RIMED, -RIMING, -RIMES to berhyme
BERINGED	*adj* adorned with rings
BERLIN	*n* pl. -S a type of carriage
BERLINE	*n* pl. -S a limousine
BERM	*n* pl. -S a ledge
BERME	*n* pl. -S berm
BERMUDAS	*n/pl* knee-length walking shorts
BERNICLE	*n* pl. -S a wild goose
BEROBED	*adj* wearing a robe
BEROUGED	*adj* obviously or thickly rouged
BERRETTA	*n* pl. -S biretta
BERRY	*v* -RIED, -RYING, -RIES to produce berries (fleshy fruits)
BERSEEM	*n* pl. -S a clover
BERSERK	*n* pl. -S a fierce warrior
BERTH	*v* -ED, -ING, -S to provide with a mooring
BERTHA	*n* pl. -S a wide collar
BERYL	*n* pl. -S a green mineral BERYLINE *adj*
BESCORCH	*v* -ED, -ING, -ES to scorch
BESCOUR	*v* -ED, -ING, -S to scour thoroughly
BESCREEN	*v* -ED, -ING, -S to screen
BESEECH	*v* -SOUGHT or -SEECHED, -SEECHING, -SEECHES to implore
BESEEM	*v* -ED, -ING, -S to be suitable
BESET	*v* -SET, -SETTING, -SETS to assail
BESETTER	*n* pl. -S one that besets
BESHADOW	*v* -ED, -ING, -S to cast a shadow on
BESHAME	*v* -SHAMED, -SHAMING, -SHAMES to put to shame
BESHIVER	*v* -ED, -ING, -S to break into small pieces
BESHOUT	*v* -ED, -ING, -S to shout at
BESHREW	*v* -ED, -ING, -S to curse
BESHROUD	*v* -ED, -ING, -S to cover
BESIDE	*prep* next to
BESIDES	*adv* in addition
BESIEGE	*v* -SIEGED, -SIEGING, -SIEGES to surround
BESIEGER	*n* pl. -S one that besieges
BESLAVED	*adj* filled with slaves
BESLIME	*v* -SLIMED, -SLIMING, -SLIMES to cover with slime
BESMEAR	*v* -ED, -ING, -S to smear over
BESMILE	*v* -SMILED, -SMILING, -SMILES to smile on
BESMIRCH	*v* -ED, -ING, -ES to dirty
BESMOKE	*v* -SMOKED, -SMOKING, -SMOKES to soil with smoke
BESMOOTH	*v* -ED, -ING, -S to smooth
BESMUDGE	*v* -SMUDGED, -SMUDGING, -SMUDGES to smudge
BESMUT	*v* -SMUTTED, -SMUTTING, -SMUTS to blacken with smut
BESNOW	*v* -ED, -ING, -S to cover with snow
BESOM	*n* pl. -S a broom
BESOOTHE	*v* -SOOTHED, -SOOTHING -SOOTHES to soothe
BESOT	*v* -SOTTED, -SOTTING, -SOTS to stupefy
BESOUGHT	a past tense of beseech
BESPEAK	*v* -SPOKE or -SPAKE, -SPOKEN, -SPEAKING, -SPEAKS to claim in advance
BESPOUSE	*v* -SPOUSED, -SPOUSING, -SPOUSES to marry
BESPREAD	*v* -SPREAD, -SPREADING, -SPREADS to spread over
BESPRENT	*adj* sprinkled over
BEST	*v* -ED, -ING, -S to outdo
BESTEAD	*v* -ED, -ING, -S to help
BESTIAL	*adj* pertaining to beasts
BESTIARY	*n* pl. -ARIES a collection of animal fables
BESTIR	*v* -STIRRED, -STIRRING, -STIRS to rouse
BESTOW	*v* -ED, -ING, -S to present as a gift
BESTOWAL	*n* pl. -S a gift
BESTREW	*v* -STREWED, -STREWN, -STREWING, -STREWS to scatter
BESTRIDE	*v* -STRODE or -STRID, -STRIDDEN, -STRIDING, -STRIDES to straddle
BESTROW	*v* -STROWED, -STROWN, -STROWING, -STROWS to bestrew
BESTUD	*v* -STUDDED, -STUDDING, -STUDS to dot
BESWARM	*v* -ED, -ING, -S to swarm all over
BET	*v* BET or BETTED, BETTING, BETS to wager
BETA	*n* pl. -S a Greek letter

BETAINE *n* pl. -S an alkaloid

BETAKE *v* -TOOK, -TAKEN, -TAKING, -TAKES to cause to go

BETATRON *n* pl. -S an electron accelerator

BETATTER *v* -ED, -ING, -S to tatter

BETAXED *adj* burdened with taxes

BETEL *n* pl. -S a climbing plant

BETELNUT *n* pl. -S a seed chewed as a stimulant

BETH *n* pl. -S a Hebrew letter

BETHANK *v* -ED, -ING, -S to thank

BETHEL *n* pl. -S a holy place

BETHESDA *n* pl. -S a chapel

BETHINK *v* -THOUGHT, -THINKING, -THINKS to consider

BETHORN *v* -ED, -ING, -S to fill with thorns

BETHUMP *v* -ED, -ING, -S to thump soundly

BETIDE *v* -TIDED, -TIDING, -TIDES to befall

BETIME *adv* betimes

BETIMES *adv* soon

BETISE *n* pl. -S stupidity

BETOKEN *v* -ED, -ING, -S to indicate

BETON *n* pl. -S a type of concrete

BETONY *n* pl. -NIES a European herb

BETOOK past tense of betake

BETRAY *v* -ED, -ING, -S to aid an enemy of

BETRAYAL *n* pl. -S the act of betraying

BETRAYER *n* pl. -S one that betrays

BETROTH *v* -ED, -ING, -S to engage to marry

BETTA *n* pl. -S a freshwater fish

BETTED a past tense of bet

BETTER *v* -ED, -ING, -S to improve

BETTING present participle of bet

BETTOR *n* pl. -S one that bets

BETWEEN *prep* in the space that separates

BETWIXT *prep* between

BEUNCLED *adj* having many uncles

BEVATRON *n* pl. -S a proton accelerator

BEVEL *v* -ELED, -ELING, -ELS or -ELLED, -ELLING, -ELS to cut at an angle

BEVELER *n* pl. -S one that bevels

BEVELLER *n* pl. -S beveler

BEVELLING a present participle of bevel

BEVERAGE *n* pl. -S a liquid for drinking

BEVIES pl. of bevy

BEVOMIT *v* -ED, -ING, -S to vomit all over

BEVOR *n* pl. -S a piece of armor for the lower face

BEVY *n* pl. BEVIES a group

BEWAIL *v* -ED, -ING, -S to lament

BEWAILER *n* pl. -S one that bewails

BEWARE *v* -WARED, -WARING, -WARES to be careful

BEWEARY *v* -WEARIED, -WEARYING, -WEARIES to make weary

BEWEEP *v* -WEPT, -WEEPING, -WEEPS to lament

BEWIG *v* -WIGGED, -WIGGING, -WIGS to adorn with a wig

BEWILDER *v* -ED, -ING, -S to confuse

BEWINGED *adj* having wings

BEWITCH *v* -ED, -ING, -ES to affect by witchcraft or magic

BEWORM *v* -ED, -ING, -S to infest with worms

BEWORRY *v* -RIED, -RYING, -RIES to worry

BEWRAP *v* -WRAPPED or -WRAPT, -WRAPPING, -WRAPS to wrap completely

BEWRAY *v* -ED, -ING, -S to divulge

BEWRAYER *n* pl. -S one that bewrays

BEY *n* pl. BEYS a Turkish ruler

BEYLIC *n* pl. -S the domain of a bey

BEYLIK *n* pl. -S beylic

BEYOND *n* pl. -S something that lies farther ahead

BEZANT *n* pl. -S a coin of ancient Rome

BEZAZZ *n* pl. -ES pizazz

BEZEL *n* pl. -S a slanted surface

BEZIL *n* pl. -S bezel

BEZIQUE *n* pl. -S a card game

BEZOAR *n* pl. -S a gastric mass

BEZZANT *n* pl. -S bezant

BHAKTA *n* pl. -S one who practices bhakti

BHAKTI *n* pl. -S a selfless devotion to a deity in Hinduism

BHANG *n* pl. -S the hemp plant

BHARAL *n* pl. -S a goatlike Asian mammal

BHEESTIE *n* pl. -S bheesty

BHEESTY *n* pl. -TIES a water carrier

BHISTIE *n* pl. -S bheesty

BHOOT *n* pl. -S bhut

BHUT *n* pl. -S a small whirlwind

BI *n* pl. -S a bisexual

BIACETYL *n* pl. -S a chemical flavor enhancer

BIALI *n* pl. -S bialy

BIALY *n* pl. -ALYS an onion roll

BIANNUAL   *adj* occurring twice a year

BIAS   *v* -ASED, -ASING, -ASES or -ASSED, -ASSING, -ASSES to prejudice **BIASEDLY** *adv*

BIASNESS   *n* pl. -ES the state of being slanted

BIATHLON   *n* pl. -S an athletic contest

BIAXAL   *adj* biaxial

BIAXIAL   *adj* having two axes

BIB   *v* BIBBED, BIBBING, BIBS to tipple

BIBASIC   *adj* dibasic

BIBB   *n* pl. -S a mast support

BIBBED   past tense of bib

BIBBER   *n* pl. -S a tippler

BIBBERY   *n* pl. -BERIES the act of bibbing

BIBBING   present participle of bib

BIBCOCK   *n* pl. -S a type of faucet

BIBELOT   *n* pl. -S a trinket

BIBLE   *n* pl. -S an authoritative publication **BIBLICAL** *adj*

BIBLESS   *adj* having no bib (a cloth covering)

BIBLIKE   *adj* resembling a bib

BIBLIST   *n* pl. -S one who takes the words of the Bible literally

BIBULOUS   *adj* given to drinking

BICARB   *n* pl. -S sodium bicarbonate

BICAUDAL   *adj* having two tails

BICE   *n* pl. -S a blue or green pigment

BICEPS   *n* pl. -ES an arm muscle

BICHROME   *adj* two-colored

BICKER   *v* -ED, -ING, -S to argue

BICKERER   *n* pl. -S one that bickers

BICOLOR   *n* pl. -S something having two colors

BICOLOUR   *n* pl. -S bicolor

BICONVEX   *adj* convex on both sides

BICORN   *adj* having two horns

BICORNE   *n* pl. -S a type of hat

BICRON   *n* pl. -S one billionth of a meter

BICUSPID   *n* pl. -S a tooth

BICYCLE   *v* -CLED, -CLING, -CLES to ride a bicycle (a two-wheeled vehicle)

BICYCLER   *n* pl. -S one that bicycles

BICYCLIC   *adj* having two cycles

BICYCLING   present participle of bicycle

BID   *v* BADE, BIDDEN, BIDDING, BIDS to make a bid (an offer of a price)

BIDARKA   *n* pl. -S an Eskimo canoe

BIDARKEE   *n* pl. -S bidarka

BIDDABLE   *adj* obedient **BIDDABLY** *adv*

BIDDEN   past participle of bid

BIDDER   *n* pl. -S one that bids

BIDDING   *n* pl. -S a command

BIDDY   *n* pl. -DIES a hen

BIDE   *v* BIDED or BODE, BIDING, BIDES to wait

BIDENTAL   *adj* having two teeth

BIDER   *n* pl. -S one that bides

BIDET   *n* pl. -S a low basin used for washing

BIDING   present participle of bide

BIELD   *v* -ED, -ING, -S to shelter

BIENNALE   *n* pl. -S a biennial show

BIENNIAL   *n* pl. -S an event that occurs every two years

BIENNIUM   *n* pl. -NIA or -NIUMS a period of two years

BIER   *n* pl. -S a coffin stand

BIFACE   *n* pl. -S a stone tool having a cutting edge

BIFACIAL   *adj* having two faces

BIFF   *v* -ED, -ING, -S to hit

BIFFIN   *n* pl. -S a cooking apple

BIFFY   *n* pl. -FIES a toilet

BIFID   *adj* divided into two parts **BIFIDLY** *adv*

BIFIDITY   *n* pl. -TIES the state of being bifid

BIFILAR   *adj* having two threads

BIFLEX   *adj* bent in two places

BIFOCAL   *n* pl. -S a type of lens

BIFOLD   *adj* twofold

BIFORATE   *adj* having two perforations

BIFORKED   *adj* divided into two branches

BIFORM   *adj* having two forms

BIFORMED   *adj* biform

BIG   *adj* BIGGER, BIGGEST of considerable size

BIGAMIES   pl. of bigamy

BIGAMIST   *n* pl. -S one who commits bigamy

BIGAMOUS   *adj* guilty of bigamy

BIGAMY   *n* pl. -MIES the crime of being married to two people simultaneously

BIGARADE   *n* pl. -S a citrus tree

BIGAROON   *n* pl. -S a type of cherry

BIGEMINY   *n* pl. -NIES the state of having a double pulse

BIGEYE   *n* pl. -S a marine fish

BIGFOOT   *n* pl. -FEET or -FOOTS a large hairy humanlike creature

BIGGER   comparative of big

BIGGEST   superlative of big

BIGGETY   *adj* biggity

BIGGIE   *n* pl. -S one that is big

BIGGIN   *n* pl. -S a house

BIGGING   *n* pl. -S biggin

BIGGISH   *adj* somewhat big

BIGGITY   *adj* conceited

BIGHEAD   *n* pl. -S a disease of animals

BIGHORN   *n* pl. -S a wild sheep

BIGHT   *v* -ED, -ING, -S to fasten with a loop of rope

BIGLY   *adv* in a big manner

BIGMOUTH   *n* pl. -S a talkative person

BIGNESS   *n* pl. -ES the state of being big

BIGNONIA   *n* pl. -S a climbing plant

BIGOT   *n* pl. -S a prejudiced person

BIGOTED   *adj* intolerant

BIGOTRY   *n* pl. -RIES prejudice

BIGWIG   *n* pl. -S an important person

BIHOURLY   *adj* occurring every two hours

BIJOU   *n* pl. -JOUX or -JOUS a jewel

BIJUGATE   *adj* two-paired

BIJUGOUS   *adj* bijugate

BIKE   *v* BIKED, BIKING, BIKES to bicycle

BIKER   *n* pl. -S one that bikes

BIKEWAY   *n* pl. -WAYS a route for bikes

BIKIE   *n* pl. -S biker

BIKING   present participle of bike

BIKINI   *n* pl. -S a type of bathing suit **BIKINIED** *adj*

BILABIAL   *n* pl. -S a sound articulated with both lips

BILANDER   *n* pl. -S a small ship

BILAYER   *n* pl. -S a film with two molecular layers

BILBERRY   *n* pl. -RIES an edible berry

BILBO   *n* pl. -BOS or -BOES a finely tempered sword

BILBOA   *n* pl. -S bilbo

BILE   *n* pl. -S a fluid secreted by the liver

BILGE   *v* BILGED, BILGING, BILGES to spring a leak

BILGY   *adj* BILGIER, BILGIEST smelling like seepage

BILIARY   *adj* pertaining to bile

BILINEAR   *adj* pertaining to two lines

BILIOUS   *adj* pertaining to bile

BILK   *v* -ED, -ING, -S to cheat

BILKER   *n* pl. -S one that bilks

BILL   *v* -ED, -ING, -S to present a statement of costs to **BILLABLE** *adj*

BILLBUG   *n* pl. -S a weevil

BILLER   *n* pl. -S one that bills

BILLET   *v* -ED, -ING, -S to lodge soldiers

BILLETER   *n* pl. -S one that billets

BILLFISH   *n* pl. -ES a fish with long, slender jaws

BILLFOLD   *n* pl. -S a wallet

BILLHEAD   *n* pl. -S a letterhead

BILLHOOK   *n* pl. -S a cutting tool

BILLIARD   *n* pl. -S a carom shot in billiards (a table game)

BILLIE   *n* pl. -S a comrade

BILLIES   pl. of billy

BILLING   *n* pl. -S the relative position in which a performer is listed

BILLION   *n* pl. -S a number

BILLON   *n* pl. -S an alloy of silver and copper

BILLOW   *v* -ED, -ING, -S to swell

BILLOWY   *adj* -LOWIER, -LOWIEST swelling; surging

BILLY   *n* pl. -LIES a short club

BILLYCAN   *n* pl. -S a pot for heating water

BILOBATE   *adj* having two lobes

BILOBED   *adj* bilobate

BILSTED   *n* pl. -S a hardwood tree

BILTONG   *n* pl. -S dried and cured meat

BIMA   *n* pl. -S bema

BIMAH   *n* pl. -S bema

BIMANOUS   *adj* two-handed

BIMANUAL   *adj* done with two hands

BIMBO   *n* pl. -BOS or -BOES a disreputable person

BIMENSAL   *adj* occurring every two months

BIMESTER   *n* pl. -S a two-month period

BIMETAL   *n* pl. -S something composed of two metals

BIMETHYL   *n* pl. -S ethane

BIMODAL   *adj* having two statistical modes

BIMORPH   *n* pl. -S a device consisting of two crystals cemented together

BIN   *v* BINNED, BINNING, BINS to store in a large receptacle

BINAL   *adj* twofold

BINARY   *n* pl. -RIES a combination of two things

BINATE   *adj* growing in pairs **BINATELY** *adv*

BINAURAL   *adj* hearing with both ears

BIND   *v* BOUND, BINDING, BINDS to tie or secure **BINDABLE** *adj*

BINDER   *n* pl. -S one that binds

BINDERY   *n* pl. -ERIES a place where books are bound

BINDI   *n* pl. -S a dot worn on the forehead by women in India

BINDING	*n* pl. -S the cover and fastenings of a book	**BIOMETRY**	*n* pl. -TRIES the statistical study of biological data
BINDLE	*n* pl. -S a bundle	**BIONICS**	*n/pl* a science joining biology and electronics **BIONIC** *adj*
BINDWEED	*n* pl. -S a twining plant		
BINE	*n* pl. -S a twining plant stem	**BIONOMY**	*n* pl. -MIES ecology **BIONOMIC** *adj*
BINGE	*v* BINGED, BINGEING or BINGING, BINGES to indulge in something without restraint	**BIONT**	*n* pl. -S a living organism **BIONTIC** *adj*
BINGER	*n* pl. -S one that binges	**BIOPIC**	*n* pl. -S a biographical movie
BINGO	*n* pl. -GOS a game of chance	**BIOPLASM**	*n* pl. -S living matter
BINIT	*n* pl. -S a unit of computer information	**BIOPSY**	*n* pl. -SIES the examination of tissue **BIOPSIC, BIOPTIC** *adj*
BINNACLE	*n* pl. -S a compass stand	**BIOSCOPE**	*n* pl. -S an early movie projector
BINNED	past tense of bin		
BINNING	present participle of bin	**BIOSCOPY**	*n* pl. -PIES a type of medical examination
BINOCLE	*n* pl. -S a binocular		
BINOCS	*n/pl* binoculars	**BIOTA**	*n* pl. -S the flora and fauna of a region
BINOMIAL	*n* pl. -S an algebraic expression	**BIOTECH**	*n* pl. -S applied biological science
BINT	*n* pl. -S a woman		
BIO	*n* pl. BIOS a biography	**BIOTIC**	*adj* pertaining to life
BIOASSAY	*v* -ED, -ING, -S to test a substance (as a drug)	**BIOTICAL**	*adj* biotic
		BIOTICS	*n/pl* a life science
BIOCHIP	*n* pl. -S a hypothetical computer component that uses proteins to store or process data	**BIOTIN**	*n* pl. -S a B vitamin
		BIOTITE	*n* pl. -S a form of mica **BIOTITIC** *adj*
		BIOTOPE	*n* pl. -S a stable habitat
BIOCIDE	*n* pl. -S a substance destructive to living organisms **BIOCIDAL** *adj*	**BIOTOXIN**	*n* pl. -S poison made by a plant or animal
		BIOTRON	*n* pl. -S a climate control chamber
BIOCLEAN	*adj* free of harmful organisms		
BIOCYCLE	*n* pl. -S a life-supporting region	**BIOTYPE**	*n* pl. -S a group of genetically similar organisms **BIOTYPIC** *adj*
BIOETHIC	*adj* pertaining to ethical questions arising from advances in biology		
		BIOVULAR	*adj* derived from two ova
		BIPACK	*n* pl. -S a pair of films
BIOGAS	*n* pl. -GASES or -GASSES fuel gas produced by organic waste	**BIPAROUS**	*adj* producing offspring in pairs
		BIPARTED	*adj* having two parts
		BIPARTY	*adj* of two parties
BIOGEN	*n* pl. -S a hypothetical protein molecule	**BIPED**	*n* pl. -S a two-footed animal **BIPEDAL** *adj*
BIOGENIC	*adj* produced by living organisms	**BIPHASIC**	*adj* having two phases
		BIPHENYL	*n* pl. -S a hydrocarbon
BIOGENY	*n* pl. -NIES the development of life from preexisting life	**BIPLANE**	*n* pl. -S a type of airplane
		BIPOD	*n* pl. -S a two-legged support
BIOHERM	*n* pl. -S a mass of marine fossils	**BIPOLAR**	*adj* having two poles
		BIRACIAL	*adj* including members of two races
BIOLOGIC	*n* pl. -S a drug obtained from an organic source		
BIOLOGY	*n* pl. -GIES the science of life	**BIRADIAL**	*adj* having dual symmetry
BIOLYSIS	*n* pl. -YSES death **BIOLYTIC** *adj*	**BIRAMOSE**	*adj* biramous
		BIRAMOUS	*adj* divided into two branches
		BIRCH	*v* -ED, -ING, -ES to whip
BIOMASS	*n* pl. -ES an amount of living matter	**BIRCHEN**	*adj* made of birch wood
		BIRD	*v* -ED, -ING, -S to hunt birds (winged, warm-blooded vertebrates)
BIOME	*n* pl. -S an ecological community		

BIRDBATH   n pl. -S a bath for birds

BIRDCAGE   n pl. -S a cage for birds

BIRDCALL   n pl. -S the call of a bird

BIRDER   n pl. -S a bird hunter

BIRDFARM   n pl. -S an aircraft carrier

BIRDIE   v BIRDIED, BIRDIEING, BIRDIES to shoot in one stroke under par in golf

BIRDING   n pl. -S bird-watching

BIRDLIKE   adj resembling a bird

BIRDLIME   v -LIMED, -LIMING, -LIMES to trap small birds

BIRDMAN   n pl. -MEN one who keeps birds

BIRDSEED   n pl. -S a mixture of seeds used for feeding birds

BIRDSEYE   n pl. -S a flowering plant

BIRDSHOT   n pl. -S small shot for shooting birds

BIRDSONG   n pl. -S the song of a bird

BIREME   n pl. -S an ancient galley

BIRETTA   n pl. -S a cap worn by clergymen

BIRK   n pl. -S a birch tree

BIRKIE   n pl. -S a lively person

BIRL   v -ED, -ING, -S to rotate a floating log

BIRLE   v BIRLED, BIRLING, BIRLES to carouse

BIRLER   n pl. -S one that birls

BIRLING   n pl. -S a lumberjack's game

BIRR   v -ED, -ING, -S to make a whirring noise

BIRR   n pl. BIRROTCH a monetary unit of Ethiopia

BIRRETTA   n pl. -S biretta

BIRSE   n pl. -S a bristle

BIRTH   v -ED, -ING, -S to originate

BIRTHDAY   n pl. -DAYS an anniversary of a birth

BIS   adv twice

BISCUIT   n pl. -S a small cake of shortened bread

BISE   n pl. -S a cold wind

BISECT   v -ED, -ING, -S to cut into two parts

BISECTOR   n pl. -S something that bisects

BISEXUAL   n pl. -S one who is attracted to both sexes

BISHOP   v -ED, -ING, -S to appoint as a bishop (the head of a diocese)

BISK   n pl. -S bisque

BISMUTH   n pl. -S a metallic element

BISNAGA   n pl. -S a type of cactus

BISON   n pl. -S an ox-like animal

BISQUE   n pl. -S a thick soup

BISTATE   adj pertaining to two states

BISTER   n pl. -S a brown pigment **BISTERED** adj

BISTORT   n pl. -S a perennial herb with roots used as astringents

BISTOURY   n pl. -RIES a surgical knife

BISTRE   n pl. -S bister **BISTRED** adj

BISTRO   n pl. -TROS a small tavern **BISTROIC** adj

BIT   v BITTED, BITTING, BITS to restrain

BITABLE   adj capable of being bitten

BITCH   v -ED, -ING, -ES to complain

BITCHERY   n pl. -ERIES bitchy behavior

BITCHY   adj BITCHIER, BITCHIEST malicious **BITCHILY** adv

BITE   v BIT, BITTEN, BITING, BITES to seize with the teeth **BITEABLE** adj

BITER   n pl. -S one that bites

BITEWING   n pl. -S a dental X-ray film

BITING   present participle of bite

BITINGLY   adv sarcastically

BITSTOCK   n pl. -S a brace on a drill

BITSY   adj tiny

BITT   v -ED, -ING, -S to secure a cable

BITTED   past tense of bit

BITTEN   a past participle of bite

BITTER   adj -TERER, -TEREST having a disagreeable taste **BITTERLY** adv

BITTER   v -ED, -ING, -S to make bitter

BITTERN   n pl. -S a wading bird

BITTIER   comparative of bitty

BITTIEST   superlative of bitty

BITTING   n pl. -S an indentation in a key

BITTOCK   n pl. -S a small amount

BITTY   adj -TIER, -TIEST fragmented

BITUMEN   n pl. -S an asphalt

BIUNIQUE   adj being a type of correspondence between two sets

BIVALENT   n pl. -S a pair of chromosomes

BIVALVE   n pl. -S a bivalved mollusk

BIVALVED   adj having a two-valved shell

BIVINYL   n pl. -S a flammable gas used in making synthetic rubber

BIVOUAC   v -OUACKED, -OUACKING, -OUACKS or -OUACS to make a camp

BIWEEKLY   n pl. -LIES a publication issued every two weeks

BIYEARLY   adj occurring every two years

BIZ *n* pl. BIZZES business

BIZARRE *n* pl. -S a strangely striped flower

BIZE *n* pl. -S bise

BIZNAGA *n* pl. -S bisnaga

BIZONE *n* pl. -S two combined zones **BIZONAL** *adj*

BLAB *v* BLABBED, BLABBING, BLABS to talk idly

BLABBER *v* -ED, -ING, -S to blab

BLABBY *adj* talkative

BLACK *adj* BLACKER, BLACKEST being of the darkest color

BLACK *v* -ED, -ING, -S to make black

BLACKBOY *n* pl. -BOYS an Australian plant

BLACKCAP *n* pl. -S a small European bird

BLACKEN *v* -ED, -ING, -S to make black

BLACKFIN *n* pl. -S a food fish

BLACKFLY *n* pl. -FLIES a biting fly

BLACKGUM *n* pl. -S a tupelo

BLACKING *n* pl. -S black shoe polish

BLACKISH *adj* somewhat black

BLACKLEG *n* pl. -S a cattle disease

BLACKLY *adv* in a black manner

BLACKOUT *n* pl. -S a power failure

BLACKTOP *v* -TOPPED, -TOPPING, -TOPS to pave with asphalt

BLADDER *n* pl. -S a saclike receptacle **BLADDERY** *adj*

BLADE *n* pl. -S a cutting edge **BLADED** *adj*

BLAE *adj* bluish-black

BLAH *n* pl. -S nonsense

BLAIN *n* pl. -S a blister

BLAM *n* pl. -S the sound of a gunshot

BLAMABLE *adj* being at fault **BLAMABLY** *adv*

BLAME *v* BLAMED, BLAMING, BLAMES to find fault with

BLAMEFUL *adj* blamable

BLAMER *n* pl. -S one that blames

BLAMING present participle of blame

BLANCH *v* -ED, -ING, -ES to whiten

BLANCHER *n* pl. -S a whitener

BLAND *adj* BLANDER, BLANDEST soothing **BLANDLY** *adv*

BLANDISH *v* -ED, -ING, -ES to coax by flattery

BLANK *adj* BLANKER, BLANKEST empty

BLANK *v* -ED, -ING, -S to delete

BLANKET *v* -ED, -ING, -S to cover uniformly

BLANKLY *adv* in a blank manner

BLARE *v* BLARED, BLARING, BLARES to sound loudly

BLARNEY *v* -NEYED, -NEYING, -NEYS to beguile with flattery

BLASE *adj* indifferent

BLAST *v* -ED, -ING, -S to use an explosive

BLASTEMA *n* pl. -MAS or -MATA a region of embryonic cells

BLASTER *n* pl. -S one that blasts

BLASTIE *n* pl. -S a dwarf

BLASTIER comparative of blasty

BLASTIEST superlative of blasty

BLASTING *n* pl. -S the act of one that blasts

BLASTOFF *n* pl. -S the launching of a rocket

BLASTOMA *n* pl. -MAS or -MATA a type of tumor

BLASTULA *n* pl. -LAS or -LAE an early embryo

BLASTY *adj* BLASTIER, BLASTIEST gusty

BLAT *v* BLATTED, BLATTING, BLATS to bleat

BLATANCY *n* pl. -CIES something blatant

BLATANT *adj* obvious

BLATE *adj* timid

BLATHER *v* -ED, -ING, -S to talk foolishly

BLATTED past tense of blat

BLATTER *v* -ED, -ING, -S to chatter

BLATTING present participle of blat

BLAUBOK *n* pl. -S an extinct antelope

BLAW *v* BLAWED, BLAWN, BLAWING, BLAWS to blow

BLAZE *v* BLAZED, BLAZING, BLAZES to burn brightly

BLAZER *n* pl. -S a lightweight jacket

BLAZON *v* -ED, -ING, -S to proclaim

BLAZONER *n* pl. -S one that blazons

BLAZONRY *n* pl. -RIES a great display

BLEACH *v* -ED, -ING, -ES to whiten

BLEACHER *n* pl. -S one that bleaches

BLEAK *adj* BLEAKER, BLEAKEST dreary

BLEAK *n* pl. -S a freshwater fish

BLEAKISH *adj* somewhat bleak

BLEAKLY *adv* in a bleak manner

BLEAR *v* -ED, -ING, -S to dim

BLEARY *adj* BLEARIER, BLEARIEST dimmed **BLEARILY** *adv*

BLEAT *v* -ED, -ING, -S to utter the cry of a sheep

BLEATER *n* pl. -S one that bleats

BLEB *n* pl. -S a blister **BLEBBY** *adj*

BLEED	*v* BLED, BLEEDING, BLEEDS to lose blood
BLEEDER	*n* pl. -S one that bleeds
BLEEDING	*n* pl. -S the act of losing blood
BLEEP	*v* -ED, -ING, -S to blip
BLELLUM	*n* pl. -S a babbler
BLEMISH	*v* -ED, -ING, -ES to mar
BLENCH	*v* -ED, -ING, -ES to flinch
BLENCHER	*n* pl. -S one that blenches
BLEND	*v* BLENDED or BLENT, BLENDING, BLENDS to mix smoothly and inseparably together
BLENDE	*n* pl. -S a shiny mineral
BLENDER	*n* pl. -S one that blends
BLENNY	*n* pl. -NIES a marine fish
BLENT	a past tense of blend
BLESBOK	*n* pl. -S a large antelope
BLESBUCK	*n* pl. -S blesbok
BLESS	*v* BLESSED or BLEST, BLESSING, BLESSES to sanctify
BLESSED	*adj* -EDER, -EDEST holy
BLESSER	*n* pl. -S one that blesses
BLESSING	*n* pl. -S a prayer
BLEST	a past tense of bless
BLET	*n* pl. -S a decay of fruit
BLETHER	*v* -ED, -ING, -S to blather
BLEW	past tense of blow
BLIGHT	*v* -ED, -ING, -S to cause decay
BLIGHTER	*n* pl. -S one that blights
BLIGHTY	*n* pl. BLIGHTIES a wound causing one to be sent home to England
BLIMEY	*interj* — used as an expression of surprise
BLIMP	*n* pl. -S a nonrigid aircraft **BLIMPISH** *adj*
BLIMY	*interj* blimey
BLIN	*n* pl. BLINI or BLINIS a blintze
BLIND	*adj* BLINDER, BLINDEST sightless
BLIND	*v* -ED, -ING, -S to make sightless
BLINDAGE	*n* pl. -S a protective screen
BLINDER	*n* pl. -S an obstruction to sight
BLINDLY	*adv* in a blind manner
BLINI	a pl. of blin
BLINIS	a pl. of blin
BLINK	*v* -ED, -ING, -S to open and shut the eyes
BLINKARD	*n* pl. -S one who habitually blinks
BLINKER	*v* -ED, -ING, -S to put blinders on
BLINTZ	*n* pl. -ES blintze
BLINTZE	*n* pl. -S a thin pancake
BLIP	*v* BLIPPED, BLIPPING, BLIPS to remove sound from a recording
BLISS	*v* -ED, -ING, -ES to experience or produce ecstasy
BLISSFUL	*adj* very happy
BLISTER	*v* -ED, -ING, -S to cause blisters (skin swellings)
BLISTERY	*adj* having blisters
BLITE	*n* pl. -S an annual herb
BLITHE	*adj* BLITHER, BLITHEST merry **BLITHELY** *adv*
BLITHER	*v* -ED, -ING, -S to blather
BLITZ	*v* -ED, -ING, -ES to subject to a sudden attack
BLIZZARD	*n* pl. -S a heavy snowstorm
BLOAT	*v* -ED, -ING, -S to swell
BLOATER	*n* pl. -S a smoked herring
BLOB	*v* BLOBBED, BLOBBING, BLOBS to splotch
BLOC	*n* pl. -S a coalition
BLOCK	*v* -ED, -ING, -S to obstruct
BLOCKADE	*v* -ADED, -ADING, -ADES to block
BLOCKAGE	*n* pl. -S the act of blocking
BLOCKER	*n* pl. -S one that blocks
BLOCKISH	*adj* blocky
BLOCKY	*adj* BLOCKIER, BLOCKIEST short and stout
BLOKE	*n* pl. -S a fellow
BLOND	*adj* BLONDER, BLONDEST light-colored
BLOND	*n* pl. -S a blond person
BLONDE	*n* pl. -S blond
BLONDISH	*adj* somewhat blond
BLOOD	*v* -ED, -ING, -S to stain with blood (the fluid circulated by the heart)
BLOODFIN	*n* pl. -S a freshwater fish
BLOODIED	past tense of bloody
BLOODIER	comparative of bloody
BLOODIES	present 3d person sing. of bloody
BLOODIEST	superlative of bloody
BLOODILY	*adv* in a bloody manner
BLOODING	*n* pl. -S a fox hunting ceremony
BLOODRED	*adj* of the color of blood
BLOODY	*adj* BLOODIER, BLOODIEST stained with blood
BLOODY	*v* BLOODIED, BLOODYING, BLOODIES to make bloody
BLOOEY	*adj* being out of order
BLOOIE	*adj* blooey

BLOOM v -ED, -ING, -S to bear flowers

BLOOMER n pl. -S a blooming plant

BLOOMERY n pl. -ERIES a furnace for smelting iron

BLOOMY adj BLOOMIER, BLOOMIEST covered with flowers

BLOOP v -ED, -ING, -S to hit a short fly ball

BLOOPER n pl. -S a public blunder

BLOSSOM v -ED, -ING, -S to bloom

BLOSSOMY adj having blossoms

BLOT v BLOTTED, BLOTTING, BLOTS to spot or stain

BLOTCH v -ED, -ING, -ES to mark with large spots

BLOTCHY adj BLOTCHIER, BLOTCHIEST blotched

BLOTLESS adj spotless

BLOTTED past tense of blot

BLOTTER n pl. -S a piece of ink-absorbing paper

BLOTTIER comparative of blotty

BLOTTIEST superlative of blotty

BLOTTING present participle of blot

BLOTTO adj drunk

BLOTTY adj -TIER, -TIEST spotty

BLOUSE v BLOUSED, BLOUSING, BLOUSES to hang loosely

BLOUSON n pl. -S a woman's garment

BLOUSY adj BLOUSIER, BLOUSIEST blowsy **BLOUSILY** adv

BLOVIATE v -ATED, -ATING, -ATES to speak pompously

BLOW v BLEW, BLOWN, BLOWING, BLOWS to drive or impel by a current of air

BLOW v BLEW, BLOWED, BLOWING, BLOWS to damn

BLOWBACK n pl. -S an escape of gases

BLOWBALL n pl. -S a fluffy seed ball

BLOWBY n pl. -BYS leakage of exhaust fumes

BLOWDOWN n pl. -S a tree blown down by the wind

BLOWER n pl. -S one that blows

BLOWFISH n pl. -ES a marine fish

BLOWFLY n pl. -FLIES a type of fly

BLOWGUN n pl. -S a tube through which darts may be blown

BLOWHARD n pl. -S a braggart

BLOWHOLE n pl. -S an air or gas vent

BLOWIER comparative of blowy

BLOWIEST superlative of blowy

BLOWN past participle of blow

BLOWOFF n pl. -S the expelling of gas

BLOWOUT n pl. -S a sudden rupture

BLOWPIPE n pl. -S a blowgun

BLOWSED adj blowsy

BLOWSY adj -SIER, -SIEST slovenly **BLOWSILY** adv

BLOWTUBE n pl. -S a blowgun

BLOWUP n pl. -S an explosion

BLOWY adj BLOWIER, BLOWIEST windy

BLOWZED adj blowzy

BLOWZY adj -ZIER, -ZIEST blowsy **BLOWZILY** adv

BLUB v BLUBBED, BLUBBING, BLUBS to blubber

BLUBBER v -ED, -ING, -S to weep noisily

BLUBBERY adj fat; swollen

BLUCHER n pl. -S a half boot

BLUDGEON v -ED, -ING, -S to hit with a club

BLUDGER n pl. -S a loafer or shirker

BLUE adj BLUER, BLUEST having the color of the clear sky

BLUE v BLUED, BLUEING or BLUING, BLUES to make blue

BLUEBALL n pl. -S a medicinal herb

BLUEBELL n pl. -S a flowering plant

BLUEBILL n pl. -S the scaup duck

BLUEBIRD n pl. -S a songbird

BLUEBOOK n pl. -S an examination booklet

BLUECAP n pl. -S a flowering plant

BLUECOAT n pl. -S a police officer

BLUED past tense of blue

BLUEFIN n pl. -S a large tuna

BLUEFISH n pl. -ES a marine fish

BLUEGILL n pl. -S an edible sunfish

BLUEGUM n pl. -S a timber tree

BLUEHEAD n pl. -S a marine fish

BLUEING n pl. -S bluing

BLUEISH adj bluish

BLUEJACK n pl. -S an oak tree

BLUEJAY n pl. -JAYS a corvine bird

BLUELINE n pl. -S a line that divides a hockey rink

BLUELY adv in a blue manner

BLUENESS n pl. -ES the state of being blue

BLUENOSE n pl. -S a puritanical person

BLUER comparative of blue

BLUESIER comparative of bluesy

BLUESIEST superlative of bluesy

BLUESMAN n pl. -MEN one who plays the blues

BLUEST superlative of blue

BLUESTEM n pl. -S a prairie grass

BLUESY *adj* BLUESIER, BLUESIEST resembling the blues (a musical form)

BLUET *n* pl. -S a meadow flower

BLUETICK *n* pl. -S a hunting dog

BLUEWEED *n* pl. -S a bristly weed

BLUEWOOD *n* pl. -S a shrub

BLUEY *n* pl. BLUEYS a bag of clothing carried in travel

BLUFF *v* -ED, -ING, -S to mislead

BLUFF *adj* BLUFFER, BLUFFEST having a broad front **BLUFFLY** *adv*

BLUFFER *n* pl. -S one that bluffs

BLUING *n* pl. -S a fabric coloring

BLUISH *adj* somewhat blue

BLUME *v* BLUMED, BLUMING, BLUMES to blossom

BLUNDER *v* -ED, -ING, -S to make a mistake

BLUNGE *v* BLUNGED, BLUNGING, BLUNGES to mix clay with water

BLUNGER *n* pl. -S one that blunges

BLUNT *adj* BLUNTER, BLUNTEST not sharp or pointed **BLUNTLY** *adv*

BLUNT *v* -ED, -ING, -S to make blunt

BLUR *v* BLURRED, BLURRING, BLURS to make unclear

BLURB *v* -ED, -ING, -S to praise in a publicity notice

BLURRY *adj* -RIER, -RIEST unclear **BLURRILY** *adv*

BLURT *v* -ED, -ING, -S to speak abruptly

BLURTER *n* pl. -S one that blurts

BLUSH *v* -ED, -ING, -ES to become red

BLUSHER *n* pl. -S one that blushes

BLUSHFUL *adj* of a red color

BLUSTER *v* -ED, -ING, -S to blow violently

BLUSTERY *adj* windy

BLYPE *n* pl. -S a shred

BO *n* pl. BOS a pal

BOA *n* pl. -S a large snake

BOAR *n* pl. -S a male pig

BOARD *v* -ED, -ING, -S to take meals for a fixed price

BOARDER *n* pl. -S one that boards

BOARDING *n* pl. -S a surface of wooden boards

BOARDMAN *n* pl. -MEN a board member

BOARFISH *n* pl. -ES a marine fish

BOARISH *adj* swinish; coarse

BOART *n* pl. -S bort

BOAST *v* -ED, -ING, -S to brag

BOASTER *n* pl. -S one that boasts

BOASTFUL *adj* given to boasting

BOAT *v* -ED, -ING, -S to travel by boat (watercraft) **BOATABLE** *adj*

BOATBILL *n* pl. -S a wading bird

BOATEL *n* pl. -S a waterside hotel

BOATER *n* pl. -S one that boats

BOATFUL *n* pl. -S as much as a boat can hold

BOATHOOK *n* pl. -S a pole with a metal hook for use aboard a boat

BOATING *n* pl. -S the sport of traveling by boat

BOATLIKE *adj* resembling a boat

BOATLOAD *n* pl. -S the amount that a boat holds

BOATMAN *n* pl. -MEN one who works on boats

BOATSMAN *n* pl. -MEN boatman

BOATYARD *n* pl. -S a marina

BOB *v* BOBBED, BOBBING, BOBS to move up and down

BOBBER *n* pl. -S one that bobs

BOBBERY *n* pl. -BERIES a disturbance

BOBBIES pl. of bobby

BOBBIN *n* pl. -S a thread holder

BOBBINET *n* pl. -S a machine-made net

BOBBING present participle of bob

BOBBLE *v* -BLED, -BLING, -BLES to fumble

BOBBY *n* pl. -BIES a police officer

BOBCAT *n* pl. -S a lynx

BOBECHE *n* pl. -S a glass collar on a candle holder

BOBOLINK *n* pl. -S a songbird

BOBSLED *v* -SLEDDED, -SLEDDING, -SLEDS to ride on a bobsled (a racing sled)

BOBSTAY *n* pl. -STAYS a steadying rope

BOBTAIL *v* -ED, -ING, -S to cut short

BOBWHITE *n* pl. -S a game bird

BOCACCIO *n* pl. -CIOS a rockfish

BOCCE *n* pl. -S boccie

BOCCI *n* pl. -S boccie

BOCCIA *n* pl. -S boccie

BOCCIE *n* pl. -S an Italian bowling game

BOCK *n* pl. -S a dark beer

BOD *n* pl. -S a body

BODE *v* BODED, BODING, BODES to be an omen of

BODEGA *n* pl. -S a grocery store

BODEMENT *n* pl. -S an omen

BODHRAN *n* pl. -S an Irish drum

BODICE *n* pl. -S a corset

BODIED past tense of body

BODIES present 3d person sing. of body

BODILESS *adj* lacking material form

BODILY *adj* of the body

BODING *n* pl. -S an omen

BODINGLY *adv* ominously

BODKIN *n* pl. -S a sharp instrument

BODY *v* BODIED, BODYING, BODIES to give form to

BODYSUIT *n* pl. -S a one-piece garment for the torso

BODYSURF *v* -ED, -ING, -S to ride a wave without a surfboard

BODYWORK *n* pl. -S a vehicle body

BOEHMITE *n* pl. -S a mineral

BOFF *n* pl. -S a hearty laugh

BOFFIN *n* pl. -S a scientific expert

BOFFO *n* pl. -FOS a boff

BOFFOLA *n* pl. -S a boff

BOG *v* BOGGED, BOGGING, BOGS to impede

BOGAN *n* pl. -S a backwater or tributary

BOGBEAN *n* pl. -S a marsh plant

BOGEY *v* -GEYED, -GEYING, -GEYS to shoot in one stroke over par in golf

BOGEYMAN *n* pl. -MEN a terrifying creature

BOGGED past tense of bog

BOGGIER comparative of boggy

BOGGIEST superlative of boggy

BOGGING present participle of bog

BOGGISH *adj* boggy

BOGGLE *v* -GLED, -GLING, -GLES to hesitate

BOGGLER *n* pl. -S one that causes another to boggle

BOGGY *adj* -GIER, -GIEST marshy

BOGIE *n* pl. -S bogy

BOGIES pl. of bogy

BOGLE *n* pl. -S a bogy

BOGUS *adj* not genuine; fake

BOGWOOD *n* pl. -S preserved tree wood

BOGY *n* pl. -GIES a goblin

BOGYISM *n* pl. -S behavior characteristic of a bogy

BOGYMAN *n* pl. -MEN bogeyman

BOHEA *n* pl. -S a black tea

BOHEMIA *n* pl. -S a community of bohemians

BOHEMIAN *n* pl. -S an unconventional person

BOHUNK *n* pl. -S an unskilled laborer

BOIL *v* -ED, -ING, -S to vaporize liquid BOILABLE *adj*

BOILER *n* pl. -S a vessel for boiling

BOILOFF *n* pl. -S the vaporization of a liquid

BOING *interj* — used to express the sound of reverberation or vibration

BOISERIE *n* pl. -S wood paneling on a wall

BOITE *n* pl. -S a nightclub

BOLA *n* pl. -S a throwing weapon

BOLAR *adj* pertaining to bole

BOLAS *n* pl. -ES bola

BOLD *adj* BOLDER, BOLDEST daring BOLDLY *adv*

BOLDFACE *v* -FACED, -FACING, -FACES to print in thick type

BOLDNESS *n* pl. -ES the quality of being bold

BOLE *n* pl. -S a fine clay

BOLERO *n* pl. -ROS a Spanish dance

BOLETE *n* pl. -S boletus

BOLETUS *n* pl. -TUSES or -TI a fungus

BOLIDE *n* pl. -S an exploding meteor

BOLIVAR *n* pl. -S or -ES a monetary unit of Venezuela

BOLIVIA *n* pl. -S a soft fabric

BOLL *v* -ED, -ING, -S to form pods

BOLLARD *n* pl. -S a thick post on a ship or wharf

BOLLIX *v* -ED, -ING, -ES to bungle

BOLLOCKS *n/pl* testicles

BOLLOX *v* -ED, -ING, -ES to bollix

BOLLWORM *n* pl. -S the larva of a certain moth

BOLO *n* pl. -LOS a machete

BOLOGNA *n* pl. -S a seasoned sausage

BOLONEY *n* pl. -NEYS bologna

BOLSHIE *n* pl. -S a Bolshevik

BOLSHY *n* pl. -SHIES bolshie

BOLSON *n* pl. -S a flat arid valley

BOLSTER *v* -ED, -ING, -S to support

BOLT *v* -ED, -ING, -S to sift

BOLTER *n* pl. -S a sifting machine

BOLTHEAD *n* pl. -S a matrass

BOLTHOLE *n* pl. -S a place or way of escape

BOLTONIA *n* pl. -S a perennial herb

BOLTROPE *n* pl. -S a rope sewn to a sail

BOLUS *n* pl. -ES a large pill

BOMB *v* -ED, -ING, -S to attack with bombs (explosive projectiles)

BOMBARD *v* -ED, -ING, -S to bomb

BOMBAST *n* pl. -S pompous language

BOMBAX *adj* pertaining to a family of tropical trees
BOMBE *n* pl. -S a frozen dessert
BOMBER *n* pl. -S one that bombs
BOMBESIN *n* pl. -S a combination of amino acids
BOMBING *n* pl. -S an attack with bombs
BOMBLOAD *n* pl. -S the quantity of bombs being carried
BOMBYCID *n* pl. -S a moth
BOMBYX *n* pl. -ES a silkworm
BONACI *n* pl. -S an edible fish
BONANZA *n* pl. -S a rich mine
BONBON *n* pl. -S a sugared candy
BOND *v* -ED, -ING, -S to join together **BONDABLE** *adj*
BONDAGE *n* pl. -S slavery
BONDER *n* pl. -S one that bonds
BONDING *n* pl. -S the formation of a close personal relationship
BONDMAID *n* pl. -S a female slave
BONDMAN *n* pl. -MEN a male slave
BONDSMAN *n* pl. -MEN bondman
BONDUC *n* pl. -S a prickly seed
BONE *v* BONED, BONING, BONES to debone
BONEFISH *n* pl. -ES a slender marine fish
BONEHEAD *n* pl. -S a stupid person
BONELESS *adj* having no bones (hard connective tissue)
BONEMEAL *n* pl. -S fertilizer or feed made from crushed bone
BONER *n* pl. -S a blunder
BONESET *n* pl. -S a perennial herb
BONEY *adj* BONIER, BONIEST bony
BONEYARD *n* pl. -S a junkyard
BONFIRE *n* pl. -S an open fire
BONG *v* -ED, -ING, -S to make a deep, ringing sound
BONGO *n* pl. -GOS or -GOES a small drum
BONGOIST *n* pl. -S a bongo player
BONHOMIE *n* pl. -S friendliness
BONIER comparative of bony or boney
BONIEST superlative of bony or boney
BONIFACE *n* pl. -S an innkeeper
BONINESS *n* pl. -ES the state of being bony
BONING present participle of bone
BONITA *n* pl. -S bonito
BONITO *n* pl. -TOS or -TOES a marine food fish
BONK *v* -ED, -ING, -S to hit on the head with a hollow blow
BONKERS *adj* crazy
BONNE *n* pl. -S a housemaid

BONNET *v* -ED, -ING, -S to provide with a bonnet (a type of hat)
BONNIE *adj* bonny
BONNOCK *n* pl. -S bannock
BONNY *adj* -NIER, -NIEST pretty **BONNILY** *adv*
BONSAI *n* pl. BONSAI a potted shrub that has been dwarfed
BONSPELL *n* pl. -S bonspiel
BONSPIEL *n* pl. -S a curling match or tournament
BONTEBOK *n* pl. -S an antelope
BONUS *n* pl. -ES an additional payment
BONY *adj* BONIER, BONIEST full of bones
BONZE *n* pl. -S a Buddhist monk
BONZER *adj* very good
BOO *v* -ED, -ING, -S to cry "boo"
BOOB *v* -ED, -ING, -S to make a foolish mistake
BOOBISH *adj* doltish
BOOBOO *n* pl. -BOOS a mistake
BOOBY *n* pl. -BIES a dolt
BOODLE *v* -DLED, -DLING, -DLES to take bribes
BOODLER *n* pl. -S one that boodles
BOOGER *n* pl. -S a bogeyman
BOOGEY *v* -GEYED, -GEYING, -GEYS boogie
BOOGIE *v* -GIED, -GYING, -GIES to dance to rock music
BOOGY *v* -GIED, -GYING, -GIES boogie
BOOGYMAN *n* pl. -MEN bogeyman
BOOHOO *v* -ED, -ING, -S to weep noisily
BOOK *v* -ED, -ING, -S to engage services **BOOKABLE** *adj*
BOOKCASE *n* pl. -S a case which holds books (literary volumes)
BOOKEND *n* pl. -S a support for a row of books
BOOKER *n* pl. -S one that books
BOOKFUL *n* pl. -S as much as a book can hold
BOOKIE *n* pl. -S a bet taker
BOOKING *n* pl. -S an engagement
BOOKISH *adj* pertaining to books
BOOKLET *n* pl. -S a small book
BOOKLICE *n/pl* wingless insects that damage books
BOOKLORE *n* pl. -S book learning
BOOKMAN *n* pl. -MEN a scholar
BOOKMARK *n* pl. -S a marker for finding a place in a book

BOOKRACK n pl. -S a support for an open book

BOOKREST n pl. -S a bookrack

BOOKSHOP n pl. -S a store where books are sold

BOOKWORM n pl. -S an avid book reader

BOOM v -ED, -ING, -S to make a deep, resonant sound

BOOMBOX n pl. -ES a portable radio and tape or compact disc player

BOOMER n pl. -S one that booms

BOOMIER comparative of boomy

BOOMIEST superlative of boomy

BOOMKIN n pl. -S a bumkin

BOOMLET n pl. -S a small increase in prosperity

BOOMTOWN n pl. -S a prospering town

BOOMY adj BOOMIER, BOOMIEST prospering

BOON n pl. -S a timely benefit

BOONDOCK adj pertaining to a backwoods area

BOONIES n/pl a backwoods area

BOOR n pl. -S a rude person

BOORISH adj rude

BOOST v -ED, -ING, -S to support

BOOSTER n pl. -S one that boosts

BOOT v -ED, -ING, -S to load a program into a computer **BOOTABLE** adj

BOOTEE n pl. -S a baby's sock

BOOTERY n pl. -ERIES a shoe store

BOOTH n pl. -S a small enclosure

BOOTIE n pl. -S bootee

BOOTIES pl. of booty

BOOTJACK n pl. -S a device for pulling off boots

BOOTLACE n pl. -S a shoelace

BOOTLEG v -LEGGED, -LEGGING, -LEGS to smuggle

BOOTLESS adj useless

BOOTLICK v -ED, -ING, -S to flatter servilely

BOOTY n pl. -TIES a rich gain or prize

BOOZE v BOOZED, BOOZING, BOOZES to drink liquor excessively

BOOZER n pl. -S one that boozes

BOOZY adj BOOZIER, BOOZIEST drunken **BOOZILY** adv

BOP v BOPPED, BOPPING, BOPS to hit or strike

BOPEEP n pl. -S a game of peekaboo

BOPPER n pl. -S a bebopper

BORA n pl. -S a cold wind

BORACES a pl. of borax

BORACIC adj boric

BORACITE n pl. -S a mineral

BORAGE n pl. -S a medicinal herb

BORAL n pl. -S a mixture of boron carbide and aluminum

BORANE n pl. -S a chemical compound

BORATE v -RATED, -RATING, -RATES to mix with borax or boric acid

BORAX n pl. -RAXES or -RACES a white crystalline compound

BORDEAUX n pl. BORDEAUX a red or white wine

BORDEL n pl. -S a brothel

BORDELLO n pl. -LOS a brothel

BORDER v -ED, -ING, -S to put a border (an edge) on

BORDERER n pl. -S one that borders

BORDURE n pl. -S a border around a shield

BORE v BORED, BORING, BORES to pierce with a rotary tool

BOREAL adj pertaining to the north

BORECOLE n pl. -S kale

BORED past tense of bore

BOREDOM n pl. -S tedium

BOREEN n pl. -S a lane in Ireland

BOREHOLE n pl. -S a hole bored in the earth

BORER n pl. -S one that bores

BORESOME adj tedious

BORIC adj pertaining to boron

BORIDE n pl. -S a boron compound

BORING n pl. -S an inner cavity

BORINGLY adv tediously

BORN adj having particular qualities from birth

BORNE a past participle of bear

BORNEOL n pl. -S an alcohol

BORNITE n pl. -S an ore of copper

BORON n pl. -S a nonmetallic element **BORONIC** adj

BOROUGH n pl. -S an incorporated town

BORROW v -ED, -ING, -S to take on loan

BORROWER n pl. -S one that borrows

BORSCH n pl. -ES borscht

BORSCHT n pl. -S a beet soup

BORSHT n pl. -S borscht

BORSTAL n pl. -S a reformatory

BORT n pl. -S a low-quality diamond **BORTY** adj

BORTZ n pl. -ES bort

BORZOI n pl. -S a Russian hound

BOSCAGE n pl. -S a thicket

BOSCHBOK n pl. -S bushbuck

BOSH n pl. -ES nonsense

BOSHBOK   *n* pl. -S bushbuck
BOSHVARK   *n* pl. -S a wild hog
BOSK   *n* pl. -S a small wooded area
BOSKAGE   *n* pl. -S boscage
BOSKER   *adj* fine; very good
BOSKET   *n* pl. -S a thicket
BOSKY   *adj* BOSKIER, BOSKIEST wooded; bushy
BOSOM   *v* -ED, -ING, -S to embrace
BOSOMY   *adj* swelling outward
BOSON   *n* pl. -S a subatomic particle
BOSQUE   *n* pl. -S bosk
BOSQUET   *n* pl. -S bosket
BOSS   *v* -ED, -ING, -ES to supervise
BOSSDOM   *n* pl. -S the domain of a political boss
BOSSIER   comparative of bossy
BOSSIES   pl. of bossy
BOSSISM   *n* pl. -S control by political bosses
BOSSY   *adj* BOSSIER, BOSSIEST domineering **BOSSILY** *adv*
BOSSY   *n* pl. BOSSIES a cow
BOSTON   *n* pl. -S a card game
BOSUN   *n* pl. -S a boatswain
BOT   *n* pl. -S the larva of a botfly
BOTA   *n* pl. -S a leather bottle
BOTANIC   *adj* pertaining to botany
BOTANICA   *n* pl. -S a shop that sells herbs and magic charms
BOTANIES   pl. of botany
BOTANISE   *v* -NISED, -NISING, -NISES to botanize
BOTANIST   *n* pl. -S one skilled in botany
BOTANIZE   *v* -NIZED, -NIZING, -NIZES to study plants
BOTANY   *n* pl. -NIES the science of plants
BOTCH   *v* -ED, -ING, -ES to bungle
BOTCHER   *n* pl. -S one that botches
BOTCHERY   *n* pl. -ERIES something botched
BOTCHY   *adj* BOTCHIER, BOTCHIEST badly done **BOTCHILY** *adv*
BOTEL   *n* pl. -S boatel
BOTFLY   *n* pl. -FLIES a type of fly
BOTH   *adj* being the two
BOTHER   *v* -ED, -ING, -S to annoy
BOTHRIUM   *n* pl. -RIA or -RIUMS a groove on a tapeworm
BOTHY   *n* pl. BOTHIES a hut in Scotland
BOTONEE   *adj* having arms ending in a trefoil — used of a heraldic cross
BOTONNEE   *adj* botonee

BOTRYOID   *adj* resembling a cluster of grapes
BOTRYOSE   *adj* botryoid
BOTRYTIS   *n* pl. -TISES a plant disease
BOTT   *n* pl. -S bot
BOTTLE   *v* -TLED, -TLING, -TLES to put into a bottle (a rigid container)
BOTTLER   *n* pl. -S one that bottles
BOTTLING   *n* pl. -S a bottled beverage
BOTTOM   *v* -ED, -ING, -S to comprehend
BOTTOMER   *n* pl. -S one that bottoms
BOTTOMRY   *n* pl. -RIES a maritime contract
BOTULIN   *n* pl. -S a nerve poison
BOTULISM   *n* pl. -S botulin poisoning
BOUBOU   *n* pl. -S a long flowing garment
BOUCHEE   *n* pl. -S a small patty shell
BOUCLE   *n* pl. -S a knitted fabric
BOUDOIR   *n* pl. -S a woman's bedroom
BOUFFANT   *n* pl. -S a woman's hairdo
BOUFFE   *n* pl. -S a comic opera
BOUGH   *n* pl. -S a tree branch
     BOUGHED *adj*
BOUGHPOT   *n* pl. -S a large vase
BOUGHT   past tense of buy
BOUGHTEN   *adj* purchased
BOUGIE   *n* pl. -S a wax candle
BOUILLON   *n* pl. -S a clear broth
BOULDER   *n* pl. -S a large rock
     BOULDERY *adj*
BOULE   *n* pl. -S buhl
BOULLE   *n* pl. -S buhl
BOUNCE   *v* BOUNCED, BOUNCING, BOUNCES to spring back
BOUNCER   *n* pl. -S one that bounces
BOUNCY   *adj* BOUNCIER, BOUNCIEST tending to bounce **BOUNCILY** *adv*
BOUND   *v* -ED, -ING, -S to leap
BOUNDARY   *n* pl. -ARIES a dividing line
BOUNDEN   *adj* obliged
BOUNDER   *n* pl. -S one that bounds
BOUNTY   *n* pl. -TIES a reward
     BOUNTIED *adj*
BOUQUET   *n* pl. -S a bunch of flowers
BOURBON   *n* pl. -S a whiskey
BOURDON   *n* pl. -S a part of a bagpipe
BOURG   *n* pl. -S a medieval town
BOURGEON   *v* -ED, -ING, -S to burgeon
BOURN   *n* pl. -S a stream
BOURNE   *n* pl. -S bourn
BOURREE   *n* pl. -S an old French dance
BOURRIDE   *n* pl. -S a fish stew
BOURSE   *n* pl. -S a stock exchange

BOURTREE *n* pl. -S a European tree

BOUSE *v* BOUSED, BOUSING, BOUSES to haul by means of a tackle

BOUSOUKI *n* pl. -KIA or -KIS bouzouki

BOUSY *adj* boozy

BOUT *n* pl. -S a contest

BOUTIQUE *n* pl. -S a small shop

BOUTON *n* pl. -S an enlarged end of a nerve fiber

BOUVIER *n* pl. -S a large dog

BOUZOUKI *n* pl. -KIA or -KIS a stringed musical instrument

BOVID *n* pl. -S a bovine

BOVINE *n* pl. -S an ox-like animal

BOVINELY *adv* stolidly

BOVINITY *n* pl. -TIES the state of being a bovine

BOW *v* -ED, -ING, -S to bend forward

BOWEL *v* -ELED, -ELING, -ELS or -ELLED, -ELLING, -ELS to disbowel

BOWER *v* -ED, -ING, -S to embower

BOWERY *n* -ERIES a colonial Dutch farm

BOWFIN *n* pl. -S a freshwater fish

BOWFRONT *adj* having a curved front

BOWHEAD *n* pl. -S an arctic whale

BOWING *n* pl. -S the technique of managing the bow of a stringed instrument

BOWINGLY *adv* in a bowing manner

BOWKNOT *n* pl. -S a type of knot

BOWL *v* -ED, -ING, -S to play at bowling

BOWLDER *n* pl. -S boulder

BOWLEG *n* pl. -S an outwardly curved leg

BOWLER *n* pl. -S one that bowls

BOWLESS *adj* being without an archery bow

BOWLFUL *n* pl. -S as much as a bowl can hold

BOWLIKE *adj* curved

BOWLINE *n* pl. -S a type of knot

BOWLING *n* pl. -S a game in which balls are rolled at objects

BOWLLIKE *adj* concave

BOWMAN *n* pl. -MEN an archer

BOWPOT *n* pl. -S boughpot

BOWSE *v* BOWSED, BOWSING, BOWSES to bouse

BOWSHOT *n* pl. -S the distance an arrow is shot

BOWSPRIT *n* pl. -S a ship's spar

BOWWOW *v* -ED, -ING, -S to bark like a dog

BOWYER *n* pl. -S a maker of archery bows

BOX *v* -ED, -ING, -ES to put in a box (a rectangular container)

BOXBERRY *n* pl. -RIES an evergreen plant

BOXBOARD *n* pl. -S stiff paperboard

BOXCAR *n* pl. -S a roofed freight car

BOXER *n* pl. -S one that packs boxes

BOXFISH *n* pl. -ES a marine fish

BOXFUL *n* pl. -S as much as a box can hold

BOXHAUL *v* -ED, -ING, -S to veer a ship around

BOXIER comparative of boxy

BOXIEST superlative of boxy

BOXINESS *n* pl. -ES the state of being boxy

BOXING *n* pl. -S a casing

BOXLIKE *adj* resembling a box

BOXTHORN *n* pl. -S a thorny shrub

BOXWOOD *n* pl. -S an evergreen shrub

BOXY *adj* BOXIER, BOXIEST resembling a box

BOY *n* pl. BOYS a male child

BOYAR *n* pl. -S a former Russian aristocrat

BOYARD *n* pl. -S boyar

BOYARISM *n* pl. -S the rule of boyars

BOYCHICK *n* pl. -S boychik

BOYCHIK *n* pl. -S a young man

BOYCOTT *v* -ED, -ING, -S to refuse to buy

BOYHOOD *n* pl. -S the state of being a boy

BOYISH *adj* resembling a boy

BOYISHLY *adv*

BOYLA *n* pl. -S a witch doctor

BOYO *n* pl. BOYOS a boy

BOZO *n* pl. -ZOS a fellow

BRA *n* pl. -S a brassiere

BRABBLE *v* -BLED, -BLING, -BLES to quarrel noisily

BRABBLER *n* pl. -S one that brabbles

BRACE *v* BRACED, BRACING, BRACES to support

BRACELET *n* pl. -S a wrist ornament

BRACER *n* pl. -S one that braces

BRACERO *n* pl. -ROS a Mexican laborer

BRACH *n* pl. -ES or -S a hound bitch

BRACHET *n* pl. -S a brach

BRACHIAL *n* pl. -S a part of the arm

BRACHIUM *n* pl. -IA the upper part of arm

BRACING *n* pl. -S a brace or reinforcement

BRACIOLA *n* pl. -S a thin slice of meat
BRACIOLE *n* pl. -S braciola
BRACKEN *n* pl. -S a large fern
BRACKET *v* -ED, -ING, -S to classify
BRACKISH *adj* salty
BRACONID *n* pl. -S any of a family of flies
BRACT *n* pl. -S a leaflike plant part **BRACTEAL, BRACTED** *adj*
BRACTLET *n* pl. -S a small bract
BRAD *v* BRADDED, BRADDING, BRADS to fasten with thin nails
BRADAWL *n* pl. -S a type of awl
BRADOON *n* pl. -S bridoon
BRAE *n* pl. -S a hillside
BRAG *adj* BRAGGER, BRAGGEST first-rate
BRAG *v* BRAGGED, BRAGGING, BRAGS to speak vainly of one's deeds
BRAGGART *n* pl. -S one who brags
BRAGGER *n* pl. -S a braggart
BRAGGEST superlative of brag
BRAGGING present participle of brag
BRAGGY *adj* -GIER, -GIEST tending to brag
BRAHMA *n* pl. -S a large domestic fowl
BRAID *v* -ED, -ING, -S to weave together
BRAIDER *n* pl. -S one that braids
BRAIDING *n* pl. -S something made of braided material
BRAIL *v* -ED, -ING, -S to haul in a sail
BRAILLE *v* BRAILLED, BRAILLING, BRAILLES to write in braille (raised writing for the blind)
BRAIN *v* -ED, -ING, -S to hit on the head
BRAINIER comparative of brainy
BRAINIEST superlative of brainy
BRAINILY *adv* in a brainy manner
BRAINISH *adj* impetuous
BRAINPAN *n* pl. -S the skull
BRAINY *adj* BRAINIER, BRAINIEST smart
BRAISE *v* BRAISED, BRAISING, BRAISES to cook in fat
BRAIZE *n* pl. -S a marine fish
BRAKE *v* BRAKED, BRAKING, BRAKES to slow down or stop
BRAKEAGE *n* pl. -S the act of braking
BRAKEMAN *n* pl. -MEN a trainman
BRAKING present participle of brake
BRAKY *adj* BRAKIER, BRAKIEST abounding in shrubs or ferns

BRALESS *adj* wearing no bra
BRAMBLE *v* -BLED, -BLING, -BLES to gather berries
BRAMBLY *adj* -BLIER, -BLIEST prickly
BRAN *v* BRANNED, BRANNING, BRANS to soak in water mixed with bran (the outer coat of cereals)
BRANCH *v* -ED, -ING, -ES to form branches
BRANCHIA *n* pl. -CHIAE a respiratory organ of aquatic animals
BRANCHY *adj* BRANCHIER, BRANCHIEST having many branches
BRAND *v* -ED, -ING, -S to mark with a hot iron
BRANDER *n* pl. -S one that brands
BRANDISH *v* -ED, -ING, -ES to wave menacingly
BRANDY *v* -DIED, -DYING, -DIES to mix with brandy (a liquor)
BRANK *n* pl. -S a device used to restrain the tongue
BRANNED past tense of bran
BRANNER *n* pl. -S one that brans
BRANNING present participle of bran
BRANNY *adj* -NIER, -NIEST containing bran
BRANT *n* pl. -S a wild goose
BRANTAIL *n* pl. -S a singing bird
BRASH *adj* BRASHER, BRASHEST rash; hasty **BRASHLY** *adv*
BRASH *n* pl. -ES a mass of fragments
BRASHY *adj* BRASHIER, BRASHIEST brash
BRASIER *n* pl. -S brazier
BRASIL *n* pl. -S brazil
BRASILIN *n* pl. -S brazilin
BRASS *v* -ED, -ING, -ES to coat with brass (an alloy of copper and zinc)
BRASSAGE *n* pl. -S a fee for coining money
BRASSARD *n* pl. -S an insignia
BRASSART *n* pl. -S brassard
BRASSICA *n* pl. -S a tall herb
BRASSIE *n* pl. -S a golf club
BRASSISH *adj* resembling brass
BRASSY *adj* BRASSIER, BRASSIEST resembling brass **BRASSILY** *adv*
BRAT *n* pl. -S a spoiled child **BRATTISH** *adj*
BRATTICE *v* -TICED, -TICING, -TICES to partition

BRATTLE	v -TLED, -TLING, -TLES to clatter
BRATTY	adj -TIER, -TIEST resembling a brat
BRAUNITE	n pl. -S a mineral
BRAVA	n pl. -S a shout of approval
BRAVADO	n pl. -DOS or -DOES false bravery
BRAVE	adj- BRAVER, BRAVEST showing courage **BRAVELY** adv
BRAVE	v BRAVED, BRAVING, BRAVES to face with courage
BRAVER	n pl. -S one that braves
BRAVERY	n pl. -ERIES courage
BRAVEST	superlative of brave
BRAVI	a pl. of bravo
BRAVING	present participle of brave
BRAVO	n pl. -VOS or -VOES or -VI a hired killer
BRAVO	v -ED, -ING, -ES to applaud by shouting "bravo"
BRAVURA	n pl. -RAS or -RE fine musical technique
BRAW	adj BRAWER, BRAWEST splendid
BRAWL	v -ED, -ING, -S to fight
BRAWLER	n pl. -S a fighter
BRAWLIE	adv splendidly
BRAWLY	adj BRAWLIER, BRAWLIEST inclined to brawl
BRAWN	n pl. -S muscular strength
BRAWNY	adj BRAWNIER, BRAWNIEST muscular **BRAWNILY** adv
BRAWS	n/pl fine clothes
BRAXY	n pl. BRAXIES a fever of sheep
BRAY	v BRAYED, BRAYING, BRAYS to utter a harsh cry
BRAYER	n pl. -S a roller used to spread ink
BRAZA	n pl. -S a Spanish unit of length
BRAZE	v BRAZED, BRAZING, BRAZES to solder together
BRAZEN	v -ED, -ING, -S to face boldly
BRAZENLY	adv boldly
BRAZER	n pl. -S one that brazes
BRAZIER	n pl. -S one who works in brass
BRAZIL	n pl. -S a dyewood
BRAZILIN	n pl. -S a chemical compound
BRAZING	present participle of braze
BREACH	v -ED, -ING, -ES to break through
BREACHER	n pl. -S one that breaches
BREAD	v -ED, -ING, -S to cover with crumbs of bread (a baked foodstuff made from flour)
BREADBOX	n pl. -ES a container for bread
BREADNUT	n pl. -S a tropical fruit
BREADTH	n pl. -S width
BREADY	adj resembling or characteristic of bread
BREAK	v BROKE, BROKEN, BREAKING, BREAKS to reduce to fragments
BREAKAGE	n pl. -S the act of breaking
BREAKER	n pl. -S one that breaks
BREAKING	n pl. -S the change of a pure vowel to a diphthong
BREAKOUT	n pl. -S an escape
BREAKUP	n pl. -S the act of breaking up
BREAM	v -ED, -ING, -S to clean a ship's bottom
BREAST	v -ED, -ING, -S to confront boldly
BREATH	n pl. -S air inhaled and exhaled
BREATHE	v BREATHED, BREATHING, BREATHES to inhale and exhale air
BREATHER	n pl. -S one that breathes
BREATHY	adj BREATHIER, BREATHIEST marked by loud breathing
BRECCIA	n pl. -S a type of rock **BRECCIAL** adj
BRECHAM	n pl. -S a collar for a horse
BRECHAN	n pl. -S brecham
BRED	past tense of breed
BREDE	n pl. -S a braid
BREE	n pl. -S broth
BREECH	v -ED, -ING, -ES to clothe with breeches (trousers)
BREED	v BRED, BREEDING, BREEDS to cause to give birth
BREEDER	n pl. -S one that breeds
BREEDING	n pl. -S upbringing
BREEKS	n/pl breeches
BREEZE	v BREEZED, BREEZING, BREEZES to move swiftly
BREEZY	adj BREEZIER, BREEZIEST windy **BREEZILY** adv
BREGMA	n pl. -MATA a junction point of the skull **BREGMATE** adj
BREN	n pl. -S a submachine gun
BRENT	n pl. -S brant
BRETHREN	a pl. of brother
BREVE	n pl. -S a symbol used to indicate a short vowel

BREVET   v -VETED, -VETING, -VETS or -VETTED, -VETTING, -VETS to confer an honorary rank upon

BREVETCY   n pl. -CIES an honorary rank

BREVIARY   n pl. -RIES a prayer book

BREVIER   n pl. -S a size of type

BREVITY   n pl. -TIES shortness of duration

BREW   v -ED, -ING, -S to make beer or the like

BREWAGE   n pl. -S a brewed beverage

BREWER   n pl. -S one that brews

BREWERY   n pl. -ERIES a place for brewing

BREWING   n pl. -S a quantity brewed at one time

BREWIS   n pl. BREWISES broth

BRIAR   n pl. -S brier **BRIARY** adj

BRIARD   n pl. -S a large dog

BRIBE   v BRIBED, BRIBING, BRIBES to practice bribery **BRIBABLE** adj

BRIBEE   n pl. -S one that is bribed

BRIBER   n pl. -S one that bribes

BRIBERY   n pl. -ERIES an act of influencing corruptly

BRIBING   present participle of bribe

BRICK   v -ED, -ING, -S to build with bricks (blocks of clay)

BRICKBAT   n pl. -S a piece of brick

BRICKLE   n pl. -S a brittle candy

BRICKY   adj BRICKIER, BRICKIEST made of bricks

BRICOLE   n pl. -S a cushion shot in billiards

BRIDAL   n pl. -S a wedding

BRIDALLY   adv in a manner befitting a bride

BRIDE   n pl. -S a woman just married or about to be married

BRIDGE   v BRIDGED, BRIDGING, BRIDGES to connect

BRIDGING   n pl. -S a bracing

BRIDLE   v -DLED, -DLING, -DLES to control with a restraint

BRIDLER   n pl. -S one that bridles

BRIDOON   n pl. -S a device used to control a horse

BRIE   n pl. -S bree

BRIEF   adj BRIEFER, BRIEFEST short

BRIEF   v -ED, -ING, -S to summarize

BRIEFER   n pl. -S one that briefs

BRIEFING   n pl. -S a short lecture

BRIEFLY   adv in a brief manner

BRIER   n pl. -S a thorny shrub **BRIERY** adj

BRIG   n pl. -S a two-masted ship

BRIGADE   v -GADED, -GADING, -GADES to group together

BRIGAND   n pl. -S a bandit

BRIGHT   adj BRIGHTER, BRIGHTEST emitting much light **BRIGHTLY** adv

BRIGHT   n pl. -S a light-hued tobacco

BRIGHTEN   v -ED, -ING, -S to make bright

BRILL   n pl. -S an edible flatfish

BRIM   v BRIMMED, BRIMMING, BRIMS to fill to the top

BRIMFUL   adj ready to overflow

BRIMFULL   adj brimful

BRIMLESS   adj having no brim (an upper edge)

BRIMMED   past tense of brim

BRIMMER   n pl. -S a brimming cup or glass

BRIMMING   present participle of brim

BRIN   n pl. -S a rib of a fan

BRINDED   adj brindled

BRINDLE   n pl. -S a brindled color

BRINDLED   adj streaked

BRINE   v BRINED, BRINING, BRINES to treat with brine (salted water)

BRINER   n pl. -S one that brines

BRING   v BROUGHT, BRINGING, BRINGS to take with oneself to a place

BRINGER   n pl. -S one that brings

BRINIER   comparative of briny

BRINIES   pl. of briny

BRINIEST   superlative of briny

BRINING   present participle of brine

BRINISH   adj resembling brine

BRINK   n pl. -S an extreme edge

BRINY   n pl. BRINIES the sea

BRINY   adj BRINIER, BRINIEST salty

BRIO   n pl. BRIOS liveliness

BRIOCHE   n pl. -S a rich roll

BRIONY   n pl. -NIES bryony

BRIQUET   v -QUETTED, -QUETTING, -QUETS to mold into small bricks

BRIS   n pl. BRISSES a Jewish circumcision rite

BRISANCE   n pl. -S the shattering effect of an explosive **BRISANT** adj

BRISK   adj BRISKER, BRISKEST lively

BRISK   v -ED, -ING, -S to make brisk

BRISKET *n* pl. -S the breast of an animal

BRISKLY *adv* in a brisk manner

BRISLING *n* pl. -S a small herring

BRISSES pl. of bris

BRISTLE *v* -TLED, -TLING, -TLES to rise stiffly

BRISTLY *adj* -TLIER, -TLIEST stiffly erect

BRISTOL *n* pl. -S a smooth cardboard

BRIT *n* pl. -S a young herring

BRITCHES *n/pl* breeches; trousers

BRITSKA *n* pl. -S an open carriage

BRITT *n* pl. -S brit

BRITTLE *adj* -TLER, -TLEST likely to break

BRITTLE *v* -TLED, -TLING, -TLES to become brittle

BRITTLY *adv* in a brittle manner

BRITZKA *n* pl. -S britska

BRITZSKA *n* pl. -S britska

BRO *n* pl. BROS a brother

BROACH *v* -ED, -ING, -ES to pierce so as to withdraw a liquid

BROACHER *n* pl. -S one that broaches

BROAD *adj* BROADER, BROADEST wide

BROAD *n* pl. -S an expansion of a river

BROADAX *n* pl. -ES a broad-edged ax

BROADAXE *n* pl. -S broadax

BROADEN *v* -ED, -ING, -S to make broad

BROADISH *adj* somewhat broad

BROADLY *adv* in a broad manner

BROCADE *v* -CADED, -CADING, -CADES to weave with a raised design

BROCATEL *n* pl. -S a heavy fabric

BROCCOLI *n* pl. -S a vegetable related to the cabbage

BROCHE *adj* brocaded

BROCHURE *n* pl. -S a pamphlet

BROCK *n* pl. -S a badger

BROCKAGE *n* pl. -S an imperfectly minted coin

BROCKET *n* pl. -S a small, red deer

BROCOLI *n* pl. -S broccoli

BROGAN *n* pl. -S a heavy shoe

BROGUE *n* pl. -S an Irish accent

BROGUERY *n* pl. -ERIES the use of an Irish accent

BROGUISH *adj* resembling a brogue

BROIDER *v* -ED, -ING, -S to adorn with needlework

BROIDERY *n* pl. -DERIES the act of broidering

BROIL *v* -ED, -ING, -S to cook by direct heat

BROILER *n* pl. -S a device for broiling

BROKAGE *n* pl. -S the business of a broker

BROKE past tense of break

BROKEN *adj* shattered **BROKENLY** *adv*

BROKER *v* -ED, -ING, -S to act as a broker (an agent who buys and sells stocks)

BROLLY *n* pl. -LIES an umbrella

BROMAL *n* pl. -S a medicinal liquid

BROMATE *v* -MATED, -MATING, -MATES to combine with bromine

BROME *n* pl. -S a tall grass

BROMELIN *n* pl. -S an enzyme

BROMIC *adj* containing bromine

BROMID *n* pl. -S bromide

BROMIDE *n* pl. -S a bromine compound

BROMIDIC *adj* commonplace; trite

BROMIN *n* pl. -S bromine

BROMINE *n* pl. -S a volatile liquid element

BROMISM *n* pl. -S a diseased condition of the skin

BROMIZE *v* -MIZED, -MIZING, -MIZES to treat with bromine or a bromide

BROMO *n* pl. -MOS a medicinal compound

BRONC *n* pl. -S bronco

BRONCHI pl. of bronchus

BRONCHIA *n/pl* the main air passages of the lungs

BRONCHO *n* pl. -CHOS bronco

BRONCHUS *n* pl. -CHI a tracheal branch

BRONCO *n* pl. -COS a wild horse

BRONZE *v* BRONZED, BRONZING, BRONZES to make brown or tan

BRONZER *n* pl. -S one that bronzes

BRONZING *n* pl. -S a brownish coloring

BRONZY *adj* BRONZIER, BRONZIEST of a brownish color

BROO *n* pl. BROOS a bree

BROOCH *n* pl. -ES a decorative pin

BROOD *v* -ED, -ING, -S to ponder gloomily

BROODER *n* pl. -S one that broods

BROODY *adj* BROODIER, BROODIEST tending to brood **BROODILY** *adv*

BROOK *v* -ED, -ING, -S to tolerate

BROOKIE *n* pl. -S a brook trout

BROOKITE *n* pl. -S a mineral

BROOKLET *n* pl. -S a small brook or creek

BROOM *v* -ED, -ING, -S to sweep

BROOMY *adj* BROOMIER, BROOMIEST abounding in broom (a type of shrub)

BROS pl. of bro

BROSE *n* pl. -S a porridge

BROSY *adj* smeared with brose

BROTH *n* pl. -S a thin clear soup

BROTHEL *n* pl. -S a house of prostitution

BROTHER *n* pl. -S or BRETHREN a male sibling

BROTHER *v* -ED, -ING, -S to treat like a brother

BROTHY *adj* resembling broth

BROUGHAM *n* pl. -S a type of carriage

BROUGHT past tense of bring

BROUHAHA *n* pl. -S an uproar

BROW *n* pl. -S the forehead **BROWED** *adj*

BROWBAND *n* pl. -S a band designed to cross the forehead

BROWBEAT *v* -BEAT, -BEATEN, -BEATING, -BEATS to intimidate

BROWLESS *adj* lacking eyebrows

BROWN *adj* BROWNER, BROWNEST of a dark color

BROWN *v* -ED, -ING, -S to make brown

BROWNIE *n* pl. -S a small sprite

BROWNIER comparative of browny

BROWNIEST superlative of browny

BROWNISH *adj* somewhat brown

BROWNOUT *n* pl. -S a power reduction

BROWNY *adj* BROWNIER, BROWNIEST somewhat brown

BROWSE *v* BROWSED, BROWSING, BROWSES to look at casually

BROWSER *n* pl. -S one that browses

BRR *interj* brrr

BRRR *interj* — used to indicate that one feels cold

BRUCELLA *n* pl. -LAE or -LAS any of a genus of harmful bacteria

BRUCIN *n* pl. -S brucine

BRUCINE *n* pl. -S a poisonous alkaloid

BRUGH *n* pl. -S a borough

BRUIN *n* pl. -S a bear

BRUISE *v* BRUISED, BRUISING, BRUISES to injure without breaking the surface of the skin

BRUISER *n* pl. -S a big, husky man

BRUIT *v* -ED, -ING, -S to spread news of

BRUITER *n* pl. -S one that bruits

BRULOT *n* pl. -S a biting fly

BRULYIE *n* pl. -S a noisy quarrel

BRULZIE *n* pl. -S brulyie

BRUMAL *adj* wintry

BRUMBY *n* pl. -BIES a wild horse

BRUME *n* pl. -S fog **BRUMOUS** *adj*

BRUNCH *v* -ED, -ING, -ES to eat a late morning meal

BRUNET *n* pl. -S a dark-haired male

BRUNETTE *n* pl. -S a dark-haired female

BRUNIZEM *n* pl. -S a prairie soil

BRUNT *n* pl. -S the main impact

BRUSH *v* -ED, -ING, -ES to touch lightly

BRUSHER *n* pl. -S one that brushes

BRUSHIER comparative of brushy

BRUSHIEST superlative of brushy

BRUSHOFF *n* pl. -S an abrupt dismissal

BRUSHUP *n* pl. -S a quick review

BRUSHY *adj* BRUSHIER, BRUSHIEST shaggy; rough

BRUSK *adj* BRUSKER, BRUSKEST brusque

BRUSQUE *adj* BRUSQUER, BRUSQUEST abrupt in manner

BRUT *adj* very dry

BRUTAL *adj* cruel; savage **BRUTALLY** *adv*

BRUTE *v* BRUTED, BRUTING, BRUTES to shape a diamond by rubbing it with another diamond

BRUTELY *adv* in a brutal manner

BRUTIFY *v* -FIED, -FYING, -FIES to make brutal

BRUTING present participle of brute

BRUTISH *adj* brutal

BRUTISM *n* pl. -S the state of being brutal

BRUXISM *n* pl. -S a nervous grinding of the teeth

BRYOLOGY *n* pl. -GIES the study of mosses

BRYONY *n* pl. -NIES a climbing plant

BRYOZOAN *n* pl. -S a type of small aquatic animal

BUB *n* pl. -S young fellow

BUBAL *n* pl. -S a large antelope

BUBALE *n* pl. -S bubal

BUBALINE *adj* pertaining to the bubal

BUBALIS *n* pl. -LISES bubal

BUBBLE   v -BLED, -BLING, -BLES to form bubbles (bodies of gas contained within a liquid)

BUBBLER   n pl. -S a drinking fountain

BUBBLY   n pl. -BLIES champagne

BUBBLY   adj -BLIER, -BLIEST full of bubbles

BUBINGA   n pl. -S an African tree

BUBO   n pl. -BOES a swelling of a lymph gland **BUBOED** adj

BUBONIC   adj pertaining to a bubo

BUCCAL   adj pertaining to the cheek **BUCCALLY** adv

BUCK   v -ED, -ING, -S to leap forward and upward suddenly

BUCKAROO n pl. -ROOS a cowboy

BUCKAYRO n pl. -ROS buckaroo

BUCKBEAN n pl. -S a marsh plant

BUCKEEN   n pl. -S a poor man who acts as if wealthy

BUCKER   n pl. -S a bucking horse

BUCKEROO n pl. -ROOS buckaroo

BUCKET   v -ED, -ING, -S to hurry

BUCKEYE   n pl. -S a nut-bearing tree

BUCKISH   adj foppish

BUCKLE   v -LED, -LING, -LES to bend under pressure

BUCKLER   v -ED, -ING, -S to shield

BUCKO   n pl. BUCKOES a bully

BUCKRAM   v -ED, -ING, -S to stiffen

BUCKSAW   n pl. -S a wood-cutting saw

BUCKSHEE   n pl. -S something extra obtained free

BUCKSHOT   n pl. -S a large lead shot

BUCKSKIN   n pl. -S the skin of a male deer

BUCKTAIL   n pl. -S a fishing lure

BUCOLIC   n pl. -S a pastoral poem

BUD   v BUDDED, BUDDING, BUDS to put forth buds (undeveloped plant parts)

BUDDER   n pl. -S one that buds

BUDDIED   past tense of buddy

BUDDIES   present 3d person sing. of buddy

BUDDING   n pl. -S a type of asexual reproduction

BUDDLE   n pl. -S an apparatus on which crushed ore is washed

BUDDLEIA   n pl. -S a tropical shrub

BUDDY   v -DIED, -DYING, -DIES to become close friends

BUDGE   v BUDGED, BUDGING, BUDGES to move slightly

BUDGER   n pl. -S one that budges

BUDGET   v -ED, -ING, -S to estimate expenditures

BUDGETER   n pl. -S one that budgets

BUDGIE   n pl. -S a small parrot

BUDGING   present participle of budge

BUDLESS   adj being without buds

BUDLIKE   adj resembling a bud

BUDWORM   n pl. -S a caterpillar that eats buds

BUFF   v -ED, -ING, -S to polish **BUFFABLE** adj

BUFFALO   n pl. -LOES or -LOS an ox-like animal

BUFFALO   v -ED, -ING, -ES to intimidate

BUFFER   v -ED, -ING, -S to cushion

BUFFET   v -ED, -ING, -S to hit sharply

BUFFETER   n pl. -S one that buffets

BUFFI   a pl. of buffo

BUFFIER   comparative of buffy

BUFFIEST   superlative of buffy

BUFFO   n pl. -FI or -FOS an operatic clown

BUFFOON   n pl. -S a clown

BUFFY   adj BUFFIER, BUFFIEST of a yellowish-brown color

BUG   v BUGGED, BUGGING, BUGS to annoy

BUGABOO   n pl. -BOOS a bugbear

BUGBANE   n pl. -S a perennial herb

BUGBEAR   n pl. -S an object or source of dread

BUGEYE   n pl. -S a small boat

BUGGED   past tense of bug

BUGGER   v -ED, -ING, -S to damn

BUGGERY   n pl. -GERIES sodomy

BUGGING   present participle of bug

BUGGY   n pl. -GIES a light carriage

BUGGY   adj -GIER, -GIEST infested with bugs

BUGHOUSE   n pl. -S an insane asylum

BUGLE   v -GLED, -GLING, -GLES to play a bugle (a brass wind instrument)

BUGLER   n pl. -S one that plays a bugle

BUGLOSS   n pl. -ES a coarse plant

BUGSEED   n pl. -S an annual herb

BUGSHA   n pl. -S buqsha

BUHL   n pl. -S a style of furniture decoration

BUHLWORK n pl. -S buhl

BUHR   n pl. -S a heavy stone

BUILD   v BUILT or BUILDED, BUILDING, BUILDS to construct

BUILDER   n pl. -S one that builds

BUILDING   n pl. -S something that is built

BUILDUP   *n* pl. -S an accumulation

BUILT   a past tense of build

BUIRDLY   *adj* burly

BULB   *n* pl. -S an underground bud **BULBAR, BULBED** *adj*

BULBEL   *n* pl. -S bulbil

BULBIL   *n* pl. -S a small bulb

BULBLET   *n* pl. -S a small bulb

BULBOUS   *adj* bulb-shaped; bulging

BULBUL   *n* pl. -S a songbird

BULGE   *v* BULGED, BULGING, BULGES to swell out

BULGER   *n* pl. -S a golf club

BULGUR   *n* pl. -S crushed wheat

BULGY   *adj* BULGIER, BULGIEST bulging

BULIMIA   *n* pl. -S insatiable appetite **BULIMIC, BULIMIAC** *adj*

BULK   *v* -ED, -ING, -S to gather into a mass

BULKAGE   *n* pl. -S a peristaltic stimulant

BULKHEAD   *n* pl. -S an upright partition in a ship

BULKY   *adj* BULKIER, BULKIEST massive **BULKILY** *adv*

BULL   *v* -ED, -ING, -S to push ahead

BULLA   *n* pl. -LAE a large blister

BULLACE   *n* pl. -S a purple plum

BULLATE   *adj* having a blistered appearance

BULLBAT   *n* pl. -S a nocturnal bird

BULLDOG   *v* -DOGGED, -DOGGING, -DOGS to throw a steer

BULLDOZE   *v* -DOZED, -DOZING, -DOZES to bully

BULLET   *v* -ED, -ING, -S to move swiftly

BULLETIN   *v* -ED, -ING, -S to issue a news item

BULLFROG   *n* pl. -S a large frog

BULLHEAD   *n* pl. -S a freshwater catfish

BULLHORN   *n* pl. -S an electric megaphone

BULLIED   past tense of bully

BULLIER   comparative of bully

BULLIES   present 3d person sing. of bully

BULLIEST   superlative of bully

BULLION   *n* pl. -S uncoined gold or silver

BULLISH   *adj* stubborn

BULLNECK   *n* pl. -S a thick neck

BULLNOSE   *n* pl. -S a disease of swine

BULLOCK   *n* pl. -S a castrated bull **BULLOCKY** *adj*

BULLOUS   *adj* resembling bullae

BULLPEN   *n* pl. -S an enclosure for bulls

BULLPOUT   *n* pl. -S a bullhead

BULLRING   *n* pl. -S a bullfight arena

BULLRUSH   *n* pl. -ES bulrush

BULLSHOT   *n* pl. -S a drink made of vodka and bouillon

BULLWEED   *n* pl. -S knapweed

BULLWHIP   *v* -WHIPPED, -WHIPPING, -WHIPS to strike with a long whip

BULLY   *v* -LIED, -LYING, -LIES to treat abusively

BULLY   *adj* -LIER, -LIEST wonderful

BULLYBOY   *n* pl. -BOYS a ruffian

BULLYRAG   *v* -RAGGED, -RAGGING, -RAGS to bully

BULRUSH   *n* pl. -ES a tall marsh plant

BULWARK   *v* -ED, -ING, -S to fortify with a defensive wall

BUM   *v* BUMMED, BUMMING, BUMS to live idly

BUM   *adj* BUMMER, BUMMEST of little value; worthless

BUMBLE   *v* -BLED, -BLING, -BLES to bungle

BUMBLER   *n* pl. -S one that bumbles

BUMBLING   *n* pl. -S an instance of clumsiness

BUMBOAT   *n* pl. -S a boat used to peddle wares to larger ships

BUMF   *n* pl. -S paperwork

BUMKIN   *n* pl. -S a ship's spar

BUMMED   past tense of bum

BUMMER   *n* pl. -S one that bums

BUMMEST   superlative of bum

BUMMING   present participle of bum

BUMP   *v* -ED, -ING, -S to knock against

BUMPER   *v* -ED, -ING, -S to fill to the brim

BUMPH   *n* pl. -S bumf

BUMPKIN   *n* pl. -S an unsophisticated rustic

BUMPY   *adj* BUMPIER, BUMPIEST of uneven surface **BUMPILY** *adv*

BUN   *n* pl. -S a small bread roll

BUNCH   *v* -ED, -ING, -ES to group together

BUNCHY   *adj* BUNCHIER, BUNCHIEST clustered **BUNCHILY** *adv*

BUNCO   *v* -ED, -ING, -S to swindle

BUNCOMBE   *n* pl. -S nonsense

BUND   *n* pl. -S a political association

BUNDIST   *n* pl. -S a member of a bund

BUNDLE   *v* -DLED, -DLING, -DLES to fasten a group of objects together

BUNDLER   *n* pl. -S one that bundles

BUNDLING   *n* pl. -S a former courtship custom

BUNDT   *n* pl. -S a type of cake pan

BUNG   *v* -ED, -ING, -S to plug with a cork or stopper

BUNGALOW   *n* pl. -S a small cottage

BUNGHOLE   *n* pl. -S a hole in a keg or barrel

BUNGLE   *v* -GLED, -GLING, -GLES to work, make, or do clumsily

BUNGLER   *n* pl. -S one that bungles

BUNGLING   *n* pl. -S an instance of clumsiness

BUNION   *n* pl. -S a painful swelling of the foot

BUNK   *v* -ED, -ING, -S to go to bed

BUNKER   *v* -ED, -ING, -S to store in a large bin

BUNKMATE   *n* pl. -S a person with whom sleeping quarters are shared

BUNKO   *v* -ED, -ING, -S to bunco

BUNKUM   *n* pl. -S nonsense

BUNN   *n* pl. -S bun

BUNNY   *n* pl. -NIES a rabbit

BUNRAKU   *n* pl. -S a Japanese puppet show

BUNT   *v* -ED, -ING, -S to butt

BUNTER   *n* pl. -S one that bunts

BUNTING   *n* pl. -S a fabric used for flags

BUNTLINE   *n* pl. -S a rope used to haul up a sail

BUNYA   *n* pl. -S an evergreen tree

BUOY   *v* -ED, -ING, -S to mark with a buoy (a warning float)

BUOYAGE   *n* pl. -S a group of buoys

BUOYANCE   *n* pl. -S buoyancy

BUOYANCY   *n* pl. -CIES the tendency to float

BUOYANT   *adj* having buoyancy

BUPPIE   *n* pl. -S a black professional person working in a city

BUQSHA   *n* pl. -S a monetary unit of Yemen

BUR   *v* BURRED, BURRING, BURS to burr

BURA   *n* pl. -S buran

BURAN   *n* pl. -S a violent windstorm

BURBLE   *v* -BLED, -BLING, -BLES to speak quickly and excitedly

BURBLER   *n* pl. -S one that burbles

BURBLY   *adj* -BLIER, -BLIEST burbling

BURBOT   *n* pl. -S a freshwater fish

BURBS   *n/pl* the suburbs

BURD   *n* pl. -S a maiden

BURDEN   *v* -ED, -ING, -S to load heavily

BURDENER   *n* pl. -S one that burdens

BURDIE   *n* pl. -S burd

BURDOCK   *n* pl. -S a coarse weed

BUREAU   *n* pl. -REAUS or -REAUX a chest of drawers

BURET   *n* pl. -S burette

BURETTE   *n* pl. -S a measuring tube

BURG   *n* pl. -S a city or town

BURGAGE   *n* pl. -S a feudal tenure

BURGEE   *n* pl. -S a small flag

BURGEON   *v* -ED, -ING, -S to develop rapidly

BURGER   *n* pl. -S a hamburger

BURGESS   *n* pl. -ES a citizen of an English borough

BURGH   *n* pl. -S a Scottish borough **BURGHAL** *adj*

BURGHER   *n* pl. -S a citizen of a borough

BURGLAR   *n* pl. -S one who commits burglary

BURGLARY   *n* pl. -GLARIES a felonious theft

BURGLE   *v* -GLED, -GLING, -GLES to commit burglary

BURGONET   *n* pl. -S an open helmet

BURGOO   *n* pl. -GOOS a thick oatmeal

BURGOUT   *n* pl. -S burgoo

BURGRAVE   *n* pl. -S a German nobleman

BURGUNDY   *n* pl. -DIES a red wine

BURIAL   *n* pl. -S the act of burying

BURIED   past tense of bury

BURIER   *n* pl. -S one that buries

BURIES   present 3d person sing. of bury

BURIN   *n* pl. -S an engraving tool

BURKE   *v* BURKED, BURKING, BURKES to murder by suffocation

BURKER   *n* pl. -S one that burkes

BURKITE   *n* pl. -S a burker

BURL   *v* -ED, -ING, -S to finish cloth by removing lumps

BURLAP   *n* pl. -S a coarse fabric

BURLER   *n* pl. -S one that burls

BURLESK   *n* pl. -S a type of stage show

BURLEY   *n* pl. -LEYS a light tobacco

BURLY   *adj* -LIER, -LIEST heavy and muscular **BURLILY** *adv*

BURN   *v* BURNED or BURNT, BURNING, BURNS to destroy by fire

BURNABLE   *n* pl. -S something that can be burned

BURNER   *n* pl. -S one that burns

BURNET   *n* pl. -S a perennial herb

BURNIE   *n* pl. -S a brooklet

BURNING   *n* pl. -S the firing of ceramic materials

BURNISH *v* -ED, -ING, -ES to polish

BURNOOSE *n* pl. -S a hooded cloak

BURNOUS *n* pl. -ES burnoose

BURNOUT *n* pl. -S a destructive fire

BURNT a past tense of burn

BURP *v* -ED, -ING, -S to belch

BURR *v* -ED, -ING, -S to remove a rough edge from

BURRED past tense of bur

BURRER *n* pl. -S one that burrs

BURRIER comparative of burry

BURRIEST superlative of burry

BURRING present participle of bur

BURRITO *n* pl. -TOS a tortilla rolled around a filling

BURRO *n* pl. -ROS a small donkey

BURROW *v* -ED, -ING, -S to dig a hole or tunnel in the ground

BURROWER *n* pl. -S one that burrows

BURRY *adj* -RIER, -RIEST prickly

BURSA *n* pl. -SAS or -SAE a bodily pouch **BURSAL** *adj*

BURSAR *n* pl. -S a college treasurer

BURSARY *n* pl. -RIES a college treasury

BURSATE *adj* pertaining to a bursa

BURSE *n* pl. -S a small bag or pouch

BURSEED *n* pl. -S a coarse weed

BURSERA *adj* designating a family of shrubs and trees

BURSITIS *n* pl. -TISES inflammation of a bursa

BURST *v* BURST or BURSTED, BURSTING, BURSTS to break open suddenly or violently

BURSTER *n* pl. -S one that bursts

BURSTONE *n* pl. -S a heavy stone

BURTHEN *v* -ED, -ING, -S to burden

BURTON *n* pl. -S a hoisting tackle

BURWEED *n* pl. -S a coarse weed

BURY *v* BURIED, BURYING, BURIES to put in the ground and cover with earth

BUS *v* BUSED, BUSING, BUSES or BUSSED, BUSSING, BUSSES to transport by bus (a large motor vehicle)

BUSBAR *n* pl. -S a type of electrical conductor

BUSBOY *n* pl. -BOYS a waiter's assistant

BUSBY *n* pl. -BIES a tall fur hat

BUSH *v* -ED, -ING, -ES to cover with bushes (shrubs)

BUSHBUCK *n* pl. -S a small antelope

BUSHEL *v* -ELED, -ELING, -ELS or -ELLED, -ELLING, -ELS to mend clothing

BUSHELER *n* pl. -S one that bushels

BUSHER *n* pl. -S a minor league baseball player

BUSHFIRE *n* pl. -S a fire in a wooded area

BUSHGOAT *n* pl. -S a bushbuck

BUSHIDO *n* pl. -DOS the code of the samurai

BUSHIER comparative of bushy

BUSHIEST superlative of bushy

BUSHILY *adv* in a bushy manner

BUSHING *n* pl. -S a lining for a hole

BUSHLAND *n* pl. -S unsettled forest land

BUSHLESS *adj* having no bushes

BUSHLIKE *adj* resembling a bush

BUSHMAN *n* pl. -MEN a woodsman

BUSHPIG *n* pl. -S a wild African pig

BUSHTIT *n* pl. -S a titmouse

BUSHWA *n* pl. -S nonsense

BUSHWAH *n* pl. -S bushwa

BUSHY *adj* BUSHIER, BUSHIEST covered with bushes

BUSIED past tense of busy

BUSIER comparative of busy

BUSIES present 3d person sing. of busy

BUSIEST superlative of busy

BUSILY *adv* in a busy manner

BUSINESS *n* pl. -ES an occupation, profession, or trade

BUSING *n* pl. -S the act of transporting by bus

BUSK *v* -ED, -ING, -S to prepare

BUSKER *n* pl. -S a roaming entertainer

BUSKIN *n* pl. -S a high shoe **BUSKINED** *adj*

BUSMAN *n* pl. -MEN a bus operator

BUSS *v* -ED, -ING, -ES to kiss

BUSSED a past tense of bus

BUSSES a present 3d person sing. of bus

BUSSING *n* pl. -S busing

BUST *v* -ED, -ING, -S to burst

BUSTARD *n* pl. -S a game bird

BUSTER *n* pl. -S one that breaks up something

BUSTIC *n* pl. -S a tropical tree

BUSTIER *n* pl. -S a woman's undergarment

BUSTLE *v* -TLED, -TLING, -TLES to move energetically

BUSTLINE *n* pl. -S the distance around the bust (the upper torso of a woman)

BUSLOAD *n* pl. -S a load that fills a bus

BUSTY *adj* BUSTIER, BUSTIEST full-bosomed

BUSULFAN *n* pl. -S a medicine

BUSY *adj* BUSIER, BUSIEST occupied

BUSY *v* BUSIED, BUSYING, BUSIES to make busy

BUSYBODY *n* pl. -BODIES a nosy person

BUSYNESS *n* pl. -ES the state of being busy

BUSYWORK *n* pl. -S active but valueless work

BUT *n* pl. -S a flatfish

BUTANE *n* pl. -S a flammable gas

BUTANOL *n* pl. -S a flammable alcohol

BUTANONE *n* pl. -S a flammable ketone

BUTCH *n* pl. -ES a lesbian with mannish traits

BUTCHER *v* -ED, -ING, -S to slaughter

BUTCHERY *n* pl. -ERIES wanton or cruel killing

BUTE *n* pl. BUTE a pain-relieving drug

BUTENE *n* pl. -S butylene

BUTEO *n* pl. -TEOS a hawk

BUTLE *v* -LED, -LING, -LES to serve as a butler

BUTLER *n* pl. -S a male servant

BUTLERY *n* pl. -LERIES a storage room

BUTLES present 3d person sing. of butle

BUTLING present participle of butle

BUTT *v* -ED, -ING, -S to hit with the head

BUTTALS *n/pl* boundary lines

BUTTE *n* pl. -S an isolated hill

BUTTER *v* -ED, -ING, -S to spread with butter (a milk product)

BUTTERY *adj* -TERIER, -TERIEST containing butter

BUTTERY *n* pl. -TERIES a wine cellar

BUTTIES pl. of butty

BUTTOCK *n* pl. -S either of the two rounded parts of the rump

BUTTON *v* -ED, -ING, -S to fasten with a button (a small disk)

BUTTONER *n* pl. -S one that buttons

BUTTONY *adj* resembling a button

BUTTRESS *v* -ED, -ING, -ES to prop up

BUTTY *n* pl. -TIES a fellow workman

BUTUT *n* pl. -S a monetary unit of Gambia

BUTYL *n* pl. -S a hydrocarbon radical

BUTYLATE *v* -ATED, -ATING, -ATES to add a butyl to

BUTYLENE *n* pl. -S a gaseous hydrocarbon

BUTYRAL *n* pl. -S a chemical compound

BUTYRATE *n* pl. -S a chemical salt

BUTYRIC *adj* derived from butter

BUTYRIN *n* pl. -S a chemical compound

BUTYROUS *adj* resembling butter

BUTYRYL *n* pl. -S a radical of butyric acid

BUXOM *adj* -OMER, -OMEST healthily plump BUXOMLY *adv*

BUY *v* BOUGHT, BUYING, BUYS to purchase BUYABLE *adj*

BUYBACK *n* pl. -S the repurchase by a corporation of its own stock

BUYER *n* pl. -S one that buys

BUYOUT *n* pl. -S the purchase of a business

BUZUKI *n* pl. -KIA or -KIS bouzouki

BUZZ *v* -ED, -ING, -ES to make a vibrating sound

BUZZARD *n* pl. -S a large bird of prey

BUZZER *n* pl. -S a signaling device

BUZZWIG *n* pl. -S a large, thick wig

BUZZWORD *n* pl. -S a word used to impress someone

BWANA *n* pl. -S master; boss

BY *n* pl. BYS a pass in certain card games

BYE *n* pl. -S a side issue

BYELAW *n* pl. -S bylaw

BYGONE *n* pl. -S a past occurrence

BYLAW *n* pl. -S a secondary law

BYLINE *v* -LINED, -LINING, -LINES to write under a byline (a line giving the author's name)

BYLINER *n* pl. -S one that writes under a byline

BYNAME *n* pl. -S a secondary name

BYPASS *v* -ED, -ING, -ES to avoid by going around

BYPAST *adj* past; gone by

BYPATH *n* pl. -S an indirect road

BYPLAY *n* pl. -PLAYS secondary action

BYRE *n* pl. -S a cowshed

BYRL *v* -ED, -ING, -S to birle

BYRNIE *n* pl. -S an armored shirt

BYROAD *n* pl. -S a side road

BYSSUS *n* pl. BYSSUSES or BYSSI a fine linen

BYSTREET *n* pl. -S a side street

BYTALK	*n* pl. -S small talk	**BYWORD**	*n* pl. -S a well-known saying
BYTE	*n* pl. -S a group of adjacent binary digits	**BYWORK**	*n* pl. -S work done during leisure time
BYWAY	*n* pl. -WAYS a side road	**BYZANT**	*n* pl. -S bezant

C₃

CAB	*v* CABBED, CABBING, CABS to take or drive a taxicab
CABAL	*v* -BALLED, -BALLING, -BALS to conspire
CABALA	*n* pl. -S an occult or secret doctrine
CABALISM	*n* pl. -S adherence to a cabala
CABALIST	*n* pl. -S one who practices cabalism
CABALLED	past tense of cabal
CABALLING	present participle of cabal
CABANA	*n* pl. -S a small cabin
CABARET	*n* pl. -S a music hall
CABBAGE	*v* -BAGED, -BAGING, -BAGES to steal
CABBALA	*n* pl. -S cabala
CABBALAH	*n* pl. -S cabala
CABBED	past tense of cab
CABBIE	*n* pl. -S cabby
CABBING	present participle of cab
CABBY	*n* pl. -BIES a driver of a cab
CABER	*n* pl. -S a heavy pole thrown as a trial of strength
CABERNET	*n* pl. -S a dry red wine
CABESTRO	*n* pl. -TROS a lasso
CABEZON	*n* pl. -S a large, edible fish
CABEZONE	*n* pl. -S cabezon
CABILDO	*n* pl. -DOS a town council
CABIN	*v* -ED, -ING, -S to live in a cabin (a roughly built house)
CABINET	*n* pl. -S a piece of furniture with shelves and drawers
CABLE	*v* -BLED, -BLING, -BLES to fasten with a cable (a heavy rope)
CABLET	*n* pl. -S a small cable
CABLEWAY	*n* pl. -WAYS a suspended cable
CABLING	present participle of cable
CABMAN	*n* pl. -MEN a driver of a cab
CABOB	*n* pl. -S kabob
CABOCHED	*adj* full-faced — used of an animal's head in heraldry
CABOCHON	*n* pl. -S a precious stone
CABOMBA	*n* pl. -S an aquatic plant
CABOODLE	*n* pl. -S a collection
CABOOSE	*n* pl. -S the last car of a freight train
CABOSHED	*adj* caboched
CABOTAGE	*n* pl. -S coastal trade
CABRESTA	*n* pl. -S cabestro
CABRESTO	*n* pl. -TOS cabestro
CABRETTA	*n* pl. -S a soft leather
CABRILLA	*n* pl. -S a sea bass
CABRIOLE	*n* pl. -S a curved furniture leg
CABSTAND	*n* pl. -S a place where cabs await hire
CACA	*n* pl. -S excrement
CACAO	*n* pl. -CAOS a tropical tree
CACHALOT	*n* pl. -S a large whale
CACHE	*v* CACHED, CACHING, CACHES to store in a hiding place
CACHEPOT	*n* pl. -S an ornamental container for a flowerpot
CACHET	*v* -ED, -ING, -S to print a design on an envelope
CACHEXIA	*n* pl. -S general ill health **CACHEXIC** *adj*
CACHEXY	*n* pl. -CHEXIES cachexia
CACHING	present participle of cache
CACHOU	*n* pl. -S catechu
CACHUCHA	*n* pl. -S a Spanish dance
CACIQUE	*n* pl. -S a tropical oriole
CACKLE	*v* -LED, -LING, -LES to make the sound of a hen
CACKLER	*n* pl. -S one that cackles
CACODYL	*n* pl. -S a poisonous liquid

CACOMIXL *n* pl. -S a raccoon-like mammal

CACTUS *n* pl. -TI or -TUSES a plant native to arid regions **CACTOID** *adj*

CAD *n* pl. -S an ungentlemanly man

CADASTER *n* pl. -S a public record of land ownership

CADASTRE *n* pl. -S cadaster

CADAVER *n* pl. -S a corpse

CADDICE *n* pl. -S caddis

CADDIE *v* -DIED, -DYING, -DIES to serve as a golfer's assistant

CADDIS *n* pl. -DISES a coarse woolen fabric

CADDISH *adj* resembling a cad

CADDY *v* -DIED, -DYING, -DIES to caddie

CADE *n* pl. -S a European shrub

CADELLE *n* pl. -S a small, black beetle

CADENCE *v* -DENCED, -DENCING, -DENCES to make rhythmic

CADENCY *n* pl. -CIES a rhythm

CADENT *adj* having rhythm

CADENZA *n* pl. -S an elaborate musical passage

CADET *n* pl. -S a student at a military school

CADGE *v* CADGED, CADGING, CADGES to get by begging

CADGER *n* pl. -S one that cadges

CADGY *adj* cheerful

CADI *n* pl. -S a Muslim judge

CADMIUM *n* pl. -S a metallic element **CADMIC** *adj*

CADRE *n* pl. -S a nucleus of trained personnel

CADUCEUS *n* pl. -CEI a heraldic wand or staff **CADUCEAN** *adj*

CADUCITY *n* pl. -TIES senility

CADUCOUS *adj* transitory; perishable

CAECUM *n* pl. -CA cecum **CAECAL** *adj* **CAECALLY** *adv*

CAEOMA *n* pl. -S a spore-forming organ of a fungus

CAESAR *n* pl. -S an emperor

CAESIUM *n* pl. -S cesium

CAESTUS *n* pl. -ES cestus

CAESURA *n* pl. -RAS or -RAE a pause in a line of verse **CAESURAL, CAESURIC** *adj*

CAFE *n* pl. -S a small restaurant

CAFF *n* pl. -S a cafe

CAFFEIN *n* pl. -S caffeine

CAFFEINE *n* pl. -S a bitter alkaloid used as a stimulant

CAFTAN *n* pl. -S a full-length tunic

CAGE *v* CAGED, CAGING, CAGES to confine

CAGEFUL *n* pl. -S the number held in a cage (an enclosure)

CAGELING *n* pl. -S a caged bird

CAGER *n* pl. -S a basketball player

CAGEY *adj* CAGIER, CAGIEST shrewd

CAGIER comparative of cagy

CAGIEST superlative of cagy

CAGILY *adv* in a cagey manner

CAGINESS *n* pl. -ES the quality of being cagey

CAGING present participle of cage

CAGY *adj* CAGIER, CAGIEST cagey

CAHIER *n* pl. -S a notebook

CAHOOT *n* pl. -S partnership

CAHOW *n* pl. -S a sea bird

CAID *n* pl. -S a Muslim leader

CAIMAN *n* pl. -S a tropical reptile

CAIN *n* pl. -S kain

CAIQUE *n* pl. -S a long, narrow rowboat

CAIRD *n* pl. -S a gypsy

CAIRN *n* pl. -S a mound of stones set up as a memorial **CAIRNED, CAIRNY** *adj*

CAISSON *n* pl. -S a watertight chamber

CAITIFF *n* pl. -S a despicable person

CAJAPUT *n* pl. -S cajeput

CAJEPUT *n* pl. -S an Australian tree

CAJOLE *v* -JOLED, -JOLING, -JOLES to persuade by flattery

CAJOLER *n* pl. -S one that cajoles

CAJOLERY *n* pl. -ERIES persuasion by flattery

CAJOLING present participle of cajole

CAJON *n* pl. -ES a steep-sided canyon

CAJUPUT *n* pl. -S cajeput

CAKE *v* CAKED, CAKING, CAKES to form into a hardened mass

CAKEWALK *v* -ED, -ING, -S to step stylishly

CAKEY *adj* CAKIER, CAKIEST tending to form lumps

CAKY *adj* CAKIER, CAKIEST cakey

CALABASH *n* pl. -ES a gourd

CALADIUM *n* pl. -S a tropical plant

CALAMAR *n* pl. -S calamary

CALAMARI *n* pl. -S squid used as food

CALAMARY *n* pl. -MARIES a squid

CALAMI pl. of calamus

CALAMINE v -MINED, -MINING, -MINES to apply an ointment for skin ailments

CALAMINT n pl. -S a perennial herb

CALAMITE n pl. -S an extinct treelike plant

CALAMITY n pl. -TIES a grievous misfortune

CALAMUS n pl. -MI a marsh plant

CALANDO adj gradually diminishing

CALASH n pl. -ES a light carriage

CALATHOS n pl. -THI a fruit basket

CALATHUS n pl. -THI calathos

CALCANEA n/pl calcanei

CALCANEI n/pl bones of the heel

CALCAR n pl. -CARIA an anatomical projection

CALCAR n pl. -S a type of oven

CALCEATE adj wearing shoes

CALCES a pl. of calx

CALCIC adj pertaining to lime or calcium

CALCIFIC adj containing salts of calcium

CALCIFY v -FIED, -FYING, -FIES to harden

CALCINE v -CINED, -CINING, -CINES to reduce to a calx by heat

CALCITE n pl. -S a mineral **CALCITIC** adj

CALCIUM n pl. -S a metallic element

CALCSPAR n pl. -S a calcite

CALCTUFA n pl. -S a mineral deposit

CALCTUFF n pl. -S calctufa

CALCULUS n pl. -LI or -LUSES a branch of mathematics

CALDARIA n/pl rooms for taking hot baths

CALDERA n pl. -S a large crater

CALDRON n pl. -S a large kettle or boiler

CALECHE n pl. -S calash

CALENDAL adj pertaining to calends

CALENDAR v -ED, -ING, -S to schedule

CALENDER v -ED, -ING, -S to smooth by pressing between rollers

CALENDS n pl. CALENDS the first day of the Roman month

CALESA n pl. -S a calash

CALF n pl. CALVES or CALFS a young cow or bull **CALFLIKE** adj

CALFSKIN n pl. -S the skin of a calf

CALIBER n pl. -S the diameter of a gun barrel

CALIBRE n pl. -S caliber **CALIBRED** adj

CALICES pl. of calix

CALICHE n pl. -S a mineral deposit

CALICLE n pl. -S a cup-shaped, anatomical structure

CALICO n pl. -COES or -COS a cotton fabric

CALIF n pl. -S caliph

CALIFATE n pl. -S the domain of a calif

CALIPASH n pl. -ES an edible part of a turtle

CALIPEE n pl. -S an edible part of a turtle

CALIPER v -ED, -ING, -S to use a type of measuring device

CALIPH n pl. -S a Muslim leader **CALIPHAL** adj

CALISAYA n pl. -S the medicinal bark of the cinchona

CALIX n pl. -LICES a cup

CALK v -ED, -ING, -S to caulk

CALKER n pl. -S one that calks

CALKIN n pl. -S a gripping projection on a horseshoe

CALL v -ED, -ING, -S to summon **CALLABLE** adj

CALLA n pl. -S a tropical plant

CALLALOO n pl. -LOOS a crabmeat soup

CALLAN n pl. -S callant

CALLANT n pl. -S a lad

CALLBACK n pl. -S a recall of a defective product

CALLBOY n pl. -BOYS a bellboy

CALLER n pl. -S one that calls

CALLET n pl. -S a prostitute

CALLING n pl. -S a vocation or profession

CALLIOPE n pl. -S a keyboard musical instrument

CALLIPEE n pl. -S calipee

CALLIPER v -ED, -ING, -S to caliper

CALLOSE n pl. -S a part of a plant cell wall

CALLOUS v -ED, -ING, -ES to make or become hard

CALLOW adj -LOWER, -LOWEST immature

CALLUS v -ED, -ING, -ES to form a hard growth

CALM adj CALMER, CALMEST free from agitation **CALMLY** adv

CALM v -ED, -ING, -S to make calm

CALMNESS n pl. -ES the state of being calm

CALO n pl. CALO a Spanish argot used by Chicano youths

CALOMEL n pl. -S a chemical compound used as a purgative

CALORIC n pl. -S heat

CALORIE   n pl. -S a unit of heat

CALORIZE   v -RIZED, -RIZING, -RIZES to coat steel with aluminum

CALORY   n pl. -RIES calorie

CALOTTE   n pl. -S a skullcap

CALOTYPE   n pl. -S a kind of photograph

CALOYER   n pl. -S a monk of the Eastern Church

CALPAC   n pl. -S a sheepskin hat

CALPACK   n pl. -S calpac

CALQUE   v CALQUED, CALQUING, CALQUES to model a word's meaning upon that of an analogous word in another language

CALTHROP   n pl. -S caltrop

CALTRAP   n pl. -S caltrop

CALTROP   n pl. -S a spiny plant

CALUMET   n pl. -S a ceremonial pipe

CALUMNY   n pl. -NIES a false and malicious accusation

CALUTRON   n pl. -S a device used for separating isotopes

CALVADOS   n pl. -ES a dry apple brandy

CALVARIA   n pl. -S the dome of the skull

CALVARY   n pl. -RIES a representation of the Crucifixion

CALVE   v CALVED, CALVING, CALVES to give birth to a calf

CALVES   a pl. of calf

CALX   n pl. -ES or CALCES a mineral residue

CALYCATE   adj calycine

CALYCEAL   adj calycine

CALYCES   a pl. of calyx

CALYCINE   adj pertaining to a calyx

CALYCLE   n pl. -S an outer calyx

CALYCULI   n/pl small, cup-shaped structures

CALYPSO   n pl. -SOS or -SOES an improvised song

CALYPTER   n pl. -S calyptra

CALYPTRA   n pl. -S a hood-shaped organ of flowers

CALYX   n pl. -LYXES or -LYCES the outer protective covering of a flower

CALZONE   n pl. -S a turnover with a savory filling

CAM   n pl. -S a rotating or sliding piece of machinery

CAMAIL   n pl. -S a piece of armor for the neck CAMAILED adj

CAMAS   n pl. -ES camass

CAMASS   n pl. -ES a perennial herb

CAMBER   v -ED, -ING, -S to arch slightly

CAMBIA   a pl. of cambium

CAMBIAL   adj pertaining to cambium

CAMBISM   n pl. -S the theory and practice of exchange in commerce

CAMBIST   n pl. -S a dealer in bills of exchange

CAMBIUM   n pl. -BIUMS or -BIA a layer of plant tissue

CAMBOGIA   n pl. -S a gum resin

CAMBRIC   n pl. -S a fine linen

CAME   n pl. -S a leaden window rod

CAMEL   n pl. -S a large, humped mammal

CAMELEER   n pl. -S a camel driver

CAMELIA   n pl. -S camellia

CAMELLIA   n pl. -S a tropical shrub

CAMEO   v -ED, -ING, -S to portray in sharp, delicate relief

CAMERA   n pl. -ERAS or -ERAE a judge's chamber CAMERAL adj

CAMION   n pl. -S a military truck

CAMISA   n pl. -S a shirt or chemise

CAMISADE   n pl. -S camisado

CAMISADO   n pl. -DOS or -DOES an attack made at night

CAMISE   n pl. -S a loose shirt or gown

CAMISIA   n pl. -S camise

CAMISOLE   n pl. -S a brief negligee

CAMLET   n pl. -S a durable fabric

CAMOMILE   n pl. -S a medicinal herb

CAMORRA   n pl. -S an unscrupulous secret society

CAMP   v -ED, -ING, -S to live in the open

CAMPAGNA   n pl. -PAGNE a flat, open plain

CAMPAIGN   v -ED, -ING, -S to conduct a series of operations to reach a specific goal

CAMPER   n pl. -S one that camps

CAMPFIRE   n pl. -S an outdoor fire

CAMPHENE   n pl. -S camphine

CAMPHINE   n pl. -S an explosive liquid

CAMPHIRE   n pl. -S a flowering plant

CAMPHOL   n pl. -S borneol

CAMPHOR   n pl. -S a volatile compound

CAMPI   pl. of campo

CAMPIER   comparative of campy

CAMPIEST   superlative of campy

CAMPILY   adv in a campy manner

CAMPING   n pl. -S the act of living outdoors

CAMPION   n pl. -S an herb

CAMPO   *n* pl. -PI an open space in a town

CAMPO   *n* pl. -POS a level, grassy plain

CAMPONG   *n* pl. -S kampong

CAMPOREE   *n* pl. -S a gathering of Boy Scouts

CAMPSITE   *n* pl. -S an area suitable for camping

CAMPUS   *v* -ED, -ING, -ES to restrict a student to the school grounds

CAMPY   *adj* CAMPIER, CAMPIEST comically exaggerated

CAMSHAFT   *n* pl. -S a shaft fitted with cams

CAN   *v* CANNED, CANNING, CANS to put in a can (a cylindrical container)

CAN   *v* present sing. 2d person CAN or CANST, past sing. 2d person COULD, COULDEST, or COULDST — used as an auxiliary to express ability

CANAILLE   *n* pl. -S the common people

CANAKIN   *n* pl. -S cannikin

CANAL   *v* -NALLED, -NALLING, -NALS or -NALED, -NALING, -NALS to dig an artificial waterway through

CANALISE   *v* -ISED, -ISING, -ISES to canalize

CANALIZE   *v* -IZED, -IZING, -IZES to canal

CANALLED   a past tense of canal

CANALLER   *n* pl. -S a freight boat

CANALLING   a present participle of canal

CANAPE   *n* pl. -S a food served before a meal

CANARD   *n* pl. -S a false story

CANARY   *n* pl. -NARIES a songbird

CANASTA   *n* pl. -S a card game

CANCAN   *n* pl. -S a dance marked by high kicking

CANCEL   *v* -CELED, -CELING, -CELS or -CELLED, -CELLING, -CELS to annul

CANCELER   *n* pl. -S one that cancels

CANCER   *n* pl. -S a malignant growth

CANCHA   *n* pl. -S a jai alai court

CANCROID   *n* pl. -S a skin cancer

CANDELA   *n* pl. -S a unit of luminous intensity

CANDENT   *adj* glowing

CANDID   *adj* -DIDER, -DIDEST frank and sincere

CANDID   *n* pl. -S an unposed photograph

CANDIDA   *n* pl. -S a parasitic fungus

CANDIDLY   *adv* in a candid manner

CANDIED   past tense of candy

CANDIES   present 3d person sing. of candy

CANDLE   *v* -DLED, -DLING, -DLES to examine eggs in front of a light

CANDLER   *n* pl. -S one that candles

CANDOR   *n* pl. -S frankness; sincerity

CANDOUR   *n* pl. -S candor

CANDY   *v* -DIED, -DYING, -DIES to coat with sugar

CANE   *v* CANED, CANING, CANES to beat with a rod

CANELLA   *n* pl. -S a medicinal tree bark

CANEPHOR   *n* pl. -S a Greek maiden bearing a basket on her head

CANER   *n* pl. -S one that canes

CANEWARE   *n* pl. -S a yellowish stoneware

CANFIELD   *n* pl. -S a card game

CANFUL   *n* pl. CANFULS or CANSFUL as much as a can holds

CANGUE   *n* pl. -S an ancient Chinese punishing device

CANID   *n* pl. -S a dog

CANIKIN   *n* pl. -S cannikin

CANINE   *n* pl. -S a dog

CANING   present participle of cane

CANINITY   *n* pl. -TIES the state of being a canine

CANISTER   *n* pl. -S a small, metal box

CANITIES   *n* pl. CANITIES the turning gray of the hair

CANKER   *v* -ED, -ING, -S to affect with ulcerous sores

CANNA   *n* pl. -S a tropical plant

CANNABIC   *adj* pertaining to cannabis

CANNABIN   *n* pl. -S a resin extracted from cannabis

CANNABIS   *n* pl. -BISES hemp

CANNED   past tense of can

CANNEL   *n* pl. -S an oily, compact coal

CANNELON   *n* pl. -S a stuffed roll

CANNER   *n* pl. -S one who cans food

CANNERY   *n* pl. -NERIES a place where food is canned

CANNIBAL   *n* pl. -S one who eats his own kind

CANNIE   *adj* -NIER, -NIEST canny

CANNIER   comparative of canny

CANNIEST   superlative of canny

CANNIKIN   *n* pl. -S a small can or cup

CANNILY   *adv* in a canny manner

CANNING   *n* pl. -S the business of preserving food in airtight containers

CANNOLI   *n/pl* a tube of pastry

CANNON   *v* -ED, -ING, -S to fire a cannon (a heavy firearm)

CANNONRY   *n* pl. -RIES artillery

CANNOT   the negative form of can

CANNULA   *n* pl. -LAS or -LAE a tube inserted into a bodily cavity **CANNULAR** *adj*

CANNY   *adj* -NIER, -NIEST prudent

CANOE   *v* -NOED, -NOEING, -NOES to paddle a canoe (a light, slender boat)

CANOEIST   *n* pl. -S one who canoes

CANOLA   *n* pl. CANOLA an oil from the seeds of a kind of herb

CANON   *n* pl. -S a law decreed by a church council **CANONIC** *adj*

CANONESS   *n* pl. -ES a woman who lives according to a canon

CANONISE   *v* -ISED, -ISING, -ISES to canonize

CANONIST   *n* pl. -S a specialist in canon law

CANONIZE   *v* -IZED, -IZING, -IZES to declare to be a saint

CANONRY   *n* pl. -RIES a clerical office

CANOODLE   *v* -DLED, -DLING, -DLES to caress

CANOPY   *v* -PIED, -PYING, -PIES to cover from above

CANOROUS   *adj* melodic

CANSFUL   a pl. of canful

CANSO   *n* pl. -SOS a love song

CANST   a present 2d person sing. of can

CANT   *v* -ED, -ING, -S to tilt or slant

CANTALA   *n* pl. -S a tropical plant

CANTATA   *n* pl. -S a vocal composition

CANTDOG   *n* pl. -S a device used to move logs

CANTEEN   *n* pl. -S a small container for carrying water

CANTER   *v* -ED, -ING, -S to ride a horse at a moderate pace

CANTHUS   *n* pl. -THI a corner of the eye **CANTHAL** *adj*

CANTIC   *adj* slanted

CANTICLE   *n* pl. -S a hymn

CANTINA   *n* pl. -S a saloon

CANTLE   *n* pl. -S the rear part of a saddle

CANTO   *n* pl. -TOS a division of a long poem

CANTON   *v* -ED, -ING, -S to divide into cantons (districts)

CANTONAL   *adj* pertaining to a canton

CANTOR   *n* pl. -S a religious singer

CANTRAIP   *n* pl. -S cantrip

CANTRAP   *n* pl. -S cantrip

CANTRIP   *n* pl. -S a magic spell

CANTUS   *n* pl. CANTUS a style of church music

CANTY   *adj* cheerful

CANULA   *n* pl. -LAS or -LAE cannula

CANULATE   *v* -LATED, -LATING, -LATES to insert a canula into

CANVAS   *v* -ED, -ING, -ES to canvass

CANVASER   *n* pl. -S one that canvases

CANVASS   *v* -ED, -ING, -ES to examine thoroughly

CANYON   *n* pl. -S a deep valley with steep sides

CANZONA   *n* pl. -S canzone

CANZONE   *n* pl. -NI or -NES a form of lyric poetry

CANZONET   *n* pl. -S a short song

CAP   *v* CAPPED, CAPPING, CAPS to provide with a cap (a type of head covering)

CAPABLE   *adj* -BLER, -BLEST having ability **CAPABLY** *adv*

CAPACITY   *n* pl. -TIES the ability to receive or contain

CAPE   *n* pl. -S a sleeveless garment **CAPED** *adj*

CAPELAN   *n* pl. -S capelin

CAPELET   *n* pl. -S a small cape

CAPELIN   *n* pl. -S a small, edible fish

CAPER   *v* -ED, -ING, -S to frolic

CAPERER   *n* pl. -S one that capers

CAPESKIN   *n* pl. -S a soft leather

CAPEWORK   *n* pl. -S a bullfighting technique

CAPFUL   *n* pl. -S as much as a cap can hold

CAPH   *n* pl. -S kaph

CAPIAS   *n* pl. -ES a judicial writ

CAPITA   pl. of caput

CAPITAL   *n* pl. -S the upper part of a column

CAPITATE   *adj* head-shaped

CAPITOL   *n* pl. -S a building occupied by a state legislature

CAPITULA   *n/pl* flower clusters

CAPLESS   *adj* being without a cap

CAPLET   *n* pl. -S a coated tablet

CAPLIN   *n* pl. -S capelin

CAPMAKER   *n* pl. -S one that makes caps

CAPO   n pl. -POS a pitch-raising device for fretted instruments
CAPON   n pl. -S a gelded rooster
CAPONATA   n pl. -S a relish made with eggplant
CAPONIER   n pl. -S a type of defense
CAPONIZE   v -IZED, -IZING, -IZES to geld a rooster
CAPORAL   n pl. -S a coarse tobacco
CAPOTE   n pl. -S a hooded cloak or overcoat
CAPOUCH   n pl. -ES capuche
CAPPED   past tense of cap
CAPPER   n pl. -S a capmaker
CAPPING   n pl. -S a wax covering in a honeycomb
CAPRIC   adj pertaining to a goat
CAPRICCI   n/pl caprices
CAPRICE   n pl. -S a whim
CAPRIFIG   n pl. -S a European tree
CAPRINE   adj capric
CAPRIOLE   v -OLED, -OLING, -OLES to leap
CAPRIS   n/pl pants for women
CAPROCK   n pl. -S an overlying rock layer
CAPSICIN   n pl. -S a liquid used as a flavoring
CAPSICUM   n pl. -S a tropical herb
CAPSID   n pl. -S the outer shell of a virus particle CAPSIDAL adj
CAPSIZE   v -SIZED, -SIZING, -SIZES to overturn
CAPSOMER   n pl. -S a protein forming the capsid
CAPSTAN   n pl. -S a machine used to hoist weights
CAPSTONE   n pl. -S the top stone of a structure
CAPSULAR   adj enclosed and compact
CAPSULE   v -SULED, -SULING, -SULES to condense into a brief form
CAPTAIN   v -ED, -ING, -S to lead or command
CAPTAN   n pl. -S a fungicide
CAPTION   v -ED, -ING, -S to provide with a title
CAPTIOUS   adj tending to find fault
CAPTIVE   n pl. -S a prisoner
CAPTOR   n pl. -S one who takes or holds a captive
CAPTURE   v -TURED, -TURING, -TURES to take by force or cunning
CAPTURER   n pl. -S one that captures
CAPUCHE   n pl. -S a hood or cowl CAPUCHED adj
CAPUCHIN   n pl. -S a long-tailed monkey

CAPUT   n pl. CAPITA a head or head-like part
CAPYBARA   n pl. -S a large rodent
CAR   n pl. -S an automobile
CARABAO   n pl. -BAOS a water buffalo
CARABID   n pl. -S a predatory beetle
CARABIN   n pl. -S carbine
CARABINE   n pl. -S carbine
CARACAL   n pl. -S an African lynx
CARACARA   n pl. -S a large hawk
CARACK   n pl. -S carrack
CARACOL   v -COLLED, -COLLING, -COLS to caracole
CARACOLE   v -COLED, -COLING, -COLES to perform a half turn on a horse
CARACUL   n pl. -S karakul
CARAFE   n pl. -S a glass bottle
CARAGANA   n pl. -S an Asian shrub
CARAGEEN   n pl. -S an edible seaweed
CARAMBA   interj — used to express surprise or dismay
CARAMEL   n pl. -S a chewy candy
CARANGID   n pl. -S a marine fish
CARAPACE   n pl. -S a hard, protective outer covering
CARAPAX   n pl. -ES carapace
CARASSOW   n pl. -S curassow
CARAT   n pl. -S a unit of weight for gems
CARATE   n pl. -S a tropical skin disease
CARAVAN   v -VANED, -VANING, -VANS or -VANNED, -VANNING, -VANS to travel in a group
CARAVEL   n pl. -S a small sailing ship
CARAWAY   n pl. -WAYS an herb used in cooking
CARB   n pl. -S a carburetor
CARBAMIC   adj pertaining to a type of acid
CARBAMYL   n pl. -S a chemical radical
CARBARN   n pl. -S a garage for buses
CARBARYL   n pl. -S an insecticide
CARBIDE   n pl. -S a carbon compound
CARBINE   n pl. -S a light rifle
CARBINOL   n pl. -S an alcohol
CARBO   n pl. -S a carbohydrate
CARBOLIC   n pl. -S an acidic compound
CARBON   n pl. -S a nonmetallic element CARBONIC adj
CARBONYL   n pl. -S a chemical compound
CARBORA   n pl. -S a wood-boring worm
CARBOXYL   n pl. -S a univalent acid radical
CARBOY   n pl. -BOYS a large bottle CARBOYED adj

CARBURET v -RETED, -RETING, -RETS or -RETTED, -RETTING, -RETS to combine chemically with carbon

CARCAJOU n pl. -S a carnivorous mammal

CARCANET n pl. -S a jeweled necklace

CARCASE n pl. -S carcass

CARCASS n pl. -ES the body of a dead animal

CARCEL n pl. -S a unit of illumination

CARD v -ED, -ING, -S to provide with a card (a stiff piece of paper)

CARDAMOM n pl. -S a tropical herb

CARDAMON n pl. -S cardamom

CARDAMUM n pl. -S cardamom

CARDCASE n pl. -S a case for holding cards

CARDER n pl. -S one that does carding

CARDIA n pl. -DIAS or -DIAE an opening of the esophagus

CARDIAC n pl. -S a person with a heart disorder

CARDIGAN n pl. -S a type of sweater

CARDINAL n pl. -S a bright red bird

CARDING n pl. -S the process of combing and cleaning cotton fibers; cleaned and combed fibers

CARDIOID n pl. -S a heart-shaped curve

CARDITIS n pl. -TISES inflammation of the heart **CARDITIC** adj

CARDOON n pl. -S a perennial plant

CARE v CARED, CARING, CARES to be concerned or interested

CAREEN v -ED, -ING, -S to lurch while moving

CAREENER n pl. -S one that careens

CAREER v -ED, -ING, -S to go at full speed

CAREERER n pl. -S one that careers

CAREFREE adj being without worry or anxiety

CAREFUL adj -FULLER, -FULLEST cautious

CARELESS adj inattentive; negligent

CARER n pl. -S one that cares

CARESS v -ED, -ING, -ES to touch lovingly

CARESSER n pl. -S one that caresses

CARET n pl. -S a proofreaders' symbol

CARETAKE v -TOOK, -TAKEN, -TAKING, -TAKES to take care of someone else's house or land

CAREWORN adj haggard

CAREX n pl. CARICES a marsh plant

CARFARE n pl. -S payment for a bus or car ride

CARFUL n pl. -S as much as a car can hold

CARGO n pl. -GOS or -GOES conveyed merchandise

CARHOP n pl. -S a waitress at a drive-in restaurant

CARIBE n pl. -S the piranha

CARIBOU n pl. -S a large deer

CARICES pl. of carex

CARIES n pl. CARIES tooth decay **CARIED** adj

CARILLON v -LONNED, -LONNING, -LONS to play a set of bells

CARINA n pl. -NAS or -NAE a carinate anatomical part **CARINAL** adj

CARINATE adj shaped like the keel of a ship

CARING present participle of care

CARIOCA n pl. -S a South American dance

CARIOLE n pl. -S a small, open carriage

CARIOUS adj decayed

CARITAS n -ES love for all people

CARK v -ED, -ING, -S to worry

CARL n pl. -S a peasant

CARLE n pl. -S carl

CARLESS adj being without a car

CARLIN n pl. -S an old woman

CARLINE n pl. -S carling

CARLING n pl. -S a beam supporting a ship's deck

CARLISH adj resembling a carl

CARLOAD n pl. -S as much as a car can hold

CARMAKER n pl. -S an automobile manufacturer

CARMAN n pl. -MEN a streetcar driver

CARMINE n pl. -S a vivid red color

CARN n pl. -S cairn

CARNAGE n pl. -S great and bloody slaughter

CARNAL adj pertaining to bodily appetites **CARNALLY** adv

CARNAUBA n pl. -S a palm tree

CARNET n pl. -S an official permit

CARNEY n pl. -NEYS carny

CARNIE n pl. -S carny

CARNIES pl. of carny

CARNIFY v -FIED, -FYING, -FIES to form into flesh

CARNIVAL n pl. -S a traveling amusement show

CARNY n pl. -NIES a carnival

CAROACH n pl. -ES caroche

CAROB n pl. -S an evergreen tree

CAROCH n pl. -ES caroche

CAROCHE n pl. -S a stately carriage

CAROL v -OLED, -OLING, -OLS or -OLLED, -OLLING, -OLS to sing joyously

CAROLER n pl. -S one that carols

CAROLI a pl. of carolus

CAROLLED a past tense of carol

CAROLLER n pl. -S caroler

CAROLLING a present participle of carol

CAROLUS n pl. -LUSES or -LI an old English coin

CAROM v -ED, -ING, -S to collide with and rebound

CAROTENE n pl. -S a plant pigment

CAROTID n pl. -S an artery in the neck

CAROTIN n pl. -S carotene

CAROUSAL n pl. -S a boisterous drinking party

CAROUSE v -ROUSED, -ROUSING, -ROUSES to engage in a carousal

CAROUSEL n pl. -S an amusement park ride

CAROUSER n pl. -S one that carouses

CAROUSING present participle of carouse

CARP v -ED, -ING, -S to find fault unreasonably

CARPAL n pl. -S carpale

CARPALE n pl. -LIA a bone of the wrist

CARPEL n pl. -S a simple pistil

CARPER n pl. -S one that carps

CARPET v -ED, -ING, -S to cover a floor with a heavy fabric

CARPI pl. of carpus

CARPING n pl. -S the act of one who carps

CARPOOL v -ED, -ING, -S to take turns driving a group of commuters

CARPORT n pl. -S a shelter for a car

CARPUS n pl. -PI the wrist

CARR n pl. -S a marsh

CARRACK n pl. -S a type of merchant ship

CARREL n pl. -S a desk in a library stack for solitary study

CARRELL n pl. -S carrel

CARRIAGE n pl. -S a wheeled, horse-drawn vehicle

CARRIED past tense of carry

CARRIER n pl. -S one that carries

CARRIES present 3d person sing. of carry

CARRIOLE n pl. -S cariole

CARRION n pl. -S dead and putrefying flesh

CARRITCH n pl. -ES a religious handbook

CARROCH n pl. -ES caroche

CARROM v -ED, -ING, -S to carom

CARROT n pl. -S an edible orange root

CARROTIN n pl. -S carotene

CARROTY adj -ROTIER, -ROTIEST resembling a carrot in color

CARRY v -RIED, -RYING, -RIES to convey from one place to another

CARRYALL n pl. -S a light covered carriage

CARRYON n pl. -S a small piece of luggage

CARRYOUT n pl. -S a take-out order of food

CARSE n pl. -S low, fertile land along a river

CARSICK adj nauseated from riding in a car

CART v -ED, -ING, -S to convey in a cart (a two-wheeled vehicle) **CARTABLE** adj

CARTAGE n pl. -S the act of carting

CARTE n pl. -S a menu

CARTEL n pl. -S a business organization

CARTER n pl. -S one that carts

CARTLOAD n pl. -S as much as a cart can hold

CARTON v -ED, -ING, -S to pack in a cardboard box

CARTOON v -ED, -ING, -S to sketch a cartoon (a humorous representation) of

CARTOONY adj resembling a cartoon

CARTOP adj able to fit on top of a car

CARTOUCH n pl. -ES a scroll-like tablet

CARUNCLE n pl. -S a fleshy outgrowth

CARVE v CARVED, CARVING, CARVES to form by cutting

CARVEL n pl. -S caravel

CARVEN adj carved

CARVER n pl. -S one that carves

CARVING n pl. -S a carved figure or design

CARWASH n pl. -ES an establishment equipped to wash automobiles

CARYATIC adj resembling a caryatid

CARYATID n pl. -S or -ES a sculptured female figure used as a column

CARYOTIN n pl. -S karyotin

CASA n pl. -S a dwelling

CASABA   *n* pl. -S a variety of melon
CASAVA   *n* pl. -S cassava
CASBAH   *n* pl. -S the old section of a North African city
CASCABEL   *n* pl. -S the rear part of a cannon
CASCABLE   *n* pl. -S cascabel
CASCADE   *v* -CADED, -CADING, -CADES to fall like a waterfall
CASCARA   *n* pl. -S a medicinal tree bark
CASE   *v* CASED, CASING, CASES to put in a case (a container or receptacle)
CASEASE   *n* pl. -S an enzyme
CASEATE   *v* -ATED, -ATING, -ATES to become cheesy
CASEBOOK   *n* pl. -S a law textbook
CASED   past tense of case
CASEFY   *v* -FIED, -FYING, -FIES to caseate
CASEIN   *n* pl. -S a milk protein **CASEIC** *adj*
CASELOAD   *n* pl. -S the number of cases being handled
CASEMATE   *n* pl. -S a bombproof shelter
CASEMENT   *n* pl. -S a type of window
CASEOSE   *n* pl. -S a proteose
CASEOUS   *adj* cheesy
CASERN   *n* pl. -S a barracks for soldiers
CASERNE   *n* pl. -S casern
CASETTE   *n* pl. -S cassette
CASEWORK   *n* pl. -S a form of social work
CASEWORM   *n* pl. -S an insect larva
CASH   *v* -ED, -ING, -ES to convert into cash (ready money) **CASHABLE** *adj*
CASHAW   *n* pl. -S cushaw
CASHBOOK   *n* pl. -S a book of monetary records
CASHBOX   *n* pl. -ES a container for money
CASHEW   *n* pl. -S a nut-bearing tree
CASHIER   *v* -ED, -ING, -S to dismiss in disgrace
CASHLESS   *adj* having no cash
CASHMERE   *n* pl. -S a fine wool
CASHOO   *n* pl. -SHOOS catechu
CASIMERE   *n* pl. -S a woolen fabric
CASIMIRE   *n* pl. -S casimere
CASING   *n* pl. -S a protective outer covering
CASINO   *n* pl. -NOS or -NI a gambling room
CASITA   *n* pl. -S a small house
CASK   *v* -ED, -ING, -S to store in a cask (a strong barrel)

CASKET   *v* -ED, -ING, -S to place in a casket (a burial case)
CASKY   *adj* resembling a cask
CASQUE   *n* pl. -S a helmet **CASQUED** *adj*
CASSABA   *n* pl. -S casaba
CASSATA   *n* pl. -S an Italian ice cream
CASSAVA   *n* pl. -S a tropical plant
CASSETTE   *n* pl. -S a small case containing audiotape or videotape
CASSIA   *n* pl. -S a variety of cinnamon
CASSINO   *n* pl. -NOS a card game
CASSIS   *n* pl. -SISES a European bush
CASSOCK   *n* pl. -S a long garment worn by clergymen
CAST   *v* CAST, CASTING, CASTS to throw with force **CASTABLE** *adj*
CASTANET   *n* pl. -S a rhythm instrument
CASTAWAY   *n* pl. -WAYS an outcast
CASTE   *n* pl. -S a system of distinct social classes
CASTEISM   *n* pl. -S the use of a caste system
CASTER   *n* pl. -S a small, swiveling wheel
CASTING   *n* pl. -S something made in a mold
CASTLE   *v* -TLED, -TLING, -TLES to make a certain move in chess
CASTOFF   *n* pl. -S a discarded person or thing
CASTOR   *n* pl. -S caster
CASTRATE   *v* -TRATED, -TRATING, -TRATES to remove the testes of
CASTRATO   *n* pl. -TI a singer castrated in boyhood
CASUAL   *n* pl. -S one who works occasionally
CASUALLY   *adv* informally
CASUALTY   *n* pl. -TIES a victim of war or disaster
CASUIST   *n* pl. -S one who resolves ethical problems
CASUS   *n* pl. CASUS a legal occurrence or event
CAT   *v* CATTED, CATTING, CATS to hoist an anchor to the cathead
CATACOMB   *n* pl. -S an underground cemetery
CATALASE   *n* pl. -S an enzyme
CATALO   *n* pl. -LOS or -LOES a hybrid between a buffalo and a cow

CATALOG v -ED, -ING, -S to classify information descriptively

CATALPA n pl. -S a tree

CATALYST n pl. -S a substance that accelerates a chemical reaction

CATALYZE v -LYZED, -LYZING, -LYZES to act as a catalyst

CATAMITE n pl. -S a boy used in sodomy

CATAPULT v -ED, -ING, -S to hurl through the air

CATARACT n pl. -S a tremendous waterfall

CATARRH n pl. -S inflammation of a mucous membrane

CATAWBA n pl. -S a variety of fox grape

CATBIRD n pl. -S a songbird

CATBOAT n pl. -S a small sailboat

CATBRIER n pl. -S a thorny vine

CATCALL v -ED, -ING, -S to deride by making shrill sounds

CATCH v CAUGHT, CATCHING, CATCHES to capture after pursuit

CATCHALL n pl. -S a container for odds and ends

CATCHER n pl. -S one that catches

CATCHFLY n pl. -FLIES an insect-catching plant

CATCHUP n pl. -S ketchup

CATCHY adj CATCHIER, CATCHIEST pleasing and easily remembered

CATCLAW n pl. -S a flowering shrub

CATE n pl. -S a choice food

CATECHIN n pl. -S a chemical used in dyeing

CATECHOL n pl. -S a chemical used in photography

CATECHU n pl. -S a resin used in tanning

CATEGORY n pl. -RIES a division in any system of classification

CATENA n pl. -NAS or -NAE a closely linked series

CATENARY n pl. -NARIES a mathematical curve

CATENATE v -NATED, -NATING, -NATES to link together

CATENOID n pl. -S a geometric surface

CATER v -ED, -ING, -S to provide food and service for

CATERAN n pl. -S a brigand

CATERER n pl. -S one that caters

CATERESS n pl. -ES a woman who caters

CATFACE n pl. -S a deformity of fruit

CATFALL n pl. -S an anchor line

CATFIGHT n pl. -S a fight between two women

CATFISH n pl. -ES a scaleless, large-headed fish

CATGUT n pl. -S a strong cord

CATHEAD n pl. -S a beam projecting from a ship's bow

CATHECT v -ED, -ING, -S to invest with psychic energy

CATHEDRA n pl. -DRAS or -DRAE a bishop's throne

CATHETER n pl. -S a medical instrument

CATHEXIS n pl. -THEXES the concentration of psychic energy on a person or idea

CATHODE n pl. -S a negatively charged electrode **CATHODAL, CATHODIC** adj

CATHOLIC n pl. -S a member of the early Christian church

CATHOUSE n pl. -S a brothel

CATION n pl. -S a positively charged ion **CATIONIC** adj

CATKIN n pl. -S a flower cluster

CATLIKE adj resembling a cat; stealthy; silent

CATLIN n pl. -S catling

CATLING n pl. -S a surgical knife

CATMINT n pl. -S catnip

CATNAP v -NAPPED, -NAPPING, -NAPS to doze

CATNAPER n pl. -S one that steals cats

CATNIP n pl. -S an aromatic herb

CATSPAW n pl. -S a light wind

CATSUP n pl. -S ketchup

CATTAIL n pl. -S a marsh plant

CATTALO n pl. -LOS or -LOES catalo

CATTED past tense of cat

CATTERY n pl. -TERIES an establishment for breeding cats

CATTIE n pl. -S an Asian unit of weight

CATTIER comparative of catty

CATTIET superlative of catty

CATTILY adv in a catty manner

CATTING present participle of cat

CATTISH adj catty

CATTLE n/pl domesticated bovines

CATTLEYA n pl. -S a tropical orchid

CATTY adj -TIER, -TIEST catlike; spiteful

CATWALK n pl. -S a narrow walkway

CAUCUS v -CUSED, -CUSING, -CUSES or -CUSSED, -CUSSING, -CUSSES to hold a political meeting

CAUDAD adv toward the tail

CAUDAL *adj* taillike **CAUDALLY** *adv*
CAUDATE *n* pl. -S a basal ganglion of the brain
CAUDATED *adj* having a tail
CAUDEX *n* pl. -DICES or -DEXES the woody base of some plants
CAUDILLO *n* pl. -LLOS a military dictator
CAUDLE *n* pl. -S a warm beverage
CAUGHT past tense of catch
CAUL *n* pl. -S a fetal membrane
CAULD *n* pl. -S cold
CAULDRON *n* pl. -S caldron
CAULES pl. of caulis
CAULICLE *n* pl. -S a small stem
CAULINE *adj* pertaining to a stem
CAULIS *n* pl. -LES a plant stem
CAULK *v* -ED, -ING, -S to make the seams of a ship watertight
CAULKER *n* pl. -S one that caulks
CAULKING *n* pl. -S the material used to caulk
CAUSABLE *adj* capable of being caused
CAUSAL *n* pl. -S a word expressing cause or reason
CAUSALLY *adv* by way of causing
CAUSE *v* CAUSED, CAUSING, CAUSES to bring about
CAUSER *n* pl. -S one that causes
CAUSERIE *n* pl. -S an informal conversation
CAUSEWAY *v* -ED, -ING, -S to build a causeway (a raised roadway) over
CAUSEY *n* pl. -SEYS a paved road
CAUSING present participle of cause
CAUSTIC *n* pl. -S a corrosive substance
CAUTERY *n* pl. -TERIES something used to destroy tissue
CAUTION *v* -ED, -ING, -S to warn
CAUTIOUS *adj* exercising prudence to avoid danger
CAVALERO *n* pl. -ROS a horseman
CAVALIER *v* -ED, -ING, -S to behave haughtily
CAVALLA *n* pl. -S a large food fish
CAVALLY *n* pl. -LIES cavalla
CAVALRY *n* pl. -RIES a mobile army unit
CAVATINA *n* pl. -NAS or -NE a simple song
CAVE *v* CAVED, CAVING, CAVES to hollow out
CAVEAT *v* -ED, -ING, -S to enter a type of legal notice
CAVEATOR *n* pl. -S one that files a caveat
CAVED past tense of cave
CAVEFISH *n* pl. -ES a sightless fish

CAVELIKE *adj* resembling a cave (an underground chamber)
CAVEMAN *n* pl. -MEN a cave dweller
CAVER *n* pl. -S one that caves
CAVERN *v* -ED, -ING, -S to hollow out
CAVETTO *n* pl. -TOS or -TI a concave molding
CAVIAR *n* pl. -S the roe of sturgeon
CAVIARE *n* pl. -S caviar
CAVICORN *adj* having hollow horns
CAVIE *n* pl. -S a hencoop
CAVIES pl of cavy
CAVIL *v* -ILED, -ILING, -ILS or -ILLED, -ILLING, -ILS to carp
CAVILER *n* pl. -S one that cavils
CAVILLER *n* pl. -S caviler
CAVILLING a present participle of cavil
CAVING *n* pl. -S the sport of exploring caves
CAVITARY *adj* pertaining to the formation of cavities in tissue
CAVITATE *v* -TATED, -TATING, -TATES to form cavities
CAVITY *n* pl. -TIES an unfilled space within a mass **CAVITIED** *adj*
CAVORT *v* -ED, -ING, -S to frolic
CAVORTER *n* pl. -S one that cavorts
CAVY *n* pl. -VIES a short-tailed rodent
CAW *v* -ED, -ING, -S to utter the sound of a crow
CAY *n* pl. CAYS a small low island
CAYENNE *n* pl. -S a hot seasoning **CAYENNED** *adj*
CAYMAN *n* pl. -S caiman
CAYUSE *n* pl. -S an Indian pony
CAZIQUE *n* pl. -S cacique
CEASE *v* CEASED, CEASING, CEASES to stop
CEBID *n* pl. -S ceboid
CEBOID *n* pl. -S one of a family of monkeys
CECUM *n* pl. CECA a bodily cavity with one opening **CECAL** *adj* **CECALLY** *adv*
CEDAR *n* pl. -S an everygreen tree **CEDARN** *adj*
CEDE *v* CEDED, CEDING, CEDES to yield
CEDER *n* pl. -S one that cedes
CEDI *n* pl. -S a monetary unit of Ghana
CEDILLA *n* pl. -S a pronunciation mark
CEDING present participle of cede
CEDULA *n* pl. -S a Philippine tax
CEE *n* pl. -S the letter C

CEIBA	n pl. -S a tropical tree
CEIL	v -ED, -ING, -S to furnish with a ceiling
CEILER	n pl. -S one that ceils
CEILING	n pl. -S the overhead lining of a room
CEINTURE	n pl. -S a belt for the waist
CEL	n pl. -S a sheet of celluloid used in animation
CELADON	n pl. -S a pale green color
CELEB	n pl. -S a celebrity; a famous person
CELERIAC	n pl. -S a variety of celery
CELERITY	n pl. -TIES swiftness
CELERY	n pl. -ERIES a plant with edible stalks
CELESTA	n pl. -S a keyboard instrument
CELESTE	n pl. -S celesta
CELIAC	n pl. -S one that has a chronic nutritional disturbance
CELIBACY	n pl. -CIES abstention from sexual intercourse
CELIBATE	n pl. -S one who lives a life of celibacy
CELL	v -ED, -ING, -S to store in a honeycomb
CELLA	n pl. -LAE the interior of an ancient temple
CELLAR	v -ED, -ING, -S to store in an underground room
CELLARER	n pl. -S the steward of a monastery
CELLARET	n pl. -S a cabinet for wine bottles
CELLIST	n pl. -S one who plays the cello
CELLMATE	n pl. -S one of two or more prisoners sharing a cell
CELLO	n pl. -LOS or -LI a stringed muscial instrument
CELLULAR	adj pertaining to a cell (a basic unit of life)
CELLULE	n pl. -S a small cell
CELOM	n pl. -LOMS or -LOMATA coelom
CELOSIA	n pl. -S a flowering plant
CELT	n pl. -S a primitive ax
CEMBALO	n pl. -LI or -LOS a harpsichord
CEMENT	v -ED, -ING, -S to bind firmly
CEMENTER	n pl. -S one that cements
CEMENTUM	n pl. -TA the hard tissue covering the roots of the teeth
CEMETERY	n pl. -TERIES a burial ground
CENACLE	n pl. -S a small dining room
CENOBITE	n pl. -S a member of a religious order

CENOTAPH	n pl. -S an empty tomb
CENOTE	n pl. -S a sinkhole in limestone
CENSE	v CENSED, CENSING, CENSES to perfume with incense
CENSER	n pl. -S a vessel for burning incense
CENSOR	v -ED, -ING, -S to delete an objectionable word or passage
CENSUAL	adj pertaining to the act of censusing
CENSURE	v -SURED, -SURING, -SURES to criticize severely
CENSURER	n pl. -S one that censures
CENSUS	v -ED, -ING, -ES to take an official count of
CENT	n pl. -S the 100th part of a dollar
CENTAL	n pl. -S a unit of weight
CENTARE	n pl. -S a measure of land area
CENTAUR	n pl. -S a mythological creature
CENTAURY	n pl. -RIES a medicinal herb
CENTAVO	n pl. -VOS a coin of various Spanish-American nations
CENTER	v -ED, -ING, -S to place at the center (the midpoint)
CENTESIS	n pl. -TESES a surgical puncture
CENTIARE	n pl. -S centare
CENTILE	n pl. -S a value of a statistical variable
CENTIME	n pl -S the 100th part of a franc
CENTIMO	n pl. -MOS any of various small coins
CENTNER	n pl. -S a unit of weight
CENTO	n pl. -TONES or -TOS a literary work made up of parts from other works
CENTRA	a pl. of centrum
CENTRAL	n pl. -S a telephone exchange
CENTRAL	adj -TRALER, -TRALEST situated at, in, or near the center
CENTRE	v -TRED, -TRING, -TRES to center
CENTRIC	adj situated at the center
CENTRING	n pl. -S a temporary framework for an arch
CENTRISM	n pl. -S moderate political philosophy
CENTRIST	n pl. -S an advocate of centrism

CENTROID *n* pl. -S the center of mass of an object

CENTRUM *n* pl. -TRUMS or -TRA the body of a vertebra

CENTUM *n* pl. -S one hundred

CENTUPLE *v* -PLED, -PLING, -PLES to increase a hundredfold

CENTURY *n* pl. -RIES a period of 100 years

CEORL *n* pl. -S a freeman of low birth CEORLISH *adj*

CEP *n* pl. -S cepe

CEPE *n* pl. -S a large mushroom

CEPHALAD *adv* toward the head

CEPHALIC *adj* pertaining to the head

CEPHALIN *n* pl. -S a bodily chemical

CEPHEID *n* pl. -S a giant star

CERAMAL *n* pl. -S a heat-resistant alloy

CERAMIC *n* pl. -S an item made of baked clay

CERAMIST *n* pl. -S one who makes ceramics

CERASTES *n* pl. CERASTES a venomous snake

CERATE *n* pl. -S a medicated ointment

CERATED *adj* covered with wax

CERATIN *n* pl. -S keratin

CERATOID *adj* hornlike

CERCARIA *n* pl. -IAE or -IAS a parasitic worm

CERCIS *n* pl. -CISES a shrub

CERCUS *n* pl. CERCI a sensory appendage of an insect

CERE *v* CERED, CERING, CERES to wrap in a waxy cloth

CEREAL *n* pl. -S a food made from grain

CEREBRAL *n* pl. -S a kind of consonant

CEREBRUM *n* pl. -BRUMS or -BRA a part of the brain CEREBRIC *adj*

CERED past tense of cere

CEREMENT *n* pl. -S a waxy cloth

CEREMONY *n* pl. -NIES a formal observance

CEREUS *n* pl. -ES a tall cactus

CERIA *n* pl. -S a chemical compound

CERIC *adj* containing cerium

CERING present participle of cere

CERIPH *n* pl. -S serif

CERISE *n* pl. -S a red color

CERITE *n* pl. -S a mineral

CERIUM *n* pl. -S a metallic element

CERMET *n* pl. -S ceramal

CERNUOUS *adj* drooping or nodding

CERO *n* pl. CEROS a large food fish

CEROTIC *adj* pertaining to beeswax

CEROTYPE *n* pl. -S a process of engraving using wax

CEROUS *adj* pertaining to cerium

CERTAIN *adj* -TAINER, -TAINEST absolutely confident

CERTES *adv* in truth

CERTIFY *v* -FIED, -FYING, -FIES to confirm

CERULEAN *n* pl. -S a blue color

CERUMEN *n* pl. -S a waxy secretion of the ear

CERUSE *n* pl. -S a lead compound

CERUSITE *n* pl. -S a lead ore

CERVELAS *n* pl. -ES cervelat

CERVELAT *n* pl. -S a smoked sausage

CERVICAL *adj* pertaining to the cervix

CERVID *adj* of the deer family

CERVINE *adj* pertaining to deer

CERVIX *n* pl. -VICES or -VIXES the neck

CESAREAN *n* pl. -S a method of child delivery

CESARIAN *n* pl. -S cesarean

CESIUM *n* pl. -S a metallic element

CESS *v* -ED, -ING, -ES to tax or assess

CESSION *n* pl. -S the act of ceding

CESSPIT *n* pl. -S a cesspool

CESSPOOL *n* pl. -S a covered well or pit for sewage

CESTA *n* pl. -S a basket used in jai alai

CESTI pl. of cestus

CESTODE *n* pl. -S a tapeworm

CESTOID *n* pl. -S cestode

CESTOS *n* pl. -TOI cestus

CESTUS *n* pl. -TI a belt or girdle

CESTUS *n* pl. -ES a hand covering for ancient Roman boxers

CESURA *n* pl. -RAS or -RAE caesura

CETACEAN *n* pl. -S an aquatic mammal

CETANE *n* pl. -S a diesel fuel

CETE *n* pl. -S a group of badgers

CETOLOGY *n* pl. -GIES the study of whales

CEVICHE *n* pl. -S seviche

CHABLIS *n* pl. CHABLIS a dry white wine

CHABOUK *n* pl. -S a type of whip

CHABUK *n* pl. -S chabouk

CHACMA *n* pl. -S a large baboon

CHACONNE *n* pl. -S an ancient dance

CHAD *n* pl. -S a scrap of paper CHADLESS *adj*

CHADAR *n* pl. -DARS or -DRI chador

CHADARIM a pl. of cheder

CHADOR n pl. -DORS or -DRI a large shawl

CHAETA n pl. -TAE a bristle or seta **CHAETAL** adj

CHAFE v CHAFED, CHAFING, CHAFES to warm by rubbing

CHAFER n pl. -S a large beetle

CHAFF v -ED, -ING, -S to poke fun at

CHAFFER v -ED, -ING, -S to bargain or haggle

CHAFFY adj CHAFFIER, CHAFFIEST worthless

CHAFING present participle of chafe

CHAGRIN v -GRINED, -GRINING, -GRINS or -GRINNED, -GRINNING, -GRINS to humiliate

CHAIN v -ED, -ING, -S to bind with a chain (a series of connected rings)

CHAINE n pl. -S a series of ballet turns

CHAINMAN n pl. -MEN a surveyor's assistant who uses a measuring chain

CHAINSAW v -SAWED, -SAWING, -SAWS to cut with a chain saw

CHAIR v -ED, -ING, -S to install in office

CHAIRMAN n pl. -MEN the presiding officer of a meeting

CHAIRMAN v -MANED, -MANING, -MANS or -MANNED, -MANNING, -MANS to act as chairman of

CHAISE n pl. -S a light carriage

CHAKRA n pl. -S a body center in yoga

CHALAH n pl. -LAHS, -LOTH or -LOT challah

CHALAZA n pl. -ZAS or -ZAE a band of tissue in an egg **CHALAZAL** adj

CHALAZIA n/pl tumors of the eyelid

CHALCID n pl. -S a tiny fly

CHALDRON n pl. -S a unit of dry measure

CHALEH n pl. -S challah

CHALET n pl. -S a Swiss cottage

CHALICE n pl. -S a drinking cup **CHALICED** adj

CHALK v -ED, -ING, -S to mark with chalk (a soft limestone)

CHALKY adj CHALKIER, CHALKIEST resembling chalk

CHALLA n pl. -S challah

CHALLAH n pl. -LAHS, -LOTH, or -LOT a kind of bread

CHALLIE n pl. -S challis

CHALLIES pl. of chally

CHALLIS n pl. -LISES a light fabric

CHALLOT a pl. of challah

CHALLOTH a pl. of challah

CHALLY n pl. -LIES challis

CHALONE n pl. -S a hormone

CHALOT a pl. of chalah

CHALOTH a pl. of chalah

CHALUTZ n pl. -LUTZIM halutz

CHAM n pl. -S a khan

CHAMADE n pl. -S a signal made with a drum

CHAMBER v -ED, -ING, -S to put in a chamber (a room)

CHAMBRAY n pl. -BRAYS a fine fabric

CHAMFER v -ED, -ING, -S to groove

CHAMFRON n pl. -S armor for a horse's head

CHAMISE n pl. -S chamiso

CHAMISO n pl. -SOS a flowering shrub

CHAMMY v -MIED, -MYING, -MIES to chamois

CHAMOIS n pl. -OIX a soft leather

CHAMOIS v -ED, -ING, -ES to prepare leather like chamois

CHAMP v -ED, -ING, -S to chew noisily

CHAMPAC n pl. -S champak

CHAMPAK n pl. -S an East Indian tree

CHAMPER n pl. -S one that champs

CHAMPION v -ED, -ING, -S to defend or support

CHAMPY adj broken up by the trampling of beasts

CHANCE v CHANCED, CHANCING, CHANCES to risk

CHANCEL n pl. -S an area around a church altar

CHANCERY n pl. -CERIES a court of public record

CHANCIER comparative of chancy

CHANCIEST superlative of chancy

CHANCILY adv in a chancy manner

CHANCING present participle of chance

CHANCRE n pl. -S a hard-based sore

CHANCY adj CHANCIER, CHANCIEST risky

CHANDLER n pl. -S a dealer in provisions

CHANFRON n pl. -S chamfron

CHANG n pl. -S a cattie

CHANGE v CHANGED, CHANGING, CHANGES to make different

CHANGER n pl. -S one that changes

CHANNEL v -NELED, -NELING, -NELS or -NELLED, -NELLING, -NELS to direct along some desired course

CHANSON n pl. -S a song

CHANT v -ED, -ING, -S to sing

CHANTAGE n pl. -S blackmail

CHANTER n pl. -S one that chants

CHANTEY n pl. -TEYS a sailor's song

CHANTIES pl. of chanty

CHANTOR n pl. -S chanter

CHANTRY n pl. -TRIES an endowment given to a church

CHANTY n pl. -TIES chantey

CHAO n pl. CHAO a monetary unit of Vietnam

CHAOS n pl. -ES a state of total disorder; a confused mass **CHAOTIC** adj

CHAP v CHAPPED or CHAPT, CHAPPING, CHAPS to split, crack, or redden

CHAPATI n pl. -S an unleavened bread of India

CHAPATTI n pl. -S chapati

CHAPBOOK n pl. -S a small book of popular tales

CHAPE n pl. -S a part of a scabbard

CHAPEAU n pl. -PEAUX or -PEAUS a hat

CHAPEL n pl. -S a place of worship

CHAPERON v -ED, -ING, -S to accompany

CHAPITER n pl. -S the capital of a column

CHAPLAIN n pl. -S a clergyman attached to a chapel

CHAPLET n pl. -S a wreath for the head

CHAPMAN n pl. -MEN a peddler

CHAPPED a past tense of chap

CHAPPING present participle of chap

CHAPT a past tense of chap

CHAPTER v -ED, -ING, -S to divide a book into chapters (main sections)

CHAQUETA n pl. -S a jacket worn by cowboys

CHAR v CHARRED, CHARRING, CHARS to burn slightly

CHARACID n pl. -S characin

CHARACIN n pl. -S a tropical fish

CHARADE n pl. -S a word represented by pantomime

CHARAS n pl. -ES hashish

CHARCOAL v -ED, -ING, -S to blacken with charcoal (a dark, porous carbon)

CHARD n pl. -S a variety of beet

CHARE v CHARED, CHARING, CHARES to do small jobs

CHARGE v CHARGED, CHARGING, CHARGES to accuse formally

CHARGER n pl. -S one that charges

CHARIER comparative of chary

CHARIEST superlative of chary

CHARILY adv in a chary manner

CHARING present participle of chare

CHARIOT v -ED, -ING, -S to ride in a chariot (a type of cart)

CHARISM n pl. -S charisma

CHARISMA n pl. -MATA a special magnetic appeal

CHARITY n pl. -TIES something given to the needy

CHARK v -ED, -ING, -S to char

CHARKA n pl. -S charkha

CHARKHA n pl. -S a spinning wheel

CHARLADY n pl. -DIES a cleaning woman

CHARLEY n pl. -LEYS charlie

CHARLIE n pl. -LIES a fool

CHARLOCK n pl. -S a troublesome weed

CHARM v -ED, -ING, -S to attract irresistibly

CHARMER n pl. -S one that charms

CHARMING adj -INGER, -INGEST pleasing

CHARNEL n pl. -S a room where corpses are placed

CHARPAI n pl. -S charpoy

CHARPOY n pl. -POYS a bed used in India

CHARQUI n pl. -S a type of meat **CHARQUID** adj

CHARR n pl. -S a small-scaled trout

CHARRED past tense of char

CHARRIER comparative of charry

CHARRIEST superlative of charry

CHARRING present participle of char

CHARRO n pl. -ROS a cowboy

CHARRY adj -RIER, -RIEST resembling charcoal

CHART v -ED, -ING, -S to map out

CHARTER v -ED, -ING, -S to lease or hire

CHARTIST n pl. -S a stock market specialist

CHARY adj CHARIER, CHARIEST cautious

CHASE v CHASED, CHASING, CHASES to pursue

CHASER n pl. -S one that chases

CHASING n pl. -S a design engraved on metal

CHASM n pl. -S a deep cleft in the earth **CHASMAL, CHASMED, CHASMIC, CHASMY** adj

CHASSE v CHASSED, CHASSEING, CHASSES to perform a dance movement

CHASSEUR *n* pl. -S a cavalry soldier
CHASSIS *n* pl. CHASSIS the frame of a car
CHASTE *adj* CHASTER, CHASTEST morally pure **CHASTELY** *adv*
CHASTEN *v* -ED, -ING, -S to chastise
CHASTISE *v* -TISED, -TISING, -TISES to discipline by punishment
CHASTITY *n* pl. -TIES moral purity
CHASUBLE *n* pl. -S a sleeveless vestment
CHAT *v* CHATTED, CHATTING, CHATS to converse informally
CHATCHKA *n* pl. -S a knickknack
CHATCHKE *n* pl. -S chatchka
CHATEAU *n* pl. -TEAUX or -TEAUS a large country house
CHATTED past tense of chat
CHATTEL *n* pl. -S a slave
CHATTER *v* -ED, -ING, -S to talk rapidly and trivially **CHATTERY** *adj*
CHATTING present participle of chat
CHATTY *adj* -TIER, -TIEST talkative **CHATTILY** *adv*
CHAUFER *n* pl. -S chauffer
CHAUFFER *n* pl. -S a small furnace
CHAUNT *v* -ED, -ING, -S to chant
CHAUNTER *n* pl. -S one that chaunts
CHAUSSES *n/pl* medieval armor
CHAW *v* -ED, -ING, -S to chew
CHAWER *n* pl. -S one that chaws
CHAY *n* pl. CHAYS the root of an East Indian herb
CHAYOTE *n* pl. -S a tropical vine
CHAZAN *n* pl. -ZANS or -ZANIM a cantor
CHAZZAN *n* pl. -ZANS or -ZANIM chazan
CHAZZEN *n* pl. -ZENS or -ZENIM chazan
CHEAP *adj* CHEAPER, CHEAPEST inexpensive
CHEAP *n* pl. -S a market
CHEAPEN *v* -ED, -ING, -S to make cheap
CHEAPIE *n* pl. -S one that is cheap
CHEAPISH *adj* somewhat cheap
CHEAPLY *adv* in a cheap manner
CHEAPO *n* pl. CHEAPOS a cheapie
CHEAT *v* -ED, -ING, -S to defraud
CHEATER *n* pl. -S one that cheats
CHEBEC *n* pl. -S a small bird
CHECHAKO *n* pl. -KOS a newcomer
CHECK *v* -ED, -ING, -S to inspect
CHECKER *v* -ED, -ING, -S to mark with squares
CHECKOFF *n* pl. -S a method of collecting union dues
CHECKOUT *n* pl. -S a test of a machine

CHECKROW *v* -ED, -ING, -S to plant in rows which divide the land into squares
CHECKUP *n* pl. -S an examination
CHEDDAR *n* pl. -S a type of cheese
CHEDDITE *n* pl. -S chedite
CHEDER *n* pl. CHADARIM or CHEDERS heder
CHEDITE *n* pl. -S an explosive
CHEEK *v* -ED, -ING, -S to speak impudently to
CHEEKFUL *n* pl. -S the amount held in one's cheek
CHEEKY *adj* CHEEKIER, CHEEKIEST impudent **CHEEKILY** *adv*
CHEEP *v* -ED, -ING, -S to chirp
CHEEPER *n* pl. -S one that cheeps
CHEER *v* -ED, -ING, -S to applaud with shouts of approval
CHEERER *n* pl. -S one that cheers
CHEERFUL *adj* -FULLER, -FULLEST full of spirits
CHEERIER comparative of cheery
CHEERIEST superlative of cheery
CHEERILY *adv* in a cheery manner
CHEERIO *n* pl. -IOS a greeting
CHEERLED past tense of cheerlead
CHEERLY *adv* cheerily
CHEERO *n* pl. CHEEROS cheerio
CHEERY *adj* CHEERIER, CHEERIEST cheerful
CHEESE *v* CHEESED, CHEESING, CHEESES to stop
CHEESY *adj* CHEESIER, CHEESIEST resembling cheese (a food made from milk curds) **CHEESILY** *adv*
CHEETAH *n* pl. -S a swift-running wildcat
CHEF *v* CHEFFED, CHEFFING, CHEFS to work as a chef (a chief cook)
CHEFDOM *n* pl. -S the status or function of a chef
CHEGOE *n* pl. -S chigoe
CHELA *n* pl. -LAE a pincerlike claw
CHELA *n* pl. -S a pupil of a guru
CHELATE *v* -LATED, -LATING, -LATES to combine a metal ion with a compound
CHELATOR *n* pl. -S one that chelates
CHELOID *n* pl. -S keloid
CHEMIC *n* pl. -S a chemist
CHEMICAL *n* pl. -S a substance obtained by a process of chemistry
CHEMISE *n* pl. -S a loose dress
CHEMISM *n* pl. -S chemical attraction

CHEMIST *n* pl. -S one versed in chemistry

CHEMURGY *n* pl. -GIES a branch of applied chemistry

CHENILLE *n* pl. -S a soft fabric

CHENOPOD *n* pl. -S a flowering plant

CHEQUE *n* pl. -S a written order directing a bank to pay money

CHEQUER *v* -ED, -ING, -S to checker

CHERISH *v* -ED, -ING, -ES to hold dear

CHEROOT *n* pl. -S a square-cut cigar

CHERRY *n* pl. -RIES a fruit

CHERT *n* pl. -S a compact rock

CHERTY *adj* CHERTIER, CHERTIEST resembling chert

CHERUB *n* pl. -UBS or -UBIM or -UBIMS an angel CHERUBIC *adj*

CHERVIL *n* pl. -S an aromatic herb

CHESS *n* pl. -ES a weed

CHESSMAN *n* pl. -MEN one of the pieces used in chess (a board game for two players)

CHEST *n* pl. -S a part of the body CHESTED *adj*

CHESTFUL *n* pl. -S as much as a chest or box can hold

CHESTNUT *n* pl. -S an edible nut

CHESTY *adj* CHESTIER, CHESTIEST proud

CHETAH *n* pl. -S cheetah

CHETH *n* pl. -S heth

CHETRUM *n* pl. -S a monetary unit of Bhutan

CHEVALET *n* pl. -S a part of a stringed instrument

CHEVERON *n* pl. -S chevron

CHEVIED past tense of chevy

CHEVIES present 3d person sing. of chevy

CHEVIOT *n* pl. -S a coarse fabric

CHEVRE *n* pl. -S a cheese made from goat's milk

CHEVRON *n* pl. -S a V-shaped pattern

CHEVY *v* CHEVIED, CHEVYING, CHEVIES to chase about

CHEW *v* -ED, -ING, -S to crush or grind with the teeth CHEWABLE *adj*

CHEWER *n* pl. -S one that chews

CHEWINK *n* pl. -S a common finch

CHEWY *adj* CHEWIER, CHEWIEST not easily chewed

CHEZ *prep* at the home of

CHI *n* pl. -S a Greek letter

CHIA *n* pl. -S a Mexican herb

CHIAO *n* pl. CHIAO a monetary unit of China

CHIASM *n* pl. -S chiasma

CHIASMA *n* pl. -MATA or -MAS an anatomical junction CHIASMAL, CHIASMIC *adj*

CHIASMUS *n* pl. -MI a reversal of word order between parallel phrases CHIASTIC *adj*

CHIAUS *n* pl. -ES a Turkish messenger

CHIBOUK *n* pl. -S a tobacco pipe

CHIC *n* pl. -S elegance

CHIC *adj* CHICER, CHICEST smartly stylish

CHICANE *v* -CANED, -CANING, -CANES to trick

CHICANER *n* pl. -S one that chicanes

CHICANO *n* pl. -NOS an American of Mexican descent

CHICCORY *n* pl. -RIES chicory

CHICHI *n* pl. -S elaborate ornamentation

CHICK *n* pl. -S a young bird

CHICKEE *n* pl. -S a stilt house of the Seminole Indians

CHICKEN *v* -ED, -ING, -S to lose one's nerve

CHICKORY *n* pl. -RIES chicory

CHICKPEA *n* pl. -S an Asian herb

CHICLE *n* pl. -S a tree gum

CHICLY *adv* in an elegant manner

CHICNESS *n* pl. -ES elegance

CHICO *n* pl. -COS a prickly shrub

CHICORY *n* pl. -RIES a perennial herb

CHIDE *v* CHIDED or CHID, CHIDDEN, CHIDING, CHIDES to scold

CHIDER *n* pl. -S one that chides

CHIEF *adj* CHIEFER, CHIEFEST highest in authority

CHIEF *n* pl. -S the person highest in authority

CHIEFDOM *n* pl. -S the domain of a chief

CHIEFLY *adv* above all

CHIEL *n* pl. -S chield

CHIELD *n* pl. -S a young man

CHIFFON *n* pl. -S a sheer fabric

CHIGETAI *n* pl. -S a wild ass

CHIGGER *n* pl. -S a parasitic mite

CHIGNON *n* pl. -S a woman's hairdo

CHIGOE *n* pl. -S a tropical flea

CHILD *n* pl. CHILDREN a young person

CHILDBED *n* pl. -S the state of a woman giving birth

CHILDE *n* pl. -S a youth of noble birth

CHILDING *adj* pregnant
CHILDISH *adj* resembling a child
CHILDLY *adj* -LIER, -LIEST resembling a child
CHILDREN pl. of child
CHILE *n* pl. -S chili
CHILI *n* pl. -ES a hot pepper
CHILIAD *n* pl. -S a group of one thousand
CHILIASM *n* pl. -S a religious doctrine
CHILIAST *n* pl. -S a supporter of chiliasm
CHILIDOG *n* pl. -S a hot dog topped with chili
CHILL *v* -ED, -ING, -S to make cold
CHILL *adj* CHILLER, CHILLEST cool
CHILLER *n* pl. -S one that chills
CHILLI *n* pl. -ES chili
CHILLUM *n* pl. -S a part of a water pipe
CHILLY *adj* CHILLIER, CHILLIEST cool CHILLILY *adv*
CHILOPOD *n* pl. -S a multi-legged insect
CHIMAERA *n* pl. -S a marine fish
CHIMAR *n* pl. -S chimere
CHIMB *n* pl. -S the rim of a cask
CHIMBLEY *n* pl. -BLEYS chimley
CHIMBLY *n* pl. -BLIES chimley
CHIME *v* CHIMED, CHIMING, CHIMES to ring harmoniously
CHIMER *n* pl. -S one that chimes
CHIMERA *n* pl. -S an imaginary monster
CHIMERE *n* pl. -S a bishop's robe
CHIMERIC *adj* imaginary; unreal
CHIMING present participle of chime
CHIMLA *n* pl. -S chimley
CHIMLEY *n* pl. -LEYS a chimney
CHIMNEY *n* pl. -NEYS a flue
CHIMP *n* pl. -S a chimpanzee
CHIN *v* CHINNED, CHINNING, CHINS to hold with the chin (the lower part of the face)
CHINA *n* pl. -S fine porcelain ware
CHINBONE *n* pl. -S the lower jaw
CHINCH *n* pl. -ES a bedbug
CHINCHY *adj* CHINCHIER, CHINCHIEST stingy
CHINE *v* CHINED, CHINING, CHINES to cut through the backbone of
CHINK *v* -ED, -ING, -S to fill cracks or fissures in
CHINKY *adj* CHINKIER, CHINKIEST full of cracks
CHINLESS *adj* lacking a chin
CHINNED past tense of chin
CHINNING present participle of chin
CHINO *n* pl. -NOS a strong fabric

CHINONE *n* pl. -S quinone
CHINOOK *n* pl. -S a warm wind
CHINTS *n* pl. -ES chintz
CHINTZ *n* pl. -ES a cotton fabric
CHINTZY *adj* CHINTZIER, CHINTZIEST gaudy; cheap
CHIP *v* CHIPPED, CHIPPING, CHIPS to break a small piece from
CHIPMUCK *n* pl. -S a chipmunk
CHIPMUNK *n* pl. -S a small rodent
CHIPPED past tense of chip
CHIPPER *v* -ED, -ING, -S to chirp
CHIPPIE *n* pl. -S chippy
CHIPPING present participle of chip
CHIPPY *n* pl. -PIES a prostitute
CHIPPY *adj* -PIER, -PIEST belligerent
CHIRAL *adj* pertaining to an asymmetrical molecule
CHIRK *v* -ED, -ING, -S to make a shrill noise
CHIRK *adj* CHIRKER, CHIRKEST cheerful
CHIRM *v* -ED, -ING, -S to chirp
CHIRO *n* pl. -ROS a marine fish
CHIRP *v* -ED, -ING, -S to utter a short, shrill sound
CHIRPER *n* pl. -S one that chirps
CHIRPY *adj* CHIRPIER, CHIRPIEST cheerful CHIRPILY *adv*
CHIRR *v* -ED, -ING, -S to make a harsh, vibrant sound
CHIRRE *v* CHIRRED, CHIRRING, CHIRRES to chirr
CHIRRUP *v* -ED, -ING, -S to chirp repeatedly CHIRRUPY *adj*
CHISEL *v* -ELED, -ELING, -ELS or -ELLED, -ELLING, -ELS to use a chisel (a cutting tool)
CHISELER *n* pl. -S one that chisels
CHIT *n* pl. -S a short letter
CHITAL *n* pl. CHITAL an Asian deer
CHITCHAT *v* -CHATTED, -CHATTING, -CHATS to indulge in small talk
CHITIN *n* pl. -S the main component of insect shells
CHITLIN *n* pl. -S chitling
CHITLING *n* pl. -S a part of the small intestine of swine
CHITON *n* pl. -S a tunic worn in ancient Greece
CHITOSAN *n* pl. -S a compound derived from chitin
CHITTER *v* -ED, -ING, -S to twitter
CHITTY *n* pl. -TIES a chit

CHIVALRY *n* pl. -RIES knightly behavior and skill

CHIVAREE *v* -REED, -REEING, -REES to perform a mock serenade

CHIVARI *v* -RIED, -RIING, -RIES to chivaree

CHIVE *n* pl. -S an herb used as a seasoning

CHIVVY *v* -VIED, -VYING, -VIES to chevy

CHIVY *v* CHIVIED, CHIVYING, CHIVIES to chevy

CHLAMYS *n* pl. -MYSES or -MYDES a garment worn in ancient Greece

CHLOASMA *n* pl. -MATA a skin discoloration

CHLORAL *n* pl. -S a chemical compound

CHLORATE *n* pl. -S a chemical salt

CHLORDAN *n* pl. -S a toxic compound of chlorine

CHLORIC *adj* pertaining to chlorine

CHLORID *n* pl. -S chloride

CHLORIDE *n* pl. -S a chlorine compound

CHLORIN *n* pl. -S chlorine

CHLORINE *n* pl. -S a gaseous element

CHLORITE *n* pl. -S a mineral group

CHLOROUS *adj* pertaining to chlorine

CHOANA *n* pl. -NAE a funnel-shaped opening

CHOCK *v* -ED, -ING, -S to secure with a wedge of wood or metal

CHOCKFUL *adj* full to the limit

CHOICE *n* pl. -S one that is chosen

CHOICE *adj* CHOICER, CHOICEST of fine quality **CHOICELY** *adv*

CHOIR *v* -ED, -ING, -S to sing in unison

CHOIRBOY *n* pl. -BOYS a boy who sings in a choir (a body of church singers)

CHOKE *v* CHOKED, CHOKING, CHOKES to impede the breathing of

CHOKER *n* pl. -S one that chokes

CHOKEY *adj* CHOKIER, CHOKIEST choky

CHOKING present participle of choke

CHOKY *adj* CHOKIER, CHOKIEST tending to cause choking

CHOLATE *n* pl. -S a chemical salt

CHOLENT *n* pl. -S a traditional Jewish stew

CHOLER *n* pl. -S anger

CHOLERA *n* pl. -S an acute disease

CHOLERIC *adj* bad-tempered

CHOLINE *n* pl. -S a B vitamin

CHOLLA *n* pl. -S a treelike cactus

CHOLO *n* pl. -LOS a pachuco

CHOMP *v* -ED, -ING, -S to champ

CHOMPER *n* pl. -S one that chomps

CHON *n* pl. CHON a monetary unit of South Korea

CHOOK *n* pl. -S a chicken

CHOOSE *v* CHOSE, CHOSEN, CHOOSING, CHOOSES to take by preference

CHOOSER *n* pl. -S one that chooses

CHOOSEY *adj* CHOOSIER, CHOOSIEST choosy

CHOOSING present participle of choose

CHOOSY *adj* CHOOSIER, CHOOSIEST hard to please

CHOP *v* CHOPPED, CHOPPING, CHOPS to sever with a sharp tool

CHOPIN *n* pl. -S chopine

CHOPINE *n* pl. -S a type of shoe

CHOPPED past tense of chop

CHOPPER *v* -ED, -ING, -S to travel by helicopter

CHOPPING present participle of chop

CHOPPY *adj* CHOPPIER, CHOPPIEST full of short, rough waves **CHOPPILY** *adv*

CHORAGUS *n* pl. -GI or -GUSES the leader of a chorus or choir **CHORAGIC** *adj*

CHORAL *n* pl. -S chorale

CHORALE *n* pl. -S a hymn that is sung in unison

CHORALLY *adv* harmoniously

CHORD *v* -ED, -ING, -S to play a chord (a combination of three or more musical tones)

CHORDAL *adj* pertaining to a chord

CHORDATE *n* pl. -S any of a large phylum of animals

CHORE *v* CHORED, CHORING, CHORES to do small jobs

CHOREA *n* pl. -S a nervous disorder **CHOREAL, CHOREIC** *adj*

CHOREGUS *n* pl. -GI or -GUSES choragus

CHOREMAN *n* pl. -MEN a menial worker

CHOREOID *adj* resembling chorea

CHORIAL *adj* pertaining to the chorion

CHORIAMB *n* pl. -S a type of metrical foot

CHORIC *adj* pertaining to a chorus

CHORINE *n* pl. -S a chorus girl

CHORING present participle of chore

CHORIOID *n* pl. -S choroid

CHORION n pl. -S an embryonic membrane

CHORIZO n pl. -ZOS a highly seasoned sausage

CHOROID n pl. -S a membrane of the eye

CHORTLE v -TLED, -TLING, -TLES to chuckle with glee

CHORTLER n pl. -S one that chortles

CHORUS v -RUSED, -RUSING, -RUSES or -RUSSED, -RUSSING, -RUSSES to sing in unison

CHOSE n pl. -S an item of personal property

CHOSEN past participle of choose

CHOTT n pl. -S a saline lake

CHOUGH n pl. -S a crow-like bird

CHOUSE v CHOUSED, CHOUSING, CHOUSES to swindle

CHOUSER n pl. -S one that chouses

CHOUSH n pl. -ES chiaus

CHOUSING present participle of chouse

CHOW v -ED, -ING, -S to eat

CHOWCHOW n pl. -S a relish of mixed pickles in mustard

CHOWDER v -ED, -ING, -S to make a thick soup of

CHOWSE v CHOWSED, CHOWSING, CHOWSES to chouse

CHOWTIME n pl. -S mealtime

CHRESARD n pl. -S the available water of the soil

CHRISM n pl. -S a consecrated oil CHRISMAL adj

CHRISMON n pl. -MA or -MONS a Christian monogram

CHRISOM n pl. -S chrism

CHRISTEN v -ED, -ING, -S to baptise

CHRISTIE n pl. -S christy

CHRISTY n pl. -TIES a skiing turn

CHROMA n pl. -S the purity of a color

CHROMATE n pl. -S a chemical salt

CHROME v CHROMED, CHROMING, CHROMES to plate with chromium

CHROMIC adj pertaining to chromium

CHROMIDE n pl. -S a tropical fish

CHROMING n pl. -S a chromium ore

CHROMITE n pl. -S a chromium ore

CHROMIUM n pl. -S a metallic element

CHROMIZE v -MIZED, -MIZING, -MIZES to chrome

CHROMO n pl. -MOS a type of color picture

CHROMOUS adj pertaining to chromium

CHROMYL n pl. -S a bivalent radical

CHRONAXY n pl. -AXIES the time required to excite a nerve cell electrically

CHRONIC n pl. -S one that suffers from a long-lasting disease

CHRONON n pl. -S a hypothetical unit of time

CHTHONIC adj pertaining to the gods of the underworld

CHUB n pl. -S a freshwater fish

CHUBASCO n pl. -COS a violent thunderstorm

CHUBBY adj -BIER, -BIEST plump CHUBBILY adv

CHUCK v -ED, -ING, -S to throw

CHUCKIES pl. of chucky

CHUCKLE v -LED, -LING, -LES to laugh quietly

CHUCKLER n pl. -S one that chuckles

CHUCKY n pl. CHUCKIES a little chick

CHUDDAH n pl. -S chuddar

CHUDDAR n pl. -S a large, square shawl

CHUDDER n pl. -S chuddar

CHUFA n pl. -S a European sedge

CHUFF adj CHUFFER, CHUFFEST gruff

CHUFF v -ED, -ING, -S to chug

CHUFFY adj -FIER, -FIEST plump

CHUG v CHUGGED, CHUGGING, CHUGS to move with a dull explosive sound

CHUGALUG v -LUGGED, -LUGGING, -LUGS to drink without pause

CHUGGER n pl. -S one that chugs

CHUKAR n pl. -S a game bird

CHUKKA n pl. -S a type of boot

CHUKKAR n pl. -S a chukker

CHUKKER n pl. -S a period of play in polo

CHUM v CHUMMED, CHUMMING, CHUMS to be close friends with someone

CHUMMY adj -MIER, -MIEST friendly CHUMMILY adv

CHUMP v -ED, -ING, -S to munch

CHUMSHIP n pl. -S friendship

CHUNK v -ED, -ING, -S to make a dull explosive sound

CHUNKY adj CHUNKIER, CHUNKIEST stocky CHUNKILY adv

CHUNTER v -ED, -ING, -S to mutter

CHURCH v -ED, -ING, -ES to bring to church (a building for Christian worship)

CHURCHLY adj -LIER, -LIEST pertaining to a church

CHURCHY *adj* CHURCHIER, CHURCHIEST churchy

CHURL *n* pl. -S a rude person **CHURLISH** *adj*

CHURN *v* -ED, -ING, -S to stir briskly in order to make butter

CHURNER *n* pl. -S one that churns

CHURNING *n* pl. -S the butter churned at one time

CHURR *v* -ED, -ING, -S to make a vibrant sound

CHUTE *v* CHUTED, CHUTING, CHUTES to convey by chute (a vertical passage)

CHUTIST *n* pl. -S a parachutist

CHUTNEE *n* pl. -S chutney

CHUTNEY *n* pl. -NEYS a sweet and sour sauce

CHUTZPA *n* pl. -S chutzpah

CHUTZPAH *n* pl. -S supreme self-confidence

CHYLE *n* pl. -S a digestive fluid **CHYLOUS** *adj*

CHYME *n* pl. -S semi-digested food

CHYMIC *n* pl. -S chemic

CHYMIST *n* pl. -S chemist

CHYMOSIN *n* pl. -S rennin

CHYMOUS *adj* pertaining to chyme

CIAO *interj* — used as an expression of greeting and farewell

CIBOL *n* pl. -S a variety of onion

CIBORIUM *n* pl. -RIA a vessel for holding holy bread

CIBOULE *n* pl. -S cibol

CICADA *n* pl. -DAS or -DAE a winged insect

CICALA *n* pl. -LAS or -LE cicada

CICATRIX *n* pl. -TRICES or -TRIXES scar tissue

CICELY *n* pl. -LIES a fragrant herb

CICERO *n* pl. -ROS a unit of measure in printing

CICERONE *n* pl. -NES or -NI a tour guide

CICHLID *n* pl. -LIDS or -LIDAE a tropical fish

CICISBEO *n* pl. -BEI or -BEOS a lover of a married woman

CICOREE *n* pl. -S a perennial herb

CIDER *n* pl. -S the juice pressed from apples

CIGAR *n* pl. -S a roll of tobacco leaf for smoking

CIGARET *n* pl. -S a narrow roll of finely cut tobacco for smoking

CILANTRO *n* pl. -TROS an herb used in cooking

CILIA pl. of cilium

CILIARY *adj* pertaining to cilia

CILIATE *n* pl. -S one of a class of ciliated protozoans

CILIATED *adj* having cilia

CILICE *n* pl. -S a coarse cloth

CILIUM *n* pl. CILIA a short, hairlike projection

CIMBALOM *n* pl. -S a Hungarian dulcimer

CIMEX *n* pl. -MICES a bedbug

CINCH *v* -ED, -ING, -ES to girth

CINCHONA *n* pl. -S a Peruvian tree

CINCTURE *v* -TURED, -TURING, -TURES to gird or encircle

CINDER *v* -ED, -ING, -S to reduce to cinders (ashes)

CINDERY *adj* containing cinders

CINE *n* pl. -S a motion picture

CINEAST *n* pl. -S a devotee of motion pictures

CINEASTE *n* pl. -S cineast

CINEMA *n* pl. -S a motion-picture theater

CINEOL *n* pl. -S a liquid used as an antiseptic

CINEOLE *n* pl. -S cineol

CINERARY *adj* used for cremated ashes

CINERIN *n* pl. -S a compound used in insecticides

CINGULUM *n* pl. -LA an anatomical band or girdle

CINNABAR *n* pl. -S the principal ore of mercury

CINNAMON *n* pl. -S a spice obtained from tree bark **CINNAMIC** *adj*

CINNAMYL *n* pl. -S a chemical used to make soap

CINQUAIN *n* pl. -S a stanza of five lines

CINQUE *n* pl. -S the number five

CION *n* pl. -S a cutting from a plant or tree

CIOPPINO *n* pl. -NOS a spicy fish stew

CIPHER *v* -ED, -ING, -S to solve problems in arithmetic

CIPHONY *n* pl. -NIES the electronic scrambling of voice transmissions

CIPOLIN *n* pl. -S a type of marble

CIRCA *prep* about; around

CIRCLE *v* -CLED, -CLING, -CLES to move or revolve around

CIRCLER *n* pl. -S one that circles

CIRCLET *n* pl. -S a small ring or ring-shaped object

CIRCLING present participle of circle

CIRCUIT v -ED, -ING, -S to move around

CIRCUITY n pl. -ITIES lack of straightforwardness

CIRCULAR n pl. -S a leaflet intended for wide distribution

CIRCUS n pl. -ES a public entertainment CIRCUSY adj

CIRE n pl. -S a highly glazed finish for fabrics

CIRQUE n pl. -S a deep, steep-walled basin on a mountain

CIRRATE adj having cirri

CIRRI pl. of cirrus

CIRRIPED n pl. -S any of an order of crustaceans

CIRROSE adj cirrous

CIRROUS adj having cirri

CIRRUS n pl. -RI a tendril or similar part

CIRSOID adj varicose

CIS adj having certain atoms on the same side of the molecule

CISCO n pl. -COS or -COES a freshwater fish

CISLUNAR adj situated between the earth and the moon

CISSOID n pl. -S a type of geometric curve

CISSY n pl. -SIES sissy

CIST n pl. -S a prehistoric stone coffin

CISTERN n pl. -S a water tank

CISTERNA n pl. -NAE a fluid-containing sac

CISTRON n pl. -S a segment of DNA

CISTUS n pl. -ES a flowering shrub

CITABLE adj citeable

CITADEL n pl. -S a fortress or stronghold

CITATION n pl. -S the act of citing CITATORY adj

CITATOR n pl. -S one that cites

CITE v CITED, CITING, CITES to quote as an authority or example

CITEABLE adj suitable for citation

CITER n pl. -S one that cites

CITHARA n pl. -S an ancient stringed instrument

CITHER n pl. -S cittern

CITHERN n pl. -S cittern

CITHREN n pl. -S cittern

CITIED adj having cities

CITIES pl. of city

CITIFY v -FIED, -FYING, -FIES to urbanize

CITING present participle of cite

CITIZEN n pl. -S a resident of a city or town

CITOLA n pl. -S a cittern

CITOLE n pl. -S citola

CITRAL n pl. -S a lemon flavoring

CITRATE n pl. -S a salt of citric acid CITRATED adj

CITREOUS adj having a lemonlike color

CITRIC adj derived from citrus fruits

CITRIN n pl. -S a citric vitamin

CITRINE n pl. -S a variety of quartz

CITRININ n pl. -S an antibiotic

CITRON n pl. -S a lemonlike fruit

CITROUS adj pertaining to a citrus tree

CITRUS n pl. -ES any of a genus of tropical, fruit-bearing trees CITRUSY adj

CITTERN n pl. -S a pear-shaped guitar

CITY n pl. CITIES a large town

CITYFIED adj having the customs and manners of city people

CITYWARD adv toward the city

CITYWIDE adj including all parts of a city

CIVET n pl. -S a catlike mammal

CIVIC adj pertaining to a city

CIVICISM n pl. -S a system of government based upon individual rights

CIVICS n/pl the science of civic affairs

CIVIE n pl. -S civvy

CIVIL adj pertaining to citizens

CIVILIAN n pl. -S a nonmilitary person

CIVILISE v -LISED, -LISING, -LISES to civilize

CIVILITY n pl. -TIES courtesy; politeness

CIVILIZE v -LIZED, -LIZING, -LIZES to bring out of savagery

CIVILLY adv politely

CIVISM n pl -S good citizenship

CIVVY n pl. -VIES a civilian

CLABBER v -ED, -ING, -S to curdle

CLACH n pl. -S clachan

CLACHAN n pl. -S a hamlet

CLACK v -ED, -ING, -S to make an abrupt, dry sound

CLACKER n pl. -S one that clacks

CLAD v CLAD, CLADDING, CLADS to coat one metal over another

CLADDING n pl. -S something that overlays

CLADE n pl. -S a group of biological taxa

CLADIST *n* pl. -S a taxonomist who uses clades in classifying life-forms

CLADODE *n* pl. -S a leaflike part of a stem

CLAG *v* CLAGGED, CLAGGING, CLAGS to clog

CLAIM *v* -ED, -ING, -S to demand as one's due

CLAIMANT *n* pl. -S one that asserts a right or title

CLAIMER *n* pl. -S one that claims

CLAM *v* CLAMMED, CLAMMING, CLAMS to dig for clams (bivalve mollusks)

CLAMANT *adj* noisy

CLAMBAKE *n* pl. -S a beach picnic

CLAMBER *v* -ED, -ING, -S to climb awkwardly

CLAMMED past tense of clam

CLAMMER *n* pl. -S one that clams

CLAMMING present participle of clam

CLAMMY *adj* CLAMMIER, CLAMMIEST cold and damp **CLAMMILY** *adv*

CLAMOR *v* -ED, -ING, -S to make loud outcries

CLAMORER *n* pl. -S one that clamors

CLAMOUR *v* -ED, -ING, -S to clamor

CLAMP *v* -ED, -ING, -S to fasten with a clamp (a securing device)

CLAMPER *n* pl. -S a device worn on shoes to prevent slipping on ice

CLAMWORM *n* pl. -S a marine worm

CLAN *n* pl. -S a united group of families

CLANG *v* -ED, -ING, -S to ring loudly

CLANGER *n* pl. -S a blunder

CLANGOR *v* -ED, -ING, -S to clang repeatedly

CLANGOUR *v* -ED, -ING, -S to clangor

CLANK *v* -ED, -ING, -S to make a sharp, metallic sound

CLANNISH *adj* characteristic of a clan

CLANSMAN *n* pl. -MEN a member of a clan

CLAP *v* CLAPPED or CLAPT, CLAPPING, CLAPS to strike one palm against the other

CLAPPER *n* p. -S one that claps

CLAPTRAP *n* pl. -S pretentious language

CLAQUE *n* pl. -S a group of hired applauders

CLAQUER *n* pl. -S claqueur

CLAQUEUR *n* pl. -S a member of a claque

CLARENCE *n* pl. -S a closed carriage

CLARET *n* pl. -S a dry red wine

CLARIES pl. of clary

CLARIFY *v* -FIED, -FYING, -FIES to make clear

CLARINET *n* pl. -S a woodwind instrument

CLARION *v* -ED, -ING, -S to proclaim by blowing a medieval trumpet

CLARITY *n* pl. -TIES the state of being clear

CLARKIA *n* pl. -S an annual herb

CLARO *n* pl. -ROS or -ROES a mild cigar

CLARY *n* pl. CLARIES an aromatic herb

CLASH *v* -ED, -ING, -ES to conflict or disagree

CLASHER *n* pl. -S one that clashes

CLASP *v* CLASPED or CLASPT, CLASPING, CLASPS to embrace tightly

CLASPER *n* pl. -S one that clasps

CLASS *v* -ED, -ING, -ES to classify

CLASSER *n* pl. -S one that classes

CLASSES pl. of classis

CLASSIC *n* pl. -S a work of enduring excellence

CLASSICO *adj* made from grapes grown in a certain part of Italy

CLASSIER comparative of classy

CLASSIEST superlative of classy

CLASSIFY *v* -FIED, -FYING, -FIES to arrange according to characteristics

CLASSILY *adv* in a classy manner

CLASSIS *n* pl. CLASSES a governing body in certain churches

CLASSISM *n* pl. -S discrimination based on social class

CLASSIST *n* pl. -S an advocate of classism

CLASSY *adj* CLASSIER, CLASSIEST stylish; elegant

CLAST *n* pl. -S a fragment of rock

CLASTIC *n* pl. -S a rock made up of other rocks

CLATTER *v* -ED, -ING, -S to move with a rattling noise

CLATTERY *adj* having a rattling noise

CLAUCHT a past tense of cleek

CLAUGHT *v* -ED, -ING, -S to clutch

CLAUSE *n* pl. -S a distinct part of a composition **CLAUSAL** *adj*

CLAUSTRA *n/pl* basal ganglia in the brain

CLAVATE *adj* shaped like a club

CLAVE *n pl.* -S one of a pair of percussion sticks

CLAVER *v* -ED, -ING, -S to gossip

CLAVI *pl.* of clavus

CLAVICLE *n pl.* -S a bone of the shoulder

CLAVIER *n pl.* -S a keyboard instrument

CLAVUS *n pl.* -VI a horny thickening of the skin

CLAW *v* -ED, -ING, -S to scratch with claws (sharp, curved toenails)

CLAWER *n pl.* -S one that claws

CLAWLESS *adj* having no claws

CLAWLIKE *adj* resembling a claw

CLAXON *n pl.* -S klaxon

CLAY *v* -ED, -ING, -S to treat with clay (a fine-grained, earthy material)

CLAYBANK *n pl.* -S a yellow-brown color

CLAYEY *adj* CLAYIER, CLAYIEST resembling clay

CLAYISH *adj* resembling or containing clay

CLAYLIKE *adj* resembling clay

CLAYMORE *n pl.* -S a type of sword

CLAYPAN *n pl.* -S a shallow natural depression

CLAYWARE *n pl.* -S pottery

CLEAN *adj* CLEANER, CLEANEST free from dirt or stain

CLEAN *v* -ED, -ING, -S to rid of dirt or stain

CLEANER *n pl.* -S one that cleans

CLEANLY *adj* -LIER, -LIEST habitually clean

CLEANSE *v* CLEANSED, CLEANSING, CLEANSES to clean

CLEANSER *n pl.* -S one that cleanses

CLEANUP *n pl.* -S an act of cleaning

CLEAR *adj* CLEARER, CLEAREST clean and pure

CLEAR *v* -ED, -ING, -S to remove obstructions

CLEARER *n pl.* -S one that clears

CLEARING *n pl.* -S an open space

CLEARLY *adv* in a clear manner

CLEAT *v* -ED, -ING, -S to strengthen with a strip of wood or iron

CLEAVAGE *n pl.* -S the act of cleaving

CLEAVE *v* CLEAVED, CLEFT, CLOVE or CLAVE, CLOVEN, CLEAVING, CLEAVES to split or divide

CLEAVER *n pl.* -S a heavy knife

CLEEK *v* CLAUGHT or CLEEKED, CLEEKING, CLEEKS to clutch

CLEF *n pl.* -S a musical symbol

CLEFT *v* -ED, -ING, -S to insert a scion into the stock of a plant

CLEIDOIC *adj* enclosed in a shell

CLEMATIS *n pl.* -TISES a flowering vine

CLEMENCY *n pl.* -CIES mercy

CLEMENT *adj* merciful

CLENCH *v* -ED, -ING, -ES to grasp firmly

CLENCHER *n pl.* -S one that clenches

CLEOME *n pl.* -S a tropical plant

CLEPE *v* CLEPED or CLEPT, CLEPING, CLEPES to call by name

CLERGY *n pl.* -GIES the body of persons ordained for religious service

CLERIC *n pl.* -S a member of the clergy

CLERICAL *n pl.* -S a cleric

CLERID *n pl.* -S a predatory beetle

CLERIHEW *n pl.* -S a humorous poem

CLERISY *n pl.* -SIES the well-educated class

CLERK *v* -ED, -ING, -S to serve as a clerk (an office worker)

CLERKDOM *n pl.* -S the status or function of a clerk

CLERKISH *adj* resembling or suitable to a clerk

CLERKLY *adj* -LIER, -LIEST pertaining to a clerk

CLEVEITE *n pl.* -S a radioactive mineral

CLEVER *adj* -ERER, -EREST mentally keen **CLEVERLY** *adv*

CLEVIS *n pl.* -ISES a metal fastening device

CLEW *v* -ED, -ING, -S to roll into a ball

CLICHE *n pl.* -S a trite expression **CLICHED** *adj*

CLICK *v* -ED, -ING, -S to make a short, sharp sound

CLICKER *n pl.* -S one that clicks

CLIENT *n pl.* -S a customer **CLIENTAL** *adj*

CLIFF *n pl.* -S a high, steep face of rock

CLIFFY *adj* CLIFFIER, CLIFFIEST abounding in cliffs

CLIFT *n pl.* -S cliff

CLIMATE *n pl.* -S the weather conditions characteristic of an area **CLIMATAL, CLIMATIC** *adj*

CLIMAX *v* -ED, -ING, -ES to reach a high or dramatic point

CLIMB   *v* CLIMBED or CLOMB, CLIMBING, CLIMBS to ascend

CLIMBER   *n* pl. -S one that climbs

CLIME   *n* pl. -S climate

CLINAL   *adj* pertaining to a cline

CLINALLY   *adv* in a clinal manner

CLINCH   *v* -ED, -ING, -ES to settle a matter decisively

CLINCHER   *n* pl. -S a decisive fact or remark

CLINE   *n* pl. -S a series of changes within a species

CLING   *v* CLUNG, CLINGING, CLINGS to adhere closely

CLING   *v* -ED, -ING, -S to make a high-pitched ringing sound

CLINGER   *n* pl. -S one that clings

CLINGY   *adj* CLINGIER, CLINGIEST adhesive

CLINIC   *n* pl. -S a medical facility **CLINICAL** *adj*

CLINK   *v* -ED, -ING, -S to make a soft, sharp, ringing sound

CLINKER   *v* -ED, -ING, -S to form fused residue in burning

CLIP   *v* CLIPPED, CLIPT, CLIPPING, CLIPS to trim by cutting

CLIPPER   *n* pl. -S one that clips

CLIPPING   *n* pl. -S something that is clipped out or off

CLIPT   a past participle of clip

CLIQUE   *v* CLIQUED, CLIQUING, CLIQUES to form a clique (an exclusive group of persons)

CLIQUEY   *adj* CLIQUIER, CLIQUIEST inclined to form cliques

CLIQUISH   *adj* cliquey

CLIQUY   *adj* CLIQUIER, CLIQUIEST cliquey

CLITELLA   *n/pl* regions in the body walls of certain annelids

CLITIC   *n* pl. -S a word pronounced as part of a neighboring word

CLITORIS   *n* pl. -RISES or -RIDES a sex organ **CLITORAL, CLITORIC** *adj*

CLIVERS   *n* pl. CLIVERS an annual herb

CLIVIA   *n* pl. -S a flowering plant

CLOACA   *n* pl. -ACAE or -ACAS a sewer **CLOACAL** *adj*

CLOAK   *v* -ED, -ING, -S to conceal

CLOBBER   *v* -ED, -ING, -S to trounce

CLOCHARD   *n* pl. -S a vagrant

CLOCHE   *n* pl. -S a bell-shaped hat

CLOCK   *v* -ED, -ING, -S to time with a stopwatch

CLOCKER   *n* pl. -S one that clocks

CLOD   *n* pl. -S a dolt **CLODDISH** *adj*

CLODDY   *adj* -DIER, -DIEST lumpy

CLODPATE   *n* pl. -S a stupid person

CLODPOLE   *n* pl. -S clodpate

CLODPOLL   *n* pl. -S clodpate

CLOG   *v* CLOGGED, CLOGGING, CLOGS to block up or obstruct

CLOGGER   *n* pl. -S one that clogs

CLOGGY   *adj* -GIER, -GIEST clogging or able to clog

CLOISTER   *v* -ED, -ING, -S to seclude

CLOMB   a past tense of climb

CLOMP   *v* -ED, -ING, -S to walk heavily and clumsily

CLON   *n* pl. -S a group of asexually derived organisms **CLONAL** *adj* **CLONALLY** *adv*

CLONE   *v* CLONED, CLONING, CLONES to reproduce by asexual means

CLONER   *n* pl. -S one that clones

CLONIC   *adj* pertaining to clonus

CLONING   *n* pl. -S a technique for reproducing by asexual means

CLONISM   *n* pl. -S the condition of having clonus

CLONK   *v* -ED, -ING, -S to make a dull thumping sound

CLONUS   *n* pl. -ES a form of muscular spasm

CLOOT   *n* pl. -S a cloven hoof

CLOP   *v* CLOPPED, CLOPPING, CLOPS to make the sound of a hoof striking pavement

CLOQUE   *n* pl. -S a fabric with an embossed design

CLOSE   *adj* CLOSER, CLOSEST near **CLOSELY** *adv*

CLOSE   *v* CLOSED, CLOSING, CLOSES to block against entry or passage **CLOSABLE** *adj*

CLOSEOUT   *n* pl. -S a clearance sale

CLOSER   *n* pl. -S one that closes

CLOSEST   superlative of close

CLOSET   *v* -ED, -ING, -S to enclose in a private room

CLOSING   *n* pl. -S a concluding part

CLOSURE   *v* -SURED, -SURING, -SURES to cloture

CLOT   *v* CLOTTED, CLOTTING, CLOTS to form into a clot (a thick mass)

CLOTH   *n* pl. -S fabric

CLOTHE v CLOTHED or CLAD, CLOTHING, CLOTHES to provide with clothing

CLOTHIER n pl. -S one who makes or sells clothing

CLOTHING n pl. -S wearing apparel

CLOTTED past tense of clot

CLOTTING present participle of clot

CLOTTY adj tending to clot

CLOTURE v -TURED, -TURING, -TURES to end a debate by calling for a vote

CLOUD v -ED, -ING, -S to cover with clouds (masses of visible vapor)

CLOUDLET n pl. -S a small cloud

CLOUDY adj CLOUDIER, CLOUDIEST overcast with clouds **CLOUDILY** adv

CLOUGH n pl. -S a ravine

CLOUR v -ED, -ING, -S to knock or bump

CLOUT v -ED, -ING, -S to hit with the hand

CLOUTER n pl. -S one that clouts

CLOVE n pl. -S a spice

CLOVEN adj split; divided

CLOVER n pl. -S a plant

CLOWDER n pl. -S a group of cats

CLOWN v -ED, -ING, -S to act like a clown (a humorous performer)

CLOWNERY n pl. -ERIES clownish behavior

CLOWNISH adj resembling or befitting a clown

CLOY v -ED, -ING, -S to gratify beyond desire

CLOZE n pl. -S a test of reading comprehension

CLUB v CLUBBED, CLUBBING, CLUBS to form a club (an organized group of persons)

CLUBABLE adj sociable

CLUBBER n pl.-S a member of a club

CLUBBING present participle of club

CLUBBISH adj clubby

CLUBBY adj -BIER, -BIEST characteristic of a club

CLUBFOOT n pl. -FEET a deformed foot

CLUBHAND n pl. -S a deformed hand

CLUBHAUL v -ED, -ING, -S to put a vessel about

CLUBMAN n pl. -MEN a male member of a club

CLUBROOM n pl. -S a room for a club's meetings

CLUBROOT n pl. -S a plant disease

CLUCK v -ED, -ING, -S to make the sound of a hen

CLUE v CLUED, CLUEING or CLUING, CLUES to give guiding information

CLUELESS adj hopelessly confused or ignorant

CLUMBER n pl. -S a stocky spaniel

CLUMP v -ED, -ING, -S to form into a thick mass

CLUMPISH adj resembling a clump (a thick mass)

CLUMPY adj CLUMPIER, CLUMPIEST lumpy

CLUMSY adj -SIER, -SIEST awkward **CLUMSILY** adv

CLUNG past tense of cling

CLUNK v -ED, -ING, -S to thump

CLUNKER n pl. -S a jalopy

CLUNKY adj CLUNKIER, CLUNKIEST clumsy in style

CLUPEID n pl. -S a fish of the herring family

CLUPEOID n pl. -S a clupeid

CLUSTER v -ED, -ING, -S to form into a cluster (a group of similar objects)

CLUSTERY adj pertaining to a cluster

CLUTCH v -ED, -ING, -ES to grasp and hold tightly

CLUTCHY adj tending to clutch

CLUTTER v -ED, -ING, -S to pile in a disorderly state

CLUTTERY adj characterized by disorder

CLYPEUS n pl. CLYPEI a shield-like structure **CLYPEAL, CLYPEATE** adj

CLYSTER n pl. -S an enema

COACH v -ED, -ING, -ES to tutor or train

COACHER n pl. -S one that coaches

COACHMAN n pl. -MEN one who drives a coach or carriage

COACT v -ED, -ING, -S to act together

COACTION n pl. -S joint action

COACTIVE adj mutually active

COACTOR n pl. -S a fellow actor in a production

COADMIRE v -MIRED, -MIRING, -MIRES to admire together

COADMIT v -MITTED, -MITTING, -MITS to admit several things equally

COAEVAL n pl. -S coeval

COAGENCY n pl. -CIES a joint agency

COAGENT *n* pl. -S a person, force, or other agent working together with another

COAGULUM *n* pl. -LA or -LUMS a clot

COAL *v* -ED, -ING, -S to supply with coal (a carbon fuel)

COALA *n* pl. -S koala

COALBIN *n* pl. -S a bin for storing coal

COALBOX *n* pl. -ES a box for storing coal

COALER *n* pl. -S one that supplies coal

COALESCE *v* -ALESCED, -ALESCING, -ALESCES to blend

COALFISH *n* pl. -ES a blackish fish

COALHOLE *n* pl. -S a compartment for storing coal

COALIER comparative of coaly

COALIEST superlative of coaly

COALIFY *v* -FIED, -FYING, -FIES to convert into coal

COALLESS *adj* lacking coal

COALPIT *n* pl. -S a pit from which coal is obtained

COALSACK *n* pl. -S a dark region of the Milky Way

COALSHED *n* pl. -S a shed for storing coal

COALY *adj* COALIER, COALIEST containing coal

COALYARD *n* pl. -S a yard for storing coal

COAMING *n* pl. -S a raised border

COANCHOR *v* -ED, -ING, -S to present televised news reports jointly

COANNEX *v* -ED, -ING, -ES to annex jointly

COAPPEAR *v* -ED, -ING, -S to appear together or at the same time

COAPT *v* -ED, -ING, -S to fit together and make fast

COARSE *adj* COARSER, COARSEST rough **COARSELY** *adv*

COARSEN *v* -ED, -ING, -S to make coarse

COASSIST *v* -ED, -ING, -S to assist jointly

COASSUME *v* -SUMED, -SUMING, -SUMES to assume together

COAST *v* -ED, -ING, -S to slide down a hill

COASTAL *adj* pertaining to or located near a seashore

COASTER *n* pl. -S a sled

COASTING *n* pl. -S coastal trade

COAT *v* -ED, -ING, -S to cover with a coat (an outer garment)

COATEE *n* pl. -S a small coat

COATER *n* pl. -S one that coats

COATI *n* pl. -S a tropical mammal

COATING *n* pl. -S a covering layer

COATLESS *adj* lacking a coat

COATRACK *n* pl. -S a rack or stand for coats

COATROOM *n* pl. -S a room for storing coats

COATTAIL *n* pl. -S the back lower portion of a coat

COATTEND *v* -ED, -ING, -S to attend together

COATTEST *v* -ED, -ING, -S to attest jointly

COAUTHOR *v* -ED, -ING, -S to write together

COAX *v* -ED, -ING, -ES to cajole

COAXAL *adj* coaxial

COAXER *n* pl. -S one that coaxes

COAXIAL *adj* having a common axis

COB *n* pl. -S a corncob

COBALT *n* pl. -S a metallic element **COBALTIC** *adj*

COBB *n* pl. -S a sea gull

COBBER *n* pl. -S a comrade

COBBIER comparative of cobby

COBBIEST superlative of cobby

COBBLE *v* -BLED, -BLING, -BLES to mend

COBBLER *n* pl. -S a mender of shoes

COBBY *adj* -BIER, -BIEST stocky

COBIA *n* pl. -S a large game fish

COBLE *n* pl. -S a small fishing boat

COBNUT *n* pl. -S an edible nut

COBRA *n* pl. -S a venomous snake

COBWEB *v* -WEBBED, -WEBBING, -WEBS to cover with cobwebs (spider webs)

COBWEBBY *adj* -BIER, -BIEST covered with cobwebs

COCA *n* pl. -S a South American shrub

COCAIN *n* pl. -S cocaine

COCAINE *n* pl. -S a narcotic alkaloid

COCCAL *adj* pertaining to a coccus

COCCI pl. of coccus

COCCIC *adj* coccal

COCCID *n* pl. -S an insect

COCCIDIA *n/pl* parasitic protozoans

COCCOID *n* pl. -S a spherical cell or body

COCCUS *n* pl. COCCI a spherical bacterium **COCCOUS** *adj*

COCCYX *n* pl. -CYGES or -CYXES a bone of the spine

COCHAIR *v* -ED, -ING, -S to serve jointly as chairman of

COCHIN *n* pl. -S a large domestic chicken

COCHLEA *n* pl. -CHLEAE or -CHLEAS a part of the ear **COCHLEAR** *adj*

COCINERA *n* pl. -S a cook

COCK *v* -ED, -ING, -S to tilt to one side

COCKADE *n* pl. -S an ornament worn on a hat **COCKADED** *adj*

COCKAPOO *n* pl. -POOS a hybrid between a cocker spaniel and a poodle

COCKATOO *n* pl. -TOOS a parrot

COCKBILL *v* -ED, -ING, -S to raise the yardarm on a ship

COCKBOAT *n* pl. -S a small boat

COCKCROW *n* pl. -S daybreak

COCKER *v* -ED, -ING, -S to pamper

COCKEREL *n* pl. -S a young rooster

COCKEYE *n* pl. -S a squinting eye **COCKEYED** *adj*

COCKIER comparative of cocky

COCKIEST superlative of cocky

COCKILY *adv* in a cocky manner

COCKISH *adj* cocky

COCKLE *v* -LED, -LING, -LES to wrinkle or pucker

COCKLIKE *adj* resembling a rooster

COCKLOFT *n* pl. -S a small attic

COCKNEY *n* pl. -NEYS a resident of the East End of London

COCKPIT *n* pl. -S a pilot's compartment in certain airplanes

COCKSHUT *n* pl. -S the close of day

COCKSHY *n* pl. -SHIES a target in a throwing contest

COCKSPUR *n* pl. -S a thorny plant

COCKSURE *adj* certain

COCKTAIL *v* -ED, -ING, -S to drink alcoholic beverages

COCKUP *n* pl. -S a turned-up part of something

COCKY *adj* COCKIER, COCKIEST arrogantly self-confident

COCO *n* pl. -COS a tall palm tree

COCOA *n* pl. -S chocolate

COCOANUT *n* pl. -S coconut

COCOBOLA *n* pl. -S cocobolo

COCOBOLO *n* pl. -LOS a tropical tree

COCOMAT *n* pl. -S a matting made from coir

COCONUT *n* pl. -S the fruit of the coco

COCOON *v* -ED, -ING, -S to wrap or envelop tightly

COCOTTE *n* pl. -S a prostitute

COCOYAM *n* pl. -S a tropical tuber

COCREATE *v* -ATED, -ATING, -ATES to create together

COD *v* CODDED, CODDING, CODS to fool

CODA *n* pl. -S a passage at the end of a musical composition

CODABLE *adj* capable of being coded

CODDED past tense of cod

CODDER *n* pl. -S a cod fisherman

CODDING present participle of cod

CODDLE *v* -DLED, -DLING, -DLES to pamper

CODDLER *n* pl. -S one that coddles

CODE *v* CODED, CODING, CODES to convert into symbols

CODEBOOK *n* pl. -S a book listing words and their coded equivalents

CODEBTOR *n* pl. -S one that shares a debt

CODEC *n* pl. -S an integrated circuit

CODED past tense of code

CODEIA *n* pl. -S codeine

CODEIN *n* pl. -S codeine

CODEINA *n* pl. -S codeine

CODEINE *n* pl. -S a narcotic alkaloid

CODELESS *adj* being without a set of laws

CODEN *n* pl. -S a coding classification

CODER *n* pl. -S one that codes

CODERIVE *v* -RIVED, -RIVING, -RIVES to derive jointly

CODESIGN *v* -ED, -ING, -S to design jointly

CODEX *n* pl. -DICES an ancient manuscript

CODFISH *n* pl. -ES the cod (a marine food fish)

CODGER *n* pl. -S an old man

CODICES pl. of codex

CODICIL *n* pl. -S a supplement to a will

CODIFIER *n* pl. -S one that codifies

CODIFY *v* -FIED, -FYING, -FIES to arrange or systematize

CODING present participle of code

CODIRECT *v* -ED, -ING, -S to direct jointly

CODLIN *n* pl. -S codling

CODLING *n* pl. -S an unripe apple

CODON *n* pl. -S a triplet of nucleotides (basic components of DNA)

CODPIECE *n* pl. -S a cover for the crotch in men's breeches

CODRIVE *v* -DROVE, -DRIVEN, -DRIVING, -DRIVES to work as a codriver

CODRIVER *n* pl. -S one who takes turns driving a vehicle

COED *n* pl. -S a female student

COEDIT *v* -ED, -ING, -S to edit with another person

COEDITOR *n* pl. -S one that coedits

COEFFECT *n* pl. -S an accompanying effect

COELIAC *adj* celiac

COELOM *n* pl. -LOMS or -LOMATA a body cavity in some animals **COELOMIC** *adj*

COELOME *n* pl. -S coelom

COEMBODY *v* -BODIED, -BODYING, -BODIES to embody jointly

COEMPLOY *v* -ED, -ING, -S to employ together

COEMPT *v* -ED, -ING, -S to buy up the entire supply of a product

COENACT *v* -ED, -ING, -S to enact jointly or at the same time

COENAMOR *v* -ED, -ING, -S to inflame with mutual love

COENDURE *v* -DURED, -DURING, -DURES to endure together

COENURE *n* pl. -S coenurus

COENURUS *n* pl. -RI a tapeworm larva

COENZYME *n* pl. -S a substance necessary for the functioning of certain enzymes

COEQUAL *n* pl. -S one who is equal with another

COEQUATE *v* -QUATED, -QUATING, -QUATES to equate with something else

COERCE *v* -ERCED, -ERCING, -ERCES to compel by force or threat

COERCER *n* pl. -S one that coerces

COERCION *n* pl. -S the act of coercing

COERCIVE *adj* serving to coerce

COERECT *v* -ED, -ING, -S to erect together

COESITE *n* pl. -S a type of silica

COEVAL *n* pl. -S one of the same era or period as another

COEVALLY *adv* contemporarily

COEVOLVE *v* -VOLVED, -VOLVING, -VOLVES to evolve together

COEXERT *v* -ED, -ING, -S to exert jointly

COEXIST *v* -ED, -ING, -S to exist together

COEXTEND *v* -ED, -ING, -S to extend through the same space or time as another

COFACTOR *n* pl. -S a coenzyme

COFF *v* COFT, COFFING, COFFS to buy

COFFEE *n* pl. -S an aromatic, mildly stimulating beverage

COFFER *v* -ED, -ING, -S to put in a strongbox

COFFIN *v* -ED, -ING, -S to put in a coffin (a burial case)

COFFLE *v* -FLED, -FLING, -FLES to chain slaves together

COFFRET *n* pl. -S a small strongbox

COFOUND *v* -ED, -ING, -S to found jointly

COFT past tense of coff

COG *v* COGGED, COGGING, COGS to cheat at dice

COGENCY *n* pl. -CIES the state of being cogent

COGENT *adj* convincing **COGENTLY** *adv*

COGGED past tense of cog

COGGING present participle of cog

COGITATE *v* -TATED, -TATING, -TATES to ponder

COGITO *n* pl. -TOS a philosophical principle

COGNAC *n* pl. -S a brandy

COGNATE *n* pl. -S one that is related to another

COGNISE *v* -NISED, -NISING, -NISES to cognize

COGNIZE *v* -NIZED, -NIZING, -NIZES to become aware of in one's mind

COGNIZER *n* pl. -S one that cognizes

COGNOMEN *n* pl. -MENS or -MINA a family name

COGNOVIT *n* pl. -S a written admission of liability

COGON *n* pl. -S a tall tropical grass

COGWAY *n* pl. -WAYS a railway operating on steep slopes

COGWHEEL *n* pl. -S a toothed wheel

COHABIT *v* -ED, -ING, -S to live together as man and wife while unmarried

COHEAD *v* -ED, -ING, -S to head jointly

COHEIR *n* pl. -S a joint heir

COHERE *v* -HERED, -HERING, -HERES to stick together

COHERENT *adj* sticking together

COHERER *n* pl. -S a device used to detect radio waves

COHERING present participle of cohere

COHESION *n* pl. -S the act or state of cohering **COHESIVE** *adj*

COHO *n* pl. -HOS a small salmon

COHOBATE *v* -BATED, -BATING, -BATES to distill again

COHOG *n* pl. -S a quahog

COHOLDER *n* pl. -S an athlete who holds a record with another

COHORT *n* pl. -S a companion or associate

COHOSH *n* pl. -ES a medicinal plant

COHOST *v* -ED, -ING, -S to host jointly

COHUNE *n* pl. -S a palm tree

COIF *v* -ED, -ING -S to style the hair

COIFFE *v* COIFFED, COIFFING, COIFFES to coif

COIFFEUR *n* pl. -S a male hairdresser

COIFFURE *v* -FURED, -FURING, -FURES to coif

COIGN *v* -ED, -ING, -S to quoin

COIGNE *v* COIGNED, COIGNING, COIGNES to quoin

COIL *v* -ED, -ING, -S to wind in even rings

COILER *n* pl. -S one that coils

COIN *v* -ED, -ING, -S to make coins (metal currency) **COINABLE** *adj*

COINAGE *n* pl. -S the act of making coins

COINCIDE *v* -CIDED, -CIDING, -CIDES to be in the same place

COINER *n* pl. -S one that coins

COINFER *v* -FERRED, -FERRING, -FERS to infer jointly

COINHERE *v* -HERED, -HERING, -HERES to inhere jointly

COINMATE *n* pl. -S a fellow inmate

COINSURE *v* -SURED, -SURING, -SURES to insure with another

COINTER *v* -TERRED, -TERRING, -TERS to bury together

COINVENT *v* -ED, -ING, -S to invent together

COIR *n* pl. -S a fiber obtained from coconut husks

COISTREL *n* pl. -S a knave

COISTRIL *n* pl. -S coistrel

COITION *n* pl. -S coitus

COITUS *n* pl. -ES sexual intercourse **COITAL** *adj* **COITALLY** *adv*

COJOIN *v* -ED, -ING, -S to join together

COKE *v* COKED, COKING, COKES to change into a carbon fuel

COKEHEAD *n* pl. -S a cocaine addict

COL *n* pl. -S a depression between two mountains

COLA *n* pl. -S a carbonated beverage

COLANDER *n* pl. -S a kitchen utensil for draining off liquids

COLD *adj* COLDER, COLDEST having little or no warmth

COLD *n* pl. -S the relative lack of heat; a chill

COLDCOCK *v* -ED, -ING, -S to knock unconscious

COLDISH *adj* somewhat cold

COLDLY *adv* in a cold manner

COLDNESS *n* pl. -ES the state of being cold

COLE *n* pl. -S a plant of the cabbage family

COLEAD *v* -LED, -LEADING, -LEADS to lead jointly

COLEADER *n* pl. -S one that coleads

COLESEED *n* pl. -S colza

COLESLAW *n* pl. -S a salad made of shredded raw cabbage

COLESSEE *n* pl. -S a joint lessee

COLESSOR *n* pl. -S a joint lessor

COLEUS *n* pl. -ES a tropical plant

COLEWORT *n* pl. -S cole

COLIC *n* pl. -S acute abdominal pain

COLICIN *n* pl. -S an antibacterial substance

COLICINE *n* pl. -S colicin

COLICKY *adj* pertaining to or associated with colic

COLIES pl. of coly

COLIFORM *n* pl. -S a bacillus of the colon

COLIN *n* pl. -S the bobwhite

COLINEAR *adj* lying in the same straight line

COLISEUM *n* pl. -S a large structure for public entertainment

COLISTIN *n* pl. -S an antibiotic

COLITIS *n* pl. -TISES inflammation of the colon **COLITIC** *adj*

COLLAGE *v* -LAGED, -LAGING, -LAGES to arrange materials in a collage (a kind of artistic composition)

COLLAGEN *n* pl. -S a protein

COLLAPSE *v* -LAPSED, -LAPSING, -LAPSES to crumble suddenly

COLLAR *v* -ED, -ING, -S to provide with a collar (something worn around the neck)

COLLARD *n* pl. -S a variety of kale

COLLARET *n* pl. -S a small collar

COLLATE *v* -LATED, -LATING, -LATES to compare critically

COLLATOR *n* pl. -S one that collates

COLLECT *v* -ED, -ING, -S to bring together in a group

COLLEEN *n* pl. -S an Irish girl

COLLEGE *n* pl. -S a school of higher learning

COLLEGER *n* pl. -S a student supported by funds from his college

COLLEGIA   *n/pl* soviet executive councils

COLLET   *v* -ED, -ING, -S to set a gem in a rim or ring

COLLIDE   *v* -LIDED, -LIDING, -LIDES to come together with violent impact

COLLIDER   *n* pl. -S a type of particle accelerator

COLLIE   *n* pl. -S a large dog

COLLIED   past tense of colly

COLLIER   *n* pl. -S a coal miner

COLLIERY   *n* pl. -LIERIES a coal mine

COLLIES   present 3d person sing. of colly

COLLINS   *n* pl. -ES an alcoholic beverage

COLLOGUE   *v* -LOGUED, -LOGUING, -LOGUES to conspire

COLLOID   *n* pl. -S a type of chemical suspension

COLLOP   *n* pl. -S a small portion of meat

COLLOQUY   *n* pl. -QUIES a conversation

COLLUDE   *v* -LUDED, -LUDING, -LUDES to conspire

COLLUDER   *n* pl. -S one that colludes

COLLUVIA   *n/pl* rock debris

COLLY   *v* -LIED, -LYING, -LIES to blacken with coal dust

COLLYRIA   *n/pl* medicinal lotions

COLOBOMA   *n* pl. -MATA a lesion of the eye

COLOBUS   *n* pl. -BI a long-tailed monkey

COLOCATE   *v* -CATED, -CATING, -CATES to place two or more housing units in close proximity

COLOG   *n* pl. -S the logarithm of the reciprocal of a number

COLOGNE   *n* pl. -S a scented liquid **COLOGNED** *adj*

COLON   *n* pl. -S a section of the large intestine

COLON   *n* pl. -ES a monetary unit of Costa Rica

COLONE   *n* pl. -S colon

COLONEL   *n* pl. -S a military officer

COLONI   pl. of colonus

COLONIAL   *n* pl. -S a citizen of a colony

COLONIC   *n* pl. -S irrigation of the colon

COLONIES   pl. of colony

COLONISE   *v* -NISED, -NISING, -NISES to colonize

COLONIST   *n* pl. -S one who settles a colony

COLONIZE   *v* -NIZED, -NIZING, -NIZES to establish a colony

COLONUS   *n* pl. -NI a freeborn serf

COLONY   *n* pl. -NIES a group of emigrants living in a new land

COLOPHON   *n* pl. -S an inscription placed at the end of a book

COLOR   *v* -ED, -ING, -S to give color (a visual attribute of objects) to

COLORADO   *adj* of medium strength and color — used of cigars

COLORANT   *n* pl. -S a pigment or dye

COLORED   *adj* having color

COLORER   *n* pl. -S one that colors

COLORFUL   *adj* full of color

COLORING   *n* pl. -S appearance in regard to color

COLORISM   *n* pl. -S coloring

COLORIST   *n* pl. -S a person skilled in the use of color

COLORIZE   *v* -IZED, -IZING, -IZES to give color to a black-and-white film

COLORMAN   *n* pl. -MEN a sportscaster who provides commentary during a game

COLOSSAL   *adj* gigantic

COLOSSUS   *n* pl. -LOSSI or -LOSSUSES a gigantic statue

COLOTOMY   *n* pl. -MIES a surgical incision of the colon

COLOUR   *v* -ED, -ING, -S to color

COLOURER   *n* pl. -S colorer

COLPITIS   *n* pl. -TISES a vaginal inflammation

COLT   *n* pl. -S a young male horse **COLTISH** *adj*

COLTER   *n* pl. -S a blade on a plow

COLUBRID   *n* pl. -S any of a large family of snakes

COLUGO   *n* pl. -GOS a small mammal

COLUMBIC   *adj* pertaining to niobium

COLUMEL   *n* pl. -S a small column-like anatomical part

COLUMN   *n* pl. -S a vertical cylindrical support **COLUMNAL, COLUMNAR, COLUMNED** *adj*

COLURE   *n* pl. -S an astronomical circle

COLY   *n* pl. COLIES an African bird

COLZA   *n* pl. -S a plant of the cabbage family

COMA   *n* pl. -S a condition of prolonged unconsciousness

COMA   *n* pl. -MAE a tuft of silky hairs

COMAKE   *v* -MADE, -MAKING, -MAKES to serve as comaker for another's loan

COMAKER   *n* pl. -S one who assumes financial responsibility for another's default

COMAL *adj* comose

COMANAGE *v* -AGED, -AGING, -AGES to manage jointly

COMATE *n* pl. -S a companion

COMATIC *adj* having blurred vision as a result of coma

COMATIK *n* pl. -S komatik

COMATOSE *adj* affected with coma

COMATULA *n* pl. -LAE a marine animal

COMB *v* -ED, -ING, -S to arrange or clean with a comb (a toothed instrument)

COMBAT *v* -BATED, -BATING, -BATS or -BATTED, -BATTING, -BATS to fight against

COMBATER *n* pl. -S one that combats

COMBE *n* pl. -S a narrow valley

COMBER *n* pl. -S one that combs

COMBINE *v* -BINED, -BINING, -BINES to blend

COMBINER *n* pl. -S one that combines

COMBINGS *n/pl* hair removed by a comb

COMBINING present participle of combine

COMBLIKE *adj* resembling a comb

COMBO *n* pl. -BOS a small jazz band

COMBUST *v* -ED, -ING, -S to burn

COME *v* CAME, COMING, COMES or COMETH to move toward something or someone

COMEBACK *n* pl. -S a return to former prosperity

COMEDIAN *n* pl. -S a humorous entertainer

COMEDIC *adj* pertaining to comedy

COMEDIES pl. of comedy

COMEDO *n* pl. -DOS or -DONES a skin blemish

COMEDOWN *n* pl. -S a drop in status

COMEDY *n* pl. -DIES a humorous play, movie, or other work

COMELY *adj* -LIER, -LIEST pleasing to look at **COMELILY** *adv*

COMEMBER *n* pl. -S one that shares membership

COMER *n* pl. -S one showing great promise

COMET *n* pl. -S a celestial body **COMETARY** *adj*

COMETH a present 3d person sing. of come

COMETHER *n* pl. -S an affair or matter

COMETIC *adj* pertaining to a comet

COMFIER comparative of comfy

COMFIEST superlative of comfy

COMFIT *n* pl. -S a candy

COMFORT *v* -ED, -ING, -S to soothe in time of grief

COMFREY *n* pl. -FREYS a coarse herb

COMFY *adj* -FIER, -FIEST comfortable

COMIC *n* pl. -S a comedian

COMICAL *adj* funny

COMING *n* pl. -S arrival

COMINGLE *v* -GLED, -GLING, -GLES to blend thoroughly

COMITIA *n* pl. COMITIA a public assembly in ancient Rome **COMITIAL** *adj*

COMITY *n* pl. -TIES civility

COMIX *n/pl* comic books or strips

COMMA *n* pl. -MAS or -MATA a fragment of a few words or feet in ancient prosody

COMMAND *v* -ED, -ING, -S to direct with authority

COMMANDO *n* pl. -DOES or -DOS a military unit

COMMATA a pl. of comma

COMMENCE *v* -MENCED, -MENCING, -MENCES to begin

COMMEND *v* -ED, -ING, -S to praise

COMMENT *v* -ED, -ING, -S to remark

COMMERCE *v* -MERCED, -MERCING, -MERCES to commune

COMMIE *n* pl. -S a Communist

COMMIES pl. of commy

COMMIT *v* -MITTED, -MITTING, -MITS to do, perform, or perpetrate

COMMIX *v* -MIXED or -MIXT, -MIXING, -MIXES to mix together

COMMODE *n* pl. -S a cabinet

COMMON *adj* -MONER, -MONEST ordinary

COMMON *n* pl. -S a tract of publicly used land

COMMONER *n* pl. -S one of the common people

COMMONLY *adv* in a common manner

COMMOVE *v* -MOVED, -MOVING, -MOVES to move violently

COMMUNAL *adj* belonging to a community; public

COMMUNE *v* -MUNED, -MUNING, -MUNES to converse intimately

COMMUTE *v* -MUTED, -MUTING, -MUTES to exchange

COMMUTER *n* pl. -S one that commutes

COMMY *n* pl. -MIES commie

COMOSE *adj* bearing a tuft of silky hairs

COMOUS *adj* comose

COMP *v* -ED, -ING, -S to play a jazz accompaniment

COMPACT *adj* -PACTER, -PACTEST closely and firmly united

COMPACT *v* -ED, -ING, -S to pack closely together

COMPADRE *n* pl. -S a close friend

COMPANY *v* -NIED, -NYING, -NIES to associate with

COMPARE *v* -PARED, -PARING, -PARES to represent as similar

COMPARER *n* pl. -S one that compares

COMPART *v* -ED, -ING, -S to divide into parts

COMPASS *v* -ED, -ING, -ES to go around

COMPEER *v* -ED, -ING, -S to equal or match

COMPEL *v* -PELLED, -PELLING, -PELS to urge forcefully

COMPEND *n* pl. -S a brief summary

COMPERE *v* -PERED, -PERING, -PERES to act as master of ceremonies

COMPETE *v* -PETED, -PETING, -PETES to vie

COMPILE *v* -PILED, -PILING, -PILES to collect into a volume

COMPILER *n* pl. -S one that compiles

COMPLAIN *v* -ED, -ING, -S to express discontent

COMPLEAT *adj* highly skilled

COMPLECT *v* -ED, -ING, -S to weave together

COMPLETE *adj* -PLETER, -PLETEST having all necessary parts

COMPLETE *v* -PLETED, -PLETING, -PLETES to bring to an end

COMPLEX *adj* -PLEXER, -PLEXEST complicated

COMPLEX *v* -ED, -ING, -ES to make complex

COMPLICE *n* pl. -S an associate

COMPLIED past tense of comply

COMPLIER *n* pl. -S one that complies

COMPLIES present 3d person sing. of comply

COMPLIN *n* pl. -S compline

COMPLINE *n* pl. -S the last liturgical prayer of the day

COMPLOT *v* -PLOTTED, -PLOTTING, -PLOTS to conspire

COMPLY *v* -PLIED, -PLYING, -PLIES to obey

COMPO *n* pl. -POS a mixed substance

COMPONE *adj* compony

COMPONY *adj* composed of squares of alternating colors

COMPORT *v* -ED, -ING -S to conduct oneself in a certain way

COMPOSE *v* -POSED, -POSING, -POSES to form the substance of

COMPOSER *n* pl. -S one that writes music

COMPOST *v* -ED, -ING, -S to fertilize

COMPOTE *n* pl. -S fruit stewed in syrup

COMPOUND *v* -ED, -ING, -S to add to

COMPRESS *v* -ED, -ING, -ES to compact

COMPRISE *v* -PRISED, -PRISING, -PRISES to include or contain

COMPRIZE *v* -PRIZED, -PRIZING, -PRIZES to comprise

COMPT *v* -ED, -ING, -S to count

COMPUTE *v* -PUTED, -PUTING, -PUTES to calculate

COMPUTER *n* pl. -S a machine that computes automatically

COMRADE *n* pl. -S a close friend

COMTE *n* pl. -S a French nobleman

CON *v* CONNED, CONNING, CONS to study carefully

CONATION *n* pl. -S the inclination to act purposefully **CONATIVE** *adj*

CONATUS *n* pl. CONATUS an effort

CONCAVE *v* -CAVED, -CAVING, -CAVES to make concave (curving inward)

CONCEAL *v* -ED, -ING, -S to keep from sight or discovery

CONCEDE *v* -CEDED, -CEDING, -CEDES to acknowledge as true

CONCEDER *n* pl. -S one that concedes

CONCEIT *v* -ED, -ING, -S to imagine

CONCEIVE *v* -CEIVED, -CEIVING, -CEIVES to understand

CONCENT *n* pl. -S harmony

CONCEPT *n* pl. -S a general idea

CONCERN *v* -ED, -ING, -S to be of interest to

CONCERT *v* -ED, -ING, -S to plan

CONCERTO *n* pl. -TOS or -TI a musical composition

CONCH *n* pl. -S or -ES a marine mollusk

CONCHA *n* pl. -CHAE an anatomical shell-like structure **CONCHAL** *adj*

CONCHIE *n* pl. -S conchy

CONCHOID *n* pl. -S a type of geometric curve

CONCHY *n* pl. -CHIES a conscientious objector

CONCISE *adj* -CISER, -CISEST succinct

CONCLAVE *n* pl. -S a secret meeting
CONCLUDE *v* -CLUDED, -CLUDING, -CLUDES to finish
CONCOCT *v* -ED, -ING, -S to prepare by combining ingredients
CONCORD *n* pl. -S a state of agreement
CONCRETE *v* -CRETED, -CRETING, -CRETES to solidify
CONCUR *v* -CURRED, -CURRING, -CURS to agree
CONCUSS *v* -ED, -ING, -ES to injure the brain by a violent blow
CONDEMN *v* -ED, -ING, -S to criticize severely
CONDENSE *v* -DENSED, -DENSING, -DENSES to compress
CONDIGN *adj* deserved; appropriate
CONDO *n* pl. -DOS or -DOES an individually owned unit in a multiunit structure
CONDOLE *v* -DOLED, -DOLING, -DOLES to mourn
CONDOLER *n* pl. -S one that condoles
CONDOM *n* pl. -S a prophylactic
CONDONE *v* -DONED, -DONING, -DONES to forgive or overlook
CONDONER *n* pl. -S one that condones
CONDOR *n* pl. -S or -ES a coin of Chile
CONDUCE *v* -DUCED, -DUCING, -DUCES to contribute to a result
CONDUCER *n* pl. -S one that conduces
CONDUCT *v* -ED, -ING, -S to lead or guide
CONDUIT *n* pl. -S a channel or pipe for conveying fluids
CONDYLE *n* pl. -S a protuberance on a bone CONDYLAR *adj*
CONE *v* CONED, CONING, CONES to shape like a cone (a geometric solid)
CONELRAD *n* pl. -S a system of defense in the event of air attack
CONENOSE *n* pl. -S a bloodsucking insect
CONEPATE *n* pl. -S a skunk
CONEPATL *n* pl. -S conepate
CONEY *n* pl. -NEYS cony
CONFAB *v* -FABBED, -FABBING, -FABS to chat
CONFECT *v* -ED, -ING, -S to prepare from various ingredients
CONFER *v* -FERRED, -FERRING, -FERS to bestow
CONFEREE *n* pl. -S one upon whom something is conferred

CONFERVA *n* pl. -VAE or -VAS a freshwater alga
CONFESS *v* -ED, -ING, -ES to acknowledge or disclose
CONFETTO *n* pl. -TI a bonbon
CONFIDE *v* -FIDED, -FIDING, -FIDES to reveal in trust or confidence
CONFIDER *n* pl. -S one that confides
CONFINE *v* -FINED, -FINING, -FINES to shut within an enclosure
CONFINER *n* pl. -S one that confines
CONFIRM *v* -ED, -ING, -S to assure the validity of
CONFIT *n* pl. -S meat cooked and preserved in its own fat
CONFLATE *v* -FLATED, -FLATING, -FLATES to blend
CONFLICT *v* -ED, -ING, -S to come into opposition
CONFLUX *n* pl. -ES a flowing together of streams
CONFOCAL *adj* having the same focus or foci
CONFORM *v* -ED, -ING, -S to become the same or similar
CONFOUND *v* -ED, -ING, -S to confuse
CONFRERE *n* pl. -S a colleague
CONFRONT *v* -ED, -ING, -S to face defiantly
CONFUSE *v* -FUSED, -FUSING, -FUSES to mix up mentally
CONFUTE *v* -FUTED, -FUTING, -FUTES to disprove
CONFUTER *n* pl. -S one that confutes
CONGA *v* -ED, -ING, -S to perform a conga (Latin American dance)
CONGE *n* pl. -S permission to depart
CONGEAL *v* -ED, -ING, -S to change from a fluid to a solid
CONGEE *v* -GEED, -GEEING, -GEES to bow politely
CONGENER *n* pl. -S one of the same kind or class
CONGER *n* pl. -S a marine eel
CONGEST *v* -ED, -ING, -S to fill to excess
CONGIUS *n* pl. -GII an ancient unit of measure
CONGLOBE *v* -GLOBED, -GLOBING, -GLOBES to become a globule
CONGO *n* pl. -GOS congou
CONGO *n* pl. -GOES an eellike amphibian
CONGOU *n* pl. -S a Chinese tea
CONGRATS *n/pl* congratulations

CONGRESS   v -ED, -ING, -ES to assemble together

CONI   pl. of conus

CONIC   n pl. -S a geometric curve

CONICAL   adj shaped like a cone

CONICITY   n pl. -TIES the state of being conical

CONIDIUM   n pl. -NIDIA a fungus spore CONIDIAL, CONIDIAN adj

CONIES   pl. of cony

CONIFER   n pl. -S an evergreen tree

CONIINE   n pl. -S a poisonous alkaloid

CONIN   n pl. -S coniine

CONINE   n pl. -S coniine

CONING   present participle of cone

CONIOSIS   n pl. -OSES an infection caused by the inhalation of dust

CONIUM   n pl. -S a poisonous herb

CONJOIN   v -ED, -ING, -S to join together CONJOINT adj

CONJUGAL   adj pertaining to marriage

CONJUNCT   n pl. -S one that is joined with another

CONJURE   v -JURED, -JURING, -JURES to summon a spirit

CONJURER   n pl. -S a sorcerer

CONJUROR   n pl. -S conjurer

CONK   v -ED, -ING, -S to hit on the head

CONKER   n pl. -S a chestnut used in a British game

CONKY   adj full of a tree fungus

CONN   v -ED, -ING, -S to direct the steering of a ship

CONNATE   adj innate

CONNECT   v -ED, -ING, -S to join together

CONNED   past tense of con

CONNER   n pl. -S one that cons

CONNING   present participle of con

CONNIVE   v -NIVED, -NIVING, -NIVES to feign ignorance of wrongdoing

CONNIVER   n pl. -S one that connives

CONNOTE   v -NOTED, -NOTING, -NOTES to imply another meaning besides the literal one

CONODONT   n pl. -S a fossil

CONOID   n pl. -S a geometric solid CONOIDAL adj

CONQUER   v -ED, -ING, -S to overcome by force

CONQUEST   n pl. -S the act of conquering

CONQUIAN   n pl. -S a card game

CONSENT   v -ED, -ING, -S to permit or approve

CONSERVE   v -SERVED, -SERVING, -SERVES to protect from loss or depletion

CONSIDER   v -ED, -ING, -S to think about

CONSIGN   v -ED, -ING, -S to give over to another's care

CONSIST   v -ED, -ING, -S to be made up or composed

CONSOL   n pl. -S a government bond

CONSOLE   v -SOLED, -SOLING, -SOLES to comfort

CONSOLER   n pl. -S one that consoles

CONSOMME   n pl. -S a clear soup

CONSORT   v -ED, -ING, -S to keep company

CONSPIRE   v -SPIRED, -SPIRING, -SPIRES to plan secretly with another

CONSTANT   n pl. -S something that does not vary

CONSTRUE   v -STRUED, -STRUING, -STRUES to interpret

CONSUL   n pl. -S an official serving abroad CONSULAR adj

CONSULT   v -ED, -ING, -S to ask an opinion of

CONSUME   v -SUMED, -SUMING, -SUMES to use up

CONSUMER   n pl. -S one that consumes

CONTACT   v -ED, -ING, -S to communicate with

CONTAGIA   n/pl causative agents of infectious diseases

CONTAIN   v -ED, -ING, -S to hold within

CONTE   n pl. -S a short story

CONTEMN   v -ED, -ING, -S to scorn

CONTEMPT   n pl. -S the feeling of one who views something as mean, vile, or worthless

CONTEND   v -ED, -ING, -S to vie

CONTENT   v -ED, -ING, -S to satisfy

CONTEST   v -ED, -ING, -S to compete for

CONTEXT   n pl. -S the part of a discourse in which a particular word or phrase appears

CONTINUA   n/pl mathematical sets

CONTINUE   v -UED, -UING, -UES to go on with

CONTINUO   n pl. -UOS a type of instrumental part

CONTO   n pl. -TOS a Portuguese money of account

CONTORT   v -ED, -ING, -S to twist out of shape

CONTOUR   v -ED, -ING, -S to make the outline of

CONTRA	*n* pl. -S a Nicaraguan revolutionary
CONTRACT	*v* -ED, -ING, -S to decrease in size or volume
CONTRAIL	*n* pl. -S a visible trail of water vapor from an aircraft
CONTRARY	*n* pl. -TRARIES an opposite
CONTRAST	*v* -ED, -ING, -S to place in opposition to set off differences
CONTRITE	*adj* deeply sorry for one's sins
CONTRIVE	*v* -TRIVED, -TRIVING, -TRIVES to devise
CONTROL	*v* -TROLLED, -TROLLING, -TROLS to exercise authority over
CONTUSE	*v* -TUSED, -TUSING, -TUSES to bruise
CONUS	*n* pl. CONI an anatomical part in mammals
CONVECT	*v* -ED, -ING, -S to transfer heat by a process of circulation
CONVENE	*v* -VENED, -VENING, -VENES to assemble
CONVENER	*n* pl. -S one that convenes
CONVENOR	*n* pl. -S convener
CONVENT	*v* -ED, -ING, -S to convene
CONVERGE	*v* -VERGED, -VERGING, -VERGES to come together
CONVERSE	*v* -VERSED, -VERSING, -VERSES to speak together
CONVERT	*v* -ED, -ING, -S to change into another form
CONVEX	*n* pl. -ES a surface or body that is convex (curving outward)
CONVEXLY	*adv* in a convex manner
CONVEY	*v* -ED, -ING, -S to transport
CONVEYER	*n* pl. -S one that conveys
CONVEYOR	*n* pl. -S conveyer
CONVICT	*v* -ED, -ING, -S to prove guilty
CONVINCE	*v* -VINCED, -VINCING, -VINCES to cause to believe something
CONVOKE	*v* -VOKED, -VOKING, -VOKES to cause to assemble
CONVOKER	*n* pl. -S one that convokes
CONVOLVE	*v* -VOLVED, -VOLVING, -VOLVES to roll together
CONVOY	*v* -ED, -ING, -S to escort
CONVULSE	*v* -VULSED, -VULSING, -VULSES to shake violently
CONY	*n* pl. CONIES a rabbit
COO	*v* COOED, COOING, COOS to make the sound of a dove
COOCH	*n* pl. -ES a sinuous dance
COOCOO	*adj* crazy
COOEE	*v* COOEED, COOEEING, COOEES to cry out shrilly
COOER	*n* pl. -S one that coos
COOEY	*v* -EYED, -EYING, -EYS to cooee
COOF	*n* pl. -S a dolt
COOINGLY	*adv* in the manner of cooing doves; affectionately
COOK	*v* -ED, -ING, -S to prepare food by heating **COOKABLE** *adj*
COOKBOOK	*n* pl. -S a book of recipes
COOKER	*n* pl. -S one that cooks
COOKERY	*n* pl. -ERIES the art of cooking
COOKEY	*n* pl. -EYS cookie
COOKIE	*n* pl. -S a small, flat cake
COOKING	*n* pl. -S the act of one that cooks
COOKLESS	*adj* having no person that cooks
COOKOUT	*n* pl. -S a meal eaten and prepared outdoors
COOKSHOP	*n* pl. -S a shop that sells cooked food
COOKTOP	*n* pl. -S a counter-top cooking apparatus
COOKWARE	*n* pl. -S utensils used in cooking
COOKY	*n* pl. COOKIES cookie
COOL	*adj* COOLER, COOLEST moderately cold
COOL	*v* -ED, -ING, -S to make less warm
COOLANT	*n* pl. -S a fluid used to cool engines
COOLDOWN	*n* pl. -S a gradual return of physiological functions to normal levels after strenuous exercise
COOLER	*n* pl. -S something that cools
COOLIE	*n* pl. -S an Oriental laborer
COOLIES	pl. of cooly
COOLISH	*adj* somewhat cool
COOLLY	*adv* in a cool manner
COOLNESS	*n* pl. -ES the state of being cool
COOLTH	*n* pl. -S coolness
COOLY	*n* pl. COOLIES coolie
COOMB	*n* pl. -S combe
COOMBE	*n* pl. -S combe
COON	*n* pl. -S a raccoon
COONCAN	*n* pl. -S conquian
COONSKIN	*n* pl. -S the pelt of a raccoon
COONTIE	*n* pl. -S a tropical plant
COOP	*v* -ED, -ING, -S to confine

COOPER   v -ED, -ING, -S to make or mend barrels

COOPERY   n pl. -ERIES the trade of coopering

COOPT   v -ED, -ING, -S to elect or appoint

COOPTION   n pl. -S the act of coopting

COOT   n pl. -S an aquatic bird

COOTER   n pl. -S a turtle

COOTIE   n pl. -S a body louse

COP   v COPPED, COPPING, COPS to steal

COPAIBA   n pl. -S a resin

COPAL   n pl. -S a resin

COPALM   n pl. -S a hardwood tree

COPARENT   n pl. -S a fellow parent

COPASTOR   n pl. -S one that shares the duties of a pastor

COPATRON   n pl. -S a fellow patron

COPE   v COPED, COPING, COPES to contend or strive

COPECK   n pl. -S kopeck

COPEMATE   n pl. -S an antagonist

COPEN   n pl. -S a blue color

COPEPOD   n pl. -S a minute crustacean

COPER   n pl. -S a horse dealer

COPIED   past tense of copy

COPIER   n pl. -S one that copies

COPIES   present 3d person sing. of copy

COPIHUE   n -pl. -S a climbing vine

COPILOT   n pl. -S an assistant pilot

COPING   n pl. -S the top part of a wall

COPIOUS   adj abundant

COPLANAR   adj lying in the same plane

COPLOT   v -PLOTTED, -PLOTTING, -PLOTS to plot together

COPPED   past tense of cop

COPPER   v -ED, -ING, -S to cover with copper (a metallic element)

COPPERAH   n pl. -S copra

COPPERAS   n pl. -ES a compound used in making inks

COPPERY   adj resembling copper

COPPICE   v -PICED, -PICING, -PICES to cause to grow in the form of a coppice (a thicket)

COPPING   present participle of cop

COPPRA   n pl. -S copra

COPRA   n pl. -S dried coconut meat

COPRAH   n pl. -S copra

COPREMIA   n pl. -S a form of blood poisoning COPREMIC adj

COPRINCE   n pl. -S one of two princes ruling jointly

COPSE   n pl. -S a coppice

COPTER   n pl. -S a helicopter

COPULA   n pl. -LAS or -LAE something that links COPULAR adj

COPULATE   v -LATED, -LATING, -LATES to engage in coitus

COPURIFY   v -FIED, -FYING, -FIES to become purified with another substance

COPY   v COPIED, COPYING, COPIES to imitate

COPYBOOK   n pl. -S a book used in teaching penmanship

COPYBOY   n pl. -BOYS an office boy

COPYCAT   v -CATTED, -CATTING, -CATS to imitate

COPYDESK   n pl. -S an editor's desk in a newspaper office

COPYEDIT   v -ED, -ING, -S to prepare copy for the printer

COPYHOLD   n pl. -S a type of ownership of land

COPYIST   n pl. -S an imitator

COPYREAD   v -READ, -READING, -READS to copyedit

COQUET   v -QUETTED, -QUETTING, -QUETS to flirt

COQUETRY   n pl. -TRIES flirtatious behavior

COQUETTE   v -QUETTED, -QUETTING, -QUETTES to coquet

COQUILLE   n pl. -S a cooking utensil

COQUINA   n pl. -S a small marine clam

COQUITO   n pl. -TOS a palm tree

COR   interj — used to express surprise, admiration, or irritation

CORACLE   n pl. -S a small boat

CORACOID   n pl. -S a bone of the shoulder girdle

CORAL   n pl. -S a mass of marine animal skeletons

CORANTO   n pl. -TOS or -TOES courante

CORBAN   n pl. -S an offering to God

CORBEIL   n pl. -S a sculptured fruit basket

CORBEL   v -BELED, -BELING, -BELS or -BELLED, -BELLING, -BELS to provide a wall with a bracket

CORBIE   n pl. -S a raven or crow

CORBINA   n pl. -S a food and game fish

CORBY   n pl. CORBIES corbie

CORD   v -ED, -ING, -S to fasten with a cord (a thin rope)

CORDAGE   n pl. -S the amount of wood in an area

CORDATE   adj heart-shaped

CORDELLE v -DELLED, -DELLING, -DELLES to tow a boat with a cordelle (a towrope)

CORDER n pl. -S one that cords

CORDIAL n pl. -S a liqueur

CORDING n pl. -S the ribbed surface of cloth

CORDITE n pl. -S an explosive powder

CORDLESS adj having no cord

CORDLIKE adj resembling a cord

CORDOBA n pl. -S a monetary unit of Nicaragua

CORDON v -ED, -ING, -S to form a barrier around

CORDOVAN n pl. -S a fine leather

CORDUROY v -ED, -ING, -S to build a type of road

CORDWAIN n pl. -S cordovan

CORDWOOD n pl. -S wood used for fuel

CORE v CORED, CORING, CORES to remove the core (the central part) of

COREDEEM v -ED, -ING, -S to redeem jointly

COREIGN n pl. -S a joint reign

CORELATE v -LATED, -LATING, -LATES to place into mutual or reciprocal relation

CORELESS adj having no core

COREMIUM n pl. -MIA an organ of certain fungi

CORER n pl. -S a utensil for coring apples

CORF n pl. CORVES a wagon used in a mine

CORGI n pl. -S a short-legged dog

CORING present participle of core

CORIUM n pl. -RIA a skin layer

CORK v -ED, -ING, -S to stop up

CORKAGE n pl. -S a charge for wine in a restaurant

CORKER n pl. -S one that corks

CORKIER comparative of corky

CORKIEST superlative of corky

CORKLIKE adj resembling cork (a porous tree bark)

CORKWOOD n pl. -S a small tree

CORKY adj CORKIER, CORKIEST corklike

CORM n pl. -S a stem of certain plants CORMOID, CORMOUS, CORMLIKE adj

CORMEL n pl. -S a small corm

CORN v -ED, -ING, -S to preserve with salt

CORNBALL n pl. -S a hick

CORNCAKE n pl. -S a cake made of cornmeal

CORNCOB n pl. -S the woody core of an ear of corn

CORNCRIB n pl. -S a building in which corn is stored

CORNEA n pl. -S a part of the eye **CORNEAL** adj

CORNEL n pl. -S a hardwood tree or shrub

CORNEOUS adj of a hornlike texture

CORNER v -ED, -ING, -S to gain control of

CORNET n pl. -S a trumpetlike instrument

CORNETCY n -CIES a rank in the British cavalry

CORNFED adj fed on corn

CORNHUSK n pl. -S the husk covering an ear of corn

CORNICE v -NICED, -NICING, -NICES to decorate with a molding

CORNICHE n pl. -S a road built along a cliff

CORNICLE n pl. -S a part of an aphid

CORNIER comparative of corny

CORNIEST superlative of corny

CORNILY adv in a corny manner

CORNMEAL n pl. -S meal made from corn

CORNPONE adj having simple, folksy qualities

CORNROW v -ED, -ING, -S to braid hair tightly in rows close to the scalp

CORNU n pl. -NUA a hornlike bone formation **CORNUAL** adj

CORNUS n pl. -ES a cornel

CORNUTE adj horn-shaped

CORNUTED adj cornute

CORNUTO n pl. -TOS the husband of an unfaithful wife

CORNY adj CORNIER, CORNIEST trite

CORODY n pl. -DIES an allowance of food or clothes

COROLLA n pl. -S a protective covering of a flower

CORONA n pl. -NAS or -NAE a luminous circle around a celestial body

CORONACH n pl. -S a dirge

CORONAL n pl. -S a wreath worn on the head

CORONARY n pl. -NARIES an artery supplying blood to the heart

CORONATE v -NATED, -NATING, -NATES to crown

CORONEL   *n* pl. -S coronal
CORONER   *n* pl. -S an officer who investigates questionable deaths
CORONET   *n* pl. -S a small crown
CORONOID   *adj* crown-shaped
COROTATE   *v* -TATED, -TATING, -TATES to rotate together
CORPORA   pl. of corpus
CORPORAL   *n* pl. -S a military rank
CORPS   *n* pl. CORPS a military unit
CORPSE   *n* pl. -S a dead body
CORPSMAN   *n* pl. -MEN an enlisted man trained in first aid
CORPUS   *n* pl. -PORA a human or animal body
CORRADE   *v* -RADED, -RADING, -RADES to erode
CORRAL   *v* -RALLED, -RALLING, -RALS to place livestock in a corral (an enclosure)
CORRECT   *v* -ED, -ING, -S to make free from error
CORRECT   *adj* -RECTER, -RECTEST free from error
CORRIDA   *n* pl. -S a bullfight
CORRIDOR   *n* pl. -S a narrow hallway
CORRIE   *n* pl. -S a cirque
CORRIVAL   *n* pl. -S a rival or opponent
CORRODE   *v* -RODED, -RODING, -RODES to eat away gradually
CORRODY   *n* pl. -DIES corody
CORRUPT   *adj* -RUPTER, -RUPTEST dishonest and venal
CORRUPT   *v* -ED, -ING, -S to subvert the honesty or integrity of
CORSAC   *n* pl. -S an Asian fox
CORSAGE   *n* pl. -S a small bouquet of flowers
CORSAIR   *n* pl. -S a pirate
CORSE   *n* pl. -S a corpse
CORSELET   *n* pl. -S a piece of body armor
CORSET   *v* -ED, -ING, -S to fit with a corset (a supporting undergarment)
CORSETRY   *n* pl. -RIES the work of making corsets
CORSLET   *n* pl. -S corselet
CORTEGE   *n* pl. -S a retinue
CORTEX   *n* pl. -TICES or -TEXES the outer layer of an organ CORTICAL *adj*
CORTIN   *n* pl. -S a hormone
CORTISOL   *n* pl. -S a hormone
CORULER   *n* pl. -S one that rules jointly
CORUNDUM   *n* pl. -S a hard mineral

CORVEE   *n* pl. -S an obligation to perform feudal service
CORVES   pl. of corf
CORVET   *n* pl. -S corvette
CORVETTE   *n* pl. -S a small, swift warship
CORVINA   *n* pl. -S corbina
CORVINE   *adj* pertaining or belonging to the crow family of birds
CORY   *n* pl. CORY a former monetary unit of Guinea
CORYBANT   *n* pl. -BANTS or -BANTES a reveler
CORYMB   *n* pl. -S a flower cluster CORYMBED *adj*
CORYPHEE   *n* pl. -S a ballet dancer
CORYZA   *n* pl. -S a head cold CORYZAL *adj*
COS   *n* pl. -ES a variety of lettuce
COSCRIPT   *v* -ED, -ING, -S to collaborate in preparing a script for
COSEC   *n* pl. -S cosecant
COSECANT   *n* pl. -S a trigonometric function of an angle
COSET   *n* pl. -S a mathematical subset
COSEY   *n* pl. -SEYS a cozy
COSH   *v* -ED, -ING, -ES to bludgeon
COSHER   *v* -ED, -ING, -S to coddle
COSIE   *n* pl. -S a cozy
COSIED   past tense of cosy
COSIER   comparative of cosy
COSIES   present 3d person sing. of cosy
COSIEST   superlative of cosy
COSIGN   *v* -ED, -ING, -S to sign jointly
COSIGNER   *n* pl. -S one that cosigns
COSILY   *adv* in a cosy manner
COSINE   *n* pl. -S a trigonometric function of an angle
COSINESS   *n* pl. -ES coziness
COSMETIC   *n* pl. -S a beauty preparation
COSMIC   *adj* pertaining to the cosmos
COSMICAL   *adj* cosmic
COSMISM   *n* pl. -S a philosophical theory
COSMIST   *n* pl. -S a supporter of cosmism
COSMOS   *n* pl. -ES the universe regarded as an orderly system
COSS   *n* pl. COSS kos
COSSACK   *n* pl. -S a Russian cavalryman
COSSET   *v* -ED, -ING, -S to fondle
COST   *v* COST or COSTED, COSTING, COSTS to estimate a price for production of
COSTA   *n* pl. -TAE a rib COSTAL *adj*

COSTAR	*v* -STARRED, -STARRING, -STARS to star with another actor
COSTARD	*n* pl. -S a large cooking apple
COSTATE	*adj* having a rib or ribs
COSTER	*n* pl. -S a hawker of fruit or vegetables
COSTIVE	*adj* constipated
COSTLESS	*adj* free of charge
COSTLY	*adj* -LIER, -LIEST expensive
COSTMARY	*n* pl. -MARIES an herb used in salads
COSTREL	*n* pl. -S a flask
COSTUME	*v* -TUMED, -TUMING, -TUMES to supply with a costume (a style of dress)
COSTUMER	*n* pl. -S one that costumes
COSTUMEY	*adj* of or pertaining to a costume
COSTUMING	present participle of costume
COSY	*v* COSIED, COSYING, COSIES cozy
COSY	*adj* COSIER, COSIEST cozy
COT	*n* pl. -S a light, narrow bed
COTAN	*n* pl. -S a trigonometric function of an angle
COTE	*v* COTED, COTING, COTES to pass by
COTEAU	*n* pl. -TEAUX the higher ground of a region
COTENANT	*n* pl. -S one who is a tenant with another in the same place
COTERIE	*n* pl. -S a clique
COTHURN	*n* pl. -S a buskin worn by ancient Roman actors
COTHURNI	*n/pl* cothurns
COTIDAL	*adj* indicating coincidence of the tides
COTILLON	*n* pl. -S a ballroom dance
COTING	present participle of cote
COTQUEAN	*n* pl. -S a vulgar woman
COTTA	*n* pl. -TAE or -TAS a short surplice
COTTAGE	*n* pl. -S a small house **COTTAGEY** *adj*
COTTAGER	*n* pl. -S one that lives in a cottage
COTTAR	*n* pl. -S cotter
COTTER	*n* pl. -S a pin or wedge used for fastening parts together **COTTERED** *adj*
COTTIER	*n* pl. -S cotter
COTTON	*v* -ED, -ING, -S to take a liking
COTTONY	*adj* resembling cotton (a soft, fibrous material)
COTYLOID	*adj* cup-shaped
COTYPE	*n* pl. -S a taxonomic type
COUCH	*v* -ED, -ING, -ES to put into words
COUCHANT	*adj* lying down
COUCHER	*n* pl. -S one that couches
COUCHING	*n* pl. -S a form of embroidery
COUDE	*adj* pertaining to a type of telescope
COUGAR	*n* pl. -S a mountain lion
COUGH	*v* -ED, -ING, -S to expel air from the lungs noisily
COUGHER	*n* pl. -S one that coughs
COULD	past tense of can
COULDEST	a past 2d person sing. of can
COULDST	a past 2d person sing. of can
COULEE	*n* pl. -S a small ravine
COULIS	*n* pl. -LISES a thick sauce of pureed vegetable or fruit
COULISSE	*n* pl. -S a side scene of a theatre stage
COULOIR	*n* pl. -S a deep gorge or gully
COULOMB	*n* pl. -S an electrical measure
COULTER	*n* pl. -S colter
COUMARIN	*n* pl. -S a chemical compound **COUMARIC** *adj*
COUMAROU	*n* pl. -S the seed of a tropical tree
COUNCIL	*n* pl. -S a group of persons appointed for a certain function
COUNSEL	*v* -SELED, -SELING, -SELS or -SELLED, -SELLING, -SELS to advise
COUNT	*v* -ED, -ING, -S to list or mention the units of one by one to ascertain the total
COUNTER	*v* -ED, -ING, -S to oppose
COUNTESS	*n* pl. -ES a noblewoman
COUNTIAN	*n* pl. -S a resident of a county
COUNTRY	*n* pl. -TRIES the territory of a nation
COUNTY	*n* pl. -TIES an administrative division of a state
COUP	*v* -ED, -ING, -S to overturn
COUPE	*n* pl. -S an automobile with two doors
COUPLE	*v* -PLED, -PLING, -PLES to unite in pairs
COUPLER	*n* pl. -S one that couples
COUPLET	*n* pl. -S a pair of successive lines of verse
COUPLING	*n* pl. -S a joining device
COUPON	*n* pl. -S a certificate entitling the holder to certain benefits
COURAGE	*n* pl. -S the quality that enables one to face danger fearlessly; spirit

COURANT n pl. -S courante
COURANTE n pl. -S an old, lively dance
COURANTO n pl. -TOS or -TOES courante
COURIER n pl. -S a messenger
COURLAN n pl. -S a wading bird
COURSE v COURSED, COURSING, COURSES to cause hounds to chase game
COURSER n pl. -S one that courses
COURSING n pl. -S the pursuit of game by hounds
COURT v -ED, -ING, -S to woo
COURTER n pl. -S one that courts
COURTESY v -SIED, -SYING, -SIES to curtsy
COURTIER n pl. -S one who attends a royal court
COURTLY adj -LIER, -LIEST stately
COUSCOUS n pl. -ES a North African cereal
COUSIN n pl. -S a child of one's aunt or uncle COUSINLY adj
COUSINRY n pl. -RIES cousins collectively
COUTEAU n pl. -TEAUX a knife
COUTER n pl. -S a piece of armor for the elbow
COUTH adj COUTHER, COUTHEST sophisticated
COUTH n pl. -S refinement
COUTHIE adj COUTHIER, COUTHIEST friendly
COUTURE n pl. -S the business of dressmaking
COUVADE n pl. -S a primitive birth ritual
COVALENT adj sharing electron pairs
COVE v COVED, COVING, COVES to curve over or inward
COVEN n pl. -S a group of witches
COVENANT v -ED, -ING, -S to enter into a binding agreement
COVER v -ED, -ING, -S to place something over or upon
COVERAGE n pl. -S the extent to which something is covered
COVERALL n pl. -S a one-piece work garment
COVERER n pl. -S one that covers
COVERING n pl. -S something that covers
COVERLET n pl. -S a bed covering
COVERLID n pl. -S a coverlet
COVERT n pl. -S a hiding place
COVERTLY adv secretly
COVERUP n pl. -S something used to conceal improper activity

COVET v -ED, -ING, -S to desire greatly
COVETER n pl. -S one that covets
COVETOUS adj excessively desirous
COVEY n pl. -EYS a flock of birds
COVIN n pl. -S a conspiracy to defraud
COVING n pl. -S a concave molding
COW n pl. -S or KINE a farm animal
COW v -ED, -ING, -S to intimidate
COWAGE n pl. -S a tropical vine
COWARD n pl. -S one who lacks courage
COWARDLY adj lacking courage
COWBANE n pl. -S a poisonous plant
COWBELL n pl. -S a bell around a cow's neck
COWBERRY n pl. -RIES a pasture shrub
COWBIND n pl. -S a species of bryony
COWBIRD n pl. -S a blackbird
COWBOY n pl. -BOYS a ranch worker
COWEDLY adv in a cowed manner
COWER v -ED, -ING, -S to cringe
COWFISH n pl. -ES an aquatic mammal
COWFLAP n pl. -S cowflop
COWFLOP n pl. -S a cowpat
COWGIRL n pl. -S a female ranch worker
COWHAGE n pl. -S cowage
COWHAND n pl. -S a cowboy
COWHERB n pl. -S an annual herb
COWHERD n pl. -S one who tends cattle
COWHIDE v -HIDED, -HIDING, -HIDES to flog with a leather whip
COWIER comparative of cowy
COWIEST superlative of cowy
COWINNER n pl. -S one of two or more winners
COWL v -ED, -ING, -S to cover with a hood
COWLICK n pl. -S a lock of unruly hair
COWLING n pl. -S a covering for an aircraft engine
COWMAN n pl. -MEN one who owns cattle
COWORKER n pl. -S a fellow worker
COWPAT n pl. -S a dropping of cow dung
COWPEA n pl. -S a black-eyed pea
COWPIE n pl. -S a cowpat
COWPLOP n pl. -S a cowpat
COWPOKE n pl. -S a cowboy
COWPOX n pl. -ES a cattle disease
COWRIE n pl. -S cowry
COWRITE v -WROTE, -WRITTEN, -WRITING, -WRITES to collaborate in writing

COWRY   n pl. -RIES a glossy seashell
COWSHED   n pl. -S a shelter for cows
COWSKIN   n pl. -S the hide of a cow
COWSLIP   n pl. -S a flowering plant
COWY   adj COWIER, COWIEST
            suggestive of a cow
COX   v -ED, -ING, -ES to coxswain
COXA   n pl. COXAE the hip or hip
            joint COXAL adj
COXALGIA   n pl. -S pain in the hip
            COXALGIC adj
COXALGY   n pl. -GIES coxalgia
COXCOMB   n pl. -S a conceited dandy
COXITIS   n pl. COXITIDES inflammation
            of the hip joint
COXSWAIN   v -ED, -ING, -S to steer a
            racing rowboat
COY   adj COYER, COYEST shy
COY   v -ED, -ING, -S to caress
COYDOG   n pl. -S a hybrid between a
            coyote and a wild dog
COYISH   adj somewhat coy
COYLY   adv in a coy manner
COYNESS   n pl. -ES the state of being
            coy
COYOTE   n pl. -S a small wolf
COYPOU   n pl. -S a coypu
COYPU   n pl. -S an aquatic rodent
COZ   n pl. COZES or COZZES a
            cousin
COZEN   v -ED, -ING, -S to deceive
COZENAGE   n pl. -S the practice of
            cozening
COZENER   n pl. -S one that cozens
COZEY   n pl. -ZEYS a cozy
COZIE   n pl. S a cozy
COZIED   past tense of cozy
COZIER   comparative of cozy
COZIES   present 3d person sing. of
            cozy
COZIEST   superlative of cozy
COZINESS   n pl. -ES the state of being
            cozy
COZY   v COZIED, COZYING,
            COZIES to attempt to get on
            friendly terms
COZY   adj COZIER, COZIEST snug
            and comfortable COZILY adv
COZZES   a pl. of coz
CRAAL   v -ED, -ING, -S to kraal
CRAB   v CRABBED, CRABBING,
            CRABS to complain
CRABBER   n pl. -S one that crabs
CRABBY   adj -BIER, -BIEST grumpy
            CRABBILY adv

CRABMEAT   n pl. -S the edible part of a
            crab
CRABWISE   adv sideways
CRACK   v -ED, -ING, -S to break
            without dividing into parts
CRACKER   n pl. -S a thin, crisp biscuit
CRACKING   n pl. -S a chemical process
CRACKLE   v -LED, -LING, -ES to make a
            succession of snapping
            sounds
CRACKLY   adj -LIER, -LIEST brittle
CRACKNEL   n pl. -S a hard, crisp biscuit
CRACKPOT   n pl. -S an eccentric person
CRACKUP   n pl. -S a collision
CRACKY   interj — used to express
            surprise
CRADLE   v -DLED, -DLING, -DLES to
            nurture during infancy
CRADLER   n pl. -S one that cradles
CRAFT   v -ED, -ING, -S to make by
            hand
CRAFTY   adj CRAFTIER, CRAFTIEST
            skillful in deceiving CRAFTILY
            adv
CRAG   n pl. -S a large jagged rock
            CRAGGED adj
CRAGGY   adj -GIER, -GIEST full of
            crags CRAGGILY adv
CRAGSMAN   n pl. -MEN one who climbs
            crags
CRAKE   n pl. -S a small, harsh-voiced
            bird
CRAM   v CRAMMED, CRAMMING,
            CRAMS to fill or pack tightly
CRAMBE   n pl. -S an annual herb
CRAMBO   n pl. -BOS or -BOES a word
            game
CRAMMED   past tense of cram
CRAMMER   n pl. -S one that crams
CRAMMING   present participle of cram
CRAMOISY   n pl. -SIES crimson cloth
CRAMP   v -ED, -ING, -S to restrain or
            confine
CRAMPIT   n pl. -S a piece of equipment
            used in curling
CRAMPON   n pl. -S a device for raising
            heavy objects
CRAMPOON   n pl. -S crampon
CRANCH   v -ED, -ING, -ES to craunch
CRANE   v CRANED, CRANING,
            CRANES to stretch out one's
            neck
CRANIA   a pl. of cranium
CRANIAL   adj pertaining to the skull
CRANIATE   n pl. -S one that has a skull
CRANING   present participle of crane

CRANIUM n pl. -NIUMS or -NIA the skull
CRANK v -ED, -ING, -S to start manually
CRANK adj CRANKER, CRANKEST lively
CRANKIER comparative of cranky
CRANKIEST superlative of cranky
CRANKILY adv in a cranky manner
CRANKISH adj eccentric
CRANKLE v -KLED, -KLING, -KLES to crinkle
CRANKLY adv in a crank manner
CRANKOUS adj cranky
CRANKPIN n pl. -S the handle of a crank
CRANKY adj CRANKIER, CRANKIEST grumpy
CRANNIED adj having crannies
CRANNIES pl. of cranny
CRANNOG n pl. -S an artificial island
CRANNOGE n pl. -S crannog
CRANNY n pl. -NIES a crevice CRANNIED adj
CRAP v CRAPPED, CRAPPING, CRAPS to throw a 2, 3, or 12 in a dice game
CRAPE v CRAPED, CRAPING, CRAPES to crepe
CRAPPIE n pl. -S an edible fish
CRAPPING present participle of crap
CRAPPY adj -PIER, -PIEST markedly inferior in quality
CRASES pl. of crasis
CRASH v -ED, -ING, -ES to collide noisily
CRASHER n pl. -S one that crashes
CRASIS n pl. CRASES a vowel contraction
CRASS adj CRASSER, CRASSEST grossly vulgar or stupid CRASSLY adv
CRATCH n pl. -ES a manger
CRATE v CRATED, CRATING, CRATES to put in a packing box
CRATER v -ED, -ING, -S to form cavities in a surface
CRATON n pl. -S a part of the earth's crust CRATONIC adj
CRAUNCH v -ED, -ING, -ES to crunch
CRAVAT n pl. -S a necktie
CRAVE v CRAVED, CRAVING, CRAVES to desire greatly
CRAVEN v -ED, -ING, -S to make cowardly
CRAVENLY adv in a cowardly manner
CRAVER n pl. -S one that craves

CRAVING n pl. -S a great desire
CRAW n pl. -S the stomach of an animal
CRAWDAD n pl. -S a crayfish
CRAWFISH v -ED, -ING, -ES to back out or retreat
CRAWL v -ED, -ING, -S to move with the body on or near the ground
CRAWLER n pl. -S one that crawls
CRAWLWAY n pl. -WAYS a small, low tunnel
CRAWLY adj CRAWLIER, CRAWLIEST creepy
CRAYFISH n pl. -ES a crustacean
CRAYON v -ED, -ING, -S to use a drawing implement
CRAZE v CRAZED, CRAZING, CRAZES to make insane
CRAZY adj -ZIER, -ZIEST insane CRAZILY adv
CRAZY n pl. -ZIES a crazy person
CREAK v -ED, -ING, -S to squeak
CREAKY adj CREAKIER, CREAKIEST creaking CREAKILY adv
CREAM v -ED, -ING, -S to form cream (a part of milk)
CREAMER n pl. -S a cream pitcher
CREAMERY n pl. -ERIES a dairy
CREAMY adj CREAMIER, CREAMIEST rich in cream CREAMILY adv
CREASE v CREASED, CREASING, CREASES to make a fold or winkle in
CREASER n pl. -S one that creases
CREASY adj CREASIER, CREASIEST having folds or wrinkles
CREATE v -ATED, -ATING, -ATES to cause to exist
CREATIN n pl. -S creatine
CREATINE n pl. -S a chemical compound
CREATION n pl. -S something created
CREATIVE adj having the ability to create
CREATOR n pl. -S one that creates
CREATURE n pl. -S a living being
CRECHE n pl. -S a day nursery
CREDAL adj pertaining to a creed
CREDENCE n pl. -S belief
CREDENDA n/pl articles of faith
CREDENT adj believing
CREDENZA n pl. -S a piece of furniture
CREDIBLE adj believable CREDIBLY adv
CREDIT v -ED, -ING, -S to accept as true
CREDITOR n pl. -S one to whom money is owed
CREDO n pl. -DOS a creed

CREED *n* pl. -S a statement of belief
CREEDAL *adj*

CREEK *n* pl. -S a watercourse smaller than a river

CREEL *v* -ED, -ING, -S to put fish in a creel (a fish basket)

CREEP *v* CREPT, CREEPING, CREEPS to crawl

CREEPAGE *n* pl. -S gradual movement

CREEPER *n* pl. -S one that creeps

CREEPIE *n* pl. -S a low stool

CREEPY *adj* CREEPIER, CREEPIEST repugnant **CREEPILY** *adv*

CREESE *n* pl. -S kris

CREESH *v* -ED, -ING, -ES to grease

CREMAINS *n/pl* the ashes of a cremated body

CREMATE *v* -MATED, -MATING, -MATES to reduce to ashes by burning

CREMATOR *n* pl. -S one that cremates

CREME *n* pl. -S cream

CRENATE *adj* having an edge with rounded projections

CRENATED *adj* crenate

CRENEL *v* -ELED, -ELING, -ELS or -ELLED, -ELLING, -ELS to provide with crenelles

CRENELLE *n* pl. -S a rounded projection

CREODONT *n* pl. -S an extinct carnivore

CREOLE *n* pl. -S a type of mixed language

CREOLISE *v* -ISED, -ISING, -ISES to creolize

CREOLIZE *v* -IZED, -IZING, -IZES to cause a language to become a creole

CREOSOL *n* pl. -S a chemical compound

CREOSOTE *v* -SOTED, -SOTING, -SOTES to treat with a wood preservative

CREPE *v* CREPED, CREPING, CREPES to frizz the hair

CREPEY *adj* CREPIER, CREPIEST crinkly

CREPON *n* pl. -S a crinkled fabric

CREPT past tense of creep

CREPY *adj* CREPIER, CREPIEST crepey

CRESCENT *n* pl. -S the figure of the moon in its first or last quarter

CRESCIVE *adj* increasing

CRESOL *n* pl. -S a chemical disinfectant

CRESS *n* pl. -ES a plant used in salads

CRESSET *n* pl. -S a metal cup for burning oil

CREST *v* -ED, -ING, -S to reach a crest (a peak)

CRESTAL *adj* pertaining to a crest (a peak)

CRESTING *n* pl. -S a decorative coping

CRESYL *n* pl. -S tolyl

CRESYLIC *adj* pertaining to cresol

CRETIC *n* pl. -S a type of metrical foot

CRETIN *n* pl. -S an idiot

CRETONNE *n* pl. -S a heavy fabric

CREVALLE *n* pl. -S a food and game fish

CREVASSE *v* -VASSED, -VASSING, -VASSES to fissure

CREVICE *n* pl. -S a cleft **CREVICED** *adj*

CREW *v* -ED, -ING, -S to serve aboard a ship

CREWEL *n* pl. -S a woolen yarn

CREWLESS *adj* without any crewmen

CREWMAN *n* pl. -MEN one who serves on a ship

CREWMATE *n* pl. -S a fellow crewman

CREWNECK *n* pl. -S a sweater with a collarless neckline

CRIB *v* CRIBBED, CRIBBING, CRIBS to confine closely

CRIBBAGE *n* pl. -S a card game

CRIBBER *n* pl. -S one that cribs

CRIBBING *n* pl. -S a supporting framework

CRIBBLED *adj* covered with dots

CRIBROUS *adj* pierced with small holes

CRIBWORK *n* pl. -S a framework of logs

CRICETID *n* pl. -S a small rodent

CRICK *v* -ED, -ING, -S to cause a spasm of the neck

CRICKET *v* -ED, -ING, -S to play cricket (a ball game)

CRICKEY *interj* — used as a mild oath

CRICOID *n* pl. -S a cartilage of the larynx

CRIED past tense of cry

CRIER *n* pl. -S one that cries

CRIES present 3d person sing. of cry

CRIKEY *interj* — used as a mild oath

CRIME *n* pl. -S a violation of the law

CRIMINAL *n* pl. -S one who has committed a crime

CRIMMER *n* pl. -S krimmer

CRIMP *v* -ED, -ING, -S to pleat

CRIMPER *n* pl. -S one that crimps

CRIMPLE *v* -PLED, -PLING, -PLES to wrinkle

CRIMPY *adj* CRIMPIER, CRIMPIEST wavy

CRIMSON v -ED, -ING, -S to make crimson (a red color)

CRINGE v CRINGED, CRINGING, CRINGES to shrink in fear

CRINGER n pl. -S one that cringes

CRINGLE· n pl. -S a small loop of rope

CRINITE n pl. -S a fossil crinoid

CRINKLE v -KLED, -KLING, -KLES to wrinkle

CRINKLY adj -KLIER, -KLIEST crinkled

CRINOID n pl. -S a marine animal

CRINUM n pl. -S a tropical herb

CRIOLLO n pl. -LLOS a person of Spanish ancestry

CRIPE interj — used as a mild oath

CRIPES interj — used as a mild oath

CRIPPLE v -PLED, -PLING, -PLES to disable or impair

CRIPPLER n pl. -S one that cripples

CRIS n pl. -ES kris

CRISIS n pl. CRISES a crucial turning point **CRISIC** adj

CRISP adj CRISPER, CRISPEST brittle

CRISP v -ED, -ING, -S to make crisp

CRISPATE adj curled

CRISPEN v -ED, -ING, -S to make crisp

CRISPER n pl. -S one that crisps

CRISPLY adv in a crisp manner

CRISPY adj CRISPIER, CRISPIEST crisp **CRISPILY** adv

CRISSUM n pl. CRISSA a region of feathers on a bird **CRISSAL** adj

CRISTA n pl. -TAE a part of a cell

CRISTATE adj having a projection on the head

CRITERIA n/pl standards of judgment

CRITIC n pl. -S one who judges the merits of something **CRITICAL** adj

CRITIQUE v -TIQUED, -TIQUING, -TIQUES to judge as a critic

CRITTER n pl. -S a creature

CRITTUR n pl. -S critter

CROAK v -ED, -ING, -S to utter a low, hoarse sound

CROAKER n pl. -S one that croaks

CROAKY adj CROAKIER, CROAKIEST low and hoarse **CROAKILY** adv

CROC n pl. -S a crocodile

CROCEIN n pl. -S a red dye

CROCEINE n pl. -S crocein

CROCHET v -ED, -ING, -S to do a type of needlework

CROCI a pl. of crocus

CROCINE adj pertaining to the crocus

CROCK v -ED, -ING, -S to stain or soil

CROCKERY n pl. -ERIES pottery

CROCKET n pl. -S an architectural ornament

CROCOITE n pl. -S a mineral

CROCUS n pl. -CUSES or -CI a flowering plant

CROFT n pl. -S a small tenant farm

CROFTER n pl. -S a tenant farmer

CROJIK n pl. -S a triangular sail

CROMLECH n pl. -S a dolmen

CRONE n pl. -S a withered old woman

CRONY n pl. CRONIES a close friend

CRONYISM n pl. -S a kind of political favoritism

CROOK v -ED, -ING, -S to bend

CROOKED adj -EDER, -EDEST dishonest

CROOKERY n pl. -ERIES crooked activity

CROON v -ED, -ING, -S to sing softly

CROONER n pl. -S one that croons

CROP v CROPPED, CROPPING, CROPS to cut off short

CROPLAND n pl. -S farmland

CROPLESS adj being without crops (agricultural produce)

CROPPED past tense of crop

CROPPER n pl. -S one that crops

CROPPIE n pl. -S crappie

CROPPING present participle of crop

CROQUET v -ED, -ING, -S to drive a ball away in a certain game

CROQUIS n pl. CROQUIS a sketch

CRORE n pl. -S a monetary unit of India

CROSIER n pl. -S a bishop's staff

CROSS v -ED, -ING, -ES to intersect

CROSS adj CROSSER, CROSSEST ill-tempered

CROSSARM n pl. -S a horizontal bar

CROSSBAR v -BARRED, -BARRING, -BARS to fasten with crossarms

CROSSBOW n pl. -S a kind of weapon

CROSSCUT v -CUT, -CUTTING, -CUTS to cut across

CROSSE n pl. -S a lacrosse stick

CROSSER n pl. -S one that crosses

CROSSING n pl. -S an intersection

CROSSLET n pl. -S a heraldic symbol

CROSSLY adv in a cross manner

CROSSTIE n pl. -S a transverse beam

CROSSWAY n pl. -WAYS a road that crosses another road

CROTCH *n* pl. -ES an angle formed by two diverging parts **CROTCHED** *adj*

CROTCHET *n* pl. -S a small hook

CROTON *n* pl. -S a tropical plant

CROUCH *v* -ED, -ING, -ES to stoop

CROUP *n* pl. -S a disease of the throat

CROUPE *n* pl. -S the rump of certain animals

CROUPIER *n* pl. -S an attendant in a casino

CROUPOUS *adj* pertaining to croup

CROUPY *adj* CROUPIER, CROUPIEST affected with croup **CROUPILY** *adv*

CROUSE *adj* lively **CROUSELY** *adv*

CROUTON *n* pl. -S a small cube of toasted bread

CROW *v* -ED, -ING, -S to boast

CROWBAR *v* -BARRED, -BARRING, -BARS to use a steel bar as a lever

CROWD *v* -ED, -ING, -S to press into an insufficient space

CROWDER *n* pl. -S one that crowds

CROWDIE *n* pl. -S crowdy

CROWDY *n* pl. -DIES porridge

CROWER *n* pl. -S one that crows

CROWFOOT *n* pl. -FOOTS or -FEET a flowering plant

CROWN *v* -ED, -ING, -S to supply with a crown (a royal headpiece)

CROWNER *n* pl. -S a coroner

CROWNET *n* pl. -S a coronet

CROWSTEP *n* pl. -S a step on top of a wall

CROZE *n* pl. -S a tool used in barrel-making

CROZER *n* pl. -S a croze

CROZIER *n* pl. -S crosier

CRUCES *a* pl. of crux

CRUCIAL *adj* of supreme importance

CRUCIAN *n* pl. -S a European fish

CRUCIATE *adj* cross-shaped

CRUCIBLE *n* pl. -S a heat-resistant vessel

CRUCIFER *n* pl. -S one who carries a cross

CRUCIFIX *n* pl. -ES a cross bearing an image of Christ

CRUCIFY *v* -FIED, -FYING, -FIES to put to death on a cross

CRUCK *n* pl. -S a curved roof timber

CRUD *v* CRUDDED, CRUDDING, CRUDS to curd

CRUDDY *adj* -DIER, -DIEST filthy; contemptible

CRUDE *adj* CRUDER, CRUDEST unrefined **CRUDELY** *adv*

CRUDE *n* pl. -S unrefined petroleum

CRUDITES *n/pl* pieces of raw vegetables served with a dip

CRUDITY *n* pl. -TIES the state of being crude

CRUEL *adj* CRUELER, CRUELEST or CRUELLER, CRUELLEST indifferent to the pain of others **CRUELLY** *adv*

CRUELTY *n* pl. -TIES a cruel act

CRUET *n* pl. -S a glass bottle

CRUISE *v* CRUISED, CRUISING, CRUISES to sail about touching at several ports

CRUISER *n* pl. -S a boat that cruises

CRUISING *n* pl. -S the act of driving around in search of fun

CRULLER *n* pl. -S a small sweet cake

CRUMB *v* -ED, -ING, -S to break into crumbs (small pieces)

CRUMBER *n* pl. -S one that crumbs

CRUMBIER comparative of crumby

CRUMBIEST superlative of crumby

CRUMBLE *v* -BLED, -BLING, -BLES to break into small pieces

CRUMBLY *adj* -BLIER, -BLIEST easily crumbled

CRUMBUM *n* pl. -S a despicable person

CRUMBY *adj* CRUMBIER, CRUMBIEST full of crumbs

CRUMHORN *n* pl. -S a double-reed woodwind instrument

CRUMMIE *n* pl. -S a cow with crooked horns

CRUMMY *adj* -MIER, -MIEST of little or no value

CRUMP *v* -ED, -ING, -S to crunch

CRUMPET *n* pl. -S a small cake cooked on a griddle

CRUMPLE *v* -PLED, -PLING, -PLES to wrinkle

CRUMPLY *adj* -PLIER, -PLIEST easily wrinkled

CRUNCH *v* -ED, -ING, -ES to chew with a crackling sound

CRUNCHER *n* pl. -S one that crunches

CRUNCHY *adj* CRUNCHIER, CRUNCHIEST crisp

CRUNODE *n* pl. -S a point at which a curve crosses itself **CRUNODAL** *adj*

CRUOR *n* pl. -S clotted blood

CRUPPER *n* pl. -S the rump of a horse

CRURAL *adj* pertaining to the thigh or leg

CRUS *n* pl. CRURA a part of the leg

CRUSADE *v* -SADED, -SADING, -SADES to engage in a holy war

CRUSADER *n* pl. -S one that crusades

CRUSADO *n* pl. -DOES or -DOS an old Portuguese coin

CRUSE *n* pl. -S a small bottle

CRUSET *n* pl. -S a melting pot

CRUSH *v* -ED, -ING, -ES to press or squeeze out of shape

CRUSHER *n* pl. -S one that crushes

CRUSILY *adj* covered with crosslets

CRUST *v* -ED, -ING, -S to form a crust (a hardened outer surface)

CRUSTAL *adj* pertaining to the earth's crust

CRUSTOSE *adj* forming a thin, brittle crust

CRUSTY *adj* CRUSTIER, CRUSTIEST surly **CRUSTILY** *adv*

CRUTCH *v* -ED, -ING, -ES to prop up or support

CRUX *n* pl. CRUXES or CRUCES a basic or decisive point

CRUZADO *n* pl. -DOES or -DOS crusado

CRUZEIRO *n* pl. -ROS a monetary unit of Brazil

CRWTH *n* pl. -S an ancient stringed musical instrument

CRY *v* CRIED, CRYING, CRIES to weep **CRYINGLY** *adv*

CRYBABY *n* pl. -BIES a person who cries easily

CRYOGEN *n* pl. -S a substance for producing low temperatures

CRYOGENY *n* pl. -NIES a branch of physics

CRYOLITE *n* pl. -S a mineral

CRYONICS *n/pl* the practice of freezing dead bodies for future revival **CRYONIC** *adj*

CRYOSTAT *n* pl. -S a refrigerating device

CRYOTRON *n* pl. -S an electronic device

CRYPT *n* pl. -S a burial vault **CRYPTAL** *adj*

CRYPTIC *adj* mysterious

CRYPTO *n* pl. -TOS one who belongs secretly to a group

CRYSTAL *n* pl. -S a transparent mineral

CTENIDIA *n/pl* comblike anatomical structures

CTENOID *adj* comblike

CUB *n* pl. -S the young of certain animals

CUBAGE *n* pl. -S cubature

CUBATURE *n* pl. -S cubical content

CUBBISH *adj* resembling a cub

CUBBY *n* pl. -BIES a small, enclosed space

CUBE *v* CUBED, CUBING, CUBES to form into a cube (a regular solid)

CUBEB *n* pl. -S a woody vine

CUBER *n* pl. -S one that cubes

CUBIC *n* pl. -S a mathematical equation or expression

CUBICAL *adj* shaped like a cube

CUBICITY *n* pl. -TIES the state of being cubical

CUBICLE *n* pl. -S a small chamber

CUBICLY *adv* in the form of a cube

CUBICULA *n/pl* burial chambers

CUBIFORM *adj* shaped like a cube

CUBING present participle of cube

CUBISM *n* pl. -S a style of art **CUBISTIC** *adj*

CUBIST *n* pl. -S an adherent of cubism

CUBIT *n* pl. -S an ancient measure of length **CUBITAL** *adj*

CUBOID *n* pl. -S a bone of the foot **CUBOIDAL** *adj*

CUCKOLD *v* -ED, -ING, -S to make a cuckold (a cornuto) of

CUCKOO *v* -ED, -ING, -S to repeat monotonously

CUCUMBER *n* pl. -S a garden vegetable

CUCURBIT *n* pl. -S a gourd

CUD *n* pl. -S a portion of food to be chewed again

CUDBEAR *n* pl. -S a red dye

CUDDIE *n* pl. -S cuddy

CUDDIES pl. of cuddy

CUDDLE *v* -DLED, -DLING, -DLES to hug tenderly

CUDDLER *n* pl. -S one that cuddles

CUDDLY *adj* -DLIER, -DLIEST fit for cuddling

CUDDY *n* pl. -DIES a donkey

CUDGEL *v* -ELED, -ELING, -ELS or -ELLED, -ELLING, -ELS to beat with a heavy club

CUDGELER *n* pl. -S one that cudgels

CUDWEED *n* pl. -S a perennial herb

CUE *v* CUED, CUING or CUEING, CUES to give a signal to an actor

CUESTA *n* pl. -S a type of land elevation

CUFF *v* -ED, -ING, -S to furnish with a cuff (a part of a sleeve)

CUFFLESS *adj* having no cuff

CUIF *n* pl. -S coof

CUING a present participle of cue

CUIRASS *v* -ED, -ING, -ES to cover with a type of armor

CUISH *n* pl. -ES cuisse

CUISINE *n* pl. -S a style of cooking

CUISSE *n* pl. -S a piece of armor for the thigh

CUITTLE *v* -TLED, -TLING, -TLES to coax

CUKE *n* pl. -S a cucumber

CULCH *n* pl. -ES an oyster bed

CULET *n* pl. -S a piece of armor for the lower back

CULEX *n* pl. CULICES a mosquito

CULICID *n* pl. -S a culicine

CULICINE *n* pl. -S a mosquito

CULINARY *adj* pertaining to cookery

CULL *v* -ED, -ING, -S to select from others

CULLAY *n* pl. -LAYS quillai

CULLER *n* pl. -S one that culls

CULLET *n* pl. -S broken glass gathered for remelting

CULLIED past tense of cully

CULLIES present 3d person sing. of cully

CULLION *n* pl. -S a vile fellow

CULLIS *n* pl. -LISES a gutter in a roof

CULLY *v* -LIED, -LYING, -LIES to trick

CULM *v* -ED, -ING, -S to form a hollow stem

CULOTTE *n* pl. -S a divided skirt

CULPA *n* pl. -PAE negligence for which one is liable

CULPABLE *adj* deserving blame or censure **CULPABLY** *adv*

CULPRIT *n* pl. -S one that is guilty

CULT *n* pl. -S a religious society **CULTISH** *adj*

CULTCH *n* pl. -ES culch

CULTI a pl. of cultus

CULTIC *adj* pertaining to a cult

CULTIGEN *n* pl. -S a cultivar

CULTISH *adj.* pertaining to a cult

CULTISM *n* pl. -S devotion to a cult

CULTIST *n* pl. -S a member of a cult

CULTIVAR *n* pl. -S a variety of plant originating under cultivation

CULTLIKE *adj* resembling a cult

CULTRATE *adj* sharp-edged and pointed

CULTURAL *adj* produced by breeding

CULTURE *v* -TURED, -TURING, -TURES to make fit for raising crops

CULTUS *n* pl. -TUSES or -TI a cult

CULVER *n* pl. -S a pigeon

CULVERIN *n* pl. -S a medieval musket

CULVERT *n* pl. -S a conduit

CUM *prep* together with

CUMARIN *n* pl. -S coumarin

CUMBER *v* -ED, -ING, -S to hinder

CUMBERER *n* pl. -S one that cumbers

CUMBROUS *adj* unwieldy

CUMIN *n* pl. -S a plant used in cooking

CUMMER *n* pl. -S a godmother

CUMMIN *n* pl. -S cumin

CUMQUAT *n* pl. -S kumquat

CUMSHAW *n* pl. -S a gift

CUMULATE *v* -LATED, -LATING, -LATES to heap

CUMULUS *n* pl. -LI a type of cloud **CUMULOUS** *adj*

CUNDUM *n* pl. -S condom

CUNEAL *adj* cuneate

CUNEATE *adj* wedge-shaped; triangular

CUNEATED *adj* cuneate

CUNEATIC *adj* cuneate

CUNIFORM *n* pl. -S wedge-shaped writing characters

CUNNER *n* pl. -S a marine fish

CUNNING *adj* -NINGER, -NINGEST crafty

CUNNING *n* pl. -S skill in deception

CUP *v* CUPPED, CUPPING, CUPS to place in a cup (a small, open container)

CUPBOARD *n* pl. -S a cabinet

CUPCAKE *n* pl. -S a small cake

CUPEL *v* -PELED, -PELING, -PELS or -PELLED, -PELLING, -PELS to refine gold or silver in a cuplike vessel

CUPELER *n* pl. -S cupeller

CUPELLER *n* pl. -S one that cupels

CUPFUL *n* pl. CUPFULS or CUPSFUL as much as a cup can hold

CUPID *n* pl. -S a naked, winged representation of the Roman god of love

CUPIDITY *n* pl. -TIES greed; lust

CUPLIKE *adj* resembling a cup

CUPOLA *v* -ED, -ING, -S to shape like a dome

CUPPA *n* pl. -S a cup of tea

CUPPED past tense of cup

CUPPER *n* pl. -S one that performs cupping

CUPPING *n* pl. -S an archaic medical process

CUPPY *adj* -PIER, -PIEST cuplike

CUPREOUS *adj* containing copper

CUPRIC *adj* containing copper

CUPRITE *n* pl. -S an ore of copper
CUPROUS *adj* containing copper
CUPRUM *n* pl. -S copper
CUPSFUL a pl. of cupful
CUPULA *n* pl. -LAE a cup-shaped anatomical structure
CUPULAR *adj* cupulate
CUPULATE *adj* cup-shaped
CUPULE *n* pl. -S a cup-shaped anatomical structure
CUR *n* pl. -S a mongrel dog
CURABLE *adj* capable of being cured **CURABLY** *adv*
CURACAO *n* pl. -S a type of liqueur
CURACOA *n* pl. -S curacao
CURACY *n* pl. -CIES the office of a curate
CURAGH *n* pl. -S currach
CURARA *n* pl. -S curare
CURARE *n* pl. -S an arrow poison
CURARI *n* pl. -S curare
CURARINE *n* pl. -S a poisonous alkaloid
CURARIZE *v* -RIZED, -RIZING, -RIZES to poison with curare
CURASSOW *n* pl. -S a turkey-like bird
CURATE *v* -RATED, -RATING, -RATES to act as curator of
CURATIVE *n* pl. -S something that cures
CURATOR *n* pl. -S a museum manager
CURB *v* -ED, -ING, -S to restrain **CURBABLE** *adj*
CURBER *n* pl. -S one that curbs
CURBING *n* pl. -S a concrete border along a street
CURBSIDE *n* pl. -S the side of a pavement bordered by a curbing
CURCH *n* pl. -ES a kerchief
CURCULIO *n* pl. -LIOS a weevil
CURCUMA *n* pl. -S a tropical plant
CURD *v* -ED, -ING, -S to curdle
CURDIER comparative of curdy
CURDIEST superlative of curdy
CURDLE *v* -DLED, -DLING, -DLES to congeal
CURDLER *n* pl. -S one that curdles
CURDY *adj* CURDIER, CURDIEST curdled
CURE *v* CURED, CURING, CURES to restore to health
CURELESS *adj* not curable
CURER *n* pl. -S one that cures
CURET *n* pl. -S a surgical instrument
CURETTE *v* -RETTED, -RETTING, -RETTES to treat with a curet

CURF *n* pl. -S an incision made by a cutting tool
CURFEW *n* pl. -S a regulation concerning the hours which one may keep
CURIA *n* pl. -RIAE a court of justice **CURIAL** *adj*
CURIE *n* pl. -S a unit of radioactivity
CURING present participle of cure
CURIO *n* pl. -RIOS an unusual art object
CURIOSA *n/pl* pornographic books
CURIOUS *adj* -OUSER, -OUSEST eager for information
CURITE *n* pl. -S a radioactive mineral
CURIUM *n* pl. -S a radioactive element
CURL *v* -ED, -ING, -S to form into ringlets
CURLER *n* pl. -S one that curls
CURLEW *n* pl. -S a shore bird
CURLICUE *v* -CUED, -CUING, -CUES to decorate with curlicues (fancy spiral figures)
CURLING *n* pl. -S a game played on ice
CURLY *adj* CURLIER, CURLIEST tending to curl **CURLILY** *adv*
CURLYCUE *n* pl. -S curlicue
CURN *n* pl. -S grain
CURR *v* -ED, -ING, -S to purr
CURRACH *n* pl. -S a coracle
CURRAGH *n* pl. -S currach
CURRAN *n* pl. -S curn
CURRANT *n* pl. -S an edible berry
CURRENCY *n* pl. -CIES money
CURRENT *n* pl. -S a continuous flow
CURRICLE *n* pl. -S a light carriage
CURRIE *v* -RIED, -RYING, -RIES to prepare food a certain way
CURRIED past tense of curry
CURRIER *n* pl. -S one that curries leather
CURRIERY *n* pl. -ERIES the shop of a currier
CURRISH *adj* resembling a cur
CURRY *v* -RIED, -RYING, -RIES to prepare leather for use or sale
CURRYING present participle of currie
CURSE *v* CURSED or CURST, CURSING, CURSES to wish evil upon
CURSED *adj* CURSEDER, CURSEDEST wicked **CURSEDLY** *adv*
CURSER *n* pl. -S one that curses
CURSING present participle of curse
CURSIVE *n* pl. -S a style of print

CURSOR	*n* pl. -S a light indicator on a computer display	**CUSSER**	*n* pl. -S one that cusses
CURSORY	*adj* hasty and superficial	**CUSSO**	*n* pl. -SOS an Ethiopian tree
CURST	a past tense of curse	**CUSSWORD**	*n* pl. -S a profane or obscene word
CURT	*adj* CURTER, CURTEST abrupt	**CUSTARD**	*n* pl. -S a thick, soft dessert **CUSTARDY** *adj*
CURTAIL	*v* -ED, -ING, -S to cut short	**CUSTODES**	pl. of custos
CURTAIN	*v* -ED, -ING, -S to provide with a hanging piece of fabric	**CUSTODY**	*n* pl. -DIES guardianship
CURTAL	*n* pl. -S an animal with a clipped tail	**CUSTOM**	*n* pl. -S a habitual practice
CURTALAX	*n* pl. -ES a cutlass	**CUSTOMER**	*n* pl. -S one who buys something
CURTATE	*adj* shortened	**CUSTOS**	*n* pl. -TODES a guardian or keeper
CURTESY	*n* pl. -SIES a type of legal tenure	**CUSTUMAL**	*n* pl. -S a written record of laws and customs
CURTLY	*adv* in a curt manner	**CUT**	*v* CUT, CUTTING, CUTS to divide into parts with a sharp-edged instrument
CURTNESS	*n* pl. -ES the quality of being curt		
CURTSEY	*v* -ED, -ING, -S to curtsy	**CUTAWAY**	*n* pl. -AWAYS a type of coat
CURTSY	*v* -SIED, -SYING, -SIES to bow politely	**CUTBACK**	*n* pl. -S a reduction
		CUTBANK	*n* pl. -S a steep stream bank
CURULE	*adj* of the highest rank	**CUTCH**	*n* pl. -ES catechu
CURVE	*v* CURVED, CURVING, CURVES to deviate from straightness **CURVEDLY** *adv*	**CUTCHERY**	*n* pl. -CHERIES a judicial office in India
		CUTDOWN	*n* pl. -S a reduction
CURVET	*v* -VETED, -VETING, -VETS or -VETTED, -VETTING, -VETS to prance	**CUTE**	*adj* CUTER, CUTEST pleasingly attractive **CUTELY** *adv*
CURVEY	*adj* CURVIER, CURVIEST curvy	**CUTENESS**	*n* pl. -ES the quality of being cute
CURVING	present participle of curve	**CUTES**	a pl. of cutis
CURVY	*adj* CURVIER, CURVIEST curved	**CUTESIE**	*adj* -SIER, -SIEST cutesy
		CUTEST	superlative of cute
CUSCUS	*n* pl. -ES an arboreal mammal	**CUTESY**	*adj* -SIER, -SIEST self-consciously cute
CUSEC	*n* pl. -S a volumetric unit of flow of liquids		
		CUTEY	*n* pl. -TEYS cutie
CUSHAT	*n* pl. -S a pigeon	**CUTGRASS**	*n* pl. -ES a swamp grass
CUSHAW	*n* pl. -S a variety of squash	**CUTICLE**	*n* pl. -S the epidermis
CUSHIER	comparative of cushy	**CUTICULA**	*n* pl. -LAE the outer hard covering of an insect
CUSHIEST	superlative of cushy		
CUSHILY	*adv* in a cushy manner	**CUTIE**	*n* pl. -S a cute person
CUSHION	*v* -ED, -ING, -S to pad with soft material	**CUTIN**	*n* pl. -S a waxy substance found on plants
CUSHIONY	*adj* soft	**CUTINISE**	*v* -ISED, -ISING, -ISES to cutinize
CUSHY	*adj* CUSHIER, CUSHIEST easy	**CUTINIZE**	*v* -IZED, -IZING, -IZES to become coated with cutin
CUSK	*n* pl. -S a marine food fish		
CUSP	*n* pl. -S a pointed end **CUSPATE, CUSPATED, CUSPED** *adj*	**CUTIS**	*n* pl. -TES or -TISES the corium
		CUTLAS	*n* pl. -ES cutlass
CUSPID	*n* pl. -S a pointed tooth	**CUTLASS**	*n* pl. -ES a short sword
CUSPIDAL	*adj* having a cusp	**CUTLER**	*n* pl. -S one who sells and repairs cutting tools
CUSPIDOR	*n* pl. -S a spittoon		
CUSPIS	*n* pl. -PIDES a cusp	**CUTLERY**	*n* pl. -LERIES the occupation of a cutler
CUSS	*v* -ED, -ING, -ES to curse		
CUSSEDLY	*adv* in a cranky manner	**CUTLET**	*n* pl. -S a slice of meat

CUTLINE *n* pl. -S a caption
CUTOFF *n* pl. -S the point at which something terminates
CUTOUT *n* pl. -S something cut out
CUTOVER *n* pl. -S land cleared of trees
CUTPURSE *n* pl. -S a pickpocket
CUTTABLE *adj* capable of being cut
CUTTAGE *n* pl. -S a means of plant propagation
CUTTER *n* pl. -S one that cuts
CUTTIES pl. of cutty
CUTTING *n* pl. -S a section cut from a plant
CUTTLE *v* -TLED, -TLING, -TLES to fold cloth in a particular fashion
CUTTY *n* pl. -TIES a thickset girl
CUTUP *n* pl. -S a mischievous person
CUTWATER *n* pl. -S the front part of a ship's prow
CUTWORK *n* pl. -S a type of embroidery
CUTWORM *n* pl. -S a caterpillar
CUVETTE *n* pl. -S a small tube or vessel
CWM *n* pl. -S a cirque
CYAN *n* pl. -S a blue color
CYANAMID *n* pl. -S a chemical compound
CYANATE *n* pl. -S a chemical salt
CYANIC *adj* blue or bluish
CYANID *n* pl. -S a compound of cyanogen
CYANIDE *v* -NIDED, -NIDING, -NIDES to treat an ore with cyanid
CYANIN *n* pl. -S cyanine
CYANINE *n* pl. -S a blue dye
CYANITE *n* pl. -S a mineral **CYANITIC** *adj*
CYANO *adj* pertaining to cyanogen
CYANOGEN *n* pl. -S a reactive compound of carbon and nitrogen
CYANOSIS *n* pl. -NOSES bluish discoloration of the skin **CYANOSED, CYANOTIC** *adj*
CYBORG *n* pl. -S a human linked to a mechanical device for life support
CYCAD *n* pl. -S a tropical plant
CYCAS *n* pl. -ES a tropical plant
CYCASIN *n* pl. -S a sugar derivative
CYCLAMEN *n* pl. -S a flowering plant
CYCLASE *n* pl. -S an enzyme
CYCLE *v* -CLED, -CLING, -CLES to ride a bicycle
CYCLECAR *n* pl. -S a type of motor vehicle
CYCLER *n* pl. -S a cyclist
CYCLERY *n* pl. -RIES a bicycle shop
CYCLIC *adj* moving in complete circles **CYCLICLY** *adv*

CYCLICAL *n* pl. -S a stock whose earnings fluctuate widely with variations in the economy
CYCLING *n* pl. -S the act of riding a bicycle
CYCLIST *n* pl. -S one who rides a bicycle
CYCLITOL *n* pl. -S a chemical compound
CYCLIZE *v* -CLIZED, -CLIZING, -CLIZES to form one or more rings in a chemical compound
CYCLO *n* pl. -CLOS a three-wheeled motor vehicle
CYCLOID *n* pl. -S a geometric curve
CYCLONE *n* pl. -S a rotating system of winds **CYCLONAL, CYCLONIC** *adj*
CYCLOPS *n* pl. CYCLOPS a freshwater animal
CYCLOSIS *n* pl. -CLOSES the circulation of protoplasm within a cell
CYDER *n* pl. -S cider
CYESIS *n* pl. CYESES pregnancy
CYGNET *n* pl. -S a young swan
CYLINDER *v* -ED, -ING, -S to furnish with a cylinder (a chamber in an engine)
CYLIX *n* pl. CYLICES kylix
CYMA *n* pl. -MAS or -MAE a curved molding
CYMAR *n* pl. -S simar
CYMATIUM *n* pl. -TIA a cyma
CYMBAL *n* pl. -S a percussion instrument
CYMBALER *n* pl. -S one that plays the cymbals
CYMBALOM *n* pl. -S cimbalom
CYMBIDIA *n/pl* tropical orchids
CYMBLING *n* pl. -S cymling
CYME *n* pl. -S a flower cluster
CYMENE *n* pl. -S a hydrocarbon
CYMLIN *n* pl. -S cymling
CYMLING *n* pl. -S a variety of squash
CYMOGENE *n* pl. -S a volatile compound
CYMOID *adj* resembling a cyma
CYMOL *n* pl. -S cymene
CYMOSE *adj* resembling a cyme **CYMOSELY** *adv*
CYMOUS *adj* cymose
CYNIC *n* pl. -S a cynical person
CYNICAL *adj* distrusting the motives of others
CYNICISM *n* pl. -S cynical quality
CYNOSURE *n* pl. -S a center of attraction
CYPHER *v* -ED, -ING, -S to cipher
CYPRES *n* pl. -ES a legal doctrine

CYPRESS   *n* pl. -ES a thin fabric
CYPRIAN   *n* pl. -S a prostitute
CYPRINID   *n* pl. -S a small freshwater fish
CYPRUS   *n* pl. -ES cypress
CYPSELA   *n* pl. -LAE an achene in certain plants
CYST   *n* pl. -S a sac
CYSTEIN   *n* pl. -S cysteine
CYSTEINE   *n* pl. -S an amino acid
CYSTIC   *adj* pertaining to a cyst
CYSTINE   *n* pl. -S an amino acid
CYSTITIS   *n* pl. -TITIDES inflammation of the urinary bladder
CYSTOID   *n* pl. -S a cyst-like structure
CYTASTER   *n* pl. -S a structure formed in a cell during mitosis
CYTIDINE   *n* pl. -S a compound containing cytosine
CYTOGENY   *n* pl. -NIES the formation of cells

CYTOKINE   *n* pl. -S a kind of substance secreted by cells of the immune system
CYTOLOGY   *n* pl. -GIES a study of cells
CYTON   *n* pl. -S the body of a nerve cell
CYTOSINE   *n* pl. -S a component of DNA and RNA
CYTOSOL   *n* pl. -S the fluid portion of cell material
CZAR   *n* pl. -S an emperor or king
CZARDAS   *n* pl. CZARDAS a Hungarian dance
CZARDOM   *n* pl. -S the domain of a czar
CZAREVNA   *n* pl. -S the daughter of a czar
CZARINA   *n* pl. -S the wife of a czar
CZARISM   *n* pl. -S autocratic government
CZARIST   *n* pl. -S a supporter of czarism
CZARITZA   *n* pl. -S a czarina

DA *prep* of; from — used in names

DAB *v* DABBED, DABBING, DABS to touch lightly

DABBER *n* pl. -S one that dabs

DABBLE *v* -BLED, -BLING, -BLES to splash

DABBLER *n* pl. -S one that dabbles

DABBLING *n* pl. -S a superficial interest

DABCHICK *n* pl. -S a small grebe

DABSTER *n* pl. -S a bungler

DACE *n* pl. -S a freshwater fish

DACHA *n* pl. -S a Russian cottage

DACKER *v* -ED, -ING, -S to waver

DACOIT *n* pl. -S a bandit in India

DACOITY *n* pl. -COITIES robbery by dacoits

DACTYL *n* pl. -S a type of metrical foot

DACTYLIC *n* pl. -S a verse consisting of dactyls

DACTYLUS *n* pl. -LI a leg joint of certain insects

DAD *n* pl. -S father

DADA *n* pl. -S an artistic and literary movement

DADAISM *n* pl. -S the dada movement

DADAIST *n* pl. -S a follower of dadaism

DADDLE *v* -DLED, -DLING, -DLES to diddle

DADDY *n* pl. -DIES father

DADO *v* -ED, -ING, -ES or -S to set into a groove

DAEDAL *adj* skillful

DAEMON *n* pl. -S demon **DAEMONIC** *adj*

DAFF *v* -ED, -ING, -S to thrust aside

DAFFODIL *n* pl. -S a flowering plant

DAFFY *adj* -FIER, -FIEST silly **DAFFILY** *adv*

DAFT *adj* DAFTER, DAFTEST insane **DAFTLY** *adv*

DAFTNESS *n* pl. -ES the quality of being daft

DAG *n* pl. -S a hanging end or shred

DAGGA *n* pl. -S marijuana

DAGGER *v* -ED, -ING, -S to stab with a small knife

DAGGLE *v* -GLED, -GLING, -GLES to drag in mud

DAGLOCK *n* pl. -S a dirty or tangled lock of wool

DAGOBA *n* pl. -S a Buddhist shrine

DAGWOOD *n* pl. -S a large sandwich

DAH *n* pl. -S a dash in Morse code

DAHABEAH *n* pl. -S a large passenger boat

DAHABIAH *n* pl. -S dahabeah

DAHABIEH *n* pl. -S dahabeah

DAHABIYA *n* pl. -S dahabeah

DAHL *n* pl. -S dal

DAHLIA *n* pl. -S a flowering plant

DAHOON *n* pl. -S an evergreen tree

DAIKER *v* -ED, -ING, -S to dacker

DAIKON *n* pl. -S a Japanese radish

DAILY *n* pl. -LIES a newspaper published every weekday

DAIMEN *adj* occasional

DAIMIO *n* pl. -MIOS a former Japanese nobleman

DAIMON *n* pl. -S or -ES an attendant spirit **DAIMONIC** *adj*

DAIMYO *n* pl. -MYOS daimio

DAINTY *n* pl. -TIES something delicious

DAINTY *adj* -TIER, -TIEST delicately pretty **DAINTILY** *adv*

DAIQUIRI *n* pl. -S a cocktail

DAIRY *n* pl. DAIRIES an establishment dealing in milk products

DAIRYING *n* pl. -S the business of a dairy

DAIRYMAN *n* pl. -MEN a man who works in or owns a dairy

DAIS *n* pl. -ISES a raised platform

DAISHIKI *n* pl. -S dashiki

DAISY *n* pl. -SIES a flowering plant **DAISIED** *adj*

DAK *n* pl. -S transportation by relays of men and horses

DAKERHEN *n* pl. -S a European bird

DAKOIT *n* pl. -S dacoit

DAKOITY *n* pl. -TIES dacoity

DAL *n* pl. -S a dish of lentils and spices in India

DALAPON *n* pl. -S an herbicide used on unwanted grasses

DALASI *n* pl. DALASI or DALASIS a unit of Gambian currency

DALE *n* pl. -S a valley

DALEDH *n* pl. -S daleth

DALESMAN *n* pl. -MEN one living in a dale

DALETH *n* pl. -S a Hebrew letter

DALLES *n/pl* rapids

DALLIER *n* pl. -S one that dallies

DALLY *v* -LIED, -LYING, -LIES to waste time

DALMATIC *n* pl. -S a wide-sleeved vestment

DALTON *n* pl. -S a unit of atomic mass

DALTONIC *adj* pertaining to a form of color blindness

DAM *v* DAMMED, DAMMING, DAMS to build a barrier to obstruct the flow of water

DAMAGE *v* -AGED, -AGING, -AGES to injure

DAMAGER *n* pl. -S one that damages

DAMAN *n* pl. -S a small mammal

DAMAR *n* pl. -S dammar

DAMASK *v* -ED, -ING, -S to weave with elaborate design

DAME *n* pl. -S a matron

DAMEWORT *n* pl. -S a flowering plant

DAMMAR *n* pl. -S a hard resin

DAMMED past tense of dam

DAMMER *n* pl. -S dammar

DAMMING present participle of dam

DAMN *v* -ED, -ING, -S to curse

DAMNABLE *adj* detestable **DAMNABLY** *adv*

DAMNDEST *n* pl. -S utmost

DAMNED *adj* DAMNEDER, DAMNEDEST or DAMNDEST damnable

DAMNER *n* pl. -S one that damns

DAMNIFY *v* -FIED, -FYING, -FIES to cause loss or damage to

DAMOSEL *n* pl. -S damsel

DAMOZEL *n* pl. -S damsel

DAMP *adj* DAMPER, DAMPEST moist

DAMP *v* -ED, -ING, -S to lessen in intensity

DAMPEN *v* -ED, -ING, -S to moisten

DAMPENER *n* pl. -S one that dampens

DAMPER *n* pl. -S one that damps

DAMPING *n* pl. -S the ability of a device to prevent instability

DAMPISH *adj* somewhat damp

DAMPLY *adv* in a damp manner

DAMPNESS *n* pl. -ES the state of being damp

DAMSEL *n* pl. -S a maiden

DAMSON *n* pl. -S a small purple plum

DANCE *v* DANCED, DANCING, DANCES to move rhythmically to music

DANCER *n* pl. -S one that dances

DANDER *v* -ED, -ING, -S to stroll

DANDIER comparative of dandy

DANDIES pl. of dandy

DANDIEST superlative of dandy

DANDIFY *v* -FIED, -FYING, -FIES to cause to resemble a dandy

DANDILY *adv* in a dandy manner

DANDLE *v* -DLED, -DLING, -DLES to fondle

DANDLER *n* pl. -S one that dandles

DANDRIFF *n* pl. -S dandruff

DANDRUFF *n* pl. -S a scurf that forms on the scalp

DANDY *adj* -DIER, -DIEST fine

DANDY *n* pl. -DIES a man who is overly concerned about his appearance

DANDYISH *adj* suggestive of a dandy

DANDYISM *n* pl. -S the style or conduct of a dandy

DANEGELD *n* pl. -S an annual tax in medieval England

DANEWEED *n* pl. -S a danewort

DANEWORT *n* pl. -S a flowering plant

DANG *v* -ED, -ING, -S to damn

DANGER *v* -ED, -ING, -S to endanger

DANGLE *v* -GLED, -GLING, -GLES to hang loosely

DANGLER *n* pl. -S one that dangles

DANIO	*n* pl. -NIOS an aquarium fish	**DARN**	*v* -ED, -ING, -S to mend with
DANISH	*n* pl. DANISH a pastry of		interlacing stitches
	raised dough	**DARNDEST**	*n* pl. -S damndest
DANK	*adj* DANKER, DANKEST	**DARNED**	*adj* DARNEDER,
	unpleasantly damp **DANKLY**		DARNEDEST or DARNDEST
	adv		damned
DANKNESS	*n* pl. -ES the state of being	**DARNEL**	*n* pl. -S an annual grass
	dank	**DARNER**	*n* pl. -S one that darns
DANSEUR	*n* pl. -S a male ballet dancer	**DARNING**	*n* pl. -S things to be darned
DANSEUSE	*n* pl. -S a female ballet dancer	**DARSHAN**	*n* pl. -S a Hindu blessing
DAP	*v* DAPPED, DAPPING, DAPS	**DART**	*v* -ED, -ING, -S to move
	to dip lightly or quickly into		suddenly or swiftly
	water	**DARTER**	*n* pl. -S one that darts
DAPHNE	*n* pl. -S a flowering shrub	**DARTLE**	*v* -TLED, -TLING, -TLES to
DAPHNIA	*n* pl. -S a minute crustacean		dart repeatedly
DAPPED	past tense of dap	**DASH**	*v* -ED, -ING, -ES to strike
DAPPER	*adj* -PERER, -PEREST		violently
	looking neat and trim	**DASHEEN**	*n* pl. -S a tropical plant
	DAPPERLY *adv*	**DASHER**	*n* pl. -S one that dashes
DAPPING	present participle of dap	**DASHI**	*n* pl. -S a fish broth
DAPPLE	*v* -PLED, -PLING, -PLES to	**DASHIER**	comparative of dashy
	mark with spots	**DASHIEST**	superlative of dashy
DAPSONE	*n* pl. -S a medicinal substance	**DASHIKI**	*n* pl. -S an African tunic
DARB	*n* pl. -S something considered	**DASHPOT**	*n* pl. -S a shock absorber
	extraordinary	**DASHY**	*adj* DASHIER, DASHIEST
DARBIES	*n/pl* handcuffs		stylish
DARE	*v* DARED or DURST,	**DASSIE**	*n* pl. -S a hyrax
	DARING, DARES to have the	**DASTARD**	*n* pl. -S a base coward
	necessary courage	**DASYURE**	*n* pl. -S a flesh-eating mammal
DAREFUL	*adj* brave	**DATA**	a pl. of datum
DARER	*n* pl. -S one that dares	**DATABANK**	*n* pl. -S a database
DARESAY	*v* to venture to say —	**DATABASE**	*n* pl. -S a collection of data in
	DARESAY is the only form of		a computer
	this verb; it is not conjugated	**DATABLE**	*adj* capable of being dated
DARIC	*n* pl. -S an ancient Persian	**DATARY**	*n* pl. -RIES a cardinal in the
	coin		Roman Catholic Church
DARING	*n* pl. -S bravery	**DATCHA**	*n* pl. -S dacha
DARINGLY	*adv* in a brave manner	**DATE**	*v* DATED, DATING, DATES to
DARIOLE	*n* pl. -S a type of pastry filled		determine or record the date of
	with cream, custard, or jelly		**DATEABLE** *adj*
DARK	*adj* DARKER, DARKEST	**DATEDLY**	*adv* in an old-fashioned
	having little or no light		manner
DARK	*v* -ED, -ING, -S to darken	**DATELESS**	*adj* having no date
DARKEN	*v* -ED, -ING, -S to make dark	**DATELINE**	*v* -LINED, -LINING, -LINES to
DARKENER	*n* pl. -S one that darkens		provide a news story with its
DARKISH	*adj* somewhat dark		date and place of origin
DARKLE	*v* -KLED, -KLING, -KLES to	**DATER**	*n* pl. -S one that dates
	become dark	**DATING**	present participle of date
DARKLY	*adv* -LIER, -LIEST in a dark	**DATIVE**	*n* pl. -S a grammatical case
	manner		**DATIVAL** *adj* **DATIVELY** *adv*
DARKNESS	*n* pl. -ES the state of being	**DATO**	*n* pl. -TOS datto
	dark	**DATTO**	*n* pl. -TOS a Philippine tribal
DARKROOM	*n* pl. -S a room in which film is		chief
	processed	**DATUM**	*n* pl. -TA or -TUMS something
DARKSOME	*adj* dark		used as a basis for calculating
DARLING	*n* pl. -S a much-loved person		

DATURA n pl. -S a flowering plant **DATURIC** adj

DAUB v -ED, -ING, -S to smear

DAUBE n pl. -S a braised meat stew

DAUBER n pl. -S one that daubs

DAUBERY n pl. -ERIES a bad or inexpert painting

DAUBRY n pl. -RIES daubery

DAUBY adj DAUBIER, DAUBIEST smeary

DAUGHTER n pl. -S a female child

DAUNDER v -ED, -ING, -S to dander

DAUNT v -ED, -ING, -S to intimidate

DAUNTER n pl. -S one that daunts

DAUPHIN n pl. -S the eldest son of a French king

DAUPHINE n pl. -S the wife of a dauphin

DAUT v -ED, -ING, -S to fondle

DAUTIE n pl. -S a small pet

DAVEN v -ED, -ING, -S to utter Jewish prayers

DAVIT n pl. -S a hoisting device on a ship

DAVY n pl. -VIES a safety lamp

DAW v DAWED, DAWEN, DAWING, DAWS to dawn

DAWDLE v -DLED, -DLING, -DLES to waste time

DAWDLER n pl. -S one that dawdles

DAWEN past participle of daw

DAWK n pl. -S dak

DAWN v -ED, -ING, -S to begin to grow light in the morning

DAWNLIKE adj suggestive of daybreak

DAWT v -ED, -ING, -S to daut

DAWTIE n pl. -S dautie

DAY n pl. DAYS the time between sunrise and sunset

DAYBED n pl. -S a couch that can be converted into a bed

DAYBOOK n pl. -S a diary

DAYBREAK n pl. -S the first appearance of light in the morning

DAYDREAM v -DREAMED or -DREAMT, -DREAMING, -DREAMS to fantasize

DAYFLY n pl. -FLIES a mayfly

DAYGLOW n pl. -S airglow seen during the day

DAYLIGHT v -LIGHTED or -LIT, -LIGHTING, -LIGHTS to illuminate with the light of day

DAYLILY n pl. -LILIES a flowering plant

DAYLONG adj lasting all day

DAYMARE n pl. -S a nightmarish fantasy experienced while awake

DAYROOM n pl. -S a room for reading and recreation

DAYSIDE n pl. -S the sun side of a planet or the moon

DAYSMAN n pl. -MEN an arbiter

DAYSTAR n pl. -S a planet visible in the east just before sunrise

DAYTIME n pl. -S day

DAYWORK n pl. -S work done on a daily basis

DAZE v DAZED, DAZING, DAZES to stun **DAZEDLY** adv

DAZZLE v -ZLED, -ZLING, -ZLES to blind by bright light

DAZZLER n pl. -S one that dazzles

DE prep of; from — used in names

DEACON v -ED, -ING, -S to read a hymn aloud

DEACONRY n pl. -RIES a clerical office

DEAD adj DEADER, DEADEST deprived of life

DEAD n pl. -S the period of greatest intensity

DEADBEAT n pl. -S a loafer

DEADBOLT n pl. -S a lock for a door

DEADEN v -ED, -ING, -S to diminish the sensitivity or vigor of

DEADENER n pl. -S one that deadens

DEADEYE n pl. -S an expert marksman

DEADFALL n pl. -S a type of animal trap

DEADHEAD v -ED, -ING, -S to travel without freight

DEADLIER comparative of deadly

DEADLIEST superlative of deadly

DEADLIFT v -ED, -ING, -S to execute a type of lift in weight lifting

DEADLINE n pl. -S a time limit

DEADLOCK v -ED, -ING, -S to come to a standstill

DEADLY adj -LIER, -LIEST fatal

DEADNESS n pl. -ES the state of being dead

DEADPAN v -PANNED, -PANNING, -PANS to act without emotion

DEADWOOD n pl. -S a reinforcement in a ship's keel

DEAERATE v -ATED, -ATING, -ATES to remove air or gas from

DEAF adj DEAFER, DEAFEST lacking the sense of hearing

DEAFEN v -ED, -ING, -S to make deaf

DEAFISH adj somewhat deaf

DEAFLY adv in a deaf manner

DEAFNESS n pl. -ES the state of being deaf

DEAIR   v -ED, -ING, -S to remove air from

DEAL   v DEALT, DEALING, DEALS to trade or do business

DEALATE   n pl. -S an insect divested of its wings **DEALATED** adj

DEALER   n pl. -S one that deals

DEALFISH   n pl. -ES a marine fish

DEALING   n pl. -S a business transaction

DEALT   past tense of deal

DEAN   v -ED, -ING, -S to serve as dean (the head of a faculty)

DEANERY   n pl. -ERIES the office of a dean

DEANSHIP   n pl. -S deanery

DEAR   adj DEARER, DEAREST greatly loved

DEAR   n pl. -S a loved one

DEARIE   n pl. -S deary

DEARIES   pl. of deary

DEARLY   adv in a dear manner

DEARNESS   n pl. -ES the state of being dear

DEARTH   n pl. -S scarcity

DEARY   n pl. DEARIES darling

DEASH   v -ED, -ING, -ES to remove ash from

DEASIL   adv clockwise

DEATH   n pl. -S the end of life

DEATHBED   n pl. -S the bed on which a person dies

DEATHCUP   n pl. -S a poisonous mushroom

DEATHFUL   adj fatal

DEATHLY   adj fatal

DEATHY   adj deathly

DEAVE   v DEAVED, DEAVING, DEAVES to deafen

DEB   n pl. -S a debutante

DEBACLE   n pl. -S a sudden collapse

DEBAR   v -BARRED, -BARRING, -BARS to exclude

DEBARK   v -ED, -ING, -S to unload from a ship

DEBASE   v -BASED, -BASING, -BASES to lower in character, quality, or value

DEBASER   n pl. -S one that debases

DEBATE   v -BATED, -BATING, -BATES to argue about

DEBATER   n pl. -S one that debates

DEBAUCH   v -ED, -ING, -ES to corrupt

DEBEAK   v -ED, -ING, -S to remove the tip of the upper beak of

DEBILITY   n pl. -TIES weakness

DEBIT   v -ED, -ING, -S to charge with a debt

DEBONAIR   adj suave

DEBONE   v -BONED, -BONING, -BONES to remove the bones from

DEBONER   n pl. -S a bone remover

DEBOUCH   v -ED, -ING, -ES to march into the open

DEBOUCHE   n pl. -S an opening for the passage of troops

DEBRIDE   v -BRIDED, -BRIDING, -BRIDES to remove dead tissue surgically

DEBRIEF   v -ED, -ING, -S to question after a mission

DEBRIS   n pl. DEBRIS fragments or scattered remains

DEBRUISE   v -BRUISED, -BRUISING, -BRUISES to cross a coat of arms

DEBT   n pl. -S something that is owed **DEBTLESS** adj

DEBTOR   n pl. -S one who owes something to another

DEBUG   v -BUGGED, -BUGGING, -BUGS to remove bugs from

DEBUGGER   n pl. -S one that debugs

DEBUNK   v -ED, -ING, -S to expose the sham or falseness of

DEBUNKER   n pl. -S one that debunks

DEBUT   v -ED, -ING, -S to make one's first public appearance

DEBUTANT   n pl. -S one who is debuting

DEBYE   n pl. -S a unit of measure for electric dipole moments

DECADE   n pl. -S a period of ten years **DECADAL** adj

DECADENT   n pl. -S one in a state of mental or moral decay

DECAF   n pl. -S decaffeinated coffee

DECAGON   n pl. -S a ten-sided polygon

DECAGRAM   n pl. -S dekagram

DECAL   n pl. -S a picture or design made to be transferred from specially prepared paper

DECALOG   n pl. -S the Ten Commandments

DECAMP   v -ED, -ING, -S to depart from a camping ground

DECANAL   adj pertaining to a dean

DECANE   n pl. -S a hydrocarbon

DECANT   v -ED, -ING, -S to pour from one container into another

DECANTER   n pl. -S a decorative bottle

DECAPOD   *n* pl. -S a ten-legged crustacean

DECARE   *n* pl. -S dekare

DECAY   *v* -ED, -ING, -S to decompose

DECAYER   *n* pl. -S one that decays

DECEASE   *v* -CEASED, -CEASING, -CEASES to die

DECEDENT   *n* pl. -S a deceased person

DECEIT   *n* pl. -S the act of deceiving

DECEIVE   *v* -CEIVED, -CEIVING, -CEIVES to mislead by falsehood

DECEIVER   *n* pl. -S one that deceives

DECEMVIR   *n* pl. -VIRS or -VIRI one of a body of ten Roman magistrates

DECENARY   *n* pl. -RIES a tithing

DECENCY   *n* pl. -CIES the state of being decent

DECENNIA   *n/pl* decades

DECENT   *adj* -CENTER, -CENTEST conforming to recognized standards of propriety **DECENTLY** *adv*

DECENTER   *v* -ED, -ING, -S to put out of center

DECENTRE   *v* -TRED, -TRING, -TRES to decenter

DECERN   *v* -ED, -ING, -S to decree by judicial sentence

DECIARE   *n* pl. -S a metric unit of area

DECIBEL   *n* pl. -S a unit of sound intensity

DECIDE   *v* -CIDED, -CIDING, -CIDES to make a choice or judgment

DECIDER   *n* pl. -S one that decides

DECIDUA   *n* pl. -UAS or -UAE a mucous membrane of the uterus **DECIDUAL** *adj*

DECIGRAM   *n* pl. -S one tenth of a gram

DECILE   *n* pl. -S a statistical interval

DECIMAL   *n* pl. -S a fraction whose denominator is some power of ten

DECIMATE   *v* -MATED, -MATING, -MATES to destroy a large part of

DECIPHER   *v* -ED, -ING, -S to determine the meaning of

DECISION   *n* pl. -S the act of deciding

DECISIVE   *adj* conclusive

DECK   *v* -ED, -ING, -S to adorn

DECKEL   *n* pl. -S deckle

DECKER   *n* pl. -S something having a specified number of levels, floors, or layers

DECKHAND   *n* pl. -S a seaman who performs manual duties

DECKING   *n* pl. -S material for a ship's deck

DECKLE   *n* pl. -S a frame used in making paper by hand

DECLAIM   *v* -ED, -ING, -S to speak formally

DECLARE   *v* -CLARED, -CLARING, -CLARES to make known clearly

DECLARER   *n* pl. -S one that declares

DECLASS   *v* -ED, -ING, -ES to lower in status

DECLASSE   *adj* lowered in status

DECLINE   *v* -CLINED, -CLINING, -CLINES to refuse

DECLINER   *n* pl. -S one that declines

DECO   *n* pl. DECOS a decorative style

DECOCT   *v* -ED, -ING, -S to extract the flavor of by boiling

DECODE   *v* -CODED, -CODING, -CODES to convert a coded message into plain language

DECODER   *n* pl. -S one that decodes

DECOLOR   *v* -ED, -ING, -S to deprive of color

DECOLOUR   *v* -ED, -ING, -S to decolor

DECOR   *n* pl. -S style or mode of decoration

DECORATE   *v* -RATED, -RATING, -RATES to adorn

DECOROUS   *adj* proper

DECORUM   *n* pl. -S conformity to social conventions

DECOUPLE   *v* -PLED, -PLING, -PLES to disconnect

DECOY   *v* -ED, -ING, -S to lure into a trap

DECOYER   *n* pl. -S one that decoys

DECREASE   *v* -CREASED, -CREASING, -CREASES to diminish

DECREE   *v* -CREED, -CREEING, -CREES to order or establish by law or edict

DECREER   *n* pl. -S one that decrees

DECREPIT   *adj* worn out by long use

DECRETAL   *n* pl. -S a papal edict

DECRIAL   *n* pl. -S the act of decrying

DECRIED   past tense of decry

DECRIER   *n* pl. -S one that decries

DECROWN   *v* -ED, -ING, -S to deprive of a crown; depose

DECRY   *v* -CRIED, -CRYING, -CRIES to denounce

DECRYPT   v -ED, -ING, -S to decode
DECUMAN   adj extremely large
DECUPLE   v -PLED, -PLING, -PLES to increase tenfold
DECURIES   pl. of decury
DECURION   n pl. -S a commander of a decury
DECURVE   v -CURVED, -CURVING, -CURVES to curve downward
DECURY   n pl. -RIES a group of ten soldiers in ancient Rome
DEDAL   adj daedal
DEDANS   n pl. DEDANS a gallery for tennis spectators
DEDICATE   v -CATED, -CATING, -CATES to set apart for some special use
DEDUCE   v -DUCED, -DUCING, -DUCES to infer
DEDUCT   v -ED, -ING, -S to subtract
DEE   n pl. -S the letter D
DEED   v -ED, -ING, -S to transfer by deed (a legal document)
DEEDLESS   adj being without deeds
DEEDY   adj DEEDIER, DEEDIEST industrious
DEEJAY   n pl. -JAYS a disc jockey
DEEM   v -ED, -ING, -S to hold as an opinion
DEEMSTER   n pl. -S a judicial officer of the Isle of Man
DEEP   adj DEEPER, DEEPEST extending far down from a surface
DEEP   n pl. -S a place or thing of great depth
DEEPEN   v -ED, -ING, -S to make deep
DEEPENER   n pl. -S one that deepens
DEEPLY   adv at or to a great depth
DEEPNESS   n pl. -ES the quality of being deep
DEER   n pl. -S a ruminant mammal DEERLIKE adj
DEERFLY   n pl. -FLIES a bloodsucking fly
DEERSKIN   n pl. -S the skin of a deer
DEERWEED   n pl. -S a bushlike herb
DEERYARD   n pl. -S an area where deer herd in winter
DEET   n pl. -S an insect repellent
DEEWAN   n pl. -S dewan
DEFACE   v -FACED, -FACING, -FACES to mar the appearance of
DEFACER   n pl. -S one that defaces
DEFAME   v -FAMED, -FAMING, -FAMES to attack the good name of

DEFAMER   n pl. -S one that defames
DEFANG   v -ED, -ING, -S to make harmless
DEFAT   v -FATTED, -FATTING, -FATS to remove fat from
DEFAULT   v -ED, -ING, -S to fail to do something required
DEFEAT   v -ED, -ING, -S to win victory over
DEFEATER   n pl. -S one that defeats
DEFECATE   v -CATED, -CATING, -CATES to discharge feces
DEFECT   v -ED, -ING, -S to desert an allegiance
DEFECTOR   n pl. -S one that defects
DEFENCE   n pl. -S something that defends
DEFEND   v -ED, -ING, -S to protect
DEFENDER   n pl. -S one that defends
DEFENSE   v -FENSED, -FENSING, -FENSES to guard against a specific attack
DEFER   v -FERRED, -FERRING, -FERS to postpone
DEFERENT   n pl. -S an imaginary circle around the earth
DEFERRAL   n pl. -S the act of deferring
DEFERRED   past tense of defer
DEFERRER   n pl. -S one that defers
DEFERRING   present participle of defer
DEFI   n pl. -S a challenge
DEFIANCE   n pl. -S bold opposition
DEFIANT   adj showing defiance
DEFICIT   n pl. -S a shortage
DEFIED   past tense of defy
DEFIER   n pl. -S one that defies
DEFIES   present 3d person sing. of defy
DEFILADE   v -LADED, -LADING, -LADES to shield from enemy fire
DEFILE   v -FILED, -FILING, -FILES to make dirty
DEFILER   n pl. -S one that defiles
DEFINE   v -FINED, -FINING, -FINES to state the meaning of
DEFINER   n pl. -S one that defines
DEFINITE   adj known for certain
DEFLATE   v -FLATED, -FLATING, -FLATES to release the air or gas from
DEFLATER   n pl. -S one that deflates
DEFLATOR   n pl. -S one that deflates
DEFLEA   v -ED, -ING, -S to rid of fleas
DEFLECT   v -ED, -ING, -S to turn aside
DEFLEXED   adj bent downward
DEFLOWER   v -ED, -ING, -S to deprive of flowers

DEFOAM v -ED, -ING, -S to remove foam from

DEFOAMER n pl. -S one that defoams

DEFOCUS v -CUSED, -CUSING, -CUSES or -CUSSED, -CUSSING, -CUSSES to cause to go out of focus

DEFOG v -FOGGED, -FOGGING, -FOGS to remove fog from

DEFOGGER n pl. -S one that defogs

DEFORCE v -FORCED, -FORCING, -FORCES to withhold by force

DEFOREST v -ED, -ING, -S to clear of forests

DEFORM v -ED, -ING, -S to spoil the form of

DEFORMER n pl. -S one that deforms

DEFRAUD v -ED, -ING, -S to swindle

DEFRAY v -ED, -ING, -S to pay

DEFRAYAL n pl. -S the act of defraying

DEFRAYER n pl. -S one that defrays

DEFROCK v -ED, -ING, -S to unfrock

DEFROST v -ED, -ING, -S to remove frost from

DEFT adj DEFTER, DEFTEST skillful DEFTLY adv

DEFTNESS n pl. -ES the quality of being deft

DEFUNCT adj deceased

DEFUND v -ED, -ING, -S to withdraw funding from

DEFUSE v -FUSED, -FUSING, -FUSES to remove the fuse from

DEFUZE v -FUZED, -FUZING, -FUZES to defuse

DEFY v -FIED, -FYING, -FIES to resist openly and boldly

DEGAGE adj free and relaxed in manner

DEGAME n pl. -S a tropical tree

DEGAMI n pl. -S degame

DEGAS v -GASSED, -GASSING, -GASSES or -GASES to remove gas from

DEGASSER n pl. -S one that degasses

DEGAUSS v -ED, -ING, -ES to demagnetize

DEGERM v -ED, -ING, -S to remove germs from

DEGLAZE v -GLAZED, -GLAZING, -GLAZES to remove the glaze from

DEGRADE v -GRADED, -GRADING, -GRADES to debase

DEGRADER n pl. -S one that degrades

DEGREASE v -GREASED, -GREASING, -GREASES to remove the grease from

DEGREE n pl. -S one of a series of stages DEGREED adj

DEGUM v -GUMMED, -GUMMING, -GUMS to free from gum

DEGUST v -ED, -ING, -S to taste with pleasure

DEHISCE v -HISCED, -HISCING, -HISCES to split open

DEHORN v -ED, -ING, -S to deprive of horns

DEHORNER n pl. -S one that dehorns

DEHORT v -ED, -ING, -S to try to dissuade

DEI prep of; from — used in names

DEICE v -ICED, -ICING, -ICES to free from ice

DEICER n pl. -S one that deices

DEICIDE n pl. -S the killing of a god DEICIDAL adj

DEICING present participle of deice

DEICTIC adj proving directly

DEIFIC adj godlike

DEIFICAL adj deific

DEIFIED past tense of deify

DEIFIER n pl. -S one that deifies

DEIFORM adj having the form of a god

DEIFY v -FIED, -FYING, -FIES to make a god of

DEIGN v -ED, -ING, -S to lower oneself to do something

DEIL n pl. -S the devil

DEIONIZE v -IZED, -IZING, -IZES to remove ions from

DEISM n pl. -S a religious philosophy

DEIST n pl. -S an adherent of deism DEISTIC adj

DEITY n pl. -TIES a god or goddess

DEIXIS n pl. DEIXISES the specifying function of some words

DEJECT v -ED, -ING, -S to depress

DEJECTA n/pl excrements

DEJEUNER n pl. -S a late breakfast

DEKAGRAM n pl. -S a measure equal to ten grams

DEKARE n pl. -S a measure equal to ten ares

DEKE v DEKED, DEKING, DEKES to feint in hockey

DEKKO n pl. -KOS a look

DEL n pl. -S an operator in differential calculus

DELAINE n pl. -S a wool fabric

DELATE v -LATED, -LATING, -LATES to accuse

DELATION n pl. -S the act of delating

DELATOR n pl. -S one that delates

DELAY v -ED, -ING, -S to put off to a later time

DELAYER n pl. -S one that delays

DELE v DELED, DELEING, DELES to delete

DELEAD v -ED, -ING, -S to remove lead from

DELEAVE v -LEAVED, -LEAVING, -LEAVES to separate the copies of

DELEGACY n pl. -CIES the act of delegating

DELEGATE v -GATED, -GATING, -GATES to appoint as one's representative

DELETE v -LETED, -LETING, -LETES to remove written or printed matter

DELETION n pl. -S the act of deleting

DELF n pl. -S delft

DELFT n pl. -S an earthenware

DELI n pl. DELIS a delicatessen

DELICACY n pl. -CIES a choice food

DELICATE n pl. -S a delicacy

DELICT n pl. -S an offense against civil law

DELIGHT v -ED, -ING, -S to give great pleasure to

DELIME v -LIMED, -LIMING, -LIMES to free from lime

DELIMIT v -ED, -ING, -S to mark the boundaries of

DELIRIUM n pl. -IUMS or -IA wild excitement

DELIST v -ED, -ING, -S to remove from a list

DELIVER v -ED, -ING, -S to take to the intended recipient

DELIVERY n pl. -ERIES the act of delivering

DELL n pl. -S a small, wooded valley

DELLY n pl. DELLIES deli

DELOUSE v -LOUSED, -LOUSING, -LOUSES to remove lice from

DELOUSER n pl. -S one that gets rid of lice

DELTA n pl. -S an alluvial deposit at the mouth of a river **DELTAIC, DELTIC** adj

DELTOID n pl. -S a shoulder muscle

DELUDE v -LUDED, -LUDING, -LUDES to mislead the mind or judgment of

DELUDER n pl. -S one that deludes

DELUGE v -UGED, -UGING, -UGES to flood

DELUSION n pl. -S the act of deluding

DELUSIVE adj tending to delude

DELUSORY adj delusive

DELUSTER v -ED, -ING, -S to lessen the sheen of

DELUXE adj of special elegance or luxury

DELVE v DELVED, DELVING, DELVES to search in depth

DELVER n pl. -S one that delves

DEMAGOG v -ED, -ING, -S to behave like a demagog (a leader who appeals to emotions and prejudices)

DEMAGOGY n pl. -GOGIES the rule of a demagog

DEMAND v -ED, -ING, -S to ask for with authority

DEMANDER n pl. -S one that demands

DEMARCHE n pl. -S a procedure

DEMARK v -ED, -ING, -S to delimit

DEMAST v -ED, -ING, -S to strip masts from

DEME n pl. -S a Greek district

DEMEAN v -ED, -ING, -S to conduct oneself in a particular manner

DEMEANOR n pl. -S the manner in which one conducts oneself

DEMENT v -ED, -ING, -S to make insane

DEMENTIA n pl. -S mental illness

DEMERARA n pl. -S a coarse light-brown sugar

DEMERGE v -MERGED, -MERGING, -MERGES to remove a division from a corporation

DEMERGER v -ED, -ING, -S to demerge

DEMERIT v -ED, -ING, -S to lower in rank or status

DEMERSAL adj found at the bottom of the sea

DEMESNE n pl. -S the legal possession of land as one's own

DEMETON n pl. -S an insecticide

DEMIES pl. of demy

DEMIGOD n pl. -S a lesser god

DEMIJOHN n pl. -S a narrow-necked jug

DEMILUNE n pl. -S a half-moon

DEMIREP n pl. -S a prostitute

DEMISE v -MISED, -MISING, -MISES to bequeath

DEMIT v -MITTED, -MITTING, -MITS to resign

DEMIURGE *n* pl. -S a magistrate of ancient Greece

DEMIVOLT *n* pl. -S a half turn made by a horse

DEMO *n* pl. DEMOS a demonstration

DEMOB *v* -MOBBED, -MOBBING, -MOBS to discharge from military service

DEMOCRAT *n* pl. -S one who believes in political and social equality

DEMODE *adj* demoded

DEMODED *adj* out-of-date

DEMOLISH *v* -ED, -ING, -ES to destroy

DEMON *n* pl. -S an evil spirit

DEMONESS *n* pl. -ES a female demon

DEMONIAC *n* pl. -S one regarded as possessed by a demon

DEMONIAN *adj* demonic

DEMONIC *adj* characteristic of a demon

DEMONISE *v* -ISED, -ISING, -ISES to demonize

DEMONISM *n* pl. -S belief in demons

DEMONIST *n* pl. -S one who believes in demons

DEMONIZE *v* -IZED, -IZING, -IZES to make a demon of

DEMOS *n* pl. -ES the people of an ancient Greek state

DEMOTE *v* -MOTED, -MOTING, -MOTES to lower in rank or grade

DEMOTIC *adj* pertaining to a simplified form of ancient Egyptian writing

DEMOTICS *n/pl* the study of people in society

DEMOTING present participle of demote

DEMOTION *n* pl. -S the act of demoting

DEMOTIST *n* pl. -S a student of demotic writings

DEMOUNT *v* -ED, -ING, -S to remove from a mounting

DEMPSTER *n* pl. -S a deemster

DEMUR *v* -MURRED, -MURRING, -MURS to object

DEMURE *adj* -MURER, -MUREST shy and modest **DEMURELY** *adv*

DEMURRAL *n* pl. -S the act of demurring

DEMURRED past tense of demur

DEMURRER *n* pl. -S one that demurs

DEMURRING present participle of demur

DEMY *n* pl. -MIES a size of paper

DEN *v* DENNED, DENNING, DENS to live in a lair

DENARIUS *n* pl. DENARII a coin of ancient Rome

DENARY *adj* containing ten

DENATURE *v* -TURED, -TURING, -TURES to deprive of natural qualities

DENAZIFY *v* -FIED, -FYING, -FIES to rid of Nazism

DENDRITE *n* pl. -S a branched part of a nerve cell

DENDROID *adj* shaped like a tree

DENDRON *n* pl. -S a dendrite

DENE *n* pl. -S a valley

DENGUE *n* pl. -S a tropical disease

DENIABLE *adj* capable of being denied **DENIABLY** *adv*

DENIAL *n* pl. -S the act of denying

DENIED past tense of deny

DENIER *n* pl. -S one that denies

DENIES present 3d person sing. of deny

DENIM *n* pl. -S a durable fabric

DENIZEN *v* -ED, -ING, -S to make a citizen of

DENNED past tense of den

DENNING present participle of den

DENOTE *v* -NOTED, -NOTING, -NOTES to indicate **DENOTIVE** *adj*

DENOUNCE *v* -NOUNCED, -NOUNCING, -NOUNCES to condemn openly

DENSE *adj* DENSER, DENSEST compact **DENSELY** *adv*

DENSIFY *v* -FIED, -FYING, -FIES to make denser

DENSITY *n* pl. -TIES the state of being dense

DENT *v* -ED, -ING, -S to make a depression in

DENTAL *n* pl. -S a dentally produced sound

DENTALIA *n/pl* mollusks with long, tapering shells

DENTALLY *adv* with the tip of the tongue against the upper front teeth

DENTATE *adj* having teeth

DENTATED *adj* dentate

DENTICLE *n* pl. -S a small tooth

DENTIL *n* pl. -S a small rectangular block **DENTILED** *adj*

DENTIN *n* pl. -S the hard substance forming the body of a tooth **DENTINAL** *adj*

DENTINE *n* pl. -S dentin

DENTIST *n* pl. -S one who treats the teeth

DENTOID *adj* resembling a tooth

DENTURE *n* pl. -S a set of teeth
DENTURAL *adj*

DENUDATE *v* -DATED, -DATING, -DATES to denude

DENUDE *v* -NUDED, -NUDING, -NUDES to strip of all covering

DENUDER *n* pl. -S one that denudes

DENY *v* -NIED, -NYING, -NIES to declare to be untrue

DEODAND *n* pl. -S property forfeited to the crown under a former English law

DEODAR *n* pl. -S an East Indian cedar

DEODARA *n* pl. -S deodar

DEONTIC *adj* pertaining to moral obligation

DEORBIT *v* -ED, -ING, -S to come out of an orbit

DEOXY *adj* having less oxygen than the compound from which it is derived

DEPAINT *v* -ED, -ING, -S to depict

DEPART *v* -ED, -ING, -S to go away

DEPARTEE *n* pl. -S one that departs

DEPEND *v* -ED, -ING, -S to rely

DEPERM *v* -ED, -ING, -S to demagnetize

DEPICT *v* -ED, -ING, -S to portray

DEPICTER *n* pl. -S one that depicts

DEPICTOR *n* pl. -S depicter

DEPILATE *v* -LATED, -LATING, -LATES to remove hair from

DEPLANE *v* -PLANED, -PLANING, -PLANES to get off an airplane

DEPLETE *v* -PLETED, -PLETING, -PLETES to lessen or exhaust the supply of

DEPLORE *v* -PLORED, -PLORING, -PLORES to regret strongly

DEPLORER *n* pl. -S one that deplores

DEPLOY *v* -ED, -ING, -S to position troops for battle

DEPLUME *v* -PLUMED, -PLUMING, -PLUMES to deprive of feathers

DEPOLISH *v* -ED, -ING, -ES to remove the gloss or polish of

DEPONE *v* -PONED, -PONING, -PONES to testify under oath

DEPONENT *n* pl. -S one that depones

DEPORT *v* -ED, -ING, -S to expel from a country

DEPORTEE *n* pl. -S one who is deported

DEPOSAL *n* pl. -S the act of deposing

DEPOSE *v* -POSED, -POSING, -POSES to remove from office

DEPOSER *n* pl. -S one that deposes

DEPOSIT *v* -ED, -ING, -S to place

DEPOT *n* pl. -S a railroad or bus station

DEPRAVE *v* -PRAVED, -PRAVING, -PRAVES to corrupt in morals

DEPRAVER *n* pl. -S one that depraves

DEPRESS *v* -ED, -ING, -ES to make sad

DEPRIVAL *n* pl. -S the act of depriving

DEPRIVE *v* -PRIVED, -PRIVING, -PRIVES to take something away from

DEPRIVER *n* pl. -S one that deprives

DEPSIDE *n* pl. -S an aromatic compound

DEPTH *n* pl. -S deepness

DEPURATE *v* -RATED, -RATING, -RATES to free from impurities

DEPUTE *v* -PUTED, -PUTING, -PUTES to delegate

DEPUTIZE *v* -TIZED, -TIZING, -TIZES to appoint as a deputy

DEPUTY *n* pl. -TIES one appointed to act for another

DERAIGN *v* -ED, -ING, -S to dispute a claim

DERAIL *v* -ED, -ING, -S to run off the rails of a track

DERANGE *v* -RANGED, -RANGING, -RANGES to disorder

DERAT *v* -RATTED, -RATTING, -RATS to rid of rats

DERATE *v* -RATED, -RATING, -RATES to lower the rated capability of

DERAY *n* pl. -RAYS disorderly revelry

DERBY *n* pl. -BIES a type of hat

DERE *adj* dire

DERELICT *n* pl. -S something abandoned

DERIDE *v* -RIDED, -RIDING, -RIDES to ridicule

DERIDER *n* pl. -S one that derides

DERINGER *n* pl. -S a short-barreled pistol

DERISION *n* pl. -S the act of deriding

DERISIVE *adj* expressing derision

DERISORY *adj* derisive

DERIVATE *n* pl. -S something derived

DERIVE *v* -RIVED, -RIVING, -RIVES to obtain or receive from a source

DERIVER *n* pl. -S one that derives

DERM *n* pl. -S derma

DERMA *n* pl. -S a layer of the skin
DERMAL *adj*

DERMIS *n* pl. -MISES derma **DERMIC** *adj*

DERMOID *n* pl. -S a cystic tumor

DERNIER *adj* last

DEROGATE *v* -GATED, -GATING, -GATES to detract

DERRICK *n* pl. -S a hoisting apparatus

DERRIERE *n* pl. -S the buttocks

DERRIS *n* pl. -RISES a climbing plant

DERRY *n* pl. -RIES a meaningless word used in the chorus of old songs

DERVISH *n* pl. -ES a member of a Muslim religious order

DES *prep* of the — used in names

DESALT *v* -ED, -ING, -S to remove the salt from

DESALTER *n* pl. -S one that desalts

DESAND *v* -ED, -ING, -S to remove sand from

DESCANT *v* -ED, -ING, -S to sing

DESCEND *v* -ED, -ING, -S to come or go down

DESCENT *n* pl. -S the act of descending

DESCRIBE *v* -SCRIBED, -SCRIBING, -SCRIBES to give a verbal account of

DESCRIER *n* pl. -S one that descries

DESCRY *v* -SCRIED, -SCRYING, -SCRIES to discern

DESELECT *v* -ED, -ING, -S to dismiss from a training program

DESERT *v* -ED, -ING, -S to abandon

DESERTER *n* pl. -S one that deserts

DESERTIC *adj* arid and barren

DESERVE *v* -SERVED, -SERVING, -SERVES to be entitled to or worthy of

DESERVER *n* pl. -S one that deserves

DESEX *v* -ED, -ING, -ES to castrate or spay

DESIGN *v* -ED, -ING, -S to conceive and plan out

DESIGNEE *n* pl. -S one who is designated

DESIGNER *n* pl. -S one that designs

DESILVER *v* -ED, -ING, -S to remove the silver from

DESINENT *adj* terminating

DESIRE *v* -SIRED, -SIRING, -SIRES to wish for

DESIRER *n* pl. -S one that desires

DESIROUS *adj* desiring

DESIST *v* -ED, -ING, -S to cease doing something

DESK *n* pl. -S a writing table

DESKMAN *n* pl. -MEN one who works at a desk

DESKTOP *n* pl. -S the top of a desk

DESMAN *n* pl. -S an aquatic mammal

DESMID *n* pl. -S a freshwater alga

DESMOID *n* pl. -S a very hard tumor

DESOLATE *v* -LATED, -LATING, -LATES to lay waste

DESORB *v* -ED, -ING, -S to remove by the reverse of absorption

DESOXY *adj* deoxy

DESPAIR *v* -ED, -ING, -S to lose all hope

DESPATCH *v* -ED, -ING, -ES to dispatch

DESPISE *v* -SPISED, -SPISING, -SPISES to loathe

DESPISER *n* pl. -S one that despises

DESPITE *v* -SPITED, -SPITING, -SPITES to treat with contempt

DESPOIL *v* -ED, -ING, -S to plunder

DESPOND *v* -ED, -ING, -S to lose spirit or hope

DESPOT *n* pl. -S a tyrant **DESPOTIC** *adj*

DESSERT *n* pl. -S something served as the last course of a meal

DESTAIN *v* -ED, -ING, -S to remove stain from

DESTINE *v* -TINED, -TINING, -TINES to determine beforehand

DESTINY *n* pl. -NIES the fate or fortune to which one is destined

DESTRIER *n* pl. -S a war horse

DESTROY *v* -ED, -ING, -S to damage beyond repair or renewal

DESTRUCT *v* -ED, -ING, -S to destroy

DESUGAR *v* -ED, -ING, -S to remove sugar from

DESULFUR *v* -ED, -ING, -S to free from sulfur

DETACH *v* -ED, -ING, -ES to unfasten and separate

DETACHER *n* pl. -S one that detaches

DETAIL *v* -ED, -ING, -S to report with complete particulars

DETAILER *n* pl. -S one that details

DETAIN *v* -ED, -ING, -S to hold in custody

DETAINEE *n* pl. -S one who is detained

DETAINER *n* pl. -S the unlawful withholding of another's property

DETASSEL *v* -SELED, -SELING, -SELS or -SELLED, -SELLING, -SELS to remove tassels from

DETECT *v* -ED, -ING, -S to discover or perceive

DETECTER *n* pl. -S detector

DETECTOR *n* pl. -S one that detects

DETENT *n* pl. -S a locking or unlocking mechanism

DETENTE *n* pl. -S an easing of international tension

DETER *v* -TERRED, -TERRING, -TERS to stop from proceeding

DETERGE *v* -TERGED, -TERGING, -TERGES to cleanse

DETERGER *n* pl. -S one that deterges

DETERRED past tense of deter

DETERRER *n* pl. -S one that deters

DETERRING present participle of deter

DETEST *v* -ED, -ING, -S to dislike intensely

DETESTER *n* pl. -S one that detests

DETHRONE *v* -THRONED, -THRONING, -THRONES to remove from a throne

DETICK *v* -ED, -ING, -S to remove ticks from

DETICKER *n* pl. -S one that deticks

DETINUE *n* pl. -S an action to recover property wrongfully detained

DETONATE *v* -NATED, -NATING, -NATES to cause to explode

DETOUR *v* -ED, -ING, -S to take an indirect route

DETOX *v* -ED, -ING, -ES to detoxify

DETOXIFY *v* -FIED, -FYING, -FIES to remove a toxin from

DETRACT *v* -ED, -ING, -S to take away

DETRAIN *v* -ED, -ING, -S to get off a railroad train

DETRITUS *n* pl. DETRITUS particles of rock **DETRITAL** *adj*

DETRUDE *v* -TRUDED, -TRUDING, -TRUDES to thrust out

DEUCE *v* DEUCED, DEUCING, DEUCES to bring a tennis score to a tie

DEUCEDLY *adv* extremely

DEUTERIC *adj* pertaining to heavy hydrogen

DEUTERON *n* pl. -S an atomic particle

DEUTZIA *n* pl. -S an ornamental shrub

DEV *n* pl. -S deva

DEVA *n* pl. -S a Hindu god

DEVALUE *v* -UED, -UING, -UES to lessen the worth of

DEVEIN *v* -ED, -ING, -S to remove the dorsal vein from

DEVEL *v* -ED, -ING, -S to strike forcibly

DEVELOP *v* -ED, -ING, -S to bring to a more advanced or effective state

DEVELOPE *v* -OPED, -OPING, -OPES to develop

DEVERBAL *adj* derived from a verb

DEVEST *v* -ED, -ING, -S to divest

DEVIANCE *n* pl. -S the behavior of a deviant

DEVIANCY *n* pl. -CIES deviance

DEVIANT *n* pl. -S one that deviates from a norm

DEVIATE *v* -ATED, -ATING, -ATES to turn aside from a course or norm

DEVIATOR *n* pl. -S one that deviates

DEVICE *n* pl. -S something devised or constructed for a specific purpose

DEVIL *v* -ILED, -ILING, -ILS or -ILLED, -ILLING, -ILS to prepare food with pungent seasoning

DEVILISH *adj* fiendish

DEVILKIN *n* pl. -S a small demon

DEVILLED a past tense of devil

DEVILLING a present participle of devil

DEVILRY *n* pl. -RIES deviltry

DEVILTRY *n* pl. -TRIES mischief

DEVIOUS *adj* indirect

DEVISAL *n* pl. -S the act of devising

DEVISE *v* -VISED, -VISING, -VISES to form in the mind

DEVISEE *n* pl. -S one to whom a will is made

DEVISER *n* pl. -S one that devises

DEVISING present participle of devise

DEVISOR *n* pl. -S one who makes a will

DEVOICE *v* -VOICED, -VOICING, -VOICES to unvoice

DEVOID *adj* completely lacking

DEVOIR *n* pl. -S an act of civility or respect

DEVOLVE *v* -VOLVED, -VOLVING, -VOLVES to transfer from one person to another

DEVON *n* pl. -S one of a breed of small, hardy cattle

DEVOTE *v* -VOTED, -VOTING, -VOTES to give oneself wholly to

DEVOTEE *n* pl. -S an ardent follower or supporter

DEVOTION *n* pl. -S the act of devoting

DEVOUR *v* -ED, -ING, -S to eat up voraciously

DEVOURER *n* pl. -S one that devours

DEVOUT *adj* -VOUTER, -VOUTEST pious **DEVOUTLY** *adv*

DEW *v* -ED, -ING, -S to wet with dew (condensed moisture)

DEWAN *n* pl. -S an official in India

DEWAR *n* pl. -S a double-walled flask
DEWATER *v* -ED, -ING, -S to remove water from
DEWAX *v* -ED, -ING, -ES to remove wax from
DEWBERRY *n* pl. -RIES an edible berry
DEWCLAW *n* pl. -S a vestigial toe
DEWDROP *n* pl. -S a drop of dew
DEWFALL *n* pl. -S the formation of dew
DEWIER comparative of dewy
DEWIEST superlative of dewy
DEWILY *adv* in a dewy manner
DEWINESS *n* pl. -ES the state of being dewy
DEWLAP *n* pl. -S a fold of loose skin under the neck
DEWLESS *adj* having no dew
DEWOOL *v* -ED, -ING, -S to remove the wool from
DEWORM *v* -ED, -ING, -S to rid of worms
DEWORMER *n* pl. -S one that deworms
DEWY *adj* DEWIER, DEWIEST moist with dew
DEX *n* pl. -ES a sulfate used as a central nervous system stimulant
DEXIE *n* pl. -S a tablet of dex
DEXIES pl. of dexy
DEXTER *adj* situated on the right
DEXTRAL *adj* pertaining to the right
DEXTRAN *n* pl. -S a substance used as a blood plasma substitute
DEXTRIN *n* pl. -S a substance used as an adhesive
DEXTRINE *n* pl. -S dextrin
DEXTRO *adj* turning to the right
DEXTROSE *n* pl. -S a form of glucose
DEXTROUS *adj* adroit
DEXY *n* pl. DEXIES dexie
DEY *n* pl. DEYS a former North African ruler
DEZINC *v* -ZINCKED, -ZINCKING, -ZINCS or -ZINCED, -ZINCING, -ZINCS to remove zinc from
DHAK *n* pl. -S an Asian tree
DHAL *n* pl. -S dal
DHARMA *n* pl. -S conformity to Hindu law DHARMIC *adj*
DHARNA *n* pl. -S a form of protest in India
DHOBI *n* pl. -S a person who does laundry in India
DHOLE *n* pl. -S a wild dog of India
DHOOLY *n* pl. -LIES dooly

DHOORA *n* pl. -S durra
DHOOTI *n* pl. -S dhoti
DHOOTIE *n* pl. -S dhoti
DHOTI *n* pl. -S a loincloth worn by Hindu men
DHOURRA *n* pl. -S durra
DHOW *n* pl. -S an Arabian sailing vessel
DHURNA *n* pl. -S dharna
DHURRIE *n* pl. -S a cotton rug made in India
DHUTI *n* pl. -S dhoti
DIABASE *n* pl. -S an igneous rock
DIABASIC *adj*
DIABETES *n* pl. DIABETES a metabolic disorder
DIABETIC *n* pl. -S one who has diabetes
DIABLERY *n* pl. -RIES sorcery
DIABOLIC *adj* devilish
DIABOLO *n* pl. -LOS a game requiring manual dexterity
DIACETYL *n* pl. -S biacetyl
DIACID *n* pl. -S a type of acid
DIACIDIC *adj*
DIACONAL *adj* pertaining to a deacon
DIADEM *v* -ED, -ING, -S to adorn with a crown
DIAGNOSE *v* -NOSED, -NOSING, -NOSES to recognize a disease by its signs and symptoms
DIAGONAL *n* pl. -S an oblique line
DIAGRAM *v* -GRAMED, -GRAMING, -GRAMS or -GRAMMED, -GRAMMING, -GRAMS to illustrate by a diagram (a graphic design)
DIAGRAPH *n* pl. -S a drawing device
DIAL *v* DIALED, DIALING, DIALS or DIALLED, DIALLING, DIALS to manipulate a calibrated disk
DIALECT *n* pl. -S a regional variety of a language
DIALER *n* pl. -S one that dials
DIALING *n* pl. -S the measurement of time by sundials
DIALIST *n* pl. -S a dialer
DIALLAGE *n* pl. -S a mineral
DIALLED a past tense of dial
DIALLEL *adj* pertaining to a genetic crossing
DIALLER *n* pl. -S dialer
DIALLING *n* pl. -S dialing
DIALLIST *n* pl. -S dialist
DIALOG *v* -ED, -ING, -S to dialogue
DIALOGER *n* pl. -S one that dialogs

DIALOGIC *adj* conversational

DIALOGUE *v* -LOGUED, -LOGUING, -LOGUES to carry on a conversation

DIALYSE *v* -LYSED, -LYSING, -LYSES to dialyze

DIALYSER *n* pl. -S dialyzer

DIALYSIS *n* pl. -YSES the separation of substances in a solution by diffusion through a membrane

DIALYTIC *adj* pertaining to dialysis

DIALYZE *v* -LYZED, -LYZING, -LYZES to subject to dialysis

DIALYZER *n* pl. -S an apparatus used for dialysis

DIAMANTE *n* pl. -S a sparkling decoration

DIAMETER *n* pl. -S a straight line passing through the center of a circle and ending at the periphery

DIAMIDE *n* pl. -S a chemical compound

DIAMIN *n* pl. -S diamine

DIAMINE *n* pl. -S a chemical compound

DIAMOND *v* -ED, -ING, -S to adorn with diamonds (precious gems)

DIANTHUS *n* pl. -ES an ornamental herb

DIAPASON *n* pl. -S a burst of harmonious sound

DIAPAUSE *v* -PAUSED, -PAUSING, -PAUSES to undergo dormancy

DIAPER *v* -ED, -ING, -S to put a diaper (a baby's breechcloth) on

DIAPHONE *n* pl. -S a low-pitched foghorn

DIAPHONY *n* pl. -NIES organum

DIAPIR *n* pl. -S a bend in a layer of rock **DIAPIRIC** *adj*

DIAPSID *adj* pertaining to a type of reptile

DIARCHY *n* pl. -CHIES a government with two rulers **DIARCHIC** *adj*

DIARIES pl. of diary

DIARIST *n* pl. -S one who keeps a diary

DIARRHEA *n* pl. -S an intestinal disorder

DIARY *n* pl. -RIES a personal journal

DIASPORA *n* pl. -S migration

DIASPORE *n* pl. -S a mineral

DIASTASE *n* pl. -S an enzyme

DIASTEM *n* pl. -S an interruption in the deposition of sediment

DIASTEMA *n* pl. -MATA a space between teeth

DIASTER *n* pl. -S a stage in mitosis **DIASTRAL** *adj*

DIASTOLE *n* pl. -S the normal rhythmical dilation of the heart

DIATOM *n* pl. -S any of a class of algae

DIATOMIC *adj* composed of two atoms

DIATONIC *adj* pertaining to a type of musical scale

DIATRIBE *n* pl. -S a bitter and abusive criticism

DIATRON *n* pl. -S a circuitry design that uses diodes

DIAZEPAM *n* pl. -S a tranquilizer

DIAZIN *n* pl. -S diazine

DIAZINE *n* pl. -S a chemical compound

DIAZINON *n* pl. -S an insecticide

DIAZO *adj* containing a certain chemical group

DIAZOLE *n* pl. -S a chemical compound

DIB *v* DIBBED, DIBBING, DIBS to fish by letting the bait bob lightly on the water

DIBASIC *adj* having two replaceable hydrogen atoms

DIBBER *n* pl. -S a planting implement

DIBBING present participle of dib

DIBBLE *v* -BLED, -BLING, -BLES to dib

DIBBLER *n* pl. -S one that dibbles

DIBBUK *n* pl. -BUKS or -BUKIM dybbuk

DICAST *n* pl. -S a judge of ancient Athens **DICASTIC** *adj*

DICE *v* DICED, DICING, DICES to cut into small cubes

DICENTRA *n* pl. -S a perennial herb

DICER *n* pl. -S a device that dices food

DICEY *adj* DICIER, DICIEST dangerous

DICHASIA *n/pl* flower clusters

DICHOTIC *adj* affecting the two ears differently

DICHROIC *adj* having two colors

DICIER comparative of dicey

DICIEST superlative of dicey

DICING present participle of dice

DICK *n* pl. -S a detective

DICKENS *n* pl. -ES devil

DICKER *v* -ED, -ING, -S to bargain

DICKEY *n* pl. -EYS a blouse front

DICKIE *n* pl. -S dickey

DICKY *n* pl. DICKIES dickey

DICKY *adj* DICKIER, DICKIEST poor in condition

DICLINY *n* pl. -NIES the state of having stamens and pistils in separate flowers

DICOT *n* pl. -S a plant with two seed leaves

DICOTYL *n* pl. -S dicot

DICROTAL *adj* dicrotic

DICROTIC *adj* having a double pulse beat

DICTA a pl. of dictum

DICTATE *v* -TATED, -TATING, -TATES to read aloud for recording

DICTATOR *n* pl. -S one that dictates

DICTIER comparative of dicty

DICTIEST superlative of dicty

DICTION *n* pl. -S choice and use of words in speech or writing

DICTUM *n* pl. -TA or -TUMS an authoritative statement

DICTY *adj* -TIER, -TIEST snobbish

DICYCLIC *adj* having two maxima of population each year

DICYCLY *n* pl. -CLIES the state of being dicyclic

DID a past tense of do

DIDACT *n* pl. -S a didactic person

DIDACTIC *adj* instructive

DIDACTYL *adj* having two digits at the end of each limb

DIDAPPER *n* pl. -S a dabchick

DIDDLE *v* -DLED, -DLING, -DLES to swindle

DIDDLER *n* pl. -S one that diddles

DIDDLEY *n* pl. -DLIES diddly

DIDDLY *n* pl. -DLIES the least amount

DIDIE *n* pl. -S didy

DIDIES pl. of didy

DIDO *n* pl. -DOS or -DOES a mischievous act

DIDST a past tense of do

DIDY *n* pl. -DIES a diaper

DIDYMIUM *n* pl. -S a mixture of rare-earth elements

DIDYMOUS *adj* occurring in pairs

DIDYNAMY *n* pl. -MIES the state of having four stamens in pairs of unequal length

DIE *v* DIED, DYING, DIES to cease living

DIE *v* DIED, DIEING, DIES to cut with a die (a device for shaping material)

DIEBACK *n* pl. -S a gradual dying of plant shoots

DIECIOUS *adj* dioicous

DIED past tense of die

DIEHARD *n* pl. -S a stubborn person

DIEL *adj* involving a full day

DIELDRIN *n* pl. -S an insecticide

DIEMAKER *n* pl. -S one that makes dies

DIENE *n* pl. -S a chemical compound

DIERESIS *n* pl. DIERESES the separation of two vowels into two syllables DIERETIC *adj*

DIESEL *v* -ED, -ING, -S to continue running after the ignition is turned off

DIESIS *n* pl. DIESES a reference mark in printing

DIESTER *n* pl. -S a type of chemical compound

DIESTOCK *n* pl. -S a frame for holding dies

DIESTRUM *n* pl. -S diestrus

DIESTRUS *n* pl. -ES a period of sexual inactivity

DIET *v* -ED, -ING, -S to regulate one's daily sustenance

DIETARY *n* pl. -ETARIES a system of dieting

DIETER *n* pl. -S one that diets

DIETETIC *adj* pertaining to diet

DIETHER *n* pl. -S a chemical compound

DIFFER *v* -ED, -ING, -S to be unlike

DIFFRACT *v* -ED, -ING, -S to separate into parts

DIFFUSE *v* -FUSED, -FUSING, -FUSES to spread widely or thinly

DIFFUSER *n* pl. -S one that diffuses

DIFFUSOR *n* pl. -S diffuser

DIG *v* DUG or DIGGED, DIGGING, DIGS to break up, turn over, or remove earth

DIGAMIES pl. of digamy

DIGAMIST *n* pl. -S one who practices digamy

DIGAMMA *n* pl. -S a Greek letter

DIGAMY *n* pl. -MIES a second legal marriage DIGAMOUS *adj*

DIGEST *v* -ED, -ING, -S to render food usable for the body

DIGESTER *n* pl. -S an apparatus in which substances are softened or decomposed

DIGESTOR *n* pl. -S digester

DIGGED a past tense of dig

DIGGER *n* pl. -S one that digs

DIGGING present participle of dig

DIGGINGS *n/pl* an excavation site

DIGHT *v* -ED, -ING, -S to adorn

DIGIT *n* pl. -S a finger or toe

DIGITAL *n* pl. -S a piano key

DIGITATE *adj* having digits

DIGITIZE *v* -TIZED, -TIZING, -TIZES to put data into digital notation

DIGLOT *n* pl. -S a bilingual book or edition

DIGNIFY   v -FIED, -FYING, -FIES to add dignity to

DIGNITY   n pl. -TIES stateliness and nobility of manner

DIGOXIN   n pl. -S a drug to improve heart function

DIGRAPH   n pl. -S a pair of letters representing a single speech sound

DIGRESS   v -ED, -ING, -ES to stray from the main topic

DIHEDRAL   n pl. -S a dihedron

DIHEDRON   n pl. -S a figure formed by two intersecting planes

DIHYBRID   n pl. -S an offspring of parents differing in two pairs of genes

DIHYDRIC   adj containing two hydroxyl radicals

DIKDIK   n pl. -S a small antelope

DIKE   v DIKED, DIKING, DIKES to furnish with an embankment

DIKER   n pl. -S one that dikes

DIKTAT   n pl. -S a harsh settlement imposed on a defeated nation

DILATANT   n pl. -S a dilator

DILATATE   adj dilated

DILATE   v -LATED, -LATING, -LATES to make wider or larger

DILATER   n pl. -S dilator

DILATION   n pl. -S the act of dilating

DILATIVE   adj tending to dilate

DILATOR   n pl. -S one that dilates

DILATORY   adj tending to delay

DILDO   n pl. -DOS an object used as a penis substitute

DILDOE   n pl. -S dildo

DILEMMA   n pl. -S a perplexing situation **DILEMMIC** adj

DILIGENT   adj persevering

DILL   n pl. -S an annual herb

DILLED   adj flavored with dill

DILLY   n pl. DILLIES something remarkable

DILUENT   n pl. -S a diluting substance

DILUTE   v -LUTED, -LUTING, -LUTES to thin or reduce the concentration of

DILUTER   n pl. -S one that dilutes

DILUTION   n pl. -S the act of diluting

DILUTIVE   adj tending to dilute

DILUTOR   n pl. -S diluter

DILUVIA   a pl. of diluvium

DILUVIAL   adj pertaining to a flood

DILUVIAN   adj diluvial

DILUVION   n pl. -S diluvium

DILUVIUM   n pl. -VIA or -VIUMS coarse rock material deposited by glaciers

DIM   adj DIMMER, DIMMEST obscure

DIM   v DIMMED, DIMMING, DIMS to make dim

DIME   n pl. -S a coin of the United States

DIMER   n pl. -S a molecule composed of two identical molecules

DIMERIC   adj dimerous

DIMERISM   n pl. -S the state of being dimerous

DIMERIZE   v -IZED, -IZING, -IZES to form a dimer

DIMEROUS   adj composed of two parts

DIMETER   n pl. -S a verse of two metrical feet

DIMETHYL   n pl. -S ethane

DIMETRIC   adj pertaining to a type of crystal system

DIMINISH   v -ED, -ING, -ES to lessen

DIMITY   n pl. -TIES a cotton fabric

DIMLY   adv in a dim manner

DIMMABLE   adj capable of being dimmed

DIMMED   past tense of dim

DIMMER   n pl. -S a device for varying the intensity of illumination

DIMMEST   superlative of dim

DIMMING   present participle of dim

DIMNESS   n pl. -ES the state of being dim

DIMORPH   n pl. -S either of two distinct forms

DIMOUT   n pl. -S a condition of partial darkness

DIMPLE   v -PLED, -PLING, -PLES to mark with indentations

DIMPLY   adj -PLIER, -PLIEST dimpled

DIMWIT   n pl. -S a dunce

DIN   v DINNED, DINNING, DINS to make a loud noise

DINAR   n pl. -S an ancient gold coin of Muslim areas

DINDLE   v -DLED, -DLING, -DLES to tingle

DINE   v DINED, DINING, DINES to eat dinner

DINER   n pl. -S one that dines

DINERIC   adj pertaining to the interface between two immiscible liquids

DINERO   n pl. -ROS a former silver coin of Peru

DINETTE   n pl. -S a small dining room

DING   v -ED, -ING, -S to ring

DINGBAT *n* pl. -S a typographical ornament

DINGDONG *v* -ED, -ING, -S to make a ringing sound

DINGE *n* pl. -S the condition of being dingy

DINGER *n* pl. -S a home run

DINGEY *n* pl. -GEYS dinghy

DINGHY *n* pl. -GHIES a small boat

DINGIER comparative of dingy

DINGIES pl. of dingy

DINGIEST superlative of dingy

DINGILY *adv* in a dingy manner

DINGLE *n* pl. -S a dell

DINGO *n* pl. -GOES a wild dog of Australia

DINGUS *n* pl. -ES a doodad

DINGY *n* pl. -GIES dinghy

DINGY *adj* -GIER, -GIEST grimy

DINING present participle of dine

DINITRO *adj* containing two nitro groups

DINK *v* -ED, -ING, -S to adorn

DINKEY *n* pl. -KEYS a small locomotive

DINKIER comparative of dinky

DINKIES pl. of dinky

DINKIEST superlative of dinky

DINKLY *adv* neatly

DINKUM *n* pl. -S the truth

DINKY *n* pl. -KIES dinkey

DINKY *adj* -KIER, -KIEST small

DINNED past tense of din

DINNER *n* pl. -S the main meal of the day

DINNING present participle of din

DINOSAUR *n* pl. -S one of a group of extinct reptiles

DINT *v* -ED, -ING, -S to dent

DIOBOL *n* pl. -S a coin of ancient Greece

DIOBOLON *n* pl. -S diobol

DIOCESAN *n* pl. -S a bishop

DIOCESE *n* pl. -S an ecclesiastical district

DIODE *n* pl. -S a type of electron tube

DIOECISM *n* pl. -S the state of being dioicous

DIOECY *n* pl. DIOECIES dioecism

DIOICOUS *adj* unisexual

DIOL *n* pl. -S a chemical compound

DIOLEFIN *n* pl. -S a hydrocarbon

DIOPSIDE *n* pl. -S a mineral

DIOPTASE *n* pl. -S a mineral

DIOPTER *n* pl. -S a measure of refractive power DIOPTRAL *adj*

DIOPTRE *n* pl. -S diopter

DIOPTRIC *adj* aiding the vision by refraction

DIORAMA *n* pl. -S a three-dimensional exhibit DIORAMIC *adj*

DIORITE *n* pl. -S an igneous rock DIORITIC *adj*

DIOXANE *n* pl. -S a flammable liquid

DIOXID *n* pl. -S dioxide

DIOXIDE *n* pl. -S a type of oxide

DIOXIN *n* pl. -S a toxic solid hydrocarbon

DIP *v* DIPPED or DIPT, DIPPING, DIPS to immerse briefly into a liquid

DIPHASE *adj* having two phases

DIPHASIC *adj* diphase

DIPHENYL *n* pl. -S biphenyl

DIPLEGIA *n* pl. -S paralysis of the same part on both sides of the body

DIPLEX *adj* pertaining to the simultaneous transmission or reception of two radio signals

DIPLEXER *n* pl. -S a coupling device

DIPLOE *n* pl. -S a bony tissue of the cranium DIPLOIC *adj*

DIPLOID *n* pl. -S a cell having the basic chromosome number doubled

DIPLOIDY *n* pl. -DIES the condition of being a diploid

DIPLOMA *n* pl. -MAS or -MATA a certificate of an academic degree

DIPLOMA *v* -ED, -ING, -S to furnish with a diploma

DIPLOMAT *n* pl. -S a governmental official

DIPLONT *n* pl. -S an organism having a particular chromosomal structure

DIPLOPIA *n* pl. -S double vision DIPLOPIC *adj*

DIPLOPOD *n* pl. -S a multi-legged insect

DIPLOSIS *n* pl. -LOSES a method of chromosome formation

DIPNET *v* -NETTED, -NETTING, -NETS to scoop fish with a type of net

DIPNOAN *n* pl. -S a lungfish

DIPODY *n* pl. -DIES a dimeter DIPODIC *adj*

DIPOLE *n* pl. -S a pair of equal and opposite electric charges DIPOLAR *adj*

DIPPABLE *adj* capable of being dipped

DIPPED a past tense of dip

DIPPER *n* pl. -S one that dips

DIPPING	present participle of dip
DIPPY	adj -PIER, -PIEST foolish
DIPSAS	n pl. DIPSADES a fabled serpent
DIPSO	n pl. -SOS a person who craves alcoholic liquors
DIPSTICK	n pl. -S a measuring rod
DIPT	a past tense of dip
DIPTERA	pl. of dipteron
DIPTERAL	adj having two rows or columns
DIPTERAN	n pl. -S a two-winged fly
DIPTERON	n pl. -TERA dipteran
DIPTYCA	n pl. -S diptych
DIPTYCH	n pl. -S an ancient writing tablet
DIQUAT	n pl. -S an herbicide
DIRDUM	n pl. -S blame
DIRE	adj DIRER, DIREST disastrous
DIRECT	v -ED, -ING, -S to control or conduct the affairs of
DIRECT	adj -RECTER, -RECTEST straightforward **DIRECTLY** adv
DIRECTOR	n pl. -S one that directs
DIREFUL	adj dreadful
DIRELY	adv in a dire manner
DIRENESS	n pl. -ES the state of being dire
DIRER	comparative of dire
DIREST	superlative of dire
DIRGE	n pl. -S a funeral song **DIRGEFUL** adj
DIRHAM	n pl. -S a monetary unit of Morocco
DIRIMENT	adj nullifying
DIRK	v -ED, -ING, -S to stab with a small knife
DIRL	v -ED, -ING, -S to tremble
DIRNDL	n pl. -S a woman's dress
DIRT	n pl. -S earth or soil
DIRTBAG	n pl. -S a dirty or contemptible person
DIRTY	adj DIRTIER, DIRTIEST unclean **DIRTILY** adv
DIRTY	v DIRTIED, DIRTYING, DIRTIES to make dirty
DIS	v DISSED, DISSING, DISSES to insult or criticize
DISABLE	v -ABLED, -ABLING, -ABLES to render incapable or unable
DISABUSE	v -ABUSED, -ABUSING, -ABUSES to free from false or mistaken ideas
DISAGREE	v -AGREED, -AGREEING, -AGREES to differ in opinion
DISALLOW	v -ED, -ING, -S to refuse to allow
DISANNUL	v -NULLED, -NULLING, -NULS to annul
DISARM	v -ED, -ING, -S to deprive of weapons
DISARMER	n pl. -S one that disarms
DISARRAY	v -ED, -ING, -S to disorder
DISASTER	n pl. -S a calamity
DISAVOW	v -ED, -ING, -S to disclaim responsibility for
DISBAND	v -ED, -ING, -S to break up
DISBAR	v -BARRED, -BARRING, -BARS to expel from the legal profession
DISBOSOM	v -ED, -ING, -S to confess
DISBOUND	adj not having a binding
DISBOWEL	v -ELED, -ELING, -ELS or -ELLED, -ELLING, -ELS to remove the intestines of
DISBUD	v -BUDDED, -BUDDING, -BUDS to remove buds from
DISBURSE	v -BURSED, -BURSING, -BURSES to pay out
DISC	v -ED, -ING, -S to disk
DISCANT	v -ED, -ING, -S to descant
DISCARD	v -ED, -ING, -S to throw away
DISCASE	v -CASED, -CASING, -CASES to remove the case of
DISCEPT	v -ED, -ING, -S to debate
DISCERN	v -ED, -ING, -S to perceive
DISCI	a pl. of discus
DISCIPLE	v -PLED, -PLING, -PLES to cause to become a follower
DISCLAIM	v -ED, -ING, -S to renounce any claim to or connection with
DISCLIKE	adj disklike
DISCLOSE	v -CLOSED, -CLOSING, -CLOSES to reveal
DISCO	v -ED, -ING, -S to dance at a discotheque
DISCOID	n pl. -S a disk
DISCOLOR	v -ED, -ING, -S to alter the color of
DISCORD	v -ED, -ING, -S to disagree
DISCOUNT	v -ED, -ING, -S to reduce the price of
DISCOVER	v -ED, -ING, -S to gain sight or knowledge of
DISCREET	adj -CREETER, -CREETEST tactful
DISCRETE	adj separate
DISCROWN	v -ED, -ING, -S to deprive of a crown
DISCUS	n pl. -CUSES or -CI a disk hurled in athletic competition

DISCUSS *v* -ED, -ING, -ES to talk over or write about

DISDAIN *v* -ED, -ING, -S to scorn

DISEASE *v* -EASED, -EASING, -EASES to make unhealthy

DISENDOW *v* -ED, -ING, -S to deprive of endowment

DISEUSE *n* pl. -S a female entertainer

DISFAVOR *v* -ED, -ING, -S to regard with disapproval

DISFROCK *v* -ED, -ING, -S to unfrock

DISGORGE *v* -GORGED, -GORGING, -GORGES to vomit

DISGRACE *v* -GRACED, -GRACING, -GRACES to bring shame or discredit upon

DISGUISE *v* -GUISED, -GUISING, -GUISES to alter the appearance of

DISGUST *v* -ED, -ING, -S to cause nausea or loathing in

DISH *v* -ED, -ING, -ES to put into a dish (a concave vessel)

DISHELM *v* -ED, -ING, -S to deprive of a helmet

DISHERIT *v* -ED, -ING, -S to deprive of an inheritance

DISHEVEL *v* -ELED, -ELING, -ELS or -ELLED, -ELLING, -ELS to make messy

DISHFUL *n* pl. -S as much as a dish can hold

DISHIER comparative of dishy

DISHIEST superlative of dishy

DISHLIKE *adj* resembling a dish

DISHONOR *v* -ED, -ING, -S to deprive of honor

DISHPAN *n* pl. -S a pan for washing dishes

DISHRAG *n* pl. -S a cloth for washing dishes

DISHWARE *n* pl. -S tableware used in serving food

DISHY *adj* DISHIER, DISHIEST attractive

DISINTER *v* -TERRED, -TERRING, -TERS to exhume

DISJECT *v* -ED, -ING, -S to disperse

DISJOIN *v* -ED, -ING, -S to separate

DISJOINT *v* -ED, -ING, -S to put out of order

DISJUNCT *n* pl. -S an alternative in a logical disjunction

DISK *v* -ED, -ING, -S to break up land with a type of farm implement

DISKETTE *n* pl. -S a floppy disk for a computer

DISKLIKE *adj* resembling a disk (a flat, circular plate)

DISLIKE *v* -LIKED, -LIKING, -LIKES to regard with aversion

DISLIKER *n* pl. -S one that dislikes

DISLIMN *v* -ED, -ING, -S to make dim

DISLODGE *v* -LODGED, -LODGING, -LODGES to remove from a firm position

DISLOYAL *adj* not loyal

DISMAL *n* pl. -S a track of swampy land

DISMAL *adj* -MALER, -MALEST cheerless and depressing **DISMALLY** *adv*

DISMAST *v* -ED, -ING, -S to remove the mast of

DISMAY *v* -ED, -ING, -S to deprive of courage or resolution

DISME *n* pl. -S a former coin of the United States

DISMISS *v* -ED, -ING, -ES to permit or cause to leave

DISMOUNT *v* -ED, -ING, -S to get down from an elevated position

DISOBEY *v* -ED, -ING, -S to fail to obey

DISOMIC *adj* having a number of chromosomes duplicated

DISORDER *v* -ED, -ING, -S to put out of order

DISOWN *v* -ED, -ING, -S to deny the ownership of

DISPART *v* -ED, -ING, -S to separate

DISPATCH *v* -ED, -ING, -ES to send off with speed

DISPEL *v* -PELLED, -PELLING, -PELS to drive off in various directions

DISPEND *v* -ED, -ING, -S to squander

DISPENSE *v* -PENSED, -PENSING, -PENSES to distribute

DISPERSE *v* -PERSED, -PERSING, -PERSES to scatter

DISPIRIT *v* -ED, -ING, -S to lower in spirit

DISPLACE *v* -PLACED, -PLACING, -PLACES to remove from the usual or proper place

DISPLANT *v* -ED, -ING, -S to dislodge

DISPLAY *v* -ED, -ING, -S to make evident or obvious

DISPLODE *v* -PLODED, -PLODING, -PLODES to explode

DISPLUME *v* -PLUMED, -PLUMING, -PLUMES to deplume

DISPORT v -ED, -ING, -S to amuse oneself

DISPOSAL n pl. -S the act of disposing

DISPOSE v -POSED, -POSING, -POSES to put in place

DISPOSER n pl. -S one that disposes

DISPREAD v -SPREAD, -SPREADING, -SPREADS to spread out

DISPRIZE v -PRIZED, -PRIZING, -PRIZES to disdain

DISPROOF n pl. -S the act of disproving

DISPROVE v -PROVED, -PROVEN, -PROVING, -PROVES to refute

DISPUTE v -PUTED, -PUTING, -PUTES to argue about

DISPUTER n pl. -S one that disputes

DISQUIET v -ED, -ING, -S to deprive of quiet, rest, or peace

DISRATE v -RATED, -RATING, -RATES to lower in rating or rank

DISROBE v -ROBED, -ROBING, -ROBES to undress

DISROBER n pl. -S one that disrobes

DISROOT v -ED, -ING, -S to uproot

DISRUPT v -ED, -ING, -S to throw into confusion

DISS v -ED, -ING, -ES to dis

DISSAVE v -SAVED, -SAVING, -SAVES to use savings for current expenses

DISSEAT v -ED, -ING, -S to unseat

DISSECT v -ED, -ING, -S to cut apart for scientific examination

DISSED past tense of dis or diss

DISSEISE v -SEISED, -SEISING, -SEISES to deprive

DISSEIZE v -SEIZED, -SEIZING, -SEIZES to disseise

DISSENT v -ED, -ING, -S to disagree

DISSERT v -ED, -ING, -S to discuss in a learned or formal manner

DISSERVE v -SERVED, -SERVING, -SERVES to treat badly

DISSEVER v -ED, -ING, -S to sever

DISSING present participle of dis or diss

DISSOLVE v -SOLVED, -SOLVING, -SOLVES to make into a solution

DISSUADE v -SUADED, -SUADING, -SUADES to persuade not to do something

DISTAFF n pl. -TAFFS or -TAVES a type of staff

DISTAIN v -ED, -ING, -S to stain

DISTAL adj located far from the point of origin **DISTALLY** adv

DISTANCE v -TANCED, -TANCING, -TANCES to leave behind

DISTANT adj far off or apart

DISTASTE v -TASTED, -TASTING, -TASTES to dislike

DISTAVES a pl. of distaff

DISTEND v -ED, -ING, -S to swell

DISTENT adj distended

DISTICH n pl. -S a couplet

DISTIL v -TILLED, -TILLING, -TILS to distill

DISTILL v -ED, -ING, -S to extract by vaporization and condensation

DISTINCT adj -TINCTER, -TINCTEST clearly different

DISTOME n pl. -S a parasitic flatworm

DISTORT v -ED, -ING, -S to twist or bend out of shape

DISTRACT v -ED, -ING, -S to divert the attention of

DISTRAIN v -ED, -ING, -S to seize and hold property as security

DISTRAIT adj absentminded

DISTRESS v -ED, -ING, -ES to cause anxiety or suffering to

DISTRICT v -ED, -ING, -S to divide into localities

DISTRUST v -ED, -ING, -S to have no trust in

DISTURB v -ED, -ING, -S to interrupt the quiet, rest, or peace of

DISULFID n pl. -S a chemical compound

DISUNION n pl. -S the state of being disunited

DISUNITE v -UNITED, -UNITING, -UNITES to separate

DISUNITY n pl. -TIES lack of unity

DISUSE v -USED, -USING, -USES to stop using

DISVALUE v -UED, -UING, -UES to treat as of little value

DISYOKE v -YOKED, -YOKING, -YOKES to free from a yoke

DIT n pl. -S a dot in Morse code

DITA n pl. -S a Philippine tree

DITCH v -ED, -ING, -ES to dig a long, narrow excavation in the ground

DITCHER n pl. -S one that ditches

DITE n pl. -S a small amount

DITHEISM n pl. -S belief in two coequal gods

DITHEIST n pl. -S an adherent of ditheism

DITHER v -ED, -ING, -S to act nervously or indecisively

DITHERER n pl. -S one that dithers

DITHERY adj nervously excited

DITHIOL adj containing two chemical groups both of which include sulfur and hydrogen

DITSY adj -SIER, -SIEST silly, eccentric

DITTANY n pl. -NIES a perennial herb

DITTO v -ED, -ING, -S to repeat

DITTY n pl. -TIES a short, simple song

DITZ n pl. -ES a ditsy person

DITZY adj -ZIER, -ZIEST ditsy

DIURESIS n pl. DIURESES excessive discharge of urine

DIURETIC n pl. -S a drug which increases urinary discharge

DIURNAL n pl. -S a diary

DIURON n pl. -S an herbicide

DIVA n pl. -S a distinguished female operatic singer

DIVAGATE v -GATED, -GATING, -GATES to wander

DIVALENT adj having a valence of two

DIVAN n pl. -S a sofa or couch

DIVE v DIVED or DOVE, DIVING, DIVES to plunge headfirst into water

DIVEBOMB v -ED, -ING, -S to drop bombs on a target from a diving airplane

DIVER n pl. -S one that dives

DIVERGE v -VERGED, -VERGING, -VERGES to move in different directions from a common point

DIVERSE adj different

DIVERT v -ED, -ING, -S to turn aside

DIVERTER n pl. -S one that diverts

DIVEST v -ED, -ING, -S to strip or deprive of anything

DIVIDE v -VIDED, -VIDING, -VIDES to separate into parts, areas, or groups

DIVIDEND n pl. -S a quantity to be divided

DIVIDER n pl. -S one that divides

DIVIDING present participle of divide

DIVIDUAL adj capable of being divided

DIVINE v -VINED, -VINING, -VINES to foretell by occult means

DIVINE adj -VINER, -VINEST pertaining to or characteristic of a god **DIVINELY** adv

DIVINER n pl. -S one that divines

DIVING present participle of dive

DIVINING present participle of divine

DIVINISE v -NISED, -NISING, -NISES to divinize

DIVINITY n pl. -TIES the state of being divine

DIVINIZE v -NIZED, -NIZING, -NIZES to make divine

DIVISION n pl. -S the act of dividing

DIVISIVE adj causing disunity or dissension

DIVISOR n pl. -S a number by which a dividend is divided

DIVORCE v -VORCED, -VORCING, -VORCES to terminate the marriage contract between

DIVORCEE n pl. -S a divorced woman

DIVORCER n pl. -S one that divorces

DIVORCING present participle of divorce

DIVOT n pl. -S a piece of turf

DIVULGE v -VULGED, -VULGING, -VULGES to reveal

DIVULGER n pl. -S one that divulges

DIVVY v -VIED, -VYING, -VIES to divide

DIWAN n pl. -S dewan

DIXIT n pl. -S a statement

DIZEN v -ED, -ING, -S to dress in fine clothes

DIZYGOUS adj developed from two fertilized ova

DIZZY adj -ZIER, -ZIEST having a sensation of whirling **DIZZILY** adv

DIZZY v -ZIED, -ZYING, -ZIES to make dizzy

DJEBEL n pl. -S jebel

DJELLABA n pl. -S a long hooded garment

DJIN n pl. -S jinni

DJINN n pl. -S jinni

DJINNI n pl. DJINN jinni

DJINNY n pl. DJINN jinni

DO v DID or DIDST, DONE, DOING, present sing. 2d person DO, DOEST or DOST, 3d person DOES, DOETH or DOTH to begin and carry through to completion

DO n pl. DOS the first tone of the diatonic musical scale

DOABLE adj able to be done

DOAT v -ED, -ING, -S to dote

DOBBER n pl. -S a float for a fishing line

DOBBIN n pl. -S a farm horse

DOBBY	n pl. -BIES a fool
DOBIE	n pl. -S adobe
DOBIES	pl. of doby
DOBLA	n pl. -S a former gold coin of Spain
DOBLON	n pl. -S or -ES a former gold coin of Spain and Spanish America
DOBRA	n pl. -S a former gold coin of Portugal
DOBSON	n pl. -S an aquatic insect larva
DOBY	n pl. -BIES dobie
DOC	n pl. -S doctor
DOCENT	n pl. -S a college or university lecturer
DOCETIC	adj pertaining to a religious doctrine
DOCILE	adj easily trained **DOCILELY** adv
DOCILITY	n pl. -TIES the quality of being docile
DOCK	v -ED, -ING, -S to bring into a dock (a wharf)
DOCKAGE	n pl. -S a charge for the use of a dock
DOCKER	n pl. -S a dock worker
DOCKET	v -ED, -ING, -S to supply with an identifying statement
DOCKHAND	n pl. -S a docker
DOCKLAND	n pl. -S the part of a port occupied by docks
DOCKSIDE	n pl. -S the area adjacent to a dock
DOCKYARD	n pl. -S a shipyard
DOCTOR	v -ED, -ING, -S to treat medically
DOCTORAL	adj pertaining to a doctor
DOCTRINE	n pl. -S a belief or set of beliefs taught or advocated
DOCUMENT	v -ED, -ING, -S to support by conclusive information or evidence
DODDER	v -ED, -ING, -S to totter
DODDERER	n pl. -S one that dodders
DODDERY	adj feeble
DODGE	v DODGED, DODGING, DODGES to evade
DODGEM	n pl. -S an amusement park ride
DODGER	n pl. -S one that dodges
DODGERY	n pl. -ERIES evasion
DODGING	present participle of dodge
DODGY	adj DODGIER, DODGIEST evasive
DODO	n pl. -DOES or -DOS an extinct flightless bird
DODOISM	n pl. -S a stupid remark
DOE	n pl. -S a female deer
DOER	n pl. -S one that does something
DOES	a present 3d person sing. of do
DOESKIN	n pl. -S the skin of a doe
DOEST	a present 2d person sing. of do
DOETH	a present 3d person sing. of do
DOFF	v -ED, -ING, -S to take off
DOFFER	n pl. -S one that doffs
DOG	v DOGGED, DOGGING, DOGS to follow after like a dog (a domesticated, carnivorous mammal)
DOGBANE	n pl. -S a perennial herb
DOGBERRY	n pl. -RIES a wild berry
DOGCART	n pl. -S a one-horse carriage
DOGDOM	n pl. -S the world of dogs
DOGE	n pl. -S the chief magistrate in the former republics of Venice and Genoa
DOGEAR	v -ED, -ING, -S to turn down a corner of a page
DOGEDOM	n pl. -S the domain of a doge
DOGESHIP	n pl. -S the office of a doge
DOGEY	n pl. -GEYS dogie
DOGFACE	n pl. -S a soldier in the U.S. Army
DOGFIGHT	v -FOUGHT, -FIGHTING, -FIGHTS to engage in an aerial battle
DOGFISH	n pl. -ES a small shark
DOGGED	past tense of dog
DOGGEDLY	adv stubbornly
DOGGER	n pl. -S a fishing vessel
DOGGEREL	n pl. -S trivial, awkwardly written verse
DOGGERY	n pl. -GERIES surly behavior
DOGGIE	n pl. -S doggy
DOGGIER	comparative of doggy
DOGGIES	pl. of doggy
DOGGIEST	superlative of doggy
DOGGING	present participle of dog
DOGGISH	adj doglike
DOGGO	adv in hiding
DOGGONE	v -GONED, -GONING, -GONES to damn
DOGGONE	adj -GONER, -GONEST damned
DOGGONED	adj -GONEDER, -GONEDEST damned
DOGGONING	present participle of doggone
DOGGREL	n pl. -S doggerel
DOGGY	n pl. -GIES a small dog
DOGGY	adj -GIER, -GIEST resembling or suggestive of a dog

DOGHOUSE *n* pl. -S a shelter for a dog
DOGIE *n* pl. -S a stray calf
DOGIES pl. of dogy
DOGLEG *v* -LEGGED, -LEGGING, -LEGS to move along a bent course
DOGLIKE *adj* resembling a dog
DOGMA *n* pl. -MAS or -MATA a principle or belief put forth as authoritative **DOGMATIC** *adj*
DOGNAP *v* -NAPED, -NAPING, -NAPS or -NAPPED, -NAPPING, -NAPS to steal a dog
DOGNAPER *n* pl. -S one that dognaps
DOGSBODY *n* pl. -BODIES a menial worker
DOGSLED *n* pl. -S a sled drawn by dogs
DOGTOOTH *n* pl. -TEETH a cuspid
DOGTROT *v* -TROTTED, -TROTTING, -TROTS to move at a steady trot
DOGVANE *n* pl. -S a small vane
DOGWATCH *n* pl. -ES a short period of watch duty on a ship
DOGWOOD *n* pl. -S a tree
DOGY *n* pl. -GIES dogie
DOILED *adj* dazed
DOILY *n* pl. -LIES a small napkin
DOING *n* pl. -S an action
DOIT *n* pl. -S a former Dutch coin
DOITED *adj* old and feeble
DOJO *n* pl. -JOS a school that teaches judo or karate
DOL *n* pl. -S a unit of pain intensity
DOLCE *n* pl. -CI a soft-toned organ stop
DOLDRUMS *n/pl* a state of inactivity or stagnation
DOLE *v* DOLED, DOLING, DOLES to distribute in small portions
DOLEFUL *adj* -FULLER, -FULLEST mournful
DOLERITE *n* pl. -S a variety of basalt
DOLESOME *adj* doleful
DOLING present participle of dole
DOLL *v* -ED, -ING, -S to dress stylishly
DOLLAR *n* pl. -S a monetary unit of the United States
DOLLIED past tense of dolly
DOLLIES present 3d person sing. of dolly
DOLLISH *adj* pretty
DOLLOP *v* -ED, -ING, -S to dispense in small amounts

DOLLY *v* -LIED, -LYING, -LIES to move on a wheeled platform
DOLMA *n* pl. -MAS or -MADES a stuffed grape leaf
DOLMAN *n* pl. -S a Turkish robe
DOLMEN *n* pl. -S a prehistoric monument
DOLOMITE *n* pl. -S a mineral
DOLOR *n* pl. -S grief
DOLOROSO *adj* having a mournful musical quality
DOLOROUS *adj* mournful
DOLOUR *n* pl. -S dolor
DOLPHIN *n* pl. -S a marine mammal
DOLT *n* pl. -S a stupid person **DOLTISH** *adj*
DOM *n* pl. -S a title given to certain monks
DOMAIN *n* pl. -S an area of control
DOMAL *adj* domical
DOME *v* DOMED, DOMING, DOMES to cover with a dome (a rounded roof)
DOMELIKE *adj* resembling a dome
DOMESDAY *n* pl. -DAYS doomsday
DOMESTIC *n* pl. -S a household servant
DOMIC *adj* domical
DOMICAL *adj* shaped like a dome
DOMICIL *v* -ED, -ING, -S to domicile
DOMICILE *v* -CILED, -CILING, -CILES to establish in a residence
DOMINANT *n* pl. -S a controlling genetic character
DOMINATE *v* -NATED, -NATING, -NATES to control
DOMINE *n* pl. -S master
DOMINEER *v* -ED, -ING, -S to tyrannize
DOMING present participle of dome
DOMINICK *n* pl. -S one of an American breed of chickens
DOMINIE *n* pl. -S a clergyman
DOMINION *n* pl. -S supreme authority
DOMINIUM *n* pl. -S the right of ownership and control of property
DOMINO *n* pl. -NOES or -NOS a small mask
DON *v* DONNED, DONNING, DONS to put on
DONA *n* pl. -S a Spanish lady
DONATE *v* -NATED, -NATING, -NATES to contribute
DONATION *n* pl. -S something donated
DONATIVE *n* pl. -S a donation
DONATOR *n* pl. -S a donor
DONE past participle of do
DONEE *n* pl. -S a recipient of a gift

DONENESS *n* pl. -ES the state of being cooked enough

DONG *n* pl. -S a deep sound like that of a large bell

DONGA *n* pl. -S a gully in a veldt

DONGOLA *n* pl. -S a type of leather

DONJON *n* pl. -S the main tower of a castle

DONKEY *n* pl. -KEYS the domestic ass

DONNA *n* pl. DONNAS or DONNE an Italian lady

DONNED past tense of don

DONNEE *n* pl. -S the set of assumptions upon which a story proceeds

DONNERD *adj* donnered

DONNERED *adj* dazed

DONNERT *adj* donnered

DONNIKER *n* pl. -S a bathroom or privy

DONNING present participle of don

DONNISH *adj* scholarly

DONOR *n* pl. -S one that donates

DONSIE *adj* unlucky

DONSY *adj* donsie

DONUT *n* pl. -S doughnut

DONZEL *n* pl. -S a young squire

DOODAD *n* pl. -S an article whose name is unknown or forgotten

DOODLE *v* -DLED, -DLING, -DLES to draw or scribble aimlessly

DOODLER *n* pl. -S one that doodles

DOOFUS *n* pl. -ES a stupid or foolish person

DOOLEE *n* pl. -S a stretcher for the sick or wounded

DOOLIE *n* pl. -S doolee

DOOLY *n* pl. -LIES doolee

DOOM *v* -ED, -ING, -S to destine to an unhappy fate

DOOMFUL *adj* ominous

DOOMSDAY *n* pl. -DAYS judgment day

DOOMSTER *n* pl. -S a judge

DOOMY *adj* doomful **DOOMILY** *adv*

DOOR *n* pl. -S a movable barrier at an entranceway

DOORBELL *n* pl. -S a bell at a door

DOORJAMB *n* pl. -S a vertical piece at the side of a doorway

DOORKNOB *n* pl. -S a handle for opening a door

DOORLESS *adj* having no door

DOORMAN *n* pl. -MEN the door attendant of a building

DOORMAT *n* pl. -S a mat placed in front of a door

DOORNAIL *n* pl. -S a large-headed nail

DOORPOST *n* pl. -S a doorjamb

DOORSILL *n* pl. -S the sill of a door

DOORSTEP *n* pl. -S a step leading to a door

DOORSTOP *n* pl. -S an object used for holding a door open

DOORWAY *n* pl. -WAYS the entranceway to a room or building

DOORYARD *n* pl. -S a yard in front of a house

DOOZER *n* pl. -S an extraordinary one of its kind

DOOZIE *n* pl. -S doozy

DOOZY *n* pl. -ZIES doozer

DOPA *n* pl. -S a drug to treat Parkinson's disease

DOPAMINE *n* pl. -S a form of dopa used to stimulate the heart

DOPANT *n* pl. -S an impurity added to a pure substance

DOPE *v* DOPED, DOPING, DOPES to give a narcotic to

DOPEHEAD *n* pl. -S a drug addict

DOPER *n* pl. -S one that dopes

DOPESTER *n* pl. -S one who predicts the outcomes of contests

DOPEY *adj* DOPIER, DOPIEST lethargic; stupid

DOPIER comparative of dopy

DOPIEST superlative of dopy

DOPINESS *n* pl. -ES the state of being dopey

DOPING present participle of dope

DOPY *adj* DOPIER, DOPIEST dopey

DOR *n* pl. -S a black European beetle

DORADO *n* pl. -DOS a marine fish

DORBUG *n* pl. -S a dor

DORE *adj* gilded

DORHAWK *n* pl. -S a nocturnal bird

DORIES pl. of dory

DORK *n* pl. -S a stupid or foolish person

DORKY *adj* DORKIER, DORKIEST stupid, foolish

DORM *n* pl. -S a dormitory

DORMANCY *n* pl. -CIES the state of being dormant

DORMANT *adj* lying asleep

DORMER *n* pl. -S a type of window

DORMICE pl. of dormouse

DORMIE *adj* being ahead by as many holes in golf as remain to be played

DORMIENT *adj* dormant

DORMIN *n* pl. -S a plant hormone

DORMOUSE *n* pl. -MICE a small rodent

DORMY *adj* dormie
DORNECK *n* pl. -S dornick
DORNICK *n* pl. -S a heavy linen fabric
DORNOCK *n* pl. -S dornick
DORP *n* pl. -S a village
DORPER *n* pl. -S one of a breed of mutton-producing sheep
DORR *n* pl. -S dor
DORSA pl. of dorsum
DORSAD *adv* dorsally
DORSAL *n* pl. -S a dorsally located anatomical part
DORSALLY *adv* toward the back
DORSEL *n* pl. -S a dossal
DORSER *n* pl. -S dosser
DORSUM *n* pl. -SA the back
DORTY *adj* sullen
DORY *n* pl. -RIES a flat-bottomed boat
DOSAGE *n* pl. -S the amount of medicine to be given
DOSE *v* DOSED, DOSING, DOSES to give a specified quantity of medicine to
DOSER *n* pl. -S one that doses
DOSS *v* -ED, -ING, -ES to sleep in any convenient place
DOSSAL *n* pl. -S an ornamental cloth hung behind an altar
DOSSEL *n* pl. -S dossal
DOSSER *n* pl. -S a basket carried on the back
DOSSERET *n* pl. -S a block resting on the capital of a column
DOSSIER *n* pl. -S a file of papers on a single subject
DOSSIL *n* pl. -S a cloth roll for wiping ink
DOST a present 2d person sing. of do
DOT *v* DOTTED, DOTTING, DOTS to cover with dots (tiny round marks)
DOTAGE *n* pl. -S a state of senility
DOTAL *adj* pertaining to a dowry
DOTARD *n* pl. -S a senile person **DOTARDLY** *adj*
DOTATION *n* pl. -S an endowment
DOTE *v* DOTED, DOTING, DOTES to show excessive affection
DOTER *n* pl. -S one that dotes
DOTH a present 3d person sing. of do
DOTIER comparative of doty
DOTIEST superlative of doty
DOTING present participle of dote
DOTINGLY *adv* in an excessively affectionate manner

DOTTED past tense of dot
DOTTEL *n* pl. -S dottle
DOTTER *n* pl. -S one that dots
DOTTEREL *n* pl. -S a shore bird
DOTTIER comparative of dotty
DOTTIEST superlative of dotty
DOTTILY *adv* in a dotty manner
DOTTING present participle of dot
DOTTLE *n* pl. -S a mass of half-burnt pipe tobacco
DOTTREL *n* pl. -S dotterel
DOTTY *adj* -TIER, -TIEST crazy
DOTY *adj* DOTIER, DOTIEST stained by decay
DOUBLE *v* -BLED, -BLING, -BLES to make twice as great
DOUBLER *n* pl. -S one that doubles
DOUBLET *n* pl. -S a close-fitting jacket
DOUBLING present participle of double
DOUBLOON *n* pl. -S a former Spanish gold coin
DOUBLURE *n* pl. -S the lining of a book cover
DOUBLY *adv* to twice the degree
DOUBT *v* -ED, -ING, -S to be uncertain about
DOUBTER *n* pl. -S one that doubts
DOUBTFUL *adj* uncertain
DOUCE *adj* sedate **DOUCELY** *adv*
DOUCEUR *n* pl. -S a gratuity
DOUCHE *v* DOUCHED, DOUCHING, DOUCHES to cleanse with a jet of water
DOUGH *n* pl. -S a flour mixture
DOUGHBOY *n* pl. -BOYS an infantryman
DOUGHIER comparative of doughy
DOUGHIEST superlative of doughy
DOUGHNUT *n* pl. -S a ring-shaped cake
DOUGHT a past tense of dow
DOUGHTY *adj* -TIER, -TIEST courageous
DOUGHY *adj* DOUGHIER, DOUGHIEST resembling dough
DOUM *n* pl. -S an African palm tree
DOUMA *n* pl. -S duma
DOUPIONI *n* pl. -S a silk yarn
DOUR *adj* DOURER, DOUREST sullen
DOURA *n* pl. -S durra
DOURAH *n* pl. -S durra
DOURINE *n* pl. -S a disease of horses
DOURLY *adv* in a dour manner
DOURNESS *n* pl. -ES the state of being dour
DOUSE *v* DOUSED, DOUSING, DOUSES to plunge into water
DOUSER *n* pl. -S one that douses

DOUX   *adj* very sweet — used of champagne

DOUZEPER   *n* pl. -S one of twelve legendary knights

DOVE   *n* pl. -S a bird of the pigeon family

DOVECOT   *n* pl. -S dovecote

DOVECOTE   *n* pl. -S a roost for domesticated pigeons

DOVEKEY   *n* pl. -KEYS dovekie

DOVEKIE   *n* pl. -S a seabird

DOVELIKE   *adj* resembling or suggestive of a dove

DOVEN   *v* -ED, -ING, -S to daven

DOVETAIL   *v* -ED, -ING, -S to fit together closely

DOVISH   *adj* not warlike

DOW   *v* DOWED or DOUGHT, DOWING, DOWS to prosper

DOWABLE   *adj* entitled to an endowment

DOWAGER   *n* pl. -S a dignified elderly woman

DOWDY   *adj* DOWDIER, DOWDIEST lacking in stylishness or neatness **DOWDILY** *adv* **DOWDYISH** *adj*

DOWDY   *n* pl. DOWDIES a dowdy woman

DOWEL   *v* -ELED, -ELING, -ELS or -ELLED, -ELLING, -ELS to fasten with wooden pins

DOWER   *v* -ED, -ING, -S to provide with a dowry

DOWERY   *n* pl. -ERIES dowry

DOWIE   *adj* dreary

DOWN   *v* -ED, -ING, -S to cause to fall

DOWNBEAT   *n* pl. -S the first beat of a musical measure

DOWNCAST   *n* pl. -S an overthrow or ruin

DOWNCOME   *n* pl. -S downfall

DOWNER   *n* pl. -S a depressant drug

DOWNFALL   *n* pl. -S a sudden fall

DOWNHAUL   *n* pl. -S a rope for hauling down sails

DOWNHILL   *n* pl. -S a downward slope

DOWNIER   comparative of downy

DOWNIEST   superlative of downy

DOWNLAND   *n* pl. -S a rolling treeless upland

DOWNLINK   *n* pl. -S a communications channel from a spacecraft

DOWNLOAD   *v* -ED, -ING, -S to transfer data from a large computer to a smaller one

DOWNPIPE   *n* pl. -S a pipe for draining water from a roof

DOWNPLAY   *v* -ED, -ING, -S to de-emphasize

DOWNPOUR   *n* pl. -S a heavy rain

DOWNSIDE   *n* pl. -S a negative aspect

DOWNSIZE   *v* -SIZED, -SIZING, -SIZES to produce in a smaller size

DOWNTICK   *n* pl. -S a stock market transaction

DOWNTIME   *n* pl. -S the time when a machine or factory is inactive

DOWNTOWN   *n* pl. -S the business district of a city

DOWNTROD   *adj* oppressed

DOWNTURN   *n* pl. -S a downward turn

DOWNWARD   *adv* from a higher to a lower place

DOWNWASH   *n* pl. -ES a downward deflection of air

DOWNWIND   *adv* in the direction that the wind blows

DOWNY   *adj* DOWNIER, DOWNIEST soft

DOWRY   *n* pl. -RIES the money or property a wife brings to her husband at marriage

DOWSABEL   *n* pl. -S a sweetheart

DOWSE   *v* DOWSED, DOWSING, DOWSES to search for underground water with a divining rod

DOWSER   *n* pl. -S one that dowses

DOXIE   *n* pl. -S doxy

DOXOLOGY   *n* pl. -GIES a hymn or verse of praise to God

DOXY   *n* pl. DOXIES a doctrine

DOYEN   *n* pl. -S the senior member of a group

DOYENNE   *n* pl. -S a female doyen

DOYLEY   *n* pl. -LEYS doily

DOYLY   *n* pl. -LIES doily

DOZE   *v* DOZED, DOZING, DOZES to sleep lightly

DOZEN   *v* -ED, -ING, -S to stun

DOZENTH   *n* pl. -S twelfth

DOZER   *n* pl. -S one that dozes

DOZIER   comparative of dozy

DOZIEST   superlative of dozy

DOZILY   *adv* in a dozy manner

DOZINESS   *n* pl. -ES the state of being dozy

DOZING   present participle of doze

DOZY   *adj* DOZIER, DOZIEST drowsy

DRAB   *adj* DRABBER, DRABBEST cheerless

DRAB   v DRABBED, DRABBING, DRABS to consort with prostitutes

DRABBET   n pl. -S a coarse linen fabric

DRABBLE   v -BLED, -BLING, -BLES to draggle

DRABLY   adv in a drab manner

DRABNESS   n pl. -ES the quality of being drab

DRACAENA   n pl. -S a tropical plant

DRACHM   n pl. -S a unit of weight

DRACHMA   n pl. -MAS, -MAE or -MAI a monetary unit of Greece

DRACONIC   adj pertaining to a dragon

DRAFF   n pl. -S the damp remains of malt after brewing

DRAFFISH   adj draffy

DRAFFY   adj DRAFFIER, DRAFFIEST worthless

DRAFT   v -ED, -ING, -S to conscript for military service

DRAFTEE   n pl, -S one that is drafted

DRAFTER   n pl. -S one that drafts

DRAFTING   n pl. -S mechanical drawing

DRAFTY   adj DRAFTIER, DRAFTIEST having or exposed to currents of air **DRAFTILY** adv

DRAG   v DRAGGED, DRAGGING, DRAGS to pull along the ground

DRAGEE   n pl. -S a sugarcoated candy

DRAGGER   n pl. -S one that drags

DRAGGIER   comparative of draggy

DRAGGIEST   superlative of draggy

DRAGGING   present participle of drag

DRAGGLE   v -GLED, -GLING, -GLES to make wet and dirty

DRAGGY   adj -GIER, -GIEST sluggish

DRAGLINE   n pl. -S a line used for dragging

DRAGNET   n pl. -S a net for trawling

DRAGOMAN   n pl. -MANS or -MEN an interpreter in Near Eastern countries

DRAGON   n pl. -S a mythical, serpentlike monster

DRAGONET   n pl. -S a marine fish

DRAGOON   v -ED, -ING, -S to harass by the use of troops

DRAGROPE   n pl. -S a rope used for dragging

DRAGSTER   n pl. -S a vehicle used in drag racing

DRAIL   n pl. -S a heavy fishhook

DRAIN   v -ED, -ING, -S to draw off a liquid

DRAINAGE   n pl. -S the act of draining

DRAINER   n pl. -S one that drains

DRAKE   n pl. -S a male duck

DRAM   v DRAMMED, DRAMMING, DRAMS to tipple

DRAMA   n pl. -S a composition written for theatrical performance

DRAMATIC   adj pertaining to drama

DRAMEDY   n pl. -DIES a sitcom having dramatic scenes

DRAMMED   past tense of dram

DRAMMING   present participle of dram

DRAMMOCK   n pl. -S raw oatmeal mixed with cold water

DRAMSHOP   n pl. -S a barroom

DRANK   past tense of drink

DRAPE   v DRAPED, DRAPING, DRAPES to arrange in graceful folds **DRAPABLE** adj

DRAPER   n pl. -S a dealer in cloth

DRAPERY   n pl. -ERIES cloth arranged in graceful folds

DRAPEY   adj characterized by graceful folds

DRAPING   present participle of drape

DRASTIC   adj extremely severe

DRAT   v DRATTED, DRATTING, DRATS to damn

DRAUGHT   v -ED, -ING, -S to draft

DRAUGHTY   adj DRAUGHTIER, DRAUGHTIEST drafty

DRAVE   a past tense of drive

DRAW   v DREW, DRAWN, DRAWING, DRAWS to move by pulling **DRAWABLE** adj

DRAWBACK   n pl. -S a hindrance

DRAWBAR   n pl. -S a railroad coupler

DRAWBORE   n pl. -S a hole for joining a mortise and tenon

DRAWDOWN   n pl. -S a lowering of a water level

DRAWEE   n pl. -S the person on whom a bill of exchange is drawn

DRAWER   n pl. -S one that draws

DRAWING   n pl. -S a portrayal in lines of a form or figure

DRAWL   v -ED, -ING, -S to speak slowly with vowels greatly prolonged

DRAWLER   n pl. -S one that drawls

DRAWLY   adj DRAWLIER, DRAWLIEST marked by drawling

DRAWN   past participle of draw

DRAWTUBE   n pl. -S a tube that slides within another tube

DRAY *v* -ED, -ING, -S to transport by dray (a low, strong cart)

DRAYAGE *n* pl. -S transportation by dray

DRAYMAN *n* pl. -MEN one who drives a dray

DREAD *v* -ED, -ING, -S to fear greatly

DREADFUL *n* pl. -S a publication containing sensational material

DREAM *v* DREAMED or DREAMT, DREAMING, DREAMS to have a dream (a series of images occurring during sleep)

DREAMER *n* pl. -S one that dreams

DREAMFUL *adj* dreamy

DREAMT a past tense of dream

DREAMY *adj* DREAMIER, DREAMIEST full of dreams **DREAMILY** *adv*

DREAR *n* pl. -S the state of being dreary

DREARY *adj* DREARIER, DREARIEST dismal **DREARILY** *adv*

DREARY *n* pl. DREARIES a dismal person

DRECK *n* pl. -S rubbish **DRECKY** *adj*

DREDGE *v* DREDGED, DREDGING, DREDGES to clear with a dredge (a machine for scooping mud)

DREDGER *n* pl. -S one that dredges

DREDGING *n* pl. -S matter that is dredged up

DREE *v* DREED, DREEING, DREES to suffer

DREG *n* pl. -S the sediment of liquors **DREGGISH** *adj*

DREGGY *adj* -GIER, -GIEST full of dregs

DREICH *adj* dreary

DREIDEL *n* pl. -S a spinning toy

DREIDL *n* pl. -S dreidel

DREIGH *adj* dreich

DREK *n* pl. -S dreck

DRENCH *v* -ED, -ING, -ES to wet thoroughly

DRENCHER *n* pl. -S one that drenches

DRESS *v* DRESSED or DREST, DRESSING, DRESSES to put clothes on

DRESSAGE *n* pl. -S the training of a horse in obedience and deportment

DRESSER *n* pl. -S one that dresses

DRESSING *n* pl. -S material applied to cover a wound

DRESSY *adj* DRESSIER, DRESSIEST stylish **DRESSILY** *adv*

DREST a past tense of dress

DREW past tense of draw

DRIB *v* DRIBBED, DRIBBING, DRIBS to drip

DRIBBLE *v* -BLED, -BLING, -BLES to drivel

DRIBBLER *n* pl. -S one that dribbles

DRIBBLET *n* pl. -S driblet

DRIBBLING present participle of dribble

DRIBBLY *adj* tending to dribble

DRIBLET *n* pl. -S a small drop of liquid

DRIED past tense of dry

DRIEGH *adj* dreary

DRIER *n* pl. -S one that dries

DRIES present 3d person sing. of dry

DRIEST a superlative of dry

DRIFT *v* -ED, -ING, -S to move along in a current

DRIFTAGE *n* pl. -S the act of drifting

DRIFTER *n* pl. -S one that drifts

DRIFTPIN *n* pl. -S a metal rod for securing timbers

DRIFTY *adj* DRIFTIER, DRIFTIEST full of drifts (masses of wind-driven snow)

DRILL *v* -ED, -ING, -S to bore a hole in

DRILLER *n* pl. -S one that drills

DRILLING *n* pl. -S a heavy twilled cotton fabric

DRILY *adv* dryly

DRINK *v* DRANK, DRUNK, DRINKING, DRINKS to swallow liquid

DRINKER *n* pl. -S one that drinks

DRIP *v* DRIPPED or DRIPT, DRIPPING, DRIPS to fall in drops

DRIPLESS *adj* designed not to drip

DRIPPER *n* pl. -S something from which a liquid drips

DRIPPING *n* pl. -S juice drawn from meat during cooking

DRIPPY *adj* -PIER, -PIEST very wet

DRIPT a past tense of drip

DRIVE *v* DROVE or DRAVE, DRIVEN, DRIVING, DRIVES to urge or propel forward **DRIVABLE** *adj*

DRIVEL *v* -ELED, -ELING, -ELS or -ELLED, -ELLING, -ELS to let saliva flow from the mouth

DRIVELER *n* pl. -S one that drivels

DRIVEN past participle of drive

DRIVER *n* pl. -S one that drives

DRIVEWAY *n* pl. -WAYS a private road providing access to a building

DRIVING   *n* pl. -S management of a motor vehicle

DRIZZLE   *v* -ZLED, -ZLING, -ZLES to rain lightly

DRIZZLY   *adj* -ZLIER, -ZLIEST characterized by light rain

DROGUE   *n* pl. -S a sea anchor

DROIT   *n* pl. -S a legal right

DROLL   *adj* DROLLER, DROLLEST comical

DROLL   *v* -ED, -ING, -S to jest

DROLLERY   *n* pl. -ERIES something droll

DROLLY   *adv* in a droll manner

DROMON   *n* pl. -S dromond

DROMOND   *n* pl. -S a large fast-sailing medieval galley

DRONE   *v* DRONED, DRONING, DRONES to make a continuous low sound

DRONER   *n* pl. -S one that drones

DRONGO   *n* pl. -GOS a tropical bird

DRONING   present participle of drone

DRONISH   *adj* habitually lazy

DROOL   *v* -ED, -ING, -S to drivel

DROOP   *v* -ED, -ING, -S to hang downward

DROOPY   *adj* DROOPIER, DROOPIEST drooping **DROOPILY** *adv*

DROP   *v* DROPPED or DROPT, DROPPING, DROPS to fall in drops (globules)

DROPHEAD   *n* pl. -S a convertible car

DROPKICK   *n* pl. -S a type of kick in football

DROPLET   *n* pl. -S a tiny drop

DROPOUT   *n* pl. -S one who quits school prematurely

DROPPED   past tense of drop

DROPPER   *n* pl. -S a tube for dispensing liquid in drops

DROPPING   *n* pl. -S something that has been dropped

DROPSHOT   *n* pl. -S a type of shot in tennis

DROPSY   *n* pl. -SIES an excessive accumulation of serous fluid **DROPSIED** *adj*

DROPT   a past tense of drop

DROPWORT   *n* pl. -S a perennial herb

DROSERA   *n* pl. -S a sundew

DROSHKY   *n* pl. -KIES an open carriage

DROSKY   *n* pl. -KIES droshky

DROSS   *n* pl. -ES waste matter

DROSSY   *adj* DROSSIER, DROSSIEST worthless

DROUGHT   *n* pl. -S a dry period

DROUGHTY   *adj* DROUGHTIER, DROUGHTIEST dry

DROUK   *v* -ED, -ING, -S to drench

DROUTH   *n* pl. -S drought

DROUTHY   *adj* DROUTHIER, DROUTHIEST droughty

DROVE   *v* DROVED, DROVING, DROVES to drive cattle or sheep

DROVER   *n* pl. -S a driver of cattle or sheep

DROWN   *v* -ED, -ING, -S to suffocate in water

DROWND   *v* -ED, -ING, -S to drown

DROWNER   *n* pl. -S one that drowns

DROWSE   *v* DROWSED, DROWSING, DROWSES to doze

DROWSY   *adj* DROWSIER, DROWSIEST sleepy **DROWSILY** *adv*

DRUB   *v* DRUBBED, DRUBBING, DRUBS to beat severely

DRUBBER   *n* pl. -S one that drubs

DRUBBING   *n* pl. -S a severe beating

DRUDGE   *v* DRUDGED, DRUDGING, DRUDGES to do hard, menial, or tedious work

DRUDGER   *n* pl. -S one that drudges

DRUDGERY   *n* pl. -ERIES hard, menial, or tedious work

DRUDGING   present participle of drudge

DRUG   *v* DRUGGED, DRUGGING, DRUGS to affect with a drug (a medicinal substance)

DRUGGET   *n* pl. -S a coarse woolen fabric

DRUGGIE   *n* pl. -S a drug addict

DRUGGIST   *n* pl. -S a pharmacist

DRUGGY   *adj* -GIER, -GIEST affected by drugs

DRUID   *n* pl. -S one of an ancient Celtic order of priests **DRUIDIC** *adj*

DRUIDESS   *n* pl. -ES a female druid

DRUIDISM   *n* pl. -S the religious system of the druids

DRUM   *v* DRUMMED, DRUMMING, DRUMS to beat a drum (a percussion instrument)

DRUMBEAT   *n* pl. -S the sound of a drum

DRUMBLE   *v* -BLED, -BLING, -BLES to move slowly

DRUMFIRE   *n* pl. -S heavy, continuous gunfire

DRUMFISH   *n* pl. -ES a fish that makes a drumming sound

DRUMHEAD *n* pl. -S the material stretched over the end of a drum
DRUMLIER comparative of drumly
DRUMLIEST superlative of drumly
DRUMLIKE *adj* resembling the head of a drum
DRUMLIN *n* pl. -S a long hill of glacial drift
DRUMLY *adj* -LIER, -LIEST dark and gloomy
DRUMMED past tense of drum
DRUMMER *n* pl. -S one that drums
DRUMMING present participle of drum
DRUMROLL *n* pl. -S a roll played on a drum
DRUNK *adj* DRUNKER, DRUNKEST intoxicated
DRUNK *n* pl. -S a drunken person
DRUNKARD *n* pl. -S one who is habitually drunk
DRUNKEN *adj* drunk
DRUPE *n* pl. -S a fleshy fruit
DRUPELET *n* pl. -S a small drupe
DRUSE *n* pl. -S a crust of small crystals lining a rock cavity
DRUTHERS *n/pl* one's preference
DRY *adj* DRIER, DRIEST or DRYER, DRYEST having no moisture
DRY *v* DRIED, DRYING, DRIES to make dry DRYABLE *adj*
DRY *n* pl. DRYS a prohibitionist
DRYAD *n* pl. -S or -ES a nymph of the woods DRYADIC *adj*
DRYER *n* pl. -S drier
DRYISH *adj* somewhat dry
DRYLAND *adj* relating to an arid region
DRYLOT *n* pl. -S an enclosure for livestock
DRYLY *adv* in a dry manner
DRYNESS *n* pl. -ES the state of being dry
DRYPOINT *n* pl. -S a method of engraving
DRYSTONE *adj* constructed of stone without mortar
DRYWALL *n* pl. -S board used instead of plaster in walls
DUAD *n* pl. -S a pair
DUAL *n* pl. -S a linguistic form
DUALISM *n* pl. -S a philosophical theory
DUALIST *n* pl. -S an adherent of dualism
DUALITY *n* pl. -TIES the state of being twofold
DUALIZE *v* -IZED, -IZING, -IZES to make twofold

DUALLY *adv* in two ways
DUB *v* DUBBED, DUBBING, DUBS to confer knighthood on
DUBBER *n* pl. -S one that dubs
DUBBIN *n* pl. -S material for softening and waterproofing leather
DUBBING *n* pl. -S dubbin
DUBIETY *n* pl. -ETIES the state of being dubious
DUBIOUS *adj* doubtful
DUBONNET *n* pl. -S a red color
DUCAL *adj* pertaining to a duke (a high-ranking nobleman) **DUCALLY** *adv*
DUCAT *n* pl. -S any of several gold coins formerly used in Europe
DUCE *n* pl. DUCES or DUCI a leader
DUCHESS *n* pl. -ES the wife or widow of a duke
DUCHY *n* pl. DUCHIES the domain of a duke
DUCI a pl. of duce
DUCK *v* -ED, -ING, -S to lower quickly
DUCKBILL *n* pl. -S a platypus
DUCKER *n* pl. -S one that ducks
DUCKIE *adj* ducky
DUCKIER comparative of ducky
DUCKIES pl. of ducky
DUCKIEST superlative of ducky
DUCKLING *n* pl. -S a young duck
DUCKPIN *n* pl. -S a type of bowling pin
DUCKTAIL *n* pl. -S a style of haircut
DUCKWALK *v* -ED, -ING, -S to walk in a squatting position
DUCKWEED *n* pl. -S an aquatic plant
DUCKY *adj* DUCKIER, DUCKIEST excellent
DUCKY *n* pl. DUCKIES a darling
DUCT *v* -ED, -ING, -S to convey through a duct (a tubular passage)
DUCTAL *adj* made up of ducts
DUCTILE *adj* easily molded or shaped
DUCTING *n* pl. -S a system of ducts
DUCTLESS *adj* being without a duct
DUCTULE *n* pl. -S a small duct
DUCTWORK *n* pl. -S a system of ducts
DUD *n* pl. -S a bomb that fails to explode
DUDDIE *adj* ragged
DUDDY *adj* duddie
DUDE *v* DUDED, DUDING, DUDES to dress up in flashy clothes
DUDEEN *n* pl. -S a short tobacco pipe

DUDGEON	*n* pl. -S a feeling of resentment
DUDING	present participle of dude
DUDISH	*adj* resembling a dude (a dandy)
DUDISHLY	*adv* in the manner of a dude
DUE	*n* pl. -S something that is owed
DUECENTO	*n* pl. -TOS the thirteenth century
DUEL	*v* DUELED, DUELING, DUELS or DUELLED, DUELLING, DUELS to fight formally
DUELER	*n* pl. -S one that duels
DUELIST	*n* pl. -S a dueler
DUELLED	a past tense of duel
DUELLER	*n* pl. -S dueler
DUELLI	a pl. of duello
DUELLING	a present participle of duel
DUELLIST	*n* pl. -S duelist
DUELLO	*n* pl. -LOS or -LI the art of dueling; a duel
DUENDE	*n* pl. -S charisma
DUENESS	*n* pl. -ES the state of being owed
DUENNA	*n* pl. -S a governess
DUET	*v* DUETTED, DUETTING, DUETS to perform a duet (a musical composition for two)
DUETTIST	*n* pl. -S a participant in a duet
DUFF	*n* pl. -S a thick pudding
DUFFEL	*n* pl. -S a coarse woolen fabric
DUFFER	*n* pl. -S a clumsy person
DUFFLE	*n* pl. -S duffel
DUG	*n* pl. -S the teat or udder of a female mammal
DUGONG	*n* pl. -S an aquatic mammal
DUGOUT	*n* pl. -S a canoe made by hollowing out a log
DUI	a pl. of duo
DUIKER	*n* pl. -S a small antelope
DUIT	*n* pl. -S doit
DUKE	*v* DUKED, DUKING, DUKES to fight
DUKEDOM	*n* pl. -S a duchy
DULCET	*n* pl. -S a soft-toned organ stop
DULCETLY	*adv* melodiously
DULCIANA	*n* pl. -S a soft-toned organ stop
DULCIFY	*v* -FIED, -FYING, -FIES to sweeten
DULCIMER	*n* pl. -S a stringed instrument
DULCINEA	*n* pl. -S a sweetheart

DULIA	*n* pl. -S veneration of saints
DULL	*adj* DULLER, DULLEST mentally slow
DULL	*v* -ED, -ING, -S to make less sharp
DULLARD	*n* pl. -S a dolt
DULLISH	*adj* somewhat dull
DULLNESS	*n* pl. -ES the state of being dull
DULLY	*adv* in a dull manner
DULNESS	*n* pl. -ES dullness
DULSE	*n* pl. -S an edible seaweed
DULY	*adv* rightfully
DUMA	*n* pl. -S a Russian council
DUMB	*adj* DUMBER, DUMBEST incapable of speech **DUMBLY** *adv*
DUMB	*v* -ED, -ING, -S to make silent
DUMBBELL	*n* pl. -S a weight lifted for muscular exercise
DUMBCANE	*n* pl. -S a tropical plant
DUMBHEAD	*n* pl. -S a stupid person
DUMBNESS	*n* pl. -ES the state of being dumb
DUMDUM	*n* pl. -S a type of bullet
DUMFOUND	*v* -ED, -ING, -S to astonish
DUMKA	*n* pl. -KY a Slavic folk ballad
DUMMKOPF	*n* pl. -S a dolt
DUMMY	*v* -MIED, -MYING, -MIES to make a representation of
DUMP	*v* -ED, -ING, -S to let fall heavily
DUMPCART	*n* pl. -S a type of cart
DUMPER	*n* pl. -S one that dumps
DUMPIER	comparative of dumpy
DUMPIEST	superlative of dumpy
DUMPILY	*adv* in a dumpy manner
DUMPING	*n* pl. -S the selling of large quantities of goods at below the market price
DUMPISH	*adj* sad
DUMPLING	*n* pl. -S a ball of dough cooked with stew or soup
DUMPY	*adj* DUMPIER, DUMPIEST short and thick
DUN	*v* DUNNED, DUNNING, DUNS to make demands upon for payment of a debt
DUN	*adj* DUNNER, DUNNEST of a dull brown color
DUNAM	*n* pl. -S a unit of land measure in Israel
DUNCE	*n* pl. -S a stupid person **DUNCICAL, DUNCISH** *adj*
DUNCH	*n* pl. -ES a push

DUNE *n* pl. -S a hill of sand **DUNELIKE** *adj*

DUNELAND *n* pl. -S an area having many dunes

DUNG *v* -ED, -ING, -S to fertilize with manure

DUNGAREE *n* pl. -S a coarse cotton fabric

DUNGEON *v* -ED, -ING, -S to confine in a dungeon (an underground prison)

DUNGHILL *n* pl. -S a heap of manure

DUNGY *adj* DUNGIER, DUNGIEST filthy

DUNITE *n* pl. -S an igneous rock **DUNITIC** *adj*

DUNK *v* -ED, -ING, -S to dip into liquid

DUNKER *n* pl. -S one that dunks

DUNLIN *n* pl. -S a wading bird

DUNNAGE *n* pl. -S packing material used to protect cargo

DUNNED past tense of dun

DUNNER comparative of dun

DUNNESS *n* pl. -ES the state of being dun

DUNNEST superlative of dun

DUNNING present participle of dun

DUNNITE *n* pl. -S an explosive

DUNT *v* -ED, -ING, -S to strike with a heavy blow

DUO *n* pl. DUOS or DUI an instrumental duet

DUODENUM *n* pl. -DENA or -DENUMS the first portion of the small intestine **DUODENAL** *adj*

DUOLOG *n* pl. -S duologue

DUOLOGUE *n* pl. -S a conversation between two persons

DUOMO *n* pl. -MOS or -MI a cathedral

DUOPOLY *n* pl. -LIES the market condition existing when there are two sellers only

DUOPSONY *n* pl. -NIES the market condition existing when there are two buyers only

DUOTONE *n* pl. -S an illustration in two tones

DUP *v* DUPPED, DUPPING, DUPS to open

DUPE *v* DUPED, DUPING, DUPES to deceive **DUPABLE** *adj*

DUPER *n* pl. -S one that dupes

DUPERY *n* pl. -ERIES the act of duping

DUPING present participle of dupe

DUPLE *adj* having two parts or elements

DUPLEX *v* -ED, -ING, -ES to make duple

DUPLEXER *n* pl. -S an electronic switching device

DUPPED past tense of dup

DUPPING present participle of dup

DURA *n* pl. -S durra

DURABLE *adj* able to withstand wear or decay **DURABLY** *adv*

DURABLES *n/pl* durable goods

DURAL *adj* of the dura mater (a brain membrane)

DURAMEN *n* pl. -S the central wood of a tree

DURANCE *n* pl. -S restraint by or as if by physical force

DURATION *n* pl. -S continuance in time

DURATIVE *n* pl. -S a type of verb

DURBAR *n* pl. -S the court of a native ruler in India

DURE *v* DURED, DURING, DURES to endure

DURESS *n* pl. -ES compulsion by threat

DURIAN *n* pl. -S an East Indian tree

DURING *prep* throughout the duration of

DURION *n* pl. -S durian

DURMAST *n* pl. -S a European oak

DURN *v* -ED, -ING, -S to damn

DURNED *adj* DURNEDER, DURNEDEST or DURNDEST damned

DURO *n* pl. -ROS a Spanish silver dollar

DUROC *n* pl. -S a large red hog

DURR *n* pl. -S durra

DURRA *n* pl. -S a cereal grain

DURRIE *n* pl. -S dhurrie

DURST a past tense of dare

DURUM *n* pl. -S a kind of wheat

DUSK *v* -ED, -ING, -S to become dark

DUSKISH *adj* dusky

DUSKY *adj* DUSKIER, DUSKIEST somewhat dark **DUSKILY** *adv*

DUST *v* -ED, -ING, -S to make free of dust (minute particles of matter)

DUSTBIN *n* pl. -S a trash can

DUSTER *n* pl. -S one that dusts

DUSTHEAP *n* pl. -S a pile of trash

DUSTIER comparative of dusty

DUSTIEST superative of dusty

DUSTILY *adv* in a dusty manner
DUSTLESS *adj* being without dust
DUSTLIKE *adj* resembling dust
DUSTMAN *n* pl. -MEN a trashman
DUSTOFF *n* pl. -S a military helicopter for evacuating the wounded
DUSTPAN *n* pl. -S a pan for holding swept dust
DUSTRAG *n* pl. -S a rag used for dusting
DUSTUP *n* pl. -S an argument
DUSTY *adj* DUSTIER, DUSTIEST full of dust
DUTCH *adv* with each person paying for himself
DUTCHMAN *n* pl. -MEN something used to hide structural defects
DUTEOUS *adj* dutiful
DUTIABLE *adj* subject to import tax
DUTIFUL *adj* obedient
DUTY *n* pl. -TIES a moral or legal obligation
DUUMVIR *n* pl. -VIRS or -VIRI a magistrate of ancient Rome
DUVET *n* pl. -S a down-filled bed covering
DUVETINE *n* pl. -S duvetyn
DUVETYN *n* pl. -S a smooth lustrous velvety fabric
DUVETYNE *n* pl. -S duvetyn
DUXELLES *n* pl. DUXELLES a garnish or sauce with minced mushrooms
DWARF *adj* DWARFER, DWARFEST extremely small
DWARF *n* pl. DWARFS or DWARVES an extremely small person
DWARF *v* -ED, -ING, -S to cause to appear small
DWARFISH *adj* resembling a dwarf
DWARFISM *n* pl. -S a condition of stunted growth
DWARVES a pl. of dwarf
DWEEB *n* pl. -S an unattractive or inept person
DWELL *v* DWELT or DWELLED, DWELLING, DWELLS to reside
DWELLER *n* pl. -S one that dwells
DWELLING *n* pl. -S a place of residence
DWELT a past tense of dwell
DWINDLE *v* -DLED, -DLING, -DLES to decrease steadily
DWINE *v* DWINED, DWINING, DWINES to pine or waste away

DYABLE *adj* dyeable
DYAD *n* pl. -S a pair of units
DYADIC *n* pl. -S a sum of mathematical dyads
DYARCHY *n* pl. -CHIES diarchy **DYARCHIC** *adj*
DYBBUK *n* pl. -BUKS or -BUKIM a wandering soul in Jewish folklore
DYE *v* DYED, DYEING, DYES to treat with a dye (a coloring matter)
DYEABLE *adj* capable of being dyed
DYEING *n* pl. -S something colored with a dye
DYER *n* pl. -S one that dyes
DYESTUFF *n* pl. -S a dye
DYEWEED *n* pl. -S a shrub that yields a yellow dye
DYEWOOD *n* pl. -S a wood from which a dye is extracted
DYING *n* pl. -S a passing out of existence
DYKE *v* DYKED, DYKING, DYKES to dike
DYNAMIC *n* pl. -S a physical force
DYNAMISM *n* pl. -S a theory that explains the universe in terms of force or energy
DYNAMIST *n* pl. -S an adherent of dynamism
DYNAMITE *v* -MITED, -MITING, -MITES to blow up with a powerful explosive
DYNAMO *n* pl. -MOS a forceful energetic person
DYNAST *n* pl. -S a ruler
DYNASTY *n* pl. -TIES a succession of rulers from the same line of descent **DYNASTIC** *adj*
DYNATRON *n* pl. -S a type of electron tube
DYNE *n* pl. -S a unit of force
DYNEIN *n* pl. DYNEIN an enzyme involved in cell movement
DYNEL *n* pl. -S a synthetic fiber
DYNODE *n* pl. -S a type of electrode
DYSGENIC *adj* causing the deterioration of hereditary qualities
DYSLEXIA *n* pl. -S impairment of the ability to read
DYSLEXIC *n* pl. -S one who is affected with dyslexia
DYSPEPSY *n* pl. -SIES indigestion

DYSPNEA   *n* pl. -S labored breathing **DYSPNEAL, DYSPNEIC** *adj*

DYSPNOEA   *n* pl. -S dyspnea **DYSPNOIC** *adj*

DYSTAXIA   *n* pl. -S a form of muscular tremor

DYSTOCIA   *n* pl. -S difficult labor and delivery in childbirth

DYSTONIA   *n* pl. -S a condition of disordered tonicity of muscle tissue **DYSTONIC** *adj*

DYSTOPIA   *n* pl. -S a wretched place

DYSURIA   *n* pl. -S painful urination **DYSURIC** *adj*

DYVOUR   *n* pl. -S one who is bankrupt

EACH   *adj* being one of two or more distinct individuals

EAGER   *adj* -GERER, -GEREST impatiently longing **EAGERLY** *adv*

EAGER   *n* pl. -S eagre

EAGLE   *n* pl. -S a large bird of prey

EAGLET   *n* pl. -S a young eagle

EAGRE   *n* pl. -S a tidal flood

EANLING   *n* pl. -S yeanling

EAR   *v* -ED, -ING, -S to form the fruiting head of a cereal

EARACHE   *n* pl. -S a pain in the ear (an organ of hearing)

EARDROP   *n* pl. -S an earring

EARDRUM   *n* pl. -S the tympanic membrane

EARED   *adj* having ears

EARFLAP   *n* pl. -S a part of a cap designed to cover the ears

EARFUL   *n* pl. -S a flow of information

EARING   *n* pl. -S a line on a ship

EARL   *n* pl. -S a British nobleman

EARLAP   *n* pl. -S an earflap

EARLDOM   *n* pl. -S the rank of an earl

EARLESS   *adj* lacking ears

EARLIER   comparative of early

EARLIEST   superlative of early

EARLOBE   *n* pl. -S a part of the ear

EARLOCK   *n* pl. -S a curl of hair by the ear

EARLSHIP   *n* pl. -S earldom

EARLY   *adv* -LIER, -LIEST near the beginning of a period of time or a series of events

EARMARK   *v* -ED, -ING, -S to designate for a specific use

EARMUFF   *n* pl. -S one of a pair of ear coverings

EARN   *v* -ED, -ING, -S to gain or deserve for one's labor or service

EARNER   *n* pl. -S one that earns

EARNEST   *n* pl. -S a down payment

EARNINGS   *n/pl* something earned

EARPHONE   *n* pl. -S a listening device worn over the ear

EARPIECE   *n* pl. -S an earphone

EARPLUG   *n* pl. -S a plug for the ear

EARRING   *n* pl. -S an ornament for the earlobe

EARSHOT   *n* pl. -S the range within which sound can be heard

EARSTONE   *n* pl. -S an otolith

EARTH   *v* -ED, -ING, -S to cover with earth (soil)

EARTHEN   *adj* made of earth

EARTHIER   comparative of earthy

EARTHIEST   superlative of earthy

EARTHILY   *adv* in an earthy manner

EARTHLY   *adj* -LIER, -LIEST worldly

EARTHMAN   *n* pl. -MEN a person from the planet earth

EARTHNUT   *n* pl. -S a European herb

EARTHPEA   *n* pl. -S a twining plant

EARTHSET   *n* pl. -S the setting of the earth as seen from the moon

EARTHY   *adj* EARTHIER, EARTHIEST composed of, resembling, or suggestive of earth

EARWAX   *n* pl. -ES cerumen

EARWIG   *v* -WIGGED, -WIGGING, -WIGS to insinuate against in secret

EARWORM   *n* pl. -S a bollworm

EASE   *v* EASED, EASING, EASES to give rest or relief to

EASEFUL   *adj* restful

EASEL   *n* pl. -S a three-legged frame
EASEMENT   *n* pl. -S relief
EASIER   comparative of easy
EASIES   pl. of easy
EASIEST   superlative of easy
EASILY   *adv* without difficulty
EASINESS   *n* pl. -ES the state of being easy
EASING   present participle of ease
EAST   *n* pl. -S a cardinal point of the compass
EASTER   *n* pl. -S a wind or storm from the east
EASTERLY   *n* pl. -LIES a wind from the east
EASTERN   *adj* being to, toward, or in the east
EASTING   *n* pl. -S a movement toward the east
EASTWARD   *n* pl. -S a direction toward the east
EASY   *adj* EASIER, EASIEST not difficult
EASY   *n* pl. EASIES a communications code word for the letter E
EAT   *v* ATE or ET, EATEN, EATING, EATS to consume food
EATABLE   *n* pl. -S an edible
EATER   *n* pl. -S one that eats
EATERY   *n* pl. -ERIES a lunchroom
EATH   *adj* easy
EATING   *n* pl. -S the act of consuming food
EAU   *n* pl. EAUX water
EAVE   *n* pl. -S the lower projecting edge of a roof **EAVED** *adj*
EBB   *v* -ED, -ING, -S to recede
EBBET   *n* pl. -S a common green newt
EBON   *n* pl. -S ebony
EBONIES   pl. of ebony
EBONISE   *v* -ISED, -ISING, -ISES to ebonize
EBONITE   *n* pl. -S a hard rubber
EBONIZE   *v* -IZED, -IZING, -IZES to stain black in imitation of ebony
EBONY   *n* pl. -NIES a hard, heavy wood
ECARTE   *n* pl. -S a card game
ECAUDATE   *adj* having no tail
ECBOLIC   *n* pl. -S a type of drug
ECCLESIA   *n* pl. -SIAE an assembly in ancient Greece

ECCRINE   *adj* producing secretions externally
ECDYSIS   *n* pl. -DYSES the shedding of an outer layer of skin **ECDYSIAL** *adj*
ECDYSON   *n* pl. -S ecdysone
ECDYSONE   *n* pl. -S an insect hormone
ECESIS   *n* pl. -SISES the establishment of a plant or animal in a new environment
ECHARD   *n* pl. -S the water in the soil not available to plants
ECHE   *v* ECHED, ECHING, ECHES to increase
ECHELLE   *n* pl. -S a device for spreading light into its component colors
ECHELON   *v* -ED, -ING, -S to group in a particular formation
ECHIDNA   *n* pl. -NAS or -NAE a spiny anteater
ECHINATE   *adj* spiny
ECHING   present participle of eche
ECHINOID   *n* pl. -S a spiny marine animal
ECHINUS   *n* pl. -NI echinoid
ECHO   *v* -ED, -ING, -ES to produce an echo
ECHO   *n* pl. ECHOES or ECHOS a repetition of sound by reflection of sound waves
ECHOER   *n* pl. -S one that echoes
ECHOEY   *adj* full of echoes
ECHOGRAM   *n* pl. -S a record produced by a device that uses ultrasonic waves
ECHOIC   *adj* resembling an echo
ECHOISM   *n* pl. -S the formation of words in imitation of sounds
ECHOLESS   *adj* producing no echo
ECLAIR   *n* pl. -S a type of pastry
ECLAT   *n* pl. -S brilliance
ECLECTIC   *n* pl. -S one who draws his beliefs from various sources
ECLIPSE   *v* ECLIPSED, ECLIPSING, ECLIPSES to obscure
ECLIPSIS   *n* pl. ECLIPSES or ECLIPSISES an ellipsis
ECLIPTIC   *n* pl. -S an astronomical plane
ECLOGITE   *n* pl. -S a type of rock
ECLOGUE   *n* pl. -S a pastoral poem
ECLOSION   *n* pl. -S the emergence of an insect larva from an egg
ECOCIDE   *n* pl. -S the destruction of the natural environment **ECOCIDAL** *adj*
ECOFREAK   *n* pl. -S a zealous environmentalist

ECOLOGY   *n* pl. -GIES an environmental science ECOLOGIC *adj*

ECONOBOX   *n* pl. -ES a small economical car

ECONOMIC   *adj* pertaining to financial matters

ECONOMY   *n* pl. -MIES thrift

ECOTONE   *n* pl. -S a type of ecological zone ECOTONAL *adj*

ECOTYPE   *n* pl. -S a subspecies adapted to specific environmental conditions ECOTYPIC *adj*

ECRASEUR   *n* pl. -S a surgical instrument

ECRU   *n* pl. -S a yellowish brown color

ECSTASY   *n* pl. -SIES a state of exaltation

ECSTATIC   *n* pl. -S one that is subject to ecstasies

ECTASIS   *n* pl. -TASES the lengthening of a usually short syllable ECTATIC *adj*

ECTHYMA   *n* pl. -MATA a virus disease

ECTODERM   *n* pl. -S the outermost germ layer of an embryo

ECTOMERE   *n* pl. -S a cell that develops into ectoderm

ECTOPIA   *n* pl. -S congenital displacement of parts or organs ECTOPIC *adj*

ECTOSARC   *n* pl. -S the outermost layer of protoplasm of certain protozoans

ECTOZOAN   *n* pl. -S ectozoon

ECTOZOON   *n* pl. -ZOA a parasite on the body of an animal

ECTYPE   *n* pl. -S a copy ECTYPAL *adj*

ECU   *n* pl. -S an old French coin

ECUMENIC   *adj* universal

ECZEMA   *n* pl. -S a skin disease

ED   *n* pl. ED education

EDACIOUS   *adj* voracious

EDACITY   *n* pl. -TIES gluttony

EDAPHIC   *adj* pertaining to the soil

EDDO   *n* pl. -DOES a tropical plant

EDDY   *v* -DIED, -DYING, -DIES to move against the main current

EDEMA   *n* pl. -MAS or -MATA an excessive accumulation of serous fluid

EDENIC   *adj* pertaining to a paradise

EDENTATE   *n* pl. -S a toothless mammal

EDGE   *v* EDGED, EDGING, EDGES to provide with an edge (a bounding or dividing line)

EDGELESS   *adj* lacking an edge

EDGER   *n* pl. -S a tool used to trim a lawn's edge

EDGEWAYS   *adv* edgewise

EDGEWISE   *adv* sideways

EDGIER   comparative of edgy

EDGIEST   superlative of edgy

EDGILY   *adv* in an edgy manner

EDGINESS   *n* pl. -ES the state of being edgy

EDGING   *n* pl. -S something that forms or serves as an edge

EDGY   *adj* EDGIER, EDGIEST tense, nervous, or irritable

EDH   *n* pl. -S an Old English letter

EDIBLE   *n* pl. -S something fit to be eaten

EDICT   *n* pl. -S an authoritative order having the force of law EDICTAL *adj*

EDIFICE   *n* pl. -S a building

EDIFIER   *n* pl. -S one that edifies

EDIFY   *v* -FIED, -FYING, -FIES to enlighten

EDILE   *n* pl. -S aedile

EDIT   *v* -ED, -ING, -S to correct and prepare for publication EDITABLE *adj*

EDITION   *n* pl. -S a particular series of printed material

EDITOR   *n* pl. -S one that edits

EDITRESS   *n* pl. -ES a female editor

EDUCABLE   *n* pl. -S a mildly retarded person

EDUCATE   *v* -CATED, -CATING, -CATES to teach

EDUCATOR   *n* pl. -S one that educates

EDUCE   *v* EDUCED, EDUCING, EDUCES to draw forth or bring out EDUCIBLE *adj*

EDUCT   *n* pl. -S something educed

EDUCTION   *n* pl. -S the act of educing EDUCTIVE *adj*

EDUCTOR   *n* pl. -S one that educes

EEL   *n* pl. -S a snakelike fish

EELGRASS   *n* pl. -ES an aquatic plant

EELIER   comparative of eely

EELIEST   superlative of eely

EELLIKE   *adj* resembling an eel

EELPOUT   *n* pl. -S a marine fish

EELWORM   *n* pl. -S a small roundworm

EELY   *adj* EELIER, EELIEST resembling an eel

EERIE   *adj* -RIER, -RIEST weird EERILY *adv*

EERINESS   *n* pl. -ES the state of being eerie

EERY	*adj* -RIER, -RIEST eerie
EF	*n* pl. -S the letter F
EFF	*n* pl. -S ef
EFFABLE	*adj* capable of being uttered or expressed
EFFACE	*v* -FACED, -FACING, -FACES to rub or wipe out
EFFACER	*n* pl. -S one that effaces
EFFECT	*v* -ED, -ING, -S to bring about
EFFECTER	*n* pl. -S effector
EFFECTOR	*n* pl. -S a bodily organ that responds to a nerve impulse
EFFENDI	*n* pl. -S a Turkish title of respect
EFFERENT	*n* pl. -S an organ or part conveying nervous impulses to an effector
EFFETE	*adj* exhausted of vigor or energy **EFFETELY** *adv*
EFFICACY	*n* pl. -CIES effectiveness
EFFIGIAL	*adj* resembling an effigy
EFFIGY	*n* pl. -GIES a likeness or representation
EFFLUENT	*n* pl. -S an outflow
EFFLUVIA	*n/pl* byproducts in the form of waste
EFFLUX	*n* pl. -ES an outflow
EFFORT	*n* pl. -S a deliberate exertion
EFFULGE	*v* -FULGED, -FULGING, -FULGES to shine forth
EFFUSE	*v* -FUSED, -FUSING, -FUSES to pour forth
EFFUSION	*n* pl. -S an outpouring of emotion
EFFUSIVE	*adj* pouring forth
EFT	*n* pl. -S a newt
EFTSOON	*adv* soon afterward
EFTSOONS	*adv* eftsoon
EGAD	*interj* — used as a mild oath
EGADS	*interj* egad
EGAL	*adj* equal
EGALITE	*n* pl. -S equality
EGER	*n* pl. -S eagre
EGEST	*v* -ED, -ING, -S to discharge from the body
EGESTA	*n/pl* egested matter
EGESTION	*n* pl. -S the act of egesting **EGESTIVE** *adj*
EGG	*v* -ED, -ING, -S to incite or urge
EGGAR	*n* pl. -S egger
EGGCUP	*n* pl. -S a cup from which an egg is eaten
EGGER	*n* pl. -S a kind of moth
EGGHEAD	*n* pl. -S an intellectual
EGGLESS	*adj* lacking eggs
EGGNOG	*n* pl. -S a beverage
EGGPLANT	*n* pl. -S a perennial herb yielding edible fruit
EGGSHELL	*n* pl. -S the hard exterior of a bird's egg
EGGY	*adj* containing eggs
EGIS	*n* pl. EGISES aegis
EGLATERE	*n* pl. -S a wild rose
EGLOMISE	*adj* made of glass with a painted picture on the back
EGO	*n* pl. EGOS the conscious self
EGOISM	*n* pl. -S extreme devotion to self-interest
EGOIST	*n* pl. -S one who practices egoism **EGOISTIC** *adj*
EGOLESS	*adj* not characterized by egoism
EGOMANIA	*n* pl. -S extreme egotism
EGOTISM	*n* pl. -S self-conceit
EGOTIST	*n* pl. -S a conceited person
EGRESS	*v* -ED, -ING, -ES to go out
EGRET	*n* pl. -S a wading bird
EGYPTIAN	*n* pl. -S a typeface with squared serifs
EH	*interj* — used to express doubt or surprise
EIDE	pl. of eidos
EIDER	*n* pl. -S a large sea duck
EIDETIC	*adj* pertaining to vivid recall
EIDOLIC	*adj* pertaining to an eidolon
EIDOLON	*n* pl. -LONS or -LA a phantom
EIDOS	*n* pl. EIDE an essence
EIGHT	*n* pl. -S a number
EIGHTEEN	*n* pl. -S a number
EIGHTH	*n* pl. -S one of eight equal parts
EIGHTHLY	*adv* in the eighth place
EIGHTVO	*n* pl. -VOS octavo
EIGHTY	*n* pl. EIGHTIES a number
EIKON	*n* pl. -S or -ES icon
EINKORN	*n* pl. -S a variety of wheat
EINSTEIN	*n* pl. -S a very intelligent person
EIRENIC	*adj* irenic
EISWEIN	*n* pl. -S a sweet German wine
EITHER	*adj* being one or the other
EJECT	*v* -ED, -ING, -S to throw out forcibly
EJECTA	*n/pl* ejected material
EJECTION	*n* pl. -S the act of ejecting
EJECTIVE	*n* pl. -S a sound produced with air compressed above the closed glottis
EJECTOR	*n* pl. -S one that ejects
EKE	*v* EKED, EKING, EKES to supplement with great effort

EKISTICS   n/pl a science dealing with human habitats EKISTIC adj
EKPWELE   n pl. -S a former monetary unit of Equatorial Guinea
EKTEXINE   n pl. -S an outer layer of the exine
EKUELE   n pl. EKUELE ekpwele
EL   n pl. -S an elevated railroad or train
ELAIN   n pl. -S olein
ELAN   n pl. -S enthusiasm
ELAND   n pl. -S a large antelope
ELAPHINE   adj pertaining to a genus of deer
ELAPID   n pl. -S a venomous snake
ELAPINE   adj pertaining to a family of snakes
ELAPSE   v ELAPSED, ELAPSING, ELAPSES to pass away
ELASTASE   n pl. -S an enzyme
ELASTIC   n pl. -S a stretchable material
ELASTIN   n pl. -S a bodily protein
ELATE   v ELATED, ELATING, ELATES to raise the spirits of ELATEDLY adv
ELATER   n pl. -S a click beetle
ELATERID   n pl. -S an elater
ELATERIN   n pl. -S a chemical compound
ELATING   present participle of elate
ELATION   n pl. -S a feeling of great joy
ELATIVE   n pl. -S an adjectival form in some languages
ELBOW   v -ED, -ING, -S to jostle
ELD   n pl. -S old age
ELDER   n pl. -S an older person
ELDERLY   n pl. -LIES a rather old person
ELDEST   adj oldest
ELDRESS   n pl. -ES a female elder (a church officer)
ELDRICH   adj eldritch
ELDRITCH   adj weird
ELECT   v -ED, -ING, -S to select by vote for an office
ELECTEE   n pl. -S a person who has been elected
ELECTION   n pl. -S the act of electing
ELECTIVE   n pl. -S an optional course of study
ELECTOR   n pl. -S one that elects
ELECTRET   n pl. -S a type of nonconductor
ELECTRIC   n pl. -S something run by electricity
ELECTRO   v -ED, -ING, -S to make a metallic copy of a page of type for printing

ELECTRON   n pl. -S an elementary particle
ELECTRUM   n pl. -S an alloy of gold and silver
ELEGANCE   n pl. -S tasteful opulence
ELEGANCY   n pl. -CIES elegance
ELEGANT   adj tastefully opulent
ELEGIAC   n pl. -S a type of verse
ELEGIES   pl. of elegy
ELEGISE   v -GISED, -GISING, -GISES to elegize
ELEGIST   n pl. -S one that writes elegies
ELEGIT   n pl. -S a type of judicial writ
ELEGIZE   v -GIZED, -GIZING, -GIZES to write an elegy
ELEGY   n pl. -GIES a mournful poem for one who is dead
ELEMENT   n pl. -S a substance that cannot be separated into simpler substances by chemical means
ELEMI   n pl. -S a fragrant resin
ELENCHUS   n pl. -CHI a logical refutation ELENCHIC, ELENCTIC adj
ELEPHANT   n pl. -S a large mammal
ELEVATE   v -VATED, -VATING, -VATES to raise
ELEVATED   n pl. -S a railway that operates on a raised structure
ELEVATOR   n pl. -S one that elevates
ELEVEN   n pl. -S a number
ELEVENTH   n pl. -S one of eleven equal parts
ELEVON   n pl. -S a type of airplane control surface
ELF   n pl. ELVES a small, often mischievous fairy ELFLIKE adj
ELFIN   n pl. -S an elf
ELFISH   adj resembling an elf ELFISHLY adv
ELFLOCK   n pl. -S a lock of tangled hair
ELHI   adj pertaining to school grades 1 through 12
ELICIT   v -ED, -ING, -S to educe
ELICITOR   n pl. -S one that elicits
ELIDE   v ELIDED, ELIDING, ELIDES to omit ELIDIBLE adj
ELIGIBLE   n pl. -S one that is qualified to be chosen
ELIGIBLY   adv in a qualified manner
ELINT   n pl. -S the gathering of intelligence by electronic devices
ELISION   n pl. -S the act of eliding
ELITE   n pl. -S a socially superior group

ELITISM *n* pl. -S belief in rule by an elite

ELITIST *n* pl. -S an adherent of elitism

ELIXIR *n* pl. -S a medicinal beverage

ELK *n* pl. -S a large deer

ELKHOUND *n* pl. -S a hunting dog

ELL *n* pl. -S the letter L

ELLIPSE *n* pl. -S a type of plane curve

ELLIPSIS *n* pl. -LIPSES an omission of a word or words in a sentence

ELLIPTIC *adj* having the shape of an ellipse

ELM *n* pl. -S a deciduous tree

ELMY *adj* -MIER, -MIEST abounding in elms

ELODEA *n* pl. -S an aquatic herb

ELOIGN *v* -ED, -ING, -S to remove to a distant place

ELOIGNER *n* pl. -S one that eloigns

ELOIN *v* -ED, -ING, -S to eloign

ELOINER *n* pl. -S one that eloins

ELONGATE *v* -GATED, -GATING, -GATES to lengthen

ELOPE *v* ELOPED, ELOPING, ELOPES to run off secretly to be married

ELOPER *n* pl. -S one that elopes

ELOQUENT *adj* fluent and convincing in speech

ELSE *adv* in a different place, time, or way

ELUANT *n* pl. -S a solvent

ELUATE *n* pl. -S the material obtained by eluting

ELUDE *v* ELUDED, ELUDING, ELUDES to evade

ELUDER *n* pl. -S one that eludes

ELUENT *n* pl. -S eluant

ELUSION *n* pl. -S the act of eluding

ELUSIVE *adj* tending to elude

ELUSORY *adj* elusive

ELUTE *v* ELUTED, ELUTING, ELUTES to remove by means of a solvent

ELUTION *n* pl. -S the act of eluting

ELUVIA a pl. of eluvium

ELUVIAL *adj* pertaining to an eluvium

ELUVIATE *v* -ATED, -ATING, -ATES to undergo a transfer of materials in the soil

ELUVIUM *n* pl. -VIA or -VIUMS a soil deposit

ELVER *n* pl. -S a young eel

ELVES pl. of elf

ELVISH *adj* elfish **ELVISHLY** *adv*

ELYSIAN *adj* delightful

ELYTRON *n* pl. -TRA a hardened forewing of certain insects **ELYTROID, ELYTROUS** *adj*

ELYTRUM *n* pl. -TRA elytron

EM *n* pl. -S the letter M

EMACIATE *v* -ATED, -ATING, -ATES to make thin

EMANATE *v* -NATED, -NATING, -NATES to send forth

EMANATOR *n* pl. -S one that emanates

EMBALM *v* -ED, -ING, -S to treat so as to protect from decay

EMBALMER *n* pl. -S one that embalms

EMBANK *v* -ED, -ING, -S to confine or protect with a raised structure

EMBAR *v* -BARRED, -BARRING, -BARS to imprison

EMBARGO *v* -ED, -ING, -ES to restrain trade by a governmental order

EMBARK *v* -ED, -ING, -S to make a start

EMBARRED past tense of embar

EMBARRING present participle of embar

EMBASSY *n* pl. -SIES the headquarters of an ambassador

EMBATTLE *v* -TLED, -TLING, -TLES to prepare for battle

EMBAY *v* -ED, -ING, -S to enclose in a bay

EMBED *v* -BEDDED, -BEDDING, -BEDS to fix firmly into a surrounding mass

EMBER *n* pl. -S a glowing fragment from a fire

EMBEZZLE *v* -ZLED, -ZLING, -ZLES to appropriate fraudulently to one's own use

EMBITTER *v* -ED, -ING, -S to make bitter

EMBLAZE *v* -BLAZED, -BLAZING, -BLAZES to set on fire

EMBLAZER *n* pl. -S one that emblazes

EMBLAZON *v* -ED, -ING, -S to decorate with brilliant colors

EMBLEM *v* -ED, -ING, -S to represent with an emblem (a graphical symbol)

EMBODIER *n* pl. -S one that embodies

EMBODY *v* -BODIED, -BODYING, -BODIES to provide with a body

EMBOLDEN *v* -ED, -ING, -S to instill with courage

EMBOLI pl. of embolus

EMBOLIES pl. of emboly

EMBOLISM *n* pl. -S the obstruction of a blood vessel by an embolus **EMBOLIC** *adj*

EMBOLUS *n* pl. -LI an abnormal particle circulating in the blood

EMBOLY *n* pl. -LIES a phase of embryonic growth

EMBORDER *v* -ED, -ING, -S to provide with a border

EMBOSK *v* -ED, -ING, -S to conceal with foliage

EMBOSOM *v* -ED, -ING, -S to embrace

EMBOSS *v* -ED, -ING, -ES to decorate with raised designs

EMBOSSER *n* pl. -S one that embosses

EMBOW *v* -ED, -ING, -S to arch

EMBOWEL *v* -ELED, -ELING, -ELS or -ELLED, -ELLING, -ELS to disbowel

EMBOWER *v* -ED, -ING, -S to surround with foliage

EMBRACE *v* -BRACED, -BRACING, -BRACES to hug

EMBRACER *n* pl. -S one that embraces

EMBROIL *v* -ED, -ING, -S to involve in conflict

EMBROWN *v* -ED, -ING, -S to make brown

EMBRUE *v* -BRUED, -BRUING, -BRUES to imbrue

EMBRUTE *v* -BRUTED, -BRUTING, -BRUTES to imbrute

EMBRYO *n* pl. -BRYOS an organism in its early stages of development

EMBRYOID *n* pl. -S a mass of tissue that resembles an embryo

EMBRYON *n* pl. -S an embryo

EMCEE *v* -CEED, -CEEING, -CEES to serve as master of ceremonies

EME *n* pl. -S an uncle

EMEER *n* pl. -S emir

EMEERATE *n* pl. -S emirate

EMEND *v* -ED, -ING, -S to correct

EMENDATE *v* -DATED, -DATING, -DATES to emend

EMENDER *n* pl. -S one that emends

EMERALD *n* pl. -S a green gem

EMERGE *v* EMERGED, EMERGING, EMERGES to come out into view

EMERGENT *n* pl. -S a type of aquatic plant

EMERIES pl. of emery

EMERITA *n* pl. -TAE a retired woman who retains an honorary title

EMERITUS *n* pl. -TI a retired person who retains an honorary title

EMEROD *n* pl. -S a tumor

EMEROID *n* pl. -S emerod

EMERSED *adj* standing out of water

EMERSION *n* pl. -S the act of emerging

EMERY *n* pl. -ERIES a granular corundum

EMESIS *n* pl. EMESES the act of vomiting

EMETIC *n* pl. -S a substance which induces vomiting

EMETIN *n* pl. -S emetine

EMETINE *n* pl. -S an alkaloid

EMEU *n* pl. -S emu

EMEUTE *n* pl. -S a riot

EMF *n* pl. -S a difference in electric potential

EMIC *adj* relating to a type of linguistic analysis

EMIGRANT *n* pl. -S one that emigrates

EMIGRATE *v* -GRATED, -GRATING, -GRATES to leave one country or region to settle in another

EMIGRE *n* pl. -S an emigrant

EMINENCE *n* pl. -S high station or rank

EMINENCY *n* pl. -CIES eminence

EMINENT *adj* of high station or rank

EMIR *n* pl. -S an Arab chieftain or prince

EMIRATE *n* pl. -S the rank of an emir

EMISSARY *n* pl. -SARIES a person sent on a mission

EMISSION *n* pl. -S the act of emitting **EMISSIVE** *adj*

EMIT *v* EMITTED, EMITTING, EMITS to send forth

EMITTER *n* pl. -S one that emits

EMMER *n* pl. -S a type of wheat

EMMET *n* pl. -S an ant

EMODIN *n* pl. -S a chemical compound

EMOTE *v* EMOTED, EMOTING, EMOTES to express emotion in an exaggerated manner

EMOTER *n* pl. -S one that emotes

EMOTION *n* pl. -S an affective state of consciousness

EMOTIVE *adj* pertaining to emotion

EMPALE *v* -PALED, -PALING, -PALES to impale

EMPALER *n* pl. -S one that empales

EMPANADA *n* pl. -S a pastry turnover

EMPANEL *v* -ELED, -ELING, -ELS or -ELLED, -ELLING, -ELS to impanel

EMPATHY *n* pl. -THIES imaginative identification with another's thoughts and feelings **EMPATHIC** *adj*

EMPEROR *n* pl. -S the ruler of an empire

EMPERY *n* pl. -PERIES absolute dominion

EMPHASIS *n* pl. -PHASES special significance imparted to something

EMPHATIC *adj* strongly expressive

EMPIRE *n* pl. -S a major political unit

EMPIRIC *n* pl. -S one who relies on practical experience

EMPLACE *v* -PLACED, -PLACING, -PLACES to position

EMPLANE *v* -PLANED, -PLANING, -PLANES to enplane

EMPLOY *v* -ED -ING, -S to hire

EMPLOYE *n* pl. -S employee

EMPLOYEE *n* pl. -S a person who is employed

EMPLOYER *n* pl. -S one that employs

EMPOISON *v* -ED, -ING, -S to embitter

EMPORIUM *n* pl. -RIUMS or -RIA a trading or market center

EMPOWER *v* -ED, -ING, -S to give legal power to

EMPRESS *n* pl. -ES a female ruler of an empire

EMPRISE *n* pl. -S an adventurous undertaking

EMPRIZE *n* pl. -S emprise

EMPTIED past tense of empty

EMPTIER *n* pl. -S one that empties

EMPTIES present 3d person sing. of empty

EMPTIEST superlative of empty

EMPTILY *adv* in an empty manner

EMPTINGS *n/pl* emptins

EMPTINS *n/pl* a liquid leavening

EMPTY *adj* -TIER, -TIEST containing nothing

EMPTY *v* -TIED, -TYING, -TIES to remove the contents of

EMPURPLE *v* -PLED, -PLING, -PLES to tinge with purple

EMPYEMA *n* pl. -EMATA or -EMAS a collection of pus in a body cavity **EMPYEMIC** *adj*

EMPYREAL *adj* pertaining to the sky

EMPYREAN *n* pl. -S the highest heaven

EMU *n* pl. -S a large, flightless bird

EMULATE *v* -LATED, -LATING, -LATES to try to equal or surpass

EMULATOR *n* pl. -S one that emulates

EMULOUS *adj* eager to equal or surpass another

EMULSIFY *v* -FIED, -FYING, -FIES to make into an emulsion

EMULSION *n* pl. -S a type of liquid mixture **EMULSIVE** *adj*

EMULSOID *n* pl. -S a liquid dispersed in another liquid

EMYD *n* pl. -S a freshwater tortoise

EMYDE *n* pi. -S emyd

EN *n* pl. -S the letter N

ENABLE *v* -BLED, -BLING, -BLES to make possible

ENABLER *n* pl. -S one that enables

ENACT *v* -ED, -ING, -S to make into a law

ENACTIVE *adj* having the power to enact

ENACTOR *n* pl. -S one that enacts

ENACTORY *adj* pertaining to the enactment of law

ENAMEL *v* -ELED, -ELING, -ELS or -ELLED, -ELLING, -ELS to cover with a hard, glossy surface

ENAMELER *n* pl. -S one that enamels

ENAMINE *n* pl. -S a type of amine

ENAMOR *v* -ED, -ING, -S to inspire with love

ENAMOUR *v* -ED, -ING, -S to enamor

ENATE *n* pl. -S a relative on the mother's side **ENATIC** *adj*

ENATION *n* pl. -S an outgrowth from the surface of an organ

ENCAENIA *n/pl* annual university ceremonies

ENCAGE *v* -CAGED, -CAGING, -CAGES to confine in a cage

ENCAMP *v* -ED, -ING, -S to set up a camp

ENCASE *v* -CASED, -CASING, -CASES to enclose in a case

ENCASH *v* -ED, -ING, -ES to cash

ENCEINTE *n* pl. -S an encircling fortification

ENCHAIN *v* -ED, -ING, -S to bind with chains

ENCHANT *v* -ED, -ING, -S to delight

ENCHASE *v* -CHASED, -CHASING, -CHASES to place in an ornamental setting

ENCHASER *n* pl. -S one that enchases

ENCHORIC *adj* belonging to a particular country

ENCINA *n* pl. -S an evergreen oak **ENCINAL** *adj*

ENCIPHER *v* -ED, -ING, -S to write in characters of hidden meaning

ENCIRCLE *v* -CLED, -CLING, -CLES to form a circle around

ENCLASP *v* -ED, -ING, -S to embrace

ENCLAVE *n* pl. -S a territorial unit enclosed within foreign territory

ENCLITIC *n* pl. -S a word pronounced as part of the preceding word

ENCLOSE *v* -CLOSED, -CLOSING, -CLOSES to close in on all sides

ENCLOSER *n* pl. -S one that encloses

ENCODE *v* -CODED, -CODING, -CODES to put into code

ENCODER *n* pl. -S one that encodes

ENCOMIUM *n* pl. -MIUMS or -MIA a eulogy

ENCORE *v* -CORED, -CORING, -CORES to call for the reappearance of a performer

ENCROACH *v* -ED, -ING, -ES to advance beyond the proper limits

ENCRUST *v* -ED, -ING, -S to cover with a crust

ENCRYPT *v* -ED, -ING, -S to encipher

ENCUMBER *v* -ED, -ING, -S to hinder in action or movement

ENCYCLIC *n* pl. -S a letter addressed by the pope to the bishops of the world

ENCYST *v* -ED, -ING, -S to enclose in a cyst

END *v* -ED, -ING, -S to terminate

ENDAMAGE *v* -AGED, -AGING, -AGES to damage

ENDAMEBA *n* pl. -BAS or -BAE a parasitic ameba

ENDANGER *v* -ED, -ING, -S to imperil

ENDARCH *adj* formed from the center outward

ENDARCHY *n* pl. -CHIES the condition of being endarch

ENDBRAIN *n* pl. -S a part of the brain

ENDEAR *v* -ED, -ING, -S to make dear or beloved

ENDEAVOR *v* -ED, -ING, -S to make an effort

ENDEMIAL *adj* peculiar to a country or people

ENDEMIC *n* pl. -S an endemial disease

ENDEMISM *n* pl. -S the state of being endemial

ENDER *n* pl. -S one that ends something

ENDERMIC *adj* acting by absorption through the skin

ENDEXINE *n* pl. -S an inner layer of the exine

ENDGAME *n* pl. -S the last stage of a chess game

ENDING *n* pl. -S a termination

ENDITE *v* -DITED, -DITING, -DITES to indite

ENDIVE *n* pl. -S an herb cultivated as a salad plant

ENDLEAF *n* pl. -LEAVES an endpaper

ENDLESS *adj* enduring forever

ENDLONG *adv* lengthwise

ENDMOST *adj* farthest

ENDNOTE *n* pl. -S a note placed at the end of the text

ENDOCARP *n* pl. -S the inner layer of a pericarp

ENDOCAST *n* pl. -S a cast of the cranial cavity

ENDODERM *n* pl. -S the innermost germ layer of an embryo

ENDOGAMY *n* pl. -MIES marriage within a particular group

ENDOGEN *n* pl. -S a type of plant

ENDOGENY *n* pl. -NIES growth from within

ENDOPOD *n* pl. -S a branch of a crustacean limb

ENDORSE *v* -DORSED, -DORSING, -DORSES to sign the back of a negotiable document

ENDORSEE *n* pl. -S one to whom a document is transferred by endorsement

ENDORSER *n* pl. -S one that endorses

ENDORSING present participle of endorse

ENDORSOR *n* pl. -S endorser

ENDOSARC *n* pl. -S a portion of a cell

ENDOSMOS *n* pl. -ES a form of osmosis

ENDOSOME *n* pl. -S a cellular particle

ENDOSTEA *n/pl* bone membranes

ENDOW *v* -ED, -ING, -S to provide with something

ENDOWER *n* pl. -S one that endows

ENDOZOIC *adj* involving passage through an animal

ENDPAPER *n* pl. -S a sheet of paper used in bookbinding

ENDPLATE *n* pl. -S a type of nerve terminal

ENDPOINT *n* pl. -S either of two points that mark the end of a line segment

ENDRIN *n* pl. -S an insecticide

ENDUE *v* -DUED, -DUING, -DUES to provide with some quality or gift

ENDURE *v* -DURED, -DURING, -DURES to last

ENDURO *n* pl. -DUROS a long race

ENDWAYS *adv* endwise

ENDWISE *adv* lengthwise

ENEMA *n* pl. -MAS or -MATA a liquid injected into the rectum

ENEMY *n* pl. -MIES one that is antagonistic toward another

ENERGID *n* pl. -S a nucleus and the body of cytoplasm with which it interacts

ENERGIES pl. of energy

ENERGISE *v* -GISED, -GISING, -GISES to energize

ENERGIZE *v* -GIZED, -GIZING, -GIZES to give energy to

ENERGY *n* -GIES the capacity for vigorous activity

ENERVATE *v* -VATED, -VATING, -VATES to deprive of strength or vitality

ENFACE *v* -FACED, -FACING, -FACES to write on the front of

ENFEEBLE *v* -BLED, -BLING, -BLES to make feeble

ENFEOFF *v* -ED, -ING, -S to invest with a feudal estate

ENFETTER *v* -ED, -ING, -S to enchain

ENFEVER *v* -ED, -ING, -S to fever

ENFILADE *v* -LADED, -LADING, -LADES to direct heavy gunfire along the length of

ENFLAME *v* -FLAMED, -FLAMING, -FLAMES to inflame

ENFOLD *v* -ED, -ING, -S to envelop

ENFOLDER *n* pl. -S one that enfolds

ENFORCE *v* -FORCED, -FORCING, -FORCES to compel obedience to

ENFORCER *n* pl. -S one that enforces

ENFRAME *v* -FRAMED, -FRAMING, -FRAMES to frame

ENG *n* pl. -S a phonetic symbol

ENGAGE *v* -GAGED, -GAGING, -GAGES to employ

ENGAGER *n* pl. -S one that engages

ENGENDER *v* -ED, -ING, -S to bring into existence

ENGILD *v* -ED, -ING, -S to brighten

ENGINE *v* -GINED, -GINING, -GINES to equip with machinery

ENGINEER *v* -ED, -ING, -S to carry through or manage by contrivance

ENGINERY *n* pl. -RIES machinery

ENGINING present participle of engine

ENGINOUS *adj* ingenious

ENGIRD *v* -GIRT or -GIRDED, -GIRDING, -GIRDS to gird

ENGIRDLE *v* -DLED, -DLING, -DLES to engird

ENGLISH *v* -ED, -ING, -ES to cause a billiard ball to spin around its vertical axis

ENGLUT *v* -GLUTTED, -GLUTTING, -GLUTS to gulp down

ENGORGE *v* -GORGED, -GORGING, -GORGES to fill with blood

ENGRAFT *v* -ED, -ING, -S to graft for propagation

ENGRAIL *v* -ED, -ING, -S to ornament the edge of with curved indentations

ENGRAIN *v* -ED, -ING, -S to ingrain

ENGRAM *n* pl. -S the durable mark caused by a stimulus upon protoplasm

ENGRAMME *n* pl. -S engram

ENGRAVE *v* -GRAVED, -GRAVING, -GRAVES to form by incision

ENGRAVER *n* pl. -S one that engraves

ENGROSS *v* -ED, -ING, -ES to occupy completely

ENGULF *v* -ED, -ING, -S to surround completely

ENHALO *v* -ED, -ING, -ES or -S to surround with a halo

ENHANCE *v* -HANCED, -HANCING, -HANCES to raise to a higher degree

ENHANCER *n* pl. -S one that enhances

ENIGMA *n* pl. -MAS or -MATA something that is hard to understand or explain

ENISLE *v* -ISLED, -ISLING, -ISLES to isolate

ENJAMBED *adj* marked by the continuation of a sentence from one line of a poem to the next

ENJOIN *v* -ED, -ING, -S to command

ENJOINER *n* pl. -S one that enjoins

ENJOY *v* -ED, -ING, -S to receive pleasure from

ENJOYER *n* pl. -S one that enjoys

ENKINDLE *v* -DLED, -DLING, -DLES to set on fire

ENLACE *v* -LACED, -LACING, -LACES to bind with laces

ENLARGE *v* -LARGED, -LARGING, -LARGES to make or become larger

ENLARGER *n* pl. -S a device used to enlarge photographs

ENLIST *v* -ED, -ING, -S to engage for military service

ENLISTEE *n* pl. -S one that is enlisted

ENLISTER *n* pl. -S one that enlists

ENLIVEN *v* -ED, -ING, -S to make lively

ENMESH *v* -ED, -ING, -ES to ensnare or entangle in a net

ENMITY *n* pl. -TIES hostility

ENNEAD *n* pl. -S a group of nine **ENNEADIC** *adj*

ENNEAGON *n* pl. -S a nonagon

ENNOBLE *v* -BLED, -BLING, -BLES to make noble

ENNOBLER *n* pl. -S one that ennobles

ENNUI *n* pl. -S a feeling of weariness and discontent

ENNUYE *adj* oppressed with ennui

ENNUYEE *adj* ennuye

ENOL *n* pl. -S a chemical compound **ENOLIC** *adj*

ENOLASE *n* pl. -S an enzyme

ENOLOGY *n* pl. -GIES oenology

ENORM *adj* enormous

ENORMITY *n* pl. -TIES a grave offense against decency

ENORMOUS *adj* huge

ENOSIS *n* pl. -SISES union

ENOUGH *n* pl. -S a sufficient supply

ENOUNCE *v* ENOUNCED, ENOUNCING, ENOUNCES to announce

ENOW *n* pl. -S enough

ENPLANE *v* -PLANED, -PLANING, -PLANES to board an airplane

ENQUIRE *v* -QUIRED, -QUIRING, -QUIRES to inquire

ENQUIRY *n* pl. -RIES inquiry

ENRAGE *v* -RAGED, -RAGING, -RAGES to make very angry

ENRAPT *adj* rapt

ENRAVISH *v* -ED, -ING, -ES to delight greatly

ENRICH *v* -ED, -ING, -ES to add desirable elements to

ENRICHER *n* pl. -S one that enriches

ENROBE *v* -ROBED, -ROBING, -ROBES to dress

ENROBER *n* pl. -S one that enrobes

ENROL *v* -ROLLED, -ROLLING, -ROLS to enroll

ENROLL *v* -ED, -ING, -S to enter the name of in a register, record, or roll

ENROLLEE *n* pl. -S one that is enrolled

ENROLLER *n* pl. -S one that enrolls

ENROLLING present participle of enrol

ENROOT *v* -ED, -ING, -S to implant

ENS *n* pl. ENTIA an entity

ENSAMPLE *n* pl. -S an example

ENSCONCE *v* -SCONCED, -SCONCING, -SCONCES to settle securely or comfortably

ENSCROLL *v* -ED, -ING, -S to write on a scroll

ENSEMBLE *n* pl. -S a group of complementary parts

ENSERF *v* -ED, -ING, -S to make a serf of

ENSHEATH *v* -ED, -ING, -S to enclose in a sheath

ENSHRINE *v* -SHRINED, -SHRINING, -SHRINES to place in a shrine

ENSHROUD *v* -ED, -ING, -S to conceal

ENSIFORM *adj* sword-shaped

ENSIGN *n* pl. -S a navy officer

ENSIGNCY *n* pl. -CIES the rank of an ensign

ENSILAGE *v* -LAGED, -LAGING, -LAGES to ensile

ENSILE *v* -SILED, -SILING, -SILES to store in a silo

ENSKY *v* -SKIED or -SKYED, -SKYING, -SKIES to raise to the skies

ENSLAVE *v* -SLAVED, -SLAVING, -SLAVES to make a slave of

ENSLAVER *n* pl. -S one that enslaves

ENSNARE *v* -SNARED, -SNARING, -SNARES to trap

ENSNARER *n* pl. -S one that ensnares

ENSNARL *v* -ED, -ING, -S to tangle

ENSORCEL *v* -ED, -ING, -S to bewitch

ENSOUL *v* -ED, -ING, -S to endow with a soul

ENSPHERE *v* -SPHERED, -SPHERING, -SPHERES to enclose in a sphere

ENSUE *v* -SUED, -SUING, -SUES to occur afterward or as a result

ENSURE *v* -SURED, -SURING, -SURES to make certain

ENSURER *n* pl. -S one that ensures

ENSWATHE *v* -SWATHED, -SWATHING, -SWATHES to swathe

ENTAIL *v* -ED, -ING, -S to restrict the inheritance of to a specified line of heirs

ENTAILER *n* pl. -S one that entails

ENTAMEBA *n* pl. -BAE or -BAS endameba

ENTANGLE *v* -TANGLED, -TANGLING, -TANGLES to tangle

ENTASIA n pl. -S spasmodic contraction of a muscle

ENTASIS n pl. -TASES a slight convexity in a column **ENTASTIC** adj

ENTELLUS n pl. -ES a hanuman

ENTENTE n pl. -S an agreement between nations

ENTER v -ED, -ING, -S to come or go into

ENTERA a pl. of enteron

ENTERAL adj enteric

ENTERER n pl. -S one that enters

ENTERIC adj pertaining to the enteron

ENTERON n pl. -TERONS or -TERA the alimentary canal

ENTHALPY n pl. -PIES a thermodynamic measure of heat

ENTHETIC adj introduced from outside

ENTHRAL v -THRALLED, -THRALLING, -THRALS to enthrall

ENTHRALL v -ED, -ING, -S to charm

ENTHRONE v -THRONED, -THRONING, -THRONES to place on a throne

ENTHUSE v -THUSED, -THUSING, -THUSES to show enthusiasm

ENTIA pl. of ens

ENTICE v -TICED, -TICING, -TICES to allure

ENTICER n pl. -S one that entices

ENTIRE n pl. -S the whole of something

ENTIRELY adv completely

ENTIRETY n pl. -TIES completeness

ENTITLE v -TLED, -TLING, -TLES to give a title to

ENTITY n pl. -TIES something that has a real existence

ENTODERM n pl. -S endoderm

ENTOIL v -ED, -ING, -S to entrap

ENTOMB v -ED, -ING, -S to place in a tomb

ENTOPIC adj situated in the normal place

ENTOZOA a pl. of entozoan and pl. of entozoon

ENTOZOAL adj entozoic

ENTOZOAN n pl. -ZOANS or -ZOA an entozoic parasite

ENTOZOIC adj living within an animal

ENTOZOON n pl. -ZOA entozoan

ENTRAILS n/pl the internal organs

ENTRAIN v -ED, -ING, -S to board a train

ENTRANCE v -TRANCED, -TRANCING, -TRANCES to fill with delight or wonder

ENTRANT n pl. -S one that enters

ENTRAP v -TRAPPED, -TRAPPING, -TRAPS to trap

ENTREAT v -ED, -ING, -S to ask for earnestly

ENTREATY n pl. -TREATIES an earnest request

ENTREE n pl. -S the principal dish of a meal

ENTRENCH v -ED, -ING, -ES to establish firmly

ENTREPOT n pl. -S a warehouse

ENTRESOL n pl. -S a mezzanine

ENTRIES pl. of entry

ENTROPY n pl. -PIES a thermodynamic measure of disorder **ENTROPIC** adj

ENTRUST v -ED, -ING, -S to give over for safekeeping

ENTRY n pl. -TRIES a place of entrance

ENTRYWAY n pl. -WAYS a passage serving as an entrance

ENTWINE v -TWINED, -TWINING, -TWINES to twine around

ENTWIST v -ED, -ING, -S to twist together

ENURE v -URED, -URING, -URES to inure

ENURESIS n pl. -SISES involuntary urination

ENURETIC n pl. -S one who is affected with enuresis

ENVELOP v -ED, -ING, -S to cover completely

ENVELOPE n pl. -S a paper container

ENVENOM v -ED, -ING, -S to put venom into

ENVIABLE adj desirable **ENVIABLY** adv

ENVIED past tense of envy

ENVIER n pl. -S one that envies

ENVIES present 3d person sing. of envy

ENVIOUS adj resentful and desirous of another's possessions or qualities

ENVIRON v -ED, -ING, -S to encircle

ENVISAGE v -AGED, -AGING, -AGES to form a mental image of

ENVISION v -ED, -ING, -S to envisage

ENVOI n pl. -S the closing of a poem or prose work

ENVOY n pl. -VOYS a representative

ENVY v -VIED, -VYING, -VIES to be envious of

ENWHEEL v -ED, -ING, -S to encircle

ENWIND v -WOUND, -WINDING, -WINDS to wind around

ENWOMB v -ED, -ING, -S to enclose as if in a womb

ENWRAP v -WRAPPED, -WRAPPING, -WRAPS to envelop

ENZOOTIC n pl. -S a type of animal disease

ENZYM n pl. -S enzyme

ENZYME n pl. -S a complex protein **ENZYMIC** adj

EOBIONT n pl. -S a type of basic organism

EOHIPPUS n pl. -ES an extinct horse

EOLIAN adj pertaining to the wind

EOLIPILE n pl. -S a type of engine

EOLITH n pl. -S a prehistoric stone tool **EOLITHIC** adj

EOLOPILE n pl. -S eolipile

EON n pl. -S an indefinitely long period of time

EONIAN adj everlasting

EONISM n pl. -S adoption of the dress and mannerisms of the opposite sex

EOSIN n pl. -S a red dye **EOSINIC** adj

EOSINE n pl. -S eosin

EPACT n pl. -S the difference between the lengths of the solar and lunar years

EPARCH n pl. -S the head of an eparchy

EPARCHY n pl. -CHIES a district of modern Greece

EPAULET n pl. -S a shoulder ornament

EPAZOTE n pl. -S an herb of the goosefoot family

EPEE n pl. -S a type of sword

EPEEIST n pl. -S one who fences with an epee

EPEIRIC adj pertaining to vertical movement of the earth's crust

EPENDYMA n pl. -S a membrane lining certain body cavities

EPERGNE n pl. -S an ornamental dish

EPHA n pl. -S ephah

EPHAH n pl. -S a Hebrew unit of dry measure

EPHEBE n pl. -S ephebus **EPHEBIC** adj

EPHEBOS n pl. -BOI ephebus

EPHEBUS n pl. -BI a young man of ancient Greece

EPHEDRA n pl. -S a desert shrub

EPHEDRIN n pl. -S an alkaloid used to treat allergies

EPHEMERA n pl. -ERAS or -ERAE something of very short life or duration

EPHOD n pl. -S an ancient Hebrew vestment

EPHOR n pl. -ORS or -ORI a magistrate of ancient Greece **EPHORAL** adj

EPHORATE n pl. -S the office of ephor

EPIBLAST n pl. -S the ectoderm

EPIBOLY n pl. -LIES the growth of one part around another **EPIBOLIC** adj

EPIC n pl. -S a long narrative poem **EPICAL** adj **EPICALLY** adv

EPICALYX n pl. -LYXES or -LYCES a set of bracts close to and resembling a calyx

EPICARP n pl. -S the outer layer of a pericarp

EPICEDIA n/pl funeral songs

EPICENE n pl. -S one having both male and female characteristics

EPICLIKE adj resembling an epic

EPICOTYL n pl. -S a part of a plant embryo

EPICURE n pl. -S a gourmet

EPICYCLE n pl. -S a circle that rolls on the circumference of another circle

EPIDEMIC n pl. -S a rapid spread of a disease

EPIDERM n pl. -S the outer layer of skin

EPIDOTE n pl. -S a mineral **EPIDOTIC** adj

EPIDURAL adj situated on the membrane that encloses the brain

EPIFAUNA n pl. -FAUNAE or -FAUNAS fauna living on a hard sea floor

EPIFOCAL adj pertaining to the point of origin of an earthquake

EPIGEAL adj epigeous

EPIGEAN adj epigeous

EPIGEIC adj epigeous

EPIGENE adj occurring near the surface of the earth

EPIGENIC adj pertaining to change in the mineral character of a rock

EPIGEOUS adj growing on or close to the ground

EPIGON n pl. -S epigone

EPIGONE *n* pl. -S an inferior imitator **EPIGONIC** *adj*

EPIGONUS *n* pl. -NI epigone

EPIGRAM *n* pl. -S a brief, witty remark

EPIGRAPH *n* pl. -S an engraved inscription

EPIGYNY *n* pl. -NIES the state of having floral organs near the top of the ovary

EPILEPSY *n* pl. -SIES a disorder of the nervous system

EPILOG *n* pl. -S a concluding section

EPILOGUE *v* -LOGUED, -LOGUING, -LOGUES to provide with a concluding section

EPIMER *n* pl. -S a type of sugar compound **EPIMERIC** *adj*

EPIMERE *n* pl. -S a part of an embryo

EPIMYSIA *n/pl* muscle sheaths

EPINAOS *n* pl. -NAOI a rear vestibule

EPINASTY *n* pl. -TIES a downward bending of plant parts

EPIPHANY *n* pl. -NIES an appearance of a deity

EPIPHYTE *n* pl. -S a plant growing upon another plant

EPISCIA *n* pl. -S a tropical herb

EPISCOPE *n* pl. -S a type of projector

EPISODE *n* pl. -S an incident in the course of a continuous experience **EPISODIC** *adj*

EPISOME *n* pl. -S a genetic determinant **EPISOMAL** *adj*

EPISTASY *n* pl. -SIES a suppression of genetic effect

EPISTLE *n* pl. -S a long or formal letter

EPISTLER *n* pl. -S one that writes epistles

EPISTOME *n* pl. -S a structure covering the mouth of various invertebrates

EPISTYLE *n* pl. -S a part of a classical building

EPITAPH *n* pl. -S an inscription on a tomb

EPITASIS *n* pl. -ASES the main part of a classical drama

EPITAXY *n* pl. -TAXIES a type of crystalline growth **EPITAXIC** *adj*

EPITHET *n* pl. -S a term used to characterize a person or thing

EPITOME *n* pl. -S a typical or ideal example **EPITOMIC** *adj*

EPITOPE *n* pl. -S a region on the surface of an antigen

EPIZOA pl. of epizoon

EPIZOIC *adj* living on the body of an animal

EPIZOISM *n* pl. -S the state of being epizoic

EPIZOITE *n* pl. -S an epizoic organism

EPIZOON *n* pl. -ZOA an epizoic parasite

EPIZOOTY *n* pl. -TIES a type of animal disease

EPOCH *n* pl. -S a particular period of time **EPOCHAL** *adj*

EPODE *n* pl. -S a type of poem

EPONYM *n* pl. -S the person for whom something is named **EPONYMIC** *adj*

EPONYMY *n* pl. -MIES the derivation of an eponymic name

EPOPEE *n* pl. -S an epic poem

EPOPOEIA *n* pl. -S epopee

EPOS *n* pl. -ES an epic poem

EPOXIDE *n* pl. -S an epoxy compound

EPOXY *v* EPOXIED or EPOXYED, EPOXYING, EPOXIES to glue with epoxy (a type of resin)

EPSILON *n* pl. -S a Greek letter

EQUABLE *adj* not changing or varying greatly **EQUABLY** *adv*

EQUAL *adj* having the same capability, quantity, or effect as another

EQUAL *v* EQUALED, EQUALING, EQUALS or EQUALLED, EQUALLING, EQUALS to be equal to

EQUALISE *v* -ISED, -ISING, -ISES to equalize

EQUALITY *n* pl. -TIES the state of being equal

EQUALIZE *v* -IZED, -IZING, -IZES to make equal

EQUALLED a past tense of equal

EQUALLING a past participle of equal

EQUALLY *adv* in an equal manner

EQUATE *v* EQUATED, EQUATING, EQUATES to make equal

EQUATION *n* pl. -S the act of equating

EQUATOR *n* pl. -S a great circle of spherical celestial bodies

EQUERRY *n* pl. -RIES an officer in charge of the care of horses

EQUID *n* pl. -S an animal of the horse family

EQUINE *n* pl. -S a horse

EQUINELY *adv* in a horselike manner

EQUINITY *n* pl. -TIES the state of being like a horse

EQUINOX *n pl.* -ES a point on the celestial sphere

EQUIP *v* EQUIPPED, EQUIPPING, EQUIPS to provide with whatever is needed

EQUIPAGE *n pl.* -S a carriage

EQUIPPER *n pl.* -S one that equips

EQUIPPING present participle of equip

EQUISETA *n/pl* rushlike plants

EQUITANT *adj* overlapping

EQUITES *n/pl* a privileged military class of ancient Rome

EQUITY *n pl.* -TIES fairness or impartiality

EQUIVOKE *n pl.* -S a play on words

ER *interj* — used to express hesitation

ERA *n pl.* -S an epoch

ERADIATE *v* -ATED, -ATING, -ATES to radiate

ERASE *v* ERASED, ERASING, ERASES to rub or scrape out ERASABLE *adj*

ERASER *n pl.* -S one that erases

ERASION *n pl.* -S an erasure

ERASURE *n pl.* -S the act of erasing

ERBIUM *n pl.* -S a metallic element

ERE *prep* previous to; before

ERECT *v* -ED, -ING, -S to build

ERECTER *n pl.* -S erector

ERECTILE *adj* capable of being raised upright

ERECTION *n pl.* -S the act of erecting

ERECTIVE *adj* tending to erect

ERECTLY *adv* in an upright manner

ERECTOR *n pl.* -S one that erects

ERELONG *adv* soon

EREMITE *n pl.* -S a hermit EREMITIC *adj*

EREMURUS *n pl.* -URI a perennial herb

ERENOW *adv* before this time

EREPSIN *n pl.* -S a mixture of enzymes in the small intestine

ERETHISM *n pl.* -S abnormal irritability ERETHIC *adj*

EREWHILE *adv* some time ago

ERG *n pl.* -S a unit of work or energy

ERGASTIC *adj* constituting the nonliving by-products of protoplasmic activity

ERGATE *n pl.* -S a worker ant

ERGATIVE *adj* pertaining to a type of language

ERGO *conj* therefore

ERGODIC *adj* pertaining to the probability that any state will recur

ERGOT *n pl.* -S a fungus ERGOTIC *adj*

ERGOTISM *n pl.* -S poisoning produced by eating ergot-infected grain

ERICA *n pl.* -S a shrub of the heath family

ERICOID *adj* resembling heath

ERIGERON *n pl.* -S an herb

ERINGO *n pl.* -GOES or -GOS eryngo

ERISTIC *n pl.* -S an expert in debate

ERLKING *n pl.* -S an evil spirit of Germanic folklore

ERMINE *n pl.* -S the fur of certain weasels ERMINED *adj*

ERN *n pl.* -S erne

ERNE *n pl.* -S a sea eagle

ERODE *v* ERODED, ERODING, ERODES to wear away by constant friction

ERODENT *adj* erosive

ERODIBLE *adj* erosible

ERODING present participle of erode

EROGENIC *adj* arousing sexual desire

EROS *n pl.* -ES sexual desire

EROSE *adj* uneven EROSELY *adv*

EROSIBLE *adj* capable of being eroded

EROSION *n pl.* -S the act of eroding

EROSIVE *adj* causing erosion

EROTIC *n pl.* -S an amatory poem EROTICAL *adj*

EROTICA *n/pl* literature or art dealing with sexual love

EROTISM *n pl.* -S sexual excitement

EROTIZE *v* -TIZED, -TIZING, -TIZES to give a sexual meaning to

ERR *v* -ED, -ING, -S to make a mistake

ERRANCY *n pl.* -CIES an instance of erring

ERRAND *n pl.* -S a short trip made for a particular purpose

ERRANT *n pl.* -S a wanderer

ERRANTLY *adv* in a wandering manner

ERRANTRY *n pl.* -RIES the state of wandering

ERRATA *n pl.* -S a list of printing errors

ERRATIC *n pl.* -S an eccentric person

ERRATUM *n pl.* -TA a printing error

ERRHINE *n pl.* -S a substance that promotes nasal discharge

ERRINGLY *adv* in a mistaken manner

ERROR *n pl.* -S a mistake

ERS *n pl.* -ES ervil

ERSATZ *n pl.* -ES a substitute

ERST *adv* formerly

ERUCT *v* -ED, -ING, -S to belch

ERUCTATE *v* -TATED, -TATING, -TATES to eruct

ERUDITE *adj* scholarly

ERUGO *n* pl. -GOS aerugo

ERUMPENT *adj* bursting forth

ERUPT *v* -ED, -ING, -S to burst forth

ERUPTION *n* pl. -S the act of erupting

ERUPTIVE *n* pl. -S a type of rock

ERVIL *n* pl. -S a European vetch

ERYNGO *n* pl. -GOES or -GOS a medicinal herb

ERYTHEMA *n* pl. -S a redness of the skin

ERYTHRON *n* pl. -S a bodily organ consisting of the red blood cells

ES *n* pl. ESES ess

ESCALADE *v* -LADED, -LADING, -LADES to enter by means of ladders

ESCALATE *v* -LATED, -LATING, -LATES to increase

ESCALLOP *v* -ED, -ING, -S to scallop

ESCALOP *v* -ED, -ING, -S to escallop

ESCAPADE *n* pl. -S a reckless adventure

ESCAPE *v* -CAPED, -CAPING, -CAPES to get away

ESCAPEE *n* pl. -S one that has escaped

ESCAPER *n* pl. -S one that escapes

ESCAPING present participle of escape

ESCAPISM *n* pl. -S the avoidance of reality by diversion of the mind

ESCAPIST *n* pl. -S one given to escapism

ESCAR *n* pl. -S esker

ESCARGOT *n* pl. -S an edible snail

ESCAROLE *n* pl. -S a variety of endive

ESCARP *v* -ED, -ING, -S to cause to slope steeply

ESCHALOT *n* pl. -S a shallot

ESCHAR *n* pl. -S a hard, dry scab

ESCHEAT *v* -ED, -ING, -S to confiscate

ESCHEW *v* -ED, -ING, -S to avoid

ESCHEWAL *n* pl. -S the act of eschewing

ESCOLAR *n* pl. -S a food fish

ESCORT *v* -ED, -ING, -S to accompany

ESCOT *v* -ED, -ING, -S to provide support for

ESCROW *v* -ED, -ING, -S to place in the custody of a third party

ESCUAGE *n* pl. -S scutage

ESCUDO *n* pl. -DOS a monetary unit of Portugal

ESCULENT *n* pl. -S something that is edible

ESERINE *n* pl. -S a toxic alkaloid

ESKAR *n* pl. -S esker

ESKER *n* pl. -S a narrow ridge of gravel and sand

ESOPHAGI *n/pl* tubes connecting the mouth to the stomach

ESOTERIC *adj* designed for a select few

ESPALIER *v* -ED, -ING, -S to furnish with a trellis

ESPANOL *n* pl. -ES a native of Spain

ESPARTO *n* pl. -TOS a perennial grass

ESPECIAL *adj* special

ESPIAL *n* pl. -S the act of espying

ESPIED past tense of espy

ESPIEGLE *adj* playful

ESPIES present 3d person sing. of espy

ESPOUSAL *n* pl. -S a marriage ceremony

ESPOUSE *v* -POUSED, -POUSING, -POUSES to marry

ESPOUSER *n* pl. -S one that espouses

ESPRESSO *n* pl. -SOS a strong coffee

ESPRIT *n* pl. -S spirit

ESPY *v* -PIED, -PYING, -PIES to catch sight of

ESQUIRE *v* -QUIRED, -QUIRING, -QUIRES to escort

ESS *n* pl. -ES the letter S

ESSAY *v* -ED, -ING, -S to try

ESSAYER *n* pl. -S one that essays

ESSAYIST *n* pl. -S a writer of essays (prose compositions)

ESSENCE *n* pl. -S a fundamental nature or quality

ESSOIN *n* pl. -S an excuse

ESSONITE *n* pl. -S a variety of garnet

ESTANCIA *n* pl. -S a cattle ranch

ESTATE *v* -TATED, -TATING, -TATES to provide with landed property

ESTEEM *v* -ED, -ING, -S to have a high opinion of

ESTER *n* pl. -S a type of chemical compound

ESTERASE *n* pl. -S a type of enzyme

ESTERIFY *v* -FIED, -FYING, -FIES to convert into an ester

ESTHESIA *n* pl. -S the ability to receive sensation

ESTHESIS *n* pl. -THESISES or -THESES esthesia

ESTHETE *n* pl. -S an esthetic person

ESTHETIC *adj* keenly appreciative of the beautiful

ESTIMATE *v* -MATED, -MATING, -MATES to make an approximate judgment of

ESTIVAL *adj* pertaining to summer

ESTIVATE *v* -VATED, -VATING, -VATES to spend the summer

ESTOP *v* -TOPPED, -TOPPING, -TOPS to impede by estoppel

ESTOPPEL *n* pl. -S a legal restraint preventing a person from contradicting his own previous statement

ESTOVERS *n/pl* necessities allowed by law

ESTRAGON *n* pl. -S tarragon

ESTRAL *adj* estrous

ESTRANGE *v* -TRANGED, -TRANGING, -TRANGES to alienate

ESTRAY *v* -ED, -ING, -S to stray

ESTREAT *v* -ED, -ING, -S to copy from court records for use in prosecution

ESTRIN *n* pl. -S estrone

ESTRIOL *n* pl. -S an estrogen

ESTROGEN *n* pl. -S a female sex hormone promoting or producing estrus

ESTRONE *n* pl. -S an estrogen

ESTROUS *adj* pertaining to estrus

ESTRUAL *adj* estrous

ESTRUM *n* pl. -S estrus

ESTRUS *n* pl. -ES the period of heat in female mammals

ESTUARY *n* pl. -ARIES an inlet of the sea at a river's lower end

ESURIENT *adj* greedy

ET a past tense of eat

ETA *n* pl. -S a Greek letter

ETAGERE *n* pl. -S an ornamental stand

ETALON *n* pl. -S an optical instrument

ETAMIN *n* pl. -S etamine

ETAMINE *n* pl. -S a loosely woven fabric

ETAPE *n* pl. -S a warehouse

ETATISM *n* pl. -S state socialism **ETATIST** *adj*

ETCETERA *n* pl. -S a number of additional items

ETCH *v* -ED, -ING, -ES to engrave with acid

ETCHANT *n* pl. -S a substance used in etching

ETCHER *n* pl. -S one that etches

ETCHING *n* pl. -S an etched design

ETERNAL *n* pl. -S something lasting forever

ETERNE *adj* everlasting

ETERNISE *v* -NISED, -NISING, -NISES to eternize

ETERNITY *n* pl. -TIES infinite time

ETERNIZE *v* -NIZED, -NIZING, -NIZES to make everlasting

ETESIAN *n* pl. -S an annually recurring wind

ETH *n* pl. -S edh

ETHANE *n* pl. -S a gaseous hydrocarbon

ETHANOL *n* pl. -S an alcohol

ETHENE *n* pl. -S ethylene

ETHEPHON *n* pl. -S a synthetic plant growth regulator

ETHER *n* pl. -S a volatile liquid used as an anesthetic **ETHERIC** *adj*

ETHEREAL *adj* airy

ETHERIFY *v* -FIED, -FYING, -FIES to convert into ether

ETHERISH *adj* resembling ether

ETHERIZE *v* -IZED, -IZING, -IZES to treat with ether

ETHIC *n* pl. -S a body of moral principles

ETHICAL *n* pl. -S a drug sold by prescription only

ETHICIAN *n* pl. -S an ethicist

ETHICIST *n* pl. -S a specialist in ethics

ETHICIZE *v* -CIZED, -CIZING, -CIZES to make ethical

ETHINYL *n* pl. -S ethynyl

ETHION *n* pl. -S a pesticide

ETHMOID *n* pl. -S a bone of the nasal cavity

ETHNARCH *n* pl. -S the ruler of a people or province

ETHNIC *n* pl. -S a member of a particular ethnos **ETHNICAL** *adj*

ETHNOS *n* pl. -ES a group of people who share a common and distinctive culture

ETHOLOGY *n* pl. -GIES the study of animal behavior

ETHOS *n* pl. -ES the fundamental character of a culture

ETHOXY *n* pl. -OXIES ethoxyl

ETHOXYL *n* pl. -S a univalent chemical radical

ETHYL *n* pl. -S a univalent chemical radical

ETHYLATE *v* -ATED, -ATING, -ATES to introduce the ethyl group into

ETHYLENE *n* pl. -S a flammable gas

ETHYLIC *adj* pertaining to ethyl

ETHYNE *n* pl. -S a flammable gas

ETHYNYL *n* pl. -S a univalent chemical radical

ETIC *adj* relating to a type of linguistic analysis

ETIOLATE	*v* -LATED, -LATING, -LATES to whiten
ETIOLOGY	*n* pl. -GIES the study of the causes of diseases
ETNA	*n* pl. -S a container for heating liquids
ETOILE	*n* pl. -S a star
ETOUFFEE	*n* pl. -S a Cajun stew
ETUDE	*n* pl. -S a piece of music for the practice of a point of technique
ETUI	*n* pl. -S a case for holding small articles
ETWEE	*n* pl. -S etui
ETYMON	*n* pl. -MA or -MONS the earliest known form of a word
EUCAINE	*n* pl. -S an anesthetic
EUCALYPT	*n* pl. -S an evergreen tree
EUCHARIS	*n* pl. -RISES a flowering plant
EUCHRE	*v* -CHRED, -CHRING, -CHRES to prevent from winning three tricks in euchre (a card game)
EUCLASE	*n* pl. -S a mineral
EUCRITE	*n* pl. -S a type of meteorite **EUCRITIC** *adj*
EUDAEMON	*n* pl. -S eudemon
EUDEMON	*n* pl. -S a good spirit
EUGENIA	*n* pl. -S a tropical evergreen tree
EUGENICS	*n/pl* the science of hereditary improvement **EUGENIC** *adj*
EUGENIST	*n* pl. -S a student of eugenics
EUGENOL	*n* pl. -S an aromatic liquid
EUGLENA	*n* pl. -S a freshwater protozoan
EULACHAN	*n* pl. -S eulachon
EULACHON	*n* pl. -S a marine food fish
EULOGIA	*n* pl. -GIAE holy bread
EULOGIA	*n* pl. -S a blessing
EULOGIES	pl. of eulogy
EULOGISE	*v* -GISED, -GISING, -GISES to eulogize
EULOGIST	*n* pl. -S one that eulogizes
EULOGIUM	*n* pl. -GIA or -GIUMS a eulogy
EULOGIZE	*v* -GIZED, -GIZING, -GIZES to praise highly
EULOGY	*n* pl. -GIES a formal expression of high praise
EUNUCH	*n* pl. -S a castrated man
EUONYMUS	*n* pl. -ES any of a genus of shrubs or small trees
EUPATRID	*n* pl. -RIDS or -RIDAE an aristocrat of ancient Athens
EUPEPSIA	*n* pl. -S good digestion **EUPEPTIC** *adj*
EUPEPSY	*n* pl. -SIES eupepsia
EUPHENIC	*adj* dealing with biological improvement
EUPHONY	*n* pl. -NIES pleasant sound **EUPHONIC** *adj*
EUPHORIA	*n* pl. -S a feeling of well-being **EUPHORIC** *adj*
EUPHOTIC	*adj* pertaining to the upper layer of a body of water
EUPHRASY	*n* pl. -SIES an annual herb
EUPHROE	*n* pl. -S a device used to adjust a shipboard awning
EUPHUISM	*n* pl. -S an artificially elegant style of speech or writing
EUPHUIST	*n* pl. -S one given to euphuism
EUPLOID	*n* pl. -S a cell having three or more identical genomes
EUPLOIDY	*n* pl. -DIES the state of being a euploid
EUPNEA	*n* pl. -S normal breathing **EUPNEIC** *adj*
EUPNOEA	*n* pl. -S eupnea **EUPNOEIC** *adj*
EUREKA	*interj* — used to express triumph upon discovering something
EURIPUS	*n* pl. -PI a swift sea channel
EURO	*n* pl. EUROS a large kangaroo
EUROKY	*n* pl. -KIES the ability of an organism to live under variable conditions **EUROKOUS** *adj*
EUROPIUM	*n* pl. -S a metallic element
EURYBATH	*n* pl. -S an organism that can live in a wide range of water depths
EURYOKY	*n* pl. -KIES euroky
EURYTHMY	*n* pl. -MIES harmony of movement or structure
EUSTACY	*n* pl. -CIES a worldwide change in sea level **EUSTATIC** *adj*
EUSTELE	*n* pl. -S a plant part
EUTAXY	*n* pl. -TAXIES good order
EUTECTIC	*n* pl. -S an alloy that has the lowest possible melting point
EUTROPHY	*n* pl. -PHIES healthful nutrition
EUXENITE	*n* pl. -S a mineral
EVACUANT	*n* pl. -S a cathartic medicine
EVACUATE	*v* -ATED, -ATING, -ATES to remove from a dangerous area
EVACUEE	*n* pl. -S one that is evacuated
EVADE	*v* EVADED, EVADING, EVADES to escape or avoid by cleverness or deceit **EVADABLE, EVADIBLE** *adj*
EVADER	*n* pl. -S one that evades

EVALUATE   v -ATED, -ATING, -ATES to determine the value of

EVANESCE   v -NESCED, -NESCING, -NESCES to fade away

EVANGEL   n pl. -S a preacher of the gospel

EVANISH   v -ED, -ING, -ES to vanish

EVASION   n pl. -S the act of evading

EVASIVE   adj tending to evade

EVE   n pl. -S evening

EVECTION   n pl. -S irregularity in the moon's motion

EVEN   adj EVENER, EVENEST flat and smooth

EVEN   v -ED, -ING, -S to make even

EVENER   n pl. -S one that evens

EVENFALL   n pl. -S twilight

EVENING   n pl. -S the latter part of the day and early part of the night

EVENLY   adv in an even manner

EVENNESS   n pl. -ES the state of being even

EVENSONG   n pl. -S an evening prayer service

EVENT   n pl. -S something that occurs

EVENTFUL   adj momentous

EVENTIDE   n pl. -S evening

EVENTUAL   adj occurring at a later time

EVER   adv at all times

EVERMORE   adv forever

EVERSION   n pl -S the act of everting

EVERT   v -ED, -ING, -S to turn outward or inside out

EVERTOR   n pl. -S a muscle that turns a part outward

EVERY   adj each without exception

EVERYDAY   adj ordinary

EVERYMAN   n pl. -MEN the typical or ordinary man

EVERYONE   pron every person

EVERYWAY   adv in every way

EVICT   v -ED, -ING, -S to expel by legal process

EVICTEE   n pl. -S one that is evicted

EVICTION   n pl. -S the act of evicting

EVICTOR   n pl. -S one that evicts

EVIDENCE   v -DENCED, -DENCING, -DENCES to indicate clearly

EVIDENT   adj clear to the vision or understanding

EVIL   adj EVILER, EVILEST or EVILLER, EVILLEST morally bad

EVIL   n pl. -S something that is evil

EVILDOER   n pl. -S one that does evil

EVILLER   a comparative of evil

EVILLEST   a superlative of evil

EVILLY   adv in an evil manner

EVILNESS   n pl. -ES the quality of being evil

EVINCE   v EVINCED, EVINCING, EVINCES to show clearly EVINCIVE adj

EVITE   v EVITED, EVITING, EVITES to avoid EVITABLE adj

EVOCABLE   adj capable of being evoked

EVOCATOR   n pl. -S one that evokes

EVOKE   v EVOKED, EVOKING, EVOKES to call forth

EVOKER   n pl. -S an evocator

EVOLUTE   n pl. -S a type of geometric curve

EVOLVE   v EVOLVED, EVOLVING, EVOLVES to develop

EVOLVER   n pl. -S one that evolves

EVONYMUS   n pl. -ES euonymus

EVULSION   n pl. -S the act of pulling out

EVZONE   n pl. -S a Greek soldier

EWE   n pl. -S a female sheep

EWER   n pl. -S a large pitcher

EX   n pl. -ES the letter X

EXACT   adj -ACTER, -ACTEST precise

EXACT   v -ED, -ING, -S to force the payment or yielding of

EXACTA   n pl. -S a type of horse racing bet

EXACTER   n pl. -S one that exacts

EXACTION   n pl. -S the act of exacting

EXACTLY   adv in an exact manner

EXACTOR   n pl. -S exacter

EXALT   v -ED, -ING, -S to raise

EXALTER   n pl. -S one that exalts

EXAM   n pl. -S an examination

EXAMEN   n pl. -S a critical study

EXAMINE   v -INED, -INING, -INES to inspect

EXAMINEE   n pl. -S one that is taking an examination

EXAMINER   n pl. -S one that examines

EXAMINING   present participle of examine

EXAMPLE   v -PLED, -PLING, -PLES to show by representation

EXANTHEM   n pl. -S a skin eruption

EXARCH   n pl. -S the ruler of a province in the Byzantine Empire EXARCHAL adj

EXARCHY   n pl. -CHIES the domain of an exarch

EXCAVATE   v -VATED, -VATING, -VATES to dig out

EXCEED   v -ED, -ING, -S to go beyond

EXCEEDER *n* pl. -S one that exceeds

EXCEL *v* -CELLED, -CELLING, -CELS to surpass others

EXCEPT *v* -ED, -ING, -S to leave out

EXCERPT *v* -ED, -ING, -S to pick out a passage from for quoting

EXCESS *v* -ED, -ING, -ES to eliminate the position of

EXCHANGE *v* -CHANGED, -CHANGING, -CHANGES to give and receive reciprocally

EXCIDE *v* -CIDED, -CIDING, -CIDES to excise

EXCIMER *n* pl. -S a dimer that exists in an excited state

EXCIPLE *n* pl. -S a rim around the hymenium of various lichens

EXCISE *v* -CISED, -CISING, -CISES to remove by cutting out

EXCISION *n* pl. -S the act of excising

EXCITANT *n* pl. -S a stimulant

EXCITE *v* -CITED, -CITING, -CITES to arouse the emotions of

EXCITER *n* pl. -S one that excites

EXCITON *n* pl. -S a phenomenon occurring in an excited crystal

EXCITOR *n* pl. -S exciter

EXCLAIM *v* -ED, -ING, -S to cry out suddenly

EXCLAVE *n* pl. -S a portion of a country which is isolated in foreign territory

EXCLUDE *v* -CLUDED, -CLUDING, -CLUDES to shut out

EXCLUDER *n* pl. -S one that excludes

EXCRETA *n/pl* excreted matter **EXCRETAL** *adj*

EXCRETE *v* -CRETED, -CRETING, -CRETES to separate and eliminate from an organic body

EXCRETER *n* pl. -S one that excretes

EXCURSUS *n* pl. -ES a long appended exposition of a topic

EXCUSE *v* -CUSED, -CUSING, -CUSES to apologize for

EXCUSER *n* pl. -S one that excuses

EXEC *n* pl. -S an executive officer

EXECRATE *v* -CRATED, -CRATING, -CRATES to curse

EXECUTE *v* -CUTED, -CUTING, -CUTES to carry out

EXECUTER *n* pl. -S executor

EXECUTOR *n* pl. -S one that executes

EXEDRA *n* pl. -DRAE a curved outdoor bench

EXEGESIS *n* pl. -GESES critical explanation or analysis **EXEGETIC** *adj*

EXEGETE *n* pl. -S one skilled in exegesis

EXEMPLAR *n* pl. -S one that is worthy of being copied

EXEMPLUM *n* pl. -PLA an example

EXEMPT *v* -ED, -ING, -S to free from an obligation required of others

EXEQUY *n* pl. -QUIES a funeral procession **EXEQUIAL** *adj*

EXERCISE *v* -CISED, -CISING, -CISES to make use of

EXERGUE *n* pl. -S a space on a coin **EXERGUAL** *adj*

EXERT *v* -ED, -ING, -S to put into action

EXERTION *n* pl. -S the act of exerting

EXERTIVE *adj* tending to exert

EXEUNT *v* they leave the stage — used as a stage direction

EXHALANT *n* pl. -S something that exhales

EXHALE *v* -HALED, -HALING, -HALES to expel air or vapor

EXHALENT *n* pl. -S exhalant

EXHAUST *v* -ED, -ING, -S to use up

EXHIBIT *v* -ED, -ING, -S to present for public viewing

EXHORT *v* -ED, -ING, -S to advise urgently

EXHORTER *n* pl. -S one that exhorts

EXHUME *v* -HUMED, -HUMING, -HUMES to dig out of the earth

EXHUMER *n* pl. -S one that exhumes

EXIGENCE *n* pl. -S exigency

EXIGENCY *n* pl. -CIES urgency

EXIGENT *adj* urgent

EXIGIBLE *adj* liable to be demanded

EXIGUITY *n* pl. -ITIES the state of being exiguous

EXIGUOUS *adj* meager

EXILE *v* -ILED, -ILING, -ILES to banish from one's own country

EXILIAN *adj* exilic

EXILIC *adj* pertaining to exile (banishment from one's own country)

EXILING present participle of exile

EXIMIOUS *adj* excellent

EXINE *n* pl. -S the outer layer of certain spores

EXIST *v* -ED, -ING, -S to be

EXISTENT *n* pl. -S something that exists

EXIT *v* -ED, -ING, -S to go out

EXITLESS *adj* lacking a way out

EXOCARP *n* pl. -S the epicarp

EXOCRINE *n* pl. -S an external secretion

EXODERM *n* pl. -S the ectoderm

EXODOS *n* pl. -DOI a concluding dramatic scene

EXODUS *n* pl. -ES a movement away

EXOERGIC *adj* releasing energy

EXOGAMY *n* pl. -MIES marriage outside of a particular group **EXOGAMIC** *adj*

EXOGEN *n* pl. -S a type of plant

EXON *n* pl. -S a sequence in the genetic code **EXONIC** *adj*

EXONUMIA *n/pl* numismatic items other than coins or paper money

EXORABLE *adj* persuadable

EXORCISE *v* -CISED, -CISING, -CISES to free of an evil spirit

EXORCISM *n* pl. -S the act of exorcising

EXORCIST *n* pl. -S one who practices exorcism

EXORCIZE *v* -CIZED, -CIZING, -CIZES to exorcise

EXORDIUM *n* pl. -DIUMS or -DIA a beginning **EXORDIAL** *adj*

EXOSMOSE *n* pl. -S a form of osmosis **EXOSMIC** *adj*

EXOSPORE *n* pl. -S the outer coat of a spore

EXOTERIC *adj* suitable for the public

EXOTIC *n* pl. -S something from another part of the world

EXOTICA *n/pl* things excitingly different or unusual

EXOTISM *n* pl. -S an exotic

EXOTOXIN *n* pl. -S an excreted toxin **EXOTOXIC** *adj*

EXPAND *v* -ED, -ING, -S to increase in size or volume

EXPANDER *n* pl. -S one that expands

EXPANDOR *n* pl. -S a type of transducer

EXPANSE *n* pl. -S a wide, continuous area

EXPAT *n* pl. -S an expatriate person

EXPECT *v* -ED, -ING, -S to anticipate

EXPEDITE *v* -DITED, -DITING, -DITES to speed up the progress of

EXPEL *v* -PELLED, -PELLING, -PELS to force out

EXPELLEE *n* pl. -S a deportee

EXPELLER *n* pl. -S one that expels

EXPELLING present participle of expel

EXPEND *v* -ED, -ING, -S to use up

EXPENDER *n* pl. -S one that expends

EXPENSE *v* -PENSED, -PENSING, -PENSES to charge with costs

EXPERT *v* -ED, -ING, -S to serve as an authority

EXPERTLY *adv* skillfully

EXPIABLE *adj* capable of being expiated

EXPIATE *v* -ATED, ATING, -ATES to atone for

EXPIATOR *n* pl. -S one that expiates

EXPIRE *v* -PIRED, -PIRING, -PIRES to come to an end

EXPIRER *n* pl. -S one that expires

EXPIRY *n* pl. -RIES a termination

EXPLAIN *v* -ED, -ING, -S to make plain or understandable

EXPLANT *v* -ED, -ING, -S to remove from the natural site of growth and place in a medium

EXPLICIT *n* pl. -S a statement formerly used at the close of a book

EXPLODE *v* -PLODED, -PLODING, -PLODES to blow up

EXPLODER *n* pl. -S one that explodes

EXPLOIT *v* -ED, -ING, -S to take advantage of

EXPLORE *v* -PLORED, -PLORING, -PLORES to travel through for the purpose of discovery

EXPLORER *n* pl. -S one that explores

EXPO *n* pl. -POS a public exhibition

EXPONENT *n* pl. -S one who expounds

EXPORT *v* -ED, -ING, -S to send to other countries for commercial purposes

EXPORTER *n* pl. -S one that exports

EXPOSAL *n* pl. -S an exposure

EXPOSE *v* -POSED, -POSING, -POSES to lay open to view

EXPOSER *n* pl. -S one that exposes

EXPOSIT *v* -ED, -ING, -S to expound

EXPOSURE *n* pl. -S the act of exposing

EXPOUND *v* -ED, -ING, -S to explain in detail

EXPRESS *v* -ED, -ING, -ES to set forth in words

EXPRESSO *n* pl. -SOS espresso

EXPULSE *v* -PULSED, -PULSING, -PULSES to expel

EXPUNGE *v* -PUNGED, -PUNGING, -PUNGES to delete

EXPUNGER *n* pl. -S one that expunges

EXSCIND *v* -ED, -ING, -S to cut out

EXSECANT *n* pl. -S a trigonometric function of an angle

EXSECT *v* -ED, -ING, -S to cut out

EXSERT *v* -ED, -ING, -S to thrust out

EXTANT *adj* still in existence

EXTEND   *v* -ED, -ING, -S to stretch out to full length

EXTENDER   *n* pl. -S a substance added to another substance

EXTENSOR   *n* pl. -S a muscle that extends a limb

EXTENT   *n* pl. -S the range over which something extends

EXTERIOR   *n* pl. -S a part or surface that is outside

EXTERN   *n* pl. -S a nonresident of an institution

EXTERNAL   *n* pl. -S an exterior

EXTERNE   *n* pl. -S extern

EXTINCT   *v* -ED, -ING, -S to extinguish

EXTOL   *v* -TOLLED, -TOLLING, -TOLS to praise highly

EXTOLL   *v* -ED, -ING, -S to extol

EXTOLLER   *n* pl. -S one that extols

EXTOLLING   present participle of extol

EXTORT   *v* -ED, -ING, -S to obtain from a person by violence or intimidation

EXTORTER   *n* pl. -S one that extorts

EXTRA   *n* pl. -S something additional

EXTRACT   *v* -ED, -ING, -S to pull or draw out

EXTRADOS   *n* pl. -ES the outer curve of an arch

EXTREMA   pl. of extremum

EXTREME   *adj* -TREMER, -TREMEST existing in a very high degree

EXTREME   *n* pl. -S the highest degree

EXTREMUM   *n* pl. -MA a maximum or a minimum of a mathematical function

EXTRORSE   *adj* facing outward

EXTRUDE   *v* -TRUDED, -TRUDING, -TRUDES to force, thrust, or push out

EXTRUDER   *n* pl. -S one that extrudes

EXTUBATE   *v* -BATED, -BATING, -BATES to remove a tube from

EXUDATE   *n* pl. -S an exuded substance

EXUDE   *v* -UDED, -UDING, -UDES to ooze forth

EXULT   *v* -ED, -ING, -S to rejoice greatly

EXULTANT   *adj* exulting

EXURB   *n* pl. -S a residential area lying beyond the suburbs of a city **EXURBAN** *adj*

EXURBIA   *n* pl. -S an exurb

EXUVIATE   *v* -ATED, -ATING, -ATES to molt

EXUVIUM   *n* pl. -VIAE or -VIA the molted covering of an animal **EXUVIAL** *adj*

EYAS   *n* pl. -ES a young hawk

EYE   *v* EYED, EYING or EYEING, EYES to watch closely **EYEABLE** *adj*

EYE   *n* pl. EYES, EYEN or EYNE the organ of sight

EYEBALL   *v* -ED, -ING, -S to eye

EYEBAR   *n* pl. -S a metal bar with a loop at one or both ends

EYEBEAM   *n* pl. -S a glance

EYEBOLT   *n* pl. -S a type of bolt or screw

EYEBROW   *n* pl. -S the ridge over the eye

EYECUP   *n* pl. -S a cup used for applying lotions to the eyes

EYED   past tense of eye

EYEDNESS   *n* pl. -ES preference for the use of one eye over the other

EYEDROPS   *n/pl* a medicated solution for the eyes applied in drops

EYEFUL   *n* pl. -S a complete view

EYEGLASS   *n* pl. -ES a lens used to aid vision

EYEHOLE   *n* pl. -S a small opening

EYEHOOK   *n* pl. -S a type of hook

EYELASH   *n* pl. -ES a hair growing on the edge of an eyelid

EYELESS   *adj* lacking eyes

EYELET   *v* -LETTED, -LETTING, -LETS to make a small hole in

EYELID   *n* pl. -S the lid of skin that can be closed over an eyeball

EYELIKE   *adj* resembling an eye

EYELINER   *n* pl. -S makeup for the eyes

EYEN   a pl. of eye

EYEPIECE   *n* pl. -S the lens or lens group nearest the eye in an optical instrument

EYEPOINT   *n* pl. -S the point at which an eye is placed in using an optical instrument

EYER   *n* pl. -S one that eyes

EYESHADE   *n* pl. -S a visor for shading the eyes

EYESHOT   *n* pl. -S the range of vision

EYESIGHT   *n* pl. -S the ability to see

EYESOME   *adj* pleasant to look at

EYESORE   *n* pl. -S something offensive to the sight

EYESPOT   *n* pl. -S a simple visual organ of lower animals

EYESTALK   *n* pl. -S a stalklike structure with an eye at its tip

EYESTONE *n* pl. -S a disk used to remove foreign matter from the eye

EYETOOTH *n* pl. -TEETH a cuspid

EYEWASH *n* pl. -ES an eye lotion

EYEWATER *n* pl. -S an eyewash

EYEWEAR *n* pl. EYEWEAR devices worn on or over the eyes

EYEWINK *n* pl. -S a wink of the eye

EYING a present participle of eye

EYNE a pl. of eye

EYRA *n* pl. -S a wild cat of tropical America

EYRE *n* pl. -S a journey

EYRIE *n* pl. -S aerie

EYRIR *n* pl. AURAR a monetary unit of Iceland

EYRY *n* pl. -RIES aerie

FA *n* pl. -S the fourth tone of the diatonic musical scale

FABLE *v* -BLED, -BLING, -BLES to compose or tell fictitious tales

FABLER *n* pl. -S one that fables

FABLIAU *n* pl. -AUX a short metrical tale popular in medieval France

FABLING present participle of fable

FABRIC *n* pl. -S a woven, felted, or knitted material

FABULAR *adj* legendary

FABULIST *n* pl. -S a liar

FABULOUS *adj* almost unbelievable

FACADE *n* pl. -S the front of a building

FACE *v* FACED, FACING, FACES to oppose or meet defiantly **FACEABLE** *adj*

FACEDOWN *adv* with the front part down

FACELESS *adj* lacking personal distinction or identity

FACER *n* pl. -S one that faces

FACET *v* -ETED, -ETING, -ETS or -ETTED, -ETTING, -ETS to cut small plane surfaces on

FACETE *adj* witty **FACETELY** *adv*

FACETIAE *n/pl* witty sayings or writings

FACETTED a past tense of facet

FACETTING a present participle of facet

FACEUP *adv* with the front part up

FACIA *n* pl. -S fascia

FACIAL *n* pl. -S a treatment for the face

FACIALLY *adv* with respect to the face

FACIEND *n* pl. -S a number to be multiplied by another

FACIES *n* pl. FACIES general appearance

FACILE *adj* easily achieved or performed **FACILELY** *adv*

FACILITY *n* pl. -TIES the quality of being facile

FACING *n* pl. -S a lining at the edge of a garment

FACT *n* pl. -S something known with certainty **FACTFUL** *adj*

FACTION *n* pl. -S a clique within a larger group

FACTIOUS *adj* promoting dissension

FACTOID *n* pl. -S a brief news item

FACTOR *v* -ED, -ING, -S to express as a product of two or more quantities

FACTORY *n* pl. -RIES a building or group of buildings in which goods are manufactured

FACTOTUM *n* pl. -S a person employed to do many kinds of work

FACTUAL *adj* pertaining to facts

FACTURE *n* pl. -S the act of making something

FACULA *n* pl. -LAE an unusually bright spot on the sun's surface **FACULAR** *adj*

FACULTY *n* pl. -TIES an inherent power or ability

FAD *n* pl. -S a practice or interest that enjoys brief popularity

FADABLE *adj* capable of fading

FADDIER comparative of faddy

FADDIEST superlative of faddy

FADDISH *adj* inclined to take up fads

FADDISM *n* pl. -S inclination to take up fads

FADDIST *n* pl. -S a faddish person

FADDY *adj* -DIER, -DIEST faddish

FADE *v* FADED, FADING, FADES to lose color or brightness **FADEDLY** *adv*

FADEAWAY *n* pl. -AWAYS a type of pitch in baseball

FADELESS *adj* not fading

FADER *n* pl. -S one that fades

FADGE *v* FADGED, FADGING, FADGES to succeed

FADING *n* pl. -S an Irish dance

FADO *n* pl. -DOS a Portuguese folk song

FAECES *n/pl* feces **FAECAL** *adj*

FAENA *n* pl. -S a series of passes made by a matador in a bullfight

FAERIE *n* pl. -S a fairy

FAERY *n* pl. -ERIES faerie

FAG *v* FAGGED, FAGGING, FAGS to make weary by hard work

FAGGOT *v* -ED, -ING, -S to fagot

FAGIN *n* pl. -S a person who instructs others in crime

FAGOT *v* -ED, -ING, -S to bind together into a bundle

FAGOTER *n* pl. -S one that fagots

FAGOTING *n* pl. -S a type of embroidery

FAHLBAND *n* pl. -S a band or stratum of rock impregnated with metallic sulfides

FAIENCE *n* pl. -S a variety of glazed pottery

FAIL *v* -ED, -ING, -S to be unsuccessful in an attempt

FAILING *n* pl. -S a minor fault or weakness

FAILLE *n* pl. -S a woven fabric

FAILURE *n* pl. -S the act of failing

FAIN *adj* FAINER, FAINEST glad

FAINEANT *n* pl. -S a lazy person

FAINT *v* -ED, -ING, -S to lose consciousness

FAINT *adj* FAINTER, FAINTEST lacking strength or vigor

FAINTER *n* pl. -S one that faints

FAINTISH *adj* somewhat faint

FAINTLY *adv* in a faint manner

FAIR *adj* FAIRER, FAIREST free from bias, dishonesty, or injustice

FAIR *v* -ED, -ING, -S to make smooth

FAIRIES pl. of fairy

FAIRING *n* pl. -S a structure on an aircraft serving to reduce drag

FAIRISH *adj* moderately good

FAIRLEAD *n* pl. -S a device used to hold a ship's rigging in place

FAIRLY *adv* in a fair manner

FAIRNESS *n* pl. -ES the quality of being fair

FAIRWAY *n* pl. -WAYS the mowed part of a golf course between tee and green

FAIRY *n* pl. FAIRIES an imaginary supernatural being

FAIRYISM *n* pl. -S the quality of being like a fairy

FAITH *v* -ED, -ING, -S to believe or trust

FAITHFUL *n* pl. -S a loyal follower or member

FAITOUR *n* pl. -S an impostor

FAJITA *n* pl. -S marinated and grilled beef, chicken, or shrimp served with a flour tortilla

FAKE *v* FAKED, FAKING, FAKES to contrive and present as genuine

FAKEER *n* pl. -S fakir

FAKER *n* pl. -S one that fakes

FAKERY *n* pl. -ERIES the practice of faking

FAKEY *adj* not genuine; phony

FAKING present participle of fake

FAKIR *n* pl. -S a Hindu ascetic

FALAFEL *n* pl. FALAFEL ground spiced vegetables formed into patties

FALBALA *n* pl. -S a trimming for a woman's garment

FALCATE *adj* curved and tapering to a point

FALCATED *adj* falcate

FALCES pl. of falx

FALCHION *n* pl. -S a broad-bladed sword

FALCON *n* pl. -S a bird of prey

FALCONER *n* pl. -S one that hunts with hawks

FALCONET *n* pl. -S a small falcon

FALCONRY *n* pl. -RIES the sport of hunting with falcons

FALDERAL *n* pl. -S nonsense

FALDEROL *n* pl. -S falderal

FALL *v* FELL, FALLEN, FALLING, FALLS to descend under the force of gravity

FALLACY *n* pl. -CIES a false idea

FALLAL *n* pl. -S a showy article of dress

FALLAWAY *n* pl. -AWAYS a shot in basketball

FALLBACK *n* pl. -S an act of retreating

FALLEN past participle of fall

FALLER *n* pl. -S one that falls

FALLFISH *n* pl. -ES a freshwater fish

FALLIBLE	*adj* capable of erring **FALLIBLY** *adv*
FALLOFF	*n* pl. -S a decline in quantity or quality
FALLOUT	*n* pl. -S radioactive debris resulting from a nuclear explosion
FALLOW	*v* -ED, -ING, -S to plow and leave unseeded
FALSE	*adj* FALSER, FALSEST contrary to truth or fact **FALSELY** *adv*
FALSETTO	*n* pl. -TOS an artificially high voice
FALSIE	*n* pl. -S a pad worn within a brassiere
FALSIFY	*v* -FIED, -FYING, -FIES to represent falsely
FALSITY	*n* pl. -TIES something false
FALTBOAT	*n* pl. -S a collapsible boat resembling a kayak
FALTER	*v* -ED, -ING, -S to hesitate
FALTERER	*n* pl. -S one that falters
FALX	*n* pl. FALCES a sickle-shaped structure
FAME	*v* FAMED, FAMING, FAMES to make famous
FAMELESS	*adj* not famous
FAMILIAL	*adj* pertaining to a family
FAMILIAR	*n* pl. -S a close friend or associate
FAMILISM	*n* pl. -S a social structure in which the family takes precedence over the individual
FAMILY	*n* pl. -LIES a group of persons related by blood or marriage
FAMINE	*n* pl. -S a widespread scarcity of food
FAMING	present participle of fame
FAMISH	*v* -ED, -ING, -ES to suffer extreme hunger
FAMOUS	*adj* well-known **FAMOUSLY** *adv*
FAMULUS	*n* pl. -LI a servant or attendant
FAN	*v* FANNED, FANNING, FANS to cool or refresh with a fan (a device for putting air into motion)
FANATIC	*n* pl. -S a zealot
FANCIED	past tense of fancy
FANCIER	*n* pl. -S one that has a special liking for something
FANCIES	present 3d person sing. of fancy
FANCIFUL	*adj* unrealistic
FANCIFY	*v* -FIED, -FYING, -FIES to make fancy
FANCY	*adj* -CIER, -CIEST ornamental **FANCILY** *adv*
FANCY	*v* -CIED, -CYING, -CIES to take a liking to
FANDANGO	*n* pl. -GOS a lively Spanish dance
FANDOM	*n* pl. -S an aggregate of enthusiastic devotees
FANE	*n* pl. -S a temple
FANEGA	*n* pl. -S a Spanish unit of dry measure
FANEGADA	*n* pl. -S a Spanish unit of area
FANFARE	*n* pl. -S a short, lively musical flourish
FANFARON	*n* pl. -S a braggart
FANFOLD	*v* -ED, -ING, -S to fold paper like a fan
FANG	*n* pl. -S a long, pointed tooth **FANGED, FANGLESS, FANGLIKE** *adj*
FANGA	*n* pl. -S fanega
FANION	*n* pl. -S a small flag
FANJET	*n* pl. -S a type of jet engine
FANLIGHT	*n* pl. -S a type of window
FANLIKE	*adj* resembling a fan
FANNED	past tense of fan
FANNER	*n* pl. -S one that fans
FANNING	present participle of fan
FANNY	*n* pl. -NIES the buttocks
FANO	*n* pl. FANOS a fanon
FANON	*n* pl. -S a cape worn by the pope
FANTAIL	*n* pl. -S a fan-shaped tail or end
FANTASIA	*n* pl. -S a free-form musical composition
FANTASIE	*n* pl. -S a fantasia
FANTASIED	past tense of fantasy
FANTASIES	present 3d person sing. of fantasy
FANTASM	*n* pl. -S phantasm
FANTAST	*n* pl. -S an impractical person
FANTASY	*v* -SIED, -SYING, -SIES to imagine
FANTOD	*n* pl. -S an emotional outburst
FANTOM	*n* pl. -S phantom
FANUM	*n* pl. -S fanon
FANWISE	*adj* spread out like an open fan
FANWORT	*n* pl. -S an aquatic plant
FANZINE	*n* pl. -S a magazine written by and for enthusiastic devotees
FAQIR	*n* pl. -S fakir
FAQUIR	*n* pl. -S fakir

FAR	adv FARTHER, FARTHEST or FURTHER, FURTHEST at or to a great distance
FARAD	n pl. -S a unit of electrical capacitance
FARADAIC	adj faradic
FARADAY	n pl. -DAYS a unit of electricity
FARADIC	adj pertaining to a type of electric current
FARADISE	v -DISED, -DISING, -DISES to faradize
FARADISM	n pl. -S the use of faradic current for therapeutic purposes
FARADIZE	v -DIZED, -DIZING, -DIZES to treat by faradism
FARAWAY	adj distant
FARCE	v FARCED, FARCING, FARCES to fill out with witty material
FARCER	n pl. -S farceur
FARCEUR	n pl. -S a joker
FARCI	adj stuffed with finely chopped meat
FARCICAL	adj absurd
FARCIE	adj farci
FARCING	present participle of farce
FARCY	n pl. -CIES a disease of horses
FARD	v -ED, -ING, -S to apply cosmetics to
FARDEL	n pl. -S a bundle
FARE	v FARED, FARING, FARES to get along
FARER	n pl. -S a traveler
FAREWELL	v -ED, -ING, -S to say goodby
FARFAL	n pl. -S farfel
FARFEL	n pl. -S noodles in the form of small pellets or granules
FARINA	n pl. -S a fine meal made from cereal grain
FARING	present participle of fare
FARINHA	n pl. -S a meal made from the root of the cassava
FARINOSE	adj resembling farina
FARL	n pl. -S a thin oatmeal cake
FARLE	n pl. -S farl
FARM	v -ED, -ING, -S to manage and cultivate as a farm (a tract of land devoted to agriculture) FARMABLE adj
FARMER	n pl. -S one that farms
FARMHAND	n pl. -S a farm laborer
FARMING	n pl. -S the business of operating a farm
FARMLAND	n pl. -S cultivated land
FARMWIFE	n pl. -WIVES a farmer's wife
FARMWORK	n pl. -S labor done on a farm
FARMYARD	n pl. -S an area surrounded by farm buildings
FARNESOL	n pl. -S an alcohol used in perfumes
FARNESS	n pl. -ES the state of being far off or apart
FARO	n pl. FAROS a card game
FAROUCHE	adj sullenly shy
FARRAGO	n pl. -GOES a confused mixture
FARRIER	n pl. -S one that shoes horses
FARRIERY	n pl. -ERIES the trade of a farrier
FARROW	v -ED, -ING, -S to give birth to a litter of pigs
FARSIDE	n pl. -S the farther side
FARTHER	a comparative of far
FARTHEST	a superlative of far
FARTHING	n pl. -S a former British coin
FASCES	n pl. FASCES an ancient Roman symbol of power
FASCIA	n pl. -CIAE or -CIAS a broad and distinct band of color FASCIAL, FASCIATE adj
FASCICLE	n pl. -S a small bundle
FASCINE	n pl. -S a bundle of sticks used in building fortifications
FASCISM	n pl. -S an oppressive political system
FASCIST	n pl. -S an advocate of fascism
FASH	v -ED, -ING, -ES to annoy
FASHION	v -ED, -ING, -S to give a particular shape or form to
FASHIOUS	adj annoying
FAST	adj FASTER, FASTEST moving or able to move quickly
FAST	v -ED, -ING, -S to abstain from eating
FASTBACK	n pl. -S a type of automobile roof
FASTBALL	n pl. -S a type of pitch in baseball
FASTEN	v -ED, -ING, -S to secure
FASTENER	n pl. -S one that fastens
FASTING	n pl. -S abstention from eating
FASTNESS	n pl. -ES the quality of being fast
FASTUOUS	adj arrogant
FAT	adj FATTER, FATTEST having an abundance of flesh
FAT	v FATTED, FATTING, FATS to make fat

FATAL *adj* causing or capable of causing death

FATALISM *n* pl. -S the doctrine that all events are predetermined

FATALIST *n* pl. -S a believer in fatalism

FATALITY *n* pl. -TIES a death resulting from an unexpected occurrence

FATALLY *adv* in a fatal manner

FATBACK *n* pl. -S a marine fish

FATBIRD *n* pl. -S a wading bird

FATE *v* FATED, FATING, FATES to destine

FATEFUL *adj* decisively important

FATHEAD *n* pl. -S a dolt

FATHER *v* -ED, -ING, -S to cause to exist

FATHERLY *adj* paternal

FATHOM *v* -ED, -ING, -S to understand

FATIDIC *adj* pertaining to prophecy

FATIGUE *v* -TIGUED, -TIGUING, -TIGUES to weary

FATING present participle of fate

FATLESS *adj* having no fat

FATLIKE *adj* resembling fat

FATLING *n* pl. -S a young animal fattened for slaughter

FATLY *adv* in the manner of one that is fat

FATNESS *n* pl. -ES the state of being fat

FATSTOCK *n* pl. -S livestock that is fat and ready for market

FATTED past tense of fat

FATTEN *v* -ED, -ING, -S to make fat

FATTENER *n* pl. -S one that fattens

FATTER comparative of fat

FATTEST superlative of fat

FATTIER comparative of fatty

FATTIES pl. of fatty

FATTIEST superlative of fatty

FATTILY *adv* in a fatty manner

FATTING present participle of fat

FATTISH *adj* somewhat fat

FATTY *adj* -TIER, -TIEST greasy; oily

FATTY *n* pl. -TIES one that is fat

FATUITY *n* pl. -ITIES something foolish or stupid

FATUOUS *adj* smugly stupid

FATWA *n* pl. -S an Islamic legal decree

FATWOOD *n* pl. -S wood used for kindling

FAUBOURG *n* pl. -S a suburb

FAUCAL *n* pl. -S a sound produced in the fauces

FAUCES *n/pl* the passage from the mouth to the pharynx

FAUCET *n* pl. -S a device for controlling the flow of liquid from a pipe

FAUCIAL *adj* pertaining to the fauces

FAUGH *interj* — used to express disgust

FAULD *n* pl. -S a piece of armor below the breastplate

FAULT *v* -ED, -ING, -S to criticize

FAULTY *adj* FAULTIER, FAULTIEST imperfect **FAULTILY** *adv*

FAUN *n* pl. -S a woodland deity of Roman mythology **FAUNLIKE** *adj*

FAUNA *n* pl. -NAS or -NAE the animal life of a particular region **FAUNAL** *adj* **FAUNALLY** *adv*

FAUTEUIL *n* pl. -S an armchair

FAUVE *n* pl. -S a fauvist

FAUVISM *n* pl. -S a movement in painting

FAUVIST *n* pl. -S an advocate of fauvism

FAUX *adj* not genuine; fake

FAVA *n* pl. -S the edible seed of a climbing vine

FAVE *n* pl. -S a favorite

FAVELA *n* pl. -S a slum area

FAVELLA *n* pl. -S favela

FAVISM *n* pl. -S an acute anemia

FAVONIAN *adj* pertaining to the west wind

FAVOR *v* -ED, -ING, -S to regard with approval

FAVORER *n* pl. -S one that favors

FAVORITE *n* pl. -S a person or thing preferred above all others

FAVOUR *v* -ED, -ING, -S to favor

FAVOURER *n* pl. -S favorer

FAVUS *n* pl. -ES a skin disease

FAWN *v* -ED, -ING, -S to seek notice or favor by servile demeanor

FAWNER *n* pl. -S one that fawns

FAWNLIKE *adj* resembling a young deer

FAWNY *adj* FAWNIER, FAWNIEST of a yellowish-brown color

FAX *v* -ED, -ING, -ES to transmit and reproduce by electronic means

FAY *v* -ED, -ING, -S to join closely

FAYALITE *n* pl. -S a mineral

FAZE *v* FAZED, FAZING, FAZES to disturb the composure of

FAZENDA *n* pl. -S a Brazilian plantation

FEAL *adj* loyal

FEALTY *n* pl. -TIES loyalty

FEAR *v* -ED, -ING, -S to be afraid of

FEARER *n* pl. -S one that fears

FEARFUL *adj* -FULLER, -FULLEST afraid

FEARLESS *adj* unafraid

FEARSOME *adj* frightening

FEASANCE *n* pl. -S the performance of a condition, obligation, or duty

FEASE *v* FEASED, FEASING, FEASES to faze

FEASIBLE *adj* capable of being done FEASIBLY *adv*

FEAST *v* -ED, -ING, -S to eat sumptuously

FEASTER *n* pl. -S one that feasts

FEASTFUL *adj* festive

FEAT *n* pl. -S a notable act or achievement

FEAT *adj* FEATER, FEATEST skillful

FEATHER *v* -ED, -ING, -S to cover with feathers (horny structures that form the principal covering of birds)

FEATHERY *adj* -ERIER, -ERIEST resembling feathers

FEATLY *adj* -LIER, -LIEST graceful

FEATURE *v* -TURED, -TURING, -TURES to give special prominence to

FEAZE *v* FEAZED, FEAZING, FEAZES to faze

FEBRIFIC *adj* feverish

FEBRILE *adj* feverish

FECAL *adj* pertaining to feces

FECES *n/pl* bodily waste discharged through the anus

FECIAL *n* pl. -S fetial

FECK *n* pl. -S value

FECKLESS *adj* worthless

FECKLY *adv* almost

FECULA *n* pl. -LAE fecal matter

FECULENT *adj* foul with impurities

FECUND *adj* fruitful

FED *n* pl. -S a federal agent

FEDAYEE *n* pl. -YEEN an Arab commando

FEDERACY *n* pl. -CIES an alliance

FEDERAL *n* pl. -S a supporter of a type of central government

FEDERATE *v* -ATED, -ATING, -ATES to unite in an alliance

FEDORA *n* pl. -S a type of hat

FEE *v* FEED, FEEING, FEES to pay a fee (a fixed charge) to

FEEBLE *adj* -BLER, -BLEST weak FEEBLY *adv*

FEEBLISH *adj* somewhat feeble

FEED *v* FED, FEEDING, FEEDS to give food to FEEDABLE *adj*

FEEDBACK *n* pl. -S the return of a portion of the output to the input

FEEDBAG *n* pl. -S a bag for feeding horses

FEEDBOX *n* pl. -ES a box for animal feed

FEEDER *n* pl. -S one that feeds

FEEDHOLE *n* pl. -S one of a series of holes in paper tape

FEEDLOT *n* pl. -S a plot of land on which livestock is fattened

FEEL *v* FELT, FEELING, FEELS to perceive through the sense of touch

FEELER *n* pl. -S a tactile organ

FEELESS *adj* requiring no fee

FEELING *n* pl. -S the function or power of perceiving by touch

FEET pl. of foot FEETLESS *adj*

FEEZE *v* FEEZED, FEEZING, FEEZES to faze

FEH *n* pl. -S peh

FEIGN *v* -ED, -ING, -S to pretend

FEIGNER *n* pl. -S one that feigns

FEIJOA *n* pl. -S a green edible fruit

FEINT *v* -ED, -ING, -S to make a deceptive movement

FEIRIE *adj* nimble

FEIST *n* pl. -S a small dog of mixed breed

FEISTY *adj* FEISTIER, FEISTIEST full of nervous energy

FELAFEL *n* pl. FELAFEL falafel

FELDSHER *n* pl. -S a medical worker in Russia

FELDSPAR *n* pl. -S a mineral

FELICITY *n* pl. -TIES happiness

FELID *n* pl. -S a feline

FELINE *n* pl. -S an animal of the cat family

FELINELY *adv* in a catlike manner

FELINITY *n* pl. -TIES the quality of being catlike

FELL *v* -ED, -ING, -S to cause to fall

FELL *adj* FELLER, FELLEST cruel

FELLA *n* pl. -S a man or boy

FELLABLE *adj* capable of being felled

FELLAH *n* pl. -LAHS, -LAHIN, or -LAHEEN a peasant or laborer in Arab countries

FELLATE *v* -LATED, -LATING, -LATES to perform fellatio

FELLATIO *n* pl. -TIOS oral stimulation of the penis

FELLATOR *n* pl. -S one that fellates

FELLER   n pl. -S one that fells
FELLIES   pl. of felly
FELLNESS   n pl. -ES extreme cruelty
FELLOE   n pl. -S the rim of a wheel
FELLOW   v -ED, -ING, -S to produce an equal to
FELLOWLY   adj friendly
FELLY   n pl. -LIES a felloe
FELON   n pl. -S a person who has committed a felony
FELONRY   n pl. -RIES the whole class of felons
FELONY   n pl. -NIES a grave crime
FELSITE   n pl. -S an igneous rock
FELSITIC adj
FELSPAR   n pl. -S feldspar
FELSTONE   n pl. -S felsite
FELT   v -ED, -ING, -S to mat together
FELTING   n pl. -S felted material
FELTLIKE   adj like a cloth made from wool
FELUCCA   n pl. -S a swift sailing vessel
FELWORT   n pl. -S a flowering plant
FEM   n pl. -S a passive homosexual
FEMALE   n pl. -S an individual that bears young or produces ova
FEME   n pl. -S a wife
FEMINACY   n pl. -CIES the state of being a female
FEMINIE   n/pl women collectively
FEMININE   n pl. -S a word or form having feminine gender
FEMINISE   v -NISED, -NISING, -NISES to feminize
FEMINISM   n pl. -S a doctrine advocating rights for women equal to those of men
FEMINIST   n pl. -S a supporter of feminism
FEMINITY   n pl. -TIES the quality of being womanly
FEMINIZE   v -NIZED, -NIZING, -NIZES to make womanly
FEMME   n pl. -S a woman
FEMORAL   adj pertaining to the femur
FEMUR   n pl. -MURS or -MORA a bone of the leg
FEN   n pl. -S a marsh
FENAGLE   v -GLED, -GLING, -GLES to finagle
FENCE   v FENCED, FENCING, FENCES to practice the art of fencing
FENCER   n pl. -S one that fences

FENCEROW   n pl. -S the land occupied by a fence
FENCIBLE   n pl. -S a soldier enlisted for home service only
FENCING   n pl. -S the art of using a sword in attack and defense
FEND   v -ED, -ING, -S to ward off
FENDER   n pl. -S a metal guard over the wheel of a motor vehicle
FENDERED adj
FENESTRA   n pl. -TRAE a small anatomical opening
FENLAND   n pl. -S marshy ground
FENNEC   n pl. -S an African fox
FENNEL   n pl. -S a perennial herb
FENNY   adj marshy
FENTHION   n pl. -S an insecticide
FENURON   n pl. -S an herbicide
FEOD   n pl. -S a fief
FEODARY   n pl. -RIES a vassal
FEOFF   v -ED, -ING, -S to grant a fief to
FEOFFEE   n pl. -S one to whom a fief is granted
FEOFFER   n pl. -S one that grants a fief to another
FEOFFOR   n pl. -S feoffer
FER   prep for
FERACITY   n pl. -TIES the state of being fruitful
FERAL   adj wild
FERBAM   n pl. -S a fungicide
FERE   n pl. -S a companion
FERETORY   n pl. -RIES a receptacle in which sacred relics are kept
FERIA   n pl. -RIAS or -RIAE a weekday of a church calendar on which no feast is celebrated
FERIAL adj
FERINE   adj feral
FERITY   n pl. -TIES wildness
FERLIE   n pl. -S a strange sight
FERLY   n pl. -LIES ferlie
FERMATA   n pl. -TAS or -TE the sustaining of a musical note, chord, or rest beyond its written time value
FERMENT   v -ED, -ING, -S to undergo a type of chemical reaction
FERMI   n pl. -S a unit of length
FERMION   n pl. -S a type of atomic particle
FERMIUM   n pl. -S a radioactive element
FERN   n pl. -S a flowerless vascular plant FERNLESS, FERNLIKE adj

FERNERY *n pl.* -ERIES a place in which ferns are grown

FERNY *adj* FERNIER, FERNIEST abounding in ferns

FEROCITY *n pl.* -TIES fierceness

FERRATE *n pl.* -S a chemical salt

FERREL *v* -RELED, -RELING, -RELS or -RELLED, -RELLING, -RELS ferrule

FERREOUS *adj* containing iron

FERRET *v* -ED, -ING, -S to search out by careful investigation

FERRETER *n pl.* -S one that ferrets

FERRETY *adj* suggestive of a ferret (a polecat)

FERRIAGE *n pl.* -S transportation by ferry

FERRIC *adj* pertaining to iron

FERRIED past tense of ferry

FERRIES present 3d person sing. of ferry

FERRITE *n pl.* -S a magnetic substance FERRITIC *adj*

FERRITIN *n pl.* -S a protein that contains iron

FERROUS *adj* pertaining to iron

FERRULE *v* -RULED, -RULING, -RULES to furnish with a metal ring or cap to prevent splitting

FERRUM *n pl.* -S iron

FERRY *v* -RIED, -RYING, -RIES to transport by ferry (a type of boat)

FERRYMAN *n pl.* -MEN one who operates a ferry

FERTILE *adj* capable of reproducing

FERULA *n pl.* -LAE or -LAS a flat piece of wood

FERULE *v* -ULED, -ULING, -ULES to ferrule

FERVENCY *n pl.* -CIES fervor

FERVENT *adj* marked by fervor

FERVID *adj* fervent FERVIDLY *adv*

FERVOR *n pl.* -S great warmth or intensity

FERVOUR *n pl.* -S fervor

FESCUE *n pl.* -S a perennial grass

FESS *v* -ED, -ING, -ES to confess

FESSE *n pl.* -S a horizontal band across the middle of a heraldic shield

FESSWISE *adv* horizontally

FESTAL *adj* festive FESTALLY *adv*

FESTER *v* -ED, -ING, -S to generate pus

FESTIVAL *n pl.* -S a day or time of celebration

FESTIVE *adj* of or befitting a festival

FESTOON *v* -ED, -ING, -S to hang decorative chains or strips on

FET *v* FETTED, FETTING, FETS to fetch

FETA *n pl.* -S a Greek cheese

FETAL *adj* pertaining to a fetus

FETATION *n pl.* -S the development of a fetus

FETCH *v* -ED, -ING, -ES to go after and bring back

FETCHER *n pl.* -S one that fetches

FETE *v* FETED, FETING, FETES to honor with a celebration

FETERITA *n pl.* -S a cereal grass

FETIAL *n pl.* -S a priest of ancient Rome

FETIALIS *n pl.* -LES fetial

FETICH *n pl.* -ES fetish

FETICIDE *n pl.* -S the killing of a fetus

FETID *adj* having an offensive odor FETIDLY *adv*

FETING present participle of fete

FETISH *n pl.* -ES an object believed to have magical power

FETLOCK *n pl.* -S a joint of a horse's leg

FETOLOGY *n pl.* -GIES the branch of medicine dealing with the fetus

FETOR *n pl.* -S an offensive odor

FETTED past tense of fet

FETTER *v* -ED, -ING, -S to shackle

FETTERER *n pl.* -S one that fetters

FETTING present participle of fet

FETTLE *v* -TLED, -TLING, -TLES to cover the hearth of with fettling

FETTLING *n pl.* -S loose material thrown on the hearth of a furnace to protect it

FETUS *n pl.* -ES the unborn organism carried within the womb in the later stages of its development

FEU *v* -ED, -ING, -S to grant land to under Scottish feudal law

FEUAR *n pl.* -S one granted land under Scottish feudal law

FEUD *v* -ED, -ING, -S to engage in a feud (a bitter, continuous hostility)

FEUDAL *adj* pertaining to a political and economic system of medieval Europe FEUDALLY *adv*

FEUDARY *n pl.* -RIES a vassal

FEUDIST *n pl.* -S one that feuds

FEVER *v* -ED, -ING, -S to affect with fever (abnormal elevation of the body temperature)

FEVERFEW *n pl.* -S a perennial herb

FEVERISH *adj* having a fever
FEVEROUS *adj* feverish
FEW *adj* FEWER, FEWEST amounting to or consisting of a small number
FEWNESS *n* pl. -ES the state of being few
FEWTRILS *n/pl* things of little value
FEY *adj* FEYER, FEYEST crazy **FEYLY** *adv*
FEYNESS *n* pl. -ES the state of being fey
FEZ *n* pl. FEZZES or FEZES a brimless cap worn by men in the Near East **FEZZED** *adj*
FIACRE *n* pl. -S a small carriage
FIANCE *n* pl. -S a man engaged to be married
FIANCEE *n* pl. -S a woman engaged to be married
FIAR *n* pl. -S the holder of a type of absolute ownership of land under Scottish law
FIASCO *n* pl. -COES or -CHI a wine bottle
FIASCO *n* pl. -COES or -COS a complete failure
FIAT *n* pl. -S an authoritative order
FIB *v* FIBBED, FIBBING, FIBS to tell a trivial lie
FIBBER *n* pl. -S one that fibs
FIBER *n* pl. -S a thread or threadlike object or structure **FIBERED** *adj*
FIBERIZE *v* -IZED, -IZING, -IZES to break into fibers
FIBRANNE *n* pl. -S a fabric made of spun-rayon yarn
FIBRE *n* pl. -S fiber
FIBRIL *n* pl. -S a small fiber
FIBRILLA *n* pl. -LAE a fibril
FIBRIN *n* pl. -S an insoluble protein
FIBROID *n* pl. -S a fibroma
FIBROIN *n* pl. -S an insoluble protein
FIBROMA *n* pl. -MAS or -MATA a benign tumor composed of fibrous tissue
FIBROSIS *n* pl. -BROSES the development of excess fibrous tissue in a bodily organ **FIBROTIC** *adj*
FIBROUS *adj* containing, consisting of, or resembling fibers
FIBULA *n* pl. -LAE or -LAS a bone of the leg **FIBULAR** *adj*
FICE *n* pl. -S a feist
FICHE *n* pl. -S a sheet of microfilm

FICHU *n* pl. -S a woman's scarf
FICIN *n* pl. -S an enzyme
FICKLE *adj* -LER, -LEST not constant or loyal **FICKLY** *adv*
FICO *n* pl. -COES something of little worth
FICTILE *adj* moldable
FICTION *n* pl. -S a literary work whose content is produced by the imagination
FICTIVE *adj* imaginary
FICUS *n* pl. -ES a tropical tree
FID *n* pl. -S a square bar used as a support for a topmast
FIDDLE *v* -DLED, -DLING, -DLES to play a violin
FIDDLER *n* pl. -S one that fiddles
FIDDLY *adj* intricately difficult to handle
FIDEISM *n* pl. -S reliance on faith rather than reason
FIDEIST *n* pl. -S a believer in fideism
FIDELITY *n* pl. -TIES loyalty
FIDGE *v* FIDGED, FIDGING, FIDGES to fidget
FIDGET *v* -ED, -ING, -S to move nervously or restlessly
FIDGETER *n* pl. -S one that fidgets
FIDGETY *adj* nervously restless
FIDGING present participle of fidge
FIDO *n* pl. -DOS a defective coin
FIDUCIAL *adj* based on faith or trust
FIE *interj* — used to express disapproval
FIEF *n* pl. -S a feudal estate
FIEFDOM *n* pl. -S a fief
FIELD *v* -ED, -ING, -S to play as a fielder
FIELDER *n* pl. -S one that catches or picks up a ball in play
FIEND *n* pl. -S a demon
FIENDISH *adj* extremely wicked or cruel
FIERCE *adj* FIERCER, FIERCEST violently hostile or aggressive **FIERCELY** *adv*
FIERY *adj* -ERIER, -ERIEST intensely hot **FIERILY** *adv*
FIESTA *n* pl. -S a festival
FIFE *v* FIFED, FIFING, FIFES to play a fife (a high-pitched flute)
FIFER *n* pl. -S one that plays a fife
FIFTEEN *n* pl. -S a number
FIFTH *n* pl. -S one of five equal parts
FIFTHLY *adv* in the fifth place
FIFTIETH *n* pl. -S one of fifty equal parts
FIFTY *n* pl. -TIES a number
FIFTYISH *adj* being about fifty years old

FIG 199 FIMBLE

FIG v FIGGED, FIGGING, FIGS to adorn

FIGEATER n pl. -S a large beetle

FIGHT v FOUGHT, FIGHTING, FIGHTS to attempt to defeat an adversary

FIGHTER n pl. -S one that fights

FIGHTING n pl. -S the act of one that fights

FIGMENT n pl. -S a product of mental invention

FIGULINE n pl. -S a piece of pottery

FIGURAL adj consisting of human or animal form

FIGURANT n pl. -S a ballet dancer who dances only in groups

FIGURATE adj having a definite shape

FIGURE v -URED, -URING, -URES to compute

FIGURER n pl. -S one that figures

FIGURINE n pl. -S a small statue

FIGURING present participle of figure

FIGWORT n pl. -S a flowering plant

FIL n pl. -S a coin of Iraq and Jordan

FILA pl. of filum

FILAGREE v -GREED, -GREEING, -GREES to filigree

FILAMENT n pl. -S a very thin thread or threadlike structure

FILAR adj pertaining to a thread

FILAREE n pl. -S a European weed

FILARIA n pl. -IAE a parasitic worm FILARIAL, FILARIAN adj

FILARIID n pl. -S filaria

FILATURE n pl. -S the reeling of silk from cocoons

FILBERT n pl. -S the edible nut of a European shrub

FILCH v -ED, -ING, -ES to steal

FILCHER n pl. -S one that filches

FILE v FILED, FILING, FILES to arrange in order for future reference FILEABLE adj

FILEFISH n pl. -ES a marine fish

FILEMOT adj of a brownish yellow color

FILER n pl. -S one that files

FILET v -ED, -ING, -S to fillet

FILIAL adj pertaining to a son or daughter FILIALLY adv

FILIATE v -ATED, -ATING, -ATES to bring into close association

FILIBEG n pl. -S a pleated skirt worn by Scottish Highlanders

FILICIDE n pl. -S the killing of one's child

FILIFORM adj shaped like a filament

FILIGREE v -GREED, -GREEING, -GREES to adorn with intricate ornamental work

FILING n pl. -S a particle removed by a file

FILISTER n pl. -S a groove on a window frame

FILL v -ED, -ING, -S to put as much as can be held into

FILLE n pl. -S a girl

FILLER n pl. -S one that fills

FILLET v -ED, -ING, -S to cut boneless slices from

FILLIES pl. of filly

FILLING n pl. -S that which is used to fill something

FILLIP v -ED, -ING, -S to strike sharply

FILLO n pl. -LOS phyllo

FILLY n pl. -LIES a young female horse

FILM v -ED, -ING, -S to make a motion picture FILMABLE adj

FILMCARD n pl. -S a fiche

FILMDOM n pl. -S the motion-picture industry

FILMER n pl. -S one that films

FILMGOER n pl. -S one that goes to see motion pictures

FILMIC adj pertaining to motion pictures

FILMIER comparative of filmy

FILMIEST superlative of filmy

FILMILY adv in a filmy manner

FILMLAND n pl. -S filmdom

FILMSET v -SET, -SETTING, -SETS to photoset

FILMY adj FILMIER, FILMIEST resembling or covered with film; hazy

FILO n pl. -LOS phyllo

FILOSE adj resembling a thread

FILTER v -ED, -ING, -S to pass through a filter (a device for removing suspended matter)

FILTERER n pl. -S one that filters

FILTH n pl. -S foul or dirty matter

FILTHY adj FILTHIER, FILTHIEST offensively dirty FILTHILY ad

FILTRATE v -TRATED, -TRATING, -TRATES to filter

FILUM n pl. -LA a threadlike anatomical structure

FIMBLE n pl. -S the male hemp plant

FIMBRIA	*n* pl. -BRIAE a fringe or fringe-like structure **FIMBRIAL** *adj*
FIN	*v* FINNED, FINNING, FINS to equip with fins (external paddle-like structures)
FINABLE	*adj* subject to the payment of a fine
FINAGLE	*v* -GLED, -GLING, -GLES to obtain by trickery
FINAGLER	*n* pl. -S one that finagles
FINAL	*n* pl. -S the last examination of an academic course
FINALE	*n* pl. -S a close or termination of something
FINALIS	*n* pl. -LES a type of tone in medieval music
FINALISM	*n* pl. -S the doctrine that all events are determined by ultimate purposes
FINALIST	*n* pl. -S a contestant who reaches the last part of a competition
FINALITY	*n* pl. -TIES the state of being conclusive
FINALIZE	*v* -IZED, -IZING, -IZES to put into finished form
FINALLY	*adv* at the end
FINANCE	*v* -NANCED, -NANCING, -NANCES to supply the money for
FINBACK	*n* pl. -S the rorqual
FINCH	*n* pl. -ES a small bird
FIND	*v* FOUND, FINDING, FINDS to come upon after a search **FINDABLE** *adj*
FINDER	*n* pl. -S one that finds
FINDING	*n* pl. -S something that is found
FINE	*adj* FINER, FINEST of excellent quality
FINE	*v* FINED, FINING, FINES to subject to a fine (a monetary penalty)
FINEABLE	*adj* finable
FINELY	*adv* in a fine manner
FINENESS	*n* pl. -ES the quality of being fine
FINER	comparative of fine
FINERY	*n* pl. -ERIES elaborate adornment
FINESPUN	*adj* developed with extreme care
FINESSE	*v* -NESSED, -NESSING, -NESSES to bring about by adroit maneuvering
FINEST	superlative of fine

FINFISH	*n* pl. -ES a true fish
FINFOOT	*n* pl. -S an aquatic bird
FINGER	*v* -ED, -ING, -S to touch with the fingers (the terminating members of the hand)
FINGERER	*n* pl. -S one that fingers
FINIAL	*n* pl. -S a crowning ornament **FINIALED** *adj*
FINICAL	*adj* finicky
FINICKIN	*adj* finicky
FINICKY	*adj* -ICKIER, -ICKIEST difficult to please
FINIKIN	*adj* finicky
FINIKING	*adj* finicky
FINING	*n* pl. -S the clarifying of wines
FINIS	*n* pl. -NISES the end
FINISH	*v* -ED, -ING, -ES to bring to an end
FINISHER	*n* pl. -S one that finishes
FINITE	*n* pl. -S something that is finite (having definite limits)
FINITELY	*adv* to a finite extent
FINITUDE	*n* pl. -S the state of being finite
FINK	*v* -ED, -ING, -S to inform to the police
FINLESS	*adj* having no fins
FINLIKE	*adj* resembling a fin
FINMARK	*n* pl. -S a monetary unit of Finland
FINNED	past tense of fin
FINNICKY	*adj* -NICKIER, -NICKIEST finicky
FINNIER	comparative of finny
FINNIEST	superlative of finny
FINNING	present participle of fin
FINNMARK	*n* pl. -S finmark
FINNY	*adj* -NIER, -NIEST having or characterized by fins
FINO	*n* pl. -NOS a very dry sherry
FINOCHIO	*n* pl. -CHIOS a perennial herb
FIORD	*n* pl. -S fjord
FIPPLE	*n* pl. -S a plug of wood at the mouth of certain wind instruments
FIQUE	*n* pl. -S a tropical plant
FIR	*n* pl. -S an evergreen tree
FIRE	*v* FIRED, FIRING, FIRES to project by discharging from a gun **FIREABLE** *adj*
FIREARM	*n* pl. -S a weapon from which a shot is discharged by gunpowder
FIREBACK	*n* pl. -S a cast-iron plate along the back of a fireplace
FIREBALL	*n* pl. -S a luminous meteor

FIREBASE *n* pl. -S a military base from which fire is directed against the enemy

FIREBIRD *n* pl. -S a brightly colored bird

FIREBOAT *n* pl. -S a boat equipped with fire-fighting apparatus

FIREBOMB *v* -ED, -ING, -S to attack with incendiary bombs

FIREBOX *n* pl. -ES a chamber in which fuel is burned

FIREBRAT *n* pl. -S a small, wingless insect

FIREBUG *n* pl. -S an arsonist

FIRECLAY *n* pl. -CLAYS a heat-resistant clay

FIRED past tense of fire

FIREDAMP *n* pl. -S a combustible gas

FIREDOG *n* pl. -S an andiron

FIREFANG *v* -ED, -ING, -S to decompose by oxidation

FIREFLY *n* pl. -FLIES a luminous insect

FIREHALL *n* pl. -S a fire station

FIRELESS *adj* having no fire

FIRELIT *adj* lighted by firelight

FIRELOCK *n* pl. -S a type of gun

FIREMAN *n* pl. -MEN a man employed to extinguish fires

FIREPAN *n* pl. -S an open pan for holding live coals

FIREPINK *n* pl. -S a flowering plant

FIREPLUG *n* pl. -S a hydrant

FIREPOT *n* pl. -S a clay pot filled with burning items

FIRER *n* pl. -S one that fires

FIREROOM *n* pl. -S a room containing a ship's boilers

FIRESIDE *n* pl. -S the area immediately surrounding a fireplace

FIRETRAP *n* pl. -S a building that is likely to catch on fire

FIREWEED *n* pl. -S a perennial herb

FIREWOOD *n* pl. -S wood used as fuel

FIREWORK *n* pl. -S a device for producing a striking display of light or a loud noise

FIREWORM *n* pl. -S a glowworm

FIRING *n* pl. -S the process of maturing ceramic products by heat

FIRKIN *n* pl. -S a British unit of capacity

FIRM *adj* FIRMER, FIRMEST unyielding to pressure

FIRM *v* -ED, -ING, -S to make firm

FIRMAN *n* pl. -S an edict issued by a Middle Eastern sovereign

FIRMER *n* pl. -S a woodworking tool

FIRMLY *adv* in a firm manner

FIRMNESS *n* pl. -ES the state of being firm

FIRMWARE *n* pl. -S computer programs permanently stored on a microchip

FIRN *n* pl. -S neve

FIRRY *adj* abounding in firs

FIRST *n* pl. -S something that precedes all others

FIRSTLY *adv* before all others

FIRTH *n* pl. -S an inlet of the sea

FISC *n* pl. -S a state or royal treasury

FISCAL *n* pl. -S a public prosecutor

FISCALLY *adv* with regard to financial matters

FISH *v* -ED, -ING, -ES to catch or try to catch fish (cold-blooded aquatic vertebrates)

FISHABLE *adj* suitable for fishing

FISHBOLT *n* pl. -S a type of bolt

FISHBONE *n* pl. -S a bone of a fish

FISHBOWL *n* pl. -S a bowl in which live fish are kept

FISHER *n* pl. -S one that fishes

FISHERY *n* pl. -ERIES a place for catching fish

FISHEYE *n* pl. -S a suspicious stare

FISHGIG *n* pl. -S a pronged implement for spearing fish

FISHHOOK *n* pl. -S a barbed hook for catching fish

FISHIER comparative of fishy

FISHIEST superlative of fishy

FISHILY *adv* in a fishy manner

FISHING *n* pl. -S the occupation or pastime of catching fish

FISHLESS *adj* having no fish

FISHLIKE *adj* resembling a fish

FISHLINE *n* pl. -S a line used in fishing

FISHMEAL *n* pl. -S ground dried fish

FISHNET *n* pl. -S a net for catching fish

FISHPOLE *n* pl. -S a fishing rod

FISHPOND *n* pl. -S a pond abounding in edible fish

FISHTAIL *v* -ED, -ING, -S to have the rear end of a moving vehicle slide from side to side

FISHWAY *n* pl. -WAYS a device for enabling fish to pass around a dam

FISHWIFE *n* pl. -WIVES a woman who sells fish

FISHWORM *n* pl. -S a worm used as bait

FISHY   *adj* FISHIER, FISHIEST of or resembling fish

FISSATE   *adj* deeply split

FISSILE   *adj* capable of being split

FISSION   *v* -ED, -ING, -S to split into parts

FISSIPED   *n* pl. -S a mammal that has separated toes

FISSURE   *v* -SURED, -SURING, -SURES to split

FIST   *v* -ED, -ING, -S to strike with the fist (the hand closed tightly)

FISTFUL   *n* pl. -S a handful

FISTIC   *adj* pertaining to pugilism

FISTNOTE   *n* pl. -S a part of a text to which attention is drawn by an index mark

FISTULA   *n* pl. -LAE or -LAS a duct formed by the imperfect closing of a wound **FISTULAR** *adj*

FIT   *adj* FITTER, FITTEST healthy

FIT   *v* FITTED, FITTING, FITS to bring to a required form and size

FITCH   *n* pl. -ES a polecat

FITCHEE   *adj* fitchy

FITCHET   *n* pl. -S a fitch

FITCHEW   *n* pl. -S a fitch

FITCHY   *adj* having the arms ending in a point — used of a heraldic cross

FITFUL   *adj* recurring irregularly **FITFULLY** *adv*

FITLY   *adv* in a fit manner

FITMENT   *n* pl. -S equipment

FITNESS   *n* pl. -ES the state of being fit

FITTABLE   *adj* capable of being fitted

FITTED   past tense of fit

FITTER   *n* pl. -S one that fits

FITTEST   superlative of fit

FITTING   *n* pl. -S a small often standardized accessory part

FIVE   *n* pl. -S a number

FIVEFOLD   *adj* five times as great

FIVEPINS   *n/pl* a bowling game

FIVER   *n* pl. -S a five-dollar bill

FIX   *v* FIXED or FIXT, FIXING, FIXES to repair **FIXABLE** *adj*

FIXATE   *v* -ATED, -ATING, -ATES to make stable or stationary

FIXATIF   *n* pl. -S fixative

FIXATION   *n* pl. -S the act of fixating

FIXATIVE   *n* pl. -S a substance for preserving paintings or drawings

FIXEDLY   *adv* firmly

FIXER   *n* pl. -S one that fixes

FIXINGS   *n/pl* accompaniments to the main dish of a meal

FIXIT   *adj* involved with fixing things

FIXITY   *n* pl. -TIES stability

FIXT   a past tense of fix

FIXTURE   *n* pl. -S a permanent part or appendage of a house

FIXURE   *n* pl. -S firmness

FIZ   *n* pl. FIZZES a hissing or sputtering sound

FIZGIG   *n* pl. -S fishgig

FIZZ   *v* -ED, -ING, -ES to make a hissing or sputtering sound

FIZZER   *n* pl. -S one that fizzes

FIZZES   pl. of fiz

FIZZLE   *v* -ZLED, -ZLING, -ZLES to fizz

FIZZY   *adj* FIZZIER, FIZZIEST fizzing

FJELD   *n* pl. -S a high, barren plateau

FJORD   *n* pl. -S a narrow inlet of the sea between steep cliffs

FLAB   *n* pl. -S flabby body tissue

FLABBY   *adj* -BIER, -BIEST flaccid **FLABBILY** *adv*

FLABELLA   *n/pl* fan-shaped anatomical structures

FLACCID   *adj* lacking firmness

FLACK   *v* -ED, -ING, -S to work as a press agent

FLACKERY   *n* pl. -ERIES publicity

FLACON   *n* pl. -S a small stoppered bottle

FLAG   *v* FLAGGED, FLAGGING, FLAGS to mark with a flag (a piece of cloth used as a symbol)

FLAGELLA   *n/pl* long, slender plant shoots

FLAGGER   *n* pl. -S one that flags

FLAGGING   *n* pl. -S a type of pavement

FLAGGY   *adj* -GIER, -GIEST drooping

FLAGLESS   *adj* having no flag

FLAGMAN   *n* pl. -MEN one who carries a flag

FLAGON   *n* pl. -S a large bulging bottle

FLAGPOLE   *n* pl. -S a pole on which a flag is displayed

FLAGRANT   *adj* extremely or deliberately conspicuous

FLAGSHIP   *n* pl. -S a ship bearing the flag of a fleet

FLAIL   *v* -ED, -ING, -S to swing freely

FLAIR   *n* pl. -S a natural aptitude

FLAK   *n* pl. FLAK antiaircraft fire

FLAKE   v FLAKED, FLAKING,
            FLAKES to peel off in flakes
            (flat, thin pieces)
FLAKER   n pl. -S one that flakes
FLAKY   adj FLAKIER, FLAKIEST
            resembling flakes FLAKILY
            adv
FLAM   v FLAMMED, FLAMMING,
            FLAMS to deceive
FLAMBE   v -BEED, -BEING, -BES to
            douse with a liqueur and ignite
FLAMBEAU   n pl. -BEAUX or -BEAUS a
            flaming torch
FLAMBEE   adj flaming
FLAME   v FLAMED, FLAMING,
            FLAMES to burn brightly
FLAMEN   n pl. -MENS or -MINES a
            priest of ancient Rome
FLAMENCO   n pl. -COS a strongly rhythmic
            style of dancing
FLAMEOUT   n pl. -S a failure of a jet
            engine in flight
FLAMER   n pl. -S one that flames
FLAMIER   comparative of flamy
FLAMIEST   superlative of flamy
FLAMINES   a pl. of flamen
FLAMING   present participle of flame
FLAMINGO   n pl. -GOS or -GOES a
            wading bird
FLAMMED   past tense of flam
FLAMMING   present participle of flam
FLAMY   adj FLAMIER, FLAMIEST
            flaming
FLAN   n pl. -S or -ES a type of
            custard
FLANCARD   n pl. -S a piece of armor for
            the side of a horse
FLANERIE   n pl. -S idleness
FLANEUR   n pl. -S an idler
FLANGE   v FLANGED, FLANGING,
            FLANGES to provide with a
            protecting rim
FLANGER   n pl. -S one that flanges
FLANK   v -ED, -ING, -S to be located
            at the side of
FLANKEN   n/pl beef cut from the sides
            that is boiled with vegetables
FLANKER   n pl. -S one that flanks
FLANNEL   v -NELED, -NELING, -NELS
            or -NELLED, -NELLING,
            -NELS to cover with flannel (a
            soft fabric)
FLAP   v FLAPPED, FLAPPING,
            FLAPS to wave up and down
FLAPJACK   n pl. -S a pancake

FLAPLESS   adj having no flap (a flat
            appendage)
FLAPPED   past tense of flap
FLAPPER   n pl. -S one that flaps
FLAPPING   present participle of flap
FLAPPY   adj -PIER, -PIEST flapping
FLARE   v FLARED, FLARING,
            FLARES to burn with a bright,
            wavering light
FLASH   v -ED, -ING, -ES to send forth
            a sudden burst of light
FLASHER   n pl. -S one that flashes
FLASHGUN   n pl. -S a photographic
            apparatus
FLASHING   n pl. -S sheet metal used in
            waterproofing a roof
FLASHY   adj FLASHIER, FLASHIEST
            gaudy FLASHILY adv
FLASK   n pl. -S a narrow-necked
            container
FLASKET   n pl. -S a small flask
FLAT   adj FLATTER, FLATTEST
            having a smooth or even
            surface
FLAT   v FLATTED, FLATTING,
            FLATS to flatten
FLATBED   n pl. -S a type of truck or
            trailer
FLATBOAT   n pl. -S a flat-bottomed boat
FLATCAP   n pl. -S a type of hat
FLATCAR   n pl. -S a railroad car without
            sides or roof
FLATFISH   n pl. -ES any of an order of
            marine fishes
FLATFOOT   n pl. -FEET a foot condition
FLATFOOT   v -ED, -ING, -S to walk with a
            dragging gait
FLATHEAD   n pl. -S a marine food fish
FLATIRON   n pl. -S a device for pressing
            clothes
FLATLAND   n pl. -S land lacking significant
            variation in elevation
FLATLET   n pl. -S a type of apartment
FLATLING   adv with a flat side or edge
FLATLONG   adv flatling
FLATLY   adv in a flat manner
FLATMATE   n pl. -S one with whom an
            apartment is shared
FLATNESS   n pl. -ES the state of being flat
FLATTED   past tense of flat
FLATTEN   v -ED, -ING, -S to make or
            become flat
FLATTER   v -ED, -ING, -S to praise
            excessively
FLATTERY   n pl. -TERIES the act of
            flattering

FLATTEST superlative of flat

FLATTING present participle of flat

FLATTISH *adj* somewhat flat

FLATTOP *n* pl. -S an aircraft carrier

FLATUS *n* pl. -ES intestinal gas

FLATWARE *n* pl. -S tableware that is fairly flat

FLATWASH *n* pl. -ES flatwork

FLATWAYS *adv* flatwise

FLATWISE *adv* with the flat side in a particular position

FLATWORK *n* pl. -S laundry that can be ironed mechanically

FLATWORM *n* pl. -S a flat-bodied worm

FLAUNT *v* -ED, -ING, -S to exhibit in a gaudy manner

FLAUNTER *n* pl. -S one that flaunts

FLAUNTY *adj* FLAUNTIER, FLAUNTIEST gaudy

FLAUTIST *n* pl. -S flutist

FLAVANOL *n* pl. -S flavonol

FLAVIN *n* pl. -S a yellow pigment

FLAVINE *n* pl. -S flavin

FLAVONE *n* pl. -S a chemical compound

FLAVONOL *n* pl. -S a derivative of flavone

FLAVOR *v* -ED, -ING, -S to give flavor (distinctive taste) to

FLAVORER *n* pl. -S one that flavors

FLAVORY *adj* full of flavor

FLAVOUR *v* -ED, -ING, -S to flavor

FLAVOURY *adj* flavory

FLAW *v* -ED, -ING, -S to produce a flaw (an imperfection) in

FLAWLESS *adj* having no flaw

FLAWY *adj* FLAWIER, FLAWIEST full of flaws

FLAX *n* pl. -ES an annual herb

FLAXEN *adj* of a pale yellow color

FLAXSEED *n* pl. -S the seed of flax

FLAXY *adj* FLAXIER, FLAXIEST flaxen

FLAY *v* -ED, -ING, -S to strip off the skin of

FLAYER *n* pl. -S one that flays

FLEA *n* pl. -S a parasitic insect

FLEABAG *n* pl. -S an inferior hotel

FLEABANE *n* pl. -S a flowering plant

FLEABITE *n* pl. -S the bite of a flea

FLEAM *n* pl. -S a surgical instrument

FLEAPIT *n* pl. -S a run-down movie theater

FLEAWORT *n* pl. -S a European herb

FLECHE *n* pl. -S a steeple

FLECK *v* -ED, -ING, -S to mark with flecks (tiny streaks or spots)

FLECKY *adj* flecked

FLECTION *n* pl. -S the act of bending

FLED past tense of flee

FLEDGE *v* FLEDGED, FLEDGING, FLEDGES to furnish with feathers

FLEDGY *adj* FLEDGIER, FLEDGIEST covered with feathers

FLEE *v* FLED, FLEEING, FLEES to run away

FLEECE *v* FLEECED, FLEECING, FLEECES to remove the coat of wool from

FLEECER *n* pl. -S one that fleeces

FLEECH *v* -ED, -ING, -ES to coax

FLEECING present participle of fleece

FLEECY *adj* FLEECIER, FLEECIEST woolly **FLEECILY** *adv*

FLEER *v* -ED, -ING, -S to deride

FLEET *adj* FLEETER, FLEETEST swift **FLEETLY** *adv*

FLEET *v* -ED, -ING, -S to move swiftly

FLEISHIG *adj* made of meat or meat products

FLEMISH *v* -ED, -ING, -ES to coil rope in a certain manner

FLENCH *v* -ED, -ING, -ES to flense

FLENSE *v* FLENSED, FLENSING, FLENSES to strip the blubber or skin from

FLENSER *n* pl. -S one that flenses

FLESH *v* -ED, -ING, -ES to plunge into the flesh (soft body tissue)

FLESHER *n* pl. -S one that removes flesh from animal hides

FLESHIER comparative of fleshy

FLESHIEST superlative of fleshy

FLESHING *n* pl. -S the distribution of the lean and fat on an animal

FLESHLY *adj* -LIER, -LIEST pertaining to the body

FLESHPOT *n* pl. -S a pot for cooking meat

FLESHY *adj* FLESHIER, FLESHIEST having much flesh

FLETCH *v* -ED, -ING, -ES to fledge

FLETCHER *n* pl. -S one that makes arrows

FLEURY *adj* having the arms terminating in three leaves — used of a heraldic cross

FLEW *n* pl. -S a fishing net

FLEX *v* -ED, -ING, -ES to bend

FLEXAGON *n* pl. -S a folded paper construction

FLEXIBLE *adj* capable of being bent **FLEXIBLY** *adv*

FLEXILE	adj flexible
FLEXION	n pl. -S flection
FLEXOR	n pl. -S a muscle that serves to bend a bodily part
FLEXTIME	n pl. -S a system that allows flexible working hours
FLEXUOSE	adj flexuous
FLEXUOUS	adj winding
FLEXURE	n pl. -S the act of bending **FLEXURAL** adj
FLEY	v -ED, -ING, -S to frighten
FLIC	n pl. -S a Parisian policeman
FLICHTER	v -ED, -ING, -S to flicker
FLICK	v -ED, -ING, -S to strike with a quick, light blow
FLICKER	v -ED, -ING, -S to move waveringly
FLICKERY	adj flickering
FLIED	a past tense of fly
FLIER	n pl. -S one that flies
FLIES	present 3d person sing. of fly
FLIEST	superlative of fly
FLIGHT	v -ED, -ING, -S to fly in a flock
FLIGHTY	adj FLIGHTIER, FLIGHTIEST fickle
FLIMFLAM	v -FLAMMED, -FLAMMING, -FLAMS to swindle
FLIMSY	adj -SIER, -SIEST lacking solidity or strength **FLIMSILY** adv
FLIMSY	n pl. -SIES a thin paper
FLINCH	v -ED, -ING, -ES to shrink back involuntarily
FLINCHER	n pl. -S one that flinches
FLINDER	n pl. -S a small fragment
FLING	v FLUNG, FLINGING, FLINGS to throw with force
FLINGER	n pl. -S one that flings
FLINKITE	n pl. -S a mineral
FLINT	v -ED, -ING, -S to provide with flint (a spark-producing rock)
FLINTY	adj FLINTIER, FLINTIEST resembling flint **FLINTILY** adv
FLIP	v FLIPPED, FLIPPING, FLIPS to throw with a brisk motion
FLIP	adj FLIPPER, FLIPPEST flippant
FLIPPANT	adj impudent
FLIPPED	past tense of flip
FLIPPER	n pl. -S a broad, flat limb adapted for swimming
FLIPPEST	superlative of flip
FLIPPING	present participle of flip
FLIPPY	adj flaring at the bottom
FLIRT	v -ED, -ING, -S to behave amorously without serious intent
FLIRTER	n pl. -S one that flirts
FLIRTY	adj FLIRTIER, FLIRTIEST given to flirting
FLIT	v FLITTED, FLITTING, FLITS to move lightly and swiftly
FLITCH	v -ED, -ING, -ES to cut into strips
FLITE	v FLITED, FLITING, FLITES to quarrel
FLITTED	past tense of flit
FLITTER	v -ED, -ING, -S to flutter
FLITTING	present participle of flit
FLIVVER	n pl. -S an old, battered car
FLOAT	v -ED, -ING, -S to rest or remain on the surface of a liquid
FLOATAGE	n pl. -S flotage
FLOATEL	n pl. -S a houseboat used as a hotel
FLOATER	n pl. -S one that floats
FLOATY	adj FLOATIER, FLOATIEST tending to float
FLOC	v FLOCCED, FLOCCING, FLOCS to aggregate into floccules
FLOCCI	pl. of floccus
FLOCCOSE	adj having woolly tufts
FLOCCULE	n pl. -S a tuft-like mass
FLOCCULI	n/pl small, loosely aggregated masses
FLOCCUS	n pl. FLOCCI a floccule
FLOCK	v -ED, -ING, -S to gather or move in a crowd
FLOCKING	n pl. -S a velvety design in short fibers on cloth or paper
FLOCKY	adj FLOCKIER, FLOCKIEST woolly
FLOE	n pl. -S a large mass of floating ice
FLOG	v FLOGGED, FLOGGING, FLOGS to beat with a whip or rod
FLOGGER	n pl. -S one that flogs
FLOGGING	n pl. -S a whipping
FLOKATI	n pl. -S a Greek handwoven rug
FLONG	n pl. -S a sheet of a certain type of paper
FLOOD	v -ED, -ING, -S to inundate
FLOODER	n pl. -S one that floods
FLOODLIT	adj illuminated by floodlights
FLOODWAY	n pl. -WAYS an overflow channel

FLOOEY   *adj* awry

FLOOIE   *adj* flooey

FLOOR   *v* -ED, -ING, -S to provide with a floor (the level base of a room)

FLOORAGE   *n* pl. -S floor space

FLOORER   *n* pl. -S one that floors

FLOORING   *n* pl. -S a floor

FLOOSIE   *n* pl. -S floozy

FLOOSY   *n* pl. -SIES floozy

FLOOZIE   *n* pl. -S floozy

FLOOZY   *n* pl. -ZIES a prostitute

FLOP   *v* FLOPPED, FLOPPING, FLOPS to fall heavily and noisily

FLOPOVER   *n* pl. -S a defect in television reception

FLOPPER   *n* pl. -S one that flops

FLOPPING   present participle of flop

FLOPPY   *n* pl. -PIES a type of computer disk

FLOPPY   *adj* -PIER, -PIEST soft and flexible FLOPPILY *adv*

FLORA   *n* pl. -RAS or -RAE the plant life of a particular region

FLORAL   *adj* pertaining to flowers FLORALLY *adv*

FLORENCE   *n* pl. -S florin

FLORET   *n* pl. -S a small flower

FLORID   *adj* ruddy FLORIDLY *adv*

FLORIGEN   *n* pl. -S a plant hormone

FLORIN   *n* pl. -S a former gold coin of Europe

FLORIST   *n* pl. -S a grower or seller of flowers

FLORUIT   *n* pl. -S a period of flourishing

FLOSS   *v* -ED, -ING, -ES to clean between the teeth with a strong thread

FLOSSIE   *n* pl. -S a floozy

FLOSSY   *adj* FLOSSIER, FLOSSIEST resembling floss (a soft, light fiber) FLOSSILY *adv*

FLOTA   *n* pl. -S a fleet of Spanish ships

FLOTAGE   *n* pl. -S the act of floating

FLOTILLA   *n* pl. -S a fleet of ships

FLOTSAM   *n* pl. -S floating wreckage of a ship or its cargo

FLOUNCE   *v* FLOUNCED, FLOUNCING, FLOUNCES to move with exaggerated motions

FLOUNCY   *adj* FLOUNCIER, FLOUNCIEST flouncing

FLOUNDER   *v* -ED, -ING, -S to struggle clumsily

FLOUR   *v* -ED, -ING, -S to cover with flour (a finely ground meal of grain)

FLOURISH   *v* -ED, -ING, -ES to thrive

FLOURY   *adj* resembling flour

FLOUT   *v* -ED, -ING, -S to treat with contempt

FLOUTER   *n* pl. -S one that flouts

FLOW   *v* -ED, -ING, -S to move steadily and smoothly along

FLOWAGE   *n* pl. -S the act of flowing

FLOWER   *v* -ED, -ING, -S to put forth flowers (reproductive structures of seed-bearing plants)

FLOWERER   *n* pl. -S a plant that flowers at a certain time

FLOWERET   *n* pl. -S a floret

FLOWERY   *adj* -ERIER, -ERIEST abounding in flowers

FLOWN   a past participle of fly

FLU   *n* pl. -S a virus disease

FLUB   *v* FLUBBED, FLUBBING, FLUBS to bungle

FLUBBER   *n* pl. -S one that flubs

FLUBDUB   *n* pl. -S pretentious nonsense

FLUE   *n* pl. -S an enclosed passageway for directing a current FLUED *adj*

FLUENCY   *n* pl. -CIES the quality of being fluent

FLUENT   *adj* spoken or written with effortless ease FLUENTLY *adv*

FLUERICS   *n/pl* fluidics FLUERIC *adj*

FLUFF   *v* -ED, -ING, -S to make fluffy

FLUFFY   *adj* FLUFFIER, FLUFFIEST light and soft FLUFFILY *adv*

FLUID   *n* pl. -S a substance that tends to flow FLUIDAL *adj*

FLUIDICS   *n/pl* a branch of mechanical engineering FLUIDIC *adj*

FLUIDISE   *v* -ISED, -ISING, -ISES to fluidize

FLUIDITY   *n* pl. -TIES the quality of being able to flow

FLUIDIZE   *v* -IZED, -IZING, -IZES to cause to flow like a fluid

FLUIDLY   *adv* with fluidity

FLUIDRAM   *n* pl. -S a unit of liquid capacity

FLUKE   *v* FLUKED, FLUKING, FLUKES to obtain by chance

FLUKEY   *adj* FLUKIER, FLUKIEST fluky

FLUKY *adj* FLUKIER, FLUKIEST happening by or depending on chance

FLUME *v* FLUMED, FLUMING, FLUMES to convey by means of an artificial water channel

FLUMMERY *n* pl. -MERIES a sweet dessert

FLUMMOX *v* -ED, -ING, -ES to confuse

FLUMP *v* -ED, -ING, -S to fall heavily

FLUNG past tense of fling

FLUNK *v* -ED, -ING, -S to fail an examination or course

FLUNKER *n* pl. -S one that flunks

FLUNKEY *n* pl. -KEYS flunky

FLUNKY *n* pl. -KIES a servile follower

FLUOR *n* pl. -S fluorite **FLUORIC** *adj*

FLUORENE *n* pl. -S a chemical compound

FLUORID *n* pl. -S fluoride

FLUORIDE *n* pl. -S a compound of fluorine

FLUORIN *n* pl. -S fluorine

FLUORINE *n* pl. -S a gaseous element

FLUORITE *n* pl. -S a mineral

FLURRY *v* -RIED, -RYING, -RIES to confuse

FLUSH *adj* FLUSHER, FLUSHEST ruddy

FLUSH *v* -ED, -ING, -ES to blush

FLUSHER *n* pl. -S one that flushes

FLUSTER *v* -ED, -ING, -S to put into a state of nervous confusion

FLUTE *v* FLUTED, FLUTING, FLUTES to play on a flute (a woodwind instrument)

FLUTER *n* pl. -S a flutist

FLUTEY *adj* FLUTIER, FLUTIEST fluty

FLUTIER comparative of fluty

FLUTIEST superlative of fluty

FLUTING *n* pl. -S a series of parallel grooves

FLUTIST *n* pl. -S one who plays the flute

FLUTTER *v* -ED, -ING, -S to wave rapidly and irregularly

FLUTTERY *adj* marked by fluttering

FLUTY *adj* FLUTIER, FLUTIEST resembling a flute in sound

FLUVIAL *adj* pertaining to a river

FLUX *v* -ED, -ING, -ES to melt

FLUXGATE *n* pl. -S a device to measure a magnetic field

FLUXION *n* pl. -S the act of flowing

FLUYT *n* pl. -S a type of ship

FLY *v* FLEW, FLOWN, FLYING, FLIES to move through the air

FLY *v* FLIED, FLYING, FLIES to hit a ball high into the air in baseball

FLY *adj* FLIER, FLIEST clever

FLYABLE *adj* suitable for flying

FLYAWAY *n* pl. -AWAYS one that is elusive

FLYBELT *n* pl. -S an area infested with tsetse flies

FLYBLOW *v* -BLEW, -BLOWN, -BLOWING, -BLOWS to taint

FLYBOAT *n* pl. -S a small, fast boat

FLYBOY *n* pl. -BOYS a pilot in an air force

FLYBY *n* pl. -BYS a flight of aircraft close to a specified place

FLYER *n* pl. -S flier

FLYING *n* pl. -S the operation of an aircraft

FLYLEAF *n* pl. -LEAVES a blank leaf at the beginning or end of a book

FLYLESS *adj* free of flies (winged insects)

FLYMAN *n* pl. -MEN a stage worker in a theater

FLYOFF *n* pl. -S a competitive testing of model aircraft

FLYOVER *n* pl. -S a flight of aircraft over a specific location

FLYPAPER *n* pl. -S paper designed to catch or kill flies

FLYPAST *n* pl. -S a flyby

FLYSCH *n* pl. -ES a sandstone deposit

FLYSPECK *v* -ED, -ING, -S to mark with minute spots

FLYTE *v* FLYTED, FLYTING, FLYTES to flite

FLYTIER *n* pl. -S a maker of fishing flies

FLYTING *n* pl. -S a dispute in verse form

FLYTRAP *n* pl. -S a trap for catching flies

FLYWAY *n* pl. -WAYS an established air route of migratory birds

FLYWHEEL *n* pl. -S a heavy disk used in machinery

FOAL *v* -ED, -ING, -S to give birth to a horse

FOAM *v* -ED, -ING, -S to form foam (a light, bubbly, gas and liquid mass) **FOAMABLE** *adj*

FOAMER *n* pl. -S one that foams

FOAMIER comparative of foamy

FOAMIEST superlative of foamy

FOAMILY *adv* in a foamy manner

FOAMLESS *adj* being without foam

FOAMLIKE *adj* resembling foam

FOAMY   adj FOAMIER, FOAMIEST covered with foam

FOB   v FOBBED, FOBBING, FOBS to deceive

FOCAL   adj pertaining to a focus

FOCALISE   v -ISED, -ISING, -ISES to focalize

FOCALIZE   v -IZED, -IZING, -IZES to focus

FOCALLY   adv with regard to focus

FOCUS   n pl. -CUSES or -CI a point at which rays converge or from which they diverge

FOCUS   v -CUSED, -CUSING, -CUSES or -CUSSED, -CUSSING, -CUSSES to bring to a focus

FOCUSER   n pl. -S one that focuses

FODDER   v -ED, -ING, -S to feed with coarse food

FODGEL   adj plump

FOE   n pl. -S an enemy

FOEHN   n pl. -S a warm, dry wind

FOEMAN   n pl. -MEN an enemy in war

FOETAL   adj fetal

FOETID   adj fetid

FOETOR   n pl. -S fetor

FOETUS   n pl. -ES fetus

FOG   v FOGGED, FOGGING, FOGS, to cover with fog (condensed water vapor near the earth's surface)

FOGBOUND   adj surrounded by fog

FOGBOW   n pl. -S a nebulous arc of light sometimes seen in a fog

FOGDOG   n pl. -S a fogbow

FOGEY   n pl. -GEYS fogy

FOGFRUIT   n pl. -S a flowering plant

FOGGAGE   n pl. -S a second growth of grass

FOGGED   past tense of fog

FOGGER   n pl. -S one that fogs

FOGGING   present participle of fog

FOGGY   adj -GIER, -GIEST filled with fog FOGGILY adv

FOGHORN   n pl. -S a horn sounded in a fog to give warning

FOGIE   n pl. -S fogy

FOGLESS   adj having no fog

FOGY   n pl. -GIES an old-fashioned person FOGYISH adj

FOGYISM   n pl. -S old-fashioned behavior

FOH   interj faugh

FOHN   n pl. -S foehn

FOIBLE   n pl. -S a minor weakness

FOIL   v -ED, -ING, -S to prevent the success of FOILABLE adj

FOILSMAN   n pl. -MEN a fencer

FOIN   v -ED, -ING, -S to thrust with a pointed weapon

FOISON   n pl. -S strength

FOIST   v -ED, -ING, -S to force upon slyly

FOLACIN   n pl. -S a B vitamin

FOLATE   n pl. -S folacin

FOLD   v -ED, -ING, -S to lay one part over another part of FOLDABLE adj

FOLDAWAY   adj designed to fold out of the way

FOLDBOAT   n pl. -S a faltboat

FOLDER   n pl. -S one that folds

FOLDEROL   n pl. -S falderal

FOLDOUT   n pl. -S a gatefold

FOLIA   a pl. of folium

FOLIAGE   n pl. -S the growth of leaves of a plant FOLIAGED adj

FOLIAR   adj pertaining to a leaf

FOLIATE   v -ATED, -ATING, -ATES to hammer into thin plates

FOLIO   v -ED, -ING, -S to number the pages of

FOLIOSE   adj having leaves

FOLIOUS   adj foliose

FOLIUM   n pl. -LIA or -LIUMS a thin layer

FOLK   n pl. -S a people or tribe

FOLKIE   n pl. -S a performer of folk music

FOLKISH   adj characteristic of the common people

FOLKLIFE   n pl. -LIVES the traditions, skills, and products of a people

FOLKLIKE   adj folkish

FOLKLORE   n pl. -S the lore of a people

FOLKMOOT   n pl. -S a general assembly of the people in early England

FOLKMOT   n pl. -S folkmoot

FOLKMOTE   n pl. -S folkmoot

FOLKSY   adj FOLKSIER, FOLKSIEST friendly FOLKSILY adv

FOLKTALE   n pl. -S a tale forming part of the oral tradition of a people

FOLKWAY   n pl. -WAYS a traditional custom of a people

FOLKY   n pl. FOLKIES folkie

FOLLES   pl. of follis

FOLLICLE   n pl. -S a small bodily cavity

FOLLIES   pl. of folly

FOLLIS   n pl. -LES a coin of ancient Rome

FOLLOW *v* -ED, -ING, -S to come or go after

FOLLOWER *n* pl. -S one that follows

FOLLY *n* pl. -LIES a foolish idea or action

FOMENT *v* -ED, -ING, -S to promote the development of

FOMENTER *n* pl. -S one that foments

FOMITE *n* pl. -S an inanimate object that serves to transmit infectious organisms

FON *n* pl. -S foehn

FOND *adj* FONDER, FONDEST having an affection

FOND *v* -ED, -ING, -S to display affection

FONDANT *n* pl. -S a soft, creamy candy

FONDLE *v* -DLED, -DLING, -DLES to caress

FONDLER *n* pl. -S one that fondles

FONDLING *n* pl. -S one that is fondled

FONDLY *adv* in a fond manner

FONDNESS *n* pl. -ES affection

FONDU *n* pl. -S fondue

FONDUE *n* pl. -S a dish of melted cheese

FONT *n* pl. -S a receptacle for the water used in baptism **FONTAL** *adj*

FONTANEL *n* pl. -S a space in the fetal and infantile skull

FONTINA *n* pl. -S an Italian cheese

FOOD *n* pl. -S a substance taken into the body to maintain life and growth **FOODLESS** *adj*

FOODIE *n* pl. -S an enthusiast of foods and their preparation

FOODWAYS *n/pl* the eating habits of a people

FOOFARAW *n* pl. -S excessive ornamentation

FOOL *v* -ED, -ING, -S to deceive

FOOLERY *n* pl. -ERIES foolish behavior or speech

FOOLFISH *n* pl. -ES a marine fish

FOOLISH *adj* -ISHER, -ISHEST lacking good sense or judgment

FOOLSCAP *n* pl. -S a paper size

FOOT *n* pl. FEET the terminal part of the leg on which the body stands and moves

FOOT *v* -ED, -ING, -S to walk

FOOTAGE *n* pl. -S a length or quantity expressed in feet

FOOTBALL *n* pl. -S a type of ball

FOOTBATH *n* pl. -S a bath for the feet

FOOTBOY *n* pl. -BOYS a serving boy

FOOTER *n* pl. -S one that walks

FOOTFALL *n* pl. -S the sound of a footstep

FOOTGEAR *n* pl. -S footwear

FOOTHILL *n* pl. -S a low hill at the foot of higher hills

FOOTHOLD *n* pl. -S a secure support for the feet

FOOTIE *n* pl. -S footsie

FOOTIER comparative of footy

FOOTIEST superlative of footy

FOOTING *n* pl. -S a foothold

FOOTLE *v* -TLED, -TLING, -TLES to waste time

FOOTLER *n* pl. -S one that footles

FOOTLESS *adj* having no feet

FOOTLIKE *adj* resembling a foot

FOOTLING present participle of footle

FOOTMAN *n* pl. -MEN a male servant

FOOTMARK *n* pl. -S a mark left by the foot on a surface

FOOTNOTE *v* -NOTED, -NOTING, -NOTES to furnish with explanatory notes

FOOTPACE *n* pl. -S a walking pace

FOOTPAD *n* pl. -S one who robs a pedestrian

FOOTPATH *n* pl. -S a path for pedestrians

FOOTRACE *n* pl. -S a race run on foot

FOOTREST *n* pl. -S a support for the feet

FOOTROPE *n* pl. -S a rope used in sailing

FOOTSIE *n* pl. -S a flirting game played with the feet

FOOTSLOG *v* -SLOGGED, -SLOGGING, -SLOGS to march through mud

FOOTSORE *adj* having sore or tired feet

FOOTSTEP *n* pl. -S a step with the foot

FOOTSY *n* pl. -SIES footsie

FOOTWALL *n* pl. -S the layer of rock beneath a vein of ore

FOOTWAY *n* pl. -WAYS a footpath

FOOTWEAR *n* pl. -S wearing apparel for the feet

FOOTWORK *n* pl. -S the use of the feet

FOOTWORN *adj* footsore

FOOTY *adj* -TIER, -TIEST paltry

FOOZLE *v* -ZLED, -ZLING, -ZLES to bungle

FOOZLER *n* pl. -S one that foozles

FOP *v* FOPPED, FOPPING, FOPS to deceive

FOPPERY *n* pl. -PERIES foppish behavior

FOPPISH *adj* characteristic of a dandy

FOR *prep* directed or sent to

FORA a pl. of forum

FORAGE v -AGED, -AGING, -AGES to search about

FORAGER n pl. -S one that forages

FORAM n pl. -S a marine rhizopod

FORAMEN n pl. -MINA or -MENS a small anatomical opening

FORAY v -ED, -ING, -S to raid

FORAYER n pl. -S one that forays

FORB n pl. -S an herb other than grass

FORBAD a past tense of forbid

FORBADE a past tense of forbid

FORBEAR v -BORE, -BORNE, -BEARING, -BEARS to refrain from

FORBID v -BADE or -BAD, -BIDDEN, -BIDDING, -BIDS to command not to do something

FORBIDAL n pl. -S the act of forbidding

FORBODE v -BODED, -BODING, -BODES to forebode

FORBORE past tense of forbear

FORBORNE past participle of forbear

FORBY prep close by

FORBYE prep forby

FORCE v FORCED, FORCING, FORCES to overcome resistance by the exertion of strength **FORCEDLY** adv

FORCEFUL adj strong

FORCEPS n pl. -CIPES an instrument for seizing and holding objects

FORCER n pl. -S one that forces

FORCIBLE adj effected by force **FORCIBLY**

FORCING present participle of force

FORCIPES pl. of forceps

FORD v -ED, -ING, -S to cross by wading **FORDABLE** adj

FORDLESS adj unable to be forded

FORDO v -DID, -DONE, -DOING, -DOES to destroy

FORE n pl. -S the front part of something

FOREARM v -ED, -ING, -S to arm in advance

FOREBAY n pl. -BAYS a reservoir from which water is taken to run equipment

FOREBEAR n pl. -S an ancestor

FOREBODE v -BODED, -BODING, -BODES to indicate in advance

FOREBODY n pl. -BODIES the forward part of a ship

FOREBOOM n pl. -S the boom of a ship's foremast

FOREBY prep forby

FOREBYE prep forby

FORECAST v -ED, -ING, -S to estimate or calculate in advance

FOREDATE v -DATED, -DATING, -DATES to antedate

FOREDECK n pl. -S the forward part of a ship's deck

FOREDO v -DID, -DONE, -DOING, -DOES to fordo

FOREDOOM v -ED, -ING, -S to doom in advance

FOREFACE n pl. -S the front part of the head of a quadruped

FOREFEEL v -FELT, -FEELING, -FEELS to have a premonition of

FOREFEND v -ED, -ING, -S to forfend

FOREFOOT n pl. -FEET one of the front feet of an animal

FOREGO v -WENT, -GONE, -GOING, -GOES to go before

FOREGOER n pl. -S one that foregoes

FOREGUT n pl. -S the front part of the embryonic alimentary canal

FOREHAND n pl. -S a type of tennis stroke

FOREHEAD n pl. -S the part of the face above the eyes

FOREHOOF n pl. -HOOFS or -HOOVES the hoof of a forefoot

FOREIGN adj situated outside a place or country

FOREKNOW v -KNEW, -KNOWN, -KNOWING, -KNOWS to know in advance

FORELADY n pl. -DIES a woman who supervises workers

FORELAND n pl. -S a projecting mass of land

FORELEG n pl. -S one of the front legs of an animal

FORELIMB n pl. -S a foreleg

FORELOCK v -ED, -ING, -S to fasten with a linchpin

FOREMAN n pl. -MEN a man who supervises workers

FOREMAST n pl. -S the forward mast of a ship

FOREMILK n pl. -S the milk secreted immediately after childbirth

FOREMOST adj first in position

FORENAME n pl. -S a first name

FORENOON n pl. -S the period of daylight before noon

FORENSIC *n pl* -S an argumentative exercise

FOREPART *n pl.* -S the front part

FOREPAST *adj* already in the past

FOREPAW *n pl.* -S the paw of a foreleg

FOREPEAK *n pl.* -S the forward part of a ship's hold

FOREPLAY *n pl.* -PLAYS erotic stimulation preceding sexual intercourse

FORERANK *n pl.* -S the first rank

FORERUN *v* -RAN, -RUNNING, -RUNS to run in advance of

FORESAID *adj* previously said

FORESAIL *n pl.* -S the lowest sail on a foremast

FORESEE *v* -SAW, -SEEN, -SEEING, -SEES to see in advance

FORESEER *n pl.* -S one that foresees

FORESHOW *v* -SHOWED, -SHOWN, -SHOWING, -SHOWS to show in advance

FORESIDE *n pl.* -S the front side

FORESKIN *n pl.* -S the prepuce

FOREST *v* -ED, -ING, -S to convert into a forest (a densely wooded area)

FORESTAL *adj* of or pertaining to a forest

FORESTAY *n pl.* -STAYS a wire or rope used to support a foremast

FORESTER *n pl.* -S one skilled in forestry

FORESTRY *n pl.* -RIES the science of planting and managing forests

FORETELL *v* -TOLD, -TELLING, -TELLS to tell of or about in advance

FORETIME *n pl.* -S the past

FORETOP *n pl.* -S a forelock

FOREVER *n pl.* -S an indefinite length of time

FOREWARN *v* -ED, -ING, -S to warn in advance

FOREWENT past tense of forego

FOREWING *n pl.* -S an anterior wing of an insect

FOREWORD *n pl.* -S an introductory statement

FOREWORN *adj* forworn

FOREYARD *n pl.* -S the lowest yard on a foremast

FORFEIT *v* -ED, -ING, -S to lose as a penalty

FORFEND *v* -ED, -ING, -S to protect

FORGAT a past tense of forget

FORGAVE past tense of forgive

FORGE *v* FORGED, FORGING, FORGES to fashion or reproduce for fraudulent purposes

FORGER *n pl.* -S one that forges

FORGERY *n pl.* -ERIES the act of forging

FORGET *v* -GOT or -GAT, -GOTTEN, -GETTING, -GETS to fail to remember

FORGING *n pl.* -S a forgery

FORGIVE *v* -GAVE, -GIVEN, -GIVING, -GIVES to pardon

FORGIVER *n pl.* -S one that forgives

FORGO *v* -WENT, -GONE, -GOING, -GOES to refrain from

FORGOER *n pl.* -S one that forgoes

FORGOT a past tense of forget

FORGOTTEN past participle of forget

FORINT *n pl.* -S a monetary unit of Hungary

FORJUDGE *v* -JUDGED, -JUDGING, -JUDGES to deprive by judgment of a court

FORK *v* -ED, -ING, -S to work with a fork (a pronged implement) **FORKEDLY** *adv*

FORKBALL *n pl.* -S a breaking pitch in baseball

FORKER *n pl.* -S one that forks

FORKFUL *n pl.* FORKFULS or FORKSFUL as much as a fork will hold

FORKIER comparative of forky

FORKIEST superlative of forky

FORKLESS *adj* having no fork

FORKLIFT *v* -ED, -ING, -S to raise or transport by means of a forklift (a machine with projecting prongs)

FORKLIKE *adj* resembling a fork

FORKSFUL a pl. of forkful

FORKY *adj* FORKIER, FORKIEST resembling a fork

FORLORN *adj* -LORNER, -LORNEST dreary

FORM *v* -ED, -ING, -S to produce **FORMABLE** *adj*

FORMAL *n pl.* -S a social event that requires evening dress

FORMALIN *n pl.* -S an aqueous solution of formaldehyde

FORMALLY *adv* in a prescribed or customary manner

FORMANT *n pl.* -S a characteristic component of the quality of a speech sound

FORMAT	v -MATTED, -MATTING, -MATS to produce in a specified style	**FORTY**	n pl. -TIES a number
		FORTYISH	adj being about forty years old
FORMATE	n pl. -S a chemical salt	**FORUM**	n pl. -RUMS or -RA a public meeting place
FORME	n pl. -S an assemblage of printing type secured in a metal frame	**FORWARD**	adj -WARDER, -WARDEST being at or near a point in advance
FORMEE	adj having the arms narrow at the center and expanding toward the ends — used of a heraldic cross	**FORWARD**	v -ED, -ING, -S to help onward
		FORWENT	past tense of forgo
FORMER	n pl. -S one that forms	**FORWHY**	adv for what reason
FORMERLY	adv previously	**FORWORN**	adj worn out
FORMFUL	adj exhibiting good form	**FORZANDO**	n pl. -DOS sforzato
FORMIC	adj pertaining to ants	**FOSS**	n pl. -ES fosse
FORMLESS	adj lacking structure	**FOSSA**	n pl. -SAE an anatomical depression **FOSSATE** adj
FORMOL	n pl. -S formalin		
FORMULA	n pl. -LAS or -LAE an exact method for doing something	**FOSSE**	n pl. -S a ditch
		FOSSETTE	n pl. -S a small fossa
FORMWORK	n pl. -S a set of forms to hold concrete until it sets	**FOSSICK**	v -ED, -ING, -S to search for gold
FORMYL	n pl. -S a univalent chemical radical	**FOSSIL**	n pl. -S the remains of an animal or plant preserved in the earth's crust
FORNIX	n pl. -NICES an arched anatomical structure **FORNICAL** adj		
		FOSTER	v -ED, -ING, -S to promote the growth of
FORRADER	adv further ahead	**FOSTERER**	n pl. -S one that fosters
FORRIT	adv toward the front	**FOU**	adj drunk
FORSAKE	v -SOOK, -SAKEN, -SAKING, -SAKES to quit or leave entirely	**FOUETTE**	n pl. -S a movement in ballet
		FOUGHT	past tense of fight
		FOUGHTEN	adj exhausted especially from fighting
FORSAKER	n pl. -S one that forsakes	**FOUL**	adj FOULER, FOULEST offensive to the senses
FORSOOTH	adv in truth		
FORSPENT	adj worn out	**FOUL**	v -ED, -ING, -S to make foul
FORSWEAR	v -SWORE, -SWORN, -SWEARING, -SWEARS to deny under oath	**FOULARD**	n pl. -S a soft fabric
		FOULING	n pl. -S a deposit or crust
		FOULLY	adv in a foul manner
FORT	n pl. -S a fortified enclosure or structure	**FOULNESS**	n pl. -ES the state of being foul
FORTE	n pl. -S a strong point	**FOUND**	v -ED, -ING, -S to establish
FORTES	pl. of fortis	**FOUNDER**	v -ED, -ING, -S to become disabled
FORTH	adv onward in time, place, or order		
		FOUNDRY	n pl. -RIES an establishment in which metal is cast
FORTIES	pl. of forty		
FORTIETH	n pl. -S one of forty equal parts	**FOUNT**	n pl. -S a fountain
		FOUNTAIN	v -ED, -ING, -S to flow like a fountain (a spring of water)
FORTIFY	v -FIED, -FYING, -FIES to strengthen against attack		
		FOUR	n pl. -S a number
FORTIS	n pl. -TES a consonant pronounced with relatively strong release of breath	**FOURCHEE**	adj having the end of each arm forked — used of a heraldic cross
		FOURFOLD	adj four times as great
FORTRESS	v -ED, -ING, -ES to fortify	**FOURGON**	n pl. -S a wagon for carrying baggage
FORTUITY	n pl. -ITIES an accidental occurrence		
		FOURPLEX	n pl. -ES quadplex
FORTUNE	v -TUNED, -TUNING, -TUNES to endow with wealth	**FOURSOME**	n pl. -S a group of four

FOURTEEN	*n* pl. -S a number
FOURTH	*n* pl. -S one of four equal parts
FOURTHLY	*adv* in the fourth place
FOVEA	*n* pl. -VEAE or -VEAS a shallow anatomical depression **FOVEAL, FOVEATE, FOVEATED** *adj*
FOVEOLA	*n* pl. -LAE or -LAS a small fovea **FOVEOLAR** *adj*
FOVEOLE	*n* pl. -S a foveola
FOVEOLET	*n* pl. -S a foveola
FOWL	*v* -ED, -ING, -S to hunt birds
FOWLER	*n* pl. -S one that fowls
FOWLING	*n* pl. -S the hunting of birds
FOWLPOX	*n* pl. -ES a virus disease of poultry
FOX	*v* -ED, -ING, -ES to outwit
FOXFIRE	*n* pl. -S a glow produced by certain fungi on decaying wood
FOXFISH	*n* pl. -ES a large shark
FOXGLOVE	*n* pl. -S a flowering plant
FOXHOLE	*n* pl. -S a small pit used for cover in a battle area
FOXHOUND	*n* pl. -S a hunting dog
FOXHUNT	*v* -ED, -ING, -S to hunt with hounds for a fox
FOXIER	comparative of foxy
FOXIEST	superlative of foxy
FOXILY	*adv* in a foxy manner
FOXINESS	*n* pl. -ES the state of being foxy
FOXING	*n* pl. -S a piece of material used to cover the upper portion of a shoe
FOXLIKE	*adj* resembling a fox (a carnivorous mammal)
FOXSKIN	*n* pl. -S the skin of a fox
FOXTAIL	*n* pl. -S the tail of a fox
FOXTROT	*v* -TROTTED, -TROTTING, -TROTS to dance the fox trot (a dance for couples)
FOXY	*adj* FOXIER, FOXIEST crafty
FOY	*n* pl. FOYS a farewell feast or gift
FOYER	*n* pl. -S an entrance room or hall
FOZINESS	*n* pl. -ES the state of being fozy
FOZY	*adj* -ZIER, -ZIEST too ripe
FRABJOUS	*adj* splendid
FRACAS	*n* pl. -ES a brawl
FRACTAL	*n* pl. -S a complex geometric curve
FRACTED	*adj* broken
FRACTI	pl. of fractus
FRACTION	*v* -ED, -ING, -S to divide into portions
FRACTUR	*n* pl. -S fraktur
FRACTURE	*v* -TURED, -TURING, -TURES to break
FRACTUS	*n* pl. -TI a ragged cloud
FRAE	*prep* from
FRAENUM	*n* pl. -NA or -NUMS frenum
FRAG	*v* FRAGGED, FRAGGING, FRAGS to injure with a type of grenade
FRAGGING	*n* pl. -S the act of one that frags
FRAGILE	*adj* easily broken or damaged
FRAGMENT	*v* -ED, -ING, -S to break into pieces
FRAGRANT	*adj* having a pleasant odor
FRAIL	*adj* FRAILER, FRAILEST fragile **FRAILLY** *adv*
FRAIL	*n* pl. -S a basket for holding dried fruits
FRAILTY	*n* pl. -TIES a weakness of character
FRAISE	*n* pl. -S a barrier of pointed stakes
FRAKTUR	*n* pl. -S a style of type
FRAME	*v* FRAMED, FRAMING, FRAMES to construct by putting together the various parts **FRAMABLE** *adj*
FRAMER	*n* pl. -S one that frames
FRAMING	*n* pl. -S framework
FRANC	*n* pl. -S a monetary unit of France
FRANCIUM	*n* pl. -S a radioactive element
FRANK	*adj* FRANKER, FRANKEST honest and unreserved in speech
FRANK	*v* -ED, -ING, -S to mark (a piece of mail) for free delivery
FRANKER	*n* pl. -S one that franks
FRANKLIN	*n* pl. -S a medieval English landowner
FRANKLY	*adv* in a frank manner
FRANTIC	*adj* wildly excited
FRAP	*v* FRAPPED, FRAPPING, FRAPS to bind firmly
FRAPPE	*n* pl. -S a partly frozen drink
FRASS	*n* pl. -ES debris made by insects
FRAT	*n* pl. -S a college fraternity
FRATER	*n* pl. -S a comrade
FRAUD	*n* pl. -S trickery
FRAUGHT	*v* -ED, -ING, -S to load down
FRAULEIN	*n* pl. -S a German governess

FRAY	v -ED, -ING, -S to wear off by rubbing
FRAYING	n pl. -S something worn off by rubbing
FRAZIL	n pl. -S tiny ice crystals formed in supercooled waters
FRAZZLE	v -ZLED, -ZLING, -ZLES to fray
FREAK	v -ED, -ING, -S to streak with color
FREAKIER	comparative of freaky
FREAKIEST	superlative of freaky
FREAKILY	adv in a freaky manner
FREAKISH	adj unusual
FREAKOUT	n pl. -S an event marked by wild excitement
FREAKY	adj FREAKIER, FREAKIEST freakish
FRECKLE	v -LED, -LING, -LES to mark with freckles (small, brownish spots)
FRECKLY	adj -LIER, -LIEST marked with freckles
FREE	adj FREER, FREEST not subject to restriction or control
FREE	v FREED, FREEING, FREES to make free
FREEBASE	v -BASED, -BASING, -BASES to use a form of cocaine that is inhaled
FREEBEE	n pl. -S freebie
FREEBIE	n pl. -S something given or received without charge
FREEBOOT	v -ED, -ING, -S to plunder
FREEBORN	adj born free
FREED	past tense of free
FREEDMAN	n pl. -MEN a man who has been freed from slavery
FREEDOM	n pl. -S the state of being free
FREEFORM	adj having a free flowing design or shape
FREEHAND	adj drawn by hand without mechanical aids
FREEHOLD	n pl. -S a form of tenure of real property
FREELOAD	v -ED, -ING, -S to live at the expense of others
FREELY	adv in a free manner
FREEMAN	n pl. -MEN one who is free
FREENESS	n pl. -ES freedom
FREER	n pl. -S one that frees
FREESIA	n pl. -S an African herb
FREEST	superlative of free
FREEWAY	n pl. -WAYS an express highway
FREEWILL	adj voluntary

FREEZE	v FROZE, FROZEN, FREEZING, FREEZES to become hardened into a solid body by loss of heat
FREEZER	n pl. -S an apparatus for freezing food
FREIGHT	v -ED, -ING, -S to load with goods for transportation
FREMD	adj strange
FREMITUS	n pl. -ES a palpable vibration
FRENA	a pl. of frenum
FRENCH	v -ED, -ING, -ES to cut into thin strips before cooking
FRENETIC	n pl. -S a frantic person
FRENULUM	n pl. -LA or -LUMS a frenum
FRENUM	n pl. -NA or -NUMS a connecting fold of membrane
FRENZILY	adv in a frantic manner
FRENZY	v -ZIED, -ZYING, -ZIES to make frantic
FREQUENT	adj -QUENTER, -QUENTEST occurring again and again
FREQUENT	v -ED, -ING, -S to be in or at often
FRERE	n pl. -S brother
FRESCO	v -ED, -ING, -ES or -S to paint on a surface of plaster
FRESCOER	n pl. -S one that frescoes
FRESH	adj FRESHER, FRESHEST new
FRESH	v -ED, -ING, -ES to freshen
FRESHEN	v -ED, -ING, -S to make or become fresh
FRESHET	n pl. -S a sudden overflow of a stream
FRESHLY	adv in a fresh manner
FRESHMAN	n pl. -MEN a first-year student
FRESNEL	n pl. -S a unit of frequency
FRET	v FRETTED, FRETTING, FRETS to worry
FRETFUL	adj inclined to fret
FRETLESS	adj having no fretwork
FRETSAW	n pl. -S a narrow-bladed saw
FRETSOME	adj fretful
FRETTED	past tense of fret
FRETTER	n pl. -S one that frets
FRETTING	present participle of fret
FRETTY	adj -TIER, -TIEST fretful
FRETWORK	n pl. -S ornamental work consisting of interlacing parts
FRIABLE	adj easily crumbled
FRIAR	n pl. -S a member of a religious order FRIARLY adj
FRIARY	n pl. -ARIES a monastery of friars

FRIBBLE   v -BLED, -BLING, -BLES to act foolishly

FRIBBLER   n pl. -S one that fribbles

FRICANDO   n pl. -DOES a roasted loin of veal

FRICTION   n pl. -S the rubbing of one body against another

FRIDGE   n pl. -S a refrigerator

FRIED   past tense of fry

FRIEND   v -ED, -ING, -S to enter into a warm association with

FRIENDLY   adj -LIER, -LIEST inclined to approve, help, or support

FRIENDLY   n pl. -LIES one who is friendly

FRIER   n pl. -S fryer

FRIES   present 3d person sing. of fry

FRIEZE   n pl. -S a coarse woolen fabric

FRIGATE   n pl. -S a sailing vessel

FRIGHT   v -ED, -ING, -S to frighten

FRIGHTEN   v -ED, -ING, -S to make afraid

FRIGID   adj very cold **FRIGIDLY** adv

FRIJOL   n pl. -ES a bean used as food

FRIJOLE   n pl. -S frijol

FRILL   v -ED, -ING, -S to provide with a frill (an ornamental ruffled edge)

FRILLER   n pl. -S one that frills

FRILLING   n pl. -S an arrangement of frills

FRILLY   adj FRILLIER, FRILLIEST having frills

FRINGE   v FRINGED, FRINGING, FRINGES to provide with a fringe (an ornamental border)

FRINGY   adj FRINGIER, FRINGIEST resembling a fringe

FRIPPERY   n pl. -PERIES excessive ornamentation

FRISE   n pl. -S frieze

FRISETTE   n pl. -S frizette

FRISEUR   n pl. -S a hairdresser

FRISK   v -ED, -ING, -S to move or leap about playfully

FRISKER   n pl. -S one that frisks

FRISKET   n pl. -S a frame used to protect paper in a printing press

FRISKY   adj FRISKIER, FRISKIEST lively and playful **FRISKILY** adv

FRISSON   n pl. -S a shudder

FRIT   v FRITTED, FRITTING, FRITS to fuse into a vitreous substance

FRITH   n pl. -S firth

FRITT   v -ED, -ING, -S to frit

FRITTATA   n pl. -S an unfolded omelet with chopped vegetables or meat

FRITTED   past tense of frit

FRITTER   v -ED, -ING, -S to squander little by little

FRITTING   present participle of frit

FRITZ   n pl. -ES a nonfunctioning state

FRIVOL   v -OLED, -OLING, -OLS or -OLLED, -OLLING, -OLS to behave playfully

FRIVOLER   n pl. -S one that frivols

FRIZ   v -ED, -ING, -ES to frizz

FRIZER   n pl. -S frizzer

FRIZETTE   n pl. -S a frizzed fringe of hair

FRIZZ   v -ED, -ING, -ES to form into small, tight curls

FRIZZER   n pl. -S one that frizzes

FRIZZIER   comparative of frizzy

FRIZZIEST   superlative of frizzy

FRIZZILY   adv in a frizzy manner

FRIZZLE   v -ZLED, -ZLING, -ZLES to frizz

FRIZZLER   n pl. -S one that frizzles

FRIZZLY   adj -ZLIER, -ZLIEST frizzy

FRIZZY   adj FRIZZIER, FRIZZIEST tightly curled

FRO   adv away

FROCK   v -ED, -ING, -S to clothe in a long, loose outer garment

FROE   n pl. -S a cleaving tool

FROG   v FROGGED, FROGGING, FROGS to hunt frogs (web-footed, tailless amphibians)

FROGEYE   n pl. -S a plant disease **FROGEYED** adj

FROGFISH   n pl. -ES a marine fish

FROGGED   past tense of frog

FROGGING   present participle of frog

FROGGY   adj -GIER, -GIEST abounding in frogs

FROGLIKE   adj resembling a frog

FROGMAN   n pl. -MEN a person equipped for extended periods of underwater swimming

FROLIC   v -ICKED, -ICKING, -ICS to play and run about merrily **FROLICKY** adj

FROM   prep starting at

FROMAGE   n pl. -S cheese

FROMENTY   n pl. -TIES frumenty

FROND   n pl. -S a type of leaf **FRONDED, FRONDOSE** adj

FRONDEUR   n pl. -S a rebel

FRONS _n_ pl. FRONTES the upper anterior portion of an insect's head

FRONT _v_ -ED, -ING, -S to provide with a front (a forward part)

FRONT _adj_ FRONTER articulated at the front of the oral passage

FRONTAGE _n_ pl. -S the front of a building or lot

FRONTAL _n_ pl. -S a bone of the skull

FRONTES pl. of frons

FRONTIER _n_ pl. -S a border between two countries

FRONTLET _n_ pl. -S a decorative band worn across the forehead

FRONTON _n_ pl. -S a jai alai arena

FRORE _adj_ frozen

FROSH _n_ pl. FROSH a freshman

FROST _v_ -ED, -ING, -S to cover with frost (a deposit of minute ice crystals)

FROSTBIT _adj_ injured by extreme cold

FROSTED _n_ pl. -S a type of milk shake

FROSTING _n_ pl. -S icing

FROSTY _adj_ FROSTIER, FROSTIEST covered with frost **FROSTILY** _adv_

FROTH _v_ -ED, -ING, -S to foam

FROTHY _adj_ FROTHIER, FROTHIEST foamy **FROTHILY** _adv_

FROTTAGE _n_ pl. -S masturbation by rubbing against another person

FROTTEUR _n_ pl. -S one who practices frottage

FROUFROU _n_ pl. -S a rustling sound

FROUNCE _v_ FROUNCED, FROUNCING, FROUNCES to pleat

FROUZY _adj_ -ZIER, -ZIEST frowzy

FROW _n_ pl. -S froe

FROWARD _adj_ disobedient

FROWN _v_ -ED, -ING, -S to contract the brow in displeasure

FROWNER _n_ pl. -S one that frowns

FROWST _v_ -ED, -ING, -S to lounge in a stuffy room

FROWSTY _adj_ -TIER, -TIEST musty

FROWSY _adj_ -SIER, -SIEST frowzy

FROWZY _adj_ -ZIER, -ZIEST unkempt **FROWZILY** _adv_

FROZE past tense of freeze

FROZEN _adj_ very cold **FROZENLY** _adv_

FRUCTIFY _v_ -FIED, -FYING, -FIES to bear fruit

FRUCTOSE _n_ pl. -S a sugar found in various fruits

FRUG _v_ FRUGGED, FRUGGING, FRUGS to perform a type of vigorous dance

FRUGAL _adj_ thrifty **FRUGALLY** _adv_

FRUIT _v_ -ED, -ING, -S to bear fruit (usually edible reproductive bodies of a seed plant)

FRUITAGE _n_ pl. -S the process of bearing fruit

FRUITER _n_ pl. -S one that grows or sells fruit

FRUITFUL _adj_ -FULLER, -FULLEST producing abundantly

FRUITIER comparative of fruity

FRUITIEST superlative of fruity

FRUITION _n_ pl. -S the accomplishment of something desired

FRUITLET _n_ pl. -S a small fruit

FRUITY _adj_ FRUITIER, FRUITIEST suggestive of fruit **FRUITILY** _adv_

FRUMENTY _n_ pl. -TIES a dish of wheat boiled in milk and sweetened with sugar

FRUMP _n_ pl. -S a dowdy woman **FRUMPISH** _adj_

FRUMPY _adj_ FRUMPIER, FRUMPIEST dowdy **FRUMPILY** _adv_

FRUSTULE _n_ pl. -S the shell of a diatom

FRUSTUM _n_ pl. -TA or -TUMS a part of a conical solid

FRY _v_ FRIED, FRYING, FRIES to cook over direct heat in hot fat or oil

FRYER _n_ pl. -S one that fries

FRYPAN _n_ pl. -S a pan for frying food

FUB _v_ FUBBED, FUBBING, FUBS to fob

FUBSY _adj_ FUBSIER, FUBSIEST chubby and somewhat squat

FUCHSIA _n_ pl. -S a flowering shrub

FUCHSIN _n_ pl. -S a red dye

FUCHSINE _n_ pl. -S fuchsin

FUCI a pl. of fucus

FUCOID _n_ pl. -S a brown seaweed **FUCOIDAL** _adj_

FUCOSE _n_ pl. -S a type of sugar

FUCOUS _adj_ of or pertaining to fucoids

FUCUS _n_ pl. -CI or -CUSES any of a genus of brown algae

FUD _n_ pl. -S an old-fashioned person

FUDDLE _v_ -DLED, -DLING, -DLES to confuse

FUDGE _v_ FUDGED, FUDGING, FUDGES to falsify

FUEHRER   n pl. -S fuhrer

FUEL   v -ELED, -ELING, -ELS or -ELLED, -ELLING, -ELS to provide with fuel (material used to produce energy)

FUELER   n pl. -S one that fuels

FUELLER   n pl. -S fueler

FUELLING   a present participle of fuel

FUELWOOD   n pl. -S firewood

FUG   v FUGGED, FUGGING, FUGS to make stuffy and odorous

FUGACITY   n pl. -TIES lack of enduring qualities

FUGAL   adj being in the style of a fugue **FUGALLY** adv

FUGATO   n pl. -TOS a fugal composition

FUGGED   past tense of fug

FUGGING   present participle of fug

FUGGY   adj -GIER, -GIEST stuffy and odorous **FUGGILY** adv

FUGIO   n pl. -GIOS a former coin of the United States

FUGITIVE   n pl. -S one who flees

FUGLE   v -GLED, -GLING, -GLES to lead

FUGLEMAN   n pl. -MEN a leader

FUGU   n pl. -S a toxin-containing fish

FUGUE   v FUGUED, FUGUING, FUGUES to compose a fugue (a type of musical composition)

FUGUIST   n pl. -S one who composes fugues

FUHRER   n pl. -S a leader

FUJI   n pl. -S a silk fabric

FULCRUM   n pl. -CRUMS or -CRA a support for a lever

FULFIL   v -FILLED, -FILLING, -FILS to fulfill

FULFILL   v -ED, -ING, -S to bring about the accomplishment of

FULGENT   adj shining brightly

FULGID   adj fulgent

FULHAM   n pl. -S a loaded die

FULL   adj FULLER, FULLEST filled completely

FULL   v -ED, -ING, -S to shrink and thicken, as cloth

FULLAM   n pl. -S fulham

FULLBACK   n pl. -S an offensive back in football

FULLER   v -ED, -ING, -S to groove with a type of hammer

FULLERY   n pl. -ERIES a place for fulling cloth

FULLFACE   n pl. -S a heavy-faced type

FULLNESS   n pl. -ES the state of being full

FULLY   adv in a full manner

FULMAR   n pl. -S an arctic seabird

FULMINE   v -MINED, -MINING, -MINES to explode loudly

FULMINIC   adj highly explosive

FULNESS   n pl. -ES fullness

FULSOME   adj repulsive

FULVOUS   adj of a brownish yellow color

FUMARASE   n pl. -S an enzyme

FUMARATE   n pl. -S a chemical salt

FUMARIC   adj pertaining to a certain acid

FUMAROLE   n pl. -S a hole from which volcanic vapors issue

FUMATORY   n pl. -RIES a fumigation chamber

FUMBLE   v -BLED, -BLING, -BLES to handle clumsily

FUMBLER   n pl. -S one that fumbles

FUME   v FUMED, FUMING, FUMES to give off fumes (gaseous exhalations)

FUMELESS   adj having no fumes

FUMELIKE   adj resembling fumes

FUMER   n pl. -S one that fumes

FUMET   n pl. -S the odor of meat while cooking

FUMETTE   n pl. -S fumet

FUMIER   comparative of fumy

FUMIEST   superlative of fumy

FUMIGANT   n pl. -S a substance used in fumigating

FUMIGATE   v -GATED, -GATING, -GATES to subject to fumes in order to destroy pests

FUMING   present participle of fume

FUMINGLY   adv angrily

FUMITORY   n pl. -RIES a climbing plant

FUMULUS   n pl. -LI a thin cloud

FUMY   adj FUMIER, FUMIEST producing or full of fumes

FUN   v FUNNED, FUNNING, FUNS to act playfully

FUN   adj FUNNER, FUNNEST providing enjoyment

FUNCTION   v -ED, -ING, -S to be in action

FUNCTOR   n pl. -S one that functions

FUND   v -ED, -ING, -S to provide money for

FUNDUS   n pl. -DI the inner basal surface of a bodily organ **FUNDIC** adj

FUNERAL   n pl. -S a ceremony held for a dead person

FUNERARY   adj pertaining to a funeral

FUNEREAL   adj funerary

FUNEST	*adj* portending death or evil
FUNFAIR	*n* pl. -S an amusement park
FUNGAL	*n* pl. -S a fungus
FUNGI	a pl. of fungus
FUNGIBLE	*n* pl. -S something that may be exchanged for an equivalent unit of the same class
FUNGIC	*adj* fungous
FUNGO	*n* pl. -GOES a fly ball hit to a fielder for practice in baseball
FUNGOID	*n* pl. -S a growth resembling a fungus
FUNGOUS	*adj* pertaining to a fungus
FUNGUS	*n* pl. -GI or -GUSES any of a major group of lower plants
FUNICLE	*n* pl. -S a cordlike anatomical structure
FUNICULI	*n/pl* funicles
FUNK	*v* -ED, -ING, -S to shrink back in fear
FUNKER	*n* pl. -S one that funks
FUNKIA	*n* pl. -S a flowering plant
FUNKY	*adj* FUNKIER, FUNKIEST having an offensive odor
FUNNED	past tense of fun
FUNNEL	*v* -NELED, -NELING, -NELS or -NELLED, -NELLING, -NELS to pass through a funnel (a cone-shaped utensil)
FUNNER	comparative of fun
FUNNEST	superlative of fun
FUNNING	present participle of fun
FUNNY	*adj* -NIER, -NIEST causing laughter or amusement FUNNILY *adv*
FUNNY	*n* pl. -NIES a comic strip
FUNNYMAN	*n* pl. -MEN a comedian
FUR	*v* FURRED, FURRING, FURS to cover with fur (a dressed animal pelt)
FURAN	*n* pl. -S a flammable liquid
FURANE	*n* pl. -S furan
FURANOSE	*n* pl. -S a type of sugar
FURBELOW	*v* -ED, -ING, -S to decorate with ruffles
FURBISH	*v* -ED, -ING, -ES to polish
FURCATE	*v* -CATED, -CATING, -CATES to divide into branches
FURCRAEA	*n* pl. -S a tropical plant
FURCULA	*n* pl. -LAE a forked bone FURCULAR *adj*
FURCULUM	*n* pl. -LA a furcula
FURFUR	*n* pl. -ES dandruff
FURFURAL	*n* pl. -S a chemical compound
FURFURAN	*n* pl. -S furan
FURIBUND	*adj* furious
FURIES	pl. of fury
FURIOSO	*adv* with great force — used as a musical direction
FURIOUS	*adj* extremely angry
FURL	*v* -ED, -ING, -S to roll up FURLABLE *adj*
FURLER	*n* pl. -S one that furls
FURLESS	*adj* having no fur
FURLONG	*n* pl. -S a unit of distance
FURLOUGH	*v* -ED, -ING, -S to grant a leave of absence to
FURMENTY	*n* pl. -TIES frumenty
FURMETY	*n* pl. -TIES frumenty
FURMITY	*n* pl. -TIES frumenty
FURNACE	*v* -NACED, -NACING, -NACES to subject to heat
FURNISH	*v* -ED, -ING, -ES to equip
FUROR	*n* pl. -S an uproar
FURORE	*n* pl. -S furor
FURRED	past tense of fur
FURRIER	*n* pl. -S one that deals in furs
FURRIERY	*n* pl. -ERIES the business of a furrier
FURRIEST	superlative of furry
FURRILY	*adv* in a furry manner
FURRINER	*n* pl. -S a foreigner
FURRING	*n* pl. -S a trimming or lining of fur
FURROW	*v* -ED, -ING, -S to make furrows (narrow depressions) in
FURROWER	*n* pl. -S one that furrows
FURROWY	*adj* marked by furrows
FURRY	*adj* -RIER, -RIEST covered with fur
FURTHER	*v* -ED, -ING, -S to help forward
FURTHEST	a superlative of far
FURTIVE	*adj* stealthy
FURUNCLE	*n* pl. -S a painful swelling of the skin
FURY	*n* pl. -RIES violent anger
FURZE	*n* pl. -S a spiny shrub
FURZY	*adj* FURZIER, FURZIEST abounding in furze
FUSAIN	*n* pl. -S a fine charcoal used in drawing
FUSCOUS	*adj* of a dusky color
FUSE	*v* FUSED, FUSING, FUSES to equip with a fuse (a detonating device)
FUSEE	*n* pl. -S a large-headed friction match
FUSEL	*n* pl. -S an oily liquid

FUSELAGE *n* pl. -S the body of an airplane

FUSELESS *adj* lacking a fuse

FUSIBLE *adj* capable of being melted **FUSIBLY** *adv*

FUSIFORM *adj* tapering toward each end

FUSIL *n* pl. -S a type of musket

FUSILE *adj* formed by melting

FUSILEER *n* pl. -S fusilier

FUSILIER *n* pl. -S a soldier armed with a fusil

FUSILLI *n* pl. -S spiral-shaped pasta

FUSING present participle of fuse

FUSION *n* pl. -S the act of melting together

FUSS *v* -ED, -ING, -ES to be overly concerned with small details

FUSSER *n* pl. -S one that fusses

FUSSPOT *n* pl. -S a fusser

FUSSY *adj* FUSSIER, FUSSIEST overly concerned with small details **FUSSILY** *adv*

FUSTIAN *n* pl. -S a cotton fabric

FUSTIC *n* pl. -S a tropical tree

FUSTY *adj* -TIER, -TIEST musty **FUSTILY** *adv*

FUTHARC *n* pl. -S futhark

FUTHARK *n* pl. -S an ancient alphabet

FUTHORC *n* pl. -S futhark

FUTHORK *n* pl. -S futhark

FUTILE *adj* having no useful result **FUTILELY** *adv*

FUTILITY *n* pl. -TIES the quality of being futile

FUTON *n* pl. -S a cotton filled mattress for use as a bed

FUTTOCK *n* pl. -S a curved timber in the frame of a wooden ship

FUTURE *n* pl. -S the time yet to come **FUTURAL** *adj*

FUTURISM *n* pl. -S an artistic and literary movement

FUTURIST *n* pl. -S an advocate of futurism

FUTURITY *n* pl. -TIES the future

FUTZ *v* -ED, -ING, -ES to spend time aimlessly

FUZE *v* FUZED, FUZING, FUZES to fuse

FUZEE *n* pl. -S fusee

FUZIL *n* pl. -S fusil

FUZING present participle of fuze

FUZZ *v* -ED, -ING, -ES to become fuzzy

FUZZY *adj* FUZZIER, FUZZIEST blurry **FUZZILY** *adv*

FYCE *n* pl. -S feist

FYKE *n* pl. -S a bag-shaped fishnet

FYLFOT *n* pl. -S a swastika

FYTTE *n* pl. -S a division of a poem or song

G₂

GAB	v GABBED, GABBING, GABS to chatter
GABBARD	n pl. -S a barge
GABBART	n pl. -S gabbard
GABBED	past tense of gab
GABBER	n pl. -S one that gabs
GABBIER	comparative of gabby
GABBIEST	superlative of gabby
GABBING	present participle of gab
GABBLE	v -BLED, -BLING, -BLES to jabber
GABBLER	n pl. -S one that gabbles
GABBRO	n pl. -BROS a type of rock **GABBROIC, GABBROID** adj
GABBY	adj -BIER, -BIEST talkative
GABELLE	n pl. -S a tax on salt **GABELLED** adj
GABFEST	n pl. -S an informal gathering for general talk
GABIES	pl. of gaby
GABION	n pl. -S a type of basket
GABLE	v -BLED, -BLING, -BLES to form a triangular section of a wall
GABOON	n pl. -S a spittoon
GABY	n pl. -BIES a dolt
GAD	v GADDED, GADDING, GADS to roam about restlessly
GADABOUT	n pl. -S one that gads about
GADARENE	adj headlong
GADDED	past tense of gad
GADDER	n pl. -S one that gads about
GADDI	n pl. -S a hassock
GADDING	present participle of gad
GADFLY	n pl. -FLIES a biting fly
GADGET	n pl. -S a mechanical device **GADGETY** adj
GADGETRY	n pl. -RIES the devising or constructing of gadgets
GADI	n pl. -S gaddi
GADID	n pl. -S gadoid
GADOID	n pl. -S a type of fish
GADROON	v -ED, -ING, -S to decorate with bands of fluted or reeded molding
GADWALL	n pl. -S a wild duck
GADZOOKS	interj — used as a mild oath
GAE	v GAED, GANE or GAEN, GAEING or GAUN, GAES to go
GAFF	v -ED, -ING, -S to catch a fish with a sharp hook
GAFFE	n pl. -S a social blunder
GAFFER	n pl. -S an old man
GAG	v GAGGED, GAGGING, GAGS to stop up the mouth
GAGA	adj crazy
GAGAKU	n pl. -S ancient court music of Japan
GAGE	v GAGED, GAGING, GAGES to pledge as security
GAGER	n pl. -S gauger
GAGGED	past tense of gag
GAGGER	n pl. -S one that gags
GAGGING	present participle of gag
GAGGLE	v -GLED, -GLING, -GLES to cackle
GAGING	present participle of gage
GAGMAN	n pl. -MEN one who writes jokes
GAGSTER	n pl. -S a gagman
GAHNITE	n pl. -S a mineral
GAIETY	n pl. -ETIES festive activity
GAIJIN	n pl. GAIJIN a foreigner in Japan
GAILY	adv in a gay manner
GAIN	v -ED, -ING, -S to acquire **GAINABLE** adj

GAINER   n pl. -S one that gains
GAINFUL   adj profitable
GAINLESS   adj profitless
GAINLY   adj -LIER, -LIEST graceful
GAINSAY   v -SAID, -SAYING, -SAYS to deny
GAINST   prep against
GAIT   v -ED, -ING, -S to train a horse to move in a particular way
GAITER   n pl. -S a covering for the lower leg
GAL   n pl. -S a girl
GALA   n pl. -S a celebration
GALABIA   n pl. -S djellaba
GALABIEH   n pl. -S djellaba
GALABIYA   n pl. -S djellaba
GALACTIC   adj pertaining to a galaxy
GALAGO   n pl. -GOS a small primate
GALAH   n pl. -S a cockatoo
GALANGAL   n pl. -S a medicinal plant
GALATEA   n pl. -S a strong cotton fabric
GALAVANT   v -ED, -ING, -S to gad about
GALAX   n pl. -ES an evergreen herb
GALAXY   n pl. -AXIES a large system of celestial bodies
GALBANUM   n pl. -S a gum resin
GALE   n pl. -S a strong wind
GALEA   n pl. -LEAE or -LEAS a helmet-shaped anatomical part GALEATE, GALEATED adj
GALENA   n pl. -S the principal ore of lead GALENIC adj
GALENITE   n pl. -S galena
GALERE   n pl. -S a group of people having a common quality
GALILEE   n pl. -S a type of porch
GALIOT   n pl. -S galliot
GALIPOT   n pl. -S a type of turpentine
GALIVANT   v -ED, -ING, -S to gad about
GALL   v -ED, -ING, -S to vex or irritate
GALLANT   v -ED, -ING, -S to court a woman
GALLATE   n pl. -S a chemical salt
GALLEASS   n pl. -ES a large war galley
GALLEIN   n pl. -S a green dye
GALLEON   n pl. -S a large sailing vessel
GALLERIA   n pl. -S a roofed promenade or court
GALLERY   v -LERIED, -LERYING, -LERIES to provide with a long covered area
GALLET   v -ED, -ING, -S to fill in mortar joints with stone chips
GALLETA   n pl. -S a perennial grass

GALLEY   n pl. -LEYS a long, low medieval ship
GALLFLY   n pl. -FLIES a small insect
GALLIARD   n pl. -S a lively dance
GALLIASS   n pl. -ES galleass
GALLIC   adj containing gallium
GALLICAN   adj pertaining to a French religious movement
GALLIED   past tense of gally
GALLIES   present 3d person sing. of gally
GALLIOT   n pl. -S a small galley
GALLIPOT   n pl. -S a small earthen jar
GALLIUM   n pl. -S a metallic element
GALLNUT   n pl. -S an abnormal swelling of plant tissue
GALLON   n pl. -S a unit of liquid measure
GALLOON   n pl. -S an ornamental braid
GALLOOT   n pl. -S galoot
GALLOP   v -ED, -ING, -S to ride a horse at full speed
GALLOPER   n pl. -S one that gallops
GALLOUS   adj containing gallium
GALLOWS   n pl. -ES a structure used for hanging a condemned person
GALLUS   n pl. -ES a suspender for trousers GALLUSED adj
GALLY   v -LIED, -LYING, -LIES to frighten
GALOOT   n pl. -S an awkward or uncouth person
GALOP   v -ED, -ING, -S to dance a galop (a lively round dance)
GALOPADE   n pl. -S a lively round dance
GALORE   n pl. -S abundance
GALOSH   n pl. -ES an overshoe GALOSHED adj
GALOSHE   n pl. -S galosh
GALUMPH   v -ED, -ING, -S to move clumsily
GALVANIC   adj pertaining to a direct electric current
GALYAC   n pl. -S galyak
GALYAK   n pl. -S a fur made from lambskin
GAM   v GAMMED, GAMMING, GAMS to visit socially
GAMA   n pl. -S a pasture grass
GAMASHES   n/pl boots worn by horseback riders
GAMAY   n pl. -MAYS a red grape
GAMB   n pl. -S a leg
GAMBA   n pl. -S a bass viol
GAMBADE   n pl. -S a gambado

GAMBADO   *n* pl. -DOES or -DOS a leap made by a horse
GAMBE   *n* pl. -S gamb
GAMBESON   *n* pl. -S a medieval coat
GAMBIA   *n* pl. -S gambier
GAMBIER   *n* pl. -S an extract obtained from an Asian vine
GAMBIR   *n* pl. -S gambier
GAMBIT   *n* pl. -S a type of chess opening
GAMBLE   *v* -BLED, -BLING, -BLES to play a game of chance for money or valuables
GAMBLER   *n* pl. -S one that gambles
GAMBOGE   *n* pl. -S a gum resin
GAMBOL   *v* -BOLED, -BOLING, -BOLS or -BOLLED, -BOLLING, -BOLS to leap about playfully
GAMBREL   *n* pl. -S a part of a horse's leg
GAMBUSIA   *n* pl. -S a small fish
GAME   *adj* GAMER, GAMEST plucky
GAME   *v* GAMED, GAMING, GAMES to gamble
GAMECOCK   *n* pl. -S a rooster trained for fighting
GAMELAN   *n* pl. -S a type of orchestra
GAMELIKE   *adj* similar to a game (a contest governed by a set of rules)
GAMELY   *adv* in a game manner
GAMENESS   *n* pl. -ES the quality of being game
GAMER   comparative of game
GAMESMAN   *n* pl. -MEN one who plays games
GAMESOME   *adj* playful
GAMEST   superlative of game
GAMESTER   *n* pl. -S a gambler
GAMETE   *n* pl. -S a mature reproductive cell **GAMETIC** *adj*
GAMEY   *adj* GAMIER, GAMIEST gamy
GAMIC   *adj* requiring fertilization
GAMIER   comparative of gamy
GAMIEST   superlative of gamy
GAMILY   *adv* in a game manner
GAMIN   *n* pl. -S an urchin
GAMINE   *n* pl. -S a tomboy
GAMINESS   *n* pl. -ES the quality of being gamy
GAMING   *n* pl. -S the practice of gambling
GAMMA   *n* pl. -S a Greek letter
GAMMADIA   *n/pl* Greek ornamental designs
GAMMED   past tense of gam
GAMMER   *n* pl. -S an old woman
GAMMIER   comparative of gammy

GAMMIEST   superlative of gammy
GAMMING   present participle of gam
GAMMON   *v* -ED, -ING, -S to mislead by deceptive talk
GAMMONER   *n* pl. -S one that gammons
GAMMY   *adj* -MIER, -MIEST lame
GAMODEME   *n* pl. -S a somewhat isolated breeding community of organisms
GAMP   *n* pl. -S a large umbrella
GAMUT   *n* pl. -S an entire range
GAMY   *adj* GAMIER, GAMIEST plucky
GAN   past tense of gin
GANACHE   *n* pl. -S creamy chocolate mixture
GANDER   *v* -ED, -ING, -S to wander
GANE   a past participle of gae
GANEF   *n* pl. -S a thief
GANEV   *n* pl. -S ganef
GANG   *v* -ED, -ING, -S to form into a gang (a group)
GANGER   *n* pl. -S a foreman of a gang of laborers
GANGLAND   *n* pl. -S the criminal underworld
GANGLIA   a pl. of ganglion
GANGLIAL   *adj* gangliar
GANGLIAR   *adj* pertaining to a ganglion
GANGLIER   comparative of gangly
GANGLIEST   superlative of gangly
GANGLING   *adj* awkwardly tall and lanky
GANGLION   *n* pl. -GLIA or -GLIONS a group of nerve cells
GANGLY   *adj* -GLIER, -GLIEST gangling
GANGPLOW   *n* pl. -S an agricultural implement
GANGREL   *n* pl. -S a vagabond
GANGRENE   *v* -GRENED, -GRENING, -GRENES to suffer the loss of tissue in part of the body
GANGSTER   *n* pl. -S a member of a criminal gang
GANGUE   *n* pl. -S the worthless rock in which valuable minerals are found
GANGWAY   *n* pl. -WAYS a passageway
GANISTER   *n* pl. -S a type of rock
GANJA   *n* pl. -S cannabis used for smoking
GANJAH   *n* pl. -S ganja
GANNET   *n* pl. -S a large seabird
GANOF   *n* pl. -S ganef
GANOID   *n* pl. -S a type of fish
GANTLET   *v* -ED, -ING, -S to overlap railroad tracks

GANTLINE *n pl.* -S a rope on a ship
GANTLOPE *n pl.* -S a former military punishment
GANTRY *n pl.* -TRIES a structure for supporting railroad signals
GANYMEDE *n pl.* -S a youth who serves liquors
GAOL *v* -ED, -ING, -S to jail
GAOLER *n pl.* -S jailer
GAP *v* GAPPED, GAPPING, GAPS to make an opening in
GAPE *v* GAPED, GAPING, GAPES to stare with open mouth
GAPER *n pl.* -S one that gapes
GAPESEED *n pl.* -S something that causes wonder
GAPEWORM *n pl.* -S a worm that causes a disease of young birds
GAPING present participle of gape
GAPINGLY *adv* in a gaping manner
GAPOSIS *n pl.* -SISES a gap in a row of buttons or snaps
GAPPED past tense of gap
GAPPING present participle of gap
GAPPY *adj* -PIER, -PIEST having openings
GAPY *adj* infested with gapeworms
GAR *v* GARRED, GARRING, GARS to cause or compel
GARAGE *v* -RAGED, -RAGING, -RAGES to put in a garage (a car shelter)
GARB *v* -ED, -ING, -S to clothe
GARBAGE *n pl.* -S food waste
GARBANZO *n pl.* -ZOS a chickpea
GARBLE *v* -BLED, -BLING, -BLES to distort the meaning of
GARBLER *n pl.* -S one that garbles
GARBLESS *adj* being without clothing
GARBOARD *n pl.* -S a plank on a ship's bottom
GARBOIL *n pl.* -S turmoil
GARCON *n pl.* -S a waiter
GARDANT *adj* turned directly toward the observer — used of a heraldic animal
GARDEN *v* -ED, -ING, -S to cultivate a plot of ground
GARDENER *n pl.* -S one that gardens
GARDENIA *n pl.* -S a tropical shrub or tree
GARDYLOO *interj* — used as a warning cry
GARFISH *n pl.* -ES a freshwater fish
GARGANEY *n pl.* -NEYS a small duck
GARGET *n pl.* -S mastitis of domestic animals GARGETY *adj*

GARGLE *v* -GLED, -GLING, -GLES to rinse the mouth or throat
GARGLER *n pl.* -S one that gargles
GARGOYLE *n pl.* -S an ornamental figure
GARIGUE *n pl.* -S a low scrubland
GARISH *adj* gaudy GARISHLY *adv*
GARLAND *v* -ED, -ING, -S to deck with wreaths of flowers
GARLIC *n pl.* -S an herb used in cooking GARLICKY *adj*
GARMENT *v* -ED, -ING, -S to clothe
GARNER *v* -ED, -ING, -S to gather and store
GARNET *n pl.* -S a mineral
GARNI *adj* garnished
GARNISH *v* -ED, -ING, -ES to decorate
GAROTE *v* -ROTED, -ROTING, -ROTES to garrote
GAROTTE *v* -ROTTED, -ROTTING, -ROTTES to garrote
GAROTTER *n pl.* -S one that garottes
GARPIKE *n pl.* -S a garfish
GARRED past tense of gar
GARRET *n pl.* -S an attic
GARRING present participle of gar
GARRISON *v* -ED, -ING, -S to assign to a military post
GARRON *n pl.* -S a small, sturdy horse
GARROTE *v* -ROTED, -ROTING, -ROTES to execute by strangling
GARROTER *n pl.* -S one that garrotes
GARROTTE *v* -ROTTED, -ROTTING, -ROTTES to garrote
GARTER *v* -ED, -ING, -S to fasten with an elastic band
GARTH *n pl.* -S a yard or garden
GARVEY *n pl.* -VEYS a small scow
GAS *v* GASSED, GASSING, GASES or GASSES to supply with gas (a substance capable of indefinite expansion)
GASALIER *n pl.* -S gaselier
GASBAG *n pl.* -S a bag for holding gas
GASCON *n pl.* -S a boaster
GASELIER *n pl.* -S a gaslight chandelier
GASEOUS *adj* pertaining to gas
GASH *v* -ED, -ING, -ES to make a long deep cut in
GASH *adj* GASHER, GASHEST knowing
GASHOUSE *n pl.* -S a gasworks
GASIFIED past tense of gasify
GASIFIER *n pl.* -S one that gasifies
GASIFORM *adj* having the form of gas

GASIFY *v* -IFIED, -IFYING, -IFIES to convert into gas

GASKET *n* pl. -S packing for making something fluid-tight

GASKIN *n* pl. -S a part of a horse's leg

GASKING *n* pl. -S a gasket

GASLESS *adj* having no gas

GASLIGHT *n* pl. -S light made by burning gas

GASLIT *adj* illuminated by gaslight

GASMAN *n* pl. -MEN an employee of a gas company

GASOGENE *n* pl. -S gazogene

GASOHOL *n* pl. -S a fuel mixture of gasoline and ethyl alcohol

GASOLENE *n* pl. -S gasoline

GASOLIER *n* pl. -S gaselier

GASOLINE *n* pl. -S a liquid fuel

GASP *v* -ED, -ING, -S to breathe convulsively

GASPER *n* pl. -S a cigarette

GASSED past tense of gas

GASSER *n* pl. -S one that gasses

GASSES a present 3d person sing. of gas

GASSING *n* pl. -S a poisoning by noxious gas

GASSY *adj* -SIER, -SIEST containing gas **GASSILY** *adv*

GAST *v* -ED, -ING, -S to scare

GASTER *n* pl. -S the enlarged part of the abdomen in some insects

GASTIGHT *adj* not allowing gas to escape or enter

GASTNESS *n* pl. -ES fright

GASTRAEA *n* pl. -S a type of metazoan

GASTRAL *adj* pertaining to the stomach

GASTREA *n* pl. -S gastraea

GASTRIC *adj* pertaining to the stomach

GASTRIN *n* pl. -S a hormone

GASTRULA *n* pl. -LAS or -LAE a metazoan embryo

GASWORKS *n* pl. GASWORKS a factory where gas is produced

GAT *n* pl. -S a pistol

GATE *v* GATED, GATING, GATES to supply with a gate (a movable barrier)

GATEAU *n* pl. -TEAUX a rich layer cake

GATEFOLD *n* pl. -S a folded insert in a book or magazine

GATELESS *adj* lacking a gate

GATELIKE *adj* resembling a gate

GATEMAN *n* pl. -MEN a person in charge of a gate

GATEPOST *n* pl. -S a post from which a gate is hung

GATEWAY *n* pl. -WAYS a passage that may be closed by a gate

GATHER *v* -ED, -ING, -S to bring together into one place or group

GATHERER *n* pl. -S one that gathers

GATING present participle of gate

GATOR *n* pl. -S an alligator

GAUCHE *adj* GAUCHER, GAUCHEST lacking social grace **GAUCHELY** *adv*

GAUCHO *n* pl. -CHOS a cowboy of the South American pampas

GAUD *n* pl. -S a showy ornament

GAUDERY *n* pl. -ERIES finery

GAUDY *adj* GAUDIER, GAUDIEST tastelessly showy **GAUDILY** *adv*

GAUDY *n* pl. -DIES a festival

GAUFFER *v* -ED, -ING, -S to goffer

GAUGE *v* GAUGED, GAUGING, GAUGES to measure precisely

GAUGER *n* pl. -S one that gauges

GAULT *n* pl. -S a heavy, thick clay soil

GAUM *v* -ED, -ING, -S to smear

GAUN present participle of gae

GAUNT *adj* GAUNTER, GAUNTEST emaciated **GAUNTLY** *adv*

GAUNTLET *v* -ED, -ING, -S to gantlet

GAUNTRY *n* pl. -TRIES gantry

GAUR *n* pl. -S a wild ox

GAUSS *n* pl. -ES a unit of magnetic induction

GAUZE *n* pl. -S a transparent fabric

GAUZY *adj* GAUZIER, GAUZIEST resembling gauze **GAUZILY** *adv*

GAVAGE *n* pl. -S introduction of material into the stomach by a tube

GAVE past tense of give

GAVEL *v* -ELED, -ELING, -ELS or -ELLED, -ELLING, -ELS to signal for attention or order by use of a gavel (a small mallet)

GAVELOCK *n* pl. -S a crowbar

GAVIAL *n* pl. -S a large reptile

GAVOT *n* pl. -S a French dance

GAVOTTE *v* -VOTTED, -VOTTING, -VOTTES to dance a gavot

GAWK *v* -ED, -ING, -S to stare stupidly

GAWKER *n* pl. -S one that gawks

GAWKIER comparative of gawky

GAWKIES pl. of gawky

GAWKISH *adj* gawky

GAWKY *adj* GAWKIER, GAWKIEST awkward **GAWKILY** *adv*

GAWKY *n* pl. GAWKIES an awkward person

GAWP *v* -ED, -ING, -S to stare stupidly

GAWPER *n* -S one that gawps

GAWSIE *adj* well-fed and healthy looking

GAWSY *adj* gawsie

GAY *adj* GAYER, GAYEST merry

GAY *n* pl. GAYS a homosexual

GAYAL *n* pl. -S a domesticated ox

GAYETY *n* pl. -ETIES gaiety

GAYLY *adv* in a gay manner

GAYNESS *n* pl. -ES gaiety

GAYWINGS *n* pl. GAYWINGS a perennial herb

GAZABO *n* pl. -BOS or -BOES a fellow

GAZANIA *n* pl. -S a South African herb

GAZAR *n* pl. -S silky sheer fabric

GAZE *v* GAZED, GAZING, GAZES to look intently

GAZEBO *n* pl. -BOS or -BOES a roofed structure open on the sides

GAZELLE *n* pl. -S a small antelope

GAZER *n* pl. -S one that gazes

GAZETTE *v* -ZETTED, -ZETTING, -ZETTES to announce in an official journal

GAZING present participle of gaze

GAZOGENE *n* pl. -S an apparatus for carbonating liquids

GAZPACHO *n* pl. -CHOS a cold, spicy soup

GAZUMP *v* -ED, -ING, -S to cheat by raising the price originally agreed upon

GAZUMPER *n* pl. -S one that gazumps

GEAR *v* -ED, -ING, -S to provide with gears (toothed machine parts)

GEARBOX *n* pl. -ES an automotive transmission

GEARCASE *n* pl. -S a casing for gears

GEARING *n* pl. -S a system of gears

GEARLESS *adj* being without gears

GECK *v* -ED, -ING, -S to mock

GECKO *n* pl. GECKOS or GECKOES a small lizard

GED *n* pl. -S a food fish

GEE *v* GEED, GEEING, GEES to turn to the right

GEEGAW *n* pl. -S gewgaw

GEEK *n* pl. -S a carnival performer

GEEKY *adj* GEEKIER, GEEKIEST socially awkward or unappealing

GEEPOUND *n* pl. -S a unit of mass

GEESE pl. of goose

GEEST *n* pl. -S old alluvial matter

GEEZ *interj* jeez

GEEZER *n* pl. -S an eccentric man

GEISHA *n* pl. -S a Japanese girl trained to entertain

GEL *v* GELLED, GELLING, GELS to become like jelly **GELABLE** *adj*

GELADA *n* pl. -S a baboon

GELANT *n* pl. -S gellant

GELATE *v* -ATED, -ATING, -ATES to gel

GELATI a pl. of gelato

GELATIN *n* pl. -S a glutinous substance

GELATINE *n* pl. -S gelatin

GELATING present participle of gelate

GELATION *n* pl. -S the process of gelling

GELATO *n* pl. -TI or -TOS Italian ice cream

GELD *v* -ED, -ING, -S to castrate

GELDER *n* pl. -S one that gelds

GELDING *n* pl. -S a castrated animal

GELEE *n* pl. -S a cosmetic gel

GELID *adj* icy **GELIDLY** *adv*

GELIDITY *n* pl. -TIES iciness

GELLANT *n* pl. -S a substance used to produce gelling

GELLED past tense of gel

GELLING present participle of gel

GELSEMIA *n/pl* medicinal plant roots

GELT *n* pl. -S money

GEM *v* GEMMED, GEMMING, GEMS to adorn with gems (precious stones)

GEMINAL *adj* of or pertaining to two substituents on the same atom

GEMINATE *v* -NATED, -NATING, -NATES to arrange in pairs

GEMLIKE *adj* resembling a gem

GEMMA *n* pl. -MAE an asexual reproductive structure

GEMMATE *v* -MATED, -MATING, -MATES to produce gemmae

GEMMED past tense of gem

GEMMIER comparative of gemmy

GEMMIEST superlative of gemmy

GEMMILY *adv* in a manner suggesting a gem

GEMMING present participle of gem

GEMMULE *n* pl. -S a small gemma

GEMMY adj -MIER, -MIEST resembling a gem

GEMOLOGY n pl. -GIES the science of gems

GEMOT n pl. -S a public meeting in Anglo-Saxon England

GEMOTE n pl. -S gemot

GEMSBOK n pl. -S a large antelope

GEMSBUCK n pl. -S gemsbok

GEMSTONE n pl. -S a precious stone

GEN n pl. -S information obtained from study

GENDARME n pl. -S a policeman

GENDER v -ED, -ING, -S to engender

GENE n pl. -S a hereditary unit

GENERA a pl. of genus

GENERAL n pl. -S a military officer

GENERATE v -ATED, -ATING, -ATES to bring into existence

GENERIC n pl. -S a type of drug

GENEROUS adj willing to give

GENESIS n pl. GENESES an origin

GENET n pl. -S a carnivorous mammal

GENETIC adj pertaining to genetics

GENETICS n/pl the science of heredity

GENETTE n pl. -S genet

GENEVA n pl. -S a liquor

GENIAL adj having a pleasant or friendly manner GENIALLY adv

GENIC adj pertaining to genes

GENIE n pl. -S jinni

GENII a pl. of genius

GENIP n pl. -S a tropical tree

GENIPAP n pl. -S a tropical tree

GENITAL adj pertaining to reproduction

GENITALS n/pl the sexual organs

GENITIVE n pl. -S a grammatical case

GENITOR n pl. -S a male parent

GENITURE n pl. -S birth

GENIUS n pl. GENIUSES or GENII an exceptional natural aptitude

GENOA n pl. -S a triangular sail

GENOCIDE n pl. -S the deliberate extermination of a national or racial group

GENOISE n pl. -S a rich spongecake

GENOM n pl. -S genome

GENOME n pl. -S a haploid set of chromosomes GENOMIC adj

GENOTYPE n pl. -S the genetic constitution of an organism

GENRE n pl. -S a type or kind

GENRO n pl. -ROS a group of elder statesmen in Japan

GENS n pl. GENTES a type of clan

GENSENG n pl. -S ginseng

GENT n pl. -S a gentleman

GENTEEL adj -TEELER, -TEELEST well-bred or refined

GENTES pl. of gens

GENTIAN n pl. -S a flowering plant

GENTIL adj kind

GENTILE n pl. -S a non-Jewish person

GENTLE adj -TLER, -TLEST mild GENTLY adv

GENTLE v -TLED, -TLING, -TLES to tame

GENTRICE n pl. -S good breeding

GENTRIFY v -FIED, -FYING, -FIES to renew a decayed urban area so as to attract middle-class residents

GENTRY n pl. -TRIES people of high social class

GENU n pl. GENUA the knee

GENUINE adj authentic

GENUS n pl. GENERA or GENUSES a kind, sort, or class

GEODE n pl. -S a type of rock

GEODESIC n pl. -S a geometric line

GEODESY n pl. -SIES geographical surveying

GEODETIC adj pertaining to geodesy

GEODIC adj of or pertaining to a geode

GEODUCK n pl. -S a large, edible clam

GEOGNOSY n pl. -SIES a branch of geology

GEOID n pl. -S a hypothetical surface of the earth GEOIDAL adj

GEOLOGER n pl. -S a specialist in geology

GEOLOGY n pl. -GIES the science that deals with the origin and structure of the earth GEOLOGIC adj

GEOMANCY n pl. -CIES a method of foretelling the future by geographical features

GEOMETER n pl. -S a specialist in geometry

GEOMETRY n pl. -TRIES a branch of mathematics

GEOPHAGY n pl. -GIES the practice of eating earthy substances

GEOPHONE n pl. -S a device that detects vibrations in the earth

GEOPHYTE n pl. -S a plant having underground buds

GEOPONIC adj pertaining to farming

GEOPROBE n pl. -S a spacecraft for exploring space near the earth

GEORGIC n pl. -S a poem about farming

GEOTAXIS n pl. -TAXES the movement of an organism in response to gravity

GERAH n pl. -S a Hebrew unit of weight

GERANIAL n pl. -S citral

GERANIOL n pl. -S an alcohol used in perfumes

GERANIUM n pl. -S a flowering plant

GERARDIA n pl. -S an herb

GERBERA n pl. -S an herb

GERBIL n pl. -S a burrowing rodent

GERBILLE n pl. -S gerbil

GERENT n pl. -S a ruler or manager

GERENUK n pl. -S a long-necked antelope

GERM n pl. -S a microorganism that causes disease

GERMAN n pl. -S an elaborate dance

GERMANE adj relevant

GERMANIC adj containing germanium (a metallic element)

GERMEN n pl. -MENS or -MINA something that serves as an origin

GERMFREE adj free from germs

GERMIER comparative of germy

GERMIEST superlative of germy

GERMINA a pl. of germen

GERMINAL adj being in the earliest stage of development

GERMY adj GERMIER, GERMIEST full of germs

GERONTIC adj pertaining to old age

GERUND n pl. -S a verbal noun

GESNERIA adj designating a type of flowering plant

GESSO n pl. -SOES a plaster mixture

GESSOED adj having gesso as a coating or constituent part

GEST n pl. -S a feat

GESTALT n pl. -STALTS or -STALTEN a unified whole

GESTAPO n pl. -POS a secret-police organization

GESTATE v -TATED, -TATING, -TATES to carry in the uterus during pregnancy

GESTE n pl. -S gest

GESTIC adj pertaining to bodily motion

GESTICAL adj gestic

GESTURAL adj pertaining to or consisting of gestures (expressive bodily motions)

GESTURE v -TURED, -TURING, -TURES to express by bodily motion

GESTURER n pl. -S one that gestures

GET v GOT, GOTTEN, GETTING, GETS to obtain or acquire GETABLE, GETTABLE adj

GETA n pl. -S a Japanese wooden clog

GETAWAY n pl. -AWAYS an escape

GETTER v -ED, -ING, -S to purify with a chemically active substance

GETTING present participle of get

GETUP n pl. -S a costume

GEUM n pl. -S a perennial herb

GEWGAW n pl. -S a showy trinket

GEY adv very

GEYSER n pl. -S a spring that ejects jets of hot water and steam

GHARIAL n pl. -S a large reptile

GHARRI n pl. -S gharry

GHARRY n pl. -RIES a carriage used in India

GHAST adj ghastly

GHASTFUL adj frightful

GHASTLY adj -LIER, -LIEST terrifying

GHAT n pl. -S a passage leading down to a river

GHAUT n pl. -S ghat

GHAZI n pl. -S or -ES a Muslim war hero

GHEE n pl. -S a kind of liquid butter made in India

GHERAO v -ED, -ING, -ES to coerce by physical means

GHERKIN n pl. -S a small cucumber

GHETTO v -ED, -ING, -S or -ES to isolate in a slum

GHI n pl. -S ghee

GHIBLI n pl. -S a hot desert wind

GHILLIE n pl. -S a type of shoe

GHOST v -ED, -ING, -S to haunt

GHOSTING n pl. -S a false image on a television screen

GHOSTLY adj -LIER, -LIEST spectral

GHOSTY adj GHOSTIER, GHOSTIEST ghostly

GHOUL n pl. -S a demon GHOULISH adj

GHOULIE n pl. -S a ghoul

GHYLL n pl. -S a ravine

GIANT n pl. -S a person or thing of great size

GIANTESS n pl. -ES a female giant

GIANTISM n pl. -S the condition of being a giant

GIAOUR n pl. -S a non-Muslim

GIB   *v* GIBBED, GIBBING, GIBS to fasten with a wedge of wood or metal

GIBBER   *v* -ED, -ING, -S to jabber

GIBBET   *v* -BETED, -BETING, -BETS or -BETTED, -BETTING, -BETS to execute by hanging

GIBBING   present participle of gib

GIBBON   *n* pl. -S an arboreal ape

GIBBOSE   *adj* gibbous

GIBBOUS   *adj* irregularly rounded

GIBBSITE   *n* pl. -S a mineral

GIBE   *v* GIBED, GIBING, GIBES to jeer **GIBINGLY** *adv*

GIBER   *n* pl. -S one that gibes

GIBLET   *n* pl. -S an edible part of a fowl

GIBSON   *n* pl. -S a martini served with a tiny onion

GID   *n* pl. -S a disease of sheep

GIDDAP   *interj* — used as a command to a horse to go faster

GIDDY   *adj* -DIER, -DIEST dizzy **GIDDILY** *adv*

GIDDY   *v* -DIED, -DYING, -DIES to make giddy

GIDDYAP   *interj* giddap

GIDDYUP   *interj* giddap

GIE   *v* GIED, GIEN, GIEING, GIES to give

GIFT   *v* -ED, -ING, -S to present with a gift (something given without charge)

GIFTEDLY   *adv* in a talented manner

GIFTLESS   *adj* being without a gift

GIFTWARE   *n* pl. -S wares suitable for gifts

GIG   *v* GIGGED, GIGGING, GIGS to catch fish with a pronged spear

GIGA   *n* pl. GIGHE a gigue

GIGABIT   *n* pl. -S a unit of information

GIGABYTE   *n* pl. -S 1,073,741,824 bytes

GIGANTIC   *adj* huge

GIGAS   *adj* pertaining to variations in plant development

GIGATON   *n* pl. -S a unit of weight

GIGAWATT   *n* pl. -S a unit of power

GIGGED   past tense of gig

GIGGING   present participle of gig

GIGGLE   *v* -GLED, -GLING, -GLES to laugh in a silly manner

GIGGLER   *n* pl. -S one that giggles

GIGGLY   *adj* -GLIER, -GLIEST tending to giggle

GIGHE   pl. of giga

GIGLET   *n* pl. -S a playful girl

GIGLOT   *n* pl. -S giglet

GIGOLO   *n* pl. -LOS a man supported financially by a woman

GIGOT   *n* pl. -S a leg of lamb

GIGUE   *n* pl. -S a lively dance

GILBERT   *n* pl. -S a unit of magnetomotive force

GILD   *v* GILDED or GILT, GILDING, GILDS to cover with a thin layer of gold

GILDER   *n* pl. -S one that gilds

GILDHALL   *n* pl. -S a town hall

GILDING   *n* pl. -S the application of gilt

GILL   *v* -ED, -ING, -S to catch fish with a type of net

GILLER   *n* pl. -S one that gills

GILLIE   *n* pl. -S ghillie

GILLNET   *v* -NETTED, -NETTING, -NETS to gill

GILLY   *v* -LIED, -LYING, -LIES to transport on a type of wagon

GILT   *n* pl. -S the gold with which something is gilded

GILTHEAD   *n* pl. -S a marine fish

GIMBAL   *v* -BALED, -BALING, -BALS or -BALLED, -BALLING, -BALS to support on a set of rings

GIMCRACK   *n* pl. -S a gewgaw

GIMEL   *n* pl. -S a Hebrew letter

GIMLET   *n* -ED, -ING, -S to pierce with a boring tool

GIMMAL   *n* pl. -S a pair of interlocked rings

GIMME   *n* pl. -S something easily won

GIMMICK   *v* -ED, -ING, -S to provide with a gimmick (a novel or tricky feature)

GIMMICKY   *adj* having or being like a gimmick

GIMMIE   *n* pl. -MIES an easy golf putt conceded to an opponent

GIMP   *v* -ED, -ING, -S to limp

GIMPIER   comparative of gimpy

GIMPIEST   superlative of gimpy

GIMPY   *adj* GIMPIER, GIMPIEST limping

GIN   *v* GINNED, GINNING, GINS to remove seeds from cotton

GIN   *v* GAN, GUNNEN, GINNING, GINS to begin

GINGAL   *n* pl. -S jingal

GINGALL   *n* pl. -S jingal

GINGELEY   *n* pl. -LEYS gingelly

GINGELI   *n* pl. -S gingelly

GINGELIES   pl. of gingely

GINGELLI   *n* pl. -S gingelly

GINGELLY   n pl. -LIES the sesame seed or its oil

GINGELY   n pl. -LIES gingelly

GINGER   v -ED, -ING, -S to flavor with ginger (a pungent spice)

GINGERLY   adv in a careful manner

GINGERY   adj having the characteristics of ginger

GINGHAM   n pl. -S a cotton fabric

GINGILI   n pl. -LIS gingelly

GINGILLI   n pl. -S gingelly

GINGIVA   n pl. -VAE the fleshy tissue that surrounds the teeth **GINGIVAL** adj

GINGKO   n pl. -KOES ginkgo

GINK   n pl. -S a fellow

GINKGO   n pl. -GOES or -GOS an ornamental tree

GINNED   past tense of gin

GINNER   n pl. -S one that gins cotton

GINNING   n pl. -S cotton as it comes from a gin

GINNY   adj GINNIER, GINNIEST affected with gin (a strong liquor)

GINSENG   n pl. -S a perennial herb

GIP   v GIPPED, GIPPING, GIPS to gyp

GIPON   n pl. -S jupon

GIPPER   n pl. -S one that gips

GIPPING   present participle of gip

GIPSY   v -SIED, -SYING, -SIES to gypsy

GIRAFFE   n pl. -S a long-necked mammal

GIRASOL   n pl. -S a variety of opal

GIRASOLE   n pl. -S girasol

GIRD   v GIRDED or GIRT, GIRDING, GIRDS to surround

GIRDER   n pl. -S a horizontal support

GIRDLE   v -DLED, -DLING, -DLES to encircle with a belt

GIRDLER   n pl. -S one that girdles

GIRL   n pl. -S a female child

GIRLHOOD   n pl. -S the state of being a girl

GIRLIE   adj featuring scantily clothed women

GIRLISH   adj of, pertaining to, or having the characteristics of a girl

GIRLY   adj girlie

GIRN   v -ED, -ING, -S to snarl

GIRO   n pl. -ROS an autogiro

GIRON   n pl. -S gyron

GIROSOL   n pl. -S girasol

GIRSH   n pl. -ES qursh

GIRT   v -ED, -ING, -S to gird

GIRTH   v -ED, -ING, -S to encircle

GISARME   n pl. -S a medieval weapon

GISMO   n pl. -MOS a gadget

GIST   n pl. -S the main point of a matter

GIT   n pl. -S a foolish person

GITANO   n pl. -NOS a Spanish gypsy

GITTERN   n pl. -S a medieval guitar

GIVE   v GAVE, GIVEN, GIVING, GIVES to transfer freely to another's possession **GIVEABLE** adj

GIVEAWAY   n pl. -AWAYS something given away free of charge

GIVEBACK   n pl. -S a worker's benefit given back to management

GIVEN   n pl. -S something assigned as a basis for a calculation

GIVER   n pl. -S one that gives

GIVING   present participle of give

GIZMO   n pl. -MOS gismo

GIZZARD   n pl. -S a digestive organ

GJETOST   n pl. -S a hard brown cheese

GLABELLA   n pl. -BELLAE the smooth area between the eyebrows

GLABRATE   adj glabrous

GLABROUS   adj smooth

GLACE   v -CEED, -CEING, -CES to cover with icing

GLACIAL   adj of or pertaining to glaciers

GLACIATE   v -ATED, -ATING, -ATES to cover with glaciers

GLACIER   n pl. -S a huge mass of ice

GLACIS   n pl. -CISES a slope

GLAD   adj GLADDER, GLADDEST feeling pleasure

GLAD   v GLADDED, GLADDING, GLADS to gladden

GLADDEN   v -ED, -ING, -S to make glad

GLADDER   comparative of glad

GLADDEST   superlative of glad

GLADDING   present participle of glad

GLADE   n pl. -S an open space in a forest

GLADIATE   adj shaped like a sword

GLADIER   comparative of glady

GLADIEST   superlative of glady

GLADIOLA   n pl. -S a flowering plant

GLADIOLI   n/pl segments of the sternum

GLADLY   adv -LIER, -LIEST in a glad manner

GLADNESS   n pl. -ES the state of being glad

GLADSOME   adj -SOMER, -SOMEST glad

GLADY *adj* GLADIER, GLADIEST having glades

GLAIKET *adj* glaikit

GLAIKIT *adj* foolish

GLAIR *v* -ED, -ING, -S to coat with egg white

GLAIRE *v* GLAIRED, GLAIRING, GLAIRES to glair

GLAIRY *adj* GLAIRIER, GLAIRIEST resembling egg white

GLAIVE *n* pl. -S a sword **GLAIVED** *adj*

GLAMOR *n* pl. -S alluring attractiveness

GLAMOUR *v* -ED, -ING, -S to bewitch

GLANCE *v* GLANCED, GLANCING, GLANCES to look quickly

GLANCER *n* pl. -S one that glances

GLAND *n* pl. -S a secreting organ

GLANDERS *n/pl* a disease of horses

GLANDULE *n* pl. -S a small gland

GLANS *n* pl. GLANDES the tip of the penis or clitoris

GLARE *v* GLARED, GLARING, GLARES to shine with a harshly brilliant light

GLARY *adj* GLARIER, GLARIEST glaring

GLASNOST *n* pl. -S a Soviet policy of open political discussion

GLASS *v* -ED, -ING, -ES to encase in glass (a transparent substance)

GLASSFUL *n* pl. -FULS as much as a drinking glass will hold

GLASSIE *n* pl. -S a type of playing marble

GLASSIER comparative of glassy

GLASSIEST superlative of glassy

GLASSILY *adv* in a glassy manner

GLASSINE *n* pl. -S a type of paper

GLASSMAN *n* pl. -MEN a glazier

GLASSY *adj* GLASSIER, GLASSIEST resembling glass

GLAUCOMA *n* pl. -S a disease of the eye

GLAUCOUS *adj* bluish green

GLAZE *v* GLAZED, GLAZING, GLAZES to fit windows with glass panes

GLAZER *n* pl. -S a glazier

GLAZIER *n* pl. -S one that glazes

GLAZIERY *n* pl. -ZIERIES the work of a glazier

GLAZING *n* pl. -S glaziery

GLAZY *adj* GLAZIER, GLAZIEST covered with a smooth, glossy coating

GLEAM *v* -ED, -ING, -S to shine with a soft radiance

GLEAMER *n* pl. -S one that gleams

GLEAMY *adj* GLEAMIER, GLEAMIEST gleaming

GLEAN *v* -ED, -ING, -S to gather little by little

GLEANER *n* pl. -S one that gleans

GLEANING *n* pl. -S something that is gleaned

GLEBA *n* pl. -BAE a spore-bearing mass of some fungi

GLEBE *n* pl. -S the soil or earth

GLED *n* pl. -S glede

GLEDE *n* pl. -S a bird of prey

GLEE *n* pl. -S an unaccompanied song

GLEED *n* pl. -S a glowing coal

GLEEFUL *adj* merry

GLEEK *v* -ED, -ING, -S to gibe

GLEEMAN *n* pl. -MEN a minstrel

GLEESOME *adj* gleeful

GLEET *v* -ED, -ING, -S to discharge mucus from the urethra

GLEETY *adj* GLEETIER, GLEETIEST resembling mucus

GLEG *adj* alert **GLEGLY** *adv*

GLEGNESS *n* pl. -ES alertness

GLEN *n* pl. -S a small valley **GLENLIKE** *adj*

GLENOID *adj* having the shallow or slightly cupped form of a bone socket

GLEY *n* pl. GLEYS a clay soil layer **GLEYED** *adj*

GLEYING *n* pl. -S development of gley

GLIA *n* pl. -S supporting tissue that binds nerve tissue

GLIADIN *n* pl. -S a simple protein

GLIADINE *n* pl. -S gliadin

GLIAL *adj* pertaining to the supporting tissue of the central nervous system

GLIB *adj* GLIBBER, GLIBBEST fluent **GLIBLY** *adv*

GLIBNESS *n* pl. -ES the quality of being glib

GLIDE *v* GLIDED, GLIDING, GLIDES to move effortlessly

GLIDER *n* pl. -S a type of aircraft

GLIFF *n* pl. -S a brief moment

GLIM *n* pl. -S a light or lamp

GLIME *v* GLIMED, GLIMING, GLIMES to glance slyly

GLIMMER *v* -ED, -ING, -S to shine faintly or unsteadily

GLIMPSE *v* GLIMPSED, GLIMPSING, GLIMPSES to see for an instant

GLIMPSER *n pl.* -S one that glimpses

GLINT *v* -ED, -ING, -S to glitter

GLIOMA *n pl.* -MAS or -MATA a type of tumor

GLISSADE *v* -SADED, -SADING, -SADES to perform a gliding dance step

GLISTEN *v* -ED, -ING, -S to shine by reflection

GLISTER *v* -ED, -ING, -S to glisten

GLITCH *n pl.* -ES a malfunction

GLITCHY *adj* characterized by glitches

GLITTER *v* -ED, -ING, -S to sparkle

GLITTERY *adj* glittering

GLITZ *n pl.* -ES gaudy showiness

GLITZY *adj* GLITZIER, GLITZIEST showy

GLOAM *n pl.* -S twilight

GLOAMING *n pl.* -S twilight

GLOAT *v* -ED, -ING, -S to regard with great or excessive satisfaction

GLOATER *n pl.* -S one that gloats

GLOB *n pl.* -S a rounded mass

GLOBAL *adj* spherical **GLOBALLY** *adv*

GLOBATE *adj* spherical

GLOBATED *adj* spherical

GLOBBY *adj* -BIER, -BIEST full of globs

GLOBE *v* GLOBED, GLOBING, GLOBES to form into a perfectly round body

GLOBIN *n pl.* -S a simple protein

GLOBOID *n pl.* -S a spheroid

GLOBOSE *adj* spherical

GLOBOUS *adj* spherical

GLOBULAR *adj* spherical

GLOBULE *n pl.* -S a small spherical mass

GLOBULIN *n pl.* -S a simple protein

GLOCHID *n pl.* -S a barbed hair on some plants

GLOGG *n pl.* -S an alcoholic beverage

GLOM *v* GLOMMED, GLOMMING, GLOMS to steal

GLOMUS *n pl.* -MERA a type of vascular tuft

GLONOIN *n pl.* -S nitroglycerin

GLOOM *v* -ED, -ING, -S to become dark

GLOOMFUL *adj* gloomy

GLOOMING *n pl.* -S gloaming

GLOOMY *adj* GLOOMIER, GLOOMIEST dismally dark **GLOOMILY** *adv*

GLOP *v* GLOPPED, GLOPPING, GLOPS to cover with glop (a messy mass or mixture)

GLOPPY *adj* being or resembling glop

GLORIA *n pl.* -S a halo

GLORIED past tense of glory

GLORIES present 3d person sing. of glory

GLORIFY *v* -FIED, -FYING, -FIES to bestow honor or praise on

GLORIOLE *n pl.* -S a halo

GLORIOUS *adj* magnificent

GLORY *v* -RIED, -RYING, -RIES to rejoice proudly

GLOSS *v* -ED, -ING, -ES to make lustrous

GLOSSA *n pl.* -SAE or -SAS the tongue **GLOSSAL** *adj*

GLOSSARY *n pl.* -RIES a list of terms and their definitions

GLOSSEME *n pl.* -S the smallest linguistic unit that signals a meaning

GLOSSER *n pl.* -S one that glosses

GLOSSIER comparative of glossy

GLOSSIES pl. of glossy

GLOSSINA *n pl.* -S a tsetse fly

GLOSSY *adj* GLOSSIER, GLOSSIEST lustrous **GLOSSILY** *adv*

GLOSSY *n pl.* GLOSSIES a type of photograph

GLOST *n pl.* -S pottery that has been coated with a glassy surface

GLOTTIS *n pl.* -TISES or -TIDES the opening between the vocal cords **GLOTTAL, GLOTTIC** *adj*

GLOUT *v* -ED, -ING, -S to scowl

GLOVE *v* GLOVED, GLOVING, GLOVES to furnish with gloves (hand coverings)

GLOVER *n pl.* -S a maker or seller of gloves

GLOW *v* -ED, -ING, -S to emit light and heat

GLOWER *v* -ED, -ING, -S to scowl

GLOWFLY *n pl.* -FLIES a firefly

GLOWWORM *n pl.* -S a luminous insect

GLOXINIA *n pl.* -S a tropical plant

GLOZE *v* GLOZED, GLOZING, GLOZES to explain away

GLUCAGON *n pl.* -S a hormone

GLUCAN *n pl.* -S a polymer of glucose

GLUCINUM *n pl.* -S a metallic element **GLUCINIC** *adj*

GLUCOSE *n pl.* -S a sugar **GLUCOSIC** *adj*

GLUE   v GLUED, GLUING or GLUEING, GLUES to fasten with glue (an adhesive substance)

GLUELIKE   adj resembling glue

GLUEPOT   n pl. -S a pot for melting glue

GLUER   n pl. -S one that glues

GLUEY   adj GLUIER, GLUIEST resembling glue **GLUILY** adv

GLUG   v GLUGGED, GLUGGING, GLUGS to make a gurgling sound

GLUING   present participle of glue

GLUM   adj GLUMMER, GLUMMEST being in low spirits **GLUMLY** adv

GLUME   n pl. -S a bract on grassy plants

GLUMNESS   n pl. -ES the state of being glum

GLUMPY   adj GLUMPIER, GLUMPIEST glum **GLUMPILY** adv

GLUNCH   v -ED, -ING, -ES to frown

GLUON   n pl. -S a hypothetical massless particle binding quarks together

GLUT   v GLUTTED, GLUTTING, GLUTS to feed or fill to excess

GLUTEAL   adj of or pertaining to the buttock muscles

GLUTEI   pl. of gluteus

GLUTELIN   n pl. -S a plant protein

GLUTEN   n pl. -S a tough elastic plant protein substance

GLUTEUS   n pl. -TEI a buttock muscle

GLUTTED   past tense of glut

GLUTTING   present participle of glut

GLUTTON   n pl. -S a person who eats to excess

GLUTTONY   n pl. -TONIES excessive eating

GLYCAN   n pl. -S a carbohydrate

GLYCERIN   n pl. -S a glycerol **GLYCERIC** adj

GLYCEROL   n pl. -S a syrupy alcohol

GLYCERYL   n pl. -S a radical derived from glycerol

GLYCIN   n pl. -S a compound used in photography

GLYCINE   n pl. -S an amino acid

GLYCOGEN   n pl. -S a carbohydrate

GLYCOL   n pl. -S an alcohol **GLYCOLIC** adj

GLYCONIC   n pl. -S a type of verse line

GLYCOSYL   n pl. -S a radical derived from glucose

GLYCYL   n pl. -S a radical derived from glycine

GLYPH   n pl. -S an ornamental groove **GLYPHIC** adj

GLYPTIC   n pl. -S the art or process of engraving on gems

GNAR   v GNARRED, GNARRING, GNARS to snarl

GNARL   v -ED, -ING, -S to twist into a state of deformity

GNARLY   adj GNARLIER, GNARLIEST gnarled

GNARR   v -ED, -ING, -S to gnar

GNARRED   past tense of gnar

GNARRING   present participle of gnar

GNASH   v -ED, -ING, -ES to grind the teeth together

GNAT   n pl. -S a small winged insect

GNATHAL   adj gnathic

GNATHIC   adj of or pertaining to the jaw

GNATHION   n pl. -S the tip of the chin

GNATHITE   n pl. -S a jawlike appendage of an insect

GNATLIKE   adj resembling a gnat

GNATTY   adj -TIER, -TIEST infested with gnats

GNAW   v GNAWED, GNAWN, GNAWING, GNAWS to wear away by persistent biting **GNAWABLE** adj

GNAWER   n pl. -S one that gnaws

GNAWING   n pl. -S a persistent dull pain

GNAWN   a past participle of gnaw

GNEISS   n pl. -ES a type of rock **GNEISSIC** adj

GNOCCHI   n/pl dumplings made of pasta

GNOME   n pl. -S a dwarf

GNOMIC   adj resembling or containing aphorisms

GNOMICAL   adj gnomic

GNOMISH   adj resembling a gnome

GNOMIST   n pl. -S a writer of aphorisms

GNOMON   n pl. -S a part of a sundial **GNOMONIC** adj

GNOSIS   n pl. GNOSES mystical knowledge

GNOSTIC   adj possessing knowledge

GNU   n pl. -S a large antelope

GO   v WENT, GONE, GOING, GOES to move along

GOA   n pl. -S an Asian gazelle

GOAD   v -ED, -ING, -S to drive animals with a goad (a pointed stick)

GOADLIKE   adj resembling a goad

GOAL   *v* -ED, -ING, -S to score a goal (a point-scoring play in some games)

GOALIE   *n* pl. -S a player who defends against goals

GOALLESS   *adj* having no goal

GOALPOST   *n* pl. -S a post that marks a boundary of the scoring area in some games

GOALWARD   *adv* toward a goal (a point-scoring area)

GOANNA   *n* pl. -S a large monitor lizard

GOAT   *n* pl. -S a horned mammal

GOATEE   *n* pl. -S a small pointed beard **GOATEED** *adj*

GOATFISH   *n* pl. -ES a tropical fish

GOATHERD   *n* pl. -S one who tends goats

GOATISH   *adj* resembling a goat

GOATLIKE   *adj* goatish

GOATSKIN   *n* pl. -S the hide of a goat

GOB   *v* GOBBED, GOBBING, GOBS to fill a mine pit with waste material

GOBAN   *n* pl. -S gobang

GOBANG   *n* pl. -S a Japanese game

GOBBED   past tense of gob

GOBBET   *n* pl. -S a piece of raw meat

GOBBING   present participle of gob

GOBBLE   *v* -BLED, -BLING, -BLES to eat hastily

GOBBLER   *n* pl. -S a male turkey

GOBIES   pl. of goby

GOBIOID   *n* pl. -S a fish of the goby family

GOBLET   *n* pl. -S a drinking vessel

GOBLIN   *n* pl. -S an evil or mischievous creature

GOBO   *n* pl. -BOS or -BOES a device used to shield a microphone from extraneous sounds

GOBONEE   *adj* gobony

GOBONY   *adj* compony

GOBY   *n* pl. GOBIES a small fish

GOD   *v* GODDED, GODDING, GODS to treat as a god (a supernatural being)

GODCHILD   *n* pl. -CHILDREN one whom a person sponsors at baptism

GODDAM   *v* -DAMMED, -DAMMING, -DAMS goddamn

GODDAMN   *v* -ED, -ING, -S to damn

GODDED   past tense of god

GODDESS   *n* pl. -ES a female god

GODDING   present participle of god

GODET   *n* pl. -S insert of cloth in a seam

GODHEAD   *n* pl. -S godhood

GODHOOD   *n* pl. -S the state of being a god

GODLESS   *adj* worshiping no god

GODLIER   comparative of godly

GODLIEST   superlative of godly

GODLIKE   *adj* divine

GODLING   *n* pl. -S a lesser god

GODLY   *adj* -LIER, -LIEST pious **GODLILY** *adv*

GODOWN   *n* pl. -S an oriental warehouse

GODROON   *n* pl. -S gadroon

GODSEND   *n* pl. -S an unexpected boon

GODSHIP   *n* pl. -S the rank of a god

GODSON   *n* pl. -S a male godchild

GODWIT   *n* pl. -S a wading bird

GOER   *n* pl. -S one that goes

GOETHITE   *n* pl. -S an ore of iron

GOFER   *n* pl. -S an employee who runs errands

GOFFER   *v* -ED, -ING, -S to press ridges or pleats into

GOGGLE   *v* -GLED, -GLING, -GLES to stare with wide eyes

GOGGLER   *n* pl. -S one that goggles

GOGGLY   *adj* -GLIER, -GLIEST wide-eyed

GOGLET   *n* pl. -S a long-necked jar

GOGO   *n* pl. -GOS a discotheque

GOING   *n* pl. -S an advance toward an objective

GOITER   *n* pl. -S an enlargement of the thyroid gland **GOITROUS** *adj*

GOITRE   *n* pl. -S goiter

GOLCONDA   *n* pl. -S a source of great wealth

GOLD   *n* pl. -S a precious metallic element

GOLD   *adj* GOLDER, GOLDEST golden

GOLDARN   *n* pl. -S an expression of anger

GOLDBUG   *n* pl. -S a gold beetle

GOLDEN   *adj* -ENER, -ENEST of the color of gold **GOLDENLY** *adv*

GOLDEYE   *n* pl. -S a freshwater fish

GOLDFISH   *n* pl. -ES a freshwater fish

GOLDURN   *n* pl. -S goldarn

GOLEM   *n* pl. -S a legendary creature

GOLF   *v* -ED, -ING, -S to play golf (a type of ball game)

GOLFER   *n* pl. -S one that golfs

GOLFING   *n* pl. -S the game of golf

GOLGOTHA   *n* pl. -S a place of burial

GOLIARD   *n* pl. -S a wandering student

GOLLIWOG   *n* pl. -S a grotesque doll

GOLLY *interj* — used as a mild oath
GOLLYWOG *n pl.* -S golliwog
GOLOSH *n pl.* -ES galosh
GOLOSHE *n pl.* -S galosh
GOMBO *n pl.* -BOS gumbo
GOMBROON *n pl.* -S a kind of Persian pottery
GOMERAL *n pl.* -S a fool
GOMEREL *n pl.* -S gomeral
GOMERIL *n pl.* -S gomeral
GOMUTI *n pl.* -S a palm tree
GONAD *n pl.* -S a sex gland GONADAL, GONADIAL, GONADIC *adj*
GONDOLA *n pl.* -S a long, narrow boat
GONE *adj* departed
GONEF *n pl.* -S ganef
GONENESS *n pl.* -ES a state of exhaustion
GONER *n pl.* -S one who is in a hopeless situation
GONFALON *n pl.* -S a banner
GONFANON *n pl.* -S gonfalon
GONG *v* -ED, -ING, -S to make the sound of a gong (a disk-shaped percussion instrument)
GONGLIKE *adj* resembling a gong
GONIA *pl.* of gonion and of gonium
GONIDIUM *n pl.* -IA an asexual reproductive cell GONIDIAL, GONIDIC *adj*
GONIF *n pl.* -S ganef
GONIFF *n pl.* -S ganef
GONION *n pl.* -NIA a part of the lower jaw
GONIUM *n pl.* -NIA an immature reproductive cell
GONOCYTE *n pl.* -S a cell that produces gametes
GONOF *n pl.* -S ganef
GONOPH *n pl.* -S ganef
GONOPORE *n pl.* -S a genital pore
GONZO *adj* bizarre
GOO *n pl.* GOOS a sticky or viscid substance
GOOBER *n pl.* -S a peanut
GOOD *adj* BETTER, BEST having positive or desirable qualities
GOOD *n pl.* -S something that is good
GOODBY *n pl.* -BYS goodbye
GOODBYE *n pl.* -S a concluding remark or gesture at parting
GOODIE *n pl.* -S goody
GOODIES *pl.* of goody
GOODISH *adj* somewhat good
GOODLY *adj* -LIER, -LIEST of pleasing appearance

GOODMAN *n pl.* -MEN the master of a household
GOODNESS *n pl.* -ES the state of being good
GOODWIFE *n pl.* -WIVES the mistress of a household
GOODWILL *n pl.* -S an attitude of friendliness
GOODY *n pl.* GOODIES a desirable food
GOOEY *adj* GOOIER, GOOIEST sticky or viscid
GOOF *v* -ED, -ING, -S to blunder
GOOFBALL *n pl.* -S a sleeping pill
GOOFY *adj* GOOFIER, GOOFIEST silly GOOFILY *adv*
GOOGLY *n pl.* -GLIES a type of bowled ball in cricket
GOOGOL *n pl.* -S an enormous number
GOOIER *comparative* of gooey
GOOIEST *superlative* of gooey
GOOK *n pl.* -S goo GOOKY *adj*
GOOMBAH *n pl.* -S an older man who is a friend
GOOMBAY *n pl.* -BAYS calypso music of the Bahamas
GOON *n pl.* -S a hired thug
GOONEY *n pl.* -NEYS an albatross
GOONIE *n pl.* -S gooney
GOONY *n pl.* -NIES gooney
GOOP *n pl.* -S goo, gunk
GOOPY *adj* GOOPIER, GOOPIEST sticky, gooey
GOORAL *n pl.* -S goral
GOOSE *n pl.* GEESE a swimming bird
GOOSE *v* GOOSED, GOOSING, GOOSES to poke between the buttocks
GOOSEY *adj* GOOSIER, GOOSIEST goosy
GOOSY *adj* GOOSIER, GOOSIEST resembling a goose
GOPHER *n pl.* -S a burrowing rodent
GOR *interj* — used as a mild oath
GORAL *n pl.* -S a goat antelope
GORBELLY *n pl.* -LIES a potbelly
GORBLIMY *interj* blimey
GORCOCK *n pl.* -S the male red grouse
GORE *v* GORED, GORING, GORES to pierce with a horn or tusk
GORGE *v* GORGED, GORGING, GORGES to stuff with food GORGEDLY *adv*
GORGEOUS *adj* beautiful
GORGER *n pl.* -S one that gorges
GORGERIN *n pl.* -S a part of a column

GORGET n pl. -S a piece of armor for the throat **GORGETED** adj

GORGING present participle of gorge

GORGON n pl. -S an ugly woman

GORHEN n pl. -S the female red grouse

GORIER comparative of gory

GORIEST superlative of gory

GORILLA n pl. -S a large ape

GORILY adv in a gory manner

GORINESS n pl. -ES the state of being gory

GORING present participle of gore

GORMAND n pl. -S gourmand

GORMLESS adj stupid

GORP n pl. -S a snack for quick energy

GORSE n pl. -S furze

GORSY adj GORSIER, GORSIEST abounding in gorse

GORY adj GORIER, GORIEST bloody

GOSH interj — used as an exclamation of surprise

GOSHAWK n pl. -S a large hawk

GOSLING n pl. -S a young goose

GOSPEL n pl. -S the message concerning Christ, the kingdom of God, and salvation

GOSPELER n pl. -S one that teaches the gospel

GOSPORT n pl. -S a communication device in an airplane

GOSSAMER n pl. -S a fine film of cobwebs

GOSSAN n pl. -S a type of decomposed rock

GOSSIP v -SIPED, -SIPING, -SIPS or -SIPPED, -SIPPING, -SIPS to talk idly about the affairs of others

GOSSIPER n pl. -S one that gossips

GOSSIPRY n pl. -RIES the practice of gossiping

GOSSIPY adj inclined to gossip

GOSSOON n pl. -S a boy

GOSSYPOL n pl. -S a toxic pigment

GOT past tense of get

GOTHIC n pl. -S a style of printing

GOTHITE n pl. -S goethite

GOTTEN past participle of get

GOUACHE n pl. -S a method of painting

GOUGE v GOUGED, GOUGING, GOUGES to cut or scoop out

GOUGER n pl. -S one that gouges

GOULASH n pl. -ES a beef stew

GOURAMI n pl. -S or -ES a food fish

GOURD n pl. -S a hard-shelled fruit

GOURDE n pl. -S a monetary unit of Haiti

GOURMAND n pl. -S one who loves to eat

GOURMET n pl. -S a connoisseur of fine food and drink

GOUT n pl. -S a metabolic disease

GOUTY adj GOUTIER, GOUTIEST affected with gout **GOUTILY** adv

GOVERN v -ED, -ING, -S to rule or direct

GOVERNOR n pl. -S one that governs

GOWAN n pl. -S a daisy **GOWANED, GOWANY** adj

GOWD n pl. -S gold

GOWK n pl. -S a fool

GOWN v -ED, -ING, -S to dress in a gown (a long, loose outer garment)

GOWNSMAN n pl. -MEN a professional or academic person

GOX n pl. -ES gaseous oxygen

GRAAL n pl. -S grail

GRAB v GRABBED, GRABBING, GRABS to grasp suddenly

GRABBER n pl. -S one that grabs

GRABBIER comparative of grabby

GRABBIEST superlative of grabby

GRABBING present participle of grab

GRABBLE v -BLED, -BLING, -BLES to grope

GRABBLER n pl. -S one that grabbles

GRABBY adj -BIER, -BIEST tending to grab

GRABEN n pl. -S a depression of the earth's crust

GRACE v GRACED, GRACING, GRACES to give beauty to

GRACEFUL adj -FULLER, -FULLEST having beauty of form or movement

GRACILE adj gracefully slender

GRACILIS n pl. -LES a thigh muscle

GRACING present participle of grace

GRACIOSO n pl. -SOS a clown in Spanish comedy

GRACIOUS adj marked by kindness and courtesy

GRACKLE n pl. -S a blackbird

GRAD n pl. -S a graduate

GRADATE v -DATED, -DATING, -DATES to change by degrees

GRADE v GRADED, GRADING, GRADES to arrange in steps or degrees **GRADABLE** adj

GRADER n pl. -S one that grades

GRADIENT   n pl. -S a rate of inclination

GRADIN   n pl. -S gradine

GRADINE   n pl. -S one of a series of steps

GRADING   present participle of grade

GRADUAL   n pl. -S a hymn sung in alternate parts

GRADUAND   n pl. -S one who is about to graduate

GRADUATE   v -ATED, -ATING, -ATES to receive an academic degree or diploma

GRADUS   n pl. -ES a dictionary of prosody

GRAECIZE   v -CIZED, -CIZING, -CIZES to grecize

GRAFFITO   n pl. -TI an inscription or drawing made on a rock or wall

GRAFT   v -ED, -ING, -S to unite with a growing plant by insertion

GRAFTAGE   n pl. -S the process of grafting

GRAFTER   n pl. -S one that grafts

GRAHAM   n pl. -S whole-wheat flour

GRAIL   n pl. -S the object of a long quest

GRAIN   v -ED, -ING, -S to form into small particles

GRAINER   n pl. -S one that grains

GRAINY   adj GRAINIER, GRAINIEST granular

GRAM   pl. -S a unit of mass and weight

GRAMA   n pl. -S a pasture grass

GRAMARY   n pl. -RIES gramarye

GRAMARYE   n pl. -S occult learning; magic

GRAMERCY   n pl. -CIES an expression of gratitude

GRAMMAR   n pl. -S the study of the formal features of a language

GRAMME   n pl. -S gram

GRAMP   n pl. -S grandfather

GRAMPUS   n pl. -ES a marine mammal

GRAN   n pl. -S a grandmother

GRANA   pl. of granum

GRANARY   n pl. -RIES a storehouse for grain

GRAND   adj GRANDER, GRANDEST large and impressive

GRAND   n pl. -S a type of piano

GRANDAD   n pl. -S granddad

GRANDAM   n pl. -S a grandmother

GRANDAME   n pl. -S grandam

GRANDDAD   n pl. -S a grandfather

GRANDDAM   n pl. -S the female parent of an animal with offspring

GRANDEE   n pl. -S man of high social position

GRANDEUR   n pl. -S the state of being grand

GRANDKID   n pl. -S the child of one's son or daughter

GRANDLY   adv in a grand manner

GRANDMA   n pl. -S a grandmother

GRANDPA   n pl. -S a grandfather

GRANDSIR   n pl. -S a grandfather

GRANDSON   n pl. -S a son of one's son or daughter

GRANGE   n pl. -S a farm

GRANGER   n pl. -S a farmer

GRANITA   n pl. -S an iced dessert

GRANITE   n pl. -S a type of rock

GRANITIC adj

GRANNIE   n pl. -S granny

GRANNY   n pl. -NIES a grandmother

GRANOLA   n pl. -S a breakfast cereal

GRANT   v -ED, -ING, -S to bestow upon

GRANTEE   n pl. -S one to whom something is granted

GRANTER   n pl. -S one that grants

GRANTOR   n pl. -S granter

GRANULAR   adj composed of granules

GRANULE   n pl. -S a small particle

GRANUM   n pl. GRANA a part of a plant chloroplast

GRAPE   n pl. -S an edible berry

GRAPERY   n pl. -ERIES a vinery

GRAPEY   adj GRAPIER, GRAPIEST grapy

GRAPH   v -ED, -ING, -S to represent by means of a diagram

GRAPHEME   n pl. -S a unit of a writing system

GRAPHIC   n pl. -S a product of the art of representation

GRAPHITE   n pl. -S a variety of carbon

GRAPIER   comparative of grapy

GRAPIEST   superlative of grapy

GRAPLIN   n pl. -S a grapnel

GRAPLINE   n pl. -S graplin

GRAPNEL   n pl. -S a type of anchor

GRAPPA   n pl. -S an Italian brandy

GRAPPLE   v -PLED, -PLING, -PLES to struggle or contend

GRAPPLER   n pl. -S one that grapples

GRAPY   adj GRAPIER, GRAPIEST resembling grapes

GRASP   v -ED, -ING, -S to seize firmly with the hand

GRASPER   n pl. -S one that grasps

GRASS v -ED, -ING, -ES to cover with grass (herbaceous plants)

GRASSY adj GRASSIER, GRASSIEST of, resembling, or pertaining to grass **GRASSILY** adv

GRAT past tense of greet (to weep)

GRATE v GRATED, GRATING, GRATES to reduce to shreds by rubbing

GRATEFUL adj -FULLER, -FULLEST deeply thankful

GRATER n pl. -S one that grates

GRATIFY v -FIED, -FYING, -FIES to satisfy

GRATIN n pl. -S a type of food crust

GRATINE adj covered with a crust

GRATINEE adj gratine

GRATING n pl. -S a network of bars covering an opening

GRATIS adj free of charge

GRATUITY n pl. -ITIES a gift of money

GRAUPEL n pl. -S precipitation consisting of granular snow pellets

GRAVAMEN n pl. -MENS or -MINA the most serious part of an accusation

GRAVE adj GRAVER, GRAVEST extremely serious

GRAVE v GRAVED, GRAVEN, GRAVING, GRAVES to engrave

GRAVEL v -ELED, -ELING, -ELS or -ELLED, -ELLING, -ELS to pave with gravel (a mixture of rock fragments)

GRAVELLY adj containing gravel

GRAVELY adv in a grave manner

GRAVEN past participle of grave

GRAVER n pl. -S an engraver

GRAVEST superlative of grave

GRAVID adj pregnant **GRAVIDLY** adv

GRAVIDA n pl. -DAS or -DAE a pregnant woman

GRAVIES pl. of gravy

GRAVING present participle of grave

GRAVITAS n pl. -ES reserved, dignified behavior

GRAVITON n pl. -S a hypothetical particle

GRAVITY n pl. -TIES the force of attraction toward the earth's center

GRAVLAKS n pl. GRAVLAKS gravlax

GRAVLAX n pl. GRAVLAX cured salmon

GRAVURE n pl. -S a printing process

GRAVY n pl. -VIES a sauce of the fat and juices from cooked meat

GRAY adj GRAYER, GRAYEST of a color between white and black

GRAY v -ED, -ING, -S to make gray

GRAYBACK n pl. -S a gray bird

GRAYFISH n pl. -ES a dogfish

GRAYISH adj somewhat gray

GRAYLAG n pl. -S a wild goose

GRAYLING n pl. -S a food fish

GRAYLY adv in a gray manner

GRAYMAIL n pl. -S pressure on an official to reveal sensitive information

GRAYNESS n pl. -ES the state of being gray

GRAYOUT n pl. -S a temporary blurring of vision

GRAZE v GRAZED, GRAZING, GRAZES to feed on growing grass **GRAZABLE** adj

GRAZER n pl. -S one that grazes

GRAZIER n pl. -S one that grazes cattle

GRAZING n pl. -S land used for the feeding of animals

GRAZIOSO adj graceful in style

GREASE v GREASED, GREASING, GREASES to smear with grease (a lubricating substance)

GREASER n pl. -S one that greases

GREASY adj GREASIER, GREASIEST containing or resembling grease **GREASILY** adv

GREAT adj GREATER, GREATEST large

GREAT n pl. -S a distinguished or outstanding person

GREATEN v -ED, -ING, -S to make greater

GREATLY adv in a great manner

GREAVE n pl. -S a piece of armor for the leg **GREAVED** adj

GREBE n pl. -S a diving bird

GRECIZE v -CIZED, -CIZING, -CIZES to provide with a Greek style

GREE v GREED, GREEING, GREES to agree

GREED n pl. -S excessive desire for gain or wealth

GREEDY adj GREEDIER, GREEDIEST marked by greed **GREEDILY** adv

GREEGREE n pl. -S grigri

GREEK n pl. GREEK something unintelligible

GREEN adj GREENER, GREENEST of the color of growing foliage

GREEN v -ED, -ING, -S to become green
GREENBUG n pl. -S a green aphid
GREENERY n pl. -ERIES green vegetation
GREENFLY n pl. -FLIES a green aphid
GREENIE n pl. -S an amphetamine pill
GREENIER comparative of greeny
GREENIEST superlative of greeny
GREENING n pl. -S a variety of apple
GREENISH adj somewhat green
GREENLET n pl. -S a vireo
GREENLY adv in a green manner
GREENTH n pl. -S verdure
GREENWAY n pl. -WAYS piece of undeveloped land in a city
GREENY adj GREENIER, GREENIEST somewhat green
GREET v -ED, -ING, -S to address in a friendly and courteous way
GREET v GRAT, GRUTTEN, GREETING, GREETS to weep
GREETER n pl. -S one that greets
GREETING n pl. -S a salutation
GREGO n pl. -GOS a hooded coat
GREIGE n pl. -S fabric in an unfinished state
GREISEN n pl. -S a type of rock
GREMIAL n pl. -S a lap cloth used by a bishop during a service
GREMLIN n pl. -S a mischievous creature
GREMMIE n pl. -S an inexperienced surfer
GREMMY n pl. -MIES gremmie
GRENADE n pl. -S an explosive device
GREW past tense of grow
GREWSOME adj -SOMER, -SOMEST gruesome
GREY adj GREYER, GREYEST gray
GREY v -ED, -ING, -S to gray
GREYHEN n pl. -S the female black grouse
GREYISH adj grayish
GREYLAG n pl. -S graylag
GREYLY adv grayly
GREYNESS n pl. -ES grayness
GRIBBLE n pl. -S a marine isopod
GRID n pl. -S a grating
GRIDDER n pl. -S a football player
GRIDDLE v -DLED, -DLING, -DLES to cook on a flat pan
GRIDE v GRIDED, GRIDING, GRIDES to scrape harshly
GRIDIRON n pl. -S a grate for broiling food
GRIDLOCK n pl. -S a traffic jam

GRIEF n pl. -S intense mental distress
GRIEVANT n pl. -S one that submits a complaint for arbitration
GRIEVE v GRIEVED, GRIEVING, GRIEVES to feel grief
GRIEVER n pl. -S one that grieves
GRIEVOUS adj causing grief
GRIFF n pl. -S griffe
GRIFFE n pl. -S the offspring of a black person and a mulatto
GRIFFIN n pl. -S a mythological creature
GRIFFON n pl. -S griffin
GRIFT v -ED, -ING, -S to swindle
GRIFTER n pl. -S a swindler
GRIG n pl. -S a lively person
GRIGRI n pl. -S a fetish or amulet
GRILL v -ED, -ING, -S to broil on a gridiron
GRILLADE n pl. -S a dish of grilled meat
GRILLAGE n pl. -S a framework of timber
GRILLE n pl. -S a grating
GRILLER n pl. -S one that grills
GRILSE n pl. -S a young salmon
GRIM adj GRIMMER, GRIMMEST stern and unrelenting
GRIMACE v -MACED, -MACING, -MACES to contort the facial features
GRIMACER n pl. -S one that grimaces
GRIME v GRIMED, GRIMING, GRIMES to make dirty
GRIMIER comparative of grimy
GRIMIEST superlative of grimy
GRIMILY adv in a grimy manner
GRIMING present participle of grime
GRIMLY adv in a grim manner
GRIMMER comparative of grim
GRIMMEST superlative of grim
GRIMNESS n pl. -ES the quality of being grim
GRIMY adj GRIMIER, GRIMIEST dirty
GRIN v GRINNED, GRINNING, GRINS to smile broadly
GRINCH n pl. -ES one who spoils the fun of others
GRIND v GROUND or GRINDED, GRINDING, GRINDS to wear, smooth, or sharpen by friction
GRINDER n pl. -S one that grinds
GRINDERY n pl. -ERIES a place where tools are ground
GRINNED past tense of grin
GRINNER n pl. -S one that grins
GRINNING present participle of grin

GRIOT *n* pl. -S a tribal entertainer in West Africa

GRIP *v* GRIPPED or GRIPT, GRIPPING, GRIPS to grasp

GRIPE *v* GRIPED, GRIPING, GRIPES to grasp

GRIPER *n* pl. -S one that gripes

GRIPEY *adj* GRIPIER, GRIPIEST gripy

GRIPIER comparative of gripy

GRIPIEST superlative of gripy

GRIPING present participle of gripe

GRIPMAN *n* pl. -MEN a cable car operator

GRIPPE *n* pl. -S a virus disease

GRIPPED a past tense of grip

GRIPPER *n* pl. -S one that grips

GRIPPIER comparative of grippy

GRIPPIEST superlative of grippy

GRIPPING present participle of grip

GRIPPLE *adj* greedy

GRIPPY *adj* GRIPPIER, GRIPPIEST affected with the grippe

GRIPSACK *n* pl. -S a valise

GRIPT a past tense of grip

GRIPY *adj* GRIPIER, GRIPIEST causing sharp pains in the bowels

GRISEOUS *adj* grayish

GRISETTE *n* pl. -S a young French working-class girl

GRISKIN *n* pl. -S the lean part of a loin of pork

GRISLY *adj* -LIER, -LIEST horrifying

GRISON *n* pl. -S a carnivorous mammal

GRIST *n* pl. -S grain for grinding

GRISTLE *n* pl. -S the tough part of meat

GRISTLY *adj* -TLIER, -TLIEST containing gristle

GRIT *v* GRITTED, GRITTING, GRITS to press the teeth together

GRITH *n* pl. -S sanctuary for a limited period of time

GRITTY *adj* -TIER, -TIEST plucky **GRITTILY** *adv*

GRIVET *n* pl. -S a small monkey

GRIZZLE *v* -ZLED, -ZLING, -ZLES to complain

GRIZZLER *n* pl. -S one that grizzles

GRIZZLY *adj* -ZLIER, -ZLIEST grayish

GRIZZLY *n* pl. -ZLIES a large bear

GROAN *v* -ED, -ING, -S to utter a low, mournful sound

GROANER *n* pl. -S one that groans

GROAT *n* pl. -S an old English coin

GROCER *n* pl. -S a dealer in foodstuffs and household supplies

GROCERY *n* pl. -CERIES a grocer's store

GROG *n* pl. -S a mixture of liquor and water

GROGGERY *n* pl. -GERIES a barroom

GROGGY *adj* -GIER, -GIEST dazed **GROGGILY** *adv*

GROGRAM *n* pl. -S a coarse silk fabric

GROGSHOP *n* pl. -S a groggery

GROIN *v* -ED, -ING, -S to build with intersecting arches

GROMMET *n* pl. -S a reinforcing ring of metal

GROMWELL *n* pl. -S an herb

GROOM *v* -ED, -ING, -S to clean and care for

GROOMER *n* pl. -S one that grooms

GROOVE *v* GROOVED, GROOVING, GROOVES to form a groove (a long, narrow depression)

GROOVER *n* pl. -S one that grooves

GROOVY *adj* GROOVIER, GROOVIEST marvelous

GROPE *v* GROPED, GROPING, GROPES to feel about with the hands

GROPER *n* pl. -S one that gropes

GROSBEAK *n* pl. -S a finch

GROSCHEN *n* pl. GROSCHEN an Austrian coin

GROSS *adj* GROSSER, GROSSEST flagrant

GROSS *v* -ED, -ING, -ES to earn exclusive of deductions

GROSSER *n* pl. -S a product yielding a large volume of business

GROSSLY *adv* in a gross manner

GROSZ *n* pl. GROSZY a Polish coin

GROSZE *n* pl. GROSZY grosz

GROT *n* pl. -S a grotto

GROTTO *n* pl. -TOES or -TOS a cave

GROTTY *adj* -TIER, -TIEST wretched

GROUCH *v* -ED, -ING, -ES to complain

GROUCHY *adj* GROUCHIER, GROUCHIEST ill-tempered

GROUND *v* -ED, -ING, -S to place on a foundation

GROUNDER *n* pl. -S a type of batted baseball

GROUP *v* -ED, -ING, -S to arrange in a group (an assemblage of persons or things)

GROUPER *n* pl. -S a food fish

GROUPIE *n* pl. -S a female follower of rock groups

GROUPING n pl. -S a set of objects

GROUPOID n pl. -S a type of mathematical set

GROUSE v GROUSED, GROUSING, GROUSES to complain

GROUSER n pl. -S one that grouses

GROUT v -ED, -ING, -S to fill with a thin mortar

GROUTER n pl. -S one that grouts

GROUTY adj GROUTIER, GROUTIEST surly

GROVE n pl. -S a small forested area GROVED adj

GROVEL v -ELED, -ELING, -ELS or -ELLED, -ELLING, -ELS to crawl in an abject manner

GROVELER n pl. -S one that grovels

GROW v GREW, GROWN, GROWING, GROWS to cultivate GROWABLE adj

GROWER n pl. -S one that grows

GROWL v -ED, -ING, -S to utter a deep, harsh sound

GROWLER n pl. -S one that growls

GROWLY adj GROWLIER, GROWLIEST deep and harsh in speech

GROWN adj mature

GROWNUP n pl. -S a mature person

GROWTH n pl. -S development

GROWTHY adj GROWTHIER, GROWTHIEST fast-growing

GROYNE n pl. -S a structure built to protect a shore from erosion

GRUB v GRUBBED, GRUBBING, GRUBS to dig

GRUBBER n pl. -S one that grubs

GRUBBY adj -BIER, -BIEST dirty GRUBBILY adv

GRUBWORM n pl. -S the larva of some insects

GRUDGE v GRUDGED, GRUDGING, GRUDGES to be unwilling to give or admit

GRUDGER n pl. -S one that grudges

GRUE n pl. -S a shudder of fear

GRUEL v -ELED, -ELING, -ELS or -ELLED, -ELLING, -ELS to disable by hard work

GRUELER n pl. -S one that gruels

GRUELING n pl. -S an exhausting experience

GRUELLED a past tense of gruel

GRUELLER n pl. -S grueler

GRUELLING present participle of gruel

GRUESOME adj -SOMER, -SOMEST repugnant

GRUFF adj GRUFFER, GRUFFEST low and harsh in speech

GRUFF v -ED, -ING, -S to utter in a gruff voice

GRUFFIER comparative of gruffy

GRUFFIEST superlative of gruffy

GRUFFILY adv in a gruffy manner

GRUFFISH adj somewhat gruff

GRUFFLY adv in a gruff manner

GRUFFY adj GRUFFIER, GRUFFIEST gruff

GRUGRU n pl. -S a palm tree

GRUIFORM adj designating an order of birds

GRUM adj GRUMMER, GRUMMEST morose

GRUMBLE v -BLED, -BLING, -BLES to mutter in discontent GRUMBLY adj

GRUMBLER n pl. -S one that grumbles

GRUME n pl. -S a thick, viscid substance

GRUMMER comparative of grum

GRUMMEST superlative of grum

GRUMMET n pl. -S grommet

GRUMOSE adj grumous

GRUMOUS adj consisting of clustered grains

GRUMP v -ED, -ING, -S to complain

GRUMPHIE n pl. -S a pig

GRUMPHY n pl. GRUMPHIES grumphie

GRUMPISH adj grumpy

GRUMPY adj GRUMPIER, GRUMPIEST ill-tempered GRUMPILY adv

GRUNGE n pl. -S dirt

GRUNGY adj -GIER, -GIEST dirty

GRUNION n pl. -S a small food fish

GRUNT v -ED, -ING, -S to utter a deep, guttural sound

GRUNTER n pl. -S one that grunts

GRUNTLE v -TLED, -TLING, -TLES to put in a good humor

GRUSHIE adj thriving

GRUTCH v -ED, -ING, -ES to grudge

GRUTTEN past participle of greet (to weep)

GRUYERE n pl. -S a Swiss cheese

GRYPHON n pl. -S griffin

GUACHARO n pl. -ROS or -ROES a tropical bird

GUACO n pl. -COS a tropical plant

GUAIAC n pl. -S guaiacum

GUAIACOL n pl. -S a chemical compound

GUAIACUM n pl. -S a medicinal resin

GUAIOCUM *n* pl. -S guaiacum
GUAN *n* pl. -S a large bird
GUANACO *n* pl. -COS a South American mammal
GUANASE *n* pl. -S án enzyme
GUANAY *n* pl. -NAYS a Peruvian cormorant
GUANIDIN *n* pl. -S a chemical compound
GUANIN *n* pl. -S guanine
GUANINE *n* pl. -S a chemical compound
GUANO *n* pl. -NOS the accumulated excrement of sea birds
GUAR *n* pl. -S a drought-tolerant legume
GUARANI *n* pl. -NIS or -NIES a monetary unit of Paraguay
GUARANTY *v* -TIED, -TYING, -TIES to assume responsibility for the quality of
GUARD *v* -ED, -ING, -S to protect
GUARDANT *n* pl. -S a guardian
GUARDER *n* pl. -S one that guards
GUARDIAN *n* pl. -S one that guards
GUAVA *n* pl. -S a tropical shrub
GUAYULE *n* pl. -S a shrub that is a source of rubber
GUCK *n* pl. -S a messy substance
GUDE *n* pl. -S good
GUDGEON *v* -ED, -ING, -S to dupe
GUENON *n* pl. -S a long-tailed monkey
GUERDON *v* -ED, -ING, -S to reward
GUERIDON *n* pl. -S a small stand or table
GUERILLA *n* pl. -S a member of a small independent band of soldiers
GUERNSEY *n* pl. -SEYS a woolen shirt
GUESS *v* -ED, -ING, -ES to form an opinion from little or no evidence
GUESSER *n* pl. -S one that guesses
GUEST *v* -ED, -ING, -S to appear as a visitor
GUFF *n* pl. -S foolish talk
GUFFAW *v* -ED, -ING, -S to laugh loudly
GUGGLE *v* -GLED, -GLING, -GLES to gurgle
GUGLET *n* pl. -S goglet
GUID *n* pl. -S good
GUIDANCE *n* pl. -S advice
GUIDE *v* GUIDED, GUIDING, GUIDES to show the way to **GUIDABLE** *adj*
GUIDER *n* pl. -S one that guides
GUIDEWAY *n* pl. -WAYS a track for controlling the line of motion of something
GUIDON *n* pl. -S a small flag

GUILD *n* pl. -S an association of people of the same trade
GUILDER *n* pl. -S a monetary unit of the Netherlands
GUILE *v* GUILED, GUILING, GUILES to beguile
GUILEFUL *adj* cunning
GUILT *n* pl. -S the fact of having committed an offense
GUILTY *adj* GUILTIER, GUILTIEST worthy of blame for an offense **GUILTILY** *adv*
GUIMPE *n* pl. -S a short blouse
GUINEA *n* pl. -S a former British coin
GUIPURE *n* pl. -S a type of lace
GUIRO *n* pl. -ROS a percussion instrument
GUISARD *n* pl. -S a masker
GUISE *v* GUISED, GUISING, GUISES to disguise
GUITAR *n* pl. -S a stringed musical instrument
GUITGUIT *n* pl. -S a tropical American bird
GUL *n* pl. -S a design in oriental carpets
GULAG *n* pl. -S a forced-labor camp
GULAR *adj* of or pertaining to the throat
GULCH *n* pl. -ES a deep, narrow ravine
GULDEN *n* pl. -S a guilder
GULES *n* pl. GULES the color red
GULF *v* -ED, -ING, -S to swallow up
GULFIER comparative of gulfy
GULFIEST superlative of gulfy
GULFLIKE *adj* resembling a deep chasm
GULFWEED *n* pl. -S a brownish seaweed
GULFY *adj* GULFIER, GULFIEST full of whirlpools
GULL *v* -ED, -ING, -S to deceive
GULLABLE *adj* gullible **GULLABLY** *adv*
GULLET *n* pl. -S the throat
GULLEY *n* pl. -LEYS a ravine
GULLIBLE *adj* easily deceived **GULLIBLY** *adv*
GULLY *v* -LIED, -LYING, -LIES to form ravines by the action of water
GULOSITY *n* pl. -TIES gluttony
GULP *v* -ED; -ING, -S to swallow rapidly
GULPER *n* pl. -S one that gulps
GULPY *adj* GULPIER, GULPIEST marked by gulping

GUM   v GUMMED, GUMMING, GUMS to smear, seal, or clog with gum (a sticky, viscid substance)

GUMBO   n pl. -BOS the okra plant

GUMBOIL   n pl. -S an abscess in the gum

GUMBOOT   n pl. -S a rubber boot

GUMBOTIL   n pl. -S a sticky clay

GUMDROP   n pl. -S a chewy candy

GUMLESS   adj having no gum

GUMLIKE   adj resembling gum

GUMMA   n pl. -MAS or -MATA a soft tumor

GUMMED   past tense of gum

GUMMER   n pl. -S one that gums

GUMMIER   comparative of gummy

GUMMIEST   superlative of gummy

GUMMING   present participle of gum

GUMMITE   n pl. -S a mixture of various minerals

GUMMOSE   adj gummy

GUMMOSIS   n pl. -MOSES a disease of plants

GUMMOUS   adj gummy

GUMMY   adj -MIER, -MIEST resembling gum

GUMPTION   n pl. -S shrewdness

GUMSHOE   v -SHOED, -SHOEING, -SHOES to investigate stealthily

GUMTREE   n pl. -S a tree that yields gum

GUMWEED   n pl. -S a plant covered with a gummy substance

GUMWOOD   n pl. -S the wood of a gumtree

GUN   v GUNNED, GUNNING, GUNS to shoot with a gun (a portable firearm)

GUNBOAT   n pl. -S an armed vessel

GUNDOG   n pl. -S a hunting dog

GUNFIGHT   v -FOUGHT, -FIGHTING, -FIGHTS to fight with guns

GUNFIRE   n pl. -S the firing of guns

GUNFLINT   n pl. -S the flint in a flintlock

GUNFOUGHT   past tense of gunfight

GUNITE   n pl. -S a mixture of cement, sand, and water

GUNK   n pl. -S filthy, sticky, or greasy matter GUNKY adj

GUNKHOLE   v -HOLED, -HOLING, -HOLES to make a series of short boat trips

GUNLESS   adj having no gun

GUNLOCK   n pl. -S the mechanism which ignites the charge of a gun

GUNMAN   n pl. -MEN one who is armed with a gun

GUNMETAL   n pl. -S a dark gray color

GUNNED   past tense of gun

GUNNEL   n pl. -S a marine fish

GUNNEN   past participle of gin

GUNNER   n pl. -S one that operates a gun

GUNNERY   n pl. -NERIES the use of guns

GUNNING   n pl. -S the sport of hunting with a gun

GUNNY   n pl. -NIES a coarse fabric

GUNNYBAG   n pl. -S a bag made of gunny

GUNPAPER   n pl. -S a type of explosive paper

GUNPLAY   n pl. -PLAYS the shooting of guns

GUNPOINT   n pl. -S the point or aim of a gun

GUNROOM   n pl. -S a room on a British warship

GUNSEL   n pl. -S a gunman

GUNSHIP   n pl. -S an armed helicopter

GUNSHOT   n pl. -S a projectile fired from a gun

GUNSMITH   n pl. -S one who makes or repairs firearms

GUNSTOCK   n pl. -S the rear wooden part of a rifle

GUNWALE   n pl. -S the upper edge of a ship's side

GUPPY   n pl. -PIES a small, tropical fish

GURGE   v GURGED, GURGING, GURGES to swirl

GURGLE   v -GLED, -GLING, -GLES to flow unevenly

GURGLET   n pl. -S goglet

GURNARD   n pl. -S a marine fish

GURNET   n pl. -S a gurnard

GURNEY   n pl. -NEYS a wheeled cot

GURRY   n pl. -RIES fish offal

GURSH   n pl. -ES qursh

GURU   n pl. -S a Hindu spiritual teacher

GURUSHIP   n pl. -S the office of a guru

GUSH   v -ED, -ING, -ES to flow forth forcefully

GUSHER   n pl. -S a gushing oil well

GUSHY   adj GUSHIER, GUSHIEST overly sentimental GUSHILY adv

GUSSET   v -ED, -ING, -S to furnish with a reinforcing piece of material

GUSSIE   v -SIED, -SYING, -SIES gussy

GUSSY   v -SIED, -SYING, -SIES to dress up in fine or showy clothes

GUST	v -ED, -ING, -S to blow in gusts (sudden blasts of wind)	**GYMNAST**	n pl. -S one who is skilled in physical exercises
GUSTABLE	n pl. -S a savory food	**GYNAECEA**	n/pl gynecia
GUSTIER	comparative of gusty	**GYNAECIA**	n/pl gynecia
GUSTIEST	superlative of gusty	**GYNANDRY**	n pl. -DRIES the condition of
GUSTILY	adv in a gusty manner		having both male and female
GUSTLESS	adj having no gusts		sexual organs
GUSTO	n pl. -TOES vigorous enjoyment	**GYNARCHY**	n pl. -CHIES government by women
GUSTY	adj GUSTIER, GUSTIEST blowing in gusts	**GYNECIC**	adj pertaining to women
		GYNECIUM	n pl. -CIA the pistil of a flower
GUT	v GUTTED, GUTTING, GUTS to remove the guts (intestines) of	**GYNECOID**	adj resembling a woman
		GYNIATRY	n pl. -TRIES the treatment of women's diseases
GUTLESS	adj lacking courage	**GYNOECIA**	n/pl gynecia
GUTLIKE	adj resembling guts	**GYP**	v GYPPED, GYPPING, GYPS to swindle
GUTSILY	adv in a gutsy manner		
GUTSY	adj GUTSIER, GUTSIEST brave	**GYPLURE**	n pl. -S a synthetic attractant to trap gypsy moths
GUTTA	n pl. -TAE a drop of liquid	**GYPPER**	n pl. -S one that gyps
GUTTATE	adj resembling a drop	**GYPSEIAN**	adj of or pertaining to gypsies
GUTTATED	adj guttate	**GYPSEOUS**	adj containing gypsum
GUTTED	past tense of gut	**GYPSTER**	n pl. -S one that gyps
GUTTER	v -ED, -ING, -S to form channels for draining off water	**GYPSUM**	n pl. -S a mineral
		GYPSY	v -SIED, -SYING, -SIES to live like a gypsy (a wanderer)
GUTTERY	adj marked by extreme vulgarity or indecency	**GYPSYDOM**	n pl. -S the realm of gypsies
GUTTIER	comparative of gutty	**GYPSYISH**	adj resembling a gypsy
GUTTIEST	superlative of gutty	**GYPSYISM**	n pl. -S the mode of life of gypsies
GUTTING	present participle of gut		
GUTTLE	v -TLED, -TLING, -TLES to eat rapidly	**GYRAL**	adj gyratory **GYRALLY** adv
		GYRASE	n pl. -S an enzyme
GUTTLER	n pl. -S one that guttles	**GYRATE**	v -RATED, -RATING, -RATES to revolve or rotate
GUTTURAL	n pl. -S a throaty sound		
GUTTY	adj -TIER, -TIEST marked by courage	**GYRATION**	n pl. -S the act of gyrating
		GYRATOR	n pl. -S one that gyrates
GUV	n pl. -S a governor	**GYRATORY**	adj moving in a circle or spiral
GUY	v -ED, -ING, -S to ridicule	**GYRE**	v GYRED, GYRING, GYRES to move in a circle or spiral
GUYOT	n pl. -S a flat-topped seamount		
		GYRENE	n pl. -S a marine
GUZZLE	v -ZLED, -ZLING, -ZLES to drink rapidly	**GYRI**	pl. of gyrus
		GYRING	present participle of gyre
GUZZLER	n pl. -S one that guzzles	**GYRO**	n pl. -ROS a gyroscope
GWEDUC	n pl. -S geoduck	**GYROIDAL**	adj spiral in arrangement
GWEDUCK	n pl. -S geoduck	**GYRON**	n pl. -S a heraldic design
GYBE	v GYBED, GYBING, GYBES to shift from side to side while sailing	**GYROSE**	adj marked with wavy lines
		GYROSTAT	n pl. -S a type of stabilizing device
GYM	n pl. -S a room for athletic activities	**GYRUS**	n pl. -RI a ridge in the brain
GYMKHANA	n pl. -S an athletic meet	**GYVE**	v GYVED, GYVING, GYVES to shackle
GYMNASIA	n/pl gyms		

HA	*n* pl. -S a sound of surprise
HAAF	*n* pl. -S a deep-sea fishing ground
HAAR	*n* pl. -S a fog
HABANERA	*n* pl. -S a Cuban dance
HABDALAH	*n* pl. -S a Jewish ceremony
HABILE	*adj* skillful
HABIT	*v* -ED, -ING, -S to clothe or dress
HABITAN	*n* pl. -S a French settler
HABITANT	*n* pl. -S an inhabitant
HABITAT	*n* pl. -S the natural environment of an organism
HABITUAL	*adj* occurring frequently or constantly
HABITUDE	*n* pl. -S a usual course of action
HABITUE	*n* pl. -S a frequent customer
HABITUS	*n* pl. HABITUS bodily build and constitution
HABOOB	*n* pl. -S a violent sandstorm
HABU	*n* pl. -S a poisonous snake
HACEK	*n* pl. -S a mark placed over a letter to modify it
HACHURE	*v* -CHURED, -CHURING, -CHURES to make a hatching on a map
HACIENDA	*n* pl. -S an estate
HACK	*v* -ED, -ING, -S to cut or chop roughly
HACKBUT	*n* pl. -S a type of gun
HACKEE	*n* pl. -S a chipmunk
HACKER	*n* pl. -S one that hacks
HACKIE	*n* pl. -S a taxicab driver
HACKLE	*v* -LED, -LING, -LES to hack
HACKLER	*n* pl. -S one that hackles
HACKLY	*adj* -LIER, -LIEST jagged
HACKMAN	*n* pl. -MEN a hackie
HACKNEY	*v* -NEYED, -NEYING, -NEYS to make common
HACKSAW	*n* pl. -S a type of saw
HACKWORK	*n* pl. -S artistic work done according to formula
HAD	a past tense of have
HADAL	*adj* pertaining to deep parts of the ocean
HADARIM	a pl. of heder
HADDEST	a past 2d person sing. of have
HADDOCK	*n* pl. -S a food fish
HADE	*v* HADED, HADING, HADES to incline
HADITH	*n* pl. HADITH or HADITHS a record of the sayings of Muhammed
HADJ	*n* pl. -ES a pilgrimage to Mecca
HADJEE	*n* pl. -S hadji
HADJI	*n* pl. -S one who has made a hadj
HADRON	*n* pl. -S an elementary particle **HADRONIC** *adj*
HADST	a past 2d person sing. of have
HAE	*v* HAED, HAEN, HAEING, HAES to have
HAEM	*n* pl. -S heme
HAEMAL	*adj* hemal
HAEMATAL	*adj* hemal
HAEMATIC	*n* pl. -S hematic
HAEMATIN	*n* pl. -S hematin
HAEMIC	*adj* hemic
HAEMIN	*n* pl. -S hemin
HAEMOID	*adj* hemoid
HAEN	past participle of hae
HAERES	*n* pl. -REDES heres
HAET	*n* pl. -S a small amount
HAFFET	*n* pl. -S the cheekbone and temple

HAFFIT   *n* pl. -S haffet
HAFIZ   *n* pl. HAFIS a Muslim who knows the Koran by heart
HAFNIUM   *n* pl. -S a metallic element
HAFT   *v* -ED, -ING, -S to supply with a handle
HAFTARA   *n* pl. -RAS, -ROT or -ROTH haphtara
HAFTARAH   *n* pl. -RAHS, -ROT or -ROTH haphtara
HAFTER   *n* pl. -S one that hafts
HAFTORAH   *n* pl. -RAHS, -ROT or -ROTH haphtara
HAG   *v* HAGGED, HAGGING, HAGS to hack
HAGADIC   *adj* haggadic
HAGADIST   *n* pl. -S a haggadic scholar
HAGBERRY   *n* pl. -RIES a small cherry
HAGBORN   *adj* born of a witch
HAGBUSH   *n* pl. -ES a large tree
HAGBUT   *n* pl. -S hackbut
HAGDON   *n* pl. -S a seabird
HAGFISH   *n* pl. -ES an eellike fish
HAGGADA   *n* pl. -DAS, -DOT or -DOTH haggadah
HAGGADAH   *n* pl. -DAHS, -DOT or -DOTH a biblical narrative **HAGGADIC** *adj*
HAGGARD   *n* pl. -S an adult hawk
HAGGED   past tense of hag
HAGGING   present participle of hag
HAGGIS   *n* pl. -GISES a Scottish dish
HAGGISH   *adj* resembling a hag
HAGGLE   *v* -GLED, -GLING, -GLES to bargain
HAGGLER   *n* pl. -S one that haggles
HAGRIDE   *v* -RODE, -RIDDEN, -RIDING, -RIDES to harass
HAH   *n* pl. -S ha.
HAHA   *n* pl. -S a fence set in a ditch
HAHNIUM   *n* pl. -S a radioactive element
HAIK   *n* pl. HAIKS or HAIKA an outer garment worn by Arabs
HAIKU   *n* pl. HAIKU a Japanese poem
HAIL   *v* -ED, -ING, -S to welcome
HAILER   *n* pl. -S one that hails
HAIR   *n* pl. -S a threadlike growth
HAIRBALL   *n* pl. -S a ball of hair
HAIRBAND   *n* pl. -S a headband
HAIRCAP   *n* pl. -S a hat
HAIRCUT   *n* pl. -S a cutting of the hair
HAIRDO   *n* pl. -DOS a style of wearing the hair
HAIRED   *adj* having hair
HAIRIER   comparative of hairy
HAIRIEST   superlative of hairy

HAIRLESS   *adj* having no hair
HAIRLIKE   *adj* resembling a hair
HAIRLINE   *n* pl. -S a very thin line
HAIRLOCK   *n* pl. -S a lock of hair
HAIRNET   *n* pl. -S a net worn to keep the hair in place
HAIRPIN   *n* pl. -S a hair fastener
HAIRWORK   *n* pl. -S the making of articles from hair
HAIRWORM   *n* pl. -S a parasitic worm
HAIRY   *adj* HAIRIER, HAIRIEST covered with hair
HAJ   *n* pl. -ES hadj
HAJI   *n* pl. -S hadji
HAJJ   *n* pl. -ES hadj
HAJJI   *n* pl. -S hadji
HAKE   *n* pl. -S a marine fish
HAKEEM   *n* pl. -S hakim
HAKIM   *n* pl. -S a Muslim physician
HALACHA   *n* pl. -CHAS or -CHOT halakah
HALAKAH   *n* pl. -KAHS or -KOTH the legal part of the Talmud
HALAKHA   *n* pl. -KHAS or -KHOT halakah
HALAKIC   *adj* pertaining to the halakah
HALAKIST   *n* pl. -S a halakic writer
HALAKOTH   a pl. of halakah
HALALA   *n* pl. -S a Saudi Arabian coin
HALALAH   *n* pl. -S halala
HALATION   *n* pl. -S a blurring of light in photographs
HALAVAH   *n* pl. -S halvah
HALAZONE   *n* pl.-S a disinfectant for drinking water
HALBERD   *n* pl. -S an axlike weapon of the 15th and 16th centuries
HALBERT   *n* pl. -S halberd
HALCYON   *n* pl. -S a mythical bird
HALE   *adj* HALER, HALEST healthy
HALE   *v* HALED, HALING, HALES to compel to go
HALENESS   *n* pl. -ES the state of being hale
HALER   *n* pl. -LERS or -LERU a coin of the Czech Republic
HALEST   superlative of hale
HALF   *n* pl. HALVES one of two equal parts
HALFBACK   *n* pl. -S a football player
HALFBEAK   *n* pl. -S a marine fish
HALFLIFE   *n* pl. -LIVES a measure of radioactive decay
HALFNESS   *n* pl. -ES the state of being half
HALFTIME   *n* pl. -S an intermission in a football game

HALFTONE *n* pl. -S a shade between light and dark

HALFWAY *adj* being in the middle

HALIBUT *n* pl. -S a flatfish

HALID *n* pl. -S halide

HALIDE *n* pl. -S a chemical compound

HALIDOM *n* pl. -S something holy

HALIDOME *n* pl. -S halidom

HALING present participle of hale

HALITE *n* pl. -S a mineral

HALITUS *n* pl. -ES an exhalation

HALL *n* pl. -S a large room for assembly

HALLAH *n* pl. -LAHS, -LOTH or -LOT challah

HALLEL *n* pl. -S a chant of praise

HALLIARD *n* pl. -S halyard

HALLMARK *v* -ED, -ING, -S to mark with an official stamp

HALLO *v* -ED, -ING, -S or -ES to shout

HALLOA *v* -ED, -ING, -S to hallo

HALLOO *v* -ED, -ING, -S to hallo

HALLOT a pl. of hallah

HALLOTH a pl. of hallah

HALLOW *v* -ED, -ING, -S to make holy

HALLOWER *n* pl. -S one that hallows

HALLUX *n* pl. -LUCES the big toe

HALLWAY *n* pl. -WAYS a hall

HALM *n* pl. -S haulm

HALMA *n* pl. -S a board game

HALO *v* -ED, -ING, -ES or -S to form a halo (a ring of light)

HALOGEN *n* pl. -S a nonmetallic element

HALOID *n* pl. -S a chemical salt

HALOLIKE *adj* resembling a halo

HALT *v* -ED, -ING, -S to stop

HALTER *v* -ED, -ING, -S to put restraint upon

HALTERE *n* pl. -S a pair of wings of an insect

HALTLESS *adj* not hesitant

HALUTZ *n* pl. -LUTZIM an Israeli farmer

HALVA *n* pl. -S halvah

HALVAH *n* pl. -S a Turkish confection

HALVE *v* HALVED, HALVING, HALVES to divide into two equal parts

HALVERS *n* pl. HALVERS half shares

HALVES pl. of half

HALVING present participle of halve

HALYARD *n* pl. -S a line used to hoist a sail

HAM *v* HAMMED, HAMMING, HAMS to overact

HAMADA *n* pl. -S hammada

HAMAL *n* pl. -S a porter in eastern countries

HAMARTIA *n* pl. -S a defect of character

HAMATE *n* pl. -S a wrist bone

HAMAUL *n* pl. -S hamal

HAMBONE *v* -BONED, -BONING, -BONES to overact

HAMBURG *n* pl. -S a patty of ground beef

HAME *n* pl. -S a part of a horse collar

HAMLET *n* pl. -S a small town

HAMMADA *n* pl. -S a desert plateau of bedrock

HAMMAL *n* pl. -S hamal

HAMMED past tense of ham

HAMMER *v* -ED, -ING, -S to strike repeatedly

HAMMERER *n* pl. -S one that hammers

HAMMIER comparative of hammy

HAMMIEST superlative of hammy

HAMMILY *adv* in a hammy manner

HAMMING present participle of ham

HAMMOCK *n* pl. -S a hanging cot

HAMMY *adj* -MIER, -MIEST overly theatrical

HAMPER *v* -ED, -ING, -S to hinder

HAMPERER *n* pl. -S one that hampers

HAMSTER *n* pl. -S a burrowing rodent

HAMULUS *n* pl. -LI a small hook HAMULAR, HAMULATE, HAMULOSE, HAMULOUS *adj*

HAMZA *n* pl. -S an Arabic diacritical mark

HAMZAH *n* pl. -S hamza

HANAPER *n* pl. -S a wicker receptacle

HANCE *n* pl. -S a side of an arch

HAND *v* -ED, -ING, -S to present with the hand (the end of the forearm)

HANDBAG *n* pl. -S a small carrying bag

HANDBALL *n* pl. -S a small rubber ball

HANDBELL *n* pl. -S a small bell with a handle

HANDBILL *n* pl. -S a circular

HANDBOOK *n* pl. -S a manual

HANDCAR *n* pl. -S a hand-operated railroad car

HANDCART *n* pl. -S a cart pushed by hand

HANDCUFF *v* -ED, -ING, -S to fetter with restraining cuffs

HANDFAST *v* -ED, -ING, -S to grip securely

HANDFUL *n* pl. HANDFULS or HANDSFUL as much as the hand can hold

HANDGRIP   n pl. -S a grip by the hand or hands
HANDGUN   n pl. -S a small firearm
HANDHELD   n pl. -S something held in the hand
HANDHOLD   n pl. -S a handgrip
HANDICAP   v -CAPPED, -CAPPING, -CAPS to hinder
HANDIER   comparative of handy
HANDIEST   superlative of handy
HANDILY   adv in a handy manner
HANDLE   v -DLED, -DLING, -DLES to touch with the hands
HANDLER   n pl. -S one that handles
HANDLESS   adj having no hands
HANDLIKE   adj resembling a hand
HANDLING   n pl. -S the manner in which something is handled
HANDLIST   n pl. -S a reference list
HANDLOOM   n pl. -S a manually operated loom
HANDMADE   adj made by hand
HANDMAID   n pl. -S a female servant
HANDOFF   n pl. -S a play in football
HANDOUT   n pl. -S something given out free
HANDOVER   n pl. -S an instance of giving up control
HANDPICK   v -ED, -ING, -S to choose carefully
HANDRAIL   n pl. -S a railing used for support
HANDSAW   n pl. -S a saw used manually
HANDSEL   v -SELED, -SELING, -SELS or -SELLED, -SELLING, -SELS to give a gift to
HANDSET   n pl. -S a type of telephone
HANDSEWN   adj sewn by hand
HANDSFUL   a pl. of handful
HANDSOME   adj -SOMER, -SOMEST attractive
HANDWORK   n pl. -S manual labor
HANDWRIT   adj written by hand
HANDY   adj HANDIER, HANDIEST convenient for handling
HANDYMAN   n pl. -MEN a man who does odd jobs
HANG   v HUNG or HANGED, HANGING, HANGS to attach from above only HANGABLE adj
HANGAR   v -ED, -ING, -S to place in an aircraft shelter
HANGBIRD   n pl. -S a type of bird
HANGDOG   n pl. -S a sneaky person
HANGER   n pl. -S one that hangs

HANGFIRE   n pl. -S a delay in detonation
HANGING   n pl. -S an execution by strangling with a suspended noose
HANGMAN   n pl. -MEN an executioner
HANGNAIL   n pl. -S an agnail
HANGNEST   n pl. -S a hangbird
HANGOUT   n pl. -S a place often visited
HANGOVER   n pl. -S the physical effects following a drinking binge
HANGTAG   n pl. -S a type of tag used commercially
HANGUL   n the Korean alphabetic script
HANGUP   n pl. -S an inhibition or obsession
HANIWA   n/pl Japanese clay sculptures
HANK   v -ED, -ING, -S to fasten a sail
HANKER   v -ED, -ING, -S to long for
HANKERER   n pl. -S one that hankers
HANKIE   n pl. -S hanky
HANKY   n pl. -KIES a handkerchief
HANSA   n pl. -S hanse
HANSE   n pl. -S a guild of merchants
HANSEL   v -SELED, -SELING, -SELS or -SELLED, -SELLING, -SELS to handsel
HANSOM   n pl. -S a light carriage
HANT   v -ED, -ING, -S to haunt
HANTLE   n pl. -S a large amount
HANUMAN   n pl. -S an East Indian monkey
HAO   n pl. HAO a monetary unit of Vietnam
HAP   v HAPPED, HAPPING, HAPS to happen
HAPAX   n pl. -ES a word that occurs only once
HAPHTARA   n pl. -RAS, -ROT or -ROTH a biblical selection
HAPLESS   adj luckless
HAPLITE   n pl. -S aplite
HAPLOID   n pl. -S a cell having only one set of chromosomes
HAPLOIDY   n pl. -DIES the state of being a haploid
HAPLONT   n pl. -S an organism having a particular chromosomal structure
HAPLOPIA   n pl. -S normal vision
HAPLOSIS   n pl. -LOSES the halving of the chromosome number
HAPLY   adv by chance
HAPPED   past tense of hap
HAPPEN   v -ED, -ING, -S to occur
HAPPING   present participle of hap

HAPPY *adj* -PIER, -PIEST marked by joy **HAPPILY** *adv*

HAPTEN *n* pl. -S a substance similar to an antigen **HAPTENIC** *adj*

HAPTENE *n* pl. -S hapten

HAPTIC *adj* pertaining to the sense of touch

HAPTICAL *adj* haptic

HARANGUE *v* -RANGUED, -RANGUING, -RANGUES to deliver a tirade to

HARASS *v* -ED, -ING, -ES to bother persistently

HARASSER *n* pl. -S one that harasses

HARBOR *v* -ED, -ING, -S to shelter

HARBORER *n* pl. -S one that harbors

HARBOUR *v* -ED, -ING, -S to harbor

HARD *adj* HARDER, HARDEST firm and unyielding

HARDBACK *n* pl. -S a hardcover book

HARDBALL *n* pl. -S baseball

HARDBOOT *n* pl. -S a horseman

HARDCASE *adj* tough

HARDCORE *adj* unyielding

HARDEDGE *n* pl. -S a geometric painting

HARDEN *v* -ED, -ING, -S to make hard

HARDENER *n* pl. -S one that hardens

HARDHACK *n* pl. -S a woody plant

HARDHAT *n* pl. -S a conservative

HARDHEAD *n* pl. -S a practical person

HARDIER comparative of hardy

HARDIES pl. of hardy

HARDIEST superlative of hardy

HARDILY *adv* in a hardy manner

HARDLINE *adj* unyielding

HARDLY *adv* scarcely

HARDNESS *n* pl. -ES the state of being hard

HARDNOSE *n* pl. -S a stubborn person

HARDPAN *n* pl. -S a layer of hard subsoil

HARDS *n/pl* the coarse refuse of flax

HARDSET *adj* rigid

HARDSHIP *n* pl. -S a difficult, painful condition

HARDTACK *n* pl. -S a hard biscuit

HARDTOP *n* pl. -S a type of car

HARDWARE *n* pl. -S metal goods

HARDWIRE *v* -WIRED, -WIRING, -WIRES to permanently connect electronic components

HARDWOOD *n* pl. -S the hard, compact wood of various trees

HARDY *adj* -DIER, -DIEST very sturdy

HARDY *n* pl. -DIES a blacksmith's chisel

HARE *v* HARED, HARING, HARES to run

HAREBELL *n* pl. -S a perennial herb

HAREEM *n* pl. -S harem

HARELIKE *adj* resembling a hare (a long-eared mammal)

HARELIP *n* pl. -S a deformity of the upper lip

HAREM *n* pl. -S the section of a Muslim household reserved for women

HARIANA *n* pl. -S a breed of cattle

HARICOT *n* pl. -S the seed of various string beans

HARIJAN *n* pl. -S an outcaste in India

HARING present participle of hare

HARK *v* -ED, -ING, -S to listen to

HARKEN *v* -ED, -ING, -S to hearken

HARKENER *n* pl. -S one that harkens

HARL *n* pl. -S a herl

HARLOT *n* pl. -S a prostitute

HARLOTRY *n* pl. -RIES prostitution

HARM *v* -ED, -ING, -S to injure

HARMER *n* pl. -S one that harms

HARMFUL *adj* capable of harming

HARMIN *n* pl. -S harmine

HARMINE *n* pl. -S an alkaloid used as a stimulant

HARMLESS *adj* not harmful

HARMONIC *n* pl. -S an overtone

HARMONY *n* pl. -NIES agreement

HARNESS *v* -ED, -ING, -ES to put tackle on a draft animal

HARP *v* -ED, -ING, -S to play on a harp (a type of stringed musical instrument)

HARPER *n* pl. -S a harpist

HARPIES pl. of harpy

HARPIN *n* pl. -S harping

HARPING *n* pl. -S a wooden plank used in shipbuilding

HARPIST *n* pl. -S one that plays the harp

HARPOON *v* -ED, -ING, -S to strike with a harpoon

HARPY *n* pl. -PIES a shrewish person

HARRIDAN *n* pl. -S a haggard woman

HARRIED past tense of harry

HARRIER *n* pl. -S a hunting dog

HARRIES present 3d person sing. of harry

HARROW *v* -ED, -ING, -S to break up and level soil

HARROWER *n* pl. -S one that harrows

HARRUMPH *v* -ED, -ING, -S to make a guttural sound

HARRY	v -RIED, -RYING, -RIES to pillage
HARSH	adj HARSHER, HARSHEST severe **HARSHLY** adv
HARSHEN	v -ED, -ING, -S to make harsh
HARSLET	n pl. -S haslet
HART	n pl. -S a male deer
HARTAL	n pl. -S a stoppage of work
HARUMPH	v -ED, -ING, -S harrumph
HARUSPEX	n pl. -PICES a soothsayer of ancient Rome
HARVEST	v -ED, -ING, -S to gather a crop
HAS	a present 3d person sing. of have
HASH	v -ED, -ING, -ES to mince
HASHEESH	n pl. -ES hashish
HASHHEAD	n pl. -S a hashish addict
HASHISH	n pl. -ES a mild narcotic
HASLET	n pl. -S the edible viscera of an animal
HASP	v -ED, -ING, -S to fasten with a clasp
HASSEL	n pl. -S an argument
HASSLE	v -SLED, -SLING, -SLES to argue
HASSOCK	n pl. -S a footstool
HAST	a present 2d person sing. of have
HASTATE	adj triangular
HASTE	v HASTED, HASTING, HASTES to hasten
HASTEFUL	adj hasty
HASTEN	v -ED, -ING, -S to hurry
HASTENER	n pl. -S one that hastens
HASTING	present participle of haste
HASTY	adj HASTIER, HASTIEST speedy **HASTILY** adv
HAT	v HATTED, HATTING, HATS to provide with a hat (a covering for the head)
HATABLE	adj hateable
HATBAND	n pl. -S a band worn on a hat
HATBOX	n pl. -ES a box for a hat
HATCH	v -ED, -ING, -ES to bring forth young from an egg
HATCHECK	adj pertaining to the checking of hats
HATCHEL	v -ELED, -ELING, -ELS or -ELLED, -ELLING, -ELS to separate flax fibers with a comb
HATCHER	n pl. -S one that hatches
HATCHERY	n pl. -ERIES a place for hatching eggs
HATCHET	n pl. -S a small ax
HATCHING	n pl. -S a series of lines used to show shading
HATCHWAY	n pl. -WAYS an opening in the deck of a ship
HATE	v HATED, HATING, HATES to despise
HATEABLE	adj meriting hatred
HATEFUL	adj detestable
HATER	n pl. -S one that hates
HATFUL	n pl. HATSFUL or HATFULS as much as a hat can hold
HATH	a present 3d person sing. of have
HATING	present participle of hate
HATLESS	adj lacking a hat
HATLIKE	adj resembling a hat
HATMAKER	n pl. -S one that makes hats
HATPIN	n pl. -S a pin for securing a hat
HATRACK	n pl. -S a rack for hats
HATRED	n pl. -S intense dislike or aversion
HATSFUL	a pl. of hatful
HATTED	past tense of hat
HATTER	n pl. -S a hatmaker
HATTERIA	n pl. -S a reptile
HATTING	present participle of hat
HAUBERK	n pl. -S a coat of armor
HAUGH	n pl. -S a low-lying meadow
HAUGHTY	adj -TIER, -TIEST arrogant
HAUL	v -ED, -ING, -S to pull with force
HAULAGE	n pl. -S the act of hauling
HAULER	n pl. -S one that hauls
HAULIER	n pl. -S hauler
HAULM	n pl. -S a plant stem
HAULMY	adj HAULMIER, HAULMIEST having haulms
HAULYARD	n pl. -S halyard
HAUNCH	n pl. -ES the hindquarter **HAUNCHED** adj
HAUNT	v -ED, -ING, -S to visit frequently
HAUNTER	n pl. -S one that haunts
HAUSEN	n pl. -S a Russian sturgeon
HAUSFRAU	n pl. -FRAUS or -FRAUEN a housewife
HAUT	adj haute
HAUTBOIS	n pl. HAUTBOIS hautboy
HAUTBOY	n pl. -BOYS an oboe
HAUTE	adj high-class
HAUTEUR	n pl. -S haughty manner or spirit
HAVARTI	n pl. -S a Danish cheese
HAVDALAH	n pl. -S habdalah

HAVE v past 2d person sing. HAD, HADDEST or HADST, present participle HAVING, present 2d person sing. HAVE or HAST, 3d person sing. HAS or HATH to be in possession of

HAVE n pl. -S a wealthy person

HAVELOCK n pl. -S a covering for a cap

HAVEN v -ED, -ING, -S to shelter

HAVER v -ED, -ING, -S to hem and haw

HAVEREL n pl. -S a fool

HAVING present participle of have

HAVIOR n pl. -S behavior

HAVIOUR n pl. -S havior

HAVOC v -OCKED, -OCKING, -OCS to destroy

HAVOCKER n pl. -S one that havocs

HAW v -ED, -ING, -S to turn left

HAWFINCH n pl. -ES a Eurasian finch

HAWK v -ED, -ING, -S to peddle

HAWKBILL n pl. -S a sea turtle

HAWKER n pl. -S one that hawks

HAWKEY n pl. -EYS a hawkie

HAWKEYED adj having keen sight

HAWKIE n pl. -S a white-faced cow

HAWKING n pl. -S falconry

HAWKISH adj warlike

HAWKLIKE adj resembling a hawk (a bird of prey)

HAWKMOTH n pl. -S a large moth

HAWKNOSE n pl. -S a large, curved nose

HAWKSHAW n pl. -S a detective

HAWKWEED n pl. -S a weedlike herb

HAWSE n pl. -S a part of a ship's bow

HAWSER n pl. -S a mooring rope

HAWTHORN n pl. -S a thorny shrub

HAY v -ED, -ING, -S to convert into hay (grass, cut and dried for fodder)

HAYCOCK n pl. -S a pile of hay

HAYER n pl. -S one that hays

HAYFIELD n pl. -S a field where grasses for hay are grown

HAYFORK n pl. -S a tool for pitching hay

HAYING n pl. -S the season for harvesting hay

HAYLAGE n pl. -S a type of hay

HAYLOFT n pl. -S a loft for hay storage

HAYMAKER n pl. -S one that makes hay

HAYMOW n pl. -S a hayloft

HAYRACK n pl. -S a frame used in hauling hay

HAYRICK n pl. -S a haystack

HAYRIDE n pl. -S a wagon ride

HAYSEED n pl. -S a bumpkin

HAYSTACK n pl. -S a pile of hay

HAYWARD n pl. -S an officer who tends cattle

HAYWIRE n pl. -S wire used in baling hay

HAZAN n pl. -ZANIM or -ZANS a cantor

HAZARD v -ED, -ING, -S to venture

HAZE v HAZED, HAZING, HAZES to subject to a humiliating initiation

HAZEL n pl. -S a shrub

HAZELHEN n pl. -S a European grouse

HAZELLY adj yellowish brown

HAZELNUT n pl. -S an edible nut

HAZER n pl. -S one that hazes

HAZIER comparative of hazy

HAZIEST superlative of hazy

HAZILY adv in a hazy manner

HAZINESS n pl. -ES the state of being hazy

HAZING n pl. -S an attempt to embarrass or ridicule

HAZY adj HAZIER, HAZIEST unclear

HAZZAN n pl. HAZZANIM or HAZZANS hazan

HE n pl. -S a male person

HEAD v -ED, -ING, -S to be chief of

HEADACHE n pl. -S a pain inside the head

HEADACHY adj -ACHIER, -ACHIEST having a headache

HEADBAND n pl. -S a band worn on the head

HEADER n pl. -S a grain harvester

HEADFISH n pl. -ES a marine fish

HEADGATE n pl. -S a gate to control the flow of water

HEADGEAR n pl. -S a covering for the head

HEADHUNT v -ED, -ING, -S to seek out, decapitate, and preserve the heads of enemies

HEADIER comparative of heady

HEADIEST superlative of heady

HEADILY adv in a heady manner

HEADING n pl. -S a title

HEADLAMP n pl. -S a light on the front of a car

HEADLAND n pl. -S a cliff

HEADLESS adj lacking a head

HEADLINE v -LINED, -LINING, -LINES to provide with a title

HEADLOCK n pl. -S a wrestling hold

HEADLONG adj rash; impetuous

HEADMAN n pl. -MEN a foreman

HEADMOST *adj* foremost
HEADNOTE *n* pl. -S a prefixed note
HEADPIN *n* pl. -S a bowling pin
HEADRACE *n* pl. -S a water channel
HEADREST *n* pl. -S a support for the head
HEADROOM *n* pl. -S clear vertical space
HEADSAIL *n* pl. -S a type fo sail
HEADSET *n* pl. -S a pair of earphones
HEADSHIP *n* pl. -S the position of a leader
HEADSMAN *n* pl. -MEN an executioner
HEADSTAY *n* pl. -STAYS a support for a ship's foremast
HEADWAY *n* pl. -WAYS forward movement
HEADWIND *n* pl. -S an oncoming wind
HEADWORD *n* pl. -S a word put at the beginning
HEADWORK *n* pl. -S mental work
HEADY *adj* HEADIER, HEADIEST intoxicating
HEAL *v* -ED, -ING, -S to make sound or whole **HEALABLE** *adj*
HEALER *n* pl. -S one that heals
HEALTH *n* pl. -S the physical condition of an organism
HEALTHY *adj* HEALTHIER, HEALTHIEST having good health
HEAP *v* -ED, -ING -S to pile up
HEAR *v* HEARD, HEARING, HEARS to perceive by the ear **HEARABLE** *adj*
HEARER *n* pl. -S one that hears
HEARING *n* pl. -S a preliminary examination
HEARKEN *v* -ED, -ING, -S to listen to
HEARSAY *n* pl. -SAYS secondhand information
HEARSE *v* HEARSED, HEARSING, HEARSES to transport in a hearse (a vehicle for conveying corpses)
HEART *v* -ED, -ING, -S to hearten
HEARTEN *v* -ED, -ING, -S to give courage to
HEARTH *n* pl. -S the floor of a fireplace
HEARTY *adj* HEARTIER, HEARTIEST very friendly **HEARTILY** *adv*
HEARTY *n* pl. HEARTIES a comrade
HEAT *v* HEATED or HET, HEATING, HEATS to make hot **HEATABLE** *adj*
HEATEDLY *adv* in an inflamed or excited manner

HEATER *n* pl. -S an apparatus for heating
HEATH *n* pl. -S an evergreen shrub
HEATHEN *n* pl. -S an uncivilized person
HEATHER *n* pl. -S an evergreen shrub **HEATHERY** *adj*
HEATHY *adj* HEATHIER, HEATHIEST abounding in heath
HEATLESS *adj* having no warmth
HEAUME *n* pl. -S a medieval helmet
HEAVE *v* HEAVED or HOVE, HEAVING, HEAVES to lift forcefully
HEAVEN *n* pl. -S the sky
HEAVENLY *adj* -LIER, -LIEST full of beauty and peace
HEAVER *n* pl. -S one that heaves
HEAVIER comparative of heavy
HEAVIES pl. of heavy
HEAVING present participle of heave
HEAVY *adj* HEAVIER, HEAVIEST having much weight **HEAVILY** *adv*
HEAVY *n* pl. HEAVIES a villain
HEAVYSET *adj* solidly built; stocky
HEBDOMAD *n* pl. -S the number seven
HEBETATE *v* -TATED, -TATING, -TATES to make dull
HEBETIC *adj* pertaining to puberty
HEBETUDE *n* pl. -S mental dullness
HEBRAIZE *v* -IZED, -IZING, -IZES to make Hebrew
HECATOMB *n* pl. -S a great sacrifice or slaughter
HECK *n* pl. -S hell
HECKLE *v* -LED, -LING, -LES to harass a speaker
HECKLER *n* pl. -S one that heckles
HECTARE *n* pl. -S a unit of area
HECTIC *adj* filled with turmoil **HECTICLY** *adv*
HECTICAL *adj* hectic
HECTOR *v* -ED, -ING, -S to bully
HEDDLE *n* pl. -S a part of a loom
HEDER *n* pl. HEDERS or HADARIM a Jewish school
HEDGE *v* HEDGED, HEDGING, HEDGES to surround with a hedge (a dense row of shrubs)
HEDGEHOG *n* pl. -S a small mammal
HEDGEHOP *v* -HOPPED, -HOPPING, -HOPS to fly near the ground
HEDGEPIG *n* pl. -S a hedgehog
HEDGER *n* pl. -S one that hedges
HEDGEROW *n* pl. -S a row of bushes
HEDGING present participle of hedge

HEDGY *adj* HEDGIER, HEDGIEST abounding in hedges

HEDONIC *adj* pertaining to pleasure

HEDONICS *n/pl* a branch of psychology

HEDONISM *n* pl. -S the pursuit of pleasure

HEDONIST *n* pl. -S a follower of hedonism

HEED *v* -ED, -ING, -S to pay attention to

HEEDER *n* pl. -S one that heeds

HEEDFUL *adj* paying close attention

HEEDLESS *adj* paying little or no attention

HEEHAW *v* -ED, -ING, -S to guffaw

HEEL *v* -ED, -ING, -S to supply with a heel (the raised part of a shoe)

HEELBALL *n* pl. -S a composition used for polishing

HEELER *n* pl. -S one that puts heels on shoes

HEELING *n* pl. -S the act of inclining laterally

HEELLESS *adj* lacking heels

HEELPOST *n* pl. -S a post fitted to the end of something

HEELTAP *n* pl. -S material put on the heel of a shoe

HEEZE *v* HEEZED, HEEZING, HEEZES to hoist

HEFT *v* -ED, -ING, -S to lift up

HEFTER *n* pl. -S one that hefts

HEFTY *adj* HEFTIER, HEFTIEST heavy **HEFTILY** *adv*

HEGARI *n* pl. -S a grain

HEGEMONY *n* pl. -NIES great authority

HEGIRA *n* pl. -S an exodus

HEGUMEN *n* pl. -S the head of a monastery

HEGUMENE *n* pl. -S the head of a nunnery

HEGUMENY *n* pl. -NIES the office of a hegumen

HEH *n* pl. -S a Hebrew letter

HEIFER *n* pl. -S a young cow

HEIGH *interj* — used to attract attention

HEIGHT *n* pl. -S the highest point

HEIGHTEN *v* -ED, -ING, -S to raise

HEIGHTH *n* pl. -S height

HEIL *v* -ED, -ING, -S to salute

HEIMISH *adj* homelike

HEINIE *n* pl. -S the buttocks

HEINOUS *adj* very wicked

HEIR *v* -ED, -ING, -S to inherit

HEIRDOM *n* pl. -S heirship

HEIRESS *n* pl. -ES a female inheritor

HEIRLESS *adj* having no inheritors

HEIRLOOM *n* pl. -S an inherited possession

HEIRSHIP *n* pl. -S the right to inheritance

HEISHI *n/pl* tiny beads made from shells

HEIST *v* -ED, -ING, -S to steal

HEISTER *n* pl. -S one that heists

HEJIRA *n* pl. -S hegira

HEKTARE *n* pl. -S hectare

HELD past tense of hold

HELIAC *adj* heliacal

HELIACAL *adj* pertaining to the sun

HELIAST *n* pl. -S an Athenian judge

HELICAL *adj* shaped like a helix

HELICES a pl. of helix

HELICITY *n* pl. -TIES a component of a particle's spin

HELICOID *n* pl. -S a type of geometrical surface

HELICON *n* pl. -S a large bass tuba

HELICOPT *v* -ED, -ING, -S to travel by helicopter

HELILIFT *v* -ED, -ING, -S to transport by helicopter

HELIO *n* pl. -LIOS a signaling mirror

HELIPAD *n* pl. -S a heliport

HELIPORT *n* pl. -S an airport for helicopters

HELISTOP *n* pl. -S a heliport

HELIUM *n* pl. -S a gaseous element

HELIX *n* pl. -LIXES or -LICES something spiral in form

HELL *v* -ED, -ING, -S to behave raucously

HELLBENT *adj* stubbornly determined

HELLBOX *n* pl. -ES a printer's receptacle

HELLCAT *n* pl. -S a shrewish person

HELLER *n* pl. -S a hellion

HELLERI *n* pl. -ES a tropical fish

HELLERY *n* pl. -LERIES rough play

HELLFIRE *n* pl. -S the torment of hell

HELLHOLE *n* pl. -S a horrible place

HELLION *n* pl. -S a troublesome person

HELLISH *adj* horrible

HELLKITE *n* pl. -S a cruel person

HELLO *v* -ED, -ING, -ES or -S to greet

HELLUVA *adj* disagreeable

HELM *v* -ED, -ING, -S to steer a ship

HELMET *v* -ED, -ING, -S to supply with a helmet (a protective covering for the head)

HELMINTH *n* pl. -S a worm

HELMLESS *adj* lacking a helm (a steering system)

HELMSMAN *n* pl. -MEN one that steers a ship

HELO	n pl. HELOS a helicopter
HELOT	n pl. -S a slave or serf
HELOTAGE	n pl. -S helotism
HELOTISM	n pl. -S slavery or or serfdom
HELOTRY	n pl. -RIES helotism
HELP	v HELPED or HOLP, HELPED or HOLPEN, HELPING, HELPS to give assistance to HELPABLE adj
HELPER	n pl. -S one that helps
HELPFUL	adj being of service or assistance
HELPING	n pl. -S a portion of food
HELPLESS	adj defenseless
HELPMATE	n pl. -S a helpful companion
HELPMEET	n pl. -S a helpmate
HELVE	v HELVED, HELVING, HELVES to provide with a handle
HEM	v HEMMED, HEMMING, HEMS to provide with an edge
HEMAGOG	n pl. -S an agent that promotes blood flow
HEMAL	adj pertaining to the blood
HEMATAL	adj hemal
HEMATEIN	n pl. -S a chemical compound
HEMATIC	n pl. -S a medicine for a blood disease
HEMATIN	n pl. -S heme
HEMATINE	n pl. -S hematin
HEMATITE	n pl. -S an ore of iron
HEMATOID	adj resembling blood
HEMATOMA	n pl. -MAS or -MATA a swelling filled with blood
HEME	n pl. -S a component of hemoglobin
HEMIC	adj hemal
HEMIN	n pl. -S a chloride of heme
HEMIOLA	n pl. -S a rhythmic alteration in music
HEMIOLIA	n pl. -S hemiola
HEMIPTER	n pl. -S an insect
HEMLINE	n pl. -S the bottom edge of a garment
HEMLOCK	n pl. -S a poisonous herb
HEMMED	past tense of hem
HEMMER	n pl. -S one that hems
HEMMING	present participle of hem
HEMOCOEL	n pl. -S a body cavity
HEMOCYTE	n pl. -S a blood cell
HEMOID	adj hemal
HEMOLYZE	v -LYZED, -LYZING, LYZES to break down red blood cells
HEMOSTAT	n pl. -S an instrument for reducing bleeding
HEMP	n pl. -S a tall herb
HEMPEN	adj made of hemp
HEMPIE	adj HEMPIER, HEMPIEST hempy
HEMPIER	comparative of hempy
HEMPIEST	superlative of hempy
HEMPLIKE	adj resembling hemp
HEMPSEED	n pl. -S the seed of hemp
HEMPWEED	n pl. -S a climbing plant
HEMPY	adj HEMPIER, HEMPIEST mischievous
HEN	n pl. -S a female chicken
HENBANE	n pl. -S a poisonous herb
HENBIT	n pl. -S a perennial herb
HENCE	adv consequently
HENCHMAN	n pl. -MEN an unscrupulous supporter
HENCOOP	n pl. -S a cage for hens
HENEQUEN	n pl. -S a fiber used to make ropes
HENEQUIN	n pl. -S henequen
HENHOUSE	n pl. -S a shelter for poultry
HENIQUEN	n pl. -S henequen
HENLIKE	adj resembling a hen
HENNA	v -ED, -ING, -S to dye with a reddish coloring
HENNERY	n pl. -NERIES a poultry farm
HENPECK	v -ED, -ING, -S to dominate by nagging
HENRY	n pl. -RIES or -RYS a unit of inductance
HENT	v -ED, -ING, -S to grasp
HEP	adj hip
HEPARIN	n pl. -S a biochemical
HEPATIC	n pl. -S a drug acting on the liver
HEPATICA	n pl. -CAS or -CAE a perennial herb
HEPATIZE	v -TIZED, -TIZING, -TIZES to convert tissue into a firm mass
HEPATOMA	n pl. -MAS or -MATA a tumor of the liver
HEPCAT	n pl. -S a jazz enthusiast
HEPTAD	n pl. -S a group of seven
HEPTAGON	n pl. -S a seven-sided polygon
HEPTANE	n pl. -S a hydrocarbon used as a solvent
HEPTARCH	n pl. -S one of a group of seven rulers
HEPTOSE	n pl. -S a chemical compound
HER	pron the objective or possessive case of the pronoun she
HERALD	v -ED, -ING, -S to proclaim
HERALDIC	adj pertaining to heraldry
HERALDRY	n pl. -RIES the art or science of armorial bearings

HERB *n* pl. -S a flowering plant with a nonwoody stem

HERBAGE *n* pl. -S nonwoody plant life

HERBAL *n* pl. -S a book about herbs and plants

HERBARIA *n/pl* collections of dried plants

HERBED *adj* flavored with herbs

HERBIER comparative of herby

HERBIEST superlative of herby

HERBLESS *adj* lacking herbs

HERBLIKE *adj* resembling an herb

HERBY *adj* HERBIER, HERBIEST abounding in herbs

HERCULES *n* pl. -LESES any man of great size and strength

HERD *v* -ED, -ING, -S to bring together in a herd (a group of animals)

HERDER *n* pl. -S one who tends a herd

HERDIC *n* pl. -S a type of carriage

HERDLIKE *adj* resembling a herd

HERDMAN *n* pl. -MEN herdsman

HERDSMAN *n* pl. -MEN a herder

HERE *n* pl. -S this place

HEREAT *adj* at this time

HEREAWAY *adv* in this vicinity

HEREBY *adv* by this means

HEREDES pl. of heres

HEREDITY *n* pl. -TIES the genetic transmission of chracteristics

HEREIN *adv* in this

HEREINTO *adv* into this place

HEREOF *adv* of this

HEREON *adv* on this

HERES *n* pl. HEREDES an heir

HERESY *n* pl. -SIES a belief contrary to a church doctrine

HERETIC *n* pl. -S one that upholds heresy

HERETO *adv* to this matter

HERETRIX *n* pl. -TRIXES or -TRICES heritrix

HEREUNTO *adv* hereto

HEREUPON *adv* immediately following this

HEREWITH *adv* along with this

HERIOT *n* pl. -S a feudal tribute or payment

HERITAGE *n* pl. -S something that is inherited

HERITOR *n* pl. -S one that inherits

HERITRIX *n* pl. -TRIXES or -TRICES a female heritor

HERL *n* pl. -S a feathered fishing lure

HERM *n* pl. -S a type of statue

HERMA *n* pl. -MAE or -MAI a herm **HERMAEAN** *adj*

HERMETIC *adj* airtight

HERMIT *n* pl. -S a recluse **HERMITIC** *adj*

HERMITRY *n* pl. -RIES the state of being a hermit

HERN *n* pl. -S a heron

HERNIA *n* pl. -NIAS or -NIAE the protrusion of an organ through its surrounding wall **HERNIAL** *adj*

HERNIATE *v* -ATED, -ATING, -ATES to protrude through an abnormal bodily opening

HERO *n* pl. -ROES or -ROS a hoagie

HEROIC *n* pl. -S an epic verse

HEROICAL *adj* courageous; noble

HEROIN *n* pl. -S an addictive narcotic

HEROINE *n* pl. -S a brave woman

HEROISM *n* pl. -S heroic behavior

HEROIZE *v* -IZED, -IZING, -IZES to make heroic

HERON *n* pl. -S a wading bird

HERONRY *n* pl. -RIES a place where herons breed

HERPES *n* pl. HERPES a skin infection **HERPETIC** *adj*

HERRING *n* pl. -S a food fish

HERRY *v* -RIED, -RYING, -RIES to harry

HERS *pron* the possessive case of the pronoun she

HERSELF *pron* a form of the 3d person sing. feminine pronoun

HERSTORY *n* pl. -RIES history with a feminist viewpoint

HERTZ *n* pl. -ES a unit of frequency

HESITANT *adj* tending to hesitate

HESITATE *v* -TATED, -TATING, -TATES to hold back in uncertainty

HESSIAN *n* pl. -S a coarse cloth

HESSITE *n* pl. -S a mineral

HEST *n* pl. -S a command

HET *n* pl. -S heth

HETAERA *n* pl. -RAE or -RAS a concubine **HETAERIC** *adj*

HETAIRA *n* pl. -RAI or -RAS hetaera

HETERO *n* pl. -EROS a heterosexual

HETH *n* pl. -S a Hebrew letter

HETMAN *n* pl. -S a cossack leader

HEUCH *n* pl. -S heugh

HEUGH *n* pl. -S a steep cliff

HEW *v* HEWED, HEWN, HEWING, HEWS to cut with an ax **HEWABLE** *adj*

HEWER	n pl. -S one that hews
HEX	v -ED, -ING, -ES to cast an evil spell upon
HEXAD	n pl. -S a group of six HEXADIC adj
HEXADE	n pl. -S hexad
HEXAGON	n pl. -S a polygon having six sides
HEXAGRAM	n pl. -S a six-pointed star
HEXAMINE	n pl. -S a chemical compound
HEXANE	n pl. -S a volatile liquid
HEXAPLA	n pl. -S an edition in which six texts are set in parallel columns HEXAPLAR adj
HEXAPOD	n pl. -S a six-legged insect
HEXAPODY	n pl. -DIES a line of verse with six feet
HEXARCHY	n pl. -CHIES a group of six separate states
HEXER	n pl. -S one that hexes
HEXEREI	n pl. -S witchcraft
HEXONE	n pl. -S a hydrocarbon solvent
HEXOSAN	n pl. -S a carbohydrate
HEXOSE	n pl. -S a simple sugar
HEXYL	n pl. -S a hydrocarbon radical
HEY	interj — used to attract attention
HEYDAY	n pl. -DAYS the period of one's greatest success
HEYDEY	n pl. -DEYS heyday
HI	interj — used as a greeting
HIATUS	n pl. -ES a gap or missing section HIATAL adj
HIBACHI	n pl. -S a cooking device
HIBERNAL	adj pertaining to winter
HIBISCUS	n pl. -ES a tropical plant
HIC	interj — used to represent a hiccup
HICCOUGH	v -ED, -ING, -S to hiccup
HICCUP	v -CUPED, -CUPING, -CUPs or -CUPPED, -CUPPING, -CUPS to make a peculiar-sounding, spasmodic inhalation
HICK	n pl. -S a rural person HICKISH adj
HICKEY	n pl. HICKEYS or HICKIES a gadget
HICKORY	n pl. -RIES a hardwood tree
HID	a past tense of hide
HIDABLE	adj able to be hidden
HIDALGO	n pl. -GOS a minor Spanish nobleman
HIDDEN	adj concealed; obscure HIDDENLY adv
HIDE	v HID, HIDDEN, HIDING, HIDES to conceal
HIDE	v HIDED, HIDING, HIDES to flog
HIDEAWAY	n pl. -AWAYS a hideout
HIDELESS	adj lacking a skin
HIDEOUS	adj very ugly
HIDEOUT	n pl. -S a place of refuge
HIDER	n pl. -S one that hides
HIDING	n pl. -S a beating
HIDROSIS	n pl. -DROSES abnormal perspiration
HIDROTIC	n pl. -S a drug that induces perspiration
HIE	v HIED, HIEING or HYING, HIES to hurry
HIEMAL	adj pertaining to winter
HIERARCH	n pl. -S a religious leader
HIERATIC	adj pertaining to priests
HIGGLE	v GLED, -GLING, -GLES to haggle
HIGGLER	n pl. -S one that higgles
HIGH	adj HIGHER, HIGHEST reaching far upward
HIGH	n pl. -S a high level
HIGHBALL	v -ED, -ING, -S to go at full speed
HIGHBORN	adj of noble birth
HIGHBOY	n pl. -BOYS a tall chest of drawers
HIGHBRED	adj highborn
HIGHBROW	n pl. -S a person who has superior tastes
HIGHBUSH	adj forming a tall bush
HIGHJACK	v -ED, -ING, -S to hijack
HIGHLAND	n pl. -S an elevated region
HIGHLIFE	n pl. -S the lifestyle of fashionable society
HIGHLY	adv to a high degree
HIGHNESS	n pl. -ES the state of being high
HIGHROAD	n pl. -S a highway
HIGHSPOT	n pl. -S an event of major importance
HIGHT	v -ED, -ING, -S to command
HIGHTAIL	v -ED, -ING, -S to retreat rapidly
HIGHTH	n pl. -S height
HIGHWAY	n pl. -WAYS a main road
HIJACK	v -ED, -ING, -S to seize a vehicle while in transit
HIJACKER	n pl. -S one that hijacks
HIJINKS	n/pl mischievous fun
HIKE	v HIKED, HIKING, HIKES to walk a long distance
HIKER	n pl. -S one that hikes

HILA   pl. of hilum

HILAR   *adj* pertaining to a hilum

HILARITY   *n* pl. -TIES noisy merriment

HILDING   *n* pl. -S a vile person

HILI   pl. of hilus

HILL   *v* -ED, -ING, -S to form into a hill (a rounded elevation)

HILLER   *n* pl. -S one that hills

HILLIER   comparative of hilly

HILLIEST   superlative of hilly

HILLO   *v* -ED, -ING, -S or -ES to hallo

HILLOA   *v* -ED, -ING, -S to hallo

HILLOCK   *n* pl. -S a small hill **HILLOCKY** *adj*

HILLSIDE   *n* pl. -S the side of a hill

HILLTOP   *n* pl. -S the top of a hill

HILLY   *adj* HILLIER, HILLIEST abounding in hills

HILT   *v* -ED, -ING, -S to provide with a hilt (a handle for a weapon)

HILTLESS   *adj* having no hilt

HILUM   *n* pl. HILA a small opening in a bodily organ

HILUS   *n* pl. HILI hilum

HIM   *pron* the objective case of the pronoun he

HIMATION   *n* pl. -MATIA or -MATIONS a loose outer garment

HIMSELF   *pron* a form of the 3d person sing. masculine pronoun

HIN   *n* pl. -S a Hebrew unit of liquid measure

HIND   *n* pl. -S a female red deer

HINDER   *v* -ED, -ING, -S to impede

HINDERER   *n* pl. -S one that hinders

HINDGUT   *n* pl. -S the rear part of the alimentary canal

HINDMOST   *adj* farthest to the rear

HINGE   *v* HINGED, HINGING, HINGES to attach a jointed device

HINGER   *n* pl. -S one that hinges

HINNY   *v* -NIED, -NYING, -NIES to whinny

HINT   *v* -ED, -ING, -S to suggest indirectly

HINTER   *n* pl. -S one that hints

HIP   *v* HIPPED, HIPPING, HIPS to build a type of roof

HIP   *adj* HIPPER, HIPPEST aware of the most current styles and trends

HIPBONE   *n* pl. -S a pelvic bone

HIPLESS   *adj* lacking a hip (the pelvic joint)

HIPLIKE   *adj* suggestive of a hip

HIPLINE   *n* pl. -S the distance around the hips

HIPNESS   *n* pl. -ES the state of being hip

HIPPARCH   *n* pl. -S a cavalry commander in ancient Greece

HIPPED   past tense of hip

HIPPER   comparative of hip

HIPPEST   superlative of hip

HIPPIE   *n* pl. -S a nonconformist

HIPPIER   comparative of hippy

HIPPIEST   superlative of hippy

HIPPING   present participle of hip

HIPPISH   *adj* depressed; sad

HIPPO   *n* pl. -POS a hippopotamus

HIPPY   *adj* -PIER, -PIEST having big hips

HIPSHOT   *adj* lame; awkward

HIPSTER   *n* pl. -S one that is hip

HIRABLE   *adj* available for hire

HIRAGANA   *n* pl. -S a Japanese cursive script

HIRCINE   *adj* pertaining to a goat

HIRE   *v* HIRED, HIRING, HIRES to engage the services of for payment **HIREABLE** *adj*

HIRELING   *n* pl. -S one that works for money only

HIRER   *n* pl. -S one that hires

HIRING   present participle of hire

HIRPLE   *v* -PLED, -PLING, -PLES to limp

HIRSEL   *v* -SELED, -SELING, -SELS or -SELLED, -SELLING, -SELS to herd sheep

HIRSLE   *v* -SLED, -SLING, -SLES to slide along

HIRSUTE   *adj* hairy

HIRUDIN   *n* pl. -S an anticoagulant

HIS   *pron* the possessive form of the pronoun he

HISN   *pron* his

HISPID   *adj* covered with stiff hairs

HISS   *v* -ED, -ING, -ES to make a sibilant sound

HISSELF   *pron* himself

HISSER   *n* pl. -S one that hisses

HISSING   *n* pl. -S an object of scorn

HISSY   *n* pl. HISSIES a tantrum

HIST   *v* -ED, -ING, -S to hoist

HISTAMIN   *n* pl. -S an amine released in allergic reactions

HISTIDIN   *n* pl. -S an amino acid

HISTOGEN   *n* pl. -S interior plant tissue

HISTOID   *adj* pertaining to connective tissue

HISTONE   *n* pl. -S a simple protein

HISTORIC	*adj* important in history
HISTORY	*n pl.* -RIES a chronological record of past events
HIT	*v* HIT, HITTING, HITS to strike forcibly
HITCH	*v* -ED, -ING, -ES to fasten with a knot or hook
HITCHER	*n pl.* -S one that hitches
HITHER	*adv* toward this place
HITHERTO	*adv* up to now
HITLESS	*adj* being without a hit
HITTER	*n pl.* -S one that hits
HITTING	present participle of hit
HIVE	*v* HIVED, HIVING, HIVES to cause to enter a hive (a bee's nest)
HIVELESS	*adj* lacking a hive
HIZZONER	*n pl.* -S — used as a title for a mayor
HM	*interj* hmm
HMM	*interj* — used to express thoughtful consideration
HO	*interj* — used to express surprise
HOACTZIN	*n pl.* -S or -ES hoatzin
HOAGIE	*n pl.* -S a long sandwich
HOAGY	*n pl.* -GIES hoagie
HOAR	*n pl.* -S a white coating
HOARD	*v* -ED, -ING, -S to gather and store away
HOARDER	*n pl.* -S one that hoards
HOARDING	*n pl.* -S something hoarded
HOARIER	comparative of hoary
HOARIEST	superlative of hoary
HOARILY	*adv* in a hoary manner
HOARSE	*adj* HOARSER, HOARSEST low and rough in sound **HOARSELY** *adv*
HOARSEN	*v* -ED, -ING, -S to make hoarse
HOARY	*adj* HOARIER, HOARIEST white with age
HOATZIN	*n pl.* -S or -ES a tropical bird
HOAX	*v* -ED, -ING, -ES to deceive
HOAXER	*n pl.* -S one that hoaxes
HOB	*v* HOBBED, HOBBING, HOBS to furnish with hobnails
HOBBIES	pl. of hobby
HOBBIT	*n pl.* -S a fictitious creature that lives underground
HOBBLE	*v* -BLED, -BLING, -BLES to limp
HOBBLER	*n pl.* -S one that hobbles
HOBBY	*n pl.* -BIES a recreational pastime
HOBBYIST	*n pl.* -S one that pursues a hobby
HOBLIKE	*adj* suggestive of an elf
HOBNAIL	*v* -ED, -ING, -S to put hobnails (short nails with a broad head) on a shoe sole
HOBNOB	*v* -NOBBED, -NOBBING, -NOBS to associate in a friendly way
HOBO	*v* -ED, -ING, -S or -ES to live like a hobo (a vagrant or tramp)
HOBOISM	*n pl.* -S the state of being a hobo
HOCK	*v* -ED, -ING, -S to pawn
HOCKER	*n pl.* -S one that hocks
HOCKEY	*n pl.* -EYS a game played on ice
HOCKSHOP	*n pl.* -S a pawnshop
HOCUS	*v* -CUSED, -CUSING, -CUSES or -CUSSED, -CUSSING, -CUSSES to deceive or cheat
HOD	*n pl.* -S a portable trough
HODAD	*n pl.* -S a nonsurfer
HODADDY	*n pl.* -DIES hodad
HODDEN	*n pl.* -S a coarse cloth
HODDIN	*n pl.* -S hodden
HOE	*v* HOED, HOEING, HOES to use a hoe (a gardening tool)
HOECAKE	*n pl.* -S a cornmeal cake
HOEDOWN	*n pl.* -S a square dance
HOELIKE	*adj* resembling a hoe
HOER	*n pl.* -S one that hoes
HOG	*v* HOGGED, HOGGING, HOGS to take more than one's share
HOGAN	*n pl.* -S a Navaho Indian dwelling
HOGBACK	*n pl.* -S a sharp ridge
HOGFISH	*n pl.* -ES a tropical fish
HOGG	*n pl.* -S a young sheep
HOGGED	past tense of hog
HOGGER	*n pl.* -S one that hogs
HOGGET	*n pl.* -S a young unshorn sheep
HOGGING	present participle of hog
HOGGISH	*adj* coarsely selfish
HOGLIKE	*adj* hoggish
HOGMANAY	*n pl.* -NAYS a Scottish celebration
HOGMANE	*n pl.* -S hogmanay
HOGMENAY	*n pl.* -NAYS hogmanay
HOGNOSE	*n pl.* -S a nonvenomous snake
HOGNUT	*n pl.* -S a hickory nut
HOGSHEAD	*n pl.* -S a large cask

HOGTIE   *v* -TIED, -TIEING or -TYING, -TIES to tie together the legs of

HOGWASH   *n* pl. -ES meaningless talk

HOGWEED   *n* pl. -S a coarse plant

HOICK   *v* -ED, -ING, -S to change directions abruptly

HOIDEN   *v* -ED, -ING, -S to hoyden

HOISE   *v* HOISED, HOISING, HOISES to hoist

HOIST   *v* -ED, -ING, -S to haul up by some mechanical means

HOISTER   *n* pl. -S one that hoists

HOKE   *v* HOKED, HOKING, HOKES to give false value to

HOKEY   *adj* HOKIER, HOKIEST false; contrived **HOKILY** *adv*

HOKINESS   *n* pl. -ES the state of being hokey

HOKKU   *n* pl. HOKKU haiku

HOKUM   *n* pl. -S nonsense

HOKYPOKY   *n* pl. -KIES trickery

HOLARD   *n* pl. -S the total quantity of water in the soil

HOLD   *v* HELD, HOLDEN, HOLDING, HOLDS to maintain possession of **HOLDABLE** *adj*

HOLDALL   *n* pl. -S a carrying case

HOLDBACK   *n* pl. -S a restraining device

HOLDEN   a past participle of hold

HOLDER   *n* pl. -S one that holds

HOLDFAST   *n* pl. -S a fastening device

HOLDING   *n* pl. -S something held

HOLDOUT   *n* pl. -S one who delays signing a contract

HOLDOVER   *n* pl. -S something left over

HOLDUP   *n* pl. -S a delay

HOLE   *v* HOLED, HOLING, HOLES to make a hole (a cavity in a solid)

HOLELESS   *adj* lacking a hole

HOLEY   *adj* full of holes

HOLIBUT   *n* pl. -S halibut

HOLIDAY   *v* -ED, -ING, -S to take a vacation

HOLIER   comparative of holy

HOLIES   pl. of holy

HOLIEST   superlative of holy

HOLILY   *adv* in a holy manner

HOLINESS   *n* pl. -ES the state of being holy

HOLING   present participle of hole

HOLISM   *n* pl. -S a philosophical theory

HOLIST   *n* pl. -S one who adheres to the theory of holism **HOLISTIC** *adj*

HOLK   *v* -ED, -ING, -S to howk

HOLLA   *v* -ED, -ING, -S to hallo

HOLLAND   *n* pl. -S a cotton fabric

HOLLER   *v* -ED, -ING, -S to yell

HOLLIES   pl. of holly

HOLLO   *v* -ED, -ING, -S or -ES to hallo

HOLLOA   *v* -ED, -ING, -S to hallo

HOLLOO   *v* -ED, -ING, -S to hallo

HOLLOW   *adj* -LOWER, -LOWEST not solid **HOLLOWLY** *adv*

HOLLOW   *v* -ED, -ING, -S to make hollow

HOLLY   *n* pl. -LIES a tree

HOLM   *n* pl. -S an island in a river

HOLMIUM   *n* pl. -S a metallic element **HOLMIC** *adj*

HOLOGAMY   *n* pl. -MIES the state of having gametes of the same size and form as other cells

HOLOGRAM   *n* pl. -S a three-dimensional photograph

HOLOGYNY   *n* pl. -NIES a trait transmitted solely in the female line

HOLOTYPE   *n* pl. -S an animal or plant specimen

HOLOZOIC   *adj* eating solid foods

HOLP   a past tense of help

HOLPEN   a past participle of help

HOLS   *n/pl* a vacation

HOLSTEIN   *n* pl. -S a breed of cattle

HOLSTER   *n* pl. -S a case for a pistol

HOLT   *n* pl. -S a grove

HOLY   *adj* -LIER, -LIEST having a divine nature or origin

HOLY   *n* pl. -LIES a holy place

HOLYDAY   *n* pl. -DAYS a religious holiday

HOLYTIDE   *n* pl. -S a time of religious observance

HOMAGE   *v* -AGED, -AGING, -AGES to pay tribute to

HOMAGER   *n* pl. -S a feudal vassal

HOMBRE   *n* pl. -S a fellow

HOMBURG   *n* pl. -S a felt hat

HOME   *v* HOMED, HOMING, HOMES to return to one's home (place of residence)

HOMEBODY   *n* pl. -BODIES one who likes to stay at home

HOMEBOY   *n* pl. -BOYS a boy or man from one's neighborhood

HOMEBRED   *n* pl. -S a native athlete

HOMED   past tense of home

HOMELAND   *n* pl. -S one's native land

HOMELESS   *adj* lacking a home

HOMELIKE   *adj* suggestive of a home

HOMELY   *adj* -LIER, -LIEST unattractive

HOMEMADE *adj* made at home

HOMEOBOX *n* pl. -ES a short DNA sequence

HOMEOTIC *adj* being a gene producing a shift in development

HOMEPORT *v* -ED, -ING, -S to assign a ship to a port

HOMER *v* -ED, -ING, -S to hit a home run

HOMEROOM *n* pl. -S the classroom where pupils report before classes begin

HOMESICK *adj* longing for home

HOMESITE *n* pl. -S a location for a house

HOMESPUN *n* pl. -S a loosely woven fabric

HOMESTAY *n* pl. -STAYS a period during which a visitor in a foreign country lives with a local family

HOMETOWN *n* pl. -S the town of one's birth or residence

HOMEWARD *adv* toward home

HOMEWORK *n* pl. -S work done at home

HOMEY *adj* HOMIER, HOMIEST homelike

HOMICIDE *n* pl. -S the killing of one person by another

HOMIER comparative of homy

HOMIEST superlative of homy

HOMILIST *n* pl. -S one that delivers a homily

HOMILY *n* pl. -LIES a sermon

HOMINES a pl. of homo

HOMINESS *n* pl. -ES the quality of being homey

HOMING present participle of home

HOMINIAN *n* pl. -S a hominid

HOMINID *n* pl. -S a manlike creature

HOMINIES pl. of hominy

HOMININE *adj* characteristic of man

HOMINIZE *v* -NIZED, -NIZING, -NIZES to alter the environment to conform with evolving man

HOMINOID *n* pl. -S a manlike animal

HOMINY *n* pl. -NIES hulled, dried corn

HOMMOCK *n* pl. -S a ridge in an ice field

HOMMOS *n* pl. -ES hummus

HOMO *n* pl. HOMINES or HOMOS a member of the genus that includes modern man

HOMOGAMY *n* pl. -MIES the bearing of sexually similar flowers

HOMOGENY *n* pl. -NIES correspondence in form or structure

HOMOGONY *n* pl. -NIES the condition of having flowers with uniform stamens and pistils

HOMOLOG *n* pl. -S something that exhibits homology

HOMOLOGY *n* pl. -GIES similarity in structure

HOMONYM *n* pl. -S a namesake

HOMONYMY *n* pl. -MIES the condition of having the same name

HOMOSEX *n* pl. -ES homosexuality

HOMY *adj* HOMIER, HOMIEST homey

HON *n* pl. -S a honeybun

HONAN *n* pl. -S a fine silk

HONCHO *v* -ED, -ING, -S to take charge of

HONDA *n* pl. -S a part of a lariat

HONDLE *v* -DLED, -DLING, -DLIES to haggle

HONE *v* HONED, HONING, HONES to sharpen

HONER *n* pl. -S one that hones

HONEST *adj* -ESTER, -ESTEST truthful

HONESTLY *adv*

HONESTY *n* pl. -TIES the quality of being honest

HONEWORT *n* pl. -S a perennial herb

HONEY *v* -EYED or -IED, -EYING, -EYS to sweeten with honey (a sweet, viscid fluid)

HONEYBEE *n* pl. -S a type of bee

HONEYBUN *n* pl. -S a sweetheart

HONEYDEW *n* pl. -S a sweet fluid

HONEYFUL *adj* containing much honey

HONG *n* pl. -S a Chinese factory

HONIED a past tense of honey

HONING present participle of hone

HONK *v* -ED, -ING, -S to emit a cry like that of a goose

HONKER *n* pl. -S one that honks

HONOR *v* -ED, -ING, -S to treat with respect

HONORAND *n* pl. -S an honoree

HONORARY *n* pl. -ARIES an honor society

HONOREE *n* pl. -S one that receives an honor

HONORER *n* pl. -S one that honors

HONOUR *v* -ED, -ING, -S to honor

HONOURER *n* pl. -S honorer

HOOCH *n* pl. -ES cheap whiskey

HOOD *v* -ED, -ING, -S to furnish with a hood (a covering for the head)

HOODIE *n* pl. -S a gray crow of Europe

HOODLESS *adj* lacking a hood

HOODLIKE *adj* resembling a hood

HOODLUM *n* pl. -S a thug

HOODOO   v -ED, -ING, -S to bring bad luck to

HOODWINK   v -ED, -ING, -S to trick

HOOEY   n pl. -EYS something false or nonsensical

HOOF   v -ED, -ING, -S to dance

HOOF   n pl. HOOVES or HOOFS the hard covering on the feet of certain animals

HOOFBEAT   n pl. -S the sound of hooves striking the ground

HOOFER   n pl. -S a professional dancer

HOOFLESS   adj lacking hooves

HOOFLIKE   adj resembling a hoof

HOOK   v -ED, -ING, -S to catch with a hook (a bent piece of metal)

HOOKA   n pl. -S hookah

HOOKAH   n pl. -S a water pipe

HOOKER   n pl. -S a prostitute

HOOKEY   n pl. -EYS hooky

HOOKIER   comparative of hooky

HOOKIES   pl. of hooky

HOOKIEST   superlative of hooky

HOOKLESS   adj lacking a hook

HOOKLET   n pl. -S a small hook

HOOKLIKE   adj resembling a hook

HOOKNOSE   n pl. -S an aquiline nose

HOOKUP   n pl. -S an electrical assemblage

HOOKWORM n pl. -S a parasitic worm

HOOKY   n pl. HOOKIES truancy

HOOKY   adj HOOKIER, HOOKIEST full of hooks

HOOLIE   adj easy; slow

HOOLIGAN   n pl. -S a hoodlum

HOOLY   adj hoolie

HOOP   v -ED, -ING, -S to fasten with a hoop (a circular band of metal)

HOOPER   n pl. -S one that hoops

HOOPLA   n pl. -S commotion

HOOPLESS   adj lacking a hoop

HOOPLIKE   adj suggestive of a hoop

HOOPOE   n pl. -S a European bird

HOOPOO   n pl. -POOS hoopoe

HOOPSTER   n pl. -S a basketball player

HOORAH   v -ED, -ING, -S to hurrah

HOORAY   v -ED, -ING, -S to hurrah

HOOSEGOW n pl. -S a jail

HOOSGOW   n pl. -S hoosegow

HOOT   v -ED, -ING, -S to cry like an owl

HOOTCH   n pl. -ES hooch

HOOTER   n pl. -S one that hoots

HOOTY   adj HOOTIER, HOOTIEST sounding like the cry of an owl

HOOVED   adj having hooves

HOOVES   a pl. of hoof

HOP   v HOPPED, HOPPING, HOPS to move by jumping on one foot

HOPE   v HOPED, HOPING, HOPES to have a desire or expectation

HOPEFUL   n pl. -S one that seems promising

HOPELESS   adj despairing

HOPER   n pl. -S one that hopes

HOPHEAD   n pl. -S a drug addict

HOPING   present participle of hope

HOPLITE   n pl. -S a foot soldier of ancient Greece **HOPLITIC** adj

HOPPED   past tense of hop

HOPPER   n pl. -S one that hops

HOPPING   present participle of hop

HOPPLE   v -PLED, -PLING, -PLES to hobble

HOPPY   adj -PIER, -PIEST having the taste of hops (catkins of a particular vine)

HOPSACK   n pl. -S a coarse fabric

HOPTOAD   n pl. -S a toad

HORA   n pl. -S an Israeli dance

HORAH   n pl. -S hora

HORAL   adj hourly

HORARY   adj hourly

HORDE   v HORDED, HORDING, HORDES to gather in a large group

HORDEIN   n pl. -S a simple protein

HORIZON   n pl. -S the line where the sky seems to meet the earth

HORMONE   n pl. -S a secretion of the endocrine organs **HORMONAL, HORMONIC** adj

HORN   v -ED, -ING, -S to form a horn (a hard, bonelike projection of the head)

HORNBEAM n pl. -S a small tree

HORNBILL   n pl. -S a large-billed bird

HORNBOOK n pl. -S a primer

HORNET   n pl. -S a stinging insect

HORNFELS   n pl. HORNFELS a silicate rock

HORNIER   comparative of horny

HORNIEST   superlative of horny

HORNILY   adv in a horny manner

HORNIST   n pl. -S a French horn player

HORNITO   n pl. -TOS a mound of volcanic matter

HORNLESS   adj lacking a horn

HORNLIKE   adj resembling a horn

HORNPIPE   n pl. -S a musical instrument

HORNPOUT *n* pl. -S a catfish

HORNTAIL *n* pl. -S a wasplike insect

HORNWORM *n* pl. -S the larva of a hawkmoth

HORNWORT *n* pl. -S an aquatic herb

HORNY *adj* HORNIER, HORNIEST hornlike in hardness

HOROLOGE *n* pl. -S a timepiece

HOROLOGY *n* pl. -GIES the science of measuring time

HORRENT *adj* bristling; standing erect

HORRIBLE *n* pl. -S something that causes horror

HORRIBLY *adv* dreadfully

HORRID *adj* repulsive **HORRIDLY** *adv*

HORRIFIC *adj* causing horror

HORRIFY *v* -FIED, -FYING, -FIES to cause to feel horror

HORROR *n* pl. -S a feeling of intense fear or repugnance

HORSE *v* HORSED, HORSING, HORSES to provide with a horse (a large, hoofed mammal)

HORSECAR *n* pl. -S a streetcar drawn by a horse

HORSEFLY *n* pl. -FLIES a large fly

HORSEMAN *n* pl. -MEN one who rides a horse

HORSEPOX *n* pl. -ES a skin disease of horses

HORSEY *adj* HORSIER, HORSIEST horsy

HORSIER comparative of horsy

HORSIEST superlative of horsy

HORSILY *adv* in a horsy manner

HORSING present participle of horse

HORST *n* pl. -S a portion of the earth's crust

HORSTE *n* pl. -S horst

HORSY *adj* HORSIER, HORSIEST resembling a horse

HOSANNA *v* -ED, -ING, -S to praise

HOSANNAH *interj* — used to express praise to God

HOSE *v* HOSED, HOSING, HOSES to spray with water

HOSE *n* pl. HOSEN stockings or socks

HOSEL *n* pl. -S a part of a golf club

HOSEPIPE *n* -S a flexible tube for conveying fluids

HOSIER *n* pl. -S one that makes hose

HOSIERY *n* pl. -SIERIES hose

HOSING present participle of hose

HOSPICE *n* pl. -S a shelter

HOSPITAL *n* pl. -S a medical institution

HOSPITIA *n/pl* places of shelter

HOSPODAR *n* pl. -S a governor of a region under Turkish rule

HOST *v* -ED, -ING, -S to entertain socially

HOSTA *n* pl. -S a plantain lily

HOSTAGE *n* pl. -S a person held as security

HOSTEL *v* -ED, -ING, -S to stay at inns overnight while traveling

HOSTELER *n* pl. -S an innkeeper

HOSTELRY *n* pl. -RIES an inn

HOSTESS *v* -ED, -ING, -ES to act as a hostess (a woman who entertains socially)

HOSTILE *n* pl. -S an unfriendly person

HOSTLER *n* pl. -S a person who tends horses or mules

HOSTLY *adj* pertaining to one who hosts

HOT *adj* HOTTER, HOTTEST having a high temperature

HOT *v* HOTTED, HOTTING, HOTS to heat

HOTBED *n* pl. -S a bed of rich soil

HOTBLOOD *n* pl. -S a thoroughbred horse

HOTBOX *n* pl. -ES an overheated bearing of a railroad car

HOTCAKE *n* pl. -S a pancake

HOTCH *v* -ED, -ING, -ES to wiggle

HOTCHPOT *n* pl. -S the combining of properties in order to divide them equally among heirs

HOTDOG *v* -DOGGED, -DOGGING, -DOGS to perform in a showy manner

HOTEL *n* pl. -S a public lodging

HOTELDOM *n* pl. -S hotels and hotel workers

HOTELIER *n* pl. -S a hotel manager

HOTELMAN *n* pl. -MEN a hotelier

HOTFOOT *v* -FOOTED, -FOOTING, -FOOTS to hurry

HOTHEAD *n* pl. -S a quick-tempered person

HOTHOUSE *n* pl. -S a heated greenhouse

HOTLINE *n* pl. -S a direct communications system for immediate contact

HOTLY *adv* in a hot manner

HOTNESS *n* pl. -ES the state of being hot

HOTPRESS *v* -ED, -ING, -ES to subject to heat and pressure

HOTROD *n* pl. -S a car modified for high speeds

HOTSHOT	*n* pl. -S a showily skillful person	**HOWFF**	*n* pl. -S howf
HOTSPUR	*n* pl. -S a hothead	**HOWITZER**	*n* pl. -S a short cannon
HOTTED	past tense of hot	**HOWK**	*v* -ED, -ING, -S to dig
HOTTER	comparative of hot	**HOWL**	*v* -ED, -ING, -S to cry like a dog
HOTTEST	superlative of hot	**HOWLER**	*n* pl. -S one that howls
HOTTING	present participle of hot	**HOWLET**	*n* pl. -S an owl
HOTTISH	*adj* somewhat hot	**HOY**	*n* pl. HOYS a heavy barge or scow
HOUDAH	*n* pl. -S howdah		
HOUND	*v* -ED, -ING, -S to pursue relentlessly	**HOYA**	*n* pl. -S a flowering plant
		HOYDEN	*v* -ED, -ING, -S to act like a tomboy
HOUNDER	*n* pl. -S one that hounds		
HOUR	*n* pl. -S a period of sixty minutes	**HOYLE**	*n* pl. -S a rule book
		HUARACHE	*n* pl. -S a flat-heeled sandal
HOURI	*n* pl. -S a beautiful maiden in Muslim belief	**HUARACHO**	*n* pl. -CHOS huarache
		HUB	*n* pl. -S the center of a wheel
HOURLY	*adj* occurring every hour	**HUBBLY**	*adj* having an uneven surface
HOUSE	*v* HOUSED, HOUSING, HOUSES to lodge in a house (a building in which people live)	**HUBBUB**	*n* pl. -S an uproar
		HUBBY	*n* pl. -BIES a husband
		HUBCAP	*n* pl. -S a covering for the hub of a wheel
HOUSEBOY	*n* pl. -BOYS a male servant	**HUBRIS**	*n* pl. -BRISES arrogance
HOUSEFLY	*n* pl. -FLIES a common fly	**HUCK**	*n* pl. -S a durable fabric
HOUSEFUL	*n* pl. -S as much as a house will hold	**HUCKLE**	*n* pl. -S the hip
		HUCKSTER	*v* -ED, -ING, -S to peddle
HOUSEL	*v* -SELED, -SELING, -SELS or -SELLED, -SELLING, -SELS to administer the Eucharist to	**HUDDLE**	*v* -DLED, -DLING, -DLES to crowd together
		HUDDLER	*n* pl. -S one that huddles
HOUSEMAN	*n* pl. -MEN a male servant	**HUE**	*n* pl. -S color **HUED,**
HOUSER	*n* pl. -S one who organizes housing projects		**HUELESS** *adj*
		HUFF	*v* -ED, -ING, -S to breathe heavily
HOUSESIT	*v* -SAT, -SITTING, -SITS to occupy a dwelling while the tenants are away	**HUFFISH**	*adj* sulky
		HUFFY	*adj* HUFFIER, HUFFIEST easily offended **HUFFILY** *adv*
HOUSETOP	*n* pl. -S the roof of a house		
HOUSING	*n* pl. -S any dwelling place	**HUG**	*v* HUGGED, HUGGING, HUGS to clasp tightly in the arms
HOVE	a past tense of heave		
HOVEL	*v* -ELED, -ELING, -ELS or -ELLED, -ELLING, -ELS to live in a small, miserable dwelling	**HUGE**	*adj* HUGER, HUGEST very large **HUGELY** *adj*
		HUGENESS	*n* pl. -ES the quality of being huge
HOVER	*v* -ED, -ING, -S to hang suspended in the air		
		HUGEOUS	*adj* huge
HOVERER	*n* pl. -S something that hovers	**HUGER**	comparative of huge
HOW	*n* pl. -S a method of doing something	**HUGEST**	superlative of huge
		HUGGABLE	*adj* cuddlesome
HOWBEIT	*adv* nevertheless	**HUGGED**	past tense of hug
HOWDAH	*n* pl. -S a seat on an elephant or camel for riders	**HUGGER**	*n* pl. -S one that hugs
		HUGGING	present participle of hug
HOWDIE	*n* pl. -S a midwife	**HUH**	*interj* — used to express surprise
HOWDY	*v* -DIED, -DYING, -DIES to greet with the words "how do you do"		
		HUIC	*interj* — used to encourage hunting hounds
HOWE	*n* pl. -S a valley		
HOWEVER	*adv* nevertheless	**HUIPIL**	*n* pl. -S or -ES an embroidered blouse or dress of Mexico
HOWF	*n* pl. -S a place frequently visited		
		HUISACHE	*n* pl. -S a flowering plant

HULA   *n* pl. -S a Hawaiian dance
HULK   *v* -ED, -ING, -S to appear impressively large
HULKY   *adj* HULKIER, HULKIEST massive
HULL   *v* -ED, -ING, -S to remove the shell from a seed
HULLER   *n* pl. -S one that hulls
HULLO   *v* -ED, -ING, -S or -ES to hallo
HULLOA   *v* -ED, -ING, -S to hallo
HUM   *v* HUMMED, HUMMING, HUMS to sing without opening the lips or saying words
HUMAN   *n* pl. -S a person
HUMANE   *adj* -MANER, -MANEST compassionate **HUMANELY** *adv*
HUMANISE   *v* -ISED, -ISING, -ISES to humanize
HUMANISM   *n* pl. -S the quality of being human
HUMANIST   *n* pl. -S one who studies human nature
HUMANITY   *n* pl. -TIES the human race
HUMANIZE   *v* -IZED, -IZING, -IZES to make human
HUMANLY   *adv* in a human manner
HUMANOID   *n* pl. -S something having human form
HUMATE   *n* pl. -S a chemical salt
HUMBLE   *adj* -BLER, -BLEST modest
HUMBLE   *v* -BLED, -BLING, -BLES to reduce the pride of
HUMBLER   *n* pl. -S one that humbles
HUMBLEST   superlative of humble
HUMBLING   present participle of humble
HUMBLY   *adv* in a humble manner
HUMBUG   *v* -BUGGED, -BUGGING, -BUGS to deceive
HUMDRUM   *n* pl. -S a dull, boring person
HUMERAL   *n* pl. -S a bone of the shoulder
HUMERUS   *n* pl. -MERI the large bone of the upper arm
HUMIC   *adj* derived from humus
HUMID   *adj* having much humidity
HUMIDIFY   *v* -FIED, -FYING, -FIES to make humid
HUMIDITY   *n* pl. -TIES moisture of the air
HUMIDLY   *adv* in a humid manner
HUMIDOR   *n* pl. -S a cigar case
HUMIFIED   *adj* converted into humus
HUMILITY   *n* pl. -TIES the quality of being humble
HUMMABLE   *adj* capable of being hummed
HUMMED   past tense of hum
HUMMER   *n* pl. -S one that hums

HUMMING   present participle of hum
HUMMOCK   *v* -ED, -ING, -S to form into hummocks (small rounded hills)
HUMMOCKY   *adj* abounding in hummocks
HUMMUS   *n* pl. -ES a paste of pureed chickpeas and tahini
HUMOR   *v* -ED, -ING, -S to indulge
HUMORAL   *adj* pertaining to bodily fluids
HUMORFUL   *adj* humorous
HUMORIST   *n* pl. -S a humorous writer or entertainer
HUMOROUS   *adj* funny; witty
HUMOUR   *v* -ED, -ING, -S to humor
HUMP   *v* -ED, -ING, -S to arch into a hump (a rounded protuberance)
HUMPBACK   *n* pl. -S a humped back
HUMPH   *v* -ED, -ING, -S to utter a grunt
HUMPLESS   *adj* lacking a hump
HUMPY   *adj* HUMPIER, HUMPIEST full of humps
HUMUS   *n* pl. -ES decomposed organic matter
HUMVEE   *n* pl. -S a type of motor vehicle
HUN   *n* pl. -S a barbarous, destructive person
HUNCH   *v* -ED, -ING, -ES to arch forward
HUNDRED   *n* pl. -S a number
HUNG   a past tense of hang
HUNGER   *v* -ED, -ING, -S to crave
HUNGOVER   *adj* suffering from a hangover
HUNGRY   *adj* -GRIER, -GRIEST wanting food **HUNGRILY** *adv*
HUNH   *interj* — used to ask for a repetition of an utterance
HUNK   *n* pl. -S a large piece
HUNKER   *v* -ED, -ING, -S to squat
HUNKY   *adj* HUNKIER, HUNKIEST muscular and attractive
HUNNISH   *adj* resembling a hun
HUNT   *v* -ED, -ING, -S to pursue for food or sport **HUNTABLE** *adj* **HUNTEDLY** *adv*
HUNTER   *n* pl. -S one that hunts
HUNTING   *n* pl. -S an instance of searching
HUNTRESS   *n* pl. -ES a female hunter
HUNTSMAN   *n* pl. -MEN a hunter
HUP   *interj* — used to mark a marching cadence
HURDIES   *n/pl* the buttocks
HURDLE   *v* -DLED, -DLING, -DLES to jump over
HURDLER   *n* pl. -S one that hurdles

HURDS	*n/pl* hards
HURL	*v* -ED, -ING, -S to throw with great force
HURLER	*n* pl. -S one that hurls
HURLEY	*n* pl. -LEYS hurling
HURLING	*n* pl. -S an Irish game
HURLY	*n* pl. -LIES commotion
HURRAH	*v* -ED, -ING, -S to cheer
HURRAY	*v* -ED, -ING, -S to hurrah
HURRIER	*n* pl. -S one that hurries
HURRY	*v* -RIED, -RYING, -RIES to move swiftly
HURST	*n* pl. -S a small hill
HURT	*v* HURT, HURTING, HURTS to injure
HURTER	*n* pl. -S one that hurts
HURTFUL	*adj* causing injury
HURTLE	*v* -TLED, -TLING, -TLES to rush violently
HURTLESS	*adj* harmless
HUSBAND	*v* -ED, -ING, -S to spend wisely
HUSH	*v* -ED, -ING, -ES to quiet **HUSHEDLY** *adv*
HUSHABY	*v* go to sleep — used imperatively to soothe a child
HUSHFUL	*adj* quiet
HUSK	*v* -ED, -ING, -S to remove the husk (the outer covering) from
HUSKER	*n* pl. -S one that husks
HUSKIER	comparative of husky
HUSKIES	pl. of husky
HUSKIEST	superlative of husky
HUSKILY	*adv* in a husky manner
HUSKING	*n* pl. -S a gathering of families to husk corn
HUSKLIKE	*adj* resembling a husk
HUSKY	*adj* -KIER, -KIEST hoarse
HUSKY	*n* pl. -KIES an Eskimo dog
HUSSAR	*n* pl. -S a cavalry soldier
HUSSY	*n* pl. -SIES a lewd woman
HUSTINGS	*n* pl. HUSTINGS a British court
HUSTLE	*v* -TLED, -TLING, -TLES to hurry
HUSTLER	*n* pl. -S one that hustles
HUSWIFE	*n* pl. -WIFES or -WIVES a sewing kit
HUT	*v* HUTTED, HUTTING, HUTS to live in a hut (a simple shelter)
HUTCH	*v* -ED, -ING, -ES to store away
HUTLIKE	*adj* resembling a hut
HUTMENT	*n* pl. -S a group of huts
HUTTED	past tense of hut
HUTTING	present participle of hut
HUTZPA	*n* pl. -S chutzpah
HUTZPAH	*n* pl. -S chutzpah
HUZZA	*v* -ED, -ING, -S to cheer
HUZZAH	*v* -ED, -ING, -S to huzza
HWAN	*n* pl. HWAN a monetary unit of South Korea
HYACINTH	*n* pl. -S a flowering plant
HYAENA	*n* pl. -S hyena **HYAENIC** *adj*
HYALIN	*n* pl. -S hyaline
HYALINE	*n* pl. -S a transparent substance
HYALITE	*n* pl. -S a colorless opal
HYALOGEN	*n* pl. -S a substance found in animal cells
HYALOID	*n* pl. -S a membrane of the eye
HYBRID	*n* pl. -S the offspring of genetically dissimilar parents
HYBRIS	*n* pl. -BRISES hubris
HYDATID	*n* pl. -S a cyst caused by a tapeworm
HYDRA	*n* pl. -DRAS or -DRAE a freshwater polyp
HYDRACID	*n* pl. -S an acid
HYDRAGOG	*n* pl. -S a purgative causing watery discharges
HYDRANT	*n* pl. -S an outlet from a water main
HYDRANTH	*n* pl. -S the oral opening of a hydra
HYDRASE	*n* pl. -S an enzyme
HYDRATE	*v* -DRATED, -DRATING, -DRATES to combine with water
HYDRATOR	*n* pl. -S one that hydrates
HYDRIA	*n* pl. -DRIAE a water jar
HYDRIC	*adj* pertaining to moisture
HYDRID	*n* pl. -S hydride
HYDRIDE	*n* pl. -S a chemical compound
HYDRO	*n* pl. -DROS electricity produced by waterpower
HYDROGEL	*n* pl. -S a colloid
HYDROGEN	*n* pl. -S a gaseous element
HYDROID	*n* pl. -S a polyp
HYDROMEL	*n* pl. -S a mixture of honey and water
HYDRONIC	*adj* pertaining to heating and cooling by water
HYDROPIC	*adj* affected with hydropsy
HYDROPS	*n* pl. -ES hydropsy
HYDROPSY	*n* pl. -SIES dropsy
HYDROSKI	*n* pl. -S a plate attached to a seaplane to facilitate takeoffs and landings

HYDROSOL *n* pl. -S an aqueous solution of a colloid

HYDROUS *adj* containing water

HYDROXY *adj* containing hydroxyl

HYDROXYL *n* pl. -S the radical or group containing oxygen and hydrogen

HYENA *n* pl. -S a wolflike mammal **HYENIC, HYENINE, HYENOID** *adj*

HYETAL *adj* pertaining to rain

HYGEIST *n* pl. -S an expert in hygiene

HYGIEIST *n* pl. -S hygeist

HYGIENE *n* pl. -S the science of health **HYGIENIC** *adj*

HYING present participle of hie

HYLA *n* pl. -S a tree frog

HYLOZOIC *adj* pertaining to the doctrine that life and matter are inseparable

HYMEN *n* pl. -S a vaginal membrane **HYMENAL** *adj*

HYMENEAL *n* pl. -S a wedding song or poem

HYMENIUM *n* pl. -NIA or -NIUMS a layer in certain fungi **HYMENIAL** *adj*

HYMN *v* -ED, -ING, -S to sing a hymn (a song of praise to God)

HYMNAL *n* pl. -S a book of hymns

HYMNARY *n* pl. -RIES a hymnal

HYMNBOOK *n* pl. -S a hymnal

HYMNIST *n* pl. -S one who composes hymns

HYMNLESS *adj* lacking a hymn

HYMNLIKE *adj* resembling a hymn

HYMNODY *n* pl. -DIES the singing of hymns

HYOID *n* pl. -S a bone of the tongue **HYOIDAL, HYOIDEAN** *adj*

HYOSCINE *n* pl. -S a sedative

HYP *n* pl. -S hypochondria

HYPE *v* HYPED, HYPING, HYPES to promote extravagantly

HYPER *adj* very excitable

HYPERGOL *n* pl. -S a rocket fuel

HYPERON *n* pl. -S an atomic particle

HYPEROPE *n* pl. -S a farsighted person

HYPHA *n* pl. -PHAE a threadlike element of a fungus **HYPHAL** *adj*

HYPHEMIA *n* pl. -S deficiency of blood

HYPHEN *v* -ED, -ING, -S to connect words or syllables with a hyphen (a mark of punctuation)

HYPING present participle of hype

HYPNIC *adj* pertaining to sleep

HYPNOID *adj* pertaining to hypnosis or sleep

HYPNOSIS *n* pl. -NOSES an artificially induced state resembling sleep

HYPNOTIC *n* pl. -S a sleep-inducing drug

HYPO *v* -ED, -ING, -S to inject with a hypodermic needle

HYPOACID *adj* having a lower than normal degree of acidity

HYPODERM *n* pl. -S a skin layer

HYPOGEA pl. of hypogeum

HYPOGEAL *adj* underground

HYPOGEAN *adj* hypogeal

HYPOGENE *adj* formed underground

HYPOGEUM *n* pl. -GEA an underground chamber

HYPOGYNY *n* pl. -NIES the condition of having flowers with organs situated below the ovary

HYPONEA *n* pl. -S hyponoia

HYPONOIA *n* pl. -S dulled mental activity

HYPOPNEA *n* pl. -S abnormally shallow breathing

HYPOPYON *n* pl. -S an accumulation of pus in the eye

HYPOTHEC *n* pl. -S a type of mortgage

HYPOXIA *n* pl. -S a deficiency of oxygen in body tissue **HYPOXIC** *adj*

HYRACOID *n* pl. -S a hyrax

HYRAX *n* pl. -RAXES or -RACES a small, harelike mammal

HYSON *n* pl. -S a Chinese tea

HYSSOP *n* pl. -S a medicinal herb

HYSTERIA *n* pl. -S uncontrollable excitement or fear

HYSTERIC *n* pl. -S one who is subject to fits of hysteria

HYTE *adj* insane

IAMB	*n* pl. -S a type of metrical foot
IAMBIC	*n* pl. -S an iamb
IAMBUS	*n* pl. -BUSES or -BI an iamb
IATRIC	*adj* pertaining to medicine
IATRICAL	*adj* iatric
IBEX	*n* pl. IBEXES or IBICES a wild goat
IBIDEM	*adv* in the same place
IBIS	*n* pl. IBISES a wading bird
IBOGAINE	*n* pl. -S an alkaloid used as an antidepressant
ICE	*v* ICED, ICING, ICES to cover with ice (frozen water)
ICEBERG	*n* pl. -S a large floating body of ice
ICEBLINK	*n* pl. -S a glare over an ice field
ICEBOAT	*n* pl. -S a vehicle that sails on ice
ICEBOUND	*adj* surrounded by ice
ICEBOX	*n* pl. -ES a cabinet for cooling food
ICECAP	*n* pl. -S a covering of ice and snow
ICED	past tense of ice
ICEFALL	*n* pl. -S a kind of frozen waterfall
ICEHOUSE	*n* pl. -S a building for storing ice
ICEKHANA	*n* pl. -S an automotive event held on a frozen lake
ICELESS	*adj* having no ice
ICELIKE	*adj* resembling ice
ICEMAN	*n* pl. -MEN a man who supplies ice
ICH	*n* pl. ICHS a disease of certain fishes
ICHNITE	*n* pl. -S a fossil footprint

ICHOR	*n* pl. -S a watery discharge from a wound **ICHOROUS** *adj*
ICHTHYIC	*adj* pertaining to fishes
ICICLE	*n* pl. -S a hanging spike of ice **ICICLED** *adj*
ICIER	comparative of icy
ICIEST	superlative of icy
ICILY	*adv* in an icy manner
ICINESS	*n* pl. -ES the state of being icy
ICING	*n* pl. -S a sweet mixture for covering cakes
ICK	*interj* — used to express disgust
ICKER	*n* pl. -S a head of grain
ICKINESS	*n* pl. -ES the state of being icky
ICKY	*adj* ICKIER, ICKIEST repulsive **ICKILY** *adv*
ICON	*n* pl. -S or -ES a representation **ICONIC, ICONICAL** *adj*
ICTERIC	*n* pl. -S a remedy for icterus
ICTERUS	*n* pl. -ES a diseased condition of the liver
ICTUS	*n* pl. -ES a recurring stress or beat in a poetical form **ICTIC** *adj*
ICY	*adj* ICIER, ICIEST covered with ice
ID	*n* pl. -S a part of the psyche
IDEA	*n* pl. -S a conception existing in the mind **IDEALESS** *adj*
IDEAL	*n* pl. -S a standard of perfection
IDEALISE	*v* -ISED, -ISING, -ISES to idealize
IDEALISM	*n* pl. -S the pursuit of noble goals

IDEALIST *n* pl. -S an adherent of idealism

IDEALITY *n* pl. -TIES the state of being perfect; something idealized

IDEALIZE *v* -IZED, -IZING, -IZES to regard as perfect

IDEALLY *adv* perfectly

IDEALOGY *n* pl. -GIES ideology

IDEATE *v* -ATED, -ATING, -ATES to form an idea

IDEATION *n* pl. -S the act of ideating

IDEATIVE *adj* pertaining to ideation

IDEM *adj* the same

IDENTIC *adj* identical

IDENTIFY *v* -FIED, -FYING, -FIES to establish the identity of

IDENTITY *n* pl. -TIES the essential character of a person or thing

IDEOGRAM *n* pl. -S a type of written symbol

IDEOLOGY *n* pl. -GIES a systematic body of ideas

IDES *n* pl. IDES a certain day in the ancient Roman calendar

IDIOCY *n* pl. -CIES the condition of being an idiot

IDIOLECT *n* pl. -S one's speech pattern

IDIOM *n* pl. -S an expression peculiar to a language

IDIOT *n* pl. -S a mentally deficient person **IDIOTIC** *adj*

IDIOTISM *n* pl. -S idiocy

IDLE *adj* IDLER, IDLEST inactive

IDLE *v* IDLED, IDLING, IDLES to pass time idly

IDLENESS *n* pl. -ES the state of being idle

IDLER *n* pl. -S one that idles

IDLESSE *n* pl. -S idleness

IDLEST superlative of idle

IDLING present participle of idle

IDLY *adv* in an idle manner

IDOCRASE *n* pl. -S a mineral

IDOL *n* pl. -S an object of worship

IDOLATER *n* pl. -S one that worships idols

IDOLATOR *n* pl. -S idolater

IDOLATRY *n* pl. -TRIES the worship of idols

IDOLISE *v* -ISED, -ISING, -ISES to idolize

IDOLISER *n* pl. -S one that idolises

IDOLISM *n* pl. -S idolatry

IDOLIZE *v* -IZED, -IZING, -IZES to worship

IDOLIZER *n* pl. -S one that idolizes

IDONEITY *n* pl. -TIES the state of being idoneous

IDONEOUS *adj* suitable

IDYL *n* pl. -S a poem or prose work depicting scenes of rural simplicity

IDYLIST *n* pl. -S a writer of idyls

IDYLL *n* pl. -S idyl **IDYLLIC** *adj*

IDYLLIST *n* pl. -S idylist

IF *n* pl. -S a possibility

IFF *conj* if and only if

IFFINESS *n* pl. -ES the state of being iffy

IFFY *adj* IFFIER, IFFIEST full of uncertainty

IGLOO *n* pl. -LOOS an Eskimo dwelling

IGLU *n* pl. -S igloo

IGNATIA *n* pl. -S a medicinal seed

IGNEOUS *adj* pertaining to fire

IGNIFY *v* -FIED, -FYING, -FIES to burn

IGNITE *v* -NITED, -NITING, -NITES to set on fire

IGNITER *n* pl. -S one that ignites

IGNITION *n* pl. -S the act of igniting

IGNITOR *n* pl. -S igniter

IGNITRON *n* pl. -S a type of rectifier tube

IGNOBLE *adj* of low character **IGNOBLY** *adv*

IGNOMINY *n* pl. -NIES disgrace or dishonor

IGNORANT *adj* having no knowledge

IGNORE *v* -NORED, -NORING, -NORES to refuse to notice

IGNORER *n* pl. -S one that ignores

IGUANA *n* pl. -S a tropical lizard

IGUANIAN *n* pl. -S a lizard related to the iguana

IHRAM *n* pl. -S the garb worn by Muslim pilgrims

IKAT *n* pl. -S a fabric of tie-dyed yarns

IKEBANA *n* pl. -S the Japanese art of flower arranging

IKON *n* pl. -S icon

ILEA pl. of ileum

ILEAC *adj* pertaining to the ileum

ILEAL *adj* ileac

ILEITIS *n* pl. ILEITIDES inflammation of the ileum

ILEUM *n* pl. ILEA a part of the small intestine

ILEUS *n* pl. -ES intestinal obstruction

ILEX *n* pl. -ES a holly

ILIA pl. of ilium

ILIAC *adj* pertaining to the ilium

ILIAD n pl. -S a long poem
ILIAL adj iliac
ILIUM n pl. ILIA a bone of the pelvis
ILK n pl. -S a class or kind
ILKA adj each
ILL n pl. -S an evil
ILLATION n pl. -S the act of inferring
ILLATIVE n pl. -S a word or phrase introducing an inference
ILLEGAL n pl. -S a person who enters a country without authorization
ILLICIT adj not permitted
ILLINIUM n pl. -S a radioactive element
ILLIQUID adj not readily convertible into cash
ILLITE n pl. -S a group of minerals **ILLITIC** adj
ILLNESS n pl. -ES sickness
ILLOGIC n pl. -S absence of logic
ILLUME v -LUMED, -LUMING, -LUMES to illuminate
ILLUMINE v -MINED, -MINING, -MINES to illuminate
ILLUSION n pl. -S a false perception
ILLUSIVE adj illusory
ILLUSORY adj based on illusion
ILLUVIUM n pl. -VIA or -VIUMS a type of material accumulated in soil **ILLUVIAL** adj
ILLY adv badly
ILMENITE n pl. -S a mineral
IMAGE v -AGED, -AGING, -AGES to imagine
IMAGER n pl. -S one that images
IMAGERY n pl. -ERIES mental pictures
IMAGINAL adj pertaining to an imago
IMAGINE v -INED, -INING, -INES to form a mental picture of
IMAGINER n pl. -S one that imagines
IMAGING present participle of image
IMAGINING present participle of imagine
IMAGISM n pl. -S a movement in poetry
IMAGIST n pl. -S an adherent of imagism
IMAGO n pl. -GOES or -GOS an adult insect
IMAM n pl. -S a Muslim priest
IMAMATE n pl. -S the office of an imam
IMARET n pl. -S a Turkish inn
IMAUM n pl. -S imam
IMBALM v -ED, -ING, -S to embalm
IMBALMER n pl. -S embalmer
IMBARK v -ED, -ING, -S to embark
IMBECILE n pl. -S a mentally deficient person

IMBED v -BEDDED, -BEDDING, -BEDS to embed
IMBIBE v -BIBED, -BIBING, -BIBES to drink
IMBIBER n pl. -S one that imbibes
IMBITTER v -ED, -ING, -S to embitter
IMBLAZE v -BLAZED, -BLAZING, -BLAZES to emblaze
IMBODY v -BODIED, -BODYING, -BODIES to embody
IMBOLDEN v -ED, -ING, -S to embolden
IMBOSOM v -ED, -ING, -S to embosom
IMBOWER v -ED, -ING, -S to embower
IMBROWN v -ED, -ING, -S to embrown
IMBRUE v -BRUED, -BRUING, -BRUES to stain
IMBRUTE v -BRUTED, -BRUTING, -BRUTES to make brutal
IMBUE v -BUED, -BUING, -BUES to make thoroughly wet
IMID n pl. -S imide
IMIDE n pl. -S a chemical compound **IMIDIC** adj
IMIDO adj containing an imide
IMINE n pl. -S a chemical compound
IMINO adj containing an imine
IMITABLE adj capable of being imitated
IMITATE v -TATED, -TATING, -TATES to behave in the same way as
IMITATOR n pl. -S one that imitates
IMMANE adj great in size
IMMANENT adj existing within
IMMATURE n pl. -S an individual that is not fully grown or developed
IMMENSE adj -MENSER, -MENSEST great in size
IMMERGE v -MERGED, -MERGING, -MERGES to immerse
IMMERSE v -MERSED, -MERSING, -MERSES to plunge into a liquid
IMMESH v -ED, -ING, -ES to enmesh
IMMIES pl. of immy
IMMINENT adj ready to take place
IMMINGLE v -GLED, -GLING, -GLES to blend
IMMIX v -ED, -ING, -ES to mix in
IMMOBILE adj incapable of being moved
IMMODEST adj not modest
IMMOLATE v -LATED, -LATING, -LATES to kill as a sacrifice
IMMORAL adj contrary to established morality
IMMORTAL n pl. -S one who is not subject to death
IMMOTILE adj lacking mobility

IMMUNE	*n* pl. -S one who is protected from a disease	**IMPERIA**	a pl. of imperium
IMMUNISE	*v* -NISED, -NISING, -NISES to immunize	**IMPERIAL**	*n* pl. -S an emperor or empress
IMMUNITY	*n* pl. -TIES the state of being protected from a disease	**IMPERIL**	*v* -ILED, -ILING, -ILS or -ILLED, -ILLING, -ILS to place in jeopardy
IMMUNIZE	*v* -NIZED, -NIZING, -NIZES to protect from a disease	**IMPERIUM**	*n* pl. -RIUMS or -RIA absolute power
IMMURE	*v* -MURED, -MURING, -MURES to imprison	**IMPETIGO**	*n* pl. -GOS a skin disease
IMMY	*n* pl. -MIES a type of playing marble	**IMPETUS**	*n* pl. -ES an impelling force
		IMPHEE	*n* pl. -S an African grass
IMP	*v* -ED, -ING, -S to graft feathers onto a bird's wing	**IMPI**	*n* pl. -S a body of warriors
		IMPIETY	*n* pl. -TIES lack of piety
IMPACT	*v* -ED, -ING, -S to pack firmly together	**IMPING**	*n* pl. -S the process of grafting
		IMPINGE	*v* -PINGED, -PINGING, -PINGES to collide
IMPACTER	*n* pl. -S one that impacts		
IMPACTOR	*n* pl. -S impacter	**IMPINGER**	*n* pl. -S one that impinges
IMPAINT	*v* -ED, -ING, -S to paint or depict	**IMPIOUS**	*adj* not pious
		IMPISH	*adj* mischievous **IMPISHLY** *adv*
IMPAIR	*v* -ED, -ING, -S to make worse	**IMPLANT**	*v* -ED, -ING, -S to set securely
IMPAIRER	*n* pl. -S one that impairs	**IMPLEAD**	*v* -ED, -ING, -S to sue in a court of law
IMPALA	*n* pl. -S an African antelope		
IMPALE	*v* -PALED, -PALING, -PALES to pierce with a pointed object	**IMPLEDGE**	*v* -PLEDGED, -PLEDGING, -PLEDGES to pawn
IMPALER	*n* pl. -S one that impales	**IMPLICIT**	*adj* implied
IMPANEL	*v* -ELED, -ELING, -ELS or -ELLED, -ELLING, -ELS to enter on a list for jury duty	**IMPLIED**	past tense of imply
		IMPLIES	present 3d person sing. of imply
IMPARITY	*n* pl. -TIES lack of equality	**IMPLODE**	*v* -PLODED, -PLODING, -PLODES to collapse inward
IMPARK	*v* -ED, -ING, -S to confine in a park		
		IMPLORE	*v* -PLORED, -PLORING, -PLORES to beg for urgently
IMPART	*v* -ED, -ING, -S to make known		
		IMPLORER	*n* pl. -S one that implores
IMPARTER	*n* pl. -S one that imparts	**IMPLY**	*v* -PLIED, -PLYING, -PLIES to indicate or suggest indirectly
IMPASSE	*n* pl. -S a road or passage having no exit		
		IMPOLICY	*n* pl. -CIES an unwise course of action
IMPASTE	*v* -PASTED, -PASTING, -PASTES to make into a paste		
		IMPOLITE	*adj* not polite
IMPASTO	*n* pl. -TOS a painting technique	**IMPONE**	*v* -PONED, -PONING, -PONES to wager
IMPAVID	*adj* brave		
IMPAWN	*v* -ED, -ING, -S to pawn	**IMPOROUS**	*adj* extremely dense
IMPEACH	*v* -ED, -ING, -ES to charge with misconduct in office	**IMPORT**	*v* -ED, -ING, -S to bring into a country from abroad
IMPEARL	*v* -ED, -ING, -S to make pearly	**IMPORTER**	*n* pl. -S one that imports
		IMPOSE	*v* -POSED, -POSING, -POSES to establish as compulsory
IMPEDE	*v* -PEDED, -PEDING, -PEDES to obstruct the progress of		
IMPEDER	*n* pl. -S one that impedes	**IMPOSER**	*n* pl. -S one that imposes
IMPEL	*v* -PELLED, -PELLING, -PELS to force into action	**IMPOST**	*v* -ED, -ING, -S to determine customs duties
IMPELLER	*n* pl. -S one that impels	**IMPOSTER**	*n* pl. -S impostor
IMPELLOR	*n* pl. -S impeller	**IMPOSTOR**	*n* pl. -S one that poses as another for deceptive purposes
IMPEND	*v* -ED, -ING, -S to be imminent		
		IMPOTENT	*n* pl. -S one that is powerless

IMPOUND	*v* -ED, -ING, -S to seize and retain in legal custody
IMPOWER	*v* -ED, -ING, -S to empower
IMPREGN	*v* -ED, -ING, -S to make pregnant
IMPRESA	*n* pl. -S a type of emblem
IMPRESE	*n* pl. -S impresa
IMPRESS	*v* -ED, -ING, -ES to affect strongly
IMPREST	*n* pl. -S a loan or advance of money
IMPRIMIS	*adv* in the first place
IMPRINT	*v* -ED, -ING, -S to produce a mark by pressure
IMPRISON	*v* -ED, -ING, -S to confine
IMPROPER	*adj* not proper
IMPROV	*n* pl. -S improvisation
IMPROVE	*v* -PROVED, -PROVING, -PROVES to make better
IMPROVER	*n* pl. -S one that improves
IMPUDENT	*adj* offensively bold or disrespectful
IMPUGN	*v* -ED, -ING, -S to make insinuations against
IMPUGNER	*n* pl. -S one that impugns
IMPULSE	*v* -PULSED, -PULSING, -PULSES to give impetus to
IMPUNITY	*n* pl. -TIES exemption from penalty
IMPURE	*adj* not pure **IMPURELY** *adv*
IMPURITY	*n* pl. -TIES something that is impure
IMPUTE	*v* -PUTED, -PUTING, -PUTES to credit to a person or a cause
IMPUTER	*n* pl. -S one that imputes
IN	*v* INNED, INNING, INS to harvest
INACTION	*n* pl. -S lack of action
INACTIVE	*adj* not active
INANE	*adj* INANER, INANEST nonsensical **INANELY** *adv*
INANE	*n* pl. -S empty space
INANITY	*n* pl. -TIES something that is inane
INAPT	*adj* not apt **INAPTLY** *adv*
INARABLE	*adj* not arable
INARCH	*v* -ED, -ING, -ES to graft with in a certain way
INARM	*v* -ED, -ING, -S to encircle with the arms
INBEING	*n* pl. -S the state of being inherent
INBOARD	*n* pl. -S a type of boat motor
INBORN	*adj* existing in one from birth
INBOUND	*v* -ED, -ING, -S to put a basketball in play from out of bounds
INBOUNDS	*adj* being within certain boundaries
INBRED	*n* pl. -S a product of inbreeding
INBREED	*v* -BRED, -BREEDING, -BREEDS to breed closely related stock
INBUILT	*adj* forming an integral part of a structure
INBURST	*n* pl. -S the act of bursting inward
INBY	*adv* inward
INBYE	*adv* inby
INCAGE	*v* -CAGED, -CAGING, -CAGES to encage
INCANT	*v* -ED, -ING, -S to utter ritually
INCASE	*v* -CASED, -CASING, -CASES to encase
INCENSE	*v* -CENSED, -CENSING, -CENSES to make angry
INCENTER	*n* pl. -S the point where the three lines bisecting the angles of a triangle meet
INCEPT	*v* -ED, -ING, -S to take in
INCEPTOR	*n* pl. -S one that incepts
INCEST	*n* pl. -S sexual intercourse between closely related persons
INCH	*v* -ED, -ING, -ES to move very slowly
INCHMEAL	*adv* little by little
INCHOATE	*adj* being in an early stage
INCHWORM	*n* pl. -S a type of worm
INCIDENT	*n* pl. -S an event
INCIPIT	*n* pl. -S the opening words of a text
INCISAL	*adj* being the cutting edge of a tooth
INCISE	*v* -CISED, -CISING, -CISES to cut into
INCISION	*n* pl. -S the act of incising
INCISIVE	*adj* penetrating
INCISOR	*n* pl. -S a cutting tooth
INCISORY	*adj* adapted for cutting
INCISURE	*n* pl. -S a notch or cleft of a body part
INCITANT	*n* pl. -S something that incites
INCITE	*v* -CITED, -CITING, -CITES to arouse to action
INCITER	*n* pl. -S one that incites
INCIVIL	*adj* discourteous
INCLASP	*v* -ED, -ING, -S to enclasp

INCLINE	*v* -CLINED, -CLINING, -CLINES to slant
INCLINER	*n* pl. -S one that inclines
INCLIP	*v* -CLIPPED, -CLIPPING, -CLIPS to clasp
INCLOSE	*v* -CLOSED, -CLOSING, -CLOSES to enclose
INCLOSER	*n* pl. -S one that incloses
INCLUDE	*v* -CLUDED, -CLUDING, -CLUDES to have as a part
INCOG	*n* pl. -S a disguised person
INCOME	*n* pl. -S a sum of money earned regularly
INCOMER	*n* pl. -S one that comes in
INCOMING	*n* pl. -S an arrival
INCONNU	*n* pl. -S a large food fish
INCONY	*adj* pretty
INCORPSE	*v* -CORPSED, -CORPSING, -CORPSES to become combined with
INCREASE	*v* -CREASED, -CREASING, -CREASES to make or become greater
INCREATE	*adj* not created
INCROSS	*v* -ED, -ING, -ES to inbreed
INCRUST	*v* -ED, -ING, -S to encrust
INCUBATE	*v* -BATED, -BATING, -BATES to warm eggs for hatching
INCUBUS	*n* pl. -BI or -BUSES a demon
INCUDAL	*adj* pertaining to the incus
INCUDATE	*adj* incudal
INCUDES	pl. of incus
INCULT	*adj* uncultivated
INCUMBER	*v* -ED, -ING, -S to encumber
INCUR	*v* -CURRED, -CURRING, -CURS to bring upon oneself
INCURVE	*v* -CURVED, -CURVING, -CURVES to curve inward
INCUS	*n* pl. INCUDES a bone in the middle ear
INCUSE	*v* -CUSED, -CUSING, -CUSES to mark by stamping
INDABA	*n* pl. -S a meeting of South African tribes
INDAGATE	*v* -GATED, -GATING, -GATES to investigate
INDAMIN	*n* pl. -S indamine
INDAMINE	*n* pl. -S a chemical compound
INDEBTED	*adj* beholden
INDECENT	*adj* -CENTER, -CENTEST not decent
INDEED	*adv* in truth
INDENE	*n* pl. -S a hydrocarbon
INDENT	*v* -ED, -ING, -S to cut or tear irregularly
INDENTER	*n* pl. -S one that indents
INDENTOR	*n* pl. -S indenter
INDEVOUT	*adj* not devout
INDEX	*n* pl. INDEXES or INDICES a type of reference guide at the end of a book
INDEX	*v* -ED, -ING, -ES to provide with an index
INDEXER	*n* pl. -S one that indexes
INDEXING	*n* pl. -S the linking of wages and prices to cost-of-living levels
INDICAN	*n* pl. -S a chemical compound
INDICANT	*n* pl. -S something that indicates
INDICATE	*v* -CATED, -CATING, -CATES to point out
INDICES	a pl. of index
INDICIA	*n* pl. -S a distinctive mark
INDICIUM	*n* pl. -S an indicia
INDICT	*v* -ED, -ING, -S to charge with a crime
INDICTEE	*n* pl. -S one that is indicted
INDICTER	*n* pl. -S one that indicts
INDICTOR	*n* pl. -S indicter
INDIE	*n* pl. -S a person who is independent
INDIGEN	*n* pl. -S indigene
INDIGENE	*n* pl. -S a native
INDIGENT	*n* pl. -S a needy person
INDIGN	*adj* disgraceful INDIGNLY *adv*
INDIGO	*n* pl. -GOS or -GOES a blue dye
INDIGOID	*n* pl. -S a blue dye
INDIRECT	*adj* not direct
INDITE	*v* -DITED, -DITING, -DITES to write or compose
INDITER	*n* pl. -S one that indites
INDIUM	*n* pl. -S a metallic element
INDOCILE	*adj* not docile
INDOL	*n* pl. -S indole
INDOLE	*n* pl. -S a chemical compound
INDOLENT	*adj* lazy
INDOOR	*adj* pertaining to the interior of a building
INDOORS	*adv* in or into a house
INDORSE	*v* -DORSED, -DORSING, -DORSES to endorse
INDORSEE	*n* pl. -S endorsee
INDORSER	*n* pl. -S endorser
INDORSING	present participle of indorse
INDORSOR	*n* pl. -S endorsor
INDOW	*v* -ED, -ING, -S to endow
INDOXYL	*n* -S a chemical compound
INDRAFT	*n* pl. -S an inward flow or current
INDRAWN	*adj* drawn in

INDRI *n* pl. -S a short-tailed lemur

INDUCE *v* -DUCED, -DUCING, -DUCES to influence into doing something

INDUCER *n* pl. -S one that induces

INDUCT *v* -ED, -ING, -S to bring into military service

INDUCTEE *n* pl. -S one that is inducted

INDUCTOR *n* pl. -S one that inducts

INDUE *v* -DUED, -DUING, -DUES to endue

INDULGE *v* -DULGED, -DULGING, -DULGES to yield to the desire of

INDULGER *n* pl. -S one that indulges

INDULIN *n* pl. -S induline

INDULINE *n* pl. -S a blue dye

INDULT *n* pl. -S a privilege granted by the pope

INDURATE *v* -RATED, -RATING, -RATES to make hard

INDUSIUM *n* pl. -SIA an enclosing membrane **INDUSIAL** *adj*

INDUSTRY *n* pl. -TRIES a group of productive enterprises

INDWELL *v* -DWELT, -DWELLING, -DWELLS to live within

INEARTH *v* -ED, -ING, -S to bury

INEDIBLE *adj* not fit to be eaten

INEDITA *n/pl* unpublished literary works

INEDITED *adj* not published

INEPT *adj* not suitable **INEPTLY** *adv*

INEQUITY *n* pl. -TIES unfairness

INERRANT *adj* free from error

INERT *n* pl. -S something that lacks active properties

INERTIA *n* pl. -TIAS or -TIAE the tendency of a body to resist acceleration **INERTIAL** *adj*

INERTLY *adv* inactively

INEXACT *adj* not exact

INEXPERT *n* pl. -S a novice

INFALL *n* pl. -S movement under the influence of gravity toward a celestial object

INFAMOUS *adj* having a vile reputation

INFAMY *n* pl. -MIES the state of being infamous

INFANCY *n* pl. -CIES the state of being an infant

INFANT *n* pl. -S a child in the earliest stages of life

INFANTA *n* pl. -S a daughter of a Spanish or Portuguese monarch

INFANTE *n* pl. -S a younger son of a Spanish or Portuguese monarch

INFANTRY *n* pl. -TRIES a branch of the army composed of foot soldiers

INFARCT *n* pl. -S an area of dead or dying tissue

INFARE *n* pl. -S a reception for newlyweds

INFAUNA *n* pl. -NAS or -NAE fauna living on a soft sea floor **INFAUNAL** *adj*

INFECT *v* -ED, -ING, -S to contaminate with disease-producing germs

INFECTER *n* pl. -S one that infects

INFECTOR *n* pl. -S infecter

INFECUND *adj* barren

INFEOFF *v* -ED, -ING, -S to enfeoff

INFER *v* -FERRED, -FERRING, -FERS to reach or derive by reasoning

INFERIOR *n* pl. -S one of lesser rank

INFERNAL *adj* pertaining to hell

INFERNO *n* pl. -NOS a place that resembles or suggests hell

INFERRED past tense of infer

INFERRER *n* pl. -S one that infers

INFERRING present participle of infer

INFEST *v* -ED, -ING, -S to overrun in large numbers

INFESTER *n* pl. -S one that infests

INFIDEL *n* pl. -S one who has no religious faith

INFIELD *n* pl. -S a part of a baseball field

INFIGHT *v* -FOUGHT, -FIGHTING, -FIGHTS to contend with others within the same group

INFINITE *n* pl. -S something that has no limits

INFINITY *n* pl. -TIES the state of having no limits

INFIRM *v* -ED, -ING, -S to weaken or destroy the validity of

INFIRMLY *adv* in a feeble manner

INFIX *v* -ED, -ING, -ES to implant

INFIXION *n* pl. -S the act of infixing

INFLAME *v* -FLAMED, -FLAMING, -FLAMES to set on fire

INFLAMER *n* pl. -S one that inflames

INFLATE *v* -FLATED, -FLATING, -FLATES to cause to expand by filling with gas or air

INFLATER *n* pl. -S one that inflates

INFLATOR *n* pl. -S inflater

INFLECT	v -ED, -ING, -S to bend
INFLEXED	adj bent inward
INFLICT	v -ED, -ING, -S to cause to be endured; impose
INFLIGHT	adj done during an air voyage
INFLOW	n pl. -S the act of flowing in
INFLUENT	n pl. -S a tributary
INFLUX	n pl. -ES a flowing in
INFO	n pl. -FOS information
INFOLD	v -ED, -ING, -S to fold inward
INFOLDER	n pl. -S one that infolds
INFORM	v -ED, -ING, -S to supply with information
INFORMAL	adj marked by the absence of formality or ceremony
INFORMER	n pl. -S one that informs
INFOUGHT	past tense of infight
INFRA	adv below
INFRACT	v -ED, -ING, -S to break a legal rule
INFRARED	n pl. -S a part of the invisible spectrum
INFRINGE	v -FRINGED, -FRINGING, -FRINGES to violate an oath or a law
INFRUGAL	adj not frugal
INFUSE	v -FUSED, -FUSING, -FUSES to permeate with something
INFUSER	n pl. -S one that infuses
INFUSION	n pl. -S the act of infusing
INFUSIVE	adj capable of infusing
INGATE	n pl. -S a channel by which molten metal enters a mold
INGATHER	v -ED, -ING, -S to gather in
INGENUE	n pl. -S a naive young woman
INGEST	v -ED, -ING, -S to take into the body
INGESTA	n/pl ingested material
INGLE	n pl. -S a fire
INGOING	adj entering
INGOT	v -ED, -ING, -S to shape into a convenient form for storage
INGRAFT	v -ED, -ING, -S to engraft
INGRAIN	v -ED, -ING, -S to impress firmly on the mind
INGRATE	n pl. -S an ungrateful person
INGRESS	n pl. -ES the act of entering
INGROUP	n pl. -S a group united by common interests
INGROWN	adj grown into the flesh
INGROWTH	n pl. -S growth inward
INGUINAL	adj pertaining to the groin
INGULF	v -ED, -ING, -S to engulf
INHABIT	v -ED, -ING, -S to live in
INHALANT	n pl. -S something that is inhaled

INHALE	v -HALED, -HALING, -HALES to take into the lungs
INHALER	n pl. -S one that inhales
INHAUL	n pl. -S a line for bringing in a sail
INHAULER	n pl. -S an inhaul
INHERE	v -HERED, -HERING, -HERES to be inherent
INHERENT	adj existing in something as an essential characteristic
INHERIT	v -ED, -ING, -S to receive by legal succession
INHESION	n pl. -S the state of inhering
INHIBIN	n pl. -S a human hormone
INHIBIT	v -ED, -ING, -S to restrain or hold back
INHUMAN	adj lacking desirable human qualities
INHUMANE	adj not humane
INHUME	v -HUMED, -HUMING, -HUMES to bury
INHUMER	n pl. -S one that inhumes
INIMICAL	adj unfriendly
INION	n pl. INIA a part of the skull
INIQUITY	n pl. -TIES a gross injustice
INITIAL	v -TIALED, -TIALING, -TIALS or -TIALLED, -TIALLING, -TIALS to mark with the first letters of one's name
INITIATE	v -ATED, -ATING, -ATES to originate
INJECT	v -ED, -ING, -S to force a fluid into
INJECTOR	n pl. -S one that injects
INJURE	v -JURED, -JURING, -JURES to do or cause injury to
INJURER	n pl. -S one that injures
INJURY	n pl. -RIES harm inflicted or suffered
INK	v -ED, -ING, -S to mark with ink (a colored fluid used for writing)
INKBERRY	n pl. -RIES a small shrub
INKBLOT	n pl. -S a blotted pattern of spilled ink
INKER	n pl. -S one that inks
INKHORN	n pl. -S a small container for ink
INKIER	comparative of inky
INKIEST	superlative of inky
INKINESS	n pl. -ES the state of being inky
INKJET	adj being a high-speed printing process using jets of ink

INKLE *n* pl. -S a tape used for trimming

INKLESS *adj* being without ink

INKLIKE *adj* resembling ink

INKLING *n* pl. -S a slight suggestion

INKPOT *n* pl. -S an inkwell

INKSTAND *n* pl. -S an inkwell

INKSTONE *n* pl. -S a stone on which dry ink and water are mixed

INKWELL *n* pl. -S a small container for ink

INKWOOD *n* pl. -S an evergreen tree

INKY *adj* INKIER, INKIEST resembling ink

INLACE *v* -LACED, -LACING, -LACES to enlace

INLAID past tense of inlay

INLAND *n* pl. -S the interior of a region

INLANDER *n* pl. -S one living in the interior of a region

INLAY *v* -LAID, -LAYING, -LAYS to set into a surface

INLAYER *n* pl. -S one that inlays

INLET *v* -LET, -LETTING, -LETS to insert

INLIER *n* pl. -S a type of rock formation

INLY *adv* inwardly

INMATE *n* pl. -S one who is confined to an institution

INMESH *v* -ED, -ING, -ES to enmesh

INMOST *adj* farthest within

INN *v* -ED, -ING, -S to put up at an inn (a public lodging house)

INNARDS *n/pl* the internal organs

INNATE *adj* inborn INNATELY *adv*

INNED past tense of in

INNER *n* pl. -S something that is within

INNERLY *adv* inwardly

INNERVE *v* -NERVED, -NERVING, -NERVES to stimulate

INNING *n* pl. -S a division of a baseball game

INNLESS *adj* having no inns

INNOCENT *adj* -CENTER, -CENTEST free from guilt or sin

INNOCENT *n* pl. -S an innocent person

INNOVATE *v* -VATED, -VATING, -VATES to introduce something new

INNUENDO *v* -ED, -ING, -S or -ES to make a derogatory implication

INOCULUM *n* pl. -LA or -LUMS the material used in an inoculation

INOSITE *n* pl. -S inositol

INOSITOL *n* pl. -S an alcohol found in plant and animal tissue

INPHASE *adj* having matching electrical phases

INPOUR *v* -ED, -ING, -S to pour in

INPUT *v* -PUTTED, -PUTTING, -PUTS to enter data into a computer

INQUEST *n* pl. -S a legal inquiry

INQUIET *v* -ED, -ING, -S to disturb

INQUIRE *v* -QUIRED, -QUIRING, -QUIRES to ask about

INQUIRER *n* pl. -S one that inquires

INQUIRY *n* pl. -RIES a question

INRO *n* pl. INRO a Japanese ornamental container

INROAD *n* pl. -S a hostile invasion

INRUSH *n* pl. -ES a rushing in

INSANE *adj* -SANER, -SANEST mentally unsound INSANELY *adv*

INSANITY *n* pl. -TIES the state of being insane; something utterly foolish

INSCAPE *n* pl. -S the inner essential quality of something

INSCRIBE *v* -SCRIBED, -SCRIBING, -SCRIBES to write or engrave as a lasting record

INSCROLL *v* -ED, -ING, -S to enscroll

INSCULP *v* -ED, -ING, -S to engrave

INSEAM *n* pl. -S an inner seam

INSECT *n* pl. -S any of a class of small invertebrate animals

INSECTAN *adj* pertaining to insects

INSECURE *adj* unsafe

INSERT *v* -ED, -ING, -S to put in

INSERTER *n* pl. -S one that inserts

INSET *v* -SETTED, -SETTING, -SETS to insert

INSETTER *n* pl. -S one that inserts

INSHEATH *v* -ED, -ING, -S to ensheath

INSHORE *adj* near the shore

INSHRINE *v* -SHRINED, -SHRINING, -SHRINES to enshrine

INSIDE *n* pl. -S something that lies within

INSIDER *n* pl. -S an accepted member of a clique

INSIGHT *n* pl. -S a perception of the inner nature of things

INSIGNE *n* pl. INSIGNIA an insignia

INSIGNIA *n* pl. -S an emblem of authority or honor

INSIPID *adj* dull and uninteresting

INSIST   v -ED, -ING, -S to be resolute on some matter

INSISTER   n pl. -S one that insists

INSNARE   v -SNARED, -SNARING, -SNARES to ensnare

INSNARER   n pl. -S ensnarer

INSOFAR   adv to such an extent

INSOLATE   v -LATED, -LATING, -LATES to expose to sunlight

INSOLE   n pl. -S the inner sole of a boot or shoe

INSOLENT   n pl. -S an extremely rude person

INSOMNIA   n pl. -S chronic inability to sleep

INSOMUCH   adv to such a degree

INSOUL   v -ED, -ING, -S to ensoul

INSPAN   v -SPANNED, -SPANNING, -SPANS to harness or yoke to a vehicle

INSPECT   v -ED, -ING, -S to look carefully at or over

INSPHERE   v -SPHERED, -SPHERING, -SPHERES to ensphere

INSPIRE   v -SPIRED, -SPIRING, -SPIRES to animate the mind or emotions of

INSPIRER   n pl. -S one that inspires

INSPIRIT   v -ED, -ING, -S to fill with spirit or life

INSTABLE   adj unstable

INSTAL   v -STALLED, -STALLING, -STALS to install

INSTALL   v -ED, -ING, -S to place in position for use

INSTANCE   v -STANCED, -STANCING, -STANCES to cite as an example

INSTANCY   n pl. -CIES urgency

INSTANT   n pl. -S a very short time

INSTAR   v -STARRED, -STARRING, -STARS to adorn with stars

INSTATE   v -STATED, -STATING, -STATES to place in office

INSTEAD   adv as a substitute or equivalent

INSTEP   n pl. -S a part of the foot

INSTIL   v -STILLED, -STILLING, -STILS to instill

INSTILL   v -ED, -ING, -S to infuse slowly

INSTINCT   n pl. -S an inborn behavioral pattern

INSTROKE   n pl. -S an inward stroke

INSTRUCT   v -ED, -ING, -S to supply with knowledge

INSULANT   n pl. -S an insulating material

INSULAR   n pl. -S an islander

INSULATE   v -LATED, -LATING, -LATES to separate with nonconducting material

INSULIN   n pl. -S a hormone

INSULT   v -ED, -ING, -S to treat offensively

INSULTER   n pl. -S one that insults

INSURANT   n pl. -S one who is insured

INSURE   v -SURED, -SURING, -SURES to guarantee against loss

INSURED   n pl. -S one who is insured

INSURER   n pl. -S one that insures

INSURING   present participle of insure

INSWATHE   v -SWATHED, -SWATHING, -SWATHES to enswathe

INSWEPT   adj narrowed in front

INTACT   adj not damaged in any way

INTAGLIO   n pl. -GLIOS or -GLI an incised or sunken design

INTAGLIO   v -ED, -ING, -S to engrave in intaglio

INTAKE   n pl. -S the act of taking in

INTARSIA   n pl. -S a decorative technique

INTEGER   n pl. -S a whole number

INTEGRAL   n pl. -S a total unit

INTEND   v -ED, -ING, -S to have as a specific aim or purpose

INTENDED   n pl. -S one's spouse to-be

INTENDER   n pl. -S one that intends

INTENSE   adj -TENSER, -TENSEST existing in an extreme degree

INTENT   n pl. -S a purpose

INTENTLY   adv in an unwavering manner

INTER   v -TERRED, -TERRING, -TERS to bury

INTERACT   v -ED, -ING, -S to act on each other

INTERAGE   adj including persons of various ages

INTERBED   v -BEDDED, -BEDDING, -BEDS to insert between other layers

INTERCOM   n pl. -S a type of communication system

INTERCUT   v -CUT, -CUTTING, -CUTS to alternate camera shots

INTEREST   v -ED, -ING, -S to engage the attention of

INTERIM   n pl. -S an interval

INTERIOR   n pl. -S the inside

INTERLAP   v -LAPPED, -LAPPING, -LAPS to lap one over another

INTERLAY v -LAID, -LAYING, -LAYS to place between

INTERMIT v -MITTED, -MITTING, -MITS to stop temporarily

INTERMIX v -ED, -ING, -ES to mix together

INTERN v -ED, -ING, -S to confine during a war

INTERNAL n pl. -S an inner attribute

INTERNE n pl. -S a recent medical school graduate on a hospital staff

INTERNEE n pl. -S one who has been interned

INTERRED past tense of inter

INTERREX n pl. -REGES a type of sovereign

INTERRING present participle of inter

INTERROW adj existing between rows

INTERSEX n pl. -ES a person having characteristics of both sexes

INTERTIE n pl. -S a type of electrical connection

INTERVAL n pl. -S a space of time between periods or events

INTERWAR adj happening between wars

INTHRAL v -THRALLED, -THRALLING, -THRALS to enthrall

INTHRALL v -ED, -ING, -S to enthrall

INTHRONE v -THRONED, -THRONING, -THRONES to enthrone

INTI n pl. -S a monetary unit of Peru

INTIMA n pl. -MAE or -MAS the innermost layer of an organ **INTIMAL** adj

INTIMACY n pl. -CIES the state of being closely associated

INTIMATE v -MATED, -MATING, -MATES to make known indirectly

INTIME adj cozy

INTIMIST n pl. -S a writer or artist who deals with deep personal experiences

INTINE n pl. -S the inner wall of a spore

INTITLE v -TLED, -TLING, -TLES to entitle

INTITULE v -ULED, -ULING, -ULES to entitle

INTO prep to the inside of

INTOMB v -ED, -ING, -S to entomb

INTONATE v -NATED, -NATING, -NATES to intone

INTONE v -TONED, -TONING, -TONES to speak in a singing voice

INTONER n pl. -S one that intones

INTORT v -ED, -ING, -S to twist inward

INTOWN adj located in the center of a city

INTRADAY adj occurring within a single day

INTRADOS n pl. -ES the inner curve of an arch

INTRANT n pl. -S an entrant

INTREAT v -ED, -ING, -S to entreat

INTRENCH v -ED, -ING, -ES to entrench

INTREPID adj fearless

INTRIGUE v -TRIGUED, -TRIGUING, -TRIGUES to arouse the curiosity of

INTRO n pl. -TROS an introduction

INTROFY v -FIED, -FYING, -FIES to increase the wetting properties of

INTROIT n pl. -S music sung at the beginning of a worship service

INTROMIT v -MITTED, -MITTING, -MITS to put in

INTRON n pl. -S an intervening sequence in the genetic code

INTRORSE adj facing inward

INTRUDE v -TRUDED, -TRUDING, -TRUDES to thrust or force oneself in

INTRUDER n pl. -S one that intrudes

INTRUST v -ED, -ING, -S to entrust

INTUBATE v -BATED, -BATING, -BATES to insert a tube into

INTUIT v -ED, -ING, -S to know without conscious reasoning

INTURN n pl. -S a turning inward **INTURNED** adj

INTWINE v -TWINED, -TWINING, -TWINES to entwine

INTWIST v -ED, -ING, -S to entwist

INULASE n pl. -S an enzyme

INULIN n pl. -S a chemical compound

INUNDANT adj inundating

INUNDATE v -DATED, -DATING, -DATES to overwhelm with water

INURBANE adj not urbane

INURE v -URED, -URING, -URES to accustom to accept something undesirable

INURN v -ED, -ING, -S to put in an urn

INUTILE adj useless

INVADE   v -VADED, -VADING, -VADES to enter for conquest or plunder

INVADER   n pl. -S one that invades

INVALID   v -ED, -ING, -S to disable physically

INVAR   n pl. -S an iron-nickel alloy

INVASION   n pl. -S the act of invading INVASIVE adj

INVECTED   adj edged by convex curves

INVEIGH   v -ED, -ING, -S to protest angrily

INVEIGLE   v -GLED, -GLING, -GLES to induce by guile or flattery

INVENT   v -ED, -ING, -S to devise originally

INVENTER   n pl. -S inventor

INVENTOR   n pl. -S one that invents

INVERITY   n pl. -TIES lack of truth

INVERSE   n pl. -S something that is opposite

INVERT   v -ED, -ING, -S to turn upside down

INVERTER   n pl. -S one that inverts

INVERTOR   n pl. -S a type of electrical device

INVEST   v -ED, -ING, -S to commit something of value for future profit

INVESTOR   n pl. -S one that invests

INVIABLE   adj not viable INVIABLY adv

INVIRILE   adj not virile

INVISCID   adj not viscid

INVITAL   adj not vital

INVITE   v -VITED, -VITING, -VITES to request the presence of

INVITEE   n pl. -S one that is invited

INVITER   n pl. -S one that invites

INVITING   present participle of invite

INVOCATE   v -CATED, -CATING, -CATES to invoke

INVOICE   v -VOICED, -VOICING, -VOICES to bill

INVOKE   v -VOKED, -VOKING, -VOKES to appeal to for aid

INVOKER   n pl. -S one that invokes

INVOLUTE   v -LUTED, -LUTING, -LUTES to roll or curl up

INVOLVE   v -VOLVED, -VOLVING, -VOLVES to contain or include as a part

INVOLVER   n pl. -S one that involves

INWALL   v -ED, -ING, -S to surround with a wall

INWARD   adv toward the inside

INWARDLY   adv on the inside

INWARDS   adv inward

INWEAVE   v -WOVE or -WEAVED, -WOVEN, -WEAVING, -WEAVES to weave together

INWIND   v -WOUND, -WINDING, -WINDS to enwind

INWRAP   v -WRAPPED, -WRAPPING, -WRAPS to enwrap

IODATE   v -DATED, -DATING, -DATES to iodize

IODATION   n pl. -S the act of iodating

IODIC   adj pertaining to iodine

IODID   n pl. -S iodide

IODIDE   n pl. -S a compound of iodine

IODIN   n pl. -S iodine

IODINATE   v -ATED, -ATING, -ATES to iodize

IODINE   n pl. -S a nonmetallic element

IODISE   v -DISED, -DISING, -DISES iodize

IODISM   n pl. -S iodine poisoning

IODIZE   v -DIZED, -DIZING, -DIZES to treat with iodine

IODIZER   n pl. -S one that iodizes

IODOFORM   n pl. -S an iodine compound

IODOPHOR   n pl. -S an iodine compound

IODOPSIN   n pl. -S a pigment in the retina

IODOUS   adj pertaining to iodine

IOLITE   n pl. -S a mineral

ION   n pl. -S an electrically charged atom

IONIC   n pl. -S a style of type

IONICITY   n pl. -TIES the state of existing as or like an ion

IONISE   v -ISED, -ISING, -ISES to ionize

IONIUM   n pl. -S an isotope of thorium

IONIZE   v -IZED, -IZING, -IZES to convert into ions

IONIZER   n pl. -S one that ionizes

IONOGEN   n pl. -S a compound capable of forming ions

IONOMER   n pl. -S a type of plastic

IONONE   n pl. -S a chemical compound

IOTA   n pl. -S a Greek letter

IOTACISM   n pl. -S excessive use of the letter iota

IPECAC   n pl. -S a medicinal plant

IPOMOEA   n pl. -S a flowering plant

IRACUND   adj easily angered

IRADE   n pl. -S a decree of a Muslim ruler

IRATE   adj IRATER, IRATEST angry IRATELY adv

IRE   v IRED, IRING, IRES to anger

IREFUL   adj angry IREFULLY adv

IRELESS	*adj* not angry
IRENIC	*adj* peaceful in purpose
IRENICAL	*adj* irenic
IRENICS	*n/pl* a branch of theology
IRID	*n* pl. -S a plant of the iris family
IRIDES	a pl. of iris
IRIDIC	*adj* pertaining to iridium
IRIDIUM	*n* pl. -S a metallic element
IRING	present participle of ire
IRIS	*n* pl. IRISES or IRIDES a part of the eye
IRIS	*v* -ED, -ING, -ES to give the form of a rainbow to
IRITIS	*n* pl. -TISES inflammation of the iris **IRITIC** *adj*
IRK	*v* -ED, -ING, -S to annoy or weary
IRKSOME	*adj* tending to irk
IROKO	*n* pl. -KOS a large African tree
IRON	*v* -ED, -ING, -S to furnish with iron (a metallic element)
IRONBARK	*n* pl. -S a timber tree
IRONCLAD	*n* pl. -S an armored warship
IRONE	*n* pl. -S an aromatic oil
IRONER	*n* pl. -S a machine for pressing clothes
IRONIC	*adj* pertaining to irony
IRONICAL	*adj* ironic
IRONIES	pl. of irony
IRONING	*n* pl. -S clothes pressed or to be pressed
IRONIST	*n* pl. -S one who uses irony
IRONIZE	*v* -NIZED, -NIZING, -NIZES to mix with nutritional iron
IRONLIKE	*adj* resembling iron
IRONNESS	*n* pl. -ES the state of being iron
IRONSIDE	*n* pl. -S a man of great strength
IRONWARE	*n* pl. -S articles made of iron
IRONWEED	*n* pl. -S a shrub
IRONWOOD	*n* pl. -S a hardwood tree
IRONWORK	*n* pl. -S objects made of iron
IRONY	*n* pl. -NIES the use of words to express the opposite of what is literally said
IRREAL	*adj* not real
IRRIGATE	*v* -GATED, -GATING, -GATES to supply with water by artificial means
IRRITANT	*n* pl. -S something that irritates
IRRITATE	*v* -TATED, -TATING, -TATES to excite to impatience or anger
IRRUPT	*v* -ED, -ING, -S to rush in forcibly
IS	present 3d person sing. of be
ISAGOGE	*n* pl. -S a type of introduction to a branch of study
ISAGOGIC	*n* pl. -S a branch of theology
ISARITHM	*n* pl. -S an isopleth
ISATIN	*n* pl. -S a chemical compound **ISATINIC** *adj*
ISATINE	*n* pl. -S isatin
ISBA	*n* pl. -S a Russian log hut
ISCHEMIA	*n* pl. -S a type of anemia **ISCHEMIC** *adj*
ISCHIUM	*n* pl. -CHIA a pelvic bone **ISCHIAL** *adj*
ISLAND	*v* -ED, -ING, -S to make into an island (a land area entirely surrounded by water)
ISLANDER	*n* pl. -S one that lives on an island
ISLE	*v* ISLED, ISLING, ISLES to place on an isle (a small island)
ISLELESS	*adj* lacking an isle
ISLET	*n* pl. -S a small island
ISLING	present participle of isle
ISM	*n* pl. -S a distinctive theory or doctrine
ISOBAR	*n* pl. -S a type of atom **ISOBARIC** *adj*
ISOBARE	*n* pl. -S isobar
ISOBATH	*n* pl. -S a line on a map connecting points of equal water depth
ISOCHEIM	*n* pl. -S a type of isotherm
ISOCHIME	*n* pl. -S isocheim
ISOCHOR	*n* pl. -S isochore
ISOCHORE	*n* pl. -S a curve used to show a relationship between pressure and temperature
ISOCHRON	*n* pl. -S a line on a chart connecting points representing the same time
ISOCLINE	*n* pl. -S a type of rock formation
ISOCRACY	*n* pl. -CIES a form of government
ISODOSE	*adj* pertaining to zones that receive equal doses of radiation
ISOGAMY	*n* pl. -MIES the fusion of two similar gametes
ISOGENIC	*adj* genetically similar
ISOGENY	*n* pl. -NIES the state of being of similar origin

ISOGLOSS *n pl.* -ES a line on a map between linguistically varied areas

ISOGON *n pl.* -S a polygon having equal angles

ISOGONAL *n pl.* -S isogone

ISOGONE *n pl.* -S a line on a map used to show characteristics of the earth's magnetic field

ISOGONIC *n pl.* -S isogone

ISOGONY *n pl.* -NIES an equivalent relative growth of parts

ISOGRAFT *v* -ED, -ING, -S to transplant from one individual to another of the same species

ISOGRAM *n pl.* -S a line on a map connecting points of equal value

ISOGRAPH *n pl.* -S a line on a map indicating areas that are linguistically similar

ISOGRIV *n pl.* -S a line drawn on a map such that all points have equal grid variation

ISOHEL *n pl.* -S a line on a map connecting points receiving equal sunshine

ISOHYET *n pl.* -S a line on a map connecting points having equal rainfall

ISOLABLE *adj* capable of being isolated

ISOLATE *v* -LATED, -LATING, -LATES to set apart from others

ISOLATOR *n pl.* -S one that isolates

ISOLEAD *n pl.* -S a line on a ballistic graph

ISOLINE *n pl.* -S an isogram

ISOLOG *n pl.* -S isologue

ISOLOGUE *n pl.* -S a type of chemical compound

ISOMER *n pl.* -S a type of chemical compound **ISOMERIC** *adj*

ISOMETRY *n pl.* -TRIES equality of measure

ISOMORPH *n pl.* -S something similar to something else in form

ISONOMY *n pl.* -MIES equality of civil rights **ISONOMIC** *adj*

ISOPACH *n pl.* -S an isogram connecting points of equal thickness

ISOPHOTE *n pl.* -S a curve on a chart joining points of equal light intensity

ISOPLETH *n pl.* -S a type of isogram

ISOPOD *n pl.* -S a kind of crustacean

ISOPODAN *n pl.* -S an isopod

ISOPRENE *n pl.* -S a volatile liquid

ISOSPIN *n pl.* -S a type of quantum number

ISOSPORY *n pl.* -RIES the condition of producing sexual or asexual spores of but one kind

ISOSTASY *n pl.* -SIES the state of balance in the earth's crust

ISOTACH *n pl.* -S a line on a map connecting points of equal wind velocity

ISOTHERE *n pl.* -S a type of isotherm

ISOTHERM *n pl.* -S a line on a map connecting points of equal mean temperature

ISOTONE *n pl.* -S a type of atom

ISOTONIC *adj* of equal tension

ISOTOPE *n pl.* -S a form of an element **ISOTOPIC** *adj*

ISOTOPY *n pl.* -PIES the state of being an isotope

ISOTROPY *n pl.* -PIES the state of being identical in all directions

ISOTYPE *n pl.* -S a type of diagram **ISOTYPIC** *adj*

ISOZYME *n pl.* -S a type of enzyme **ISOZYMIC** *adj*

ISSEI *n pl.* -S a Japanese immigrant to the United States

ISSUABLE *adj* authorized for issuing **ISSUABLY** *adv*

ISSUANCE *n pl.* -S the act of issuing

ISSUANT *adj* coming forth

ISSUE *v* -SUED, -SUING, -SUES to come forth

ISSUER *n pl.* -S one that issues

ISTHMI a pl. of isthmus

ISTHMIAN *n pl.* -S a native of an isthmus

ISTHMIC *adj* pertaining to an isthmus

ISTHMOID *adj* isthmic

ISTHMUS *n pl.* -MUSES or -MI a strip of land connecting two larger land masses

ISTLE *n pl.* -S a strong fiber

IT *pron* the 3d person sing. neuter pronoun

ITALIC *n pl.* -S a style of print

ITCH *v* -ED, -ING, -ES to have an uneasy or tingling skin sensation

ITCHING *n pl.* -S an uneasy or tingling skin sensation

ITCHY *adj* ITCHIER, ITCHIEST causing an itching sensation **ITCHILY** *adv*

ITEM *v* -ED, -ING, -S to itemize

ITEMISE	*v* -ISED, -ISING, -ISES itemize
ITEMIZE	*v* -IZED, -IZING, -IZES to set down the particulars of
ITEMIZER	*n* pl. -S one that itemizes
ITERANCE	*n* pl. -S repetition
ITERANT	*adj* repeating
ITERATE	*v* -ATED, -ATING, -ATES to repeat
ITERUM	*adv* again; once more
ITHER	*adj* other
ITS	*pron* the possessive form of the pronoun it
ITSELF	*pron* a reflexive form of the pronoun it

IVIED	*adj* covered with ivy
IVORY	*n* pl. -RIES a hard white substance found in elephant tusks
IVY	*n* pl. IVIES a climbing vine **IVYLIKE** *adj*
IWIS	*adv* certainly
IXIA	*n* pl. -S a flowering plant
IXODID	*n* pl. -S a bloodsucking insect
IXORA	*n* pl. -S a flowering plant
IXTLE	*n* pl. -S istle
IZAR	*n* pl. -S an outer garment worn by Muslim women
IZZARD	*n* pl. -S the letter Z

JAB v JABBED, JABBING, JABS to poke sharply

JABBER v -ED, -ING, -S to talk rapidly

JABBERER n pl. -S one that jabbers

JABBING present participle of jab

JABIRU n pl. -S a wading bird

JABOT n pl. -S a decoration on a shirt

JACAL n pl. -ES or -S a hut

JACAMAR n pl. -S a tropical bird

JACANA n pl. -S a wading bird

JACINTH n pl. -S a variety of zircon

JACINTHE n pl. -S an orange color

JACK v -ED, -ING, -S to raise with a type of lever

JACKAL n pl. -S a doglike mammal

JACKAROO n pl. -ROOS jackeroo

JACKASS n pl. -ES a male donkey

JACKBOOT n pl. -S a heavy boot

JACKDAW n pl. -S a crowlike bird

JACKER n pl. -S one that jacks

JACKEROO n pl. -ROOS an inexperienced ranch hand

JACKET v -ED, -ING, -S to provide with a jacket (a short coat)

JACKFISH n pl. -ES a food fish

JACKIES pl. of jacky

JACKLEG n pl. -S an unskilled worker

JACKPOT n pl. -S a top prize or reward

JACKROLL v -ED, -ING, -S to rob a drunken or sleeping person

JACKSTAY n pl. -STAYS a rope on a ship

JACKY n pl. JACKIES a sailor

JACOBIN n pl. -S a pigeon

JACOBUS n pl. -ES an old English coin

JACONET n pl. -S a cotton cloth

JACQUARD n pl. -S a fabric of intricate weave

JACULATE v -LATED, -LATING, -LATES to throw

JADE v JADED, JADING, JADES to weary **JADEDLY** adv

JADEITE n pl. -S a mineral **JADITIC** adj

JADISH adj worn-out **JADISHLY** adv

JAEGER n pl. -S a hunter

JAG v JAGGED, JAGGING, JAGS to cut unevenly

JAGER n pl. -S jaeger

JAGG v -ED, -ING, -S to jag

JAGGARY n pl. -RIES jaggery

JAGGED adj -GEDER, -GEDEST having a sharply uneven edge or surface **JAGGEDLY** adv

JAGGER n pl. -S one that jags

JAGGERY n pl. -GERIES a coarse, dark sugar

JAGGHERY n pl. -GHERIES jaggery

JAGGING present participle of jag

JAGGY adj -GIER, -GIEST jagged

JAGLESS adj smooth and even

JAGRA n pl. -S jaggery

JAGUAR n pl. -S a large feline animal

JAIL v -ED, -ING, -S to put in jail (a place of confinement)

JAILBAIT n pl. JAILBAIT a girl under the age of consent with whom sexual intercourse constitutes statutory rape

JAILBIRD n pl. -S a prisoner

JAILER n pl. -S a keeper of a jail

JAILOR n pl. -S jailer

JAKE adj all right; fine

JAKES n/pl an outhouse

JALAP n pl. -S a Mexican plant **JALAPIC** adj.

JALAPENO n pl. -NOS a hot pepper

JALAPIN n pl. -S a medicinal substance contained in jalap

JALOP n pl. -S jalap

JALOPPY	n pl. -PIES jalopy
JALOPY	n pl. -LOPIES a decrepit car
JALOUSIE	n pl. -S a type of window
JAM	v JAMMED, JAMMING, JAMS to force together tightly
JAMB	v -ED, -ING, -S to jam
JAMBE	n pl. -S a jambeau
JAMBEAU	n pl. -BEAUX a piece of armor for the leg
JAMBOREE	n pl. -S a noisy celebration
JAMMED	past tense of jam
JAMMER	n pl. -S one that jams
JAMMIES	n/pl pajamas
JAMMING	present participle of jam
JAMMY	adj -MIER, -MIEST sticky with jam (boiled fruit and sugar)
JANE	n pl. -S a girl or woman
JANGLE	v -GLED, -GLING, -GLES to make a harsh, metallic sound
JANGLER	n pl. -S one that jangles
JANGLY	adj -GLIER, -GLIEST jangling
JANIFORM	adj hypocritical
JANISARY	n pl. -SARIES janizary
JANITOR	n pl. -S a maintenance man
JANIZARY	n pl. -ZARIES a Turkish soldier
JANTY	adj jaunty
JAPAN	v -PANNED, -PANNING, -PANS to coat with a glossy, black lacquer
JAPANIZE	v -NIZED, -NIZING, -NIZES to make Japanese
JAPANNER	n pl. -S one that japans
JAPANNING	present participle of japan
JAPE	v JAPED, JAPING, JAPES to mock
JAPER	n pl. -S one that japes
JAPERY	n pl. -ERIES mockery
JAPING	present participle of jape
JAPINGLY	adv in a japing manner
JAPONICA	n pl. -S an Asian shrub
JAR	v JARRED, JARRING, JARS to cause to shake
JARFUL	n pl. JARFULS or JARSFUL the quantity held by a jar (a cylindrical container)
JARGON	v -ED, -ING, -S to speak or write an obscure and often pretentious kind of language
JARGONEL	n pl. -S a variety of pear
JARGOON	n pl. -S a variety of zircon
JARHEAD	n -S a marine soldier
JARINA	n pl. -S the hard seed of a palm tree
JARL	n pl. -S a Scandinavian nobleman
JARLDOM	n pl. -S the domain of a jarl
JAROSITE	n pl. -S a mineral
JAROVIZE	v -VIZED, -VIZING, -VIZES to hasten the flowering of a plant
JARRAH	n pl. -S an evergreen tree
JARRED	past tense of jar
JARRING	present participle of jar
JARSFUL	a pl. of jarful
JARVEY	n pl. -VEYS the driver of a carriage for hire
JASMIN	n pl. -S jasmine
JASMINE	n pl. -S a climbing shrub
JASPER	n pl. -S a variety of quartz
JASPERY	adj
JASSID	n pl. -S any of a family of plant pests
JATO	n pl. -TOS a takeoff aided by jet propulsion
JAUK	v -ED, -ING, -S to dawdle
JAUNCE	v JAUNCED, JAUNCING, JAUNCES to prance
JAUNDICE	v -DICED, -DICING, -DICES to prejudice unfavorably
JAUNT	v -ED, -ING, -S to make a pleasure trip
JAUNTY	adj -TIER, -TIEST having a lively and self-confident manner JAUNTILY adv
JAUP	v -ED, -ING, -S to splash
JAVA	n pl. -S coffee
JAVELIN	v -ED, -ING, -S to pierce with a javelin (a light spear)
JAVELINA	n pl. -S a peccary
JAW	v -ED, -ING, -S to jabber
JAWAN	n pl. -S a soldier of India
JAWBONE	v -BONED, -BONING, -BONES to attempt to convince
JAWBONER	n pl. -S one that jawbones
JAWLIKE	adj resembling the jaw (the framework of the mouth)
JAWLINE	n pl. -S the outline of the lower jaw
JAY	n pl. JAYS a corvine bird
JAYBIRD	n pl. -S a jay
JAYGEE	n pl. -S a military officer
JAYVEE	n pl. -S a junior varsity player
JAYWALK	v -ED, -ING, -S to cross a street recklessly
JAZZ	v -ED, -ING, -ES to enliven
JAZZER	n pl. -S one that jazzes
JAZZLIKE	adj resembling a type of music
JAZZMAN	n pl. -MEN a type of musician
JAZZY	adj JAZZIER, JAZZIEST lively JAZZILY adv

JEALOUS *adj* resentful of another's advantages

JEALOUSY *n pl.* -SIES a jealous feeling

JEAN *n pl.* -S a durable cotton fabric

JEBEL *n pl.* -S a mountain

JEE *v* JEED, JEEING, JEES to gee

JEEP *v* -ED, -ING, -S to travel by a small type of motor vehicle

JEEPERS *interj* — used as a mild oath

JEEPNEY *n pl.* -NEYS a Philippine jitney

JEER *v* -ED, -ING, -S to mock

JEERER *n pl.* -S one that jeers

JEEZ *interj* — used as a mild oath

JEFE *n pl.* -S a chief

JEHAD *n pl.* -S jihad

JEHU *n pl.* -S a fast driver

JEJUNA *pl.* of jejunum

JEJUNAL *adj* pertaining to the jejunum

JEJUNE *adj* uninteresting; childish **JEJUNELY** *adv*

JEJUNITY *n pl.* -TIES something that is jejune

JEJUNUM *n pl.* -NA a part of the small intestine

JELL *v* -ED, -ING, -S to congeal

JELLABA *n pl.* -S djellaba

JELLIFY *v* -FIED, -FYING, -FIES to jelly

JELLY *v* -LIED, -LYING, -LIES to make into a jelly (a soft, semisolid substance)

JELUTONG *n pl.* -S a tropical tree

JEMADAR *n pl.* -S an officer in the army of India

JEMIDAR *n pl.* -S jemadar

JEMMY *v* -MIED, -MYING, -MIES to jimmy

JENNET *n pl.* -S a small horse

JENNY *n pl.* -NIES a female donkey

JEON *n pl.* JEON a monetary unit of South Korea

JEOPARD *v* -ED, -ING, -S to imperil

JEOPARDY *n pl.* -DIES risk of loss or injury

JERBOA *n pl.* -S a small rodent

JEREED *n pl.* -S a wooden javelin

JEREMIAD *n pl.* -S a tale of woe

JERID *n pl.* -S jereed

JERK *v* -ED, -ING, -S to move with a sharp, sudden motion

JERKER *n pl.* -S one that jerks

JERKIES *pl.* of jerky

JERKIN *n pl.* -S a sleeveless jacket

JERKY *adj* JERKIER, JERKIEST characterized by jerking movements **JERKILY** *adv*

JERKY *n pl.* -KIES dried meat

JEROBOAM *n pl.* -S a wine bottle

JERREED *n pl.* -S jereed

JERRICAN *n pl.* -S jerrycan

JERRID *n pl.* -S jereed

JERRY *n pl.* -RIES a German soldier

JERRYCAN *n pl.* -S a fuel container

JERSEY *n pl.* -SEYS a close-fitting knitted shirt **JERSEYED** *adj*

JESS *v* -ED, -ING, -ES to fasten straps around the legs of a hawk

JESSANT *adj* shooting forth

JESSE *v* JESSED, JESSING, JESSES to jess

JEST *v* -ED, -ING, -S to joke

JESTER *n pl.* -S one that jests

JESTFUL *adj* tending to jest

JESTING *n pl.* -S the act of one who jests

JET *v* JETTED, JETTING, JETS to spurt forth in a stream

JETBEAD *n pl.* -S an ornamental shrub

JETE *n pl.* -S a ballet leap

JETLIKE *adj* resembling a jet airplane

JETLINER *n pl.* -S a type of aircraft

JETON *n pl.* -S jetton

JETPORT *n pl.* -S a type of airport

JETSAM *n pl.* -S goods cast overboard

JETSOM *n pl.* -S jetsam

JETTED past tense of jet

JETTIED past tense of jetty

JETTIER comparative of jetty

JETTIES present 3d person sing. of jetty

JETTIEST superlative of jetty

JETTING present participle of jet

JETTISON *v* -ED, -ING, -S to cast overboard

JETTON *n pl.* -S a piece used in counting

JETTY *v* -TIED, -TYING, -TIES to jut

JETTY *adj* -TIER, -TIEST having the color jet black

JEU *n pl.* JEUX a game

JEWEL *v* -ELED, -ELING, -ELS or -ELLED, -ELLING, -ELS to adorn or equip with jewels (precious stones)

JEWELER *n pl.* -S a dealer or maker of jewelry

JEWELLER *n pl.* -S jeweler

JEWELLING a present participle of jewel

JEWELRY	*n* pl. -RIES an article or articles for personal adornment
JEWFISH	*n* pl. -ES a large marine fish
JEZAIL	*n* pl. -S a type of firearm
JEZEBEL	*n* pl. -S a scheming, wicked woman
JIAO	*n* pl. JIAO chiao
JIB	*v* JIBBED, JIBBING, JIBS to refuse to proceed further
JIBB	*v* -ED, -ING, -S to shift from side to side while sailing
JIBBER	*n* pl. -S a horse that jibs
JIBBING	present participle of jib
JIBBOOM	*n* pl. -S a ship's spar
JIBE	*v* JIBED, JIBING, JIBES to gibe **JIBINGLY** *adv*
JIBER	*n* pl. -S one that jibes
JICAMA	*n* pl. -S a tropical plant with edible roots
JIFF	*n* pl. -S jiffy
JIFFY	*n* pl. -FIES a short time
JIG	*v* JIGGED, JIGGING, JIGS to bob
JIGGER	*v* -ED, -ING, -S to jerk up and down
JIGGERED	*adj* damned
JIGGING	present participle of jig
JIGGLE	*v* -GLED, -GLING, -GLES to shake lightly
JIGGLY	*adj* -GLIER, -GLIEST unsteady
JIGSAW	*v* -SAWED, -SAWN, -SAWING, -SAWS to cut with a type of saw
JIHAD	*n* pl. -S a Muslim holy war
JILL	*n* pl. -S a unit of liquid measure
JILLION	*n* pl. -S a very large number
JILT	*v* -ED, -ING, -S to reject a lover
JILTER	*n* pl. -S one that jilts
JIMINY	*interj* — used to express surprise
JIMJAMS	*n/pl* violent delirium
JIMMINY	*interj* jiminy
JIMMY	*v* -MIED, -MYING, -MIES to pry open with a crowbar
JIMP	*adj* JIMPER, JIMPEST natty **JIMPLY** *adv*
JIMPY	*adj* jimp
JIN	*n* pl. -S jinn
JINGAL	*n* pl. -S a heavy musket
JINGALL	*n* pl. -S jingal
JINGKO	*n* pl. -KOES ginkgo
JINGLE	*v* -GLED, -GLING, -GLES to make a tinkling sound
JINGLER	*n* pl. -S one that jingles
JINGLY	*adj* -GLIER, -GLIEST jingling
JINGO	*n* pl. -GOES a zealous patriot
JINGOISH	*adj*
JINGOISM	*n* pl. -S the spirit or policy of jingoes
JINGOIST	*n* pl. -S a jingo
JINK	*v* -ED, -ING, -S to move quickly out of the way
JINKER	*n* pl. -S one that jinks
JINN	*n* pl. -S a supernatural being in Muslim mythology
JINNEE	*n* pl. JINN jinn
JINNI	*n* pl. JINN jinn
JINX	*v* -ED, -ING, -ES to bring bad luck to
JIPIJAPA	*n* pl. -S a tropical plant
JITNEY	*n* pl. -NEYS a small bus
JITTER	*v* -ED, -ING, -S to fidget
JITTERY	*adj* -TERIER, -TERIEST extremely nervous
JIUJITSU	*n* pl. -S jujitsu
JIUJUTSU	*n* pl. -S jujitsu
JIVE	*v* JIVED, JIVING, JIVES to play jazz or swing music
JIVEASS	*adj* insincere, phony
JIVER	*n* pl. -S one that jives
JIVEY	*adj* JIVIER, JIVIEST jazzy, lively
JNANA	*n* pl. -S knowledge acquired through meditation
JO	*n* pl. JOES a sweetheart
JOANNES	*n* pl. JOANNES johannes
JOB	*v* JOBBED, JOBBING, JOBS to work by the piece
JOBBER	*n* pl. -S a pieceworker
JOBBERY	*n* pl. -BERIES corruption in public office
JOBBING	present participle of job
JOBLESS	*adj* having no job
JOBNAME	*n* pl. -S a computer code for a job instruction
JOCK	*n* pl. -S an athletic supporter
JOCKETTE	*n* pl. -S a woman who rides horses in races
JOCKEY	*v* -EYED, -EYING, -EYS to maneuver for an advantage
JOCKO	*n* pl. JOCKOS a monkey
JOCOSE	*adj* humorous **JOCOSELY** *adv*
JOCOSITY	*n* pl. -TIES the state of being jocose
JOCULAR	*adj* given to joking
JOCUND	*adj* cheerful **JOCUNDLY** *adv*
JODHPUR	*n* pl. -S a type of boot
JOE	*n* pl. -S a fellow

JOEY   *n* pl. -EYS a young kangaroo

JOG   *v* JOGGED, JOGGING, JOGS to run at a slow, steady pace

JOGGER   *n* pl. -S one that jogs

JOGGING   *n* pl. -S the practice of running at a slow, steady pace

JOGGLE   *v* -GLED, -GLING, -GLES to shake slightly

JOGGLER   *n* pl. -S one that joggles

JOHANNES   *n* pl. JOHANNES a Portuguese coin

JOHN   *n* pl. -S a toilet

JOHNBOAT   *n* pl. -S a narrow square-ended boat

JOHNNY   *n* pl. -NIES a sleeveless hospital gown

JOIN   *v* -ED, -ING, -S to unite **JOINABLE** *adj*

JOINDER   *n* pl. -S a joining of parties in a lawsuit

JOINER   *n* pl. -S a carpenter

JOINERY   *n* pl. -ERIES the trade of a joiner

JOINING   *n* pl. -S a juncture

JOINT   *v* -ED, -ING, -S to fit together by means of a junction

JOINTER   *n* pl. -S one that joints

JOINTLY   *adv* together

JOINTURE   *v* -TURED, -TURING, -TURES to set aside property as an inheritance

JOIST   *v* -ED, -ING, -S to support with horizontal beams

JOJOBA   *n* pl. -S a small tree

JOKE   *v* JOKED, JOKING, JOKES to say something amusing

JOKER   *n* pl. -S one that jokes

JOKESTER   *n* pl. -S a practical joker

JOKEY   *adj* JOKIER, JOKIEST amusing **JOKILY** *adv*

JOKIER   comparative of jokey

JOKIEST   superlative of jokey

JOKINESS   *n* pl. -ES the state of being jokey

JOKING   present participle of joke

JOKINGLY   *adv* in a joking manner

JOKY   *adj* JOKIER, JOKIEST jokey

JOLE   *n* pl. -S jowl

JOLLIED   past tense of jolly

JOLLIER   comparative of jolly

JOLLIES   present 3d person sing. of jolly

JOLLIEST   superlative of jolly

JOLLIFY   *v* -FIED, -FYING, -FIES to make jolly

JOLLITY   *n* pl. -TIES mirth

JOLLY   *adj* -LIER, -LIEST cheerful **JOLLILY** *adv*

JOLLY   *v* -LIED, -LYING, -LIES to put in a good humor for one's own purposes

JOLT   *v* -ED, -ING, -S to jar or shake roughly

JOLTER   *n* pl. -S one that jolts

JOLTY   *adj* JOLTIER, JOLTIEST marked by a jolting motion **JOLTILY** *adv*

JONES   *n* pl. JONESES a drug addiction

JONGLEUR   *n* pl. -S a minstrel

JONQUIL   *n* pl. -S a perennial herb

JORAM   *n* pl. -S jorum

JORDAN   *n* pl. -S a type of container

JORUM   *n* pl. -S a large drinking bowl

JOSEPH   *n* pl. -S a woman's long cloak

JOSH   *v* -ED, -ING, -ES to tease

JOSHER   *n* pl. -S one that joshes

JOSS   *n* pl. -ES a Chinese idol

JOSTLE   *v* -TLED, -TLING, -TLES to bump or push roughly

JOSTLER   *n* pl. -S one that jostles

JOT   *v* JOTTED, JOTTING, JOTS to write down quickly

JOTA   *n* pl. -S a Spanish dance

JOTTER   *n* pl. -S one that jots

JOTTING   *n* pl. -S a brief note

JOTTY   *adj* written down quickly

JOUAL   *n* pl. -S a dialect of Canadian French

JOUK   *v* -ED, -ING, -S to dodge

JOULE   *n* pl. -S a unit of energy

JOUNCE   *v* JOUNCED, JOUNCING, JOUNCES to move roughly up and down

JOUNCY   *adj* JOUNCIER, JOUNCIEST marked by a jouncing motion

JOURNAL   *n* pl. -S a record of daily events

JOURNEY   *v* -ED, -ING, -S to travel

JOUST   *v* -ED, -ING, -S to engage in personal combat

JOUSTER   *n* pl. -S one that jousts

JOVIAL   *adj* good-humored **JOVIALLY** *adv*

JOVIALTY   *n* pl. -TIES the quality or state of being jovial

JOW   *v* -ED, -ING, -S to toll

JOWAR   *n* pl. -S a durra grown in India

JOWL   *n* pl. -S the fleshy part under the lower jaw **JOWLED** *adj*

JOWLY   *adj* JOWLIER, JOWLIEST having prominent jowls

JOY *v* -ED, -ING, -S to rejoice

JOYANCE *n* pl. -S gladness

JOYFUL *adj* -FULLER, -FULLEST happy **JOYFULLY** *adv*

JOYLESS *adj* being without gladness

JOYOUS *adj* joyful **JOYOUSLY** *adv*

JOYPOP *v* -POPPED, -POPPING, -POPS to use habit-forming drugs occasionally

JOYRIDE *v* -RODE, -RIDDEN, -RIDING, -RIDES to take an automobile ride for pleasure

JOYRIDER *n* pl. -S one that joyrides

JOYSTICK *n* pl. -S the control stick in an airplane

JUBA *n* pl. -S a lively dance

JUBBAH *n* pl. -S a loose outer garment

JUBE *n* pl. -S a platform in a church

JUBHAH *n* pl. -S jubbah

JUBILANT *adj* exultant

JUBILATE *v* -LATED, -LATING, -LATES to exult

JUBILE *n* pl. -S jubilee

JUBILEE *n* pl. -S a celebration

JUDAS *n* pl. -ES a peephole

JUDDER *v* -ED, -ING, -S to vibrate

JUDGE *v* JUDGED, JUDGING, JUDGES to decide on critically

JUDGER *n* pl. -S one that judges

JUDGMENT *n* pl. -S an authoritative opinion

JUDICIAL *adj* pertaining to courts of law

JUDO *n* pl. -DOS a form of jujitsu

JUDOIST *n* pl. -S one skilled in judo

JUDOKA *n* pl. -S a judoist

JUG *v* JUGGED, JUGGING, JUGS to put into a jug (a large, deep container with a narrow mouth and a handle)

JUGA a pl. of jugum

JUGAL *adj* pertaining to the cheek or cheekbone

JUGATE *adj* occurring in pairs

JUGFUL *n* pl. JUGFULS or JUGSFUL as much as a jug will hold

JUGGED past tense of jug

JUGGING present participle of jug

JUGGLE *v* -GLED, -GLING, -GLES to perform feats of manual dexterity

JUGGLER *n* pl. -S one that juggles

JUGGLERY *n* pl. -GLERIES the art of a juggler

JUGGLING *n* pl. -S jugglery

JUGHEAD *n* pl. -S a dolt

JUGSFUL a pl. of jugful

JUGULA pl. of jugulum

JUGULAR *n* pl. -S a vein of the neck

JUGULATE *v* -LATED, -LATING, -LATES to suppress a disease by extreme measures

JUGULUM *n* pl. -LA a part of a bird's neck

JUGUM *n* pl. -GA or -GUMS a pair of the opposite leaflets of a pinnate leaf

JUICE *v* JUICED, JUICING, JUICES to extract the juice (the liquid part of a fruit or vegetable) from

JUICER *n* pl. -S a juice extractor

JUICY *adj* JUICIER, JUICIEST full of juice **JUICILY** *adv*

JUJITSU *n* pl. -S a Japanese art of self-defense

JUJU *n* pl. -S an object regarded as having magical power

JUJUBE *n* pl. -S a fruit-flavored candy

JUJUISM *n* pl. -S the system of beliefs connected with jujus

JUJUIST *n* pl. -S a follower of jujuism

JUJUTSU *n* pl. -S jujitsu

JUKE *v* JUKED, JUKING, JUKES to fake out of position

JUKEBOX *n* pl. -ES a coin-operated phonograph

JULEP *n* pl. -S a sweet drink

JULIENNE *v* -ENNED, -ENNING, -ENNES to cut food into long thin strips

JUMBAL *n* pl. -S a ring-shaped cookie

JUMBLE *v* -BLED, -BLING, -BLES to mix in a disordered manner

JUMBLER *n* pl. -S one that jumbles

JUMBO *n* pl. -BOS a very large specimen of its kind

JUMBUCK *n* pl. -S a sheep

JUMP *v* -ED, -ING, -S to spring off the ground

JUMPER *n* pl. -S one that jumps

JUMPOFF *n* pl. -S a starting point

JUMPSUIT *n* pl. -S a one-piece garment

JUMPY *adj* JUMPIER, JUMPIEST nervous **JUMPILY** *adv*

JUN *n* pl. JUN a coin of North Korea

JUNCO *n* pl. -COS or -COES a small finch

JUNCTION *n* pl. -S a place where things join

JUNCTURE *n* pl. -S the act of joining

JUNGLE　　n pl. -S land covered with dense tropical vegetation JUNGLED adj

JUNGLY　　adj -GLIER, -GLIEST resembling a jungle

JUNIOR　　n pl. -S a person who is younger than another

JUNIPER　　n pl. -S an evergreen tree

JUNK　　v -ED, -ING, -S to discard as trash

JUNKER　　n pl. -S something ready for junking

JUNKET　　v -ED, -ING, -S to banquet

JUNKETER　　n pl. -S one that junkets

JUNKIE　　n pl. -S a drug addict

JUNKMAN　　n pl. -MEN one who buys and sells junk

JUNKY　　adj JUNKIER, JUNKIEST worthless

JUNKYARD　　n pl. -S a place where junk is stored

JUNTA　　n pl. -S a political or governmental council

JUNTO　　n pl. -TOS a political faction

JUPE　　n pl. -S a woman's jacket

JUPON　　n pl. -S a tunic

JURA　　pl. of jus

JURAL　　adj pertaining to law JURALLY adv

JURANT　　n pl. -S one that takes an oath

JURAT　　n pl. -S a statement on an affidavit

JURATORY　　adj pertaining to an oath

JUREL　　n pl. -S a food fish

JURIDIC　　adj pertaining to the law

JURIST　　n pl. -S one versed in the law JURISTIC adj

JUROR　　n pl. -S a member of a jury

JURY　　v -RIED, -RYING, -RIES to select material for exhibition

JURYMAN　　n pl. -MEN a juror

JUS　　n pl. JURA a legal right

JUSSIVE　　n pl. -S a word used to express command

JUST　　v -ED, -ING, -S to joust

JUST　　adj JUSTER, JUSTEST acting in conformity with what is morally good

JUSTER　　n pl. -S jouster

JUSTICE　　n pl. -S a judge

JUSTIFY　　v -FIED, -FYING, -FIES to show to be just, right, or valid

JUSTLE　　v -TLED, -TLING, -TLES to jostle

JUSTLY　　adv in a just manner

JUSTNESS　　n pl. -ES the quality of being just

JUT　　v JUTTED, JUTTING, JUTS to protrude

JUTE　　n pl. -S a strong, coarse fiber

JUTTY　　v -TIED, -TYING, -TIES to jut

JUVENAL　　n pl. -S a young bird's plumage

JUVENILE　　n pl. -S a young person

K 5

KA	*n* pl. -S the spiritual self of a human being in Egyptian religion
KAAS	*n* pl. KAAS kas
KAB	*n* pl. -S an ancient Hebrew unit of measure
KABAB	*n* pl. -S kabob
KABAKA	*n* pl. -S a Ugandan emperor
KABALA	*n* pl. -S cabala
KABAR	*n* pl. -S caber
KABAYA	*n* pl. -S a cotton jacket
KABBALA	*n* pl. -S cabala
KABBALAH	*n* pl. -S cabala
KABELJOU	*n* pl. -S a large food fish
KABIKI	*n* pl. -S a tropical tree
KABOB	*n* pl. -S cubes of meat cooked on a skewer
KABUKI	*n* pl. -S a form of Japanese theater
KACHINA	*n* pl. -S an ancestral spirit
KADDISH	*n* pl. -DISHIM a Jewish prayer
KADI	*n* pl. -S cadi
KAE	*n* pl. -S a bird resembling a crow
KAF	*n* pl. -S kaph
KAFFIR	*n* pl. -S kafir
KAFFIYEH	*n* pl. -S a large, square kerchief
KAFIR	*n* pl. -S a cereal grass
KAFTAN	*n* pl. -S caftan
KAGU	*n* pl. -S a flightless bird
KAHUNA	*n* pl. -S a medicine man
KAIAK	*n* pl. -S kayak
KAIF	*n* pl. -S kef
KAIL	*n* pl. -S kale
KAILYARD	*n* pl. -S kaleyard
KAIN	*n* pl. -S a tax paid in produce or livestock
KAINIT	*n* pl. -S kainite

KAINITE	*n* pl. -S a mineral salt
KAISER	*n* pl. -S an emperor
KAISERIN	*n* pl. -S a kaiser's wife
KAJEPUT	*n* pl. -S cajuput
KAKA	*n* pl. -S a parrot
KAKAPO	*n* pl. -POS a flightless parrot
KAKEMONO	*n* pl. -NOS a Japanese scroll
KAKI	*n* pl. -S a Japanese tree
KAKIEMON	*n* pl. -S a Japanese porcelain
KALAM	*n* pl. -S a type of Muslim theology
KALE	*n* pl. -S a variety of cabbage
KALENDS	*n* pl. KALENDS calends
KALEWIFE	*n* pl. -WIVES a female vegetable vendor
KALEYARD	*n* pl. -S a kitchen garden
KALIAN	*n* pl. -S a hookah
KALIF	*n* pl. -S caliph
KALIFATE	*n* pl. -S califate
KALIMBA	*n* pl. -S an African musical instrument
KALIPH	*n* pl. -S caliph
KALIUM	*n* pl. -S potassium
KALLIDIN	*n* pl. -S a hormone
KALMIA	*n* pl. -S an evergreen shrub
KALONG	*n* pl. -S a fruit-eating bat
KALPA	*n* pl. -S a period of time in Hindu religion
KALPAK	*n* pl. -S calpac
KALYPTRA	*n* pl. -S a thin veil
KAMAAINA	*n* pl. -S a longtime resident of Hawaii
KAMACITE	*n* pl. -S an alloy of nickel and iron
KAMALA	*n* pl. -S an Asian tree
KAME	*n* pl. -S a mound of detrital material
KAMI	*n* pl. KAMI a sacred power or force

KAMIK   *n* pl. -S a type of boot
KAMIKAZE   *n* pl. -S a plane to be flown in
               a suicide crash on a target
KAMPONG   *n* pl. -S a small village
KAMSEEN   *n* pl. -S khamsin
KAMSIN   *n* pl. -S khamsin
KANA   *n* pl. -S the Japanese syllabic
               script
KANBAN   *n* pl. -S a manufacturing
               strategy wherein parts are
               delivered only as needed
KANE   *n* pl. -S kain
KANGAROO   *n* pl. -ROOS an Australian
               mammal
KANJI   *n* pl. -S a system of Japanese
               writing
KANTAR   *n* pl. -S a unit of weight
KANTELE   *n* pl. -S a type of harp
KAOLIANG   *n* pl. -S an Asian sorghum
KAOLIN   *n* pl. -S a fine white clay
               KAOLINIC *adj*
KAOLINE   *n* pl. -S kaolin
KAON   *n* pl. -S a type of meson
KAPA   *n* pl. -S a coarse cloth
KAPH   *n* pl. -S a Hebrew letter
KAPOK   *n* pl. -S a mass of silky fibers
KAPPA   *n* pl. -S a Greek letter
KAPUT   *adj* ruined
KAPUTT   *adj* kaput
KARAKUL   *n* pl. -S an Asian sheep
KARAOKE   *n* pl. -S a musical device to
               which a user sings along
KARAT   *n* pl. -S a unit of quality for
               gold
KARATE   *n* pl. -S a Japanese art of self-
               defense
KARMA   *n* pl. -S the force generated by
               a person's actions **KARMIC**
               adj
KARN   *n* pl. -S cairn
KAROO   *n* pl. -ROOS karroo
KAROSS   *n* pl. -ES an African garment
KARROO   *n* pl. -ROOS a dry plateau
KARST   *n* pl. -S a limestone region
               KARSTIC *adj*
KART   *n* pl. -S a small motor vehicle
KARTING   *n* pl. -S the sport of racing
               karts
KARYOTIN   *n* pl. -S the nuclear material of
               a cell
KAS   *n* pl. KAS a large cupboard
KASBAH   *n* pl. -S casbah
KASHA   *n* pl. -S a cooked cereal
KASHER   *v* -ED, -ING, -S to kosher
KASHMIR   *n* pl. -S cashmere
KASHRUT   *n* pl. -S kashruth

KASHRUTH   *n* pl. -S the Jewish dietary
               laws
KAT   *n* pl. -S an evergreen shrub
KATA   *n* pl. -S an exercise of set
               movements
KATAKANA   *n* pl. -S a Japanese syllabic
               symbol
KATCHINA   *n* pl. -S kachina
KATCINA   *n* pl. -S kachina
KATHODE   *n* pl. -S cathode **KATHODAL,**
               KATHODIC *adj*
KATION   *n* pl. -S cation
KATYDID   *n* pl. -S a grasshopper
KAURI   *n* pl. -S a timber tree
KAURY   *n* pl. -RIES kauri
KAVA   *n* pl. -S a tropical shrub
KAVAKAVA   *n* pl. -S kava
KAVASS   *n* pl. -ES a Turkish policeman
KAY   *n* pl. KAYS the letter K
KAYAK   *v* -ED, -ING, -S to travel in a
               kayak (an Eskimo canoe)
KAYAKER   *n* pl. -S one that rides in a
               kayak
KAYAKING   *n* pl. -S the act or skill of
               managing a kayak
KAYLES   *n/pl* a British game
KAYO   *v* -ED, -ING, -S or -ES to
               knock out
KAZACHOK   *n* pl. -ZACHKI a Russian folk
               dance
KAZATSKI   *n* pl. -ES kazachok
KAZATSKY   *n* pl. -SKIES kazachok
KAZOO   *n* pl. -ZOOS a toy musical
               instrument
KBAR   *n* pl. -S a kilobar
KEA   *n* pl. -S a parrot
KEBAB   *n* pl. -S kabob
KEBAR   *n* pl. -S caber
KEBBIE   *n* pl. -S a rough walking stick
KEBBOCK   *n* pl. -S kebbuck
KEBBUCK   *n* pl. -S a whole cheese
KEBLAH   *n* pl. -S kiblah
KEBOB   *n* pl. -S kabob
KECK   *v* -ED, -ING, -S to retch
KECKLE   *v* -LED, -LING, -LES to wind
               with rope to prevent chafing
KEDDAH   *n* pl. -S an enclosure for
               elephants
KEDGE   *v* KEDGED, KEDGING,
               KEDGES to move a vessel
               with the use of an anchor
KEDGEREE   *n* pl. -S a food in India
KEEF   *n* pl. -S kef
KEEK   *v* -ED, -ING, -S to peep
KEEL   *v* -ED, -ING, -S to capsize

KEELAGE *n* pl. -S the amount paid to keep a boat in a harbor

KEELBOAT *n* pl. -S a freight boat

KEELHALE *v* -HALED, -HALING, -HALES to keelhaul

KEELHAUL *v* -ED, -ING, -S to rebuke severely

KEELLESS *adj* having no keel (the main structural part of a ship)

KEELSON *n* pl. -S a beam in a ship

KEEN *adj* KEENER, KEENEST enthusiastic

KEEN *v* -ED, -ING, -S to wail loudly over the dead

KEENER *n* pl. -S one that keens

KEENLY *adv* in a keen manner

KEENNESS *n* pl. -ES sharpness

KEEP *v* KEPT, KEEPING, KEEPS to continue to possess **KEEPABLE** *adj*

KEEPER *n* pl. -S one that keeps

KEEPING *n* pl. -S custody

KEEPSAKE *n* pl. -S a memento

KEESHOND *n* pl. -HONDS or -HONDEN a small, heavy-coated dog

KEESTER *n* pl. -S keister

KEET *n* pl. -S a young guinea fowl

KEEVE *n* pl. -S a tub or vat

KEF *n* pl. -S hemp smoked to produce euphoria

KEFFIYEH *n* pl. -S kaffiyeh

KEFIR *n* pl. -S a fermented beverage made from cow's milk

KEG *n* pl. -S a small barrel

KEGELER *n* pl. -S kegler

KEGLER *n* pl. -S a bowler

KEGLING *n* pl. -S bowling

KEIR *n* pl. -S kier

KEISTER *n* pl. -S the buttocks

KEITLOA *n* pl. -S a rhinoceros

KELEP *n* pl. -S a stinging ant

KELIM *n* pl. -S kilim

KELLY *n* pl. -LIES a bright green color

KELOID *n* pl. -S a scar caused by excessive growth of fibrous tissue **KELOIDAL** *adj*

KELP *v* -ED, -ING, -S to burn a type of seaweed

KELPIE *n* pl. -S a water sprite

KELPY *n* pl. -PIES kelpie

KELSON *n* pl. -S keelson

KELTER *n* pl. -S kilter

KELVIN *n* pl. -S a unit of temperature

KEMP *n* pl. -S a champion

KEMPT *adj* neatly kept

KEN *v* KENNED or KENT, KENNING, KENS to know

KENAF *n* pl. -S an East Indian plant

KENCH *n* pl. -ES a bin for salting fish

KENDO *n* pl. -DOS a Japanese sport

KENNED a past tense of ken

KENNEL *v* -NELED, -NELING, -NELS or -NELLED, -NELLING, -NELS to keep in a shelter for dogs

KENNING *n* pl. -S a metaphorical compound word or phrase

KENO *n* pl. -NOS a game of chance

KENOSIS *n* pl. -SISES the incarnation of Christ **KENOTIC** *adj*

KENOTRON *n* pl. -S a type of diode

KENT a past tense of ken

KEP *v* KEPPED, KEPPEN or KIPPEN, KEPPING, KEPS to catch

KEPHALIN *n* pl. -S cephalin

KEPI *n* pl. -S a type of cap

KEPPED past tense of kep

KEPPEN a past participle of kep

KEPPING present participle of kep

KEPT past tense of keep

KERAMIC *n* pl. -S ceramic

KERATIN *n* pl. -S a fibrous protein

KERATOID *adj* horny

KERATOMA *n* pl. -MAS or -MATA a skin disease

KERATOSE *adj* of or resembling horny tissue

KERB *v* -ED, -ING, -S to provide with curbing

KERCHIEF *n* pl. -CHIEFS or -CHIEVES a cloth worn as a head covering

KERCHOO *interj* achchoo

KERF *v* -ED, -ING, -S to make an incision with a cutting tool

KERMES *n* pl. KERMES a red dye

KERMESS *n* pl. -ES kermis

KERMESSE *n* pl. -S kermis

KERMIS *n* pl. -MISES a festival

KERN *v* -ED, -ING, -S to be formed with a projecting typeface

KERNE *n* pl. -S a medieval foot soldier

KERNEL *v* -NELED, -NELING, -NELS or -NELLED, -NELLING, -NELS to envelop as a kernel (the inner part of a nut)

KERNITE *n* pl. -S a mineral

KEROGEN *n* pl. -S a substance found in shale

KEROSENE *n* pl. -S a fuel oil

KEROSINE *n* pl. -S kerosene

KERPLUNK v -ED, -ING, -S to fall or drop with a heavy sound
KERRIA n pl. -S a Chinese shrub
KERRY n pl. -RIES one of an Irish breed of cattle
KERSEY n pl. -SEYS a woolen cloth
KERYGMA n pl. -MATA the preaching of the gospel
KESTREL n pl. -S a small falcon
KETCH n pl. -ES a sailing vessel
KETCHUP n pl. -S a spicy tomato sauce
KETENE n pl. -S a toxic gas
KETO adj of or pertaining to ketone
KETOL n pl. -S a chemical compound
KETONE n pl. -S a type of chemical compound **KETONIC** adj
KETOSE n pl. -S a simple sugar
KETOSIS n pl. -TOSES a buildup of ketones in the body **KETOTIC** adj
KETTLE n pl. -S a vessel for boiling liquids
KEV n pl. KEV a unit of energy
KEVEL n pl. -S a belaying cleat or peg
KEVIL n pl. -S kevel
KEX n pl. -ES a dry, hollow stalk
KEY v -ED, -ING, -S to provide with a key (a device used to turn the bolt in a lock)
KEYBOARD v -ED, -ING, -S to operate a machine by means of a keyset
KEYCARD n pl. -S a coded card for operating a device
KEYHOLE n pl. -S a hole for a key
KEYLESS adj being without a key
KEYNOTE v -NOTED, -NOTING, -NOTES to deliver the main speech at a function
KEYNOTER n pl. -S one that keynotes
KEYPAD n pl. -S a small keyboard
KEYPUNCH v -ED, -ING, -ES to perforate with a machine
KEYSET n pl. -S a system of finger levers
KEYSTER n pl. -S keister
KEYSTONE n pl. -S the central stone of an arch
KEYWAY n pl. -WAYS a slot for a key
KEYWORD n pl. -S a significant word
KHADDAR n pl. -S a cotton cloth
KHADI n pl. -S khaddar
KHAF n pl. -S kaph
KHAKI n pl. -S a durable cloth
KHALIF n pl. -S caliph
KHALIFA n pl. -S caliph
KHAMSEEN n pl. -S khamsin

KHAMSIN n pl. -S a hot, dry wind
KHAN n pl. -S an Asian ruler
KHANATE n pl. -S the domain of a khan
KHAPH n pl. -S kaph
KHAT n pl. -S kat
KHAZEN n pl. -ZENS or -ZENIM hazzan
KHEDA n pl. -S keddah
KHEDAH n pl. -S keddah
KHEDIVE n pl. -S a Turkish viceroy **KHEDIVAL** adj
KHET n pl. -S heth
KHETH n pl. -S heth
KHI n pl. -S chi
KHIRKAH n pl. -S a patchwork garment
KHOUM n pl. -S a monetary unit of Mauritania
KIANG n pl. -S a wild ass
KIAUGH n pl. -S trouble; worry
KIBBE n pl. -S a Near Eastern dish of ground lamb and bulgur
KIBBEH n pl. -S kibbe
KIBBI n pl. -S kibbe
KIBBITZ v -ED, -ING, -ES kibitz
KIBBLE v -BLED, -BLING, -BLES to grind coarsely
KIBBUTZ n pl. -BUTZIM a collective farm in Israel
KIBE n pl. -S a sore caused by exposure to cold
KIBEI n pl. -S one born in America of immigrant Japanese parents and educated in Japan
KIBITZ v -ED, -ING, -ES to meddle
KIBITZER n pl. -S one that kibitzes
KIBLA n pl. -S kiblah
KIBLAH n pl. -S the direction toward which Muslims face while praying
KIBOSH v -ED, -ING, -ES to stop
KICK v -ED, -ING, -S to strike out with the foot or feet **KICKABLE** adj
KICKBACK n pl. -S a strong reaction
KICKBALL n pl. -S baseball using an inflated ball that is kicked
KICKER n pl. -S one that kicks
KICKIER comparative of kicky
KICKIEST superlative of kicky
KICKOFF n pl. -S the kick that begins play in football
KICKSHAW n pl. -S a trifle or trinket
KICKUP n pl. -S a noisy argument
KICKY adj KICKIER, KICKIEST exciting
KID v KIDDED, KIDDING, KIDS to tease

KIDDER   n pl. -S one that kids
KIDDIE   n pl. -S a small child
KIDDIES   pl. of kiddy
KIDDING   present participle of kid
KIDDISH   adj childish
KIDDO   n pl. -DOS or -DOES — used as a form of familiar address
KIDDUSH   n pl. -ES a Jewish prayer
KIDDY   n pl. -DIES kiddie
KIDLIKE   adj resembling a child
KIDNAP   v -NAPED, -NAPING, -NAPS or -NAPPED, -NAPPING, -NAPS to take a person by force and often for ransom
KIDNAPEE   n pl. -S one that is kidnaped
KIDNAPER   n pl. -S one that kidnaps
KIDNAPPER   n pl. -S kidnaper
KIDNAPPING   present participle of kidnap
KIDNEY   n pl. -NEYS a bodily organ
KIDSKIN   n pl. -S a type of leather
KIDVID   n pl. -S television programs for children
KIEF   n pl. -S kef
KIELBASA   n pl. -BASAS, -BASI, or -BASY a smoked sausage
KIER   n pl. -S a vat for boiling and dyeing fabrics
KIESTER   n pl. -S keister
KIF   n pl. -S kef
KILIM   n pl. -S an oriental tapestry
KILL   v -ED, -ING, -S to cause to die
KILLDEE   n pl. -S killdeer
KILLDEER   n pl. -S a wading bird
KILLER   n pl. -S one that kills
KILLICK   n pl. -S a small anchor
KILLIE   n pl. -S a freshwater fish
KILLING   n pl. -S a sudden notable success
KILLJOY   n pl. -JOYS one who spoils the fun of others
KILLOCK   n pl. -S killick
KILN   v -ED, -ING, -S to bake in a type of oven
KILO   n pl. KILOS a kilogram or kilometer
KILOBAR   n pl. -S a unit of atmospheric pressure
KILOBASE   n pl. -S unit of measure of a nucleic-acid chain
KILOBAUD   n pl. -S a unit of data transmission speed
KILOBIT   n pl. -S a unit of computer information
KILOBYTE   n pl. -S 1,024 bytes
KILOGRAM   n pl. -S a unit of mass and weight

KILOMOLE   n pl. -S one thousand moles
KILORAD   n pl. -S a unit of nuclear radiation
KILOTON   n pl. -S a unit of weight
KILOVOLT   n pl. -S a unit of electromotive force
KILOWATT   n pl. -S a unit of power
KILT   v -ED, -ING, -S to make creases or pleats in
KILTER   n pl. -S good condition
KILTIE   n pl. -S one who wears a kilt (a type of skirt)
KILTING   n pl. -S an arrangement of kilt pleats
KILTY   n pl. KILTIES kiltie
KIMCHEE   n pl. -S kimchi
KIMCHI   n pl. -S a spicy Korean dish of pickled cabbage
KIMONO   n pl. -NOS a loose robe
KIMONOED   adj
KIN   n pl. -S a group of persons of common ancestry
KINA   n pl. -S a monetary unit of Papua New Guinea
KINASE   n pl. -S an enzyme
KIND   adj KINDER, KINDEST having a gentle, giving nature
KIND   n pl. -S a class of similar or related objects or individuals
KINDLE   v -DLED, -DLING, -DLES to cause to burn
KINDLER   n pl. -S one that kindles
KINDLESS   adj lacking kindness
KINDLING   n pl. -S material that is easily ignited
KINDLY   adj -LIER, -LIEST kind
KINDNESS   n pl. -ES the quality of being kind
KINDRED   n pl. -S a natural grouping
KINE   n pl. -S a type of television tube
KINEMA   n pl. -S cinema
KINESIC   adj pertaining to kinesics
KINESICS   n/pl the study of body motion in relation to communication
KINESIS   n pl. -NESES a type of movement
KINETIC   adj pertaining to motion
KINETICS   n/pl a branch of science dealing with motion
KINETIN   n pl. -S a substance that increases plant growth
KINFOLK   n/pl relatives
KINFOLKS   n/pl kinfolk
KING   v -ED, -ING, -S to reign as king (a male monarch)

KINGBIRD *n* pl. -S an American bird
KINGBOLT *n* pl. -S a kingpin
KINGCUP *n* pl. -S a marsh plant
KINGDOM *n* pl. -S the area ruled by a king
KINGFISH *n* pl. -ES a marine food fish
KINGHOOD *n* pl. -S the office of a king
KINGLESS *adj* having no king
KINGLET *n* pl. -S a king who rules over a small area
KINGLIKE *adj* resembling a king
KINGLY *adj* -LIER, -LIEST of or befitting a king
KINGPIN *n* pl. -S a central bolt connecting an axle to a vehicle
KINGPOST *n* pl. -S a supporting structure of a roof
KINGSHIP *n* pl. -S the power or position of a king
KINGSIDE *n* pl. -S a part of a chessboard
KINGWOOD *n* pl. -S a hardwood tree
KININ *n* pl. -S a hormone
KINK *v* -ED, -ING, -S to form a tight curl or bend in
KINKAJOU *n* pl. -S an arboreal mammal
KINKY *adj* KINKIER, KINKIEST tightly curled **KINKILY** *adv*
KINO *n* pl. -NOS a gum resin
KINSFOLK *n/pl* kinfolk
KINSHIP *n* pl. -S relationship
KINSMAN *n* pl. -MEN a male relative
KIOSK *n* pl. -S an open booth
KIP *v* KIPPED, KIPPING, KIPS to sleep
KIPPEN a past participle of kep
KIPPER *v* -ED, -ING, -S to cure fish by salting and smoking
KIPPERER *n* pl. -S one that kippers
KIPPING present participle of kip
KIPSKIN *n* pl. -S an animal hide that has not been tanned
KIR *n* pl. -S an alcoholic beverage
KIRIGAMI *n* pl. -S the Japanese art of folding paper
KIRK *n* pl. -S a church
KIRKMAN *n* pl. -MEN a member of a church
KIRMESS *n* pl. -ES kermis
KIRN *v* -ED, -ING, -S to churn
KIRSCH *n* pl. -ES a kind of brandy
KIRTLE *n* pl. -S a man's tunic or coat **KIRTLED** *adj*
KISHKA *n* pl. -S kishke
KISHKE *n* pl. -S a sausage
KISMAT *n* pl. -S kismet
KISMET *n* pl. -S destiny **KISMETIC** *adj*

KISS *v* -ED, -ING, -ES to touch with the lips as a sign of affection **KISSABLE** *adj* **KISSABLY** *adv*
KISSER *n* pl. -S one that kisses
KISSY *adj* inclined to kiss
KIST *n* pl. -S a chest, box, or coffin
KISTFUL *n* pl. -S as much as a kist can hold
KIT *v* KITTED, KITTING, KITS to equip
KITCHEN *n* pl. -S a room where food is cooked
KITE *v* KITED, KITING, KITES to obtain money or credit fraudulently
KITELIKE *adj* resembling a kite (a light, covered frame flown in the wind)
KITER *n* pl. -S one that kites
KITH *n* pl. -S one's friends and neighbors
KITHARA *n* pl. -S cithara
KITHE *v* KITHED, KITHING, KITHES to make known
KITING present participle of kite
KITLING *n* pl. -S a young animal
KITSCH *n* pl. -ES faddish art or literature **KITSCHY** *adj*
KITTED past tense of kit
KITTEL *n* pl. KITTEL a Jewish ceremonial robe
KITTEN *v* -ED, -ING, -S to bear kittens (young cats)
KITTIES pl. of kitty
KITTING present participle of kit
KITTLE *v* -TLED, -TLING, -TLES to tickle
KITTLE *adj* -TLER, -TLEST ticklish
KITTY *n* pl. -TIES a kitten or cat
KIVA *n* pl. -S an underground ceremonial chamber
KIWI *n* pl. -S a flightless bird
KLATCH *n* pl. -ES a social gathering
KLATSCH *n* pl. -ES klatch
KLAVERN *n* pl. -S a local branch of the Ku Klux Klan
KLAXON *n* pl. -S a low-pitched horn
KLEAGLE *n* pl. -S an official in the Ku Klux Klan
KLEPHT *n* pl. -S a Greek guerrilla **KLEPHTIC** *adj*
KLEZMER *n* pl. -MORIM a Jewish folk musician
KLISTER *n* pl. -S a wax for skis
KLONG *n* pl. -S a canal

KLOOF n pl. -S a ravine

KLUDGE n pl. -S a system composed of ill-fitting components

KLUGE n pl. -S kludge

KLUTZ n pl. -ES a clumsy person

KLUTZY adj KLUTZIER, KLUTZIEST clumsy

KLYSTRON n pl. -S a type of electron tube

KNACK v -ED, -ING, -S to strike sharply

KNACKER n pl. -S one that buys old livestock

KNACKERY n pl. -ERIES the place of business of a knacker

KNAP v KNAPPED, KNAPPING, KNAPS to strike sharply

KNAPPER n pl. -S one that knaps

KNAPSACK n pl. -S a bag carried on the back

KNAPWEED n pl. -S a meadow plant

KNAR n pl. -S a bump on a tree **KNARRED, KNARRY** adj

KNAUR n pl. -S knar

KNAVE n pl. -S a dishonest person **KNAVISH** adj

KNAVERY n pl. -ERIES trickery

KNAWEL n pl. -S a Eurasian plant

KNEAD v -ED, -ING, -S to work into a uniform mixture with the hands

KNEADER n pl. -S one that kneads

KNEE v KNEED, KNEEING, KNEES to strike with the knee (a joint of the leg)

KNEECAP v -CAPPED, -CAPPING, -CAPS to maim by shooting in the kneecap (a bone at the front of the knee)

KNEEHOLE n pl. -S a space for the knees

KNEEL v KNELT or KNEELED, KNEELING, KNEELS to rest on the knees

KNEELER n pl. -S one that kneels

KNEEPAD n pl. -S a covering for a knee

KNEEPAN n pl. -S the kneecap

KNEESOCK n pl. -S a sock reaching up to the knee

KNELL v -ED, -ING, -S to sound a bell

KNELT a past tense of kneel

KNESSET n pl. -S the Israeli parliament

KNEW past tense of know

KNICKERS n/pl loose-fitting pants gathered at the knee

KNIFE n pl. KNIVES a sharp-edged instrument used for cutting

KNIFE v KNIFED, KNIFING, KNIFES to cut with a knife

KNIFER n pl. -S one that knifes

KNIGHT v -ED, -ING, -S to make a knight (a medieval gentleman-soldier) of

KNIGHTLY adj of or befitting a knight

KNISH n pl. -ES dough stuffed with filling and fried

KNIT v KNITTED, KNITTING, KNITS to make a fabric or garment by joining loops of yarn

KNITTER n pl. -S one that knits

KNITTING n pl. -S work done by a knitter

KNITWEAR n pl. -S knitted clothing

KNIVES pl. of knife

KNOB n pl. -S a rounded protuberance **KNOBBED, KNOBLIKE** adj

KNOBBLY adj -BLIER, -BLIEST having very small knobs

KNOBBY adj -BIER, -BIEST full of knobs

KNOCK v -ED, -ING, -S to strike sharply

KNOCKER n pl. -S one that knocks

KNOCKOFF n pl. -S a copy that sells for less than the original

KNOCKOUT n pl. -S a blow that induces unconsciousness

KNOLL v -ED, -ING, -S to knell

KNOLLER n pl. -S one that knolls

KNOLLY adj hilly

KNOP n pl. -S a knob **KNOPPED** adj

KNOSP n pl. -S a knob

KNOT v KNOTTED, KNOTTING, KNOTS to tie in a knot (a closed loop)

KNOTHOLE n pl. -S a hole in a plank

KNOTLESS adj having no knots

KNOTLIKE adj resembling a knot

KNOTTED past tense of knot

KNOTTER n pl. -S one that knots

KNOTTING n pl. -S a fringe made of knotted threads

KNOTTY adj -TIER, -TIEST full of knots **KNOTTILY** adv

KNOTWEED n pl. -S a common weed

KNOUT v -ED, -ING, -S to flog with a leather whip

KNOW v KNEW, KNOWN, KNOWING, KNOWS to have a true understanding of **KNOWABLE** adj

KNOWER n pl. -S one that knows

KNOWING adj -INGER, -INGEST astute

KNOWING n pl. -S knowledge

KNOWN *n* pl. -S a mathematical quantity whose value is given

KNUBBY *adj* -BIER, -BIEST nubby

KNUCKLE *v* -LED, -LING, -LES to hit with the knuckles (the joints of the fingers)

KNUCKLER *n* pl. -S a type of baseball pitch

KNUCKLY *adj* -LIER, -LIEST having prominent knuckles

KNUR *n* pl. -S a bump on a tree

KNURL *v* -ED, -ING, -S to make grooves or ridges in

KNURLY *adj* KNURLIER, KNURLIEST gnarly

KOA *n* pl. -S a timber tree

KOALA *n* pl. -S an Australian mammal

KOAN *n* pl. -S a paradox meditated on by Buddhist monks

KOB *n* pl. -S a reddish brown antelope

KOBO *n* pl. KOBO a monetary unit of Nigeria

KOBOLD *n* pl. -S an elf

KOEL *n* pl. -S an Australian bird

KOHL *n* pl. -S a type of eye makeup

KOHLRABI *n* pl. -ES a variety of cabbage

KOI *n* pl. KOI a large and colorful fish

KOINE *n* pl. -S a type of dialect

KOKANEE *n* pl. -S a food fish

KOLA *n* pl. -S cola

KOLACKY *n* pl. KOLACKY a kind of pastry

KOLBASI *n* pl. -S kielbasa

KOLBASSI *n* pl. -S kielbasa

KOLHOZ *n* pl. -HOZY or -HOZES kolkhoz

KOLINSKI *n* pl. -ES kolinsky

KOLINSKY *n* pl. -SKIES an Asian mink

KOLKHOS *n* pl. -KHOSY or -KHOSES kolkhoz

KOLKHOZ *n* pl. -KHOZY or -KHOZES a collective farm in Russia

KOLKOZ *n* pl. -KOZY or -KOZES kolkhoz

KOLO *n* pl. -LOS a European folk dance

KOMATIK *n* pl. -S an Eskimo sledge

KOMONDOR *n* pl. -DORS, -DOROK, or -DOROCK a large, shaggy-coated dog

KONK *v* -ED, -ING, -S conk

KOODOO *n* pl. -DOOS kudu

KOOK *n* pl. -S an eccentric person

KOOKIE *adj* KOOKIER, KOOKIEST kooky

KOOKY *adj* KOOKIER, KOOKIEST eccentric

KOP *n* pl. -S a hill

KOPECK *n* pl. -S a Russian coin

KOPEK *n* pl. -S kopeck

KOPH *n* pl. -S a Hebrew letter

KOPJE *n* pl. -S a small hill

KOPPA *n* pl. -S a Greek letter

KOPPIE *n* pl. -S kopje

KOR *n* pl. -S a Hebrew unit of measure

KORAT *n* pl. -S a cat having a silver-blue coat

KORE *n* pl. -RAI an ancient Greek statue of a young woman

KORUNA *n* pl. KORUNAS, KORUNY, or KORUN a monetary unit of the Czech Republic

KOS *n* pl. KOS a land measure in India

KOSHER *v* -ED, -ING, -S to make fit to be eaten according to Jewish dietary laws

KOSS *n* pl. KOSS kos

KOTO *n* pl. -TOS a musical instrument

KOTOW *v* -ED, -ING, -S to kowtow

KOTOWER *n* pl. -S one that kotows

KOUMIS *n* pl. -MISES koumiss

KOUMISS *n* pl. -ES a beverage made from camel's milk

KOUMYS *n* pl. -ES koumiss

KOUMYSS *n* pl. -ES koumiss

KOUPREY *n* pl. -PREYS a short-haired ox

KOUROS *n* pl. -ROI an ancient Greek statue of a young man

KOUSSO *n* pl. -SOS cusso

KOWTOW *v* -ED, -ING, -S to behave in a servile manner

KOWTOWER *n* pl. -S one that kowtows

KRAAL *v* -ED, -ING, -S to pen in a type of enclosure

KRAFT *n* pl. -S a strong paper

KRAIT *n* pl. -S a venomous snake

KRAKEN *n* pl. -S a legendary sea monster

KRATER *n* pl. -S a type of vase

KRAUT *n* pl. -S sauerkraut

KREEP *n* pl. -S a basaltic lunar rock

KREMLIN *n* pl. -S a Russian citadel

KREPLACH *n* pl. KREPLACH dumplings filled with ground meat or cheese

KREUTZER *n* pl. -S a former monetary unit of Austria

KREUZER *n* pl. -S kreutzer

KRILL *n* pl. -S an aggregate of small marine crustaceans

KRIMMER *n* pl. -S a kind of fur

KRIS *n* pl. -ES a short sword

KRONA *n* pl. KRONUR a monetary unit of Iceland

KRONA *n* pl. KRONOR a monetary unit of Sweden

KRONE *n* pl. KRONER a monetary unit of Denmark

KRONE *n* pl. KRONEN a former monetary unit of Austria

KRONOR pl. of krona

KRONUR pl. of krona

KROON *n* pl. KROONS or KROONI a former monetary unit of Estonia

KRUBI *n* pl. -S a tropical plant

KRUBUT *n* pl. -S krubi

KRULLER *n* pl. -S cruller

KRUMHORN *n* pl. -S crumhorn

KRYOLITE *n* pl. -S cryolite

KRYOLITH *n* pl. -S cryolite

KRYPTON *n* pl. -S a gaseous element

KUCHEN *n* pl. KUCHEN a coffee cake

KUDO *n* pl. -DOS award; honor

KUDU *n* pl. -S a large antelope

KUDZU *n* pl. -S an Asian vine

KUE *n* pl. -S the letter Q

KUGEL *n* pl. -S a baked pudding of potatoes or noodles

KUKRI *n* pl. -S a long, curved knife of Nepal

KULAK *n* pl. -LAKS or -LAKI a rich Russian peasant

KULTUR *n* pl. -S culture; civilization

KUMISS *n* pl. -ES koumiss

KUMMEL *n* pl. -S a type of liqueur

KUMQUAT *n* pl. -S a citrus fruit

KUMYS *n* pl. -ES koumiss

KUNZITE *n* pl. -S a mineral

KURBASH *v* -ED, -ING, -ES to flog with a leather whip

KURGAN *n* pl. -S a mound of earth over a grave

KURTA *n* pl. -S a shirt worn in India

KURTOSIS *n* pl. -SISES the relative degree of curvature in a statistical curve

KURU *n* pl. -S a disease of the nervous system

KUSSO *n* pl. -SOS cusso

KUVASZ *n* pl. -VASZOK a large dog having a white coat

KVAS *n* pl. -ES kvass

KVASS *n* pl. -ES a Russian beer

KVETCH *v* -ED, -ING, -ES to complain

KVETCHY *adj* KVETCHIER, KVETCHIEST habitually complaining

KWACHA *n* pl. KWACHA a monetary unit of Zambia

KWANZA *n* pl. -S a monetary unit of Angola

KYACK *n* pl. -S a packsack

KYAK *n* pl. -S a kayak (an Eskimo canoe)

KYANISE *v* -ISED, -ISING, -ISES to kyanize

KYANITE *n* pl. -S cyanite

KYANIZE *v* -IZED, -IZING, -IZES to treat wood with a type of preservative

KYAR *n* pl. -S coir

KYAT *n* pl. -S a monetary unit of Myanmar

KYBOSH *v* -ED, -ING, -ES to kibosh

KYLIX *n* pl. -LIKES a drinking vessel

KYMOGRAM *n* pl. -S a record of fluid pressure

KYPHOSIS *n* pl. -PHOSES abnormal curvature of the spine **KYPHOTIC** *adj*

KYRIE *n* pl. -S a religious petition for mercy

KYTE *n* pl. -S the stomach

KYTHE *v* KYTHED, KYTHING, KYTHES to kithe

LA   *n* pl. -S the sixth tone of the diatonic musical scale

LAAGER   *v* -ED, -ING, -S to form a defensive encampment

LAARI   *n* pl. LAARI a monetary unit of the Maldives

LAB   *n* pl. -S a laboratory

LABARUM   *n* pl. -RA or -RUMS an ecclesiastical banner

LABDANUM   *n* pl. -S a fragrant resin

LABEL   *v* -BELED, -BELING, -BELS or -BELLED, -BELLING, -BELS to describe or designate

LABELER   *n* pl. -S one that labels

LABELLA   pl. of labellum

LABELLED   a past tense of label

LABELLER   *n* pl. -S labeler

LABELLING   a present participle of label

LABELLUM   *n* pl. -LA the lower petal of an orchid

LABIA   pl. of labium

LABIAL   *n* pl. -S a labially produced sound

LABIALLY   *adv* by means of the lips

LABIATE   *n* pl. -S a labiated plant

LABIATED   *adj* having corollas that are divided into two liplike parts

LABILE   *adj* likely to change

LABILITY   *n* pl. -TIES the state of being labile

LABIUM   *n* pl. -BIA a fold of the vulva

LABOR   *v* -ED, -ING, -S to work

LABORER   *n* pl. -S one that labors

LABORITE   *n* pl. -S a supporter of labor interests

LABOUR   *v* -ED, -ING, -S to labor

LABOURER   *n* pl. -S laborer

LABRA   a pl. of labrum

LABRADOR   *n* pl. -S a hunting dog

LABRET   *n* pl. -S an ornament worn in a perforation of the lip

LABROID   *n* pl. -S a marine fish

LABRUM   *n* pl. -BRA or -BRUMS a lip or liplike structure

LABRUSCA   *adj* designating a fox grape

LABURNUM   *n* pl. -S an ornamental tree

LAC   *n* pl. -S a resinous substance secreted by certain insects

LACE   *v* LACED, LACING, LACES to fasten by means of a lace (a cord for drawing together two edges)

LACELESS   *adj* lacking lace

LACELIKE   *adj* resembling lace

LACER   *n* pl. -S one that laces

LACERATE   *v* -ATED, -ATING, -ATES to tear roughly

LACERTID   *n* pl. -S a type of lizard

LACEWING   *n* pl. -S a winged insect

LACEWOOD   *n* pl. -S an Australian tree

LACEWORK   *n* pl. -S a delicate openwork fabric

LACEY   *adj* LACIER, LACIEST lacy

LACHES   *n* pl. LACHES undue delay in asserting a legal right

LACIER   comparative of lacy

LACIEST   superlative of lacy

LACILY   *adv* in a lacy manner

LACINESS   *n* pl. -ES the quality of being lacy

LACING   *n* pl. -S a contrasting marginal band of color

LACK   *v* -ED, -ING, -S to be without

LACKADAY   *interj* — used to express regret

LACKER   *v* -ED, -ING, -S to lacquer

LACKEY   *v* -ED, -ING, -S to act in a servile manner

LACONIC   *adj* using a minimum of words

LACONISM *n* pl. -S brevity of expression

LACQUER *v* -ED, -ING, -S to coat with a glossy substance

LACQUEY *v* -ED, -ING, -S to lackey

LACRIMAL *n* pl. -S a type of vase

LACROSSE *n* pl. -S a type of ball game

LACTAM *n* pl. -S a chemical compound

LACTARY *adj* pertaining to milk

LACTASE *n* pl. -S an enzyme

LACTATE *v* -TATED, -TATING, -TATES to secrete milk

LACTEAL *n* pl. -S a lymphatic vessel

LACTEAN *adj* lacteous

LACTEOUS *adj* resembling milk

LACTIC *adj* derived from milk

LACTONE *n* pl. -S any of a group of esters LACTONIC *adj*

LACTOSE *n* pl. -S a lactic sugar

LACUNA *n* pl. -NAE or -NAS an empty space or missing part LACUNAL, LACUNARY, LACUNATE *adj*

LACUNAR *n* pl. -NARS or -NARIA a ceiling with recessed panels

LACUNE *n* pl. -S lacuna

LACUNOSE *adj* marked by shallow depressions

LACY *adj* LACIER, LACIEST resembling lacework

LAD *n* pl. -S a boy or youth

LADANUM *n* pl. -S labdanum

LADDER *v* -ED, -ING, -S to cause a run in a stocking

LADDIE *n* pl. -S a lad

LADE *v* LADED, LADEN, LADING, LADES to load with a cargo

LADEN *v* -ED, -ING, -S to lade

LADER *n* pl. -S one that lades

LADIES *pl.* of lady

LADING *n* pl. -S cargo; freight

LADINO *n* pl. -NOS a fast-growing clover

LADLE *v* -DLED, -DLING, -DLES to lift out with a ladle (a type of spoon)

LADLEFUL *n* pl. -S as much as a ladle will hold

LADLER *n* pl. -S one that ladles

LADLING *present participle of ladle*

LADRON *n* pl. -S ladrone

LADRONE *n* pl. -S a thief

LADY *n* pl. -DIES a woman of refinement and gentle manners

LADYBIRD *n* pl. -S a ladybug

LADYBUG *n* pl. -S a small beetle

LADYFISH *n* pl. -ES a bonefish

LADYHOOD *n* pl. -S the state of being a lady

LADYISH *adj* somewhat ladylike

LADYKIN *n* pl. -S a small lady

LADYLIKE *adj* resembling or suitable to a lady

LADYLOVE *n* pl. -S a sweetheart

LADYPALM *n* pl. -S a palm tree

LADYSHIP *n* pl. -S the condition of being a lady

LAETRILE *n* pl. -S a drug derived from apricot pits

LAEVO *adj* levo

LAG *v* LAGGED, LAGGING, LAGS to stay or fall behind

LAGAN *n* pl. -S goods thrown into the sea with a buoy attached to enable recovery

LAGEND *n* pl. -S lagan

LAGER *v* -ED, -ING, -S to laager

LAGGARD *n* pl. -S one that lags

LAGGED *past tense of lag*

LAGGER *n* pl. -S a laggard

LAGGING *n* pl. -S an insulating material

LAGNAPPE *n* pl. -S a small gift given to a customer with his purchase

LAGOON *n* pl. -S a shallow body of water LAGOONAL *adj*

LAGUNA *n* pl. -S lagoon

LAGUNE *n* pl. -S lagoon

LAHAR *n* pl. -S a flowing mass of volcanic debris

LAIC *n* pl. -S a layman LAICAL *adj* LAICALLY *adv*

LAICH *n* pl. -S laigh

LAICISE *v* -ICISED, -ICISING, -ICISES to laicize

LAICISM *n* pl. -S a political system free from clerical control

LAICIZE *v* -ICIZED, -ICIZING, -ICIZES to free from clerical control

LAID *a past tense of lay*

LAIGH *n* pl. -S a lowland

LAIN *past participle of lie*

LAIR *v* -ED, -ING, -S to live in a lair (a wild animal's resting or dwelling place)

LAIRD *n* pl. -S the owner of a landed estate LAIRDLY *adj*

LAITANCE *n* pl. -S a milky deposit on the surface of fresh concrete

LAITH *adj* loath LAITHLY *adv*

LAITY *n* pl. -ITIES the nonclerical membership of a religious faith

LAKE *n* pl. -S a sizable inland body of water LAKELIKE *adj*

LAKED *adj* subjected to the process of laking

LAKEPORT *n* pl. -S a city located on the shore of a lake

LAKER *n* pl. -S a lake fish

LAKESIDE *n* pl. -S the land along the edge of a lake

LAKH *n* pl. -S the sum of one hundred thousand

LAKING *n* pl. -S the reddening of blood plasma by the release of hemoglobin from the red corpuscles

LAKY *adj* LAKIER, LAKIEST of the color of blood

LALL *v* -ED, -ING, -S to articulate the letter *r* as *l*

LALLAN *n* pl. -S a lowland

LALLAND *n* pl. -S a lowland

LALLYGAG *v* -GAGGED, -GAGGING, -GAGS to dawdle

LAM *v* LAMMED, LAMMING, LAMS to flee hastily

LAMA *n* pl. -S a Buddhist monk

LAMASERY *n* pl. -SERIES a monastery of lamas

LAMB *v* -ED, -ING, -S to give birth to a lamb (a young sheep)

LAMBAST *v* -ED, -ING, -S to lambaste

LAMBASTE *v* -BASTED, -BASTING, -BASTES to beat severely

LAMBDA *n* pl. -S a Greek letter
LAMBDOID *adj*

LAMBENCY *n* pl. -CIES the quality or an instance of being lambent

LAMBENT *adj* flickering lightly and gently over a surface

LAMBER *n* pl. -S a ewe that is lambing

LAMBERT *n* pl. -S a unit of brightness

LAMBIE *n* pl. -S a lambkin

LAMBIER comparative of lamby

LAMBIEST superlative of lamby

LAMBKILL *n* pl. -S an evergreen shrub

LAMBKIN *n* pl. -S a small lamb

LAMBLIKE *adj* resembling a lamb

LAMBSKIN *n* pl. -S the skin of a lamb

LAMBY *adj* LAMBIER, LAMBIEST resembling a lamb

LAME *adj* LAMER, LAMEST physically disabled

LAME *v* LAMED, LAMING, LAMES to make lame

LAMED *n* pl. -S a Hebrew letter

LAMEDH *n* pl. -S lamed

LAMELLA *n* pl. -LAE or -LAS a thin plate, scale, or membrane
LAMELLAR *adj*

LAMELY *adv* in a lame manner

LAMENESS *n* pl. -ES the state of being lame

LAMENT *v* -ED, -ING, -S to express sorrow or regret for

LAMENTER *n* pl. -S one that laments

LAMER comparative of lame

LAMEST superlative of lame

LAMIA *n* pl. -MIAS or -MIAE a female demon

LAMINA *n* pl. -NAE or -NAS a thin plate, scale, or layer
LAMINAL, LAMINAR, LAMINARY *adj*

LAMINATE *v* -NATED, -NATING, -NATES to compress into a thin plate

LAMING present participle of lame

LAMINOSE *adj* composed of laminae

LAMINOUS *adj* laminose

LAMISTER *n* pl. -S lamster

LAMMED past tense of lam

LAMMING present participle of lam

LAMP *v* -ED, -ING, -S to look at

LAMPAD *n* pl. -S a candlestick

LAMPAS *n* pl. -ES inflammation of the roof of a horse's mouth

LAMPERS *n* pl. -ES lampas

LAMPION *n* pl. -S a type of light-generating device

LAMPOON *v* -ED, -ING, -S to ridicule in a satirical composition

LAMPPOST *n* pl. -S a post supporting a streetlight

LAMPREY *n* pl. -PREYS an eellike fish

LAMPYRID *n* pl. -S any of a family of beetles

LAMSTER *n* pl. -S a fugitive

LANAI *n* pl. -S a veranda

LANATE *adj* covered with wool

LANATED *adj* lanate

LANCE *v* LANCED, LANCING, LANCES to pierce with a lance (a spearlike weapon)

LANCELET *n* pl. -S a small marine organism

LANCER *n* pl. -S a cavalryman armed with a lance

LANCET *n* pl. -S a narrow, pointed arch
LANCETED *adj*

LANCIERS *n* pl. LANCIERS a French dance

LANCING present participle of lance

LAND	*v* -ED, -ING, -S to set down upon land (solid ground)	
LANDAU	*n* pl. -S a type of carriage	
LANDER	*n* pl. -S one that lands	
LANDFALL	*n* pl. -S a sighting or approach to land	
LANDFILL	*n* pl. -S a system of waste disposal	
LANDFORM	*n* pl. -S a natural feature of the earth's surface	
LANDGRAB	*n* pl. -S a swift and often fraudulent seizure of land	
LANDING	*n* pl. -S a place for discharging or taking on passengers or cargo	
LANDLADY	*n* pl. -DIES a female landlord	
LANDLER	*n* pl. -S a slow Austrian dance	
LANDLESS	*adj* owning no land	
LANDLINE	*n* -S a line of communication on land	
LANDLORD	*n* pl. -S one who owns and rents out real estate	
LANDMAN	*n* pl. -MEN one who lives and works on land	
LANDMARK	*n* pl. -S an object that marks a boundary line	
LANDMASS	*n* pl. -ES a large area of land	
LANDMEN	pl. of landman	
LANDSIDE	*n* pl. -S a part of a plow	
LANDSKIP	*n* pl. -S landscape	
LANDSLEIT	pl. of landsman	
LANDSLID	past tense of landslide (to win an election by an overwhelming majority)	
LANDSLIP	*n* pl. -S the fall of a mass of earth	
LANDSMAN	*n* pl. LANDSLEIT a fellow Jew coming from one's own section of Eastern Europe	
LANDSMAN	*n* pl. -MEN landman	
LANDWARD	*adv* toward the land	
LANE	*n* pl. -S a narrow passageway	
LANELY	*adj* lonely	
LANEWAY	*n* pl. -WAYS a lane	
LANG	*adj* long	
LANGLAUF	*n* pl. -S a cross-country ski run	
LANGLEY	*n* pl. -LEYS a unit of illumination	
LANGRAGE	*n* pl. -S a shot formerly used in naval warfare	
LANGREL	*n* pl. -S langrage	
LANGSHAN	*n* pl. -S any of a breed of large domestic fowl	
LANGSYNE	*n* pl. -S time long past	

LANGUAGE	*n* pl. -S a body of words and systems serving as a means of communication
LANGUE	*n* pl. -S a type of language
LANGUET	*n* pl. -S a tonguelike part
LANGUID	*adj* lacking in vigor or vitality
LANGUISH	*v* -ED, -ING, -ES to lose vigor or vitality
LANGUOR	*n* pl. -S the state of being languid
LANGUR	*n* pl. -S an Asian monkey
LANIARD	*n* pl. -S lanyard
LANIARY	*n* pl. -ARIES a cuspid
LANITAL	*n* pl. -S a woollike fiber
LANK	*adj* LANKER, LANKEST long and slender **LANKLY** *adv*
LANKNESS	*n* pl. -ES the state of being lank
LANKY	*adj* LANKIER, LANKIEST ungracefully tall and thin **LANKILY** *adv*
LANNER	*n* pl. -S a falcon of Europe and Asia
LANNERET	*n* pl. -S a male lanner
LANOLIN	*n* pl. -S a fatty substance obtained from wool
LANOLINE	*n* pl. -S lanolin
LANOSE	*adj* lanate
LANOSITY	*n* pl. -TIES the state of being lanose
LANTANA	*n* pl. -S a tropical shrub
LANTERN	*n* pl. -S a protective case for a light
LANTHORN	*n* pl. -S a lantern
LANUGO	*n* pl. -GOS fine, soft hair
LANYARD	*n* pl. -S a fastening rope on a ship
LAP	*v* LAPPED, LAPPING, LAPS to fold over or around something
LAPBOARD	*n* pl. -S a flat board used as a table or desk
LAPDOG	*n* pl. -S a small dog
LAPEL	*n* pl. -S an extension of the collar of a garment **LAPELED, LAPELLED** *adj*
LAPFUL	*n* pl. -S as much as the lap can hold
LAPIDARY	*n* pl. -DARIES one who works with precious stones
LAPIDATE	*v* -DATED, -DATING, -DATES to hurl stones at
LAPIDES	pl. of lapis
LAPIDIFY	*v* -FIED, -FYING, -FIES to turn to stone
LAPIDIST	*n* pl. -S a lapidary

LAPILLUS   *n* pl. -LI a small fragment of lava

LAPIN   *n* pl. -S a rabbit

LAPIS   *n* pl. LAPIDES a stone

LAPIS   *n* pl. -PISES a mineral

LAPPED   past tense of lap

LAPPER   *v* -ED, -ING, -S to lopper

LAPPET   *n* pl. -S a decorative flap on a garment **LAPPETED** *adj*

LAPPING   present participle of lap

LAPSE   *v* LAPSED, LAPSING, LAPSES to fall from a previous standard **LAPSABLE, LAPSIBLE** *adj*

LAPSER   *n* pl. -S one that lapses

LAPSUS   *n* pl. LAPSUS a mistake

LAPTOP   *n* pl. -S a small computer for use on one's lap

LAPWING   *n* pl. -S a shore bird

LAR   *n* pl. -ES or -S a tutelary god or spirit of an ancient Roman household

LARBOARD   *n* pl. -S the left-hand side of a ship

LARCENER   *n* pl. -S one that commits larceny

LARCENY   *n* pl. -NIES the felonious taking and removal of another's personal goods

LARCH   *n* pl. -ES a coniferous tree

LARD   *v* -ED, -ING, -S to coat with lard (the melted fat of hogs)

LARDER   *n* pl. -S a place where food is stored

LARDIER   comparative of lardy

LARDIEST   superlative of lardy

LARDLIKE   *adj* resembling lard

LARDON   *n* pl. -S a thin slice of bacon or pork

LARDOON   *n* pl. -S lardon

LARDY   *adj* LARDIER, LARDIEST resembling lard

LAREE   *n* pl. -S lari

LARES   a pl. of lar

LARGANDO   *adj* becoming gradually slower — used as a musical direction

LARGE   *adj* LARGER, LARGEST of considerable size or quantity **LARGELY** *adv*

LARGE   *n* pl. -S generosity

LARGESS   *n* pl. -ES generosity

LARGESSE   *n* pl. -S largess

LARGEST   superlative of large

LARGISH   *adj* somewhat large

LARGO   *n* pl. -GOS a slow musical movement

LARI   *n* pl. -S a monetary unit of Maldives

LARIAT   *v* -ED, -ING, -S to lasso

LARINE   *adj* resembling a gull

LARK   *v* -ED, -ING, -S to behave playfully

LARKER   *n* pl. -S one that larks

LARKIER   comparative of larky

LARKIEST   superlative of larky

LARKISH   *adj* playful

LARKSOME   *adj* playful

LARKSPUR   *n* pl. -S a flowering plant

LARKY   *adj* LARKIER, LARKIEST playful

LARRIGAN   *n* pl. -S a type of moccasin

LARRIKIN   *n* pl. -S a rowdy

LARRUP   *v* -ED, -ING, -S to beat or thrash

LARRUPER   *n* pl. -S one that larrups

LARUM   *n* pl. -S an alarm

LARVA   *n* pl. -VAE or -VAS the immature form of various insects and animals when newly hatched **LARVAL** *adj*

LARYNX   *n* pl. LARYNGES or LARYNXES an organ of the respiratory tract **LARYNGAL** *adj*

LASAGNA   *n* pl. -S an Italian baked dish

LASAGNE   *n* pl. -S lasagna

LASCAR   *n* pl. -S an East Indian sailor

LASE   *v* LASED, LASING, LASES to function as a laser

LASER   *n* pl. -S a device that amplifies light waves

LASH   *v* -ED, -ING, -ES to strike with a whip

LASHER   *n* pl. -S one that lashes

LASHING   *n* pl. -S a flogging

LASHINS   *n/pl* an abundance

LASHKAR   *n* pl. -S lascar

LASING   present participle of lase

LASS   *n* pl. -ES a young woman

LASSIE   *n* pl. -S a lass

LASSO   *v* -ED, -ING, -S or -ES to catch with a lasso (a long rope with a running noose)

LASSOER   *n* pl. -S one that lassos

LAST   *v* -ED, -ING, -S to continue in existence

LASTER   *n* pl. -S one that lasts

LASTING   *n* pl. -S a durable fabric

LASTLY   *adv* in conclusion

LAT   *n* pl. LATS or LATI a former monetary unit of Latvia

LATAKIA *n* pl. -S a variety of Turkish tobacco

LATCH *v* -ED, -ING, -ES to close with a type of fastening device

LATCHET *n* pl. -S a thong used to fasten a shoe

LATCHKEY *n* pl. -KEYS a key for opening a latched door

LATE *adj* LATER, LATEST coming or occurring after the expected time

LATED *adj* belated

LATEEN *n* pl. -S a sailing vessel

LATEENER *n* pl. -S a lateen

LATELY *adv* not long ago

LATEN *v* -ED, -ING, -S to become late

LATENCY *n* pl. -CIES the state of being present but not manifest

LATENESS *n* pl. -ES the state of being late

LATENT *n* pl. -S a barely visible fingerprint that can be developed for study

LATENTLY *adv* dormantly

LATER comparative of late

LATERAD *adv* toward the side

LATERAL *v* -ED, -ING, -S to throw a sideward pass in football

LATERITE *n* pl. -S a type of soil

LATERIZE *v* -IZED, -IZING, -IZES to convert to laterite

LATEST *n* pl. -S the most recent development

LATEWOOD *n* pl. -S a part of an annual ring of wood

LATEX *n* pl. LATICES or LATEXES a milky liquid of certain plants

LATH *v* -ED, -ING, -S to cover with laths (thin strips of wood)

LATHE *v* LATHED, LATHING, LATHES to cut or shape on a type of machine

LATHER *v* -ED, -ING, -S to cover with lather (a light foam)

LATHERER *n* pl. -S one that lathers

LATHERY *adj* covered with lather

LATHI *n* pl. -S a heavy stick of bamboo and iron in India

LATHIER comparative of lathy

LATHIEST superlative of lathy

LATHING *n* pl. -S work made of or using laths

LATHWORK *n* pl. -S lathing

LATHY *adj* LATHIER, LATHIEST long and slender

LATI *a* pl. of lat

LATICES *a* pl. of latex

LATIGO *n* pl. -GOS or -GOES a strap used to fasten a saddle

LATINITY *n* pl. -TIES a manner of writing or speaking Latin

LATINIZE *v* -IZED, -IZING, -IZES to translate into Latin

LATINO *n* pl. -NOS a Latin American

LATISH *adj* somewhat late

LATITUDE *n* pl. -S freedom from narrow restrictions

LATKE *n* pl. -S a potato pancake

LATOSOL *n* pl. -S a tropical soil

LATRIA *n* pl. -S the supreme worship given to God only, in Roman Catholicism

LATRINE *n* pl. -S a type of toilet

LATTEN *n* pl. -S a brass-like alloy

LATTER *adj* being the second mentioned of two

LATTERLY *adv* lately

LATTICE *v* -TICED, -TICING, -TICES to form a structure consisting of interlaced strips of material

LATTIN *n* pl. -S latten

LAUAN *n* pl. -S a Philippine timber

LAUD *v* -ED, -ING, -S to praise

LAUDABLE *adj* worthy of praise
LAUDABLY *adv*

LAUDANUM *n* pl. -S a type of opium preparation

LAUDATOR *n* pl. -S a lauder

LAUDER *n* pl. -S one that lauds

LAUGH *v* -ED, -ING, -S to express emotion, typically mirth, by a series of inarticulate sounds

LAUGHER *n* pl. -S one that laughs

LAUGHING *n* pl. -S laughter

LAUGHTER *n* pl. -S the act or sound of one that laughs

LAUNCE *n* pl. -S a marine fish

LAUNCH *v* -ED, -ING, -ES to set in motion

LAUNCHER *n* pl. -S a launching device

LAUNDER *v* -ED, -ING, -S to wash clothes

LAUNDRY *n* pl. -DRIES a collection of clothes to be washed

LAURA *n* pl. -RAS or -RAE a type of monastery

LAUREATE *v* -ATED, -ATING, -ATES to laurel

LAUREL v -RELED, -RELING, -RELS or -RELLED, -RELLING, -RELS to crown with a wreath of evergreen leaves

LAUWINE n pl. -S an avalanche

LAV n pl. -S a lavatory

LAVA n pl. -S molten rock that issues from a volcano

LAVABO n pl. -BOES or -BOS a ceremonial washing in certain Christian churches

LAVAGE n pl. -S a washing

LAVALAVA n pl. -S a Polynesian garment

LAVALIER n pl. -S a pendant worn on a chain around the neck

LAVALIKE adj resembling lava

LAVATION n pl. -S the acting of washing

LAVATORY n pl. -RIES a room equipped with washing and toilet facilities

LAVE v LAVED, LAVING, LAVES to wash

LAVEER v -ED, -ING, -S to sail against the wind

LAVENDER v -ED, -ING, -S to sprinkle with a type of perfume

LAVER n pl. -S a vessel used for ancient Hebrew ceremonial washings

LAVEROCK n pl. -S a songbird

LAVING present participle of lave

LAVISH adj -ISHER, -ISHEST expending or giving in great amounts **LAVISHLY** adv

LAVISH v -ED, -ING, -ES to expend or give in great amounts

LAVISHER n pl. -S one that lavishes

LAVROCK n pl. -S laverock

LAW v -ED, -ING, -S to take a complaint to court for settlement

LAWBOOK n pl. -S a book containing or dealing with laws

LAWFUL adj allowed by law (the body of rules governing the affairs of a community) **LAWFULLY** adv

LAWGIVER n pl. -S one who institutes a legal system

LAWINE n pl. -S lauwine

LAWING n pl. -S a bill for food or drink in a tavern

LAWLESS adj having no system of laws

LAWLIKE adj being like the law

LAWMAKER n pl. -S a legislator

LAWMAN n pl. -MEN a law-enforcement officer

LAWN n pl. -S an area of grass-covered land **LAWNY** adj

LAWSUIT n pl. -S a legal action

LAWYER v -ED, -ING, -S to work as a member of the legal profession

LAWYERLY adj befitting a member of the legal profession

LAX adj LAXER, LAXEST not strict or stringent

LAXATION n pl. -S the act of relaxing

LAXATIVE n pl. -S a drug that stimulates evacuation of the bowels

LAXITY n pl. -ITIES the state of being lax

LAXLY adv in a lax manner

LAXNESS n pl. -ES laxity

LAY v LAID or LAYED, LAYING, LAYS to deposit as a wager

LAYABOUT n pl. -S a lazy person

LAYAWAY n pl. -AWAYS an item that has been reserved with a down payment

LAYER v -ED, -ING, -S to form a layer (a single thickness, coating, or covering)

LAYERAGE n pl. -S a method of plant propagation

LAYERING n pl. -S layerage

LAYETTE n pl. -S an outfit of clothing and equipment for a newborn child

LAYMAN n pl. -MEN a member of the laity

LAYOFF n pl. -S the suspension or dismissal of employees

LAYOUT n pl. -S an arrangement or plan

LAYOVER n pl. -S a stopover

LAYUP n pl. -S a shot in basketball

LAYWOMAN n pl. -WOMEN a female member of the laity

LAZAR n pl. -S a beggar afflicted with a loathsome disease

LAZARET n pl. -S a hospital treating contagious diseases

LAZE v LAZED, LAZING, LAZES to pass time lazily

LAZIED past tense of lazy

LAZIER comparative of lazy

LAZIES present 3d person sing. of lazy

LAZIEST superlative of lazy

LAZILY adv in a lazy manner

LAZINESS n pl. -ES the state of being lazy

LAZING present participle of laze

LAZULI n pl. -S a mineral

LAZULITE   *n* pl. -S a mineral

LAZURITE   *n* pl. -S a mineral

LAZY   *adj* LAZIER, LAZIEST disinclined toward work or exertion

LAZY   *v* LAZIED, LAZYING, LAZIES to move or lie lazily

LAZYISH   *adj* somewhat lazy

LEA   *n* pl. -S a meadow

LEACH   *v* -ED, -ING, -ES to subject to the filtering action of a liquid

LEACHATE   *n* pl. -S a solution obtained by leaching

LEACHER   *n* pl. -S one that leaches

LEACHY   *adj* LEACHIER, LEACHIEST porous

LEAD   *v* LED, LEADING, LEADS to show the way to by going in advance

LEAD   *v* -ED, -ING, -S to cover with lead (a heavy metallic element)

LEADEN   *adj* oppressively heavy **LEADENLY** *adv*

LEADER   *n* pl. -S one that leads or guides

LEADIER   comparative of leady

LEADIEST   superlative of leady

LEADING   *n* pl. -S a covering or border of lead

LEADLESS   *adj* having no lead

LEADMAN   *n* pl. -MEN a worker in charge of other workers

LEADOFF   *n* pl. -S an opening play or move

LEADSMAN   *n* pl. -MEN a seaman who measures the depth of water

LEADWORK   *n* pl. -S something made of lead

LEADWORT   *n* pl. -S a tropical plant

LEADY   *adj* LEADIER, LEADIEST resembling lead

LEAF   *n* pl. LEAVES a usually green, flattened organ of vascular plants

LEAF   *v* -ED, -ING, -S to turn pages rapidly

LEAFAGE   *n* pl. -S foliage

LEAFIER   comparative of leafy

LEAFIEST   superlative of leafy

LEAFLESS   *adj* having no leaves

LEAFLET   *v* -LETED, -LETING, -LETS or -LETTED, -LETTING, -LETS to distribute printed sheets of paper

LEAFLIKE   *adj* resembling a leaf

LEAFWORM   *n* pl. -S a moth larva that feeds on leaves

LEAFY   *adj* LEAFIER, LEAFIEST covered with leaves

LEAGUE   *v* LEAGUED, LEAGUING, LEAGUES to come together for a common purpose

LEAGUER   *v* -ED, -ING, -S to besiege

LEAK   *v* -ED, -ING, -S to permit the escape of something through a breach or flaw

LEAKAGE   *n* pl. -S the act or an instance of leaking

LEAKER   *n* pl. -S one that leaks

LEAKLESS   *adj* designed not to leak

LEAKY   *adj* LEAKIER, LEAKIEST tending to leak **LEAKILY** *adv*

LEAL   *adj* loyal **LEALLY** *adv*

LEALTY   *n* pl. -TIES loyalty

LEAN   *v* LEANED or LEANT, LEANING, LEANS to deviate from a vertical position

LEAN   *adj* LEANER, LEANEST having little fat **LEANLY** *adv*

LEANER   *n* pl. -S one that leans

LEANING   *n* pl. -S a tendency

LEANNESS   *n* pl. -ES the state of being lean

LEANT   a past tense of lean

LEAP   *v* LEAPED or LEAPT or LEPT, LEAPING, LEAPS to spring off the ground

LEAPER   *n* pl. -S one that leaps

LEAPFROG   *v* -FROGGED, -FROGGING, -FROGS to jump over with the legs wide apart

LEAPT   a past tense of leap

LEAR   *n* pl. -S learning

LEARIER   comparative of leary

LEARIEST   superlative of leary

LEARN   *v* LEARNED or LEARNT, LEARNING, LEARNS to gain knowledge by experience, instruction, or study

LEARNER   *n* pl. -S one that learns

LEARNING   *n* pl. -S acquired knowledge

LEARNT   a past tense of learn

LEARY   *adj* LEARIER, LEARIEST leery

LEASE   *v* LEASED, LEASING, LEASES to grant temporary use of in exchange for rent **LEASABLE** *adj*

LEASER   *n* pl. -S one that leases

LEASH   *v* -ED, -ING, -ES to restrain an animal with a line or thong

LEASING *n* pl. -S a falsehood

LEAST *n* pl. -S something that is smallest in size or degree

LEATHER *v* -ED, -ING, -S to cover with leather (the dressed or tanned hide of an animal)

LEATHERN *adj* made of leather

LEATHERY *adj* resembling leather

LEAVE *v* LEFT, LEAVING, LEAVES to go away from

LEAVED *adj* having a leaf or leaves

LEAVEN *v* -ED, -ING, -S to produce fermentation in

LEAVER *n* pl. -S one that leaves

LEAVES pl. of leaf

LEAVING *n* pl. -S a leftover

LEAVY *adj* LEAVIER, LEAVIEST leafy

LEBEN *n* pl. -S a type of liquid food

LECH *v* -ED, -ING, -ES to engage in lechery

LECHAYIM *n* pl. -S lehayim

LECHER *v* -ED, -ING, -S to engage in lechery

LECHERY *n* pl. -ERIES excessive sexual indulgence

LECHWE *n* pl. -S an African antelope

LECITHIN *n* pl. -S any of a group of fatty substances found in plant and animal tissues

LECTERN *n* pl. -S a reading desk

LECTIN *n* pl. -S a protein that binds to a sugar molecule

LECTION *n* pl. -S a portion of sacred writing read in a church service

LECTOR *n* pl. -S a reader of the lessons in a church service

LECTURE *v* -TURED, -TURING, -TURES to expound on a specific subject

LECTURER *n* pl. -S one that lectures

LECYTHIS *adj* designating a family of tropical shrubs

LECYTHUS *n* pl. -THI lekythos

LED past tense of lead

LEDGE *n* pl. -S a narrow, shelflike projection

LEDGER *n* pl. -S an account book of final entry

LEDGY *adj* LEDGIER, LEDGIEST abounding in ledges

LEE *n* pl. -S shelter from the wind

LEEBOARD *n* pl. -S a board attached to a sailing vessel to prevent leeway

LEECH *v* -ED, -ING, -ES to cling to and feed upon or drain

LEEK *n* pl. -S an herb used in cookery

LEER *v* -ED, -ING, -S to look with a sideways glance

LEERY *adj* LEERIER, LEERIEST suspicious **LEERILY** *adv*

LEET *n* pl. -S a former English court for petty offenses

LEEWARD *n* pl. -S the direction toward which the wind is blowing

LEEWAY *n* pl. -WAYS the lateral drift of a ship

LEFT *adj* LEFTER, LEFTEST pertaining to the side of the body to the north when one faces east

LEFT *n* pl. -S the left side or hand

LEFTIES pl. of lefty

LEFTISH *adj* inclined to be a leftist

LEFTISM *n* pl. -S a liberal political philosophy

LEFTIST *n* pl. -S an advocate of leftism

LEFTOVER *n* pl. -S an unused or unconsumed portion

LEFTWARD *adv* toward the left

LEFTWING *adj* favoring leftism

LEFTY *n* pl. LEFTIES a left-handed person

LEG *v* LEGGED, LEGGING, LEGS to move with the legs (appendages that serve as a means of support and locomotion)

LEGACY *n* pl. -CIES something bequeathed

LEGAL *n* pl. -S an authorized investment that may be made by investors such as savings banks

LEGALESE *n* pl. -S the specialized language of lawyers

LEGALISE *v* -ISED, -ISING, -ISES to legalize

LEGALISM *n* pl. -S strict conformity to the law

LEGALIST *n* pl. -S an adherent of legalism

LEGALITY *n* pl. -TIES the condition of being lawful

LEGALIZE *v* -IZED, -IZING, -IZES to make lawful

LEGALLY *adv* in a lawful manner

LEGATE *v* -GATED, -GATING, -GATES to bequeath

LEGATEE *n* pl. -S the inheritor of a legacy

LEGATINE *adj* pertaining to an official envoy

LEGATING present participle of legate

LEGATION *n* pl. -S the sending of an official envoy

LEGATO *n* pl. -TOS a smooth and flowing musical style

LEGATOR *n* pl. -S one that legates

LEGEND *n* pl. -S an unverified story from earlier times

LEGENDRY *n* pl. -RIES a collection of legends

LEGER *n* pl. -S fishing bait made to lie on the bottom

LEGERITY *n* pl. -TIES quickness of the mind or body

LEGES pl. of lex

LEGGED past tense of leg

LEGGIER comparative of leggy

LEGGIERO *adv* in a light or graceful manner — used as a musical direction

LEGGIEST superlative of leggy

LEGGIN *n* pl. -S legging

LEGGING *n* pl. -S a covering for the leg

LEGGY *adj* -GIER, -GIEST having long legs

LEGHORN *n* pl. -S a smooth, plaited straw

LEGIBLE *adj* capable of being read **LEGIBLY** *adv*

LEGION *n* pl. -S a large military force

LEGIST *n* pl. -S one learned or skilled in the law

LEGIT *n* pl. -S legitimate drama

LEGLESS *adj* having no legs

LEGLIKE *adj* resembling a leg

LEGMAN *n* pl. -MEN a newspaperman assigned to gather information

LEGONG *n* pl. -S a Balinese dance

LEGROOM *n* pl. -S space in which to extend the legs

LEGUME *n* pl. -S a type of plant

LEGUMIN *n* pl. -S a plant protein

LEGWORK *n* pl. -S work that involves extensive walking

LEHAYIM *n* pl. -S a traditional Jewish toast

LEHR *n* pl. -S a type of oven

LEHUA *n* pl. -S a tropical tree

LEI *n* pl. -S a wreath of flowers

LEISTER *v* -ED, -ING, -S to spear with a three-pronged fishing implement

LEISURE *n* pl. -S freedom from the demands of work or duty **LEISURED** *adj*

LEK *n* pl. LEKS or LEKE or LEKU a monetary unit of Albania

LEKVAR *n* pl. -S a prune butter

LEKYTHOS *n* pl. -THOI an oil jar used in ancient Greece

LEKYTHUS *n* pl. -THI lekythos

LEMAN *n* pl. -S a lover

LEMMA *n* pl. -MAS or -MATA a type of proposition in logic

LEMMING *n* pl. -S a mouselike rodent

LEMNISCI *n/pl* bands of nerve fibers

LEMON *n* pl. -S a citrus fruit **LEMONISH, LEMONY** *adj*

LEMONADE *n* pl. -S a beverage

LEMPIRA *n* pl. -S a monetary unit of Honduras

LEMUR *n* pl. -S an arboreal mammal related to the monkeys

LEMURES *n/pl* the ghosts of the dead in ancient Roman religion

LEMURINE *adj* pertaining to a lemur

LEMUROID *n* pl. -S a lemur

LEND *v* LENT, LENDING, LENDS to give the temporary use of **LENDABLE** *adj*

LENDER *n* pl. -S one that lends

LENES pl. of lenis

LENGTH *n* pl. -S the longer or longest dimension of an object

LENGTHEN *v* -ED, -ING, -S to make or become longer

LENGTHY *adj* LENGTHIER, LENGTHIEST very long

LENIENCE *n* pl. -S leniency

LENIENCY *n* pl. -CIES the quality of being lenient

LENIENT *adj* gently tolerant

LENIS *n* pl. LENES a speech sound pronounced with little or no aspiration

LENITION *n* pl. -S a change in articulation

LENITIVE *n* pl. -S a soothing medicine

LENITY *n* pl. -TIES leniency

LENO *n* pl. -NOS a style of weaving

LENS *n* pl. -ES a piece of transparent material used in changing the convergence of light rays **LENSLESS** *adj*

LENS *v* -ED, -ING, -ES to make a film of

LENSE *n* pl. -S lens

LENSMAN *n* pl. -MEN a photographer

LENT	past tense of lend
LENTANDO	adv becoming slower — used as a musical direction
LENTEN	adj meager
LENTIC	adj pertaining to still water
LENTICEL	n pl. -S a mass of cells on a plant stem
LENTIGO	n pl. -TIGINES a freckle
LENTIL	n pl. -S a Eurasian annual plant
LENTISK	n pl. -S an evergreen tree
LENTO	n pl. -TOS a slow musical movement
LENTOID	adj lens-shaped
LEONE	n pl. -S a monetary unit of Sierra Leone
LEONINE	adj pertaining to a lion
LEOPARD	n pl. -S a large, carnivorous feline mammal
LEOTARD	n pl. -S a close-fitting garment
LEPER	n pl. -S one affected with leprosy
LEPIDOTE	adj covered with small scales
LEPORID	n pl. -RIDS or -RIDAE a gnawing mammal
LEPORINE	adj resembling a rabbit or hare
LEPROSE	adj leprous
LEPROSY	n pl. -SIES a chronic disease characterized by skin lesions and deformities
LEPROTIC	adj leprous
LEPROUS	adj affected with leprosy
LEPT	a past tense of leap
LEPTON	n pl. -TA a monetary unit of Greece
LEPTON	n pl. -S an subatomic particle **LEPTONIC** adj
LESBIAN	n pl. -S a female homosexual
LESION	n pl. -S an abnormal change in the structure of an organ or tissue **LESIONED** adj
LESS	adj LESSER, LEAST not as great in quantity or degree
LESSEE	n pl. -S one to whom a lease is granted
LESSEN	v -ED, -ING, -S to make or become less
LESSER	adj not as large or important
LESSON	v -ED, -ING, -S to instruct
LESSOR	n pl. -S one that grants a lease
LEST	conj for fear that
LET	v LETTED, LETTING, LETS to hinder
LETCH	v -ED, -ING, -ES lech
LETDOWN	n pl. -S a decrease
LETHAL	n pl. -S a death-causing genetic defect
LETHALLY	adv in a deadly manner
LETHARGY	n pl. -GIES drowsiness; sluggishness
LETHE	n pl. -S forgetfulness **LETHEAN** adj
LETTED	past tense of let
LETTER	v -ED, -ING, -S to mark with letters (written symbols representing speech sounds)
LETTERER	n pl. -S one that letters
LETTING	present participle of let
LETTUCE	n pl. -S an herb cultivated as a salad plant
LETUP	n pl. -S a lessening or relaxation
LEU	n pl. LEI a monetary unit of Romania
LEUCEMIA	n pl. -S leukemia **LEUCEMIC** adj
LEUCIN	n pl. -S leucine
LEUCINE	n pl. -S an amino acid
LEUCITE	n pl. -S a mineral **LEUCITIC** adj
LEUCOMA	n pl. -S leukoma
LEUD	n pl. -S or -ES a feudal vassal
LEUKEMIA	n pl. -S a disease of the blood-forming organs
LEUKEMIC	n pl. -S one affected with leukemia
LEUKOMA	n pl. -S an opacity of the cornea
LEUKON	n pl. -S a bodily organ consisting of the white blood cells
LEUKOSIS	n pl. -KOSES leukemia **LEUKOTIC** adj
LEV	n pl. LEVA a monetary unit of Bulgaria
LEVANT	v -ED, -ING, -S to avoid a debt
LEVANTER	n pl. -S an easterly Mediterranean wind
LEVATOR	n pl. -ES or -S a muscle that raises an organ or part
LEVEE	v LEVEED, LEVEEING, LEVEES to provide with an embankment
LEVEL	v -ELED, -ELING, -ELS or -ELLED, -ELLING, -ELS to make even
LEVELER	n pl. -S one that levels
LEVELLER	n pl. -S leveler
LEVELLING	a present participle of level
LEVELLY	adv in an even manner

LEVER v -ED, -ING, -S to move with a lever (a rigid body used to lift weight)

LEVERAGE v -AGED, -AGING, -AGES to provide with a type of economic advantage

LEVERET n pl. -S a young hare

LEVIABLE adj liable to be levied

LEVIED past tense of levy

LEVIER n pl. -S one that levies

LEVIES present 3d person sing. of levy

LEVIGATE v -GATED, -GATING, -GATES to reduce to a fine powder

LEVIN n pl. -S lightning

LEVIRATE n pl. -S the custom of marrying the widow of one's brother

LEVITATE v -TATED, -TATING, -TATES to rise and float in the air

LEVITY n pl. -TIES conduct characterized by a lack of seriousness

LEVO adj turning toward the left

LEVODOPA n pl. -S a form of dopa

LEVOGYRE adj turning toward the left

LEVULIN n pl. -S a chemical compound

LEVULOSE n pl. -S a very sweet sugar

LEVY v LEVIED, LEVYING, LEVIES to impose or collect by legal authority

LEWD adj LEWDER, LEWDEST obscene **LEWDLY** adv

LEWDNESS n pl. -ES the state of being lewd

LEWIS n pl. -ISES a hoisting device

LEWISITE n pl. -S a vesicant liquid

LEWISSON n pl. -S lewis

LEX n pl. LEGES law

LEXEME n pl. -S a linguistic unit **LEXEMIC** adj

LEXICAL adj pertaining to the words of a language

LEXICON n pl. -CA or -CONS a dictionary

LEXIS n pl. LEXES the vocabulary of a language, a group, or a subject field

LEY n pl. LEYS lea

LI n pl. -S a Chinese unit of distance

LIABLE adj subject or susceptible to something possible or likely

LIAISE v LIAISED, LIAISING, LIAISES to establish liaison

LIAISON n pl. -S a means for maintaining communication

LIANA n pl. -S a tropical vine

LIANE n pl. -S liana

LIANG n pl. -S a Chinese unit of weight

LIANOID adj pertaining to a liana

LIAR n pl. -S one that speaks falsely

LIARD n pl. -S a former silver coin of France

LIB n pl. -S liberation

LIBATION n pl. -S a ceremonial pouring of a liquid

LIBECCIO n pl. -CIOS a southwest wind

LIBEL v -BELED, -BELING, -BELS or -BELLED, -BELLING, -BELS to make or publish a defamatory statement about

LIBELANT n pl. -S a plaintiff in a type of lawsuit

LIBELEE n pl. -S a defendant in a type of lawsuit

LIBELER n pl. -S one that libels

LIBELIST n pl. -S a libeler

LIBELLED a past tense of libel

LIBELLEE n pl. -S libelee

LIBELLER n pl. -S libeler

LIBELLING a present participle of libel

LIBELOUS adj defamatory

LIBER n pl. LIBRI or LIBERS a book of public records

LIBERAL n pl. -S a person favorable to progress or reform

LIBERATE v -ATED, -ATING, -ATES to set free

LIBERTY n pl. -TIES the state of being free

LIBIDO n pl. -DOS the energy derived from instinctual biological drives

LIBLAB n pl. -S a person supporting a coalition of liberal and labor groups

LIBRA n pl. -BRAE an ancient Roman unit of weight

LIBRA n pl. -S a former gold coin of Peru

LIBRARY n pl. -BRARIES a place where literary materials are kept for reading and reference

LIBRATE v -BRATED, -BRATING, -BRATES to move from side to side

LIBRETTO n pl. -TOS or -TI the text of an opera

LIBRI a pl. of liber

LICE pl. of louse

LICENCE	v -CENCED, -CENCING, -CENCES to license	**LIERNE**	n pl. -S a connecting part in Gothic vaulting
LICENCEE	n pl. -S licensee	**LIEU**	n pl. -S place; stead
LICENCER	n pl. -S licenser	**LIEVE**	adv LIEVER, LIEVEST gladly
LICENSE	v -CENSED, -CENSING, -CENSES to issue or grant authoritative permission to	**LIFE**	n pl. LIVES the quality that distinguishes animals and plants from inanimate matter
LICENSEE	n pl. -S one that is licensed	**LIFEBOAT**	n pl. -S a small rescue boat
LICENSER	n pl. -S one that licenses	**LIFEFUL**	adj full of life
LICENSOR	n pl. -S licenser	**LIFELESS**	adj having no life
LICENTE	n/pl lisente	**LIFELIKE**	adj resembling a living thing
LICH	n pl. -ES a corpse	**LIFELINE**	n pl. -S a rope used to aid a person in distress
LICHEE	n pl. -S litchi	
LICHEN	v -ED, -ING, -S to cover with lichens (flowerless plants)	**LIFELONG**	adj lasting for a lifetime
		LIFER	n pl. -S a prisoner serving a life sentence
LICHENIN	n pl. -S a chemical compound	
LICHI	n pl. -S litchi	**LIFETIME**	n pl. -S the period of living existence
LICHT	v -ED, -ING, -S to light	
LICHTLY	adv lightly	**LIFEWAY**	n pl. -WAYS a way of living
LICIT	adj lawful **LICITLY** adv	**LIFEWORK**	n pl. -S the major work of one's lifetime
LICK	v -ED, -ING, -S to pass the tongue over the surface of	**LIFT**	v -ED, -ING, -S to move to a higher position **LIFTABLE** adj
LICKER	n pl. -S one that licks	
LICKING	n pl. -S a thrashing or beating	**LIFTER**	n pl. -S one that lifts
LICKSPIT	n pl. -S a fawning person	**LIFTGATE**	n pl. -S a rear panel on a station wagon that opens upward
LICORICE	n pl. -S a perennial herb	
LICTOR	n pl. -S a magistrate's attendant in ancient Rome	
		LIFTMAN	n pl. -MEN an elevator operator
LID	v LIDDED, LIDDING, LIDS to provide with a lid (a movable cover)	**LIFTOFF**	n pl. -S the vertical takeoff of a rocket
LIDAR	n pl. -S an electronic locating device	**LIGAMENT**	n pl. -S a band of firm, fibrous tissue
LIDLESS	adj having no lid	**LIGAN**	n pl. -S lagan
LIDO	n pl. -DOS a fashionable beach resort	**LIGAND**	n pl. -S a type of ion or molecule
LIE	v LIED, LYING, LIES to speak falsely	**LIGASE**	n pl. -S an enzyme
		LIGATE	v -GATED, -GATING, -GATES to bind
LIE	v LAY, LAIN, LYING, LIES to be in or get into a horizontal position	**LIGATION**	n pl. -S the act of ligating **LIGATIVE** adj
LIED	n pl. LIEDER a German song	**LIGATURE**	v -TURED, -TURING, -TURES to ligate
LIEF	adj LIEFER, LIEFEST willing **LIEFLY** adv	**LIGER**	n pl. -S the offspring of a male lion and a female tiger
LIEGE	n pl. -S a feudal lord	**LIGHT**	adj LIGHTER, LIGHTEST having little weight
LIEGEMAN	n pl. -MEN a feudal vassal	
LIEN	n pl. -S a legal right to hold or sell a debtor's property	**LIGHT**	v LIGHTED or LIT, LIGHTING, LIGHTS to illuminate
LIENABLE	adj capable of being subjected to a lien	**LIGHTEN**	v -ED, -ING, -S to reduce the weight of
LIENAL	adj pertaining to the spleen	**LIGHTER**	v -ED, -ING, -S to convey in a type of barge
LIENTERY	n pl. -TERIES a form of diarrhea	
		LIGHTFUL	adj brightly illuminated
LIER	n pl. -S one that lies or reclines	**LIGHTING**	n pl. -S illumination
		LIGHTISH	adj somewhat light

LIGHTLY *adv* to a moderate degree
LIGNEOUS *adj* of or resembling wood
LIGNIFY *v* -FIED, -FYING, -FIES to convert into wood
LIGNIN *n* pl. -S an essential part of woody tissue
LIGNITE *n* pl. -S a type of coal **LIGNITIC** *adj*
LIGROIN *n* pl. -S a flammable liquid
LIGROINE *n* pl. -S ligroin
LIGULA *n* pl. -LAE or -LAS a strap-shaped organ or part **LIGULAR, LIGULATE, LIGULOID** *adj*
LIGULE *n* pl. -S a strap-shaped plant part
LIGURE *n* pl. -S a precious stone
LIKABLE *adj* pleasant
LIKE *v* LIKED, LIKING, LIKES to find pleasant
LIKE *adj* LIKER, LIKEST possessing the same or almost the same characteristics
LIKEABLE *adj* likable
LIKED past tense of like
LIKELY *adj* -LIER, -LIEST probable
LIKEN *v* -ED, -ING, -S to represent as similar
LIKENESS *n* pl. -ES a pictorial representation
LIKER *n* pl. -S one that likes
LIKEST superlative of like
LIKEWISE *adv* in a similar manner
LIKING *n* pl. -S a feeling of attraction or affection
LIKUTA *n* pl. MAKUTA a monetary unit of Zaire
LILAC *n* pl. -S a flowering shrub
LILIED *adj* covered with lilies
LILIES pl. of lily
LILLIPUT *n* pl. -S a very small person
LILT *v* -ED, -ING, -S to sing or speak rhythmically
LILY *n* pl. LILIES a flowering plant **LILYLIKE** *adj*
LIMA *n* pl. -S the edible seed of a tropical American plant
LIMACINE *adj* resembling a type of mollusk
LIMACON *n* pl. -S a type of geometric curve
LIMAN *n* pl. -S a lagoon
LIMB *v* -ED, -ING, -S to cut off the arms or legs of
LIMBA *n* pl. -S an African tree

LIMBATE *adj* having an edge of a different color
LIMBECK *n* pl. -S alembic
LIMBER *adj* -BERER, -BEREST flexible **LIMBERLY** *adv*
LIMBER *v* -ED, -ING, -S to make flexible
LIMBI a pl. of limbus
LIMBIC *adj* pertaining to a system of the brain
LIMBIER comparative of limby
LIMBIEST superlative of limby
LIMBLESS *adj* having no arms or legs
LIMBO *n* pl. -BOS a condition of oblivion or neglect
LIMBUS *n* pl. -BUSES or -BI a distinctive border
LIMBY *adj* LIMBIER, LIMBIEST having many large branches
LIME *v* LIMED, LIMING, LIMES to treat with lime (a calcium compound)
LIMEADE *n* pl. -S a beverage
LIMEKILN *n* pl. -S a furnace in which shells are burned to produce lime
LIMELESS *adj* having no lime
LIMEN *n* pl. -MENS or -MINA a sensory threshold
LIMERICK *n* pl. -S a humorous verse
LIMES *n* pl. LIMITES a fortified boundary
LIMEY *n* pl. -EYS a British sailor
LIMIER comparative of limy
LIMIEST superlative of limy
LIMINA a pl. of limen
LIMINAL *adj* pertaining to the limen
LIMINESS *n* pl. -ES the state of being limy
LIMING present participle of lime
LIMIT *v* -ED, -ING, -S to restrict
LIMITARY *adj* limiting
LIMITED *n* pl. -S a train or bus making few stops
LIMITER *n* pl. -S one that limits
LIMITES pl. of limes
LIMMER *n* pl. -S a scoundrel
LIMN *v* -ED, -ING, -S to depict by painting or drawing
LIMNER *n* pl. -S one that limns
LIMNETIC *adj* pertaining to the open water of a lake or pond
LIMNIC *adj* limnetic
LIMO *n* pl. LIMOS a limousine
LIMONENE *n* pl. -S a chemical compound
LIMONITE *n* pl. -S a major ore of iron

LIMP	*v* -ED, -ING, -S to walk lamely	**LINEN**	*n* pl. -S a fabric woven from
LIMP	*adj* LIMPER, LIMPEST lacking rigidity		the fibers of flax **LINENY** *adj*
LIMPA	*n* pl. -S rye bread made with molasses	**LINER**	*n* pl. -S a commercial ship or airplane
LIMPER	*n* pl. -S one that limps	**LINESMAN**	*n* pl. -MEN a football official
LIMPET	*n* pl. -S a type of mollusk	**LINEUP**	*n* pl. -S a row of persons
LIMPID	*adj* transparent **LIMPIDLY** *adv*	**LINEY**	*adj* LINIER, LINIEST liny
LIMPKIN	*n* pl. -S a wading bird	**LING**	*n* pl. -S a heath plant
LIMPLY	*adv* in a limp manner	**LINGA**	*n* pl. -S lingam
LIMPNESS	*n* pl. -ES the state of being limp	**LINGAM**	*n* pl. -S a Hindu phallic symbol
LIMPSEY	*adj* -SIER, -SIEST limpsy	**LINGCOD**	*n* pl. -S a marine food fish
LIMPSY	*adj* -SIER, -SIEST lacking strength or vigor	**LINGER**	*v* -ED, -ING, -S to delay leaving
LIMULOID	*n* pl. -S a horseshoe crab	**LINGERER**	*n* pl. -S one that lingers
LIMULUS	*n* pl. -LI a horseshoe crab	**LINGERIE**	*n* pl. -S women's underwear
LIMY	*adj* LIMIER, LIMIEST resembling or containing lime	**LINGIER**	comparative of lingy
		LINGIEST	superlative of lingy
LIN	*n* pl. -S linn	**LINGO**	*n* pl. -GOES strange or incomprehensible language
LINABLE	*adj* lineable		
LINAC	*n* pl. -S a device for imparting high velocities to charged particles	**LINGUA**	*n* pl. -GUAE the tongue or a tonguelike part
		LINGUAL	*n* pl. -S a sound articulated with the tongue
LINAGE	*n* pl. -S the number of lines of printed material	**LINGUINE**	*n* pl. -S linguini
LINALOL	*n* pl. -S linalool	**LINGUINI**	*n* pl. -S a type of pasta
LINALOOL	*n* pl. -S a fragrant alcohol	**LINGUIST**	*n* pl. -S a person skilled in several languages
LINCHPIN	*n* pl. -S a locking pin inserted in the end of a shaft	**LINGY**	*adj* LINGIER, LINGIEST covered with heaths
LINDANE	*n* pl. -S an insecticide	**LINIER**	comparative of liney and liny
LINDEN	*n* pl. -S a tall forest tree	**LINIEST**	superlative of liney and liny
LINDY	*n* pl. -DIES a lively dance	**LINIMENT**	*n* pl. -S a medicinal liquid
LINE	*v* LINED, LINING, LINES to mark with lines (slender, continuous marks)	**LININ**	*n* pl. -S a substance in the nucleus of a cell
		LINING	*n* pl. -S an inner layer
LINEABLE	*adj* lying in a straight line	**LINK**	*v* -ED, -ING, -S to connect **LINKABLE** *adj*
LINEAGE	*n* pl. -S direct descent from an ancestor	**LINKAGE**	*n* pl. -S the act of linking
		LINKBOY	*n* pl. -BOYS a man or boy hired to carry a torch to light the way along dark streets
LINEAL	*adj* being directly descended from an ancestor **LINEALLY** *adv*		
		LINKER	*n* pl. -S one that links
LINEAR	*adj* of or resembling a straight line **LINEARLY** *adv*	**LINKMAN**	*n* pl. -MEN a linkboy
		LINKSMAN	*n* pl. -MEN a golfer
LINEATE	*adj* marked with lines	**LINKUP**	*n* pl. -S something that serves as a linking device
LINEATED	*adj* lineate		
LINEBRED	*adj* produced by interbreeding within a particular line of descent	**LINKWORK**	*n* pl. -S something composed of interlocking rings
		LINKY	*adj* full of interlocking rings
		LINN	*n* pl. -S a waterfall
LINECUT	*n* pl. -S a type of printing plate	**LINNET**	*n* pl. -S a European songbird
LINED	past tense of line	**LINO**	*n* pl. -NOS linoleum
LINELESS	*adj* having no lines	**LINOCUT**	*n* pl. -S a print made from a design cut into linoleum
LINELIKE	*adj* resembling a line		
LINEMAN	*n* pl. -MEN one who installs or repairs telephone wires	**LINOLEUM**	*n* pl. -S a durable material used as a floor covering

LINSANG *n* pl. -S a carnivorous mammal
LINSEED *n* pl. -S flaxseed
LINSEY *n* pl. -SEYS a coarse fabric
LINSTOCK *n* pl. -S a stick having one end divided to hold a match
LINT *n* pl. -S an accumulation of bits of fiber
LINTEL *n* pl. -S a horizontal supporting beam
LINTER *n* pl. -S a machine for removing fibers from cotton seeds
LINTIER comparative of linty
LINTIEST superlative of linty
LINTLESS *adj* free from lint
LINTOL *n* pl. -S lintel
LINTY *adj* LINTIER, LINTIEST covered with lint
LINUM *n* pl. -S a plant of the flax family
LINURON *n* pl. -S a herbicide
LINY *adj* LINIER, LINIEST resembling a line
LION *n* pl. -S a large, carnivorous feline mammal
LIONESS *n* pl. -ES a female lion
LIONFISH *n* pl. -ES a tropical fish
LIONISE *v* -ISED, -ISING, -ISES to lionize
LIONISER *n* pl. -S one that lionises
LIONIZE *v* -IZED, -IZING, -IZES to treat or regard as a celebrity
LIONIZER *n* pl. -S one that lionizes
LIONLIKE *adj* resembling a lion
LIP *v* LIPPED, LIPPING, LIPS to touch with the lips (the folds of flesh around the mouth)
LIPASE *n* pl. -S an enzyme
LIPID *n* pl. -S any of a class of fatty substances **LIPIDIC** *adj*
LIPIDE *n* pl. -S lipid
LIPIN *n* pl. -S a lipid
LIPLESS *adj* having no lips
LIPLIKE *adj* resembling a lip
LIPOCYTE *n* pl. -S a fat-producing cell
LIPOID *n* pl. -S a lipid **LIPOIDAL** *adj*
LIPOMA *n* pl. -MAS or -MATA a tumor of fatty tissue
LIPOSOME *n* pl. -S a microscopic globule composed of lipids
LIPPED past tense of lip
LIPPEN *v* -ED, -ING, -S to trust
LIPPER *v* -ED, -ING, -S to ripple
LIPPING *n* pl. -S a liplike outgrowth of bone
LIPPY *adj* -PIER, -PIEST impudent

LIPSTICK *n* pl. -S a cosmetic used to color the lips
LIQUATE *v* -QUATED, -QUATING, -QUATES to purify metal by heating
LIQUEFY *v* -FIED, -FYING, -FIES to make or become liquid
LIQUEUR *n* pl. -S a sweetened alcoholic beverage
LIQUID *n* pl. -S a substance that flows freely
LIQUIDLY *adv* in a free-flowing manner
LIQUIFY *v* -FIED, -FYING, -FIES to liquefy
LIQUOR *v* -ED, -ING, -S to intoxicate with liquor (an alcoholic beverage)
LIRA *n* pl. LIRI a monetary unit of Malta
LIRA *n* pl. LIRE or LIRAS a monetary unit of Italy
LIRA *n* pl. LIROTH or LIROT a former monetary unit of Israel
LIRIPIPE *n* pl. -S a long scarf
LISENTE pl. of sente
LISLE *n* pl. -S a fine, tightly twisted cotton thread
LISP *v* -ED, -ING, -S to pronounce the letters *s* and *z* imperfectly
LISPER *n* pl. -S one that lisps
LISSOM *adj* lissome **LISSOMLY** *adv*
LISSOME *adj* lithe
LIST *v* -ED, -ING, -S to write down in a particular order **LISTABLE** *adj*
LISTEE *n* pl. -S one that is on a list
LISTEL *n* pl. -S a narrow molding
LISTEN *v* -ED, -ING, -S to make conscious use of the sense of hearing
LISTENER *n* pl. -S one that listens
LISTER *n* pl. -S a type of plow
LISTING *n* pl. -S something that is listed
LISTLESS *adj* languid
LIT *n* pl. -S the litas
LITANY *n* pl. -NIES a ceremonial form of prayer
LITAS *n* pl. LITAI or LITU a former monetary unit of Lithuania
LITCHI *n* pl. -S the edible fruit of a Chinese tree
LITE *adj* lower in calories or having less of some ingredient
LITER *n* pl. -S a unit of capacity

LITERACY   *n* pl. -CIES the ability to read and write

LITERAL   *n* pl. -S a small error in printing or writing

LITERARY   *adj* of, pertaining to, or having the characteristics of books and writings

LITERATE   *n* pl. -S one who can read and write

LITERATI   *n/pl* scholars collectively

LITHARGE   *n* pl. -S a monoxide of lead

LITHE   *adj* LITHER, LITHEST bending easily **LITHELY** *adv*

LITHEMIA   *n* pl. -S an excess of uric acid in the blood **LITHEMIC** *adj*

LITHIA   *n* pl. -S an oxide of lithium

LITHIC   *adj* pertaining to lithium

LITHIFY   *v* -FIED, -FYING, -FIES to petrify

LITHIUM   *n* pl. -S a metallic element

LITHO   *v* -ED, -ING, -S to make prints by lithography

LITHOID   *adj* resembling stone

LITHOSOL   *n* pl. -S a type of soil

LITIGANT   *n* pl. -S one who is engaged in a lawsuit

LITIGATE   *v* -GATED, -GATING, -GATES to subject to legal proceedings

LITMUS   *n* pl. -ES a blue coloring matter

LITORAL   *adj* pertaining to a coastal region

LITOTES   *n* pl. LITOTES a figure of speech in which an assertion is made by the negation of its opposite **LITOTIC** *adj*

LITRE   *n* pl. -S liter

LITTEN   *adj* lighted

LITTER   *v* -ED, -ING, -S to scatter rubbish about

LITTERER   *n* pl. -S one that litters

LITTERY   *adj* covered with rubbish

LITTLE   *adj* -TLER, -TLEST small

LITTLE   *n* pl. -S a small amount

LITTLISH   *adj* somewhat little

LITTORAL   *n* pl. -S a coastal region

LITU   a pl. of litas

LITURGY   *n* pl. -GIES a prescribed system of public worship **LITURGIC** *adj*

LIVABLE   *adj* suitable for living in

LIVE   *v* LIVED, LIVING, LIVES to function as an animal or plant

LIVE   *adj* LIVER, LIVEST having life

LIVEABLE   *adj* livable

LIVELONG   *adj* long in passing

LIVELY   *adj* -LIER, -LIEST full of energy **LIVELILY** *adv*

LIVEN   *v* -ED, -ING, -S to make lively

LIVENER   *n* pl. -S one that livens

LIVENESS   *n* pl. -ES the state of being live

LIVER   *n* pl. -S a secreting organ

LIVERIED   *adj* wearing a livery

LIVERISH   *adj* having a liver disorder

LIVERY   *n* pl. -ERIES a uniform worn by servants

LIVES   pl. of life

LIVEST   superlative of live

LIVETRAP   *v* -TRAPPED, -TRAPPING, -TRAPS to capture in a type of animal trap

LIVID   *adj* having the skin abnormally discolored **LIVIDLY** *adv*

LIVIDITY   *n* pl. -TIES the state of being livid

LIVIER   *n* pl. -S livyer

LIVING   *n* pl. -S a means of subsistence

LIVINGLY   *adv* realistically

LIVRE   *n* pl. -S a former monetary unit of France

LIVYER   *n* pl. -S a permanent resident of Newfoundland

LIXIVIUM   *n* pl. -IA or -IUMS a solution obtained by leaching **LIXIVIAL** *adj*

LIZARD   *n* pl. -S any of a suborder of reptiles

LLAMA   *n* pl. -S a ruminant mammal

LLANO   *n* pl. -NOS an open, grassy plain

LO   *interj* — used to attract attention or to express surprise

LOACH   *n* pl. -ES a freshwater fish

LOAD   *v* -ED, -ING, -S to place in or on a means of conveyance

LOADER   *n* pl. -S one that loads

LOADING   *n* pl. -S a burden

LOADSTAR   *n* pl. -S lodestar

LOAF   *n* pl. LOAVES a shaped mass of bread

LOAF   *v* -ED, -ING, -S to pass time idly

LOAFER   *n* pl. -S one that loafs

LOAM   *v* -ED, -ING, -S to cover with loam (a type of soil)

LOAMLESS   *adj* having no loam

LOAMY   *adj* LOAMIER, LOAMIEST resembling loam

LOAN   *v* -ED, -ING, -S to lend **LOANABLE** *adj*

LOANER	*n* pl. -S one that loans
LOANING	*n* pl. -S a lane
LOANWORD	*n* pl. -S a word taken from another language
LOATH	*adj* unwilling
LOATHE	*v* LOATHED, LOATHING, LOATHES to detest greatly
LOATHER	*n* pl. -S one that loathes
LOATHFUL	*adj* repulsive
LOATHING	*n* pl. -S extreme dislike
LOATHLY	*adj* repulsive
LOAVES	pl. of loaf
LOB	*v* LOBBED, LOBBING, LOBS to throw or hit in a high arc
LOBAR	*adj* pertaining to a lobe
LOBATE	*adj* having lobes **LOBATELY** *adv*
LOBATED	*adj* lobate
LOBATION	*n* pl. -S the formation of lobes
LOBBED	past tense of lob
LOBBER	*n* pl. -S one that lobs
LOBBING	present participle of lob
LOBBY	*v* -BIED, -BYING, -BIES to attempt to influence legislators
LOBBYER	*n* pl. -S a lobbyist
LOBBYGOW	*n* pl. -S an errand boy
LOBBYISM	*n* pl. -S the practice of lobbying
LOBBYIST	*n* pl. -S one who lobbies
LOBE	*n* pl. -S a rounded, projecting anatomical part **LOBED** *adj*
LOBEFIN	*n* pl. -S a bony fish
LOBELIA	*n* pl. -S a flowering plant
LOBELINE	*n* pl. -S a poisonous alkaloid
LOBLOLLY	*n* pl. -LIES a pine tree
LOBO	*n* pl. -BOS the timber wolf
LOBOTOMY	*n* pl. -MIES a type of surgical operation
LOBSTER	*v* -ED, -ING, -S to fish for lobsters (marine crustaceans)
LOBSTICK	*n* pl. -S a tree with its lower branches trimmed
LOBULE	*n* pl. -S a small lobe **LOBULAR, LOBULATE, LOBULOSE** *adj*
LOBWORM	*n* pl. -S a lugworm
LOCA	a pl. of locus
LOCAL	*n* pl. -S a train or bus making all stops
LOCALE	*n* pl. -S a locality
LOCALISE	*v* -ISED, -ISING, -ISES to localize
LOCALISM	*n* pl. -S a custom or mannerism peculiar to a locality
LOCALIST	*n* pl. -S one who is strongly concerned with the matters of a locality
LOCALITE	*n* pl. -S a resident of a locality
LOCALITY	*n* pl. -TIES an area or neighborhood
LOCALIZE	*v* -IZED, -IZING, -IZES to confine to a particular area
LOCALLY	*adv* in a particular area
LOCATE	*v* -CATED, -CATING, -CATES to determine the position of
LOCATER	*n* pl. -S one that locates
LOCATION	*n* pl. -S the place where something is at a given moment
LOCATIVE	*n* pl. -S a type of grammatical case
LOCATOR	*n* pl. -S locater
LOCH	*n* pl. -S a lake
LOCHAN	*n* pl. -S a small lake
LOCHIA	*n* pl. LOCHIA a vaginal discharge following childbirth **LOCHIAL** *adj*
LOCI	a pl. of locus
LOCK	*v* -ED, -ING, -S to secure by means of a mechanical fastening device **LOCKABLE** *adj*
LOCKAGE	*n* pl. -S a toll on a ship passing through a canal
LOCKBOX	*n* pl. -ES a box that locks
LOCKDOWN	*n* pl. -S the confinement of prisoners to their cells
LOCKER	*n* pl. -S an enclosure that may be locked
LOCKET	*n* pl. -S a small ornamental case
LOCKJAW	*n* pl. -S a form of tetanus
LOCKNUT	*n* pl. -S a nut which keeps another from loosening
LOCKOUT	*n* pl. -S a closing of a business to coerce employees to agree to terms
LOCKRAM	*n* pl. -S a coarse, linen fabric
LOCKSTEP	*n* pl. -S a mode of marching in close file
LOCKUP	*n* pl. -S a jail
LOCO	*n* pl. -COS or -COES locoweed
LOCO	*v* -ED, -ING, -S to poison with locoweed
LOCOFOCO	*n* pl. -COS a type of friction match
LOCOISM	*n* pl. -S a disease of livestock
LOCOMOTE	*v* -MOTED, -MOTING, -MOTES to move about

LOCOWEED *n* pl. -S a plant that causes poisoning when eaten by livestock

LOCULAR *adj* having or divided into loculi

LOCULATE *adj* locular

LOCULE *n* pl. -S loculus **LOCULED** *adj*

LOCULUS *n* pl. -LI a small, cell-like chamber

LOCUM *n* pl. -S a temporary substitute

LOCUS *n* pl. LOCI or LOCA a place

LOCUST *n* pl. -S a migratory grasshopper

LOCUSTA *n* pl. -TAE a spikelet **LOCUSTAL** *adj*

LOCUTION *n* pl. -S a particular form of expression

LOCUTORY *n* pl. -RIES a room in a monastery

LODE *n* pl. -S a deposit of ore

LODEN *n* pl. -S a thick, woolen fabric

LODESTAR *n* pl. -S a star used as a point of reference

LODGE *v* LODGED, LODGING, LODGES to furnish with temporary quarters

LODGER *n* pl. -S one that resides in rented quarters

LODGING *n* pl. -S a temporary place to live

LODGMENT *n* pl. -S a lodging

LODICULE *n* pl. -S a scale at the base of the ovary of a grass

LOESS *n* pl. -ES a soil deposit **LOESSAL, LOESSIAL** *adj*

LOFT *v* -ED, -ING, -S to store in a loft (an upper room)

LOFTER *n* pl. -S a type of golf club

LOFTIER comparative of lofty

LOFTIEST superlative of lofty

LOFTILY *adv* in a lofty manner

LOFTLESS *adj* having no loft

LOFTLIKE *adj* resembling a loft

LOFTY *adj* LOFTIER, LOFTIEST extending high in the air

LOG *v* LOGGED, LOGGING, LOGS to cut down trees for timber

LOGAN *n* pl. -S a stone balanced to permit easy movement

LOGANIA *adj* designating a family of flowering plants

LOGBOOK *n* pl. -S a record book of a ship or aircraft

LOGE *n* pl. -S a small compartment

LOGGATS *n/pl* loggets

LOGGED past tense of log

LOGGER *n* pl. -S one that logs

LOGGETS *n/pl* an old English throwing game

LOGGIA *n* pl. -GIAS or -GIE an open gallery

LOGGING *n* pl. -S the business of cutting down trees for timber

LOGGY *adj* -GIER, -GIEST logy

LOGIA a pl. of logion

LOGIC *n* pl. -S the science of reasoning

LOGICAL *adj* pertaining to logic

LOGICIAN *n* pl. -S one who is skilled in logic

LOGICISE *v* -CISED, -CISING, -CISES to logicize

LOGICIZE *v* -CIZED, -CIZING, -CIZES to reason

LOGIER comparative of logy

LOGIEST superlative of logy

LOGILY *adv* in a logy manner

LOGINESS *n* pl. -ES the state of being logy

LOGION *n* pl. -GIA or -GIONS a saying attributed to Jesus

LOGISTIC *n* pl. -S symbolic logic

LOGJAM *n* pl. -S a tangled mass of logs

LOGO *n* pl. LOGOS an identifying symbol

LOGOGRAM *n* pl. -S a symbol used to represent an entire word

LOGOMACH *n* pl. -S one given to arguing about words

LOGOS *n* pl. LOGOI the rational principle that governs the universe in ancient Greek philosophy

LOGOTYPE *n* pl. -S a piece of type bearing a syllable, word, or words

LOGOTYPY *n* pl. -TYPIES the use of logotypes

LOGROLL *v* -ED, -ING, -S to obtain passage of by exchanging political favors

LOGWAY *n* pl. -WAYS a ramp used in logging

LOGWOOD *n* pl. -S a tropical tree

LOGY *adj* -GIER, -GIEST sluggish

LOIN *n* pl. -S a part of the side and back between the ribs and the hipbone

LOITER *v* -ED, -ING, -S to stand idly about

LOITERER *n* pl. -S one that loiters

LOLL   *v* -ED, -ING, -S to lounge
LOLLER   *n* pl. -S one that lolls
LOLLIES   pl. of lolly
LOLLIPOP   *n* pl. -S a piece of candy on the end of a stick
LOLLOP   *v* -ED, -ING, -S to loll
LOLLY   *n* pl. -LIES a lollipop
LOLLYGAG   *v* -GAGGED, -GAGGING, -GAGS to lallygag
LOLLYPOP   *n* pl. -S lollipop
LOMEIN   *n* pl. -S a Chinese dish of noodles, meat, and vegetables
LOMENT   *n* pl. -S a type of plant pod
LOMENTUM   *n* pl. -TA or -TUMS loment
LONE   *adj* having no companions
LONELY   *adj* -LIER, -LIEST sad from lack of companionship **LONELILY** *adv*
LONENESS   *n* pl. -ES the state of being lone
LONER   *n* pl. -S one that avoids others
LONESOME   *n* pl. -S self
LONG   *adj* LONGER, LONGEST extending for a considerable distance
LONG   *v* -ED, -ING, -S to desire strongly
LONGAN   *n* pl. -S the edible fruit of a Chinese tree
LONGBOAT   *n* pl. -S the largest boat carried by a sailing vessel
LONGBOW   *n* pl. -S a type of archery bow
LONGE   *v* LONGED, LONGEING, LONGES to guide a horse by means of a long rope
LONGER   *n* pl. -S one that longs
LONGERON   *n* pl. -S a longitudinal support of an airplane
LONGHAIR   *n* pl. -S an intellectual
LONGHAND   *n* pl. -S ordinary handwriting
LONGHEAD   *n* pl. -S a person having a long skull
LONGHORN   *n* pl. -S one of a breed of long-horned cattle
LONGIES   *n/pl* long underwear
LONGING   *n* pl. -S a strong desire
LONGISH   *adj* somewhat long
LONGLEAF   *n* pl. -LEAVES an evergreen tree
LONGLINE   *n* pl. -S a type of fishing line
LONGLY   *adv* for a considerable distance
LONGNESS   *n* pl. -ES the state of being long
LONGSHIP   *n* pl. -S a medieval ship
LONGSOME   *adj* tediously long

LONGSPUR   *n* pl. -S a long-clawed finch
LONGTIME   *adj* of long duration
LONGUEUR   *n* pl. -S a dull and tedious section
LONGWAYS   *adv* longwise
LONGWISE   *adv* lengthwise
LOO   *v* -ED, -ING, -S to subject to a forfeit at loo (a card game)
LOOBY   *n* pl. -BIES a large, awkward person
LOOEY   *n* pl. -EYS looie
LOOF   *n* pl. -S the palm of the hand
LOOFA   *n* pl. -S loofah
LOOFAH   *n* pl. -S a tropical vine
LOOIE   *n* pl. -S a lieutenant of the armed forces
LOOK   *v* -ED, -ING, -S to use one's eyes in seeing
LOOKDOWN   *n* pl. -S a marine fish
LOOKER   *n* pl. -S one that looks
LOOKOUT   *n* pl. -S one engaged in keeping watch
LOOKUP   *n* pl. -S the process of looking something up
LOOM   *v* -ED, -ING, -S to appear in an enlarged and indistinct form
LOON   *n* pl. -S a diving waterfowl
LOONEY   *adj* -NIER, -NIEST loony
LOONEY   *n* pl. -EYS loony
LOONY   *adj* -NIER, -NIEST crazy
LOONY   *n* pl. -NIES a loony person
LOOP   *v* -ED, -ING, -S to form loops (circular or oval openings)
LOOPER   *n* pl. -S one that loops
LOOPHOLE   *v* -HOLED, -HOLING, -HOLES to make small openings in
LOOPY   *adj* LOOPIER, LOOPIEST full of loops
LOOSE   *adj* LOOSER, LOOSEST not firm, taut, or rigid **LOOSELY** *adv*
LOOSE   *v* LOOSED, LOOSING, LOOSES to set free
LOOSEN   *v* -ED, -ING, -S to make looser
LOOSENER   *n* pl. -S one that loosens
LOOSER   comparative of loose
LOOSEST   superlative of loose
LOOSING   present participle of loose
LOOT   *v* -ED, -ING, -S to plunder
LOOTER   *n* pl. -S one that loots
LOP   *v* LOPPED, LOPPING, LOPS to cut off branches or twigs from
LOPE   *v* LOPED, LOPING, LOPES to run with a steady, easy gait

LOPER	*n* pl. -S one that lopes
LOPPED	past tense of lop
LOPPER	*v* -ED, -ING, -S to curdle
LOPPING	present participle of lop
LOPPY	*adj* -PIEST hanging limply
LOPSIDED	*adj* leaning to one side
LOPSTICK	*n* pl. -S lobstick
LOQUAT	*n* pl. -S a small evergreen tree
LORAL	*adj* pertaining to the space between the eye and bill of a bird
LORAN	*n* pl. -S a type of navigational system
LORD	*v* -ED, -ING, -S to invest with the power of a lord (a person having dominion over others)
LORDING	*n* pl. -S a lordling
LORDLESS	*adj* having no lord
LORDLIER	comparative of lordly
LORDLIEST	superlative of lordly
LORDLIKE	*adj* lordly
LORDLING	*n* pl. -S a young or unimportant lord
LORDLY	*adj* -LIER, -LIEST of or befitting a lord
LORDOMA	*n* pl. -S lordosis
LORDOSIS	*n* pl. -DOSES a curvature of the spinal column **LORDOTIC** *adj*
LORDSHIP	*n* pl. -S the power of a lord
LORE	*n* pl. -S traditional knowledge or belief
LOREAL	*adj* loral
LORGNON	*n* pl. -S a pair of eyeglasses with a handle
LORICA	*n* pl. -CAE a protective covering or shell
LORICATE	*n* pl. -S an animal having a lorica
LORIES	pl. of lory
LORIKEET	*n* pl. -S a small parrot
LORIMER	*n* pl. -S a maker of implements for harnesses and saddles
LORINER	*n* pl. -S lorimer
LORIS	*n* pl. -RISES an Asian lemur
LORN	*adj* abandoned
LORNNESS	*n* pl. -ES the state of being lorn
LORRY	*n* pl. -RIES a type of wagon or truck
LORY	*n* pl. -RIES a small parrot
LOSE	*v* LOST, LOSING, LOSES to come to be without and be unable to find **LOSABLE** *adj*
LOSEL	*n* pl. -S a worthless person
LOSER	*n* pl. -S one that loses
LOSING	*n* pl. -S a loss
LOSINGLY	*adv* in a manner characterized by defeat
LOSS	*n* pl. -ES the act of one that loses
LOSSY	*adj* causing dissipation of electrical energy
LOST	*adj* not to be found or recovered
LOSTNESS	*n* pl. -ES the state of being lost
LOT	*v* LOTTED, LOTTING, LOTS to distribute proportionately
LOTA	*n* pl. -S lotah
LOTAH	*n* pl. -S a small water vessel used in India
LOTH	*adj* loath
LOTHARIO	*n* pl. -IOS a seducer of women
LOTHSOME	*adj* repulsive
LOTI	*n* pl. MALOTI a monetary unit of Lesotho
LOTIC	*adj* pertaining to moving water
LOTION	*n* pl. -S a liquid preparation for external application
LOTOS	*n* pl. -ES lotus
LOTTE	*n* pl. -S a monkfish
LOTTED	past tense of lot
LOTTERY	*n* pl. -TERIES a type of gambling game
LOTTING	present participle of lot
LOTTO	*n* pl. -TOS a game of chance
LOTUS	*n* pl. -ES an aquatic plant
LOUCHE	*adj* not reputable
LOUD	*adj* LOUDER, LOUDEST strongly audible
LOUDEN	*v* -ED, -ING, -S to make or become louder
LOUDISH	*adj* somewhat loud
LOUDLY	*adv* -LIER, -LIEST in a loud manner
LOUDNESS	*n* pl. -ES the quality of being loud
LOUGH	*n* pl. -S a lake
LOUIE	*n* pl. -S looie
LOUIS	*n* pl. LOUIS a former gold coin of France
LOUNGE	*v* LOUNGED, LOUNGING, LOUNGES to recline or lean in a relaxed, lazy manner
LOUNGER	*n* pl. -S one that lounges
LOUNGY	*adj* suitable for lounging
LOUP	*v* LOUPED, LOUPEN, LOUPING, LOUPS to leap
LOUPE	*n* pl. -S a small magnifying glass
LOUR	*v* -ED, -ING, -S to lower

LOURY   adj lowery
LOUSE   n pl. LICE a parasitic insect
LOUSE   v LOUSED, LOUSING,
            LOUSES to spoil or bungle
LOUSY   adj LOUSIER, LOUSIEST
            mean or contemptible
            LOUSILY adv
LOUT   v -ED, -ING, -S to bow in
            respect
LOUTISH   adj clumsy
LOUVER   n pl. -S a type of window
            LOUVERED adj
LOUVRE   n pl. -S louver
LOVABLE   adj having qualities that attract
            love LOVABLY adv
LOVAGE   n pl. -S a perennial herb
LOVAT   n pl. -S a chiefly green color
            mixture in fabrics
LOVE   v LOVED, LOVING, LOVES to
            feel great affection for
LOVEABLE   adj lovable LOVEABLY adv
LOVEBIRD   n pl. -S a small parrot
LOVEBUG   n pl. -S a small black fly that
            swarms along highways
LOVED   past tense of love
LOVELESS   adj feeling no love
LOVELIER   comparative of lovely
LOVELIES   pl. of lovely
LOVELIEST   superlative of lovely
LOVELILY   adv in a lovely manner
LOVELOCK   n pl. -S a lock of hair hanging
            separately
LOVELORN   adj not loved
LOVELY   adj -LIER, -LIEST beautiful
LOVELY   n pl. -LIES a beautiful woman
LOVER   n pl. -S one that loves another
            LOVERLY adj
LOVESICK   adj languishing with love
LOVESOME   adj lovely
LOVEVINE   n pl. -S a twining herb
LOVING   adj affectionate
LOVINGLY   adv in a loving manner
LOW   adj LOWER, LOWEST having
            relatively little upward
            extension
LOW   v -ED, -ING, -S to utter the
            sound characteristic of cattle
LOWBALL   v -ED, -ING, -S to give a
            customer a deceptively low
            price
LOWBORN   adj of humble birth
LOWBOY   n pl. -BOYS a low chest of
            drawers
LOWBRED   adj lowborn
LOWBROW   n pl. -S an uncultivated person
LOWDOWN   n pl. -S the whole truth

LOWE   v LOWED, LOWING, LOWES
            to blaze
LOWER   v -ED, -ING, -S to appear dark
            and threatening
LOWERY   adj dark and threatening
LOWING   n pl. -S the sound
            characteristic of cattle
LOWISH   adj somewhat low
LOWLAND   n pl. -S an area of land lying
            lower than the adjacent
            country
LOWLIFE   n pl. -LIFES or -LIVES a
            despicable person
LOWLIFER   n pl. -S a lowlife
LOWLIGHT   n pl. -S an unpleasant event,
            detail, or part
LOWLY   adj -LIER, -LIEST low in
            position or rank
LOWN   adj peaceful
LOWNESS   n pl. -ES the state of being
            low
LOWRIDER   n pl. -S a car having a lowered
            suspension
LOWSE   adj loose
LOX   v -ED, -ING, -ES to supply
            with lox (liquid oxygen)
LOYAL   adj -ALER, -ALEST faithful to
            one's allegiance
LOYALISM   n pl. -S loyalty
LOYALIST   n pl. -S one who is loyal
LOYALLY   adv in a loyal manner
LOYALTY   n pl. -TIES the state of being
            loyal
LOZENGE   n pl. -S a small, often
            medicated candy
LUAU   n pl. -S a Hawaiian feast
LUBBER   n pl. -S a clumsy person
            LUBBERLY adj
LUBE   n pl. -S a lubricant
LUBRIC   adj slippery
LUBRICAL   adj lubric
LUCARNE   n pl. -S a type of window
LUCE   n pl. -S a freshwater fish
LUCENCE   n pl. -S lucency
LUCENCY   n pl. -CIES the quality of being
            lucent
LUCENT   adj giving off light LUCENTLY
            adv
LUCERN   n pl. -S lucerne
LUCERNE   n pl. -S alfalfa
LUCES   a pl. of lux
LUCID   adj easily understood
            LUCIDLY adv
LUCIDITY   n pl. -TIES the quality of being
            lucid
LUCIFER   n pl. -S a friction match

LUCK   v -ED, -ING, -S to succeed by chance or good fortune

LUCKIE   n pl. -S an old woman

LUCKLESS   adj unlucky

LUCKY   adj LUCKIER, LUCKIEST having good fortune **LUCKILY** adv

LUCRE   n pl. -S monetary gain

LUCULENT   adj lucid

LUDE   n pl. -S a methaqualone pill

LUDIC   adj aimlessly playful

LUES   n pl. LUES syphilis

LUETIC   n pl. -S one infected with syphilis

LUFF   v -ED, -ING, -S to steer a sailing vessel nearer into the wind

LUFFA   n pl. -S loofah

LUG   v LUGGED, LUGGING, LUGS to carry or pull with effort

LUGE   v LUGED, LUGEING, LUGES to race on a luge (a small sled)

LUGER   n -S one that luges

LUGGAGE   n pl. -S articles containing a traveler's belongings

LUGGED   past tense of lug

LUGGER   n pl. -S a small sailing vessel

LUGGIE   n pl. -S a small wooden dish or pail

LUGGING   present participle of lug

LUGSAIL   n pl. -S a type of sail

LUGWORM   n pl. -S a burrowing marine worm

LUKEWARM   adj moderately warm

LULL   v -ED, -ING, -S to cause to sleep or rest

LULLABY   v -BIED, -BYING, -BIES to lull with a soothing song

LULU   n pl. -S something remarkable

LUM   n pl. -S a chimney

LUMBAGO   n pl. -GOS pain in the lower back

LUMBAR   n pl. -S an anatomical part situated near the loins

LUMBER   v -ED, -ING, -S to cut down and prepare timber for market

LUMBERER   n pl. -S one that lumbers

LUMEN   n pl. -MENS or -MINA the inner passage of a tubular organ **LUMENAL, LUMINAL** adj

LUMINARY   n pl. -NARIES a body that gives light

LUMINISM   n -S a style of painting

LUMINIST   n pl. -S a painter who uses the effects of light

LUMINOUS   adj giving off light

LUMMOX   n pl. -ES a clumsy person

LUMP   v -ED, -ING, -S to make into lumps (shapeless masses)

LUMPEN   n pl. -S an uprooted individual

LUMPER   n pl. -S a laborer employed to load and unload ships

LUMPFISH   n pl. -ES a marine fish

LUMPISH   adj stupid

LUMPY   adj LUMPIER, LUMPIEST full of lumps **LUMPILY** adv

LUNA   n pl. -S an alchemical designation for silver

LUNACY   n pl. -CIES insanity

LUNAR   n pl. -S an observation of the moon taken for navigational purposes

LUNARIAN   n pl. -S a supposed inhabitant of the moon

LUNATE   adj crescent-shaped **LUNATELY** adv

LUNATED   adj lunate

LUNATIC   n pl. -S an insane person

LUNATION   n pl. -S the interval between two successive new moons

LUNCH   v -ED, -ING, -ES to eat a noonday meal

LUNCHEON   n pl. -S a noonday meal

LUNCHER   n pl. -S one that lunches

LUNE   n pl. -S a crescent-shaped figure

LUNET   n pl. -S lunette

LUNETTE   n pl. -S a crescent-shaped object

LUNG   n pl. -S a respiratory organ

LUNGAN   n pl. -S longan

LUNGE   v LUNGED, LUNGING, LUNGES to make a forceful forward movement

LUNGEE   n pl. -S lungi

LUNGER   n pl. -S one that lunges

LUNGFISH   n pl. -ES a type of fish

LUNGFUL   n pl. -S as much as the lungs can hold

LUNGI   n pl. -S a loincloth worn by men in India

LUNGING   present participle of lunge

LUNGWORM   n pl. -S a parasitic worm

LUNGWORT   n pl. -S a European herb

LUNGYI   n pl. -S lungi

LUNIER   comparative of luny

LUNIES   pl. of luny

LUNIEST   superlative of luny

LUNK   n pl. -S a lunkhead

LUNKER   n pl. -S a large game fish

LUNKHEAD   n pl. -S a stupid person

LUNT   v -ED, -ING, -S to emit smoke

LUNULA   n pl. -LAE a small crescent-shaped structure **LUNULAR, LUNULATE** adj

LUNULE   n pl. -S lunula

LUNY   adj -NIER, -NIEST loony

LUNY   n pl. -NIES a loony

LUPANAR   n pl. -S a brothel

LUPIN   n pl. -S lupine

LUPINE   n pl. -S a flowering plant

LUPOUS   adj pertaining to lupus

LUPULIN   n pl. -S a medicinal powder obtained from the hop plant

LUPUS   n pl. -ES a skin disease

LURCH   v -ED, -ING, -ES to sway abruptly

LURCHER   n pl. -S one that lurks or prowls

LURDAN   n pl. -S a lazy or stupid person

LURDANE   n pl. -S lurdan

LURE   v LURED, LURING, LURES to attract with something desirable

LURER   n pl. -S one that lures

LURID   adj causing shock or horror **LURIDLY** adv

LURING   present participle of lure

LURK   v -ED, -ING, -S to wait in concealment

LURKER   n pl. -S one that lurks

LUSCIOUS   adj having a very pleasing taste or smell

LUSH   adj LUSHER, LUSHEST abounding in vegetation **LUSHLY** adv

LUSH   v -ED, -ING, -ES to drink to excess

LUSHNESS   n pl. -ES the state of being lush

LUST   v -ED, -ING, -S to have an intense desire

LUSTER   v -ED, -ING, -S to make or become lustrous

LUSTFUL   adj marked by excessive sexual desire

LUSTIER   comparative of lusty

LUSTIEST   superlative of lusty

LUSTILY   adv in a lusty manner

LUSTRA   a pl. of lustrum

LUSTRAL   adj pertaining to a lustrum

LUSTRATE   v -TRATED, -TRATING, -TRATES to purify ceremonially

LUSTRE   v -TRED, -TRING, -TRES to luster

LUSTRING   n pl. -S a glossy silk fabric

LUSTROUS   adj reflecting light evenly and efficiently

LUSTRUM   n pl. -TRUMS or -TRA a ceremonial purification of the population in ancient Rome

LUSTY   adj LUSTIER, LUSTIEST full of vigor

LUSUS   n pl. -ES an abnormality

LUTANIST   n pl. -S one who plays the lute

LUTE   v LUTED, LUTING, LUTES to play a lute (a stringed musical instrument)

LUTEA   pl. of luteum

LUTEAL   adj pertaining to the luteum

LUTECIUM   n pl. -S lutetium

LUTED   past tense of lute

LUTEFISK   n pl. -S dried codfish

LUTEIN   n pl. -S a yellow pigment

LUTENIST   n pl. -S lutanist

LUTEOLIN   n pl. -S a yellow pigment

LUTEOUS   adj light to moderate greenish yellow in color

LUTETIUM   n pl. -S a metallic element

LUTEUM   n pl. -TEA a hormone-secreting body

LUTHERN   n pl. -S a type of window

LUTHIER   n pl. -S one who makes stringed instruments

LUTING   n pl. -S a substance used as a sealant

LUTIST   n pl. -S a lutanist

LUTZ   n pl. -ES a jump in figure skating

LUV   n pl. -S a sweetheart

LUX   n pl. LUXES or LUCES a unit of illumination

LUXATE   v -ATED, -ATING, -ATES to put out of joint

LUXATION   n pl. -S the act of luxating

LUXE   n pl. -S luxury

LUXURY   n pl. -RIES free indulgence in that which affords pleasure or comfort

LWEI   n pl. -S a monetary unit of Angola

LYARD   adj streaked with gray

LYART   adj lyard

LYASE   n pl. -S an enzyme

LYCEE   n pl. -S a French secondary school

LYCEUM   n pl. -CEUMS or -CEA a hall for public lectures or discussions

LYCHEE   n pl. -S litchi

LYCHNIS   n pl. -NISES a flowering plant

LYCOPENE   n pl. -S a red pigment

LYCOPOD   *n* pl. -S an evergreen plant

LYDDITE   *n* pl. -S an explosive

LYE   *n* pl. -S a solution used in making soap

LYING   *n* pl. -S the act of telling lies

LYINGLY   *adv* falsely

LYMPH   *n* pl. -S a body fluid containing white blood cells **LYMPHOID** *adj*

LYMPHOMA   *n* pl. -MAS or -MATA a type of tumor

LYNCEAN   *adj* of or resembling a lynx

LYNCH   *v* -ED, -ING, -ES to put to death without legal sanction

LYNCHER   *n* pl. -S one that lynches

LYNCHING   *n* pl. -S the act of one who lynches

LYNCHPIN   *n* pl. -S linchpin

LYNX   *n* pl. -ES a short-tailed wildcat

LYOPHILE   *adj* pertaining to a type of colloid

LYRATE   *adj* having the shape of a lyre **LYRATELY** *adv*

LYRATED   *adj* lyrate

LYRE   *n* pl. -S an ancient harp-like instrument

LYREBIRD   *n* pl. -S an Australian bird

LYRIC   *n* pl. -S a lyrical poem

LYRICAL   *adj* having the form of a song

LYRICISE   *v* -CISED, -CISING, -CISES to lyricize

LYRICISM   *n* pl. -S the quality of being lyrics

LYRICIST   *n* pl. -S one who writes the words for songs

LYRICIZE   *v* -CIZED, -CIZING, -CIZES to write lyrics

LYRIFORM   *adj* lyrate

LYRISM   *n* pl. -S lyricism

LYRIST   *n* pl. -S one who plays the lyre

LYSATE   *n* pl. -S a product of lysis

LYSE   *v* LYSED, LYSING, LYSES to cause to undergo lysis

LYSIN   *n* pl. -S a substance capable of disintegrating blood cells or bacteria

LYSINE   *n* pl. -S an amino acid

LYSING   present participle of lyse

LYSIS   *n* pl. LYSES the disintegration of cells by lysins

LYSOGEN   *n* pl. -S a type of antigen

LYSOGENY   *n* pl. -NIES the state of being like a lysogen

LYSOSOME   *n* pl. -S a saclike part of a cell

LYSOZYME   *n* pl. -S an enzyme

LYSSA   *n* pl. -S rabies

LYTIC   *adj* pertaining to lysis

LYTTA   *n* pl. -TAE or -TAS a fibrous band in the tongue of certain carnivorous mammals

MA	*n* pl. -S mother	**MACING**	present participle of mace
MAAR	*n* pl. -S a volcanic crater	**MACK**	*n* pl. -S mac
MABE	*n* pl. -S a cultured pearl	**MACKEREL**	*n* pl. -S a marine food fish
MAC	*n* pl. -S a raincoat	**MACKINAW**	*n* pl. -S a woolen fabric
MACABER	*adj* macabre	**MACKLE**	*v* -LED, -LING, -LES to blur in
MACABRE	*adj* gruesome		printing
MACACO	*n* pl. -COS a lemur	**MACLE**	*n* pl. -S a spot or discoloration
MACADAM	*n* pl. -S a type of pavement		in a mineral **MACLED** *adj*
MACAQUE	*n* pl. -S a short-tailed monkey	**MACON**	*n* pl. -S a red or white French
MACARONI	*n* pl. -NIS or -NIES a tubular		wine
	pasta	**MACRAME**	*n* pl. -S a trimming of knotted
MACAROON	*n* pl. -S a type of cookie		thread or cord
MACAW	*n* pl. -S a large parrot	**MACRO**	*n* pl. -ROS a type of computer
MACCABAW	*n* pl. -S maccaboy		instruction
MACCABOY	*n* pl. -BOYS a type of snuff	**MACRON**	*n* pl. -S a symbol placed over
MACCHIA	*n* pl. -CHIE a dense growth of		a vowel to show that it has a
	small trees and shrubs		long sound
MACCOBOY	*n* pl. -BOYS maccaboy	**MACRURAL**	*adj* pertaining to macruran
MACE	*v* MACED, MACING, MACES	**MACRURAN**	*n* pl. -S any of a suborder of
	to attack with a clublike		crustaceans
	weapon	**MACULA**	*n* pl. -LAE or -LAS a spot
MACER	*n* pl. -S an official who carries		**MACULAR** *adj*
	a ceremonial staff	**MACULATE**	*v* -LATED, -LATING, -LATES
MACERATE	*v* -ATED, -ATING, -ATES to		to mark with spots
	soften by soaking in liquid	**MACULE**	*v* -ULED, -ULING, -ULES to
MACH	*n* pl. -S a number indicating		mackle
	the ratio of the speed of a body	**MACUMBA**	*n* pl. -S a religion practiced in
	to the speed of sound		Brazil
MACHE	*n* pl. S a European herb	**MAD**	*adj* MADDER, MADDEST
MACHETE	*n* pl. -S a large, heavy knife		insane
MACHINE	*v* -CHINED, -CHINING,	**MAD**	*v* MADDED, MADDING,
	-CHINES to process by		MADS to madden
	machine (a mechanical device)	**MADAM**	*n* pl. -S a woman who
MACHISMO	*n* pl. -MOS strong masculinity		manages a brothel
MACHO	*n* pl. -CHOS a person who	**MADAME**	*n* pl. -S madam
	exhibits machismo	**MADAME**	*n* pl. MESDAMES the French
MACHREE	*n* pl. -S dear		title of respect for a married
MACHZOR	*n* pl. -ZORIM or -ZORS		woman
	mahzor	**MADCAP**	*n* pl. -S an impulsive person

MADDED   past tense of mad
MADDEN   v -ED, -ING, -S to make or become mad
MADDER   n pl. -S a perennial herb
MADDEST   superlative of mad
MADDING   present participle of mad
MADDISH   adj somewhat mad
MADE   past tense of make
MADEIRA   n pl. -S a white wine
MADHOUSE   n pl. -S an insane asylum
MADLY   adv in a mad manner
MADMAN   n pl. -MEN a man who is insane
MADNESS   n pl. -ES the state of being mad
MADONNA   n pl. -S a former Italian title of respect for a woman
MADRAS   n pl. -ES a cotton fabric
MADRE   n pl. -S mother
MADRIGAL   n pl. -S a short lyric poem
MADRONA   n pl. -S an evergreen tree
MADRONE   n pl. -S madrona
MADRONO   n pl. -NOS madrona
MADURO   n pl. -ROS a dark-colored, relatively strong cigar
MADWOMAN   n pl. -WOMEN a woman who is insane
MADWORT   n pl. -S a flowering plant
MADZOON   n pl. -S matzoon
MAE   n pl. -S more
MAENAD   n pl. -S or -ES a female participant in ancient Greek orgies MAENADIC adj
MAESTOSO   n pl. -SOS a stately musical passage
MAESTRO   n pl. -STROS or -STRI a master of an art
MAFFIA   n pl. -S mafia
MAFFICK   v -ED, -ING, -S to celebrate boisterously
MAFIA   n pl. -S a secret criminal organization
MAFIC   adj pertaining to minerals rich in magnesium and iron
MAFIOSO   n pl. -SI a member of the mafia
MAFTIR   n pl. -S the concluding section of a parashah
MAG   n pl. -S a magazine
MAGAZINE   n pl. -S a type of periodical publication
MAGDALEN   n pl. -S a reformed prostitute
MAGE   n pl. -S a magician
MAGENTA   n pl. -S a purplish red dye
MAGGOT   n pl. -S the legless larva of certain insects MAGGOTY adj

MAGI   pl. of magus
MAGIAN   n pl. -S a magus
MAGIC   v -ICKED, -ICKING, -ICS to affect by magic (sorcery)
MAGICAL   adj resembling magic
MAGICIAN   n pl. -S one skilled in magic
MAGICKED   past tense of magic
MAGICKING present participle of magic
MAGILP   n pl. -S megilp
MAGISTER   n pl. -S a master or teacher
MAGLEV   adj pertaining to a railroad system using magnets to move a train above the tracks
MAGMA   n pl. -MAS or -MATA the molten matter from which igneous rock is formed MAGMATIC adj
MAGNATE   n pl. -S a powerful or influential person
MAGNESIA   n pl. -S a medicinal compound MAGNESIC adj
MAGNET   n pl. -S a body that possesses the property of attracting iron
MAGNETIC   n pl. -S a magnet
MAGNETO   n pl. -TOS a type of electric generator
MAGNETON   n pl. -S a unit of magnetic moment
MAGNIFIC   adj magnificent
MAGNIFY   v -FIED, -FYING, -FIES to increase the perceived size of
MAGNOLIA   n pl. -S a flowering shrub or tree
MAGNUM   n pl. -S a large wine bottle
MAGOT   n pl. -S a tailless ape
MAGPIE   n pl. -S a corvine bird
MAGUEY   n pl. -GUEYS a tropical plant
MAGUS   n pl. -GI a magician
MAHARAJA   n pl. -S a king or prince in India
MAHARANI   n pl. -S the wife of a maharaja
MAHATMA   n pl. -S a Hindu sage
MAHIMAHI   n pl. MAHIMAHI a food fish in Hawaii
MAHJONG   n pl. -S a game of Chinese origin
MAHJONGG   n pl. -S mahjong
MAHOE   n pl. -S a tropical tree
MAHOGANY   n pl. -NIES a tropical tree
MAHONIA   n pl. -S a flowering shrub
MAHOUT   n pl. -S the keeper and driver of an elephant
MAHUANG   n pl. -S an Asian plant
MAHZOR   n pl. -ZORIM or -ZORS a Jewish prayer book

MAID   *n* pl. -S a maiden **MAIDISH** *adj*

MAIDEN   *n* pl. -S a young unmarried woman **MAIDENLY** *adj*

MAIDHOOD   *n* pl. -S the state of being a maiden

MAIEUTIC   *adj* pertaining to a method of eliciting knowledge

MAIGRE   *adj* containing neither flesh nor its juices

MAIHEM   *n* pl. -S mayhem

MAIL   *v* -ED, -ING, -S to send by a governmental postal system. **MAILABLE** *adj*

MAILBAG   *n* pl. -S a bag for carrying mail (postal material)

MAILBOX   *n* pl. -ES a box for depositing mail

MAILE   *n* pl. -S a Pacific island vine

MAILER   *n* pl. -S one that mails

MAILING   *n* pl. -S a rented farm

MAILL   *n* pl. -S a payment

MAILLESS   *adj* having no armor

MAILLOT   *n* pl. -S a woman's one-piece bathing suit

MAILMAN   *n* pl. -MEN a man who carries and delivers mail

MAIM   *v* -ED, -ING, -S to injure so as to cause lasting damage

MAIMER   *n* pl. -S one that maims

MAIN   *n* pl. -S the principal part

MAINLAND   *n* pl. -S a principal land mass

MAINLINE   *v* -LINED, -LINING, -LINES to inject a narcotic into a major vein

MAINLY   *adv* for the most part

MAINMAST   *n* pl. -S the principal mast of a vessel

MAINSAIL   *n* pl. -S the principal sail of a vessel

MAINSTAY   *n* pl. -STAYS a principal support

MAINTAIN   *v* -ED, -ING, -S to keep in proper condition

MAINTOP   *n* pl. -S a platform at the head of a mainmast

MAIOLICA   *n* pl. -S majolica

MAIR   *n* pl. -S more

MAIST   *n* pl. -S most

MAIZE   *n* pl. -S an American cereal grass

MAJAGUA   *n* pl. -S a tropical tree

MAJESTIC   *adj* having majesty

MAJESTY   *n* pl. -TIES regal dignity

MAJOLICA   *n* pl. -S a type of pottery

MAJOR   *v* -ED, -ING, -S to pursue a specific principal course of study

MAJORITY   *n* pl. -TIES the greater number or part

MAJORLY   *adv* mainly

MAKAR   *n* pl. -S a poet

MAKE   *v* MADE, MAKING, MAKES to cause to exist **MAKABLE, MAKEABLE** *adj*

MAKEBATE   *n* pl. -S one that encourages quarrels

MAKEFAST   *n* pl. -S an object to which a boat is tied

MAKEOVER   *n* pl. -S a changing of appearance

MAKER   *n* pl. -S one that makes

MAKEUP   *n* pl. -S the way in which the parts or ingredients of something are put together

MAKIMONO   *n* pl. -NOS a Japanese ornamental scroll

MAKING   *n* pl. -S material from which something can be developed

MAKO   *n* pl. -KOS a large shark

MAKUTA   pl. of likuta

MALACCA   *n* pl. -S the cane of an Asian rattan palm

MALADY   *n* pl. -DIES an illness

MALAISE   *n* pl. -S a feeling of vague discomfort

MALAMUTE   *n* pl. -S an Alaskan sled dog

MALANGA   *n* pl. -S a yautia

MALAPERT   *n* pl. -S an impudent person

MALAPROP   *n* pl. -S a humorous misuse of a word

MALAR   *n* pl. -S the cheekbone

MALARIA   *n* pl. -S an infectious disease **MALARIAL, MALARIAN** *adj*

MALARKEY   *n* pl. -KEYS nonsense

MALARKY   *n* pl. -KIES malarkey

MALAROMA   *n* pl. -S a malodor

MALATE   *n* pl. -S a chemical salt

MALE   *n* pl. -S an individual that begets young by fertilizing the female

MALEATE   *n* pl. -S a chemical salt

MALEDICT   *v* -ED, -ING, -S to curse

MALEFIC   *adj* producing or causing evil

MALEMIUT   *n* pl. -S malamute

MALEMUTE   *n* pl. -S malamute

MALENESS   *n* pl. -ES the quality of being a male

MALFED   *adj* badly fed

MALGRE   *prep* in spite of

MALIC   *adj* pertaining to apples

MALICE   n pl. -S a desire to injure another

MALIGN   v -ED, -ING, -S to speak evil of

MALIGNER   n pl. -S one that maligns

MALIGNLY   adv in an evil manner

MALIHINI   n pl. -S a newcomer to Hawaii

MALINE   n pl. -S a delicate net used for veils

MALINGER   v -ED, -ING, -S to feign illness in order to avoid duty or work

MALISON   n pl. -S a curse

MALKIN   n pl. -S an untidy woman

MALL   v -ED, -ING, -S to maul

MALLARD   n pl. -S a wild duck

MALLEE   n pl. -S an evergreen tree

MALLEI   pl. of malleus

MALLEOLI   n/pl bony protuberances of the ankle

MALLET   n pl. -S a type of hammer

MALLEUS   n pl. -LEI a bone of the middle ear

MALLOW   n pl. -S a flowering plant

MALM   n pl. -S a soft, friable limestone

MALMSEY   n pl. -SEYS a white wine

MALMY   adj MALMIER, MALMIEST resembling malm

MALODOR   n pl. -S an offensive odor

MALOTI   pl. of loti

MALPOSED   adj being in the wrong position

MALT   v -ED, -ING, -S to treat or combine with malt (germinated grain)

MALTASE   n pl. -S an enzyme

MALTED   n pl. -S a sweet beverage

MALTHA   n pl. -S a natural tar

MALTIER   comparative of malty

MALTIEST   superlative of malty

MALTOL   n pl. -S a chemical compound

MALTOSE   n pl. -S a type of sugar

MALTREAT   v -ED, -ING, -S to treat badly

MALTSTER   n pl. -S one that makes malt

MALTY   adj MALTIER, MALTIEST resembling malt

MALVASIA   n pl. -S malmsey

MAMA   n pl. -S mother

MAMALIGA   n pl. -S a cornmeal porridge

MAMBA   n pl. -S a venomous snake

MAMBO   v -ED, -ING, -ES or -S to perform a ballroom dance

MAMELUKE   n pl. -S a slave in Muslim countries

MAMEY   n pl. -MEYS or -MEYES a tropical tree

MAMIE   n pl. -S mamey

MAMLUK   n pl. -S mameluke

MAMMA   n pl. -S mama

MAMMA   n pl. -MAE a milk-secreting organ

MAMMAL   n pl. -S any of a class of warm-blooded vertebrates

MAMMARY   adj pertaining to the mammae

MAMMATE   adj having mammae

MAMMATUS   n pl. -TI a type of cloud

MAMMEE   n pl. -S mamey

MAMMER   v -ED, -ING, -S to hesitate

MAMMET   n pl. -S maumet

MAMMEY   n pl. -MEYS mamey

MAMMIE   n pl. -S mammy

MAMMIES   pl. of mammy

MAMMILLA   n pl. -LAE a nipple

MAMMITIS   n pl. -MITIDES mastitis

MAMMOCK   v -ED, -ING, -S to shred

MAMMON   n pl. -S material wealth

MAMMOTH   n pl. -S an extinct elephant

MAMMY   n pl. -MIES mother

MAN   n pl. MEN an adult human male

MAN   v MANNED, MANNING, MANS to supply with men

MANA   n pl. -S a supernatural force in certain Pacific island religions

MANACLE   v -CLED, -CLING, -CLES to handcuff

MANAGE   v -AGED, -AGING, -AGES to control or direct

MANAGER   n pl. -S one that manages

MANAKIN   n pl. -S a tropical bird

MANANA   n pl. -S tomorrow

MANATEE   n pl. -S an aquatic mammal
            MANATOID adj

MANCHE   n pl. -S a heraldic design

MANCHET   n pl. -S a small loaf of fine white bread

MANCIPLE   n pl. -S an officer authorized to purchase provisions

MANDALA   n pl. -S a Hindu or Buddhist graphic symbol of the universe
            MANDALIC adj

MANDAMUS   v -ED, -ING, -ES to command by means of writ issued by a superior court

MANDARIN   n pl. -S a citrus fruit

MANDATE   v -DATED, -DATING, -DATES to authorize or decree

MANDATOR   n pl. -S one that mandates

MANDIBLE   n pl. -S the bone of the lower jaw

MANDIOCA   n pl. -S manioc

MANDOLA   n pl. -S an ancient lute

MANDOLIN *n* pl. -S a stringed musical instrument

MANDRAKE *n* pl. -S a European herb

MANDREL *n* pl. -S a shaft on which a tool is mounted

MANDRIL *n* pl. -S mandrel

MANDRILL *n* pl. -S a large baboon

MANE *n* pl. -S the long hair growing on and about the neck of some animals **MANED, MANELESS** *adj*

MANEGE *n* pl. -S the art of training and riding horses

MANEUVER *v* -ED, -ING, -S to change the position of for a specific purpose

MANFUL *adj* courageous **MANFULLY** *adv*

MANGABEY *n* pl. -BEYS a long-tailed monkey

MANGABY *n* pl. -BIES mangabey

MANGANIC *adj* containing manganese (a metallic element)

MANGE *n* pl. -S a skin disease of domestic animals

MANGEL *n* pl. -S a variety of beet

MANGER *n* pl. -S a trough or box from which horses or cattle eat

MANGEY *adj* **MANGIER, MANGIEST** mangy

MANGIER comparative of mangy

MANGIEST superlative of mangy

MANGILY *adv* in a mangy manner

MANGLE *v* -GLED, -GLING, -GLES to cut, slash, or crush so as to disfigure

MANGLER *n* pl. -S one that mangles

MANGO *n* pl. -GOES or -GOS an edible tropical fruit

MANGOLD *n* pl. -S mangel

MANGONEL *n* pl. -S a medieval military device for hurling stones

MANGROVE *n* pl. -S a tropical tree or shrub

MANGY *adj* **MANGIER, MANGIEST** affected with mange

MANHOLE *n* pl. -S a hole providing entrance to an underground or enclosed structure

MANHOOD *n* pl. -S the state of being a man

MANHUNT *n* pl. -S an intensive search for a person

MANIA *n* pl. -S an excessive interest or enthusiasm

MANIAC *n* pl. -S an insane person **MANIACAL** *adj*

MANIC *n* pl. -S one that is affected with mania

MANICURE *v* -CURED, -CURING, -CURES to trim and polish the fingernails of

MANIFEST *v* -ED, -ING, -S to show clearly

MANIFOLD *v* -ED, -ING, -S to make several copies of

MANIHOT *n* pl. -S a tropical plant

MANIKIN *n* pl. -S an anatomical model of the human body

MANILA *n* pl. -S a strong paper

MANILLA *n* pl. -S manila

MANILLE *n* pl. -S the second highest trump in certain card games

MANIOC *n* pl. -S a tropical plant

MANIOCA *n* pl. -S manioc

MANIPLE *n* pl. -S a silk band worn on the left arm as a vestment

MANITO *n* pl. -TOS manitou

MANITOU *n* pl. -S an Algonquian Indian deity

MANITU *n* pl. -S manitou

MANKIND *n* pl. MANKIND the human race

MANLESS *adj* destitute of men

MANLIKE *adj* resembling a man

MANLY *adj* -LIER, -LIEST having the qualities of a man **MANLILY** *adv*

MANMADE *adj* made by man

MANNA *n* pl. -S divinely supplied food

MANNAN *n* pl. -S a type of sugar

MANNED past tense of man

MANNER *n* pl. -S a way of acting **MANNERED** *adj*

MANNERLY *adj* polite

MANNIKIN *n* pl. -S manikin

MANNING present participle of man

MANNISH *adj* resembling or characteristic of a man

MANNITE *n* pl. -S mannitol **MANNITIC** *adj*

MANNITOL *n* pl. -S an alcohol

MANNOSE *n* pl. -S a type of sugar

MANO *n* pl. -NOS a stone used for grinding foods

MANOR *n* pl. -S a landed estate or territorial unit **MANORIAL** *adj*

MANPACK *adj* designed to be carried by one person

MANPOWER *n* pl. -S the number of men available for service

MANQUE *adj* frustrated in the fulfillment of one's aspirations

MANROPE *n* pl. -S a rope used as a handrail

MANSARD *n* pl. -S a type of roof

MANSE *n* pl. -S a clergyman's house

MANSION *n* pl. -S a large, impressive house

MANTA *n* pl. -S a cotton fabric

MANTEAU *n* pl. -TEAUS or -TEAUX a loose cloak

MANTEL *n* pl. -S a shelf above a fireplace

MANTELET *n* pl. -S a mobile screen used to protect soldiers

MANTES a pl. of mantis

MANTIC *adj* having powers of prophecy

MANTID *n* pl. -S mantis

MANTILLA *n* pl. -S a woman's scarf

MANTIS *n* pl. -TISES or -TES a predatory insect

MANTISSA *n* pl. -S the decimal part of a logarithm

MANTLE *v* -TLED, -TLING, -TLES to cloak

MANTLET *n* pl. -S mantelet

MANTLING *n* pl. -S an ornamental cloth

MANTRA *n* pl. -S a mystical formula of prayer or incantation in Hinduism **MANTRIC** *adj*

MANTRAP *n* pl. -S a trap for catching men

MANTUA *n* pl. -S a woman's gown

MANUAL *n* pl. -S a small reference book

MANUALLY *adv* by means of the hands

MANUARY *adj* involving the hands

MANUBRIA *n/pl* handle-shaped anatomical parts

MANUMIT *v* -MITTED, -MITTING, -MITS to free from slavery

MANURE *v* -NURED, -NURING, -NURES to fertilize with manure (animal excrement)

MANURER *n* pl. -S one that manures

MANURIAL *adj* of or pertaining to manure

MANURING present participle of manure

MANUS *n* pl. MANUS the end of the forelimb in vertebrates

MANWARD *adv* toward man

MANWARDS *adv* manward

MANWISE *adv* in a manner characteristic of man

MANY *adj* MORE, MOST consisting of or amounting to a large number

MANYFOLD *adv* by many times

MAP *v* MAPPED, MAPPING, MAPS to delineate on a map (a representation of a region)

MAPLE *n* pl. -S a hardwood tree

MAPLIKE *adj* resembling a map

MAPMAKER *n* pl. -S one that makes maps

MAPPABLE *adj* capable of being mapped

MAPPED past tense of map

MAPPER *n* pl. -S one that maps

MAPPING *n* pl. -S a mathematical correspondence

MAQUETTE *n* pl. -S a small preliminary model

MAQUI *n* pl. -S maquis

MAQUIS *n* pl. MAQUIS a thick underbrush

MAR *v* MARRED, MARRING, MARS to detract from the perfection or wholeness of

MARABOU *n* pl. -S an African stork

MARABOUT *n* pl. -S a marabou

MARACA *n* pl. -S a percussion instrument

MARANTA *n* pl. -S a tropical plant

MARASCA *n* pl. -S a wild cherry

MARASMUS *n* pl. -ES a wasting away of the body **MARASMIC** *adj*

MARATHON *n* pl. -S a long-distance race

MARAUD *v* -ED, -ING, -S to rove in search of booty

MARAUDER *n* pl. -S one that marauds

MARAVEDI *n* pl. -S a former coin of Spain

MARBLE *v* -BLED, -BLING, -BLES to give a mottled appearance to

MARBLER *n* pl. -S one that marbles

MARBLING *n* pl. -S an intermixture of fat and lean in meat

MARBLY *adj* -BLIER, -BLIEST mottled

MARC *n* pl. -S the residue remaining after a fruit has been pressed

MARCATO *adv* with strong accentuation — used as a musical direction

MARCEL *v* -CELLED, -CELLING, -CELS to make a deep, soft wave in the hair

MARCH *v* -ED, -ING, -ES to walk in a formal military manner

MARCHEN *n* pl. MARCHEN a folktale

MARCHER *n* pl. -S one that marches

MARCHESA *n* pl. -CHESE the wife or widow of a marchese

MARCHESE *n* p. -CHESI an Italian nobleman

MARE *n* pl. -S a mature female horse

MARE *n* pl. -RIA a dark area on the surface of the moon or Mars

MAREMMA *n* pl. -REMME a marshy coastal region

MARENGO *adj* served with a sauce of mushrooms, tomatoes, oil, and wine

MARGARIC *adj* pearly

MARGARIN *n* pl. -S a butter substitute

MARGAY *n* pl. -GAYS a small American wildcat

MARGE *n* pl. -S a margin

MARGENT *v* -ED, -ING, -S to margin

MARGIN *v* -ED, -ING, -S to provide with a margin (a border)

MARGINAL *adj* of or pertaining to a margin

MARGRAVE *n* pl. -S the military governor of a medieval German border province

MARIA pl. of mare

MARIACHI *n* pl. -S a Mexican musical band

MARIGOLD *n* pl. -S a flowering plant

MARIMBA *n* pl. -S a percussion instrument

MARINA *n* pl. -S a docking area for small boats

MARINADE *v* -NADED, -NADING, -NADES to marinate

MARINARA *n* pl. -S a seasoned tomato sauce

MARINATE *v* -NATED, -NATING, -NATES to soak in a seasoned liquid before cooking

MARINE *n* pl. -S a soldier trained for service at sea and on land

MARINER *n* pl. -S a sailor

MARIPOSA *n* pl. -S a flowering plant

MARISH *n* pl. -ES a marsh

MARITAL *adj* pertaining to marriage

MARITIME *adj* pertaining to navigation or commerce on the sea

MARJORAM *n* pl. -S fragrant herb

MARK *v* -ED, -ING, -S to make a visible impression on

MARKDOWN *n* pl. -S a reduction in price

MARKEDLY *adv* in an evident manner

MARKER *n* pl. -S one that marks

MARKET *v* -ED, -ING, -S to offer for sale

MARKETER *n* pl. -S one that markets

MARKHOOR *n* pl. -S markhor

MARKHOR *n* pl. -S a wild goat

MARKING *n* pl. -S a pattern of marks

MARKKA *n* pl. -KAA or -KAS a monetary unit of Finland

MARKSMAN *n* pl. -MEN a person skillful at hitting a target

MARKUP *n* pl. -S an increase in price

MARL *v* -ED, -ING, -S to fertilize with marl (an earthy deposit containing lime, clay, and sand)

MARLIER comparative of marly

MARLIEST superlative of marly

MARLIN *n* pl. -S a marine game fish

MARLINE *n* pl. -S a rope used on a ship

MARLING *n* pl. -S marline

MARLITE *n* pl. -S a type of marl

MARLITIC *adj*

MARLY *adj* MARLIER, MARLIEST abounding with marl

MARMITE *n* pl. -S a large soup kettle

MARMOSET *n* pl. -S a small monkey

MARMOT *n* pl. -S a burrowing rodent

MAROCAIN *n* pl. -S a light crinkled fabric

MAROON *v* -ED, -ING, -S to abandon in an isolated place

MARPLOT *n* pl. -S one that ruins a plan by meddling

MARQUE *n* pl. -S reprisal

MARQUEE *n* pl. -S a rooflike structure projecting over an entrance

MARQUESS *n* pl. -ES marquis

MARQUIS *n* pl. -ES a European nobleman

MARQUISE *n* pl. -S the wife or widow of a marquis

MARRAM *n* pl. -S a beach grass

MARRANO *n* pl. -NOS a Jew in Spain who professed Christianity to avoid persecution

MARRED past tense of mar

MARRER *n* pl. -S one that mars

MARRIAGE *n* pl. -S the legal union of a man and woman

MARRIED *n* pl. -S one who has entered into marriage

MARRIER *n* pl. -S one that marries

MARRIES present 3d person sing. of marry

MARRING present participle of mar

MARRON *n* pl. -S a variety of chestnut

MARROW *v* -ED, -ING, -S to marry

MARROWY *adj* pithy

MARRY *v* -RIED, -RYING, -RIES to enter into marriage

MARSALA *n* pl. -S a Sicilian wine

MARSE *n* pl. -S master

MARSH *n* pl. -ES a tract of low, wet land

MARSHAL *v* -ED, -ING, -S to put in proper order

MARSHALL *v* -ED, -ING, -S to marshal

MARSHY *adj* MARSHIER, MARSHIEST resembling a marsh

MARSUPIA *n/pl* abdominal pouches of certain mammals

MART *v* -ED, -ING, -S to market

MARTAGON *n* pl. -S a flowering plant

MARTELLO *n* pl. -LOS a circular fort

MARTEN *n* pl. -S a carnivorous mammal

MARTIAL *adj* pertaining to war

MARTIAN *n* pl. -S a supposed inhabitant of the planet Mars

MARTIN *n* pl. -S a small bird

MARTINET *n* pl. -S one who demands rigid adherence to rules

MARTINI *n* pl. -S an alcoholic beverage

MARTLET *n* pl. -S a martin

MARTYR *v* -ED, -ING, -S to put to death for adhering to a belief

MARTYRLY *adj* resembling a martyr

MARTYRY *n* pl. -TYRIES a shrine erected in honor of a martyred person

MARVEL *v* -VELED, -VELING, -VELS or -VELLED, -VELLING, -VELS to be filled with wonder or astonishment

MARVY *adj* marvelous

MARYJANE *n* pl. -S marijuana

MARZIPAN *n* pl. -S an almond candy

MASCARA *v* -ED, -ING, -S to color the eyelashes or eyebrows with a cosmetic

MASCON *n* pl. -S a concentration of dense mass beneath the moon's surface

MASCOT *n* pl. -S a person, animal, or object believed to bring good luck

MASER *n* pl. -S a device for amplifying electrical impulses

MASH *v* -ED, -ING, -ES to reduce to a pulpy mass

MASHER *n* pl. -S one that mashes

MASHIE *n* pl. -S a golf club

MASHY *n* pl. MASHIES mashie

MASJID *n* pl. -S a mosque

MASK *v* -ED, -ING, -S to cover with a mask (a covering used to disguise the face) MASKABLE *adj*

MASKEG *n* pl. -S muskeg

MASKER *n* pl. -S one that wears a mask

MASKING *n* pl. -S a piece of scenery used to conceal parts of a stage from the audience

MASKLIKE *adj* suggestive of a mask

MASON *v* -ED, -ING, -S to build with stone or brick

MASONIC *adj* pertaining to masonry

MASONRY *n* pl. -RIES a structure built of stone or brick

MASQUE *n* pl. -S a dramatic entertainment formerly popular in England

MASQUER *n* pl. -S masker

MASS *v* -ED, -ING, -ES to assemble in a mass (a body of coherent matter)

MASSA *n* pl. -S master

MASSACRE *v* -CRED, -CRING, -CRES to kill indiscriminately

MASSAGE *v* -SAGED, -SAGING, -SAGES to manipulate parts of the body for remedial or hygienic purposes

MASSAGER *n* pl. -S one that massages

MASSCULT *n* pl. -S culture as popularized by the mass media

MASSE *n* pl. -S a type of shot in billiards

MASSEDLY *adv* in a massed manner

MASSETER *n* pl. -S a muscle that raises the lower jaw

MASSEUR *n* pl. -S a man who massages

MASSEUSE *n* pl. -S a woman who massages

MASSICOT *n* pl. -S a yellow pigment

MASSIER comparative of massy

MASSIEST superlative of massy

MASSIF *n* pl. -S a principal mountain mass

MASSIVE *adj* of considerable size

MASSLESS *adj* having no mass

MASSY *adj* MASSIER, MASSIEST massive

MAST *v* -ED, -ING, -S to provide with a mast (a long pole on a ship that supports the sails and rigging)

MASTABA *n* pl. -S an ancient Egyptian tomb

MASTABAH *n* pl. -S mastaba

MASTER *v* -ED, -ING, -S to become skilled in

MASTERLY *adj* very skillful

MASTERY *n* pl. -TERIES superior knowledge or skill

MASTHEAD *v* -ED, -ING, -S to raise to the top of a mast

MASTIC *n* pl. -S an aromatic resin

MASTICHE *n* pl. -S mastic

MASTIFF *n* pl. -S a large, short-haired dog

MASTITIS *n* pl. -TITIDES inflammation of the breast **MASTITIC** *adj*

MASTIX *n* pl. -ES mastic

MASTLESS *adj* having no mast

MASTLIKE *adj* resembling a mast

MASTODON *n* pl. -S an extinct elephant-like mammal

MASTOID *n* pl. -S the rear portion of the temporal bone

MASURIUM *n* pl. -S a metallic element

MAT *v* MATTED, MATTING, MATS to pack down so as to form a dense mass

MATADOR *n* pl. -S the bullfighter who kills the bull in a bullfight

MATAMBALA a pl. of tambala

MATCH *v* -ED, -ING, -ES to set in competition or opposition

MATCHBOX *n* pl. -ES a small box

MATCHER *n* pl. -S one that matches

MATCHUP *n* pl. -S a setting of two players against each other

MATE *v* MATED, MATING, MATES to join as mates (partners in a union)

MATELESS *adj* having no mate

MATELOTE *n* pl. -S a fish stew

MATER *n* pl. -TERS or -TRES mother

MATERIAL *n* pl. -S the substance of which anything is or may be composed

MATERIEL *n* pl. -S the aggregate of equipment and supplies used by an organization

MATERNAL *adj* pertaining to a mother

MATESHIP *n* pl. -S the state of being a mate

MATEY *n* pl. -EYS a friend

MATH *n* pl. -S mathematics

MATILDA *n* pl. -S a hobo's bundle

MATIN *n* pl. -S a morning song, as of birds

MATINAL *adj* pertaining to the morning

MATINEE *n* pl. -S a daytime performance

MATINESS *n* pl. -ES friendliness

MATING *n* pl. -S the period during which a seasonal-breeding animal can mate

MATLESS *adj* having no mats (small floor coverings)

MATRASS *n* pl. -ES a long-necked glass vessel

MATRES a pl. of mater

MATRIX *n* pl. -TRICES or -TRIXES something within which something else originates or develops

MATRON *n* pl. -S a married woman of established social position **MATRONAL, MATRONLY** *adj*

MATSAH *n* pl. -S matzo

MATT *v* -ED, -ING, -S to matte

MATTE *v* MATTED, MATTING, MATTES to produce a dull finish on

MATTED past tense of mat, matt, and matte

MATTEDLY *adv* in a tangled manner

MATTER *v* -ED, -ING, -S to be of importance

MATTERY *adj* producing pus

MATTIN *n* pl. -S matin

MATTING *n* pl. -S a woven fabric used as a floor covering

MATTOCK *n* pl. -S a digging tool

MATTOID *n* pl. -S a mentally unbalanced person

MATTRASS *n* pl. -ES matrass

MATTRESS *n* pl. -ES a large pad filled with resilient material used on or as a bed

MATURATE *v* -RATED, -RATING, -RATES to mature

MATURE *adj* -TURER, -TUREST fully developed **MATURELY** *adv*

MATURE *v* -TURED, -TURING, -TURES to make or become mature

MATURITY *n* pl. -TIES the state of being mature

MATZA *n* pl. -S matzo

MATZAH *n* pl. -S matzo

MATZO *n* pl. -ZOS, -ZOT, or -ZOTH an unleavened bread

MATZOH *n* pl. -S matzo

MATZOON *n* pl. -S a food made from milk

MATZOT a pl. of matzo

MATZOTH a pl. of matzo

MAUD *n* pl. -S a Scottish gray and black plaid

MAUDLIN *adj* excessively emotional

MAUGER *prep* maugre

MAUGRE *prep* in spite of

MAUL *v* -ED, -ING, -S to injure by beating

MAULER *n* pl. -S one that mauls

MAUMET *n* pl. -S an idol

MAUMETRY *n* pl. -RIES idolatry

MAUN   v must — MAUN is the only form of this verb; it cannot be conjugated

MAUND   n pl. -S an Asian unit of weight

MAUNDER   v -ED, -ING, -S to talk incoherently

MAUNDY   n pl. -DIES the religious ceremony of washing the feet of the poor

MAUSOLEA   n/pl large, stately tombs

MAUT   n pl. -S malt

MAUVE   n pl. -S a purple color

MAVEN   n pl. -S mavin

MAVERICK   n pl. -S an unbranded range animal

MAVIE   n pl. -S mavis

MAVIN   n pl. -S an expert

MAVIS   n pl. -VISES a songbird

MAW   v MAWED, MAWN, MAWING, MAWS to mow

MAWKISH   adj offensively sentimental

MAX   n pl. -ES maximum

MAXI   n pl. -S a long skirt or coat

MAXICOAT   n pl. -S a long coat

MAXILLA   n pl. -LAE or -LAS the upper jaw or jawbone

MAXIM   n pl. -S a brief statement of a general truth or principle

MAXIMA   a pl. of maximum

MAXIMAL   n pl. -S an element of a mathematical set that is followed by no other

MAXIMIN   n pl. -S the maximum of a set of minima

MAXIMISE   v -MISED, -MISING, -MISES to maximize

MAXIMITE   n pl. -S a powerful explosive

MAXIMIZE   v -MIZED, -MIZING, -MIZES to make as great as possible

MAXIMUM   n pl. -MUMS or -MA the greatest possible amount, quantity, or degree

MAXIXE   n pl. -S a Brazilian dance

MAXWELL   n pl. -S a unit of magnetic flux

MAY   v present 2d person sing. MAY, MAYEST, or MAYST, past tense MIGHT — used as an auxiliary to express permission

MAY   v -ED, -ING, -S to gather flowers in the spring

MAYA   n pl. -S the power to produce illusions, in Hindu philosophy **MAYAN** adj

MAYAPPLE   n pl. -S a perennial herb

MAYBE   n pl. -S an uncertainty

MAYBUSH   n pl. -ES a flowering shrub

MAYDAY   n pl. -DAYS a radio distress call

MAYEST   a present 2d person sing. of may

MAYFLY   n pl. -FLIES a winged insect

MAYHAP   adv maybe

MAYHEM   n pl. -S the offense of willfully maiming a person

MAYING   n pl. -S the gathering of spring flowers

MAYO   n pl. -YOS mayonnaise

MAYOR   n pl. -S the chief executive official of a city or borough **MAYORAL** adj

MAYORESS   n pl. -ES a female mayor

MAYPOLE   n pl. -S a decorated pole used in a spring celebration

MAYPOP   n pl. -S a flowering vine

MAYST   a present 2d person sing. of may

MAYVIN   n pl. -S mavin

MAYWEED   n pl. -S a malodorous weed

MAZAEDIA   n/pl spore-producing organs of certain lichens

MAZARD   n pl. -S the head or face

MAZE   v MAZED, MAZING, MAZES to bewilder **MAZEDLY** adv

MAZELIKE   adj mazy

MAZER   n pl. -S a large drinking bowl

MAZIER   comparative of mazy

MAZIEST   superlative of mazy

MAZILY   adv in a mazy manner

MAZINESS   n pl. -ES the quality of being mazy

MAZING   present participle of maze

MAZOURKA   n pl. -S mazurka

MAZUMA   n pl. -S money

MAZURKA   n pl. -S a Polish dance

MAZY   adj MAZIER, MAZIEST full of confusing turns and passages

MAZZARD   n pl. -S a wild cherry

MBIRA   n pl. -S an African musical instrument

ME   pron the objective case of the pronoun I

MEAD   n pl. -S an alcoholic beverage

MEADOW   n pl. -S a tract of grassland **MEADOWY** adj

MEAGER   adj deficient in quantity or quality **MEAGERLY** adv

MEAGRE   adj meager **MEAGRELY** adv

MEAL   n pl. -S the food served and eaten in one sitting

MEALIE   n pl. -S an ear of corn

MEALIER   comparative of mealy

MEALIEST superlative of mealy

MEALLESS adj lacking a meal

MEALTIME n pl. -S the usual time for a meal

MEALWORM n pl. -S the destructive larva of certain beetles

MEALY adj MEALIER, MEALIEST soft, dry, and friable

MEALYBUG n pl. -S a destructive insect

MEAN v MEANT, MEANING, MEANS to intend

MEAN adj MEANER, MEANEST inferior in grade, quality, or character

MEANDER v -ED, -ING, -S to wander

MEANER n pl. -S one that means

MEANIE n pl. -S a nasty person

MEANIES pl. of meany

MEANING n pl. -S something that one intends to convey by language

MEANLY adv in a mean manner

MEANNESS n pl. -ES the state of being mean

MEANT past tense of mean

MEANTIME n pl. -S the intervening time

MEANY n pl. MEANIES meanie

MEASLE n pl. -S a tapeworm larva **MEASLED** adj

MEASLY adj -SLIER, -SLIEST meager

MEASURE v -SURED, -SURING, -SURES to ascertain the dimensions, quantity, or capacity of

MEASURER n pl. -S one that measures

MEAT n pl. -S animal flesh used as food **MEATED** adj

MEATAL adj pertaining to a meatus

MEATBALL n pl. -S a small ball of chopped meat

MEATHEAD n pl. -S a dolt

MEATIER comparative of meaty

MEATIEST superlative of meaty

MEATILY adv in a meaty manner

MEATLESS adj having no meat

MEATLOAF n pl. -LOAVES a baked loaf of ground meat

MEATMAN n pl. -MEN a vendor of meat

MEATUS n pl. -ES a natural body passage

MEATY adj MEATIER, MEATIEST full of meat

MECCA n pl. -S a place visited by many people

MECHANIC n pl. -S a person who works with machines

MECONIUM n pl. -S the first fecal excretion of a newborn child

MED adj medical

MEDAKA n pl. -S a Japanese fish

MEDAL v -ALED, -ALING, -ALS or -ALLED, -ALLING, -ALS to honor with a medal (a commemorative piece of metal)

MEDALIST n pl. -S a person to whom a medal has been awarded

MEDALLIC adj of or pertaining to a medal

MEDALLING a present participle of medal

MEDDLE v -DLED, -DLING, -DLES to interest oneself in what is not one's concern

MEDDLER n pl. -S one that meddles

MEDEVAC v -VACKED, -VACKING, -VACS to evacuate the wounded from a battlefield by helicopter

MEDFLY n pl. -FLIES a Mediterranean fruit fly

MEDIA n pl. -DIAE the middle layer of a blood or lymph vessel

MEDIA n pl. -S a channel of communication

MEDIACY n pl. -CIES the act of mediating

MEDIAD adv toward the middle of a body or part

MEDIATE pl. of media

MEDIAL n pl. -S a sound, syllable, or letter in the middle of a word

MEDIALLY adv in a central manner

MEDIAN n pl. -S a central part

MEDIANLY adv medially

MEDIANT n pl. -S a type of musical tone

MEDIATE v -ATED, -ATING, -ATES to act between disputing parties in order to bring about a settlement

MEDIATOR n pl. -S one that mediates

MEDIC n pl. -S one engaged in medical work

MEDICAID n pl. -S a type of governmental health program

MEDICAL n pl. -S a physical examination

MEDICARE n pl. -S a type of governmental health program

MEDICATE v -CATED, -CATING, -CATES to treat with medicine

MEDICINE v -CINED, -CINING, -CINES to administer medicine (a substance used in the treatment of disease) to

MEDICK *n* pl. -S a flowering plant

MEDICO *n* pl. -COS a doctor or medical student

MEDIEVAL *n* pl. -S a person belonging to the Middle Ages

MEDII pl. of medius

MEDINA *n* pl. -S the native quarter of a North African city

MEDIOCRE *adj* neither good nor bad

MEDITATE *v* -TATED, -TATING, -TATES to ponder

MEDIUM *n* pl. -DIA or -DIUMS a surrounding environment in which something functions and thrives

MEDIUS *n* pl. -DII the middle finger

MEDLAR *n* pl. -S a Eurasian tree

MEDLEY *n* pl. -LEYS a mixture

MEDULLA *n* pl. -LAS or -LAE the central tissue in the stems of certain plants **MEDULLAR** *adj*

MEDUSA *n* pl. -SAE or -SAS a jellyfish **MEDUSAL** *adj*

MEDUSAN *n* pl. -S medusa

MEDUSOID *n* pl. -S medusa

MEED *n* pl. -S a deserved reward

MEEK *adj* MEEKER, MEEKEST lacking in spirit and courage **MEEKLY** *adv*

MEEKNESS *n* pl. -ES the quality of being meek

MEERKAT *n* pl. -S an African mongoose

MEET *v* MET, MEETING, MEETS to come into the company or presence of

MEETER *n* pl. -S one that meets

MEETING *n* pl. -S an assembly for a common purpose

MEETLY *adv* suitably

MEETNESS *n* pl. -ES suitability

MEGABAR *n* pl. -S a unit of pressure

MEGABIT *n* pl. -S a unit of computer information

MEGABUCK *n* pl. -S one million dollars

MEGABYTE *n* pl. -S 1,048,576 bytes

MEGACITY *n* pl. -CITIES a very large city

MEGADEAL *n* pl. -S a business deal involving a lot of money

MEGADOSE *n* pl. -S an abnormally large dose

MEGADYNE *n* pl. -S a unit of force

MEGAHIT *n* pl. -S something extremely successful

MEGALITH *n* pl. -S a huge stone used in prehistoric monuments

MEGALOPS *n* pl. -LOPSES a larval stage of most crabs

MEGAPOD *n* pl. -S megapode

MEGAPODE *n* pl. -S a large-footed bird

MEGASS *n* pl. -ES a bagasse

MEGASSE *n* pl. -S megass

MEGASTAR *n* pl. -S an extremely successful performer

MEGATON *n* pl. -S a unit of explosive force

MEGAVOLT *n* pl. -S a unit of electromotive force

MEGAWATT *n* pl. -S a unit of power

MEGILLAH *n* pl. -S a long, involved story

MEGILP *n* pl. -S a substance with which pigments are mixed in painting

MEGILPH *n* pl. -S megilp

MEGOHM *n* pl. -S a unit of electrical resistance

MEGRIM *n* pl. -S a migraine

MEIKLE *adj* large

MEINIE *n* pl. -S meiny

MEINY *n* pl. -NIES a retinue

MEIOSIS *n* pl. -OSES a type of cell division **MEIOTIC** *adj*

MEL *n* pl. -S honey

MELAMED *n* pl. -LAMDIM a teacher in a Jewish school

MELAMINE *n* pl. -S a chemical compound

MELANGE *n* pl. -S a mixture

MELANIAN *adj* pertaining to dark pigmentation

MELANIC *n* pl. -S one who is affected with melanism

MELANIN *n* pl. -S a dark pigment

MELANISM *n* pl. -S abnormally dark pigmentation of the skin

MELANIST *n* pl. -S a melanic

MELANITE *n* pl. -S a black variety of garnet

MELANIZE *v* -NIZED, -NIZING, -NIZES to make dark

MELANOID *n* pl. -S a dark pigment

MELANOMA *n* pl. -MAS or -MATA a darkly pigmented tumor

MELANOUS *adj* having dark skin and hair

MELD *v* -ED, -ING, -S to blend

MELDER *n* pl. -S the amount of grain ground at one time

MELEE *n* pl. -S a confused struggle

MELIC *adj* pertaining to song

MELILITE *n* pl. -S a mineral group

MELILOT *n* pl. -S a flowering plant

MELINITE *n* pl. -S a powerful explosive

MELISMA *n* pl. -MAS or -MATA melodic embellishment

MELL *v* -ED, -ING, -S to mix

MELLIFIC *adj* producing honey

MELLOW *adj* -LOWER, -LOWEST soft and full-flavored from ripeness **MELLOWLY** *adv*

MELLOW *v* -ED, -ING, -S to make or become mellow

MELODEON *n* pl. -S a musical instrument

MELODIA *n* pl. -S a type of organ stop

MELODIC *adj* pertaining to melody

MELODICA *n* pl. -S a harmonica with a small keyboard at one end

MELODIES pl. of melody

MELODISE *v* -DISED, -DISING, -DISES to melodize

MELODIST *n* pl. -S a composer of melodies

MELODIZE *v* -DIZED, -DIZING, -DIZES to compose a melody

MELODY *n* pl. -DIES an agreeable succession of musical sounds

MELOID *n* pl. -S a type of beetle

MELON *n* pl. -S any of various gourds

MELT *v* -ED, -ING, -S to change from a solid to a liquid state by heat **MELTABLE** *adj*

MELTAGE *n* pl. -S the process of melting

MELTDOWN *n* pl. -S the melting of the core of a nuclear reactor

MELTER *n* pl. -S one that melts

MELTON *n* pl. -S a heavy woolen fabric

MEM *n* pl. -S a Hebrew letter

MEMBER *n* pl. -S a distinct part of a whole **MEMBERED** *adj*

MEMBRANE *n* pl. -S a thin, pliable layer of tissue

MEMENTO *n* pl. -TOS or -TOES something that serves as a reminder of the past

MEMO *n* pl. MEMOS a note designating something to be remembered

MEMOIR *n* pl. -S a biography

MEMORIAL *n* pl. -S something that serves as a remembrance of a person or event

MEMORISE *v* -ISED, -ISING, -ISES memorize

MEMORIZE *v* -RIZED, -RIZING, -RIZES to commit to memory

MEMORY *n* pl. -RIES the mental faculty of retaining and recalling past experience

MEMSAHIB *n* pl. -S a European woman living in colonial India

MEN pl. of man

MENACE *v* -ACED, -ACING, -ACES to theaten

MENACER *n* pl. -S one that menaces

MENAD *n* pl. -S maenad

MENAGE *n* pl. -S a household

MENARCHE *n* pl. -S the first occurrence of menstruation

MENAZON *n* pl. -S an insecticide

MEND *v* -ED, -ING, -S to repair **MENDABLE** *adj*

MENDER *n* pl. -S one that mends

MENDIGO *n* pl. -GOS a freshwater fish

MENDING *n* pl. -S an accumulation of articles to be mended

MENFOLK *n/pl* the men of a family or community

MENFOLKS *n/pl* menfolk

MENHADEN *n* pl. -S a marine fish

MENHIR *n* pl. -S a prehistoric monument

MENIAL *n* pl. -S a domestic servant

MENIALLY *adv* in a servile manner

MENINX *n* pl. -NINGES any of the membranes enclosing the brain and spinal cord

MENISCUS *n* pl. -CI or -CUSES a crescent-shaped body **MENISCAL** *adj*

MENO *adv* less — used as a musical direction

MENOLOGY *n* pl. -GIES an ecclesiastical calendar

MENORAH *n* pl. -S a candleholder used in Jewish worship

MENSA *n* pl. -SAS or -SAE the grinding surface of a tooth

MENSAL *adj* pertaining to or used at the table

MENSCH *n* pl. MENSCHES or MENSCHEN an admirable person

MENSE *v* MENSED, MENSING, MENSES to do honor to

MENSEFUL *adj* proper

MENSTRUA *n/pl* solvents

MENSURAL *adj* pertaining to measure

MENSWEAR *n* pl. -S clothing for men

MENTA pl. of mentum

MENTAL *adj* pertaining to the mind **MENTALLY** *adv*

MENTHENE *n* pl. -S a liquid hydrocarbon

MENTHOL *n* pl. -S an alcohol

MENTION *v* -ED, -ING, -S to refer to in a casual manner

MENTOR *v* -ED, -ING, -S to serve as a friend and teacher to

MENTUM *n* pl. -TA the chin

MENU *n* pl. -S a list of the dishes available in a restaurant

MEOU *v* -ED, -ING, -S meow

MEOW *v* -ED, -ING, -S to make the crying sound of a cat

MEPHITIS *n* pl. -TISES an offensive odor **MEPHITIC** *adj*

MERCAPTO *adj* containing a particular chemical group

MERCER *n* pl. -S a dealer in textiles

MERCERY *n* pl. -CERIES a mercer's shop

MERCHANT *v* -ED, -ING, -S to buy and sell goods for profit

MERCIES pl. of mercy

MERCIFUL *adj* full of mercy

MERCURY *n* pl. -RIES a metallic element **MERCURIC** *adj*

MERCY *n* pl. -CIES compassion shown to an offender or enemy

MERE *n* pl. -S a pond or lake

MERE *adj* MERER, MEREST being nothing more than **MERELY** *adv*

MERENGUE *n* pl. -S a ballroom dance

MERGE *v* MERGED, MERGING, MERGES to combine

MERGENCE *n* pl. -S the act of merging

MERGER *n* pl. -S the union of two or more businesses into a single enterprise

MERGING present participle of merge

MERIDIAN *n* pl. -S a circle around the earth passing through both poles

MERINGUE *n* pl. -S a topping for pastries

MERINO *n* pl. -NOS a fine wool

MERISIS *n* pl. MERISES growth

MERISTEM *n* pl. -S formative plant tissue

MERISTIC *adj* made up of segments

MERIT *v* -ED, -ING, -S to earn

MERK *n* pl. -S a former coin of Scotland

MERL *n* pl. -S merle

MERLE *n* pl. -S a blackbird

MERLIN *n* pl. -S a European falcon

MERLON *n* pl. -S the solid part of an indented parapet

MERLOT *n* pl. -S a dry red wine

MERMAID *n* pl. -S a legendary marine creature

MERMAN *n* pl. -MEN a legendary marine creature

MEROPIA *n* pl. -S partial blindness **MEROPIC** *adj*

MERRY *adj* -RIER, -RIEST cheerful **MERRILY** *adv*

MESA *n* pl. -S a land formation having a flat top and steep sides

MESALLY *adv* medially

MESARCH *adj* originating in a mesic habitat

MESCAL *n* pl. -S a cactus

MESDAMES pl. of madame

MESEEMS *v* past tense MESEEMED present 3d person sing. MESEEMETH it seems to me — MESEEMS is an impersonal verb and is used only in the 3d person sing.

MESH *v* -ED, -ING, -ES to entangle

MESHIER comparative of meshy

MESHIEST superlative of meshy

MESHUGA *adj* crazy

MESHUGAH *adj* meshuga

MESHUGGA *adj* meshuga

MESHUGGE *adj* meshuga

MESHWORK *n* pl. -S a network

MESHY *adj* MESHIER, MESHIEST netty

MESIAL *adj* situated in the middle **MESIALLY** *adv*

MESIAN *adj* mesial

MESIC *adj* characterized by a medium supply of moisture

MESMERIC *adj* pertaining to hypnotism

MESNALTY *n* pl. -TIES a type of feudal estate

MESNE *n* pl. -S a feudal lord holding land from a superior

MESOCARP *n* pl. -S the middle layer of a pericarp

MESODERM *n* pl. -S the middle germ layer of an embryo

MESOGLEA *n* pl. -S a gelatinous material in sponges

MESOMERE *n* pl. -S an embryonic segment

MESON *n* pl. -S a subatomic particle **MESONIC** *adj*

MESOPHYL *n* pl. -S the soft tissue of a leaf

MESOSOME *n* pl. -S a specialized cellular part

MESOTRON *n* pl. -S a meson

MESQUIT *n* pl. -S mesquite

MESQUITE *n* pl. -S a spiny tree or shrub

MESS   v -ED, -ING, -ES to make dirty or untidy

MESSAGE   v -SAGED, -SAGING, -SAGES to send as a message (an oral, written, or signaled communication)

MESSAN   n pl. -S a lapdog

MESSIAH   n pl. -S an expected liberator

MESSIER   comparative of messy

MESSIEST   superlative of messy

MESSIEURS   pl. of monsieur

MESSILY   adv in a messy manner

MESSMAN   n pl. -MEN a serviceman who works in a dining facility

MESSMATE   n pl. -S a person with whom one eats regularly

MESSUAGE   n pl. -S a dwelling house with its adjacent buildings and land

MESSY   adj MESSIER, MESSIEST dirty or untidy

MESTEE   n pl. -S mustee

MESTESO   n pl. -SOS or -SOES mestizo

MESTINO   n pl. -NOS or -NOES mestizo

MESTIZA   n pl. -S a female mestizo

MESTIZO   n pl. -ZOS or -ZOES a person of mixed ancestry

MET   past tense of meet

META   adj pertaining to positions in a benzene ring separated by one carbon atom

METAGE   n pl. -S an official measurement of weight or contents

METAL   v -ALED, -ALING, -ALS or -ALLED, -ALLING, -ALS to cover with metal (any of various ductile, fusible, and lustrous substances)

METALISE   v -ISED, -ISING, -ISES to metalize

METALIST   n pl. -S one who works with metals

METALIZE   v -IZED, -IZING, -IZES to treat with metal

METALLED   a past tense of metal

METALLIC   n pl. -S a fabric or yarn made of or coated with metal

METALLING   a present participle of metal

METAMER   n pl. -S a type of chemical compound

METAMERE   n pl. -S a somite

METAPHOR   n pl. -S a type of figure of speech

METATE   n pl. -S a stone used for grinding grains

METAZOAN   n pl. -S any of a major division of multicellular animals **METAZOAL, METAZOIC** adj

METAZOON   n pl. -ZOA a metazoan

METE   v METED, METING, METES to distribute by measure

METEOR   n pl. -S a small celestial body that enters the earth's atmosphere **METEORIC** adj

METEPA   n pl. -S a chemical compound

METER   v -ED, -ING, -S to measure by mechanical means

METERAGE   n pl. -S the process of metering

METH   n pl. -S a stimulant drug

METHADON   n pl. -S a narcotic drug

METHANE   n pl. -S a flammable gas

METHANOL   n pl. -S a toxic alcohol

METHINKS   v past tense METHOUGHT it seems to me — METHINKS is an impersonal verb and is used only in the 3d person sing.

METHOD   n pl. -S a means of procedure

METHODIC   adj systematic

METHOUGHT   past tense of methinks

METHOXY   adj containing a certain chemical group

METHOXYL   adj methoxy

METHYL   n pl. -S a univalent radical **METHYLIC** adj

METHYLAL   n pl. -S a flammable liquid

METICAL   n pl. -CAIS or -CALS a monetary unit of Mozambique

METIER   n pl. -S a vocation

METING   present participle of mete

METIS   n pl. METIS a person of mixed ancestry

METISSE   n pl. -S a female metis

METONYM   n pl. -S a word used in metonymy

METONYMY   n pl. -MIES a type of figure of speech

METOPE   n pl. -PES or -PAE a space between two triglyphs

METOPIC   adj pertaining to the forehead

METOPON   n pl. -S a narcotic drug

METRE   v -TRED, -TRING, -TRES to meter

METRIC   n pl. -S a standard of measurement

METRICAL   adj pertaining to or composed in a system of arranged and measured rhythm

METRIFY   v -FIED, -FYING, -FIES to compose in metrical form

METRING   present participle of metre
METRIST   n pl. -S one who metrifies
METRITIS   n pl. -TISES inflammation of
             the uterus
METRO   n pl. -ROS a subway
METTLE   n pl. -S quality of character
             METTLED adj
METUMP   n pl. -S a tumpline
MEUNIERE   adj cooked in browned butter
MEW   v -ED, -ING, -S to confine
MEWL   v -ED, -ING, -S to whimper
MEWLER   n pl. -S one that mewls
MEZCAL   n pl. -S mescal
MEZE   n pl. -S a Greek or Middle
             Eastern appetizer
MEZEREON   n pl. -S a flowering shrub
MEZEREUM   n pl. -S mezereon
MEZQUIT   n pl. -S mesquite
MEZQUITE   n pl. -S mesquite
MEZUZA   n pl. -S mezuzah
MEZUZAH   n pl. -ZAHS, -ZOT, or -ZOTH
             a Judaic scroll
MEZZO   n pl. -ZOS a female voice of a
             full, deep quality
MHO   n pl. MHOS a unit of electrical
             conductance
MI   n pl. -S the third tone of the
             diatonic musical scale
MIAOU   v -ED, -ING, -S to meow
MIAOW   v -ED, -ING, -S to meow
MIASM   n pl. -S miasma
MIASMA   n pl. -MAS or -MATA a
             noxious vapor MIASMAL,
             MIASMIC adj
MIAUL   v -ED, -ING, -S to meow
MIB   n pl. -S a type of playing
             marble
MICA   n pl. -S a mineral
MICAWBER   n pl. -S a person who remains
             hopeful despite adversity
MICE   pl. of mouse
MICELL   n pl. -S micelle
MICELLA   n pl. -LAE micelle
MICELLE   n pl. -S a coherent strand or
             structure in a fiber MICELLAR
             adj
MICHE   v MICHED, MICHING,
             MICHES to skulk
MICKEY   n pl. -EYS a drugged drink
MICKLE   adj -LER, -LEST large
MICKLE   n pl. -S a large amount
MICRA   a pl. of micron
MICRIFY   v -FIED, -FYING, -FIES to
             make small
MICRO   adj very small

MICROBAR   n pl. -S a unit of atmospheric
             pressure
MICROBE   n pl. -S a minute life form
             MICROBIC adj
MICROBUS   n pl. -BUSES or -BUSSES a
             small bus
MICRODOT   n pl. -S a copy of printed
             matter reduced to the size of a
             dot
MICROHM   n pl. -S a unit of electrical
             resistance
MICROLUX   n pl. -LUXES or -LUCES a
             unit of illumination
MICROMHO   n pl. -S a unit of electrical
             conductance
MICRON   n pl. -CRONS or -CRA a unit
             of length
MICRURGY   n pl. -GIES the use of minute
             tools under high magnification
MID   n pl. -S the middle
MIDAIR   n pl. -S a region in the middle
             of the air
MIDBRAIN   n pl. -S the middle region of
             the brain
MIDCULT   n pl. -S middle-class culture
MIDDAY   n pl. -DAYS the middle of the
             day
MIDDEN   n pl. -S a dunghill
MIDDIES   pl. of middy
MIDDLE   v -DLED, -DLING, -DLES to
             place in the middle (the area or
             point equidistant from
             extremes or limits)
MIDDLER   n pl. -S a student in an
             intermediate grade
MIDDLING   n pl. -S a cut of pork
MIDDY   n pl. -DIES a loosely fitting
             blouse
MIDFIELD   n pl. -S the middle portion of a
             playing field
MIDGE   n pl. -S a small winged insect
MIDGET   n pl. -S a very small person
MIDGUT   n pl. -S the middle part of the
             embryonic digestive tract
MIDI   n pl. -S a skirt or coat that
             extends to the middle of the
             calf
MIDIRON   n pl. -S a golf club
MIDLAND   n pl. -S the middle part of a
             country
MIDLEG   n pl. -S the middle of the leg
MIDLIFE   n pl. -LIVES middle age
MIDLINE   n pl. -S a median line
MIDMONTH   n pl. -S the middle of the
             month

MIDMOST *n* pl. -S a part exactly in the middle

MIDNIGHT *n* pl. -S the middle of the night

MIDNOON *n* pl. -S midday

MIDPOINT *n* pl. -S a point at the middle

MIDRANGE *n* pl. -S the middle of a range

MIDRASH *n* pl. -RASHIM or -RASHOTH an early Jewish interpretation of a biblical text

MIDRIB *n* pl. -S the central vein of a leaf

MIDRIFF *n* pl. -S the middle part of the body

MIDSHIP *adj* pertaining to the middle of a ship

MIDSHIPS *adv* toward the middle of a ship

MIDSIZE *adj* of intermediate size

MIDSIZED *adj* midsize

MIDSOLE *n* pl. -S a middle layer of the sole of a shoe

MIDSPACE *n* pl. -S the middle of a space

MIDST *n* pl. -S the middle

MIDSTORY *n* pl. -RIES the middle of a story

MIDTERM *n* pl. -S an examination given in the middle of an academic semester

MIDTOWN *n* pl. -S the central part of a city

MIDWATCH *n* pl. -ES a watch on a ship between midnight and 4 A.M.

MIDWAY *n* pl. -WAYS an avenue at a fair or carnival for concessions and amusements

MIDWEEK *n* pl. -S the middle of the week

MIDWIFE *v* -WIFED, -WIFING, -WIFES or -WIVED, -WIVING, -WIVES to assist a woman in childbirth

MIDYEAR *n* pl. -S the middle of the year

MIEN *n* pl. -S demeanor

MIFF *v* -ED, -ING, -S to annoy

MIFFY *adj* MIFFIER, MIFFIEST easily annoyed

MIG *n* pl. -S a type of playing marble

MIGG *n* pl. -S mig

MIGGLE *n* pl. -S a mig

MIGHT *n* pl. -S strength

MIGHTY *adj* MIGHTIER, MIGHTIEST strong **MIGHTILY** *adv*

MIGNON *n* pl. -S a cut of beef

MIGNONNE *adj* daintily small

MIGRAINE *n* pl. -S a severe headache

MIGRANT *n* pl. -S one that migrates

MIGRATE *v* -GRATED, -GRATING, -GRATES to move from one region to another

MIGRATOR *n* pl. -S a migrant

MIHRAB *n* pl. -S a niche in a mosque

MIJNHEER *n* pl. -S mynheer

MIKADO *n* pl. -DOS an emperor of Japan

MIKE *v* MIKED, MIKING, MIKES to amplify or record by use of a microphone

MIKRON *n* pl. -KRONS or -KRA micron

MIKVAH *n* pl. -VAHS or -VOTH a place for ritual bathing by Orthodox Jews

MIKVEH *n* pl. -S mikvah

MIL *n* pl. -S a unit of length

MILADI *n* pl. -S milady

MILADY *n* pl. -DIES an English gentlewoman

MILAGE *n* pl. -S mileage

MILCH *adj* giving milk

MILCHIG *adj* made of or derived from milk

MILD *adj* MILDER, MILDEST not harsh or rough

MILDEN *v* -ED, -ING, -S to make or become mild

MILDEW *v* -ED, -ING, -S to affect with mildew (a whitish growth produced by fungi)

MILDEWY *adj* affected with or resembling mildew

MILDLY *adj* in a mild manner

MILDNESS *n* pl. -ES the quality of being mild

MILE *n* pl. -S a unit of distance

MILEAGE *n* pl. -S total distance expressed in miles

MILEPOST *n* pl. -S a post indicating distance in miles

MILER *n* pl. -S one that runs a mile race

MILESIMO *n* pl. -MOS a former monetary unit of Chile

MILFOIL *n* pl. -S a perennial herb

MILIA pl. of milium

MILIARIA *n* pl. -S a skin disease

MILIARY *adj* made up of many small projections

MILIEU *n* pl. -LIEUS or -LIEUX environment

MILITANT *n* pl. -S a person who is aggressively engaged in a cause

MILITARY *n* pl. -TARIES armed forces

MILITATE	v -TATED, -TATING, -TATES to have influence or effect	**MILLINE**	n pl. -S a unit of advertising space
MILITIA	n pl. -S a citizen army	**MILLINER**	n pl. -S one who makes or sells women's hats
MILIUM	n pl. -IA a small, whitish lump in the skin		
MILK	v -ED, -ING, -S to draw milk (a whitish, nutritious liquid) from the udder of	**MILLING**	n pl. -S a corrugated edge on a coin
		MILLIOHM	n pl. -S a unit of electrical resistance
MILKER	n pl. -S one that milks	**MILLION**	n pl. -S a number
MILKFISH	n pl. -ES a marine food fish	**MILLIPED**	n pl. -S a multi-legged arthropod
MILKIER	comparative of milky		
MILKIEST	superlative of milky	**MILLIREM**	n pl. -S a quantity of ionizing radiation
MILKILY	adv in a milky manner		
MILKMAID	n pl. -S a woman who milks cows	**MILLPOND**	n pl. -S a pond for supplying water to run a mill wheel (a type of waterwheel)
MILKMAN	n pl. -MEN a man who sells or delivers milk		
		MILLRACE	n pl. -S the current of water that drives a mill wheel
MILKSHED	n pl. -S a region supplying milk to a particular community	**MILLRUN**	n pl. -S a millrace
MILKSOP	n pl. -S an effeminate man	**MILLWORK**	n pl. -S woodwork produced by milling
MILKWEED	n pl. -S a plant that secretes a milky juice		
		MILNEB	n pl. -S a fungicide
MILKWOOD	n pl. -S a tropical tree	**MILO**	n pl. -LOS a cereal grass
MILKWORT	n pl. -S a flowering plant	**MILORD**	n pl. -S an English gentleman
MILKY	adj MILKIER, MILKIEST resembling or suggestive of milk	**MILPA**	n pl. -S a field that is cleared from a jungle for farming purposes
MILL	v -ED, -ING, -S to grind by mechanical means **MILLABLE** adj	**MILREIS**	n pl. MILREIS a former monetary unit of Portugal
MILLAGE	n pl. -S a type of monetary rate	**MILT**	v -ED, -ING, -S to impregnate with milt (fish sperm)
MILLCAKE	n pl. -S a residue from pressed linseed	**MILTER**	n pl. -S a male fish at breeding time
MILLDAM	n pl. -S a dam built to form a millpond	**MILTY**	adj MILTIER, MILTIEST full of milt
MILLE	n pl. -S a thousand	**MIM**	adj primly demure
MILLEPED	n pl. -S milliped	**MIMBAR**	n pl. -S a pulpit in a mosque
MILLER	n pl. -S one that mills	**MIME**	v MIMED, MIMING, MIMES to mimic
MILLET	n pl. -S a cereal grass		
MILLIARD	n pl. -S a billion	**MIMEO**	v -ED, -ING, -S to make copies of by use of a mimeograph
MILLIARE	n pl. -S a unit of area		
MILLIARY	n pl. -ARIES an ancient Roman milestone	**MIMER**	n pl. -S one that mimes
		MIMESIS	n pl. -SISES mimicry **MIMETIC** adj
MILLIBAR	n pl. -S a unit of atmospheric pressure		
		MIMETITE	n pl. -S an ore of lead
MILLIEME	n pl. -S unit of value of Egypt and Sudan	**MIMIC**	v -ICKED, -ICKING, -ICS to imitate closely
MILLIER	n pl. -S a unit of weight	**MIMICAL**	adj of the nature of mimicry
MILLIGAL	n pl. -S a unit of acceleration	**MIMICKER**	n pl. -S one that mimics
MILLILUX	n pl. -LUXES or -LUCES a unit of illumination	**MIMICKING**	present participle of mimic
		MIMICRY	n pl. -RIES an instance of mimicking
MILLIME	n pl. -S a coin of Tunisia		
MILLIMHO	n pl. -MHOS a unit of electrical conductance	**MIMING**	present participle of mime
		MIMOSA	n pl. -S a tropical plant

MINA *n* pl. -NAS or -NAE an ancient unit of weight and value

MINABLE *adj* capable of being mined

MINACITY *n* pl. -TIES the state of being threatening

MINAE a pl. of mina

MINARET *n* pl. -S a slender tower attached to a mosque

MINATORY *adj* threatening

MINCE *v* MINCED, MINCING, MINCES to cut into very small pieces

MINCER *n* pl. -S one that minces

MINCY *adj* MINCIER, MINCIEST affectedly dainty

MIND *v* -ED, -ING, -S to heed

MINDER *n* pl. -S one that minds

MINDFUL *adj* heedful

MINDLESS *adj* lacking intelligence

MINDSET *n* pl. -S a fixed mental attitude

MINE *v* MINED, MINING, MINES to dig into for valuable materials

MINEABLE *adj* minable

MINER *n* pl. -S one that mines

MINERAL *n* pl. -S a naturally occurring inorganic substance having a characteristic set of physical properties

MINGIER comparative of mingy

MINGIEST superlative of mingy

MINGLE *v* -GLED, -GLING, -GLES to mix together

MINGLER *n* pl. -S one that mingles

MINGY *adj* -GIER, -GIEST mean and stingy

MINI *n* pl. -S something distinctively smaller than others of its kind

MINIBIKE *n* pl. -S a small motorcycle

MINIBUS *n* pl. -BUSES or -BUSSES a small bus

MINICAB *n* pl. -S a small taxicab

MINICAMP *n* pl. -S a short training camp for football players

MINICAR *n* pl. -S a small automobile

MINIFY *v* -FIED, -FYING, -FIES to make small or smaller

MINIKIN *n* pl. -S a small or dainty creature

MINILAB *n* pl. -S a retail outlet offering rapid on-site film development

MINIM *n* pl. -S a unit of liquid measure

MINIMA a pl. of minimum

MINIMAL *n* pl. -S an element of a mathematical set that precedes all others

MINIMAX *n* pl. -ES the minimum of a set of maxima

MINIMILL *n* pl. -S a small-scale steel mill

MINIMISE *v* -MISED, -MISING, -MISES to minimize

MINIMIZE *v* -MIZED, -MIZING, -MIZES to make as small as possible

MINIMUM *n* pl. -MUMS or -MA the least possible amount, quantity, or degree

MINING *n* pl. -S the process or business of working mines (excavations in the earth)

MINION *n* pl. -S a servile follower

MINIPARK *n* pl. -S a small city park

MINISH *v* -ED, -ING, -ES to diminish

MINISKI *n* pl. -S a short ski

MINISTER *v* -ED, -ING, -S to give aid or service

MINISTRY *n* pl. -TRIES the act of ministering

MINIUM *n* pl. -S a red pigment

MINIVAN *n* pl. -S a small van

MINIVER *n* pl. -S a white fur

MINK *n* pl. -S a carnivorous mammal

MINKE *n* pl. -S a small whale

MINNOW *n* pl. -S a small fish

MINNY *n* pl. -NIES minnow

MINOR *v* -ED, -ING, -S to pursue a specific subordinate course of study

MINORCA *n* pl. -S any of a breed of large domestic fowls

MINORITY *n* pl. -TIES the smaller number or part

MINSTER *n* pl. -S a large or important church

MINSTREL *n* pl. -S a medieval musician

MINT *v* -ED, -ING, -S to produce by stamping metal, as coins

MINTAGE *n* pl. -S the act of minting

MINTER *n* pl. -S one that mints

MINTY *adj* MINTIER, MINTIEST having the flavor mint (an aromatic herb)

MINUEND *n* pl. -S a number from which another is to be subtracted

MINUET *n* pl. -S a slow, stately dance

MINUS *n* pl. -ES a negative quantity

MINUTE *v* -UTED, -UTING, -UTES to make a brief note of

MINUTE *adj* -NUTER, -NUTEST very small **MINUTELY** *adv*

MINUTIA *n* pl. -TIAE a small detail **MINUTIAL** *adj*

MINUTING present participle of minute

MINX   *n* pl. -ES a pert girl **MINXISH** *adj*

MINYAN   *n* pl. -YANS or -YANIM the minimum number required to be present for the conduct of a Jewish service

MIOSIS   *n* pl. -OSES excessive contraction of the pupil of the eye

MIOTIC   *n* pl. -S an agent that causes miosis

MIQUELET   *n* pl. -S a former Spanish or French soldier

MIR   *n* pl. MIRS or MIRI a Russian peasant commune

MIRACLE   *n* pl. -S an event ascribed to supernatural or divine origin

MIRADOR   *n* pl. -S an architectural feature designed to afford an extensive view

MIRAGE   *n* pl. -S a type of optical illusion

MIRE   *v* MIRED, MIRING, MIRES to cause to stick in swampy ground

MIREX   *n* pl. -ES an insecticide

MIRI   a pl. of mir

MIRIER   comparative of miry

MIRIEST   superlative of miry

MIRINESS   *n* pl. -ES the state of being miry

MIRING   present participle of mire

MIRK   *adj* MIRKER, MIRKEST murk

MIRK   *n* pl. -S murk

MIRKY   *adj* MIRKIER, MIRKIEST murky **MIRKILY** *adv*

MIRLITON   *n* pl. -S a chayote

MIRROR   *v* -ED, -ING, -S to reflect an image of

MIRTH   *n* pl. -S spirited gaiety **MIRTHFUL** *adj*

MIRY   *adj* MIRIER, MIRIEST swampy

MIRZA   *n* pl. -S a Persian title of honor

MISACT   *v* -ED, -ING, -S to act badly

MISADAPT   *v* -ED, -ING, -S to adapt wrongly

MISADD   *v* -ED, -ING, -S to add incorrectly

MISAGENT   *n* pl. -S a bad agent

MISAIM   *v* -ED, -ING, -S to aim badly

MISALIGN   *v* -ED, -ING, -S to align improperly

MISALLY   *v* -LIED, -LYING, -LIES to ally badly

MISALTER   *v* -ED, -ING, -S to alter wrongly

MISANDRY   *n* pl. -DRIES hatred of men

MISAPPLY   *v* -PLIED, -PLYING, -PLIES to apply wrongly

MISASSAY   *v* -ED, -ING, -S to attempt unsuccessfully

MISATE   past tense of miseat

MISATONE   *v* -ATONED, -ATONING, -ATONES to atone wrongly

MISAVER   *v* -AVERRED, -AVERRING, -AVERS to speak erroneously

MISAWARD   *v* -ED, -ING, -S to award wrongly

MISBEGIN   *v* -GAN, -GUN, -GINNING, -GINS to begin wrongly

MISBEGOT   *adj* born out of wedlock

MISBIAS   *v* -ASED, -ASING, -ASES or -ASSED, -ASSING, -ASSES to bias wrongly

MISBILL   *v* -ED, -ING, -S to bill wrongly

MISBIND   *v* -BOUND, -BINDING, -BINDS to bind imperfectly

MISBRAND   *v* -ED, -ING, -S to brand incorrectly

MISBUILD   *v* -BUILT, -BUILDING, -BUILDS to build imperfectly

MISCALL   *v* -ED, -ING, -S to call by a wrong name

MISCARRY   *v* -RIED, -RYING, -RIES to be unsuccessful

MISCAST   *v* -CAST, -CASTING, -CASTS to cast in an unsuitable role

MISCHIEF   *n* pl. -S action that causes irritation, harm, or trouble

MISCIBLE   *adj* capable of being mixed

MISCITE   *v* -CITED, -CITING, -CITES to misquote

MISCLAIM   *v* -ED, -ING, -S to claim wrongfully

MISCLASS   *v* -ED, -ING, -ES to put in the wrong class

MISCODE   *v* -CODED, -CODING, -CODES to code wrongly

MISCOIN   *v* -ED, -ING, -S to coin improperly

MISCOLOR   *v* -ED, -ING, -S to color incorrectly

MISCOOK   *v* -ED, -ING, -S to cook badly

MISCOPY   *v* -COPIED, -COPYING, -COPIES to copy incorrectly

MISCOUNT   *v* -ED, -ING, -S to count incorrectly

MISCUE   *v* -CUED, -CUING, -CUES to make a faulty stroke in billiards

MISCUT v -CUT, -CUTTING, -CUTS to cut incorrectly

MISDATE v -DATED, -DATING, -DATES to date incorrectly

MISDEAL v -DEALT, -DEALING, -DEALS to deal cards incorrectly

MISDEED n pl. -S an evil act

MISDEEM v -ED, -ING, -S to judge unfavorably

MISDIAL v -DIALED, -DIALING, -DIALS or -DIALLED, -DIALLING, -DIALS to dial wrongly

MISDO v -DID, -DONE, -DOING, -DOES to do wrongly

MISDOER n pl. -S one that misdoes

MISDOING n pl. -S an instance of doing wrong

MISDONE past participle of misdo

MISDOUBT v -ED, -ING, -S to doubt

MISDRAW v -DREW, -DRAWN, -DRAWING, -DRAWS to draw incorrectly

MISDRIVE v -DROVE, -DRIVEN, -DRIVING, -DRIVES to drive wrongly or improperly

MISE n pl. -S an agreement or settlement

MISEASE n pl. -S discomfort

MISEAT v -ATE, -EATEN, -EATING, -EATS to eat improperly

MISEDIT v -ED, -ING, -S to edit incorrectly

MISENROL v -ROLLED, -ROLLING, -ROLS to misenroll

MISENROLL v -ED, -ING, -S to enroll improperly

MISENTER v -ED, -ING, -S to enter erroneously

MISENTRY n pl. -TRIES an erroneous entry

MISER n pl. -S one who hoards money greedily

MISERERE n pl. -S a part of a church seat

MISERLY adj characteristic of a miser

MISERY n pl. -ERIES a state of great suffering

MISEVENT n pl. -S a mishap

MISFAITH n pl. -S lack of faith; disbelief

MISFIELD v -ED, -ING, -S to field badly

MISFILE v -FILED, -FILING, -FILES to file in the wrong place

MISFIRE v -FIRED, -FIRING, -FIRES to fail to fire

MISFIT v -FITTED, -FITTING, -FITS to fit badly

MISFOCUS v -CUSED, -CUSING, -CUSES or -CUSSED, -CUSSING, -CUSSES to focus badly

MISFORM v -ED, -ING, -S to misshape

MISFRAME v -FRAMED, -FRAMING, -FRAMES to frame badly

MISGAUGE v -GAUGED, -GAUGING, -GAUGES to gauge wrongly or inaccurately

MISGIVE v -GAVE, -GIVEN, -GIVING, -GIVES to make doubtful or fearful

MISGRADE v -GRADED, -GRADING, -GRADES to grade incorrectly

MISGRAFT v -ED, -ING, -S to graft wrongly

MISGROW v -GREW, -GROWN, -GROWING, -GROWS to grow abnormally

MISGUESS v -ED, -ING, -ES to guess wrongly

MISGUIDE v -GUIDED, -GUIDING, -GUIDES to guide wrongly

MISHAP n pl. -S an unfortunate accident

MISHEAR v -HEARD, -HEARING, -HEARS to hear incorrectly

MISHIT v -HIT, -HITTING, -HITS to hit poorly

MISHMASH n pl. -ES a confused mixture

MISHMOSH n pl. -ES mishmash

MISINFER v -FERRED, -FERRING, -FERS to infer wrongly

MISINTER v -TERRED, -TERRING, -TERS to inter improperly

MISJOIN v -ED, -ING, -S to join improperly

MISJUDGE v -JUDGED, -JUDGING, -JUDGES to judge wrongly

MISKAL n pl. -S an Oriental unit of weight

MISKEEP v -KEPT, -KEEPING, -KEEPS to keep wrongly

MISKICK v -ED, -ING, -S to kick badly

MISKNOW v -KNEW, -KNOWN, -KNOWING, -KNOWS to fail to understand or recognize

MISLABEL v -BELED, -BELING, -BELS or -BELLED, -BELLING, -BELS to label incorrectly or falsely

MISLABOR v -ED, -ING, -S to labor badly

MISLAIN past participle of mislie

MISLAY v -LAID, -LAYING, -LAYS to put in a forgotten place

MISLAYER n pl. -S one that mislays

MISLEAD v -LED, -LEADING, -LEADS to lead astray

MISLEARN v -LEARNED or -LEARNT, -LEARNING, -LEARNS to learn wrongly

MISLIE v -LAY, -LAIN, -LYING, -LIES to lie in a wrong position

MISLIGHT v -LIGHTED or -LIT, -LIGHTING, -LIGHTS to lead astray by its light

MISLIKE v -LIKED, -LIKING, -LIKES to dislike

MISLIKER n pl. -S one that mislikes

MISLIT a past tense of mislight

MISLIVE v -LIVED, -LIVING, -LIVES to live a bad life

MISLODGE v -LODGED, -LODGING, -LODGES to lodge in a wrong place

MISLYING present participle of mislie

MISMAKE v -MADE, -MAKING, -MAKES to make incorrectly

MISMARK v -ED, -ING, -S to mark wrongly

MISMATCH v -ED, -ING, -ES to match badly

MISMATE v -MATED, -MATING, -MATES to mate unsuitably

MISMEET v -MET, -MEETING, -MEETS to meet under unfortunate circumstances

MISMOVE v -MOVED, -MOVING, -MOVES to move wrongly

MISNAME v -NAMED, -NAMING, -NAMES to call by a wrong name

MISNOMER n pl. -S a name wrongly used

MISO n pl. -SOS a type of food paste

MISOGAMY n pl. -MIES a hatred of marriage

MISOGYNY n pl. -NIES a hatred of women

MISOLOGY n pl. -GIES a hatred of debate or reasoning

MISORDER v -ED, -ING, -S to order incorrectly

MISPAGE v -PAGED, -PAGING, -PAGES to page incorrectly

MISPAINT v -ED, -ING, -S to paint wrongly

MISPARSE v -PARSED, -PARSING, -PARSES to parse incorrectly

MISPART v -ED, -ING, -S to part badly

MISPATCH v -ED, -ING, -ES to patch badly

MISPEN v -PENNED, -PENNING, -PENS to write incorrectly

MISPLACE v -PLACED, -PLACING, -PLACES to put in a wrong place

MISPLAN v -PLANNED, -PLANNING, -PLANS to plan badly

MISPLANT v -ED, -ING, -S to plant wrongly

MISPLAY v -ED, -ING, -S to make a bad play in a game

MISPLEAD v -PLEADED or -PLED, -PLEADING, -PLEADS to plead wrongly or falsely

MISPOINT v -ED, -ING, -S to point improperly

MISPOISE v -POISED, -POISING, -POISES to poise incorrectly

MISPRICE v PRICED, -PRICING, PRICES to price incorrectly

MISPRINT v -ED, -ING, -S to print incorrectly

MISPRIZE v -PRIZED, -PRIZING, -PRIZES to despise

MISQUOTE v -QUOTED, -QUOTING, -QUOTES to quote incorrectly

MISRAISE v -RAISED, -RAISING, -RAISES to raise wrongly

MISRATE v -RATED, -RATING, -RATES to rate incorrectly

MISREAD v -READ, -READING, -READS to read incorrectly

MISREFER v -FERRED, -FERRING, -FERS to refer incorrectly

MISRELY v -LIED, -LYING, -LIES to rely wrongly

MISROUTE v -ROUTED, -ROUTING, -ROUTES to route incorrectly

MISRULE v -RULED, -RULING, -RULES to rule unwisely or unjustly

MISS v -ED, -ING, -ES to fail to make contact with

MISSABLE adj able to be missed

MISSAL n pl. -S a prayer book

MISSAY v -SAID, -SAYING, -SAYS to say incorrectly

MISSEAT v -ED, -ING, -S to seat wrongly

MISSEL n pl. -S a European thrush

MISSEND v -SENT, -SENDING, -SENDS to send incorrectly

MISSENSE n pl. -S a form of genetic mutation

MISSET v -SET, -SETTING, -SETS to set incorrectly

MISSHAPE   v -SHAPED, -SHAPEN, -SHAPING, -SHAPES to shape badly

MISSHOD   adj improperly shod

MISSIES   pl. of missy

MISSILE   n pl. -S an object or weapon that is thrown or projected

MISSILRY   n pl. -RIES the science of designing and operating guided missiles

MISSION   v -ED, -ING, -S to send to perform a specific task

MISSIS   n pl. -SISES a wife

MISSIVE   n pl. -S a written communication

MISSORT   v -ED, -ING, -S to sort badly or improperly

MISSOUND   v -ED, -ING, -S to sound wrongly

MISSOUT   n pl. -S a losing throw of dice

MISSPACE   v -SPACED, -SPACING, -SPACES to space incorrectly

MISSPEAK   v -SPOKE, -SPOKEN, -SPEAKING, -SPEAKS to speak incorrectly

MISSPELL   v -SPELLED or -SPELT, -SPELLING, -SPELLS to spell incorrectly

MISSPEND   v -SPENT, -SPENDING, -SPENDS to spend wrongly

MISSPOKE   past tense of misspeak

MISSPOKEN   past participle of misspeak

MISSTART   v -ED, -ING, -S to start off badly

MISSTATE   v -STATED, -STATING, -STATES to state wrongly

MISSTEER   v -ED, -ING, -S to steer wrongly

MISSTEP   n pl. -S a false step

MISSTOP   v -STOPPED, -STOPPING, -STOPS to stop wrongly

MISSTYLE   v -STYLED, -STYLING, -STYLES to style or call wrongly

MISSUIT   v -ED, -ING, -S to suit badly

MISSUS   n pl. -ES missis

MISSY   n pl. MISSIES a young girl

MIST   v -ED, -ING, -S to become blurry

MISTAKE   v -TOOK or -TEUK, -TAKEN, -TAKING, -TAKES to interpret wrongly

MISTAKER   n pl. -S one that mistakes

MISTBOW   n pl. -S a fogbow

MISTEACH   v -TAUGHT, -TEACHING, -TEACHES to teach wrongly or badly

MISTEND   v -ED, -ING, -S to tend to improperly

MISTER   n pl. -S sir

MISTERM   v -ED, -ING, -S to call by a wrong name

MISTEUK   a past tense of mistake

MISTHINK   v -THOUGHT, -THINKING, -THINKS to think wrongly

MISTHROW   v -THREW, -THROWN, -THROWING, -THROWS to throw errantly

MISTIER   comparative of misty

MISTIEST   superlative of misty

MISTILY   adv in a misty manner

MISTIME   v -TIMED, -TIMING, -TIMES to time wrongly

MISTITLE   v -TLED, -TLING, -TLES to call by a wrong title

MISTOOK   a past tense of mistake

MISTOUCH   v -ED, -ING, -ES to touch improperly

MISTRACE   v -TRACED, -TRACING, -TRACES to trace wrongly

MISTRAIN   v -ED, -ING, -S to train improperly

MISTRAL   n pl. -S a cold, dry wind

MISTREAT   v -ED, -ING, -S to treat badly

MISTRESS   n pl. -ES a woman in a position of authority

MISTRIAL   n pl. -S a trial made invalid because of some error in procedure

MISTRUST   v -ED, -ING, -S to distrust

MISTRUTH   n pl. -S a lie

MISTRYST   v -ED, -ING, -S to fail to keep an appointment with

MISTUNE   v -TUNED, -TUNING, -TUNES to tune incorrectly

MISTUTOR   v -ED, -ING, -S to instruct or bring up badly

MISTY   adj MISTIER, MISTIEST blurry

MISTYPE   v -TYPED, -TYPING, -TYPES to type incorrectly

MISUNION   n pl. -S a bad union

MISUSAGE   n pl. -S incorrect use

MISUSE   v -USED, -USING, -USES to use incorrectly

MISUSER   n pl. -S one that misuses

MISVALUE   v -UED, -UING, -UES to value incorrectly

MISWORD   v -ED, -ING, -S to word wrongly

MISWRITE	*v* -WROTE or -WRIT, -WRITTEN, -WRITING, -WRITES to write incorrectly
MISYOKE	*v* -YOKED, -YOKING, -YOKES to yoke improperly
MITE	*n* pl. -S a small arachnid
MITER	*v* -ED, -ING, -S to raise to the rank of a bishop
MITERER	*n* pl. -S one that miters
MITHER	*n* pl. -S mother
MITICIDE	*n* pl. -S a substance used to kill mites
MITIER	comparative of mity
MITIEST	superlative of mity
MITIGATE	*v* -GATED, -GATING, -GATES to make less severe
MITIS	*n* pl. -TISES a type of wrought iron
MITOGEN	*n* pl. -S a substance that induces mitosis
MITOSIS	*n* pl. -TOSES a type of cell division **MITOTIC** *adj*
MITRAL	*adj* pertaining to a valve of the heart
MITRE	*v* -TRED, -TRING, -TRES to miter
MITSVAH	*n* pl. -VAHS or -VOTH mitzvah
MITT	*n* pl. -S a type of baseball glove
MITTEN	*n* pl. -S a type of covering for the hand
MITTIMUS	*n* pl. -ES a warrant committing a person to prison
MITY	*adj* MITIER, MITIEST infested with mites
MITZVAH	*n* pl. -VAHS or -VOTH a commandment of Jewish law
MIX	*v* MIXED or MIXT, MIXING, MIXES to put together into one mass **MIXABLE, MIXIBLE** *adj*
MIXER	*n* pl. -S one that mixes
MIXOLOGY	*n* pl. -GIES the art of making mixed drinks
MIXT	a past tense of mix
MIXTURE	*n* pl. -S something produced by mixing
MIXUP	*n* pl. -S a state of confusion
MIZEN	*n* pl. -S mizzen
MIZZEN	*n* pl. -S a type of sail
MIZZLE	*v* -ZLED, -ZLING, -ZLES to rain in fine droplets
MIZZLY	*adj* characterized by a fine rain
MM	*interj* — used to express assent or satisfaction
MNEMONIC	*n* pl. -S a device to assist the memory
MO	*n* pl. MOS a moment
MOA	*n* pl. -S an extinct flightless bird
MOAN	*v* -ED, -ING, -S to utter a low, mournful sound
MOANER	*n* pl. -S one that moans
MOANFUL	*adj* moaning
MOAT	*v* -ED, -ING, -S to surround with a moat (a water-filled trench)
MOATLIKE	*adj* suggestive of a moat
MOB	*v* MOBBED, MOBBING, MOBS to crowd about
MOBBER	*n* pl. -S one that mobs
MOBBISH	*adj* characteristic of a mob (a disorderly crowd of people)
MOBCAP	*n* pl. -S a woman's cap
MOBILE	*n* pl. -S a form of sculpture
MOBILISE	*v* -LISED, -LISING, -LISES to mobilize
MOBILITY	*n* pl. -TIES the ability to move
MOBILIZE	*v* -LIZED, -LIZING, -LIZES to put into movement
MOBLED	*adj* wrapped in or as if in a hood
MOBOCRAT	*n* pl. -S a supporter of mob rule
MOBSTER	*n* pl. -S a gangster
MOC	*n* pl. -S a moccasin
MOCCASIN	*n* pl. -S a type of shoe
MOCHA	*n* pl. -S a choice, pungent coffee
MOCHILA	*n* pl. -S a leather covering for a saddle
MOCK	*v* -ED, -ING, -S to ridicule **MOCKABLE** *adj*
MOCKER	*n* pl. -S one that mocks
MOCKERY	*n* pl. -ERIES the act of mocking
MOCKUP	*n* pl. -S a full-sized model
MOD	*n* pl. -S one who wears boldly stylish clothes
MODAL	*adj* pertaining to a mode **MODALLY** *adv*
MODALITY	*n* pl. -TIES the state of being modal
MODE	*n* pl. -S a method of doing or acting
MODEL	*v* -ELED, -ELING, -ELS or -ELLED, -ELLING, -ELS to plan or form after a pattern
MODELER	*n* pl. -S one that models
MODELING	*n* pl. -S the treatment of volume in sculpture

MODELIST *n* pl. -S one who makes models

MODELLED a past tense of model

MODELLER *n* pl. -S modeler

MODELLING a present participle of model

MODEM *n* pl. -S a device for converting signals from one form to another

MODERATE *v* -ATED, -ATING, -ATES to make less extreme

MODERATO *n* pl. -TOS a musical passage played at a medium tempo

MODERN *adj* -ERNER, -ERNEST pertaining to present or recent time MODERNLY *adv*

MODERN *n* pl. -S a person of modern times or views

MODERNE *adj* pretentiously modern

MODEST *adj* -ESTER, -ESTEST having a moderate regard for oneself MODESTLY *adv*

MODESTY *n* pl. -TIES the quality of being modest

MODI pl. of modus

MODICUM *n* pl. -CA or -CUMS a small amount

MODIFIER *n* pl. -S one that modifies

MODIFY *v* -FIED, -FYING, -FIES to change in form or character

MODIOLUS *n* pl. -LI a bony shaft of the inner ear

MODISH *adj* stylish MODISHLY *adv*

MODISTE *n* pl. -S a dealer in stylish women's clothing

MODULAR *adj* pertaining to a module

MODULATE *v* -LATED, -LATING, -LATES to adjust to a certain proportion

MODULE *n* pl. -S a standard of measurement

MODULO *adv* with respect to a modulus

MODULUS *n* pl. -LI a number that produces the same remainder when divided into each of two numbers

MODUS *n* pl. -DI a mode

MOFETTE *n* pl. -S a noxious emanation from a fissure in the earth

MOFFETTE *n* pl. -S mofette

MOG *v* MOGGED, MOGGING, MOGS to move away

MOGGIE *n* pl. -S moggy

MOGGY *n* pl. -GIES a cat

MOGUL *n* pl. -S an important person

MOHAIR *n* pl. -S the long, silky hair of the Angora goat

MOHEL *n* pl. -HALIM, -HELM or -HELS a person who performs Jewish ritual circumcisions

MOHUR *n* pl. -S a former gold coin of India

MOIDORE *n* pl. -S a former gold coin of Portugal

MOIETY *n* pl. -ETIES a half

MOIL *v* -ED, -ING, -S to work hard

MOILER *n* pl. -S one that moils

MOIRA *n* pl. -RAI fate or destiny, in ancient Greek religion

MOIRE *n* pl. -S a fabric having a wavy pattern

MOIST *adj* MOISTER, MOISTEST slightly wet

MOISTEN *v* -ED, -ING, -S to make or become moist

MOISTFUL *adj* moist

MOISTLY *adv* in a moist manner

MOISTURE *n* pl. -S condensed or diffused liquid

MOJARRA *n* pl. -S a marine fish

MOJO *n* pl. -JOS or -JOES a magic charm

MOKE *n* pl. -S a donkey

MOL *n* pl. -S mole

MOLA *n* pl. -S a marine fish

MOLAL *adj* pertaining to a mole

MOLALITY *n* pl. -TIES the number of moles of solute per liter of solvent

MOLAR *n* pl. -S a grinding tooth

MOLARITY *n* pl. -TIES the number of moles of solute per liter of solution

MOLASSES *n* pl. -LASSESES a thick syrup

MOLD *v* -ED, -ING, -S to work into a particular shape MOLDABLE *adj*

MOLDER *v* -ED, -ING, -S to turn to dust by natural decay

MOLDIER comparative of moldy

MOLDIEST superlative of moldy

MOLDING *n* pl. -S a long, narrow strip used to decorate a surface

MOLDWARP *n* pl. -S a burrowing mammal

MOLDY *adj* MOLDIER, MOLDIEST musty

MOLE *n* pl. -S the quantity of a compound that has a weight equal to the compound's molecular weight

MOLECULE *n* pl. -S the smallest physical unit of an element

MOLEHILL   *n* pl. -S a small mound of earth
MOLESKIN   *n* pl. -S a cotton fabric
MOLEST   *v* -ED, -ING, -S to disturb or annoy
MOLESTER   *n* pl. -S one that molests
MOLIES   pl. of moly
MOLINE   *adj* having arms forked and curved at the ends — used of a heraldic cross
MOLL   *n* pl. -S a gangster's girlfriend
MOLLAH   *n* pl. -S mullah
MOLLIE   *n* pl. -S a tropical fish
MOLLIES   pl. of molly
MOLLIFY   *v* -FIED, -FYING, -FIES to soothe
MOLLUSC   *n* pl. -S mollusk
MOLLUSK   *n* pl. -S any of a phylum of soft-bodied invertebrates
MOLLY   *n* pl. -LIES mollie
MOLOCH   *n* pl. -S a spiny lizard
MOLT   *v* -ED, -ING, -S to cast off an outer covering
MOLTEN   *adj* made liquid by heat **MOLTENLY** *adv*
MOLTER   *n* pl. -S one that molts
MOLTO   *adv* very — used in musical directions
MOLY   *n* pl. -LIES a wild garlic
MOLYBDIC   *adj* pertaining to a certain metallic element
MOM   *n* pl. -S mother
MOME   *n* pl. -S a fool
MOMENT   *n* pl. -S a brief period of time
MOMENTA   a pl. of momentum
MOMENTLY   *adv* from moment to moment
MOMENTO   *n* pl. -TOS or -TOES memento
MOMENTUM   *n* pl. -TA or -TUMS force of movement
MOMI   a pl. of momus
MOMISM   *n* pl. -S an excessive dependence on mothers
MOMMA   *n* pl. -S mother
MOMMY   *n* pl. -MIES mother
MOMSER   *n* pl. -S a bastard
MOMUS   *n* pl. -MUSES or -MI a carping person
MOMZER   *n* pl. -S momser
MON   *n* pl. MEN man
MONACHAL   *adj* pertaining to monks
MONACID   *n* pl. -S monoacid
MONAD   *n* pl. -S a single-celled organism **MONADAL, MONADIC** *adj*
MONADES   pl. of monas

MONADISM   *n* pl. -S a philosophical doctrine
MONANDRY   *n* pl. -DRIES the condition of having one husband at a time
MONARCH   *n* pl. -S an absolute ruler
MONARCHY   *n* pl. -CHIES rule by a monarch
MONARDA   *n* pl. -S an aromatic herb
MONAS   *n* pl. MONADES a monad
MONASTIC   *n* pl. -S a monk
MONAURAL   *adj* pertaining to sound transmission, recording, or reproduction involving a single transmission path
MONAXIAL   *adj* having one axis
MONAXON   *n* pl. -S a straight spicule in sponges
MONAZITE   *n* pl. -S a mineral
MONDE   *n* pl. -S the world
MONDO   *n* pl. -DOS a rapid question and answer technique employed in Zen Buddhism
MONECIAN   *adj* having both male and female sex organs in the same individual
MONELLIN   *n* pl. -S a protein extracted from a West African red berry
MONERAN   *n* pl. -S a cellular organism that does not have a distinct nucleus
MONETARY   *adj* pertaining to money
MONETISE   *v* -TISED, -TISING, -TISES to monetize
MONETIZE   *v* -TIZED, -TIZING, -TIZES to coin into money
MONEY   *n* pl. MONEYS or MONIES an official medium of exchange and measure of value
MONEYBAG   *n* pl. -S a bag for holding money
MONEYED   *adj* having much money
MONEYER   *n* pl. -S one that coins money
MONEYMAN   *n* pl. -MEN a person who invests large sums of money
MONGEESE   a pl. of mongoose
MONGER   *v* -ED, -ING, -S to peddle
MONGO   *n* pl. -GOS mungo
MONGOE   *n* pl. -S mungo
MONGOL   *n* pl. -S a person affected with a form of mental deficiency
MONGOOSE   *n* pl. -GOOSES or -GEESE a carnivorous mammal
MONGREL   *n* pl. -S an animal or plant of mixed breed
MONGST   *prep* amongst
MONICKER   *n* pl. -S moniker

MONIE   adj many
MONIED   adj moneyed
MONIES   a pl. of money
MONIKER   n pl. -S a name
MONISH   v -ED, -ING, -ES to warn
MONISM   n pl. -S a philosophical theory
MONIST   n pl. -S an adherent of monism MONISTIC adj
MONITION   n pl. -S a warning
MONITIVE   adj giving warning
MONITOR   v -ED, -ING, -S to keep track of
MONITORY   n pl. -RIES a letter of warning
MONK   n pl. -S a man who is a member of a secluded religious order
MONKERY   n pl. -ERIES the mode of life of monks
MONKEY   v -ED, -ING, -S to mimic
MONKFISH   n pl. -ES a marine fish
MONKHOOD   n pl. -S the state of being a monk
MONKISH   adj pertaining to monks
MONO   n pl. MONOS an infectious disease
MONOACID   n pl. -S a type of acid
MONOCARP   n pl. -S a plant that yields fruit only once before dying
MONOCLE   n pl. -S an eyeglass for one eye MONOCLED adj
MONOCOT   n pl. -S a type of seed plant
MONOCRAT   n pl. -S an autocrat
MONOCYTE   n pl. -S a type of white blood cell
MONODIST   n pl. -S one who writes monodies
MONODY   n pl. -DIES an elegy performed by one person MONODIC adj
MONOECY   n pl. -CIES the condition of being monecian
MONOFIL   n pl. -S a single filament of synthetic fiber
MONOFUEL   n pl. -S a type of rocket propellant
MONOGAMY   n pl. -MIES marriage with one person at a time
MONOGENY   n pl. -NIES asexual reproduction
MONOGERM   adj being a fruit that produces a single plant
MONOGLOT   n pl. -S a person speaking or writing only one language

MONOGRAM   v -GRAMED, -GRAMING, -GRAMS or -GRAMMED, -GRAMMING, -GRAMS to mark with a design of one's initials
MONOGYNY   n pl. -NIES the condition of having one wife at a time
MONOHULL   n pl. -S a vessel with a single hull
MONOLITH   n pl. -S a large block of stone
MONOLOG   n pl. -S a lengthy speech by one person
MONOLOGY   n pl. -GIES the act of uttering a monolog
MONOMER   n pl. -S a type of chemical compound
MONOMIAL   n pl. -S an algebraic expression consisting of a single term
MONOPODE   n pl. -S a creature having one foot
MONOPODY   n pl. -DIES a measure consisting of a single metrical foot
MONOPOLE   n pl. -S a type of radio antenna
MONOPOLY   n pl. -LIES exclusive control of a commodity or service in a particular market
MONORAIL   n pl. -S a single rail serving as a track for a wheeled vehicle
MONOSOME   n pl. -S an unpaired chromosome
MONOSOMY   n pl. -MIES a condition of having one unpaired chromosome
MONOTINT   n pl. -S a painting done in different shades of one color
MONOTONE   n pl. -S a vocal utterance in one unvaried tone
MONOTONY   n pl. -NIES tedious sameness
MONOTYPE   n pl. -S the only representative of its group
MONOXIDE   n pl. -S a type of oxide
MONS   n pl. MONTES a protuberance of the body
MONSIEUR   n pl. MESSIEURS a French title of courtesy for a man
MONSOON   n pl. -S a seasonal wind
MONSTER   n pl. -S a strange or terrifying creature
MONSTERA   n pl. -S a tropical American plant
MONTAGE   v -TAGED, -TAGING, -TAGES to combine into a composite picture

MONTANE *n* pl. -S the lower vegetation belt of a mountain

MONTE *n* pl. -S a card game

MONTEITH *n* pl. -S a large punch bowl

MONTERO *n* pl. -ROS a type of cap

MONTES pl. of mons

MONTH *n* pl. -S a period of approximately 30 days

MONTHLY *n* pl. -LIES a publication issued once a month

MONUMENT *n* pl. -S a structure built as a memorial

MONURON *n* pl. -S an herbicide

MONY *adj* many

MOO *v* -ED, -ING, -S to make the deep, moaning sound of a cow

MOOCH *v* -ED, -ING, -ES to obtain without paying

MOOCHER *n* pl. -S one that mooches

MOOD *n* pl. -S a person's emotional state at a particular moment

MOODY *adj* MOODIER, MOODIEST given to changing moods
MOODILY *adv*

MOOL *n* pl. -S soft soil

MOOLA *n* pl. -S moolah

MOOLAH *n* pl. -S money

MOOLEY *n* pl. -EYS muley

MOON *v* -ED, -ING, -S to spend time idly

MOONBEAM *n* pl. -S a ray of light from the moon (the earth's natural satellite)

MOONBOW *n* pl. -S a rainbow formed by light from the moon

MOONCALF *n* pl. -CALVES a foolish person

MOONDUST *n* pl. -S dust on the moon

MOONEYE *n* pl. -S a freshwater fish

MOONFISH *n* pl. -ES a marine fish

MOONIER comparative of moony

MOONIEST superlative of moony

MOONILY *adv* in a moony manner

MOONISH *adj* fickle

MOONLESS *adj* lacking the light of the moon

MOONLET *n* pl. -S a small satellite

MOONLIKE *adj* resembling the moon

MOONLIT *adj* lighted by the moon

MOONPORT *n* pl. -S a facility for launching spacecraft to the moon

MOONRISE *n* pl. -S the rising of the moon above the horizon

MOONSAIL *n* pl. -S a light, square sail

MOONSEED *n* pl. -S a climbing plant

MOONSET *n* pl. -S the setting of the moon below the horizon

MOONSHOT *n* pl. -S the launching of a spacecraft to the moon

MOONWALK *n* pl. -S an instance of walking on the moon

MOONWARD *adv* toward the moon

MOONWORT *n* pl. -S a flowering plant

MOONY *adj* MOONIER, MOONIEST resembling the moon

MOOR *v* -ED, -ING, -S to secure a vessel by means of cables

MOORAGE *n* pl. -S the act of mooring

MOORCOCK *n* pl. -S the male moorfowl

MOORFOWL *n* pl. -S a game bird

MOORHEN *n* pl. -S the female moorfowl

MOORIER comparative of moory

MOORIEST superlative of moory

MOORING *n* pl. -S a place where a vessel may be moored

MOORISH *adj* marshy

MOORLAND *n* pl. -S a tract of marshy land

MOORWORT *n* pl. -S a marsh plant

MOORY *adj* MOORIER, MOORIEST marshy

MOOSE *n* pl. MOOSE a ruminant mammal

MOOT *v* -ED, -ING, -S to bring up for discussion

MOOTER *n* pl. -S one that moots

MOP *v* MOPPED, MOPPING, MOPS to wipe with a mop (an implement for cleaning floors)

MOPBOARD *n* pl. -S a board at the base of a wall

MOPE *v* MOPED, MOPING, MOPES to act in a dejected or gloomy manner

MOPED *n* pl. -S a type of motorbike

MOPER *n* pl. -S one that mopes

MOPERY *n* pl. -PERIES an act of dawdling

MOPEY *adj* MOPIER, MOPIEST dejected

MOPIER comparative of mopy

MOPIEST superlative of mopy

MOPING present participle of mope

MOPINGLY *adv* in a moping manner

MOPISH *adj* given to moping
MOPISHLY *adv*

MOPOKE *n* pl. -S an Australian bird

MOPPED past tense of mop

MOPPER *n* pl. -S one that mops

MOPPET *n* pl. -S a child

MOPPING present participle of mop

MOPY *adj* MOPIER, MOPIEST mopey

MOQUETTE *n* pl. -S a woolen fabric

MOR *n* pl. -S a forest humus

MORA *n* pl. -RAE or -RAS a unit of metrical time in prosody

MORAINE *n* pl. -S an accumulation of debris deposited by a glacier **MORAINAL, MORAINIC** *adj*

MORAL *adj* pertaining to principles of right and wrong **MORALLY** *adv*

MORALE *n* pl. -S the state of the spirits of an individual or group

MORALISE *v* -ISED, -ISING, -ISES to moralize

MORALISM *n* pl. -S the practice of moralizing

MORALIST *n* pl. -S a teacher of morality

MORALITY *n* pl. -TIES conformity to the rules of right conduct

MORALIZE *v* -IZED, -IZING, -IZES to explain in a moral sense

MORALS *n/pl* rules of conduct with respect to right and wrong

MORASS *n* pl. -ES a marsh **MORASSY** *adj*

MORATORY *adj* authorizing delay of payment

MORAY *n* pl. -RAYS a tropical eel

MORBID *adj* gruesome **MORBIDLY** *adv*

MORBIFIC *adj* causing disease

MORBILLI *n/pl* a virus disease

MORCEAU *n* pl. -CEAUX a short literary or musical composition

MORDANCY *n* pl. -CIES a sarcastic quality

MORDANT *v* -ED, -ING, -S to treat with a caustic substance

MORDENT *n* pl. -S a melodic embellishment

MORE *n* pl. -S a greater amount

MOREEN *n* pl. -S a heavy fabric

MOREL *n* pl. -S an edible mushroom

MORELLE *n* pl. -S a flowering plant

MORELLO *n* pl. -LOS a variety of sour cherry

MOREOVER *adv* in addition

MORESQUE *n* pl. -S an ancient decorative style

MORGAN *n* pl. -S a unit of distance between genes

MORGEN *n* pl. -S a Dutch unit of land area

MORGUE *n* pl. -S a place where dead bodies are kept for identification

MORIBUND *adj* being about to die

MORION *n* pl. -S a type of helmet

MORN *n* pl. -S morning

MORNING *n* pl. -S the early part of the day

MOROCCO *n* pl. -COS a soft leather

MORON *n* pl. -S a mentally deficient person **MORONIC** *adj*

MORONISM *n* pl. -S the condition of being a moron

MORONITY *n* pl. -TIES moronism

MOROSE *adj* sullen **MOROSELY** *adv*

MOROSITY *n* pl. -TIES the state of being morose

MORPH *n* pl. -S a type of phoneme

MORPHEME *n* pl. -S a linguistic unit

MORPHIA *n* pl. -S morphine

MORPHIC *adj* pertaining to form

MORPHIN *n* pl. -S morphine

MORPHINE *n* pl. -S a narcotic alkaloid

MORPHO *n* pl. -PHOS a tropical butterfly

MORRION *n* pl. -S morion

MORRIS *n* pl. -RISES an English folk dance

MORRO *n* pl. -ROS a rounded elevation

MORROW *n* pl. -S the next day

MORSE *adj* designating a code used in telegraphy

MORSEL *v* -SELED, -SELING, -SELS or -SELLED, -SELLING, -SELS to divide into small pieces

MORT *n* pl. -S a note sounded on a hunting horn to announce the killing of an animal

MORTAL *n* pl. -S a human being

MORTALLY *adv* fatally

MORTAR *v* -ED, -ING, -S to secure with mortar (a type of cement)

MORTARY *adj* containing or resembling mortar

MORTGAGE *v* -GAGED, -GAGING, -GAGES to pledge to a creditor as security

MORTICE *v* -TICED, -TICING, -TICES to mortise

MORTIFY *v* -FIED, -FYING, -FIES to humiliate

MORTISE *v* -TISED, -TISING, -TISES to join or fasten securely

MORTISER *n* pl. -S one that mortises

MORTMAIN *n* pl. -S perpetual ownership of land

MORTUARY *n* pl. -ARIES a place where dead bodies are kept until burial

MORULA   *n* pl. -LAE or -LAS an embryonic mass of cells **MORULAR** *adj*

MOSAIC   *v* -ICKED, -ICKING, -ICS to form into a mosaic (a type of inlaid surface decoration)

MOSASAUR   *n* pl. -S an extinct lizard

MOSCHATE   *adj* musky

MOSEY   *v* -ED, -ING, -S to saunter

MOSHAV   *n* pl. -SHAVIM a cooperative settlement of small farms in Israel

MOSK   *n* pl. -S mosque

MOSQUE   *n* pl. -S a Muslim house of worship

MOSQUITO   *n* pl. -TOES or -TOS a winged insect

MOSS   *v* -ED, -ING, -ES to cover with moss (a growth of small, leafy-stemmed plants)

MOSSBACK   *n* pl. -S a large, old fish

MOSSER   *n* pl. -S one that gathers or works with moss

MOSSIER   comparative of mossy

MOSSIEST   superlative of mossy

MOSSLIKE   *adj* resembling moss

MOSSO   *adv* rapidly — used as a musical direction

MOSSY   *adj* MOSSIER, MOSSIEST covered with moss

MOST   *n* pl. -S the greatest amount

MOSTE   past tense of mote

MOSTEST   *n* pl. -S most

MOSTLY   *adv* mainly

MOT   *n* pl. -S a witty saying

MOTE   *v* past tense MOSTE may

MOTE   *n* pl. -S a small particle

MOTEL   *n* pl. -S a roadside hotel

MOTET   *n* pl. -S a type of choral composition

MOTEY   *adj* full of motes

MOTH   *n* pl. -S a winged insect

MOTHBALL   *v* -ED, -ING, -S to put into storage

MOTHER   *v* -ED, -ING, -S to give birth to

MOTHERLY   *adj* maternal

MOTHERY   *adj* slimy

MOTHLIKE   *adj* resembling a moth

MOTHY   *adj* MOTHIER, MOTHIEST full of moths

MOTIF   *n* pl. -S a recurring thematic element in an artistic work **MOTIFIC** *adj*

MOTILE   *n* pl. -S one whose mental imagery consists chiefly of inner feelings of action

MOTILITY   *n* pl. -TIES the ability to move

MOTION   *v* -ED, -ING, -S to signal by a bodily movement

MOTIONAL   *adj* pertaining to movement

MOTIONER   *n* pl. -S one that motions

MOTIVATE   *v* -VATED, -VATING, -VATES to provide with an incentive

MOTIVE   *v* -TIVED, -TIVING, -TIVES to motivate

MOTIVIC   *adj* pertaining to a musical motif

MOTIVITY   *n* pl. -TIES the ability to move

MOTLEY   *adj* -LEYER, -LEYEST or -LIER, -LIEST composed of diverse elements

MOTLEY   *n* pl. -LEYS a garment of various colors

MOTMOT   *n* pl. -S a tropical bird

MOTOR   *v* -ED, -ING, -S to travel by automobile

MOTORBUS   *n* pl. -BUSES or -BUSSES a bus

MOTORCAR   *n* pl. -S an automobile

MOTORDOM   *n* pl. -S the motor vehicle industry

MOTORIC   *adj* pertaining to muscular movement

MOTORING   *n* pl. -S the recreation of traveling by automobile

MOTORISE   *v* -ISED, -ISING, -ISES to motorize

MOTORIST   *n* pl. -S one who travels by automobile

MOTORIZE   *v* -IZED, -IZING, -IZES to equip with motor vehicles

MOTORMAN   *n* pl. -MEN one who operates an electric streetcar or subway train

MOTORWAY   *n* pl. -WAYS a type of highway

MOTT   *n* pl. -S motte

MOTTE   *n* pl. -S a small growth of trees on a prairie

MOTTLE   *v* -TLED, -TLING, -TLES to mark with spots or streaks of different colors

MOTTLER   *n* pl. -S one that mottles

MOTTO   *n* pl. -TOES or -TOS a short expression of a guiding principle

MOUCH   *v* -ED, -ING, -ES to mooch

MOUCHOIR   *n* pl. -S a small handkerchief

MOUE   *n* pl. -S a pouting grimace

MOUFFLON   *n* pl. -S mouflon

MOUFLON   *n* pl. -S a wild sheep

MOUILLE *adj* pronounced with the front of the tongue against the palate

MOUJIK *n* pl. -S muzhik

MOULAGE *n* pl. -S the making of a cast or mold of a mark for use in a criminal investigation

MOULD *v* -ED, -ING, -S to mold

MOULDER *v* -ED, -ING, -S to molder

MOULDING *n* pl. -S molding

MOULDY *adj* MOULDIER, MOULDIEST moldy

MOULIN *n* pl. -S a vertical cavity in a glacier

MOULT *v* -ED, -ING, -S to molt

MOULTER *n* pl. -S molter

MOUND *v* -ED, -ING, -S to pile

MOUNT *v* -ED, -ING, -S to get up on

MOUNTAIN *n* pl. -S a large, natural elevation of the earth's surface

MOUNTER *n* pl. -S one that mounts

MOUNTING *n* pl. -S something that provides a backing or appropriate setting for something else

MOURN *v* -ED, -ING, -S to feel or express grief or sorrow

MOURNER *n* pl. -S one that mourns

MOURNFUL *adj* -FULLER, -FULLEST expressing grief or sorrow

MOURNING *n* pl. -S an outward sign of grief

MOUSE *n* pl. MICE a small rodent

MOUSE *v* MOUSED, MOUSING, MOUSES to catch mice

MOUSER *n* pl. -S an animal that catches mice

MOUSEY *adj* MOUSIER, MOUSIEST mousy

MOUSIER comparative of mousy

MOUSIEST superlative of mousy

MOUSILY *adv* in a mousy manner

MOUSING *n* pl. -S a wrapping around the shank end of a hook

MOUSSAKA *n* pl. -S a Middle Eastern dish of meat and eggplant

MOUSSE *v* MOUSSED, MOUSSING, MOUSSES to style with mousse (foamy preparation used in styling hair)

MOUSY *adj* MOUSIER, MOUSIEST resembling a mouse

MOUTH *v* -ED, -ING, -S to put into the mouth

MOUTHER *n* pl. -S a speaker

MOUTHFUL *n* pl. -S as much as the mouth can hold

MOUTHY *adj* MOUTHIER, MOUTHIEST very talkative **MOUTHILY** *adv*

MOUTON *n* pl. -S sheepskin processed to resemble seal or beaver

MOVABLE *n* pl. -S something that can be moved

MOVABLY *adv* so as to be capable of being moved

MOVE *v* MOVED, MOVING, MOVES to change from one position to another

MOVEABLE *n* pl. -S movable

MOVEABLY *adv* movably

MOVED past tense of move

MOVELESS *adj* incapable of movement

MOVEMENT *n* pl. -S the act of moving

MOVER *n* pl. -S one that moves

MOVIE *n* pl. -S a motion picture

MOVIEDOM *n* pl. -S filmdom

MOVIEOLA *n* pl. -S a device for viewing and editing film

MOVING present participle of move

MOVINGLY *adv* so as to affect the emotions

MOVIOLA *n* pl. -S movieola

MOW *v* MOWED, MOWN, MOWING, MOWS to cut down standing herbage

MOWER *n* pl. -S one that mows

MOWING *n* pl. -S the act of cutting down standing herbage

MOXA *n* pl. -S a Chinese plant

MOXIE *n* pl. -S spirit or courage

MOZETTA *n* pl. -TAS or -TE mozzetta

MOZO *n* pl. -ZOS a manual laborer

MOZZETTA *n* pl. -TAS or -TE a hooded cape worn by bishops

MRIDANGA *n* pl. -S a drum of India

MU *n* pl. -S a Greek letter

MUCH *n* pl. -ES a great amount

MUCHACHO *n* pl. -CHOS a young man

MUCHLY *adv* very much

MUCHNESS *n* pl. -ES the quality of being great

MUCID *adj* musty

MUCIDITY *n* pl. -TIES the state of being mucid

MUCILAGE *n* pl. -S an adhesive substance

MUCIN *n* pl. -S a protein secreted by the mucous membranes **MUCINOID, MUCINOUS** *adj*

MUCK *v* -ED, -ING, -S to fertilize with manure

MUCKER   *n* pl. -S a vulgar person

MUCKIER   comparative of mucky

MUCKIEST   superlative of mucky

MUCKILY   *adv* in a mucky manner

MUCKLE   *n* pl. -S a large amount

MUCKLUCK   *n* pl. -S mukluk

MUCKRAKE   *v* -RAKED, -RAKING, -RAKES to search for and expose corruption

MUCKWORM   *n* pl. -S a worm found in manure

MUCKY   *adj* MUCKIER, MUCKIEST filthy

MUCLUC   *n* pl. -S mukluk

MUCOID   *n* pl. -S a complex protein **MUCOIDAL** *adj*

MUCOR   *n* pl. -S a type of fungus

MUCOSA   *n* pl. -SAE or -SAS a mucous membrane **MUCOSAL** *adj*

MUCOSE   *adj* mucous

MUCOSITY   *n* pl. -TIES the state of being mucous

MUCOUS   *adj* secreting or containing mucus

MUCRO   *n* pl. -CRONES a sharp point at the end of certain plant and animal organs

MUCUS   *n* pl. -ES a viscid bodily fluid

MUD   *v* MUDDED, MUDDING, MUDS to cover with mud (soft, wet earth)

MUDCAP   *v* -CAPPED, -CAPPING, -CAPS to cover an explosive with mud before detonating

MUDCAT   *n* pl. -S a type of catfish

MUDDER   *n* pl. -S a racehorse that runs well on a muddy track

MUDDIED   past tense of muddy

MUDDIER   comparative of muddy

MUDDIES   present 3d person sing. of muddy

MUDDIEST   superlative of muddy

MUDDILY   *adv* in a muddy manner

MUDDING   present participle of mud

MUDDLE   *v* -DLED, -DLING, -DLES to mix in a disordered manner

MUDDLER   *n* pl. -S one that muddles

MUDDLY   *adj* disordered

MUDDY   *adj* -DIER, -DIEST covered or filled with mud

MUDDY   *v* -DIED, -DYING, -DIES to make or become muddy

MUDFISH   *n* pl. -ES a fish found in mud or muddy water

MUDFLAT   *n* pl. -S a level tract alternately covered and left bare by the tide

MUDFLOW   *n* pl. -S a moving mass of mud

MUDGUARD   *n* pl. -S a fender

MUDHOLE   *n* pl. -S a hole or hollow place full of mud

MUDLARK   *n* pl. -S a street urchin

MUDPACK   *n* pl. -S cosmetic paste for the face

MUDPUPPY   *n* pl. -PIES a large salamander

MUDRA   *n* pl. -S a hand gesture in East Indian classical dancing

MUDROCK   *n* pl. -S pelite

MUDROOM   *n* pl. -S a room for shedding muddy clothing or footwear

MUDSILL   *n* pl. -S the lowest supporting timber of a structure

MUDSLIDE   *n* pl. -S a mudflow down a slope

MUDSTONE   *n* pl. -S a type of rock

MUEDDIN   *n* pl. -S muezzin

MUENSTER   *n* pl. -S a mild cheese

MUESLI   *n* pl. -S a breakfast cereal

MUEZZIN   *n* pl. -S a Muslim crier who calls the faithful to prayer

MUFF   *v* -ED, -ING, -S to bungle

MUFFIN   *n* pl. -S a small, round bread

MUFFLE   *v* -FLED, -FLING, -FLES to wrap with something to deaden sound

MUFFLER   *n* pl. -S a device for deadening sound

MUFTI   *n* pl. -S a judge who interprets Muslim religious law

MUG   *v* MUGGED, MUGGING, MUGS to assault with intent to rob

MUGFUL   *n* pl. -S as much as a mug can hold

MUGG   *v* -ED, -ING, -S to make funny faces

MUGGAR   *n* pl. -S mugger

MUGGED   past tense of mug

MUGGEE   *n* pl. -S one who is mugged

MUGGER   *n* pl. -S a large Asian crocodile

MUGGIER   comparative of muggy

MUGGIEST   superlative of muggy

MUGGILY   *adv* in a muggy manner

MUGGING   *n* pl. -S a street assault or beating

MUGGINS   *n* pl. MUGGINS a card game

MUGGUR   *n* pl. -S mugger

MUGGY   *adj* -GIER, -GIEST warm and humid

MUGWORT   n pl. -S a flowering plant
MUGWUMP   n pl. -S a political independent
MUHLY   n pl. MUHLIES a perennial grass
MUJIK   n pl. -S muzhik
MUKLUK   n pl. -S a soft boot worn by Eskimos
MUKTUK   n pl. -S whale skin used for food
MULATTO   n pl. -TOES or -TOS the offspring of one white and one black parent
MULBERRY   n pl. -RIES a tree bearing an edible, berrylike fruit
MULCH   v -ED, -ING, -ES to provide with a protective covering for the soil
MULCT   v -ED, -ING, -S to defraud
MULE   v MULED, MULING, MULES to strike from dies belonging to two different issues, as a coin
MULETA   n pl. -S a red cloth used by a matador
MULETEER   n pl. -S one who drives mules (hoofed work animals)
MULEY   n pl. -LEYS a hornless cow
MULING   present participle of mule
MULISH   adj stubborn MULISHLY adv
MULL   v -ED, -ING, -S to ponder
MULLA   n pl. -S mullah
MULLAH   n pl. -S a Muslim religious leader or teacher
MULLEIN   n pl. -S a Eurasian herb
MULLEN   n pl. -S mullein
MULLER   n pl. -S a grinding implement
MULLET   n pl. -S an edible fish
MULLEY   n pl. -LEYS muley
MULLIGAN   n pl. -S a stew of various meats and vegetables
MULLION   v -ED, -ING, -S to provide with vertical dividing strips
MULLITE   n pl. -S a mineral
MULLOCK   n pl. -S waste earth or rock from a mine MULLOCKY adj
MULTIAGE   adj including people of various ages
MULTICAR   adj owning or involving several cars
MULTIFID   adj divided into many parts
MULTIJET   adj having more than two jets
MULTIPED   n pl. -S an animal having many feet
MULTIPLE   n pl. -S the product of a quantity by an integer
MULTIPLY   v -PLIED, -PLYING, -PLIES to increase in number

MULTITON   adj weighing many tons
MULTIUSE   adj having many uses
MULTURE   n pl. -S a fee paid to a miller for grinding grain
MUM   v MUMMED, MUMMING, MUMS to act in a disguise
MUMBLE   v -BLED, -BLING, -BLES to speak unclearly
MUMBLER   n pl. -S one that mumbles
MUMBLY   adj given to mumbling
MUMM   v -ED, -ING, -S to mum
MUMMED   past tense of mum and mumm
MUMMER   n pl. -S one that mums
MUMMERY   n pl. -MERIES a performance by mummers
MUMMIED   past tense of mummy
MUMMIES   present 3d person sing. of mummy
MUMMIFY   v -FIED, -FYING, -FIES to preserve by embalming
MUMMING   present participle of mum
MUMMY   v -MIED, -MYING, -MIES to mummify
MUMP   v -ED, -ING, -S to beg
MUMPER   n pl. -S one that mumps
MUMU   n pl. -S muumuu
MUN   n pl. -S man; fellow
MUNCH   v -ED, -ING, -ES to chew with a crackling sound
MUNCHER   n pl. -S one that munches
MUNCHIES   n/pl hunger pangs
MUNCHKIN   n pl. -S a small friendly person
MUNDANE   adj ordinary
MUNDUNGO   n pl. -GOS a foul-smelling tobacco
MUNGO   n pl. -GOS a low-quality wool
MUNGOOSE   n pl. -S mongoose
MUNI   n pl. -S a security issued by a state or local government
MUNIMENT   n pl. -S a means of defense
MUNITION   v -ED, -ING, -S to furnish with war materiel
MUNNION   n pl. -S a muntin
MUNSTER   n pl. -S muenster
MUNTIN   n pl. -S a dividing strip for window panes
MUNTING   n pl. -S muntin
MUNTJAC   n pl. -S a small Asian deer
MUNTJAK   n pl. -S muntjac
MUON   n pl. -S a subatomic particle MUONIC adj
MUONIUM   n pl. -S an electron and a positive muon bound together
MURA   n pl. -S a Japanese village
MURAENID   n pl. -S a moray

MURAL   *n* pl. -S a painting applied directly to a wall or ceiling

MURALIST   *n* pl. -S a painter of murals

MURDER   *v* -ED, -ING, -S to kill unlawfully with premediated malice

MURDEREE   *n* pl. -S one that is murdered

MURDERER   *n* pl. -S one that murders

MURE   *v* MURED, MURING, MURES to immure

MUREIN   *n* pl. -S a type of polymer

MUREX   *n* pl. -RICES or -REXES a marine mollusk

MURIATE   *n* pl. -S chloride

MURIATED   *adj* pickled

MURICATE   *adj* covered with short, sharp points

MURICES   a pl. of murex

MURID   *n* pl. -S a murine

MURINE   *n* pl. -S any of a family of small rodents

MURING   present participle of mure

MURK   *adj* MURKER, MURKEST dark **MURKLY** *adv*

MURK   *n* pl. -S darkness

MURKY   *adj* MURKIER, MURKIEST dark **MURKILY** *adv*

MURMUR   *v* -ED, -ING, -S to speak unclearly

MURMURER   *n* pl. -S one that murmurs

MURPHY   *n* pl. -PHIES a potato

MURR   *n* pl. -S murre

MURRA   *n* pl. -S a substance used to make fine vases and cups in ancient Rome

MURRAIN   *n* pl. -S a disease of cattle

MURRE   *n* pl. -S a diving bird

MURRELET   *n* pl. -S a small diving bird

MURREY   *n* pl. -REYS a dark purple color

MURRHA   *n* pl. -S murra **MURRHINE** *adj*

MURRINE   *adj* pertaining to murra

MURRY   *n* pl. -RIES a moray

MURTHER   *v* -ED, -ING, -S to murder

MUSCA   *n* pl. -CAE any of a genus of flies

MUSCADEL   *n* pl. -S muscatel

MUSCADET   *n* pl. -S a dry white French wine

MUSCAT   *n* pl. -S a sweet, white grape

MUSCATEL   *n* pl. -S a wine made from muscat grapes

MUSCID   *n* pl. -S musca

MUSCLE   *v* -CLED, -CLING, -CLES to proceed by force

MUSCLY   *adj* composed of muscle (tissue that produces bodily movement)

MUSCULAR   *adj* pertaining to muscle

MUSE   *v* MUSED, MUSING, MUSES to ponder

MUSEFUL   *adj* pensive

MUSER   *n* pl. -S one that muses

MUSETTE   *n* pl. -S a small bagpipe

MUSEUM   *n* pl. -S a place where objects of lasting interest or value are cared for and exhibited

MUSH   *v* -ED, -ING, -ES to travel over snow with a dog sled

MUSHER   *n* pl. -S one that mushes

MUSHROOM   *v* -ED, -ING, -S to grow or spread rapidly

MUSHY   *adj* MUSHIER, MUSHIEST pulpy **MUSHILY** *adv*

MUSIC   *n* pl. -S vocal or instrumental sounds organized to produce a unified composition

MUSICAL   *n* pl. -S a play in which dialogue is interspersed with songs and dances

MUSICALE   *n* pl. -S a program of music performed at a social gathering

MUSICIAN   *n* pl. -S one who performs or composes music

MUSING   *n* pl. -S contemplation

MUSINGLY   *adv* in a pensive manner

MUSJID   *n* pl. -S a mosque

MUSK   *n* pl. -S a strongly odorous substance secreted by certain animals

MUSKEG   *n* pl. -S a marsh

MUSKET   *n* pl. -S a type of firearm

MUSKETRY   *n* pl. -RIES the technique of firing small arms

MUSKIE   *n* pl. -S a freshwater fish

MUSKIER   comparative of musky

MUSKIEST   superlative of musky

MUSKILY   *adv* in a musky manner

MUSKIT   *n* pl. -S mesquite

MUSKRAT   *n* pl. -S an aquatic rodent

MUSKY   *adj* MUSKIER, MUSKIEST resembling musk

MUSLIN   *n* pl. -S a cotton fabric

MUSPIKE   *n* pl. -S a freshwater fish

MUSQUASH   *n* pl. -ES the muskrat

MUSS   *v* -ED, -ING, -ES to mess

MUSSEL   *n* pl. -S a bivalve mollusk

MUSSY   *adj* MUSSIER, MUSSIEST messy **MUSSILY** *adv*

MUST   *v* -ED, -ING, -S to become musty

MUSTACHE *n pl.* -S a growth of hair on the upper lip

MUSTANG *n pl.* -S a wild horse

MUSTARD *n pl.* -S a pungent seasoning

MUSTARDY *adj* resembling mustard

MUSTEE *n pl.* -S an octoroon

MUSTER *v* -ED, -ING, -S to summon or assemble

MUSTH *n pl.* -S a state of frenzy occurring in male elephants

MUSTY *adj* MUSTIER, MUSTIEST having a stale odor MUSTILY *adv*

MUT *n pl.* -S mutt

MUTABLE *adj* capable of change MUTABLY *adv*

MUTAGEN *n pl.* -S a substance that causes biological mutation

MUTANT *n pl.* -S something that undergoes mutation

MUTASE *n pl.* -S an enzyme

MUTATE *v* -TATED, -TATING, -TATES to undergo mutation

MUTATION *n pl.* -S the act of changing MUTATIVE *adj*

MUTCH *n pl.* -ES a close-fitting cap

MUTCHKIN *n pl.* -S a Scottish unit of liquid measure

MUTE *adj* MUTER, MUTEST characterized by an absence of speech MUTELY *adv*

MUTE *v* MUTED, MUTING, MUTES to deaden the sound of MUTEDLY *adv*

MUTENESS *n pl.* -ES the state of being mute

MUTER comparative of mute

MUTEST superlative of mute

MUTICOUS *adj* lacking a point

MUTILATE *v* -LATED, -LATING, -LATES to deprive of a limb or other essential part

MUTINE *v* -TINED, -TINING, -TINES to mutiny

MUTINEER *v* -ED, -ING, -S to mutiny

MUTING present participle of mute

MUTINIED past tense of mutiny

MUTINIES present 3d person sing. of mutiny

MUTINING present participle of mutine

MUTINOUS *adj* disposed to mutiny

MUTINY *v* -NIED, -NYING, -NIES to revolt against constituted authority

MUTISM *n pl.* -S muteness

MUTON *n pl.* -S a unit of nucleic acid

MUTT *n pl.* -S a mongrel dog

MUTTER *v* -ED, -ING, -S to speak unclearly

MUTTERER *n pl.* -S one that mutters

MUTTON *n pl.* -S the flesh of sheep used as food MUTTONY *adj*

MUTUAL *adj* shared in common MUTUALLY *adv*

MUTUEL *n pl.* -S a system of betting on races

MUTULE *n pl.* -S an ornamental block used in classical Greek architecture MUTULAR *adj*

MUUMUU *n pl.* -S a long, loose dress

MUZHIK *n pl.* -S a Russian peasant

MUZJIK *n pl.* -S muzhik

MUZZIER comparative of muzzy

MUZZIEST superlative of muzzy

MUZZILY *adv* in a muzzy manner

MUZZLE *v* -ZLED, -ZLING, -ZLES to put a covering over the mouth of to prevent biting or eating

MUZZLER *n pl.* -S one that muzzles

MUZZY *adj* -ZIER, -ZIEST confused

MY *pron* the possessive form of the pronoun I

MYALGIA *n pl.* -S muscular pain MYALGIC *adj*

MYASIS *n pl.* MYASES myiasis

MYCELE *n pl.* -S mycelium

MYCELIUM *n pl.* -LIA the vegetative portion of a fungus MYCELIAL, MYCELIAN, MYCELOID *adj*

MYCETOMA *n pl.* -MAS or -MATA a fungous infection

MYCOLOGY *n pl.* -GIES the branch of botany dealing with fungi

MYCOSIS *n pl.* -COSES a disease caused by a fungus MYCOTIC *adj*

MYELIN *n pl.* -S a fatty substance that encases certain nerve fibers MYELINIC *adj*

MYELINE *n pl.* -S myelin

MYELITIS *n pl.* -LITIDES inflammation of the bone marrow

MYELOID *adj* pertaining to bone marrow

MYELOMA *n pl.* -MAS or -MATA a tumor of the bone marrow

MYIASIS *n pl.* MYIASES infestation of human tissue by fly maggots

MYLONITE *n pl.* -S a type of rock

MYNA *n pl.* -S an Asian bird

MYNAH *n pl.* -S myna

MYNHEER *n* pl. -S a Dutch title of courtesy for a man

MYOBLAST *n* pl. -S a cell capable of giving rise to muscle cells

MYOGENIC *adj* originating in muscle tissue

MYOGRAPH *n* pl. -S an instrument for recording muscular contractions

MYOID *adj* resembling muscle

MYOLOGY *n* pl. -GIES the study of muscles **MYOLOGIC** *adj*

MYOMA *n* pl. -MAS or -MATA a tumor composed of muscle tissue

MYOPATHY *n* pl. -THIES a disorder of muscle tissue

MYOPE *n* pl. -S one who is affected with myopia

MYOPIA *n* pl. -S a visual defect **MYOPIC** *adj*

MYOPY *n* pl. -PIES myopia

MYOSCOPE *n* pl. -S an instrument for observing muscular contractions

MYOSIN *n* pl. -S a protein found in muscle tissue

MYOSIS *n* pl. MYOSES miosis

MYOSITIS *n* pl. -TISES muscular pain from infection

MYOSOTE *n* pl. -S myosotis

MYOSOTIS *n* pl. -TISES a flowering plant

MYOTIC *n* pl. -S miotic

MYOTOME *n* pl. -S a portion of an embryonic somite

MYOTONIA *n* pl. -S temporary muscular rigidity **MYOTONIC** *adj*

MYRIAD *n* pl. -S a very large number

MYRIAPOD *n* pl. -S a multi-legged arthropod

MYRICA *n* pl. -S a medicinal tree bark

MYRIOPOD *n* pl. -S myriapod

MYRMIDON *n* pl. -S a loyal follower

MYRRH *n* pl. -S an aromatic gum resin **MYRRHIC** *adj*

MYRTLE *n* pl. -S an evergreen shrub

MYSELF *pron* a form of the 1st person sing. pronoun

MYSID *n* pl. -S a small crustacean

MYSOST *n* pl. -S a mild cheese

MYSTAGOG *n* pl. -S a teacher of religious mysteries

MYSTERY *n* pl. -TERIES something that is not or cannot be known, understood, or explained

MYSTIC *n* pl. -S one who professes to have had mystical experiences

MYSTICAL *adj* spiritually significant or symbolic

MYSTICLY *adv* in a mystical manner

MYSTIFY *v* -FIED, -FYING, -FIES to perplex

MYSTIQUE *n* pl. -S an aura of mystery or mystical power surrounding a particular person or thing

MYTH *n* pl. -S a type of traditional story

MYTHIC *adj* mythical

MYTHICAL *adj* based on or described in a myth

MYTHOS *n* pl. -THOI a myth

MYTHY *adj* MYTHIER, MYTHIEST resembling myth

MYXEDEMA *n* pl. -S a disease caused by decreased activity of the thyroid gland

MYXOCYTE *n* pl. -S a large cell found in mucous tissue

MYXOID *adj* containing mucus

MYXOMA *n* pl. -MAS or -MATA a tumor composed of mucous tissue

NA *adv* no; not

NAAN *n* pl. -S nan

NAB *v* NABBED, NABBING, NABS to capture or arrest

NABBER *n* pl. -S one that nabs

NABE *n* pl. -S a neighborhood movie theater

NABIS *n* pl. NABIS a group of French artists

NABOB *n* pl. -S one who becomes rich and prominent **NABOBISH** *adj*

NABOBERY *n* pl. -ERIES the state of being a nabob

NABOBESS *n* pl. -ES a female nabob

NABOBISM *n* pl. -S great wealth and luxury

NACELLE *n* pl. -S a shelter on an aircraft

NACHAS *n* pl. NACHAS pride in another's accomplishments

NACHES *n* pl. NACHES nachas

NACHO *n* pl. -CHOS a tortilla chip topped with cheese and a savory mixture and broiled

NACRE *n* pl. -S the pearly internal layer of certain shells **NACRED, NACREOUS** *adj*

NADA *n* pl. -S nothing

NADIR *n* pl. -S a point on the celestial sphere **NADIRAL** *adj*

NAE *adv* no; not

NAETHING *n* pl. -S nothing

NAEVUS *n* pl. -VI nevus **NAEVOID** *adj*

NAG *v* NAGGED, NAGGING, NAGS to find fault incessantly

NAGANA *n* pl. -S a disease of horses in Africa

NAGGER *n* pl. -S one that nags

NAGGING present participle of nag

NAGGY *adj* -GIER, -GIEST given to nagging

NAH *adv* no

NAIAD *n* pl. -S or -ES a water nymph

NAIF *n* pl. -S a naive person

NAIL *v* -ED, -ING, -S to fasten with a nail (a slender piece of metal)

NAILER *n* pl. -S one that nails

NAILFOLD *n* pl. -S a fold of skin around the fingernail

NAILHEAD *n* pl. -S the top of a nail

NAILSET *n* pl. -S a steel rod for driving a nail into something

NAINSOOK *n* pl. -S a cotton fabric

NAIRA *n* pl. NAIRA a monetary unit of Nigeria

NAIVE *adj* NAIVER, NAIVEST lacking sophistication **NAIVELY** *adv*

NAIVE *n* pl. -S a naive person

NAIVETE *n* pl. -S the quality of being naive

NAIVETY *n* pl. -TIES naivete

NAKED *adj* -KEDER, -KEDEST being without clothing or covering **NAKEDLY** *adv*

NALED *n* pl. -S an insecticide

NALOXONE *n* pl. -S a chemical compound

NAM a past tense of nim

NAME *v* NAMED, NAMING, NAMES to give a title to **NAMABLE, NAMEABLE** *adj*

NAMELESS *adj* lacking distinction or fame

NAMELY *adv* that is to say

NAMER *n* pl. -S one that names

NAMESAKE *n* pl. -S one who is named after another

NAMETAG *n* pl. -S a tag bearing one's name worn for identification

NAMING	present participle of name
NAN	*n* pl. -S a round flat bread
NANA	*n* pl. -S a grandmother
NANDIN	*n* pl. -S an evergreen shrub
NANDINA	*n* pl. -S an Asian shrub
NANISM	*n* pl. -S abnormal smallness
NANKEEN	*n* pl. -S a cotton fabric
NANKIN	*n* pl. -S nankeen
NANNIE	*n* pl. -S nanny
NANNY	*n* pl. -NIES a children's nurse
NANOGRAM	*n* pl. -S a unit of mass and weight
NANOWATT	*n* pl. -S a unit of power
NAOS	*n* pl. NAOI an ancient temple
NAP	*v* NAPPED, NAPPING, NAPS to sleep briefly
NAPALM	*v* -ED, -ING, -S to assault with a type of incendiary bomb
NAPE	*n* pl. -S the back of the neck
NAPERY	*n* pl. -PERIES table linen
NAPHTHA	*n* pl. -S a volatile liquid
NAPHTHOL	*n* pl. -S a chemical compound
NAPHTHYL	*n* pl. -S a radical derived from naphthalene
NAPHTOL	*n* pl. -S naphthol
NAPIFORM	*adj* shaped like a turnip
NAPKIN	*n* pl. -S a piece of material used to wipe the hands and mouth
NAPLESS	*adj* threadbare
NAPOLEON	*n* pl. -S a type of pastry
NAPPE	*n* pl. -S a type of rock formation
NAPPED	past tense of nap
NAPPER	*n* pl. -S one that naps
NAPPIE	*n* pl. -S a diaper
NAPPING	present participle of nap
NAPPY	*adj* -PIER, -PIEST kinky
NARC	*n* pl. -S an undercover drug agent
NARCEIN	*n* pl. -S narceine
NARCEINE	*n* pl. -S an opium derivative
NARCISM	*n* pl. -S excessive love of oneself
NARCISSI	*n/pl* bulbous flowering plants
NARCIST	*n* pl. -S one given to narcism
NARCO	*n* pl. -COS narc
NARCOSE	*adj* characterized by stupor
NARCOSIS	*n* pl. -COSES a drug-induced stupor
NARCOTIC	*n* pl. -S a drug that dulls the senses
NARD	*n* pl. -S a fragrant ointment NARDINE *adj*
NARES	pl. of naris
NARGHILE	*n* pl. -S a hookah
NARGILE	*n* pl. -S narghile
NARGILEH	*n* pl. -S narghile
NARIS	*n* pl. NARES a nostril NARIAL, NARIC, NARINE *adj*
NARK	*v* -ED, -ING, -S to spy or inform
NARKY	*adj* irritable
NARRATE	*v* -RATED, -RATING, RATES to tell a story
NARRATER	*n* pl. -S narrator
NARRATOR	*n* pl. -S one that narrates
NARROW	*adj* -ROWER, -ROWEST of little width NARROWLY *adv*
NARROW	*v* -ED, -ING, -S to make narrow
NARTHEX	*n* pl. -ES a vestibule in a church
NARWAL	*n* pl. -S narwhal
NARWHAL	*n* pl. -S an arctic aquatic mammal
NARWHALE	*n* pl. -S narwhal
NARY	*adj* not one
NASAL	*n* pl. -S a sound uttered through the nose
NASALISE	*v* -ISED, -ISING, -ISES to nasalize
NASALITY	*n* pl. -TIES the quality or an instance of being produced nasally
NASALIZE	*v* -IZED, -IZING, -IZES to produce sounds nasally
NASALLY	*adv* through the nose
NASCENCE	*n* pl. -S nascency
NASCENCY	*n* pl. -CIES birth; origin
NASCENT	*adj* coming into existence
NASION	*n* pl. -S a point in the skull NASIAL *adj*
NASTIC	*adj* pertaining to an automatic response of plants
NASTY	*adj* -TIER, -TIEST offensive to the senses NASTILY *adv*
NASTY	*n* pl. -TIES something that is nasty
NATAL	*adj* pertaining to one's birth
NATALITY	*n* pl. -TIES birth rate
NATANT	*adj* floating or swimming NATANTLY *adv*
NATATION	*n* pl. -S the act of swimming
NATATORY	*adj* pertaining to swimming
NATCH	*adv* naturally
NATES	*n/pl* the buttocks
NATHLESS	*adv* nevertheless

NATION *n* pl. -S a politically organized people who share a territory, customs, and history

NATIONAL *n* pl. -S a citizen of a nation

NATIVE *n* pl. -S an original inhabitant of an area

NATIVELY *adv* in an inborn manner

NATIVISM *n* pl. -S a policy of favoring the interests of native inhabitants

NATIVIST *n* pl. -S an advocate of nativism

NATIVITY *n* pl. -TIES the process of being born

NATRIUM *n* pl. -S sodium

NATRON *n* pl. -S a chemical compound

NATTER *v* -ED, -ING, -S to chatter

NATTY *adj* -TIER, -TIEST neatly dressed **NATTILY** *adv*

NATURAL *n* pl. -S a type of musical note

NATURE *n* pl. -S the essential qualities of a person or thing **NATURED** *adj*

NATURISM *n* pl. -S nudism

NATURIST *n* pl. -S a nudist

NAUGHT *n* pl. -S a zero

NAUGHTY *adj* -TIER, -TIEST disobedient

NAUMACHY *n* pl. -CHIES a mock sea battle

NAUPLIUS *n* pl. -PLII a form of certain crustaceans **NAUPLIAL.** *adj*

NAUSEA *n* pl. -S a stomach disturbance

NAUSEANT *n* pl. -S an agent that induces nausea

NAUSEATE *v* -ATED, -ATING, -ATES to affect with nausea

NAUSEOUS *adj* affected with nausea

NAUTCH *n* pl. -ES a dancing exhibition in India

NAUTICAL *adj* pertaining to ships

NAUTILUS *n* pl. -LUSES or -LI a spiral-shelled mollusk

NAVAID *n* pl. -S a navigational device

NAVAL *adj* pertaining to ships **NAVALLY** *adv*

NAVAR *n* pl. -S a system of air navigation

NAVE *n* pl. -S the main part of a church

NAVEL *n* pl. -S a depression in the abdomen

NAVETTE *n* pl. -S a gem cut in a pointed oval form

NAVICERT *n* pl. -S a document permitting a vessel passage through a naval blockade

NAVIES pl. of navy

NAVIGATE *v* -GATED, -GATING, -GATES to plan and control the course of

NAVVY *n* pl. -VIES a manual laborer

NAVY *n* pl. -VIES a nation's warships

NAW *adv* no

NAWAB *n* pl. -S a nabob

NAY *n* pl. NAYS a negative vote

NAYSAYER *n* pl. -S one that denies or opposes something

NAZI *n* pl. -S a type of fascist

NAZIFY *v* -FIED, -FYING, -FIES to cause to be like a nazi

NE *adj* born with the name of

NEAP *n* pl. -S a tide of lowest range

NEAR *ad* NEARER, NEAREST situated within a short distance

NEAR *v* -ED, -ING, -S to approach

NEARBY *adj* near

NEARLY *adv* -LIER, -LIEST with close approximation

NEARNESS *n* pl. -ES the state of being near

NEARSIDE *n* pl. -S the left side

NEAT *adj* NEATER, NEATEST being in a state of cleaniness and order

NEAT *n* pl. -S a bovine

NEATEN *v* -ED, -ING, -S to make neat

NEATH *prep* beneath

NEATHERD *n* pl. -S a cowherd

NEATLY *adv* in a neat manner

NEATNESS *n* pl. -ES the state of being neat

NEB *n* pl. -S the beak of a bird

NEBBISH *n* pl. -ES a meek person **NEBBISHY** *adj*

NEBULA *n* pl. -LAS or -LAE a cloud-like interstellar mass **NEBULAR** *adj*

NEBULE *adj* composed of successive short curves

NEBULISE *v* -LISED, -LISING, -LISES to nebulize

NEBULIZE *v* -LIZED, -LIZING, -LIZES to reduce to a fine spray

NEBULOSE *adj* nebulous

NEBULOUS *adj* unclear

NEBULY *adj* nebule

NECK *v* -ED, -ING, -S to kiss and caress in lovemaking

NECKBAND *n* pl. -S a band worn around the neck (the part of the body joining the head to the trunk)

NECKER   *n* pl. -S one that necks

NECKING   *n* pl. -S a small molding near the top of a column

NECKLACE   *n* pl. -S an ornament worn around the neck

NECKLESS   *adj* having no neck

NECKLIKE   *adj* resembling the neck

NECKLINE   *n* pl. -S the line formed by the neck opening of a garment

NECKTIE   *n* pl. -S a strip of fabric worn around the neck

NECKWEAR   *n* pl. -S something that is worn around the neck

NECROPSY   *v* -SIED, -SYING, -SIES to perform an autopsy on

NECROSE   *v* -CROSED, -CROSING, -CROSES to affect with necrosis

NECROSIS   *n* pl. -CROSES the death of living tissue **NECROTIC** *adj*

NECTAR   *n* pl. -S a delicious drink

NECTARY   *n* pl. -TARIES a plant gland

NEE   *adj* born with the name of

NEED   *v* -ED, -ING, -S to have an urgent or essential use for

NEEDER   *n* pl. -S one that needs

NEEDFUL   *n* pl. -S something that is needed

NEEDIER   comparative of needy

NEEDIEST   superlative of needy

NEEDILY   *adv* in a needy manner

NEEDLE   *v* -DLED, -DLING, -DLES to sew with a slender, pointed instrument

NEEDLER   *n* pl. -S one that needles

NEEDLESS   *adj* not necessary

NEEDLING   *n* pl. -S the act of one who needles

NEEDY   *adj* NEEDIER, NEEDIEST in a state of poverty

NEEM   *n* pl. -S an East Indian tree

NEEP   *n* pl. -S a turnip

NEGATE   *v* -GATED, -GATING, -GATES to nullify

NEGATER   *n* pl. -S one that negates

NEGATION   *n* pl. -S the act of negating

NEGATIVE   *v* -TIVED, -TIVING, -TIVES to veto

NEGATON   *n* pl. -S negatron

NEGATOR   *n* pl. -S negater

NEGATRON   *n* pl. -S an electron

NEGLECT   *v* -ED, -ING, -S to fail to pay attention to

NEGLIGE   *n* pl. -S negligee

NEGLIGEE   *n* pl. -S a woman's dressing gown

NEGROID   *n* pl. -S member of the black race

NEGRONI   *n* pl. -S an alcoholic beverage

NEGUS   *n* pl. -ES an alcoholic beverage

NEIF   *n* pl. -S nieve

NEIGH   *v* -ED, -ING, -S to utter the cry of a horse

NEIGHBOR   *v* -ED, -ING, -S to live close to

NEIST   *adj* next

NEITHER   *adj* not one or the other

NEKTON   *n* pl. -S free-swimming marine animals **NEKTONIC** *adj*

NELLIE   *n* pl. -S an effeminate male

NELLY   *n* pl. -LIES nellie

NELSON   *n* pl. -S a wrestling hold

NELUMBO   *n* pl. -BOS an aquatic herb

NEMA   *n* pl. -S a nematode

NEMATIC   *adj* pertaining to a phase of a liquid crystal

NEMATODE   *n* pl. -S a kind of worm

NEMESIS   *n* pl. NEMESES an unbeatable opponent

NENE   *n* pl. NENE a Hawaiian goose

NEOLITH   *n* pl. -S an ancient stone implement

NEOLOGY   *n* pl. -GIES a new word or phrase **NEOLOGIC** *adj*

NEOMORPH   *n* pl. -S a type of biological structure

NEOMYCIN   *n* pl. -S an antibiotic drug

NEON   *n* pl. -S a gaseous element **NEONED** *adj*

NEONATE   *n* pl. -S a newborn child **NEONATAL** *adj*

NEOPHYTE   *n* pl. -S a novice

NEOPLASM   *n* pl. -S a tumor

NEOPRENE   *n* pl. -S a synthetic rubber

NEOTENY   *n* pl. -NIES attainment of sexual maturity in the larval stage **NEOTENIC** *adj*

NEOTERIC   *n* pl. -S a modern author

NEOTYPE   *n* pl. -S a specimen of a species

NEPENTHE   *n* pl. -S a drug that induces forgetfulness

NEPHEW   *n* pl. -S a son of one's brother or sister

NEPHRIC   *adj* renal

NEPHRISM   *n* pl. -S ill health caused by a kidney disease

NEPHRITE   *n* pl. -S a mineral

NEPHRON   *n* pl. -S an excretory unit of a kidney

NEPOTISM   *n* pl. -S favoritism shown to a relative **NEPOTIC** *adj*

NEPOTIST *n* pl. -S one who practices nepotism

NERD *n* pl. -S a socially inept person

NERDY *adj* NERDIER, NERDIEST socially inept

NEREID *n* pl. -S a sea nymph

NEREIS *n* pl. -REIDES a marine worm

NERITIC *adj* pertaining to shallow water

NEROL *n* pl. -S a fragrant alcohol

NEROLI *n* pl. -S a fragrant oil

NERTS *interj* — used to express defiance or disgust

NERTZ *interj* nerts

NERVATE *adj* having veins

NERVE *v* NERVED, NERVING, NERVES to give courage to

NERVIER comparative of nervy

NERVIEST superlative of nervy

NERVILY *adv* in a nervy manner

NERVINE *n* pl. -S a soothing medicine

NERVING *n* pl. -S a type of veterinary operation

NERVOUS *adj* easily excited

NERVULE *n* pl. -S nervure

NERVURE *n* pl. -S a vascular ridge on a leaf

NERVY *adj* NERVIER, NERVIEST impudent

NESCIENT *n* pl. -S one who is ignorant

NESS *n* pl. -ES a headland

NEST *v* -ED, -ING, -S to build a nest (a structure for holding bird eggs)

NESTABLE *adj* capable of being fitted closely within another container

NESTER *n* pl. -S one that nests

NESTLE *v* -TLED, -TLING, -TLES to lie snugly

NESTLER *n* pl. -S one that nestles

NESTLIKE *adj* resembling a nest

NESTLING *n* pl. -S a young bird

NESTOR *n* pl. -S a wise old man

NET *v* NETTED, NETTING, NETS to catch in a net (a type of openwork fabric)

NETHER *adj* situated below

NETLESS *adj* having no net

NETLIKE *adj* resembling a net

NETOP *n* pl. -S friend; companion

NETSUKE *n* pl. -S a button-like fixture on Japanese clothing

NETT *v* -ED, -ING, -S to net

NETTABLE *adj* capable of being netted

NETTED past tense of net, nett

NETTER *n* pl. -S one that nets

NETTIER comparative of netty

NETTIEST superlative of netty

NETTING *n* pl. -S a net

NETTLE *v* -TLED, -TLING, -TLES to make angry

NETTLER *n* pl. -S one that nettles

NETTLY *adj* -TLIER, -TLIEST prickly

NETTY *adj* -TIER, -TIEST resembling a net

NETWORK *v* -ED, -ING, -S to cover with or as if with crossing lines

NEUK *n* pl. -S nook

NEUM *n* pl. -S neume

NEUME *n* pl. -S a sign used in musical notation **NEUMATIC, NEUMIC** *adj*

NEURAL *adj* pertaining to the nervous system **NEURALLY** *adv*

NEURAXON *n* pl. -S a part of a neuron

NEURINE *n* pl. -S a ptomaine poison

NEURITIC *n* pl. -S one affected with neuritis

NEURITIS *n. pl.* -RITIDES *or* -RITISES inflammation of a nerve

NEUROID *adj* resembling a nerve

NEUROMA *n* pl. -MAS *or* -MATA a type of tumor

NEURON *n* pl. -S the basic cellular unit of the nervous system **NEURONAL, NEURONIC** *adj*

NEURONE *n* pl. -S neuron

NEUROSIS *n* pl. -ROSES a type of emotional disturbance **NEUROSAL** *adj*

NEUROTIC *n* pl. -S one affected with a neurosis

NEURULA *n* pl. -LAE *or* LAS a vertebrate embryo

NEUSTON *n* pl. -S an aggregate of small aquatic organisms

NEUTER *v* -ED, -ING, -S to castrate

NEUTRAL *n* pl. -S one that is impartial

NEUTRINO *n* pl. -NOS a subatomic particle

NEUTRON *n* pl. -S a subatomic particle

NEVE *n* pl. -S a granular snow

NEVER *adv* at no time

NEVUS *n* pl. -VI a birthmark **NEVOID** *adj*

NEW *adj* NEWER, NEWEST existing only a short time

NEW *n* pl. -S something that is new

NEWBORN *n* pl. -S a recently born infant

NEWCOMER *n* pl. -S one that has recently arrived

NEWEL *n* pl. -S a staircase support

NEWFOUND *adj* newly found

NEWIE *n* pl. -S something new

NEWISH *adj* somewhat new

NEWLY *adv* recently

NEWLYWED *n* pl. -S a person recently married

NEWMOWN *adj* recently mown

NEWNESS *n* pl. -ES the state of being new

NEWS *n/pl* a report of recent events

NEWSBOY *n* pl. -BOYS a boy who delivers or sells newspapers

NEWSCAST *n* pl. -S a news broadcast

NEWSHAWK *n* pl. -S a newspaper reporter

NEWSIE *n* pl. -S newsy

NEWSIER comparative of newsy

NEWSIES pl. of newsy

NEWSIEST superlative of newsy

NEWSLESS *adj* having no news

NEWSMAN *n* pl. -MEN a news reporter

NEWSPEAK *n* pl. -S a deliberately ambiguous language

NEWSREEL *n* pl. -S a short movie presenting current events

NEWSROOM *n* pl. -S a room where the news is gathered

NEWSY *adj* NEWSIER, NEWSIEST full of news

NEWSY *n* pl. NEWSIES a newsboy

NEWT *n* pl. -S a small salamander

NEWTON *n* pl. -S a unit of force

NEXT *adj* coming immediately after; adjoining

NEXTDOOR *adj* located in the next building or room

NEXUS *n* pl. -ES a connection or link

NGULTRUM *n* pl. -S a monetary unit of Bhutan

NGWEE *n* pl. NGWEE a monetary unit of Zambia

NIACIN *n* pl. -S a B vitamin

NIB *v* NIBBED, NIBBING, NIBS to provide with a penpoint

NIBBLE *v* -BLED, -BLING, -BLES to eat with small bites

NIBBLER *n* pl. -S one that nibbles

NIBLICK *n* pl. -S a golf club

NIBLIKE *adj* resembling a penpoint

NICAD *n* pl. -S nickel cadmium

NICE *adj* NICER, NICEST pleasing to the senses **NICELY** *adv*

NICENESS *n* pl. -ES the quality of being nice

NICETY *n* pl. -TIES a fine point or distinction

NICHE *v* NICHED, NICHING, NICHES to place in a receding space or hollow

NICK *v* -ED, -ING, -S to make a shallow cut in

NICKEL *v* -ELED, -ELING, -ELS or -ELLED, -ELLING, -ELS to plate with nickel (a metallic element)

NICKELIC *adj* pertaining to or containing nickel

NICKER *v* -ED, -ING, -S to neigh

NICKLE *v* -LED, -LING, -LES nickel

NICKNACK *n* pl. -S a trinket

NICKNAME *v* -NAMED, -NAMING, -NAMES to give an alternate name to

NICOL *n* pl. -S a type of prism

NICOTIN *n* pl. -S nicotine

NICOTINE *n* pl. -S a poisonous alkaloid in tobacco

NICTATE *n* -TATED, -TATING, -TATES to wink

NIDAL *adj* pertaining to a nidus

NIDE *n* NIDED, NIDING, NIDES to nest

NIDERING *n* pl. -S a coward

NIDGET *n* pl. -S an idiot

NIDI a pl. of nidus

NIDIFY *v* -FIED, -FYING, -FIES to nest

NIDING present participle of nide

NIDUS *n* pl. NIDI or NIDUSES a nest or breeding place

NIECE *n* pl. -S a daughter of one's brother or sister

NIELLIST *n* pl. -S one that niellos

NIELLO *n* pl. -LI or -LOS a black metallic substance

NIELLO *v* -ED, -ING, -S to decorate with niello

NIEVE *n* pl. -S the fist or hand

NIFFER *v* -ED, -ING, -S to barter

NIFTY *adj* -TIER, -TIEST stylish; pleasing **NIFTILY** *adv*

NIFTY *n* pl. -TIES something that is nifty

NIGGARD *v* -ED, -ING, -S to act stingily

NIGGLE *v* -GLED, -GLING, -GLES to worry over petty details

NIGGLER *n* pl. -S one that niggles

NIGGLING *n* pl. -S petty or meticulous work

NIGH *adj* NIGHER, NIGHEST near

NIGH *v* -ED, -ING, -S to approach

NIGHNESS *n* pl. -ES the state of being nigh

NIGHT *n* pl. -S the period from sunset to sunrise

NIGHTCAP *n* pl. -S a cap worn to bed

NIGHTIE *n* pl. -S a nightgown

NIGHTIES pl. of nighty

NIGHTJAR *n* pl. -S a nocturnal bird

NIGHTLY *adv* every night; at night

NIGHTY *n* pl. NIGHTIES nightie

NIGRIFY *v* -FIED, -FYING, -FIES to make black

NIGROSIN *n* pl. -S a type of dye

NIHIL *n* pl. -S nothing

NIHILISM *n* pl. -S a doctrine that denies traditional values

NIHILIST *n* pl. -S an adherent of nihilism

NIHILITY *n* pl. -TIES the state of being nothing

NIL *n* pl. -S nothing

NILGAI *n* pl. -S a large antelope

NILGAU *n* pl. -S nilgai

NILGHAI *n* pl. -S nilgai

NILGHAU *n* pl. -S nilgai

NILL *v* -ED, -ING, -S to be unwilling

NIM *v* NAM or NIMMED, NIMMING, NIMS to steal

NIMBLE *adj* -BLER, -BLEST agile NIMBLY *adv*

NIMBUS *n* pl. -BI or -BUSES a luminous cloud NIMBUSED *adj*

NIMIETY *n* pl. -ETIES excess NIMIOUS *adj*

NIMMED past tense of nim

NIMMING present participle of nim

NIMROD *n* pl. -S a hunter

NINE *n* pl. -S a number

NINEBARK *n* pl. -S a flowering shrub

NINEFOLD *adj* nine times as great

NINEPIN *n* pl. -S a wooden pin used in a bowling game

NINETEEN *n* pl. -S a number

NINETY *n* pl. -TIES a number

NINJA *n* pl. -S a feudal Japanese warrior

NINNY *n* pl. -NIES a fool NINNYISH *adj*

NINON *n* pl. -S a sheer fabric

NINTH *n* pl. -S one of nine equal parts

NINTHLY *adv* in the ninth place

NIOBATE *n* pl. -S a chemical salt

NIOBIUM *n* pl. -S a metallic element NIOBIC, NIOBOUS *adj*

NIP *v* NIPPED, NIPPING, NIPS to pinch

NIPA *n* pl. -S a palm tree

NIPPER *n* pl. -S one that nips

NIPPIER comparative of nippy

NIPPIEST superlative of nippy

NIPPILY *adv* in a nippy manner

NIPPING present participle of nip

NIPPLE *n* pl. -S a protuberance on the breast NIPPLED *adj*

NIPPY *adj* -PIER, -PIEST sharp or biting

NIRVANA *n* pl. -S a blessed state in Buddhism NIRVANIC *adj*

NISEI *n* pl. -S one born in America of immigrant Japanese parents

NISI *adj* not yet final

NISUS *n* pl. NISUS an effort

NIT *n* pl. -S the egg of a parasitic insect

NITE *n* pl. -S night

NITER *n* pl. -S a chemical salt

NITERIE *n* pl. -S nitery

NITERY *n* pl. -ERIES a nightclub

NITID *adj* bright

NITINOL *n* pl. -S an alloy of nickel and titanium

NITON *n* pl. -S radon

NITPICK *v* -ED, -ING, -S to fuss over petty details

NITPICKY *adj* -PICKIER, -PICKIEST tending to nitpick

NITRATE *v* -TRATED, -TRATING, -TRATES to treat with nitric acid

NITRATOR *n* pl. -S one that nitrates

NITRE *n* pl. -S niter

NITRIC *adj* containing nitrogen

NITRID *n* pl. -S nitride

NITRIDE *v* -TRIDED, -TRIDING, -TRIDES to convert into a nitride (a compound of nitrogen)

NITRIFY *v* -FIED, -FYING, -FIES to combine with nitrogen

NITRIL *n* pl. -S nitrile

NITRILE *n* pl. -S a chemical compound

NITRITE *n* pl. -S a salt of nitrous acid

NITRO *n* pl. -TROS a nitrated product

NITROGEN *n* pl. -S a gaseous element

NITROLIC *adj* pertaining to a class of acids

NITROSO *adj* containing nitrosyl

NITROSYL *n* pl. -S a univalent radical

NITROUS *adj* containing nitrogen

NITTY *adj* -TIER, -TIEST full of nits

NITWIT	*n* pl. -S a stupid person	**NODDING**	present participle of nod
NIVAL	*adj* pertaining to snow	**NODDLE**	*v* -DLED, -DLING, -DLES to
NIVEOUS	*adj* resembling snow		nod frequently
NIX	*v* -ED, -ING, -ES to veto	**NODDY**	*n* pl. -DIES a fool
NIX	*n* pl. NIXES or NIXE a water	**NODE**	*n* pl. -S a swollen enlargement
	sprite	**NODI**	pl. of nodus
NIXIE	*n* pl. -S a female water sprite	**NODICAL**	*adj* pertaining to an
NIXY	*n* pl. NIXIES an undeliverable		astronomical point
	piece of mail	**NODOSE**	*adj* having nodes
NIZAM	*n* pl. -S a former sovereign of	**NODOSITY**	*n* pl. -TIES the state of being
	India		nodose
NIZAMATE	*n* pl. -S the territory of a nizam	**NODOUS**	*adj* nodose
NO	*n* pl. NOS or NOES a negative	**NODULE**	*n* pl. -S a small node
	reply		**NODULAR, NODULOSE,**
NOB	*n* pl. -S a wealthy person		**NODULOUS** *adj*
NOBBIER	comparative of nobby	**NODUS**	*n* pl. -DI a difficulty
NOBBIEST	superlative of nobby	**NOEL**	*n* pl. -S a Christmas carol
NOBBILY	*adv* in a nobby manner	**NOES**	a pl. of no
NOBBLE	*v* -BLED, -BLING, -BLES to	**NOESIS**	*n* pl. -SISES the process of
	disable a racehorse		reason
NOBBLER	*n* pl. -S one that nobbles	**NOETIC**	*adj* pertaining to reason
NOBBY	*adj* -BIER, -BIEST elegant	**NOG**	*v* NOGGED, NOGGING,
NOBELIUM	*n* pl. -S a radioactive element		NOGS to fill in a space in a
NOBILITY	*n* pl. -TIES the social class		wall with bricks
	composed of nobles	**NOGG**	*n* pl. -S a strong ale
NOBLE	*adj* -BLER, -BLEST	**NOGGIN**	*n* pl. -S a small cup
	possessing qualities of	**NOGGING**	*n* pl. -S a type of masonry
	excellence	**NOH**	*n* pl. NOH the classical drama
NOBLE	*n* pl. -S a person of high birth,		of Japan
	rank, or title	**NOHOW**	*adv* in no manner
NOBLEMAN	*n* pl. -MEN a noble	**NOIL**	*n* pl. -S a kind of short fiber
NOBLER	comparative of noble		**NOILY** *adj*
NOBLESSE	*n* pl. -S the nobility	**NOIR**	*n* pl. -S a bleak type of crime
NOBLEST	superlative of noble		fiction **NOIRISH** *adj*
NOBLY	*adv* in a noble manner	**NOISE**	*v* NOISED, NOISING,
NOBODY	*n* pl. -BODIES an unimportant		NOISES to spread as a rumor
	person		or report
NOCENT	*adj* harmful	**NOISETTE**	*n* pl. -S a small round piece of
NOCK	*v* -ED, -ING, -S to notch a bow		meat
	or arrow	**NOISOME**	*adj* disgusting; harmful
NOCTUID	*n* pl. -S a night-flying moth	**NOISY**	*adj* NOISIER, NOISIEST
	NOCTUOID *adj*		making loud sounds **NOISILY**
NOCTULE	*n* pl. -S a large bat		*adv*
NOCTURN	*n* pl. -S a religious service	**NOLO**	*n* pl. -LOS a type of legal plea
NOCTURNE	*n* pl. -S a musical composition	**NOM**	*n* pl. -S a name
NOCUOUS	*adj* harmful	**NOMA**	*n* pl. -S a severe inflammation
NOD	*v* NODDED, NODDING,		of the mouth
	NODS to briefly lower the head	**NOMAD**	*n* pl. -S a wanderer **NOMADIC**
	forward		*adj*
NODAL	*adj* of the nature of a node	**NOMADISM**	*n* pl. -S the mode of life of a
	NODALLY *adv*		nomad
NODALITY	*n* pl. -TIES the state of being	**NOMARCH**	*n* pl. -S the head of a nome
	nodal	**NOMARCHY**	*n* pl. -ARCHIES a nome
NODDED	past tense of nod	**NOMBLES**	*n/pl* numbles
NODDER	*n* pl. -S one that nods	**NOMBRIL**	*n* pl. -S a point on a heraldic
NODDIES	pl. of noddy		shield

NOME *n* pl. -S a province of modern Greece

NOMEN *n* pl. -MINA the second name of an ancient Roman

NOMINAL *n* pl. -S a word functioning as a noun

NOMINATE *v* -NATED, -NATING, -NATES to name as a candidate

NOMINEE *n* pl. -S one that is nominated

NOMISM *n* pl. -S strict adherence to moral law **NOMISTIC** *adj*

NOMOGRAM *n* pl. -S a type of graph

NOMOLOGY *n* pl. -GIES the science of law

NOMOS *n* pl. NOMOI law

NONA *n* pl. -S a virus disease

NONACID *n* pl. -S a substance that is not an acid

NONACTOR *n* pl. -S a person who is not an actor

NONADULT *n* pl. -S a person who is not an adult

NONAGE *n* pl. -S a period of immaturity

NONAGON *n* pl. -S a nine-sided polygon

NONART *n* pl. -S something that is not art

NONBANK *adj* not involving a bank

NONBASIC *adj* not basic

NONBEING *n* pl. -S lack of being

NONBLACK *n* pl. -S one that is not black

NONBODY *n* pl. -BODIES a person's nonphysical nature

NONBOOK *n* pl. -S a book of little literary merit

NONBRAND *adj* lacking a brand name

NONCASH *adj* other than cash

NONCE *n* pl. -S the present occasion

NONCLASS *n* pl -ES a lack of class

NONCLING *adj* not clinging

NONCOLA *adj* being a drink that is not a cola

NONCOLOR *n* pl. -S a lack of color

NONCOM *n* pl. -S a noncommissioned officer

NONCRIME *n* pl. -S something that is not a crime

NONDAIRY *adj* having no milk products

NONDANCE *n* pl. -S an unrhythmic dance

NONDRUG *adj* not involving drugs

NONE *n* pl. -S one of seven canonical daily periods for prayer and devotion

NONEGO *n* pl. -GOS all that is not part of the ego

NONELECT *adj* not chosen

NONELITE *adj* not belonging to an elite group

NONEMPTY *adj* not empty

NONENTRY *n* pl. -TRIES the fact of not entering

NONEQUAL *n* pl. -S one that is not equal

NONESUCH *n* pl. -ES a person or thing without an equal

NONET *n* pl. -S a composition for nine instruments or voices

NONEVENT *n* pl. -S an expected event that does not occur

NONFACT *n* pl. -S a statement not based on fact

NONFAN *n* pl. -S a person who is not a fan (an enthusiast)

NONFARM *adj* not pertaining to the farm

NONFAT *adj* having no fat solids

NONFATAL *adj* not fatal

NONFATTY *adj* not fatty

NONFINAL *adj* not being the last

NONFLUID *n* pl. -S a substance that is not a fluid

NONFOCAL *adj* not focal

NONFOOD *adj* pertaining to something other than food

NONFUEL *adj* not used as a fuel

NONGAME *adj* not hunted for food, sport, or fur

NONGAY *n* pl. -S a person who is not a homosexual

NONGLARE *adj* that does not glare

NONGREEN *adj* not green

NONGUEST *n* pl. -S one who is not a guest

NONGUILT *n* pl. -S the absence of guilt

NONHARDY *adj* not hardy

NONHEME *adj* not containing iron that is bound like that of heme

NONHERO *n* pl. -ROES an antihero

NONHOME *adj* not taking place in the home

NONHUMAN *adj* not human

NONIDEAL *adj* not ideal

NONIMAGE *adj* not having an image

NONIONIC *adj* not ionic

NONIRON *adj* not needing to be ironed

NONISSUE *n* pl. -S a topic that is not controversial

NONJUROR *n* pl. -S one who refuses to take a required oath

NONJURY *adj* not involving a jury

NONLABOR *adj* not pertaining to labor

NONLEAFY *adj* not having leaves

NONLEGAL *adj* not legal

NONLIFE *n* pl. -LIVES the absence of life

NONLOCAL *n* pl. -S one that is not local

NONMAJOR *n* pl. -S a student who is not majoring in a specified subject

NONMAN *n* pl. -MEN a being that is not a man

NONMEAT *adj* not containing meat

NONMETAL *n* pl. -S an element that lacks metallic properties

NONMETRO *adj* not metropolitan

NONMODAL *adj* not modal

NONMONEY *adj* not involving money

NONMORAL *adj* not pertaining to morals

NONMUSIC *n* pl. -S inferior music

NONNAVAL *adj* not naval

NONNEWS *adj* not being news

NONNOVEL *n* pl. -S a literary work that is not a novel

NONOBESE *adj* not obese

NONOHMIC *adj* not measured in ohms

NONOILY *adj* not oily

NONOWNER *n* pl. -S one who is not the owner

NONPAGAN *n* pl. -S one who is not a pagan

NONPAID *adj* not paid

NONPAPAL *adj* not papal

NONPAR *adj* being a stock that has no face value

NONPARTY *adj* not affiliated with any political party

NONPAST *n* pl. -S a verb form that lacks an inflection for a past tense

NONPEAK *adj* being a time when something is not at its highest level

NONPLAY *n* pl. -PLAYS a theatrical work that is not a play

NONPLUS *v* -PLUSED, -PLUSING, -PLUSES or -PLUSSED, -PLUSSING, -PLUSSES to baffle

NONPOINT *adj* not occurring at a definite single site

NONPOLAR *adj* not polar

NONPOOR *adj* not being poor

NONPRINT *adj* not involving printed material

NONPROS *v* -PROSSED, -PROSSING, -PROSSES to enter a judgment against a plaintiff who fails to prosecute

NONQUOTA *adj* not included in or subject to a quota

NONRATED *adj* not rated

NONRIGID *adj* not rigid

NONRIVAL *n* pl. -S an unimportant rival

NONROYAL *adj* not royal

NONRURAL *adj* not rural

NONSELF *n* pl. -SELVES foreign material in a body

NONSENSE *n* pl. -S behavior or language that is meaningless or absurd

NONSKED *n* pl. -S an airline without scheduled flying times

NONSKID *adj* designed to inhibit skidding

NONSKIER *n* pl. -S one that does not ski

NONSLIP *adj* designed to prevent slipping

NONSOLAR *adj* not solar

NONSOLID *n* pl. -S a substance that is not a solid

NONSTICK *adj* allowing of easy removal of cooked food particles

NONSTOP *adj* making no stops

NONSTORY *n* pl. -RIES an insignificant news story

NONSTYLE *n* pl. -S a style that is not identifiable

NONSUCH *n* pl. -ES nonesuch

NONSUGAR *n* pl. -S a substance that is not a sugar

NONSUIT *v* -ED, -ING, -S to dismiss the lawsuit of

NONTAX *n* pl. -ES a tax of little consequence

NONTIDAL *adj* not tidal

NONTITLE *adj* pertaining to an athletic contest in which a title is not at stake

NONTONAL *adj* lacking tonality

NONTOXIC *adj* not toxic

NONTRUMP *adj* not having a trump

NONTRUTH *n* pl. -S something that is not true

NONUNION *n* pl. -S failure of a broken bone to heal

NONUPLE *n* pl. -S a number nine times as great as another

NONURBAN *adj* not urban

NONUSE *n* pl. -S failure to use

NONUSER *n* pl. -S one that is not a user

NONUSING *adj* not using

NONVALID *adj* not valid

NONVIRAL *adj* not viral

NONVOCAL *adj* not vocal

NONVOTER *n* pl. -S one that does not vote

NONWAR *n* pl. -S a war that is not officially declared

NONWHITE *n* pl. -S a person who is not of the white race

NONWOODY *adj* not woody

NONWORD *n* pl. -S a word that has no meaning

NONWORK   *adj* not involving work
NONWOVEN   *n* pl. -S a fabric not made by weaving
NONYL   *n* pl. -S an alkyl radical
NONZERO   *adj* having a value other than zero
NOO   *adv* now
NOODGE   *v* NOODGED, NOODGING, NOODGES to nag
NOODLE   *v* -DLED, -DLING, -DLES to play idly on a musical instrument
NOOK   *n* pl. -S a corner, as in a room
NOOKLIKE *adj*
NOON   *n* pl. -S midday
NOONDAY   *n* pl. -DAYS noon
NOONING   *n* pl. -S a meal eaten at noon
NOONTIDE   *n* pl. -S noon
NOONTIME   *n* pl. -S noon
NOOSE   *v* NOOSED, NOOSING, NOOSES to secure with a type of loop
NOOSER   *n* pl. -S one that nooses
NOPAL   *n* pl. -S a cactus
NOPE   *adv* no
NOR   *conj* and not
NORDIC   *adj* pertaining to cross-country ski racing and ski jumping
NORI   *n* pl. -S dried seaweed pressed into sheets
NORIA   *n* pl. -S a type of waterwheel
NORITE   *n* pl. -S a granular rock
NORITIC *adj*
NORLAND   *n* pl. -S a region in the north
NORM   *n* pl. -S a standard regarded as typical for a specific group
NORMAL   *n* pl. -S the usual or expected state or form
NORMALCY   *n* pl. -CIES conformity with the norm
NORMALLY   *adv* as a rule; usually
NORMANDE   *adj* prepared with foods associated with Normandy
NORMED   *adj* having a norm
NORMLESS   *adj* having no norm
NORTH   *n* pl. -S a point of the compass
NORTHER   *n* pl. -S a wind or storm from the north
NORTHERN   *n* pl. -S a person living in the north
NORTHING   *n* pl. -S movement toward the north
NOSE   *v* NOSED, NOSING, NOSES to sniff with the nose (the organ of smell)
NOSEBAG   *n* pl. -S a feedbag
NOSEBAND   *n* pl. -S a part of a horse's bridle
NOSED   past tense of nose
NOSEDIVE   *n* pl. -S a steep downward plunge
NOSEGAY   *n* pl. -GAYS a bouquet
NOSELESS   *adj* having no nose
NOSELIKE   *adj* resembling a nose
NOSEY   *adj* NOSIER, NOSIEST nosy
NOSH   *v* -ED, -ING, -ES to eat snacks between meals
NOSHER   *n* pl. -S one that noshes
NOSIER   comparative of nosy, nosey
NOSIEST   superlative of nosy, nosey
NOSILY   *adv* in a nosy manner
NOSINESS   *n* pl. -ES the quality of being nosy
NOSING   *n* pl. -S a projecting edge
NOSOLOGY   *n* pl. -GIES a classification of diseases
NOSTOC   *n* pl. -S a freshwater alga
NOSTRIL   *n* pl. -S an external opening of the nose
NOSTRUM   *n* pl. -S a medicine of one's own invention
NOSY   *adj* NOSIER, NOSIEST unduly curious
NOT   *adv* in no way
NOTA   pl. of notum
NOTABLE   *n* pl. -S a person of distinction
NOTABLY   *adv* in a distinguished manner
NOTAL   *adj* pertaining to a notum
NOTARIAL   *adj* pertaining to a notary
NOTARIZE   *v* -RIZED, -RIZING, -RIZES to certify through a notary
NOTARY   *n* pl. -RIES a public officer who certifies documents
NOTATE   *v* -TATED, -TATING, -TATES to put into notation
NOTATION   *n* pl. -S a system of symbols
NOTCH   *v* -ED, -ING, -ES to make an angular cut in
NOTCHER   *n* pl. -S one that notches
NOTE   *v* NOTED, NOTING, NOTES to write down
NOTEBOOK   *n* pl. -S a book in which to write
NOTECASE   *n* pl. -S a billfold
NOTED   past tense of note
NOTEDLY   *adv* in a famous manner
NOTELESS   *adj* undistinguished
NOTEPAD   *n* pl. -S a number of sheets of paper glued together at one end
NOTER   *n* pl. -S one that notes
NOTHER   *adj* different

NOTHING   *n* pl. -S the absence of all quantity or magnitude

NOTICE   *v* -TICED, -TICING, -TICES to become aware of

NOTICER   *n* pl. -S one that notices

NOTIFIER   *n* pl. -S one that notifies

NOTIFY   *v* -FIED, -FYING, -FIES to inform

NOTING   present participle of note

NOTION   *n* pl. -S a general idea **NOTIONAL** *adj*

NOTORNIS   *n* pl. NOTORNIS a flightless bird

NOTTURNO   *n* pl. -NI a nocturne

NOTUM   *n* pl. -TA a part of the thorax of an insect

NOUGAT   *n* pl. -S a chewy candy

NOUGHT   *n* pl. -S naught

NOUMENON   *n* pl. -MENA an object of intellectual intuition **NOUMENAL** *adj*

NOUN   *n* pl. -S a word used to denote the name of something **NOUNAL, NOUNLESS** *adj* **NOUNALLY** *adv*

NOURISH   *v* -ED, -ING, -ES to sustain with food

NOUS   *n* pl. -ES mind, reason, or intellect

NOUVEAU   *adj* newly arrived or developed

NOUVELLE   *adj* pertaining to a form of French cooking

NOVA   *n* pl. -VAS or -VAE a type of star **NOVALIKE** *adj*

NOVATION   *n* pl. -S the substitution of a new legal obligation for an old one

NOVEL   *n* pl. -S a fictional prose narrative

NOVELISE   *v* -ISED, -ISING, -ISES to novelize

NOVELIST   *n* pl. -S a writer of novels

NOVELIZE   *v* -IZED, -IZING, -IZES to put into the form of a novel

NOVELLA   *n* pl. -LAS or -LE a short novel

NOVELLY   *adv* in a new or unusual manner

NOVELTY   *n* pl. -TIES something new or unusual

NOVENA   *n* pl. -NAS or -NAE a religious devotion lasting nine days

NOVERCAL   *adj* pertaining to a stepmother

NOVICE   *n* pl. -S a person new to any field or activity

NOW   *n* pl. -S the present time

NOWADAYS   *adv* in these times

NOWAY   *adv* in no way

NOWAYS   *adv* noway

NOWHERE   *n* pl. -S a nonexistent place

NOWISE   *adv* not at all

NOWNESS   *n* pl. -ES the state of existing at the present time

NOWT   *n* pl. -S naught

NOXIOUS   *adj* harmful to health

NOYADE   *n* pl. -S an execution by drowning

NOZZLE   *n* pl. -S a projecting spout

NTH   *adj* pertaining to an indefinitely large ordinal number

NU   *n* pl. -S a Greek letter

NUANCE   *n* pl. -S a slight variation **NUANCED** *adj*

NUB   *n* pl. -S a protuberance or knob

NUBBIER   comparative of nubby

NUBBIEST   superlative of nubby

NUBBIN   *n* pl. -S an undeveloped fruit

NUBBLE   *n* pl. -S a small nub

NUBBLY   *adj* -BLIER, -BLIEST having nubbles

NUBBY   *adj* -BIER, -BIEST having nubs

NUBIA   *n* pl. -S a woman's scarf

NUBILE   *adj* suitable for marriage

NUBILITY   *n* pl. -TIES the quality of being nubile

NUBILOSE   *adj* nubilous

NUBILOUS   *adj* cloudy

NUCELLUS   *n* pl. -LI the essential part of a plant ovule **NUCELLAR** *adj*

NUCHA   *n* pl. -CHAE the nape of the neck

NUCHAL   *n* pl. -S an anatomical part lying in the region of the nape

NUCLEAL   *adj* nuclear

NUCLEAR   *adj* pertaining to a nucleus

NUCLEASE   *n* pl. -S an enzyme

NUCLEATE   *v* -ATED, -ATING, -ATES to form into a nucleus

NUCLEI   a pl. of nucleus

NUCLEIN   *n* pl. -S a protein found in nuclei

NUCLEOID   *n* pl. -S the DNA-containing area of certain cells

NUCLEOLE   *n* pl. -S a part of a nucleus

NUCLEOLI   *n/pl* nucleoles

NUCLEON   *n* pl. -S a subatomic particle

NUCLEUS   *n* pl. -CLEI or -CLEUSES an essential part of a cell

NUCLIDE   *n* pl. -S a species of atom **NUCLIDIC** *adj*

NUDE   *adj* NUDER, NUDEST being without clothing or covering NUDELY *adv*

NUDE   *n* pl. -S a nude figure

NUDENESS   *n* pl. -ES nudity

NUDER   comparative of nude

NUDEST   superlative of nude

NUDGE   *v* NUDGED, NUDGING, NUDGES to push gently

NUDGER   *n* pl. -S one that nudges

NUDICAUL   *adj* having leafless stems

NUDIE   *n* pl. -S a movie featuring nude performers

NUDISM   *n* pl. -S the practice of going nude

NUDIST   *n* pl. -S an advocate of nudism

NUDITY   *n* pl. -TIES the state of being nude

NUDNICK   *n* pl. -S nudnik

NUDNIK   *n* pl. -S an annoying person

NUDZH   *v* -ED, -ING, -ES to noodge

NUGATORY   *adj* having no power

NUGGET   *n* pl. -S a mass of solid matter NUGGETY *adj*

NUISANCE   *n* pl. -S a source of annoyance

NUKE   *v* NUKED, NUKING, NUKES to attack with nuclear weapons

NULL   *v* -ED, -ING, -S to reduce to nothing

NULLAH   *n* pl. -S a ravine

NULLIFY   *v* -FIED, -FYING, -FIES to make useless or ineffective

NULLITY   *n* pl. -TIES something of no legal force

NUMB   *adj* NUMBER, NUMBEST lacking sensation

NUMB   *v* -ED, -ING, -S to make numb

NUMBAT   *n* pl. -S a small Australian mammal

NUMBER   *v* -ED, -ING, -S to count

NUMBERER   *n* pl. -S one that numbers

NUMBFISH   *n* pl. -ES a fish capable of emitting electric shocks

NUMBLES   *n/pl* animal entrails

NUMBLY   *adv* in a numb manner

NUMBNESS   *n* pl. -ES the state of being numb

NUMEN   *n* pl. -MINA a deity

NUMERACY   *n* pl. -CIES the ability to understand basic mathematics

NUMERAL   *n* pl. -S a symbol that expresses a number

NUMERARY   *adj* pertaining to numbers

NUMERATE   *v* -ATED, -ATING, -ATES to count

NUMERIC   *n* pl. -S a numeral

NUMEROUS   *adj* many

NUMINA   pl. of numen

NUMINOUS   *n* pl. -ES the presence or revelation of the numen

NUMMARY   *adj* pertaining to coins

NUMMULAR   *adj* shaped like a coin

NUMSKULL   *n* pl. -S a dunce

NUN   *n* pl. -S a woman belonging to a religious order

NUNATAK   *n* pl. -S a mountain peak completely surrounded by glacial ice

NUNCHAKU   *n* pl. -S a Japanese weapon

NUNCIO   *n* pl. -CIOS an ambassador from the pope

NUNCLE   *n* pl. -S an uncle

NUNLIKE   *adj* resembling a nun

NUNNERY   *n* pl. -NERIES a religious house for nuns

NUNNISH   *adj* of, pertaining to, or characteristic of a nun

NUPTIAL   *n* pl. -S a wedding

NURD   *n* pl. -S nerd

NURL   *n* -ED, -ING, -S to knurl

NURSE   *v* NURSED, NURSING, NURSES to care for the sick or infirm

NURSER   *n* pl. -S a baby's bottle

NURSERY   *n* pl. -ERIES a room for young children

NURSING   *n* pl. -S the profession of one who nurses

NURSLING   *n* pl. -S an infant

NURTURAL   *adj* pertaining to the process of nurturing

NURTURE   *v* -TURED, -TURING, -TURES to nourish

NURTURER   *n* pl. -S one that nurtures

NUT   *v* NUTTED, NUTTING, NUTS to gather nuts (hard-shelled dry fruits)

NUTANT   *adj* drooping

NUTATE   *v* -TATED, -TATING, -TATES to exhibit nutation

NUTATION   *n* pl. -S an oscillatory movement of the axis of a rotating body

NUTBROWN   *adj* of a dark brown

NUTCASE   *n* pl. -S a crazy person

NUTGALL   *n* pl. -S a gallnut

NUTGRASS   *n* pl. -ES a perennial herb

NUTHATCH   *n* pl. -ES a small bird

NUTHOUSE   *n* pl. -S an insane asylum

NUTLET   *n* pl. -S a small nut

NUTLIKE   *adj* resembling a nut

NUTMEAT   n pl. -S the edible kernel of a nut

NUTMEG   n pl. -S an aromatic seed used as a spice

NUTPICK   n pl. -S a device for extracting the kernels from nuts

NUTRIA   n pl. -S the coypu

NUTRIENT   n pl. -S a nourishing substance

NUTSEDGE   n pl. -S nutgrass

NUTSHELL   n pl. -S the shell of a nut

NUTSY   adj NUTSIER, NUTSIEST crazy

NUTTED   past tense of nut

NUTTER   n pl. -S one that gathers nuts

NUTTING   n pl. -S the act of gathering nuts

NUTTY   adj -TIER, -TIEST silly; crazy **NUTTILY** adv

NUTWOOD   n pl. -S a nut-bearing tree

NUZZLE   v -ZLED, -ZLING, -ZLES to push with the nose

NUZZLER   n pl. -S one that nuzzles

NYALA   n pl. -S an antelope

NYLGHAI   n pl. -S nilgai

NYLGHAU   n pl. -S nilgai

NYLON   n pl. -S a synthetic material

NYMPH   n pl. -S a female spirit

NYMPHAL, NYMPHEAN adj

NYMPHA   n pl. -PHAE a fold of the vulva

NYMPHET   n pl. -S a young nymph

NYMPHO   n pl. -PHOS a woman obsessed by sexual desire

NYSTATIN   n pl. -S an antibiotic

OAF *n* pl. OAFS or OAVES a clumsy, stupid person **OAFISH** *adj* **OAFISHLY** *adv*

OAK *n* pl. -S a hardwood tree or shrub **OAKEN, OAKLIKE** *adj*

OAKMOSS *n* pl. -ES a lichen that grows on oak trees

OAKUM *n* pl. -S loosely twisted hemp fiber

OAR *v* -ED, -ING, -S to propel with oars (long, broad-bladed poles)

OARFISH *n* pl. -ES a marine fish

OARLESS *adj* having no oars

OARLIKE *adj* resembling an oar

OARLOCK *n* pl. -S a device for holding an oar in place

OARSMAN *n* pl. -MEN a person who rows a boat

OASIS *n* pl. OASES a green area in a desert region

OAST *n* pl. -S a type of kiln

OAT *n* pl. -S a cereal grass

OATCAKE *n* pl. -S a cake made of oatmeal

OATEN *adj* pertaining to oats

OATER *n* pl. -S a cowboy movie

OATH *n* pl. -S a formal declaration or promise to fulfill a pledge

OATLIKE *adj* resembling oats

OATMEAL *n* pl. -S meal made from oats

OAVES a pl. of oaf

OBCONIC *adj* conical with the apex below

OBDURACY *n* pl. -CIES the quality or an instance of being obdurate

OBDURATE *adj* stubborn

OBE *n* pl. -S obeah

OBEAH *n* pl. -S a form of sorcery of African origin

OBEAHISM *n* pl. -S the use of obeah

OBEDIENT *adj* obeying or willing to obey

OBEISANT *adj* showing reverence or respect

OBELI pl. of obelus

OBELIA *n* pl. -S a marine hydroid

OBELISE *v* -LISED, -LISING, -LISES to obelize

OBELISK *n* pl. -S a four-sided shaft of stone with a pyramidal top

OBELISM *n* pl. -S the act of obelizing

OBELIZE *v* -LIZED, -LIZING, -LIZES to mark with an obelus

OBELUS *n* pl. -LI a symbol used in ancient manuscripts to indicate a doubtful passage

OBESE *adj* very fat **OBESELY** *adv*

OBESITY *n* pl. -TIES the state or condition of being obese

OBEY *v* -ED, -ING, -S to follow the commands or guidance of **OBEYABLE** *adj*

OBEYER *n* pl. -S one that obeys

OBI *n* pl. -S obeah

OBIA *n* pl. -S obeah

OBIISM *n* pl. -S obeahism

OBIT *n* pl. -S an obituary

OBITUARY *n* pl. -ARIES a published notice of a death

OBJECT *v* -ED, -ING, -S to argue in opposition

OBJECTOR *n* pl. -S one that objects

OBLAST *n* pl. -LASTS or -LASTI an administrative division of Russia

OBLATE *n* pl. -S a layman residing in a monastery

OBLATELY *adv* elliptically

OBLATION *n* pl. -S the act of making a religious offering **OBLATORY** *adj*

OBLIGATE *v* -GATED, -GATING, -GATES to oblige

OBLIGATO *n* pl. -TI or -TOS an important musical part

OBLIGE *v* OBLIGED, OBLIGING, OBLIGES to put in one's debt by a favor or service

OBLIGEE *n* pl. -S one that is obliged

OBLIGER *n* pl. -S one that obliges

OBLIGING present participle of oblige

OBLIGOR *n* pl. -S one who places himself under a legal obligation

OBLIQUE *v* OBLIQUED, OBLIQUING, OBLIQUES to slant

OBLIVION *n* pl. -S the state of being forgotten; the act of forgetting

OBLONG *n* pl. -S something that is oblong (elongated)

OBLONGLY *adv* in an oblong manner

OBLOQUY *n* pl. -QUIES abusive language

OBOE *n* pl. -S a woodwind instrument

OBOIST *n* pl. -S one who plays the oboe

OBOL *n* pl. -S a coin of ancient Greece

OBOLE *n* pl. -S a coin of medieval France

OBOLUS *n* pl. -LI an obol

OBOVATE *adj* ovate with the narrow end at the base

OBOVOID *adj* ovoid with the narrow end at the base

OBSCENE *adj* -SCENER, -SCENEST indecent

OBSCURE *adj* -SCURER, -SCUREST dark or indistinct

OBSCURE *v* -SCURED, -SCURING, -SCURES to make obscure

OBSEQUY *n* pl. -QUIES a funeral rite

OBSERVE *v* -SERVED, -SERVING, -SERVES to look attentively

OBSERVER *n* pl. -S one that observes

OBSESS *v* -ED, -ING, -ES to dominate the thoughts of

OBSESSOR *n* pl. -S something that obsesses

OBSIDIAN *n* pl. -S a volcanic glass

OBSOLETE *v* -LETED, -LETING, -LETES to make out-of-date

OBSTACLE *n* pl. -S something that obstructs

OBSTRUCT *v* -ED, -ING, -S to get in the way of

OBTAIN *v* -ED, -ING, -S to gain possession of

OBTAINER *n* pl. -S one that obtains

OBTECT *adj* covered by a hardened secretion

OBTECTED *adj* obtect

OBTEST *v* -ED, -ING, -S to beseech

OBTRUDE *v* -TRUDED, -TRUDING, -TRUDES to thrust forward

OBTRUDER *n* pl. -S one that obtrudes

OBTUND *v* -ED, -ING, -S to deaden

OBTURATE *v* -RATED, -RATING, -RATES to close or stop up

OBTUSE *adj* -TUSER, -TUSEST dull **OBTUSELY** *adv*

OBTUSITY *n* pl. -TIES the state of being obtuse

OBVERSE *n* pl. -S the side of a coin bearing the main design

OBVERT *v* -ED, -ING, -S to turn so as to show a different surface

OBVIATE *v* -ATED, -ATING, -ATES to prevent or eliminate by effective measures **OBVIABLE** *adj*

OBVIATOR *n* pl. -S one that obviates

OBVIOUS *adj* easily perceived or understood

OBVOLUTE *adj* rolled or tuned in

OCA *n* pl. -S a South American herb

OCARINA *n* pl. -S a wind instrument

OCCASION *v* -ED, -ING, -S to cause

OCCIDENT *n* pl. -S the west

OCCIPUT *n* pl. -PITA or -PUTS the back part of the skull

OCCLUDE *v* -CLUDED, -CLUDING, -CLUDES to close or stop up

OCCLUSAL *adj* pertaining to the biting surface of a tooth

OCCULT *v* -ED, -ING, -S to conceal

OCCULTER *n* pl -S one that occults

OCCULTLY *adv* secretly

OCCUPANT *n* pl. -S a resident

OCCUPIER *n* pl. -S one that occupies

OCCUPY *v* -PIED, -PYING, -PIES to engage the attention or energies of

OCCUR *v* -CURRED, -CURRING, -CURS to take place

OCEAN *n* pl. -S the vast body of salt water that covers most of the earth's surface **OCEANIC** *adj*

OCEANAUT *n* pl. -S an aquanaut

OCELLAR	adj pertaining to an ocellus	OCTUPLET	n pl. -S a group of eight related items
OCELLATE	adj having ocelli		
OCELLUS	n pl. -LI a minute simple eye	OCTUPLEX	adj being eight times as great
OCELOT	n pl. -S an American wildcat OCELOID adj	OCTUPLING	present participle of octuple
OCHER	v -ED, -ING, -S to color with ocher (a red or yellow iron ore used as a pigment)	OCTUPLY	adv to eight times the degree
		OCTYL	n pl. -S a univalent radical
		OCULAR	n pl. -S an eyepiece
		OCULARLY	adv by means of the eyes or sight
OCHEROUS	adj containing or resembling ocher	OCULIST	n pl. -S a physician who treats diseases of the eye
OCHERY	adj ocherous		
OCHONE	interj — used to express grief	OCULUS	n pl. -LI a circular window
OCHRE	v OCHRED, OCHRING, OCHRES to ocher	OD	n pl. -S a hypothetical force of natural power
OCHREA	n pl. -REAE ocrea	ODALISK	n pl. -S a female slave in a harem
OCHREOUS	adj ocherous		
OCHRING	present participle of ochre	ODD	adj ODDER, ODDEST unusual
OCHROID	adj ocherous		
OCHROUS	adj ocherous	ODD	n pl. -S one that is odd
OCHRY	adj ochery	ODDBALL	n pl. -S an eccentric person
OCKER	n pl. -S a boorish person	ODDISH	adj somewhat odd
OCOTILLO	n pl. -LOS a Mexican shrub	ODDITY	n pl. -TIES one that is odd
OCREA	n pl. -REAE a sheathing plant part	ODDLY	adv in an odd manner
		ODDMENT	n pl. -S a remnant
OCREATE	adj having ocreae	ODDNESS	n pl. -ES the state of being odd
OCTAD	n pl. -S a group of eight OCTADIC adj		
		ODE	n pl. -S a lyric poem
OCTAGON	n pl. -S an eight-sided polygon	ODEON	n pl. -S odeum
OCTAL	adj pertaining to a number system with a base of eight	ODEUM	n pl. ODEA or ODEUMS a theater or concert hall
OCTAN	n pl. -S a fever recurring every eighth day	ODIC	adj pertaining to an ode
		ODIOUS	adj deserving or causing hatred ODIOUSLY adv
OCTANE	n pl. -S a liquid hydrocarbon		
OCTANGLE	n pl. -S an octagon	ODIST	n pl. -S one who writes odes
OCTANOL	n pl. -S an alcohol	ODIUM	n pl. -S hatred
OCTANT	n pl. -S an eighth of a circle OCTANTAL adj	ODOGRAPH	n pl. -S an odometer
		ODOMETER	n pl. -S a device for measuring distance traveled
OCTARCHY	n pl. -TARCHIES a government by eight persons	ODOMETRY	n pl. -TRIES the process of using an odometer
OCTAVE	n pl. -S a type of musical interval OCTAVAL adj	ODONATE	n pl. -S any of an order of predacious insects
OCTAVO	n pl. -VOS a page size		
OCTET	n pl. -S a group of eight	ODONTOID	n pl. -S a toothlike vertebral projection
OCTETTE	n pl. -S octet		
OCTONARY	n pl. -NARIES a stanza of eight lines	ODOR	n pl. -S the property of a substance that affects the sense of smell ODORED, ODORFUL adj
OCTOPOD	n pl. -S any of an order of eight-armed mollusks		
OCTOPUS	n pl. -PUSES, -PI, or -PODES a nocturnal octopod	ODORANT	n pl. -S an odorous substance
		ODORIZE	v -IZED, -IZING, -IZES to make odorous
OCTOROON	n pl. -S a person of one-eighth black ancestry	ODORLESS	adj having no odor
		ODOROUS	adj having an odor
OCTROI	n pl. -S a tax on certain articles brought into a city	ODOUR	n pl. -S odor ODOURFUL adj
		ODYL	n pl. -S an od
OCTUPLE	v -PLED, -PLING, -PLES to multiply by eight	ODYLE	n pl. -S odyl

ODYSSEY   *n* pl. -SEYS a long, wandering journey

OE   *n* pl. -S a whirlwind off the Faeroe islands

OECOLOGY   *n* pl. -GIES ecology

OEDEMA   *n* pl. -MAS or -MATA edema

OEDIPAL   *adj* pertaining to the libidinal feelings in a child toward the parent of the opposite sex

OEDIPEAN   *adj* oedipal

OEILLADE   *n* pl. -S an amorous look

OENOLOGY   *n* pl. -GIES the study of wines

OENOMEL   *n* pl. -S an ancient Greek beverage of wine and honey

OERSTED   *n* pl. -S a unit of magnetic intensity

OESTRIN   *n* pl. -S estrin

OESTRIOL   *n* pl. -S estriol

OESTRONE   *n* pl. -S estrone

OESTROUS   *adj* estrous

OESTRUM   *n* pl. -S estrum

OESTRUS   *n* pl. -ES estrus

OEUVRE   *n* pl. -S a work of art

OF   *prep* coming from

OFF   *v* -ED, -ING, -S to go away

OFFAL   *n* pl. -S waste material

OFFBEAT   *n* pl. -S an unaccented beat in a musical measure

OFFCAST   *n* pl. -S a castoff

OFFCUT   *n* pl. -S something that is cut off

OFFENCE   *n* pl. -S offense

OFFEND   *v* -ED, -ING, -S to commit an offense

OFFENDER   *n* pl. -S one that offends

OFFENSE   *n* pl. -S a violation of a moral or social code

OFFER   *v* -ED, -ING, -S to present for acceptance or rejection

OFFERER   *n* pl. -S one that offers

OFFERING   *n* pl. -S a contribution

OFFEROR   *n* pl. -S offerer

OFFHAND   *adv* without preparation

OFFICE   *n* pl. -S a position of authority

OFFICER   *v* -ED, -ING, -S to furnish with officers (persons holding positions of authority)

OFFICIAL   *n* pl. -S one that holds a position of authority

OFFING   *n* pl. -S the near future

OFFISH   *adj* aloof **OFFISHLY** *adv*

OFFKEY   *adj* pitched higher or lower than the correct musical tone

OFFLOAD   *v* -ED, -ING, -S to unload

OFFPRINT   *v* -ED, -ING, -S to reprint an excerpt

OFFRAMP   *n* pl. -S a road leading off an expressway

OFFSET   *v* -SET, -SETTING, -SETS to compensate for

OFFSHOOT   *n* pl. -S a lateral shoot from a main stem

OFFSHORE   *adv* away from the shore

OFFSIDE   *n* pl. -S an improper football play

OFFSTAGE   *n* pl. -S a part of a stage not visible to the audience

OFFTRACK   *adj* away from a racetrack

OFT   *adv* OFTER, OFTEST often

OFTEN   *adv* -ENER, -ENEST frequently

OFTTIMES   *adv* often

OGAM   *n* pl. -S ogham

OGDOAD   *n* pl. -S a group of eight

OGEE   *n* pl. -S an S-shaped molding

OGHAM   *n* pl. -S an Old Irish alphabet **OGHAMIC** *adj*

OGHAMIST   *n* pl. -S one who writes in ogham

OGIVE   *n* pl. -S a pointed arch **OGIVAL** *adj*

OGLE   *v* OGLED, OGLING, OGLES to stare at

OGLER   *n* pl. -S one that ogles

OGRE   *n* pl. -S a monster

OGREISH   *adj* resembling an ogre

OGREISM   *n* pl. -S the state of being ogreish

OGRESS   *n* pl. -ES a female ogre

OGRISH   *adj* ogreish **OGRISHLY** *adv*

OGRISM   *n* pl. -S ogreism

OH   *v* -ED, -ING, -S to exclaim in surprise, pain, or desire

OHIA   *n* pl. -S lehua

OHM   *n* pl. -S a unit of electrical resistance **OHMIC** *adj*

OHMAGE   *n* pl. -S electrical resistance expressed in ohms

OHMMETER   *n* pl. -S an instrument for measuring ohmage

OHO   *interj* — used to express surprise or exultation

OIDIUM   *n* pl. OIDIA a type of fungus

OIL   *v* -ED, -ING, -S to supply with oil (a greasy liquid used for lubrication, fuel, or illumination)

OILBIRD   *n* pl. -S a tropical bird

OILCAMP   *n* pl. -S a living area for workers at an oil well

OILCAN   *n* pl. -S a can for applying lubricating oil

OILCLOTH   *n* pl. -S a waterproof fabric

OILCUP   *n* pl. -S a closed cup for supplying lubricant

OILER   *n* pl. -S one that oils

OILHOLE   *n* pl. -S a hole through which lubricating oil is injected

OILIER   comparative of oily

OILIEST   superlative of oily

OILILY   *adv* in an oily manner

OILINESS   *n* pl. -ES the state of being oily

OILMAN   *n* pl. -MEN one who owns or operates oil wells

OILPAPER   *n* pl. -S a water-resistant paper

OILPROOF   *adj* impervious to oil

OILSEED   *n* pl. -S a seed from which oil is pressed out

OILSKIN   *n* pl. -S a waterproof fabric

OILSTONE   *n* pl. -S a stone for sharpening tools

OILTIGHT   *adj* being so tight as to prevent the passage of oil

OILWAY   *n* pl. -WAYS a channel for the passage of oil

OILY   *adj* OILIER, OILIEST covered or soaked with oil

OINK   *v* -ED, -ING, -S to utter the natural grunt of a hog

OINOLOGY   *n* pl. -GIES oenology

OINOMEL   *n* pl. -S oenomel

OINTMENT   *n* pl. -S a viscous preparation applied to the skin as a medicine or cosmetic

OITICICA   *n* pl. -S a South American tree

OKA   *n* pl. -S a Turkish unit of weight

OKAPI   *n* pl. -S an African ruminant mammal

OKAY   *v* -ED, -ING, -S to approve

OKE   *n* pl. -S oka

OKEH   *n* pl. -S approval

OKEYDOKE   *adj* perfectly all right

OKRA   *n* pl. -S a tall annual herb

OLD   *adj* OLDER, OLDEST or ELDER, ELDEST living or existing for a relatively long time

OLD   *n* pl. -S an individual of a specified age

OLDEN   *adj* pertaining to a bygone era

OLDIE   *n* pl. -S a popular song of an earlier day

OLDISH   *adj* somewhat old

OLDNESS   *n* pl. -ES the state of being old

OLDSQUAW   *n* pl. -S a sea duck

OLDSTER   *n* pl. -S an old person

OLDSTYLE   *n* pl. -S a style of printing type

OLDWIFE   *n* pl. -WIVES a marine fish

OLDY   *n* pl. OLDIES oldie

OLE   *n* pl. -S a shout of approval

OLEA   pl. of oleum

OLEANDER   *n* pl. -S a flowering shrub

OLEASTER   *n* pl. -S a flowering shrub

OLEATE   *n* pl. -S a chemical salt

OLEFIN   *n* pl. -S an alkene OLEFINIC *adj*

OLEFINE   *n* pl. -S olefin

OLEIC   *adj* pertaining to oil

OLEIN   *n* pl. -S the liquid portion of a fat

OLEINE   *n* pl. -S olein

OLEO   *n* pl. OLEOS margarine

OLEUM   *n* pl. OLEA oil

OLEUM   *n* pl. -S a corrosive liquid

OLIBANUM   *n* pl. -S a fragrant resin

OLIGARCH   *n* pl. -S a ruler in a government by the few

OLIGOMER   *n* pl. -S a type of polymer

OLIGURIA   *n* pl. -S reduced excretion of urine

OLIO   *n* pl. OLIOS a miscellaneous collection

OLIVARY   *adj* shaped like an olive

OLIVE   *n* pl. -S the small oval fruit of a Mediterranean tree

OLIVINE   *n* pl. -S a mineral OLIVINIC *adj*

OLLA   *n* pl. -S a wide-mouthed pot or jar

OLOGIST   *n* pl. -S an expert in a particular ology

OLOGY   *n* pl. -GIES a branch of knowledge

OLOROSO   *n* pl. -SOS a dark sherry

OLYMPIAD   *n* pl. -S a celebration of the Olympic Games

OM   *n* pl. -S a mantra used in contemplation of ultimate reality

OMASUM   *n* pl. -SA the third stomach of a ruminant

OMBER   *n* pl. -S ombre

OMBRE   *n* pl. -S a card game

OMEGA   *n* pl. -S a Greek letter

OMELET   *n* pl. -S a dish of beaten eggs cooked and folded around a filling

OMELETTE   *n* pl. -S omelet

OMEN   *v* -ED, -ING, -S to be an omen (a prophetic sign) of

OMENTUM   *n* pl. -TA or -TUMS a fold in an abdominal membrane **OMENTAL** *adj*

OMER   *n* pl. -S a Hebrew unit of dry measure

OMICRON   *n* pl. -S a Greek letter

OMIKRON   *n* pl. -S omicron

OMINOUS   *adj* portending evil

OMISSION   *n* pl. -S something left undone

OMISSIVE   *adj* marked by omission

OMIT   *v* OMITTED, OMITTING, OMITS to leave out

OMITTER   *n* pl. -S one that omits

OMNIARCH   *n* pl. -S an almighty ruler

OMNIBUS   *n* pl. -ES a bus

OMNIFIC   *adj* unlimited in creative power

OMNIFORM   *adj* of all forms

OMNIMODE   *adj* of all modes

OMNIVORA   *n/pl* omnivores

OMNIVORE   *n* pl. -S an animal that eats all kinds of food

OMOPHAGY   *n* pl. -GIES the eating of raw flesh

OMPHALOS   *n* pl. -LI a central point

ON   *n* pl. -S the side of the wicket where a batsman stands in cricket

ONAGER   *n* pl. -GERS or -GRI a wild ass of central Asia

ONANISM   *n* pl. -S coitus deliberately interrupted to prevent insemination

ONANIST   *n* pl. -S one who practices onanism

ONBOARD   *adj* carried aboard a vehicle

ONCE   *n* one single time

ONCIDIUM   *n* pl. -S a tropical orchid

ONCOGENE   *n* pl. -S a gene that causes a cell to become cancerous

ONCOLOGY   *n* pl. -GIES the science of tumors

ONCOMING   *n* pl. -S an approach

ONDOGRAM   *n* pl. -S a graph of electric wave forms

ONE   *n* pl. -S a number

ONEFOLD   *adj* constituting a single, undivided whole

ONEIRIC   *adj* pertaining to dreams

ONENESS   *n* pl. -ES unity

ONEROUS   *adj* burdensome or oppressive

ONERY   *adj* -ERIER, -ERIEST ornery

ONESELF   *pron* a person's self

ONETIME   *adj* former

ONGOING   *adj* continuing without interruption

ONION   *n* pl. -S the edible bulb of a cultivated herb **ONIONY** *adj*

ONIUM   *adj* characterized by a complex cation

ONLOOKER   *n* pl. -S a spectator

ONLY   *adv* with nothing or no one else

ONRUSH   *n* pl. -ES a forward rush or flow

ONSET   *n* pl. -S a beginning

ONSHORE   *adv* toward the shore

ONSIDE   *adj* not offside

ONSTAGE   *adj* being on a part of the stage visible to the audience

ONSTREAM   *adv* in or into production

ONTIC   *adj* having real being or existence

ONTO   *prep* to a position upon

ONTOGENY   *n* pl. -NIES the development of an individual organism

ONTOLOGY   *n* pl. -GIES the branch of philosophy that deals with being

ONUS   *n* pl. -ES a burden or responsibility

ONWARD   *adv* toward a point ahead or in front

ONWARDS   *adv* onward

ONYX   *n* pl. -ES a variety of quartz

OOCYST   *n* pl. -S a zygote

OOCYTE   *n* pl. -S an egg before maturation

OODLES   *n* pl. OODLES a large amount

OODLINS   *n* pl. OODLINS oodles

OOGAMETE   *n* pl. -S a female gamete of certain protozoa

OOGAMOUS   *adj* having structurally dissimilar gametes

OOGAMY   *n* pl. -MIES the state of being oogamous

OOGENY   *n* pl. -NIES the development of ova

OOGONIUM   *n* pl. -NIA or -NIUMS a female sexual organ in certain algae and fungi **OOGONIAL** *adj*

OOH   *v* -ED, -ING, -S to exclaim in amazement, joy, or surprise

OOLACHAN   *n* pl. -S eulachon

OOLITE   *n* pl. -S a variety of limestone **OOLITIC** *adj*

OOLITH   *n* pl. -S oolite

OOLOGIST   *n* pl. -S an expert in oology

OOLOGY   *n* pl. -GIES the study of birds' eggs **OOLOGIC** *adj*

OOLONG   *n* pl. -S a dark Chinese tea

OOMIAC   *n* pl. -S umiak

OOMIACK *n* pl. -S umiak

OOMIAK *n* pl. -S umiak

OOMPAH *v* -ED, -ING, -S to play a repeated rhythmic bass accompaniment

OOMPH *n* pl. -S spirited vigor

OOPHYTE *n* pl. -S a stage of development in certain plants **OOPHYTIC** *adj*

OOPS *interj* — used to express mild apology, surprise, or dismay

OORALI *n* pl. -S curare

OORIE *adj* ourie

OOSPERM *n* pl. -S a fertilized egg

OOSPHERE *n* pl. -S an unfertilized egg within an oogonium

OOSPORE *n* pl. -S a fertilized egg within an oogonium **OOSPORIC** *adj*

OOT *n* pl. -S out

OOTHECA *n* pl. -CAE an egg case of certain insects **OOTHECAL** *adj*

OOTID *n* pl. -S one of the four sections into which a mature ovum divides

OOZE *v* OOZED, OOZING, OOZES to flow or leak out slowly

OOZINESS *n* pl. -ES the state of being oozy

OOZY *adj* OOZIER, OOZIEST containing or resembling soft mud or slime **OOZILY** *adv*

OP *n* pl. -S a style of abstract art

OPACIFY *v* -FIED, -FYING, -FIES to make opaque

OPACITY *n* pl. -TIES something that is opaque

OPAH *n* pl. -S a marine fish

OPAL *n* pl. -S a mineral

OPALESCE *v* -ESCED, -ESCING, -ESCES to emit an iridescent shimmer of colors

OPALINE *n* pl. -S an opaque white glass

OPAQUE *adj* OPAQUER, OPAQUEST impervious to light **OPAQUELY** *adv*

OPAQUE *v* OPAQUED, OPAQUING, OPAQUES to make opaque

OPE *v* OPED, OPING, OPES to open

OPEN *adj* OPENER, OPENEST affording unobstructed access, passage, or view

OPEN *v* -ED, -ING, -S to cause to become open **OPENABLE** *adj*

OPENCAST *adj* worked from a surface open to the air

OPENER *n* pl. -S one that opens

OPENING *n* pl. -S a vacant or unobstructed space

OPENLY *adv* in an open manner

OPENNESS *n* pl. -ES the state of being open

OPENWORK *n* pl. -S ornamental or structural work containing numerous openings

OPERA *n* pl. -S a form of musical drama

OPERABLE *adj* usable **OPERABLY** *adv*

OPERAND *n* pl. -S a quantity on which a mathematical operation is performed

OPERANT *n* pl. -S one that operates

OPERATE *v* -ATED, -ATING, -ATES to perform a function

OPERATIC *n* pl. -S the technique of staging operas

OPERATOR *n* pl. -S a symbol that represents a mathematical function

OPERCELE *n* pl. -S opercule

OPERCULA *n/pl* opercules

OPERCULE *n* pl. -S an anatomical part that serves as a lid or cover

OPERETTA *n* pl. -S a light musical drama with spoken dialogue

OPERON *n* pl. -S a type of gene cluster

OPEROSE *adj* involving great labor

OPHIDIAN *n* pl. -S a snake

OPHITE *n* pl. -S an igneous rock **OPHITIC** *adj*

OPIATE *v* -ATED, -ATING, -ATES to treat with opium

OPINE *v* OPINED, OPINING, OPINES to hold or state as an opinion

OPING present participle of ope

OPINION *n* pl. -S a conclusion or judgment one holds to be true

OPIOID *n* pl. -S a peptide that acts like opium

OPIUM *n* pl. -S an addictive narcotic

OPIUMISM *n* pl. -S opium addiction

OPOSSUM *n* pl. -S an arboreal mammal

OPPIDAN *n* pl. -S a townsman

OPPILATE *v* -LATED, -LATING, -LATES to obstruct **OPPILANT** *adj*

OPPONENT *n* pl. -S one that opposes another

OPPOSE　　　*v* -POSED, -POSING, -POSES to be in contention or conflict with

OPPOSER　　*n* pl. -S one that opposes

OPPOSITE　　*n* pl. -S one that is radically different from another in some related way

OPPOSSUM　*n* pl. -S an arboreal mammal

OPPRESS　　*v* -ED, -ING, -ES to burden by abuse of power or authority

OPPUGN　　*v* -ED, -ING, -S to assail with argument

OPPUGNER　*n* pl. -S one that oppugns

OPSIN　　　*n* pl. -S a type of protein

OPSONIC　　*adj* pertaining to opsonin

OPSONIFY　　*v* -FIED, -FYING, -FIES to opsonize

OPSONIN　　*n* pl. -S an antibody of blood serum

OPSONIZE　　*v* -NIZED, -NIZING, -NIZES to form opsonins in

OPT　　　　*v* -ED, -ING, -S to choose

OPTATIVE　　*n* pl. -S a mood of verbs that expresses a wish or desire

OPTIC　　　*n* pl. -S an eye

OPTICAL　　*adj* pertaining to sight

OPTICIAN　　*n* pl. -S one who makes or deals in optical goods

OPTICIST　　*n* pl. -S one engaged in the study of light and vision

OPTIMA　　　a pl. of optimum

OPTIMAL　　*adj* most desirable

OPTIME　　　*n* pl. -S an honor student in mathematics at Cambridge University

OPTIMISE　　*v* -MISED, -MISING, -MISES to optimize

OPTIMISM　　*n* pl. -S a disposition to look or the favorable side of things

OPTIMIST　　*n* pl. -S one who exhibits optimism

OPTIMIZE　　*v* -MIZED, -MIZING, -MIZES to make as perfect, useful, or effective as possible

OPTIMUM　　*n* pl. -MA or -MUMS the most favorable condition for obtaining a given result

OPTION　　　*v* -ED, -ING, -S to grant an option (a right to buy or sell something at a specified price within a specified time) on

OPTIONAL　　*n* pl. -S an elective course of study

OPTIONEE　　*n* pl. -S one who holds a legal option

OPULENCE　　*n* pl. -S wealth

OPULENCY　　*n* pl. -CIES opulence

OPULENT　　*adj* wealthy

OPUNTIA　　*n* pl. -S an American cactus

OPUS　　　　*n* pl. OPERA or OPUSES a literary of musical work

OPUSCULA　　*n/pl* opuscules

OPUSCULE　　*n* pl. -S a minor work

OQUASSA　　*n* pl. -S a small lake trout

OR　　　　　*n* pl. -S the heraldic color gold

ORA　　　　　pl. of os

ORACH　　　*n* pl. -ES a cultivated plant

ORACHE　　　*n* pl. -S orach

ORACLE　　　*n* pl. -S a person through whom a deity is believed to speak ORACULAR *adj*

ORAD　　　　*adv* toward the mouth

ORAL　　　　*n* pl. -S an examination requiring spoken answers

ORALISM　　*n* pl. -S the use of oral methods of teaching the deaf

ORALIST　　*n* pl. -S an advocate of oralism

ORALITY　　*n* pl. -TIES the state of being produced orally

ORALLY　　　*adv* through the mouth

ORANG　　　*n* pl. -S a large ape

ORANGE　　　*n* pl. -S a citrus fruit

ORANGERY　　*n* pl. -RIES a place where orange trees are cultivated

ORANGEY　　*adj* -ANGIER, -ANGIEST orangy

ORANGISH　　*adj* of a somewhat orange color

ORANGY　　　*adj* -ANGIER, -ANGIEST resembling or suggestive of an orange

ORATE　　　*v* ORATED, ORATING, ORATES to speak formally

ORATION　　*n* pl. -S a formal speech

ORATOR　　　*n* pl. -S one that orates

ORATORIO　　*n* pl. -RIOS a type of musical composition

ORATORY　　*n* pl. -RIES the art of public speaking

ORATRESS　　*n* pl. -ES oratrix

ORATRIX　　*n* pl. -TRICES a female orator

ORB　　　　*v* -ED, -ING, -S to form into a circle or sphere

ORBIER　　　comparative of orby

ORBIEST　　superlative of orby

ORBIT　　　*v* -ED, -ING, -S to move or revolve around

ORBITAL　　*n* pl. -S a subdivision of a nuclear shell

ORBITER　　*n* pl. -S one that orbits

ORBY　　　　*adj* ORBIER, ORBIEST resembling a circle or sphere

ORC	n pl. -S a marine mammal
ORCA	n pl. -S orc
ORCEIN	n pl. -S a reddish brown dye
ORCHARD	n pl. -S an area for the cultivation of fruit trees
ORCHID	n pl. -S a flowering plant
ORCHIL	n pl. -S a purple dye
ORCHIS	n pl. -CHISES an orchid
ORCHITIS	n pl. -TISES inflammation of the testicle ORCHITIC adj
ORCIN	n pl. -S orcinol
ORCINOL	n pl. -S a chemical compound
ORDAIN	v -ED, -ING, -S to invest with holy authority
ORDAINER	n pl. -S one that ordains
ORDEAL	n pl. -S a severely difficult or painful experience
ORDER	v -ED, -ING, -S to give a command or instruction to
ORDERER	n pl. -S one that orders
ORDERLY	n pl. -LIES a male attendant
ORDINAL	n pl. -S a number designating position in a series
ORDINAND	n pl. -S a person about to be ordained
ORDINARY	adj -NARIER, -NARIEST of a kind to be expected in the normal order of events
ORDINARY	n pl. -NARIES something that is ordinary
ORDINATE	n pl. -S a particular geometric coordinate
ORDINES	a pl. of ordo
ORDNANCE	n pl. -S artillery; a cannon
ORDO	n pl. -DINES or -DOS a calendar of religious directions
ORDURE	n pl. -S manure
ORE	n pl. -S a mineral or rock containing a valuable metal
OREAD	n pl. -S a mountain nymph in Greek mythology
ORECTIC	adj pertaining to appetites or desires
ORECTIVE	adj orectic
OREGANO	n pl. -NOS an aromatic herb used as a seasoning
OREIDE	n pl. -S oroide
ORFRAY	n pl. -FRAYS orphrey
ORGAN	n pl. -S a differentiated part of an organism performing a specific function
ORGANA	a pl. of organon and organum
ORGANDIE	n pl. -S organdy
ORGANDY	n pl. -DIES a cotton fabric
ORGANIC	n pl. -S a substance of animal or vegetable origin

ORGANISE	v -NISED, -NISING, -NISES to organize
ORGANISM	n pl. -S any form of animal or plant life
ORGANIST	n pl. -S one who plays the organ (a keyboard musical instrument)
ORGANIZE	v -NIZED, -NIZING, -NIZES to form into an orderly whole
ORGANON	n pl. -GANA or -GANONS a system of rules for scientific investigation
ORGANUM	n pl. -GANA or -GANUMS organon
ORGANZA	n pl. -S a sheer fabric
ORGASM	n pl. -S the climax of sexual excitement ORGASMIC, ORGASTIC adj
ORGEAT	n pl. -S an almond-flavored syrup
ORGIAC	adj of the nature of an orgy
ORGIC	adj orgiac
ORGONE	n pl. -S a postulated energy pervading the universe
ORGULOUS	adj proud
ORGY	n pl. -GIES a party marked by unrestrained sexual indulgence
ORIBATID	n pl. -S any of a family of eyeless mites
ORIBI	n pl. -S an African antelope
ORIEL	n pl. -S a type of projecting window
ORIENT	v -ED, -ING, -S to adjust in relation to something else
ORIENTAL	n pl. -S an inhabitant of an eastern country
ORIFICE	n pl. -S a mouth or mouthlike opening
ORIGAMI	n pl. -S the Japanese art of paper folding
ORIGAN	n pl. -S marjoram
ORIGANUM	n pl. -S an aromatic herb
ORIGIN	n pl. -S a coming into being
ORIGINAL	n pl. -S the first form of something
ORINASAL	n pl. -S a sound pronounced through both the mouth and nose
ORIOLE	n pl. -S an American songbird
ORISON	n pl. -S a prayer
ORLE	n pl. -S a heraldic border
ORLOP	n pl. -S the lowest deck of a ship
ORMER	n pl. -S an abalone
ORMOLU	n pl. -S an alloy used to imitate gold

ORNAMENT *v* -ED, -ING, -S to decorate

ORNATE *adj* elaborately or excessively ornamented **ORNATELY** *adv*

ORNERY *adj* -NERIER, -NERIEST stubborn and mean-spirited

ORNIS *n* pl. ORNITHES avifauna

ORNITHIC *adj* pertaining to birds

OROGENY *n* pl. -NIES the process of mountain formation **OROGENIC** *adj*

OROIDE *n* pl. -S an alloy used to imitate gold

OROLOGY *n* pl. -GIES the study of mountains

OROMETER *n* pl. -S a type of barometer

OROTUND *adj* full and clear in sound

ORPHAN *v* -ED, -ING, -S to deprive of both parents

ORPHIC *adj* mystical

ORPHICAL *adj* orphic

ORPHREY *n* pl. -PHREYS an ornamental band or border

ORPIMENT *n* pl. -S a yellow dye

ORPIN *n* pl. -S orpine

ORPINE *n* pl. -S a perennial herb

ORRA *adj* occasional

ORRERY *n* pl. -RERIES a mechanical model of the solar system

ORRICE *n* pl. -S orris

ORRIS *n* pl. -RISES a flowering plant

ORT *n* pl. -S a scrap of food

ORTHICON *n* pl. -S a type of television camera tube

ORTHO *adj* pertaining to reproduction in a photograph of the full range of colors in nature

ORTHODOX *n* pl. -ES one holding traditional beliefs

ORTHOEPY *n* pl. -EPIES the study of correct pronunciation

ORTHOSIS *n* pl. -THOSES an orthotic

ORTHOTIC *n* pl. -S a brace for weak joints or muscles

ORTOLAN *n* pl. -S a European bird

ORYX *n* pl. -ES an African antelope

ORZO *n* pl. -zos rice-shaped pasta

OS *n* pl. ORA an orifice

OS *n* pl. OSSA a bone

OS *n* pl. OSAR an esker

OSCINE *n* pl. -S any of a family of songbirds **OSCININE** *adj*

OSCITANT *adj* yawning

OSCULA pl. of osculum

OSCULANT *adj* adhering closely

OSCULAR *adj* pertaining to the mouth

OSCULATE *v* -LATED, -LATING, -LATES to kiss

OSCULE *n* pl. -S osculum

OSCULUM *n* pl. -LA an opening in a sponge

OSE *n* pl. -S an esker

OSIER *n* pl. -S a European tree

OSMATIC *adj* depending mainly on the sense of smell

OSMICS *n/pl* the study of the sense of smell

OSMIUM *n* pl. -S a metallic element **OSMIC, OSMIOUS** *adj*

OSMOL *n* pl. -S a unit of osmotic pressure **OSMOLAL** *adj*

OSMOLAR *adj* osmotic

OSMOLE *n* pl. -S osmol

OSMOSE *v* -MOSED, -MOSING, -MOSES to undergo osmosis

OSMOSIS *n* pl. -MOSES a form of diffusion of a fluid through a membrane

OSMOTIC *adj* pertaining to osmosis

OSMOUS *adj* containing osmium

OSMUND *n* pl. -S any of a genus of large ferns

OSMUNDA *n* pl. -S osmund

OSNABURG *n* pl. -S a cotton fabric

OSPREY *n* pl. -PREYS an American hawk

OSSA pl. of os

OSSEIN *n* pl. -S a protein substance in bone

OSSEOUS *adj* resembling bone

OSSIA *conj* or else — used as a musical direction

OSSICLE *n* pl. -S a small bone

OSSIFIC *adj* pertaining to the formation of bone

OSSIFIER *n* pl. -S one that ossifies

OSSIFY *v* -FIED, -FYING, -FIES to convert into bone

OSSUARY *n* pl. -ARIES a receptacle for the bones of the dead

OSTEAL *adj* osseous

OSTEITIS *n* pl. -ITIDES inflammation of bone **OSTEITIC** *adj*

OSTEOID *n* pl. -S uncalcified bone matrix

OSTEOMA *n* pl. -MAS or -MATA a tumor of bone tissue

OSTEOSIS *n* pl. -OSES or -OSISES the formation of bone

OSTIA pl. of ostium

OSTIARY *n* pl. -ARIES a doorkeeper at a church

OSTINATO *n* pl. -TOS a constantly recurring musical phrase

OSTIOLE *n* pl. -S a small bodily opening **OSTIOLAR** *adj*

OSTIUM *n* pl. OSTIA an opening in a bodily organ

OSTLER *n* pl. -S hostler

OSTMARK *n* pl. -S a former East German monetary unit

OSTOMY *n* pl. -MIES a type of surgical operation

OSTOSIS *n* pl. -TOSES or -TOSISES the formation of bone

OSTRACOD *n* pl. -S a minute freshwater crustacean

OSTRACON *n* pl. -CA a fragment containing an inscription

OSTRICH *n* pl. -ES a large, flightless bird

OTALGIA *n* pl. -S pain in the ear **OTALGIC** *adj*

OTALGY *n* pl. -GIES otalgia

OTHER *n* pl. -S one that remains of two or more

OTIC *adj* pertaining to the ear

OTIOSE *adj* lazy **OTIOSELY** *adv*

OTIOSITY *n* pl. -TIES the state of being otiose

OTITIS *n* pl. OTITIDES inflammation of the ear **OTITIC** *adj*

OTOCYST *n* pl. -S an organ of balance in many invertebrates

OTOLITH *n* pl. -S a hard mass that forms in the inner ear

OTOLOGY *n* pl. -GIES the science of the ear

OTOSCOPE *n* pl. -S an instrument for examining the ear

OTOSCOPY *n* pl. -PIES the use of an otoscope

OTOTOXIC *adj* adversely affecting hearing or balance

OTTAR *n* pl. -S attar

OTTAVA *n* pl. -S an octave

OTTER *n* pl. -S a carnivorous mammal

OTTO *n* pl. -TOS attar

OTTOMAN *n* pl. -S a type of sofa

OUABAIN *n* pl. -S a cardiac stimulant

OUCH *v* -ED, -ING, -ES to ornament with ouches (settings for precious stones)

OUD *n* pl. -S a stringed instrument of northern Africa

OUGHT *v* -ED, -ING, -S to owe

OUGUIYA *n* pl. OUGUIYA a monetary unit of Mauritania

OUISTITI *n* pl. -S a South American monkey

OUNCE *n* pl. -S a unit of weight

OUPH *n* pl. -S ouphe

OUPHE *n* pl. -S an elf

OUR *pron* a possessive form of the pronoun we

OURANG *n* pl. -S orang

OURARI *n* pl. -S curare

OUREBI *n* pl. -S oribi

OURIE *adj* shivering with cold

OURS *pron* a possessive form of the pronoun we

OURSELF *pron* myself — used in formal or regal contexts

OUSEL *n* pl. -S ouzel

OUST *v* -ED, -ING, -S to expel or remove from a position or place

OUSTER *n* pl. -S the act of ousting

OUT *v* -ED, -ING, -S to be revealed

OUTACT *v* -ED, -ING, -S to surpass in acting

OUTADD *v* -ED, -ING, -S to surpass in adding

OUTAGE *n* pl. -S a failure or interruption in use or functioning

OUTARGUE *v* -GUED, -GUING, -GUES to get the better of by arguing

OUTASK *v* -ED, -ING, -S to surpass in asking

OUTATE past tense of outeat

OUTBACK *n* pl. -S isolated rural country

OUTBAKE *v* -BAKED, -BAKING, -BAKES to surpass in baking

OUTBARK *v* -ED, -ING, -S to surpass in barking

OUTBAWL *v* -ED, -ING, -S to surpass in bawling

OUTBEAM *v* -ED, -ING, -S to surpass in beaming

OUTBEG *v* -BEGGED, -BEGGING, -BEGS to surpass in begging

OUTBID *v* -BID, -BIDDEN, -BIDDING, -BIDS to bid higher than

OUTBITCH *v* -ED, -ING, -ES to surpass in bitching

OUTBLAZE *v* -BLAZED, -BLAZING, -BLAZES to surpass in brilliance of light

OUTBLEAT *v* -ED, -ING, -S to surpass in bleating

OUTBLESS *v* -ED, -ING, -ES to surpass in blessing

OUTBLOOM *v* -ED, -ING, -S to surpass in blooming

OUTBLUFF *v* -ED, -ING, -S to surpass in bluffing

OUTBLUSH *v* -ED, -ING, -ES to surpass in blushing

OUTBOARD *n* pl. -S a type of motor

OUTBOAST *v* -ED, -ING, -S to surpass in boasting

OUTBOUGHT past tense of outbuy

OUTBOUND *adj* outward bound

OUTBOX *v* -ED, -ING, -ES to surpass in boxing

OUTBRAG *v* -BRAGGED, -BRAGGING, -BRAGS to surpass in bragging

OUTBRAVE *v* -BRAVED, -BRAVING, -BRAVES to surpass in courage

OUTBRAWL *v* -ED, -ING, -S to surpass in brawling

OUTBREAK *n* pl. -S a sudden eruption

OUTBREED *v* -BRED, -BREEDING, -BREEDS to interbreed relatively unrelated stocks

OUTBRIBE *v* -BRIBED, -BRIBING, -BRIBES to surpass in bribing

OUTBUILD *v* -BUILT, -BUILDING, -BUILDS to surpass in building

OUTBULK *v* -ED, -ING, -S to surpass in bulking

OUTBULLY *v* -LIED, -LYING, -LIES to surpass in bullying

OUTBURN *v* -BURNED or -BURNT, -BURNING, -BURNS to burn longer than

OUTBURST *n* pl. -S a sudden and violent outpouring

OUTBUY *v* -BOUGHT, -BUYING, -BUYS to surpass in buying

OUTBY *adv* outdoors

OUTBYE *adv* outby

OUTCAPER *v* -ED, -ING, -S to surpass in capering

OUTCAST *n* pl. -S one that is cast out

OUTCASTE *n* pl. -S a Hindu who has been expelled from his caste

OUTCATCH *v* -CAUGHT, -CATCHING, -CATCHES to surpass in catching

OUTCAVIL *v* -ILED, -ILING, -ILS or -ILLED, -ILLING, -ILS to surpass in caviling

OUTCHARM *v* -ED, -ING, -S to surpass in charming

OUTCHEAT *v* -ED, -ING, -S to surpass in cheating

OUTCHIDE *v* -CHIDED or -CHID, -CHIDDEN, -CHIDING, -CHIDES to surpass in chiding

OUTCLASS *v* -ED, -ING, -ES to surpass so decisively as to appear of a higher class

OUTCLIMB *v* -CLIMBED or -CLOMB, -CLIMBING, -CLIMBS to surpass in climbing

OUTCOACH *v* -ED, -ING, -ES to surpass in coaching

OUTCOME *n* pl. -S a result

OUTCOOK *v* -ED, -ING, -S to surpass in cooking

OUTCOUNT *v* -ED, -ING, -S to surpass in counting

OUTCRAWL *v* -ED, -ING, -S to surpass in crawling

OUTCRIED past tense of outcry

OUTCRIES present 3d person sing. of outcry

OUTCROP *v* -CROPPED, -CROPPING, -CROPS to protrude above the soil

OUTCROSS *v* -ED, -ING, -ES to cross with a relatively unrelated individual

OUTCROW *v* -ED, -ING, -S to surpass in crowing

OUTCRY *v* -CRIED, -CRYING, -CRIES to cry louder than

OUTCURSE *v* -CURSED, -CURSING, -CURSES to surpass in cursing

OUTCURVE *n* pl. -S a type of pitch in baseball

OUTDANCE *v* -DANCED, -DANCING, -DANCES to surpass in dancing

OUTDARE *v* -DARED, -DARING, -DARES to surpass in daring

OUTDATE *v* -DATED, -DATING, -DATES to make out-of-date

OUTDO *v* -DID, -DONE, -DOING, -DOES to exceed in performance

OUTDODGE *v* -DODGED, -DODGING, -DODGES to surpass in dodging

OUTDOER *n* pl. -S one that outdoes

OUTDONE past participle of outdo

OUTDOOR *adj* pertaining to the open air

OUTDOORS *adv* in the open air

OUTDRAG *v* -DRAGGED, DRAGGING, -DRAGS to surpass in drag racing

OUTDRANK past tense of outdrink

OUTDRAW v -DREW, -DRAWN, -DRAWING, -DRAWS to attract a larger audience than

OUTDREAM v -DREAMED or -DREAMT, -DREAMING, -DREAMS to surpass in dreaming

OUTDRESS v -ED, -ING, -ES to surpass in dressing

OUTDREW past tense of outdraw

OUTDRINK v -DRANK, -DRUNK, -DRINKING, -DRINKS to surpass in drinking

OUTDRIVE v -DROVE, -DRIVEN, -DRIVING, -DRIVES to drive a golf ball farther than

OUTDROP v -DROPPED, -DROPPING, -DROPS to surpass in dropping

OUTDRUNK past participle of outdrink

OUTDUEL v -DUELED, -DUELING, -DUELS or -DUELLED, -DUELLING, -DUELS to surpass in dueling

OUTEARN v -ED, -ING, -S to surpass in earning

OUTEAT v -ATE, -EATEN, -EATING, -EATS to surpass in eating

OUTECHO v -ED, -ING, -ES to surpass in echoing

OUTER n pl. -S a part of a target

OUTFABLE v -BLED, -BLING, -BLES to surpass in fabling

OUTFACE v -FACED, -FACING, -FACES to confront unflinchingly

OUTFALL n pl. -S the outlet of a body of water

OUTFAST v -ED, -ING, -S to surpass in fasting

OUTFAWN v -ED, -ING, -S to surpass in fawning

OUTFEAST v -ED, -ING, -S to surpass in feasting

OUTFEEL v -FELT, -FEELING, -FEELS to surpass in feeling

OUTFIELD n pl. -S a part of a baseball field

OUTFIGHT v -FOUGHT, -FIGHTING, -FIGHTS to defeat

OUTFIND v -FOUND, -FINDING, -FINDS to surpass in finding

OUTFIRE v -FIRED, -FIRING, -FIRES to surpass in firing

OUTFISH v -ED, -ING, -ES to surpass in fishing

OUTFIT v -FITTED, -FITTING, -FITS to equip

OUTFLANK v -ED, -ING, -S to gain a tactical advantage over

OUTFLOW v -ED, -ING, -S to flow out

OUTFLY v -FLEW, -FLOWN, -FLYING, -FLIES to surpass in speed of flight

OUTFOOL v -ED, -ING, -S to surpass in fooling

OUTFOOT v -ED, -ING, -S to surpass in speed

OUTFOUGHT past tense of outfight

OUTFOUND past tense of outfind

OUTFOX v -ED, -ING, -ES to outwit

OUTFROWN v -ED, -ING, -S to frown more than

OUTGAIN v -ED, -ING, -S to gain more than

OUTGAS v -GASSED, -GASSING, -GASSES to remove gas from

OUTGIVE v -GAVE, -GIVEN, -GIVING, -GIVES to give more than

OUTGLARE v -GLARED, -GLARING, -GLARES to surpass in glaring

OUTGLOW v -ED, -ING, -S to surpass in glowing

OUTGNAW v -GNAWED, -GNAWN, -GNAWING, -GNAWS to surpass in gnawing

OUTGO v -WENT, -GONE, -GOING, -GOES to go beyond

OUTGOING n pl. -S a departure

OUTGREW past tense of outgrow

OUTGRIN v -GRINNED, -GRINNING, -GRINS to surpass in grinning

OUTGROSS v -ED, -ING, -ES to surpass in gross earnings

OUTGROUP n pl. -S a group of people outside one's own group

OUTGROW v -GREW, -GROWN, -GROWING, -GROWS to grow too large for

OUTGUESS v -ED, -ING, -ES to anticipate the actions of

OUTGUIDE v -GUIDED, -GUIDING, -GUIDES to surpass in guiding

OUTGUN v -GUNNED, -GUNNING, -GUNS to surpass in firepower

OUTGUSH n pl. -ES a gushing out

OUTHAUL n pl. -S a rope for extending a sail along a spar

OUTHEAR v -HEARD, -HEARING, -HEARS to surpass in hearing

OUTHIT v -HIT, -HITTING, -HITS to get more hits than

OUTHOMER v -ED, -ING, -S to surpass in hitting home runs

OUTHOUSE *n* pl. -S a toilet housed in a small structure

OUTHOWL *v* -ED, -ING, -S to surpass in howling

OUTHUMOR *v* -ED, -ING, -S to surpass in humoring

OUTHUNT *v* -ED, -ING, -S to surpass in hunting

OUTING *n* pl. -S a short pleasure trip

OUTJINX *v* -ED, -ING, -ES to surpass in jinxing

OUTJUMP *v* -ED, -ING, -S to surpass in jumping

OUTJUT *v* -JUTTED, -JUTTING, -JUTS to stick out

OUTKEEP *v* -KEPT, -KEEPING, -KEEPS to surpass in keeping

OUTKICK *v* -ED, -ING, -S to surpass in kicking

OUTKILL *v* -ED, -ING, -S to surpass in killing

OUTKISS *v* -ED, -ING, -ES to surpass in kissing

OUTLAID past tense of outlay

OUTLAIN past participle of outlie

OUTLAND *n* pl. -S a foreign land

OUTLAST *v* -ED, -ING, -S to last longer than

OUTLAUGH *v* -ED, -ING, -S to surpass in laughing

OUTLAW *v* -ED, -ING, -S to prohibit

OUTLAWRY *n* pl. -RIES habitual defiance of the law

OUTLAY *n* -LAID, -LAYING, -LAYS to pay out

OUTLEAP *v* -LEAPED or -LEAPT, -LEAPING, -LEAPS to surpass in leaping

OUTLEARN *v* -LEARNED or -LEARNT, -LEARNING, -LEARNS to surpass in learning

OUTLET *n* pl. -S a passage for escape or discharge

OUTLIE *v* -LAY, -LAIN, -LYING, -LIES to lie beyond

OUTLIER *n* pl. -S an outlying area or portion

OUTLINE *v* -LINED, -LINING, -LINES to indicate the main features or different parts of

OUTLINER *n* pl. -S one that outlines

OUTLIVE *v* -LIVED, -LIVING, -LIVES to live longer than

OUTLIVER *n* pl. -S one that outlives

OUTLOOK *n* pl. -S a point of view

OUTLOVE *v* -LOVED, -LOVING, -LOVES to surpass in loving

OUTLYING present participle of outlie

OUTMAN *v* -MANNED, -MANNING, -MANS to surpass in manpower

OUTMARCH *v* -ED, -ING, -ES to surpass in marching

OUTMATCH *v* -ED, -ING, -ES to outdo

OUTMODE *v* -MODED, -MODING, -MODES to outdate

OUTMOST *adj* farthest out

OUTMOVE *v* -MOVED, -MOVING, -MOVES to move faster or farther than

OUTPACE *v* -PACED, -PACING, -PACES to surpass in speed

OUTPAINT *v* -ED, -ING, -S to surpass in painting

OUTPASS *v* -ED, -ING, -ES to excel in passing a football

OUTPITCH *v* -ED, -ING, -ES to surpass in pitching

OUTPITY *v* -PITIED, -PITYING, -PITIES to surpass in pitying

OUTPLAN *v* -PLANNED, -PLANNING, -PLANS to surpass in planning

OUTPLAY *v* -ED, -ING, -S to excel or defeat in a game

OUTPLOD *v* -PLODDED, -PLODDING, -PLODS to surpass in plodding

OUTPLOT *v* -PLOTTED, -PLOTTING, -PLOTS to surpass in plotting

OUTPOINT *v* -ED, -ING, -S to score more points than

OUTPOLL *v* -ED, -ING, -S to get more votes than

OUTPORT *n* pl. -S a port of export or departure

OUTPOST *n* pl. -S a body of troops stationed at a distance from the main body

OUTPOUR *v* -ED, -ING, -S to pour out

OUTPOWER *v* -ED, -ING, -S to surpass in power

OUTPRAY *v* -ED, -ING, -S to surpass in praying

OUTPREEN *v* -ED, -ING, -S to surpass in preening

OUTPRESS *v* -ED, -ING, -ES to surpass in pressing

OUTPRICE *v* -PRICED, -PRICING, -PRICES to surpass in pricing

OUTPULL *v* -ED, -ING, -S to attract a larger audience or following than

OUTPUNCH   v -ED, -ING, -ES to surpass in punching

OUTPUSH   v -ED, -ING, -ES to surpass in pushing

OUTPUT   v -PUTTED, -PUTTING, -PUTS to produce

OUTQUOTE   v -QUOTED, -QUOTING, -QUOTES to surpass in quoting

OUTRACE   v -RACED, -RACING, -RACES to run faster or farther than

OUTRAGE   v -RAGED, -RAGING, -RAGES to arouse anger or resentment in

OUTRAISE   v -RAISED, -RAISING, -RAISES to surpass in raising

OUTRAN   past tense of outrun

OUTRANCE   n pl. -S the last extremity

OUTRANG   past tense of outring

OUTRANGE   v -RANGED, -RANGING, -RANGES to surpass in range

OUTRANK   v -ED, -ING, -S to rank higher than

OUTRATE   v -RATED, -RATING, -RATES to surpass in a rating

OUTRAVE   v -RAVED, -RAVING, -RAVES to surpass in raving

OUTRE   adj deviating from what is usual or proper

OUTREACH   v -ED, -ING, -ES to reach beyond

OUTREAD   v -READ, -READING, -READS to surpass in reading

OUTRIDE   v -RODE, -RIDDEN, -RIDING, -RIDES to ride faster or better than

OUTRIDER   n pl. -S a mounted attendant who rides before or beside a carriage

OUTRIGHT   adj being without limit or reservation

OUTRING   v -RANG, -RUNG, -RINGING, -RINGS to ring louder than

OUTRIVAL   v -VALED, -VALING, -VALS or -VALLED, -VALLING, -VALS to outdo in a competition or rivalry

OUTROAR   v -ED, -ING, -S to roar louder than

OUTROCK   v -ED, -ING, -S to surpass in rocking

OUTRODE   past tense of outride

OUTROLL   v -ED, -ING, -S to roll out

OUTROOT   v -ED, -ING, -S to pull up by the roots

OUTROW   v -ED, -ING, -S to surpass in rowing

OUTRUN   v -RAN, -RUNNING, -RUNS to run faster than

OUTRUNG   past participle of outring

OUTRUSH   v -ED, -ING, -ES to surpass in rushing

OUTSAIL   v -ED, -ING, -S to sail faster than

OUTSANG   past tense of outsing

OUTSAT   past tense of outsit

OUTSAVOR   v -ED, -ING, -S to surpass in a distinctive taste or smell

OUTSAW   past tense of outsee

OUTSCOLD   v -ED, -ING, -S to surpass in scolding

OUTSCOOP   v -ED, -ING, -S to surpass in scooping

OUTSCORE   v -SCORED, -SCORING, -SCORES to score more points than

OUTSCORN   v -ED, -ING, -S to surpass in scorning

OUTSEE   v -SAW, -SEEN, -SEEING, -SEES to see beyond

OUTSELL   v -SOLD, -SELLING, -SELLS to sell more than

OUTSERT   n pl. -S a folded sheet placed around a folded section of printed matter

OUTSERVE   v -SERVED, -SERVING, -SERVES to surpass in serving

OUTSET   n pl. -S a beginning

OUTSHAME   v -SHAMED, -SHAMING, -SHAMES to surpass in shaming

OUTSHINE   v -SHONE or -SHINED, -SHINING, -SHINES to shine brighter than

OUTSHOOT   v -SHOT, -SHOOTING, -SHOOTS to shoot better than

OUTSHOUT   v -ED, -ING, -S to shout louder than

OUTSIDE   n pl. -S the outer side, surface, or part

OUTSIDER   n pl. -S one that does not belong to a particular group

OUTSIGHT   n pl. -S the power of perceiving external things

OUTSIN   v -SINNED, -SINNING, -SINS to surpass in sinning

OUTSING   v -SANG, -SUNG, -SINGING, -SINGS to surpass in singing

OUTSIT   v -SAT, -SITTING, -SITS to remain sitting or in session longer than

OUTSIZE *n* pl. -S an unusual size
OUTSIZED *adj*

OUTSKATE *v* -SKATED, -SKATING,
-SKATES to surpass in skating

OUTSKIRT *n* pl. -S an outlying area

OUTSLEEP *v* -SLEPT, -SLEEPING,
-SLEEPS to sleep later than

OUTSLICK *v* -ED, -ING, -S to get the
better of by trickery or cunning

OUTSMART *v* -ED, -ING, -S to outwit

OUTSMILE *v* -SMILED, -SMILING,
-SMILES to surpass in smiling

OUTSMOKE *v* -SMOKED, -SMOKING,
-SMOKES to surpass in
smoking

OUTSNORE *v* -SNORED, -SNORING,
-SNORES to surpass in
snoring

OUTSOAR *v* -ED, -ING, -S to soar
beyond

OUTSOLD past tense of outsell

OUTSOLE *n* pl. -S the outer sole of a
boot or shoe

OUTSPAN *v* -SPANNED, -SPANNING,
-SPANS to unharness a draft
animal

OUTSPEAK *v* -SPOKE, -SPOKEN,
-SPEAKING, -SPEAKS to
outdo in speaking

OUTSPEED *v* -SPED or -SPEEDED,
-SPEEDING, -SPEEDS to go
faster than

OUTSPELL *v* -SPELLED or -SPELT,
-SPELLING, -SPELLS to
surpass in spelling

OUTSPEND *v* -SPENT, -SPENDING,
-SPENDS to exceed the limits
of in spending

OUTSPOKE past tense of outspeak
OUTSPOKEN past participle of outspeak

OUTSTAND *v* -STOOD, -STANDING,
-STANDS to endure beyond

OUTSTARE *v* -STARED, -STARING,
-STARES to outface

OUTSTART *v* -ED, -ING, -S to get ahead
of at the start

OUTSTATE *v* -STATED, -STATING,
-STATES to surpass in stating

OUTSTAY *v* -ED, -ING, -S to surpass in
staying power

OUTSTEER *v* -ED, -ING, -S to surpass in
steering

OUTSTOOD past tense of outstand

OUTSTRIP *v* -STRIPPED, -STRIPPING,
-STRIPS to go faster or farther
than

OUTSTUDY *v* -STUDIED, -STUDYING,
-STUDIES to surpass in
studying

OUTSTUNT *v* -ED, -ING, -S to surpass in
stunting

OUTSULK *v* -ED, -ING, -S to surpass in
sulking

OUTSUNG past participle of outsing

OUTSWEAR *v* -SWORE or -SWARE,
-SWORN, -SWEARING,
-SWEARS to surpass in
swearing

OUTSWIM *v* -SWAM, -SWUM,
-SWIMMING, -SWIMS to swim
faster or farther than

OUTTAKE *n* pl. -S a passage outwards

OUTTALK *v* -ED, -ING, -S to surpass in
talking

OUTTASK *v* -ED, -ING, -S to surpass in
tasking

OUTTELL *v* -TOLD, -TELLING, -TELLS
to say openly

OUTTHANK *v* -ED, -ING, -S to surpass in
thanking

OUTTHINK *v* -THOUGHT, -THINKING,
-THINKS to get the better of by
thinking

OUTTHROB *v* -THROBBED,
-THROBBING, -THROBS to
surpass in throbbing

OUTTHROW *v* -THREW, -THROWN,
-THROWING, -THROWS to
throw farther or more
accurately than

OUTTOLD past tense of outtell

OUTTOWER *v* -ED, -ING, -S to tower
above

OUTTRADE *v* -TRADED, -TRADING,
-TRADES to get the better of
in a trade

OUTTRICK *v* -ED, -ING, -S to get the
better of by trickery

OUTTROT *v* -TROTTED, -TROTTING,
-TROTS to surpass in trotting

OUTTRUMP *v* -ED, -ING, -S to outplay

OUTTURN *n* pl. -S a quantity produced

OUTVALUE *v* -UED, -UING, -UES to be
worth more than

OUTVAUNT *v* -ED, -ING, -S to surpass in
vaunting

OUTVIE *v* -VIED, -VYING, -VIES to
surpass in a competition

OUTVOICE *v* -VOICED, -VOICING,
-VOICES to surpass in
loudness of voice

OUTVOTE *v* -VOTED, -VOTING, -VOTES to defeat by a majority of votes

OUTVYING present participle of outvie

OUTWAIT *v* -ED, -ING, -S to exceed in patience

OUTWALK *v* -ED, -ING, -S to surpass in walking

OUTWAR *v* -WARRED, -WARRING, -WARS to surpass in warring

OUTWARD *adv* toward the outside

OUTWARDS *adv* outward

OUTWARRED past tense of outwar

OUTWARRING present participle of outwar

OUTWASH *n* pl. -ES detritus washed from a glacier

OUTWASTE *v* -WASTED, -WASTING, -WASTES to surpass in wasting

OUTWATCH *v* -ED, -ING, -ES to watch longer than

OUTWEAR *v* -WORE, -WORN, -WEARING, -WEARS to last longer than

OUTWEARY *v* -RIED, -RYING, -RIES to surpass in wearying

OUTWEEP *v* -WEPT, -WEEPING, -WEEPS to weep more than

OUTWEIGH *v* -ED, -ING, -S to weigh more than

OUTWENT past tense of outgo

OUTWEPT past tense of outweep

OUTWHIRL *v* -ED, -ING, -S to surpass in whirling

OUTWILE *v* -WILED, -WILING, -WILES to surpass in wiling

OUTWILL *v* -ED, -ING, -S to surpass in willpower

OUTWIND *v* -ED, -ING, -S to cause to be out of breath

OUTWISH *v* -ED, -ING, -ES to surpass in wishing

OUTWIT *v* -WITTED, -WITTING, -WITS to get the better of by superior cleverness

OUTWORE past tense of outwear

OUTWORK *v* -WORKED or -WROUGHT, -WORKING, -WORKS to work faster or better than

OUTWORN past participle of outwear

OUTWRITE *v* -WROTE or -WRIT, -WRITTEN, -WRITING, -WRITES to write better than

OUTWROUGHT a past tense of outwork

OUTYELL *v* -ED, -ING, -S to yell louder than

OUTYELP *v* -ED, -ING, -S to surpass in yelping

OUTYIELD *v* -ED, -ING, -S to surpass in yield

OUZEL *n* pl. -S a European bird

OUZO *n* pl. -ZOS a Greek liqueur

OVA pl. of ovum

OVAL *n* pl. -S an oval (egg-shaped) figure or object

OVALITY *n* pl. -TIES ovalness

OVALLY *adv* in the shape of an oval

OVALNESS *n* pl. -ES the state of being oval

OVARIAL *adj* ovarian

OVARIAN *adj* pertaining to an ovary

OVARIES pl. of ovary

OVARIOLE *n* pl. -S one of the tubes of which the ovaries of most insects are composed

OVARITIS *n* pl. -RITIDES inflammation of an ovary

OVARY *n* pl. -RIES a female reproductive gland

OVATE *adj* egg-shaped **OVATELY** *adv*

OVATION *n* pl. -S an expression or demonstration of popular acclaim

OVEN *n* pl. -S an enclosed compartment in which substances are heated **OVENLIKE** *adj*

OVENBIRD *n* pl. -S an American songbird

OVENWARE *n* pl. -S heat-resistant dishes for baking and serving food

OVER *v* -ED, -ING, -S to leap above and to the other side of

OVERABLE *adj* excessively able

OVERACT *v* -ED, -ING, -S to act with exaggeration

OVERAGE *n* pl. -S an amount in excess

OVERAGED *adj* too old to be useful

OVERALL *n* pl. -S a loose outer garment

OVERAPT *adj* excessively apt

OVERARCH *v* -ED, -ING, -ES to form an arch over

OVERARM *adj* done with the arm above the shoulder

OVERATE past tense of overeat

OVERAWE *v* -AWED, -AWING, -AWES to subdue by inspiring awe

OVERBAKE *v* -BAKED, -BAKING, -BAKES to bake too long

OVERBEAR v -BORE, -BORNE or -BORN, -BEARING, -BEARS to bring down by superior weight or force

OVERBEAT v -BEAT, -BEATEN, -BEATING, -BEATS to beat too much

OVERBED adj spanning a bed

OVERBET v -BET or -BETTED, -BETTING, -BETS to bet too much

OVERBID v -BID, -BID or -BIDDEN, -BIDDING, -BIDS to bid higher than

OVERBIG adj too big

OVERBILL v -ED, -ING, -S to bill too much

OVERBITE n pl. -S a faulty closure of the teeth

OVERBLOW v -BLEW, -BLOWN, -BLOWING, -BLOWS to give excessive importance to

OVERBOIL v -ED, -ING, -S to boil too long

OVERBOLD adj excessively bold or forward

OVERBOOK v -ED, -ING, -S to issue reservations in excess of the space available

OVERBORE past tense of overbear

OVERBORN a past participle of overbear

OVERBORNE a past participle of overbear

OVERBOUGHT past tense of overbuy

OVERBRED adj bred too finely or to excess

OVERBURN v -BURNED or -BURNT, -BURNING, -BURNS to burn too long

OVERBUSY adj too busy

OVERBUY v -BOUGHT, -BUYING, -BUYS to buy in quantities exceeding need or demand

OVERCALL v -ED, -ING, -S to overbid

OVERCAME past tense of overcome

OVERCAST v -CAST or -CASTED, -CASTING, -CASTS to become cloudy or dark

OVERCOAT n pl. -S a warm coat worn over indoor clothing

OVERCOLD adj too cold

OVERCOME v -CAME, -COMING, -COMES to get the better of

OVERCOOK v -ED, -ING, -S to cook too long

OVERCOOL v -ED, -ING, -S to make too cool

OVERCOY adj too coy

OVERCRAM v -CRAMMED, -CRAMMING, -CRAMS to stuff or cram to excess

OVERCROP v -CROPPED, -CROPPING, -CROPS to exhaust the fertility of by cultivating to excess

OVERCURE v -CURED, -CURING, -CURES to cure too long

OVERCUT v -CUT, -CUTTING, -CUTS to cut too much

OVERDARE v -DARED, -DARING, -DARES to become too daring

OVERDEAR adj too dear; too costly

OVERDECK v -ED, -ING, -S to adorn extravagantly

OVERDO v -DID, -DONE, -DOING, -DOES to do to excess

OVERDOER n pl. -S one that overdoes

OVERDOG n pl. -S one that is dominant or victorious

OVERDOSE v -DOSED, -DOSING, -DOSES to give an excessive dose to

OVERDRAW v -DREW, -DRAWN, -DRAWING, -DRAWS to draw checks on in excess of the balance

OVERDRY v -DRIED, -DRYING, -DRIES to dry too much

OVERDUB v -DUBBED, -DUBBING, -DUBS to add sound to an existing recording

OVERDUE adj not paid when due

OVERDYE v -DYED, -DYEING, -DYES to dye with too much color

OVEREASY adj too easy

OVEREAT v -ATE, -EATEN, -EATING, -EATS to eat to excess

OVEREDIT v -ED, -ING, -S to edit more than necessary

OVERFAR adj too great in distance, extent, or degree

OVERFAST adj too fast

OVERFAT adj too fat

OVERFEAR v -ED, -ING, -S to fear too much

OVERFEED v -FED, -FEEDING, -FEEDS to feed too much

OVERFILL v -ED, -ING, -S to fill to overflowing

OVERFISH v -ED, -ING, -ES to deplete the supply of fish in an area by fishing to excess

OVERFLOW v -FLOWED, -FLOWN, -FLOWING, -FLOWS to flow over the top of

OVERFLY *v* -FLEW, -FLOWN, -FLYING, -FLIES to fly over

OVERFOND *adj* too fond or affectionate

OVERFOUL *adj* too foul

OVERFREE *adj* too free

OVERFULL *adj* too full

OVERFUND *v* -ED, -ING, -S to fund more than required

OVERGILD *v* -GILDED or -GILT, -GILDING, -GILDS to gild over

OVERGIRD *v* -GIRDED or -GIRT, -GIRDING, -GIRDS to gird to excess

OVERGLAD *adj* too glad

OVERGOAD *v* -ED, -ING, -S to goad too much

OVERGROW *v* -GREW, -GROWN, -GROWING, -GROWS to grow over

OVERHAND *v* -ED, -ING, -S to sew with short, vertical stitches

OVERHANG *v* -HUNG, -HANGING, -HANGS to hang or project over

OVERHARD *adj* too hard

OVERHATE *v* -HATED, -HATING, -HATES to hate to excess

OVERHAUL *v* -ED, -ING, -S to examine carefully for needed repairs

OVERHEAD *n* pl. -S the general cost of running a business

OVERHEAP *v* -ED, -ING, -S to heap up or accumulate to excess

OVERHEAR *v* -HEARD, -HEARING, -HEARS to hear without the speaker's knowledge or intention

OVERHEAT *v* -ED, -ING, -S to heat to excess

OVERHIGH *adj* too high

OVERHOLD *v* -HELD, -HOLDING, -HOLDS to rate too highly

OVERHOLY *adj* too holy

OVERHOPE *v* -HOPED, -HOPING, -HOPES to hope exceedingly

OVERHOT *adj* too hot

OVERHUNG past tense of overhang

OVERHUNT *v* -ED, -ING, -S to deplete the supply of game in an area by hunting to excess

OVERHYPE *v* -HYPED, -HYPING, -HYPES to hype to excess

OVERIDLE *adj* too idle

OVERJOY *v* -ED, -ING, -S to fill with great joy

OVERJUST *adj* too just

OVERKEEN *adj* too keen

OVERKILL *v* -ED, -ING, -S to destroy with more nuclear force than required

OVERKIND *adj* too kind

OVERLADE *v* -LADED, -LADEN, -LADING, -LADES to load with too great a burden

OVERLAID past tense of overlay

OVERLAIN past participle of overlie

OVERLAND *n* pl. -S a train or stagecoach that travels over land

OVERLAP *v* -LAPPED, -LAPPING, -LAPS to extend over and cover a part of

OVERLATE *adj* too late

OVERLAX *adj* too lax

OVERLAY *v* -LAID, -LAYING, -LAYS to lay over

OVERLEAF *adv* on the other side of the page

OVERLEAP *v* -LEAPED or -LEAPT, -LEAPING, -LEAPS to leap over

OVERLEND *v* -LENT, -LENDING, -LENDS to lend too much

OVERLET *v* -LET, -LETTING, -LETS to let to excess

OVERLEWD *adj* too lewd

OVERLIE *v* -LAY, -LAIN, -LYING, -LIES to lie over

OVERLIT a past tense of overlight

OVERLIVE *v* -LIVED, -LIVING, -LIVES to outlive

OVERLOAD *v* -ED, -ING, -S to load to excess

OVERLONG *adj* too long

OVERLOOK *v* -ED, -ING, -S to fail to notice

OVERLORD *v* -ED, -ING, -S to rule tyrannically

OVERLOUD *adj* too loud

OVERLOVE *v* -LOVED, -LOVING, -LOVES to love to excess

OVERLUSH *adj* excessively lush

OVERLY *adv* to an excessive degree

OVERLYING present participle of overlie

OVERMAN *n* pl. -MEN a foreman

OVERMAN *v* -MANNED, -MANNING, -MANS to provide with more men than are needed

OVERMANY *adj* too many

OVERMEEK *adj* excessively meek

OVERMELT *v* -ED, -ING, -S to melt too much

OVERMEN pl. of overman

OVERMILD *adj* too mild

OVERMILK v -ED, -ING, -S to milk to excess

OVERMINE v -MINED, -MINING, -MINES to mine to excess

OVERMIX v -ED, -ING, -ES to mix too much

OVERMUCH n pl. -ES an excess

OVERNEAR adj too near

OVERNEAT adj too neat

OVERNEW adj too new

OVERNICE adj excessively nice

OVERPASS v -PASSED or -PAST, -PASSING, -PASSES to pass over

OVERPAY v -PAID, -PAYING, -PAYS to pay too much

OVERPERT adj too pert

OVERPLAN v -PLANNED, -PLANNING, -PLANS to plan to excess

OVERPLAY v -ED, -ING, -S to exaggerate

OVERPLOT v -PLOTTED, -PLOTTING, -PLOTS to devise an overly complex plot for

OVERPLUS n pl. -ES a surplus

OVERPLY v -PLIED, -PLYING, -PLIES to ply to excess; overwork

OVERPUMP v -ED, -ING, -S to pump to excess

OVERRAN past tense of overrun

OVERRANK adj too luxuriant in growth

OVERRASH adj too rash

OVERRATE v -RATED, -RATING, -RATES to rate too highly

OVERRICH adj too rich

OVERRIDE v -RODE, -RIDDEN, -RIDING, -RIDES to ride over

OVERRIFE adj too rife

OVERRIPE adj too ripe

OVERRODE past tense of override

OVERRUDE adj excessively rude

OVERRUFF v -ED, -ING, -S to trump with a higher trump card than has already been played

OVERRULE v -RULED, -RULING, -RULES to disallow the arguments of

OVERRUN v -RAN, -RUNNING, -RUNS to spread or swarm over

OVERSAD adj excessively sad

OVERSALE n pl. -S the act of overselling

OVERSALT v -ED, -ING, -S to salt to excess

OVERSAVE v -SAVED, -SAVING, -SAVES to save too much

OVERSAW past tense of oversee

OVERSEA adv overseas

OVERSEAS adv beyond or across the sea

OVERSEE v -SAW, -SEEN, -SEEING, -SEES to watch over and direct

OVERSEED v -ED, -ING, -S to seed to excess

OVERSEER n pl. -S one that oversees

OVERSELL v -SOLD, -SELLING, -SELLS to sell more of than can be delivered

OVERSET v -SET, -SETTING, -SETS to turn or tip over

OVERSEW v -SEWED, -SEWN, -SEWING, -SEWS to overhand

OVERSHOE n pl. -S a protective outer shoe

OVERSHOT n pl. -S a type of fabric weave

OVERSICK adj too sick

OVERSIDE n pl. -S the other side of a phonograph record

OVERSIZE n pl. -S an unusually large size

OVERSLIP v -SLIPPED or -SLIPT, -SLIPPING, -SLIPS to leave out

OVERSLOW adj too slow

OVERSOAK v -ED, -ING, -S to soak too much

OVERSOFT adj too soft

OVERSOLD past tense of oversell

OVERSOON adv too soon

OVERSOUL n pl. -S a supreme reality or mind in transcendentalism

OVERSPIN n pl. -S a forward spin imparted to a ball

OVERSTAY v -ED, -ING, -S to stay beyond the limits or duration of

OVERSTEP v -STEPPED, -STEPPING, -STEPS to go beyond

OVERSTIR v -STIRRED, -STIRRING, -STIRS to stir too much

OVERSUDS v -ED, -ING, -ES to form an excessive amount of suds

OVERSUP v -SUPPED, -SUPPING, -SUPS to sup to excess

OVERSURE adj too sure

OVERT adj open to view

OVERTAKE v -TOOK, -TAKEN, -TAKING, -TAKES to catch up with

OVERTALK v -ED, -ING, -S to talk to excess

OVERTAME adj too tame

OVERTART adj too tart

OVERTASK v -ED, -ING, -S to task too severely

OVERTAX v -ED, -ING, -ES to tax too heavily

OVERTHIN *adj* too thin

OVERTIME *v* -TIMED, -TIMING, -TIMES to exceed the desired timing for

OVERTIP *v* -TIPPED, -TIPPING, -TIPS to tip more than what is customary

OVERTIRE *v* -TIRED, -TIRING, -TIRES to tire excessively

OVERTLY *adj* in an overt manner

OVERTOIL *v* -ED, -ING, -S to wear out or exhaust by excessive toil

OVERTONE *n* pl. -S a higher partial tone

OVERTOOK past tense of overtake

OVERTOP *v* -TOPPED, -TOPPING, -TOPS to rise above the top of

OVERTRIM *v* -TRIMMED, -TRIMMING, -TRIMS to trim too much

OVERTURE *v* -TURED, -TURING, -TURES to propose

OVERTURN *v* -ED, -ING, -S to turn over

OVERURGE *v* -URGED, -URGING, -URGES to urge too much

OVERUSE *v* -USED, -USING, -USES to use too much

OVERVIEW *n* pl. -S a summary

OVERVOTE *v* -VOTED, -VOTING, -VOTES to defeat by a majority of votes

OVERWARM *v* -ED, -ING, -S to warm too much

OVERWARY *adj* too wary

OVERWEAK *adj* too weak

OVERWEAR *v* -WORE, -WORN, -WEARING, -WEARS to wear out

OVERWEEN *v* -ED, -ING, -S to be arrogant

OVERWET *v* -WETTED, -WETTING, -WETS to wet too much

OVERWIDE *adj* too wide

OVERWILY *adj* too wily

OVERWIND *v* -WOUND, -WINDING, -WINDS to wind too much, as a watch

OVERWISE *adj* too wise

OVERWORD *n* pl. -S a word or phrase repeated at intervals in a song

OVERWORE past tense of overwear

OVERWORK *v* -WORKED or -WROUGHT, -WORKING, -WORKS to cause to work too hard

OVERWORN past participle of overwear

OVERWOUND past tense of overwind

OVERWROUGHT a past tense of overwork

OVERZEAL *n* pl. -S excess of zeal

OVIBOS *n* pl. OVIBOS a wild ox

OVICIDE *n* pl. -S an agent that kills eggs **OVICIDAL** *adj*

OVIDUCT *n* pl. -S a tube through which ova travel from an ovary **OVIDUCAL** *adj*

OVIFORM *adj* shaped like an egg

OVINE *n* pl. -S a sheep or a closely related animal

OVIPARA *n/pl* egg-laying animals

OVIPOSIT *v* -ED, -ING, -S to lay eggs

OVISAC *n* pl. -S a sac containing an ovum or ova

OVOID *n* pl. -S an egg-shaped body **OVOIDAL** *adj*

OVOLO *n* pl. -LI or -LOS a convex molding

OVONIC *n* pl. -S an electronic device

OVULATE *v* -LATED, -LATING, -LATES to produce ova

OVULE *n* pl. -S a rudimentary seed **OVULAR, OVULARY** *adj*

OVUM *n* pl. OVA the female reproductive cell of animals

OW *interj* — used to express sudden pain

OWE *v* OWED, OWING, OWES to be under obligation to pay or repay

OWL *n* pl. -S a nocturnal bird

OWLET *n* pl. -S a young owl

OWLISH *adj* resembling an owl **OWLISHLY** *adv*

OWLLIKE *adj* owlish

OWN *v* -ED, -ING, -S to have as a belonging **OWNABLE** *adj*

OWNER *n* pl. -S one that owns

OWSE *n* pl. OWSEN ox

OX *n* pl. OXEN a hoofed mammal

OX *n* pl. -ES a clumsy person

OXALATE *v* -LATED, -LATING, -LATES to treat with an oxalate (a chemical salt)

OXALIS *n* pl. -ALISES a flowering plant **OXALIC** *adj*

OXAZEPAM *n* pl. -S a tranquilizing drug

OXAZINE *n* pl. -S a chemical compound

OXBLOOD *n* pl. -S a deep red color

OXBOW *n* pl. -S a U-shaped piece of wood in an ox yoke

OXCART *n* pl. -S an ox-drawn cart

OXEN pl. of ox

OXEYE *n* pl. -S a flowering plant

OXFORD *n* pl. -S a type of shoe

OXHEART *n* pl. -S a variety of sweet cherry

OXID *n* pl. -S oxide

OXIDABLE *adj* capable of being oxidized

OXIDANT *n* pl. -S an oxidizing agent

OXIDASE *n* pl. -S an oxidizing enzyme **OXIDASIC** *adj*

OXIDATE *v* -DATED, -DATING, -DATES to oxidize

OXIDE *n* pl. -S a binary compound of oxygen with another element or radical **OXIDIC** *adj*

OXIDISE *v* -DISED, -DISING, -DISES to oxidize

OXIDISER *n* pl. -S oxidizer

OXIDIZE *v* -DIZED, -DIZING, -DIZES to combine with oxygen

OXIDIZER *n* pl. -S an oxidant

OXIM *n* pl. -S oxime

OXIME *n* pl. -S a chemical compound

OXLIP *n* pl. -S a flowering plant

OXO *adj* containing oxygen

OXPECKER *n* pl. -S an African bird

OXTAIL *n* pl. -S the tail of an ox

OXTER *n* pl. -S the armpit

OXTONGUE *n* pl. -S a European herb

OXY *adj* containing oxygen

OXYACID *n* pl. -S an acid that contains oxygen

OXYGEN *n* pl. -S a gaseous element **OXYGENIC** *adj*

OXYMORON *n* pl. -MORA a combination of contradictory or incongruous words

OXYPHIL *n* pl. -S oxyphile

OXYPHILE *n* pl. -S an organism that thrives in a relatively acid environment

OXYSALT *n* pl. -S a salt of an oxyacid

OXYSOME *n* pl. -S a structural unit of cellular cristae

OXYTOCIC *n* pl. -S a drug that hastens the process of childbirth

OXYTOCIN *n* pl. -S a pituitary hormone

OXYTONE *n* pl. -S a word having heavy stress on the last syllable

OY *interj* — used to express dismay or pain

OYER *n* pl. -S a type of legal writ

OYES *n* pl. OYESSES oyez

OYEZ *n* pl. OYESSES a cry used to introduce the opening of a court of law

OYSTER *v* -ED, -ING, -S to gather oysters (edible mollusks)

OYSTERER *n* pl. -S one that gathers or sells oysters

OZONATE *v* -ATED, -ATING, -ATES to treat or combine with ozone

OZONE *n* pl. -S a form of oxygen **OZONIC** *adj*

OZONIDE *n* pl. -S a compound of ozone

OZONISE *v* -ISED, -ISING, -ISES to ozonize

OZONIZE *v* -IZED, -IZING, -IZES to convert into ozone

OZONIZER *n* pl. -S a device for converting oxygen into ozone

OZONOUS *adj* pertaining to ozone

PA   *n* pl. -S a father

PABULUM   *n* pl. -S food **PABULAR** *adj*

PAC   *n* pl. -S a shoe patterned after a moccasin

PACA   *n* pl. -S a large rodent

PACE   *v* PACED, PACING, PACES to walk with a regular step

PACER   *n* pl. -S a horse whose gait is a pace

PACHA   *n* pl. -S pasha

PACHADOM   *n* pl. -S pashadom

PACHALIC   *n* pl. -S pashalik

PACHINKO   *n* pl. -KOS a Japanese pinball game

PACHISI   *n* pl. -S a board game of India

PACHOULI   *n* pl. -S an East Indian herb

PACHUCO   *n* pl. -COS a flashy Mexican-American youth

PACIFIC   *adj* peaceful

PACIFIED   past tense of pacify

PACIFIER   *n* pl. -S one that pacifies

PACIFIES   present 3d person sing. of pacify

PACIFISM   *n* pl. -S opposition to war or violence

PACIFIST   *n* pl. -S an advocate of pacifism

PACIFY   *v* -FIED, -FYING, -FIES to make peaceful

PACING   present participle of pace

PACK   *v* -ED, -ING, -S to put into a receptacle for transportation or storage **PACKABLE** *adj*

PACKAGE   *v* -AGED, -AGING, -AGES to make into a package (a wrapped or boxed object)

PACKAGER   *n* pl. -S one that packages

PACKER   *n* pl. -S one that packs

PACKET   *v* -ED, -ING, -S to make into a small package

PACKING   *n* pl. -S material used to pack

PACKLY   *adv* intimately

PACKMAN   *n* pl. -MEN a peddler

PACKNESS   *n* pl. -ES intimacy

PACKSACK   *n* pl. -S a carrying bag to be worn on the back

PACKWAX   *n* pl. -ES paxwax

PACT   *n* pl. -S an agreement

PACTION   *n* pl. -S a pact

PAD   *v* PADDED, PADDING, PADS to line or stuff with soft material

PADAUK   *n* pl. -S a tropical tree

PADDER   *n* pl. -S one that pads

PADDIES   pl. of paddy

PADDING   *n* pl. -S material with which to pad

PADDLE   *v* -DLED, -DLING, -DLES to propel with a broad-bladed implement

PADDLER   *n* pl. -S one that paddles

PADDLING   *n* pl. -S the act of one who paddles

PADDOCK   *v* -ED, -ING, -S to confine in an enclosure for horses

PADDY   *n* pl. -DIES a rice field

PADI   *n* pl. -S paddy

PADISHAH   *n* pl. -S a sovereign

PADLE   *n* pl. -S a hoe

PADLOCK   *v* -ED, -ING, -S to secure with a type of lock

PADNAG   *n* pl. -S a horse that moves along at an easy pace

PADOUK   *n* pl. -S padauk

PADRE   *n* pl. PADRES or PADRI a Christian clergyman

PADRONE   *n* pl. -NES or -NI a master

PADSHAH   *n* pl. -S padishah

PADUASOY *n* pl. -SOYS a strong silk fabric

PAEAN *n* pl. -S a song of joy

PAEANISM *n* pl. -S the chanting of a paean

PAELLA *n* pl. -S a saffron-flavored stew

PAEON *n* pl. -S a metrical foot of four syllables

PAESAN *n* pl. -S paesano

PAESANO *n* pl. -NI or -NOS a fellow countryman

PAGAN *n* pl. -S an irreligious person

PAGANDOM *n* pl. -S the realm of pagans

PAGANISE *v* -ISED, -ISING, -ISES to paganize

PAGANISH *adj* resembling a pagan

PAGANISM *n* pl. -S an irreligious attitude

PAGANIST *n* pl. -S a pagan

PAGANIZE *v* -IZED, -IZING, -IZES to make irreligious

PAGE *v* PAGED, PAGING, PAGES to summon by calling out the name of

PAGEANT *n* pl. -S an elaborate public spectacle

PAGEBOY *n* pl. -BOYS a woman's hairstyle

PAGED past tense of page

PAGER *n* pl. -S a beeper

PAGINAL *adj* pertaining to the pages of a book

PAGINATE *v* -NATED, -NATING, -NATES to number the pages of

PAGING *n* pl. -S a transfer of computer pages

PAGOD *n* pl. -S pagoda

PAGODA *n* pl. -S a Far Eastern temple

PAGURIAN *n* pl. -S a hermit crab

PAGURID *n* pl. -S pagurian

PAH *interj* — used as an exclamation of disgust

PAHLAVI *n* pl. -S a former coin of Iran

PAHOEHOE *n* pl. -S smooth solidified lava

PAID a past tense of pay

PAIK *v* -ED, -ING, -S to beat or strike

PAIL *n* pl. -S a watertight cylindrical container

PAILFUL *n* pl. PAILFULS or PAILSFUL as much as a pail can hold

PAILLARD *n* pl. -S a slice of meat pounded thin and grilled

PAIN *v* -ED, -ING, -S to cause pain (suffering or distress)

PAINCH *n* pl. -ES paunch

PAINFUL *adj* -FULLER, -FULLEST causing pain

PAINLESS *adj* not causing pain

PAINT *v* -ED, -ING, -S to make a representation of with paints (coloring substances)

PAINTER *n* pl. -S one that paints

PAINTING *n* pl. -S a picture made with paints

PAINTY *adj* PAINTIER, PAINTIEST covered with paint

PAIR *v* -ED, -ING, -S to arrange in sets of two

PAIRING *n* pl. -S a matching of two opponents in a tournament

PAISA *n* pl. PAISE or PAISAS a coin of Pakistan

PAISAN *n* pl. -S paisano

PAISANA *n* pl. -S a female compatriot

PAISANO *n* pl. -NOS a fellow countryman

PAISE a pl. of paisa

PAISLEY *n* pl. -LEYS a patterned wool fabric

PAJAMA *n* pl. -S a garment for sleeping or lounging

PAJAMAED *adj* wearing pajamas

PAKEHA *n* pl. -S a person who is not of Maori descent

PAL *v* PALLED, PALLING, PALS to associate as friends

PALABRA *n* pl. -S a word

PALACE *n* pl. -S a royal residence **PALACED** *adj*

PALADIN *n* pl. -S a knightly champion

PALAIS *n* pl. PALAIS a palace

PALATAL *n* pl. -S a bone of the palate

PALATE *n* pl. -S the roof of the mouth

PALATIAL *adj* resembling a palace

PALATINE *n* pl. -S a high officer of an empire

PALAVER *v* -ED, -ING, -S to chatter

PALAZZO *n* pl. -ZI an impressive building

PALAZZOS *n/pl* wide-legged pants for women

PALE *adj* PALER, PALEST lacking intensity of color

PALE *v* PALED, PALING, PALES to make or become pale

PALEA *n* pl. -LEAE a small bract **PALEAL** *adj*

PALEFACE *n* pl. -S a white person

PALELY *adv* in a pale manner

PALENESS *n* pl. -ES the quality of being pale

PALEOSOL *n* pl. -S a layer of ancient soil

PALER	comparative of pale
PALEST	superlative of pale
PALESTRA	*n* pl. -TRAS or -TRAE a school for athletics in ancient Greece
PALET	*n* pl. -S a palea
PALETOT	*n* pl. -S a loose overcoat
PALETTE	*n* pl. -S a board on which an artist mixes colors
PALEWAYS	*adv* palewise
PALEWISE	*adv* vertically
PALFREY	*n* pl. -FREYS a riding horse
PALIER	comparative of paly
PALIEST	superlative of paly
PALIKAR	*n* pl. -S a Greek soldier
PALIMONY	*n* pl. -NIES an allowance paid to one member of an unmarried couple who have separated
PALING	*n* pl. -S a picket fence
PALINODE	*n* pl. -S a formal retraction
PALISADE	*v* -SADED, -SADING, -SADES to fortify with a heavy fence
PALISH	*adj* somewhat pale
PALL	*v* -ED, -ING, -S to become insipid
PALLADIA	*n/pl* safeguards
PALLADIC	*adj* pertaining to the metallic element palladium
PALLED	past tense of pal
PALLET	*n* pl. -S a bed or mattress of straw
PALLETTE	*n* pl. -S a piece of armor protecting the armpit
PALLIA	a pl. of pallium
PALLIAL	*adj* pertaining to a part of the brain
PALLIATE	*v* -ATED, -ATING, -ATES to conceal the seriousness of
PALLID	*adj* pale **PALLIDLY** *adv*
PALLIER	comparative of pally
PALLIEST	superlative of pally
PALLING	present participle of pal
PALLIUM	*n* pl. -LIA or -LIUMS a cloak worn in ancient Rome
PALLOR	*n* pl. -S paleness
PALLY	*adj* -LIER, -LIEST marked by close friendship
PALM	*v* -ED, -ING, -S to touch with the palm (inner surface) of the hand
PALMAR	*adj* pertaining to the palm
PALMARY	*adj* worthy of praise
PALMATE	*adj* resembling an open hand
PALMATED	*adj* palmate
PALMER	*n* pl. -S a religious pilgrim
PALMETTE	*n* pl. -S a type of ornament
PALMETTO	*n* pl. -TOS or -TOES a tropical tree
PALMIER	comparative of palmy
PALMIEST	superlative of palmy
PALMIST	*n* pl. -S a fortune-teller
PALMITIN	*n* pl. -S a chemical compound
PALMLIKE	*adj* resembling a palm tree
PALMY	*adj* PALMIER, PALMIEST marked by prosperity
PALMYRA	*n* pl. -S a tropical tree
PALOMINO	*n* pl. -NOS a slender-legged horse
PALOOKA	*n* pl. -S an inferior boxer
PALP	*n* pl. -S a palpus
PALPABLE	*adj* capable of being felt **PALPABLY** *adv*
PALPAL	*adj* pertaining to a palpus
PALPATE	*v* -PATED, -PATING, -PATES to examine by touch
PALPATOR	*n* pl. -S one that palpates
PALPEBRA	*n* pl. -BRAE an eyelid
PALPUS	*n* pl. -PI a sensory organ of an arthropod
PALSHIP	*n* pl. -S the relation existing between close friends
PALSY	*v* -SIED, -SYING, -SIES to paralyze
PALTER	*v* -ED, -ING, -S to talk or act insincerely
PALTERER	*n* pl. -S one that palters
PALTRY	*adj* -TRIER, -TRIEST petty **PALTRILY** *adv*
PALUDAL	*adj* pertaining to a marsh
PALUDISM	*n* pl. -S malaria
PALY	*adj* PALIER, PALIEST somewhat pale
PAM	*n* pl. -S the jack of clubs in certain card games
PAMPA	*n* pl. -S a grassland of South America
PAMPEAN	*n* pl. -S a native of the pampas
PAMPER	*v* -ED, -ING, -S to treat with extreme or excessive indulgence
PAMPERER	*n* pl. -S one that pampers
PAMPERO	*n* pl. -ROS a cold, dry wind
PAMPHLET	*n* pl. -S a printed work with a paper cover
PAN	*v* PANNED, PANNING, PANS to criticize harshly
PANACEA	*n* pl. -S a remedy for all diseases or ills **PANACEAN** *adj*

PANACHE   n pl. -S an ornamental tuft of feathers

PANADA   n pl. -S a thick sauce

PANAMA   n pl. -S a lightweight hat

PANATELA   n pl. -S a long, slender cigar

PANBROIL   v -ED, -ING, -S to fry in a pan with little or no fat

PANCAKE   v -CAKED, -CAKING, -CAKES to land an airplane in a certain manner

PANCETTA   n pl. -S unsmoked Italian bacon

PANCHAX   n pl. -ES a tropical fish

PANCREAS   n pl. -ES a large gland

PANDA   n pl. -S a carnivorous mammal

PANDANUS   n pl. -NI or -NUSES a tropical plant

PANDECT   n pl. -S a complete body of laws

PANDEMIC   n pl. -S a widespread disease

PANDER   v -ED, -ING, -S to provide gratification for others' desires

PANDERER   n pl. -S one that panders

PANDIED   past tense of pandy

PANDIES   present 3d person sing. of pandy

PANDIT   n pl. -S a wise or learned man in India

PANDOOR   n pl. -S pandour

PANDORA   n pl. -S bandore

PANDORE   n pl. -S bandore

PANDOUR   n pl. -S a marauding soldier

PANDOWDY   n pl. -DIES an apple dessert

PANDURA   n pl. -S bandore

PANDY   v -DIED, -DYING, -DIES to punish by striking the hand

PANE   n pl. -S a sheet of glass for a window PANED adj

PANEL   v -ELED, -ELING, -ELS or -ELLED, -ELLING, -ELS to decorate with thin sheets of material

PANELING   n pl. -S material with which to panel

PANELIST   n pl. -S a member of a discussion or advisory group

PANELLED   a past tense of panel

PANELLING   a present participle of panel

PANETELA   n pl. -S panatela

PANFISH   n pl. -ES any small fish that can be fried whole

PANFRY   v -FRIED, -FRYING, -FRIES to fry in a frying pan

PANFUL   n pl. -S as much as a pan will hold

PANG   v -ED, -ING, -S to cause to have spasms of pain

PANGA   n pl. -S a large knife

PANGEN   n pl. -S a hypothetical heredity-controlling particle of protoplasm

PANGENE   n pl. -S pangen

PANGOLIN   n pl. -S a toothless mammal

PANHUMAN   adj pertaining to all humanity

PANIC   v -ICKED, -ICKING, -ICS to be overwhelmed by fear

PANICKY   adj -ICKIER, -ICKIEST tending to panic

PANICLE   n pl. -S a loosely branched flower cluster PANICLED adj

PANICUM   n pl. -S a grass

PANIER   n pl. -S pannier

PANMIXIA   n pl. -S random mating within a breeding population

PANMIXIS   n pl. -MIXES panmixia

PANNE   n pl. -S a lustrous velvet

PANNED   past tense of pan

PANNIER   n pl. -S a large basket

PANNIKIN   n pl. -S a small saucepan

PANNING   present participle of pan

PANOCHA   n pl. -S a coarse Mexican sugar

PANOCHE   n pl. -S panocha

PANOPLY   n pl. -PLIES a suit of armor

PANOPTIC   adj including everything visible in one view

PANORAMA   n pl. -S a complete view

PANPIPE   n pl. -S a musical instrument

PANSOPHY   n pl. -PHIES universal knowledge

PANSY   n pl. -SIES a flowering plant

PANT   v -ED, -ING, -S to breathe quickly and with difficulty

PANTHEON   n pl. -S a temple dedicated to all the gods

PANTHER   n pl. -S a leopard

PANTIE   n pl. -S a woman's or child's undergarment

PANTIES   pl. of panty

PANTILE   n pl. -S a roofing tile PANTILED adj

PANTO   n pl. -TOS a pantomime

PANTOFLE   n pl. -S a slipper

PANTOUM   n pl. -S a verse form

PANTRY   n pl. -TRIES a closet or room for storing kitchen utensils

PANTSUIT   n pl. -S a type of woman's suit

PANTY   n pl. PANTIES pantie

PANZER   n pl. -S an armored combat vehicle

PAP   n pl. -S a soft food for infants

PAPA n pl. -S a father

PAPACY n pl. -CIES the office of the pope

PAPAIN n pl. -S an enzyme

PAPAL adj pertaining to the pope **PAPALLY** adv

PAPAW n pl. -S a fleshy fruit

PAPAYA n pl. -S a melon-like fruit **PAPAYAN** adj

PAPER v -ED, -ING, -S to cover or wrap with paper (a thin sheet material made of cellulose pulp)

PAPERBOY n pl. -BOYS a newsboy

PAPERER n pl. -S one that papers

PAPERY adj resembling paper

PAPHIAN n pl. -S a prostitute

PAPILLA n pl. -LAE a nipple-like projection **PAPILLAR** adj

PAPILLON n pl. -S a small dog having large ears

PAPOOSE n pl. -S an American Indian baby

PAPPI a pl. of pappus

PAPPIER comparative of pappy

PAPPIES pl. of pappy

PAPPIEST superlative of pappy

PAPPOOSE n pl. -S papoose

PAPPUS n pl. -PI a tuft of bristles on the achene of certain plants **PAPPOSE, PAPPOUS** adj

PAPPY adj -PIER, -PIEST resembling pap

PAPPY n pl. -PIES a father

PAPRICA n pl. -S paprika

PAPRIKA n pl. -S a seasoning made from red peppers

PAPULA n pl. -LAE papule

PAPULE n pl. -S a pimple **PAPULAR, PAPULOSE** adj

PAPYRUS n pl. -RUSES or -RI a tall aquatic plant **PAPYRAL, PAPYRIAN, PAPYRINE** adj

PAR v PARRED, PARRING, PARS to shoot in a standard number of strokes in golf

PARA n pl. -S a monetary unit of Yugoslavia

PARABLE n pl. -S a simple story conveying a moral or religious lesson

PARABOLA n pl. -S a conic section

PARACHOR n pl. -S a mathematical constant that relates molecular volume to surface tension

PARADE v -RADED, -RADING, -RADES to march in a public procession

PARADER n pl. -S one that parades

PARADIGM n pl. -S a pattern or example

PARADING present participle of parade

PARADISE n pl. -S a place of extreme beauty or delight

PARADOR n pl. -S a government-owned hotel in Spain

PARADOS n pl. -ES a protective embankment

PARADOX n pl. -ES a statement seemingly contradictory or absurd yet perhaps true

PARADROP v -DROPPED, -DROPPING, -DROPS to deliver by parachute

PARAFFIN v -ED, -ING, -S to coat with a waxy substance

PARAFORM n pl. -S a substance used as an antiseptic

PARAGOGE n pl. -S the addition of a sound or sounds at the end of a word

PARAGON v -ED, -ING, -S to compare with

PARAKEET n pl. -S a small parrot

PARAKITE n pl. -S a parachute kite for towing a person through the air by a motorboat

PARALLAX n pl. -ES an apparent optical displacement of an object

PARALLEL v -LELED, -LELING, -LELS or -LELLED, -LELLING, -LELS to be similar or analogous to

PARALYSE v -LYSED, -LYSING, -LYSES to paralyze

PARALYZE v -LYZED, -LYZING, -LYZES to render incapable of movement

PARAMENT n pl. -MENTS or -MENTA an ornamental vestment

PARAMO n pl. -MOS a plateau region of South America

PARAMOUR n pl. -S an illicit lover

PARANG n pl. -S a heavy knife

PARANOEA n pl. -S paranoia

PARANOIA n pl. -S a mental disorder

PARANOIC n pl. -S a paranoid

PARANOID n pl. -S one affected with paranoia

PARAPET n pl. -S a protective wall

PARAPH n pl. -S a flourish at the end of a signature

PARAQUAT n pl. -S a weed killer

PARAQUET *n* pl. -S parakeet

PARASANG *n* pl. -S a Persian unit of distance

PARASHAH *n* pl. -SHOTH or -SHIOTH a passage in Jewish scripture

PARASITE *n* pl. -S an organism that lives and feeds on or in another organism

PARASOL *n* pl. -S a small, light umbrella

PARAVANE *n* pl. -S an underwater device used to cut cables

PARAWING *n* pl. -S a winglike parachute

PARAZOAN *n* pl. -S any of a major division of multicellular animals

PARBOIL *v* -ED, -ING, -S to cook partially by boiling for a short time

PARCEL *v* -CELED, -CELING, -CELS or -CELLED, -CELLING, -CELS to divide into parts or shares

PARCENER *n* pl. -S a joint heir

PARCH *v* -ED, -ING, -ES to make very dry

PARCHESI *n* pl. -S pachisi

PARCHISI *n* pl. -S pachisi

PARD *n* pl. -S a leopard

PARDAH *n* pl. -S purdah

PARDEE *interj* pardi

PARDI *interj* — used as a mild oath

PARDIE *interj* pardi

PARDINE *adj* pertaining to a leopard

PARDNER *n* pl. -S chum; friend

PARDON *v* -ED, -ING, -S to release from liability for an offense

PARDONER *n* pl. -S one that pardons

PARDY *interj* pardi

PARE *v* PARED, PARING, PARES to cut off the outer covering of

PARECISM *n* pl. -S the state of having the male and female sexual organs beside or near each other

PAREIRA *n* pl. -S a medicinal plant root

PARENT *v* -ED, -ING, -S to exercise the functions of a parent (a father or mother)

PARENTAL *adj* pertaining to a parent

PAREO *n* pl. -REOS pareu

PARER *n* pl. -S one that pares

PARERGON *n* pl. -GA a composition derived from a larger work

PARESIS *n* pl. -RESES partial loss of the ability to move

PARETIC *n* pl. -S one affected with paresis

PAREU *n* pl. -S a Polynesian garment

PAREVE *adj* parve

PARFAIT *n* pl. -S a frozen dessert

PARFLESH *n* pl. -ES a rawhide soaked in lye to remove the hair and dried

PARFOCAL *adj* having lenses with the corresponding focal points in the same plane

PARGE *v* PARGED, PARGING, PARGES to parget

PARGET *v* -GETED, -GETING, -GETS or -GETTED, -GETTING, -GETS to cover with plaster

PARGING *n* pl. -S a thin coat of mortar or plaster for sealing masonry

PARGO *n* pl. -GOS a food fish

PARHELIA *n/pl* bright circular spots appearing on a solar halo

PARHELIC *adj* pertaining to parhelia

PARIAH *n* pl. -S a social outcast

PARIAN *n* pl. -S a hard, white porcelain

PARIES *n* pl. PARIETES the wall of an organ

PARIETAL *n* pl. -S a bone of the skull

PARING *n* pl. -S something pared off

PARIS *n* pl. -ISES a European herb

PARISH *n* pl. -ES an ecclesiastical district

PARITY *n* pl. -TIES equality

PARK *v* -ED, -ING, -S to leave a vehicle in a location for a time

PARKA *n* pl. -S a hooded garment

PARKER *n* pl. -S one that parks

PARKING *n* pl. -S an area in which vehicles may be left

PARKLAND *n* pl. -S a grassland region with isolated or grouped trees

PARKLIKE *adj* resembling an outdoor recreational area

PARKWAY *n* pl. -WAYS a wide highway

PARLANCE *n* pl. -S a manner of speaking

PARLANDO *adj* sung in a manner suggestive of speech

PARLANTE *adj* parlando

PARLAY *v* -ED, -ING, -S to bet an original wager and its winnings on a subsequent event

PARLE *v* PARLED, PARLING, PARLES to parley

PARLEY *v* -LEYED, -LEYING, -LEYS to discuss terms with an enemy

PARLEYER *n* pl. -S one that parleys

PARLING present participle of parle

PARLOR *n* pl. -S a room for the entertainment of visitors

PARLOUR *n* pl. -S parlor
PARLOUS *adj* dangerous
PARODIC *adj* comically imitative
PARODIED past tense of parody
PARODIES present 3d person sing. of parody
PARODIST *n* pl. -S one who parodies
PARODOS *n* pl. -DOI an ode sung in ancient Greek drama
PARODY *v* -DIED, -DYING, -DIES to imitate a serious literary work for comic effect
PAROL *n* pl. -S an utterance
PAROLE *v* -ROLED, -ROLING, -ROLES to release from prison before completion of the imposed sentence
PAROLEE *n* pl. -S one who is paroled
PARONYM *n* pl. -S a word having the same root as another
PAROQUET *n* pl. -S parakeet
PAROTIC *adj* situated near the ear
PAROTID *n* pl. -S a salivary gland
PAROTOID *n* pl. -S a gland of certain toads and frogs
PAROUS *adj* having produced offspring
PAROXYSM *n* pl. -S a sudden fit or attack
PARQUET *v* -ED, -ING, -S to furnish with a floor of inlaid design
PARR *n* pl. -S a young salmon
PARRAL *n* pl. -S parrel
PARRED past tense of par
PARREL *n* pl. -S a sliding loop of rope or chain used on a ship
PARRIDGE *n* pl. -S porridge
PARRIED past tense of parry
PARRIES present 3d person sing. of parry
PARRING present participle of par
PARRITCH *n* pl. -ES porridge
PARROKET *n* pl. -S parakeet
PARROT *v* -ED, -ING, -S to repeat or imitate without thought or understanding
PARROTER *n* pl. -S one that parrots
PARROTY *adj* resembling a parrot (a hook-billed tropical bird)
PARRY *v* -RIED, -RYING, -RIES to ward off a blow
PARSE *v* PARSED, PARSING, PARSES to describe and analyze grammatically **PARSABLE** *adj*
PARSEC *n* pl. -S a unit of astronomical distance
PARSER *n* pl. -S one that parses

PARSING present participle of parse
PARSLEY *n* pl. -LEYS a cultivated herb **PARSLEYED, PARSLIED** *adj*
PARSNIP *n* pl. -S a European herb
PARSON *n* pl. -S a clergyman **PARSONIC** *adj*
PART *v* -ED, -ING, -S to divide or break into separate pieces
PARTAKE *v* -TOOK, -TAKEN, -TAKING, -TAKES to participate
PARTAKER *n* pl. -S one that partakes
PARTAN *n* pl. -S an edible crab
PARTERRE *n* pl. -S a section of a theater
PARTIAL *n* pl. -S a simple component of a complex tone
PARTIBLE *adj* divisible
PARTICLE *n* pl. -S a very small piece or part
PARTIED past tense of party
PARTIER *n* pl. -S partyer
PARTIES present 3d person sing. of party
PARTING *n* pl. -S a division or separation
PARTISAN *n* pl. -S a firm supporter of a person, party, or cause
PARTITA *n* pl. -S a set of related instrumental pieces
PARTITE *adj* divided into parts
PARTIZAN *n* pl. -S partisan
PARTLET *n* pl. -S a woman's garment
PARTLY *adv* in some measure or degree
PARTNER *v* -ED, -ING, -S to associate with in some activity of common interest
PARTON *n* pl. -S a hypothetical atomic particle
PARTOOK past tense of partake
PARTWAY *adv* to some extent
PARTY *v* -TIED, -TYING, -TIES to attend a social gathering
PARTYER *n* pl. -S one that parties
PARURA *n* pl. -S parure
PARURE *n* pl. -S a set of matched jewelry
PARVE *adj* made without milk or meat
PARVENU *n* pl. -S one who has suddenly risen above his class
PARVENUE *adj* characteristic of a parvenu
PARVIS *n* pl. -VISES an enclosed area in front of a church
PARVISE *n* pl. -S parvis
PARVO *n* pl. -VOS a contagious disease of dogs

PARVOLIN   *n* pl. -S an oily liquid obtained from fish

PAS   *n* pl. PAS a dance step

PASCAL   *n* pl. -S a unit of pressure

PASCHAL   *n* pl. -S a candle used in certain religious ceremonies

PASE   *n* pl. -S a movement of a matador's cape

PASEO   *n* pl. -SEOS a leisurely stroll

PASH   *v* -ED, -ING, -ES to strike violently

PASHA   *n* pl. -S a former Turkish high official

PASHADOM   *n* pl. -S the rank of a pasha

PASHALIC   *n* pl. -S pashalik

PASHALIK   *n* pl. -S the territory of a pasha

PASQUIL   *n* pl. -S a satire or lampoon

PASS   *v* -ED, -ING, -ES to go by

PASSABLE   *adj* fairly good or acceptable **PASSABLY** *adv*

PASSADE   *n* pl. -S a turn of a horse backward or forward on the same ground

PASSADO   *n* pl. -DOS or -DOES a forward thrust in fencing

PASSAGE   *v* -SAGED, -SAGING, -SAGES to make a voyage

PASSANT   *adj* walking with the farther forepaw raised — used of a heraldic animal

PASSBAND   *n* pl. -S a frequency band that permits transmission with maximum efficiency

PASSBOOK   *n* pl. -S a bankbook

PASSE   *adj* outmoded

PASSEE   *adj* passe

PASSEL   *n* pl. -S a large quantity or number

PASSER   *n* pl. -S one that passes

PASSERBY   *n* pl. PASSERSBY one who passes by

PASSIBLE   *adj* capable of feeling or suffering

PASSIM   *adv* here and there

PASSING   *n* pl. -S a death

PASSION   *n* pl. -S an intense emotion

PASSIVE   *n* pl. -S a verb form

PASSKEY   *n* pl. -KEYS a key that opens several different locks

PASSLESS   *adj* incapable of being traveled over or through

PASSOVER   *n* pl. -S the lamb eaten at the feast of a Jewish holiday

PASSPORT   *n* pl. -S a document allowing travel from one country to another

PASSUS   *n* pl. -ES a section of a story or poem

PASSWORD   *n* pl. -S a secret word that must be spoken to gain admission

PAST   *n* pl. -S time gone by

PASTA   *n* pl. -S a food made of dough

PASTE   *v* PASTED, PASTING, PASTES to fasten with a sticky mixture

PASTEL   *n* pl. -S a soft, delicate hue

PASTER   *n* pl. -S one that pastes

PASTERN   *n* pl. -S a part of a horse's foot

PASTEUP   *n* pl. -S a finished copy to be photographed for making a printing plate

PASTICCI   *n/pl* pastiches

PASTICHE   *n* pl. -S an artistic work made of fragments from various sources

PASTIE   *n* pl. -S pasty

PASTIER   comparative of pasty

PASTIES   pl. of pasty

PASTIEST   superlative of pasty

PASTIL   *n* pl. -S pastille

PASTILLE   *n* pl. -S a lozenge

PASTIME   *n* pl. -S a recreational activity

PASTINA   *n* pl. -S a type of macaroni

PASTING   present participle of paste

PASTIS   *n* pl. -TISES a French liqueur

PASTLESS   *adj* having no past

PASTNESS   *n* pl. -ES the state of being past or gone by

PASTOR   *v* -ED, -ING, -S to serve as the spiritual overseer of

PASTORAL   *n* pl. -S a literary or artistic work that depicts country life

PASTRAMI   *n* pl. -S a highly seasoned smoked beef

PASTROMI   *n* pl. -S pastrami

PASTRY   *n* pl. -TRIES a sweet baked food

PASTURAL   *adj* pertaining to a pasture

PASTURE   *v* -TURED, -TURING, -TURES to put in a pasture (a grazing area)

PASTURER   *n* pl. -S one that pastures livestock

PASTY   *adj* PASTIER, PASTIEST pale and unhealthy in appearance

PASTY   *n* pl. PASTIES a meat pie

PAT   *v* PATTED, PATTING, PATS to touch lightly

PATACA   *n* pl. -S a monetary unit of Macao

PATAGIAL   *adj* pertaining to a patagium

PATAGIUM *n* pl. -GIA a wing membrane of a bat

PATAMAR *n* pl. -S a sailing vessel

PATCH *v* -ED, -ING, -ES to mend or cover a hole or weak spot in

PATCHER *n* pl. -S one that patches

PATCHY *adj* PATCHIER, PATCHIEST uneven in quality **PATCHILY** *adv*

PATE *n* pl. -S the top of the head **PATED** *adj*

PATELLA *n* pl. -LAE or -LAS the flat movable bone at the front of the knee **PATELLAR** *adj*

PATEN *n* pl. -S a plate

PATENCY *n* pl. -CIES the state of being obvious

PATENT *v* -ED, -ING, -S to obtain a patent (a government grant protecting the rights of an inventor) on

PATENTEE *n* pl. -S one that holds a patent

PATENTLY *adv* obviously

PATENTOR *n* pl. -S one that grants a patent

PATER *n* pl. -S a father

PATERNAL *adj* pertaining to a father

PATH *n* pl. -S a trodden way or track

PATHETIC *adj* arousing pity

PATHLESS *adj* having no path

PATHOGEN *n* pl. -S any disease-producing organism

PATHOS *n* pl. -ES a quality that arouses feelings of pity or compassion

PATHWAY *n* pl. -WAYS a path

PATIENCE *n* pl. -S the quality of being patient

PATIENT *adj* -TIENTER, -TIENTEST able to endure disagreeable circumstances without complaint

PATIENT *n* pl. -S one who is under medical treatment

PATIN *n* pl. -S paten

PATINA *n* pl. -NAE or -NAS a green film that forms on bronze

PATINATE *v* -NATED, -NATING, -NATES to give a patina to

PATINE *v* -TINED, -TINING, -TINES to cover with a patina

PATINIZE *v* -NIZED, -NIZING, -NIZES to patinate

PATIO *n* pl. -TIOS an outdoor paved area adjoining a house

PATLY *adv* suitably

PATNESS *n* pl. -ES suitability

PATOIS *n* pl. PATOIS a dialect

PATRIOT *n* pl. -S one who loves his country

PATROL *v* -TROLLED, -TROLLING, -TROLS to pass through an area for the purposes of observation or security

PATRON *n* pl. -S a regular customer **PATRONAL, PATRONLY** *adj*

PATROON *n* pl. -S a landowner granted manorial rights under old Dutch law

PATSY *n* pl. -SIES a person who is easily fooled

PATTAMAR *n* pl. -S patamar

PATTED past tense of pat

PATTEE *adj* paty

PATTEN *n* pl. -S a shoe having a thick wooden sole

PATTER *v* -ED, -ING, -S to talk glibly or rapidly

PATTERER *n* pl. -S one that patters

PATTERN *v* -ED, -ING, -S to make according to a prescribed design

PATTIE *n* pl. -S patty

PATTING present participle of pat

PATTY *n* pl. -TIES a small, flat cake of chopped food

PATTYPAN *n* pl. -S a pan in which patties are baked

PATULENT *adj* patulous

PATULOUS *adj* spreading; open

PATY *adj* formee

PATZER *n* pl. -S an inept chess player

PAUCITY *n* pl. -TIES smallness of number or quantity

PAUGHTY *adj* arrogant

PAULDRON *n* pl. -S a piece of armor for the shoulder

PAULIN *n* pl. -S a sheet of waterproof material

PAUNCH *n* pl. -ES the belly or abdomen **PAUNCHED** *adj*

PAUNCHY *adj* PAUNCHIER, PAUNCHIEST having a protruding belly

PAUPER *v* -ED, -ING, -S to reduce to poverty

PAUSAL *adj* pertaining to a break or rest in speaking or writing

PAUSE *v* PAUSED, PAUSING, PAUSES to stop temporarily

PAUSER *n* pl. -S one that pauses

PAVAN n pl. -S a slow, stately dance

PAVANE n pl. -S pavan

PAVE v PAVED, PAVING, PAVES to cover with material that forms a firm, level surface

PAVEED adj set close together to conceal a metal base

PAVEMENT n pl. -S a paved surface

PAVER n pl. -S one that paves

PAVID adj timid

PAVILION v -ED, -ING, -S to cover with a large tent

PAVILLON n pl. -S the bell of a wind instrument

PAVIN n pl. -S pavan

PAVING n pl. -S pavement

PAVIOR n pl. -S a paver

PAVIOUR n pl. -S a paver

PAVIS n pl. -ISES a large medieval shield

PAVISE n pl. -S pavis

PAVISER n pl. -S a soldier carrying a pavis

PAVLOVA n pl. -S a meringue dessert

PAVONINE adj resembling a peacock

PAW v -ED, -ING, -S to strike or scrape with a beating motion

PAWER n pl. -S one that paws

PAWKY adj PAWKIER, PAWKIEST sly **PAWKILY** adv

PAWL n pl. -S a hinged mechanical part

PAWN v -ED, -ING, -S to give as security for something borrowed **PAWNABLE** adj

PAWNAGE n pl. -S an act of pawning

PAWNEE n pl. -S one to whom something is pawned

PAWNER n pl. -S one that pawns something

PAWNOR n pl. -S pawner

PAWNSHOP n pl. -S a place where things are pawned

PAWPAW n pl. -S papaw

PAX n pl. -ES a ceremonial embrace given to signify Christian love and unity

PAXWAX n pl. -ES the nuchal ligament of a quadruped

PAY v PAID or PAYED, PAYING, PAYS to give money or something of value in exchange for goods or services

PAYABLE adj profitable **PAYABLY** adv

PAYABLES n/pl accounts payable

PAYBACK n pl. -S a return on an investment equal to the original capital outlay

PAYCHECK n pl. -S a check in payment of wages or salary

PAYDAY n pl. -DAYS the day on which wages are paid

PAYEE n pl. -S one to whom money is paid

PAYER n pl. -S one that pays

PAYGRADE n pl. -S the grade of military personnel according to a base pay scale

PAYLOAD n pl. -S the part of a cargo producing income

PAYMENT n pl. -S something that is paid

PAYNIM n pl. -S a pagan

PAYOFF n pl. -S the act of distributing gains

PAYOLA n pl. -S a secret payment for favors

PAYOR n pl. -S payer

PAYOUT n pl. -S money that is paid out

PAYROLL n pl. -S a list of employees entitled to payment

PAZAZZ n pl. -ES pizazz

PDQ adv immediately

PE n pl. -S a Hebrew letter

PEA n pl. -S the edible seed of an annual herb

PEACE v PEACED, PEACING, PEACES to be or become silent

PEACEFUL adj -FULLER, -FULLEST undisturbed; calm

PEACENIK n pl. -S one who demonstrates against a war

PEACH v -ED, -ING, -ES to inform against someone

PEACHER n pl. -S one that peaches

PEACHY adj PEACHIER, PEACHIEST dandy

PEACING present participle of peace

PEACOAT n pl. -S a heavy woolen jacket

PEACOCK v -ED, -ING, -S to strut vainly

PEACOCKY adj -COCKIER, -COCKIEST vain

PEAFOWL n pl. -S a large pheasant

PEAG n pl. -S wampum

PEAGE n pl. -S peag

PEAHEN n pl. -S a female peafowl

PEAK v -ED, -ING, -S to reach a maximum

PEAKIER comparative of peaky

PEAKIEST superlative of peaky

PEAKISH adj somewhat sickly

PEAKLESS	*adj* having no peak (a pointed top)
PEAKLIKE	*adj* resembling a peak
PEAKY	*adj* PEAKIER, PEAKIEST sickly
PEAL	*v* -ED, -ING, -S to ring out
PEALIKE	*adj* resembling a pea
PEAN	*n* pl. -S paean
PEANUT	*n* pl. -S the nutlike seed or pod of an annual vine
PEAR	*n* pl. -S a fleshy fruit
PEARL	*v* -ED, -ING, -S to adorn with pearls (smooth, rounded masses formed in certain mollusks)
PEARLASH	*n* pl. -ES an alkaline compound
PEARLER	*n* pl. -S one that dives for pearls
PEARLITE	*n* pl. -S a cast-iron alloy
PEARLY	*adj* PEARLIER, PEARLIEST resembling a pearl
PEARMAIN	*n* pl. -S a variety of apple
PEART	*adj* PEARTER, PEARTEST lively PEARTLY *adv*
PEASANT	*n* pl. -S a person of inferior social rank
PEASCOD	*n* pl. -S peasecod
PEASE	*n* pl. PEASEN or PEASES a pea
PEASECOD	*n* pl. -S a pea pod
PEAT	*n* pl. -S a substance composed of partially decayed vegetable matter
PEATY	*adj* PEATIER, PEATIEST resembling or containing peat
PEAVEY	*n* pl. -VEYS a lever used to move logs
PEAVY	*n* pl. -VIES peavey
PEBBLE	*v* -BLED, -BLING, -BLES to cover with pebbles (small, rounded stones)
PEBBLY	*adj* -BLIER, -BLIEST resembling pebbles
PEC	*n* pl. -S a chest muscle
PECAN	*n* pl. -S a nut-bearing tree
PECCABLE	*adj* liable to sin
PECCANCY	*n* pl. -CIES the state of being peccant
PECCANT	*adj* sinful
PECCARY	*n* pl. -RIES a hoofed mammal
PECCAVI	*n* pl. -S a confession of sin
PECH	*v* -ED, -ING, -S to pant
PECHAN	*n* pl. -S the stomach
PECK	*v* -ED, -ING, -S to strike with the beak or something pointed
PECKER	*n* pl. -S one that pecks
PECKISH	*adj* irritable
PECKY	*adj* PECKIER, PECKIEST marked by decay caused by fungi
PECORINO	*n* pl. -NOS a hard cheese made from sheep's milk
PECS	*n/pl* pectoral muscles
PECTASE	*n* pl. -S an enzyme
PECTATE	*n* pl. -S a chemical salt
PECTEN	*n* pl. -TENS or -TINES a comblike anatomical part
PECTIN	*n* pl. -S a carbohydrate derivative PECTIC *adj*
PECTIZE	*v* -TIZED, -TIZING, -TIZES to change into a jelly
PECTORAL	*n* pl. -S something worn on the breast
PECULATE	*v* -LATED, -LATING, -LATES to embezzle
PECULIAR	*n* pl. -S something belonging exclusively to a person
PECULIUM	*n* pl. -LIA private property
PED	*n* pl. -S a natural soil aggregate
PEDAGOG	*n* pl. -S a teacher
PEDAGOGY	*n* pl. -GIES the work of a teacher
PEDAL	*v* -ALED, -ALING, -ALS or -ALLED, -ALLING, -ALS to operate by means of foot levers
PEDALFER	*n* pl. -S a type of soil
PEDALIER	*n* pl. -S the pedal keyboard of an organ
PEDALLED	a past tense of pedal
PEDALLING	a present participle of pedal
PEDALO	*n* pl. -LOS a paddleboat powered by pedals
PEDANT	*n* pl. -S one who flaunts his knowledge PEDANTIC *adj*
PEDANTRY	*n* pl. -RIES ostentatious display of knowledge
PEDATE	*adj* resembling a foot PEDATELY *adv*
PEDDLE	*v* -DLED, -DLING, -DLES to travel about selling wares
PEDDLER	*n* pl. -S one that peddles
PEDDLERY	*n* pl. -RIES the trade of a peddler
PEDDLING	present tense of peddle
PEDERAST	*n* pl. -S a man who engages in sexual activities with boys
PEDES	pl. of pes

PEDESTAL	v -TALED, -TALING, -TALS or -TALLED, -TALLING, -TALS to provide with an architectural support or base	**PEERAGE**	n pl. -S the rank of a nobleman
PEDICAB	n pl. -S a passenger vehicle that is pedaled	**PEERESS**	n pl. -ES a noblewoman
		PEERIE	n pl. -S peery
PEDICEL	n pl. -S a slender basal part of an organism	**PEERLESS**	adj having no equal
		PEERY	n pl. PEERIES a child's toy
PEDICLE	n pl. -S pedicel **PEDICLED** adj	**PEESWEEP**	n pl. -S a lapwing
		PEETWEET	n pl. -S a wading bird
PEDICURE	v -CURED, -CURING, -CURES to administer a cosmetic treatment to the feet and toenails	**PEEVE**	v PEEVED, PEEVING, PEEVES to annoy
		PEEVISH	adj irritable
		PEEWEE	n pl. -S an unusually small person or thing
PEDIFORM	adj shaped like a foot	**PEEWIT**	n pl. -S pewit
PEDIGREE	n pl. -S a line of ancestors	**PEG**	v PEGGED, PEGGING, PEGS to fasten with a peg (a wooden pin)
PEDIMENT	n pl. -S a triangular architectural part		
PEDIPALP	n pl. -S an appendage of an arachnid	**PEGBOARD**	n pl. -S a board with holes for pegs
		PEGBOX	n pl. -ES a part of a stringed instrument
PEDLAR	n pl. -S peddler		
PEDLARY	n pl. -LARIES peddlery	**PEGGED**	past tense of peg
PEDLER	n pl. -S peddler	**PEGGING**	present participle of peg
PEDLERY	n pl. -LERIES peddlery	**PEGLESS**	adj lacking a peg
PEDOCAL	n pl. -S a type of soil	**PEGLIKE**	adj resembling a peg
PEDOLOGY	n pl. -GIES the scientific study of the behavior and development of children	**PEH**	n pl. -S pe
		PEIGNOIR	n pl. -S a woman's gown
		PEIN	v -ED, -ING, -S to peen
PEDRO	n pl. -DROS a card game	**PEISE**	v PEISED, PEISING, PEISES to weigh
PEDUNCLE	n pl. -S a flower stalk		
PEE	n pl. -S the letter P	**PEKAN**	n pl. -S a carnivorous mammal
PEEBEEN	n pl. -S a large hardwood evergreen tree	**PEKE**	n pl. -S a small, long-haired dog
PEEK	v -ED, -ING, -S to look furtively or quickly	**PEKIN**	n pl. -S a silk fabric
		PEKOE	n pl. -S a black tea
PEEKABOO	n pl. -BOOS a children's game	**PELAGE**	n pl. -S the coat or covering of a mammal **PELAGIAL** adj
PEEL	v -ED, -ING, -S to strip off an outer covering of **PEELABLE** adj		
		PELAGIC	adj oceanic
		PELE	n pl. -S a medieval fortified tower
PEELER	n pl. -S one that peels		
PEELING	n pl. -S a piece or strip that has been peeled off	**PELERINE**	n pl. -S a woman's cape
		PELF	n pl. -S money or wealth
PEEN	v -ED, -ING, -S to beat with the non-flat end of a hammerhead	**PELICAN**	n pl. -S a large, web-footed bird
		PELISSE	n pl. -S a long outer garment
PEEP	v -ED, -ING, -S to utter a short, shrill cry	**PELITE**	n pl. -S a rock composed of fine fragments **PELITIC** adj
		PELLAGRA	n pl. -S a niacin-deficiency disease
PEEPER	n pl. -S one that peeps		
PEEPHOLE	n pl. -S a small opening through which one may look	**PELLET**	v -ED, -ING, -S to strike with pellets (small rounded masses)
PEEPSHOW	n pl. -S an exhibition viewed through a small opening	**PELLETAL**	adj resembling a pellet
		PELLICLE	n pl. -S a thin skin or film
PEEPUL	n pl. -S pipal	**PELLMELL**	n pl. -S a jumbled mass
PEER	v -ED, -ING, -S to look narrowly or searchingly	**PELLUCID**	adj transparent
		PELMET	n pl. -S a decorative cornice

PELON   adj hairless
PELORIA   n pl. -S abnormal regularity of
            a flower form PELORIAN,
            PELORIC adj
PELORUS   n pl. -ES a navigational
            instrument
PELOTA   n pl. -S a court game of
            Spanish origin
PELT   v -ED, -ING, -S to strike
            repeatedly with blows or
            missiles
PELTAST   n pl. -S a soldier of ancient
            Greece
PELTATE   adj shaped like a shield
PELTER   v -ED, -ING, -S to pelt
PELTRY   n pl. -RIES an animal skin
PELVIC   n pl. -S a bone of the pelvis
PELVIS   n pl. -VES or -VISES a part of
            the skeleton
PEMBINA   n pl. -S a variety of cranberry
PEMICAN   n pl. -S pemmican
PEMMICAN   n pl. -S a food prepared by
            North American Indians
PEMOLINE   n pl. -S a drug used as a
            stimulant
PEMPHIX   n pl. -ES a skin disease
PEN   v PENNED, PENNING, PENS
            to write with a pen (an
            instrument for writing with fluid
            ink)
PENAL   adj pertaining to punishment
PENALISE   v -ISED, -ISING, -ISES to
            penalize
PENALITY   n pl. -TIES liability to
            punishment
PENALIZE   v -IZED, -IZING, -IZES to
            subject to a penalty
PENALLY   adv in a penal manner
PENALTY   n pl. -TIES a punishment
            imposed for violation of a law,
            rule, or agreement
PENANCE   v -ANCED, -ANCING,
            -ANCES to impose a type of
            punishment upon
PENANG   n pl. -S a cotton fabric
PENATES   n/pl the Roman gods of the
            household
PENCE   a pl. of penny
PENCEL   n pl. -S a small flag
PENCHANT   n pl. -S a strong liking for
            something
PENCIL   v -CILED, -CILING, -CILS or
            -CILLED, -CILLING, -CILS to
            produce by using a pencil (a
            writing and drawing implement)
PENCILER   n pl. -S one that pencils

PEND   v -ED, -ING, -S to remain
            undecided or unsettled
PENDANT   n pl. -S a hanging ornament
PENDENCY   n pl. -CIES a pending state
PENDENT   n pl. -S pendant
PENDULUM   n pl. -S a type of free swinging
            body PENDULAR adj
PENES   a pl. of penis
PENGO   n pl. -GOS a former monetary
            unit of Hungary
PENGUIN   n pl. -S a flightless, aquatic
            bird
PENICIL   n pl. -S a small tuft of hairs
PENIS   n pl. -NES or -NISES the male
            organ of copulation PENIAL,
            PENILE adj
PENITENT   n pl. -S a person who repents
            his sins
PENKNIFE   n pl. -KNIVES a small
            pocketknife
PENLIGHT   n pl. -S a small flashlight
PENLITE   n pl. -S penlight
PENMAN   n pl. -MEN an author
PENNA   n pl. -NAE any of the feathers
            that determine a bird's shape
PENNAME   n pl. -S a name used by an
            author instead of his real name
PENNANT   n pl. -S a long, narrow flag
PENNATE   adj having wings or feathers
PENNATED   adj pennate
PENNE   n pl. PENNE short tubular
            pasta
PENNED   past tense of pen
PENNER   n pl. -S one that pens
PENNI   n pl. -NIA or -NIS a Finnish
            coin
PENNIES   a pl. of penny
PENNINE   n pl. -S a mineral
PENNING   present participle of pen
PENNON   n pl. -S a pennant
            PENNONED adj
PENNY   n pl. PENNIES or PENCE a
            coin of the United Kingdom
PENOCHE   n pl. -S penuche
PENOLOGY   n pl. -GIES the science of the
            punishment of crime
PENONCEL   n pl. -S a small pennon
PENPOINT   n pl. -S the point of a pen
PENSEE   n pl. -S a thought
PENSIL   n pl. -S pencel
PENSILE   adj hanging loosely
PENSION   v -ED, -ING, -S to grant a
            retirement allowance to
PENSIONE   n pl. -S a boarding house
PENSIVE   adj engaged in deep thought
PENSTER   n pl. -S a writer

PENSTOCK *n* pl. -S a conduit for conveying water to a waterwheel

PENT *adj* confined

PENTACLE *n* pl. -S a five-pointed star

PENTAD *n* pl. -S a group of five

PENTAGON *n* pl. -S a five-sided polygon

PENTANE *n* pl. -S a volatile liquid

PENTANOL *n* pl. -S an alcohol

PENTARCH *n* pl. -S one of five joint rulers

PENTENE *n* pl. -S a liquid hydrocarbon

PENTODE *n* pl. -S a type of electron tube

PENTOMIC *adj* made up of five battle groups

PENTOSAN *n* pl. -S a complex carbohydrate

PENTOSE *n* pl. -S a sugar having five carbon atoms per molecule

PENTYL *n* pl. -S amyl

PENUCHE *n* pl. -S a fudge-like candy

PENUCHI *n* pl. -S penuche

PENUCHLE *n* pl. -S pinochle

PENUCKLE *n* pl. -S pinochle

PENULT *n* pl. -S the next to last syllable in a word

PENUMBRA *n* pl. -BRAE or -BRAS a partial shadow

PENURY *n* pl. -RIES extreme poverty

PEON *n* pl. -S or -ES an unskilled laborer

PEONAGE *n* pl. -S the condition of being a peon

PEONISM *n* pl. -S peonage

PEONY *n* pl. -NIES a flowering plant

PEOPLE *v* -PLED, -PLING, -PLES to furnish with inhabitants

PEOPLER *n* pl. -S one that peoples

PEP *v* PEPPED, PEPPING, PEPS to fill with energy

PEPERONI *n* pl. -S a highly seasoned sausage

PEPLOS *n* pl. -ES a garment worn by women in ancient Greece

PEPLUM *n* pl. -LUMS or -LA a short section attached to the waistline of a garment **PEPLUMED** *adj*

PEPLUS *n* pl. -ES peplos

PEPO *n* pl. -POS a fruit having a fleshy interior and a hard rind

PEPONIDA *n* pl. -S pepo

PEPONIUM *n* pl. -S pepo

PEPPED past tense of pep

PEPPER *v* -ED, -ING, -S to season with pepper (a pungent condiment)

PEPPERER *n* pl. -S one that peppers

PEPPERY *adj* resembling pepper

PEPPING present participle of pep

PEPPY *adj* -PIER, -PIEST full of energy **PEPPILY** *adv*

PEPSIN *n* pl. -S a digestive enzyme of the stomach

PEPSINE *n* pl. -S pepsin

PEPTIC *n* pl. -S a substance that promotes digestion

PEPTID *n* pl. -S peptide

PEPTIDE *n* pl. -S a combination of amino acids **PEPTIDIC** *adj*

PEPTIZE *v* -TIZED, -TIZING, -TIZES to increase the colloidal dispersion of

PEPTIZER *n* pl. -S one that peptizes

PEPTONE *n* pl. -S a protein compound **PEPTONIC** *adj*

PER *prep* for each

PERACID *n* pl. -S a type of acid

PERCALE *n* pl. -S a cotton fabric

PERCEIVE *v* -CEIVED, -CEIVING, -CEIVES to become aware of through the senses

PERCENT *n* pl. -S one part in a hundred

PERCEPT *n* pl. -S something that is perceived

PERCH *v* -ED, -ING, -ES to sit or rest on an elevated place

PERCHER *n* pl. -S one that perches

PERCOID *n* pl. -S a spiny-finned fish

PERCUSS *v* -ED, -ING, -ES to strike with force

PERDIE *interj* pardi

PERDU *n* pl. -S a soldier sent on a dangerous mission

PERDURE *v* -DURED, -DURING, -DURES to continue to exist

PERDY *interj* pardi

PEREGRIN *n* pl. -S a swift falcon much used in falconry

PEREION *n* pl. -REIA the thorax of some crustaceans

PEREON *n* pl. -REA pereion

PEREOPOD *n* pl. -S an appendage of the pereion

PERFECT *adj* -FECTER, -FECTEST lacking fault or defect; of an extreme kind

PERFECT *v* -ED, -ING, -S to make perfect

PERFECTA *n* pl. -S a system of betting

PERFECTO *n* pl. -TOS a medium-sized cigar

PERFIDY *n* pl. -DIES deliberate breach of faith or trust

PERFORCE *adv* of necessity

PERFORM *v* -ED, -ING, -S to begin and carry through to completion

PERFUME *v* -FUMED, -FUMING, -FUMES to fill with a fragrant odor

PERFUMER *n* pl. -S one that perfumes

PERFUSE *v* -FUSED, -FUSING, -FUSES to spread over or through something

PERGOLA *n* pl. -S a shaded shelter or passageway

PERHAPS *n* pl. -ES something open to doubt or conjecture

PERI *n* pl. -S a supernatural being of Persian mythology

PERIANTH *n* pl. -S an outer covering of a flower

PERIAPT *n* pl. -S an amulet

PERIBLEM *n* pl. -S a region of plant tissue

PERICARP *n* pl. -S the wall of a ripened plant ovary or fruit

PERICOPE *n* pl. -PES or -PAE a selection from a book

PERIDERM *n* pl. -S an outer layer of plant tissue

PERIDIUM *n* pl. -IA the covering of the spore-bearing organ in many fungi **PERIDIAL** *adj*

PERIDOT *n* pl. -S a mineral

PERIGEE *n* pl. -S the point in the orbit of a celestial body which is nearest to the earth **PERIGEAL, PERIGEAN** *adj*

PERIGON *n* pl. -S an angle equal to 360 degrees

PERIGYNY *n* pl. -NIES the state of being situated on a cuplike organ surrounding the pistil

PERIL *v* -ILED, -ILING, -ILS or -ILLED, -ILLING, -ILS to imperil

PERILLA *n* pl. -S an Asian herb

PERILOUS *adj* dangerous

PERILUNE *n* pl. -S the point in the orbit of a celestial body which is nearest to the moon

PERINEUM *n* pl. -NEA a region of the body at the lower end of the trunk **PERINEAL** *adj*

PERIOD *n* pl. -S a portion of time

PERIODIC *adj* recurring at regular intervals

PERIODID *n* pl. -S an iodide

PERIOTIC *adj* surrounding the ear

PERIPETY *n* pl. -TIES a sudden change in a course of events

PERIPTER *n* pl. -S a structure with a row of columns around all sides

PERIQUE *n* pl. -S a dark tobacco

PERISARC *n* pl. -S a protective covering of certain hydrozoans

PERISH *v* -ED, -ING, -ES to die

PERIWIG *n* pl. -S a wig

PERJURE *v* -JURED, -JURING, -JURES to make a perjurer of

PERJURER *n* pl. -S one guilty of perjury

PERJURY *n* pl. -RIES the willful giving of false testimony under oath in a judicial proceeding

PERK *v* -ED, -ING, -S to carry oneself jauntily

PERKISH *adj* somewhat perky

PERKY *adj* PERKIER, PERKIEST jaunty **PERKILY** *adv*

PERLITE *n* pl. -S a volcanic glass **PERLITIC** *adj*

PERM *v* -ED, -ING, -S to give hair a permanent wave

PERMEANT *adj* that permeates

PERMEASE *n* pl. -S a catalyzing agent

PERMEATE *v* -ATED, -ATING, -ATES to spread through

PERMIT *v* -MITTED, -MITTING, -MITS to allow

PERMUTE *v* -MUTED, -MUTING, -MUTES to change the order of

PERONEAL *adj* pertaining to the fibula

PERORAL *adj* occurring through the mouth

PERORATE *v* -RATED, -RATING, -RATES to make a lengthy speech

PEROXID *n* pl. -S peroxide

PEROXIDE *v* -IDED, -IDING, -IDES to treat with peroxide (a bleaching agent)

PEROXY *adj* containing the bivalent group O_2

PERPEND *v* -ED, -ING, -S to ponder

PERPENT *n* pl. -S a large building stone

PERPLEX *v* -ED, -ING, -ES to make mentally uncertain

PERRON *n* pl. -S an outdoor stairway

PERRY *n* pl. -RIES a beverage of pear juice often fermented

PERSALT *n* pl. -S a chemical salt

PERSE *n* pl. -S a blue color

PERSIST *v* -ED, -ING, -S to continue resolutely in some activity

PERSON *n* pl. -S a human being

PERSONA	*n* pl. -NAE a character in a literary work
PERSONA	*n* pl. -S the public role that a person assumes
PERSONAL	*n* pl. -S a brief, private notice in a newspaper
PERSPIRE	*v* -SPIRED, -SPIRING, -SPIRES to give off moisture through the pores of the skin **PERSPIRY** *adj*
PERSUADE	*v* -SUADED, -SUADING, -SUADES to cause to do something by means of argument, reasoning, or entreaty
PERT	*adj* PERTER, PERTEST impudent **PERTLY** *adv*
PERTAIN	*v* -ED, -ING, -S to have reference or relation
PERTNESS	*n* pl. -ES the quality of being pert
PERTURB	*v* -ED, -ING, -S to disturb greatly
PERUKE	*n* pl. -S a wig **PERUKED** *adj*
PERUSAL	*n* pl. -S the act of perusing
PERUSE	*v* -RUSED, -RUSING, -RUSES to read
PERUSER	*n* pl. -S one that peruses
PERVADE	*v* -VADED, -VADING, -VADES to spread through every part of
PERVADER	*n* pl. -S one that pervades
PERVERSE	*adj* willfully deviating from desired or expected conduct
PERVERT	*v* -ED, -ING, -S to turn away from the right course of action
PERVIOUS	*adj* capable of being penetrated
PES	*n* pl. PEDES a foot or footlike part
PESADE	*n* pl. -S the position of a horse when rearing
PESETA	*n* pl. -S a monetary unit of Spain
PESEWA	*n* pl. -S a monetary unit of Ghana
PESKY	*adj* -KIER, -KIEST annoying **PESKILY** *adv*
PESO	*n* pl. -SOS a monetary unit of various Spanish-speaking countries
PESSARY	*n* pl. -RIES a contraceptive device worn in the vagina
PEST	*n* pl. -S an annoying person or thing
PESTER	*v* -ED, -ING, -S to bother
PESTERER	*n* pl. -S one that pesters

PESTHOLE	*n* pl. -S a place liable to epidemic disease
PESTLE	*v* -TLED, -TLING, -TLES to crush with a club-shaped hand tool
PESTO	*n* pl. -TOS a sauce of basil, garlic, and olive oil
PET	*v* PETTED, PETTING, PETS to caress with the hand
PETAL	*n* pl. -S a leaflike part of a corolla **PETALED, PETALLED** *adj*
PETALINE	*adj* resembling a petal
PETALODY	*n* pl. -DIES the metamorphosis of various floral organs into petals
PETALOID	*adj* resembling a petal
PETALOUS	*adj* having petals
PETARD	*n* pl. -S an explosive device
PETASOS	*n* pl. -ES petasus
PETASUS	*n* pl. -ES a broad-brimmed hat worn in ancient Greece
PETCOCK	*n* pl. -S a small valve or faucet
PETECHIA	*n* pl. -CHIAE a small hemorrhagic spot on a body surface
PETER	*v* -ED, -ING, -S to diminish gradually
PETIOLAR	*adj* pertaining to a petiole
PETIOLE	*n* pl. -S the stalk of a leaf **PETIOLED** *adj*
PETIT	*adj* small; minor
PETITE	*n* pl. -S a clothing size for short women
PETITION	*v* -ED, -ING, -S to make a formal request
PETNAP	*v* -NAPPED, -NAPPING, -NAPS to steal a pet for profit
PETREL	*n* pl. -S a small seabird
PETRIFY	*v* -FIED, -FYING, -FIES to convert into stone or a stony substance
PETROL	*n* pl. -S gasoline
PETROLIC	*adj* derived from petroleum
PETRONEL	*n* pl. -S a portable firearm
PETROSAL	*adj* petrous
PETROUS	*adj* resembling stone in hardness
PETSAI	*n* pl. -S Chinese cabbage
PETTED	past tense of pet
PETTEDLY	*adv* peevishly
PETTER	*n* pl. -S one that pets
PETTI	pl. of petto
PETTIER	comparative of petty
PETTIEST	superlative of petty

PETTIFOG	*v* -FOGGED, -FOGGING, -FOGS to quibble
PETTILY	*adv* in a petty manner
PETTING	*n* pl. -S amorous caressing and kissing
PETTISH	*adj* peevish
PETTLE	*v* -TLED, -TLING, -TLES to caress
PETTO	*n* pl. -TI the breast
PETTY	*adj* -TIER, -TIEST insignificant
PETULANT	*adj* peevish
PETUNIA	*n* pl. -S a tropical herb
PETUNTSE	*n* pl. -S a mineral
PETUNTZE	*n* pl. -S petuntse
PEW	*n* pl. -S a bench for seating people in church
PEWEE	*n* pl. -S a small bird
PEWIT	*n* pl. -S the lapwing
PEWTER	*n* pl. -S a tin alloy
PEWTERER	*n* pl. -S one that makes articles of pewter
PEYOTE	*n* pl. -S a cactus
PEYOTL	*n* pl. -S peyote
PEYTRAL	*n* pl. -S a piece of armor for the breast of a horse
PEYTREL	*n* pl. -S peytral
PFENNIG	*n* pl. -NIGS or -NIGE a bronze coin of Germany
PFFT	*interj* — used to express a sudden ending
PFUI	*interj* phooey
PHAETON	*n* pl. -S a light carriage
PHAGE	*n* pl. -S an organism that destroys bacteria
PHALANGE	*n* pl. -S any bone of a finger or toe
PHALANX	*n* pl. -ES a formation of infantry in ancient Greece
PHALLI	a pl. of phallus
PHALLIC	*adj* pertaining to a phallus
PHALLISM	*n* pl. -S worship of the phallus as symbolic of nature's creative power
PHALLIST	*n* pl. -S one who practices phallism
PHALLUS	*n* pl. -LI or -LUSES the penis
PHANTASIED	past tense of phantasy
PHANTASIES	present 3d person sing. of phantasy
PHANTASM	*n* pl. -S a creation of the imagination
PHANTAST	*n* pl. -S fantast
PHANTASY	*v* -SIED, -SYING, -SIES to fantasy
PHANTOM	*n* pl. -S something existing in appearance only

PHARAOH	*n* pl. -S a ruler of ancient Egypt
PHARISEE	*n* pl. -S a hypocritically self-righteous person
PHARMACY	*n* pl. -CIES a drugstore
PHAROS	*n* pl. -ES a lighthouse or beacon to guide seamen
PHARYNX	*n* pl. -YNGES or -YNXES a section of the digestive tract
PHASE	*v* PHASED, PHASING, PHASES to plan or carry out by phases (distinct stages of development) **PHASEAL**, **PHASIC** *adj*
PHASEOUT	*n* pl. -S a gradual stopping of operations
PHASIS	*n* pl. PHASES a phase
PHASMID	*n* pl. -S a tropical insect
PHAT	*adj* susceptible of easy and rapid typesetting
PHATIC	*adj* sharing feelings rather than ideas
PHEASANT	*n* pl. -S a large, long-tailed bird
PHELLEM	*n* pl. -S a layer of plant cells
PHELONIA	*n/pl* liturgical vestments
PHENATE	*n* pl. -S a salt of carbolic acid
PHENAZIN	*n* pl. -S a chemical compound
PHENETIC	*adj* pertaining to a type of classificatory system
PHENETOL	*n* pl. -S a volatile liquid
PHENIX	*n* pl. -ES phoenix
PHENOL	*n* pl. -S a caustic compound
PHENOLIC	*n* pl. -S a synthetic resin
PHENOM	*n* pl. -S a person of extraordinary ability or promise
PHENOXY	*adj* containing a radical derived from phenol
PHENYL	*n* pl. -S a univalent chemical radical **PHENYLIC** *adj*
PHEW	*interj* — used to express relief, fatigue, or disgust
PHI	*n* pl. -S a Greek letter
PHIAL	*n* pl. -S a vial
PHILABEG	*n* pl. -S filibeg
PHILIBEG	*n* pl. -S filibeg
PHILOMEL	*n* pl. -S a songbird
PHILTER	*v* -ED, -ING, -S to put under the spell of a love potion
PHILTRE	*v* -TRED, -TRING, -TRES to philter
PHILTRUM	*n* pl. -TRA the indentation between the upper lip and the nose

PHIMOSIS *n* pl. -MOSES the abnormal constriction of the opening of the prepuce **PHIMOTIC** *adj*

PHIZ *n* pl. -ES a face or facial expression

PHLEGM *n* pl. -S a thick mucus secreted in the air passages

PHLEGMY *adj* PHLEGMIER, PHLEGMIEST resembling phlegm

PHLOEM *n* pl. -S a complex plant tissue

PHLOX *n* pl. -ES a flowering plant

PHOBIA *n* pl. -S an obsessive or irrational fear

PHOBIC *n* pl. -S one affected with a phobia

PHOCINE *adj* pertaining to seals

PHOEBE *n* pl. -S a small bird

PHOEBUS *n* pl. -ES the sun

PHOENIX *n* pl. -ES a mythical bird

PHON *n* pl. -S a unit of loudness

PHONAL *adj* pertaining to speech sounds

PHONATE *v* -NATED, -NATING, -NATES to produce speech sounds

PHONE *v* PHONED, PHONING, PHONES to telephone

PHONEME *n* pl. -S a unit of speech **PHONEMIC** *adj*

PHONETIC *adj* pertaining to speech sounds

PHONEY *v* -ED, -ING, -S to phony

PHONEY *adj* pl. -NIER, -NIEST phony

PHONIC *adj* pertaining to the nature of sound

PHONICS *n/pl* the science of sound

PHONIED past tense of phony

PHONIER comparative of phoney and phony

PHONIES present 3d person sing. of phony

PHONIEST superlative of phoney and phony

PHONILY *adv* in a phony manner

PHONING present participle of phone

PHONO *n* pl. -NOS a record player

PHONON *n* pl. -S a quantum of vibrational energy

PHONY *adj* pl. -NIER -NIEST not genuine or real

PHONY *v* -NIED, -NYING, -NIES to alter so as to make appear genuine

PHOOEY *interj* — used as an exclamation of disgust or contempt

PHORATE *n* pl. -S an insecticide

PHORONID *n* pl. -S a wormlike marine animal

PHOSGENE *n* pl. -S a poisonous gas

PHOSPHID *n* pl. -S a chemical compound

PHOSPHIN *n* pl. -S a poisonous gas

PHOSPHOR *n* pl. -S a substance that will emit light when exposed to radiation

PHOT *n* pl. -S a unit of illumination

PHOTIC *adj* pertaining to light

PHOTICS *n/pl* the science of light

PHOTO *v* -ED, -ING, -S to photograph

PHOTOG *n* pl. -S one who takes photographs

PHOTOMAP *v* -MAPPED, -MAPPING, -MAPS to map by means of aerial photography

PHOTON *n* pl. -S an elementary particle **PHOTONIC** *adj*

PHOTOPIA *n* pl. -S vision in bright light **PHOTOPIC** *adj*

PHOTOSET *v* -SET, -SETTING, -SETS to prepare for printing by photographic means

PHPHT *interj* pht

PHRASAL *adj* pertaining to a group of two or more associated words

PHRASE *v* PHRASED, PHRASING, PHRASES to express in words

PHRASING *n* pl. -S manner or style of verbal expression

PHRATRY *n* pl. -TRIES a tribal unit among primitive peoples **PHRATRAL, PHRATRIC** *adj*

PHREATIC *adj* pertaining to underground waters

PHRENIC *adj* pertaining to the mind

PHRENSY *v* -SIED, -SYING, -SIES to frenzy

PHT *interj* — used as an expression of mild anger or annoyance

PHTHALIC *adj* pertaining to a certain acid

PHTHALIN *n* pl. -S a chemical compound

PHTHISIC *n* pl. -S phthisis

PHTHISIS *n* pl. PHTHISES a disease of the lungs

PHUT *n* pl. -S a dull, abrupt sound

PHYLA pl. of phylon and phylum

PHYLAE pl. of phyle

PHYLAR *adj* pertaining to a phylum

PHYLAXIS *n* pl. -AXISES an inhibiting of infection by the body

PHYLE *n* pl. -LAE a political subdivision in ancient Greece **PHYLIC** *adj*

PHYLESIS *n* pl. -LESES or -LESISES the course of evolutionary development **PHYLETIC** *adj*

PHYLLARY *n* pl. -RIES a bract of certain plants

PHYLLITE *n* pl. -S a foliated rock

PHYLLO *n* pl. -LOS very thin pastry dough

PHYLLODE *n* pl. -S a flattened petiole that serves as a leaf

PHYLLOID *n* pl. -S a leaflike plant part

PHYLLOME *n* pl. -S a leaf of a plant

PHYLON *n* pl. -LA a genetically related group

PHYLUM *n* pl. -LA a taxonomic division

PHYSED *n* pl. -S physical education

PHYSES pl. of physis

PHYSIC *v* -ICKED, -ICKING, -ICS to treat with medicine

PHYSICAL *n* pl. -S a medical examination of the body

PHYSIQUE *n* pl. -S the form or structure of the body

PHYSIS *n* pl. PHYSES the principle of growth or change in nature

PHYTANE *n* pl. -S a chemical compound

PHYTOID *adj* resembling a plant

PHYTOL *n* pl. -S an alcohol

PHYTON *n* pl. -S a structural unit of a plant **PHYTONIC** *adj*

PI *n* pl. -S a Greek letter

PI *v* PIED, PIEING or PIING, PIES to jumble or disorder

PIA *n* pl. -S a membrane of the brain

PIACULAR *adj* atoning

PIAFFE *v* PIAFFED, PIAFFING, PIAFFES to perform a piaffer

PIAFFER *n* pl. -S a movement in horsemanship

PIAL *adj* pertaining to a pia

PIAN *n* pl. -S a tropical disease **PIANIC** *adj*

PIANISM *n* pl. -S performance on the piano

PIANIST *n* pl. -S one who plays the piano

PIANO *n* pl. -NOS a musical instrument

PIASABA *n* pl. -S piassava

PIASAVA *n* pl. -S piassava

PIASSABA *n* pl. -S piassava

PIASSAVA *n* pl. -S a coarse, stiff fiber

PIASTER *n* pl. -S a monetary unit of several Arab countries

PIASTRE *n* pl. -S piaster

PIAZZA *n* pl. -ZAS or -ZE a public square in an Italian town

PIBAL *n* pl. -S a small balloon for determining the direction and speed of the wind

PIBROCH *n* pl. -S a musical piece played on the bagpipe

PIC *n* pl. -S a photograph

PICA *n* pl. -S a craving for unnatural food

PICACHO *n* pl. -CHOS an isolated peak of a hill

PICADOR *n* pl. -ES or -S a horseman in a bullfight

PICAL *adj* resembling a pica

PICARA *n* pl. -S a female picaro

PICARO *n* pl. -ROS a vagabond

PICAROON *v* -ED, -ING, -S to act as a pirate

PICAYUNE *n* pl. -S a former Spanish-American coin

PICCOLO *n* pl. -LOS a small flute

PICE *n* pl. PICE a former coin of India and Pakistan

PICEOUS *adj* glossy-black in color

PICIFORM *adj* pertaining to an order of birds

PICK *v* -ED, -ING, -S to select

PICKADIL *n* pl. -S a type of collar

PICKAX *v* -ED, -ING, -ES to use a pickax (a tool for breaking hard surfaces)

PICKAXE *v* -AXED, -AXING, -AXES to pickax

PICKEER *v* -ED, -ING, -S to skirmish in advance of an army

PICKER *n* pl. -S one that picks

PICKEREL *n* pl. -S a freshwater fish

PICKET *v* -ED, -ING, -S to stand outside of some location, as a business, to publicize one's grievances against it

PICKETER *n* pl. -S one who pickets

PICKIER comparative of picky

PICKIEST superlative of picky

PICKING *n* pl. -S the act of one that picks

PICKLE *v* -LED, -LING, -LES to preserve or flavor in a solution of brine or vinegar

PICKLOCK *n* pl. -S a tool for opening locks

PICKOFF *n* pl. -S a play in baseball

PICKUP *n* pl. -S a small truck

PICKWICK *n* pl. -S a device for raising wicks in oil lamps

PICKY	*adj* PICKIER, PICKIEST fussy	**PIETIES**	pl. of piety
PICLORAM	*n* pl. -S an herbicide	**PIETISM**	*n* pl. -S piety
PICNIC	*v* -NICKED, -NICKING, -NICS to go on a picnic (an outdoor excursion with food)	**PIETIST**	*n* pl. -S a pious person
		PIETY	*n* pl. -TIES the quality or state of being pious
PICNICKY	*adj* pertaining to a picnic	**PIFFLE**	*v* -FLED, -FLING, -FLES to babble
PICOGRAM	*n* pl. -S one trillionth of a gram		
PICOLIN	*n* pl. -S picoline	**PIG**	*v* PIGGED, PIGGING, PIGS to bear pigs (cloven-hoofed mammals)
PICOLINE	*n* pl. -S a chemical compound		
PICOMOLE	*n* pl. -S one trillionth of a mole		
PICOT	*v* -ED, -ING, -S to edge with ornamental loops	**PIGBOAT**	*n* pl. -S a submarine
		PIGEON	*n* pl. -S a short-legged bird
PICOTEE	*n* pl. -S a variety of carnation	**PIGFISH**	*n* pl. -ES a marine fish
PICQUET	*n* pl. -S piquet	**PIGGED**	past tense of pig
PICRATE	*n* pl. -S a chemical salt PICRATED *adj*	**PIGGERY**	*n* pl. -GERIES a pigpen
		PIGGIE	*n* pl. -S piggy
PICRIC	*adj* having a very bitter taste	**PIGGIER**	comparative of piggy
PICRITE	*n* pl. -S an igneous rock PICRITIC *adj*	**PIGGIES**	pl. of piggy
		PIGGIEST	superlative of piggy
PICTURE	*v* -TURED, -TURING, -TURES to make a visual representation of	**PIGGIN**	*n* pl. -S a small wooden pail
		PIGGING	present participle of pig
		PIGGISH	*adj* greedy or dirty
PICUL	*n* pl. -S an Asian unit of weight	**PIGGY**	*n* pl. -GIES a small pig
PIDDLE	*v* -DLED, -DLING, -DLES to waste time	**PIGGY**	*adj* -GIER, -GIEST piggish
		PIGLET	*n* pl. -S a small pig
PIDDLER	*n* pl. -S one that piddles	**PIGLIKE**	*adj* resembling a pig
PIDDLY	*adj* insignificant	**PIGMENT**	*v* -ED, -ING, -S to add a coloring matter to
PIDDOCK	*n* pl. -S a bivalve mollusk		
PIDGIN	*n* pl. -S a mixed language	**PIGMY**	*n* pl. -MIES pygmy
PIE	*v* PIED, PIEING, PIES to pi	**PIGNOLI**	*n* pl. -S pignolia
PIEBALD	*n* pl. -S a spotted animal	**PIGNOLIA**	*n* pl. -S the edible seed of nut pines
PIECE	*v* PIECED, PIECING, PIECES to join into a whole		
		PIGNUS	*n* pl. -NORA property held as security for a debt
PIECER	*n* pl. -S one that pieces		
PIECING	*n* pl. -S material to be sewn together	**PIGNUT**	*n* pl. -S a hickory nut
		PIGOUT	*n* pl. -S an instance of eating to excess
PIECRUST	*n* pl. -S the crust of a pie		
PIED	past tense of pie	**PIGPEN**	*n* pl. -S a place where pigs are kept
PIEDFORT	*n* pl. -S piefort		
PIEDMONT	*n* pl. -S an area lying at the foot of a mountain	**PIGSKIN**	*n* pl. -S the skin of a pig
		PIGSNEY	*n* pl. -NEYS a darling
PIEFORT	*n* pl. -S an unusually thick coin	**PIGSTICK**	*v* -ED, -ING, -S to hunt for wild boar
PIEING	a present participle of pi		
PIEPLANT	*n* pl. -S a rhubarb	**PIGSTY**	*n* pl. -STIES a pigpen
PIER	*n* pl. -S a structure extending from land out over water	**PIGTAIL**	*n* pl. -S a tight braid of hair
		PIGWEED	*n* pl. -S a weedy plant
PIERCE	*v* PIERCED, PIERCING, PIERCES to cut or pass into or through	**PIING**	a present participle of pi
		PIKA	*n* pl. -S a small mammal
		PIKAKE	*n* pl. -S an East Indian vine
PIERCER	*n* pl. -S one that pierces	**PIKE**	*v* PIKED, PIKING, PIKES to pierce with a pike (a long spear)
PIEROGI	*n* pl. -ES a small dumpling with a filling		
PIERROT	*n* pl. -S a clown	**PIKEMAN**	*n* pl. -MEN a soldier armed with a pike
PIETA	*n* pl. -S a representation of the Virgin Mary mourning over the body of Christ		
		PIKER	*n* pl. -S a stingy person

PIKI *n* pl. -S thin blue cornmeal bread

PIKING present participle of pike

PILAF *n* pl. -S a dish made of seasoned rice and often meat

PILAFF *n* pl. -S pilaf

PILAR *adj* pertaining to hair

PILASTER *n* pl. -S a rectangular column

PILAU *n* pl. -S pilaf

PILAW *n* pl. -S pilaf

PILCHARD *n* pl. -S a small marine fish

PILE *v* PILED, PILING, PILES to lay one upon the other

PILEA pl. of pileum

PILEATE *adj* having a pileus

PILEATED *adj* pileate

PILED past tense of pile

PILEI pl. of pileus

PILELESS *adj* not having a raised surface of yarn

PILEOUS *adj* pilose

PILEUM *n* pl. -LEA the top of a bird's head

PILEUP *n* pl. -S a collision involving several motor vehicles

PILEUS *n* pl. -LEI the umbrella-shaped portion of a mushroom

PILEWORT *n* pl. -S a medicinal plant

PILFER *v* -ED, -ING, -S to steal

PILFERER *n* pl. -S one that pilfers

PILGRIM *n* pl. -S a traveler or wanderer

PILI *n* pl. -S a Philippine tree

PILIFORM *adj* resembling a hair

PILING *n* pl. -S a structure of building supports

PILL *v* -ED, -ING, -S to dose with pills (small, rounded masses of medicine)

PILLAGE *v* -LAGED, -LAGING, -LAGES to plunder

PILLAGER *n* pl. -S one that pillages

PILLAR *v* -ED, -ING, -S to provide with vertical building supports

PILLBOX *n* pl. -ES a small box for pills

PILLION *n* pl. -S a pad or cushion for an extra rider on a horse or motorcycle

PILLORY *v* -RIED, -RYING, -RIES to expose to public ridicule or abuse

PILLOW *v* -ED, -ING, -S to rest on a pillow (a cushion for the head)

PILLOWY *adj* resembling a pillow

PILOSE *adj* covered with hair

PILOSITY *n* pl. -TIES the state of being pilose

PILOT *v* -ED, -ING, -S to control the course of

PILOTAGE *n* pl. -S the act of piloting

PILOTING *n* pl. -S a branch of navigation

PILOUS *adj* pilose

PILSENER *n* pl. -S pilsner

PILSNER *n* pl. -S a light beer

PILULE *n* pl. -S a small pill **PILULAR** *adj*

PILUS *n* pl. -LI a hair or hairlike structure

PILY *adj* divided into a number of wedge-shaped heraldic designs

PIMA *n* pl. -S a strong, high-grade cotton

PIMENTO *n* pl. -TOS pimiento

PIMIENTO *n* pl. -TOS a sweet pepper

PIMP *v* -ED, -ING, -S to solicit clients for a prostitute

PIMPLE *n* pl. -S an inflamed swelling of the skin **PIMPLED** *adj*

PIMPLY *adj* -PLIER, -PLIEST covered with pimples

PIN *v* PINNED, PINNING, PINS to fasten with a pin (a slender, pointed piece of metal)

PINA *n* pl. -S a pineapple

PINAFORE *n* pl. -S a child's apron

PINANG *n* pl. -S a palm tree

PINASTER *n* pl. -S a pine tree

PINATA *n* pl. -S a pottery jar used in a Mexican game

PINBALL *n* pl. -S an electric game

PINBONE *n* pl. -S the hipbone

PINCER *n* pl. -S one of the two pivoted parts of a grasping tool

PINCH *v* -ED, -ING, -ES to squeeze between two edges or surfaces

PINCHBUG *n* pl. -S a large beetle

PINCHECK *n* pl. -S a fabric design

PINCHER *n* pl. -S one that pinches

PINDER *n* pl. -S an official who formerly impounded stray animals

PINDLING *adj* puny or sickly

PINE *v* PINED, PINING, PINES to yearn intensely

PINEAL *adj* shaped like a pinecone

PINECONE *n* pl. -S a cone-shaped fruit of a pine tree

PINED past tense of pine

PINELAND *n* pl. -S land forested with pine

PINELIKE *adj* resembling a pine (an evergreen tree)

PINENE   *n* pl. -S the main constituent of turpentine

PINERY   *n* pl. -ERIES an area where pineapples are grown

PINESAP   *n* pl. -S a fragrant herb

PINETUM   *n* pl. -TA a plantation of pine trees

PINEWOOD   *n* pl. -S the wood of a pine tree

PINEY   *adj* PINIER, PINIEST piny

PINFISH   *n* pl. -ES a small marine fish

PINFOLD   *v* -ED, -ING, -S to confine in an enclosure for stray animals

PING   *v* -ED, -ING, -S to produce a brief, high-pitched sound

PINGER   *n* pl. -S a device for producing pulses of sound

PINGO   *n* pl. -GOS a hill forced up by the effects of frost

PINGRASS   *n* pl. -ES a European weed

PINGUID   *adj* greasy

PINHEAD   *n* pl. -S the head of a pin

PINHOLE   *n* pl. -S a small hole made by a pin

PINIER   comparative of piney and piny

PINIEST   superlative of piney and piny

PINING   present participle of pine

PINION   *v* -ED, -ING, -S to remove or bind the wing feathers of to prevent flight

PINITE   *n* pl. -S a mineral

PINITOL   *n* pl. -S an alcohol

PINK   *adj* PINKER, PINKEST of a pale reddish hue

PINK   *v* -ED, -ING, -S to cut a saw-toothed edge on cloth

PINKEN   *v* -ED, -ING, -S to become pink

PINKER   *n* pl. -S one that pinks

PINKEY   *n* pl. -EYS a ship with a narrow overhanging stern

PINKEYE   *n* pl. -S an inflammation of the eye

PINKIE   *n* pl. -S the little finger

PINKIES   pl. of pinky

PINKING   *n* pl. -S a method of cutting or decorating

PINKISH   *adj* somewhat pink

PINKLY   *adv* with a pink hue

PINKNESS   *n* pl. -ES the state of being pink

PINKO   *n* pl. PINKOS or PINKOES a person who holds somewhat radical political views

PINKROOT   *n* pl. -S a medicinal plant root

PINKY   *n* pl. PINKIES pinkie

PINNA   *n* pl. -NAE or -NAS a feather, wing, or winglike part

PINNACE   *n* pl. -S a small sailing ship

PINNACLE   *v* -CLED, -CLING, -CLES to place on a summit

PINNAE   a pl. of pinna

PINNAL   *adj* pertaining to a pinna

PINNATE   *adj* resembling a feather

PINNATED   *adj* pinnate

PINNED   past tense of pin

PINNER   *n* pl. -S one that pins

PINNIES   pl. of pinny

PINNING   present participle of pin

PINNIPED   *n* pl. -S a mammal with limbs modified into flippers

PINNULA   *n* pl. -LAE pinnule PINNULAR *adj*

PINNULE   *n* pl. -S a pinnate part or organ

PINNY   *n* pl. -NIES a pinafore

PINOCHLE   *n* pl. -S a card game

PINOCLE   *n* pl. -S pinochle

PINOLE   *n* pl. -S a finely ground flour

PINON   *n* pl. -S or -ES a pine tree

PINOT   *n* pl. -S a red or white grape

PINPOINT   *v* -ED, -ING, -S to locate precisely

PINPRICK   *v* -ED, -ING, -S to puncture with a pin

PINSCHER   *n* pl. -S a large, short-haired dog

PINT   *n* pl. -S a liquid and dry measure of capacity

PINTA   *n* pl. -S a skin disease

PINTADA   *n* pl. -S pintado

PINTADO   *n* pl. -DOS or -DOES a large food fish

PINTAIL   *n* pl. -S a river duck

PINTANO   *n* pl. -NOS a tropical fish

PINTLE   *n* pl. -S a pin on which something turns

PINTO   *n* pl. -TOS or -TOES a spotted horse

PINTSIZE   *adj* small

PINUP   *n* pl. -S a picture that may be pinned up on a wall

PINWALE   *n* pl. -S a type of fabric

PINWEED   *n* pl. -S a perennial herb

PINWHEEL   *n* pl. -S a child's toy resembling a windmill

PINWORK   *n* pl. -S a type of embroidery

PINWORM   *n* pl. -S a parasitic worm

PINY   *adj* PINIER, PINIEST suggestive of or covered with pine trees

PINYIN   *n* a system for transliterating Chinese ideograms into the Latin alphabet

PINYON   *n* pl. -S pinon

PIOLET   *n* pl. -S an ice ax

PION   *n* pl. -S a subatomic particle PIONIC *adj*

PIONEER   *v* -ED, -ING, -S to take part in the beginnings of

PIOSITY   *n* pl. -TIES an excessive show of piety

PIOUS   *adj* marked by religious reverence PIOUSLY *adv*

PIP   *v* PIPPED, PIPPING, PIPS to break through the shell of an egg

PIPAGE   *n* pl. -S a system of pipes

PIPAL   *n* pl. -S a fig tree of India

PIPE   *v* PIPED, PIPING, PIPES to convey by means of a pipe (a hollow cylinder)

PIPEAGE   *n* pl. -S pipage

PIPEFISH   *n* pl. -ES a slender fish

PIPEFUL   *n* pl. -S a quantity sufficient to fill a tobacco pipe

PIPELESS   *adj* having no pipe

PIPELIKE   *adj* resembling a pipe

PIPELINE   *v* -LINED, -LINING, -LINES to convey by a line of pipe

PIPER   *n* pl. -S one that plays on a tubular musical instrument

PIPERINE   *n* pl. -S a chemical compound

PIPESTEM   *n* pl. -S the stem of a tobacco pipe

PIPET   *v* -PETTED, -PETTING, -PETS to pipette

PIPETTE   *v* -PETTED, -PETTING, -PETTES to measure liquid with a calibrated tube

PIPIER   comparative of pipy

PIPIEST   superlative of pipy

PIPINESS   *n* pl. -ES the quality of being pipy

PIPING   *n* pl. -S a system of pipes

PIPINGLY   *adv* shrilly

PIPIT   *n* pl. -S a songbird

PIPKIN   *n* pl. -S a small pot

PIPPED   past tense of pip

PIPPIN   *n* pl. -S any of several varieties of apple

PIPPING   present participle of pip

PIPY   *adj* PIPIER, PIPIEST shrill

PIQUANCY   *n* pl. -CIES the quality of being piquant

PIQUANT   *adj* having an agreeably sharp taste

PIQUE   *v* PIQUED, PIQUING, PIQUES to arouse anger or resentment in

PIQUET   *n* pl. -S a card game

PIRACY   *n* pl. -CIES robbery on the high seas

PIRAGUA   *n* pl. -S a dugout canoe

PIRANA   *n* pl. -S piranha

PIRANHA   *n* pl. -S a voracious fish

PIRARUCU   *n* pl. -S a large food fish

PIRATE   *v* -RATED, -RATING, -RATES to commit piracy

PIRATIC   *adj* pertaining to piracy

PIRAYA   *n* pl. -S piranha

PIRIFORM   *adj* pyriform

PIRN   *n* pl. -S a spinning-wheel bobbin

PIROG   *n* pl. -ROGEN, -ROGHI or -ROGI a large Russian pastry

PIROGI   *n* pl. -ES pierogi

PIROGUE   *n* pl. -S piragua

PIROQUE   *n* pl. -S piragua

PIROZHOK   *n* pl. -ROZHKI, -ROSHKI or -ROJKI a small Russian pastry

PISCARY   *n* pl. -RIES a place for fishing

PISCATOR   *n* pl. -S a fisherman

PISCINA   *n* pl. -NAE or -NAS a basin used in certain church ceremonies PISCINAL *adj*

PISCINE   *adj* pertaining to fish

PISCO   *n* pl. -COS a Peruvian brandy

PISH   *v* -ED, -ING, -ES to express contempt

PISHOGE   *n* pl. -S pishogue

PISHOGUE   *n* pl. -S an evil spell

PISIFORM   *n* pl. -S a small bone of the wrist

PISMIRE   *n* pl. -S an ant

PISO   *n* pl. -SOS the Philippine peso

PISOLITE   *n* pl. -S a limestone

PISSOIR   *n* pl. -S a public urinal

PISTACHE   *n* pl. -S a shade of green

PISTE   *n* pl. -S a downhill ski trail

PISTIL   *n* pl. -S the seed-bearing organ of flowering plants

PISTOL   *v* -TOLED, -TOLING, -TOLS or -TOLLED, -TOLLING, -TOLS to shoot with a small firearm

PISTOLE   *n* pl. -S a former European gold coin

PISTON   *n* pl. -S a part of an engine

PIT *v* PITTED, PITTING, PITS to mark with cavities or depressions

PITA *n* pl. -S a strong fiber

PITAPAT *v* -PATTED, -PATTING, -PATS to make a repeated tapping sound

PITCH *v* -ED, -ING, -ES to throw

PITCHER *n* pl. -S a container for holding and pouring liquids

PITCHIER comparative of pitchy

PITCHIEST superlative of pitchy

PITCHILY *adv* in a very dark manner

PITCHMAN *n* pl. -MEN a salesman of small wares

PITCHOUT *n* pl. -S a type of pitch in baseball

PITCHY *adj* PITCHIER, PITCHIEST tarry

PITEOUS *adj* pitiful

PITFALL *n* pl. -S a hidden danger or difficulty

PITH *v* -ED, -ING, -S to sever the spinal cord of

PITHEAD *n* pl. -S a mine entrance

PITHLESS *adj* lacking force

PITHY *adj* PITHIER, PITHIEST concise **PITHILY** *adv*

PITIABLE *adj* pitiful **PITIABLY** *adv*

PITIED past tense of pity

PITIER *n* pl. -S one that pities

PITIES present 3d person sing. of pity

PITIFUL *adj* -FULLER, -FULLEST arousing pity

PITILESS *adj* having no pity

PITMAN *n* pl. -MEN a mine worker

PITMAN *n* pl. -S a connecting rod

PITON *n* pl. -S a metal spike used in mountain climbing

PITSAW *n* pl. -S a large saw for cutting logs

PITTANCE *n* pl. -S a small allowance of money

PITTED past tense of pit

PITTING *n* pl. -S an arrangement of cavities or depressions

PITY *v* PITIED, PITYING, PITIES to feel pity (sorrow aroused by another's misfortune)

PIU *adv* more — used as a musical direction

PIVOT *v* -ED, -ING, -S to turn on a shaft or rod

PIVOTAL *adj* critically important

PIVOTMAN *n* pl. -MEN a center on a basketball team

PIX *n* pl. -ES pyx

PIXEL *n* pl. -S a basic unit of a video image

PIXIE *n* pl. -S pixy **PIXIEISH** *adj*

PIXINESS *n* pl. -ES the state of being playfully mischievous

PIXY *n* pl. PIXIES a playfully mischievous fairy or elf **PIXYISH** *adj*

PIZAZZ *n* pl. -ES the quality of being exciting or attractive

PIZAZZY *adj* having pizazz

PIZZA *n* pl. -S an Italian open pie

PIZZERIA *n* pl. -S a place where pizzas are made and sold

PIZZLE *n* pl. -S the penis of an animal

PLACABLE *adj* capable of being placated **PLACABLY** *adv*

PLACARD *v* -ED, -ING, -S to publicize by means of posters

PLACATE *v* -CATED, -CATING, -CATES to soothe or mollify

PLACATER *n* pl. -S one that placates

PLACE *v* PLACED, PLACING, PLACES to set in a particular position

PLACEBO *n* pl. -BOS or -BOES a substance containing no medication that is given for its psychological effect

PLACEMAN *n* pl. -MEN a political appointee to a public office

PLACENTA *n* pl. -TAS or -TAE a vascular organ in most mammals

PLACER *n* pl. -S one that places

PLACET *n* pl. -S a vote of assent

PLACID *adj* calm or peaceful **PLACIDLY** *adv*

PLACING present participle of place

PLACK *n* pl. -S a former coin of Scotland

PLACKET *n* pl. -S a slit in a garment

PLACOID *n* pl. -S a fish having platelike scales

PLAFOND *n* pl. -S an elaborately decorated ceiling

PLAGAL *adj* designating a medieval musical mode

PLAGE *n* pl. -S a bright region on the sun

PLAGIARY *n* pl. -RIES the act of passing off another's work as one's own

PLAGUE *v* PLAGUED, PLAGUING, PLAGUES to harass or torment

PLAGUER   *n* pl. -S one that plagues

PLAGUEY   *adj* plaguy

PLAGUING   present participle of plague

PLAGUY   *adj* troublesome **PLAGUILY** *adv*

PLAICE   *n* pl. -S a European flatfish

PLAID   *n* pl. -S a woolen scarf of a checkered pattern **PLAIDED** *adj*

PLAIN   *adj* PLAINER, PLAINEST evident **PLAINLY** *adv*

PLAIN   *v* -ED, -ING, -S to complain

PLAINT   *n* pl. -S a complaint

PLAISTER   *v* -ED, -ING, -S to plaster

PLAIT   *v* -ED, -ING, -S to braid

PLAITER   *n* pl. -S one that plaits

PLAITING   *n* pl. -S something that is plaited

PLAN   *v* PLANNED, PLANNING, PLANS to formulate a plan (a method for achieving an end)

PLANAR   *adj* flat

PLANARIA   *n* pl. -S an aquatic flatworm

PLANATE   *adj* having a flat surface

PLANCH   *n* pl. -ES a plank

PLANCHE   *n* pl. -S planch

PLANCHET   *n* pl. -S a flat piece of metal for stamping into a coin

PLANE   *v* PLANED, PLANING, PLANES to make smooth or even

PLANER   *n* pl. -S one that planes

PLANET   *n* pl. -S a celestial body

PLANFORM   *n* pl. -S the contour of an object as viewed from above

PLANGENT   *adj* resounding loudly

PLANING   present participle of plane

PLANISH   *v* -ED, -ING, -ES to toughen and smooth by hammering lightly

PLANK   *v* -ED, -ING, -S to cover with planks (long, flat pieces of lumber)

PLANKING   *n* pl. -S covering made of planks

PLANKTER   *n* pl. -S any organism that is an element of plankton

PLANKTON   *n* pl. -S the minute animal and plant life of a body of water

PLANLESS   *adj* having no plan

PLANNED   past tense of plan

PLANNER   *n* pl. -S one that plans

PLANNING   *n* pl. -S the establishment of goals or policies

PLANOSOL   *n* pl. -S a type of soil

PLANT   *v* -ED, -ING, -S to place in the ground for growing

PLANTAIN   *n* pl. -S a short-stemmed herb

PLANTAR   *adj* pertaining to the sole of the foot

PLANTER   *n* pl. -S one that plants

PLANTING   *n* pl. -S an area where plants are grown

PLANTLET   *n* pl. -S a small plant

PLANULA   *n* pl. -LAE the free-swimming larva of certain organisms **PLANULAR** *adj*

PLAQUE   *n* pl. -S an ornamental plate or disk

PLASH   *v* -ED, -ING, -ES to weave together

PLASHER   *n* pl. -S one that plashes

PLASHY   *adj* PLASHIER, PLASHIEST marshy

PLASM   *n* pl. -S plasma

PLASMA   *n* pl. -S the liquid part of blood **PLASMIC** *adj*

PLASMID   *n* pl. -S a hereditary structure of a cell

PLASMIN   *n* pl. -S an enzyme

PLASMOID   *n* pl. -S a type of high energy particle

PLASMON   *n* pl. -S a determinant of inheritance believed to exist in cells

PLASTER   *v* -ED, -ING, -S to cover with plaster (a mixture of lime, sand, and water)

PLASTERY   *adj* resembling plaster

PLASTIC   *n* pl. -S any of a group of synthetic or natural moldable materials

PLASTID   *n* pl. -S a structure in plant cells

PLASTRON   *n* pl. -S a part of the shell of a turtle **PLASTRAL** *adj*

PLASTRUM   *n* pl. -S plastron

PLAT   *v* PLATTED, PLATTING, PLATS to plait

PLATAN   *n* pl. -S a large tree

PLATANE   *n* pl. -S platan

PLATE   *v* PLATED, PLATING, PLATES to coat with a thin layer of metal

PLATEAU   *n* pl. -TEAUS or -TEAUX a level stretch of elevated land

PLATEAU   *v* -ED, -ING, -S to reach a period or condition of stability

PLATED   past tense of plate

PLATEFUL *n pl.* PLATEFULS or PLATESFUL the quantity that fills a plate (a shallow dish)

PLATELET *n pl.* -S a small, flattened body

PLATEN *n pl.* -S the roller of a typewriter

PLATER *n pl.* -S one that plates

PLATESFUL a *pl.* of plateful

PLATFORM *n pl.* -S a raised floor or flat surface

PLATIER comparative of platy

PLATIES a *pl.* of platy

PLATIEST superlative of platy

PLATINA *n pl.* -S platinum

PLATING *n pl.* -S a thin layer of metal

PLATINIC *adj* pertaining to platinum

PLATINUM *n pl.* -S a metallic element

PLATONIC *adj* purely spiritual and free from sensual desire

PLATOON *v* -ED, -ING, -S to alternate with another player at the same position

PLATTED past tense of plat

PLATTER *n pl.* -S a large, shallow dish

PLATTING present participle of plat

PLATY *adj* PLATIER, PLATIEST split into thin, flat pieces

PLATY *n pl.* PLATYS or PLATIES a small tropical fish

PLATYPUS *n pl.* -PUSES or -PI an aquatic mammal

PLAUDIT *n pl.* -S an expression of praise

PLAUSIVE *adj* expressing praise

PLAY *v* -ED, -ING, -S to engage in amusement or sport PLAYABLE *adj*

PLAYA *n pl.* -S the bottom of a desert basin

PLAYACT *v* -ED, -ING, -S to take part in a theatrical performance

PLAYBACK *n pl.* -S the act of replaying a newly made recording

PLAYBILL *n pl.* -S a program for a theatrical performance

PLAYBOOK *n pl.* -S a book containing one or more literary works for the stage

PLAYBOY *n pl.* -BOYS a man devoted to pleasurable activities

PLAYDATE *n pl.* -S the scheduled date for showing a theatrical production

PLAYDAY *n pl.* -DAYS a holiday

PLAYDOWN *n pl.* -S a playoff

PLAYER *n pl.* -S one who plays

PLAYFUL *adj* frolicsome

PLAYGIRL *n pl.* -S a women devoted to pleasurable activities

PLAYGOER *n pl.* -S one who attends the theater

PLAYLAND *n pl.* -S a recreational area

PLAYLESS *adj* lacking playfulness

PLAYLET *n pl.* -S a short theatrical performance

PLAYLIKE *adj* resembling a theatrical performance

PLAYLIST *n pl.* -S a list of recordings to be played on the air

PLAYMATE *n pl.* -S a companion in play

PLAYOFF *n pl.* -S a series of games played to determine a championship

PLAYPEN *n pl.* -S an enclosure in which a young child may play

PLAYROOM *n pl.* -S a recreation room

PLAYSUIT *n pl.* -S a sports outfit for women and children

PLAYTIME *n pl.* -S a time for play or amusement

PLAYWEAR *n pl.* -S clothing worn for leisure activities

PLAZA *n pl.* -S a public square

PLEA *n pl.* -S an entreaty

PLEACH *v* -ED, -ING, -ES to weave together

PLEAD *v* PLEADED or PLED, PLEADING, PLEADS to ask for earnestly

PLEADER *n pl.* -S one that pleads

PLEADING *n pl.* -S an allegation in a legal action

PLEASANT *adj* -ANTER, -ANTEST pleasing

PLEASE *v* PLEASED, PLEASING, PLEASES to give enjoyment or satisfaction to

PLEASER *n pl.* -S one that pleases

PLEASURE *v* -SURED, -SURING, -SURES to please

PLEAT *v* -ED, -ING, -S to fold in an even manner

PLEATER *n pl.* -S one that pleats

PLEB *n pl.* -S a commoner

PLEBE *n pl.* -S a freshman at a military or naval academy

PLEBEIAN *n pl.* -S a commoner

PLECTRON *n pl.* -TRONS or -TRA plectrum

PLECTRUM *n pl.* -TRUMS or -TRA an implement used to pluck the strings of a stringed instrument

PLED a past tense of plead

PLEDGE   *v* PLEDGED, PLEDGING, PLEDGES to give as security for something borrowed

PLEDGEE   *n* pl. -S one to whom something is pledged

PLEDGEOR   *n* pl. -S pledger

PLEDGER   *n* pl. -S one that pledges something

PLEDGET   *n* pl. -S a pad of absorbent cotton

PLEDGING   present participle of pledge

PLEDGOR   *n* pl. -S pledger

PLEIAD   *n* pl. -S or -ES a group of seven illustrious persons

PLENA   a pl. of plenum

PLENARY   *adj* complete in every respect

PLENCH   *n* pl. -ES a tool serving as pliers and a wrench

PLENISH   *v* -ED, -ING, -ES to fill up

PLENISM   *n* pl. -S the doctrine that space is fully occupied by matter

PLENIST   *n* pl. -S an advocate of plenism

PLENTY   *n* pl. -TIES a sufficient or abundant amount

PLENUM   *n* pl. -NUMS or -NA space considered as fully occupied by matter

PLEONASM   *n* pl. -S the use of needless words

PLEOPOD   *n* pl. -S an appendage of crustaceans

PLESSOR   *n* pl. -S plexor

PLETHORA   *n* pl. -S an excess

PLEURA   *n* pl. -RAE or -RAS a membrane that envelops the lungs PLEURAL *adj*

PLEURISY   *n* pl. -SIES inflammation of the pleura

PLEURON   *n* pl. -RA a part of a thoracic segment of an insect

PLEUSTON   *n* pl. -S aquatic vegetation

PLEW   *n* pl. -S a beaver skin

PLEXAL   *adj* pertaining to a plexus

PLEXOR   *n* pl. -S a small, hammer-like medical instrument

PLEXUS   *n* pl. -ES an interlacing of parts

PLIABLE   *adj* easily bent PLIABLY *adv*

PLIANCY   *n* pl. -CIES the quality of being pliant

PLIANT   *adj* easily bent PLIANTLY *adv*

PLICA   *n* pl. -CAE a fold of skin PLICAL *adj*

PLICATE   *adj* pleated

PLICATED   *adj* plicate

PLIE   *n* pl. -S a movement in ballet

PLIED   past tense of ply

PLIER   *n* pl. -S one that plies

PLIES   present 3d person sing. of ply

PLIGHT   *v* -ED, -ING, -S to promise or bind by a solemn pledge

PLIGHTER   *n* pl. -S one that plights

PLIMSOL   *n* pl. -S plimsoll

PLIMSOLE   *n* pl. -S plimsoll

PLIMSOLL   *n* pl. -S a rubber-soled cloth shoe

PLINK   *v* -ED, -ING, -S to shoot at random targets

PLINKER   *n* pl. -S one that plinks

PLINTH   *n* pl. -S a stone or slab upon which a column or pedestal rests

PLIOTRON   *n* pl. -S a type of vacuum tube

PLISKIE   *n* pl. -S a practical joke

PLISKY   *n* pl. -KIES pliskie

PLISSE   *n* pl. -S a puckered texture of cloth

PLOD   *v* PLODDED, PLODDING, PLODS to walk heavily

PLODDER   *n* pl. -S one that plods

PLOIDY   *n* pl. -DIES the extent of repetition of the basic number of chromosomes

PLONK   *v* -ED, -ING, -S to plunk

PLOP   *v* PLOPPED, PLOPPING, PLOPS to drop or fall heavily

PLOSION   *n* pl. -S a release of breath after the articulation of certain consonants

PLOSIVE   *n* pl. -S a sound produced by plosion

PLOT   *v* PLOTTED, PLOTTING, PLOTS to plan secretly

PLOTLESS   *adj* planless

PLOTLINE   *n* pl. -S the main story of a book

PLOTTAGE   *n* pl. -S an area of land

PLOTTED   past tense of plot

PLOTTER   *n* pl. -S one that plots

PLOTTIER   comparative of plotty

PLOTTIES   pl. of plotty

PLOTTING   present participle of plot

PLOTTY   *adj* -TIER, -TIEST full of intrigue, as a novel

PLOTTY   *n* pl. -TIES a hot, spiced beverage

PLOTZ   *v* -ED, -ING, -ES to be overwhelmed by an emotion

PLOUGH   *v* -ED, -ING, -S to plow

PLOUGHER   *n* pl. -S one that ploughs

PLOVER	n pl. -S a shore bird
PLOW	v -ED, -ING, -S to turn up land with a plow (a farm implement) **PLOWABLE** adj
PLOWBACK	n pl. -S a reinvestment of profits in a business
PLOWBOY	n pl. -BOYS a boy who leads a plow team
PLOWER	n pl. -S one that plows
PLOWHEAD	n pl. -S the clevis of a plow
PLOWLAND	n pl. -S land suitable for cultivation
PLOWMAN	n pl. -MEN a man who plows
PLOY	v -ED, -ING, -S to move from a line into column
PLUCK	v -ED, -ING, -S to pull out or off
PLUCKER	n pl. -S one that plucks
PLUCKY	adj PLUCKIER, PLUCKIEST brave and spirited **PLUCKILY** adv
PLUG	v PLUGGED, PLUGGING, PLUGS to seal or close with a plug (a piece of material used to fill a hole)
PLUGGER	n pl. -S one that plugs
PLUGLESS	adj having no plug
PLUGOLA	n pl. -S free incidental advertising on radio or television
PLUGUGLY	n pl. -LIES a hoodlum
PLUM	n pl. -S a fleshy fruit
PLUMAGE	n pl. -S the feathers of a bird **PLUMAGED** adj
PLUMATE	adj resembling a feather
PLUMB	v -ED, -ING, -S to determine the depth of
PLUMBAGO	n pl. -GOS graphite
PLUMBER	n pl. -S one who installs and repairs plumbing
PLUMBERY	n pl. -ERIES the work of a plumber
PLUMBIC	adj containing lead
PLUMBING	n pl. -S the pipe system of a building
PLUMBISM	n pl. -S lead poisoning
PLUMBOUS	adj containing lead
PLUMBUM	n pl. -S lead
PLUME	v PLUMED, PLUMING, PLUMES to cover with feathers
PLUMELET	n pl. -S a small feather
PLUMERIA	n pl. -S a flowering shrub
PLUMIER	comparative of plumy
PLUMIEST	superlative of plumy
PLUMING	present participle of plume

PLUMIPED	n pl. -S a bird having feathered feet
PLUMLIKE	adj resembling a plum
PLUMMET	v -ED, -ING, -S to drop straight down
PLUMMY	adj -MIER, -MIEST full of plums
PLUMOSE	adj having feathers
PLUMP	adj PLUMPER, PLUMPEST well-rounded and full in form
PLUMP	v -ED, -ING, -S to make plump
PLUMPEN	v -ED, -ING, -S to plump
PLUMPER	n pl. -S a heavy fall
PLUMPISH	adj somewhat plump
PLUMPLY	adv in a plump way
PLUMULE	n pl. -S the primary bud of a plant embryo **PLUMULAR** adj
PLUMY	adj PLUMIER, PLUMIEST covered with feathers
PLUNDER	v -ED, -ING, -S to rob of goods by force
PLUNGE	v PLUNGED, PLUNGING, PLUNGES to throw or thrust suddenly or forcibly into something
PLUNGER	n pl. -S one that plunges
PLUNK	v -ED, -ING, -S to fall or drop heavily
PLUNKER	n pl. -S one that plunks
PLURAL	n pl. -S a word that expresses more than one
PLURALLY	adv in a manner or form that expresses more than one
PLUS	n pl. PLUSES or PLUSSES an additional quantity
PLUSH	adj PLUSHER, PLUSHEST luxurious **PLUSHLY** adv
PLUSH	n pl. -ES a fabric with a long pile
PLUSHY	adj PLUSHIER, PLUSHIEST luxurious **PLUSHILY** adv
PLUSSAGE	n pl. -S an amount over and above another
PLUSSES	a pl. of plus
PLUTEUS	n pl. -TEI the larva of a sea urchin
PLUTON	n pl. -S a formation of igneous rock **PLUTONIC** adj
PLUVIAL	n pl. -S a prolonged period of wet climate
PLUVIAN	adj characterized by much rain
PLUVIOSE	adj pluvious
PLUVIOUS	adj pertaining to rain

PLY	*v* PLIED, PLYING, PLIES to supply with or offer repeatedly **PLYINGLY** *adv*	**POET**	*n* pl. -S one who writes poems
PLYER	*n* pl. -S plier	**POETESS**	*n* pl. -ES a female poet
PLYWOOD	*n* pl. -S a building material	**POETIC**	*adj* pertaining to poetry
PNEUMA	*n* pl. -S the soul or spirit	**POETICAL**	*adj* poetic
POACEOUS	*adj* pertaining to plants of the grass family	**POETICS**	*n/pl* poetic theory or practice
		POETISE	*v* -ISED, -ISING, -ISES to poetize
POACH	*v* -ED, -ING, -ES to trespass for the purpose of taking game or fish	**POETISER**	*n* pl. -S poetizer
		POETIZE	*v* -IZED, -IZING, -IZES to write poetry
POACHER	*n* pl. -S one that poaches	**POETIZER**	*n* pl. -S one that poetizes
POACHY	*adj* POACHIER, POACHIEST swampy	**POETLESS**	*adj* lacking a poet
		POETLIKE	*adj* resembling a poet
POCHARD	*n* pl. -S a sea duck	**POETRY**	*n* pl. -RIES literary work in metrical form
POCK	*v* -ED, -ING, -S to mark with pocks (pustules caused by an eruptive disease)	**POGEY**	*n* pl. -GEYS any form of government relief
		POGIES	pl. of pogy
POCKET	*v* -ED, -ING, -S to place in a pouch sewed into a garment	**POGONIA**	*n* pl. -S a small orchid
		POGONIP	*n* pl. -S a dense fog of suspended ice particles
POCKETER	*n* pl. -S one that pockets		
POCKMARK	*v* -ED, -ING, -S to mark with scars caused by an eruptive disease	**POGROM**	*v* -ED, -ING, -S to massacre systematically
		POGY	*n* pl. -GIES a marine fish
POCKY	*adj* POCKIER, POCKIEST covered with pocks **POCKILY** *adv*	**POH**	*interj* — used to express disgust
		POI	*n* pl. -S a Hawaiian food
POCO	*adv* a little — used as a musical direction	**POIGNANT**	*adj* emotionally distressing
		POILU	*n* pl. -S a French soldier
POCOSIN	*n* pl. -S an upland swamp	**POIND**	*v* -ED, -ING, -S to seize and sell the property of to satisfy a debt
POD	*v* PODDED, PODDING, PODS to produce seed vessels		
		POINT	*v* -ED, -ING, -S to indicate direction with the finger
PODAGRA	*n* pl. -S gout in the foot **PODAGRAL, PODAGRIC** *adj*	**POINTE**	*n* pl. -S a ballet position
PODESTA	*n* pl. -S an Italian magistrate	**POINTER**	*n* pl. -S one that points
PODGY	*adj* PODGIER, PODGIEST pudgy **PODGILY** *adv*	**POINTMAN**	*n* pl. -MEN a certain player in hockey
PODIA	*a* pl. of podium	**POINTY**	*adj* POINTIER, POINTIEST coming to a sharp, tapering end
PODIATRY	*n* pl. -TRIES the study and treatment of the human foot		
PODITE	*n* pl. -S a limb segment of an arthropod **PODITIC** *adj*	**POISE**	*v* POISED, POISING, POISES to hold in a state of equilibrium
PODIUM	*n* pl. -DIUMS or -DIA a small platform	**POISER**	*n* pl. -S one that poises
		POISHA	*n* pl. POISHA the paisa of Bangladesh
PODLIKE	*adj* resembling a pod (a seed vessel)		
PODOCARP	*adj* designating a family of evergreen trees	**POISON**	*v* -ED, -ING, -S to administer a harmful substance to
PODOMERE	*n* pl. -S a podite	**POISONER**	*n* pl. -S one that poisons
PODSOL	*n* pl. -S podzol **PODSOLIC** *adj*	**POITREL**	*n* pl. -S peytral
PODZOL	*n* pl. -S an infertile soil **PODZOLIC** *adj*	**POKE**	*v* POKED, POKING, POKES to push or prod
POECHORE	*n* pl. -S a semiarid region	**POKER**	*n* pl. -S one that pokes
POEM	*n* pl. -S a composition in verse	**POKEROOT**	*n* pl. -S pokeweed
POESY	*n* pl. -ESIES poetry	**POKEWEED**	*n* pl. -S a perennial herb

POKEY   n pl. -KEYS poky
POKIER   comparative of poky
POKIES   pl. of poky
POKIEST   superlative of poky
POKILY   adv in a poky manner
POKINESS   n pl. -ES the state of being
            poky
POKING   present participle of poke
POKY   n pl. POKIES a jail
POKY   adj POKIER, POKIEST slow
POL   n pl. -S a politician
POLAR   n pl. -S a straight line related
            to a point
POLARISE   v -ISED, -ISING, -ISES to
            polarize
POLARITY   n pl. -TIES the possession of
            two opposite qualities
POLARIZE   v -IZED, -IZING, -IZES to give
            polarity to
POLARON   n pl. -S a type of electron
POLDER   n pl. -S a tract of low land
            reclaimed from a body of water
POLE   v POLED, POLING, POLES to
            propel with a pole (a long, thin
            piece of wood or metal)
POLEAX   v -ED, -ING, -ES to strike with
            an axlike weapon
POLEAXE   v -AXED, -AXING, -AXES to
            poleax
POLECAT   n pl. -S a carnivorous mammal
POLED   past tense of pole
POLEIS   pl. of polis
POLELESS   adj having no pole
POLEMIC   n pl. -S a controversial
            argument
POLEMIST   n pl. -S one who engages in
            polemics
POLEMIZE   v -MIZED, -MIZING, -MIZES
            to engage in polemics
POLENTA   n pl. -S a thick mush of
            cornmeal
POLER   n pl. -S one that poles
POLESTAR   n pl. -S a guiding principle
POLEWARD   adv in the direction of either
            extremity of the earth's axis
POLEYN   n pl. -S a protective piece of
            leather for the knee
POLICE   v -LICED, -LICING, -LICES to
            make clean or orderly
POLICY   n pl. -CIES an action or a
            procedure considered with
            reference to prudence or
            expediency
POLING   present participle of pole
POLIO   n pl. -LIOS an infectious virus
            disease

POLIS   n pl. -LEIS an ancient Greek
            city-state
POLISH   v -ED, -ING, -ES to make
            smooth and lustrous by
            rubbing
POLISHER   n pl. -S one that polishes
POLITE   adj -LITER, -LITEST showing
            consideration for others
            POLITELY adv
POLITIC   adj shrewd
POLITICK   v -ED, -ING, -S to engage in
            politics
POLITICO   n pl. -COS or -COES one who
            politicks
POLITICS   n/pl the art or science of
            government
POLITY   n pl. -TIES a form or system
            of government
POLKA   v -ED, -ING, -S to perform a
            lively dance
POLL   v -ED, -ING, -S to question for
            the purpose of surveying public
            opinion
POLLACK   n pl. -S a marine food fish
POLLARD   v -ED, -ING, -S to cut the top
            branches of a tree back to the
            trunk
POLLEE   n pl. -S one who is polled
POLLEN   v -ED, -ING, -S to convey
            pollen (the fertilizing element in
            a seed plant) to
POLLER   n pl. -S one that polls
POLLEX   n pl. -LICES the innermost
            digit of the forelimb POLLICAL
            adj
POLLINIA   n/pl masses of pollen grains
POLLINIC   adj pertaining to pollen
POLLIST   n pl. -S a poller
POLLIWOG   n pl. -S a tadpole
POLLOCK   n pl. -S pollack
POLLSTER   n pl. -S a poller
POLLUTE   v -LUTED, -LUTING, -LUTES
            to make unclean or impure
POLLUTER   n pl. -S one that pollutes
POLLYWOG   n pl. -S polliwog
POLO   n pl. -LOS a game played on
            horseback
POLOIST   n pl. -S a polo player
POLONIUM   n pl. -S a radioactive element
POLTROON   n pl. -S a base coward
POLY   n pl. POLYS a type of white
            blood cell
POLYBRID   n pl. -S a type of hybrid plant
POLYCOT   n pl. -S a type of plant
POLYENE   n pl. -S a chemical compound
            POLYENIC adj

POLYGALA *n* pl. -S a flowering plant

POLYGAMY *n* pl. -MIES the condition of having more than one spouse at the same time

POLYGENE *n* pl. -S a type of gene

POLYGLOT *n* pl. -S one that speaks or writes several languages

POLYGON *n* pl. -S a closed plane figure bounded by straight lines

POLYGONY *n* pl. -NIES an herb

POLYGYNY *n* pl. -NIES the condition of having more than one wife at the same time

POLYMATH *n* pl. -S a person of great and varied learning

POLYMER *n* pl. -S a complex chemical compound

POLYNYA *n* pl. -YAS or -YI an area of open water surrounded by sea ice

POLYOMA *n* pl. -S a type of virus

POLYP *n* pl. -S an invertebrate

POLYPARY *n* pl. -ARIES the common supporting structure of a polyp colony

POLYPI a pl. of polypus

POLYPIDE *n* pl. -S a polyp

POLYPNEA *n* pl. -S rapid breathing

POLYPOD *n* pl. -S a many-footed organism

POLYPODY *n* pl. -DIES a fern

POLYPOID *adj* resembling a polyp

POLYPORE *n* pl. -S a type of fungus

POLYPOUS *adj* pertaining to a polyp

POLYPUS *n* pl. -PI or -PUSES a growth protruding from the mucous lining of an organ

POLYSEMY *n* pl. -MIES diversity of meanings

POLYSOME *n* pl. -S a cluster of protein particles

POLYTENE *adj* having chromosomes of a certain type

POLYTENY *n* pl. -NIES the state of being polytene

POLYTYPE *n* pl. -S a crystal structure

POLYURIA *n* pl. -S excessive urination **POLYURIC** *adj*

POLYZOAN *n* pl. -S a bryozoan

POLYZOIC *adj* composed of many zooids

POMACE *n* pl. -S the pulpy residue of crushed fruits

POMADE *v* -MADED, -MADING, -MADES to apply a perfumed hair dressing to

POMANDER *n* pl. -S a mixture of aromatic substances

POMATUM *n* pl. -S a perfumed hair dressing

POME *n* pl. -S a fleshy fruit with a core

POMELO *n* pl. -LOS a grapefruit

POMFRET *n* pl. -S a marine fish

POMMEE *adj* having arms with knoblike ends — used of a heraldic cross

POMMEL *v* -MELED, -MELING, -MELS or -MELLED, -MELLING, -MELS to strike with the fists

POMOLOGY *n* pl. -GIES the study of fruits

POMP *n* pl. -S stately or splendid display

POMPANO *n* pl. -NOS a marine food fish

POMPOM *n* pl. -S an antiaircraft cannon

POMPON *n* pl. -S an ornamental tuft or ball

POMPOUS *adj* marked by exaggerated self-importance

PONCE *v* PONCED, PONCING, PONCES to pimp

PONCHO *n* pl. -CHOS a type of cloak

POND *v* -ED, -ING, -S to collect into a pond (a small body of water)

PONDER *v* -ED, -ING, -S to consider something deeply and thoroughly

PONDERER *n* pl. -S one that ponders

PONDWEED *n* pl. -S an aquatic plant

PONE *n* pl. -S a corn bread

PONENT *adj* affirmative

PONG *v* -ED, -ING, -S to stink

PONGEE *n* pl. -S a type of silk

PONGID *n* pl. -S an anthropoid ape

PONIARD *v* -ED, -ING, -S to stab with a dagger

PONIED past tense of pony

PONIES present 3d person sing. of pony

PONS *n* pl. PONTES a band of nerve fibers in the brain

PONTIFEX *n* pl. -FICES an ancient Roman priest

PONTIFF *n* pl. -S a pope or bishop

PONTIFIC *adj* pertaining to a pope or bishop

PONTIFICES pl. of pontifex

PONTIL *n* pl. -S a punty

PONTINE *adj* pertaining to bridges

PONTON *n* pl. -S pontoon

PONTOON *n* pl. -S a flat-bottomed boat

PONY	*v* -NIED, -NYING, -NIES to prepare lessons with the aid of a literal translation
PONYTAIL	*n* pl. -S a hairstyle
POOCH	*v* -ED, -ING, -ES to bulge
POOD	*n* pl. -S a Russian unit of weight
POODLE	*n* pl. -S a heavy-coated dog
POOF	*interj* — used to indicate an instantaneous occurrence
POOH	*v* -ED, -ING, -S to express contempt for
POOL	*v* -ED, -ING, -S to combine in a common fund
POOLHALL	*n* pl. -S a poolroom
POOLROOM	*n* pl. -S an establishment for the playing of billiards
POOLSIDE	*n* pl. -S the area surrounding a swimming pool
POON	*n* pl. -S an East Indian tree
POOP	*v* -ED, -ING, -S to tire out
POOR	*adj* POORER, POOREST lacking the means of support
POORI	*n* pl. -S a light, flat wheat cake
POORISH	*adj* somewhat poor
POORLY	*adv* in a poor manner
POORNESS	*n* pl. -ES the state of being poor
POORTITH	*n* pl. -S poverty
POP	*v* POPPED, POPPING, POPS to make a sharp, explosive sound
POPCORN	*n* pl. -S a variety of corn
POPE	*n* pl. -S the head of the Roman Catholic Church POPELESS, POPELIKE *adj*
POPEDOM	*n* pl. -S the office of a pope
POPEYED	*adj* having bulging eyes
POPGUN	*n* pl. -S a toy gun
POPINJAY	*n* pl. -JAYS a vain person
POPLAR	*n* pl. -S a fast-growing tree
POPLIN	*n* pl. -S a durable fabric
POPLITIC	*adj* pertaining to the part of the leg behind the knee
POPOVER	*n* pl. -S a very light egg muffin
POPPA	*n* pl. -S papa
POPPED	past tense of pop
POPPER	*n* pl. -S one that pops
POPPET	*n* pl. -S a mechanical valve
POPPIED	*adj* covered with poppies
POPPIES	pl. of poppy
POPPING	present participle of pop
POPPLE	*v* -PLED, -PLING, -PLES to move in a bubbling or rippling manner
POPPY	*n* pl. -PIES a flowering plant
POPSIE	*n* pl. -S popsy
POPSY	*n* pl. -SIES a girlfriend
POPULACE	*n* pl. -S the common people
POPULAR	*adj* liked by many people
POPULATE	*v* -LATED, -LATING, -LATES to inhabit
POPULISM	*n* pl. -S populists' doctrines
POPULIST	*n* pl. -S a member of a party which represents the common people
POPULOUS	*adj* containing many inhabitants
PORCH	*n* pl. -ES a covered structure at the entrance to a building
PORCINE	*adj* pertaining to swine
PORCINO	*n* pl. -NI an edible mushroom
PORE	*v* PORED, PORING, PORES to gaze intently
PORGY	*n* pl. -GIES a marine food fish
PORISM	*n* pl. -S a type of mathematical proposition
PORK	*n* pl. -S the flesh of swine used as food
PORKER	*n* pl. -S a pig
PORKIER	comparative of porky
PORKIES	pl. of porky
PORKIEST	superlative of porky
PORKPIE	*n* pl. -S a man's hat
PORKWOOD	*n* pl. -S a tropical tree
PORKY	*adj* PORKIER, PORKIEST resembling pork
PORKY	*n* pl. -KIES a porcupine
PORN	*n* pl. -S pornography
PORNO	*n* pl. -NOS pornography
PORNY	*adj* PORNIER, PORNIEST pornographic
POROSE	*adj* porous
POROSITY	*n* pl. -TIES the state of being porous
POROUS	*adj* having minute openings POROUSLY *adv*
PORPHYRY	*n* pl. -RIES an igneous rock
PORPOISE	*n* pl. -S an aquatic mammal
PORRECT	*adj* extended forward
PORRIDGE	*n* pl. -S a soft food PORRIDGY *adj*
PORT	*v* -ED, -ING, -S to shift to the left side
PORTABLE	*n* pl. -S something that can be carried
PORTABLY	*adv* so as to be capable of being carried
PORTAGE	*v* -TAGED, -TAGING, -TAGES to transport from one navigable waterway to another

PORTAL *n* pl. -S a door, gate, or entrance **PORTALED** *adj*

PORTANCE *n* pl. -S demeanor

PORTAPAK *n* pl. -S a portable combined video recorder and camera

PORTEND *v* -ED, -ING, -S to serve as an omen of

PORTENT *n* pl. -S an omen

PORTER *n* pl. -S a person employed to carry luggage

PORTHOLE *n* pl. -S a small window in a ship's side

PORTICO *n* pl. -COS or -COES a type of porch

PORTIERE *n* pl. -S a curtain for a doorway

PORTION *v* -ED, -ING, -S to divide into shares for distribution

PORTLESS *adj* having no place for ships to load or unload

PORTLY *adj* -LIER, -LIEST rather heavy or fat

PORTRAIT *n* pl. -S a likeness of a person

PORTRAY *v* -ED, -ING, -S to represent pictorially

PORTRESS *n* pl. -ES a female doorkeeper

POSADA *n* pl. -S an inn

POSE *v* POSED, POSING, POSES to assume a fixed position

POSER *n* pl. -S one that poses

POSEUR *n* pl. -S an affected or insincere person

POSH *adj* POSHER, POSHEST stylish or elegant **POSHLY** *adv*

POSHNESS *n* pl. -ES the quality of being posh

POSIES pl. of posy

POSING present participle of pose

POSINGLY *adv* in a posing manner

POSIT *v* -ED, -ING, -S to place

POSITION *v* -ED, -ING, -S to put in a particular location

POSITIVE *adj* -TIVER, -TIVEST certain

POSITIVE *n* pl. -S a quantity greater than zero

POSITRON *n* pl. -S a subatomic particle

POSOLOGY *n* pl. -GIES a branch of medicine that deals with drug dosages

POSSE *n* pl. -S a body of men summoned to aid a peace officer

POSSESS *v* -ED, -ING, -ES to have as property

POSSET *n* pl. -S a hot, spiced drink

POSSIBLE *adj* -BLER, -BLEST capable of happening or proving true **POSSIBLY** *adv*

POSSUM *n* pl. -S opossum

POST *v* -ED, -ING, -S to affix in a public place

POSTAGE *n* pl. -S the charge for mailing an item

POSTAL *n* pl. -S a postcard

POSTALLY *adv* in a manner pertaining to the mails

POSTANAL *adj* situated behind the anus

POSTBAG *n* pl. -S a mailbag

POSTBASE *adj* following a base word

POSTBOX *n* pl. -ES a mailbox

POSTBOY *n* pl. -BOYS a boy who carries mail

POSTBURN *adj* following a burn

POSTCARD *n* pl. -S a card for use in the mail

POSTCAVA *n* pl. -VAE a vein in higher vertebrates

POSTCODE *n* pl. -S a code of numbers and letters used in a mailing address

POSTCOUP *adj* following a coup

POSTDATE *v* -DATED, -DATING, -DATES to give a date later than the actual date to

POSTDIVE *adj* following a dive

POSTDOC *n* pl. -S one engaged in postdoctoral study

POSTDRUG *adj* following the taking of a drug

POSTEEN *n* pl. -S an Afghan outer garment

POSTER *n* pl. -S a printed or written notice for posting

POSTERN *n* pl. -S a rear door or gate

POSTFACE *n* pl. -S a brief note placed at the end of a publication

POSTFIX *v* -ED, -ING, -ES to affix at the end of something

POSTFORM *v* -ED, -ING, -S to shape subsequently

POSTGAME *adj* following a game

POSTHEAT *n* pl. -S heat applied to a metal after welding

POSTHOLE *n* pl. -S a hole dug to secure a fence post

POSTICHE *n* pl. -S an imitation

POSTIN *n* pl. -S posteen

POSTING *n* pl. -S the act of transferring to a ledger

POSTIQUE *n* pl. -S postiche

POSTLUDE *n* pl. -S a closing musical piece

POSTMAN *n* pl. -MEN a mailman

POSTMARK *v* -ED, -ING, -S to stamp mail with an official mark

POSTORAL *adj* situated behind the mouth

POSTPAID *adv* with the postage prepaid

POSTPONE *v* -PONED, -PONING, -PONES to put off to a future time

POSTRACE *adj* following a race

POSTRIOT *adj* following a riot

POSTSYNC *v* -ED, -ING, -S to add sound to a film after a scene has been photographed

POSTTEEN *adj* occurring after one's teenage years

POSTTEST *n* pl. -S a test given after the completion of an instructional program

POSTURAL *adj* pertaining to the position of the body

POSTURE *v* -TURED, -TURING, -TURES to assume a particular position

POSTURER *n* pl. -S one that postures

POSTWAR *adj* occurring or existing after a war

POSY *n* pl. -SIES a flower or bouquet

POT *v* POTTED, POTTING, POTS to put in a pot (a round, fairly deep container)

POTABLE *n* pl. -S a liquid suitable for drinking

POTAGE *n* pl. -S a thick soup

POTAMIC *adj* pertaining to rivers

POTASH *n* pl. -ES an alkaline compound

POTASSIC *adj* pertaining to potassium (a metallic element)

POTATION *n* pl. -S the act of drinking

POTATO *n* pl. -TOES the edible tuber of a cultivated plant

POTATORY *adj* pertaining to drinking

POTBELLY *n* pl. -LIES a protruding abdominal region

POTBOIL *v* -ED, -ING, -S to produce a literary or artistic work of poor quality

POTBOY *n* pl. -BOYS a boy who serves customers in a tavern

POTEEN *n* pl. -S Irish whiskey that is distilled unlawfully

POTENCE *n* pl. -S potency

POTENCY *n* pl. -CIES the quality of being potent

POTENT *adj* powerful **POTENTLY** *adv*

POTFUL *n* pl. -S as much as a pot can hold

POTHEAD *n* pl. -S one who smokes marijuana

POTHEEN *n* pl. -S poteen

POTHER *v* -ED, -ING, -S to trouble

POTHERB *n* pl. -S any herb used as a food or seasoning

POTHOLE *n* pl. -S a deep hole in a road **POTHOLED** *adj*

POTHOOK *n* pl. -S a hook for lifting or hanging pots

POTHOUSE *n* pl. -S a tavern

POTICHE *n* pl. -S a type of vase

POTION *n* pl. -S a magical or medicinal drink

POTLACH *n* pl. -ES a ceremonial feast

POTLACHE *n* pl. -S potlach

POTLATCH *v* -ED, -ING, -ES to hold a ceremonial feast for

POTLIKE *adj* resembling a pot

POTLINE *n* pl. -S a row of electrolytic cells

POTLUCK *n* pl. -S food which is incidentally available

POTMAN *n* pl. -MEN a man who serves customers in a tavern

POTPIE *n* pl. -S a deep-dish pie containing meat and vegetables

POTSHARD *n* pl. -S potsherd

POTSHERD *n* pl. -S a fragment of broken pottery

POTSHOT *v* -SHOT, -SHOTTING, -SHOTS to shoot randomly at

POTSIE *n* pl. -S potsy

POTSTONE *n* pl. -S a variety of steatite

POTSY *n* pl. -SIES a children's game

POTTAGE *n* pl. -S a thick soup

POTTED past tense of pot

POTTEEN *n* pl. -S poteen

POTTER *v* -ED, -ING, -S to putter

POTTERER *n* pl. -S one that potters

POTTERY *n* pl. -TERIES ware molded from clay and hardened by heat

POTTIER comparative of potty

POTTIES pl. of potty

POTTIEST superlative of potty

POTTING present participle of pot

POTTLE *n* pl. -S a drinking vessel

POTTO *n* pl. -TOS a lemur of tropical Africa

POTTY *adj* -TIER, -TIEST of little importance

POTTY *n* pl. -TIES a small toilet seat

POTZER *n* pl. -S patzer

POUCH *v* -ED, -ING, -ES to put in a pouch (a small, flexible receptacle)

POUCHY *adj* POUCHIER, POUCHIEST resembling a pouch

POUF *n* pl. -S a loose roll of hair POUFED *adj*

POUFF *n* pl. -S pouf POUFFED *adj*

POUFFE *n* pl. -S pouf

POULARD *n* pl. -S a spayed hen

POULARDE *n* pl. -S poulard

POULT *n* pl. -S a young domestic fowl

POULTER *n* pl. -S one that deals in poultry

POULTICE *v* -TICED, -TICING, -TICES to apply a healing substance to

POULTRY *n* pl. -TRIES domestic fowls kept for eggs or meat

POUNCE *v* POUNCED, POUNCING, POUNCES to make a sudden assault or approach

POUNCER *n* pl. -S one that pounces

POUND *v* -ED, -ING, -S to strike heavily and repeatedly

POUNDAGE *n* pl. -S the act of impounding

POUNDAL *n* pl. -S a unit of force

POUNDER *n* pl. -S one that pounds

POUR *v* -ED, -ING, -S to cause to flow POURABLE *adj*

POURER *n* pl. -S one that pours

POUSSIE *n* pl. -S pussy

POUT *v* -ED, -ING, -S to protrude the lips in ill humor

POUTER *n* pl. -S one that pouts

POUTFUL *adj* pouty

POUTY *adj* POUTIER, POUTIEST tending to pout

POVERTY *n* pl. -TIES the state of being poor

POW *n* pl. -S an explosive sound

POWDER *v* -ED, -ING, -S to reduce to powder (matter in a finely divided state)

POWDERER *n* pl. -S one that powders

POWDERY *adj* resembling powder

POWER *v* -ED, -ING, -S to provide with means of propulsion

POWERFUL *adj* possessing great force

POWTER *n* pl. -S a domestic pigeon

POWWOW *v* -ED, -ING, -S to hold a conference

POX *v* -ED, -ING, -ES to infect with syphilis

POXVIRUS *n* pl. -ES a type of virus

POYOU *n* pl. -S an armadillo of Argentina

POZZOLAN *n* pl. -S a finely divided material used to make cement

PRAAM *n* pl. -S pram

PRACTIC *adj* practical

PRACTICE *v* -TICED, -TICING, -TICES to perform often so as to acquire skill

PRACTISE *v* -TISED, -TISING, -TISES to practice

PRAECIPE *n* pl. -S a legal writ

PRAEDIAL *adj* pertaining to land

PRAEFECT *n* pl. -S prefect

PRAELECT *v* -ED, -ING, -S to prelect

PRAETOR *n* pl. -S an ancient Roman magistrate

PRAHU *n* pl. -S prau

PRAIRIE *n* pl. -S a tract of grassland

PRAISE *v* PRAISED, PRAISING, PRAISES to express approval or admiration of

PRAISER *n* pl. -S one that praises

PRALINE *n* pl. -S a confection made of nuts cooked in sugar

PRAM *n* pl. -S a flat-bottomed boat

PRANCE *v* PRANCED, PRANCING, PRANCES to spring forward on the hind legs

PRANCER *n* pl. -S one that prances

PRANDIAL *adj* pertaining to a meal

PRANG *v* -ED, -ING, -S to cause to crash

PRANK *v* -ED, -ING, -S to adorn gaudily

PRANKISH *adj* mischievous

PRAO *n* pl. PRAOS prau

PRASE *n* pl. -S a mineral

PRAT *n* pl. -S the buttocks

PRATE *v* PRATED, PRATING, PRATES to chatter

PRATER *n* pl. -S one that prates

PRATFALL *n* pl. -S a fall on the buttocks

PRATING present participle of prate

PRATIQUE *n* pl. -S clearance given a ship by the health authority of a port

PRATTLE *v* -TLED, -TLING, -TLES to babble

PRATTLER *n* pl. -S one that prattles

PRAU *n* pl. -S a swift Malaysian sailing vessel

PRAWN *v* -ED, -ING, -S to fish for prawns (edible shellfish)

PRAWNER *n* pl. -S one that prawns

PRAXIS   *n* pl. PRAXISES or PRAXES practical use of a branch of learning

PRAY   *v* -ED, -ING, -S to address prayers to

PRAYER   *n* pl. -S a devout petition to a deity

PREACH   *v* -ED, -ING, -ES to advocate or recommend urgently

PREACHER   *n* pl. -S one that preaches

PREACHY   *adj* PREACHIER, PREACHIEST tending to preach

PREACT   *v* -ED, -ING, -S to act beforehand

PREADAPT   *v* -ED, -ING, -S to adapt beforehand

PREADMIT   *v* -MITTED, -MITTING, -MITS to admit beforehand

PREADOPT   *v* -ED, -ING, -S to adopt beforehand

PREADULT   *adj* preceding adulthood

PREAGED   *adj* previously aged

PREALLOT   *v* -LOTTED, -LOTTING, -LOTS to allot beforehand

PREAMBLE   *n* pl. -S an introductory statement

PREAMP   *n* pl. -S an amplifier

PREANAL   *adj* situated in front of the anus

PREARM   *v* -ED, -ING, -S to arm beforehand

PREAUDIT   *n* pl. -S an audit made prior to a final settlement of a transaction

PREAVER   *v* -VERRED, -VERRING, -VERS to aver or assert beforehand

PREAXIAL   *adj* situated in front of an axis

PREBASAL   *adj* situated in front of a base

PREBEND   *n* pl. -S a clergyman's stipend

PREBILL   *v* -ED, -ING, -S to bill beforehand

PREBIND   *v* -BOUND, -BINDING, -BINDS to bind in durable materials for library use

PREBLESS   *v* -ED, -ING, -ES to bless beforehand

PREBOIL   *v* -ED, -ING, -S to boil beforehand

PREBOOM   *adj* preceding a sudden expansion of business

PREBOUND   past tense of prebind

PRECAST   *v* -CAST, -CASTING, -CASTS to cast and finish before placing into position

PRECAVA   *n* pl. -VAE a vein in higher vertebrates **PRECAVAL** *adj*

PRECEDE   *v* -CEDED, -CEDING, -CEDES to go before

PRECENT   *v* -ED, -ING, -S to lead a church choir in singing

PRECEPT   *n* pl. -S a rule of conduct

PRECESS   *v* -ED, -ING, -ES to rotate with a complex motion

PRECHECK   *v* -ED, -ING, -S to check beforehand

PRECHILL   *v* -ED, -ING, -S to chill beforehand

PRECIEUX   *adj* excessively refined

PRECINCT   *n* pl. -S a subdivision of a city or town

PRECIOUS   *n* pl. -ES a darling

PRECIPE   *n* pl. -S praecipe

PRECIS   *v* -ED, -ING, -ES to make a concise summary of

PRECISE   *adj* -CISER, -CISEST sharply and clearly defined or stated

PRECITED   *adj* previously cited

PRECLEAN   *v* -ED, -ING, -S to clean beforehand

PRECLEAR   *v* -ED, -ING, -S to clear beforehand

PRECLUDE   *v* -CLUDED, -CLUDING, -CLUDES to make impossible by previous action

PRECODE   *v* -CODED, -CODING, -CODES to code beforehand

PRECOOK   *v* -ED, -ING, -S to cook beforehand

PRECOOL   *v* -ED, -ING, -S to cool beforehand

PRECOUP   *adj* preceding a coup

PRECRASH   *adj* preceding a crash

PRECURE   *v* -CURED, -CURING, -CURES to cure beforehand

PRECUT   *v* -CUT, -CUTTING, -CUTS to cut beforehand

PREDATE   *v* -DATED, -DATING, -DATES to date before the actual or a specified time

PREDATOR   *n* pl. -S one that plunders

PREDAWN   *n* pl. -S the time just before dawn

PREDIAL   *adj* praedial

PREDICT   *v* -ED, -ING, -S to tell of or about in advance

PREDIVE   *adj* preceding a dive

PREDRILL   *v* -ED, -ING, -S to drill beforehand

PREDUSK   *n* pl. -S the time just before dusk

PREE   v PREED, PREEING, PREES
            to test by tasting
PREEDIT   v -ED, -ING, -S to edit
            beforehand
PREELECT   v -ED, -ING, -S to elect or
            choose beforehand
PREEMIE   n pl. -S an infant born
            prematurely
PREEMPT   v -ED, -ING, -S to acquire by
            prior right
PREEN   v -ED, -ING, -S to smooth or
            clean with the beak or tongue
PREENACT   v -ED, -ING, -S to enact
            beforehand
PREENER   n pl. -S one that preens
PREERECT   v -ED, -ING,-S to erect
            beforehand
PREEXIST   v -ED, -ING, -S to exist before
PREFAB   v -FABBED, -FABBING,
            FABS to construct beforehand
PREFACE   v -ACED, -ACING, -ACES to
            provide with an introductory
            statement
PREFACER   n pl. -S one that prefaces
PREFADE   v -FADED, -FADING, -FADES
            to fade beforehand
PREFECT   n pl. -S an ancient Roman
            official
PREFER   v -FERRED, -FERRING,
            -FERS to hold in higher regard
            or esteem
PREFIGHT   adj preceding a fight
PREFILE   v -FILED, -FILING, -FILES to
            file beforehand
PREFIRE   v -FIRED, -FIRING, -FIRES to
            fire beforehand
PREFIX   v -ED, -ING, -ES to add as a
            prefix (a form affixed to the
            beginning of a root word)
PREFIXAL   adj pertaining to or being a
            prefix
PREFLAME   adj preceding a flame
PREFOCUS   v -CUSED, -CUSING,
            -CUSES or -CUSSED,
            -CUSSING, -CUSSES to focus
            beforehand
PREFORM   v -ED, -ING, -S to form
            beforehand
PREFRANK   v -ED, -ING, -S to frank
            beforehand
PREFREEZE   v -FROZE, -FROZEN,
            -FREEZING, -FREEZES to
            freeze beforehand
PREGAME   adj preceding a game
PREGGERS   adj pregnant

PREGNANT   adj carrying a developing fetus
            in the uterus
PREHEAT   v -ED, -ING, -S to heat
            beforehand
PREHUMAN   n pl. -S a prototype of man
PREJUDGE   v -JUDGED, -JUDGING,
            -JUDGES to judge beforehand
PRELACY   n pl. -CIES the office of a
            prelate
PRELATE   n pl. -S a high-ranking
            clergyman PRELATIC adj
PRELECT   v -ED, -ING, -S to lecture
PRELEGAL   adj occurring before the
            commencement of studies in
            law
PRELIFE   n pl. -LIVES a life conceived
            as lived before one's earthly
            life
PRELIM   n pl. -S a minor match
            preceding the main event
PRELIMIT   v -ED, -ING, -S to limit
            beforehand
PRELUDE   v -LUDED, -LUDING, -LUDES
            to play a musical introduction
PRELUDER   n pl. -S one that preludes
PRELUNCH   adj preceding lunch
PREMAN   n pl. -MEN a hypothetical
            ancestor of man
PREMEAL   adj preceding a meal
PREMED   n pl. -S a student preparing for
            the study of medicine
PREMEDIC   n pl. -S a premed
PREMEET   adj preceding a meet
PREMEN   pl. of preman
PREMIE   n pl. -S preemie
PREMIER   n pl. -S a prime minister
PREMIERE   v -MIERED, -MIERING,
            -MIERES to present publicly
            for the first time
PREMISE   v -MISED, -MISING, -MISES
            to state in advance
PREMISS   n pl. -ES a proposition in logic
PREMIUM   n pl. -S an additional payment
PREMIX   v -ED, -ING, -ES to mix before
            use
PREMOLAR   n pl. -S a tooth
PREMOLD   v -ED, -ING, -S to mold
            beforehand
PREMOLT   adj preceding a molt
PREMORAL   adj preceding the
            development of a moral code
PREMORSE   adj ending abruptly, as if bitten
            off
PREMUNE   adj resistant to a disease
PRENAME   n pl. -S a forename
PRENATAL   adj prior to birth

PRENOMEN *n pl.* -MENS or -MINA the first name of an ancient Roman

PRENOON *adj* preceding noon

PRENTICE *v* -TICED, -TICING, -TICES to place with an employer for instruction in a trade

PREORDER *v* -ED, -ING, -S to order beforehand

PREP *v* PREPPED, PREPPING, PREPS to attend a preparatory school

PREPACK *v* -ED, -ING, -S to package before retail distribution

PREPAID past tense of prepay

PREPARE *v* -PARED, -PARING, -PARES to put in proper condition or readiness

PREPARER *n pl.* -S one that prepares

PREPASTE *v* -PASTED, -PASTING, -PASTES to paste beforehand

PREPAY *v* -PAID, -PAYING, -PAYS to pay in advance

PREPENSE *adj* planned in advance

PREPILL *adj* preceding the development of a contraceptive pill

PREPLACE *v* -PLACED, -PLACING, -PLACES to place beforehand

PREPLAN *v* -PLANNED, -PLANNING, -PLANS to plan in advance

PREPLANT *adj* occurring before planting

PREPPED past tense of prep

PREPPIE *n pl.* -S one who preps

PREPPING present participle of prep

PREPPY *adj* -PIER, -PIEST associated with the style and behavior of preparatory school students **PREPPILY** *adv*

PREPREG *n pl.* -S reinforcing material already impregnated with a synthetic resin

PREPRICE *v* -PRICED, -PRICING, -PRICES to price beforehand

PREPRINT *v* -ED, -ING, -S to print in advance

PREPUCE *n pl.* -S a fold of skin covering the penis

PREPUNCH *v* -ED, -ING, -ES to punch in advance

PREPUPAL *adj* preceding the pupal stage

PREQUEL *n pl.* -S a book whose story precedes that of an earlier work

PRERACE *adj* preceding a race

PRERENAL *adj* situated in front of the kidney

PRERINSE *n pl.* -S a rinsing beforehand

PRERIOT *adj* preceding a riot

PREROCK *adj* preceding the development of rock music

PRESA *n pl.* -SE a musical symbol

PRESAGE *v* -SAGED, -SAGING, -SAGES to foretell

PRESAGER *n pl.* -S one that presages

PRESALE *adj* preceding a sale

PRESCIND *v* -ED, -ING, -S to consider separately

PRESCORE *v* -SCORED, -SCORING, -SCORES to record the sound of before filming

PRESE *pl.* of presa

PRESELL *v* -SOLD, -SELLING, -SELLS to promote a product not yet being sold to the public

PRESENCE *n pl.* -S close proximity

PRESENT *v* -ED, -ING, -S to bring into the presence of someone

PRESERVE *v* -SERVED, -SERVING, -SERVES to keep free from harm or danger

PRESET *v* -SET, -SETTING, -SETS to set beforehand

PRESHAPE *v* -SHAPED, -SHAPING, -SHAPES to shape beforehand

PRESHOW *v* -SHOWED, -SHOWN, -SHOWING, -SHOWS to show beforehand

PRESIDE *v* -SIDED, -SIDING, -SIDES to occupy the position of authority

PRESIDER *n pl.* -S one that presides

PRESIDIA *n/pl* Soviet executive committees

PRESIDIO *n pl.* -DIOS a Spanish fort

PRESIFT *v* -ED, -ING, -S to sift beforehand

PRESLEEP *adj* preceding sleep

PRESLICE *v* -SLICED, -SLICING, -SLICES to slice beforehand

PRESOAK *v* -ED, -ING, -S to soak beforehand

PRESOLD past tense of presell

PRESONG *adj* preceding a song

PRESORT *v* -ED, -ING, -S to sort beforehand

PRESPLIT *adj* preceding a split

PRESS *v* -ED, -ING, -ES to act upon with steady force

PRESSER *n pl.* -S one that presses

PRESSING *n pl.* -S an instance of stamping with a press

PRESSMAN *n pl.* -MEN a printing press operator

PRESSOR   *n* pl. -S a substance that raises blood pressure

PRESSRUN   *n* pl. -S a continuous operation of a printing press

PRESSURE   *v* -SURED, -SURING, -SURES to apply force to

PREST   *n* pl. -S a loan

PRESTAMP   *v* -ED, -ING, -S to stamp beforehand

PRESTER   *n* pl. -S a priest

PRESTIGE   *n* pl. -S distinction or reputation in the eyes of people

PRESTO   *n* pl. -TOS a musical passage played in rapid tempo

PRESUME   *v* -SUMED, -SUMING, -SUMES to take for granted

PRESUMER   *n* pl. -S one that presumes

PRETAPE   *v* -TAPED, -TAPING, -TAPES to tape beforehand

PRETASTE   *v* -TASTED, -TASTING, -TASTES to taste beforehand

PRETAX   *adj* existing before provision for taxes

PRETEEN   *n* pl. -S a child under the age of thirteen

PRETENCE   *n* pl. -S pretense

PRETEND   *v* -ED, -ING, -S to assume or display a false appearance of

PRETENSE   *n* pl. -S the act of pretending

PRETERIT   *n* pl. -S a past tense in grammar

PRETERM   *adj* pertaining to premature birth

PRETEST   *v* -ED, -ING, -S to give a preliminary test to

PRETEXT   *v* -ED, -ING, -S to allege as an excuse

PRETOR   *n* pl. -S praetor

PRETRAIN   *v* -ED, -ING, -S to train beforehand

PRETREAT   *v* -ED, -ING, -S to treat beforehand

PRETRIAL   *n* pl. -S a proceeding that precedes a trial

PRETRIM   *v* -TRIMMED, -TRIMMING, -TRIMS to trim beforehand

PRETTIED   past tense of pretty

PRETTIER   comparative of pretty

PRETTIES   present 3d person sing. of pretty

PRETTIEST   superlative of pretty

PRETTIFY   *v* -FIED, -FYING, -FIES to make pretty

PRETTY   *v* -TIED, -TYING, -TIES to make pretty

PRETTY   *adj* -TIER, -TIEST pleasing to the eye PRETTILY *adv*

PRETYPE   *v* -TYPED, -TYPING, -TYPES to type beforehand

PRETZEL   *n* pl. -S a glazed, salted cracker

PREUNION   *n* pl. -S a union beforehand

PREUNITE   *v* -UNITED, -UNITING, -UNITES to unite beforehand

PREVAIL   *v* -ED, -ING, -S to triumph

PREVENT   *v* -ED, -ING, -S to keep from happening

PREVIEW   *v* -ED, -ING, -S to view or exhibit in advance

PREVIOUS   *adj* coming or occurring before in time or order

PREVISE   *v* -VISED, -VISING, -VISES to foresee

PREVISOR   *n* pl. -S one that previses

PREVUE   *v* -VUED, -VUING, -VUES to preview

PREWAR   *adj* occurring or existing before a war

PREWARM   *v* -ED, -ING, -S to warm beforehand

PREWARN   *v* -ED, -ING, -S to warn in advance

PREWASH   *v* -ED, -ING, -ES to wash beforehand

PREWORK   *adj* preceding work

PREWRAP   *v* -WRAPPED, -WRAPPING, -WRAPS to wrap beforehand

PREX   *n* pl. -ES prexy

PREXY   *n* pl. PREXIES a president

PREY   *v* -ED, -ING, -S to seize and devour animals for food

PREYER   *n* pl. -S one that preys

PREZ   *n* pl. -ES a president

PRIAPEAN   *adj* priapic

PRIAPI   a pl. of priapus

PRIAPIC   *adj* phallic

PRIAPISM   *n* pl. -S a persistent erection of the penis

PRIAPUS   *n* pl. -PUSES or -PI a representation of the phallus

PRICE   *v* PRICED, PRICING, PRICES to set a value on

PRICER   *n* pl. -S one that prices

PRICEY   *adj* PRICIER, PRICIEST expensive

PRICIER   comparative of pricey and pricy

PRICIEST   superlative of pricey and pricy

PRICING   present participle of price

PRICK   *v* -ED, -ING, -S to puncture slightly

PRICKER   *n* pl. -S one that pricks

PRICKET   n pl. -S a spike for holding a candle upright

PRICKIER   comparative of pricky

PRICKIEST   superlative of pricky

PRICKING   n pl. -S a prickly feeling

PRICKLE   v -LED, -LING, -LES to prick

PRICKLY   adj -LIER, -LIEST having many sharp points

PRICKY   adj PRICKIER, PRICKIEST prickly

PRICY   adj PRICIER, PRICIEST pricey

PRIDE   v PRIDED, PRIDING, PRIDES to feel pride (a feeling of self-esteem)

PRIDEFUL   adj full of pride

PRIED   past tense of pry

PRIEDIEU   n pl. -DIEUS or -DIEUX a piece of furniture for kneeling on during prayer

PRIER   n pl. -S one that pries

PRIES   present 3d person sing. of pry

PRIEST   v -ED, -ING, -S to ordain as a priest (one authorized to perform religious rites)

PRIESTLY   adj -LIER, -LIEST characteristic of or befitting a priest

PRIG   v PRIGGED, PRIGGING, PRIGS to steal

PRIGGERY   n pl. -GERIES priggism

PRIGGISH   adj marked by priggism

PRIGGISM   n pl. -S prim adherence to convention

PRILL   v -ED, -ING, -S to convert into pellets

PRIM   adj PRIMMER, PRIMMEST formally precise or proper

PRIM   v PRIMMED, PRIMMING, PRIMS to give a prim expression to

PRIMA   n pl. -S primo

PRIMACY   n pl. -CIES the state of being first

PRIMAGE   n pl. -S an amount paid as an addition to freight charges

PRIMAL   adj being at the beginning or foundation

PRIMARY   n pl. -RIES a preliminary election

PRIMATAL   n pl. -S a primate

PRIMATE   n pl. -S any of an advanced order of mammals

PRIME   v PRIMED, PRIMING, PRIMES to make ready

PRIMELY   adv excellently

PRIMER   n pl. -S a book that covers the basics of a subject

PRIMERO   n pl. -ROS a card game

PRIMEVAL   adj pertaining to the earliest ages

PRIMI   a pl. of primo

PRIMINE   n pl. -S the outer covering of an ovule

PRIMING   n pl. -S the act of one that primes

PRIMLY   adv in a prim manner

PRIMMED   past tense of prim

PRIMMER   comparative of prim

PRIMMEST   superlative of prim

PRIMMING   present participle of prim

PRIMNESS   n pl. -ES the state of being prim

PRIMO   n pl. -MOS or -MI the main part in a musical piece

PRIMP   v -ED, -ING, -S to dress or adorn carefully

PRIMROSE   n pl. -S a perennial herb

PRIMSIE   adj prim

PRIMULA   n pl. -S primrose

PRIMUS   n pl. -ES the head bishop of Scotland

PRINCE   n pl. -S a non-reigning male member of a royal family

PRINCELY   adj -LIER, -LIEST of or befitting a prince

PRINCESS   n pl. -ES a non-reigning female member of a royal family

PRINCIPE   n pl. -PI a prince

PRINCOCK   n pl. -S a coxcomb

PRINCOX   n pl. -ES princock

PRINK   v -ED, -ING, -S to dress or adorn in a showy manner

PRINKER   n pl. -S one that prinks

PRINT   v -ED, -ING, -S to produce by pressed type on a surface

PRINTER   n pl. -S one that prints

PRINTERY   n pl. -ERIES a place where printing is done

PRINTING   n pl. -S a reproduction from a printing surface

PRINTOUT   n pl. -S the printed output of a computer

PRION   n -S a protein particle

PRIOR   n pl. -S an officer in a monastery

PRIORATE   n pl. -S the office of a prior

PRIORESS   n pl. -ES a nun corresponding in rank to a prior

PRIORIES   pl. of priory

PRIORITY *n* pl. -TIES precedence established by importance

PRIORLY *adv* previously

PRIORY *n* pl. -RIES a religious house

PRISE *v* PRISED, PRISING, PRISES to raise or force with a lever

PRISERE *n* pl. -S a succession of vegetational stages

PRISM *n* pl. -S a solid which disperses light into a spectrum

PRISMOID *n* pl. -S a geometric solid

PRISON *v* -ED, -ING, -S to imprison

PRISONER *n* pl. -S one that is imprisoned

PRISS *v* -ED, -ING, -ES to act in a prissy manner

PRISSY *adj* -SIER, -SIEST excessively or affectedly proper **PRISSILY** *adv*

PRISSY *n* pl. -SIES one who is prissy

PRISTANE *n* pl. -S a chemical compound

PRISTINE *adj* pertaining to the earliest time or state

PRITHEE *interj* — used to express a wish or request

PRIVACY *n* pl. -CIES the state of being private

PRIVATE *adj* -VATER, -VATEST secluded from the sight, presence, or intrusion of others

PRIVATE *n* pl. -S a soldier of lower rank

PRIVET *n* pl. -S an ornamental shrub

PRIVIER comparative of privy

PRIVIES pl. of privy

PRIVITY *n* pl. -TIES private knowledge

PRIVY *adj* PRIVIER, PRIVIEST private **PRIVILY** *adv*

PRIVY *n* pl. PRIVIES an outhouse

PRIZE *v* PRIZED, PRIZING, PRIZES to value highly

PRIZER *n* pl. -S one who vies for a reward

PRO *n* pl. PROS an argument or vote in favor of something

PROA *n* pl. -S prau

PROBABLE *adj* likely to occur or prove true **PROBABLY** *adv*

PROBAND *n* pl. -S one whose reactions or responses are studied

PROBANG *n* pl. -S a surgical rod

PROBATE *v* -BATED, -BATING, -BATES to establish the validity of

PROBE *v* PROBED, PROBING, PROBES to investigate or examine thoroughly

PROBER *n* pl. one that probes

PROBIT *n* pl. -S a unit of statistical probability

PROBITY *n* pl. -TIES complete and confirmed integrity

PROBLEM *n* pl. -S a perplexing question or situation

PROCAINE *n* pl. -S a compound used as a local anesthetic

PROCARP *n* pl. -S a female sexual organ in certain algae

PROCEED *v* -ED, -ING, -S to go forward or onward

PROCESS *v* -ED, -ING, -ES to treat or prepare by a special method

PROCHAIN *adj* prochein

PROCHEIN *adj* nearest in time, relation, or degree

PROCLAIM *v* -ED, -ING, -S to make known publicly or officially

PROCTOR *v* -ED, -ING, -S to supervise

PROCURAL *n* pl. -S the act of procuring

PROCURE *v* -CURED, -CURING, -CURES to obtain by effort

PROCURER *n* pl. -S one that procures

PROD *v* PRODDED, PRODDING, PRODS to jab with something pointed

PRODDER *n* pl. -S one that prods

PRODIGAL *n* pl. -S one who spends lavishly and foolishly

PRODIGY *n* pl. -GIES a child having exceptional talent or ability

PRODROME *n* pl. -DROMES or -DROMATA a sign of impending disease

PRODUCE *v* -DUCED, -DUCING, -DUCES to bring into existence

PRODUCER *n* pl. -S one that produces

PRODUCT *n* pl. -S something produced by labor or effort

PROEM *n* pl. -S an introductory statement **PROEMIAL** *adj*

PROETTE *n* pl. -S a female professional athlete

PROF *n* pl. -S a professor

PROFANE *v* -FANED, -FANING, -FANES to treat with irreverence or abuse

PROFANER *n* pl. -S one that profanes

PROFESS *v* -ED, -ING, -ES to affirm openly

PROFFER *v* -ED, -ING, -S to present for acceptance

PROFILE *v* -FILED, -FILING, -FILES to draw an outline of

PROFILER *n* pl. -S one that profiles

PROFIT	*v* -ED, -ING, -S to gain an advantage or benefit
PROFITER	*n* pl. -S one that profits
PROFOUND	*adj* -FOUNDER, -FOUNDEST intellectually deep and penetrating
PROFOUND	*n* pl. -S something that is very deep
PROFUSE	*adj* pouring forth generously
PROG	*v* PROGGED, PROGGING, PROGS to prowl about for food or plunder
PROGENY	*n* pl. -NIES a descendant or offspring
PROGERIA	*n* pl. -S premature aging
PROGGER	*n* pl. -S one that progs
PROGGING	present participle of prog
PROGNOSE	*v* -NOSED, -NOSING, -NOSES to forecast the probable course of a disease
PROGRADE	*adj* pertaining to the orbital motion of a body
PROGRAM	*v* -GRAMED, -GRAMING, -GRAMS or -GRAMMED, -GRAMMING, -GRAMS to arrange in a plan of proceedings
PROGRESS	*v* -ED, -ING, -ES to move forward or onward
PROHIBIT	*v* -ED, -ING, -S to forbid by authority
PROJECT	*v* -ED, -ING, -S to extend outward
PROJET	*n* pl. -S a plan or outline
PROLABOR	*adj* favoring organized labor
PROLAMIN	*n* pl. -S a simple protein
PROLAN	*n* pl. -S a sex hormone
PROLAPSE	*v* -LAPSED, -LAPSING, -LAPSES to fall or slip out of place
PROLATE	*adj* extended lengthwise
PROLE	*n* pl. -S a member of the working class
PROLEG	*n* pl. -S an abdominal leg of certain insect larvae
PROLIFIC	*adj* producing abundantly
PROLINE	*n* pl. -S an amino acid
PROLIX	*adj* tediously long and wordy **PROLIXLY** *adv*
PROLOG	*v* -ED, -ING, -S to prologue
PROLOGUE	*v* -LOGUED, -LOGUING, -LOGUES to preface
PROLONG	*v* -ED, -ING, -S to lengthen in duration
PROLONGE	*n* pl. -S a rope used for pulling a gun carriage
PROM	*n* pl. -S a formal dance
PROMINE	*n* pl. -S a substance that promotes growth
PROMISE	*v* -ISED, -ISING, -ISES to make a declaration of assurance
PROMISEE	*n* pl. -S one who is promised something
PROMISER	*n* pl. -S promisor
PROMISING	present participle of promise
PROMISOR	*n* pl. -S one that promises
PROMO	*n* pl. -MOS a promotional presentation
PROMOTE	*v* -MOTED, -MOTING, -MOTES to contribute to the progress of
PROMOTER	*n* pl. -S one that promotes
PROMPT	*adj* PROMPTER, PROMPTEST quick to act or respond
PROMPT	*v* -ED, -ING, -S to induce to action
PROMPTER	*n* pl. -S one that prompts
PROMPTLY	*adv* in a prompt manner
PROMULGE	*v* -MULGED, -MULGING, -MULGES to proclaim
PRONATE	*v* -NATED, -NATING, -NATES to turn the palm downward or backward
PRONATOR	*n* pl. -S or -ES a forearm or forelimb muscle
PRONE	*adj* lying with the front or face downward **PRONELY** *adv*
PRONG	*v* -ED, -ING, -S to pierce with a pointed projection
PRONOTUM	*n* pl. -NOTA a hard outer plate of an insect
PRONOUN	*n* pl. -S a word that may be used in place of a noun
PRONTO	*adv* quickly
PROOF	*v* -ED, -ING, -S to examine for errors
PROOFER	*n* pl. -S one that proofs
PROP	*v* PROPPED, PROPPING, PROPS to keep from falling
PROPANE	*n* pl. -S a flammable gas
PROPEL	*v* -PELLED, -PELLING, -PELS to cause to move forward or onward
PROPEND	*v* -ED, -ING, -S to have a tendency toward
PROPENE	*n* pl. -S a flammable gas
PROPENOL	*n* pl. -S a flammable liquid
PROPENSE	*adj* tending toward
PROPENYL	*adj* pertaining to a certain chemical group

PROPER _adj_ -ERER, -EREST suitable **PROPERLY** _adv_

PROPER _n_ pl. -S a portion of the Mass

PROPERTY _n_ pl. -TIES something owned

PROPHAGE _n_ pl. -S a form of virus

PROPHASE _n_ pl. -S the first stage in mitosis

PROPHECY _n_ pl. -CIES a prediction

PROPHESY _v_ -SIED, -SYING, -SIES to predict

PROPHET _n_ pl. -S one who predicts

PROPINE _v_ -PINED, -PINING, -PINES to offer as a gift

PROPJET _n_ pl. -S a type of airplane

PROPMAN _n_ pl. -MEN a man in charge of stage properties

PROPOLIS _n_ pl. -LISES a resinous substance used as a cement by bees

PROPONE _v_ -PONED, -PONING, -PONES to propose

PROPOSAL _n_ pl. -S something that is proposed

PROPOSE _v_ -POSED, -POSING, -POSES to put forward for consideration or acceptance

PROPOSER _n_ pl. -S one that proposes

PROPOUND _v_ -ED, -ING, -S to propose

PROPPED past tense of prop

PROPPING present participle of prop

PROPYL _n_ pl. -S a univalent radical **PROPYLIC** _adj_

PROPYLON _n_ pl. -LA an entrance to a temple

PRORATE _v_ -RATED, -RATING, -RATES to divide proportionately

PROROGUE _v_ -ROGUED, -ROGUING, -ROGUES to discontinue a session of

PROSAIC _adj_ pertaining to prose

PROSAISM _n_ pl. -S a prosaic style

PROSAIST _n_ pl. -S a writer of prose

PROSE _v_ PROSED, PROSING, PROSES to write prose (writing without metrical structure)

PROSECT _v_ -ED, -ING, -S to dissect

PROSER _n_ pl. -S a prosaist

PROSIER comparative of prosy

PROSIEST superlative of prosy

PROSILY _adv_ in a prosy manner

PROSING present participle of prose

PROSIT _interj_ — used as a drinking toast

PROSO _n_ pl. -SOS millet

PROSODY _n_ pl. -DIES the study of poetical forms **PROSODIC** _adj_

PROSOMA _n_ pl. -S the front region of the body of an invertebrate **PROSOMAL** _adj_

PROSPECT _v_ -ED, -ING, -S to explore for mineral deposits

PROSPER _v_ -ED, -ING, -S to be successful or fortunate

PROSS _n_ pl. -ES a prostitute

PROSSIE _n_ pl. -S a prostitute

PROST _interj_ prosit

PROSTATE _n_ pl. -S a gland in male mammals

PROSTIE _n_ pl. -S a prostitute

PROSTYLE _n_ pl. -S a building having a row of columns across the front only

PROSY _adj_ PROSIER, PROSIEST prosaic

PROTAMIN _n_ pl. -S a simple protein

PROTASIS _n_ pl. -ASES the introductory part of a classical drama **PROTATIC** _adj_

PROTEA _n_ pl. -S an evergreen shrub

PROTEAN _n_ pl. -S a type of protein

PROTEASE _n_ pl. -S an enzyme

PROTECT _v_ -ED, -ING, -S to keep from harm, attack, or injury

PROTEGE _n_ pl. -S one whose career is promoted by an influential person

PROTEGEE _n_ pl. -S a female protege

PROTEI pl. of proteus

PROTEID _n_ pl. -S protein

PROTEIDE _n_ pl. -S proteid

PROTEIN _n_ pl. -S a nitrogenous organic compound

PROTEND _v_ -ED, -ING, -S to extend

PROTEOSE _n_ pl. -S a water-soluble protein

PROTEST _v_ -ED, -ING, -S to express strong objection

PROTEUS _n_ pl. -TEI any of a genus of aerobic bacteria

PROTEUS _n_ pl. -ES one that readily changes his appearance or principles

PROTIST _n_ pl. -S any of a group of unicellular organisms

PROTIUM _n_ pl. -S an isotope of hydrogen

PROTOCOL _v_ -COLED, -COLING, -COLS or -COLLED, -COLLING, -COLS to form a preliminary draft of an official document

PROTON *n* pl. -S a subatomic particle **PROTONIC** *adj*

PROTOPOD *n* pl. -S a part of a crustacean appendage

PROTOXID *n* pl. -S an oxide

PROTOZOA *n/pl* unicellular microscopic organisms

PROTRACT *v* -ED, -ING, -S to prolong

PROTRUDE *v* -TRUDED, -TRUDING, -TRUDES to extend beyond the main portion

PROTYL *n* pl. -S protyle

PROTYLE *n* pl. -S a hypothetical substance from which all the elements are supposedly derived

PROUD *adj* PROUDER, PROUDEST having or displaying pride **PROUDLY** *adv*

PROUDFUL *adj* prideful

PROUNION *adj* favoring labor unions

PROVE *v* PROVED, PROVEN, PROVING, PROVES to establish the truth or validity of **PROVABLE** *adj* **PROVABLY** *adv*

PROVENLY *adv* without doubt

PROVER *n* pl. -S one that proves

PROVERB *v* -ED, -ING, -S to make a byword of

PROVIDE *v* -VIDED, -VIDING, -VIDES to supply

PROVIDER *n* pl. -S one that provides

PROVINCE *n* pl. -S an administrative division of a country

PROVING present participle of prove

PROVIRUS *n* pl. -ES a form of virus **PROVIRAL** *adj*

PROVISO *n* pl. -SOS or -SOES a clause in a document introducing a condition or restriction

PROVOKE *v* -VOKED, -VOKING, -VOKES to incite to anger or resentment

PROVOKER *n* pl. -S one that provokes

PROVOST *n* pl. -S a high-ranking university official

PROW *n* pl. -S the forward part of a ship

PROW *adj* PROWER, PROWEST brave

PROWAR *adj* favoring war

PROWESS *n* pl. -ES exceptional ability

PROWL *v* -ED, -ING, -S to move about stealthily

PROWLER *n* pl. -S one that prowls

PROXEMIC *adj* pertaining to a branch of environmental study

PROXIES pl. of proxy

PROXIMAL *adj* located near the point of origin

PROXIMO *adj* of or occurring in the following month

PROXY *n* pl. PROXIES a person authorized to act for another

PRUDE *n* pl. -S a prudish person

PRUDENCE *n* pl. -S the quality of being prudent

PRUDENT *adj* having, showing, or exercising good judgment

PRUDERY *n* pl. -ERIES excessive regard for propriety, modesty, or morality

PRUDISH *adj* marked by prudery

PRUINOSE *adj* having a powdery covering

PRUNE *v* PRUNED, PRUNING, PRUNES to cut off branches or parts from **PRUNABLE** *adj*

PRUNELLA *n* pl. -S a strong woolen fabric

PRUNELLE *n* pl. -S a plum-flavored liqueur

PRUNELLO *n* pl. -LOS prunella

PRUNER *n* pl. -S one that prunes

PRUNING present participle of prune

PRUNUS *n* pl. -ES a flowering tree

PRURIENT *adj* having lustful thoughts or desires

PRURIGO *n* pl. -GOS a skin disease

PRURITUS *n* pl. -ES intense itching **PRURITIC** *adj*

PRUSSIC *adj* pertaining to a type of acid

PRUTA *n* pl. PRUTOT prutah

PRUTAH *n* pl. PRUTOTH a monetary unit of Israel

PRY *v* PRIED, PRYING, PRIES to inquire impertinently into private matters **PRYINGLY** *adv*

PRYER *n* pl. -S prier

PRYTHEE *interj* prithee

PSALM *v* -ED, -ING, -S to praise in psalms (sacred songs)

PSALMIC *adj* of or pertaining to a psalm

PSALMIST *n* pl. -S a writer of psalms

PSALMODY *n* pl. -DIES the use of psalms in worship

PSALTER *n* pl. -S a book of psalms

PSALTERY *n* pl. -TERIES an ancient stringed musical instrument

PSALTRY *n* pl. -TRIES psaltery

PSAMMITE *n* pl. -S a fine-grained rock

PSAMMON *n* pl. -S a group of microorganisms living in waterlogged sands

PSCHENT *n* pl. -S a crown worn by ancient Egyptian kings

PSEPHITE *n* pl, -S a rock composed of small pebbles

PSEUD *n* pl. -S a person pretending to be an intellectual

PSEUDO *n* pl. PSEUDOS a pseud

PSHAW *v* -ED, -ING, -S to utter an expression of disapproval

PSI *n* pl. -S a Greek letter

PSILOCIN *n* pl. -S a hallucinogenic drug

PSILOSIS *n* pl. -LOSES a tropical disease **PSILOTIC** *adj*

PSOAS *n* pl. PSOAI or PSOAE a muscle of the loin **PSOATIC** *adj*

PSOCID *n* pl. -S a minute winged insect

PSORALEA *n* pl. -S a plant of the bean family

PSORALEN *n* pl. -S a drug used to treat psoriasis

PSST *interj* — used to attract someone's attention

PSYCH *v* -ED, -ING, -S to put into the proper frame of mind

PSYCHE *n* pl. -S the mental structure of a person

PSYCHIC *n* pl. -S one sensitive to extrasensory phenomena

PSYCHO *n* pl. -CHOS a mentally unstable person

PSYLLA *n* pl. -S any of various plant lice

PSYLLID *n* pl. -S psylla

PSYLLIUM *n* pl. -S the seed of a fleawort

PSYWAR *n* pl. -S psychological warfare

PTERIN *n* pl. -S a chemical compound

PTEROPOD *n* pl. -S a type of mollusk

PTERYGIA *n/pl* fleshy growths over the cornea

PTERYLA *n* pl. -LAE a feathered area on the skin of a bird

PTISAN *n* pl. -S a tea of herbs or barley

PTOMAIN *n* pl. -S ptomaine

PTOMAINE *n* pl. -S a compound produced by the decomposition of protein

PTOSIS *n* pl. PTOSES a drooping of the upper eyelid **PTOTIC** *adj*

PTYALIN *n* pl. -S a salivary enzyme

PTYALISM *n* pl. -S an excessive flow of saliva

PUB *n* pl. -S a tavern

PUBERTY *n* pl. -TIES a period of sexual maturation **PUBERAL, PUBERTAL** *adj*

PUBES *n* pl. PUBES the lower part of the abdomen

PUBIC *adj* pertaining to the pubes or pubis

PUBIS *n* pl. PUBES the forward portion of either of the hipbones

PUBLIC *n* pl. -S the community or the people as a whole

PUBLICAN *n* pl. -S one who owns or manages a pub

PUBLICLY *adv* by the public

PUBLISH *v* -ED, -ING, -ES to print and issue to the public

PUCCOON *n* pl. -S an herb that yields a red dye

PUCE *n* pl. -S a dark red color

PUCK *n* pl. -S a rubber disk used in ice hockey

PUCKA *adj* pukka

PUCKER *v* -ED, -ING, -S to gather into small wrinkles or folds

PUCKERER *n* pl. -S one that puckers

PUCKERY *adj* -ERIER, -ERIEST having a tendency to pucker

PUCKISH *adj* impish

PUD *n* pl. -S pudding

PUDDING *n* pl. -S a thick, soft dessert

PUDDLE *v* -DLED, -DLING, -DLES to strew with puddles (small pools of water)

PUDDLER *n* pl. -S one who subjects iron to puddling

PUDDLING *n* pl. -S the process of converting pig iron to wrought iron

PUDDLY *adj* -DLIER, -DLIEST full of puddles

PUDENCY *n* pl. -CIES modesty

PUDENDUM *n* pl. -DA the external genital organs of a woman **PUDENDAL** *adj*

PUDGY *adj* PUDGIER, PUDGIEST short and fat **PUDGILY** *adv*

PUDIBUND *adj* prudish

PUDIC *adj* to the pudendum

PUEBLO *n* pl. -LOS a communal dwelling of certain Indian tribes

PUERILE *adj* childish

PUFF	*v* -ED, -ING, -S to blow in short gusts
PUFFBALL	*n* pl. -S any of various globular fungi
PUFFER	*n* pl. -S one that puffs
PUFFERY	*n* pl. -ERIES excessive public praise
PUFFIN	*n* pl. -S a sea bird
PUFFY	*adj* -FIER, -FIEST swollen **PUFFILY** *adv*
PUG	*v* PUGGED, PUGGING, PUGS to fill in with clay or mortar
PUGAREE	*n* pl. -S pugree
PUGGAREE	*n* pl. -S pugree
PUGGED	past tense of pug
PUGGIER	comparative of puggy
PUGGIEST	superlative of puggy
PUGGING	present participle of pug
PUGGISH	*adj* somewhat stubby
PUGGREE	*n* pl. -S pugree
PUGGRY	*n* pl. -GRIES pugree
PUGGY	*adj* -GIER, -GIEST puggish
PUGH	*interj* — used to express disgust
PUGILISM	*n* pl. -S the art or practice of fighting with the fists
PUGILIST	*n* pl. -S one who fights with his fists
PUGMARK	*n* pl. -S a footprint
PUGREE	*n* pl. -S a cloth band wrapped around a hat
PUISNE	*n* pl. -S one of lesser rank
PUISSANT	*adj* powerful
PUJA	*n* pl. -S a Hindu prayer ritual
PUJAH	*n* pl. -S puja
PUKE	*v* PUKED, PUKING, PUKES to vomit
PUKKA	*adj* genuine
PUL	*n* pl. PULS or PULI a coin of Afghanistan
PULA	*n* pl. PULA a monetary unit of Botswana
PULE	*v* PULED, PULING, PULES to whine
PULER	*n* pl. -S one that pules
PULI	*n* pl. -LIK or -LIS a long-haired sheepdog
PULICENE	*adj* pertaining to fleas
PULICIDE	*n* pl. -S an agent used for destroying fleas
PULIK	a pl. of puli
PULING	*n* pl. -S a plaintive cry
PULINGLY	*adv* in a whining manner

PULL	*v* -ED, -ING, -S to exert force in order to cause motion toward the force
PULLBACK	*n* pl. -S a restraint or drawback
PULLER	*n* pl. -S one that pulls
PULLET	*n* pl. -S a young hen
PULLEY	*n* pl. -LEYS a device used for lifting weight
PULLMAN	*n* pl. -S a railroad sleeping car
PULLOUT	*n* pl. -S a withdrawal
PULLOVER	*n* pl. -S a garment that is put on by being drawn over the head
PULLUP	*n* pl. -S the act of raising oneself while hanging by the hands
PULMONIC	*adj* pertaining to the lungs
PULMOTOR	*n* pl. -S a respiratory device
PULP	*v* -ED, -ING, -S to reduce to pulp (a soft, moist mass of matter)
PULPAL	*adj* pertaining to pulp **PULPALLY** *adv*
PULPER	*n* pl. -S one that pulps
PULPIER	comparative of pulpy
PULPIEST	superlative of pulpy
PULPILY	*adv* in a pulpy manner
PULPIT	*n* pl. -S a platform in a church **PULPITAL** *adj*
PULPLESS	*adj* having no pulp
PULPOUS	*adj* pulpy
PULPWOOD	*n* pl. -S soft wood used in making paper
PULPY	*adj* PULPIER, PULPIEST resembling pulp
PULQUE	*n* pl. -S a fermented Mexican beverage
PULSANT	*adj* pulsating
PULSAR	*n* pl. -S a celestial source of radio waves
PULSATE	*v* -SATED, -SATING, -SATES to expand and contract rhythmically
PULSATOR	*n* pl. -S something that pulsates
PULSE	*v* PULSED, PULSING, PULSES to pulsate
PULSEJET	*n* pl. -S a type of engine
PULSER	*n* pl. -S a device that causes pulsations
PULSING	present participle of pulse
PULSION	*n* pl. -S propulsion
PULSOJET	*n* pl. -S pulsejet
PULVILLI	*n/pl* pads between the claws of an insect's foot

PULVINUS *n* pl. -NI a swelling at the base of a leaf **PULVINAR** *adj*

PUMA *n* pl. -S a cougar

PUMELO *n* pl. -LOS pomelo

PUMICE *v* -ICED, -ICING, -ICES to polish with a porous volcanic rock

PUMICER *n* pl. -S one that pumices

PUMICITE *n* pl. -S a porous volcanic rock

PUMMEL *v* -MELED, -MELING, -MELS or -MELLED, -MELLING, -MELS to pommel

PUMMELO *n* pl. -LOS a shaddock

PUMP *v* -ED, -ING, -S to cause to flow by means of a pump (a device for moving fluids)

PUMPER *n* pl. -S one that pumps

PUMPKIN *n* pl. -S a large, edible fruit

PUMPLESS *adj* lacking a pump

PUMPLIKE *adj* resembling a pump

PUN *v* PUNNED, PUNNING, PUNS to make a pun (a play on words)

PUNA *n* pl. -S a cold, arid plateau

PUNCH *v* -ED, -ING, -ES to perforate with a type of tool

PUNCHEON *n* pl. -S a vertical supporting timber

PUNCHER *n* pl. -S one that punches

PUNCHY *adj* PUNCHIER, PUNCHIEST dazed **PUNCHILY** *adv*

PUNCTATE *adj* covered with dots

PUNCTUAL *adj* being on time

PUNCTURE *v* -TURED, -TURING, -TURES to pierce with a pointed object

PUNDIT *n* pl. -S a Hindu scholar **PUNDITIC** *adj*

PUNDITRY *n* pl. -RIES the learning of pundits

PUNG *n* pl. -S a box-shaped sleigh

PUNGENCY *n* pl. -CIES the state of being pungent

PUNGENT *adj* sharply affecting the organs of taste or smell

PUNGLE *v* -GLED, -GLING, -GLES to contribute

PUNIER comparative of puny

PUNIEST superlative of puny

PUNILY *adv* in a puny manner

PUNINESS *n* pl. -ES the state of being puny

PUNISH *v* -ED, -ING, -ES to impose a penalty on in requital for wrongdoing

PUNISHER *n* pl. -S one that punishes

PUNITION *n* pl. -S the act of punishing; punishment

PUNITIVE *adj* inflicting punishment

PUNITORY *adj* punitive

PUNK *n* pl. -S dry, decayed wood used as tinder

PUNK *adj* PUNKER, PUNKEST of inferior quality

PUNKA *n* pl. -S a ceiling fan used in India

PUNKAH *n* pl. -S punka

PUNKER *n* pl. -S a punk rock musician

PUNKEY *n* pl. -KEYS punkie

PUNKIE *n* pl. -S a biting gnat

PUNKIN *n* pl. -S pumpkin

PUNKISH *adj* pertaining to a style inspired by punk rock

PUNKY *adj* PUNKIER, PUNKIEST resembling punk

PUNNED past tense of pun

PUNNER *n* pl. -S a punster

PUNNET *n* pl. -S a small basket

PUNNING present participle of pun

PUNNY *adj* -NIER, -NIEST being or involving a pun

PUNSTER *n* pl. -S one who is given to punning

PUNT *v* -ED, -ING, -S to propel through water with a pole

PUNTER *n* pl. -S one that punts

PUNTO *n* pl. -TOS a hit or thrust in fencing

PUNTY *n* pl. -TIES an iron rod used in glassmaking

PUNY *adj* PUNIER, PUNIEST of inferior size, strength, or significance

PUP *v* PUPPED, PUPPING, PUPS to give birth to puppies

PUPA *n* pl. -PAS or -PAE an intermediate stage of a metamorphic insect **PUPAL** *adj*

PUPARIUM *n* pl. -IA a pupal shell **PUPARIAL** *adj*

PUPATE *v* -PATED, -PATING, -PATES to pass through the pupal stage

PUPATION *n* pl. -S the act of pupating

PUPFISH *n* pl. -ES a small, freshwater fish

PUPIL *n* pl. -S a student under the close supervision of a teacher

PUPILAGE *n* pl. -S the state of being a pupil

PUPILAR *adj* pertaining to a part of the eye

PUPILARY *adj* pupilar

PUPPED past tense of pup

PUPPET *n* pl. -S a small figure, as of a person or animal, manipulated by the hand

PUPPETRY *n* pl. -RIES the art of making or manipulating puppets

PUPPING present participle of pup

PUPPY *n* pl. -PIES a young dog **PUPPYISH** *adj*

PUPPYDOM *n* pl. -S the world of puppies

PUR *v* PURRED, PURRING, PURS to purr

PURANA *n* pl. -S a Hindu scripture **PURANIC** *adj*

PURBLIND *adj* partially blind

PURCHASE *v* -CHASED, -CHASING, -CHASES to acquire by the payment of money

PURDA *n* pl. -S purdah

PURDAH *n* pl. -S a curtain used in India to seclude women

PURE *adj* PURER, PUREST free from anything different, inferior, or contaminating

PUREBRED *n* pl. -S an animal of unmixed stock

PUREE *v* -REED, -REEING, -REES to reduce to a thick pulp by cooking and sieving

PURELY *adv* in a pure manner

PURENESS *n* pl. -ES the quality of being pure

PURER comparative of pure

PUREST superlative of pure

PURFLE *v* -FLED, -FLING, -FLES to decorate the border of

PURFLING *n* pl. -S an ornamental border

PURGE *v* PURGED, PURGING, PURGES to purify

PURGER *n* pl. -S one that purges

PURGING *n* pl. -S the act of purifying

PURI *n* pl. -S poori

PURIFIER *n* pl. -S one that purifies

PURIFY *v* -FIED, -FYING, -FIES to free from impurities

PURIN *n* pl. -S purine

PURINE *n* pl. -S a chemical compound

PURISM *n* pl. -S strict adherence to traditional correctness

PURIST *n* pl. -S one who practices purism **PURISTIC** *adj*

PURITAN *n* pl. -S a rigorously moral or religious person

PURITY *n* pl. -TIES the quality of being pure

PURL *v* -ED, -ING, -S to knit with a particular stitch

PURLIEU *n* pl. -S an outlying or neighboring area

PURLIN *n* pl. -S a horizontal supporting timber

PURLINE *n* pl. -S purlin

PURLOIN *v* -ED, -ING, -S to steal

PURPLE *adj* -PLER, -PLEST of a color intermediate between red and blue

PURPLE *v* -PLED, -PLING, -PLES to make purple

PURPLISH *adj* somewhat purple

PURPLY *adj* purplish

PURPORT *v* -ED, -ING, -S to profess or claim

PURPOSE *v* -POSED, -POSING, -POSES to resolve to perform or accomplish

PURPURA *n* pl. -S a disease characterized by purple spots on the skin

PURPURE *n* pl. -S the heraldic color purple

PURPURIC *adj* pertaining to purpura

PURPURIN *n* pl. -S a reddish dye

PURR *v* -ED, -ING, -S to utter a low, vibrant sound

PURRED past tense of pur and purr

PURRING present participle of pur and purr

PURSE *v* PURSED, PURSING, PURSES to pucker

PURSER *n* pl. -S an officer in charge of a ship's accounts

PURSIER comparative of pursy

PURSIEST superlative of pursy

PURSILY *adv* in a pursy manner

PURSING present participle of purse

PURSLANE *n* pl. -S a common garden herb

PURSUANT *adv* in accordance

PURSUE *v* -SUED, -SUING, -SUES to follow in order to overtake or capture

PURSUER *n* pl. -S one that pursues

PURSUIT *n* pl. -S the act of pursuing

PURSY *adj* PURSIER, PURSIEST short of breath

PURULENT *adj* secreting pus

PURVEY *v* -ED, -ING, -S to supply

PURVEYOR *n* pl. -S one that purveys

PURVIEW *n* pl. -S the extent of operation, authority, or concern

PUS *n* pl. -ES a viscous fluid formed in infected tissue

PUSH *v* -ED, -ING, -ES to exert force in order to cause motion away from the force

PUSHBALL *n* pl. -S a type of ball game

PUSHCART *n* pl. -S a light cart pushed by hand

PUSHDOWN *n* pl. -S a store of computer data

PUSHER *n* pl. -S one that pushes

PUSHFUL *adj* pushy

PUSHIER comparative of pushy

PUSHIEST superlative of pushy

PUSHILY *adv* in a pushy manner

PUSHOVER *n* pl. -S an easily defeated person or team

PUSHPIN *n* pl. -S a large-headed pin

PUSHROD *n* pl. -S a rod for operating the valves in an engine

PUSHUP *n* pl. -S a type of exercise

PUSHY *adj* PUSHIER, PUSHIEST offensively aggressive

PUSLEY *n* pl. -LEYS pussley

PUSLIKE *adj* resembling pus

PUSS *n* pl. -ES a cat

PUSSIER comparative of pussy

PUSSIES pl. of pussy

PUSSIEST superlative of pussy

PUSSLEY *n* pl. -LEYS purslane

PUSSLIKE *adj* catlike

PUSSLY *n* pl. -LIES pussley

PUSSY *n* pl. PUSSIES a cat

PUSSY *adj* -SIER, -SIEST full of pus

PUSSYCAT *n* pl. -S a cat

PUSTULE *n* pl. -S a small elevation of the skin containing pus **PUSTULAR, PUSTULED** *adj*

PUT *v* PUT, PUTTING, PUTS to place in a particular position

PUTAMEN *n* pl. -MINA the hard covering of the kernel of certain fruits

PUTATIVE *adj* generally regarded as such

PUTLOG *n* pl. -S a horizontal supporting timber

PUTOFF *n* pl. -S an excuse

PUTON *n* pl. -S a hoax or deception

PUTOUT *n* pl. -S an act of causing an out in baseball

PUTREFY *v* -FIED, -FYING, -FIES to make or become putrid

PUTRID *adj* being in a decomposed, foul-smelling state **PUTRIDLY** *adv*

PUTSCH *n* pl. -ES a suddenly executed attempt to overthrow a government

PUTT *v* -ED, -ING, -S to hit with a light stroke in golf

PUTTEE *n* pl. -S a strip of cloth wound around the leg

PUTTER *v* -ED, -ING, -S to occupy oneself in a leisurely or ineffective manner

PUTTERER *n* pl. -S one that putters

PUTTI pl. of putto

PUTTIED past tense of putty

PUTTIER *n* pl. -S one that putties

PUTTING present participle of put

PUTTO *n* pl. -TI an infant boy in art

PUTTY *v* -TIED, -TYING, -TIES to fill with a type of cement

PUTZ *v* -ED, -ING, -ES to waste time

PUZZLE *v* -ZLED, -ZLING, -ZLES to cause uncertainty and indecision in

PUZZLER *n* pl. -S something that puzzles

PYA *n* pl. -S a copper coin of Burma

PYAEMIA *n* pl. -S pyemia **PYAEMIC** *adj*

PYCNIDIA *n/pl* spore-bearing organs of certain fungi

PYCNOSIS *n* pl. -NOSES pyknosis

PYCNOTIC *adj* pyknotic

PYE *n* pl. -S a book of ecclesiastical rules in the pre-Reformation English church

PYELITIS *n* pl. -TISES inflammation of the pelvis or the kidney **PYELITIC** *adj*

PYEMIA *n* pl. -S the presence of pus in the blood **PYEMIC** *adj*

PYGIDIUM *n* pl. -IA the posterior region of certain invertebrates **PYGIDIAL** *adj*

PYGMY *n* pl. -MIES a small person **PYGMAEAN, PYGMEAN, PYGMOID, PYGMYISH** *adj*

PYGMYISM *n* pl. -S a stunted or dwarfish condition

PYIC *adj* pertaining to pus

PYIN *n* pl. -S a protein compound contained in pus

PYJAMAS *n* pl. PYJAMAS pajamas

PYKNIC *n* pl. -S a person having a broad, stocky build

PYKNOSIS *n* pl. -NOSES a shrinking and thickening of a cell nucleus

PYKNOTIC *adj* exhibiting pyknosis

PYLON *n* pl. -S a tall structure marking an entrance or approach

PYLORUS *n* pl. -RI or -RUSES the opening between the stomach and the duodenum **PYLORIC** *adj*

PYODERMA *n* pl. -S a pus-causing skin disease

PYOGENIC *adj* producing pus

PYOID *adj* puslike

PYORRHEA *n* pl. -S a discharge of pus

PYOSIS *n* pl. -OSES the formation of pus

PYRALID *n* pl. -S a long-legged moth

PYRAMID *v* -ED, -ING, -S to raise or increase by adding amounts gradually

PYRAN *n* pl. -S a chemical compound **PYRANOID** *adj*

PYRANOSE *n* pl. -S a simple sugar

PYRE *n* pl. -S a pile of combustible material

PYRENE *n* pl. -S a putamen

PYRENOID *n* pl. -S a protein body of certain lower organisms

PYRETIC *adj* pertaining to fever

PYREXIA *n* pl. -S fever **PYREXIAL, PYREXIC** *adj*

PYRIC *adj* pertaining to burning

PYRIDINE *n* pl. -S a flammable liquid **PYRIDIC** *adj*

PYRIFORM *adj* pear-shaped

PYRITE *n* pl. -S a metallic sulfide **PYRITIC, PYRITOUS** *adj*

PYROGEN *n* pl. -S a substance that produces fever

PYROLA *n* pl. -S a perennial herb

PYROLOGY *n* pl. -GIES the scientific examination of materials by heat

PYROLYZE *v* -LYZED, -LYZING, -LYZES to affect compounds by the application of heat

PYRONE *n* pl. -S a chemical compound

PYRONINE *n* pl. -S a dye

PYROPE *n* pl. -S a variety of garnet

PYROSIS *n* pl. -SISES heartburn

PYROSTAT *n* pl. -S a thermostat

PYROXENE *n* pl. -S any of a group of minerals common in igneous rocks

PYRRHIC *n* pl. -S a type of metrical foot

PYRROL *n* pl. -S pyrrole

PYRROLE *n* pl. -S a chemical compound **PYRROLIC** *adj*

PYRUVATE *n* pl. -S a chemical salt

PYTHON *n* pl. -S a large snake **PYTHONIC** *adj*

PYURIA *n* pl. -S the presence of pus in the urine

PYX *n* pl. -ES a container in which the eucharistic bread is kept

PYXIDES pl. of pyxis

PYXIDIUM *n* pl. -IA a type of seed vessel

PYXIE *n* pl. -S an evergreen shrub

PYXIS *n* pl. PYXIDES a pyxidium

Q 10

QAID	*n* pl. -S caid
QANAT	*n* pl. -S a system of underground tunnels and wells in the Middle East
QAT	*n* pl. -S kat
QINDAR	*n* pl. -DARS or -DARKA qintar
QINTAR	*n* pl. -S a monetary unit of Albania
QIVIUT	*n* pl. -S the wool of a musk-ox
QOPH	*n* pl. -S koph
QUA	*adv* in the capacity of
QUAALUDE	*n* pl. -S a sedative drug
QUACK	*v* -ED, -ING, -S to utter the characteristic cry of a duck
QUACKERY	*n* pl. -ERIES fraudulent practice
QUACKISH	*adj* fraudulent
QUACKISM	*n* pl. -S quackery
QUAD	*v* QUADDED, QUADDING, QUADS to space out by means of quadrats
QUADPLEX	*n* pl. -ES a building having four units
QUADRANS	*n* pl. -RANTES an ancient Roman coin
QUADRANT	*n* pl. -S a quarter section of a circle
QUADRAT	*n* pl. -S a piece of type metal used for filling spaces
QUADRATE	*v* -RATED, -RATING, -RATES to correspond or agree
QUADRIC	*n* pl. -S a type of geometric surface
QUADRIGA	*n* pl. -GAE a chariot drawn by four horses
QUADROON	*n* pl. -S a person of one-quarter black ancestry
QUAERE	*n* pl. -S a question
QUAESTOR	*n* pl. -S an ancient Roman magistrate
QUAFF	*v* -ED, -ING, -S to drink deeply
QUAFFER	*n* pl. -S one that quaffs
QUAG	*n* pl. -S a quagmire
QUAGGA	*n* pl. -S an extinct zebralike mammal
QUAGGY	*adj* -GIER, -GIEST marshy
QUAGMIRE	*n* pl. -S an area of marshy ground
QUAGMIRY	*adj* -MIRIER, -MIRIEST marshy
QUAHAUG	*n* pl. -S quahog
QUAHOG	*n* pl. -S an edible clam
QUAI	*n* pl. -S quay
QUAICH	*n* pl. -ES or -S a small drinking vessel
QUAIGH	*n* pl. -S quaich
QUAIL	*v* -ED, -ING, -S to cower
QUAINT	*adj* QUAINTER, QUAINTEST pleasingly old-fashioned or unfamiliar **QUAINTLY** *adv*
QUAKE	*v* QUAKED, QUAKING, QUAKES to shake or vibrate
QUAKER	*n* pl. -S one that quakes
QUAKY	*adj* QUAKIER, QUAKIEST tending to quake **QUAKILY** *adv*
QUALE	*n* pl. -LIA a property considered apart from things having the property
QUALIFY	*v* -FIED, -FYING, -FIES to make suitable or capable
QUALITY	*n* pl. -TIES a characteristic or attribute
QUALM	*n* pl. -S a feeling of doubt or misgiving
QUALMISH	*adj* having qualms

QUALMY *adj* QUALMIER, QUALMIEST qualmish

QUAMASH *n* pl. -ES camass

QUANDANG *n* pl. -S quandong

QUANDARY *n* pl. -RIES a dilemma

QUANDONG *n* pl. -S an Australian tree

QUANGO *n* pl. -GOS a public administrative board

QUANT *v* -ED, -ING, -S to propel through water with a pole

QUANTA pl. of quantum

QUANTAL *adj* pertaining to a quantum

QUANTIC *n* pl. -S a type of mathematical function

QUANTIFY *v* -FIED, -FYING, -FIES to determine the quantity of

QUANTILE *n* pl. -S any of the values of a random variable that divides a frequency distribution

QUANTITY *n* pl. -TIES a specified or indefinite amount or number

QUANTIZE *v* -TIZED, -TIZING, -TIZES to limit the possible values of to a discrete set

QUANTONG *n* pl. -S quandong

QUANTUM *n* pl. -TA a fundamental unit of energy

QUARE *adj* queer

QUARK *n* pl. -S a hypothetical atomic particle

QUARREL *v* -RELED, -RELING, -RELS or -RELLED, -RELLING, -RELS to engage in an angry dispute

QUARRIER *n* pl. -S one that quarries

QUARRY *v* -RIED, -RYING, -RIES to dig stone from an excavation

QUART *n* pl. -S a liquid measure of capacity

QUARTAN *n* pl. -S a recurrent malarial fever

QUARTE *n* pl. -S a fencing thrust

QUARTER *v* -ED, -ING, -S to divide into four equal parts

QUARTERN *n* pl. -S one-fourth of something

QUARTET *n* pl. -S a group of four

QUARTIC *n* pl. -S a type of mathematical function

QUARTILE *n* pl. -S a portion of a frequency distribution

QUARTO *n* pl. -TOS the size of a piece of paper cut four from a sheet

QUARTZ *n* pl. -ES a mineral

QUASAR *n* pl. -S a distant celestial object emitting strong radio waves

QUASH *v* -ED, -ING, -ES to suppress completely

QUASHER *n* pl. -S one that quashes

QUASI *adj* similar but not exactly the same

QUASS *n* pl. -ES kvass

QUASSIA *n* pl. -S a tropical tree

QUASSIN *n* pl. -S a medicinal compound obtained from the wood of a quassia

QUATE *adj* quiet

QUATORZE *n* pl. -S a set of four cards of the same denomination scoring fourteen points

QUATRAIN *n* pl. -S a stanza of four lines

QUATRE *n* pl. -S the four at cards or dice

QUAVER *v* -ED, -ING, -S to quiver

QUAVERER *n* pl. -S one that quavers

QUAVERY *adj* quivery

QUAY *n* pl. QUAYS a wharf **QUAYLIKE** *adj*

QUAYAGE *n* pl. -S a charge for the use of a quay

QUAYSIDE *n* pl. -S the area adjacent to a quay

QUEAN *n* pl. -S a harlot

QUEASY *adj* -SIER, -SIEST easily nauseated **QUEASILY** *adv*

QUEAZY *adj* -ZIER, -ZIEST queasy

QUEEN *v* -ED, -ING, -S to make a queen (a female monarch) of

QUEENDOM *n* pl. -S the area ruled by a queen

QUEENLY *adj* -LIER, -LIEST of or befitting a queen

QUEER *adj* QUEERER, QUEEREST deviating from the expected or normal

QUEER *v* -ED, -ING, -S to spoil the effect or success of

QUEERISH *adj* somewhat queer

QUEERLY *adv* in a queer manner

QUELL *v* -ED, -ING, -S to suppress

QUELLER *n* pl. -S one that quells

QUENCH *v* -ED, -ING, -ES to put out or extinguish

QUENCHER *n* pl. -S one that quenches

QUENELLE *n* pl. -S a type of dumpling

QUERCINE *adj* pertaining to oaks

QUERIDA *n* pl. -S a female sweetheart

QUERIED past tense of query

QUERIER *n* pl. -S a querist

QUERIES present 3d person sing. of query

QUERIST *n* pl. -S one who queries

QUERN *n* pl. -S a hand-turned grain mill

QUERY *v* -RIED, -RYING, -RIES to question

QUEST *v* -ED, -ING, -S to make a search

QUESTER *n* pl. -S one that quests

QUESTION *v* -ED, -ING, -S to put a question (an inquiry) to

QUESTOR *n* pl. -S quaestor

QUETZAL *n* pl. -S or -ES a tropical bird

QUEUE *v* QUEUED, QUEUING or QUEUEING, QUEUES to line up

QUEUER *n* pl. -S one that queues

QUEY *n* pl. QUEYS a young cow

QUEZAL *n* pl. -S or -ES quetzal

QUIBBLE *v* -BLED, -BLING, -BLES to argue over trivialities

QUIBBLER *n* pl. -S one that quibbles

QUICHE *n* pl. -S a custard-filled pastry

QUICK *adj* QUICKER, QUICKEST acting or capable of acting with speed

QUICK *n* pl. -S a sensitive area of flesh

QUICKEN *v* -ED, -ING, -S to speed up

QUICKIE *n* pl. -S something done quickly

QUICKLY *adv* in a quick manner

QUICKSET *n* pl. -S a plant suitable for hedges

QUID *n* pl. -S a portion of something to be chewed

QUIDDITY *n* pl. -TIES the true nature of a thing

QUIDNUNC *n* pl. -S a nosy person

QUIET *adj* -ETER, -ETEST making little or no noise

QUIET *v* -ED, -ING, -S to cause to be quiet

QUIETEN *v* -ED, -ING, -S to quiet

QUIETER *n* pl. -S one that quiets

QUIETISM *n* pl. -S a form of religious mysticism

QUIETIST *n* pl. -S an advocate of quietism

QUIETLY *adv* in a quiet manner

QUIETUDE *n* pl. -S a state of tranquillity

QUIETUS *n* pl. -ES a final settlement

QUIFF *n* pl. -S a forelock

QUILL *v* -ED, -ING, -S to press small ridges in

QUILLAI *n* pl. -S an evergreen tree

QUILLAIA *n* pl. -S a quillai

QUILLAJA *n* pl. -S a quillai

QUILLET *n* pl. -S a trivial distinction

QUILLING *n* pl. -S material that is quilled

QUILT *v* -ED, -ING, -S to stitch together with padding in between

QUILTER *n* pl. -S one that quilts

QUILTING *n* pl. -S material that is used for making quilts

QUIN *n* pl. -S a quintuplet

QUINARY *n* pl. -RIES a group of five

QUINATE *adj* arranged in groups of five

QUINCE *n* pl. -S an apple-like fruit

QUINCUNX *n* pl. -ES an arrangement of five objects

QUINELA *n* pl. -S quinella

QUINELLA *n* pl. -S a type of bet in horse racing

QUINIC *adj* pertaining to quinine

QUINIELA *n* pl. -S quinella

QUININ *n* pl. -S quinine

QUININA *n* pl. -S quinine

QUININE *n* pl. -S a medicinal alkaloid

QUINNAT *n* pl. -S a food fish

QUINOA *n* pl. -S a weedy plant

QUINOID *n* pl. -S a chemical compound

QUINOL *n* pl. -S a chemical compound

QUINOLIN *n* pl. -S a chemical compound

QUINONE *n* pl. -S a chemical compound

QUINSY *n* pl. -SIES an inflammation of the tonsils

QUINT *n* pl. -S a group of five

QUINTA *n* pl. -S a country estate in Portugal or Latin America

QUINTAIN *n* pl. -S an object used as a target in a medieval sport

QUINTAL *n* pl. -S a unit of weight

QUINTAN *n* pl. -S a recurrent fever

QUINTAR *n* pl. -S qintar

QUINTE *n* pl. -S a position in fencing

QUINTET *n* pl. -S a group of five

QUINTIC *n* pl. -S a type of mathematical function

QUINTILE *n* pl. -S a portion of a frequency distribution

QUINTIN *n* pl. -S a fine linen

QUIP *v* QUIPPED, QUIPPING, QUIPS to make witty remarks

QUIPPER *n* pl. -S one that quips

QUIPPISH *adj* witty

QUIPPU *n* pl. -S quipu

QUIPSTER *n* pl. -S one that quips

QUIPU *n* pl. -S an ancient calculating device

QUIRE *v* QUIRED, QUIRING, QUIRES to arrange sheets of paper in sets of twenty-four

QUIRK *v* -ED, -ING, -S to twist

QUIRKISH *adj* quirky

QUIRKY *adj* QUIRKIER, QUIRKIEST peculiar **QUIRKILY** *adv*

QUIRT *v* -ED, -ING, -S to strike with a riding whip

QUISLING *n* pl. -S a traitor who aids the invaders of his country

QUIT *v* QUITTED, QUITTING, QUITS to end one's engagement in or occupation with

QUITCH *n* pl. -ES a perennial grass

QUITE *adv* to the fullest extent

QUITRENT *n* pl. -S a fixed rent due from a socage tenant

QUITTED past tense of quit

QUITTER *n* pl. -S one that quits

QUITTING present participle of quit

QUITTOR *n* pl. -S an inflammation of an animal's hoof

QUIVER *v* -ED, -ING, -S to shake with a slight but rapid motion

QUIVERER *n* pl. -S one that quivers

QUIVERY *adj* marked by quivering

QUIXOTE *n* pl. -S a quixotic person

QUIXOTIC *adj* extremely idealistic

QUIXOTRY *n* pl. -TRIES quixotic action or thought

QUIZ *v* QUIZZED, QUIZZING, QUIZZES to test the knowledge of by asking questions

QUIZZER *n* pl. -S one that quizzes

QUOD *n* pl. -S a prison

QUOHOG *n* pl. -S quahog

QUOIN *v* -ED, -ING, -S to secure with a type of wedge

QUOIT *v* -ED, -ING, -S to play a throwing game similar to ringtoss

QUOKKA *n* pl. -S a short-tailed wallaby

QUOMODO *n* pl. -DOS a means or manner

QUONDAM *adj* that once was

QUORUM *n* pl. -S a particularly chosen group

QUOTA *n* pl. -S a proportional part or share

QUOTE *v* QUOTED, QUOTING, QUOTES to repeat the words of **QUOTABLE** *adj* **QUOTABLY** *adv*

QUOTER *n* pl. -S one that quotes

QUOTH *v* said — QUOTH is the only accepted form of this verb; it cannot be conjugated

QUOTHA *interj* — used to express surprise or sarcasm

QUOTIENT *n* pl. -S the number resulting from the division of one number by another

QUOTING present participle of quote

QURSH *n* pl. -ES a monetary unit of Saudi Arabia

QURUSH *n* pl. -ES qursh

R₁

RABAT *n* pl. -S a dickey attached to a clerical collar

RABATO *n* pl. -TOS a wide, lace-edged collar

RABBET *v* -ED, -ING, -S to cut a groove in

RABBI *n* pl. -S or -ES a Jewish spiritual leader

RABBIN *n* pl. -S rabbi

RABBINIC *adj* pertaining to rabbis

RABBIT *v* -ED, -ING, -S to hunt rabbits (rodent-like mammals)

RABBITER *n* pl. -S one that rabbits

RABBITRY *n* pl. -RIES a place where rabbits are kept

RABBITY *adj* resembling a rabbit

RABBLE *v* -BLED, -BLING, -BLES to mob

RABBLER *n* pl. -S an iron bar used in puddling

RABBONI *n* pl. -S master; teacher — used as a Jewish title of respect

RABIC *adj* pertaining to rabies

RABID *adj* affected with rabies **RABIDLY** *adv*

RABIDITY *n* pl. -TIES the state of being rabid

RABIES *n* pl. RABIES an infectious virus disease **RABIETIC** *adj*

RACCOON *n* pl. -S a carnivorous mammal

RACE *v* RACED, RACING, RACES to compete in a contest of speed

RACEMATE *n* pl. -S a chemical salt

RACEME *n* pl. -S a mode of arrangement of flowers along an axis **RACEMED** *adj*

RACEMIC *adj* pertaining to a racemate

RACEMISM *n* pl. -S the state of being racemic

RACEMIZE *v* -MIZED, -MIZING, -MIZES to convert into a racemic compound

RACEMOID *adj* pertaining to a raceme

RACEMOSE *adj* having the form of a raceme

RACEMOUS *adj* racemose

RACER *n* pl. -S one that races

RACEWAY *n* pl. -WAYS a channel for conducting water

RACHET *n* pl. -S ratchet

RACHILLA *n* pl. -LAE the central stalk of a grass spikelet

RACHIS *n* pl. -CHISES or -CHIDES the spinal column **RACHIAL** *adj*

RACHITIS *n* pl. -TIDES rickets **RACHITIC** *adj*

RACIAL *adj* pertaining to an ethnic group **RACIALLY** *adv*

RACIER comparative of racy

RACIEST superlative of racy

RACILY *adv* in a racy manner

RACINESS *n* pl. -ES the quality of being racy

RACING *n* pl. -S the sport of engaging in contests of speed

RACISM *n* pl. -S a doctrine of racial superiority

RACIST *n* pl. -S an advocate of racism

RACK *v* -ED, -ING, -S to place in a type of framework

RACKER *n* pl. -S one that racks

RACKET *v* -ED, -ING, -S to make a loud noise

RACKETY *adj* -ETIER, -ETIEST noisy

RACKFUL *n* pl. -S as much as a rack can hold

RACKLE *adj* impetuous; rash

RACKWORK *n* pl. -S a type of mechanism

RACLETTE *n* pl. -S a cheese dish

RACON *n* pl. -S a type of radar transmitter

RACOON *n* pl. -S raccoon

RACQUET *n* pl. -S a lightweight implement used in various ball games

RACY *adj* RACIER, RACIEST bordering on impropriety or indecency

RAD *v* RADDED, RADDING, RADS to fear

RADAR *n* pl. -S an electronic locating device

RADDLE *v* -DLED, -DLING, -DLES to weave together

RADIABLE *adj* capable of radiating

RADIAL *n* pl. -S a part diverging from a center

RADIALE *n* pl. -LIA a bone of the carpus

RADIALLY *adv* in a diverging manner

RADIAN *n* pl. -S a unit of angular measure

RADIANCE *n* pl. -S brightness

RADIANCY *n* pl. -CIES radiance

RADIANT *n* pl. -S a point from which rays are emitted

RADIATE *v* -ATED, -ATING, -ATES to emit rays

RADIATOR *n* pl. -S a heating device

RADICAL *n* pl. -S a group of atoms that acts as a unit in chemical compounds

RADICAND *n* pl. -S a quantity in mathematics

RADICATE *v* -CATED, -CATING, -CATES to cause to take root

RADICEL *n* pl. -S a rootlet

RADICES a pl. of radix

RADICLE *n* pl. -S a part of a plant embryo

RADII a pl. of radius

RADIO *v* -ED, -ING, -S to transmit by radio (an apparatus for wireless communication)

RADIOMAN *n* pl. -MEN a radio operator or technician

RADISH *n* pl. -ES a pungent, edible root

RADIUM *n* pl. -S a radioactive element

RADIUS *n* pl. -DII or -DIUSES a straight line from the center of a circle to the circumference

RADIX *n* pl. -DICES or -DIXES the root of a plant

RADOME *n* pl. -S a domelike device used to shelter a radar antenna

RADON *n* pl. -S a radioactive element

RADULA *n* pl. -LAE or -LAS a tonguelike organ of mollusks **RADULAR** *adj*

RADWASTE *n* pl. -S radioactive waste

RAFF *n* pl. -S riffraff

RAFFIA *n* pl. -S a palm tree

RAFFISH *adj* tawdry

RAFFLE *v* -FLED, -FLING, -FLES to dispose of by a form of lottery

RAFFLER *n* pl. -S one that raffles

RAFT *v* -ED, -ING, -S to transport on a raft (a type of buoyant structure)

RAFTER *n* pl. -S a supporting beam

RAFTERED *adj* furnished with rafters

RAFTSMAN *n* pl. -MEN one who manages a raft

RAG *v* RAGGED, RAGGING, RAGS to scold

RAGA *n* pl. -S a Hindu musical form

RAGBAG *n* pl. -S a bag for storing scraps of cloth

RAGE *v* RAGED, RAGING, RAGES to act or speak with violent anger

RAGEE *n* pl. -S ragi

RAGGED *adj* -GEDER, -GEDEST tattered **RAGGEDLY** *adv*

RAGGEDY *adj* somewhat ragged

RAGGEE *n* pl. -S ragi

RAGGIES pl. of raggy

RAGGING present participle of rag

RAGGLE *n* pl. -S a groove cut in masonry

RAGGY *n* pl. -GIES ragi

RAGI *n* pl. -S an East Indian cereal grass

RAGING present participle of rage

RAGINGLY *adv* in a furious manner

RAGLAN *n* pl. -S a type of overcoat

RAGMAN *n* pl. -MEN one who gathers and sells scraps of cloth

RAGOUT *v* -ED, -ING, -S to make into a highly seasoned stew

RAGTAG *n* pl. -S riffraff

RAGTIME *n* pl. -S a style of American dance music

RAGTOP *n* pl. -S a convertible automobile

RAGWEED *n* pl. -S a weedy herb

RAGWORT *n* pl. -S a flowering plant

RAH *interj* — used to cheer on a team or player

RAIA *n* pl. -S rayah

RAID *v* -ED, -ING, -S to make a sudden assault on

RAIDER *n* pl. -S one that raids

RAIL *v* -ED, -ING, -S to scold in abusive or insolent language

RAILBIRD *n* pl. -S a racing enthusiast

RAILBUS *n* pl. -BUSES or -BUSSES a passenger car equipped for operation on rails

RAILCAR *n* pl. -S a railroad car

RAILER *n* pl. -S one that rails

RAILHEAD *n* pl. -S the end of a railroad line

RAILING *n* pl. -S a fence-like barrier

RAILLERY *n* pl. -LERIES good-natured teasing

RAILROAD *v* -ED, -ING, -S to transport by railroad (a type of road on which locomotives are run)

RAILWAY *n* pl. -WAYS a railroad

RAIMENT *n* pl. -S clothing

RAIN *v* -ED, -ING, -S to fall like rain (drops of water condensed from atmospheric vapor)

RAINBAND *n* pl. -S a dark band in the solar spectrum

RAINBIRD *n* pl. -S a type of bird

RAINBOW *n* pl. -S an arc of spectral colors formed in the sky

RAINCOAT *n* pl. -S a waterproof coat

RAINDROP *n* pl. -S a drop of rain

RAINFALL *n* pl. -S a fall of rain

RAINIER comparative of rainy

RAINIEST superlative of rainy

RAINILY *adv* in a rainy manner

RAINLESS *adj* having no rain

RAINOUT *n* pl. -S atomic fallout occurring in precipitation

RAINWASH *v* -ED, -ING, -ES to wash material downhill by rain

RAINWEAR *n* pl. -S waterproof clothing

RAINY *adj* RAINIER, RAINIEST marked by rain

RAISE *v* RAISED, RAISING, RAISES to move to a higher position **RAISABLE** *adj*

RAISER *n* pl. -S one that raises

RAISIN *n* pl. -S a dried grape **RAISINY** *adj*

RAISING *n* pl. -S an elevation

RAISONNE *adj* arranged systematically

RAJ *n* pl. -ES dominion; sovereignty

RAJA *n* pl. -S rajah

RAJAH *n* pl. -S a king or prince in India

RAKE *v* RAKED, RAKING, RAKES to gather with a toothed implement

RAKEE *n* pl. -S raki

RAKEHELL *n* pl. -S a man lacking in moral restraint

RAKEOFF *n* pl. -S a share of profits

RAKER *n* pl. -S one that rakes

RAKI *n* pl. -S a Turkish liqueur

RAKING present participle of rake

RAKISH *adj* dapper **RAKISHLY** *adv*

RALE *n* pl. -S an abnormal respiratory sound

RALLIED past tense of rally

RALLIER *n* pl. -S one that rallies

RALLINE *adj* pertaining to a family of marsh birds

RALLY *v* -LIED, -LYING, -LIES to call together for a common purpose

RALLYE *n* pl. -S a type of automobile race

RALLYING *n* pl. -S the sport of driving in rallyes

RALLYIST *n* pl. -S a participant in a rallye

RALPH *v* -ED, -ING, -S to vomit

RAM *v* RAMMED, RAMMING, RAMS to strike with great force

RAMATE *adj* having branches

RAMBLE *v* -BLED, -BLING, -BLES to wander

RAMBLER *n* pl. -S one that rambles

RAMBUTAN *n* pl. -S the edible fruit of a Malayan tree

RAMEE *n* pl. -S ramie

RAMEKIN *n* pl. -S a cheese dish

RAMENTUM *n* pl. -TA a scale formed on the surface of leaves

RAMEQUIN *n* pl. -S ramekin

RAMET *n* pl. -S an independent member of a clone

RAMI pl. of ramus

RAMIE *n* pl. -S an Asian shrub

RAMIFORM *adj* shaped like a branch

RAMIFY *v* -FIED, -FYING, -FIES to divide into branches

RAMILIE *n* pl. -S ramillie

RAMILLIE *n* pl. -S a type of wig

RAMJET *n* pl. -S a type of engine

RAMMED past tense of ram

RAMMER *n* pl. -S one that rams

RAMMIER	comparative of rammy
RAMMIEST	superlative of rammy
RAMMING	present participle of ram
RAMMISH	*adj* resembling a ram (a male sheep)
RAMMY	*adj* -MIER, -MIEST rammish
RAMOSE	*adj* having many branches RAMOSELY *adv*
RAMOSITY	*n* pl. -TIES the state of being ramose
RAMOUS	*adj* ramose
RAMP	*v* -ED, -ING, -S to rise or stand on the hind legs
RAMPAGE	*v* -PAGED, -PAGING, -PAGES to move about wildly or violently
RAMPAGER	*n* pl. -S one that rampages
RAMPANCY	*n* pl. -CIES the state of being rampant
RAMPANT	*adj* unrestrained
RAMPART	*v* -ED, -ING, -S to furnish with a fortifying embankment
RAMPIKE	*n* pl. -S a standing dead tree
RAMPION	*n* pl. -S a European plant
RAMPOLE	*n* pl. -S rampike
RAMROD	*v* -RODDED, -RODDING, -RODS to supervise
RAMSHORN	*n* pl. -S a snail used as an aquarium scavenger
RAMSON	*n* pl. -S a broad-leaved garlic
RAMTIL	*n* pl. -S a tropical plant
RAMULOSE	*adj* having many small branches
RAMULOUS	*adj* ramulose
RAMUS	*n* pl. -MI a branch-like part of a structure
RAN	past tense of run and rin
RANCE	*n* pl. -S a variety of marble
RANCH	*v* -ED, -ING, -ES to work on a ranch (an establishment for raising livestock)
RANCHER	*n* pl. -S one that owns or works on a ranch
RANCHERO	*n* pl. -ROS a rancher
RANCHMAN	*n* pl. -MEN a rancher
RANCHO	*n* pl. -CHOS a ranch
RANCID	*adj* having an unpleasant odor or taste RANCIDLY *adv*
RANCOR	*n* pl. -S bitter and vindictive enmity RANCORED *adj*
RANCOUR	*n* pl. -S rancor
RAND	*n* pl. -S a strip of leather at the heel of a shoe
RANDAN	*n* pl. -S a boat rowed by three persons
RANDIER	comparative of randy
RANDIES	pl. of randy
RANDIEST	superlative of randy
RANDOM	*n* pl. -S a haphazard course
RANDOMLY	*adv* in a haphazard manner
RANDY	*adj* -DIER, -DIEST lustful
RANDY	*n* pl. RANDIES a rude person
RANEE	*n* pl. -S rani
RANG	past tense of ring
RANGE	*v* RANGED, RANGING, RANGES to place in a particular order
RANGER	*n* pl. -S an officer supervising the care of a forest
RANGY	*adj* RANGIER, RANGIEST tall and slender
RANI	*n* pl. -S the wife of a rajah
RANID	*n* pl. -S any of a large family of frogs
RANK	*v* -ED, -ING, -S to determine the relative position of
RANK	*adj* RANKER, RANKEST strong and disagreeable in odor or taste
RANKER	*n* pl. -S an enlisted soldier
RANKING	*n* pl. -S a listing of ranked individuals
RANKISH	*adj* somewhat rank
RANKLE	*v* -KLED, -KLING, -KLES to cause irritation or resentment in
RANKLY	*adv* in a rank manner
RANKNESS	*n* pl. -ES the state of being rank
RANPIKE	*n* pl. -S rampike
RANSACK	*v* -ED, -ING, -S to search thoroughly
RANSOM	*v* -ED, -ING, -S to obtain the release of by paying a demanded price
RANSOMER	*n* pl. -S one that ransoms
RANT	*v* -ED, -ING, -S to speak in a loud or vehement manner
RANTER	*n* pl. -S one that rants
RANULA	*n* pl. -S a cyst formed under the tongue
RAP	*v* RAPPED, RAPPING, RAPS to strike sharply
RAPACITY	*n* pl. -TIES the quality of being ravenous
RAPE	*v* RAPED, RAPING, RAPES to force to submit to sexual intercourse
RAPER	*n* pl. -S a rapist
RAPESEED	*n* pl. -S the seed of a European herb

RAPHE n pl. RAPHAE or RAPHES a seamlike ridge between two halves of an organ or part

RAPHIA n pl. -S raffia

RAPHIDE n pl. -S a needle-shaped crystal occurring in plant cells

RAPHIS n pl. -PHIDES raphide

RAPID adj -IDER, -IDEST moving or acting with great speed **RAPIDLY** adv

RAPID n pl. -S a fast-moving part of a river

RAPIDITY n pl. -TIES the state of being rapid

RAPIER n pl. -S a long, slender sword **RAPIERED** adj

RAPINE n pl. -S the taking of property by force

RAPING present participle of rape

RAPIST n pl. -S one who rapes

RAPPAREE n pl. -S a plunderer

RAPPED past tense of rap

RAPPEE n pl. -S a strong snuff

RAPPEL v -PELLED, -PELLING, -PELS to descend from a steep height by means of a rope

RAPPEN n pl. RAPPEN a monetary unit of Switzerland

RAPPER n pl. -S one that raps

RAPPING present participle of rap

RAPPINI n/pl immature turnip plants

RAPPORT n pl. -S a harmonious relationship

RAPT adj deeply engrossed **RAPTLY** adv

RAPTNESS n pl. -ES the state of being rapt

RAPTOR n pl. -S a bird of prey

RAPTURE v -TURED, -TURING, -TURES to fill with great joy

RARE adj RARER, RAREST occurring infrequently

RARE v RARED, RARING, RARES to be enthusiastic

RAREBIT n pl. -S a cheese dish

RAREFIER n pl. -S one that rarefies

RAREFY v -EFIED, -EFYING, -EFIES to make less dense

RARELY adv not often

RARENESS n pl. -ES the quality of being rare

RARER comparative of rare

RARERIPE n pl. -S a fruit that ripens early

RAREST superlative of rare

RARIFY v -FIED, -FYING, -FIES to rarefy

RARING adj full of enthusiasm

RARITY n pl. -TIES rareness

RAS n pl. -ES an Ethiopian prince

RASBORA n pl. -S a tropical fish

RASCAL n pl. -S an unscrupulous or dishonest person

RASCALLY adj characteristic of a rascal

RASE v RASED, RASING, RASES to raze

RASER n pl. -S one that rases

RASH adj RASHER, RASHEST acting without due caution or forethought

RASH n pl. -ES a skin eruption **RASHLIKE** adj

RASHER n pl. -S a thin slice of meat

RASHLY adv in a rash manner

RASHNESS n pl. -ES the state of being rash

RASING present participle of rase

RASORIAL adj habitually scratching the ground for food

RASP v -ED, -ING, -S to rub with something rough

RASPER n pl. -S one that rasps

RASPISH adj irritable

RASPY adj RASPIER, RASPIEST rough

RASSLE v -SLED, -SLING, -SLES to wrestle

RASTER n pl. -S the area reproducing images on the picture tube of a television set

RASURE n pl. -S erasure

RAT v RATTED, RATTING, RATS to hunt rats (long-tailed rodents)

RATABLE adj capable of being rated **RATABLY** adv

RATAFEE n pl. -S ratafia

RATAFIA n pl. -S an almond-flavored liqueur

RATAL n pl. -S an amount on which rates are assessed

RATAN n pl. -S rattan

RATANY n pl. -NIES rhatany

RATAPLAN v -PLANNED, -PLANNING, -PLANS to make a rapidly repeating sound

RATATAT n pl. -S a quick, sharp rapping sound

RATBAG n pl. -S an eccentric or disagreeable person

RATCH n pl. -ES a ratchet

RATCHET	*n* pl. -S a mechanism which allows motion in one direction only
RATE	*v* RATED, RATING, RATES to estimate the value of
RATEABLE	*adj* ratable **RATEABLY** *adv*
RATEL	*n* pl. -S a carnivorous mammal
RATER	*n* pl. -S one that rates
RATFINK	*n* pl. -S a contemptible person
RATFISH	*n* pl. -ES a marine fish
RATH	*adj* rathe
RATHE	*adj* appearing or ripening early
RATHER	*adv* preferably
RATHOLE	*n* pl. -S a hole made by a rat
RATICIDE	*n* pl. -S a substance for killing rats
RATIFIER	*n* pl. -S one that ratifies
RATIFY	*v* -FIED, -FYING, -FIES to approve and sanction formally
RATINE	*n* pl. -S a heavy fabric
RATING	*n* pl. -S relative estimate or evaluation
RATIO	*n* pl. -TIOS a proportional relationship
RATION	*v* -ED, -ING, -S to distribute in fixed portions
RATIONAL	*n* pl. -S a number that can be expressed as a quotient of integers
RATITE	*n* pl. -S a flightless bird
RATLIKE	*adj* resembling a rat
RATLIN	*n* pl. -S ratline
RATLINE	*n* pl. -S one of the ropes forming the steps of a rope ladder on a ship
RATO	*n* pl. -TOS a rocket-assisted airplane takeoff
RATOON	*v* -ED, -ING, -S to sprout from a root planted the previous year
RATOONER	*n* pl. -S a plant that ratoons
RATSBANE	*n* pl. -S rat poison
RATTAIL	*n* pl. -S a marine fish
RATTAN	*n* pl. -S a palm tree
RATTED	past tense of rat
RATTEEN	*n* pl. -S a coarse woolen fabric
RATTEN	*v* -ED, -ING, -S to harass
RATTENER	*n* pl. -S one that rattens
RATTER	*n* pl. -S an animal used for catching rats
RATTIER	comparative of ratty
RATTIEST	superlative of ratty
RATTING	present participle of rat
RATTISH	*adj* ratlike
RATTLE	*v* -TLED, -TLING, -TLES to make a quick succession of short, sharp sounds
RATTLER	*n* pl. -S one that rattles
RATTLING	*n* pl. -S ratline
RATTLY	*adj* tending to rattle
RATTON	*n* pl. -S a rat
RATTOON	*v* -ED, -ING, -S to ratoon
RATTRAP	*n* pl. -S a trap for catching rats
RATTY	*adj* -TIER, -TIEST infested with rats
RAUCITY	*n* pl. -TIES the state of being raucous
RAUCOUS	*adj* loud and unruly
RAUNCHY	*adj* -CHIER, -CHIEST slovenly
RAVAGE	*v* -AGED, -AGING, -AGES to destroy
RAVAGER	*n* pl. -S one that ravages
RAVE	*v* RAVED, RAVING, RAVES to speak irrationally or incoherently
RAVEL	*v* -ELED, -ELING, -ELS or -ELLED, -ELLING, -ELS to separate the threads of
RAVELER	*n* pl. -S one that ravels
RAVELIN	*n* pl. -S a type of fortification
RAVELING	*n* pl. -S a loose thread
RAVELLED	a past tense of ravel
RAVELLER	*n* pl. -S raveler
RAVELLING	*n* pl. -S raveling
RAVELLY	*adj* tangled
RAVEN	*v* -ED, -ING, -S to eat in a ravenous manner
RAVENER	*n* pl. -S one that ravens
RAVENING	*n* pl. -S rapacity
RAVENOUS	*adj* extremely hungry
RAVER	*n* pl. -S one that raves
RAVIGOTE	*n* pl. -S a spiced vinegar sauce
RAVIN	*v* -ED, -ING, -S to raven
RAVINE	*n* pl. -S a narrow, steep-sided valley
RAVING	*n* pl. -S irrational, incoherent speech
RAVINGLY	*adv* in a delirious manner
RAVIOLI	*n* pl. -S an Italian pasta dish
RAVISH	*v* -ED, -ING, -ES to seize and carry off by force
RAVISHER	*n* pl. -S one that ravishes
RAW	*adj* RAWER, RAWEST uncooked
RAW	*n* pl. -S a sore or irritated spot
RAWBONED	*adj* having little flesh
RAWHIDE	*v* -HIDED, -HIDING, -HIDES to beat with a type of whip

RAWIN   *n* pl. -S a wind measurement made by tracking a balloon with radar

RAWISH   *adj* somewhat raw

RAWLY   *adv* in a raw manner

RAWNESS   *n* pl. -ES the state of being raw

RAX   *v* -ED, -ING, -ES to stretch out

RAY   *v* -ED, -ING, -S to emit rays (narrow beams of light)

RAYA   *n* pl. -S rayah

RAYAH   *n* pl. -S a non-Muslim inhabitant of Turkey

RAYGRASS   *n* pl. -ES ryegrass

RAYLESS   *adj* having no rays

RAYLIKE   *adj* resembling a narrow beam of light

RAYON   *n* pl. -S a synthetic fiber

RAZE   *v* RAZED, RAZING, RAZES to tear down or demolish

RAZEE   *v* -ZEED, -ZEEING, -ZEES to make lower by removing the upper deck, as a ship

RAZER   *n* pl. -S one that razes

RAZING   present participle of raze

RAZOR   *v* -ED, -ING, -S to shave or cut with a sharp-edged instrument

RAZZ   *v* -ED, -ING, -ES to deride

RE   *n* pl. -S the second tone of the diatonic musical scale

R₁ E₁

Following is a list of self-explanatory verbs containing the prefix RE- (again):

REABSORB   *v* -ED, -ING, -S

REACCEDE   *v* -CEDED, -CEDING, -CEDES

REACCENT   *v* -ED, -ING, -S

REACCEPT   *v* -ED, -ING, -S

REACCUSE   *v* -CUSED, -CUSING, -CUSES

READAPT   *v* -ED, -ING, -S

READD   *v* -ED, -ING, -S

READDICT   *v* -ED, -ING, -S

READJUST   *v* -ED, -ING, -S

READMIT   *v* -MITTED, -MITTING, -MITS

READOPT   *v* -ED, -ING, -S

READORN   *v* -ED, -ING, -S

REAFFIRM   *v* -ED, -ING, -S

REAFFIX   *v* -ED, -ING, -ES

REALIGN   *v* -ED, -ING, -S

REALLOT   *v* -LOTTED, -LOTTING, -LOTS

REALTER   *v* -ED, -ING, -S

REANNEX   *v* -ED, -ING, -ES

REANOINT   *v* -ED, -ING, -S

REAPPEAR   *v* -ED, -ING, -S

REAPPLY   *v* -PLIED, -PLYING, -PLIES

REARGUE   *v* -GUED, -GUING, -GUES

REARM   *v* -ED, -ING, -S

REAROUSE   *v* -AROUSED, -AROUSING, -AROUSES

REARREST   *v* -ED, -ING, -S

REASCEND   *v* -ED, -ING, -S

REASSAIL   *v* -ED, -ING, -S

REASSERT   *v* -ED, -ING, -S

REASSESS   *v* -ED, -ING, -ES

REASSIGN   *v* -ED, -ING, -S

REASSORT   *v* -ED, -ING, -S

REASSUME   *v* -SUMED, -SUMING, -SUMES

REASSURE   *v* -SURED, -SURING, -SURES

REATTACH   *v* -ED, -ING, -ES

REATTACK   *v* -ED, -ING, -S

REATTAIN   *v* -ED, -ING, -S

REAVAIL   *v* -ED, -ING, -S

REAVOW   *v* -ED, -ING, -S

REAWAKE   *v* -AWAKED or -AWOKE, -AWOKEN, -AWAKING, -AWAKES

REAWAKEN   *v* -ED, -ING, -S

REBAIT   *v* -ED, -ING, -S

REBEGIN   *v* -GAN, -GUN, -GINNING, -GINS

REBID   *v* -BID, -BIDDEN, -BIDDING, -BIDS

REBILL   *v* -ED, -ING, -S

REBIND   *v* -BOUND, -BINDING, -BINDS

REBLEND   *v* -ED, -ING, -S

REBLOOM   *v* -ED, -ING, -S

REBOARD   *v* -ED, -ING, -S

REBODY   *v* -BODIED, -BODYING, -BODIES

REBOIL   *v* -ED, -ING, -S

REBOOK   *v* -ED, -ING, -S

REBOOT   *v* -ED, -ING, -S

REBORE   *v* -BORED, -BORING, -BORES

REBOTTLE   *v* -TLED, -TLING, -TLES

REBOUGHT   past tense of rebuy

REBOUND   past tense of rebind

REBREED   *v* -BRED, -BREEDING, -BREEDS

REBUILD   v -BUILT or -BUILDED,
-BUILDING, -BUILDS

REBURY   v -BURIED, -BURYING,
-BURIES

REBUTTON   v -ED, -ING, -S

REBUY   v -BOUGHT, -BUYING,
-BUYS

RECANE   v -CANED, -CANING,
-CANES

RECARRY   v -RIED, -RYING, -RIES

RECAST   v -CAST, -CASTING, -CASTS

RECHANGE   v -CHANGED, -CHANGING,
-CHANGES

RECHARGE   v -CHARGED, -CHARGING,
-CHARGES

RECHART   v -ED, -ING, -S

RECHECK   v -ED, -ING, -S

RECHEW   v -ED, -ING, -S

RECHOOSE   v -CHOSE, -CHOSEN,
-CHOOSING, -CHOOSES

RECIRCLE   v -CLED, -CLING, -CLES

RECLAD   a past tense of reclothe

RECLASP   v -ED, -ING, -S

RECLEAN   v -ED, -ING, -S

RECLOTHE   v -CLOTHED or -CLAD,
-CLOTHING, -CLOTHES

RECOAL   v -ED, -ING, -S

RECOCK   v -ED, -ING, -S

RECODE   v -CODED, -CODING,
-CODES

RECODIFY   v -FIED, -FYING, -FIES

RECOIN   v -ED, -ING, -S

RECOLOR   v -ED, -ING, -S

RECOMB   v -ED, -ING, -S

RECOMMIT   v -MITTED, -MITTING, -MITS

RECOOK   v -ED, -ING, -S

RECOPY   v -COPIED, -COPYING,
-COPIES

RECORK   v -ED, -ING, -S

RECOUPLE   v -PLED, -PLING, -PLES

RECRATE   v -CRATED, -CRATING,
-CRATES

RECROSS   v -ED, -ING, -ES

RECROWN   v -ED, -ING, -S

RECUT   v -CUT, -CUTTING, -CUTS

REDAMAGE   v -AGED, -AGING, -AGES

REDATE   v -DATED, -DATING, -DATES

REDECIDE   v -CIDED, -CIDING, -CIDES

REDEFEAT   v -ED, -ING, -S

REDEFECT   v -ED, -ING, -S

REDEFINE   v -FINED, -FINING, -FINES

REDEFY   v -FIED, -FYING, -FIES

REDEMAND   v -ED, -ING, -S

REDENY   v -NIED, -NYING, -NIES

REDEPLOY   v -ED, -ING, -S

REDESIGN   v -ED, -ING, -S

REDIAL   v -DIALED, -DIALING,
-DIALS or -DIALLED,
-DIALLING, -DIALS

REDID   past tense of redo

REDIGEST   v -ED, -ING, -S

REDIP   v -DIPPED or -DIPT,
-DIPPING, -DIPS

REDIVIDE   v -VIDED, -VIDING, -VIDES

REDO   v -DID, -DONE, -DOING,
-DOES

REDOCK   v -ED, -ING, -S

REDON   v -DONNED, -DONNING,
DONS

REDONE   past participle of redo

REDRAW   v -DREW, -DRAWN,
-DRAWING, -DRAWS

REDREAM   v -DREAMED or -DREAMT,
-DREAMING, -DREAMS

REDRIED   past tense of redry

REDRIES   present 3d person sing. of
redry

REDRILL   v -ED, -ING, -S

REDRIVE   v -DROVE, -DRIVEN,
-DRIVING, -DRIVES

REDRY   v -DRIED, -DRYING, -DRIES

REDUB   v -DUBBED, -DUBBING,
-DUBS

REDYE   v -DYED, -DYEING, -DYES

REEARN   v -ED, -ING, -S

REECHO   v -ED, -ING, -ES

REEDIT   v -ED, -ING, -S

REEJECT   v -ED, -ING, -S

REELECT   v -ED, -ING, -S

REEMBARK   v -ED, -ING, -S

REEMBODY   v -BODIED, -BODYING,
-BODIES

REEMERGE   v -EMERGED, -EMERGING,
-EMERGES

REEMIT   v -EMITTED, -EMITTING,
-EMITS

REEMPLOY   v -ED, -ING, -S

REENACT   v -ED, -ING, -S

REENDOW   v -ED, -ING, -S

REENGAGE   v -GAGED, -GAGING,
-GAGES

REENJOY   v -ED, -ING, -S

REENLIST   v -ED, -ING, -S

REENROLL   v -ED, -ING, -S

REENTER   v -ED, -ING, -S

REEQUIP   v -EQUIPPED, -EQUIPPING,
-EQUIPS

REERECT   v -ED, -ING, -S

REEVOKE   v -EVOKED, -EVOKING,
-EVOKES

REEXPEL   v -PELLED, -PELLING, -PELS

REEXPORT   v -ED, -ING, -S

REEXPOSE v -POSED, -POSING, -POSES

REFALL v -FELL, -FALLEN, -FALLING, -FALL

REFASTEN v -ED, -ING, -S

REFEED v -FED, -FEEDING, -FEEDS

REFEEL v -FELT, -FEELING, -FEELS

REFELL past tense of refall

REFENCE v -FENCED, -FENCING, -FENCES

REFIGHT v -FOUGHT, -FIGHTING, -FIGHTS

REFIGURE v -URED, -URING, -URES

REFILE v -FILED, -FILING, -FILES

REFILL v -ED, -ING, -S

REFILM v -ED, -ING, -S

REFILTER v -ED, -ING, -S

REFIND v -FOUND, -FINDING, -FINDS

REFIRE v -FIRED, -FIRING, -FIRES

REFIX v -ED, -ING, -ES

REFLEW past tense of refly

REFLIES present 3d person sing. of refly

REFLOAT v -ED, -ING, -S

REFLOOD v -ED, -ING, -S

REFLOW v -ED, -ING, -S

REFLOWER v -ED, -ING, -S

REFLY v -FLEW, -FLOWN, -FLYING, -FLIES

REFOCUS v -CUSED, -CUSING, -CUSES or -CUSSED, -CUSSING, -CUSSES

REFOLD v -ED, -ING, -S

REFORGE v -FORGED, -FORGING, -FORGES

REFORMAT v -MATTED, -MATTING, -MATS

REFOUGHT past tense of refight

REFOUND v -ED, -ING, -S

REFRAME v -FRAMED, -FRAMING, -FRAMES

REFREEZE v -FROZE, -FROZEN, -FREEZING, -FREEZES

REFRONT v -ED, -ING, -S

REFRY v -FRIED, -FRYING, -FRIES

REFUEL v -ELED, -ELING, -ELS or -ELLED, -ELLING, -ELS

REGAIN v -ED, -ING, -S

REGATHER v -ED, -ING, -S

REGAUGE v -GAUGED, -GAUGING, -GAUGES

REGAVE past tense of regive

REGEAR v -ED, -ING, -S

REGILD v -GILDED or -GILT, -GILDING, -GILDS

REGIVE v -GAVE, -GIVEN, -GIVING, -GIVES

REGLAZE v -GLAZED, -GLAZING, -GLAZES

REGLOSS v -ED, -ING, -ES

REGLOW v -ED, -ING, -S

REGLUE v -GLUED, -GLUING, -GLUES

REGRADE v -GRADED, -GRADING, -GRADES

REGRAFT v -ED, -ING, -S

REGRANT v -ED, -ING, -S

REGREEN v -ED, -ING, -S

REGREW past tense of regrow

REGRIND v -GROUND, -GRINDING, -GRINDS

REGROOM v -ED, -ING, -S

REGROOVE v -GROOVED, -GROOVING, -GROOVES

REGROUND past tense of regrind

REGROUP v -ED, -ING, -S

REGROW v -GREW, -GROWN, -GROWING, -GROWS

REHAMMER v -ED, -ING, -S

REHANDLE v -DLED, -DLING, -DLES

REHANG v -HUNG or -HANGED, -HANGING, -HANGS

REHARDEN v -ED, -ING, -S

REHASH v -ED, -ING, -ES

REHEAR v -HEARD, -HEARING, -HEARS

REHEAT v -ED, -ING, -S

REHEEL v -ED, -ING, -S

REHEM v -HEMMED, -HEMMING, -HEMS

REHINGE v -HINGED, -HINGING, -HINGES

REHIRE v -HIRED, -HIRING, -HIRES

REHUNG a past tense of rehang

REIGNITE v -NITED, -NITING, -NITES

REIMAGE v -AGED, -AGING, -AGES

REIMPORT v -ED, -ING, -S

REIMPOSE v -POSED, -POSING, -POSES

REINCITE v -CITED, -CITING, -CITES

REINCUR v -CURRED, -CURRING, -CURS

REINDEX v -ED, -ING, -ES

REINDICT v -ED, -ING, -S

REINDUCE v -DUCED, -DUCING, -DUCES

REINDUCT v -ED, -ING, -S

REINFECT v -ED, -ING, -S

REINFORM v -ED, -ING, -S

REINFUSE v -FUSED, -FUSING, -FUSES

REINJECT v -ED, -ING, -S

REINJURE v -JURED, -JURING, -JURES

REINK v -ED, -ING, -S

REINSERT v -ED, -ING, -S

REINSURE	v -SURED, -SURING, -SURES
REINTER	v -TERRED, -TERRING, -TERS
REINVADE	v -VADED, -VADING, -VADES
REINVENT	v -ED, -ING, -S
REINVEST	v -ED, -ING, -S
REINVITE	v -VITED, -VITING, -VITES
REINVOKE	v -VOKED, -VOKING, -VOKES
REISSUE	v -SUED, -SUING, -SUES
REJACKET	v -ED, -ING, -S
REJOIN	v -ED, -ING, -S
REJUDGE	v -JUDGED, -JUDGING, -JUDGES
REJUGGLE	v -GLED, -GLING, -GLES
REKEY	v -ED, -ING, -S
REKINDLE	v -DLED, -DLING, -DLES
REKNIT	v -KNITTED, -KNITTING, -KNITS
RELABEL	v -BELED, -BELING, -BELS or -BELLED, -BELLING, -BELS
RELACE	v -LACED, -LACING, -LACES
RELAUNCH	v -ED, -ING, -ES
RELAY	v -LAID, -LAYING, -LAYS
RELEARN	v -LEARNED or -LEARNT, -LEARNING, -LEARNS
RELEND	v -LENT, -LENDING, -LENDS
RELET	v -LET, -LETTING, -LETS
RELETTER	v -ED, -ING, -S
RELIGHT	v -LIGHTED or -LIT, -LIGHTING, -LIGHTS
RELINE	v -LINED, -LINING, -LINES
RELINK	v -ED, -ING, -S
RELIST	v -ED, -ING, -S
RELIT	a past tense of relight
RELOAD	v -ED, -ING, -S
RELOAN	v -ED, -ING, -S
RELOCK	v -ED, -ING, -S
RELOOK	v -ED, -ING, -S
REMAIL	v -ED, -ING, -S
REMAKE	v -MADE, -MAKING, -MAKES
REMAP	v -MAPPED, -MAPPING, -MAPS
REMARKET	v -ED, -ING, -S
REMARRY	v -RIED, -RYING, -RIES
REMASTER	v -ED, -ING, -S
REMATCH	v -ED, -ING, -ES
REMATE	v -MATED, -MATING, -MATES
REMEET	v -MET, -MEETING, -MEETS
REMELT	v -ED, -ING, -S
REMEND	v -ED, -ING, -S
REMERGE	v -MERGED, -MERGING, -MERGES
REMET	past tense of remeet
REMET	past tense of remeet
REMIX	v -MIXED or -MIXT, -MIXING, -MIXES
REMODIFY	v -FIED, -FYING, -FIES
REMOLD	v -ED, -ING, -S
REMOUNT	v -ED, -ING, -S
RENAIL	v -ED, -ING, -S
RENAME	v -NAMED, -NAMING, -NAMES
RENEST	v -ED, -ING, -S
RENOTIFY	v -FIED, -FYING, -FIES
RENUMBER	v -ED, -ING, -S
REOBJECT	v -ED, -ING, -S
REOBTAIN	v -ED, -ING, -S
REOCCUPY	v -PIED, -PYING, -PIES
REOCCUR	v -CURRED, -CURRING, -CURS
REOIL	v -ED, -ING, -S
REOPEN	v -ED, -ING, -S
REOPPOSE	v -POSED, -POSING, -POSES
REORDAIN	v -ED, -ING, -S
REORDER	v -ED, -ING, -S
REORIENT	v -ED, -ING, -S
REOUTFIT	v -FITTED, -FITTING, -FITS
REPACIFY	v -FIED, -FYING, -FIES
REPACK	v -ED, -ING, -S
REPAINT	v -ED, -ING, -S
REPANEL	v -ELED, -ELING, -ELS or -ELLED, -ELLING, -ELS
REPAPER	v -ED, -ING, -S
REPARK	v -ED, -ING, -S
REPASS	v -ED, -ING, -ES
REPATCH	v -ED, -ING, -ES
REPAVE	v -PAVED, -PAVING, -PAVES
REPEG	v -PEGGED, -PEGGING, -PEGS
REPEOPLE	v -PLED, -PLING, -PLES
REPERK	v -ED, -ING, -S
REPHRASE	v -PHRASED, -PHRASING, PHRASES
REPIN	v -PINNED, -PINNING, -PINS
REPLAN	v -PLANNED, -PLANNING, -PLANS
REPLANT	v -ED, -ING, -S
REPLATE	v -PLATED, -PLATING -PLATES
REPLAY	v -ED, -ING, -S
REPLEAD	v -PLEADED or -PLED, -PLEADING, -PLEADS
REPLEDGE	v -PLEDGED, -PLEDGING, -PLEDGES
REPLOT	v -PLOTTED, -PLOTTING, -PLOTS
REPLUMB	v -ED, -ING, -S

REPLUNGE	v -PLUNGED, -PLUNGING, -PLUNGES
REPOLISH	v -ED, -ING, -ES
REPOLL	v -ED, -ING, -S
REPOT	v -POTTED, -POTTING, -POTS
REPOUR	v -ED, -ING, -S
REPOWER	v -ED, -ING, -S
REPRICE	v -PRICED, -PRICING, -PRICES
REPRINT	v -ED, -ING, -S
REPROBE	v -PROBED, -PROBING, -PROBES
REPUMP	v -ED, -ING, -S
REPURIFY	v -FIED, -FYING, -FIES
REPURSUE	v -SUED, -SUING, -SUES
RERACK	v -ED, -ING, -S
RERAISE	v -RAISED, -RAISING, -RAISES
REREAD	v -READ, -READING, -READS
RERECORD	v -ED, -ING, -S
REREMIND	v -ED, -ING, -S
REREPEAT	v -ED, -ING, -S
REREVIEW	v -ED, -ING, -S
RERIG	v -RIGGED, -RIGGING, -RIGS
RERISE	v -ROSE, -RISEN, -RISING, -RISES
REROLL	v -ED, -ING, -S
REROOF	v -ED, -ING, -S
REROSE	past tense of rerise
REROUTE	v -ROUTED, -ROUTING, -ROUTES
RESADDLE	v -DLED, -DLING, -DLES
RESAID	past tense of resay
RESAIL	v -ED, -ING, -S
RESALUTE	v -LUTED, -LUTING, -LUTES
RESAMPLE	v -PLED, -PLING, -PLES
RESAW	v -SAWED, -SAWN, -SAWING, -SAWS
RESAY	v -SAID, -SAYING, -SAYS
RESCHOOL	v -ED, -ING, -S
RESCORE	v -SCORED, -SCORING, -SCORES
RESCREEN	v -ED, -ING, -S
RESCULPT	v -ED, -ING, -S
RESEAL	v -ED, -ING, -S
RESEASON	v -ED, -ING, -S
RESEAT	v -ED, -ING, -S
RESECURE	v -CURED, -CURING, -CURES
RESEE	v -SAW, -SEEN, -SEEING, -SEES
RESEED	v -ED, -ING, -S
RESEEK	v -SOUGHT, -SEEKING, -SEEKS
RESEEN	past participle of resee
RESEIZE	v -SEIZED, -SEIZING, -SEIZES
RESELL	v -SOLD, -SELLING, -SELLS
RESEND	v -SENT, -SENDING, -SENDS
RESET	v -SET, -SETTING, -SETS
RESETTLE	v -TLED, -TLING, -TLES
RESEW	v -SEWED, -SEWN, -SEWING, -SEWS
RESHAPE	v -SHAPED, -SHAPING, -SHAPES
RESHAVE	v -SHAVED, -SHAVEN, -SHAVING, -SHAVES
RESHINE	v -SHONE or -SHINED, -SHINING, -SHINES
RESHIP	v -SHIPPED, -SHIPPING, -SHIPS
RESHOE	v -SHOD, -SHOEING, -SHOES
RESHONE	a past tense of reshine
RESHOOT	v -SHOT, -SHOOTING, -SHOOTS
RESHOW	v -SHOWED, -SHOWN, -SHOWING, -SHOWS
RESIFT	v -ED, -ING, -S
RESIGHT	v -ED, -ING, -S
RESILVER	v -ED, -ING, -S
RESITE	v -SITED, -SITING, -SITES
RESIZE	v -SIZED, -SIZING, -SIZES
RESKETCH	v -ED, -ING, -ES
RESLATE	v -SLATED, -SLATING, -SLATES
RESMELT	v -ED, -ING, -S
RESMOOTH	v -ED, -ING, -S
RESOAK	v -ED, -ING, -S
RESOD	v -SODDED, -SODDING, -SODS
RESOLD	past tense of resell
RESOLDER	v -ED, -ING, -S
RESOLE	v -SOLED, -SOLING, -SOLES
RESOUGHT	past tense of reseek
RESOW	v -SOWED, -SOWN, -SOWING, -SOWS
RESPACE	v -SPACED, -SPACING, -SPACES
RESPADE	v -SPADED, -SPADING, -SPADES
RESPEAK	v -SPOKE, -SPOKEN, -SPEAKING, -SPEAKS
RESPELL	v -SPELLED or -SPELT, -SPELLING, -SPELLS
RESPLICE	v -SPLICED, -SPLICING, -SPLICES

RESPLIT	v -SPLIT, -SPLITTING, -SPLITS
RESPOKE	past tense of respeak
RESPOKEN	past participle of respeak
RESPOT	v -SPOTTED, -SPOTTING, -SPOTS
RESPRANG	a past tense of respring
RESPRAY	v -ED, -ING, -S
RESPREAD	v -SPREAD, -SPREADING, -SPREADS
RESPRING	v -SPRANG or -SPRUNG, -SPRINGING, -SPRINGS
RESPROUT	v -ED, -ING, -S
RESTACK	v -ED, -ING, -S
RESTAFF	v -ED, -ING, -S
RESTAGE	v -STAGED, -STAGING, -STAGES
RESTAMP	v -ED, -ING, -S
RESTART	v -ED, -ING, -S
RESTATE	v -STATED, -STATING, -STATES
RESTITCH	v -ED, -ING, -ES
RESTOCK	v -ED, -ING, -S
RESTOKE	v -STOKED, -STOKING, -STOKES
RESTRESS	v -ED, -ING, -ES
RESTRIKE	v -STRUCK, -STRICKEN, -STRIKING, -STRIKES
RESTRING	v -STRUNG, -STRINGING, -STRINGS
RESTRIVE	v -STROVE, -STRIVEN, -STRIVING, -STRIVES
RESTRUCK	past tense of restrike
RESTRUNG	past tense of restring
RESTUDY	v -STUDIED, -STUDYING, -STUDIES
RESTUFF	v -ED, -ING, -S
RESTYLE	v -STYLED, -STYLING, -STYLES
RESUBMIT	v -MITTED, -MITTING, -MITS
RESUMMON	v -ED, -ING, -S
RESUPPLY	v -PLIED, -PLYING, -PLIES
RESURVEY	v -ED, -ING, -S
RETACK	v -ED, -ING, -S
RETACKLE	v -LED, -LING, -LES
RETAG	v -TAGGED, -TAGGING, -TAGS
RETAILOR	v -ED, -ING, -S
RETAPE	v -TAPED, -TAPING, -TAPES
RETARGET	v -ED, -ING, -S
RETASTE	v -TASTED, -TASTING, -TASTES
RETAX	v -ED, -ING, -ES
RETEACH	v -TAUGHT, -TEACHING, -TEACHES
RETEAM	v -ED, -ING, -S
RETEAR	v -TORE, -TORN, -TEARING, -TEARS
RETELL	v -TOLD, -TELLING, -TELLS
RETEMPER	v -ED, -ING, -S
RETEST	v -ED, -ING, -S
RETHINK	v -THOUGHT, -THINKING, -THINKS
RETHREAD	v -ED, -ING, -S
RETIE	v -TIED, -TYING, -TIES
RETILE	v -TILED, -TILING, -TILES
RETIME	v -TIMED, -TIMING, -TIMES
RETINT	v -ED, -ING, -S
RETITLE	v -TLED, -TLING, -TLES
RETOLD	past tense of retell
RETORE	past tense of retear
RETORN	past participle of retear
RETRACK	v -ED, -ING, -S
RETRAIN	v -ED, -ING, -S
RETRIM	v -TRIMMED, -TRIMMING, -TRIMS
RETRY	v -TRIED, -TRYING, -TRIES
RETUNE	v -TUNED, -TUNING, -TUNES
RETWIST	v -ED, -ING, -S
RETYING	present participle of retie
RETYPE	v -TYPED, -TYPING, -TYPES
REUNIFY	v -FIED, -FYING, -FIES
REUNITE	v -UNITED, -UNITING, -UNITES
REUSE	v -USED, -USING, -USES
REUTTER	v -ED, -ING, -S
REVALUE	v -UED, -UING, -UES
REVERIFY	v -FIED, -FYING, -FIES
REVEST	v -ED, -ING, -S
REVIEW	v -ED, -ING, -S
REVISIT	v -ED, -ING, -S
REVOICE	v -VOICED, -VOICING, -VOICES
REVOTE	v -VOTED, -VOTING, -VOTES
REWAKE	v -WAKED or -WOKE, -WOKEN, -WAKING, -WAKES
REWAKEN	v -ED, -ING, -S
REWAN	a past tense of rewin
REWARM	v -ED, -ING, -S
REWASH	v -ED, -ING, -ES
REWAX	v -ED, -ING, -ES
REWEAVE	v -WOVE or -WEAVED, -WOVEN, -WEAVING, -WEAVES
REWED	v -WEDDED, -WEDDING, -WEDS
REWEIGH	v -ED, -ING, -S
REWELD	v -ED, -ING, -S
REWET	v -WETTED, -WETTING, -WETS
REWIDEN	v -ED, -ING, -S

REWIN	v -WON or -WAN, -WINNING, -WINS	**REAGIN**	n pl. -S a type of antibody **REAGINIC** adj
REWIND	v -WOUND or -WINDED, -WINDING, -WINDS	**REAL**	adj REALER, REALEST having actual existence
REWIRE	v -WIRED, -WIRING, -WIRES	**REAL**	n pl. -S or -ES a former
REWOKE	a past tense of rewake		monetary unit of Spain
REWOKEN	past participle of rewake	**REAL**	n pl. REIS a former monetary
REWON	a past tense of rewin		unit of Portugal and Brazil
REWORK	v -WORKED or -WROUGHT, -WORKING, -WORKS	**REALGAR**	n pl. -S a mineral
		REALIA	n/pl objects used by a teacher
REWOUND	a past tense of rewind		to illustrate everyday living
REWOVE	a past tense of reweave	**REALISE**	v -ISED, -ISING, -ISES to
REWOVEN	past participle of reweave		realize
REWRAP	v -WRAPPED, or -WRAPT, -WRAPPING, -WRAPS	**REALISER**	n pl. -S one that realises
		REALISM	n pl. -S concern with fact or
REWRITE	v -WROTE, -WRITTEN, -WRITING, -WRITES		reality
		REALIST	n pl. -S one who is concerned
REWROUGHT a past tense of rework		with fact or reality
REZONE	v -ZONED, -ZONING, -ZONES	**REALITY**	n pl. -TIES something that is real
		REALIZE	v -IZED, -IZING, -IZES to understand completely
		REALIZER	n pl. -S one that realizes
REACH	v -ED, -ING, -ES to stretch out or put forth	**REALLY**	adv actually
		REALM	n pl. -S a kingdom
REACHER	n pl. -S one that reaches	**REALNESS**	n pl. -ES the state of being
REACT	v -ED, -ING, -S to respond to a stimulus		real
		REALTY	n pl. -TIES property in
REACTANT	n pl. -S one that reacts		buildings and land
REACTION	n pl. -S the act of reacting	**REAM**	v -ED, -ING, -S to enlarge with
REACTIVE	adj tending to react		a reamer
REACTOR	n pl. -S one that reacts	**REAMER**	n pl. -S a tool used to enlarge
READ	v READ, READING, READS to look at so as to take in the meaning of, as something written or printed **READABLE** adj **READABLY** adv		holes
		REAP	v -ED, -ING, -S to cut for harvest **REAPABLE** adj
		REAPER	n pl. -S one that reaps
		REAPHOOK	n pl. -S an implement used in reaping
READER	n pl. -S one that reads		
READERLY	adj typical of a reader	**REAR**	v -ED, -ING, -S to lift upright
READIED	past tense of ready	**REARER**	n pl. -S one that rears
READIER	comparative of ready	**REARMICE**	n/pl reremice
READIES	present 3d person sing. of ready	**REARMOST**	adj coming or situated last
		REARWARD	n pl. -S the rearmost division
READIEST	superlative of ready		of an army
READILY	adv in a ready manner	**REASCENT**	n pl. -S a new or second
READING	n pl. -S material that is read		ascent
READOUT	n pl. -S a presentation of computer data	**REASON**	v -ED, -ING, -S to derive inferences or conclusions from known or presumed facts
READY	adj READIER, READIEST prepared		
		REASONER	n pl. -S one that reasons
READY	v READIED, READYING, READIES to make ready	**REATA**	n pl. -S riata
		REAVE	v REAVED or REFT, -REAVING, REAVES to plunder
REAGENT	n pl. -S a substance used in a chemical reaction to ascertain the nature or composition of another		
		REAVER	n pl. -S one that reaves
		REB	n pl. -S a Confederate soldier

REBAR n pl. -S a steel rod for use in reinforced concrete

REBATE v -BATED, -BATING, -BATES to deduct or return from a payment or bill

REBATER n pl. -S one that rebates

REBATO n pl. -TOS rabato

REBBE n pl. -S a rabbi

REBEC n pl. -S an ancient stringed instrument

REBECK n pl. -S rebec

REBEL v -BELLED, -BELLING, -BELS to oppose the established government of one's land

REBELDOM n pl. -S an area controlled by rebels

REBIRTH n pl. -S a new or second birth

REBOANT adj resounding loudly

REBOP n pl. -S a type of music

REBORN adj born again

REBOUND v -ED, -ING, -S to spring back

REBOZO n pl. -ZOS a long scarf

REBRANCH v -ED, -ING, -ES to form secondary branches

REBUFF v -ED, -ING, -S to reject or refuse curtly

REBUKE v -BUKED, -BUKING, -BUKES to criticize sharply

REBUKER n pl. -S one that rebukes

REBURIAL n pl. -S a second burial

REBUS n pl. -ES a type of puzzle

REBUT v -BUTTED, -BUTTING, -BUTS to refute

REBUTTAL n pl. -S argument or proof that rebuts

REBUTTER n pl. -S one that rebuts

REBUTTING present participle of rebut

REC n pl. -S recreation

RECALL v -ED, -ING, -S to call back

RECALLER n pl. -S one that recalls

RECAMIER n pl. -S a backless couch

RECANT v -ED, -ING, -S to make a formal retraction or disavowal of

RECANTER n pl. -S one that recants

RECAP v -CAPPED, -CAPPING, -CAPS to review by a brief summary

RECCE n pl. -S a recon

RECEDE v -CEDED, -CEDING, -CEDES to move back or away

RECEIPT v -ED, -ING, -S to mark as having been paid

RECEIVE v -CEIVED, -CEIVING, -CEIVES to come into possession of

RECEIVER n pl. -S one that receives

RECENCY n pl. -CIES the state of being recent

RECENT adj -CENTER, -CENTEST of or pertaining to a time not long past **RECENTLY** adv

RECEPT n pl. -S a type of mental image

RECEPTOR n pl. -S a nerve ending specialized to receive stimuli

RECESS v -ED, -ING, -ES to place in a receding space or hollow

RECHEAT n pl. -S a hunting call

RECIPE n pl. -S a set of instructions for making something

RECISION n pl. -S a cancellation

RECITAL n pl. -S a detailed account

RECITE v -CITED, -CITING, -CITES to declaim or say from memory

RECITER n pl. -S one that recites

RECK v -ED, -ING, -S to be concerned about

RECKLESS adj foolishly heedless of danger

RECKON v -ED, -ING, -S to count or compute

RECKONER n pl. -S one that reckons

RECLAIM v -ED, -ING, -S to make suitable for cultivation or habitation

RECLAME n pl. -S publicity

RECLINE v -CLINED, -CLINING, -CLINES to lean or lie back

RECLINER n pl. -S one that reclines

RECLUSE n pl. -S one who lives in solitude and seclusion

RECOIL v -ED, -ING, -S to draw back in fear or disgust

RECOILER n pl. -S one that recoils

RECON n pl. -S a preliminary survey

RECONVEY v -ED, -ING, -S to convey back to a previous position

RECORD v -ED, -ING, -S to set down for preservation

RECORDER n pl. -S one that records

RECOUNT v -ED, -ING, -S to relate in detail

RECOUP v -ED, -ING, -S to get back the equivalent of

RECOUPE adj divided twice

RECOURSE n pl. -S a turning or applying to someone or something for aid

RECOVER v -ED, -ING, -S to obtain again after losing

RECOVERY   *n* pl. -ERIES an economic upturn

RECREANT   *n* pl. -S a coward

RECREATE   *v* -ATED, -ATING, -ATES to refresh mentally or physically

RECRUIT   *v* -ED, -ING, -S to engage for military service

RECTA   a pl. of rectum

RECTAL   *adj* pertaining to the rectum **RECTALLY** *adv*

RECTI   pl. of rectus

RECTIFY   *v* -FIED, -FYING, -FIES to correct

RECTO   *n* pl. -TOS a right-hand page of a book

RECTOR   *n* pl. -S a clergyman in charge of a parish

RECTORY   *n* pl. -RIES a rector's dwelling

RECTRIX   *n* pl. -TRICES a feather of a bird's tail

RECTUM   *n* pl. -TUMS or -TA the terminal portion of the large intestine

RECTUS   *n* pl. -TI a straight muscle

RECUR   *v* -CURRED, -CURRING, -CURS to happen again

RECURVE   *v* -CURVED, -CURVING, -CURVES to curve backward or downward

RECUSAL   *n* pl. -S the act of recusing

RECUSANT   *n* pl. -S one who refuses to accept established authority

RECUSE   *v* -CUSED, -CUSING, -CUSES to disqualify or challenge as judge in a particular case

RECYCLE   *v* -CLED, -CLING, -CLES to process in order to extract useful materials

RECYCLER   *n* pl. -S one that recycles

RED   *adj* REDDER, REDDEST of the color of blood

RED   *v* REDDED, REDDING, REDS to redd

REDACT   *v* -ED, -ING, -S to prepare for publication

REDACTOR   *n* pl. -S one that redacts

REDAN   *n* pl. -S a type of fortification

REDARGUE   *v* -GUED, -GUING, -GUES to disprove

REDBAIT   *v* -ED, -ING, -S to denounce as Communist

REDBAY   *n* pl. -BAYS a small tree

REDBIRD   *n* pl. -S a bird with red plummage

REDBONE   *n* pl. -S a hunting dog

REDBRICK   *n* pl. -S a modern British university

REDBUD   *n* pl. -S a small tree

REDBUG   *n* pl. -S a chigger

REDCAP   *n* pl. -S a porter

REDCOAT   *n* pl. -S a British soldier during the American Revolution

REDD   *v* -ED, -ING, -S to put in order

REDDED   past tense of red and redd

REDDEN   *v* -ED, -ING, -S to make or become red

REDDER   *n* pl. -S one that redds

REDDEST   superlative of red

REDDING   present participle of red and redd

REDDISH   *adj* somewhat red

REDDLE   *v* -DLED, -DLING, -DLES to ruddle

REDE   *v* REDED, REDING, REDES to advise

REDEAR   *n* pl. -S a common sunfish

REDEEM   *v* -ED, -ING, -S to buy back

REDEEMER   *n* pl. -S one that redeems

REDEYE   *n* pl. -S a railroad danger signal

REDFIN   *n* pl. -S a freshwater fish

REDFISH   *n* pl. -ES an edible rockfish

REDHEAD   *n* pl. -S a person with red hair

REDHORSE   *n* pl. -S a freshwater fish

REDIA   *n* pl. -DIAE or -DIAS the larva of certain flatworms **REDIAL** *adj*

REDING   present participle of rede

REDIRECT   *v* -ED, -ING, -S to change the course or direction of

REDLEG   *n* pl. -S a bird with red legs

REDLINE   *v* -LINED, -LINING, -LINES to withhold loans or insurance from certain neighborhoods

REDLY   *adv* with red color

REDNESS   *n* pl. -ES the state of being red

REDO   *n* pl. -DOS something that is done again

REDOLENT   *adj* fragrant

REDOUBLE   *v* -BLED, -BLING, -BLES to double

REDOUBT   *n* pl. -S an enclosed fortification

REDOUND   *v* -ED, -ING, -S to have an effect or consequence

REDOUT   *n* pl. -S a condition in which blood is driven to the head

REDOWA   *n* pl. -S a lively dance

REDOX   *n* pl. -ES a type of chemical reaction

REDPOLL *n* pl. -S a small finch

REDRAFT *v* -ED, -ING, -S to make a revised copy of

REDRAWER *n* pl. -S one that redraws

REDRESS *v* -ED, -ING, -ES to set right

REDROOT *n* pl. -S a perennial herb

REDSHANK *n* pl. -S a shore bird

REDSHIFT *n* pl. -S a displacement of the spectrum of a celestial body toward the longer wavelengths

REDSHIRT *v* -ED, -ING, -S to keep a college athlete out of varsity play in order to extend his eligibility

REDSTART *n* pl. -S a small songbird

REDTOP *n* pl. -S a type of grass

REDUCE *v* -DUCED, -DUCING, -DUCES to diminish

REDUCER *n* pl. -S one that reduces

REDUCTOR *n* pl. -S an apparatus for the reduction of metallic ions in solution

REDUVIID *n* pl. -S a bloodsucking insect

REDUX *adj* brought back

REDWARE *n* pl. -S an edible seaweed

REDWING *n* pl. -S a European thrush

REDWOOD *n* pl. -S a very tall evergreen tree

REE *n* pl. -S the female Eurasian sandpiper

REECHY *adj* REECHIER, REECHIEST foul, rancid

REED *v* -ED, -ING, -S to fasten with reeds (the stalks of tall grasses)

REEDBIRD *n* pl. -S the bobolink

REEDBUCK *n* pl. -S an African antelope

REEDIER comparative of reedy

REEDIEST superlative of reedy

REEDIFY *v* -FIED, -FYING, -FIES to rebuild

REEDILY *adv* with a thin, piping sound

REEDING *n* pl. -S a convex molding

REEDLIKE *adj* resembling a reed

REEDLING *n* pl. -S a marsh bird

REEDMAN *n* pl. -MEN one who plays a reed instrument

REEDY *adj* REEDIER, REEDIEST abounding in reeds

REEF *v* -ED, -ING, -S to reduce the area of a sail **REEFABLE** *adj*

REEFER *n* pl. -S one that reefs

REEFY *adj* REEFIER, REEFIEST abounding in ridges of rock

REEK *v* -ED, -ING, -S to give off a strong, unpleasant odor

REEKER *n* pl. -S one that reeks

REEKY *adj* REEKIER, REEKIEST reeking

REEL *v* -ED, -ING, -S to wind on a type of rotary device **REELABLE** *adj*

REELER *n* pl. -S one that reels

REENTRY *n* pl. -TRIES a new or second entry

REEST *v* -ED, -ING, -S to balk

REEVE *v* REEVED or ROVE, ROVEN, REEVING, REEVES to fasten by passing through or around something

REF *v* REFFED, REFFING, REFS to referee

REFACE *v* -FACED, -FACING, -FACES to repair the outer surface of

REFECT *v* -ED, -ING, -S to refresh with food and drink

REFEL *v* -FELLED, -FELLING, -FELS to reject

REFER *v* -FERRED, -FERRING, -FERS to direct to a source for help or information

REFEREE *v* -EED, -EEING, -EES to supervise the play in certain sports

REFERENT *n* pl. -S something referred to

REFERRAL *n* pl. -S one that is referred

REFERRED past tense of refer

REFERRER *n* pl. -S one that refers

REFERRING present participle of refer

REFFED past tense of ref

REFFING present participle of ref

REFINE *v* -FINED, -FINING, -FINES to free from impurities

REFINER *n* pl. -S one that refines

REFINERY *n* pl. -ERIES a place where crude material is refined

REFINING present participle of refine

REFINISH *v* -ED, -ING, -ES to give a new surface to

REFIT *v* -FITTED, -FITTING, -FITS to prepare and equip for additional use

REFLATE *v* -FLATED, -FLATING, -FLATES to inflate again

REFLECT *v* -ED, -ING, -S to turn or throw back from a surface

REFLET *n* pl. -S special brilliance of surface

REFLEX *v* -ED, -ING, -ES to bend back

REFLEXLY *adv* in a reflexed manner

REFLUENT *adj* flowing back

REFLUX   *v* -ED, -ING, -ES to cause to flow back

REFOREST   *v* -ED, -ING, -S to replant with trees

REFORM   *v* -ED, -ING, -S to change to a better state

REFORMER   *n* pl. -S one that reforms

REFRACT   *v* -ED, -ING, -S to deflect in a particular manner, as a ray of light

REFRAIN   *v* -ED, -ING, -S to keep oneself back

REFRESH   *v* -ED, -ING, -ES to restore the well-being and vigor of

REFT   a past tense of reave

REFUGE   *v* -UGED, -UGING, -UGES to give or take shelter

REFUGEE   *n* pl. -S one who flees for safety

REFUGIUM   *n* pl. -GIA a stable area during a period of continental climactic change

REFUND   *v* -ED, -ING, -S to give back

REFUNDER   *n* pl. -S one that refunds

REFUSAL   *n* pl. -S the act of refusing

REFUSE   *v* -FUSED, -FUSING, -FUSES to express oneself as unwilling to accept, do, or comply with

REFUSER   *n* pl. -S one that refuses

REFUSNIK   *n* pl. -S a Soviet citizen who is refused permission to emigrate

REFUTAL   *n* pl. -S the act of refuting

REFUTE   *v* -FUTED, -FUTING, -FUTES to prove to be false or erroneous

REFUTER   *n* pl. -S one that refutes

REG   *n* pl. -S a regulation

REGAINER   *n* pl. -S one that regains

REGAL   *adj* of or befitting a king

REGALE   *v* -GALED, -GALING, -GALES to delight

REGALER   *n* pl. -S one that regales

REGALIA   *n/pl* the rights and privileges of a king

REGALITY   *n* pl. -TIES regal authority

REGALLY   *adv* in a regal manner

REGARD   *v* -ED, -ING, -S to look upon with a particular feeling

REGATTA   *n* pl. -S a boat race

REGELATE   *v* -LATED, -LATING, -LATES to refreeze ice by reducing the pressure

REGENCY   *n* pl. -CIES the office of a regent

REGENT   *n* pl. -S one who rules in the place of a sovereign **REGENTAL** *adj*

REGES   pl. of rex

REGGAE   *n* pl. -S a form of popular Jamaican music

REGICIDE   *n* pl. -S the killing of a king

REGIME   *n* pl. -S a system of government

REGIMEN   *n* pl. -S a systematic plan

REGIMENT   *v* -ED, -ING, -S to form into military units

REGINA   *n* pl. -NAE or -NAS queen **REGINAL** *adj*

REGION   *n* pl. -S an administrative area or division

REGIONAL   *n* pl. -S something that serves as a region

REGISTER   *v* -ED, -ING, -S to record officially

REGISTRY   *n* pl. -TRIES the act of registering

REGIUS   *adj* holding a professorship founded by the sovereign

REGLET   *n* pl. -S a flat, narrow molding

REGMA   *n* pl. -MATA a type of fruit

REGNA   pl. of regnum

REGNAL   *adj* pertaining to a king or his reign

REGNANCY   *n* pl. -CIES the state of being regnant

REGNANT   *adj* reigning

REGNUM   *n* pl. -NA dominion

REGOLITH   *n* pl. -S a layer of loose rock

REGORGE   *v* -GORGED, -GORGING, -GORGES to vomit

REGOSOL   *n* pl. -S a type of soil

REGRATE   *v* -GRATED, -GRATING, -GRATES to buy up in order to sell for a higher price in the same area

REGREET   *v* -ED, -ING, -S to greet in return

REGRESS   *v* -ED, -ING, -ES to go back

REGRET   *v* -GRETTED, -GRETTING, -GRETS to look back upon with sorrow or remorse

REGROWTH   *n* pl. -S a new or second growth

REGULAR   *n* pl. -S an habitual customer

REGULATE   *v* -LATED, -LATING, -LATES to control according to rule

REGULUS   *n* pl. -LI or -LUSES a mass that forms beneath the slag in a furnace **REGULINE** *adj*

REHAB   *v* -HABBED, -HABBING, -HABS to restore to a good condition

REHABBER   *n* pl. -S one that rehabs

REHEARSE   *v* -HEARSED, -HEARSING, -HEARSES to practice in preparation for a public appearance

REHEATER   *n* pl. -S one that reheats

REHOBOAM   *n* pl. -S a wine bottle

REHOUSE   *v* -HOUSED, -HOUSING, -HOUSES to establish in a new housing unit

REI   *n* pl. -S an erroneous English form for a former Portuguese coin

REIF   *n* pl. -S robbery

REIFIER   *n* pl. -S one that reifies

REIFY   *v* -IFIED, -IFYING, -IFIES to regard as real or concrete

REIGN   *v* -ED, -ING, -S to exercise sovereign power

REIN   *v* -ED, -ING, -S to restrain

REINDEER   *n* pl. -S a large deer

REINJURY   *n* pl. -RIES a second injury

REINLESS   *adj* unrestrained

REINSMAN   *n* pl. -MEN a skilled rider of horses

REIS   pl. of real

REISSUER   *n* pl. -S one that reissues

REITBOK   *n* pl. -S the reedbuck

REIVE   *v* REIVED, REIVING, REIVES to plunder

REIVER   *n* pl. -S one that reives

REJECT   *v* -ED, -ING, -S to refuse to accept, consider, or make use of

REJECTEE   *n* pl. -S one that is rejected

REJECTER   *n* pl. -S one that rejects

REJECTOR   *n* pl. -S rejecter

REJIGGER   *v* -ED, -ING, -S to alter

REJOICE   *v* -JOICED, -JOICING, -JOICES to feel joyful

REJOICER   *n* pl. -S one that rejoices

RELAPSE   *v* -LAPSED, -LAPSING, -LAPSES to fall or slip back into a former state

RELAPSER   *n* pl. -S one that relapses

RELATE   *v* -LATED, -LATING, -LATES to give an account of

RELATER   *n* pl. -S one that relates

RELATION   *n* pl. -S a significant association between two or more things

RELATIVE   *n* pl. -S one who is connected with another by blood or marriage

RELATOR   *n* pl. -S relater

RELAX   *v* -ED, -ING, -ES to make less tense or rigid

RELAXANT   *n* pl. -S a drug that relieves muscular tension

RELAXER   *n* pl. -S one that relaxes

RELAXIN   *n* pl. -S a female hormone

RELAY   *v* -ED, -ING, -S to send along by using fresh sets to replace tired ones

RELEASE   *v* -LEASED, -LEASING, -LEASES to set free

RELEASER   *n* pl. -S one that releases

RELEGATE   *v* -GATED, -GATING, -GATES to assign

RELENT   *v* -ED, -ING, -S to become less severe

RELEVANT   *adj* pertaining to the matter at hand

RELEVE   *n* pl. -S a raising onto the toe in ballet

RELIABLE   *n* pl. -S one that can be relied on

RELIABLY   *adv* In a manner that can be relied on

RELIANCE   *n* pl. -S confident or trustful dependence

RELIANT   *adj* showing reliance

RELIC   *n* pl. -S a surviving memorial of something past

RELICT   *n* pl. -S an organism surviving in a changed environment

RELIED   past tense of rely

RELIEF   *n* pl. -S aid in the form of money or necessities

RELIER   *n* pl. -S one that relies

RELIES   present 3d person sing. of rely

RELIEVE   *v* -LIEVED, -LIEVING, -LIEVES to lessen or free from pain or discomfort

RELIEVER   *n* pl. -S one that relieves

RELIEVO   *n* pl. -VOS the projection of figures or forms from a flat background

RELIGION   *n* pl. -S the worship of a god or the supernatural

RELIQUE   *n* pl. -S relic

RELISH   *v* -ED, -ING, -ES to enjoy

RELIVE   *v* -LIVED, -LIVING, -LIVES to experience again

RELOADER   *n* pl. -S one that reloads

RELOCATE   *v* -CATED, -CATING, -CATES to establish in a new place

RELUCENT *adj* reflecting light

RELUCT *v* -ED, -ING, -S to show opposition

RELUME *v* -LUMED, -LUMING, -LUMES to light again

RELUMINE *v* -MINED, -MINING, -MINES to relume

RELY *v* -LIED, -LYING, -LIES to place trust or confidence

REM *n* pl. -S a quantity of ionizing radiation

REMAIN *v* -ED, -ING, -S to continue in the same state

REMAKER *n* pl. -S one that remakes

REMAN *v* -MANNED, -MANNING, -MANS to furnish with a fresh supply of men

REMAND *v* -ED, -ING, -S to send back

REMANENT *adj* remaining

REMANNED past tense of reman

REMANNING present participle of reman

REMARK *v* -ED, -ING, -S to say or write briefly or casually

REMARKER *n* pl. -S one that remarks

REMARQUE *n* pl. -S a mark made in the margin of an engraved plate

REMEDIAL *adj* intended to correct something

REMEDY *v* -DIED, -DYING, -DIES to relieve or cure

REMEMBER *v* -ED, -ING, -S to bring to mind again

REMEX *n* pl. REMIGES a flight feather of a bird's wing **REMIGIAL** *adj*

REMIND *v* -ED, -ING, -S to cause to remember

REMINDER *n* pl. -S one that reminds

REMINT *v* -ED, -ING, -S to melt down and make into new coin

REMISE *v* -MISED, -MISING, -MISES to give up a claim to

REMISS *adj* careless **REMISSLY** *adv*

REMIT *v* -MITTED, -MITTING, -MITS to send money in payment

REMITTAL *n* pl. -S the act of remitting

REMITTER *n* pl. -S one that remits

REMITTING present participle of remit

REMITTOR *n* pl. -S remitter

REMNANT *n* pl. -S something remaining

REMODEL *v* -ELED, -ELING, -ELS or -ELLED, -ELLING, -ELS to make over

REMOLADE *n* pl. -S a piquant sauce

REMORA *n* pl. -S a type of marine fish **REMORID** *adj*

REMORSE *n* pl. -S deep anguish caused by a sense of guilt

REMOTE *adj* -MOTER, -MOTEST situated far away **REMOTELY** *adv*

REMOTE *n* pl. -S a broadcast originating outside a studio

REMOTION *n* pl. -S the act of removing

REMOVAL *n* pl. -S the act of removing

REMOVE *v* -MOVED, -MOVING, -MOVES to take or move away

REMOVER *n* pl. -S one that removes

REMUDA *n* pl. -S a herd of horses

RENAL *adj* pertaining to the kidneys

RENATURE *v* -TURED, -TURING, -TURES to restore natural qualities

REND *v* RENT or RENDED, RENDING, RENDS to tear apart forcibly

RENDER *v* -ED, -ING, -S to cause to be or become

RENDERER *n* pl. -S one that renders

RENDIBLE *adj* capable of being rent

RENDZINA *n* pl. -S a type of soil

RENEGADE *v* -GADED, -GADING, -GADES to become a traitor

RENEGADO *n* pl. -DOS or -DOES a traitor

RENEGE *v* -NEGED, -NEGING, -NEGES to fail to carry out a promise or commitment

RENEGER *n* pl. -S one that reneges

RENEW *v* -ED, -ING, -S to make new or as if new again

RENEWAL *n* pl. -S the act of renewing

RENEWER *n* pl. -S one that renews

RENIFORM *adj* kidney-shaped

RENIG *v* -NIGGED, -NIGGING, -NIGS to renege

RENIN *n* pl. -S an enzyme

RENITENT *adj* resisting physical pressure

RENMINBI *n* pl. RENMINBI currency in the People's Republic of China

RENNASE *n* pl. -S rennin

RENNET *n* pl. -S a lining membrane in the stomach of certain young animals

RENNIN *n* pl. -S an enzyme

RENOGRAM *n* pl. -S a photographic depiction of the course of renal excretion

RENOUNCE *v* -NOUNCED, -NOUNCING, -NOUNCES to disown

RENOVATE *v* -VATED, -VATING, -VATES to make like new

RENOWN   v -ED, -ING, -S to make famous

RENT   v -ED, -ING, -S to obtain temporary use of in return for compensation RENTABLE adj

RENTAL   n pl. -S an amount paid or collected as rent

RENTE   n pl. -S annual income under French law

RENTER   n pl. -S one that rents

RENTIER   n pl. -S one that receives a fixed income

RENVOI   n pl. -S the expulsion by a government of an alien

REOFFER   v -ED, -ING, -S to offer for public sale

REOVIRUS   n pl. -ES a type of virus

REP   n pl. -S a cross-ribbed fabric

REPAID   past tense of repay

REPAIR   v -ED, -ING, -S to restore to good condition

REPAIRER   n pl. -S one that repairs

REPAND   adj having a wavy margin REPANDLY adv

REPARTEE   n pl. -S a quick, witty reply

REPAST   v -ED, -ING, -S to eat or feast

REPAY   v -PAID, -PAYING, -PAYS to pay back

REPEAL   v -ED, -ING, -S to revoke

REPEALER   n pl. -S one that repeals

REPEAT   v -ED, -ING, -S to say or do again

REPEATER   n pl. -S one that repeats

REPEL   v -PELLED, -PELLING, -PELS to drive back

REPELLER   n pl. -S one that repels

REPENT   v -ED, -ING, -S to feel remorse or self-reproach for a past action

REPENTER   n pl. -S one that repents

REPETEND   n pl. -S a phrase or sound that is repeated

REPINE   v -PINED, -PINING, -PINES to express discontent

REPINER   n pl. -S one that repines

REPLACE   v -PLACED, -PLACING, -PLACES to take the place of

REPLACER   n pl. -S one that replaces

REPLETE   adj abundantly supplied

REPLEVIN   v -ED, -ING, -S to replevy

REPLEVY   v -PLEVIED, -PLEVYING, -PLEVIES to regain possession of by legal action

REPLICA   n pl. -S a close copy or reproduction

REPLICON   n pl. -S a section of nucleic acid that replicates as a unit

REPLIER   n pl. -S one that replies

REPLY   v -PLIED, -PLYING, -PLIES to answer

REPO   n pl. -POS something repossessed

REPORT   v -ED, -ING, -S to give an account of

REPORTER   n pl. -S one that reports

REPOSAL   n pl. -S the act of reposing

REPOSE   v -POSED, -POSING, -POSES to lie at rest

REPOSER   n pl. -S one that reposes

REPOSIT   v -ED, -ING, -S to put away

REPOUSSE   n pl. -S a raised design hammered in metal

REPP   n pl. -S rep

REPPED   adj resembling rep

REPRESS   v -ED, -ING, -ES to keep under control

REPRIEVE   v -PRIEVED, -PRIEVING, -PRIEVES to postpone the punishment of

REPRISAL   n pl. -S an act of retaliation

REPRISE   v -PRISED, -PRISING, -PRISES to take back by force

REPRO   n pl. -PROS a trial sheet of printed material suitable for photographic reproduction

REPROACH   v -ED, -ING, -ES to find fault with

REPROOF   n pl. -S criticism for a fault

REPROVAL   n pl. -S reproof

REPROVE   v -PROVED, -PROVING, -PROVES to rebuke

REPROVER   n pl. -S one that reproves

REPTANT   adj creeping or crawling

REPTILE   n pl. -S any of a class of cold-blooded, air-breathing vertebrates

REPUBLIC   n pl. -S a constitutional form of government

REPUGN   v -ED, -ING, -S to oppose

REPULSE   v -PULSED, -PULSING, -PULSES to drive back

REPULSER   n pl. -S one that repulses

REPUTE   v -PUTED, -PUTING, -PUTES to consider to be as specified

REQUEST   v -ED, -ING, -S to express a desire for

REQUIEM   n pl. -S a musical composition for the dead

REQUIN   n pl. -S a voracious shark

REQUIRE   v -QUIRED, -QUIRING, -QUIRES to have need of

REQUIRER *n* pl. -S one that requires

REQUITAL *n* pl. -S something given in return, compensation, or retaliation

REQUITE *v* -QUITED, -QUITING, -QUITES to make equivalent return for

REQUITER *n* pl. -S one that requites

RERAN past tense of rerun

REREDOS *n* pl. -ES an ornamental screen behind an altar

REREMICE *n/pl* a bat (a flying mammal)

REREWARD *n* pl. -S rearward

REROLLER *n* pl. -S one that rerolls

RERUN *v* -RAN, -RUNNING, -RUNS to present a repetition of a recorded performance

RES *n* pl. RES a particular thing or matter

RESALE *n* pl. -S the act of selling again

RESCALE *v* -SCALED, -SCALING, -SCALES to plan on a new scale

RESCIND *v* -ED, -ING, -S to annul

RESCRIPT *n* pl. -S something rewritten

RESCUE *v* -CUED, -CUING, -CUES to free from danger

RESCUER *n* pl. -S one that rescues

RESEARCH *v* -ED, -ING, -ES to investigate thoroughly

RESEAU *n* pl. -SEAUS or -SEAUX a filter screen for making color films

RESECT *v* -ED, -ING, -S to excise part of an organ or structure surgically

RESEDA *n* pl. -S a flowering plant

RESELLER *n* pl. -S one that resells

RESEMBLE *v* -BLED, -BLING, -BLES to be similar to

RESENT *v* -ED, -ING, -S to feel or express annoyance or ill will at

RESERVE *v* -SERVED, -SERVING, -SERVES to keep back for future use

RESERVER *n* pl. -S one that reserves

RESETTER *n* pl. -S one that resets

RESH *n* pl. -ES a Hebrew letter

RESHAPER *n* pl. -S one that reshapes something

RESID *n* pl. -S a type of fuel oil

RESIDE *v* -SIDED, -SIDING, -SIDES to dwell permanently or continuously

RESIDENT *n* pl. -S one who resides

RESIDER *n* pl. -S a resident

RESIDUA a pl. of residuum

RESIDUAL *n* pl. -S something left over

RESIDUE *n* pl. -S something remaining after the removal of a part

RESIDUUM *n* pl. -SIDUA or -SIDUUMS residue

RESIGN *v* -ED, -ING, -S to give up one's office or position

RESIGNER *n* pl. -S one that resigns

RESILE *v* -SILED, -SILING, -SILES to spring back

RESIN *v* -ED, -ING, -S to treat with resin (a viscous substance obtained from certain plants)

RESINATE *v* -ATED, -ATING, -ATES to resin

RESINIFY *v* -FIED, -FYING, -FIES to convert into resin

RESINOID *n* pl. -S a resinous substance

RESINOUS *adj* resembling resin

RESINY *adj* resinous

RESIST *v* -ED, -ING, -S to strive against

RESISTER *n* pl. -S one that resists

RESISTOR *n* pl. -S a device in an electric circuit

RESOJET *n* pl. -S a pulsejet

RESOLUTE *adj* -LUTER, -LUTEST characterized by firmness or determination

RESOLUTE *n* pl. -S one who is resolute

RESOLVE *v* -SOLVED, -SOLVING, -SOLVES to make a firm decision about

RESOLVER *n* pl. -S one that resolves

RESONANT *n* pl. -S a resounding sound

RESONATE *v* -NATED, -NATING, -NATES to resound

RESORB *v* -ED, -ING, -S to absorb again

RESORCIN *n* pl. -S a chemical compound

RESORT *v* -ED, -ING, -S to go frequently or habitually

RESORTER *n* pl. -S one that resorts

RESOUND *v* -ED, -ING, -S to make a loud, long, or echoing sound

RESOURCE *n* pl. -S an available supply

RESPECT *v* -ED, -ING, -S to have a high regard for

RESPIRE *v* -SPIRED, -SPIRING, -SPIRES to breathe

RESPITE *v* -SPITED, -SPITING, -SPITES to relieve temporarily

RESPOND *v* -ED, -ING, -S to say or act in return

RESPONSA *n/pl* written rabbinic decisions

RESPONSE *n* pl. -S a reply or reaction

REST *v* -ED, -ING, -S to refresh oneself by ceasing work or activity

RESTER *n* pl. -S one that rests

RESTFUL *adj* -FULLER, -FULLEST tranquil

RESTIVE *adj* difficult to control

RESTLESS *adj* unable or disinclined to remain at rest

RESTORAL *n* pl. -S the act of restoring

RESTORE *v* -STORED, -STORING, -STORES to bring back to a former or original condition

RESTORER *n* pl. -S one that restores

RESTRAIN *v* -ED, -ING, -S to hold back from action

RESTRICT *v* -ED, -ING, -S to keep within certain boundaries

RESTROOM *n* pl. -S a room furnished with toilets and sinks

RESULT *v* -ED, -ING, -S to occur as a consequence

RESUME *v* -SUMED, -SUMING, -SUMES to take up again after interruption

RESUMER *n* pl. -S one that resumes

RESUPINE *adj* lying on the back

RESURGE *v* -SURGED, -SURGING, -SURGES to rise again

RET *v* RETTED, RETTING, RETS to soak in order to loosen the fiber from the woody tissue

RETABLE *n* pl. -S a raised shelf above an altar

RETAIL *v* -ED, -ING, -S to sell in small quantities

RETAILER *n* pl. -S one that retails

RETAIN *v* -ED, -ING, -S to keep possession of

RETAINER *n* pl. -S one that retains

RETAKE *v* -TOOK, -TAKEN, -TAKING, -TAKES to take back

RETAKER *n* pl. -S one that retakes

RETARD *v* -ED, -ING, -S to slow the progress of

RETARDER *n* pl. -S one that retards

RETCH *v* -ED, -ING, -ES to make an effort to vomit

RETE *n* pl. -TIA an anatomical mesh or network

RETEM *n* pl. -S a desert shrub

RETENE *n* pl. -S a chemical compound

RETIA pl. of rete

RETIAL *adj* pertaining to a rete

RETIARII *n/pl* ancient Roman gladiators

RETIARY *adj* resembling a net

RETICENT *adj* tending to be silent

RETICLE *n* pl. -S a network of lines in the eyepiece of an optical instrument

RETICULA *n/pl* netlike structures

RETICULE *n* pl. -S a woman's handbag

RETIFORM *adj* arranged like a net

RETINA *n* pl. -NAS or -NAE a membrane of the eye

RETINAL *n* pl. -S retinene

RETINE *n* pl. -S a substance in cells that retards growth and cell division

RETINENE *n* pl. -S a pigment in the retina

RETINITE *n* pl. -S a fossil resin

RETINOID *n* pl. -S a compound analogous to vitamin A

RETINOL *n* pl. -S a liquid hydrocarbon

RETINUE *n* pl. -S a group of attendants RETINUED *adj*

RETINULA *n* pl. -LAE or -LAS a neural receptor of an arthropod's eye

RETIRANT *n* pl. -S a retiree

RETIRE *v* -TIRED, -TIRING, -TIRES to go away or withdraw

RETIREE *n* pl. -S one who has retired from his vocation

RETIRER *n* pl. -S one that retires

RETIRING *adj* shy

RETOOK past tense of retake

RETOOL *v* -ED, -ING, -S to reequip with tools

RETORT *v* -ED, -ING, -S to answer back sharply

RETORTER *n* pl. -S one that retorts

RETOUCH *v* -ED, -ING, -ES to add new details or touches to

RETRACE *v* -TRACED, -TRACING, -TRACES to go back over

RETRACT *v* -ED, -ING, -S to take back

RETRAL *adj* situated toward the back RETRALLY *adv*

RETREAD *v* -ED, -ING, -S to furnish with a new tread

RETREAT *v* -ED, -ING, -S to go back or backward

RETRENCH *v* -ED, -ING, -ES to curtail

RETRIAL *n* pl. -S a second trial

RETRIEVE *v* -TRIEVED, -TRIEVING, -TRIEVES to get back

RETRO *n* pl. -ROS a rocket on a spacecraft that produces thrust in a direction opposite to the line of flight

RETROACT *v* -ED, -ING, -S to act in return

RETROFIT	v -FITTED, -FITTING, -FITS to furnish with new parts not originally available
RETRORSE	adj bent backward
RETSINA	n pl. -S a resin-flavored Greek wine
RETTED	past tense of ret
RETTING	present participle of ret
RETURN	v -ED, -ING, -S to come or go back
RETURNEE	n pl. -S one that has returned
RETURNER	n pl. -S one that returns
RETUSE	adj having a rounded apex with a shallow notch — used of leaves
REUNION	n pl. -S a reuniting of persons after separation
REUNITER	n pl. -S one that reunites
REUSABLE	adj capable of being used again
REV	v REVVED, REVVING, REVS to increase the speed of
REVAMP	v -ED, -ING, -S to make over
REVAMPER	n pl. -S one that revamps
REVANCHE	n pl. -S a political policy designed to regain lost territory
REVEAL	v -ED, -ING, -S to make known
REVEALER	n pl. -S one that reveals
REVEHENT	adj carrying back
REVEILLE	n pl. -S a morning bugle call
REVEL	v -ELED, -ELING, -ELS or -ELLED, -ELLING, -ELS to engage in revelry
REVELER	n pl. -S one that revels
REVELLER	n pl. -S reveler
REVELLING	present participle of revel
REVELRY	n pl. -RIES noisy merrymaking
REVENANT	n pl. -S one that returns
REVENGE	v -VENGED, -VENGING, -VENGES to inflict injury in return for
REVENGER	n pl. -S one that revenges
REVENUE	n pl. -S the income of a government REVENUAL, REVENUED adj
REVENUER	n pl. -S a revenue officer
REVERB	v -ED, -ING, -S to continue in a series of echoes
REVERE	v -VERED, -VERING, -VERES to regard with great respect
REVEREND	n pl. -S a clergyman
REVERENT	adj deeply respectful
REVERER	n pl. -S one that reveres
REVERIE	n pl. -S a daydream
REVERIES	pl. of revery

REVERING	present participle of revere
REVERS	n pl. REVERS a part of a garment turned back to show the inside
REVERSAL	n pl. -S the act of reversing
REVERSE	v -VERSED, -VERSING, -VERSES to turn or move in the opposite direction
REVERSER	n pl. -S one that reverses
REVERSO	n pl. -VERSOS verso
REVERT	v -ED, -ING, -S to return to a former state
REVERTER	n pl. -S one that reverts
REVERY	n pl. -ERIES reverie
REVET	v -VETTED, -VETTING, -VETS to face with masonry
REVIEWAL	n pl. -S the act of reviewing
REVIEWER	n pl. -S one that reviews
REVILE	v -VILED, -VILING, -VILES to denounce with abusive language
REVILER	n pl. -S one that reviles
REVISAL	n pl. -S a revision
REVISE	v -VISED, -VISING, -VISES to make a new or improved version of
REVISER	n pl. -S one that revises
REVISION	n pl. -S a revised version
REVISOR	n pl. -S reviser
REVISORY	adj pertaining to revision
REVIVAL	n pl. -S renewed attention to or interest in something
REVIVE	v -VIVED, -VIVING, -VIVES to bring back to life or consciousness
REVIVER	n pl. -S one that revives
REVIVIFY	v -FIED, -FYING, -FIES to give new life to
REVIVING	present participle of revive
REVOKE	v -VOKED, -VOKING, -VOKES to annul by taking back
REVOKER	n pl. -S one that revokes
REVOLT	v -ED, -ING, -S to rise up against authority
REVOLTER	n pl. -S one that revolts
REVOLUTE	adj rolled backward or downward
REVOLVE	v -VOLVED, -VOLVING, -VOLVES to turn about an axis
REVOLVER	n pl. -S a type of handgun
REVUE	n pl. -S a type of musical show
REVUIST	n pl. -S a writer of revues
REVULSED	adj affected with revulsion
REVVED	past tense of rev

REVVING present participle of rev

REWARD v -ED, -ING, -S to give recompense to for worthy behavior

REWARDER n pl. -S one that rewards

REWINDER n pl. -S one that rewinds

REWORD v -ED, -ING, -S to state again in other words

REWRITER n pl. -S one that rewrites

REX n pl. REGES king

REX n pl. -ES an animal with a single wavy layer of hair

REYNARD n pl. -S a fox

RHABDOM n pl. -S a rodlike structure in the retinula

RHABDOME n pl. -S rhabdom

RHACHIS n pl. -CHISES or -CHIDES rachis

RHAMNOSE n pl. -S a sugar found in plants

RHAMNUS n pl. -ES a thorny tree or shrub

RHAPHE n pl. -PHAE or -PHES raphe

RHAPSODE n pl. -S a reciter of epic poetry in ancient Greece

RHAPSODY n pl. -DIES an exalted expression of feeling

RHATANY n pl. -NIES a South American shrub

RHEA n pl. -S a flightless bird

RHEBOK n pl. -S a large antelope

RHEMATIC adj pertaining to a verb

RHENIUM n pl. -S a metallic element

RHEOBASE n pl. -S the smallest amount of electricity required to stimulate a nerve

RHEOLOGY n pl. -GIES the study of matter in the fluid state

RHEOPHIL adj living in flowing water

RHEOSTAT n pl. -S a resistor used to control electric current

RHESUS n pl. -ES an Asian monkey

RHETOR n pl. -S a teacher of rhetoric

RHETORIC n pl. -S the study of effective speech and writing

RHEUM n pl. -S a watery discharge from the eyes or nose **RHEUMIC** adj

RHEUMY adj RHEUMIER, RHEUMIEST marked by rheum

RHINAL adj pertaining to the nose

RHINITIS n pl. RHINITIDES inflammation of the mucous membranes of the nose

RHINO n pl. -NOS a rhinoceros

RHIZOBIA n/pl rod-shaped bacteria

RHIZOID n pl. -S a rootlike structure

RHIZOMA n pl. -MATA rhizome

RHIZOME n pl. -S a rootlike, underground stem **RHIZOMIC** adj

RHIZOPOD n pl. -S any of a class of protozoans

RHIZOPUS n pl. -PI or -PUSES any of a genus of mold fungi

RHO n pl. RHOS a Greek letter

RHODAMIN n pl. -S a red dye

RHODIUM n pl. -S a metallic element **RHODIC** adj

RHODORA n pl. -S a flowering shrub

RHOMB n pl. -S a rhombus

RHOMBI a pl. of rhombus

RHOMBIC adj having the shape of a rhombus

RHOMBOID n pl. -S a type of geometric figure

RHOMBUS n pl. -BUSES or -BI a type of geometric figure

RHONCHUS n pl. -CHI a rattling respiratory sound **RHONCHAL** adj

RHUBARB n pl. -S a perennial herb

RHUMB n pl. -S a point of the mariner's compass

RHUMBA v -ED, -ING, -S to rumba

RHUS n pl. -ES any of a genus of shrubs and trees

RHYME v RHYMED, RHYMING, RHYMES to compose verse with corresponding terminal sounds

RHYMER n pl. -S one that rhymes

RHYOLITE n pl. -S a volcanic rock

RHYTA pl. of rhyton

RHYTHM n pl. -S movement or procedure with uniform recurrence of strong and weak elements

RHYTHMIC n pl. -S the science of rhythm

RHYTON n pl. -TA an ancient Greek drinking horn

RIA n pl. -S a long, narrow inlet

RIAL n pl. -S a monetary unit of Iran

RIALTO n pl. -TOS a marketplace

RIANT adj cheerful **RIANTLY** adv

RIATA n pl. -S a lasso

RIB v RIBBED, RIBBING, RIBS to poke fun at

RIBALD n pl. -S one who uses crude language

RIBALDLY adv crudely

RIBALDRY n pl. -RIES crude language

RIBAND n pl. -S a ribbon

RIBBAND   *n* pl. -S a long, narrow strip used in shipbuilding
RIBBED   past tense of rib
RIBBER   *n* pl. -S one that ribs
RIBBIER   comparative of ribby
RIBBIEST   superlative of ribby
RIBBING   *n* pl. -S the act of one that ribs
RIBBON   *v* -ED, -ING, -S to decorate with ribbons (narrow strips of fine fabric)
RIBBONY   *adj* resembling ribbon
RIBBY   *adj* -BIER, -BIEST marked by prominent ribs (curved bony rods in the body)
RIBES   *n* pl. RIBES a flowering shrub
RIBGRASS   *n* pl. -ES a weedy plant
RIBIER   *n* pl. -S a large, black grape
RIBLESS   *adj* having no ribs
RIBLET   *n* pl. -S the rib end in a breast of lamb or veal
RIBLIKE   *adj* resembling a rib
RIBOSE   *n* pl. -S a pentose sugar
RIBOSOME   *n* pl. -S a particle composed of protein and ribonucleic acid
RIBWORT   *n* pl. -S ribgrass
RICE   *v* RICED, RICING, RICES to press through a ricer
RICEBIRD   *n* pl. -S the bobolink
RICER   *n* pl. -S a kitchen utensil consisting of a container perforated with small holes
RICERCAR   *n* pl. -S an instrumental composition
RICH   *adj* RICHER, RICHEST having wealth
RICHEN   *v* -ED, -ING, -S to make rich
RICHES   *n/pl* wealth
RICHLY   *adv* in a rich manner
RICHNESS   *n* pl. -ES the state of being rich
RICHWEED   *n* pl. -S a flowering plant
RICIN   *n* pl. -S a poisonous protein
RICING   present participle of rice
RICINUS   *n* pl. -ES a large-leaved plant
RICK   *v* -ED, -ING, -S to pile hay in stacks
RICKETS   *n/pl* a disease resulting from vitamin D deficiency
RICKETY   *adj* -ETIER, -ETIEST likely to fall or collapse
RICKEY   *n* pl. -EYS an alcoholic beverage containing lime juice, sugar, and soda water
RICKRACK   *n* pl. -S a flat braid used as a trimming
RICKSHA   *n* pl. -S rickshaw

RICKSHAW   *n* pl. -S a small, two-wheeled passenger vehicle
RICOCHET   *v* -CHETED, -CHETING, -CHETS or -CHETTED, -CHETTING, -CHETS to rebound from a surface
RICOTTA   *n* pl. -S an Italian cheese
RICRAC   *n* pl. -S rickrack
RICTUS   *n* pl. -ES the expanse of the open mouth **RICTAL** *adj*
RID   *v* RID or RIDDED, RIDDING, RIDS to free from something objectionable
RIDABLE   *adj* capable of being ridden
RIDDANCE   *n* pl. -S deliverance
RIDDED   a past tense of rid
RIDDEN   past participle of ride
RIDDER   *n* pl. -S one that rids
RIDDING   present participle of rid
RIDDLE   *v* -DLED, -DLING, -DLES to pierce with many holes
RIDDLER   *n* pl. -S one that riddles
RIDE   *v* RODE, RIDDEN, RIDING, RIDES to sit on, control, and be conveyed by an animal or machine
RIDEABLE   *adj* ridable
RIDENT   *adj* laughing
RIDER   *n* pl. -S one that rides
RIDGE   *v* RIDGED, RIDGING, RIDGES to form into ridges (long, narrow elevations)
RIDGEL   *n* pl. -S a ridgling
RIDGIER   comparative of ridgy
RIDGIEST   superlative of ridgy
RIDGIL   *n* pl. -S a ridgling
RIDGING   present participle of ridge
RIDGLING   *n* pl. -S a male animal with undescended testicles
RIDGY   *adj* RIDGIER, RIDGIEST having ridges
RIDICULE   *v* -CULED, -CULING, -CULES to make fun of
RIDING   *n* pl. -S the act of one that rides
RIDLEY   *n* pl. -LEYS a sea turtle
RIDOTTO   *n* pl. -TOS a public musical entertainment in 18th century England
RIEL   *n* pl. -S a monetary unit of Cambodia
RIESLING   *n* pl. -S a white Rhine wine
RIEVER   *n* pl. -S reaver
RIF   *v* RIFFED, RIFFING, RIFS to dismiss from employment
RIFAMPIN   *n* pl. -S an antibiotic

RIFE	*adj* RIFER, RIFEST abundant RIFELY *adv*	**RIGIDITY**	*n* pl. -TIES the state of being rigid
RIFENESS	*n* pl. -ES the state of being rife	**RIGIDLY**	*adv* in a rigid manner
RIFF	*v* -ED, -ING, -S to riffle	**RIGOR**	*n* pl. -S strictness or severity
RIFFED	past tense of rif	**RIGORISM**	*n* pl. -S strictness or severity
RIFFING	present participle of rif		in conduct or attitude
RIFFLE	*v* -FLED, -FLING, -FLES to flip through hastily	**RIGORIST**	*n* pl. -S one that professes rigorism
RIFFLER	*n* pl. -S a filing and scraping tool	**RIGOROUS**	*adj* characterized by rigor
		RIGOUR	*n* pl. -S rigor
RIFFRAFF	*n* pl. -S the disreputable element of society	**RIKISHA**	*n* pl. -S rickshaw
		RIKSHAW	*n* pl. -S rickshaw
RIFLE	*v* -FLED, -FLING, -FLES to search through and rob	**RILE**	*v* RILED, RILING, RILES to anger
RIFLEMAN	*n* pl. -MEN a soldier armed with a rifle (a type of firearm)	**RILEY**	*adj* angry
		RILIEVO	*n* pl. -VI relievo
RIFLER	*n* pl. -S one that rifles	**RILING**	present participle of rile
RIFLERY	*n* pl. -RIES the practice of shooting at targets with a rifle	**RILL**	*v* -ED, -ING, -S to flow like a rill (a small brook)
RIFLING	*n* pl. -S the system of grooves in a gun barrel	**RILLE**	*n* pl. -S a valley on the moon's surface
RIFT	*v* -ED, -ING, -S to form rifts (clefts)	**RILLET**	*n* pl. -S a small rill
RIFTLESS	*adj* having no rift	**RIM**	*v* RIMMED, RIMMING, RIMS to provide with a rim (an outer edge)
RIG	*v* RIGGED, RIGGING, RIGS to put in proper condition for use	**RIME**	*v* RIMED, RIMING, RIMES to rhyme
RIGADOON	*n* pl. -S a lively dance	**RIMER**	*n* pl. -S one that rimes
RIGATONI	*n* pl. -S a tubular pasta	**RIMESTER**	*n* pl. -S a rimer
RIGAUDON	*n* pl. -S rigadoon	**RIMFIRE**	*n* pl. -S a cartridge having the primer set in the rim of the shell
RIGGED	past tense of rig		
RIGGER	*n* pl. -S one that rigs	**RIMIER**	comparative of rimy
RIGGING	*n* pl. -S the system of lines, chains, and tackle used aboard a ship	**RIMIEST**	superlative of rimy
		RIMINESS	*n* pl. -ES the condition of being rimy
RIGHT	*adj* RIGHTER, RIGHTEST being in accordance with what is good, proper, or just	**RIMING**	present participle of rime
		RIMLAND	*n* pl. -S an outlying area
		RIMLESS	*adj* having no rim
RIGHT	*v* -ED, -ING, -S to put in proper order or condition	**RIMMED**	past tense of rim
		RIMMER	*n* pl. -S a reamer
RIGHTER	*n* pl. -S one that rights	**RIMMING**	present participle of rim
RIGHTFUL	*adj* just or proper	**RIMOSE**	*adj* marked by cracks RIMOSELY *adv*
RIGHTIES	pl. of righty		
RIGHTISM	*n* pl. -S a conservative political philosophy	**RIMOSITY**	*n* pl. -TIES the state of being rimose
RIGHTIST	*n* pl. -S an advocate of rightism	**RIMOUS**	*adj* rimose
		RIMPLE	*v* -PLED, -PLING, -PLES to wrinkle
RIGHTLY	*adv* in a right manner		
RIGHTO	*interj* — used to express cheerful consent	**RIMROCK**	*n* pl. -S a type of rock formation
RIGHTY	*n* pl. RIGHTIES a right-handed person	**RIMY**	*adj* RIMIER, RIMIEST frosty
		RIN	*v* RAN, RINNING, RINS to run or melt
RIGID	*adj* not flexible		
RIGIDIFY	*v* -FIED, -FYING, -FIES to make rigid	**RIND**	*n* pl. -S a thick and firm outer covering RINDED *adj*

RING   *v* -ED, -ING, -S to form a ring (a circular band) around

RING   *v* RANG, RUNG, RINGING, RINGS to give forth a clear, resonant sound

RINGBARK   *v* -ED, -ING, -S to make an encircling cut through the bark of

RINGBOLT   *n* pl. -S a type of eyebolt

RINGBONE   *n* pl. -S a bony growth on a horse's foot

RINGDOVE   *n* pl. -S a European pigeon

RINGENT   *adj* having open liplike parts

RINGER   *n* pl. -S one that rings

RINGGIT   *n* pl. RINGGIT a monetary unit of Malaysia

RINGHALS   *n* pl. -ES a venomous snake

RINGLET   *n* pl. -S a small ring

RINGLIKE   *adj* resembling a ring

RINGNECK   *n* pl. -S a bird having a ring of color around the neck

RINGSIDE   *n* pl. -S the area just outside a boxing or wrestling ring (a square enclosure)

RINGTAIL   *n* pl. -S an animal having a tail with ringlike markings

RINGTAW   *n* pl. -S a game of marbles

RINGTOSS   *n* pl. -ES a game in which the object is to toss a ring onto an upright stick

RINGWORM   *n* pl. -S a skin disease

RINK   *n* pl. -S a surface of ice for skating

RINNING   present participle of rin

RINSE   *v* RINSED, RINSING, RINSES to cleanse with clear water **RINSABLE, RINSIBLE** *adj*

RINSER   *n* pl. -S one that rinses

RINSING   *n* pl. -S the act of one that rinses

RIOJA   *n* pl. -S a dry red Spanish wine

RIOT   *v* -ED, -ING, -S to take part in a violent public disturbance

RIOTER   *n* pl. -S one that riots

RIOTOUS   *adj* characterized by rioting

RIP   *v* RIPPED, RIPPING, RIPS to tear or cut apart roughly

RIPARIAN   *adj* pertaining to the bank of a river

RIPCORD   *n* pl. -S a cord pulled to release a parachute

RIPE   *adj* RIPER, RIPEST fully developed **RIPELY** *adv*

RIPE   *v* RIPED, RIPING, RIPES to cleanse

RIPEN   *v* -ED, -ING, -S to become ripe

RIPENER   *n* pl. -S one that ripens

RIPENESS   *n* pl. -ES the state of being ripe

RIPER   comparative of ripe

RIPEST   superlative of ripe

RIPIENO   *n* pl. -NI or -NOS tutti

RIPING   present participle of ripe

RIPOFF   *n* pl. -S an instance of stealing

RIPOST   *v* -ED, -ING, -S to riposte

RIPOSTE   *v* -POSTED, -POSTING, -POSTES to make a return thrust in fencing

RIPPABLE   *adj* capable of being ripped

RIPPED   past tense of rip

RIPPER   *n* pl. -S one that rips

RIPPING   *adj* excellent

RIPPLE   *v* -PLED, -PLING, -PLES to form ripples (small waves)

RIPPLER   *n* pl. -S a toothed tool for cleaning flax fiber

RIPPLET   *n* pl. -S a small ripple

RIPPLING   present participle of ripple

RIPPLY   *adj* -PLIER, -PLIEST marked by ripples

RIPRAP   *v* -RAPPED, -RAPPING, -RAPS to strengthen with a foundation of broken stones

RIPSAW   *n* pl. -S a type of saw

RIPSTOP   *n* pl. -S a fabric woven so that small tears do not spread

RIPTIDE   *n* pl. -S a tide that opposes other tides

RISE   *v* ROSE, RISEN, RISING, RISES to move upward

RISER   *n* pl. -S one that rises

RISHI   *n* pl. -S a Hindu sage

RISIBLE   *adj* inclined to laugh **RISIBLY** *adv*

RISIBLES   *n/pl* a sense of the ridiculous

RISING   *n* pl. -S the act of one that rises

RISK   *v* -ED, -ING, -S to expose to a risk (a chance of injury or loss)

RISKER   *n* pl. -S one that risks

RISKLESS   *adj* free of risk

RISKY   *adj* RISKIER, RISKIEST dangerous **RISKILY** *adv*

RISOTTO   *n* pl. -TOS a rice dish

RISQUE   *adj* bordering on impropriety or indecency

RISSOLE   *n* pl. -S a small roll filled with meat or fish

RISUS   *n* pl. -ES a grin or laugh

RITARD   *n* pl. -S a musical passage with a gradual slackening in tempo

RITE   *n* pl. -S a ceremonial act or procedure

RITTER   *n* pl. -S a knight

RITUAL   *n* pl. -S a system of rites

RITUALLY   *adv* ceremonially

RITZ   *n* pl. -ES pretentious display

RITZY   *adj* RITZIER, RITZIEST elegant **RITZILY** *adv*

RIVAGE   *n* pl. -S a coast, shore, or bank

RIVAL   *v* -VALED, -VALING, -VALS or -VALLED, -VALLING, -VALS to strive to equal or surpass

RIVALRY   *n* pl. -RIES competition

RIVE   *v* RIVED, RIVEN, RIVING, RIVES to tear apart

RIVER   *n* pl. -S a large, natural stream of water

RIVERBED   *n* pl. -S the area covered or once covered by a river

RIVERINE   *adj* pertaining to a river

RIVET   *v* -ETED, -ETING, -ETS or -ETTED, -ETTING, -ETS to fasten with a type of metal bolt

RIVETER   *n* pl. -S one that rivets

RIVIERA   *n* pl. -S a coastal resort area

RIVIERE   *n* pl. -S a necklace of precious stones

RIVING   present participle of rive

RIVULET   *n* pl. -S a small stream

RIVULOSE   *adj* having narrow, winding lines

RIYAL   *n* pl. -S a monetary unit of Saudi Arabia

ROACH   *v* -ED, -ING, -ES to cause to arch

ROAD   *n* pl. -S an open way for public passage

ROADBED   *n* pl. -S the foundation for a railroad track

ROADEO   *n* pl. -EOS a competition for truck drivers

ROADIE   *n* pl. -S a person who works for traveling entertainers

ROADKILL   *n* pl. -S an animal that has been killed on a road

ROADLESS   *adj* having no roads

ROADSHOW   *n* pl. -S a theatrical show on tour

ROADSIDE   *n* pl. -S the area along the side of a road

ROADSTER   *n* pl. -S a light, open automobile

ROADWAY   *n* pl. -WAYS a road

ROADWORK   *n* pl. -S outdoor running as a form of physical conditioning

ROAM   *v* -ED, -ING, -S to move about without purpose or plan

ROAMER   *n* pl. -S one that roams

ROAN   *n* pl. -S an animal having a coat sprinkled with white or gray

ROAR   *v* -ED, -ING, -S to utter a loud, deep sound

ROARER   *n* pl. -S one that roars

ROARING   *n* pl. -S a loud, deep sound

ROAST   *v* -ED, -ING, -S to cook with dry heat

ROASTER   *n* pl. -S one that roasts

ROB   *v* ROBBED, ROBBING, ROBS to take property from illegally

ROBALO   *n* pl. -LOS a marine food fish

ROBAND   *n* pl. -S a piece of yarn used to fasten a sail

ROBBED   past tense of rob

ROBBER   *n* pl. -S one that robs

ROBBERY   *n* pl. -BERIES the act of one who robs

ROBBIN   *n* pl. -S a roband

ROBBING   present participle of rob

ROBE   *v* ROBED, ROBING, ROBES to cover with a robe (a long, loose outer garment)

ROBIN   *n* pl. -S a songbird

ROBLE   *n* pl. -S an oak tree

ROBORANT   *n* pl. -S an invigorating drug

ROBOT   *n* pl. -S a humanlike machine that performs various functions **ROBOTIC** *adj*

ROBOTICS   *n/pl* a field of interest concerned with robots

ROBOTISM   *n* pl. -S the state of being a robot

ROBOTIZE   *v* -IZED, -IZING, -IZES to make automatic

ROBOTRY   *n* pl. -RIES the science of robots

ROBUST   *adj* -BUSTER, -BUSTEST strong and healthy **ROBUSTLY** *adv*

ROBUSTA   *n* pl. -S a coffee grown in Africa

ROC   *n* pl. -S a legendary bird of prey

ROCAILLE   *n* pl. -S rococo

ROCHET   *n* pl. -S a linen vestment

ROCK   *v* -ED, -ING, -S to move back and forth

ROCKABY *n* pl. -BIES a song used to lull a child to sleep

ROCKABYE *n* pl. -S rockaby

ROCKAWAY *n* pl. -WAYS a light carriage

ROCKER *n* pl. -S a rocking chair

ROCKERY *n* pl. -ERIES a rock garden

ROCKET *v* -ED, -ING, -S to convey by means of a rocket (a device propelled by the reaction of escaping gases)

ROCKETER *n* pl. -S one that designs or launches rockets

ROCKETRY *n* pl. -RIES the science of rockets

ROCKFALL *n* pl. -S a mass of fallen rocks

ROCKFISH *n* pl. -ES a fish living around rocks

ROCKIER comparative of rocky

ROCKIEST superlative of rocky

ROCKLESS *adj* having no rocks

ROCKLIKE *adj* resembling a rock (a large mass of stone)

ROCKLING *n* pl. -S a marine fish

ROCKOON *n* pl. -S a small rocket

ROCKROSE *n* pl. -S a flowering plant

ROCKWEED *n* pl. -S a brown seaweed

ROCKWORK *n* pl. -S a natural mass of rocks

ROCKY *adj* ROCKIER, ROCKIEST unsteady

ROCOCO *n* pl. -COS a style of architecture and decoration

ROD *v* RODDED, RODDING, RODS to provide with a rod (a straight, slender piece of wood, metal, or other material)

RODE past tense of ride

RODENT *n* pl. -S a gnawing mammal

RODEO *n* pl. -DEOS a public exhibition of cowboy skills

RODLESS *adj* having no rod

RODLIKE *adj* resembling a rod

RODMAN *n* pl. -MEN a surveyor's assistant

RODSMAN *n* pl. -MEN rodman

ROE *n* pl. -S the mass of eggs within a female fish

ROEBUCK *n* pl. -S the male of a small Eurasian deer

ROENTGEN *n* pl. -S a unit of radiation dosage

ROGATION *n* pl. -S the proposal of a law in ancient Rome

ROGATORY *adj* requesting information

ROGER *n* pl. -S the pirate flag bearing the skull and crossbones

ROGUE *v* ROGUED, ROGUEING or ROGUING, ROGUES to defraud

ROGUERY *n* pl. -ERIES roguish conduct

ROGUISH *adj* dishonest

ROIL *v* -ED, -ING, -S to make muddy

ROILY *adj* ROILIER, ROILIEST muddy

ROISTER *v* -ED, -ING, -S to revel

ROLAMITE *n* pl. -S a nearly frictionless mechanical device

ROLE *n* pl. -S a part played by an actor

ROLL *v* -ED, -ING, -S to move along by repeatedly turning over

ROLLAWAY *adj* mounted on rollers for easy movement

ROLLBACK *n* pl. -S a return to a lower level of prices or wages

ROLLER *n* pl. -S a cylindrical device that rolls or rotates

ROLLICK *v* -ED, -ING, -S to frolic

ROLLICKY *adj* given to rollicking

ROLLING *n* pl. -S the act of one that rolls

ROLLMOP *n* pl. -S a fillet of herring

ROLLOUT *n* pl. -S a type of play in football

ROLLOVER *n* pl. -S a motor vehicle accident in which the vehicle overturns

ROLLTOP *adj* having a flexible, sliding cover

ROLLWAY *n* pl. -WAYS an incline for rolling logs

ROM *n* pl. -S a Gypsy man or boy

ROMAINE *n* pl. -S a variety of lettuce

ROMAN *n* pl. -S a metrical narrative of medieval France

ROMANCE *v* -MANCED, -MANCING, -MANCES to woo

ROMANCER *n* pl. -S one that romances

ROMANISE *v* -ISED, -ISING, -ISES to romanize

ROMANIZE *v* -IZED, -IZING, -IZES to write in the Roman alphabet

ROMANO *n* pl. -NOS an Italian cheese

ROMANTIC *n* pl. -S a fanciful person

ROMAUNT *n* pl. -S a long, medieval narrative

ROMEO *n* pl. -MEOS a male lover

ROMP *v* -ED, -ING, -S to play boisterously

ROMPER *n* pl. -S one that romps

ROMPISH *adj* inclined to romp

RONDEAU *n* pl. -DEAUX a short poem of fixed form

RONDEL *n* pl. -S a rondeau of 14 lines

RONDELET *n* pl. -S a rondeau of 5 or 7 lines

RONDELLE *n* pl. -S rondel

RONDO *n* pl. -DOS a type of musical composition

RONDURE *n* pl. -S a circle or sphere

RONION *n* pl. -S a mangy animal or person

RONNEL *n* pl. -S an insecticide

RONTGEN *n* pl. -S roentgen

RONYON *n* pl. -S ronion

ROOD *n* pl. -S a crucifix

ROOF *v* -ED, -ING, -S to provide with a roof (the external upper covering of a building)

ROOFER *n* pl. -S one that builds or repairs roofs

ROOFING *n* pl. -S material for a roof

ROOFLESS *adj* having no roof

ROOFLIKE *adj* resembling a roof

ROOFLINE *n* pl. -S the profile of a roof

ROOFTOP *n* pl. -S a roof

ROOFTREE *n* pl. -S a horizontal timber in a roof

ROOK *v* -ED, -ING, -S to swindle

ROOKERY *n* pl. -ERIES a colony of rooks (European crows)

ROOKIE *n* pl. -S a novice

ROOKY *adj* ROOKIER, ROOKIEST abounding in rooks

ROOM *v* -ED, -ING, -S to occupy a room (a walled space within a building)

ROOMER *n* pl. -S a lodger

ROOMETTE *n* pl. -S a small room

ROOMFUL *n* pl. -S as much as a room can hold

ROOMIE *n* pl. -S a roommate

ROOMMATE *n* pl. -S one with whom a room is shared

ROOMY *adj* ROOMIER, ROOMIEST spacious **ROOMILY** *adv*

ROORBACH *n* pl. -S roorback

ROORBACK *n* pl. -S a false story used for political advantage

ROOSE *v* ROOSED, ROOSING, ROOSES to praise

ROOSER *n* pl. -S one that rooses

ROOST *v* -ED, -ING, -S to settle down for rest or sleep

ROOSTER *n* pl. -S a male chicken

ROOT *v* -ED, -ING, -S to put forth a root (an underground portion of a plant)

ROOTAGE *n* pl. -S a system of roots

ROOTER *n* pl. -S one that gives encouragement or support

ROOTHOLD *n* pl. -S the embedding of a plant to soil through the growing of roots

ROOTIER comparative of rooty

ROOTIEST superlative of rooty

ROOTLESS *adj* having no roots

ROOTLET *n* pl. -S a small root

ROOTLIKE *adj* resembling a root

ROOTY *adj* ROOTIER, ROOTIEST full of roots

ROPE *v* ROPED, ROPING, ROPES to bind with a rope (a thick line of twisted fibers) **ROPABLE** *adj*

ROPELIKE *adj* resembling a rope

ROPER *n* pl. -S one that ropes

ROPERY *n* pl. -ERIES a place where ropes are made

ROPEWALK *n* pl. -S a long path where ropes are made

ROPEWAY *n* pl. -WAYS an aerial cable used to transport freight

ROPEY *adj* ROPIER, ROPIEST ropy

ROPIER comparative of ropy

ROPIEST superlative of ropy

ROPILY *adv* in a ropy manner

ROPINESS *n* pl. -ES the quality of being ropy

ROPING present participle of rope

ROPY *adj* ROPIER, ROPIEST resembling a rope or ropes

ROQUE *n* pl. -S a form of croquet

ROQUET *v* -ED, -ING, -S to cause one's own ball to hit another in croquet

RORQUAL *n* pl. -S a large whale

ROSARIAN *n* pl. -S a cultivator of roses

ROSARIUM *n* pl. -IA or -IUMS a rose garden

ROSARY *n* pl. -RIES a series of prayers in the Roman Catholic Church

ROSCOE *n* pl. -S a pistol

ROSE *v* ROSED, ROSING, ROSES to make the color of a rose (a reddish flower)

ROSEATE *adj* rose-colored

ROSEBAY *n* pl. -BAYS an evergreen shrub

ROSEBUD *n* pl. -S the bud of a rose

ROSEBUSH *n* pl. -ES a shrub that bears roses

ROSED past tense of rose

ROSEFISH *n* pl. -ES a marine food fish

ROSELIKE *adj* resembling a rose

ROSELLE *n* pl. -S a tropical plant

ROSEMARY *n* pl. -MARIES an evergreen shrub

ROSEOLA *n* pl. -S a rose-colored skin rash ROSEOLAR *adj*

ROSEROOT *n* pl. -S a perennial herb

ROSERY *n* pl. -ERIES a place where roses are grown

ROSESLUG *n* pl. -S a larval sawfly that eats rose leaves

ROSET *n* pl..-S resin

ROSETTE *n* pl. -S an ornament resembling a rose

ROSEWOOD *n* pl. -S a tropical tree

ROSIER comparative of rosy

ROSIEST superlative of rosy

ROSILY *adv* in a rosy manner

ROSIN *v* -ED, -ING, -S to treat with rosin (a brittle resin)

ROSINESS *n* pl. -ES the state of being rosy

ROSING present participle of rose

ROSINOL *n* pl. -S rosin oil

ROSINOUS *adj* resembling rosin

ROSINY *adj* rosinous

ROSOLIO *n* pl. -LIOS a liqueur made from raisins and brandy

ROSTELLA *n/pl* small, beaklike structures

ROSTER *n* pl. -S a list of names

ROSTRA a pl. of rostrum

ROSTRAL *adj* pertaining to a rostrum

ROSTRATE *adj* having a rostrum

ROSTRUM *n* pl. -TRA or -TRUMS a beaklike process or part

ROSULATE *adj* arranged in the form of a rosette

ROSY *adj* ROSIER, ROSIEST rose-colored

ROT *v* ROTTED, ROTTING, ROTS to decompose

ROTA *n* pl. -S a roster

ROTARY *n* pl. -RIES a rotating part or device

ROTATE *v* -TATED, -TATING, -TATES to turn about an axis

ROTATION *n* pl. -S the act or an instance of rotating ROTATIVE *adj*

ROTATOR *n* pl. -S one that rotates

ROTATOR *n* pl. -ES a muscle serving to rotate a part of the body

ROTATORY *adj* pertaining to rotation

ROTCH *n* pl. -ES rotche

ROTCHE *n* pl. -S a seabird

ROTE *n* pl. -S mechanical routine

ROTENONE *n* pl. -S an insecticide

ROTGUT *n* pl. -S inferior liquor

ROTI *n* pl. -S an unleavened bread

ROTIFER *n* pl. -S a microscopic aquatic organism

ROTIFORM *adj* shaped like a wheel

ROTL *n* pl. ROTLS or ARTAL a unit of weight in Muslim countries

ROTO *n* pl. -TOS a type of printing process

ROTOR *n* pl. -S a rotating part of a machine

ROTOTILL *v* -ED, -ING, -S to till soil with a type of farming implement

ROTTE *n* pl. -S a medieval stringed instrument

ROTTED past tense of rot

ROTTEN *adj* -TENER, -TENEST being in a state of decay ROTTENLY *adv*

ROTTER *n* pl. -S a scoundrel

ROTTING present participle of rot

ROTUND *adj* marked by roundness ROTUNDLY *adv*

ROTUNDA *n* pl. -S a round building

ROTURIER *n* pl. -S a commoner

ROUBLE *n* pl. -S ruble

ROUCHE *n* pl. -S ruche

ROUE *n* pl. -S a lecherous man

ROUEN *n* pl. -S any of a breed of domestic ducks

ROUGE *v* ROUGED, ROUGING, ROUGES to color with a red cosmetic

ROUGH *adj* ROUGHER, ROUGHEST having an uneven surface

ROUGH *v* -ED, -ING, -S to make rough

ROUGHAGE *n* pl. -S coarse, bulky food

ROUGHDRY *v* -DRIED, -DRYING, -DRIES to dry without ironing, as washed clothes

ROUGHEN *v* -ED, -ING, -S to make rough

ROUGHER *n* pl. -S one that roughs

ROUGHHEW *v* -HEWED, -HEWN, -HEWING, -HEWS to shape roughly

ROUGHISH *adj* somewhat rough

ROUGHLEG *n* pl. -S a large hawk

ROUGHLY *adv* in a rough manner

ROUGING present participle of rouge

ROUILLE *n* pl. -S a peppery garlic sauce

ROULADE *n* pl. -S a musical embellishment

ROULEAU *n* pl. -LEAUX or -LEAUS a roll of coins wrapped in paper

ROULETTE *v* -LETTED, -LETTING, -LETTES to make tiny slits in

ROUND *adj* ROUNDER, ROUNDEST shaped like a sphere

ROUND *v* -ED, -ING, -S to make round

ROUNDEL *n* pl. -S a round figure or object

ROUNDER *n* pl. -S a tool for rounding

ROUNDISH *adj* somewhat round

ROUNDLET *n* pl. -S a small circle

ROUNDLY *adv* in a round manner

ROUNDUP *n* pl. -S the driving together of cattle scattered over a range

ROUP *v* -ED, -ING, -S to auction

ROUPET *adj* roupy

ROUPY *adj* ROUPIER, ROUPIEST hoarse **ROUPILY** *adv*

ROUSE *v* ROUSED, ROUSING, ROUSES to bring out of a state of sleep or inactivity

ROUSER *n* pl. -S one that rouses

ROUSSEAU *n* pl. -S fried pemmican

ROUST *v* -ED, -ING, -S to arouse and drive out

ROUSTER *n* pl. -S a wharf laborer and deckhand

ROUT *v* -ED, -ING, -S to defeat overwhelmingly

ROUTE *v* ROUTED, ROUTING, ROUTES to send on a particular course

ROUTEMAN *n* pl. -MEN one who conducts business on a customary course

ROUTER *n* pl. -S a scooping tool

ROUTEWAY *n* pl. -WAYS an established course of travel

ROUTH *n* pl. -S an abundance

ROUTINE *n* pl. -S a regular course of procedure

ROUTING present participle of route

ROUX *n* pl. ROUX a mixture of butter and flour

ROVE *v* ROVED, ROVING, ROVES to roam

ROVEN a past participle of reeve

ROVER *n* pl. -S one that roves

ROVING *n* pl. -S a roll of textile fibers

ROVINGLY *adv* in a roving manner

ROW *v* -ED, -ING, -S to propel by means of oars **ROWABLE** *adj*

ROWAN *n* pl. -S a Eurasian tree

ROWBOAT *n* pl. -S a small boat designed to be rowed

ROWDY *adj* -DIER, -DIEST disorderly in behavior **ROWDILY** *adv*

ROWDY *n* pl. -DIES a rowdy person

ROWDYISH *adj* tending to be rowdy

ROWDYISM *n* pl. -S disorderly behavior

ROWEL *v* -ELED, -ELING, -ELS or -ELLED, -ELLING, -ELS to prick with a spiked wheel in order to urge forward

ROWEN *n* pl. -S a second growth of grass

ROWER *n* pl. -S one that rows

ROWING *n* pl. -S the sport of racing in light, long, and narrow rowboats

ROWLOCK *n* pl. -S an oarlock

ROWTH *n* pl. -S routh

ROYAL *n* pl. -S a size of printing paper

ROYALISM *n* pl. -S support of a monarch or monarchy

ROYALIST *n* pl. -S a supporter of a monarch or monarchy

ROYALLY *adv* in a kingly manner

ROYALTY *n* pl. -TIES the status or power of a monarch

ROYSTER *v* -ED, -ING, -S to roister

ROZZER *n* pl. -S a policeman

RUANA *n* pl. -S a woolen poncho

RUB *v* RUBBED, RUBBING, RUBS to move along the surface of a body with pressure

RUBABOO *n* pl. -BOOS a type of soup

RUBACE *n* pl. -S rubasse

RUBAIYAT *n* pl. RUBAIYAT four-lined stanzas in Persian poetry

RUBASSE *n* pl. -S a variety of quartz

RUBATO *n* pl. -TOS a fluctuation of speed within a musical phrase

RUBBABOO *n* pl. -BOOS rubaboo

RUBBED past tense of rub

RUBBER *v* -ED, -ING, -S to stretch one's neck in looking at something

RUBBERY *adj* resembling rubber (an elastic substance)

RUBBING *n* pl. -S an image produced by rubbing

RUBBISH *n* pl. -ES worthless, unwanted matter **RUBBISHY** *adj*

RUBBLE *v* -BLED, -BLING, -BLES to reduce to rubble (broken pieces)

RUBBLY *adj* -BLIER, -BLIEST abounding in rubble

RUBDOWN   *n* pl. -S a brisk rubbing of the body
RUBE   *n* pl. -S a rustic
RUBELLA   *n* pl. -S a virus disease
RUBEOLA   *n* pl. -S a virus disease **RUBEOLAR** *adj*
RUBICUND   *adj* ruddy
RUBIDIUM   *n* pl. -S a metallic element **RUBIDIC** *adj*
RUBIED   past tense of ruby
RUBIER   comparative of ruby
RUBIES   present 3d person sing. of ruby
RUBIEST   superlative of ruby
RUBIGO   *n* pl. -GOS red iron oxide
RUBIOUS   *adj* ruby-colored
RUBLE   *n* pl. -S a monetary unit of the Soviet Union
RUBOFF   *n* pl. -S a deep impression made by close contact
RUBOUT   *n* pl. -S an instance of obliterating something
RUBRIC   *n* pl. -S a part of a manuscript or book that appears in red **RUBRICAL** *adj*
RUBUS   *n* pl. RUBUS a plant of the rose family
RUBY   *v* -BIED, -BYING, -BIES to tint with the color of a ruby (a deep-red precious stone)
RUBY   *adj* -BIER, -BIEST of a deep-red color
RUBYLIKE   *adj* resembling a ruby
RUCHE   *n* pl. -S a pleated strip of fine fabric
RUCHED   *adj* trimmed with a ruche
RUCHING   *n* pl. -S a ruche
RUCK   *v* -ED, -ING, -S to wrinkle or crease
RUCKLE   *v* -LED, -LING, -LES to ruck
RUCKSACK   *n* pl. -S a knapsack
RUCKUS   *n* pl. -ES a noisy disturbance
RUCTION   *n* pl. -S a ruckus
RUCTIOUS   *adj* quarrelsome
RUDD   *n* pl. -S a freshwater fish
RUDDER   *n* pl. -S a vertical blade used to direct the course of a vessel
RUDDIER   comparative of ruddy
RUDDIEST   superlative of ruddy
RUDDILY   *adv* in a ruddy manner
RUDDLE   *v* -DLED, -DLING, -DLES to color with a red dye
RUDDOCK   *n* pl. -S a European bird
RUDDY   *adj* -DIER, -DIEST having a healthy, reddish color

RUDE   *adj* RUDER, RUDEST discourteous or impolite **RUDELY** *adv*
RUDENESS   *n* pl. -ES the quality of being rude
RUDERAL   *n* pl. -S a plant growing in poor land
RUDESBY   *n* pl. -BIES a rude person
RUDEST   superlative of rude
RUDIMENT   *n* pl. -S a basic principle or element
RUE   *v* RUED, RUING, RUES to feel sorrow or remorse for
RUEFUL   *adj* feeling sorrow or remorse **RUEFULLY** *adv*
RUER   *n* pl. -S one that rues
RUFF   *v* -ED, -ING, -S to trump
RUFFE   *n* pl. -S a freshwater fish
RUFFIAN   *n* pl. -S a tough, lawless person
RUFFLE   *v* -FLED, -FLING, -FLES to destroy the smoothness of
RUFFLER   *n* pl. -S one that ruffles
RUFFLIER   comparative of ruffly
RUFFLIEST   superlative of ruffly
RUFFLIKE   *adj* resembling a ruff (a pleated collar)
RUFFLING   present participle of ruffle
RUFFLY   *adj* -FLIER, -FLIEST not smooth
RUFIYAA   *n* pl. RUFIYAA a monetary unit of the Maldives
RUFOUS   *adj* reddish
RUG   *v* RUGGED, RUGGING, RUGS to tear roughly
RUGA   *n* pl. -GAE an anatomical fold or wrinkle **RUGAL, RUGATE** *adj*
RUGBY   *n* pl. -BIES a form of football
RUGGED   *adj* -GEDER, -GEDEST having an uneven surface **RUGGEDLY** *adv*
RUGGER   *n* pl. -S rugby
RUGGING   present participle of rug
RUGLIKE   *adj* resembling a rug (a thick fabric used as a floor covering)
RUGOLA   *n* pl. -S a pungent salad herb
RUGOSE   *adj* full of wrinkles **RUGOSELY** *adv*
RUGOSITY   *n* pl. -TIES the state of being rugose
RUGOUS   *adj* rugose
RUGULOSE   *adj* having small wrinkles
RUIN   *v* -ED, -ING, -S to destroy **RUINABLE** *adj*

RUINATE	v -ATED, -ATING, -ATES to ruin
RUINER	n pl. -S one that ruins
RUING	present participle of rue
RUINOUS	adj destructive
RULE	v RULED, RULING, RULES to exercise control over **RULABLE** adj
RULELESS	adj not restrained or regulated by law
RULER	n pl. -S one that rules
RULING	n pl. -S an authoritative decision
RULY	adj RULIER, RULIEST orderly
RUM	n pl. -S an alcoholic liquor
RUM	adj RUMMER, RUMMEST odd
RUMAKI	n pl. -S chicken liver wrapped together with water chestnuts in a bacon slice
RUMBA	v -ED, -ING, -S to perform a ballroom dance
RUMBLE	v -BLED, -BLING, -BLES to make a deep, thunderous sound
RUMBLER	n pl. -S one that rumbles
RUMBLING	n pl. -S a deep, thunderous sound
RUMBLY	adj tending to rumble
RUMEN	n pl. -MINA or -MENS a part of the stomach of a ruminant **RUMINAL** adj
RUMINANT	n pl. -S a hoofed, even-toed mammal
RUMINATE	v -NATED, -NATING, -NATES to chew again
RUMMAGE	v -MAGED, -MAGING, -MAGES to search thoroughly through
RUMMAGER	n pl. -S one that rummages
RUMMER	n pl. -S a large drinking glass
RUMMEST	superlative of rum
RUMMY	n pl. -MIES a card game
RUMMY	adj -MIER, -MIEST odd
RUMOR	v -ED, -ING, -S to spread by hearsay
RUMOUR	v -ED, -ING, -S to rumor
RUMP	n pl. -S the lower and back part of the trunk **RUMPLESS** adj
RUMPLE	v -PLED, -PLING, -PLES to wrinkle
RUMPLY	adj -PLIER, -PLIEST rumpled
RUMPUS	n pl. -ES a noisy disturbance
RUN	v RAN, RUNNING, RUNS to move by rapid steps
RUNABOUT	n pl. -S a small, open auto
RUNAGATE	n pl. -S a deserter
RUNAWAY	n pl. -AWAYS one that runs away
RUNBACK	n pl. -S a type of run in football
RUNDLE	n pl. -S a rung
RUNDLET	n pl. -S a small barrel
RUNDOWN	n pl. -S a summary
RUNE	n pl. -S a letter of an ancient alphabet **RUNELIKE** adj
RUNG	n pl. -S a crosspiece forming a step of a ladder **RUNGLESS** adj
RUNIC	adj pertaining to a rune
RUNKLE	v -KLED, -KLING, -KLES to wrinkle
RUNLESS	adj scoring no runs in baseball
RUNLET	n pl. -S a small stream
RUNNEL	n pl. -S a small stream
RUNNER	n pl. -S one that runs
RUNNING	n pl. -S a race
RUNNY	adj -NIER, -NIEST tending to drip
RUNOFF	n pl. -S rainfall that is not absorbed by the soil
RUNOUT	n pl. -S the end of a film strip
RUNOVER	n pl. -S matter for publication that exceeds the allotted space
RUNROUND	n pl. -S evasive action
RUNT	n pl. -S a small person or animal **RUNTISH** adj
RUNTY	adj RUNTIER, RUNTIEST small
RUNWAY	n pl. -WAYS a landing and takeoff strip for aircraft
RUPEE	n pl. -S a monetary unit of India
RUPIAH	n pl. -S a monetary unit of Indonesia
RUPTURE	v -TURED, -TURING, -TURES to burst
RURAL	adj pertaining to the country
RURALISE	v -ISED, -ISING, -ISES to ruralize
RURALISM	n pl. -S the state of being rural
RURALIST	n pl. -S one who lives in the country
RURALITE	n pl. -S a ruralist
RURALITY	n pl. -TIES the state of being rural
RURALIZE	v -IZED, -IZING, -IZES to make rural
RURALLY	adv in a rural manner
RURBAN	adj partially rural and urban
RUSE	n pl. -S a deception

RUSH	v -ED, -ING, -ES to move swiftly
RUSHEE	n pl. -S a college student seeking admission to a fraternity or sorority
RUSHER	n pl. -S one that rushes
RUSHIER	comparative of rushy
RUSHIEST	superlative of rushy
RUSHING	n pl. -S yardage gained in football by running plays
RUSHLIKE	adj resembling a rush (a grasslike marsh plant)
RUSHY	adj RUSHIER, RUSHIEST abounding in rushes
RUSINE	adj pertaining to a genus of deer
RUSK	n pl. -S a sweetened biscuit
RUSSET	n pl. -S a reddish or yellowish brown color RUSSETY adj
RUSSIFY	v -FIED, -FYING, -FIES to make Russian
RUST	v -ED, -ING, -S to form rust (a reddish coating that forms on iron) RUSTABLE adj
RUSTIC	n pl. -S one who lives in the country
RUSTICAL	n pl. -S a rustic
RUSTICLY	adv in a rural manner
RUSTIER	comparative of rusty
RUSTIEST	superlative of rusty
RUSTILY	adv in a rusty manner
RUSTLE	v -TLED, -TLING, -TLES to make a succession of slight, soft sounds
RUSTLER	n pl. -S one that rustles
RUSTLESS	adj free from rust
RUSTLING	present participle of rustle
RUSTY	adj RUSTIER, RUSTIEST covered with rust
RUT	v RUTTED, RUTTING, RUTS to make ruts (grooves) in
RUTABAGA	n pl. -S a plant having a thick, edible root
RUTH	n pl. -S compassion
RUTHENIC	adj pertaining to a rare, metallic element
RUTHFUL	adj full of compassion
RUTHLESS	adj having no compassion
RUTILANT	adj having a reddish glow
RUTILE	n pl. -S a mineral
RUTIN	n pl. -S a chemical compound
RUTTED	past tense of rut
RUTTIER	comparative of rutty
RUTTIEST	superlative of rutty
RUTTILY	adv in a rutty manner
RUTTING	present participle of rut
RUTTISH	adj lustful
RUTTY	adj -TIER, -TIEST marked by ruts
RYA	n pl. -S a Scandinavian handwoven rug
RYE	n pl. -S a cereal grass
RYEGRASS	n pl. -ES a European grass
RYKE	v RYKED, RYKING, RYKES to reach
RYND	n pl. -S an iron support
RYOKAN	n pl. -S a Japanese inn
RYOT	n pl. -S a tenant farmer in India

SAB   *v* SABBED, SABBING, SABS to sob

SABATON   *n* pl. -S a piece of armor for the foot

SABAYON   *n* pl. -S a sauce of whipped egg yolks, sugar, and wine

SABBAT   *n* pl. -S an assembly of demons and witches

SABBATH   *n* pl. -S sabbat

SABBATIC   *adj* bringing a period of rest

SABBED   past tense of sab

SABBING   present participle of sab

SABE   *v* SABED, SABEING, SABES to savvy

SABER   *v* -ED, -ING, -S to strike with a saber (a type of sword)

SABIN   *n* pl. -S a unit of sound absorption

SABINE   *n* pl. -S savin

SABIR   *n* pl. -S a French-based pidgin language

SABLE   *n* pl. -S a carnivorous mammal

SABOT   *n* pl. -S a wooden shoe

SABOTAGE   *v* -TAGED, -TAGING, -TAGES to destroy maliciously

SABOTEUR   *n* pl. -S one who sabotages

SABRA   *n* pl. -S a native Israeli

SABRE   *v* -BRED, -BRING, -BRES to saber

SABULOSE   *adj* sabulous

SABULOUS   *adj* sandy

SAC   *n* pl. -S a pouchlike structure in an animal or plant

SACATON   *n* pl. -S a perennial grass

SACBUT   *n* pl. -S sackbut

SACCADE   *n* pl. -S a rapid, jerky movement of the eye **SACCADIC** *adj*

SACCATE   *adj* having a sac

SACCULAR   *adj* resembling a sac

SACCULE   *n* pl. -S a small sac

SACCULUS   *n* pl. -LI saccule

SACHEM   *n* pl. -S a North American Indian chief **SACHEMIC** *adj*

SACHET   *n* pl. -S a small bag containing perfumed powder **SACHETED** *adj*

SACK   *v* -ED, -ING, -S to put into a sack (a large bag)

SACKBUT   *n* pl. -S a medieval trombone

SACKER   *n* pl. -S one that sacks

SACKFUL   *n* pl. SACKFULS or SACKSFUL as much as a sack can hold

SACKING   *n* pl. -S material for making sacks

SACKLIKE   *adj* resembling a sack

SACKSFUL   a pl. of sackful

SACLIKE   *adj* resembling a sac

SACQUE   *n* pl. -S a loose-fitting dress

SACRA   pl. of sacrum

SACRAL   *n* pl. -S a vertebra or nerve situated near the sacrum

SACRARIA   *n/pl* ancient Roman shrines

SACRED   *adj* dedicated to or set apart for the worship of a deity **SACREDLY** *adv*

SACRING   *n* pl. -S the consecration of bread and wine of the Eucharist

SACRIST   *n* pl. -S a person in charge of a sacristy

SACRISTY   *n* pl. -TIES a room in which sacred vessels and vestments are kept

SACRUM   *n* pl. -CRA or -CRUMS a bone of the pelvis

SAD	adj SADDER, SADDEST unhappy	**SAGE**	adj SAGER, SAGEST wise **SAGELY** adv
SADDEN	v -ED, -ING, -S to make sad	**SAGE**	n pl. -S an aromatic herb used
SADDHU	n pl. -S sadhu		as seasoning
SADDLE	v -DLED, -DLING, -DLES to put a saddle (a leather seat for a rider) on	**SAGENESS**	n pl. -ES wisdom
		SAGER	comparative of sage
		SAGEST	superlative of sage
SADDLER	n pl. -S one that makes, repairs, or sells saddles	**SAGGAR**	v -ED, -ING, -S to bake in a saggar (a protective clay casing)
SADDLERY	n pl. -DLERIES the shop of a saddler		
		SAGGARD	n pl. -S a saggar
SADDLING	present participle of saddle	**SAGGED**	past tense of sag
SADE	n pl. -S a Hebrew letter	**SAGGER**	v -ED, -ING, -S to saggar
SADHE	n pl. -S sade	**SAGGING**	present participle of sag
SADHU	n pl. -S a Hindu holy man	**SAGGY**	adj -GIER, -GIEST characterized by sagging
SADI	n pl. -S sade		
SADIRON	n pl. -S a heavy flatiron	**SAGIER**	comparative of sagy
SADISM	n pl. -S a tendency to take delight in inflicting pain	**SAGIEST**	superlative of sagy
		SAGITTAL	adj resembling an arrow or arrowhead
SADIST	n pl. -S one marked by sadism **SADISTIC** adj		
		SAGO	n pl. -GOS a tropical tree
SADLY	adv in a sad manner	**SAGUARO**	n pl. -ROS a tall cactus
SADNESS	n pl. -ES the state of being sad	**SAGUM**	n pl. -GA a cloak worn by ancient Roman soldiers
SAE	adv so	**SAGY**	adj SAGIER, SAGIEST flavored with sage
SAFARI	v -ED, -ING, -S to go on a hunting expedition		
		SAHIB	n pl. -S sir; master — used as a term of respect in colonial India
SAFE	adj SAFER, SAFEST free from danger **SAFELY** adv		
SAFE	n pl. -S a metal receptacle for storing valuables	**SAHIWAL**	n pl. -S any of a breed of humped dairy cattle
SAFENESS	n pl. -ES the quality of being safe	**SAHUARO**	n pl. -ROS saguaro
		SAICE	n pl. -S syce
SAFER	comparative of safe	**SAID**	n pl. -S sayyid
SAFEST	superlative of safe	**SAIGA**	n pl. -S a small antelope
SAFETY	v -TIED, -TYING, -TIES to protect against failure, breakage, or accident	**SAIL**	v -ED, -ING, -S to move across the surface of water by the action of wind **SAILABLE** adj
SAFFRON	n pl. -S a flowering plant		
SAFRANIN	n pl. -S a red dye	**SAILBOAT**	n pl. -S a boat that sails
SAFROL	n pl. -S safrole	**SAILER**	n pl. -S a vessel that sails
SAFROLE	n pl. -S a poisonous liquid	**SAILFISH**	n pl. -ES a large marine fish
SAG	v SAGGED, SAGGING, SAGS to bend or sink downward from weight or pressure	**SAILING**	n pl. -S the act of one that sails
		SAILOR	n pl. -S a member of a ship's crew **SAILORLY** adj
SAGA	n pl. -S a medieval Scandinavian narrative	**SAIMIN**	n pl. -S a Hawaiian noodle soup
		SAIN	v -ED, -ING, -S to make the sign of the cross on
SAGACITY	n pl. -TIES wisdom		
SAGAMAN	n pl. -MEN a writer of sagas	**SAINFOIN**	n pl. -S a perennial herb
SAGAMORE	n pl. -S an Algonquian Indian chief	**SAINT**	v -ED, -ING, -S to declare to be a saint (a person of exceptional holiness)
SAGANASH	n pl. -ES a white man — an Algonquian Indian term		
		SAINTDOM	n pl. -S the condition of being a saint
SAGBUT	n pl. -S sackbut		

SAINTLY *adj* -LIER, -LIEST of or befitting a saint

SAITH a present 3d person sing. of say

SAITHE *n* pl. SAITHE a marine food fish

SAIYID *n* pl. -S sayyid

SAJOU *n* pl. -S a capuchin

SAKE *n* pl. -S benefit, interest, or advantage

SAKER *n* pl. -S a Eurasian falcon

SAKI *n* pl. -S a Japanese liquor

SAL *n* pl. -S salt

SALAAM *v* -ED, -ING, -S to greet with a low bow

SALABLE *adj* capable of being or fit to be sold **SALABLY** *adv*

SALACITY *n* pl. -TIES lewdness

SALAD *n* pl. -S a dish of green, raw vegetables

SALADANG *n* pl. -S a wild ox

SALAL *n* pl. -S a small shrub

SALAMI *n* pl. -S a seasoned sausage

SALARIAT *n* pl. -S the class of salaried persons

SALARY *v* -RIED, -RYING, -RIES to pay a periodic, fixed compensation to

SALCHOW *n* pl. -S a figure-skating jump

SALE *n* pl. -S the act or an instance of selling

SALEABLE *adj* salable **SALEABLY** *adv*

SALEP *n* pl. -S a starchy meal ground from the roots of certain orchids

SALEROOM *n* pl. -S a room in which goods are displayed for sale

SALESMAN *n* pl. -MEN a man who sells merchandise

SALIC *adj* pertaining to a group of igneous rocks

SALICIN *n* pl. -S a chemical compound

SALICINE *n* pl. -S salicin

SALIENCE *n* pl. -S a projecting feature or detail

SALIENCY *n* pl. -CIES salience

SALIENT *n* pl. -S the part of a fortification projecting closest to the enemy

SALIFY *v* -FIED, -FYING, -FIES to combine with a salt

SALINA *n* pl. -S a pond, marsh, or lake containing salt water

SALINE *n* pl. -S a salt solution

SALINITY *n* pl. -TIES a concentration of salt

SALINIZE *v* -NIZED, -NIZING, -NIZES to treat with salt

SALIVA *n* pl. -S a fluid secreted by the glands of the mouth **SALIVARY** *adj*

SALIVATE *v* -VATED, -VATING, -VATES to secrete saliva

SALL *v* shall — SALL is the only form of this verb; it cannot be conjugated

SALLET *n* pl. -S a light medieval helmet

SALLIED past tense of sally

SALLIER *n* pl. -S one that sallies

SALLIES present 3d person sing. of sally

SALLOW *adj* -LOWER, -LOWEST of a sickly yellowish color **SALLOWLY** *adv*

SALLOW *v* -ED, -ING, -S to make sallow

SALLOWY *adj* abounding in willow trees

SALLY *v* -LIED, -LYING, -LIES to rush out suddenly

SALMI *n* pl. -S a dish of roasted game birds

SALMON *n* pl. -S a food fish

SALMONID *n* pl. -S a fish of the salmon family

SALOL *n* pl. -S a chemical compound

SALON *n* pl. -S a large room in which guests are received

SALOON *n* pl. -S a tavern

SALOOP *n* pl. -S a hot drink made from an infusion of aromatic herbs

SALP *n* pl. -S salpa

SALPA *n* pl. -PAE or -PAS a free-swimming tunicate

SALPIAN *n* pl. -S salpa

SALPID *n* pl. -S salpa

SALPINX *n* pl. -PINGES an anatomical tube

SALSA *n* pl. -S a spicy sauce of tomatoes, onions, and peppers

SALSIFY *n* pl. -FIES a European herb

SALSILLA *n* pl. -S a tropical plant

SALT *v* -ED, -ING, -S to treat with salt (a crystalline compound used as a seasoning and preservative)

SALT *adj* SALTER, SALTEST salty

SALTANT *adj* jumping or dancing

SALTBOX *n* pl. -ES a type of house

SALTBUSH *n* pl. -ES a salt-tolerant plant

SALTER *n* pl. -S one that salts

SALTERN *n* pl. -S a place where salt is produced

SALTIE *n* pl. -S a deep-sea vessel sailing the Great Lakes

SALTIER *n* pl. -S saltire

SALTIEST superlative of salty

SALTILY *adv* in a salty manner

SALTINE *n* pl. -S a salted cracker

SALTING *n* pl. -S land regularly flooded by tides

SALTIRE *n* pl. -S a heraldic design

SALTISH *adj* somewhat salty

SALTLESS *adj* having no salt

SALTLIKE *adj* resembling salt

SALTNESS *n* pl. -ES the state of being salty

SALTPAN *n* pl. -S a large pan for making salt by evaporation

SALTWORK *n* pl. -S a saltern

SALTWORT *n* pl. -S a seaside herb

SALTY *adj* SALTIER, SALTIEST tasting of or containing salt

SALUKI *n* pl. -S a tall, slender dog

SALUTARY *adj* producing a beneficial effect

SALUTE *v* -LUTED, -LUTING, -LUTES to greet with a sign of welcome or respect

SALUTER *n* pl. -S one that salutes

SALVABLE *adj* capable of being saved SALVABLY *adv*

SALVAGE *v* -VAGED, -VAGING, -VAGES to save from loss or destruction

SALVAGEE *n* pl. -S one in whose favor salvage has been effected

SALVAGER *n* pl. -S one that salvages

SALVAGING present participle of salvage

SALVE *v* SALVED, SALVING, SALVES to soothe

SALVER *n* pl. -S a tray or serving platter

SALVIA *n* pl. -S a flowering plant

SALVIFIC *adj* having the power to save

SALVING present participle of salve

SALVO *v* -ED, -ING, -S or -ES to discharge firearms simultaneously

SALVOR *n* pl. -S a salvager

SAMARA *n* pl. -S a dry, one-seeded fruit

SAMARIUM *n* pl. -S a metallic element

SAMBA *v* -ED, -ING, -S to perform a Brazilian dance

SAMBAR *n* pl. -S a large Asian deer

SAMBHAR *n* pl. -S sambar

SAMBHUR *n* pl. -S sambar

SAMBO *n* pl. -BOS a Latin American of mixed black and Indian ancestry

SAMBUCA *n* pl. -S an ancient stringed instrument

SAMBUKE *n* pl. -S sambuca

SAMBUR *n* pl. -S sambar

SAME *adj* resembling in every relevant respect

SAMECH *n* pl. -S samek

SAMEK *n* pl. -S a Hebrew letter

SAMEKH *n* pl. -S samek

SAMENESS *n* pl. -ES lack of change or variety

SAMIEL *n* pl. -S the simoom

SAMISEN *n* pl. -S a Japanese stringed instrument

SAMITE *n* pl. -S a silk fabric

SAMIZDAT *n* pl. -S a system in the Soviet Union for printing and distributing unauthorized literature

SAMLET *n* pl. -S a young salmon

SAMOSA *n* pl. -S a filled pastry turnover

SAMOVAR *n* pl. -S a metal urn for heating water

SAMP *n* pl. -S coarsely ground corn

SAMPAN *n* pl. -S a flat-bottomed Chinese skiff

SAMPHIRE *n* pl. -S a European herb

SAMPLE *v* -PLED, -PLING, -PLES to test a representative portion of a whole

SAMPLER *n* pl. -S one that samples

SAMPLING *n* pl. -S a small part selected for analysis

SAMSARA *n* pl. -S the cycle of birth, death, and rebirth in Buddhism

SAMSHU *n* pl. -S a Chinese liquor

SAMURAI *n* pl. -S a Japanese warrior

SANATIVE *adj* having the power to cure or heal

SANCTA a pl. of sanctum

SANCTIFY *v* -FIED, -FYING, -FIES to make holy

SANCTION *v* -ED, -ING, -S to authorize

SANCTITY *n* pl. -TIES holiness

SANCTUM *n* pl. -TUMS or -TA a sacred place

SAND *v* -ED, -ING, -S to cover with sand (a loose, granular rock material)

SANDAL *v* -DALED, -DALING, -DALS or -DALLED, -DALLING, -DALS to provide with sandals (light, open shoes)

SANDARAC *n* pl. -S an aromatic resin

SANDBAG *v* -BAGGED, -BAGGING, -BAGS to surround with bags of sand

SANDBANK *n* pl. -S a large mass of sand

SANDBAR *n* pl. -S a ridge of sand formed in a river or sea

SANDBOX *n* pl. -ES a box containing sand for children to play in

SANDBUR *n* pl. -S an annual herb

SANDBURR *n* pl. -S sandbur

SANDDAB *n* pl. -S a small flatfish

SANDER *n* pl. -S one that sands

SANDFISH *n* pl. -ES a marine fish

SANDFLY *n* pl. -FLIES a biting fly

SANDHI *n* pl. -S a process of phonetic modification

SANDHOG *n* pl. -S a worker who digs or works in sand

SANDIER comparative of sandy

SANDIEST superlative of sandy

SANDLIKE *adj* resembling sand

SANDLING *n* pl. -S a marine fish

SANDLOT *n* pl. -S a vacant lot

SANDMAN *n* pl. -MEN a mythical person who makes children sleepy by sprinkling sand in their eyes

SANDPEEP *n* pl. -S a wading bird

SANDPILE *n* pl. -S a pile of sand

SANDPIT *n* pl. -S a pit dug in sandy soil

SANDSHOE *n* pl. -S a lightweight sneaker

SANDSOAP *n* pl. -S a type of soap

SANDSPUR *n* pl. -S a sandbur

SANDWICH *v* -ED,.-ING, -ES to place between two layers or objects

SANDWORM *n* pl. -S a sand-dwelling worm

SANDWORT *n* pl. -S a flowering plant

SANDY *adj* SANDIER, SANDIEST containing or covered with sand

SANE *adj* SANER, SANEST mentally sound SANELY *adv*

SANE *v* SANED, SANING, SANES to sain

SANENESS *n* pl. -ES sanity

SANER comparative of sane

SANEST superlative of sane

SANG past tense of sing

SANGA *n* pl. -S sangar

SANGAR *n* pl. -S a temporary fortification for two or three men

SANGAREE *n* pl. -S an alcoholic beverage

SANGER *n* pl. -S sangar

SANGH *n* pl. -S an association promoting unity between the different groups in Hinduism

SANGRIA *n* pl. -S an alcoholic beverage

SANGUINE *n* pl. -S a red color

SANICLE *n* pl. -S a medicinal herb

SANIES *n* pl. SANIES a fluid discharged from wounds SANIOUS *adj*

SANING present participle of sane

SANITARY *n* pl. -TARIES a public urinal

SANITATE *v* -TATED, -TATING, -TATES to sanitize

SANITIES pl. of sanity

SANITISE *v* -TISED, -TISING, -TISES to sanitize

SANITIZE *v* -TIZED, -TIZING, -TIZES to guard against infection or disease by cleaning or sterilizing

SANITY *n* pl. -TIES the state of being sane

SANJAK *n* pl. -S an administrative district of Turkey

SANK past tense of sink

SANNOP *n* pl. -S sannup

SANNUP *n* pl. -S a married male American Indian

SANNYASI *n* pl. -S a Hindu monk

SANS *prep* without

SANSAR *n* pl. -S sarsar

SANSEI *n* pl. -S a grandchild of Japanese immigrants to the United States

SANSERIF *n* pl. -S a typeface without serifs

SANTALIC *adj* pertaining to sandalwood

SANTALOL *n* pl. -S sandalwood oil

SANTIMS *n* pl. -TIMI a former coin of Latvia

SANTIR *n* pl. -S a Persian dulcimer

SANTO *n* pl. -TOS a wooden image of a saint

SANTOL *n* pl. -S a tropical tree

SANTONIN *n* pl. -S a chemical compound

SANTOUR *n* pl. -S santir

SANTUR *n* pl. -S santir

SAP *v* SAPPED, SAPPING, SAPS to deplete or weaken gradually

SAPAJOU *n* pl. -S a capuchin

SAPHEAD *n* pl. -S a foolish, stupid, or gullible person

SAPHENA *n* pl. -NAE a vein of the leg

SAPID *adj* pleasant to the taste

SAPIDITY *n* pl. -TIES the state of being sapid

SAPIENCE   n pl. -S wisdom
SAPIENCY   n pl. -CIES sapience
SAPIENS   adj pertaining to recent man
SAPIENT   adj wise
SAPLESS   adj lacking vitality
SAPLING   n pl. -S a young tree
SAPONIFY   v -FIED, -FYING, -FIES to convert into soap
SAPONIN   n pl. -S a soapy substance obtained from plants
SAPONINE   n pl. -S saponin
SAPONITE   n pl. -S a mineral found in veins and cavities of rocks
SAPOR   n pl. -S flavor SAPOROUS adj
SAPOTA   n pl. -S an evergreen tree
SAPOTE   n pl. -S a tropical American tree
SAPOUR   n pl. -S sapor
SAPPED   past tense of sap
SAPPER   n pl. -S a military engineer
SAPPHIC   n pl. -S a type of verse form
SAPPHIRE   n pl. -S a blue gem
SAPPHISM   n pl. -S lesbianism
SAPPHIST   n pl. -S a lesbian
SAPPING   present participle of sap
SAPPY   adj -PIER, -PIEST silly SAPPILY adv
SAPREMIA   n pl. -S a form of blood poisoning SAPREMIC adj
SAPROBE   n pl. -S an organism that derives its nourishment from decaying organic matter SAPROBIC adj
SAPROPEL   n pl. -S mud consisting chiefly of decaying organic matter
SAPSAGO   n pl. -GOS a hard green cheese
SAPWOOD   n pl. -S the newly formed outer wood of a tree
SARABAND   n pl. -S a stately Spanish dance
SARAN   n pl. -S a thermoplastic resin
SARAPE   n pl. -S serape
SARCASM   n pl. -S a sharply mocking or contemptuous remark
SARCENET   n pl. -S a silk fabric
SARCOID   n pl. -S a disease of horses
SARCOMA   n pl. -MAS or -MATA a type of tumor
SARCOUS   adj composed of flesh or muscle
SARD   n pl. -S a variety of quartz
SARDANA   n pl. -S a Spanish folk dance
SARDAR   n pl. -S sirdar
SARDINE   n pl. -S a small food fish
SARDIUS   n pl. -ES sard

SARDONIC   adj mocking
SARDONYX   n pl. -ES a variety of quartz
SAREE   n pl. -S sari
SARGASSO   n pl. -GASSOS a brownish seaweed
SARGE   n pl. -S sergeant
SARI   n pl. -S an outer garment worn by Hindu women
SARIN   n pl. -S a toxic gas
SARK   n pl. -S a shirt
SARKY   adj SARKIER, SARKIEST sarcastic
SARMENT   n pl. -S a type of plant stem
SARMENTA   n/pl sarments
SAROD   n pl. -S a lute of northern India
SARODE   n pl. -S sarod
SARODIST   n pl. -S one who plays the sarod
SARONG   n pl. -S an outer garment worn in the Pacific islands
SAROS   n pl. -ES the eclipse cycle of the sun and moon
SARSAR   n pl. -S a cold, whistling wind
SARSEN   n pl. -S a large sandstone block
SARSENET   n pl. -S sarcenet
SARTOR   n pl. -S a tailor
SARTORII   n/pl flat, narrow thigh muscles
SASH   v -ED, -ING, -ES to furnish with a frame in which glass is set
SASHAY   v -ED, -ING, -S to flounce
SASHIMI   n pl. -S a Japanese dish of sliced raw fish
SASIN   n pl. -S an antelope of India
SASS   v -ED, -ING, -ES to talk impudently to
SASSABY   n pl. -BIES an African antelope
SASSIER   comparative of sassy
SASSIES   pl. of sassy
SASSIEST   superlative of sassy
SASSILY   adv in a sassy manner
SASSWOOD   n pl. -S an African tree
SASSY   n pl. -SIES sasswood
SASSY   adj SASSIER, SASSIEST impudent
SASTRUGA   n pl. -GI a ridge of snow formed by the wind in polar regions
SAT   past tense of sit
SATANG   n pl. -S a monetary unit of Thailand
SATANIC   adj extremely evil
SATANISM   n pl. -S worship of the powers of evil

SATANIST	*n* pl. -S one who practices satanism
SATARA	*n* pl. -S a woolen fabric
SATAY	*n* pl. -TAYS marinated meat that is skewered and broiled and dipped in peanut sauce
SATCHEL	*n* pl. -S a small carrying bag
SATE	*v* SATED, SATING, SATES to satiate
SATEEN	*n* pl. -S a cotton fabric
SATEM	*adj* pertaining to a group of Indo-European languages
SATI	*n* pl. -S suttee
SATIABLE	*adj* capable of being satiated **SATIABLY** *adv*
SATIATE	*v* -ATED, -ATING, -ATES to satisfy to or beyond capacity
SATIETY	*n* pl. -ETIES the state of being satiated
SATIN	*n* pl. -S a smooth fabric
SATINET	*n* pl. -S a thin satin
SATING	present participle of sate
SATINPOD	*n* pl. -S a flowering plant
SATINY	*adj* resembling satin
SATIRE	*n* pl. -S the use of derisive wit to attack folly or wickedness **SATIRIC** *adj*
SATIRISE	*v* -RISED, -RISING, -RISES to satirize
SATIRIST	*n* pl. -S one who satirizes
SATIRIZE	*v* -RIZED, -RIZING, -RIZES to subject to satire
SATISFY	*v* -FIED, -FYING, -FIES to provide fully with what is desired, expected, or needed
SATORI	*n* pl. -S the illumination of spirit sought by Zen Buddhists
SATRAP	*n* pl. -S a governor of a province in ancient Persia
SATRAPY	*n* pl. -PIES the territory of a satrap
SATSUMA	*n* pl. -S a variety of orange
SATURANT	*n* pl. -S a substance used to saturate
SATURATE	*v* -RATED, -RATING, -RATES to fill completely with something that permeates
SATYR	*n* pl. -S a woodland deity of Greek mythology **SATYRIC** *adj*
SATYRID	*n* pl. -S a brownish butterfly
SAU	*n* pl. SAU xu
SAUCE	*v* SAUCED, SAUCING, SAUCES to season with sauce (a flavorful liquid dressing)
SAUCEBOX	*n* pl. -ES a saucy person
SAUCEPAN	*n* pl. -S a cooking utensil
SAUCER	*n* pl. -S a small, shallow dish
SAUCH	*n* pl. -S saugh
SAUCING	present participle of sauce
SAUCY	*adj* SAUCIER, SAUCIEST impudent **SAUCILY** *adv*
SAUGER	*n* pl. -S a freshwater fish
SAUGH	*n* pl. -S a willow tree **SAUGHY** *adj*
SAUL	*n* pl. -S soul
SAULT	*n* pl. -S a waterfall
SAUNA	*n* pl. -S a Finnish steam bath
SAUNTER	*v* -ED, -ING, -S to walk in a leisurely manner
SAUREL	*n* pl. -S a marine fish
SAURIAN	*n* pl. -S any of a suborder of reptiles
SAUROPOD	*n* pl. -S any of a suborder of large dinosaurs
SAURY	*n* pl. -RIES a marine fish
SAUSAGE	*n* pl. -S finely chopped and seasoned meat stuffed into a casing
SAUTE	*v* -TEED or -TED, -TEING, -TES to fry in a small amount of fat
SAUTERNE	*n* pl. -S a sweet white wine
SAUTOIR	*n* pl. -S a saltire
SAUTOIRE	*n* pl. -S sautoir
SAVABLE	*adj* capable of being saved
SAVAGE	*adj* -AGER, -AGEST fierce **SAVAGELY** *adv*
SAVAGE	*v* -AGED, -AGING, -AGES to attack or treat brutally
SAVAGERY	*n* pl. -RIES the quality of being savage
SAVAGEST	superlative of savage
SAVAGING	present participle of savage
SAVAGISM	*n* pl. -S savagery
SAVANNA	*n* pl. -S a flat, treeless grassland
SAVANNAH	*n* pl. -S savanna
SAVANT	*n* pl. -S a man of profound learning
SAVARIN	*n* pl. -S a yeast cake baked in a ring mold
SAVATE	*n* pl. -S a pugilistic sport
SAVE	*v* SAVED, SAVING, SAVES to rescue from danger, injury, or loss **SAVEABLE** *adj*
SAVELOY	*n* pl. -LOYS a highly seasoned sausage
SAVER	*n* pl. -S one that saves
SAVIN	*n* pl. -S an evergreen shrub
SAVINE	*n* pl. -S savin
SAVING	*n* pl. -S the act or an instance of saving

SAVINGLY *adv* in a thrifty manner
SAVIOR *n* pl. -S one that saves
SAVIOUR *n* pl. -S savior
SAVOR *v* -ED, -ING, -S to taste or smell with pleasure
SAVORER *n* pl. -S one that savors
SAVORIER comparative of savory
SAVORIES pl. of savory
SAVOROUS *adj* savory
SAVORY *adj* -VORIER, -VORIEST pleasant to the taste or smell **SAVORILY** *adv*
SAVORY *n* pl. -VORIES a savory dish served before or after a meal
SAVOUR *v* -ED, -ING, -S to savor
SAVOURER *n* pl. -S savorer
SAVOURY *adj* -VOURIER, -VOURIEST savory
SAVOURY *n* pl. -VOURIES a savory
SAVOY *n* pl. -VOYS a variety of cabbage
SAVVY *v* -VIED, -VYING, -VIES to understand
SAVVY *adj* -VIER, -VIEST shrewd
SAW *v* SAWED, SAWN, SAWING, SAWS to cut or divide with a saw (a type of cutting tool)
SAWBILL *n* pl. -S a tropical bird
SAWBONES *n* pl. -BONESES a surgeon
SAWBUCK *n* pl. -S a sawhorse
SAWDUST *n* pl. -S small particles of wood produced in sawing
SAWER *n* pl. -S one that saws
SAWFISH *n* pl. -ES a marine fish
SAWFLY *n* pl. -FLIES a winged insect
SAWHORSE *n* pl. -S a rack used to support a piece of wood being sawed
SAWLIKE *adj* resembling a saw
SAWLOG *n* pl. -S a log large enough to saw into boards
SAWMILL *n* pl. -S a place where logs are sawed
SAWN a past participle of saw
SAWNEY *n* pl. -NEYS a foolish person
SAWTOOTH *n* pl. -TEETH a cutting edge on a saw
SAWYER *n* pl. -S one that saws wood for a living
SAX *n* pl. -ES a saxophone
SAXATILE *adj* living or growing among rocks
SAXHORN *n* pl. -S a brass wind instrument
SAXONY *n* pl. -NIES a woolen fabric
SAXTUBA *n* pl. -S a bass saxhorn

SAY *v* SAID, SAYING, present sing. 2d person SAY, SAYEST, or SAYST, 3d person SAYS or SAITH to utter **SAYABLE** *adj*
SAYER *n* pl. -S one that says
SAYID *n* pl. -S sayyid
SAYING *n* pl. -S a maxim
SAYONARA *n* pl. -S goodby
SAYST a present 2d person sing. of say
SAYYID *n* pl. -S lord; sir — used as a title of respect for a Muslim dignitary
SCAB *v* SCABBED, SCABBING, SCABS to become covered with a scab (a crust that forms over a healing wound)
SCABBARD *v* -ED, -ING, -S to put into a sheath, as a sword
SCABBLE *v* -BLED, -BLING, -BLES to shape roughly
SCABBY *adj* -BIER, -BIEST covered with scabs **SCABBILY** *adv*
SCABIES *n* pl. SCABIES a skin disease
SCABIOSA *n* pl. -S scabious
SCABIOUS *n* pl. -ES a flowering plant
SCABLAND *n* pl. -S rocky land with little soil cover
SCABLIKE *adj* resembling a scab
SCABROUS *adj* roughened with small projections
SCAD *n* pl. -S a marine fish
SCAFFOLD *v* -ED, -ING, -S to provide with a scaffold (a temporary platform for workmen)
SCAG *n* pl. -S heroin
SCALABLE *adj* capable of being scaled **SCALABLY** *adv*
SCALADE *n* pl. -S an act of scaling the walls of a fortification
SCALADO *n* pl. -DOS scalade
SCALAGE *n* pl. -S a percentage deduction to compensate for shrinkage
SCALAR *n* pl. -S a mathematical quantity possessing only magnitude
SCALARE *n* pl. -S a tropical fish
SCALAWAG *n* pl. -S a rascal
SCALD *v* -ED, -ING, -S to burn with hot liquid or steam
SCALDIC *adj* skaldic
SCALE *v* SCALED, SCALING, SCALES to climb up or over

SCALENE *adj* designating a triangle having no two sides equal

SCALENUS *n* pl. -NI a muscle of the neck

SCALEPAN *n* pl. -S a pan on a weighing scale

SCALER *n* pl. -S one that scales

SCALEUP *n* pl. -S an increase based on a fixed ratio

SCALIER comparative of scaly

SCALIEST superlative of scaly

SCALING present participle of scale

SCALL *n* pl. -S a scaly eruption of the skin

SCALLION *n* pl. -S an onion-like plant

SCALLOP *v* -ED, -ING, -S to bake in a sauce topped with bread crumbs

SCALP *v* -ED, -ING, -S to remove an upper part from

SCALPEL *n* pl. -S a small surgical knife

SCALPER *n* pl. -S one that scalps

SCALY *adj* SCALIER, SCALIEST peeling off in flakes

SCAM *v* SCAMMED, SCAMMING, SCAMS to cheat or swindle

SCAMMONY *n* pl. -NIES a climbing plant

SCAMP *v* -ED, -ING, -S to perform in a hasty or careless manner

SCAMPER *v* -ED, -ING, -S to run playfully about

SCAMPI *n* pl. SCAMPI or SCAMPIES large shrimp used in Italian cooking

SCAMPISH *adj* rascally

SCAN *v* SCANNED, SCANNING, SCANS to examine closely

SCANDAL *v* -DALED, -DALING, -DALS or -DALLED, -DALLING, -DALS to defame

SCANDENT *adj* climbing, as a plant

SCANDIA *n* pl. -S an oxide of scandium

SCANDIUM *n* pl. -S a metallic element **SCANDIC** *adj*

SCANNED past tense of scan

SCANNER *n* pl. -S one that scans

SCANNING *n* pl. -S close examination

SCANSION *n* pl. -S the analysis of verse into metrical feet and rhythm patterns

SCANT *adj* SCANTER, SCANTEST meager

SCANT *v* -ED, -ING, -S to provide with a meager portion

SCANTIER comparative of scanty

SCANTIES *n/pl* brief panties for women

SCANTLY *adv* in a scant manner

SCANTY *adj* SCANTIER, SCANTIEST meager **SCANTILY** *adv*

SCAPE *v* SCAPED, SCAPING, SCAPES to escape

SCAPHOID *n* pl. -S a bone of the wrist

SCAPOSE *adj* bearing a leafless stalk

SCAPULA *n* pl. -LAE or -LAS a bone of the shoulder

SCAPULAR *n* pl. -S a sleeveless outer garment worn by monks

SCAR *v* SCARRED, SCARRING, SCARS to form a scar (a mark left by the healing of injured tissue)

SCARAB *n* pl. -S a large, black beetle

SCARCE *adj* SCARCER, SCARCEST infrequently seen or found

SCARCELY *adv* by a narrow margin

SCARCITY *n* pl. -TIES the quality of being scarce

SCARE *v* SCARED, SCARING, SCARES to frighten

SCARER *n* pl. -S one that scares

SCAREY *adj* SCARIER, SCARIEST scary

SCARF *n* pl. SCARFS or SCARVES a piece of cloth worn for warmth or protection

SCARF *v* -ED, -ING, -S to cover with a scarf

SCARFPIN *n* pl. -S a tiepin

SCARIER comparative of scarey and scary

SCARIEST superlative of scarey and scary

SCARIFY *v* -FIED, -FYING, -FIES to make superficial cuts in

SCARILY *adv* in a scary manner

SCARING present participle of scare

SCARIOSE *adj* scarious

SCARIOUS *adj* thin, dry, and membranous

SCARLESS *adj* having no scars

SCARLET *n* pl. -S a red color

SCARP *v* -ED, -ING, -S to cut or make into a steep slope

SCARPER *v* -ED, -ING, -S to flee

SCARPH *v* -ED, -ING, -S to unite by means of a type of joint

SCARRED past tense of scar

SCARRING present participle of scar

SCARRY *adj* -RIER, -RIEST marked with scars

SCART *v* -ED, -ING, -S to scratch

SCARVES a pl. of scarf

SCARY *adj* SCARIER, SCARIEST frightening

SCAT	*v* SCATTED, SCATTING, SCATS to leave hastily
SCATBACK	*n* pl. -S a type of player in football
SCATHE	*v* SCATHED, SCATHING, SCATHES to criticize severely
SCATT	*n* pl. -S a tax
SCATTED	past tense of scat
SCATTER	*v* -ED, -ING, -S to go or send in various directions
SCATTING	present participle of scat
SCATTY	*adj* -TIER, -TIEST crazy
SCAUP	*n* pl. -S a sea duck
SCAUPER	*n* pl. -S an engraving tool
SCAUR	*n* pl. -S a protruding, isolated rock
SCAVENGE	*v* -ENGED, -ENGING, -ENGES to search through rubbish for usable items
SCENA	*n* pl. -S an elaborate composition for a single voice
SCENARIO	*n* pl. -IOS a summary of the plot of a dramatic work
SCEND	*v* -ED, -ING, -S to rise upward, as a ship on a wave
SCENE	*n* pl. -S the place where some action or event occurs
SCENERY	*n* pl. -ERIES a picturesque landscape or view
SCENIC	*adj* pertaining to scenery
SCENICAL	*adj* scenic
SCENT	*v* -ED, -ING, -S to fill with an odor
SCEPTER	*v* -ED, -ING, -S to invest with royal authority
SCEPTIC	*n* pl. -S skeptic
SCEPTRAL	*adj* pertaining to royal authority
SCEPTRE	*v* -TRED, -TRING, -TRES to scepter
SCHAPPE	*n* pl. -S a silk fabric
SCHAV	*n* pl. -S a chilled soup
SCHEDULE	*v* -ULED, -ULING, -ULES to assign to a certain date or time
SCHEMA	*n* pl. -MATA or -MAS a generalized diagram or plan
SCHEME	*v* SCHEMED, SCHEMING, SCHEMES to plan or plot
SCHEMER	*n* pl. -S one that schemes
SCHERZO	*n* pl. -ZOS or -ZI a lively musical movement
SCHILLER	*n* pl. -S a brownish luster occurring on certain minerals
SCHISM	*n* pl. -S a division into opposing parties
SCHIST	*n* pl. -S a rock that readily splits into parallel layers
SCHIZIER	comparative of schizy
SCHIZIEST	superlative of schizy
SCHIZO	*n* pl. SCHIZOS a schizoid
SCHIZOID	*n* pl. -S a person affected with a type of psychotic disorder
SCHIZONT	*n* pl. -S an organism that reproduces by a form of asexual reproduction
SCHIZY	*adj* SCHIZIER, SCHIZIEST affected with schizophrenia
SCHIZZY	*adj* SCHIZZIER, SCHIZZIEST schizy
SCHLEP	*v* SCHLEPPED, SCHLEPPING, SCHLEPS to lug or drag
SCHLEPP	*v* -ED, -ING, -S to schlep
SCHLIERE	*n* pl. -REN a small streak in an igneous rock
SCHLOCK	*n* pl. -S inferior merchandise
SCHLOCKY	*adj* of inferior quality
SCHLUMP	*v* -ED, -ING, -S to go about lazily or sloppily dressed
SCHMALTZ	*n* pl. -ES excessive sentimentality
SCHMALZ	*n* pl. -ES schmaltz
SCHMALZY	*adj* SCHMALZIER, SCHMALZIEST characterized by schmaltz
SCHMEAR	*n* pl. -S an aggregate of related things
SCHMEER	*v* -ED, -ING, -S to bribe
SCHMELZE	*n* pl. -S a type of decorative glass
SCHMO	*n* pl. SCHMOES or SCHMOS a stupid person
SCHMOE	*n* pl. -S schmo
SCHMOOS	*v* -ED, -ING, -ES to schmooze
SCHMOOSE	*v* SCHMOOSED, SCHMOOSING, SCHMOOSES to schmooze
SCHMOOZE	*v* SCHMOOZED, SCHMOOZING, SCHMOOZES to gossip
SCHMUCK	*n* pl. -S a foolish or clumsy person
SCHNAPPS	*n* pl. SCHNAPPS a strong liquor
SCHNAPS	*n* pl. SCHNAPS schnapps
SCHNECKE	*n* pl. -KEN a sweet roll
SCHNOOK	*n* pl. -S an easily deceived person
SCHNOZ	*n* pl. SCHNOZZES the nose
SCHNOZZ	*n* pl. -ES schnoz
SCHOLAR	*n* pl. -S a learned person

SCHOLIUM *n* pl. -LIA or -LIUMS an explanatory marginal note

SCHOOL *v* -ED, -ING, -S to educate in an institution of learning

SCHOONER *n* pl. -S a sailing vessel

SCHORL *n* pl. -S a mineral

SCHRIK *n* pl. -S sudden fright

SCHROD *n* pl. -S scrod

SCHTICK *n* pl. -S shtick

SCHTIK *n* pl. -S shtick

SCHUIT *n* pl. -S a Dutch sailing vessel

SCHUL *n* pl. SCHULN shul

SCHUSS *v* -ED, -ING, -ES to make a fast, straight run in skiing

SCHUSSER *n* pl. -S one that schusses

SCHWA *n* pl. -S a type of vowel sound

SCIAENID *n* pl. -S a carnivorous fish

SCIATIC *n* pl. -S a nerve, vein, or artery situated near the hip

SCIATICA *n* pl. -S a painful disorder of the hip and adjoining areas

SCIENCE *n* pl. -S a department of systematized knowledge

SCILICET *adv* namely

SCILLA *n* pl. -S a flowering plant

SCIMETAR *n* pl. -S scimitar

SCIMITAR *n* pl. -S a curved Oriental sword

SCIMITER *n* pl. -S scimitar

SCINCOID *n* pl. -S one of a family of smooth, short-limbed lizards

SCIOLISM *n* pl. -S superficial knowledge

SCIOLIST *n* pl. -S one whose knowledge is superficial

SCION *n* pl. -S a child or descendant

SCIROCCO *n* pl. -COS sirocco

SCIRRHUS *n* pl. -RHI or -RHUSES a hard tumor

SCISSILE *adj* capable of being cut or split easily

SCISSION *n* pl. -S the act of cutting or splitting

SCISSOR *v* -ED, -ING, -S to cut with a two-bladed cutting implement

SCISSURE *n* pl. -S a lengthwise cut

SCIURID *n* pl. -S a sciurine

SCIURINE *n* pl. -S a rodent of the squirrel family

SCIUROID *adj* resembling a squirrel

SCLAFF *v* -ED, -ING, -S to strike the ground with the club before hitting the ball in golf

SCLAFFER *n* pl. -S one that sclaffs

SCLERA *n* pl. -RAS or -RAE the white, fibrous outer coat of the eyeball **SCLERAL** *adj*

SCLEREID *n* pl. -S a type of plant cell

SCLERITE *n* pl. -S one of the hard plates forming the outer covering of an arthropod

SCLEROID *adj* sclerous

SCLEROMA *n* pl. -MATA a hardened patch of cellular tissue

SCLEROSE *v* -ROSED, -ROSING, -ROSES to become hard, as tissue

SCLEROUS *adj* hardened

SCOFF *v* -ED, -ING, -S to express rude doubt or derision

SCOFFER *n* pl. -S one that scoffs

SCOFFLAW *n* pl. -S an habitual law violator

SCOLD *v* -ED, -ING, -S to rebuke harshly

SCOLDER *n* pl. -S one that scolds

SCOLDING *n* pl. -S a harsh reproof

SCOLEX *n* pl. -LECES or -LICES the knoblike head of a tapeworm

SCOLIOMA *n* pl. -S abnormal curvature of the spine

SCOLLOP *v* -ED, -ING, -S to scallop

SCONCE *v* SCONCED, SCONCING, SCONCES to fine

SCONE *n* pl. -S a flat, round cake

SCOOP *v* -ED, -ING, -S to take up with a scoop (a spoonlike utensil)

SCOOPER *n* pl. -S one that scoops

SCOOPFUL *n* pl. SCOOPFULS or SCOOPSFUL as much as a scoop will hold

SCOOT *v* -ED, -ING, -S to go quickly

SCOOTER *n* pl. -S a two-wheeled vehicle

SCOP *n* pl. -S an Old English poet

SCOPE *v* SCOPED, SCOPING, SCOPES to look at in order to evaluate

SCOPULA *n* pl. -LAE or -LAS a dense tuft of hairs

SCORCH *v* -ED, -ING, -ES to burn slightly so as to alter the color or taste

SCORCHER *n* pl. -S one that scorches

SCORE *v* SCORED, SCORING, SCORES to make a point in a game or contest

SCOREPAD *n* pl. -S a pad on which scored points are recorded

SCORER *n* pl. -S one that scores

SCORIA *n* pl. -RIAE the refuse of a smelted metal or ore

SCORIFY *v* -FIED, -FYING, -FIES to reduce to scoria

SCORING	present participle of score
SCORN	v -ED, -ING, -S to treat or regard with contempt
SCORNER	n pl. -S one that scorns
SCORNFUL	adj feeling or expressing contempt
SCORPION	n pl. -S a stinging arachnid
SCOT	n pl. -S a tax
SCOTCH	v -ED, -ING, -ES to put a definite end to
SCOTER	n pl. -S a sea duck
SCOTIA	n pl. -S a concave molding
SCOTOMA	n pl. -MAS or -MATA a blind spot in the field of vision
SCOTOPIA	n pl. -S vision in dim light **SCOTOPIC** adj
SCOTTIE	n pl. -S a short-legged terrier
SCOUR	v -ED, -ING, -S to cleanse or polish by hard rubbing
SCOURER	n pl. -S one that scours
SCOURGE	v SCOURGED, SCOURGING, SCOURGES to punish severely
SCOURGER	n pl. -S one that scourges
SCOURING	n pl. -S material removed by scouring
SCOUSE	n pl. -S a type of meat stew
SCOUT	v -ED, -ING, -S to observe for the purpose of obtaining information
SCOUTER	n pl. -S one that scouts
SCOUTH	n pl. -S plenty
SCOUTHER	v -ED, -ING, -S to scorch
SCOUTING	n pl. -S the act of one that scouts
SCOW	v -ED, -ING, -S to transport by scow (a flat-bottomed boat)
SCOWDER	v -ED, -ING, -S to scouther
SCOWL	v -ED, -ING, -S to frown angrily
SCOWLER	n pl. -S one that scowls
SCRABBLE	v -BLED, -BLING, -BLES to claw or grope about frantically
SCRABBLY	adj -BLIER, -BLIEST raspy
SCRAG	v SCRAGGED, SCRAGGING, SCRAGS to wring the neck of
SCRAGGLY	adj -GLIER, -GLIEST uneven
SCRAGGY	adj -GIER, -GIEST scrawny
SCRAICH	v -ED, -ING, -S to utter a shrill cry
SCRAIGH	v -ED, -ING, -S to scraich
SCRAM	v SCRAMMED, SCRAMMING, SCRAMS to leave quickly
SCRAMBLE	v -BLED, -BLING, -BLES to move or climb hurriedly
SCRAMJET	n pl. -S a type of aircraft engine
SCRANNEL	n pl. -S a thin person
SCRAP	v SCRAPPED, SCRAPPING, SCRAPS to discard
SCRAPE	v SCRAPED, SCRAPING, SCRAPES to rub so as to remove an outer layer
SCRAPER	n pl. -S one that scrapes
SCRAPIE	n pl. -S a disease of sheep
SCRAPING	n pl. -S something scraped off
SCRAPPED	past tense of scrap
SCRAPPER	n pl. -S a fighter
SCRAPPIER	comparative of scrappy
SCRAPPIEST	superlative of scrappy
SCRAPPING	present participle of scrap
SCRAPPLE	n pl. -S a seasoned mixture of ground meat and cornmeal
SCRAPPY	adj -PIER, -PIEST marked by fighting spirit
SCRATCH	v -ED, -ING, -ES to make a thin, shallow cut or mark on
SCRATCHY	adj SCRATCHIER, SCRATCHIEST made by scratching
SCRAWL	v -ED, -ING, -S to write hastily or illegibly
SCRAWLER	n pl. -S one that scrawls
SCRAWLY	adj SCRAWLIER, SCRAWLIEST written hastily or illegibly
SCRAWNY	adj -NIER, -NIEST extremely thin
SCREAK	v -ED, -ING, -S to screech
SCREAKY	adj screechy
SCREAM	v -ED, -ING, -S to utter a prolonged, piercing cry
SCREAMER	n pl. -S one that screams
SCREE	n pl. -S a mass of rocks at the foot of a slope
SCREECH	v -ED, -ING, -ES to utter a harsh, shrill cry
SCREECHY	adj SCREECHIER, SCREECHIEST screeching
SCREED	v -ED, -ING, -S to shred
SCREEN	v -ED, -ING, -S to provide with a screen (a device designed to divide, conceal, or protect)
SCREENER	n pl. -S one that screens
SCREW	v -ED, -ING, -S to attach with a screw (a type of metal fastener)
SCREWER	n pl. -S one that screws
SCREWUP	n pl. -S an instance of bungling

SCREWY *adj* SCREWIER, SCREWIEST crazy

SCRIBAL *adj* pertaining to a public clerk or secretary

SCRIBBLE *v* -BLED, -BLING, -BLES to write hastily or carelessly

SCRIBE *v* SCRIBED, SCRIBING, SCRIBES to mark with a scriber

SCRIBER *n* pl. -S a pointed instrument used for marking off material to be cut

SCRIED past tense of scry

SCRIES present 3d person sing. of scry

SCRIEVE *v* SCRIEVED, SCRIEVING, SCRIEVES to move along swiftly and smoothly

SCRIM *n* pl. -S a cotton fabric

SCRIMP *v* -ED, -ING, -S to be very or overly thrifty

SCRIMPER *n* pl. -S one that scrimps

SCRIMPIT *adj* meager

SCRIMPY *adj* SCRIMPIER, SCRIMPIEST meager

SCRIP *n* pl. -S a small piece of paper

SCRIPT *v* -ED, -ING, -S to prepare a written text for, as a play or motion picture

SCRIPTER *n* pl. -S one that scripts

SCRIVE *v* SCRIVED, SCRIVING, SCRIVES to engrave

SCROD *n* pl. -S a young cod

SCROFULA *n* pl. -S a disease of the lymph glands

SCROGGY *adj* -GIER, -GIEST of stunted growth

SCROLL *v* -ED, -ING, -S to move text across a display screen

SCROOCH *v* -ED, -ING, -ES to crouch

SCROOGE *n* pl. -S a miserly person

SCROOP *v* -ED, -ING, -S to make a harsh, grating sound

SCROOTCH *v* -ED, -ING, -ES to scrooch

SCROTUM *n* pl. -TA or -TUMS the pouch of skin that contains the testes **SCROTAL** *adj*

SCROUGE *v* SCROUGED, SCROUGING, SCROUGES to crowd

SCROUNGE *v* SCROUNGED, SCROUNGING, SCROUNGES to gather by foraging

SCROUNGY *adj* SCROUNGIER, SCROUNGIEST dirty

SCRUB *v* SCRUBBED, SCRUBBING, SCRUBS to rub hard in order to clean

SCRUBBER *n* pl. -S one that scrubs

SCRUBBY *adj* -BIER, -BIEST inferior in size or quality

SCRUFF *n* pl. -S the back of the neck

SCRUFFY *adj* -FIER, -FIEST shabby

SCRUM *v* SCRUMMED, SCRUMMING, SCRUMS to engage in a scrummage (a formation around the ball in rugby)

SCRUNCH *v* -ED, -ING, -ES to crush

SCRUPLE *v* -PLED, -PLING, -PLES to hesitate because of ethical considerations

SCRUTINY *n* pl. -NIES a close examination

SCRY *v* SCRIED, SCRYING, SCRIES to engage in crystal gazing

SCUBA *n* pl. -S an underwater breathing device

SCUD *v* SCUDDED, SCUDDING, SCUDS to run or move swiftly

SCUDO *n* pl. -DI a former Italian coin

SCUFF *v* -ED, -ING, -S to walk without lifting the feet

SCUFFLE *v* -FLED, -FLING, -FLES to struggle in a rough, confused manner

SCUFFLER *n* pl. -S one that scuffles

SCULK *v* -ED, -ING, -S to skulk

SCULKER *n* pl. -S skulker

SCULL *v* -ED, -ING, -S to propel with a type of oar

SCULLER *n* pl. -S one that sculls

SCULLERY *n* pl. -LERIES a room in which kitchen utensils are cleaned and stored

SCULLION *n* pl. -S a kitchen servant who does menial work

SCULP *v* -ED, -ING, -S to sculpt

SCULPIN *n* pl. -S a freshwater fish

SCULPT *v* -ED, -ING, -S to form an image or representation of from solid material

SCULPTOR *n* pl. -S one that sculpts

SCUM *v* SCUMMED, SCUMMING, SCUMS to remove the scum (impure or extraneous matter) from

SCUMBAG *n* pl. -S a dirtbag

SCUMBLE	*v* -BLED, -BLING, -BLES to soften the outlines or colors of by rubbing lightly
SCUMLIKE	*adj* resembling scum
SCUMMED	past tense of scum
SCUMMER	*n* pl. -S one that scums
SCUMMING	present participle of scum
SCUMMY	*adj* -MIER, -MIEST covered with scum
SCUNNER	*v* -ED, -ING, -S to feel loathing or disgust
SCUP	*n* pl. -S a marine food fish
SCUPPAUG	*n* pl. -S scup
SCUPPER	*v* -ED, -ING, -S to ambush
SCURF	*n* pl. -S scaly or shredded dry skin
SCURFY	*adj* SCURFIER, SCURFIEST covered with scurf
SCURRIED	past tense of scurry
SCURRIES	present 3d person sing. of scurry
SCURRIL	*adj* scurrile
SCURRILE	*adj* expressed in coarse and abusive language
SCURRY	*v* -RIED, -RYING, -RIES to move hurriedly
SCURVY	*adj* -VIER, -VIEST base or contemptible **SCURVILY** *adv*
SCURVY	*n* pl. -VIES a disease resulting from vitamin C deficiency
SCUT	*n* pl. -S a short tail, as of a rabbit
SCUTA	pl. of scutum
SCUTAGE	*n* pl. -S a tax exacted by a feudal lord in lieu of military service
SCUTATE	*adj* shaped like a shield
SCUTCH	*v* -ED, -ING, -ES to separate the woody fiber from by beating
SCUTCHER	*n* pl. -S one that scutches
SCUTE	*n* pl. -S a horny plate or scale
SCUTELLA	*n/pl* small, scutate organs or parts
SCUTTER	*v* -ED, -ING, -S to scurry
SCUTTLE	*v* -TLED, -TLING, -TLES to scurry
SCUTUM	*n* pl. -TA scute
SCUZZY	*adj* -ZIER, -ZIEST dirty or shabby
SCYPHATE	*adj* shaped like a cup
SCYPHUS	*n* pl. -PHI a Greek cup with two handles

SCYTHE	*v* SCYTHED, SCYTHING, SCYTHES to cut with a scythe (a single-bladed cutting implement)
SEA	*n* pl. -S the ocean
SEABAG	*n* pl. -S a bag used by a sailor
SEABEACH	*n* pl. -ES a beach lying along the sea
SEABED	*n* pl. -S a seafloor
SEABIRD	*n* pl. -S a bird frequenting the ocean or seacoast
SEABOARD	*n* pl. -S the seacoast
SEABOOT	*n* pl. -S a waterproof boot
SEABORNE	*adj* carried on or over the sea
SEACOAST	*n* pl. -S land bordering on the sea
SEACOCK	*n* pl. -S a valve in a ship's hull
SEACRAFT	*n* pl. -S skill in sea navigation
SEADOG	*n* pl. -S a fogbow
SEADROME	*n* pl. -S an airport in the sea
SEAFARER	*n* pl. -S a sailor
SEAFLOOR	*n* pl. -S the bottom of a sea
SEAFOOD	*n* pl. -S edible fish or shellfish from the sea
SEAFOWL	*n* pl. -S a seabird
SEAFRONT	*n* pl. -S an area along the edge of the sea
SEAGIRT	*adj* surrounded by the sea
SEAGOING	*adj* designed for use on the sea
SEAGULL	*n* pl. -S a gull frequenting the sea
SEAL	*v* -ED, -ING, -S to close or make secure against access, leakage, or passage **SEALABLE** *adj*
SEALANT	*n* pl. -S a sealing agent
SEALER	*n* pl. -S one that seals
SEALERY	*n* pl. -ERIES the occupation of hunting seals
SEALLIKE	*adj* resembling a seal (an aquatic mammal)
SEALSKIN	*n* pl. -S the skin of a seal
SEAM	*v* -ED, -ING, -S to join with a seam (a line formed by sewing two pieces of fabric together)
SEAMAN	*n* pl. -MEN a sailor **SEAMANLY** *adj*
SEAMARK	*n* pl. -S a landmark serving as a navigational guide to mariners
SEAMER	*n* pl. -S one that seams
SEAMIER	comparative of seamy
SEAMIEST	superlative of seamy
SEAMLESS	*adj* having no seam
SEAMLIKE	*adj* resembling a seam

SEAMOUNT *n* pl. -S an undersea mountain

SEAMSTER *n* pl. -S a person whose occupation is sewing

SEAMY *adj* SEAMIER, SEAMIEST unpleasant

SEANCE *n* pl. -S a meeting of persons seeking spiritualistic messages

SEAPIECE *n* pl. -S a seascape

SEAPLANE *n* pl. -S an airplane designed to take off from or land on the water

SEAPORT *n* pl. -S a harbor or town accessible to seagoing ships

SEAQUAKE *n* pl. -S an undersea earthquake

SEAR *adj* SEARER, SEAREST sere

SEAR *v* -ED, -ING, -S to burn the surface of

SEARCH *v* -ED, -ING, -ES to look through or over carefully in order to find something

SEARCHER *n* pl. -S one that searches

SEAROBIN *n* pl. -S a marine fish

SEASCAPE *n* pl. -S a picture of the sea

SEASCOUT *n* pl. -S a boy scout trained in water activities

SEASHELL *n* pl. -S the shell of a marine mollusk

SEASHORE *n* pl. -S land bordering on the sea

SEASICK *adj* affected with nausea caused by the motion of a vessel at sea

SEASIDE *n* pl. -S the seashore

SEASON *v* -ED, -ING, -S to heighten or improve the flavor of by adding savory ingredients

SEASONAL *adj* occurring at a certain time of the year

SEASONER *n* pl. -S one that seasons

SEAT *v* -ED, -ING, -S to place on a seat (something on which one sits)

SEATER *n* pl. -S one that seats

SEATING *n* pl. -S material for covering seats

SEATLESS *adj* having no seat

SEATMATE *n* pl. -S one with whom one shares a seat

SEATRAIN *n* pl. -S a ship equipped to carry railroad cars

SEATWORK *n* pl. -S work done at one's seat

SEAWALL *n* pl. -S a wall to protect a shoreline from erosion

SEAWAN *n* pl. -S wampum

SEAWANT *n* pl. -S seawan

SEAWARD *n* pl. -S the direction toward the open sea

SEAWARE *n* pl. -S seaweed used as fertilizer

SEAWATER *n* pl. -S water from the sea

SEAWAY *n* pl. -WAYS the headway made by a ship

SEAWEED *n* pl. -S a plant growing in the sea

SEBACIC *adj* derived from a certain acid

SEBASIC *adj* sebacic

SEBUM *n* pl. -S a fatty matter secreted by certain glands of the skin

SEC *n* pl. -S secant

SECALOSE *n* pl. -S a complex carbohydrate

SECANT *n* pl. -S a trigonometric function of an angle

SECANTLY *adv* in an intersecting manner

SECATEUR *n* pl. -S a pruning tool

SECCO *n* pl. -COS the art of painting on dry plaster

SECEDE *v* -CEDED, -CEDING, -CEDES to withdraw formally from an alliance or association

SECEDER *n* pl. -S one that secedes

SECERN *v* -ED, -ING, -S to discern as separate

SECLUDE *v* -CLUDED, -CLUDING, -CLUDES to remove or set apart from others

SECOND *v* -ED, -ING, -S to give support or encouragement to

SECONDE *n* pl. -S a position in fencing

SECONDER *n* pl. -S one that seconds

SECONDLY *adv* in the next place after the first

SECONDO *n* pl. -DI the lower part in a piano duet

SECPAR *n* pl. -S a parsec

SECRECY *n* pl. -CIES the condition of being secret

SECRET *adj* -CRETER, -CRETEST kept from knowledge or view

SECRET *n* pl. -S something kept from the knowledge of others

SECRETE *v* -CRETED, -CRETING, -CRETES to generate and separate out from cells or bodily fluids

SECRETIN *n* pl. -S a hormone

SECRETLY *adv* in a secret manner

SECRETOR *n* pl. -S one that secretes

SECT n pl. -S a group of people united by common beliefs or interests

SECTARY n pl. -RIES a member of a sect

SECTILE adj capable of being cut smoothly

SECTION v -ED, -ING, -S to divide into sections (distinct parts)

SECTOR v -ED, -ING, -S to divide into sectors (sections)

SECTORAL adj of or pertaining to a sector

SECULAR n pl. -S a layman

SECUND adj having the parts or organs arranged on one side only **SECUNDLY** adv

SECUNDUM adv according to

SECURE adj -CURER, -CUREST free from danger **SECURELY** adv

SECURE v -CURED, -CURING, -CURES to make firm or tight

SECURER n pl. -S one that secures

SECUREST superlative of secure

SECURING present participle of secure

SECURITY n pl. -TIES the state of being secure

SEDAN n pl. -S a type of automobile

SEDARIM a pl. of seder

SEDATE adj -DATER, -DATEST calm **SEDATELY** adv

SEDATE v -DATED, -DATING, -DATES to administer a sedative to

SEDATION n pl. -S the reduction of stress or excitement by the use of sedatives

SEDATIVE n pl. -S a drug that induces a calm state

SEDER n pl. -DARIM or -DERS a Jewish ceremonial dinner

SEDERUNT n pl. -S a prolonged sitting

SEDGE n pl. -S a marsh plant

SEDGY adj SEDGIER, SEDGIEST abounding in sedge

SEDILE n pl. -LIA one of the seats in a church for the use of the officiating clergy

SEDILIUM n pl. -LIA sedile

SEDIMENT v -ED, -ING, -S to settle to the bottom of a liquid

SEDITION n pl. -S incitement of rebellion against a government

SEDUCE v -DUCED, -DUCING, -DUCES to lead astray **SEDUCIVE** adj

SEDUCER n pl. -S one that seduces

SEDULITY n pl. -TIES the state of being sedulous

SEDULOUS adj diligent

SEDUM n pl. -S a flowering plant

SEE v SAW, SEEN, SEEING, SEES to perceive with the eyes **SEEABLE** adj

SEECATCH n pl. -CATCHIE an adult male fur seal

SEED v -ED, -ING, -S to plant seeds (propagative plant structures) in

SEEDBED n pl. -S land prepared for seeding

SEEDCAKE n pl. -S a sweet cake containing aromatic seeds

SEEDCASE n pl. -S a pericarp

SEEDER n pl. -S one that seeds

SEEDIER comparative of seedy

SEEDIEST superlative of seedy

SEEDILY adv in a seedy manner

SEEDLESS adj having no seeds

SEEDLIKE adj resembling a seed

SEEDLING n pl. -S a young plant

SEEDMAN n pl. -MEN seedsman

SEEDPOD n pl. -S a type of seed vessel

SEEDSMAN n pl. -MEN a dealer in seeds

SEEDTIME n pl. -S the season for sowing seeds

SEEDY adj SEEDIER, SEEDIEST containing seeds; inferior in condition or quality

SEEING n pl. -S the act of one that sees

SEEK v SOUGHT, SEEKING, SEEKS to go in search of

SEEKER n pl. -S one that seeks

SEEL v -ED, -ING, -S to stitch closed the eyes of, as a falcon during training

SEELY adj frail

SEEM v -ED, -ING, -S to give the impression of being

SEEMER n pl. -S one that seems

SEEMING n pl. -S outward appearance

SEEMLY adj -LIER, -LIEST of pleasing appearance

SEEN past participle of see

SEEP v -ED, -ING, -S to pass slowly through small openings

SEEPAGE n pl. -S the quantity of fluid that has seeped

SEEPY adj SEEPIER, SEEPIEST soaked or oozing with water

SEER n pl. -S a prophet

SEERESS n pl. -ES a female seer

SEESAW	v -ED, -ING, -S to move up and down or back and forth	**SEJANT**	adj represented in a sitting position — used of a heraldic animal
SEETHE	v SEETHED, SEETHING, SEETHES to surge or foam as if boiling	**SEJEANT**	adj sejant
		SEL	n pl. -S self
SEG	n pl. -S one who advocates racial segregation	**SELADANG**	n pl. -S saladang
		SELAH	n pl. -S a word of unknown meaning often marking the end of a verse in the Psalms
SEGETAL	adj growing in fields of grain		
SEGGAR	n pl. -S a saggar		
SEGMENT	v -ED, -ING, -S to divide into sections	**SELAMLIK**	n pl. -S the portion of a Turkish house reserved for men
SEGNO	n pl. -GNI or -GNOS a musical sign		
		SELCOUTH	adj unusual
SEGO	n pl. -GOS a perennial herb	**SELDOM**	adj infrequent **SELDOMLY** adv
SEGUE	v -GUED, -GUEING, -GUES to proceed without pause from one musical theme to another		
		SELECT	v -ED, -ING, -S to choose
		SELECTEE	n pl. -S one that is selected
SEI	n pl. -S a rorqual	**SELECTLY**	adv by selection
SEICENTO	n pl. -TOS the seventeenth century	**SELECTOR**	n pl. -S one that selects
		SELENATE	n pl. -S a chemical salt
SEICHE	n pl. -S an oscillation of the surface of a lake or landlocked sea	**SELENIC**	adj pertaining to selenium
		SELENIDE	n pl. -S a compound of selenium
SEIDEL	n pl. -S a large beer glass	**SELENITE**	n pl. -S a variety of gypsum
SEIF	n pl. -S a long, narrow sand dune	**SELENIUM**	n pl. -S a nonmetallic element **SELENOUS** adj
SEIGNEUR	n pl. -S seignior	**SELF**	n pl. SELVES the total, essential, or particular being of one person
SEIGNIOR	n pl. -S a feudal lord		
SEIGNORY	n pl. -GNORIES the power of a seignior		
		SELF	v -ED, -ING, -S to inbreed
SEINE	v SEINED, SEINING, SEINES to catch fish with a large, vertically hanging net	**SELFDOM**	n pl. -S selfhood
		SELFHEAL	n pl. -S a perennial herb
		SELFHOOD	n pl. -S the state of being an individual person
SEINER	n pl. -S one that seines		
SEISE	v SEISED, SEISING, SEISES to seize **SEISABLE** adj	**SELFISH**	adj concerned chiefly or only with oneself
		SELFLESS	adj unselfish
SEISER	n pl. -S seizer	**SELFNESS**	n pl. -ES selfhood
SEISIN	n pl. -S seizin	**SELFSAME**	adj identical
SEISING	n pl. -S seizing	**SELFWARD**	adv toward oneself
SEISM	n pl. -S an earthquake **SEISMAL, SEISMIC** adj	**SELL**	v SOLD, SELLING, SELLS to give up to another for money or other valuable consideration **SELLABLE** adj
SEISMISM	n pl. -S the natural activity involved in earthquakes		
SEISOR	n pl. -S seizor	**SELLE**	n pl. -S a saddle
SEISURE	n pl. -S seizure	**SELLER**	n pl. -S one that sells
SEIZE	v SEIZED, SEIZING, SEIZES to take hold of suddenly and forcibly **SEIZABLE** adj	**SELLOUT**	n pl. -S a performance for which all seats have been sold
		SELSYN	n pl. -S a type of remote-control device
SEIZER	n pl. -S one that seizes		
SEIZIN	n pl. -S legal possession of land	**SELTZER**	n pl. -S carbonated mineral water
SEIZING	n pl. -S the act of one that seizes	**SELVA**	n pl. -S a tropical rain forest
		SELVAGE	n pl. -S the edge of a woven fabric finished to prevent raveling **SELVAGED** adj
SEIZOR	n pl. -S one that takes seizin		
SEIZURE	n pl. -S the act of seizing		

SELVEDGE *n* pl. -S selvage

SELVES pl. of self

SEMANTIC *adj* pertaining to meaning

SEMATIC *adj* serving as a warning

SEME *n* pl. -S a type of ornamental pattern

SEMEME *n* pl. -S the meaning of a morpheme **SEMEMIC** *adj*

SEMEN *n* pl. -MINA or -MENS a fluid produced in the male reproductive organs

SEMESTER *n* pl. -S a period constituting half of an academic year

SEMI *n* pl. -S a freight trailer

SEMIARID *adj* characterized by light rainfall

SEMIBALD *adj* partly bald

SEMICOMA *n* pl. -S a coma from which a person can be aroused

SEMIDEAF *adj* partly deaf

SEMIDOME *n* pl. -S a half dome

SEMIDRY *adj* moderately dry

SEMIFIT *adj* conforming somewhat to the lines of the body

SEMIGALA *adj* somewhat gala

SEMIHARD *adj* moderately hard

SEMIHIGH *adj* moderately high

SEMIHOBO *n* pl. -BOS or -BOES a person having some of the characteristics of a hobo

SEMILOG *adj* having one scale logarithmic and the other arithmetic

SEMIMAT *adj* having a slight luster

SEMIMATT *adj* semimat

SEMIMUTE *adj* having partially lost the faculty of speech

SEMINA a pl. of semen

SEMINAL *adj* pertaining to semen

SEMINAR *n* pl. -S an advanced study group at a college or university

SEMINARY *n* pl. -NARIES a school for the training of priests, ministers, or rabbis

SEMINUDE *adj* partly nude

SEMIOSIS *n* pl. -OSES a process in which something functions as a sign to an organism

SEMIOTIC *n* pl. -S a general theory of signs and symbolism

SEMIPRO *n* pl. -PROS one who is engaged in some field or sport for pay on a part-time basis

SEMIRAW *adj* somewhat raw

SEMIS *n* pl. -MISES a coin of ancient Rome

SEMISOFT *adj* moderately soft

SEMITIST *n* pl. -S one who favors Jewish interests

SEMITONE *n* pl. -S a type of musical tone

SEMIWILD *adj* somewhat wild

SEMOLINA *n* pl. -S a granular product of wheat used for pasta

SEMPLE *adj* of humble birth

SEMPLICE *adj* simple — used as a musical direction

SEMPRE *adv* in the same manner throughout — used as a musical direction

SEN *n* pl. SEN a monetary unit of Japan

SENARIUS *n* pl. -NARII a Greek or Latin verse consisting of six metrical feet

SENARY *adj* pertaining to the number six

SENATE *n* pl. -S an assembly having high deliberative and legislative functions

SENATOR *n* pl. -S a member of a senate

SEND *v* SENT, SENDING, SENDS to cause to go **SENDABLE** *adj*

SEND *v* -ED, -ING, -S to scend

SENDAL *n* pl. -S a silk fabric

SENDER *n* pl. -S one that sends

SENDOFF *n* pl. -S a farewell celebration

SENDUP *n* pl. -S a parody

SENE *n* pl. SENE a monetary unit of Western Samoa

SENECA *n* pl. -S senega

SENECIO *n* pl. -CIOS a flowering plant

SENEGA *n* pl. -S a medicinal plant root

SENGI *n* pl. SENGI a monetary unit of Zaire

SENHOR *n* pl. -S or -ES a Portuguese or Brazilian gentleman

SENHORA *n* pl. -S a married Portuguese or Brazilian woman

SENILE *n* pl. -S one who exhibits senility

SENILELY *adv* in a senile manner

SENILITY *n* pl. -TIES mental and physical infirmity due to old age

SENIOR *n* pl. -S a person who is older than another

SENITI *n* pl. SENITI a monetary unit of Tonga

SENNA *n* pl. -S a medicinal plant

SENNET *n* pl. -S a call sounded on a trumpet signaling the entrance or exit of actors

SENNIGHT *n* pl. -S a week

SENNIT *n* pl. -S braided straw used in making hats

SENOPIA *n* pl. -S an improvement of near vision

SENOR *n* pl. -S or -ES a Spanish gentleman

SENORA *n* pl. -S a married Spanish woman

SENORITA *n* pl. -S an unmarried Spanish girl or woman

SENRYU *n* pl. SENRYU a Japanese poem

SENSA pl. of sensum

SENSATE *v* -SATED, -SATING, -SATES to sense

SENSE *v* SENSED, SENSING, SENSES to perceive by the senses (any of certain agencies through which an individual receives impressions of the external world)

SENSEFUL *adj* sensible

SENSIBLE *adj* -BLER, -BLEST having or showing good judgment SENSIBLY *adv*

SENSIBLE *n* pl. -S something that can be sensed

SENSILLA *n* pl. -LAE a simple sense organ

SENSING present participle of sense

SENSOR *n* pl. -S a device that receives and responds to a stimulus

SENSORIA *n/pl* the parts of the brain concerned with the reception and interpretation of sensory stimuli

SENSORY *adj* pertaining to the senses or sensation

SENSUAL *adj* pertaining to the physical senses

SENSUM *n* pl. -SA an object of perception or sensation

SENSUOUS *adj* pertaining to or derived from the senses

SENT past tense of send (to cause to go)

SENTE *n* pl. LICENTE or LISENTE a monetary unit of Lesotho

SENTENCE *v* -TENCED, -TENCING, -TENCES to declare judicially the extent of punishment to be imposed

SENTI *n* pl. SENTI a former monetary unit of Tanzania

SENTIENT *n* pl. -S a person or thing capable of sensation

SENTIMO *n* pl. -MOS a monetary unit of the Philippines

SENTINEL *v* -NELED, -NELING, -NELS or -NELLED, -NELLING, -NELS to stand guard

SENTRY *n* pl. -TRIES one who stands guard

SEPAL *n* pl. -S one of the individual leaves of a calyx SEPALED, SEPALINE, SEPALLED, SEPALOID, SEPALOUS *adj*

SEPARATE *v* -RATED, -RATING, -RATES to set or keep apart

SEPIA *n* pl. -S a brown pigment SEPIC *adj*

SEPOY *n* pl. -POYS a native of India serving in the British army

SEPPUKU *n* pl. -S a Japanese form of suicide

SEPSIS *n* pl. SEPSES bacterial invasion of the body

SEPT *n* pl. -S a clan

SEPTA pl. of septum

SEPTAL *adj* pertaining to a septum

SEPTARIA *n/pl* limestone nodules

SEPTATE *adj* having a septum

SEPTET *n* pl. -S a group of seven

SEPTETTE *n* pl. -S septet

SEPTIC *n* pl. -S an agent producing sepsis SEPTICAL *adj*

SEPTIME *n* pl. -S a position in fencing

SEPTUM *n* pl. -TA or -TUMS a dividing membrane or partition

SEPTUPLE *v* -PLED, -PLING, -PLES to make seven times as great

SEQUEL *n* pl. -S something that follows and serves as a continuation

SEQUELA *n* pl. -QUELAE an abnormal condition resulting from a preceding disease

SEQUENCE *v* -QUENCED, -QUENCING, -QUENCES to arrange in consecutive order

SEQUENCY *n* pl. -CIES the following of one thing after another

SEQUENT *n* pl. -S something that follows

SEQUIN *n* pl. -S a shiny ornamental disk SEQUINED *adj*

SEQUITUR *n* pl. -S the conclusion of an inference

SEQUOIA *n* pl. -S a large evergreen tree

SER *n* pl. -S a unit of weight of India

SERA a pl. of serum

SERAC *n* pl. -S a large mass of ice broken off of a glacier

SERAGLIO *n* pl. -GLIOS a harem

SERAI *n* pl. -S a Turkish palace

SERAIL *n* pl. -S a seraglio

SERAL *adj* pertaining to a series of ecological changes

SERAPE *n* pl. -S a colorful woolen shawl

SERAPH *n* pl. -APHS, -APHIM, or -APHIN a winged celestial being **SERAPHIC** *adj*

SERAPHIM *n* pl. -S seraph

SERDAB *n* pl. -S a chamber within an ancient Egyptian tomb

SERE *adj* SERER, SEREST withered; dry

SERE *v* SERED, SERING, SERES to sear

SEREIN *n* pl. -S a fine rain falling from an apparently clear sky

SERENADE *v* -NADED, -NADING, -NADES to perform an honorific evening song for

SERENATA *n* pl. -TAS or -TE a dramatic cantata

SERENE *adj* SERENER, SERENEST calm; tranquil **SERENELY** *adv*

SERENE *n* pl. -S a serene condition or expanse

SERENITY *n* pl. -TIES the state of being serene

SERER comparative of sere

SEREST superlative of sere

SERF *n* pl. -S a feudal slave

SERFAGE *n* pl. -S serfdom

SERFDOM *n* pl. -S the state of being a serf

SERFHOOD *n* pl. -S serfdom

SERFISH *adj* characteristic of a serf

SERFLIKE *adj* serfish

SERGE *n* pl. -S a twilled fabric

SERGEANT *n* pl. -S a noncommissioned military officer

SERGING *n* pl. -S a process of finishing the raw edges of a fabric

SERIAL *n* pl. -S a literary or dramatic work presented in successive installments

SERIALLY *adv* in the manner or form of a serial

SERIATE *v* -ATED, -ATING, -ATES to put into a series

SERIATIM *adv* serially

SERICIN *n* pl. -S a kind of protein

SERIEMA *n* pl. -S a Brazilian bird

SERIES *n* pl. SERIES an arrangement of one after another

SERIF *n* pl. -S a fine line used to finish off the main stroke of a letter **SERIFED, SERIFFED** *adj*

SERIN *n* pl. -S a European finch

SERINE *n* pl. -S an amino acid

SERING present participle of sere

SERINGA *n* pl. -S a Brazilian tree

SERIOUS *adj* thoughtful or subdued in appearance or manner

SERJEANT *n* pl. -S sergeant

SERMON *n* pl. -S a religious discourse **SERMONIC** *adj*

SEROLOGY *n* pl. -GIES the science of serums

SEROSA *n* pl. -SAS or -SAE a thin membrane lining certain bodily cavities **SEROSAL** *adj*

SEROSITY *n* pl. -TIES the quality or state of being serous

SEROTINE *n* pl. -S a European bat

SEROTYPE *n* pl. -S a group of closely related organisms distinguished by a common set of antigens

SEROUS *adj* of or resembling serum

SEROW *n* pl. -S an Asian antelope

SERPENT *n* pl. -S a snake

SERPIGO *n* pl. -GOES or -GINES a spreading skin eruption

SERRANID *n* pl. -S a marine fish

SERRANO *n* pl. -NOS a small hot pepper

SERRATE *v* -RATED, -RATING, -RATES to furnish with toothlike projections

SERRY *v* -RIED, -RYING, -RIES to crowd together

SERUM *n* pl. -RUMS or -RA the watery portion of whole blood **SERUMAL** *adj*

SERVABLE *adj* capable of serving or being served

SERVAL *n* pl. -S an African wildcat

SERVANT *n* pl. -S one that serves others

SERVE *v* SERVED, SERVING, SERVES to work for

SERVER *n* pl. -S one that serves another

SERVICE *v* -VICED, -VICING, -VICES to repair

SERVICER *n* pl. -S one that services

SERVILE *adj* slavishly submissive

SERVING *n* pl. -S a portion of food

SERVITOR *n* pl. -S a male servant

SERVO	*n pl.* -VOS an automatic device used to control another mechanism
SESAME	*n pl.* -S an East Indian plant
SESAMOID	*n pl.* -S a nodular mass of bone or cartilage
SESSILE	*adj* permanently attached
SESSION	*n pl.* -S a meeting of a legislative or judicial body for the transaction of business
SESSPOOL	*n pl.* -S cesspool
SESTERCE	*n pl.* -S a coin of ancient Rome
SESTET	*n pl.* -S a stanza of six lines
SESTINA	*n pl.* -S a type of verse form
SESTINE	*n pl.* -S sestina
SET	*v* SET, SETTING, SETS to put in a particular position
SETA	*n pl.* -TAE a coarse, stiff hair **SETAL** *adj*
SETBACK	*n pl.* -S a defeat
SETENANT	*n pl.* -S a postage stamp that differs in design from others in the same sheet
SETIFORM	*adj* having the form of a seta
SETLINE	*n pl.* -S a strong fishing line
SETOFF	*n pl.* -S something that offsets something else
SETON	*n pl.* -S a type of surgical thread
SETOSE	*adj* covered with setae
SETOUS	*adj* setose
SETOUT	*n pl.* -S a display
SETSCREW	*n pl.* -S a type of screw
SETT	*n pl.* -S the burrow of a badger
SETTEE	*n pl.* -S a long seat with a high back
SETTER	*n pl.* -S one that sets
SETTING	*n pl.* -S the scenery used in a dramatic production
SETTLE	*v* -TLED, -TLING, -TLES to place in a desired state or order
SETTLER	*n pl.* -S one that settles
SETTLING	*n pl.* -S sediment
SETTLOR	*n pl.* -S one that makes a legal settlement
SETULOSE	*adj* covered with seta
SETULOUS	*adj* setulose
SETUP	*n pl.* -S the way something is arranged
SEVEN	*n pl.* -S a number
SEVENTH	*n pl.* -S one of seven equal parts
SEVENTY	*n pl.* -TIES a number
SEVER	*v* -ED, -ING, -S to divide or cut into parts
SEVERAL	*n pl.* -S a few persons or things
SEVERE	*adj* -VERER, -VEREST unsparing in the treatment of others **SEVERELY** *adv*
SEVERITY	*n pl.* -TIES the quality or state of being severe
SEVICHE	*n pl.* -S a dish of raw fish
SEW	*v* SEWED, SEWN, SEWING, SEWS to mend or fasten with a needle and thread **SEWABLE** *adj*
SEWAGE	*n pl.* -S the waste matter carried off by sewers
SEWAN	*n pl.* -S seawan
SEWAR	*n pl.* -S a medieval servant
SEWER	*v* -ED, -ING, -S to clean or maintain sewers (underground conduits for waste)
SEWERAGE	*n pl.* -S sewage
SEWING	*n pl.* -S material that has been or is to be sewed
SEWN	a past participle of sew
SEX	*v* -ED, -ING, -ES to determine the sex (the property by which organisms are classified according to reproductive functions) of
SEXIER	comparative of sexy
SEXIEST	superlative of sexy
SEXILY	*adv* in a sexy manner
SEXINESS	*n pl.* -ES the quality or state of being sexy
SEXISM	*n pl.* -S prejudice or discrimination against women
SEXIST	*n pl.* -S one that practices sexism
SEXLESS	*adj* lacking sexual characteristics
SEXOLOGY	*n pl.* -GIES the study of human sexual behavior
SEXPOT	*n pl.* -S a sexually attractive woman
SEXT	*n pl.* -S one of seven canonical daily periods for prayer and devotion
SEXTAIN	*n pl.* -S a stanza of six lines
SEXTAN	*n pl.* -S a recurrent malarial fever
SEXTANT	*n pl.* -S an instrument for measuring angular distances
SEXTARII	*n/pl* ancient Roman units of liquid measure
SEXTET	*n pl.* -S a group of six

SEXTETTE	n pl. -S sextet
SEXTILE	n pl. -S the position of two celestial bodies when they are sixty degrees apart
SEXTO	n pl. -TOS sixmo
SEXTON	n pl. -S a maintenance worker of a church
SEXTUPLE	v -PLED, -PLING, -PLES to make six times as great
SEXTUPLY	adv to six times as much or as many
SEXUAL	adj pertaining to sex **SEXUALLY** adv
SEXY	adj SEXIER, SEXIEST arousing sexual desire
SFERICS	n/pl an electronic detector of storms
SFORZATO	n pl. -TOS the playing of a tone or chord with sudden force
SFUMATO	n pl. -TOS a technique used in painting
SH	interj — used to urge silence
SHA	interj — used to urge silence
SHABBY	adj -BIER, -BIEST ragged **SHABBILY** adv
SHACK	n pl. -S a shanty
SHACKLE	v -LED, -LING, -LES to confine with metal fastenings placed around the wrists or ankles
SHACKLER	n pl. -S one that shackles
SHACKO	n pl. -KOS or -KOES shako
SHAD	n pl. -S a food fish
SHADBLOW	n pl. -S a shadbush
SHADBUSH	n pl. -ES a flowering tree or shrub
SHADCHAN	n pl. -CHANIM or -CHANS a Jewish marriage broker
SHADDOCK	n pl. -S a citrus fruit
SHADE	v SHADED, SHADING, SHADES to screen from light or heat
SHADER	n pl. -S one that shades
SHADFLY	n pl. -FLIES a winged insect
SHADIER	comparative of shady
SHADIEST	superlative of shady
SHADILY	adv in a shady manner
SHADING	n pl. -S protection against light or heat
SHADOOF	n pl. -S a device used in Egypt for raising water for irrigation
SHADOW	v -ED, -ING, -S to make dark or gloomy
SHADOWER	n pl. -S one that shadows
SHADOWY	adj -OWIER, -OWIEST dark

SHADRACH	n pl. -S a mass of unfused material in the hearth of a blast furnace
SHADUF	n pl. -S shadoof
SHADY	adj SHADIER, SHADIEST shaded
SHAFT	v -ED, -ING, -S to push or propel with a pole
SHAFTING	n pl. -S a system of rods for transmitting motion or power
SHAG	v SHAGGED, SHAGGING, SHAGS to make shaggy
SHAGBARK	n pl. -S a hardwood tree
SHAGGY	adj -GIER, -GIEST covered with long, coarse hair **SHAGGILY** adv
SHAGREEN	n pl. -S the rough skin of certain sharks
SHAH	n pl. -S an Iranian ruler
SHAHDOM	n pl. -S the territory ruled by a shah
SHAIRD	n pl. -S shard
SHAIRN	n pl. -S sharn
SHAITAN	n pl. -S an evil spirit
SHAKE	v SHOOK, SHAKEN, SHAKING, SHAKES to move to and fro with short, rapid movements **SHAKABLE** adj
SHAKEOUT	n pl. -S a minor economic recession
SHAKER	n pl. -S one that shakes
SHAKEUP	n pl. -S a total reorganization
SHAKIER	comparative of shaky
SHAKIEST	superlative of shaky
SHAKILY	adv in a shaky manner
SHAKING	present participle of shake
SHAKO	n pl. -KOS or -KOES a type of military hat
SHAKY	adj SHAKIER, SHAKIEST shaking
SHALE	n pl. -S a fissile rock
SHALED	adj having a shell or husk
SHALEY	adj SHALIER, SHALIEST shaly
SHALIER	comparative of shaly
SHALIEST	superlative of shaly
SHALL	v present sing. 2d person SHALL or SHALT, past sing. 2d person SHOULD, SHOULDST, or SHOULDEST — used as an auxiliary to express futurity, inevitability, or command
SHALLOON	n pl. -S a woolen fabric
SHALLOP	n pl. -S a small, open boat

SHALLOT   *n* pl. -S a plant resembling an onion

SHALLOW   *adj* -LOWER, -LOWEST having little depth

SHALLOW   *v* -ED, -ING, -S to make shallow

SHALOM   *n* pl. -S a word used as a Jewish greeting or farewell

SHALT   a present 2d person sing. of shall

SHALY   *adj* SHALIER, SHALIEST resembling shale

SHAM   *v* SHAMMED, SHAMMING, SHAMS to feign

SHAMABLE   *adj* capable of being shamed

SHAMAN   *n* pl. -S a medicine man among certain North American Indians **SHAMANIC** *adj*

SHAMAS   *n* pl. -MOSIM shammes

SHAMBLE   *v* -BLED, -BLING, -BLES to walk awkwardly

SHAME   *v* SHAMED, SHAMING, SHAMES to cause to feel a painful sense of guilt or degradation

SHAMEFUL   *adj* disgraceful

SHAMES   *n* pl. -MOSIM shammes

SHAMING   present participle of shame

SHAMMAS   *n* pl. -MASIM shammes

SHAMMASH   *n* pl. -MASHIM shammes

SHAMMED   past tense of sham

SHAMMER   *n* pl. -S one that shams

SHAMMES   *n* pl. -MOSIM a minor official of a synagogue

SHAMMIED   past tense of shammy

SHAMMIES   present 3d person sing. of shammy

SHAMMING   present participle of sham

SHAMMOS   *n* pl. -MOSIM shammes

SHAMMOSIM   pl. of shammes

SHAMMY   *v* -MIED, -MYING, -MIES to chamois

SHAMOIS   *n* pl. SHAMOIS chamois

SHAMOS   *n* pl. -MOSIM shammes

SHAMOSIM   pl. of shames

SHAMOY   *v* -ED, -ING, -S to chamois

SHAMPOO   *v* -ED, -ING, -S to cleanse with a special preparation

SHAMROCK   *n* pl. -S a three-leaved plant

SHAMUS   *n* pl. -ES a private detective

SHANDY   *n* pl. -DIES an alcoholic drink

SHANGHAI   *v* -ED, -ING, -S to kidnap for service aboard a ship

SHANK   *v* -ED, -ING, -S to hit sharply to the right, as a golf ball

SHANNY   *n* pl. -NIES a marine fish

SHANTEY   *n* pl. -TEYS chantey

SHANTI   *n* pl. -S peace

SHANTIES   pl. of shanty

SHANTIH   *n* pl. -S shanti

SHANTUNG   *n* pl. -S a silk fabric

SHANTY   *n* pl. -TIES a small, crudely built dwelling

SHAPE   *v* SHAPED, SHAPEN, SHAPING, SHAPES to give shape (outward form) to **SHAPABLE** *adj*

SHAPELY   *adj* -LIER, -LIEST having a pleasing shape

SHAPER   *n* pl. -S one that shapes

SHAPEUP   *n* pl. -S a system of hiring a work crew

SHAPING   present participle of shape

SHARD   *n* pl. -S a fragment of broken pottery

SHARE   *v* SHARED, SHARING, SHARES to have, get, or use in common with another or others **SHARABLE** *adj*

SHARER   *n* pl. -S one that shares

SHARIF   *n* pl. -S sherif

SHARING   present participle of share

SHARK   *v* -ED, -ING, -S to live by trickery

SHARKER   *n* pl. -S one that sharks

SHARN   *n* pl. -S cow dung **SHARNY** *adj*

SHARP   *adj* SHARPER, SHARPEST suitable for or capable of cutting or piercing

SHARP   *v* -ED, -ING, -S to raise in pitch, as a musical tone

SHARPEN   *v* -ED, -ING, -S to make sharp

SHARPER   *n* pl. -S a swindler

SHARPIE   *n* pl. -S a very alert person

SHARPLY   *adv* in a sharp manner

SHARPY   *n* pl. SHARPIES sharpie

SHASHLIK   *n* pl. -S kabob

SHASLIK   *n* pl. -S shashlik

SHATTER   *v* -ED, -ING, -S to break into pieces

SHAUGH   *n* pl. -S a thicket

SHAUL   *v* -ED, -ING, -S to shoal

SHAVE   *v* SHAVED, SHAVEN, SHAVING, SHAVES to sever the hair close to the roots **SHAVABLE** *adj*

SHAVER   *n* pl. -S one that shaves

SHAVIE   *n* pl. -S a trick or prank

SHAVING   *n* pl. -S something shaved off

SHAW   *v* SHAWED, SHAWN, SHAWING, SHAWS to show

SHAWL   *v* -ED, -ING, -S to wrap in a shawl (a piece of cloth worn as a covering)

SHAWM   *n* pl. -S an early woodwind instrument

SHAWN   past participle of shaw

SHAY   *n* pl. SHAYS a chaise

SHE   *n* pl. -S a female person

SHEA   *n* pl. -S an African tree

SHEAF   *v* -ED, -ING, -S to sheave

SHEAL   *n* pl. -S shealing

SHEALING   *n* pl. -S a shepherd's hut

SHEAR   *v* SHEARED or SHORE, SHORN, SHEARING, SHEARS to cut the hair or wool from

SHEARER   *n* pl. -S one that shears

SHEARING   *n* pl. -S an instance of cutting hair or wool

SHEATH   *v* -ED, -ING, -S to sheathe

SHEATHE   *v* SHEATHED, SHEATHING, SHEATHES to put into a protective case

SHEATHER   *n* pl. -S one that sheathes

SHEAVE   *v* SHEAVED, SHEAVING, SHEAVES to gather into a bundle

SHEBANG   *n* pl. -S a situation, organization, or matter

SHEBEAN   *n* pl. -S shebeen

SHEBEEN   *n* pl. -S a place where liquor is sold illegally

SHED   *v* SHEDDED, SHEDDING, SHEDS to house in a shed (a small, low structure)

SHEDABLE   *adj* capable of being cast off

SHEDDER   *n* pl. -S one that casts off something

SHEDDING   present participle of shed

SHEDLIKE   *adj* resembling a shed

SHEEN   *v* -ED, -ING, -S to shine

SHEENFUL   *adj* shining

SHEENY   *adj* SHEENIER, SHEENIEST shining

SHEEP   *n* pl. SHEEP a ruminant mammal

SHEEPCOT   *n* pl. -S an enclosure for sheep

SHEEPDOG   *n* pl. -S a dog trained to guard and herd sheep

SHEEPISH   *adj* embarrassed

SHEEPMAN   *n* pl. -MEN a person who raises sheep

SHEER   *v* -ED, -ING, -S to swerve

SHEER   *adj* SHEERER, SHEEREST of very thin texture **SHEERLY** *adv*

SHEET   *v* -ED, -ING, -S to cover with a sheet (a thin, rectangular piece of material)

SHEETER   *n* pl. -S one that sheets

SHEETFED   *adj* pertaining to a type of printing press

SHEETING   *n* pl. -S material in the form of sheets

SHEEVE   *n* pl. -S a grooved pulley wheel

SHEIK   *n* pl. -S an Arab chief

SHEIKDOM   *n* pl. -S the area ruled by a sheik

SHEIKH   *n* pl. -S sheik

SHEILA   *n* pl. -S a young woman

SHEITAN   *n* pl. -S shaitan

SHEKEL   *n* pl. -S an ancient unit of weight and money

SHELDUCK   *n* pl. -S a European duck

SHELF   *n* pl. SHELVES a flat rigid structure used to support articles

SHELFFUL   *n* pl. -S as much as a shelf can hold

SHELL   *v* -ED, -ING, -S to divest of a shell (a hard outer covering)

SHELLAC   *v* -LACKED, -LACKING, -LACS to cover with a thin varnish

SHELLACK   *v* -ED, -ING, -S to shellac

SHELLER   *n* pl. -S one that shells

SHELLY   *adj* SHELLIER, SHELLIEST abounding in seashells

SHELTA   *n* pl. -S an esoteric jargon of Gaelic

SHELTER   *v* -ED, -ING, -S to provide cover or protection for

SHELTIE   *n* pl. -S a small, shaggy pony

SHELTY   *n* pl. -TIES sheltie

SHELVE   *v* SHELVED, SHELVING, SHELVES to place on a shelf

SHELVER   *n* pl. -S one that shelves

SHELVES   pl. of shelf

SHELVING   *n* pl. -S material for shelves

SHELVY   *adj* SHELVIER, SHELVIEST inclining gradually

SHEND   *v* SHENT, SHENDING, SHENDS to disgrace

SHEOL   *n* pl. -S hell

SHEPHERD   *v* -ED, -ING, -S to watch over carefully

SHEQEL   *n* pl. SHEQALIM shekel

SHERBERT   *n* pl. -S sherbet

SHERBET   *n* pl. -S a frozen fruit-flavored mixture

SHERD   *n* pl. -S shard

SHEREEF   *n* pl. -S sherif

SHERIF   *n* pl. -S an Arab ruler

SHERIFF   *n* pl. -S a law-enforcement officer of a county

SHERLOCK   *n* pl. -S a detective

SHEROOT   *n* pl. -S cheroot

SHERPA   *n* pl. -S a soft fabric for linings

SHERRIS   *n* pl. -RISES sherry

SHERRY   *n* pl. -RIES a type of wine

SHETLAND   *n* pl. -S a wool yarn

SHEUCH   *n* pl. -S sheugh

SHEUGH   *n* pl. -S a ditch

SHEW   *v* SHEWED, SHEWN, SHEWING, SHEWS to show

SHEWER   *n* pl. -S one that shews

SHH   *interj* sh

SHIATSU   *n* pl. -S a massage using finger pressure

SHIATZU   *n* pl. -S shiatsu

SHIBAH   *n* pl. -S shiva

SHICKER   *n* pl. -S a drunkard

SHICKSA   *n* pl. -S shiksa

SHIED   past tense of shy

SHIEL   *n* pl. -S shieling

SHIELD   *v* -ED, -ING, -S to provide with a protective cover or shelter

SHIELDER   *n* pl. -S one that shields

SHIELING   *n* pl. -S shealing

SHIER   *n* pl. -S a horse having a tendency to shy

SHIES   present 3d person sing. of shy

SHIEST   a superlative of shy

SHIFT   *v* -ED, -ING, -S to move from one position to another

SHIFTER   *n* pl. -S one that shifts

SHIFTY   *adj* SHIFTIER, SHIFTIEST tricky **SHIFTILY** *adv*

SHIGELLA   *n* pl. -LAE or -LAS any of a genus of aerobic bacteria

SHIITAKE   *n* pl. -S a dark Oriental mushroom

SHIKAR   *v* -KARRED, -KARRING, -KARS to hunt

SHIKAREE   *n* pl. -S a big game hunter

SHIKARI   *n* pl. -S shikaree

SHIKARRED   past tense of shikar

SHIKARRING   present participle of shikar

SHIKKER   *n* pl. -S shicker

SHILINGI   *n* pl. SHILINGI a monetary unit of Tanzania

SHILL   *v* -ED, -ING, -S to act as a decoy

SHILLALA   *n* pl. -S a short, thick club

SHILLING   *n* pl. -S a former monetary unit of Great Britain

SHILPIT   *adj* sickly

SHILY   *adv* in a shy manner

SHIM   *v* SHIMMED, SHIMMING, SHIMS to fill out or level by inserting a thin wedge

SHIMMER   *v* -ED, -ING, -S to glimmer

SHIMMERY   *adj* shimmering

SHIMMING   present participle of shim

SHIMMY   *v* -MIED, -MYING, -MIES to vibrate or wobble

SHIN   *v* SHINNED, SHINNING, SHINS to climb by gripping and pulling alternately with the hands and legs

SHINBONE   *n* pl. -S the tibia

SHINDIG   *n* pl. -S an elaborate dance or party

SHINDY   *n* pl. -DYS or -DIES a shindig

SHINE   *v* SHONE or SHINED, SHINING, SHINES to emit light

SHINER   *n* pl. -S one that shines

SHINGLE   *v* -GLED, -GLING, -GLES to cover with shingles (thin, oblong pieces of building material)

SHINGLER   *n* pl. -S one that shingles

SHINGLY   *adj* covered with small, loose stones

SHINIER   comparative of shiny

SHINIEST   superlative of shiny

SHINILY   *adv* in a shiny manner

SHINING   *adj* emitting or reflecting light

SHINLEAF   *n* pl. -LEAFS or -LEAVES a perennial herb

SHINNED   past of shin

SHINNERY   *n* pl. -NERIES a dense growth of small trees

SHINNEY   *v* -ED, -ING, -S to play a form of hockey

SHINNING   present participle of shin

SHINNY   *v* -NIED, -NYING, -NIES to shin

SHINY   *adj* SHINIER, SHINIEST filled with light

SHIP   *v* SHIPPED, SHIPPING, SHIPS to transport by ship (a vessel suitable for navigation in deep water)

SHIPLAP   *n* pl. -S an overlapping joint used in carpentry

SHIPLOAD   *n* pl. -S as much as a ship can carry

SHIPMAN   *n* pl. -MEN a sailor

SHIPMATE   *n* pl. -S a fellow sailor

SHIPMENT *n* pl. -S something that is shipped

SHIPPED past tense of ship

SHIPPEN *n* pl. -S a cowshed

SHIPPER *n* pl. -S one that ships

SHIPPING *n* pl. -S the business of one that ships

SHIPPON *n* pl. -S shippen

SHIPSIDE *n* pl. -S the area alongside a ship

SHIPWAY *n* pl. -WAYS a canal deep enough to serve ships

SHIPWORM *n* pl. -S a wormlike mollusk

SHIPYARD *n* pl. -S a place where ships are built or repaired

SHIRE *n* pl. -S a territorial division of Great Britain

SHIRK *v* -ED, -ING, -S to avoid work or duty

SHIRKER *n* pl. -S one that shirks

SHIRR *v* -ED, -ING, -S to draw into three or more parallel rows, as cloth

SHIRRING *n* pl. -S a shirred arrangement of cloth

SHIRT *n* pl. -S a garment for the upper part of the body

SHIRTING *n* pl. -S fabric used for making shirts

SHIRTY *adj* SHIRTIER, SHIRTIEST angry

SHIST *n* pl. -S schist

SHITAKE *n* pl. -S shiitake

SHITTAH *n* pl. -S a hardwood tree

SHITTIM *n* pl. -S the wood of the shittah

SHIV *n* pl. -S a knife

SHIVA *n* pl. -S a period of mourning

SHIVAH *n* pl. -S shiva

SHIVAREE *v* -REED, -REEING, -REES to chivaree

SHIVE *n* pl. -S a thin fragment

SHIVER *v* -ED, -ING, -S to tremble with fear or cold

SHIVERER *n* pl. -S one that shivers

SHIVERY *adj* shivering

SHLEMIEL *n* pl. -S an unlucky bungler

SHLEP *v* SHLEPPED, SHLEPPING, SHLEPS to schlep

SHLEPP *v* -ED, -ING, -S to schlep

SHLOCK *n* pl. -S schlock

SHLUMP *v* -ED, -ING, -S to schlump

SHLUMPY *adj* slovenly

SHMALTZ *n* pl. -ES schmaltz

SHMALTZY *adj* SHMALTZIER, SHMALTZIEST schmalzy

SHMEAR *n* pl. -S schmear

SHMO *n* pl. SHMOES schmo

SHMOOZE *v* SHMOOZED, SHMOOZING, SHMOOZES to schmooze

SHMUCK *n* pl. -S schmuck

SHNAPS *n* pl. SHNAPS schnapps

SHNOOK *n* pl. -S schnook

SHOAL *adj* SHOALER, SHOALEST shallow

SHOAL *v* -ED, -ING, -S to become shallow

SHOALY *adj* SHOALIER, SHOALIEST full of shallow areas

SHOAT *n* pl. -S a young hog

SHOCK *v* -ED, -ING, -S to strike with great surprise, horror, or disgust

SHOCKER *n* pl. -S one that shocks

SHOD a past tense of shoe

SHODDEN a past participle of shoe

SHODDY *adj* -DIER, -DIEST of inferior quality **SHODDILY** *adv*

SHODDY *n* pl. -DIES a low-quality wool

SHOE *n* pl. SHOES or SHOON a covering for the foot

SHOE *v* SHOD or SHOED, SHODDEN, SHOEING, SHOES to provide with shoes

SHOEBILL *n* pl. -S a wading bird

SHOEHORN *v* -ED, -ING, -S to force into a small space

SHOELACE *n* pl. -S a lace for fastening a shoe

SHOELESS *adj* having no shoe

SHOEPAC *n* pl. -S a waterproof boot

SHOEPACK *n* pl. -S shoepac

SHOER *n* pl. -S one that shoes horses

SHOETREE *n* pl. -S a device shaped like a foot that is inserted into a shoe to preserve its shape

SHOFAR *n* pl. SHOFARS or SHOFROTH a ram's-horn trumpet blown in certain Jewish rituals

SHOG *v* SHOGGED, SHOGGING, SHOGS to move along

SHOGUN *n* pl. -S a former military leader of Japan **SHOGUNAL** *adj*

SHOJI *n* pl. -S a paper screen used as a partition or door in a Japanese house

SHOLOM *n* pl. -S shalom

SHONE a past tense of shine

SHOO *v* -ED, -ING, -S to drive away

SHOOFLY *n* pl. -FLIES a child's rocker

SHOOK	*n* pl. -S a set of parts for assembling a barrel or packing
SHOOL	*v* -ED, -ING, -S to shovel
SHOON	a pl. of shoe
SHOOT	*v* SHOT, SHOOTING, SHOOTS to hit, wound, or kill with a missile discharged from a weapon
SHOOTER	*n* pl. -S one that shoots
SHOOTING	*n* pl. -S the act of one that shoots
SHOOTOUT	*n* pl. -S a battle fought with handguns or rifles
SHOP	*v* SHOPPED, SHOPPING, SHOPS to examine goods with intent to buy
SHOPBOY	*n* pl. -BOYS a salesclerk
SHOPGIRL	*n* pl. -S a salesgirl
SHOPHAR	*n* pl. -PHARS or -PHROTH shofar
SHOPLIFT	*v* -ED, -ING, -S to steal goods from a store
SHOPMAN	*n* pl. -MEN one who owns or operates a small store
SHOPPE	*n* pl. -S a small store
SHOPPED	past tense of shop
SHOPPER	*n* pl. -S one that shops
SHOPPING	*n* pl. -S the act of one that shops
SHOPTALK	*n* pl. -S conversation concerning one's business or occupation
SHOPWORN	*adj* worn out from being on display in a store
SHORAN	*n* pl. -S a type of navigational system
SHORE	*v* SHORED, SHORING, SHORES to prop with a supporting timber
SHORING	*n* pl. -S a system of supporting timbers
SHORL	*n* pl. -S schorl
SHORN	a past participle of shear
SHORT	*adj* SHORTER, SHORTEST having little length
SHORT	*v* -ED, -ING, -S to cause a type of electrical malfunction in
SHORTAGE	*n* pl. -S an insufficient supply or amount
SHORTCUT	*v* -CUT, -CUTTING, -CUTS to take a shorter or quicker way
SHORTEN	*v* -ED, -ING, -S to make or become shorter
SHORTIA	*n* pl. -S a perennial herb
SHORTIE	*n* pl. -S shorty
SHORTIES	pl. of shorty
SHORTISH	*adj* somewhat short
SHORTLY	*adv* in a short time
SHORTY	*n* pl. SHORTIES one that is short
SHOT	*v* SHOTTED, SHOTTING, SHOTS to load with shot (small lead or steel pellets)
SHOTE	*n* pl. -S shoat
SHOTGUN	*v* -GUNNED, -GUNNING, -GUNS to shoot with a type of gun
SHOTT	*n* pl. -S chott
SHOTTED	past tense of shot
SHOTTEN	*adj* having spawned — used of a fish
SHOTTING	present participle of shot
SHOULD	past tense of shall
SHOULDER	*v* -ED, -ING, -S to assume the burden or responsibility of
SHOULDEST	a 2d person sing. past tense of shall
SHOULDST	a 2d person sing. past tense of shall
SHOUT	*v* -ED, -ING, -S to utter loudly
SHOUTER	*n* pl. -S one that shouts
SHOVE	*v* SHOVED, SHOVING, SHOVES to push roughly
SHOVEL	*v* -ELED, -ELING, -ELS or -ELLED, -ELLING, -ELS to take up with a shovel (a digging implement)
SHOVELER	*n* pl. -S one that shovels
SHOVER	*n* pl. -S one that shoves
SHOVING	present participle of shove
SHOW	*v* SHOWED, SHOWN, SHOWING, SHOWS to cause or permit to be seen **SHOWABLE** *adj*
SHOWBIZ	*n* pl. -BIZZES show business
SHOWBOAT	*v* -ED, -ING, -S to show off
SHOWCASE	*v* -CASED, -CASING, -CASES to exhibit
SHOWDOWN	*n* pl. -S an event that forces the conclusion of an issue
SHOWER	*v* -ED, -ING, -S to bathe in a spray of water
SHOWERER	*n* pl. -S one that showers
SHOWERY	*adj* abounding with brief periods of rain
SHOWGIRL	*n* pl. -S a chorus girl
SHOWIER	comparative of showy
SHOWIEST	superlative of showy
SHOWILY	*adv* in a showy manner
SHOWING	*n* pl. -S an exhibition or display

SHOWMAN *n* pl. -MEN a theatrical producer

SHOWN past participle of show

SHOWOFF *n* pl. -S one given to pretentious display

SHOWRING *n* pl. -S a ring where animals are displayed

SHOWROOM *n* pl. -S a room used for the display of merchandise

SHOWY *adj* SHOWIER, SHOWIEST making a great or brilliant display

SHOYU *n* pl. -S soy sauce

SHRANK past tense of shrink

SHRAPNEL *n* pl. SHRAPNEL fragments from an exploding bomb, mine, or shell

SHRED *v* SHREDDED, SHREDDING, SHREDS to tear into small strips

SHREDDER *n* pl. -S one that shreds

SHREW *v* -ED, -ING, -S to curse

SHREWD *adj* SHREWDER, SHREWDEST having keen insight **SHREWDLY** *adv*

SHREWDIE *n* pl. -S a shrewd person

SHREWISH *adj* ill-tempered

SHRI *n* pl. -S sri

SHRIEK *v* -ED, -ING, -S to utter a shrill cry

SHRIEKER *n* pl. -S one that shrieks

SHRIEKY *adj* SHRIEKIER, SHRIEKIEST shrill

SHRIEVAL *adj* pertaining to a sheriff

SHRIEVE *v* SHRIEVED, SHRIEVING, SHRIEVES to shrive

SHRIFT *n* pl. -S the act of shriving

SHRIKE *n* pl. -S a predatory bird

SHRILL *adj* SHRILLER, SHRILLEST having a high-pitched and piercing quality **SHRILLY** *adv*

SHRILL *v* -ED, -ING, -S to utter a shrill sound

SHRIMP *v* -ED, -ING, -S to catch shrimps (small marine decapods)

SHRIMPER *n* pl. -S a shrimp fisher

SHRIMPY *adj* SHRIMPIER, SHRIMPIEST abounding in shrimp

SHRINE *v* SHRINED, SHRINING, SHRINES to place in a shrine (a receptacle for sacred relics)

SHRINK *v* SHRANK, SHRUNK or SHRUNKEN, SHRINKING, SHRINKS to contract or draw back

SHRINKER *n* pl. -S one that shrinks

SHRIVE *v* SHROVE or SHRIVED, SHRIVEN, SHRIVING, SHRIVES to hear the confession of and grant absolution to

SHRIVEL *v* -ELED, -ELING, -ELS or -ELLED, -ELLING, -ELS to contract into wrinkles

SHRIVER *n* pl. -S one that shrives

SHRIVING present participle of shrive

SHROFF *v* -ED, -ING, -S to test the genuineness of, as a coin

SHROUD *v* -ED, -ING, -S to wrap in burial clothing

SHROVE a past tense of shrive

SHRUB *n* pl. -S a low, woody plant

SHRUBBY *adj* -BIER, -BIEST covered with shrubs

SHRUG *v* SHRUGGED, SHRUGGING, SHRUGS to raise and contract the shoulders

SHRUNK a past tense of shrink

SHRUNKEN a past participle of shrink

SHTETEL *n* pl. SHTETLACH or SHTETELS a Jewish village

SHTETL *n* pl. SHTETLACH or SHTETLS shtetel

SHTICK *n* pl. -S an entertainment routine

SHTIK *n* pl. -S shtick

SHUCK *v* -ED, -ING, -S to remove the husk or shell from

SHUCKER *n* pl. -S one that shucks

SHUCKING *n* pl. -S the act of one that shucks

SHUDDER *v* -ED, -ING, -S to tremble

SHUDDERY *adj* shuddering

SHUFFLE *v* -FLED, -FLING, -FLES to walk without lifting the feet

SHUFFLER *n* pl. -S one that shuffles

SHUL *n* pl. SHULN or SHULS a synagogue

SHUN *v* SHUNNED, SHUNNING, SHUNS to avoid

SHUNNER *n* pl. -S one that shuns

SHUNPIKE *v* -PIKED, -PIKING, -PIKES to travel on side roads to avoid expressways

SHUNT *v* -ED, -ING, -S to turn aside

SHUNTER *n* pl. -S one that shunts

SHUSH *v* -ED, -ING, -ES to silence

SHUT _v_ SHUT, SHUTTING, SHUTS to close

SHUTDOWN _n_ pl. -S a temporary closing of an industrial plant

SHUTE _v_ SHUTED, SHUTING, SHUTES to chute

SHUTEYE _n_ pl. -S sleep

SHUTOFF _n_ pl. -S a device that shuts something off

SHUTOUT _n_ pl. -S a game in which one team fails to score

SHUTTER _v_ -ED, -ING, -S to provide with shutters (hinged window covers)

SHUTTING present participle of shut

SHUTTLE _v_ -TLED, -TLING, -TLES to move or travel back and forth

SHWANPAN _n_ pl. -S swanpan

SHY _adj_ SHIER, SHIEST or SHYER, SHYEST timid

SHY _v_ SHIED, SHYING, SHIES to move suddenly back or aside, as in fear

SHYER _n_ pl. -S shier

SHYLOCK _v_ -ED, -ING, -S to lend money at high interest rates

SHYLY _adv_ in a shy manner

SHYNESS _n_ pl. -ES the state of being shy

SHYSTER _n_ pl. -S an unscrupulous lawyer or politician

SI _n_ pl. -S ti

SIAL _n_ pl. -S a type of rock formation SIALIC _adj_

SIALID _n_ pl. -S an alderfly

SIALIDAN _n_ pl. -S sialid

SIALOID _adj_ resembling saliva

SIAMANG _n_ pl. -S a large, black gibbon

SIAMESE _n_ pl. -S a water pipe with a connection for two hoses

SIB _n_ pl. -S a sibling

SIBB _n_ pl. -S sib

SIBILANT _n_ pl. -S a speech sound produced by the fricative passage of breath through a narrow orifice

SIBILATE _v_ -LATED, -LATING, -LATES to hiss

SIBLING _n_ pl. -S one having the same parents as another

SIBYL _n_ pl. -S a female prophet SIBYLIC, SIBYLLIC _adj_

SIC _v_ SICCED, SICCING, SICS to urge to attack

SICCAN _adj_ such

SICE _n_ pl. -S syce

SICK _adj_ SICKER, SICKEST affected with disease or ill health

SICK _v_ -ED, -ING, -S to sic

SICKBAY _n_ pl. -BAYS a ship's hospital

SICKBED _n_ pl. -S a sick person's bed

SICKEE _n_ pl. -S sickie

SICKEN _v_ -ED, -ING, -S to make sick

SICKENER _n_ pl. -S one that sickens

SICKERLY _adv_ securely

SICKIE _n_ pl. -S an emotionally sick person

SICKISH _adj_ somewhat sick

SICKLE _v_ -LED, -LING, -LES to cut with an agricultural implement having a single blade

SICKLY _adj_ -LIER, -LIEST appearing as if sick SICKLILY _adv_

SICKLY _v_ -LIED, -LYING, -LIES to make sickly

SICKNESS _n_ pl. -ES the state of being sick

SICKO _n_ pl. SICKOS sickie

SICKOUT _n_ pl. -S an organized absence of workers claiming to be sick

SICKROOM _n_ pl. -S a room occupied by a sick person

SIDDUR _n_ pl. -DURIM or -DURS a Jewish prayer book

SIDE _v_ SIDED, SIDING, SIDES to agree with or support

SIDEARM _adj_ thrown with a sideways sweep of the arm

SIDEBAND _n_ pl. -S a band of radio frequencies

SIDEBAR _n_ pl. -S a short news story accompanying a major story

SIDECAR _n_ pl. -S a passenger car attached to a motorcycle

SIDED past tense of side

SIDEHILL _n_ pl. -S a hillside

SIDEKICK _n_ pl. -S a close friend

SIDELINE _v_ -LINED, -LINING, -LINES to put out of action

SIDELING _adj_ sloping

SIDELONG _adj_ directed to one side

SIDEMAN _n_ pl. -MEN a member of a jazz band

SIDEREAL _adj_ pertaining to the stars

SIDERITE _n_ pl. -S a mineral

SIDESHOW _n_ pl. -S a small show offered in addition to a main attraction

SIDESLIP _v_ -SLIPPED, -SLIPPING, -SLIPS to slip to one side

SIDESPIN _n_ pl. -S a type of spin imparted to a ball

SIDESTEP v -STEPPED, -STEPPING, -STEPS to step to one side

SIDEWALK n pl. -S a paved walk for pedestrians

SIDEWALL n pl. -S a side surface of a tire

SIDEWARD adv toward one side

SIDEWAY adv sideways

SIDEWAYS adv toward or from one side

SIDEWISE adv sideways

SIDING n pl. -S material used for surfacing a frame building

SIDLE v -DLED, -DLING, -DLES to move sideways

SIDLER n pl. -S one that sidles

SIEGE v SIEGED, SIEGING, SIEGES to attempt to capture or gain

SIEMENS n pl. SIEMENS a unit of electrical conductance

SIENITE n pl. -S syenite

SIENNA n pl. -S a brown pigment

SIEROZEM n pl. -S a type of soil

SIERRA n pl. -S a mountain range **SIERRAN** adj

SIESTA n pl. -S an afternoon nap or rest

SIEUR n pl. -S an old French title of respect for a man

SIEVE v SIEVED, SIEVING, SIEVES to pass through a sieve (a utensil for separating the coarse parts from the fine parts of loose matter)

SIFAKA n pl. -S a lemur of Madagascar

SIFFLEUR n pl. -S an animal that makes a whistling noise

SIFT v -ED, -ING, -S to sieve

SIFTER n pl. -S one that sifts

SIFTING n pl. -S the work of a sifter

SIGANID n pl. -S any of a family of fishes

SIGH v -ED, -ING, -S to let out a sigh (a deep, audible breath)

SIGHER n pl. -S one that sighs

SIGHLESS adj uttering no sigh

SIGHLIKE adj resembling a sigh

SIGHT v -ED, -ING, -S to observe or notice

SIGHTER n pl. -S one that sights

SIGHTING n pl. -S an observation

SIGHTLY adj -LIER, -LIEST pleasing to look at

SIGHTSEE v -SAW, -SEEN, -SEEING, -SEES to visit and view places of interest

SIGIL n pl. -S an official seal

SIGLOS n pl. -LOI an ancient Persian coin

SIGMA n pl. -S a Greek letter **SIGMATE** adj

SIGMOID n pl. -S an S-shaped curve in a bodily part

SIGN v -ED, -ING, -S to write one's name on

SIGNAGE n pl. -S a system of signs in a community

SIGNAL v -NALED, -NALING, -NALS or -NALLED, -NALLING, -NALS to notify by a means of communication

SIGNALER n pl. -S one that signals

SIGNALLY adv notably

SIGNEE n pl. -S a signer of a document

SIGNER n pl. -S one that signs

SIGNET v -ED, -ING, -S to mark with an official seal

SIGNIFY v -FIED, -FYING, -FIES to make known

SIGNIOR n pl. -GNIORI or -GNIORS signor

SIGNIORY n pl. -GNIORIES signory

SIGNOR n pl. -GNORI or -GNORS an Italian title of courtesy for a man

SIGNORA n pl. -GNORE or -GNORAS an Italian title of courtesy for a married woman

SIGNORE n pl. -GNORI signor

SIGNORY n pl. -GNORIES seignory

SIGNPOST v -ED, -ING, -S to provide with signposts (posts bearing signs)

SIKE n pl. -S syke

SIKER adj secure

SILAGE n pl. -S fodder that has been preserved in a silo

SILANE n pl. -S a chemical compound

SILD n pl. -S a young herring

SILENCE v -LENCED, -LENCING, -LENCES to make silent

SILENCER n pl. -S one that silences

SILENI pl. of silenus

SILENT adj -LENTER, -LENTEST making no sound or noise **SILENTLY** adv

SILENTS n/pl silent movies

SILENUS n pl. -NI a woodland deity of Greek mythology

SILESIA n pl. -S a cotton fabric

SILEX n pl. -ES silica

SILICA n pl. -S a form of silicon

SILICATE	*n* pl. -S a chemical salt
SILICIC	*adj* pertaining to silicon
SILICIDE	*n* pl. -S a silicon compound
SILICIFY	*v* -FIED, -FYING, -FIES to convert into silica
SILICIUM	*n* pl. -S silicon
SILICLE	*n* pl. -S a short, flat silique
SILICON	*n* pl. -S a nonmetallic element
SILICONE	*n* pl. -S a silicon compound
SILICULA	*n* pl. -LAE a silicle
SILIQUA	*n* pl. -QUAE silique
SILIQUE	*n* pl. -LIQUES a type of seed vessel
SILK	*v* -ED, -ING, -S to cover with silk (a soft, lustrous fabric)
SILKEN	*adj* made of silk
SILKIER	comparative of silky
SILKIEST	superlative of silky
SILKILY	*adv* in a silky manner
SILKLIKE	*adj* resembling silk
SILKWEED	*n* pl. -S milkweed
SILKWORM	*n* pl. -S a caterpillar that spins a cocoon of silk fibers
SILKY	*adj* SILKIER, SILKIEST resembling silk
SILL	*n* pl. -S the horizontal piece that bears the upright portion of a frame
SILLABUB	*n* pl. -S an alcoholic beverage or dessert
SILLER	*n* pl. -S silver
SILLIBUB	*n* pl. -S sillabub
SILLY	*adj* -LIER, -LIEST showing a lack of good sense SILLILY *adv*
SILLY	*n* pl. -LIES a silly person
SILO	*v* -ED, -ING, -S to store in a silo (a tall, cylindrical structure)
SILOXANE	*n* pl. -S a chemical compound
SILT	*v* -ED, -ING, -S to fill with silt (a sedimentary material)
SILTY	*adj* SILTIER, SILTIEST full of silt
SILURID	*n* pl. -S any of a family of catfishes
SILUROID	*n* pl. -S a silurid
SILVA	*n* pl. -VAS or -VAE sylva
SILVAN	*n* pl. -S sylvan
SILVER	*v* -ED, -ING, -S to cover with silver (a metallic element)
SILVERER	*n* pl. -S one that silvers
SILVERLY	*adv* with a silvery appearance
SILVERN	*adj* silvery
SILVERY	*adj* resembling silver
SILVEX	*n* pl. -ES an herbicide
SILVICAL	*adj* pertaining to silvics

SILVICS	*n/pl* the study of forest trees
SIM	*n* pl. -S simulation
SIMA	*n* pl. -S an igneous rock
SIMAR	*n* pl. -S a woman's light jacket or robe
SIMARUBA	*n* pl. -S a tropical tree
SIMAZINE	*n* pl. -S an herbicide
SIMIAN	*n* pl. -S an ape or monkey
SIMILAR	*adj* being like but not completely identical to
SIMILE	*n* pl. -S a figure of speech
SIMIOID	*adj* simious
SIMIOUS	*adj* pertaining to simians
SIMITAR	*n* pl. -S scimitar
SIMLIN	*n* pl. -S cymling
SIMMER	*v* -ED, -ING, -S to cook below or just at the boiling point
SIMNEL	*n* pl. -S a crisp bread
SIMOLEON	*n* pl. -S a dollar
SIMONIAC	*n* pl. -S one who practices simony
SIMONIES	pl. of simony
SIMONIST	*n* pl. -S a simoniac
SIMONIZE	*v* -NIZED, -NIZING, -NIZES to polish with wax
SIMONY	*n* pl. -NIES the buying or selling of a church office
SIMOOM	*n* pl. -S a hot, dry desert wind
SIMOON	*n* pl. -S simoom
SIMP	*n* pl. -S a foolish person
SIMPER	*v* -ED, -ING, -S to smile in a silly manner
SIMPERER	*n* pl. -S one that simpers
SIMPLE	*adj* SIMPLER, SIMPLEST not complex or complicated
SIMPLE	*n* pl. -S something that is simple
SIMPLEX	*n* pl. -PLEXES, -PLICES, or -PLICIA a simple word
SIMPLIFY	*v* -FIED, -FYING, -FIES to make simple
SIMPLISM	*n* pl. -S the tendency to oversimplify an issue or problem
SIMPLIST	*n* pl. -S a person given to simplism
SIMPLY	*adv* in a simple manner
SIMULANT	*n* pl. -S one that simulates
SIMULAR	*n* pl. -S a simulant
SIMULATE	*v* -LATED, -LATING, -LATES to take on the appearance of
SIN	*v* SINNED, SINNING, SINS to commit a sin (an offense against religious or moral law)

SINAPISM *n* pl. -S a pasty mixture applied to an irritated part of the body

SINCE *adv* from then until now

SINCERE *adj* -CERER, -CEREST free from hypocrisy or falseness

SINCIPUT *n* pl. -CIPUTS or -CIPITA the forehead

SINE *n* pl. -S a trigonometric function of an angle

SINECURE *n* pl. -S an office or position requiring little or no work

SINEW *v* -ED, -ING, -S to strengthen

SINEWY *adj* lean and muscular

SINFONIA *n* pl. -NIE a symphony

SINFUL *adj* marked by sin **SINFULLY** *adv*

SING *v* SANG, SUNG, SINGING, SINGS to utter with musical inflections of the voice **SINGABLE** *adj*

SINGE *v* SINGED, SINGEING, SINGES to burn slightly

SINGER *n* pl. -S one that sings

SINGLE *v* -GLED, -GLING, -GLES to select from a group

SINGLET *n* pl. -S a man's undershirt or jersey

SINGLY *adv* without the company of others

SINGSONG *n* pl. -S monotonous cadence in speaking or reading

SINGULAR *n* pl. -S a word form that denotes one person or thing

SINH *n* pl. -S a hyperbolic function of an angle

SINICIZE *v* -CIZED, -CIZING, -CIZES to modify by Chinese influence

SINISTER *adj* threatening or portending evil

SINK *v* SANK, SUNK or SUNKEN, SINKING, SINKS to move to a lower level **SINKABLE** *adj*

SINKAGE *n* pl. -S the act, process, or degree of sinking

SINKER *n* pl. -S one that sinks

SINKHOLE *n* pl. -S a natural depression in a land surface

SINLESS *adj* free from sin

SINNED past tense of sin

SINNER *n* pl. -S one that sins

SINNING present participle of sin

SINOLOGY *n* pl. -GIES the study of the Chinese

SINOPIA *n* pl. -PIAS or -PIE a red pigment

SINSYNE *adv* since

SINTER *v* -ED, -ING, -S to make cohesive by the combined action of heat and pressure

SINUATE *v* -ATED, -ATING, -ATES to curve in and out

SINUOUS *adj* characterized by curves, bends, or turns

SINUS *n* pl. -ES a cranial cavity

SINUSOID *n* pl. -S a mathematical curve

SIP *v* SIPPED, SIPPING, SIPS to drink in small quantities

SIPE *v* SIPED, SIPING, SIPES to seep

SIPHON *v* -ED, -ING, -S to draw off through a siphon (a type of tube)

SIPHONAL *adj* of or pertaining to a siphon

SIPHONIC *adj* siphonal

SIPING present participle of sipe

SIPPED past tense of sip

SIPPER *n* pl. -S one that sips

SIPPET *n* pl. -S a small piece of bread soaked in gravy

SIPPING present participle of sip

SIR *n* pl. -S a respectful form of address used to a man

SIRDAR *n* pl. -S a person of rank in India

SIRE *v* SIRED, SIRING, SIRES to beget

SIREE *n* pl. -S sirree

SIREN *n* pl. -S a device that produces a penetrating warning sound

SIRENIAN *n* pl. -S any of an order of aquatic mammals

SIRING present participle of sire

SIRLOIN *n* pl. -S a cut of beef

SIROCCO *n* pl. -COS a hot, dry wind

SIRRA *n* pl. -S sirrah

SIRRAH *n* pl. -S a form of address used to inferiors

SIRREE *n* pl. -S sir

SIRUP *n* pl. -S syrup **SIRUPY** *adj*

SIRVENTE *n* pl. -S a satirical medieval song or poem

SIS *n* pl. SISES sister

SISAL *n* pl. -S a strong fiber used for rope

SISKIN *n* pl. -S a Eurasian finch

SISSY *n* pl. -SIES an effeminate man or boy

SISSY *adj* SISSIER, SISSIEST sissyish

SISSYISH *adj* resembling a sissy

SISTER	*v* -ED, -ING, -S to treat like a sister (a female sibling)	**SIZAR**	*n* pl. -S a British student who receives financial assistance from his college
SISTERLY	*adj* of or resembling a sister		
SISTROID	*adj* included between the convex sides of two intersecting curves	**SIZE**	*v* SIZED, SIZING, SIZES to arrange according to size (physical proportions)
SISTRUM	*n* pl. -TRUMS or -TRA an ancient Egyptian percussion instrument	**SIZEABLE**	*adj* sizable **SIZEABLY** *adv*
		SIZER	*n* pl. -S sizar
		SIZIER	comparative of sizy
SIT	*v* SAT, SAT or SITTEN, SITTING, SITS to rest on the buttocks	**SIZIEST**	superlative of sizy
		SIZINESS	*n* pl. -ES the quality or state of being sizy
SITAR	*n* pl. -S a lute of India	**SIZING**	*n* pl. -S a substance used as a glaze or filler for porous materials
SITARIST	*n* pl. -S one who plays the sitar		
SITCOM	*n* pl. -S a television comedy series with continuing characters	**SIZY**	*adj* SIZIER, SIZIEST viscid
		SIZZLE	*v* -ZLED, -ZLING, -ZLES to burn or fry with a hissing sound
SITE	*v* SITED, SITING, SITES to place in position for operation		
SITH	*adv* since	**SIZZLER**	*n* pl. -S a very hot day
SITHENCE	*adv* since	**SJAMBOK**	*v* -ED, -ING, -S to strike with a whip used in South Africa
SITHENS	*adv* since		
SITING	present participle of site	**SKA**	*n* pl. -S a popular music of Jamaica
SITOLOGY	*n* pl. -GIES the science of nutrition and diet	**SKAG**	*n* pl. -S heroin
		SKALD	*n* pl. -S an ancient Scandinavian poet **SKALDIC** *adj*
SITTEN	a past participle of sit		
SITTER	*n* pl. -S one that sits		
SITTING	*n* pl. -S a meeting or session	**SKAT**	*n* pl. -S a card game
SITUATE	*v* -ATED, -ATING, -ATES to place in a certain position	**SKATE**	*v* SKATED, SKATING, SKATES to glide over ice or the ground on skates (shoes fitted with runners or wheels)
SITUP	*n* pl. -S an exercise in which one moves from a lying to a sitting position		
		SKATER	*n* pl. -S one that skates
SITUS	*n* pl. -TUSES a position or location	**SKATING**	*n* pl. -S the sport of gliding on skates
SITZMARK	*n* pl. -S a mark left in the snow by a skier who has fallen backward	**SKATOL**	*n* pl. -S skatole
		SKATOLE	*n* pl. -S a chemical compound
		SKEAN	*n* pl. -S a type of dagger
SIVER	*n* pl. -S a sewer	**SKEANE**	*n* pl. -S a length of yarn wound in a loose coil
SIX	*n* pl. -ES a number		
SIXFOLD	*adj* being six times as great as	**SKEE**	*v* SKEED, SKEEING, SKEES to ski
SIXMO	*n* pl. -MOS a paper size		
SIXPENCE	*n* pl. -S a British coin worth six pennies	**SKEEN**	*n* pl. -S skean
		SKEET	*n* pl. -S the sport of shooting at clay pigeons hurled in the air by spring traps
SIXPENNY	*adj* worth sixpence		
SIXTE	*n* pl. -S a fencing parry		
SIXTEEN	*n* pl. -S a number		
SIXTH	*n* pl. -S one of six equal parts	**SKEETER**	*n* pl. -S a skeet shooter
SIXTHLY	*adv* in the sixth place	**SKEG**	*n* pl. -S a timber that connects the keel and sternpost of a ship
SIXTIETH	*n* pl. -S one of sixty equal parts		
SIXTY	*n* pl. -TIES a number	**SKEIGH**	*adj* proud
SIXTYISH	*adj* being about sixty years old	**SKEIN**	*v* -ED, -ING, -S to wind into long, loose coils
SIZABLE	*adj* of considerable size **SIZABLY** *adv*		

SKELETON *n* pl. -S the supporting or protective framework of a human or animal body **SKELETAL** *adj*

SKELLUM *n* pl. -S a rascal

SKELM *n* pl. -S skellum

SKELP *v* SKELPED or SKELPIT, SKELPING, SKELPS to slap

SKELTER *v* -ED, -ING, -S to scurry

SKENE *n* pl. -S skean

SKEP *n* pl. -S a beehive

SKEPSIS *n* pl. -SISES the attitude or outlook of a skeptic

SKEPTIC *n* pl. -S a person who doubts generally accepted ideas

SKERRY *n* pl. -RIES a small, rocky island

SKETCH *v* -ED, -ING, -ES to make a rough, hasty drawing of

SKETCHER *n* pl. -S one that sketches

SKETCHY *adj* SKETCHIER, SKETCHIEST lacking in completeness or clearness

SKEW *v* -ED, -ING, -S to turn aside

SKEWBACK *n* pl. -S a sloping surface against which the end of an arch rests

SKEWBALD *n* pl. -S a horse having patches of brown and white

SKEWER *v* -ED, -ING, -S to pierce with a long pin, as meat

SKEWNESS *n* pl. -ES lack of symmetry

SKI *v* -ED, -ING, -S to travel on skis (long, narrow strips of wood or metal)

SKIABLE *adj* capable of being skied over

SKIAGRAM *n* pl. -S a picture made up of shadows or outlines

SKIBOB *n* pl. -S a vehicle used for traveling over snow

SKID *v* SKIDDED, SKIDDING, SKIDS to slide sideways as a result of a loss of traction

SKIDDER *n* pl. -S one that skids

SKIDDOO *v* -ED, -ING, -S to go away

SKIDDY *adj* -DIER, -DIEST likely to cause skidding

SKIDOO *v* -ED, -ING, -S to skiddoo

SKIDWAY *n* pl. -WAYS a platform on which logs are piled for loading or sawing

SKIED past tense of ski and sky

SKIER *n* pl. -S one that skis

SKIES present 3d person sing. of sky

SKIEY *adj* skyey

SKIFF *n* pl. -S a small, open boat

SKIFFLE *v* -FLED, -FLING, -FLES to play a particular style of music

SKIING *n* pl. -S the sport of traveling on skis

SKIJORER *n* pl. -S a skier who is drawn over snow by a horse or vehicle

SKILFUL *adj* skillful

SKILL *n* pl. -S the ability to do something well **SKILLED** *adj*

SKILLESS *adj* having no skill

SKILLET *n* pl. -S a frying pan

SKILLFUL *adj* having skill

SKILLING *n* pl. -S a former coin of Scandinavian countries

SKIM *v* SKIMMED, SKIMMING, SKIMS to remove floating matter from the surface of

SKIMMER *n* pl. -S one that skims

SKIMMING *n* pl. -S something that is skimmed from a liquid

SKIMP *v* -ED, -ING, -S to scrimp

SKIMPY *adj* SKIMPIER, SKIMPIEST scanty **SKIMPILY** *adv*

SKIN *v* SKINNED, SKINNING, SKINS to strip or deprive of skin (the membranous tissue covering the body of an animal)

SKINFUL *n* pl. -S as much as a skin container can hold

SKINHEAD *n* pl. -S one whose hair is cut very short

SKINK *v* -ED, -ING, -S to pour out or serve, as liquor

SKINKER *n* pl. -S one that skinks

SKINLESS *adj* having no skin

SKINLIKE *adj* resembling skin

SKINNED past tense of skin

SKINNER *n* pl. -S one that skins

SKINNING present participle of skin

SKINNY *adj* -NIER, -NIEST very thin

SKINT *adj* having no money

SKIORING *n* pl. -S a form of skiing

SKIP *v* SKIPPED, SKIPPING, SKIPS to move with light springing steps

SKIPJACK *n* pl. -S a marine fish

SKIPLANE *n* pl. -S an airplane designed to take off from or land on snow

SKIPPED past tense of skip

SKIPPER *v* -ED, -ING, -S to act as master or captain of

SKIPPET *n* pl. -S a small box for protecting an official seal

SKIPPING present participle of skip

SKIRL *v* -ED, -ING, -S to produce a shrill sound

SKIRMISH *v* -ED, -ING, -ES to engage in a minor battle

SKIRR *v* -ED, -ING, -S to move rapidly

SKIRRET *n* pl. -S an Asian herb

SKIRT *v* -ED, -ING, -S to go or pass around

SKIRTER *n* pl. -S one that skirts

SKIRTING *n* pl. -S a board at the base of a wall

SKIT *n* pl. -S a short dramatic scene

SKITE *v* SKITED, SKITING, SKITES to move away quickly

SKITTER *v* -ED, -ING, -S to move lightly or rapidly along a surface

SKITTERY *adj* -TERIER, -TERIEST skittish

SKITTISH *adj* easily frightened

SKITTLE *n* pl. -S a wooden pin used in a bowling game

SKIVE *v* SKIVED, SKIVING, SKIVES to pare

SKIVER *n* pl. -S one that skives

SKIVVY *v* -VIED, -VYING, -VIES to work as a female servant

SKIWEAR *n* pl. -S clothing suitable for wear while skiing

SKLENT *v* -ED, -ING, -S to slant

SKOAL *v* -ED, -ING, -S to drink to the health of

SKOOKUM *adj* excellent

SKOSH *n* pl. -ES a small amount

SKREEGH *v* -ED, -ING, -S to screech

SKREIGH *v* -ED, -ING, -S to screech

SKUA *n* pl. -S a predatory seabird

SKULK *v* -ED, -ING, -S to move about stealthily

SKULKER *n* pl. -S one that skulks

SKULL *n* pl. -S the framework of the head **SKULLED** *adj*

SKULLCAP *n* pl. -S a close-fitting cap

SKUNK *v* -ED, -ING, -S to defeat overwhelmingly

SKY *v* SKIED or SKYED, SKYING, SKIES to hit or throw toward the sky (the upper atmosphere)

SKYBORNE *adj* airborne

SKYBOX *n* pl. -ES an enclosure of seats situated high in a stadium

SKYCAP *n* pl. -S a porter at an airport

SKYDIVE *v* -DIVED or -DOVE, -DIVING, -DIVES to parachute from an airplane for sport

SKYDIVER *n* pl. -S one that skydives

SKYEY *adj* resembling the sky

SKYHOOK *n* pl. -S a hook conceived as being suspended from the sky

SKYJACK *v* -ED, -ING, -S to hijack an airplane

SKYLARK *v* -ED, -ING, -S to frolic

SKYLIGHT *n* pl. -S a window in a roof or ceiling

SKYLINE *n* pl. -S the horizon

SKYLIT *adj* having a skylight

SKYMAN *n* pl. -MEN an aviator

SKYPHOS *n* pl. -PHOI a drinking vessel used in ancient Greece

SKYSAIL *n* pl. -S a type of sail

SKYWALK *n* pl. -S an elevated walkway between two buildings

SKYWARD *adv* toward the sky

SKYWARDS *adv* skyward

SKYWAY *n* pl. -WAYS an elevated highway

SKYWRITE *v* -WROTE, -WRITTEN, -WRITING, -WRITES to write in the sky by releasing a visible vapor from an airplane

SLAB *v* SLABBED, SLABBING, SLABS to cover with slabs (broad, flat pieces of solid material)

SLABBER *v* -ED, -ING, -S to slobber

SLABBERY *adj* slobbery

SLABBING present participle of slab

SLABLIKE *adj* resembling a slab

SLACK *adj* SLACKER, SLACKEST not tight or taut

SLACK *v* -ED, -ING, -S to slacken

SLACKEN *v* -ED, -ING, -S to make less tight or taut

SLACKER *n* pl. -S a shirker

SLACKLY *adv* in a slack manner

SLAG *v* SLAGGED, SLAGGING, SLAGS to convert into slag (the fused residue of a smelted ore)

SLAGGY *adj* -GIER, -GIEST resembling slag

SLAIN past participle of slay

SLAINTE *interj* — used to toast one's health

SLAKE *v* SLAKED, SLAKING, SLAKES to quench **SLAKABLE** *adj*

SLAKER *n* pl. -S one that slakes

SLALOM *v* -ED, -ING, -S to ski in a zigzag course

SLAM *v* SLAMMED, SLAMMING, SLAMS to shut forcibly and noisily

SLAMMER *n* pl. -S a jail

SLANDER *v* -ED, -ING, -S to defame

SLANG *v* -ED, -ING, -S to use slang (extremely informal or vulgar language)

SLANGY *adj* SLANGIER, SLANGIEST being or containing slang **SLANGILY** *adv*

SLANK a past tense of slink

SLANT *v* -ED, -ING, -S to deviate from the horizontal or vertical

SLANTY *adj* deviating from the horizontal or vertical

SLAP *v* SLAPPED, SLAPPING, SLAPS to strike with the open hand

SLAPDASH *n* pl. -ES careless work

SLAPJACK *n* pl. -S a pancake

SLAPPED past tense of slap

SLAPPER *n* pl. -S one that slaps

SLAPPING present participle of slap

SLASH *v* -ED, -ING, -ES to cut with violent sweeping strokes

SLASHER *n* pl. -S one that slashes

SLASHING *n* pl. -S the act of one that slashes

SLAT *v* SLATTED, SLATTING, SLATS to provide with slats (narrow strips of wood or metal)

SLATCH *n* pl. -ES a calm between breaking waves

SLATE *v* SLATED, SLATING, SLATES to cover with slate (a roofing material)

SLATER *n* pl. -S one that slates

SLATEY *adj* SLATIER, SLATIEST slaty

SLATHER *v* -ED, -ING, -S to spread thickly

SLATIER comparative of slaty

SLATIEST superlative of slaty

SLATING *n* pl. -S the act of one that slates

SLATTED past tense of slat

SLATTERN *n* pl. -S a slovenly woman

SLATTING *n* pl. -S material for making slats

SLATY *adj* SLATIER, SLATIEST resembling slate

SLAVE *v* SLAVED, SLAVING, SLAVES to work like a slave (one who is owned by another)

SLAVER *v* -ED, -ING, -S to drool

SLAVERER *n* pl. -S one that slavers

SLAVERY *n* pl. -ERIES ownership of one person by another

SLAVEY *n* pl. -EYS a female servant

SLAVING present participle of slave

SLAVISH *adj* pertaining to or characteristic of a slave

SLAW *n* pl. -S coleslaw

SLAY *v* SLEW, SLAIN, SLAYING, SLAYS to kill violently

SLAY *v* SLAYED, SLAIN, SLAYING, SLAYS to amuse overwhelmingly

SLAYER *n* pl. -S one that slays

SLEAVE *v* SLEAVED, SLEAVING, SLEAVES to separate into filaments

SLEAZE *n* pl. -S a sleazy quality

SLEAZO *adj* sleazy

SLEAZY *adj* SLEAZIER, SLEAZIEST shoddy **SLEAZILY** *adv*

SLED *v* SLEDDED, SLEDDING, SLEDS to convey on a sled (a vehicle for carrying people or loads over snow or ice)

SLEDDER *n* pl. -S one that sleds

SLEDDING *n* pl. -S the act of one that sleds

SLEDGE *v* SLEDGED, SLEDGING, SLEDGES to convey on a type of sled

SLEEK *adj* SLEEKER, SLEEKEST smooth and glossy

SLEEK *v* -ED, -ING, -S to make sleek

SLEEKEN *v* -ED, -ING, -S to sleek

SLEEKIER comparative of sleeky

SLEEKIEST superlative of sleeky

SLEEKIT *adj* sleek

SLEEKLY *adv* in a sleek manner

SLEEKY *adj* SLEEKIER, SLEEKIEST sleek

SLEEP *v* SLEPT, SLEEPING, SLEEPS to be in a natural, periodic state of rest

SLEEPER *n* pl. -S one that sleeps

SLEEPING *n* pl. -S the act of one that sleeps

SLEEPY *adj* SLEEPIER, SLEEPIEST ready or inclined to sleep **SLEEPILY** *adv*

SLEET   v -ED, -ING, -S to shower sleet (frozen rain)

SLEETY   adj SLEETIER, SLEETIEST resembling sleet

SLEEVE   v SLEEVED, SLEEVING, SLEEVES to furnish with a sleeve (the part of a garment covering the arm)

SLEIGH   v -ED, -ING, -S to ride in a sled

SLEIGHER   n pl. -S one that sleighs

SLEIGHT   n pl. -S deftness

SLENDER   adj -DERER, -DEREST thin

SLEPT   past tense of sleep

SLEUTH   v -ED, -ING, -S to act as a detective

SLEW   v -ED, -ING, -S to slue

SLICE   v SLICED, SLICING, SLICES to cut into thin, flat pieces

SLICER   n pl. -S one that slices

SLICK   adj SLICKER, SLICKEST smooth and slippery

SLICK   v -ED, -ING, -S to make slick

SLICKER   n pl. -S an oilskin raincoat

SLICKLY   adv in a slick manner

SLIDE   v SLID, SLIDDEN, SLIDING, SLIDES to move smoothly along a surface SLIDABLE adj

SLIDER   n pl. -S one that slides

SLIDEWAY   n pl. -WAYS a route along which something slides

SLIDING   present participle of slide

SLIER   a comparative of sly

SLIEST   a superlative of sly

SLIGHT   adj SLIGHTER, SLIGHTEST small in size or amount **SLIGHTLY** adv

SLIGHT   v -ED, -ING, -S to treat with disregard

SLILY   adv in a sly manner

SLIM   adj SLIMMER, SLIMMEST slender

SLIM   v SLIMMED, SLIMMING, SLIMS to make slim

SLIME   v SLIMED, SLIMING, SLIMES to cover with slime (viscous mud)

SLIMIER   comparative of slimy

SLIMIEST   superlative of slimy

SLIMILY   adv in a slimy manner

SLIMING   present participle of slime

SLIMLY   adv in a slim manner

SLIMMED   past tense of slim

SLIMMER   comparative of slim

SLIMMEST   superlative of slim

SLIMMING   present participle of slim

SLIMNESS   n pl. -ES the state of being slim

SLIMPSY   adj -SIER, -SIEST slimsy

SLIMSY   adj -SIER, -SIEST flimsy

SLIMY   adj SLIMIER, SLIMIEST resembling slime

SLING   v SLUNG, SLINGING, SLINGS to throw with a sudden motion

SLINGER   n pl. -S one that slings

SLINK   v SLUNK or SLANK or SLINKED, SLINKING, SLINKS to move stealthily

SLINKY   adj SLINKIER, SLINKIEST stealthy **SLINKILY** adv

SLIP   v SLIPPED or SLIPT, SLIPPING, SLIPS to slide suddenly and accidentally

SLIPCASE   n pl. -S a protective box for a book

SLIPE   v SLIPED, SLIPING, SLIPES to peel

SLIPFORM   v -ED, -ING, -S to construct with the use of a mold in which concrete is placed to set

SLIPKNOT   n pl. -S a type of knot

SLIPLESS   adj free from errors

SLIPOUT   n pl. -S an insert in a newspaper

SLIPOVER   n pl. -S a pullover

SLIPPAGE   n pl. -S a falling off from a standard or level

SLIPPED   a past tense of slip

SLIPPER   n pl. -S a light, low shoe

SLIPPERY   adj -PERIER, -PERIEST causing or tending to cause slipping

SLIPPING   present participle of slip

SLIPPY   adj -PIER, -PIEST slippery

SLIPSHOD   adj carelessly done or made

SLIPSLOP   n pl. -S watery food

SLIPSOLE   n pl. -S a thin insole

SLIPT   a past tense of slip

SLIPUP   n pl. -S a mistake

SLIPWARE   n pl. -S a type of pottery

SLIPWAY   n pl. -WAYS an area sloping toward the water in a shipyard

SLIT   v SLITTED, SLITTING, SLITS to make a slit (a long, narrow cut) in

SLITHER   v -ED, -ING, -S to slide from side to side

SLITHERY   adj slippery

SLITLESS   adj having no slits

SLITTED   past tense of slit

SLITTER   n pl. -S one that slits

SLITTING	present participle of slit
SLIVER	v -ED, -ING, -S to cut into long, thin pieces
SLIVERER	n pl. -S one that slivers
SLIVOVIC	n pl. -ES a plum brandy
SLOB	n pl. -S a slovenly or boorish person
SLOBBER	v -ED, -ING, -S to drool
SLOBBERY	adj slobbering
SLOBBISH	adj resembling a slob
SLOBBY	adj SLOBBIER, SLOBBIEST characteristic of a slob
SLOE	n pl. -S a plumlike fruit
SLOG	v SLOGGED, SLOGGING, SLOGS to plod
SLOGAN	n pl. -S a motto adopted by a group
SLOGGER	n pl. -S one that slogs
SLOGGING	present participle of slog
SLOID	n pl. -S sloyd
SLOJD	n pl. -S sloyd
SLOOP	n pl. -S a type of sailing vessel
SLOP	v SLOPPED, SLOPPING, SLOPS to spill or splash
SLOPE	v SLOPED, SLOPING, SLOPES to slant
SLOPER	n pl. -S one that slopes
SLOPPED	past tense of slop
SLOPPING	present participle of slop
SLOPPY	adj -PIER, -PIEST messy **SLOPPILY** adv
SLOPWORK	n pl. -S the manufacture of cheap clothing
SLOSH	v -ED, -ING, -ES to move with a splashing motion
SLOSHY	adj SLOSHIER, SLOSHIEST slushy
SLOT	v SLOTTED, SLOTTING, SLOTS to cut a long, narrow opening in
SLOTBACK	n pl. -S a type of football player
SLOTH	n pl. -S a slow-moving arboreal mammal
SLOTHFUL	adj sluggish
SLOTTED	past tense of slot
SLOTTING	present participle of slot
SLOUCH	v -ED, -ING, -ES to sit, stand, or move with a drooping posture
SLOUCHER	n pl. -S one that slouches
SLOUCHY	adj SLOUCHIER, SLOUCHIEST slouching
SLOUGH	v -ED, -ING, -S to cast off
SLOUGHY	adj SLOUGHIER, SLOUGHIEST miry
SLOVEN	n pl. -S a slovenly person
SLOVENLY	adj -LIER, -LIEST habitually untidy or unclean
SLOW	adj SLOWER, SLOWEST moving with little speed
SLOW	v -ED, -ING, -S to lessen the speed of
SLOWDOWN	n pl. -S a lessening of pace
SLOWISH	adj somewhat slow
SLOWLY	adv in a slow manner
SLOWNESS	n pl. -ES the state of being slow
SLOWPOKE	n pl. -S a slow individual
SLOWWORM	n pl. -S a European lizard having no legs
SLOYD	n pl. -S a Swedish system of manual training
SLUB	v SLUBBED, SLUBBING, SLUBS to draw out and twist slightly
SLUBBER	v -ED, -ING, -S to stain or dirty
SLUBBING	n pl. -S a slightly twisted roll of textile fibers
SLUDGE	n pl. -S a muddy deposit
SLUDGY	adj SLUDGIER, SLUDGIEST covered with sludge
SLUE	v SLUED, SLUING, SLUES to cause to move sideways
SLUFF	v -ED, -ING, -S to discard a card or cards
SLUG	v SLUGGED, SLUGGING, SLUGS to strike heavily
SLUGABED	n pl. -S one inclined to stay in bed out of laziness
SLUGFEST	n pl. -S a vigorous fight
SLUGGARD	n pl. -S an habitually lazy person
SLUGGED	past tense of slug
SLUGGER	n pl. -S one that slugs
SLUGGING	present participle of slug
SLUGGISH	adj displaying little movement or activity
SLUICE	v SLUICED, SLUICING, SLUICES to wash with a sudden flow of water
SLUICY	adj falling in streams
SLUING	present participle of slue
SLUM	v SLUMMED, SLUMMING, SLUMS to visit slums (squalid urban areas)
SLUMBER	v -ED, -ING, -S to sleep
SLUMBERY	adj sleepy
SLUMGUM	n pl. -S the residue remaining after honey is extracted from a honeycomb

SLUMISM *n* pl. -S the prevalence of slums

SLUMLORD *n* pl. -S a landlord of slum property

SLUMMED past tense of slum

SLUMMER *n* pl. -S one that slums

SLUMMING present participle of slum

SLUMMY *adj* -MIER, -MIEST resembling a slum

SLUMP *v* -ED, -ING, -S to fall or sink suddenly

SLUNG past tense of sling

SLUNK a past tense of slink

SLUR *v* SLURRED, SLURRING, SLURS to pass over lightly or carelessly

SLURB *n* pl. -S a poorly planned suburban area **SLURBAN** *adj*

SLURP *v* -ED, -ING, -S to eat or drink noisily

SLURRED past tense of slur

SLURRING present participle of slur

SLURRY *v* -RIED, -RYING, -RIES to convert into a type of watery mixture

SLUSH *v* -ED, -ING, -ES to splash with slush (partly melted snow)

SLUSHY *adj* SLUSHIER, SLUSHIEST resembling slush **SLUSHILY** *adv*

SLUT *n* pl. -S a slovenly woman **SLUTTISH** *adj*

SLUTTY *adj* SLUTTIER, SLUTTIEST characteristic of a slut

SLY *adj* SLIER, SLIEST or SLYER, SLYEST crafty **SLYLY** *adv*

SLYBOOTS *n* pl. SLYBOOTS a sly person

SLYNESS *n* pl. -ES the quality or state of being sly

SLYPE *n* pl. -S a narrow passage in an English cathedral

SMACK *v* -ED, -ING, -S to strike sharply

SMACKER *n* pl. -S one that smacks

SMALL *adj* SMALLER, SMALLEST of limited size or quantity

SMALL *n* pl. -S a small part

SMALLAGE *n* pl. -S a wild celery

SMALLISH *adj* somewhat small

SMALLPOX *n* pl. -ES a virus disease

SMALT *n* pl. -S a blue pigment

SMALTI a pl. of smalto

SMALTINE *n* pl. -S smaltite

SMALTITE *n* pl. -S a mineral

SMALTO *n* pl. -TOS or -TI colored glass used in mosaics

SMARAGD *n* pl. -S an emerald

SMARAGDE *n* pl. -S smaragd

SMARM *n* pl. -S trite sentimentality

SMARMY *adj* SMARMIER, SMARMIEST marked by excessive flattery **SMARMILY** *adv*

SMART *v* -ED, -ING, -S to cause a sharp, stinging pain

SMART *adj* SMARTER, SMARTEST characterized by mental acuity

SMARTASS *n* pl. -ES a smarty

SMARTEN *v* -ED, -ING, -S to improve in appearance

SMARTIE *n* pl. -S smarty

SMARTLY *adv* in a smart manner

SMARTY *n* pl. SMARTIES an obnoxiously conceited person

SMASH *v* -ED, -ING, -ES to shatter violently

SMASHER *n* pl. -S one that smashes

SMASHUP *n* pl. -S a collision of motor vehicles

SMATTER *v* -ED, -ING, -S to speak with little knowledge

SMAZE *n* pl. -S an atmospheric mixture of smoke and haze

SMEAR *v* -ED, -ING, -S to spread with a sticky, greasy, or dirty substance

SMEARER *n* pl. -S one that smears

SMEARY *adj* SMEARIER, SMEARIEST smeared

SMECTIC *adj* pertaining to a phase of a liquid crystal

SMECTITE *n* pl. -S a clayey mineral

SMEDDUM *n* pl. -S ground malt powder

SMEEK *v* -ED, -ING, -S to smoke

SMEGMA *n* pl. -S sebum

SMELL *v* SMELLED or SMELT, SMELLING, SMELLS to perceive by means of the olfactory nerves

SMELLER *n* pl. -S one that smells

SMELLY *adj* SMELLIER, SMELLIEST having an unpleasant odor

SMELT *v* -ED, -ING, -S to melt or fuse, as ores

SMELTER *n* pl. -S one that smelts

SMELTERY *n* pl. -ERIES a place for smelting

SMERK *v* -ED, -ING, -S to smirk

SMEW *n* pl. -S a Eurasian duck

SMIDGE *n* pl. -S a smidgen

SMIDGEN *n* pl. -S a very small amount

SMIDGEON *n* pl. -S smidgen

SMIDGIN *n* pl. -S smidgen

SMILAX   n pl. -ES a twining plant

SMILE   v SMILED, SMILING, SMILES to upturn the corners of the mouth in pleasure

SMILER   n pl. -S one that smiles

SMILEY   adj exhibiting a smile (a facial expression)

SMIRCH   v -ED, -ING, -ES to soil

SMIRK   v -ED, -ING, -S to smile in an affected or smug manner

SMIRKER   n pl. -S one that smirks

SMIRKY   adj SMIRKIER, SMIRKIEST smirking

SMITE   v SMOTE, SMIT or SMITTEN, SMITING, SMITES to strike heavily

SMITER   n pl. -S one that smites

SMITH   n pl. -S a worker in metals

SMITHERS   n/pl small fragments

SMITHERY   n pl. -ERIES the trade of a smith

SMITHY   n pl. SMITHIES the workshop of a smith

SMITING   present participle of smite

SMITTEN   a past participle of smite

SMOCK   v -ED, -ING, -S to furnish with a smock (a loose outer garment)

SMOCKING   n pl. -S a type of embroidery

SMOG   n pl. -S an atmospheric mixture of smoke and fog **SMOGLESS** adj

SMOGGY   adj -GIER, -GIEST filled with smog

SMOKE   v SMOKED, SMOKING, SMOKES to emit smoke (the gaseous product of burning materials) **SMOKABLE** adj

SMOKEPOT   n pl. -S a container for giving off smoke

SMOKER   n pl. -S one that smokes

SMOKEY   adj SMOKIER, SMOKIEST smoky

SMOKING   present participle of smoke

SMOKY   adj SMOKIER, SMOKIEST filled with smoke **SMOKILY** adv

SMOLDER   v -ED, -ING, -S to burn with no flame

SMOLT   n pl. -S a young salmon

SMOOCH   v -ED, -ING, -ES to kiss

SMOOCHY   adj smudgy

SMOOTH   adj SMOOTHER, SMOOTHEST having a surface that is free from irregularities

SMOOTH   v -ED, -ING, -S or -ES to make smooth

SMOOTHEN   v -ED, -ING, -S to smooth

SMOOTHER   n pl. -S one that smooths

SMOOTHIE   n pl. -S a person with polished manners

SMOOTHLY   adv in a smooth manner

SMOOTHY   n pl. SMOOTHIES smoothie

SMOTE   past tense of smite

SMOTHER   v -ED, -ING, -S to prevent from breathing

SMOTHERY   adj tending to smother

SMOULDER   v -ED, -ING, -S to smolder

SMUDGE   v SMUDGED, SMUDGING, SMUDGES to smear or dirty

SMUDGY   adj SMUDGIER, SMUDGIEST smudged **SMUDGILY** adv

SMUG   adj SMUGGER, SMUGGEST highly self-satisfied

SMUGGLE   v -GLED, -GLING, -GLES to import or export illicitly

SMUGGLER   n pl. -S one that smuggles

SMUGLY   adv in a smug manner

SMUGNESS   n pl. -ES the quality or state of being smug

SMUT   v SMUTTED, SMUTTING, SMUTS to soil

SMUTCH   v -ED, -ING, -ES to smudge

SMUTCHY   adj SMUTCHIER, SMUTCHIEST smudgy

SMUTTED   past tense of smut

SMUTTING   present participle of smut

SMUTTY   adj -TIER, -TIEST obscene **SMUTTILY** adv

SNACK   v -ED, -ING, -S to eat a light meal

SNAFFLE   v -FLED, -FLING, -FLES to obtain by devious means

SNAFU   v -ED, -ING, -S to bring into a state of confusion

SNAG   v SNAGGED, SNAGGING, SNAGS to catch on a snag (a jagged protuberance)

SNAGGY   adj -GIER, -GIEST full of snags

SNAGLIKE   adj resembling a snag

SNAIL   v -ED, -ING, -S to move slowly

SNAKE   v SNAKED, SNAKING, SNAKES to move like a snake (a limbless reptile)

SNAKEBIT   adj unlucky

SNAKEY   adj SNAKIER, SNAKIEST snaky

SNAKY	*adj* SNAKIER, SNAKIEST resembling a snake **SNAKILY** *adv*	**SNEER**	*v* -ED, -ING, -S to curl the lip in contempt
SNAP	*v* SNAPPED, SNAPPING, SNAPS to make a sharp cracking sound	**SNEERER**	*n* pl. -S one that sneers
		SNEERFUL	*adj* given to sneering
		SNEESH	*n* pl. -ES snuff
SNAPBACK	*n* pl. -S a sudden rebound or recovery	**SNEEZE**	*v* SNEEZED, SNEEZING, SNEEZES to make a sudden, involuntary expiration of breath
SNAPLESS	*adj* lacking a snap (a type of fastening device)	**SNEEZER**	*n* pl. -S one that sneezes
SNAPPED	past tense of snap	**SNEEZY**	*adj* SNEEZIER, SNEEZIEST tending to sneeze
SNAPPER	*n* pl. -S one that snaps	**SNELL**	*v* -ED, -ING, -S to attach a short line to a fishhook
SNAPPIER	comparative of snappy		
SNAPPIEST	superlative of snappy	**SNELL**	*adj* SNELLER, SNELLEST keen
SNAPPILY	*adv* in a snappy manner		
SNAPPING	present participle of snap	**SNIB**	*v* SNIBBED, SNIBBING, SNIBS to latch
SNAPPISH	*adj* tending to speak in an impatient or irritable manner	**SNICK**	*v* -ED, -ING, -S to nick
SNAPPY	*adj* -PIER, -PIEST snappish	**SNICKER**	*v* -ED, -ING, -S to utter a partly stifled laugh
SNAPSHOT	*v* -SHOTTED, -SHOTTING, -SHOTS to photograph informally and quickly	**SNICKERY**	*adj* tending to snicker
		SNIDE	*adj* SNIDER, SNIDEST maliciously derogatory **SNIDELY** *adv*
SNAPWEED	*n* pl. -S a flowering plant		
SNARE	*v* SNARED, SNARING, SNARES to trap	**SNIFF**	*v* -ED, -ING, -S to inhale audibly through the nose
SNARER	*n* pl. -S one that snares	**SNIFFER**	*n* pl. -S one that sniffs
SNARK	*n* pl. -S an imaginary animal	**SNIFFIER**	comparative of sniffy
SNARKY	*adj* SNARKIER, SNARKIEST snappish	**SNIFFIEST**	superlative of sniffy
		SNIFFILY	*adv* in a sniffy manner
SNARL	*v* -ED, -ING, -S to growl viciously	**SNIFFISH**	*adj* haughty
SNARLER	*n* pl. -S one that snarls	**SNIFFLE**	*v* -FLED, -FLING, -FLES to sniff repeatedly
SNARLY	*adj* SNARLIER, SNARLIEST tangled	**SNIFFLER**	*n* pl. -S one that sniffles
SNASH	*n* pl. -ES abusive language	**SNIFFY**	*adj* -FIER, -FIEST sniffish
SNATCH	*v* -ED, -ING, -ES to seize suddenly	**SNIFTER**	*n* pl. -S a pear-shaped liquor glass
SNATCHER	*n* pl. -S one that snatches	**SNIGGER**	*v* -ED, -ING, -S to snicker
SNATCHY	*adj* SNATCHIER, SNATCHIEST occurring irregularly	**SNIGGLE**	*v* -GLED, -GLING, -GLES to fish for eels
		SNIGGLER	*n* pl. -S one that sniggles
SNATH	*n* pl. -S the handle of a scythe	**SNIP**	*v* SNIPPED, SNIPPING, SNIPS to cut with a short, quick stroke
SNATHE	*n* pl. -S snath		
SNAW	*v* -ED, -ING, -S to snow		
SNAZZY	*adj* -ZIER, -ZIEST very stylish	**SNIPE**	*v* SNIPED, SNIPING, SNIPES to shoot at individuals from a concealed place
SNEAK	*v* SNEAKED or SNUCK, SNEAKING, SNEAKS to move stealthily		
		SNIPER	*n* pl. -S one that snipes
SNEAKER	*n* pl. -S one that sneaks	**SNIPPED**	past tense of snip
SNEAKY	*adj* SNEAKIER, SNEAKIEST deceitful **SNEAKILY** *adv*	**SNIPPER**	*n* pl. -S one that snips
		SNIPPET	*n* pl. -S a small piece snipped off
SNEAP	*v* -ED, -ING, -S to chide		
SNECK	*n* pl. -S a latch	**SNIPPETY**	*adj* -PETIER, -PETIEST snippy
SNED	*v* SNEDDED, SNEDDING, SNEDS to prune		
		SNIPPING	present participle of snip

SNIPPY *adj* -PIER, -PIEST snappish **SNIPPILY** *adv*

SNIT *n pl.* -S a state of agitation

SNITCH *v* -ED, -ING, -ES to tattle

SNITCHER *n pl.* -S one that snitches

SNIVEL *v* -ELED, -ELING, -ELS or -ELLED, -ELLING, -ELS to cry or whine with sniffling

SNIVELER *n pl.* -S one that snivels

SNOB *n pl.* -S one who tends to avoid or rebuff those regarded as inferior

SNOBBERY *n pl.* -BERIES snobbish behavior

SNOBBIER comparative of snobby

SNOBBIEST superlative of snobby

SNOBBILY *adv* in a snobby manner

SNOBBISH *adj* characteristic of a snob

SNOBBISM *n pl.* -S snobbery

SNOBBY *adj* -BIER, -BIEST snobbish

SNOG *v* SNOGGED, SNOGGING, SNOGS to kiss

SNOOD *v* -ED, -ING, -S to secure with a snood (a net or fabric cap for the hair)

SNOOK *v* -ED, -ING, -S to sniff

SNOOKER *v* -ED, -ING, -S to trick

SNOOL *v* -ED, -ING, -S to yield meekly

SNOOP *v* -ED, -ING, -S to pry about

SNOOPER *n pl.* -S one that snoops

SNOOPY *adj* SNOOPIER, SNOOPIEST given to snooping **SNOOPILY** *adv*

SNOOT *v* -ED, -ING, -S to treat with disdain

SNOOTY *adj* SNOOTIER, SNOOTIEST snobbish **SNOOTILY** *adv*

SNOOZE *v* SNOOZED, SNOOZING, SNOOZES to sleep lightly

SNOOZER *n pl.* -S one that snoozes

SNOOZLE *v* -ZLED, -ZLING, -ZLES to nuzzle

SNOOZY *adj* SNOOZIER, SNOOZIEST drowsy

SNORE *v* SNORED, SNORING, SNORES to breathe loudly while sleeping

SNORER *n pl.* -S one that snores

SNORKEL *v* -ED, -ING, -S to swim underwater with a type of breathing device

SNORT *v* -ED, -ING, -S to exhale noisily through the nostrils

SNORTER *n pl.* -S one that snorts

SNOT *n pl.* -S nasal mucus

SNOTTY *adj* -TIER, -TIEST arrogant **SNOTTILY** *adv*

SNOUT *v* -ED, -ING, -S to provide with a nozzle

SNOUTISH *adj* snouty

SNOUTY *adj* SNOUTIER, SNOUTIEST resembling a long, projecting nose

SNOW *v* -ED, -ING, -S to fall as snow (precipitation in the form of ice crystals)

SNOWBALL *v* -ED, -ING, -S to increase at a rapidly accelerating rate

SNOWBANK *n pl.* -S a mound of snow

SNOWBELL *n pl.* -S a flowering shrub

SNOWBELT *n pl.* -S a region that receives an appreciable amount of snow each year

SNOWBIRD *n pl.* -S a small bird

SNOWBUSH *n pl.* -ES a flowering shrub

SNOWCAP *n pl.* -S a covering of snow

SNOWDROP *n pl.* -S a European herb

SNOWFALL *n pl.* -S a fall of snow

SNOWIER comparative of snowy

SNOWIEST superlative of snowy

SNOWILY *adv* in a snowy manner

SNOWLAND *n pl.* -S an area marked by a great amount of snow

SNOWLESS *adj* having no snow

SNOWLIKE *adj* resembling snow

SNOWMAN *n pl.* -MEN a figure of a person that is made of snow

SNOWMELT *n pl.* -S water produced by the melting of snow

SNOWMOLD *n pl.* -S a fungus disease of grasses near the edge of melting snow

SNOWPACK *n pl.* -S an accumulation of packed snow

SNOWPLOW *v* -ED, -ING, -S to execute a type of skiing maneuver

SNOWSHED *n pl.* -S a structure built to provide protection against snow

SNOWSHOE *v* -SHOED, -SHOEING, -SHOES to walk on snowshoes (oval frames that allow a person to walk on deep snow)

SNOWSUIT *n pl.* -S a child's garment for winter wear

SNOWY *adj* SNOWIER, SNOWIEST abounding in snow

SNUB *v* SNUBBED, SNUBBING, SNUBS to treat with contempt or neglect

SNUBBER	*n* pl. -S one that snubs
SNUBBY	*adj* -BIER, -BIEST blunt
SNUBNESS	*n* pl. -ES bluntness
SNUCK	a past tense of sneak
SNUFF	*v* -ED, -ING, -S to use or inhale snuff (powdered tobacco)
SNUFFBOX	*n* pl. -ES a box for holding snuff
SNUFFER	*n* pl. -S one that snuffs
SNUFFIER	comparative of snuffy
SNUFFIEST	superlative of snuffy
SNUFFILY	*adv* in a snuffy manner
SNUFFLE	*v* -FLED, -FLING, -FLES to sniffle
SNUFFLER	*n* pl. -S one that snuffles
SNUFFLY	*adj* -FLIER, -FLIEST tending to snuffle
SNUFFY	*adj* SNUFFIER, SNUFFIEST dingy
SNUG	*adj* SNUGGER, SNUGGEST warmly comfortable
SNUG	*v* SNUGGED, SNUGGING, SNUGS to make snug
SNUGGERY	*n* pl. -GERIES a snug place
SNUGGEST	superlative of snug
SNUGGIES	*n/pl* women's long underwear
SNUGGING	present participle of snug
SNUGGLE	*v* -GLED, -GLING, -GLES to lie or press closely
SNUGLY	*adv* in a snug manner
SNUGNESS	*n* pl. -ES the quality or state of being snug
SNYE	*n* pl. -S a side channel in a river or creek
SO	*n* pl. SOS sol
SOAK	*v* -ED, -ING, -S to saturate thoroughly in liquid
SOAKAGE	*n* pl. -S the act of soaking
SOAKER	*n* pl. -S one that soaks
SOAP	*v* -ED, -ING, -S to treat with soap (a cleansing agent)
SOAPBARK	*n* pl. -S a tropical tree
SOAPBOX	*n* pl. -ES a box for soap
SOAPER	*n* pl. -S a serial melodrama on radio or television
SOAPIER	comparative of soapy
SOAPIEST	superlative of soapy
SOAPILY	*adv* in a soapy manner
SOAPLESS	*adj* having no soap
SOAPLIKE	*adj* resembling soap
SOAPSUDS	*n/pl* suds (soapy water)
SOAPWORT	*n* pl. -S a perennial herb
SOAPY	*adj* SOAPIER, SOAPIEST containing or resembling soap
SOAR	*v* -ED, -ING, -S to fly at a great height
SOARER	*n* pl. -S one that soars
SOARING	*n* pl. -S the sport of flying in a heavier-than-air craft without power
SOAVE	*n* pl. -S an Italian wine
SOB	*v* SOBBED, SOBBING, SOBS to cry with a convulsive catching of the breath
SOBBER	*n* pl. -S one that sobs
SOBEIT	*conj* provided that
SOBER	*adj* SOBERER, SOBEREST having control of one's faculties
SOBER	*v* -ED, -ING, -S to make sober
SOBERIZE	*v* -IZED, -IZING, -IZES to sober
SOBERLY	*adv* in a sober manner
SOBFUL	*adj* given to sobbing
SOBRIETY	*n* pl. -ETIES the quality or state of being sober
SOCAGE	*n* pl. -S a form of feudal land tenure
SOCAGER	*n* pl. -S a tenant by socage
SOCCAGE	*n* pl. -S socage
SOCCER	*n* pl. -S a type of ball game
SOCIABLE	*n* pl. -S a social
SOCIABLY	*adv* in a friendly manner
SOCIAL	*n* pl. -S a friendly gathering
SOCIALLY	*adv* with respect to society
SOCIETY	*n* pl. -ETIES an organized group of persons **SOCIETAL** *adj*
SOCK	*n* pl. SOCKS or SOX a knitted or woven covering for the foot
SOCK	*v* -ED, -ING, -S to strike forcefully
SOCKET	*v* -ED, -ING, -S to furnish with a socket (an opening for receiving something)
SOCKEYE	*n* pl. -S a food fish
SOCKLESS	*adj* having no socks
SOCKMAN	*n* pl. -MEN socman
SOCKO	*adj* strikingly impressive
SOCLE	*n* pl. -S a block used as a base for a column or pedestal
SOCMAN	*n* pl. -MEN a socager
SOD	*v* SODDED, SODDING, SODS to cover with sod (turf)
SODA	*n* pl. -S a type of chemical compound **SODALESS** *adj*
SODALIST	*n* pl. -S a member of a sodality
SODALITE	*n* pl. -S a mineral
SODALITY	*n* pl. -TIES a society

SODAMIDE   *n pl.* -S a chemical compound

SODDED   past tense of sod

SODDEN   *v* -ED, -ING, -S to make soggy

SODDENLY   *adv* in a soggy manner

SODDING   present participle of sod

SODDY   *n pl.* -DIES a house built of sod

SODIUM   *n pl.* -S a metallic element **SODIC** *adj*

SODOM   *n pl.* -S a place notorious for vice and corruption

SODOMIST   *n pl.* -S a sodomite

SODOMITE   *n pl.* -S one who practices sodomy

SODOMIZE   *v* -IZED, -IZING, -IZES to engage in sodomy with

SODOMY   *n pl.* -OMIES unnatural copulation

SOEVER   *adv* at all

SOFA   *n pl.* -S a long, upholstered seat

SOFAR   *n pl.* -S a system for locating underwater explosions

SOFFIT   *n pl.* -S the underside of an architectural structure

SOFT   *adj* SOFTER, SOFTEST yielding readily to pressure

SOFT   *n pl.* -S a soft object or part

SOFTA   *n pl.* -S a Muslim theological student

SOFTBACK   *n pl.* -S a book bound in a flexible paper cover

SOFTBALL   *n pl.* -S a type of ball

SOFTEN   *v* -ED, -ING, -S to make soft

SOFTENER   *n pl.* -S one that softens

SOFTHEAD   *n pl.* -S a foolish person

SOFTIE   *n pl.* -S softy

SOFTIES   pl. of softy

SOFTISH   *adj* somewhat soft

SOFTLY   *adv* in a soft manner

SOFTNESS   *n pl.* -ES the quality or state of being soft

SOFTWARE   *n pl.* -S written or printed data used in computer operations

SOFTWOOD   *n pl.* -S the soft wood of various trees

SOFTY   *n pl.* SOFTIES a sentimental person

SOGGED   *adj* soggy

SOGGY   *adj* -GIER, -GIEST heavy with moisture **SOGGILY** *adv*

SOIGNE   *adj* carefully done

SOIGNEE   *adj* soigne

SOIL   *v* -ED, -ING, -S to make dirty

SOILAGE   *n pl.* -S green crops for feeding animals

SOILLESS   *adj* carried on without soil (finely divided rock mixed with organic matter)

SOILURE   *n pl.* -S a stain or smudge

SOIREE   *n pl.* -S an evening party

SOJA   *n pl.* -S the soybean

SOJOURN   *v* -ED, -ING, -S to stay temporarily

SOKE   *n pl.* -S a feudal right to administer justice within a certain territory

SOKEMAN   *n pl.* -MEN socman

SOKOL   *n pl.* -S an international group promoting physical fitness

SOL   *n pl.* -S the fifth tone of the diatonic musical scale

SOLA   a pl. of solum

SOLACE   *v* -LACED, -LACING, -LACES to console

SOLACER   *n pl.* -S one that solaces

SOLAN   *n pl.* -S a gannet

SOLAND   *n pl.* -S solan

SOLANDER   *n pl.* -S a protective box for library materials

SOLANIN   *n pl.* -S solanine

SOLANINE   *n pl.* -S a poisonous alkaloid

SOLANO   *n pl.* -NOS a strong, hot wind

SOLANUM   *n pl.* -S any of a genus of herbs and shrubs

SOLAR   *adj* pertaining to the sun

SOLARIA   a pl. of solarium

SOLARISE   *v* -ISED, -ISING, -ISES to solarize

SOLARISM   *n pl.* -S an interpretation of folk tales as concepts of the nature of the sun

SOLARIUM   *n pl.* -IA or -IUMS a room exposed to the sun

SOLARIZE   *v* -IZED, -IZING, -IZES to expose to sunlight

SOLATE   *v* -ATED, -ATING, -ATES to change to a fluid colloidal system

SOLATION   *n pl.* -S the act of solating

SOLATIUM   *n pl.* -TIA a compensation given for damage to the feelings

SOLD   past tense of sell

SOLDAN   *n pl.* -S a Muslim ruler

SOLDER   *v* -ED, -ING, -S to join closely together

SOLDERER   *n pl.* -S one that solders

SOLDI   pl. of soldo

SOLDIER   *v* -ED, -ING, -S to perform military service

SOLDIERY *n* pl. -DIERIES the military profession

SOLDO *n* pl. -DI a former coin of Italy

SOLE *v* SOLED, SOLING, SOLES to furnish with a sole (the bottom surface of a shoe or boot)

SOLECISE *v* -CISED, -CISING, -CISES to solecize

SOLECISM *n* pl. -S an ungrammatical combination of words in a sentence

SOLECIST *n* pl. -S one who solecizes

SOLECIZE *v* -CIZED, -CIZING, -CIZES to use solecisms

SOLED past tense of sole

SOLEI pl. of soleus

SOLELESS *adj* having no sole

SOLELY *adv* singly

SOLEMN *adj* -EMNER, -EMNEST serious **SOLEMNLY** *adv*

SOLENESS *n* pl. -ES the state of being the only one

SOLENOID *n* pl. -S a type of electric coil

SOLERET *n* pl. -S solleret

SOLEUS *n* pl. -LEI a leg muscle

SOLFEGE *n* pl. -S a type of singing exercise

SOLFEGGI *n/pl* solfeges

SOLGEL *adj* involving some changes in the state of a colloidal system

SOLI a pl. of solo

SOLICIT *v* -ED, -ING, -S to ask for earnestly

SOLID *adj* -IDER, -IDEST having definite shape and volume

SOLID *n* pl. -S a solid substance

SOLIDAGO *n* pl. -GOS a flowering plant

SOLIDARY *adj* united

SOLIDI pl. of solidus

SOLIDIFY *v* -FIED, -FYING, -FIES to make solid

SOLIDITY *n* pl. -TIES the quality or state of being solid

SOLIDLY *adv* in a solid manner

SOLIDUS *n* pl. -DI a coin of ancient Rome

SOLING present participle of sole

SOLION *n* pl. -S an electronic detecting and amplifying device

SOLIQUID *n* pl. -S a fluid colloidal system

SOLITARY *n* pl. -TARIES one who lives alone

SOLITON *n* pl. -S a solitary wave in physics

SOLITUDE *n* pl. -S the state of being alone

SOLLERET *n* pl. -S a sabaton

SOLO *n* pl. -LOS or -LI a musical composition for a single voice or instrument

SOLO *v* -ED, -ING, -S to perform alone

SOLOIST *n* pl. -S one that performs a solo

SOLON *n* pl. -S a wise lawgiver

SOLONETS *n* pl. -ES solonetz

SOLONETZ *n* pl. -ES a type of soil

SOLSTICE *n* pl. -S the time of the year when the sun is at its greatest distance from the celestial equator

SOLUBLE *n* pl. -S something that is soluble (capable of being dissolved)

SOLUBLY *adv* in a soluble manner

SOLUM *n* pl. -LA or -LUMS a soil layer

SOLUS *adj* alone

SOLUTE *n* pl. -S a dissolved substance

SOLUTION *n* pl. -S a homogeneous liquid mixture

SOLVABLE *adj* capable of being solved

SOLVATE *v* -VATED, -VATING, -VATES to convert into a type of ion

SOLVE *v* SOLVED, SOLVING, SOLVES to find the answer or explanation for

SOLVENCY *n* pl. -CIES the ability to pay all debts

SOLVENT *n* pl. -S a substance capable of dissolving others

SOLVER *n* pl. -S one that solves

SOLVING present participle of solve

SOMA *n* pl. -MATA or -MAS the body of an organism **SOMATIC** *adj*

SOMBER *adj* gloomy **SOMBERLY** *adv*

SOMBRE *adj* somber **SOMBRELY** *adv*

SOMBRERO *n* pl. -ROS a broad-brimmed hat

SOMBROUS *adj* somber

SOME *adj* being an unspecified number or part

SOMEBODY *n* pl. -BODIES an important person

SOMEDAY *adv* at some future time

SOMEDEAL *adv* to some degree

SOMEHOW *adv* by some means

SOMEONE *n* pl. -S a somebody

SOMERSET *v* -SETED, -SETING, -SETS or -SETTED, -SETTING, -SETS to roll the body in a complete circle, head over heels

SOMETIME	adv at some future time
SOMEWAY	adv somehow
SOMEWAYS	adv someway
SOMEWHAT	n pl. -S an unspecified number or part
SOMEWHEN	adv sometime
SOMEWISE	adv somehow
SOMITE	n pl. -S a longitudinal segment of the body of some animals . SOMITAL, SOMITIC adj
SON	n pl. -S a male child
SONANCE	n pl. -S sound
SONANT	n pl. -S a sound uttered with vibration of the vocal cords SONANTAL, SONANTIC adj
SONAR	n pl. -S an underwater locating device
SONARMAN	n pl. -MEN a person who operates sonar equipment
SONATA	n pl. -S a type of musical composition
SONATINA	n pl. -TINAS or -TINE a short sonata
SONDE	n pl. -S a device for observing atmospheric phenomena
SONDER	n pl. -S a class of small yachts
SONE	n pl. -S a unit of loudness
SONG	n pl. -S a musical composition written or adapted for singing
SONGBIRD	n pl. -S a bird that utters a musical call
SONGBOOK	n pl. -S a book of songs
SONGFEST	n pl. -S an informal gathering for group singing
SONGFUL	adj melodious
SONGLESS	adj incapable of singing
SONGLIKE	adj resembling a song
SONGSTER	n pl. -S a singer
SONHOOD	n pl. -S the state of being a son
SONIC	adj pertaining to sound
SONICATE	v -CATED, -CATING, -CATES to disrupt with sound waves
SONICS	n/pl the science dealing with the practical applications of sound
SONLESS	adj having no son
SONLIKE	adj resembling a son
SONLY	adj pertaining to a son
SONNET	v -NETED, -NETING, -NETS or -NETTED, -NETTING, -NETS to compose a sonnet (a type of poem)
SONNY	n pl. -NIES a small boy
SONOBUOY	n pl. -BUOYS a buoy that detects and transmits underwater sounds
SONOGRAM	n pl. -S an image produced by ultrasound
SONORANT	n pl. -S a type of voiced sound
SONORITY	n pl. -TIES the quality or state of being sonorous
SONOROUS	adj characterized by a full and loud sound
SONOVOX	n pl. -ES a sound effects device
SONSHIP	n pl. -S the state of being a son
SONSIE	adj -SIER, -SIEST sonsy
SONSY	adj -SIER, -SIEST comely
SOOCHONG	n pl. -S souchong
SOOEY	interj — used in calling pigs
SOOK	n pl. -S souk
SOON	adv SOONER, SOONEST in the near future
SOONER	n pl. -S one who settles on government land before it is officially opened for settlement
SOOT	v -ED, -ING, -S to cover with soot (a black substance produced by combustion)
SOOTH	adj SOOTHER, SOOTHEST true
SOOTH	n pl. -S truth
SOOTHE	v SOOTHED, SOOTHING, SOOTHES to restore to a quiet or normal state
SOOTHER	n pl. -S one that soothes
SOOTHLY	adv in truth
SOOTHSAY	v -SAID, -SAYING, -SAYS to predict
SOOTY	adj SOOTIER, SOOTIEST covered with soot SOOTILY adv
SOP	v SOPPED, SOPPING, SOPS to dip or soak in a liquid
SOPH	n pl. -S a sophomore
SOPHIES	pl. of sophy
SOPHISM	n pl. -S a plausible but fallacious argument
SOPHIST	n pl. -S one that uses sophisms
SOPHY	n pl. -PHIES a ruler of Persia
SOPITE	v -PITED, -PITING, -PITES to put to sleep
SOPOR	n pl. -S an abnormally deep sleep
SOPPED	past tense of sop
SOPPING	adj very wet
SOPPY	adj -PIER, -PIEST very wet

SOPRANO   *n* pl. -NOS or -NI the highest singing voice

SORA   *n* pl. -S a marsh bird

SORB   *v* -ED, -ING, -S to take up and hold by absorption or adsorption **SORBABLE** *adj*

SORBATE   *n* pl. -S a sorbed substance

SORBENT   *n* pl. -S a substance that sorbs

SORBET   *n* pl. -S sherbet

SORBIC   *adj* pertaining to a type of fruit

SORBITOL   *n* pl. -S a chemical compound

SORBOSE   *n* pl. -S a type of sugar

SORCERER   *n* pl. -S one who practices sorcery

SORCERY   *n* pl. -CERIES alleged use of supernatural powers

SORD   *n* pl. -S a flight of mallards

SORDID   *adj* filthy **SORDIDLY** *adv*

SORDINE   *n* pl. -S a device used to muffle the tone of a musical instrument

SORDINO   *n* pl. -NI sordine

SORDOR   *n* pl. -S a sordid state

SORE   *adj* SORER, SOREST painfully sensitive to the touch

SORE   *n* pl. -S a sore area on the body

SOREHEAD   *n* pl. -S a person who is easily angered or offended

SOREL   *n* pl. -S sorrel

SORELY   *adv* in a sore manner

SORENESS   *n* pl. -ES the quality or state of being sore

SORER   comparative of sore

SOREST   superlative of sore

SORGHO   *n* pl. -GHOS sorgo

SORGHUM   *n* pl. -S a cereal grass

SORGO   *n* pl. -GOS a variety of sorghum

SORI   pl. of sorus

SORICINE   *adj* belonging to the shrew family of mammals

SORING   *n* pl. -S the practice of making a horse's front feet sore to force high stepping

SORITES   *n* pl. SORITES a type of argument used in logic **SORITIC** *adj*

SORN   *v* -ED, -ING, -S to force oneself on others for food and lodging

SORNER   *n* pl. -S one that sorns

SOROCHE   *n* pl. -S mountain sickness

SORORAL   *adj* sisterly

SORORATE   *n* pl. -S the marriage of a man usually with his deceased wife's sister

SORORITY   *n* pl. -TIES a social club for women

SOROSIS   *n* pl. -ROSES or -ROSISES a women's club or society

SORPTION   *n* pl. -S the act or process of sorbing **SORPTIVE** *adj*

SORREL   *n* pl. -S a reddish brown color

SORRIER   comparative of sorry

SORRIEST   superlative of sorry

SORRILY   *adv* in a sorry manner

SORROW   *v* -ED, -ING, -S to grieve

SORROWER   *n* pl. -S one that sorrows

SORRY   *adj* -RIER, -RIEST feeling grief or penitence

SORT   *v* -ED, -ING, -S to arrange according to kind, class, or size SORTABLE *adj* **SORTABLY** *adv*

SORTER   *n* pl. -S one that sorts

SORTIE   *v* -TIED, -TIEING, -TIES to attack suddenly from a defensive position

SORUS   *n* pl. -RI a cluster of plant reproductive bodies

SOT   *n* pl. -S an habitual drunkard

SOTH   *n* pl. -S sooth

SOTOL   *n* pl. -S a flowering plant

SOTTED   *adj* besotted

SOTTISH   *adj* resembling a sot

SOU   *n* pl. -S a former French coin

SOUARI   *n* pl. -S a tropical tree

SOUBISE   *n* pl. -S a sauce of onions and butter

SOUCAR   *n* pl. -S a Hindu banker

SOUCHONG   *n* pl. -S a Chinese tea

SOUDAN   *n* pl. -S soldan

SOUFFLE   *n* pl. -S a light, baked dish

SOUFFLED   *adj* made puffy by beating and baking

SOUGH   *v* -ED, -ING, -S to make a moaning or sighing sound

SOUGHT   past tense of seek

SOUK   *n* pl. -S a marketplace in northern Africa and the Middle East

SOUL   *n* pl. -S the spiritual aspect of human beings **SOULED, SOULLESS, SOULLIKE** *adj*

SOULFUL   *adj* full of emotion

SOUND   *adj* SOUNDER, SOUNDEST being in good health or condition

SOUND   v -ED, -ING, -S to make a sound (something that stimulates the auditory receptors)

SOUNDBOX   n pl. -ES a resonant cavity in a musical instrument

SOUNDER   n pl. -S one that sounds

SOUNDING   n pl. -S a sampling or test of opinions

SOUNDLY   adv in a sound manner

SOUNDMAN   n pl. -MEN a person who controls the quality of sound being recorded

SOUP   v -ED, -ING, -S to increase the power or efficiency of

SOUPCON   n pl. -S a minute amount

SOUPY   adj SOUPIER, SOUPIEST foggy

SOUR   adj SOURER, SOUREST sharp or biting to the taste

SOUR   v -ED, -ING, -S to make or become sour

SOURBALL   n pl. -S a sour candy

SOURCE   n pl. -S a point of origin

SOURDINE   n pl. -S sordine

SOURISH   adj somewhat sour

SOURLY   adv in a sour manner

SOURNESS   n pl. -ES the quality or state of being sour

SOURPUSS   n pl. -ES a grouchy person

SOURSOP   n pl. -S a tropical tree

SOURWOOD   n pl. -S a flowering tree

SOUSE   v SOUSED, SOUSING, SOUSES to immerse

SOUTACHE   n pl. -S a flat, narrow braid

SOUTANE   n pl. -S a cassock

SOUTER   n pl. -S a shoemaker

SOUTH   v -ED, -ING, -S to move toward the south (a cardinal point of the compass)

SOUTHER   n pl. -S a wind or storm from the south

SOUTHERN   n pl. -S a person living in the south

SOUTHING   n pl. -S movement toward the south

SOUTHPAW   n pl. -S a left-handed person

SOUTHRON   n pl. -S a southern

SOUVENIR   n pl. -S a memento

SOUVLAKI   n pl. -S a Greek shish kebab

SOVIET   n pl. -S a legislative body in a Communist country

SOVKHOZ   n pl. -KHOZES or -KHOZY a state-owned farm in the Soviet Union

SOVRAN   n pl. -S a monarch

SOVRANLY   adv supremely

SOVRANTY   n pl. -TIES a monarchy

SOW   v SOWED, SOWN, SOWING, SOWS to scatter over land for growth, as seed SOWABLE adj

SOWANS   n pl. SOWANS sowens

SOWAR   n pl. -S a mounted native soldier in India

SOWBELLY   n pl. -LIES pork cured in salt

SOWBREAD   n pl. -S a flowering plant

SOWCAR   n pl. -S soucar

SOWENS   n pl. SOWENS porridge made from oat husks

SOWER   n pl. -S one that sows

SOWN   past participle of sow

SOX   a pl. of sock

SOY   n pl. SOYS the soybean

SOYA   n pl. -S soy

SOYBEAN   n pl. -S the seed of a cultivated Asian herb

SOYMILK   n pl. -S a milk substitute made from soybeans

SOYUZ   n pl. -ES a Soviet manned spacecraft

SOZIN   n pl. -S a type of protein

SOZINE   n pl. -S sozin

SOZZLED   adj drunk

SPA   n pl. -S a mineral spring

SPACE   v SPACED, SPACING, SPACES to set some distance apart

SPACEMAN   n pl. -MEN an astronaut

SPACER   n pl. -S one that spaces

SPACEY   adj SPACIER, SPACIEST weird in behavior

SPACIAL   adj spatial

SPACING   n pl. -S the distance between any two objects

SPACIOUS   adj vast or ample in extent

SPACKLE   v -LED, -LING, -LES to fill cracks or holes in a surface with paste

SPACY   adj SPACIER, SPACIEST spacey

SPADE   v SPADED, SPADING, SPADES to take up with a spade (a digging implement)

SPADEFUL   n pl. -S as much as a spade can hold

SPADER   n pl. -S one that spades

SPADICES   pl. of spadix

SPADILLE   n pl. -S the highest trump in certain card games

SPADING   present participle of spade

SPADIX *n* pl. -DICES or -DIXES a flower cluster

SPADO *n* pl. -DONES a castrated man or animal

SPAE *v* SPAED, SPAEING, SPAES to foretell

SPAEING *n* pl. -S the act of foretelling

SPAETZLE *n/pl* tiny dumplings

SPAGYRIC *n* pl. -S a person skilled in alchemy

SPAHEE *n* pl. -S spahi

SPAHI *n* pl. -S a Turkish cavalryman

SPAIL *n* pl. -S spale

SPAIT *n* pl. -S spate

SPAKE a past tense of speak

SPALE *n* pl. -S a splinter or chip

SPALL *v* -ED, -ING, -S to break up into fragments

SPALLER *n* pl. -S one that spalls

SPALPEEN *n* pl. -S a rascal

SPAN *v* SPANNED, SPANNING, SPANS to extend over or across

SPANCEL *v* -CELED, -CELING, -CELS or -CELLED, -CELLING, -CELS to bind or fetter with a rope

SPANDEX *n* pl. -ES a synthetic elastic fiber

SPANDREL *n* pl. -S a space between two adjoining arches

SPANDRIL *n* pl. -S spandrel

SPANG *adv* directly

SPANGLE *v* -GLED, -GLING, -GLES to adorn with spangles (bits of sparkling metal)

SPANGLY *adj* -GLIER, -GLIEST covered with spangles

SPANIEL *n* pl. -S a dog with silky hair

SPANK *v* -ED, -ING, -S to slap on the buttocks

SPANKER *n* pl. -S one that spanks

SPANKING *n* pl. -S the act of one that spanks

SPANLESS *adj* having no extent

SPANNED past tense of span

SPANNER *n* pl. -S one that spans

SPANNING present participle of span

SPANWORM *n* pl. -S an inchworm

SPAR *v* SPARRED, SPARRING, SPARS to provide with spars (stout poles used to support rigging)

SPARABLE *n* pl. -S a type of nail

SPARE *v* SPARED, SPARING, SPARES to refrain from punishing, harming, or destroying

SPARE *adj* SPARER, SPAREST meager **SPARELY** *adv*

SPARER *n* pl. -S one that spares

SPARERIB *n* pl. -S a cut of pork

SPAREST *adj* superlative of spare

SPARGE *v* SPARGED, SPARGING, SPARGES to sprinkle

SPARGER *n* pl. -S one that sparges

SPARID *n* pl. -S any of a family of marine fishes

SPARING present participle of spare

SPARK *v* -ED, -ING, -S to give off sparks (small fiery particles)

SPARKER *n* pl. -S something that sparks

SPARKIER comparative of sparky

SPARKIEST superlative of sparky

SPARKILY *adv* in a lively manner

SPARKISH *adj* jaunty

SPARKLE *v* -KLED, -KLING, -KLES to give off or reflect flashes of light

SPARKLER *n* pl. -S something that sparkles

SPARKLY *adj* -KLIER, -KLIEST tending to sparkle

SPARKY *adj* SPARKIER, SPARKIEST lively

SPARLIKE *adj* resembling a spar

SPARLING *n* pl. -S a young herring

SPAROID *n* pl. -S a sparid

SPARRED past tense of spar

SPARRIER comparative of sparry

SPARRIEST superlative of sparry

SPARRING present participle of spar

SPARROW *n* pl. -S a small bird

SPARRY *adj* -RIER, -RIEST resembling spar (a lustrous mineral)

SPARSE *adj* SPARSER, SPARSEST thinly distributed **SPARSELY** *adv*

SPARSITY *n* pl. -TIES the quality or state of being sparse

SPASM *n* pl. -S an abnormal, involuntary muscular contraction

SPASTIC *n* pl. -S one suffering from spastic paralysis (a paralysis with muscle spasms)

SPAT *v* SPATTED, SPATTING, SPATS to strike lightly

SPATE *n* pl. -S a freshet

SPATHE *n* pl. -S a leaflike organ of certain plants **SPATHAL, SPATHED, SPATHOSE** *adj*

SPATHIC *adj* sparry

SPATIAL *adj* of or pertaining to space

SPATTED past tense of spat

SPATTER *v* -ED, -ING, -S to scatter in drops

SPATTING present participle of spat

SPATULA *n* pl. -S a mixing implement **SPATULAR** *adj*

SPATZLE *n/pl* spaetzle

SPAVIE *n* pl. -S spavin **SPAVIET** *adj*

SPAVIN *n* pl. -S a disease of horses **SPAVINED** *adj*

SPAWN *v* -ED, -ING, -S to deposit eggs

SPAWNER *n* pl. -S one that spawns

SPAY *v* -ED, -ING, -S to remove the ovaries of

SPAZ *n* pl. -ES a clumsy, foolish, or incompetent person

SPEAK *v* SPOKE or SPAKE, SPOKEN, SPEAKING, SPEAKS to utter words

SPEAKER *n* pl. -S one that speaks

SPEAKING *n* pl. -S a speech or discourse

SPEAN *v* -ED, -ING, -S to wean

SPEAR *v* -ED, -ING, -S to pierce with a spear (a long, pointed weapon)

SPEARER *n* pl. -S one that spears

SPEARMAN *n* pl. -MEN a person armed with a spear

SPEC *v* SPECCED, SPECCING, SPECS to write specifications for

SPECIAL *adj* -CIALER, -CIALEST of a distinct or particular kind or character

SPECIAL *n* pl. -S a special person or thing

SPECIATE *v* -ATED, -ATING, -ATES to undergo a type of evolutionary process

SPECIE *n* pl. -S coined money

SPECIFIC *n* pl. -S a remedy intended for a particular disease

SPECIFY *v* -FIED, -FYING, -FIES to state in detail

SPECIMEN *n* pl. -S a part or individual representative of a group or whole

SPECIOUS *adj* having a false look of truth or authenticity

SPECK *v* -ED, -ING, -S to mark with small spots

SPECKLE *v* -LED, -LING, -LES to speck

SPECS *n/pl* eyeglasses

SPECTATE *v* -TATED, -TATING, -TATES to attend and view

SPECTER *n* pl. -S a visible disembodied spirit

SPECTRA a pl. of spectrum

SPECTRAL *adj* resembling a specter

SPECTRE *n* pl. -S specter

SPECTRUM *n* pl. -TRA or -TRUMS an array of the components of a light wave

SPECULUM *n* pl. -LA or -LUMS a medical instrument **SPECULAR** *adj*

SPEECH *n* pl. -ES the faculty or act of speaking

SPEED *v* SPED or SPEEDED, SPEEDING, SPEEDS to move swiftly

SPEEDER *n* pl. -S one that speeds

SPEEDIER comparative of speedy

SPEEDIEST superlative of speedy

SPEEDILY *adv* in a speedy manner

SPEEDING *n* pl. -S the act of driving faster than the law allows

SPEEDO *n* pl. SPEEDOS a speedometer

SPEEDUP *n* pl. -S an acceleration of production without an increase in pay

SPEEDWAY *n* pl. -WAYS a road designed for rapid travel

SPEEDY *adj* SPEEDIER, SPEEDIEST swift

SPEEL *v* -ED, -ING, -S to climb

SPEER *v* -ED, -ING, -S to inquire

SPEERING *n* pl. -S inquiry

SPEIL *v* -ED, -ING, -S to speel

SPEIR *v* -ED, -ING, -S to speer

SPEISE *n* pl. -S speiss

SPEISS *n* pl. -ES a metallic mixture obtained in smelting certain ores

SPELAEAN *adj* spelean

SPELEAN *adj* living in caves

SPELL *v* SPELLED or SPELT, SPELLING, SPELLS to name or write the letters of in order

SPELLER *n* pl. -S one that spells words

SPELLING *n* pl. -S a sequence of letters composing a word

SPELT *n* pl. -S a variety of wheat

SPELTER *n* pl. -S zinc in the form of ingots

SPELTZ   n pl. -ES spelt
SPELUNK   v -ED, -ING, -S to explore
              caves
SPENCE   n pl. -S a pantry
SPENCER   n pl. -S a trysail
SPEND   v SPENT, SPENDING,
              SPENDS to pay out
SPENDER   n pl. -S one that spends
SPENSE   n pl. -S spence
SPENT   past tense of spend
SPERM   n pl. -S a male gamete
              SPERMIC adj
SPERMARY   n pl. -RIES an organ in which
              sperms are formed
SPERMINE   n pl. -S a chemical compound
SPERMOUS   adj resembling or made up of
              sperms
SPEW   v -ED, -ING, -S to vomit
SPEWER   n pl. -S one that spews
SPHAGNUM   n pl. -S a grayish moss
SPHENE   n pl. -S a mineral
SPHENIC   adj shaped like a wedge
SPHENOID   n pl. -S a bone of the skull
SPHERAL   adj of, pertaining to, or having
              the form of a sphere
SPHERE   v SPHERED, SPHERING,
              SPHERES to form into a
              sphere (a type of geometric
              solid)
SPHERIC   adj spheral
SPHERICS   n/pl the geometry of figures on
              the surface of a sphere
SPHERIER   comparative of sphery
SPHERIEST   superlative of sphery
SPHERING   present participle of sphere
SPHEROID   n pl. -S a type of geometric
              solid
SPHERULE   n pl. -S a small sphere
SPHERY   adj SPHERIER, SPHERIEST
              resembling a sphere
SPHINGES   a pl. of sphinx
SPHINGID   n pl. -S the hawkmoth
SPHINX   n pl. SPHINXES or
              SPHINGES a monster in
              Egyptian mythology
SPHYGMUS   n pl. -ES the pulse
              SPHYGMIC adj
SPICA   n pl. -CAE or -CAS an ear of
              grain SPICATE, SPICATED
              adj
SPICCATO   n pl. -TOS a method of
              playing a stringed instrument
SPICE   v SPICED, SPICING, SPICES
              to season with a spice (an
              aromatic vegetable substance)
SPICER   n pl. -S one that spices

SPICERY   n pl. -ERIES a spicy quality
SPICEY   adj SPICIER, SPICIEST spicy
SPICIER   comparative of spicy
SPICIEST   superlative of spicy
SPICILY   adv in a spicy manner
SPICING   present participle of spice
SPICULA   n pl. -LAE spicule SPICULAR
              adj
SPICULE   n pl. -S a needlelike structure
SPICULUM   n pl. -LA spicule
SPICY   adj SPICIER, SPICIEST
              containing spices
SPIDER   n pl. -S a type of arachnid
SPIDERY   adj -DERIER, -DERIEST
              resembling a spider
SPIED   past tense of spy
SPIEGEL   n pl. -S a type of cast iron
SPIEL   v -ED, -ING, -S to talk at
              length
SPIELER   n pl. -S one that spiels
SPIER   v -ED, -ING, -S to speer
SPIES   present 3d person sing. of spy
SPIFF   v -ED, -ING, -S to make spiffy
SPIFFING   adj spiffy
SPIFFY   adj -FIER, -FIEST stylish
              SPIFFILY adv
SPIGOT   n pl. -S a faucet
SPIKE   v SPIKED, SPIKING, SPIKES
              to fasten with a spike (a long,
              thick nail)
SPIKELET   n pl. -S a type of flower cluster
SPIKER   n pl. -S one that spikes
SPIKEY   adj SPIKIER, SPIKIEST spiky
SPIKING   present participle of spike
SPIKY   adj SPIKIER, SPIKIEST
              resembling a spike SPIKILY
              adv
SPILE   v SPILED, SPILING, SPILES
              to stop up with a wooden plug
SPILIKIN   n pl. -S a strip of wood used in
              a game
SPILING   n pl. -S a piling
SPILL   v SPILLED or SPILT,
              SPILLING, SPILLS to cause to
              run out of a container
SPILLAGE   n pl. -S something that is
              spilled
SPILLER   n pl. -S one that spills
SPILLWAY   n pl. -WAYS a channel for
              surplus water in a reservoir
SPILT   a past tense of spill
SPILTH   n pl. -S spillage
SPIN   v SPUN, SPINNING, SPINS
              to draw out and twist into
              threads

SPINACH *n* pl. -ES a cultivated herb
SPINACHY *adj*

SPINAGE *n* pl. -S spinach

SPINAL *n* pl. -S an injection of an anesthetic into the spinal cord

SPINALLY *adv* with respect to the spine

SPINATE *adj* bearing thorns

SPINDLE *v* -DLED, -DLING, -DLES to impale on a slender rod

SPINDLER *n* pl. -S one that spindles

SPINDLY *adj* -DLIER, -DLIEST long and slender

SPINE *n* pl. -S the vertebral column
SPINED *adj*

SPINEL *n* pl. -S a mineral

SPINELLE *n* pl. -S spinel

SPINET *n* pl. -S a small piano

SPINIER comparative of spiny

SPINIEST superlative of spiny

SPINIFEX *n* pl. -ES an Australian grass

SPINLESS *adj* having no rotation

SPINNER *n* pl. -S one that spins

SPINNERY *n* pl. -NERIES a spinning mill

SPINNEY *n* pl. -NEYS a thicket

SPINNING *n* pl. -S the act of one that spins

SPINNY *n* pl. -NIES spinney

SPINOFF *n* pl. -S a new application or incidental result

SPINOR *n* pl. -S a type of mathematical vector

SPINOSE *adj* spiny

SPINOUS *adj* spiny

SPINOUT *n* pl. -S a rotational skid by an automobile

SPINSTER *n* pl. -S an unmarried woman who is past the usual age for marrying

SPINTO *n* pl. -TOS a singing voice that is lyric and dramatic

SPINULA *n* pl. -LAE spinule

SPINULE *n* pl. -S a small thorn

SPINY *adj* SPINIER, SPINIEST bearing or covered with thorns

SPIRACLE *n* pl. -S an orifice through which breathing occurs

SPIRAEA *n* pl. -S spirea

SPIRAL *v* -RALED, -RALING, -RALS or -RALLED, -RALLING, -RALS to move like a spiral (a type of plane curve)

SPIRALLY *adv* in a spiral manner

SPIRANT *n* pl. -S a speech sound produced by the forcing of breath through a narrow passage

SPIRE *v* SPIRED, SPIRING, SPIRES to rise in a tapering manner

SPIREA *n* pl. -S a flowering shrub

SPIREM *n* pl. -S spireme

SPIREME *n* pl. -S a filament forming part of a cell nucleus during mitosis

SPIRIER comparative of spiry

SPIRIEST superlative of spiry

SPIRILLA *n/pl* spirally twisted, aerobic bacteria

SPIRING present participle of spire

SPIRIT *v* -ED, -ING, -S to carry off secretly

SPIROID *adj* resembling a spiral

SPIRT *v* -ED, -ING, -S to spurt

SPIRULA *n* pl. -LAE or -LAS a spiral-shelled mollusk

SPIRY *adj* SPIRIER, SPIRIEST tall, slender, and tapering

SPIT *v* SPITTED, SPITTING, SPITS to impale on a spit (a pointed rod on which meat is turned)

SPITAL *n* pl. -S a hospital

SPITBALL *n* pl. -S a type of pitch in baseball

SPITE *v* SPITED, SPITING, SPITES to treat with malice

SPITEFUL *adj* -FULLER, -FULLEST malicious

SPITFIRE *n* pl. -S a quick-tempered person

SPITING present participle of spite

SPITTED past tense of spit

SPITTER *n* pl. -S a spitball

SPITTING present participle of spit

SPITTLE *n* pl. -S saliva

SPITTOON *n* pl. -S a receptacle for saliva

SPITZ *n* pl. -ES a dog having a heavy coat

SPIV *n* pl. -S a petty criminal

SPLAKE *n* pl. -S a freshwater fish

SPLASH *v* -ED, -ING, -ES to scatter a liquid about

SPLASHER *n* pl. -S one that splashes

SPLASHY *adj* SPLASHIER, SPLASHIEST showy

SPLAT *v* SPLATTED, SPLATTING, SPLATS to flatten on impact

SPLATTER *v* -ED, -ING, -S to spatter

SPLAY *v* -ED, -ING, -S to spread out

SPLEEN *n* pl. -S a ductless organ of the body

SPLEENY *adj* SPLEENIER, SPLEENIEST peevish

SPLENDID *adj* -DIDER, -DIDEST magnificent

SPLENDOR *n* pl. -S magnificence

SPLENIA pl. of splenium

SPLENIAL *adj* pertaining to the splenius

SPLENIC *adj* pertaining to the spleen

SPLENIUM *n* pl. -NIA a surgical bandage

SPLENIUS *n* pl. -NII a muscle of the neck

SPLENT *n* pl. -S a splint

SPLICE *v* SPLICED, SPLICING, SPLICES to join at the ends

SPLICER *n* pl. -S one that splices

SPLIFF *n* pl. -S a marijuana cigarette

SPLINE *v* SPLINED, SPLINING, SPLINES to provide with a spline (a key that connects two rotating mechanical parts)

SPLINT *v* -ED, -ING, -S to brace with a splint (a thin piece of wood)

SPLINTER *v* -ED, -ING, -S to split into sharp, slender pieces

SPLIT *v* SPLIT, SPLITTING, SPLITS to separate lengthwise

SPLITTER *n* pl. -S one that splits

SPLODGE *v* SPLODGED, SPLODGING, SPLODGES to splotch

SPLORE *n* pl. -S a carousal

SPLOSH *v* -ED, -ING, -ES to splash

SPLOTCH *v* -ED, -ING, -ES to mark with large, irregular spots

SPLOTCHY *adj* SPLOTCHIER, SPLOTCHIEST splotched

SPLURGE *v* SPLURGED, SPLURGING, SPLURGES to spend money lavishly

SPLURGER *n* pl. -S one that splurges

SPLURGY *adj* SPLURGIER, SPLURGIEST tending to splurge

SPLUTTER *v* -ED, -ING, -S to speak rapidly and confusedly

SPODE *n* pl. -S a fine china

SPOIL *v* SPOILED or SPOILT, SPOILING, SPOILS to impair the value or quality of

SPOILAGE *n* pl. -S something that is spoiled or wasted

SPOILER *n* pl. -S one that spoils

SPOILT a past tense of spoil

SPOKE *v* SPOKED, SPOKING, SPOKES to provide with spokes (rods that support the rim of a wheel)

SPOKEN past participle of speak

SPOLIATE *v* -ATED, -ATING, -ATES to plunder

SPONDAIC *n* pl. -S a spondee

SPONDEE *n* pl. -S a type of metrical foot

SPONGE *v* SPONGED, SPONGING, SPONGES to wipe with a sponge (a mass of absorbent material)

SPONGER *n* pl. -S one that sponges

SPONGIER comparative of spongy

SPONGIEST superlative of spongy

SPONGILY *adv* in a spongy manner

SPONGIN *n* pl. -S a fibrous material

SPONGING present participle of sponge

SPONGY *adj* SPONGIER, SPONGIEST resembling a sponge

SPONSAL *adj* pertaining to marriage

SPONSION *n* pl. -S the act of sponsoring

SPONSON *n* pl. -S a projection from the side of a ship

SPONSOR *v* -ED, -ING, -S to make oneself responsible for

SPONTOON *n* pl. -S a spear-like weapon

SPOOF *v* -ED, -ING, -S to ridicule in fun

SPOOFER *n* pl. -S one that spoofs

SPOOFERY *n* pl. -ERIES good-natured ridicule

SPOOFY *adj* humorously satiric

SPOOK *v* -ED, -ING, -S to scare

SPOOKERY *n* pl. -ERIES something spooky

SPOOKISH *adj* spooky

SPOOKY *adj* SPOOKIER, SPOOKIEST scary **SPOOKILY** *adv*

SPOOL *v* -ED, -ING, -S to wind on a small cylinder

SPOOLING *n* pl. -S the temporary storage of data for later output

SPOON *v* -ED, -ING, -S to take up with a spoon (a type of eating utensil)

SPOONEY *adj* SPOONIER, SPOONIEST spoony

SPOONEY *n* pl. -EYS a spoony

SPOONFUL *n* pl. SPOONFULS or SPOONSFUL as much as a spoon can hold

SPOONIER comparative of spooney

SPOONIES pl. of spoony

SPOONIEST superlative of spooney

SPOONSFUL a pl. of spoonful

SPOONY *adj* SPOONIER, SPOONIEST overly sentimental **SPOONILY** *adv*

SPOONY *n* pl. SPOONIES a spoony person

SPOOR *v* -ED, -ING, -S to track

SPORADIC *adj* occurring at irregular intervals

SPORAL *adj* of, pertaining to, or resembling a spore

SPORE *v* SPORED, SPORING, SPORES to produce spores (asexual, usually single-celled reproductive bodies)

SPOROID *adj* resembling a spore

SPOROZOA *n/pl* parasitic one-celled animals

SPORRAN *n* pl. -S a large purse worn by Scottish Highlanders

SPORT *v* -ED, -ING, -S to frolic

SPORTER *n* pl. -S one that sports

SPORTFUL *adj* sportive

SPORTIF *adj* sporty

SPORTIVE *adj* playful

SPORTY *adj* SPORTIER, SPORTIEST showy **SPORTILY** *adv*

SPORULE *n* pl. -S a small spore **SPORULAR** *adj*

SPOT *v* SPOTTED, SPOTTING, SPOTS to mark with spots (small, roundish discolorations)

SPOTLESS *adj* perfectly clean

SPOTLIT a past tense of spotlight

SPOTTER *n* pl. -S one that spots

SPOTTING present participle of spot

SPOTTY *adj* -TIER, -TIEST marked with spots **SPOTTILY** *adv*

SPOUSAL *n* pl. -S marriage

SPOUSE *v* SPOUSED, SPOUSING, SPOUSES to marry

SPOUT *v* -ED, -ING, -S to eject in a rapid stream

SPOUTER *n* pl. -S one that spouts

SPRADDLE *v* -DLED, -DLING, -DLES to straddle

SPRAG *n* pl. -S a device used to prevent a vehicle from rolling backward

SPRAIN *v* -ED, -ING, -S to weaken by a sudden and violent twisting or wrenching

SPRANG *n* pl. -S a weaving technique to form an openwork mesh

SPRAT *n* pl. -S a small herring

SPRATTLE *v* -TLED, -TLING, -TLES to struggle

SPRAWL *v* -ED, -ING, -S to stretch out ungracefully

SPRAWLER *n* pl. -S one that sprawls

SPRAWLY *adj* SPRAWLIER, SPRAWLIEST tending to sprawl

SPRAY *v* -ED, -ING, -S to disperse in fine particles

SPRAYER *n* pl. -S one that sprays

SPREAD *v* SPREAD, SPREADING, SPREADS to open or expand over a larger area

SPREADER *n* pl. -S one that spreads

SPREE *n* pl. -S an unrestrained indulgence in an activity

SPRENT *adj* sprinkled over

SPRIER a comparative of spry

SPRIEST a superlative of spry

SPRIG *v* SPRIGGED, SPRIGGING, SPRIGS to fasten with small, thin nails

SPRIGGER *n* pl. -S one that sprigs

SPRIGGY *adj* -GIER, -GIEST having small branches

SPRIGHT *n* pl. -S sprite

SPRING *v* SPRANG or SPRUNG, SPRINGING, SPRINGS to move upward suddenly and swiftly

SPRINGAL *n* pl. -S a young man

SPRINGE *v* SPRINGED, SPRINGEING, SPRINGES to catch with a type of snare

SPRINGER *n* pl. -S one that springs

SPRINGY *adj* SPRINGIER, SPRINGIEST resilient

SPRINKLE *v* -KLED, -KLING, -KLES to scatter drops or particles on

SPRINT *v* -ED, -ING, -S to run at top speed

SPRINTER *n* pl. -S one that sprints

SPRIT *n* pl. -S a ship's spar

SPRITE *n* pl. -S an elf or fairy

SPRITZ *v* -ED, -ING, -ES to spray

SPRITZER *n* pl. -S a beverage of white wine and soda water

SPROCKET *n* pl. -S a toothlike projection that engages with the links of a chain

SPROUT *v* -ED, -ING, -S to begin to grow

SPRUCE *adj* SPRUCER, SPRUCEST neat and trim in appearance **SPRUCELY** *adv*

SPRUCE *v* SPRUCED, SPRUCING, SPRUCES to make spruce

SPRUCY *adj* SPRUCIER, SPRUCIEST spruce

SPRUE *n* pl. -S a tropical disease

SPRUG *n* pl. -S a sparrow

SPRUNG a past tense of spring

SPRY	*adj* SPRYER, SPRYEST or SPRIER, SPRIEST nimble **SPRYLY** *adv*
SPRYNESS	*n pl.* -ES the quality or state of being spry
SPUD	*v* SPUDDED, SPUDDING, SPUDS to remove with a spade-like tool
SPUDDER	*n pl.* -S a tool for removing bark from trees
SPUE	*v* SPUED, SPUING, SPUES to spew
SPUME	*v* SPUMED, SPUMING, SPUMES to foam
SPUMIER	comparative of spumy
SPUMIEST	superlative of spumy
SPUMING	present participle of spume
SPUMONE	*n pl.* -S an Italian ice cream
SPUMONI	*n pl.* -S spumone
SPUMOUS	*adj* spumy
SPUMY	*adj* SPUMIER, SPUMIEST foamy
SPUN	past tense of spin
SPUNK	*v* -ED, -ING, -S to begin to burn
SPUNKIE	*n pl.* -S a light caused by the combustion of marsh gas
SPUNKY	*adj* SPUNKIER, SPUNKIEST plucky **SPUNKILY** *adv*
SPUR	*v* SPURRED, SPURRING, SPURS to urge on with a spur (a horseman's goad)
SPURGALL	*v* -ED, -ING, -S to injure with a spur
SPURGE	*n pl.* -S a tropical plant
SPURIOUS	*adj* not genuine
SPURN	*v* -ED, -ING, -S to reject with contempt
SPURNER	*n pl.* -S one that spurns
SPURRED	past tense of spur
SPURRER	*n pl.* -S one that spurs
SPURREY	*n pl.* -REYS spurry
SPURRIER	*n pl.* -S one that makes spurs
SPURRING	present participle of spur
SPURRY	*n pl.* -RIES a European weed
SPURT	*v* -ED, -ING, -S to gush forth
SPURTLE	*n pl.* -S a stick for stirring porridge
SPUTA	pl. of sputum
SPUTNIK	*n pl.* -S a Soviet artificial earth satellite
SPUTTER	*v* -ED, -ING, -S to eject particles in short bursts
SPUTUM	*n pl.* -TA saliva
SPY	*v* SPIED, SPYING, SPIES to watch secretly
SPYGLASS	*n pl.* -ES a small telescope
SQUAB	*n pl.* -S a young pigeon
SQUABBLE	*v* -BLED, -BLING, -BLES to quarrel
SQUABBY	*adj* -BIER, -BIEST short and fat
SQUAD	*v* SQUADDED, SQUADDING, SQUADS to form into squads (small organized groups)
SQUADRON	*v* -ED, -ING, -S to arrange in squadrons (units of military organization)
SQUALENE	*n pl.* -S a chemical compound
SQUALID	*adj* -IDER, -IDEST marked by filthiness caused by neglect or poverty
SQUALL	*v* -ED, -ING, -S to cry or scream loudly
SQUALLER	*n pl.* -S one that squalls
SQUALLY	*adj* SQUALLIER, SQUALLIEST gusty
SQUALOR	*n pl.* -S the quality or state of being squalid
SQUAMA	*n pl.* -MAE a scale **SQUAMATE, SQUAMOSE, SQUAMOUS** *adj*
SQUANDER	*v* -ED, -ING, -S to spend wastefully
SQUARE	*adj* SQUARER, SQUAREST having four equal sides and four right angles; rigidly conventional
SQUARE	*v* SQUARED, SQUARING, SQUARES to make square
SQUARELY	*adv* in a direct manner
SQUARER	*n pl.* -S one that squares
SQUAREST	superlative of square
SQUARING	present participle of square
SQUARISH	*adj* somewhat square
SQUASH	*v* -ED, -ING, -ES to press into a pulp or flat mass
SQUASHER	*n pl.* -S one that squashes
SQUASHY	*adj* SQUASHIER, SQUASHIEST soft and moist
SQUAT	*v* SQUATTED, SQUATTING, SQUATS to sit on one's heels
SQUAT	*adj* SQUATTER, SQUATTEST short and thick **SQUATLY** *adv*
SQUATTER	*v* -ED, -ING, -S to move through water
SQUATTING	present participle of squat
SQUATTY	*adj* -TIER, -TIEST squat
SQUAW	*n pl.* -S an American Indian woman

SQUAWK *v* -ED, -ING, -S to utter a loud, harsh cry

SQUAWKER *n* pl. -S one that squawks

SQUEAK *v* -ED, -ING, -S to make a sharp, high-pitched sound

SQUEAKER *n* pl. -S one that squeaks

SQUEAKY *adj* SQUEAKIER, SQUEAKIEST tending to squeak

SQUEAL *v* -ED, -ING, -S to utter a sharp, shrill cry

SQUEALER *n* pl. -S one that squeals

SQUEEGEE *v* -GEED, -GEEING, -GEES to wipe with a squeegee (an implement for removing water from a surface)

SQUEEZE *v* SQUEEZED, SQUEEZING, SQUEEZES to press hard upon

SQUEEZER *n* pl. -S one that squeezes

SQUEG *v* SQUEGGED, SQUEGGING, SQUEGS to oscillate in an irregular manner

SQUELCH *v* -ED, -ING, -ES to squash

SQUELCHY *adj* SQUELCHIER, SQUELCHIEST squashy

SQUIB *v* SQUIBBED, SQUIBBING, SQUIBS to lampoon

SQUID *v* SQUIDDED, SQUIDDING, SQUIDS to fish for squid (ten-armed marine mollusks)

SQUIFFED *adj* drunk

SQUIFFY *adj* -FIER, -FIEST squiffed

SQUIGGLE *v* -GLED, -GLING, -GLES to wriggle

SQUIGGLY *adj* -GLIER, -GLIEST wriggly

SQUILGEE *v* -GEED, -GEEING, -GEES to squeegee

SQUILL *n* pl. -S a Eurasian herb

SQUILLA *n* pl. -LAS or -LAE a burrowing crustacean

SQUINCH *v* -ED, -ING, -ES to squint

SQUINNY *v* -NIED, -NYING, -NIES to squint

SQUINNY *adj* -NIER, -NIEST squinty

SQUINT *adj* SQUINTER, SQUINTEST cross-eyed

SQUINT *v* -ED, -ING, -S to look with the eyes partly closed

SQUINTER *n* pl. -S one that squints

SQUINTY *adj* SQUINTIER, SQUINTIEST marked by squinting

SQUIRE *v* SQUIRED, SQUIRING, SQUIRES to serve as a squire (an escort)

SQUIREEN *n* pl. -S an owner of a small estate

SQUIRISH *adj* of, resembling, or befitting a squire

SQUIRM *v* -ED, -ING, -S to wriggle

SQUIRMER *n* pl. -S one that squirms

SQUIRMY *adj* SQUIRMIER, SQUIRMIEST wriggly

SQUIRREL *v* -RELED, -RELING, -RELS or -RELLED, -RELLING, -RELS to store up for future use

SQUIRT *v* -ED, -ING, -S to eject in a thin, swift stream

SQUIRTER *n* pl. -S one that squirts

SQUISH *v* -ED, -ING, -ES to squash

SQUISHY *adj* SQUISHIER, SQUISHIEST squashy

SQUOOSH *v* -ED, -ING, -ES to squash

SQUOOSHY *adj* SQUOOSHIER, SQUOOSHIEST squashy

SQUUSH *v* -ED, -ING, -ES to squash

SRADDHA *n* pl. -S sradha

SRADHA *n* pl. -S a Hindu ceremonial offering

SRI *n* pl. -S mister; sir — used as a Hindu title of respect

STAB *v* STABBED, STABBING, STABS to pierce with a pointed weapon

STABBER *n* pl. -S one that stabs

STABILE *n* pl. -S a stationary abstract sculpture

STABLE *adj* -BLER, -BLEST resistant to sudden change or position or condition

STABLE *v* -BLED, -BLING, -BLES to put in a stable (a shelter for domestic animals)

STABLER *n* pl. -S one that keeps a stable

STABLEST superlative of stable

STABLING *n* pl. -S accommodation for animals in a stable

STABLISH *v* -ED, -ING, -ES to establish

STABLY *adv* in a stable manner

STACCATO *n* pl. -TOS or -TI a musical passage marked by the short, clear-cut playing of tones

STACK *v* -ED, -ING, -S to pile

STACKER *n* pl. -S one that stacks

STACKUP *n* pl. -S an arrangement of circling airplanes over an airport waiting to land

STACTE *n* pl. -S a spice used by the ancient Jews in making incense

STADDLE *n* pl. -S a platform on which hay is stacked

STADE *n* pl. -S an ancient Greek unit of length

STADIA *n* pl. -S a method of surveying distances

STADIUM *n* pl. -S a structure in which athletic events are held

STAFF *v* -ED, -ING, -S to provide with a staff (a body of assistants)

STAFFER *n* pl. -S a member of a staff

STAG *v* STAGGED, STAGGING, STAGS to attend a social function without a female companion

STAGE *v* STAGED, STAGING, STAGES to produce for public view

STAGEFUL *n* pl. -S as much or as many as a stage can hold

STAGER *n* pl. -S an experienced person

STAGEY *adj* STAGIER, STAGIEST stagy

STAGGARD *n* pl. -S a full-grown male red deer

STAGGART *n* pl. -S staggard

STAGGED past tense of stag

STAGGER *v* -ED, -ING, -S to walk or stand unsteadily

STAGGERY *adj* unsteady

STAGGIE *n* pl. -S a colt

STAGGING present participle of stag

STAGGY *adj* -GIER, -GIEST having the appearance of a mature male

STAGIER comparative of stagey and stagy

STAGIEST superlative of stagey and stagy

STAGILY *adv* in a stagy manner

STAGING *n* pl. -S a temporary platform

STAGNANT *adj* not moving or flowing

STAGNATE *v* -NATED, -NATING, -NATES to become stagnant

STAGY *adj* STAGIER, STAGIEST having a theatrical quality

STAID *adj* STAIDER, STAIDEST sober and sedate **STAIDLY** *adv*

STAIG *n* pl. -S a colt

STAIN *v* -ED, -ING, -S to discolor or dirty

STAINER *n* pl. -S one that stains

STAIR *n* pl. -S a rest for the foot used in going from one level to another

STAIRWAY *n* pl. -WAYS a flight of stairs

STAITHE *n* pl. -S a wharf equipped for transferring coal from railroad cars into ships

STAKE *v* STAKED, STAKING, STAKES to fasten with a stake (a pointed piece of wood or metal)

STAKEOUT *n* pl. -S a surveillance of an area especially by the police

STALAG *n* pl. -S a German prisoner-of-war camp

STALE *adj* STALER, STALEST not fresh **STALELY** *adv*

STALE *v* STALED, STALING, STALES to become stale

STALK *v* -ED, -ING, -S to pursue stealthily

STALKER *n* pl. -S one that stalks

STALKY *adj* STALKIER, STALKIEST long and slender **STALKILY** *adv*

STALL *v* -ED, -ING, -S to stop the progress of

STALLION *n* pl. -S an uncastrated male horse

STALWART *n* pl. -S an unwavering partisan

STAMEN *n* pl. -S the pollen-bearing organ of flowering plants

STAMINA *n* pl. -S endurance **STAMINAL** *adj*

STAMMEL *n* pl. -S a red color

STAMMER *v* -ED, -ING, -S to speak with involuntary breaks and pauses

STAMP *v* -ED, -ING, -S to bring the foot down heavily

STAMPEDE *v* -PEDED, -PEDING, -PEDES to cause to run away in headlong panic

STAMPER *n* pl. -S one that stamps

STANCE *n* pl. -S a manner of standing

STANCH *adj* STANCHER, STANCHEST staunch

STANCH *v* -ED, -ING, -ES to stop the flow of blood from

STANCHER *n* pl. -S one that stanches

STANCHLY *adv* in a stanch manner

STAND *v* STOOD, STANDING, STANDS to assume or maintain an upright position

STANDARD *n* pl. -S an established measure of comparison

STANDBY   *n* pl. -BYS one that can be relied on

STANDEE   *n* pl. -S one who stands because of the lack of seats

STANDER   *n* pl. -S one that stands

STANDING   *n* pl. -S a position or condition in society

STANDISH   *n* pl. -ES a receptacle for pens and ink

STANDOFF   *n* pl. -S a tie or draw, as in a game

STANDOUT   *n* pl. -S one that shows marked superiority

STANDPAT   *adj* resisting or opposing change

STANDUP   *adj* having an upright position

STANE   *v* STANED, STANING, STANES to stone

STANG   *v* -ED, -ING, -S to sting

STANHOPE   *n* pl. -S a light, open carriage

STANINE   *n* pl. -S one of the nine classes into which a set of scores are divided

STANING   present participle of stane

STANK   *n* pl. -S a pond

STANNARY   *n* pl. -RIES a tin-mining region

STANNIC   *adj* pertaining to tin

STANNITE   *n* pl. -S an ore of tin

STANNOUS   *adj* pertaining to tin

STANNUM   *n* pl. -S tin

STANZA   *n* pl. -S a division of a poem **STANZAED, STANZAIC** *adj*

STAPEDES   pl. of stapes

STAPELIA   *n* pl. -S an African plant

STAPES   *n* pl. -PEDES a bone of the middle ear

STAPH   *n* pl. -S any of various spherical bacteria

STAPLE   *v* -PLED, -PLING, -PLES to fasten by means of a U-shaped metal loop

STAPLER   *n* pl. -S a stapling device

STAR   *v* STARRED, STARRING, STARS to shine as a star (a natural luminous body visible in the sky)

STARCH   *v* -ED, -ING, -ES to treat with starch (a solid carbohydrate)

STARCHY   *adj* STARCHIER, STARCHIEST containing starch

STARDOM   *n* pl. -S the status of a preeminent performer

STARDUST   *n* pl. -S a romantic quality

STARE   *v* STARED, STARING, STARES to gaze fixedly

STARER   *n* pl. -S one that stares

STARETS   *n* pl. STARTSY a spiritual adviser in the Eastern Orthodox Church

STARFISH   *n* pl. -ES a star-shaped marine animal

STARGAZE   *v* -GAZED, -GAZING, -GAZES to gaze at the stars

STARING   present participle of stare

STARK   *adj* STARKER, STARKEST harsh in appearance **STARKLY** *adv*

STARKERS   *adj* naked

STARLESS   *adj* having no stars

STARLET   *n* pl. -S a small star

STARLIKE   *adj* resembling a star

STARLING   *n* pl. -S a European bird

STARLIT   *adj* lighted by the stars

STARNOSE   *n* pl. -S a burrowing mammal

STARRED   past tense of star

STARRING   present participle of star

STARRY   *adj* -RIER, -RIEST abounding with stars

STARSHIP   *n* pl. -S a spaceship for interstellar travel

START   *v* -ED, -ING, -S to set out

STARTER   *n* pl. -S one that starts

STARTLE   *v* -TLED, -TLING, -TLES to frighten or surprise suddenly

STARTLER   *n* pl. -S one that startles

STARTSY   pl. of starets

STARTUP   *n* pl. -S the act of starting something

STARVE   *v* STARVED, STARVING, STARVES to die from lack of food

STARVER   *n* pl. -S one that starves

STARWORT   *n* pl. -S a flowering plant

STASES   pl. of stasis

STASH   *v* -ED, -ING, -ES to store in a secret place

STASIMON   *n* pl. -MA a choral ode in ancient Greek drama

STASIS   *n* pl. STASES a stoppage of the normal flow of bodily fluids

STAT   *n* pl. -S a statistic

STATABLE   *adj* capable of being stated

STATAL   *adj* pertaining to a national government

STATANT   *adj* standing with all feet on the ground — used of a heraldic animal

STATE   *v* STATED, STATING, STATES to set forth in words

STATEDLY   *adv* regularly

STATELY   *adj* -LIER, -LIEST dignified

STATER   *n* pl. -S one that states

STATIC   *n* pl. -S random noise produced in a radio or television receiver **STATICAL** *adj*

STATICE   *n* pl. -S a flowering plant

STATICKY   *adj* marked by static

STATING   present participle of state

STATION   *v* -ED, -ING, -S to assign to a position

STATISM   *n* pl. -S a theory of government

STATIST   *n* pl. -S an adherent of statism

STATIVE   *n* pl. -S a verb that expresses a condition

STATOR   *n* pl. -S the part of a machine about which the rotor revolves

STATUARY   *n* pl. -ARIES a group of statues

STATUE   *n* pl. -S a three-dimensional work of art **STATUED** *adj*

STATURE   *n* pl. -S the natural height of a human or animal body

STATUS   *n* pl. -ES relative position

STATUSY   *adj* conferring prestige

STATUTE   *n* pl. -S a law enacted by the legislative branch of a government

STAUMREL   *n* pl. -S a dolt

STAUNCH   *adj* STAUNCHER, STAUNCHEST firm and dependable

STAUNCH   *v* -ED, -ING, -ES to stanch

STAVE   *v* STAVED or STOVE, STAVING, STAVES to drive or thrust away

STAW   a past tense of steal

STAY   *v* STAYED or STAID, STAYING, STAYS to continue in a place or condition

STAYER   *n* pl. -S one that stays

STAYSAIL   *n* pl. -S a type of sail

STEAD   *v* -ED, -ING, -S to be of advantage to

STEADIED   past tense of steady

STEADIER   *n* pl. -S one that steadies

STEADIES   present 3d person sing. of steady

STEADING   *n* pl. -S a small farm

STEADY   *adj* STEADIER, STEADIEST firm in position **STEADILY** *adv*

STEADY   *v* STEADIED, STEADYING, STEADIES to make steady

STEAK   *n* pl. -S a slice of meat

STEAL   *v* STOLE or STAW, STOLEN, STEALING, STEALS to take without right or permission

STEALAGE   *n* pl. -S theft

STEALER   *n* pl. -S one that steals

STEALING   *n* pl. -S the act of one that steals

STEALTH   *n* pl. -S stealthy procedure

STEALTHY   *adj* STEALTHIER, STEALTHIEST intended to escape observation

STEAM   *v* -ED, -ING, -S to expose to steam (water in the form of vapor)

STEAMER   *v* -ED, -ING, -S to travel by steamship

STEAMY   *adj* STEAMIER, STEAMIEST marked by steam **STEAMILY** *adv*

STEAPSIN   *n* pl. -S an enzyme

STEARATE   *n* pl. -S a chemical salt

STEARIN   *n* pl. -S the solid portion of a fat **STEARIC** *adj*

STEARINE   *n* pl. -S stearin

STEATITE   *n* pl. -S a variety of talc

STEDFAST   *adj* staunch

STEED   *n* pl. -S a horse

STEEK   *v* -ED, -ING, -S to shut

STEEL   *v* -ED, -ING, -S to cover with steel (a tough iron alloy)

STEELIE   *n* pl. -S a steel playing marble

STEELY   *adj* STEELIER, STEELIEST resembling steel

STEENBOK   *n* pl. -S an African antelope

STEEP   *adj* STEEPER, STEEPEST inclined sharply

STEEP   *v* -ED, -ING, -S to soak in a liquid

STEEPEN   *v* -ED, -ING, -S to make steep

STEEPER   *n* pl. -S one that steeps

STEEPISH   *adj* somewhat steep

STEEPLE   *n* pl. -S a tapering structure on a church tower **STEEPLED** *adj*

STEEPLY   *adv* in a steep manner

STEER   *v* -ED, -ING, -S to direct the course of

STEERAGE   *n* pl. -S the act of steering

STEERER   *n* pl. -S one that steers

STEEVE   *v* STEEVED, STEEVING, STEEVES to stow in the hold of a ship

STEEVING   *n* pl. -S the angular elevation of a bowsprit from a ship's keel

STEGODON   *n* pl. -S an extinct elephant-like mammal

STEIN   *n* pl. -S a beer mug

STEINBOK *n* pl. -S steenbok

STELA *n* pl. -LAE or -LAI an inscribed slab used as a monument **STELAR, STELENE** *adj*

STELE *n* pl. -S the central portion of vascular tissue in a plant stem **STELIC** *adj*

STELLA *n* pl. -S a former coin of the United States

STELLAR *adj* pertaining to the stars

STELLATE *adj* shaped like a star

STELLIFY *v* -FIED, -FYING, -FIES to convert into a star

STEM *v* STEMMED, STEMMING, STEMS to remove stems (ascending axes of a plant) from

STEMLESS *adj* having no stem

STEMLIKE *adj* resembling a stem

STEMMA *n* pl. -MAS or -MATA a scroll recording the genealogy of a family in ancient Rome

STEMMED past tense of stem

STEMMER *n* pl. -S one that removes stems

STEMMERY *n* pl. -MERIES a place where tobacco leaves are stripped

STEMMING present participle of stem

STEMMY *adj* -MIER, -MIEST abounding in stems

STEMSON *n* pl. -S a supporting timber of a ship

STEMWARE *n* pl. -S a type of glassware

STENCH *n* pl. -ES a foul odor

STENCHY *adj* STENCHIER, STENCHIEST having a stench

STENCIL *v* -CILED, -CILING, -CILS or -CILLED, -CILLING, -CILS to mark by means of a perforated sheet of material

STENGAH *n* pl. -S a mixed drink

STENO *n* pl. STENOS a stenographer

STENOKY *n* pl. -KIES the ability of an organism to live only under a narrow range of conditions

STENOSED *adj* affected with stenosis

STENOSIS *n* pl. -NOSES a narrowing of a bodily passage **STENOTIC** *adj*

STENTOR *n* pl. -S a person having a very loud voice

STEP *v* STEPPED, STEPPING, STEPS to move by lifting the foot and setting it down in another place

STEPDAME *n* pl. -S a stepmother

STEPLIKE *adj* resembling a stair

STEPPE *n* pl. -S a vast treeless plain

STEPPED past tense of step

STEPPER *n* pl. -S one that steps

STEPPING present participle of step

STEPSON *n* pl. -S a son of one's spouse by a former marriage

STEPWISE *adj* marked by a gradual progression

STERE *n* pl. -S a unit of volume

STEREO *v* -ED, -ING, -S to make a type of printing plate

STERIC *adj* pertaining to the spatial relationships of atoms in a molecule

STERICAL *adj* steric

STERIGMA *n* pl. -MAS or -MATA a spore-bearing stalk of certain fungi

STERILE *adj* incapable of producing offspring

STERLET *n* pl. -S a small sturgeon

STERLING *n* pl. -S British money

STERN *adj* STERNER, STERNEST unyielding

STERN *n* pl. -S the rear part of a ship

STERNA a pl. of sternum

STERNAL *adj* pertaining to the sternum

STERNITE *n* pl. -S a somitic sclerite

STERNLY *adv* in a stern manner

STERNSON *n* pl. -S a reinforcing post of a ship

STERNUM *n* pl. -NA or -NUMS a long, flat supporting bone of most vertebrates

STERNWAY *n* pl. -WAYS the backward movement of a vessel

STEROID *n* pl. -S a type of chemical compound

STEROL *n* pl. -S a type of solid alcohol

STERTOR *n* pl. -S a deep snoring sound

STET *v* STETTED, STETTING, STETS to cancel a previously made printing correction

STEW *v* -ED, -ING, -S to cook by boiling slowly

STEWARD *v* -ED, -ING, -S to manage

STEWBUM *n* pl. -S a drunken bum

STEWPAN *n* pl. -S a pan used for stewing

STEY *adj* steep

STHENIA *n* pl. -S excessive energy **STHENIC** *adj*

STIBIAL *adj* pertaining to stibium

STIBINE *n* pl. -S a poisonous gas

STIBIUM *n* pl. -S antimony

STIBNITE *n* pl. -S an ore of antimony

STICH *n* pl. -S a line of poetry **STICHIC** *adj*

STICK   v -ED, -ING, -S to support with slender pieces of wood

STICK   v STUCK, STICKING, STICKS to pierce with a pointed object

STICKER   n pl. -S an adhesive label

STICKFUL   n pl. -S an amount of set type

STICKIER   comparative of sticky

STICKIEST   superlative of sticky

STICKILY   adv in a sticky manner

STICKIT   adj unsuccessful

STICKLE   v -LED, -LING, -LES to argue stubbornly

STICKLER   n pl. -S one that stickles

STICKMAN   n pl. -MEN one who supervises the play at a dice table

STICKOUT   n pl. -S one that is conspicuous

STICKPIN   n pl. -S a decorative tiepin

STICKUM   n pl. -S a substance that causes adhesion

STICKUP   n pl. -S a robbery at gunpoint

STICKY   adj STICKIER, STICKIEST tending to adhere

STICTION   n pl. -S the force required to begin to move a body that is in contact with another body

STIED   a past tense of sty

STIES   present 3d person sing. of sty

STIFF   adj STIFFER, STIFFEST difficult to bend or stretch

STIFF   v -ED, -ING, -S to cheat someone by not paying

STIFFEN   v -ED, -ING, -S to make stiff

STIFFISH   adj somewhat stiff

STIFFLY   adv in a stiff manner

STIFLE   v -FLED, -FLING, -FLES to smother

STIFLER   n pl. -S one that stifles

STIGMA   n pl. -MAS or -MATA a mark of disgrace **STIGMAL** adj

STILBENE   n pl. -S a chemical compound

STILBITE   n pl. -S a mineral

STILE   n pl. -S a series of steps for passing over a fence or wall

STILETTO   v -ED, -ING, -S or -ES to stab with a stiletto (a short dagger)

STILL   adj STILLER, STILLEST free from sound or motion

STILL   v -ED, -ING, -S to make still

STILLMAN   n pl. -MEN one who operates a distillery

STILLY   adj STILLIER, STILLIEST still

STILT   v -ED, -ING, -S to raise on stilts (long, slender poles)

STIME   n pl. -S a glimpse

STIMULUS   n pl. -LI something that causes a response

STIMY   v -MIED, -MYING, -MIES to stymie

STING   v STUNG, STINGING, STINGS to prick painfully

STINGER   n pl. -S one that stings

STINGIER   comparative of stingy

STINGIEST   superlative of stingy

STINGILY   adv in a stingy manner

STINGO   n pl. -GOS a strong ale or beer

STINGRAY   n pl. -RAYS a flat-bodied marine fish

STINGY   adj -GIER, -GIEST unwilling to spend or give

STINK   v STANK or STUNK, STINKING, STINKS to emit a foul odor

STINKARD   n pl. -S a despicable person

STINKBUG   n pl. -S an insect that emits a foul odor

STINKER   n pl. -S one that stinks

STINKIER   comparative of stinky

STINKIEST   superlative of stinky

STINKO   adj drunk

STINKPOT   n pl. -S a jar containing foul-smelling combustibles formerly used in warfare

STINKY   adj STINKIER, STINKIEST emitting a foul odor

STINT   v -ED, -ING, -S to limit

STINTER   n pl. -S one that stints

STIPE   n pl. -S a slender supporting part of a plant **STIPED** adj

STIPEL   n pl. -S a small stipule

STIPEND   n pl. -S a fixed sum of money paid periodically

STIPES   n pl. STIPITES a stipe

STIPPLE   v -PLED, -PLING, -PLES to draw, paint, or engrave by means of dots or short touches

STIPPLER   n pl. -S one that stipples

STIPULE   n pl. -S an appendage at the base of a leaf in certain plants **STIPULAR, STIPULED** adj

STIR   v STIRRED, STIRRING, STIRS to pass an implement through in circular motions

STIRK   n pl. -S a young cow

STIRP   n pl. -S lineage

STIRPS   n pl. STIRPES a family or branch of a family

STIRRED   past tense of stir

STIRRER   n pl. -S one that stirs

STIRRING present participle of stir

STIRRUP *n* pl. -S a support for the foot of a horseman

STITCH *v* -ED, -ING, -ES to join by making in-and-out movements with a threaded needle

STITCHER *n* pl. -S one that stitches

STITHY *v* STITHIED, STITHYING, STITHIES to forge on an anvil

STIVER *n* pl. -S a former Dutch coin

STOA *n* pl. STOAE, STOAI, or STOAS an ancient Greek covered walkway

STOAT *n* pl. -S a weasel with a black-tipped tail

STOB *v* STOBBED, STOBBING, STOBS to stab

STOCCADO *n* pl. -DOS a thrust with a rapier

STOCCATA *n* pl. -S stoccado

STOCK *v* -ED, -ING, -S to keep for future sale or use

STOCKADE *v* -ADED, -ADING, -ADES to build a type of protective fence around

STOCKCAR *n* pl. -S a boxcar for carrying livestock

STOCKER *n* pl. -S a young animal suitable for being fattened for market

STOCKIER comparative of stocky

STOCKIEST superlative of stocky

STOCKILY *adv* in a stocky manner

STOCKING *n* pl. -S a knitted or woven covering for the foot and leg

STOCKISH *adj* stupid

STOCKIST *n* pl. -S one who stocks goods

STOCKMAN *n* pl. -MEN one who owns or raises livestock

STOCKPOT *n* pl. -S a pot in which broth is prepared

STOCKY *adj* STOCKIER, STOCKIEST having a short, thick body

STODGE *v* STODGED, STODGING, STODGES to stuff full with food

STODGY *adj* STODGIER, STODGIEST boring STODGILY *adv*

STOGEY *n* pl. -GEYS stogy

STOGIE *n* pl. -S stogy

STOGY *n* pl. -GIES a long, slender cigar

STOIC *n* pl. -S one who is indifferent to pleasure or pain STOICAL *adj*

STOICISM *n* pl. -S indifference to pleasure or pain

STOKE *v* STOKED, STOKING, STOKES to supply a furnace with fuel

STOKER *n* pl. -S one that stokes

STOKESIA *n* pl. -S a perennial herb

STOKING present participle of stoke

STOLE *n* pl. -S a long-wide scarf STOLED *adj*

STOLEN past participle of steal

STOLID *adj* -IDER, -IDEST showing little or no emotion STOLIDLY *adv*

STOLLEN *n* pl. -S a sweet bread

STOLON *n* pl. -S a type of plant stem STOLONIC *adj*

STOLPORT *n* pl. -S an airport for aircraft needing comparatively short runways

STOMA *n* pl. -MAS or -MATA a minute opening in the epidermis of a plant organ

STOMACH *v* -ED, -ING, -S to tolerate

STOMACHY *adj* paunchy

STOMAL *adj* stomatal

STOMATA a pl. of stoma

STOMATAL *adj* pertaining to a stoma

STOMATE *n* pl. -S a stoma

STOMATIC *adj* pertaining to the mouth

STOMODEA *n/pl* embryonic oral cavities

STOMP *v* -ED, -ING, -S to tread heavily

STOMPER *n* pl. -S one that stomps

STONE *v* STONED, STONING, STONES to pelt with stones (pieces of concreted earthy or mineral matter) STONABLE *adj*

STONEFLY *n* pl. -FLIES a winged insect

STONER *n* pl. -S one that stones

STONEY *adj* STONIER, STONIEST stony

STONIER comparative of stony

STONIEST superlative of stony

STONILY *adv* in a stony manner

STONING present participle of stone

STONISH *v* -ED, -ING, -ES to astonish

STONY *adj* STONIER, STONIEST abounding in stones

STOOD past tense of stand

STOOGE *v* STOOGED, STOOGING, STOOGES to act as a comedian's straight man

STOOK *v* -ED, -ING, -S to stack upright in a field for drying, as bundles of grain

STOOKER *n* pl. -S one that stooks

STOOL *v* -ED, -ING, -S to defecate

STOOLIE *n* pl. -S an informer

STOOP *v* -ED, -ING, -S to bend the body forward and down

STOOPER *n* pl. -S one that stoops

STOP *v* STOPPED or STOPT, STOPPING, STOPS to discontinue the progress or motion of

STOPBANK *n* pl. -S an embankment along a river

STOPCOCK *n* pl. -S a type of faucet

STOPE *v* STOPED, STOPING, STOPES to excavate in layers, as ore

STOPER *n* pl. -S one that stopes

STOPGAP *n* pl. -S a temporary substitute

STOPING present participle of stope

STOPOVER *n* pl. -S a brief stop in the course of a journey

STOPPAGE *n* pl. -S the act of stopping

STOPPED a past tense of stop

STOPPER *v* -ED, -ING, -S to plug

STOPPING present participle of stop

STOPPLE *v* -PLED, -PLING, -PLES to stopper

STOPT a past tense of stop

STORABLE *n* pt. -S something that can be stored

STORAGE *n* pl. -S a place for storing

STORAX *n* pl. -ES a fragrant resin

STORE *v* STORED, STORING, STORES to put away for future use

STOREY *n* pl. -REYS a horizontal division of a building **STOREYED** *adj*

STORIED past tense of story

STORIES present 3d person sing. of story

STORING present participle of store

STORK *n* pl. -S a wading bird

STORM *v* -ED, -ING, -S to blow violently

STORMY *adj* STORMIER, STORMIEST storming **STORMILY** *adv*

STORY *v* -RIED, -RYING, -RIES to relate as a story (an account of an event or series of events)

STOSS *adj* facing the direction from which a glacier moves

STOTINKA *n* pl. -KI a monetary unit of Bulgaria

STOUND *v* -ED, -ING, -S to ache

STOUP *n* pl. -S a basin for holy water

STOUR *n* pl. -S dust

STOURE *n* pl. -S stour

STOURIE *adj* stoury

STOURY *adj* dusty

STOUT *adj* STOUTER, STOUTEST fat

STOUT *n* pl. -S a strong, dark ale

STOUTEN *v* -ED, -ING, -S to make stout

STOUTISH *adj* somewhat stout

STOUTLY *adv* in a stout manner

STOVE *n* pl. -S a heating apparatus

STOVER *n* pl. -S coarse food for cattle

STOW *v* -ED, -ING, -S to pack **STOWABLE** *adj*

STOWAGE *n* pl. -S goods in storage

STOWAWAY *n* pl. -AWAYS one who hides aboard a conveyance to obtain free passage

STOWP *n* pl. -S stoup

STRADDLE *v* -DLED, -DLING, -DLES to sit, stand, or walk with the legs wide apart

STRAFE *v* STRAFED, STRAFING, STRAFES to attack with machine-gun fire from an airplane

STRAFER *n* pl. -S one that strafes

STRAGGLE *v* -GLED, -GLING, -GLES to stray

STRAGGLY *adj* -GLIER, -GLIEST irregularly spread out

STRAIGHT *adj* STRAIGHTER, STRAIGHTEST extending uniformly in one direction without bends or irregularities

STRAIGHT *v* -ED, -ING, -S to make straight

STRAIN *v* -ED, -ING, -S to exert to the utmost

STRAINER *n* pl. -S a utensil used to separate liquids from solids

STRAIT *n* pl. -S a narrow waterway connecting two larger bodies of water

STRAIT *adj* STRAITER, STRAITEST narrow **STRAITLY** *adv*

STRAITEN *v* -ED, -ING, -S to make strait

STRAKE *n* pl. -S a line of planking extending along a ship's hull **STRAKED** *adj*

STRAMASH *n* pl. -ES an uproar

STRAMONY *n* pl. -NIES a poisonous weed

STRAND *v* -ED, -ING, -S to leave in an unfavorable situation

STRANDER *n* pl. -S a machine that twists fibers into rope

STRANG *adj* strong

STRANGE *adj* STRANGER, STRANGEST unusual or unfamiliar

STRANGER *v* -ED, -ING, -S to estrange

STRANGLE *v* -GLED, -GLING, -GLES to choke to death

STRAP *v* STRAPPED, STRAPPING, STRAPS to fasten with a strap (a narrow strip of flexible material)

STRAPPER *n* pl. -S one that straps

STRASS *n* pl. -ES a brilliant glass used in making imitation gems

STRATA *n* pl. -S a stratum

STRATAL *adj* pertaining to a stratum

STRATEGY *n* pl. -GIES a plan for obtaining a specific goal

STRATH *n* pl. -S a wide river valley

STRATI pl. of stratus

STRATIFY *v* -FIED, -FYING, -FIES to form or arrange in layers

STRATOUS *adj* stratal

STRATUM *n* pl. -TA or -TUMS a layer of material

STRATUS *n* pl. -TI a type of cloud

STRAVAGE *v* -VAGED, -VAGING, -VAGES to stroll

STRAVAIG *v* -ED, -ING, -S to stravage

STRAW *v* -ED, -ING, -S to cover with straw (stalks of threshed grain)

STRAWHAT *adj* pertaining to a summer theater situated in a resort area

STRAWY *adj* STRAWIER, STRAWIEST resembling straw

STRAY *v* -ED, -ING, -S to wander from the proper area or course

STRAYER *n* pl. -S one that strays

STREAK *v* -ED, -ING, -S to cover with streaks (long, narrow marks)

STREAKER *n* pl. -S one that streaks

STREAKY *adj* STREAKIER, STREAKIEST covered with streaks

STREAM *v* -ED, -ING, -S to flow in a steady current

STREAMER *n* pl. -S a long, narrow flag

STREAMY *adj* STREAMIER, STREAMIEST streaming

STREEK *v* -ED, -ING, -S to stretch

STREEKER *n* pl. -S one that streeks

STREEL *v* -ED, -ING, -S to saunter

STREET *n* pl. -S a public thoroughfare

STRENGTH *n* pl. -S capacity for exertion or endurance

STREP *n* pl. -S any of various spherical or oval bacteria

STRESS *v* -ED, -ING, -ES to place emphasis on

STRESSOR *n* pl. -S a type of stimulus

STRETCH *v* -ED, -ING, -ES to draw out or open to full length

STRETCHY *adj* STRETCHIER, STRETCHIEST having a tendency to stretch

STRETTA *n* pl. -TE or -TAS stretto

STRETTO *n* pl. -TI or -TOS a concluding musical passage played at a faster tempo

STREUSEL *n* pl. -S a topping for coffee cakes

STREW *v* STREWED, STREWN, STREWING, STREWS to scatter about

STREWER *n* pl. -S one that strews

STRIA *n* pl. STRIAE a thin groove, stripe, or streak

STRIATE *v* -ATED, -ATING, -ATES to mark with striae

STRICK *n* pl. -S a bunch of flax fibers

STRICKEN *adj* strongly affected or afflicted

STRICKLE *v* -LED, -LING, -LES to shape or smooth with a strickle (an instrument for leveling off grain)

STRICT *adj* STRICTER, STRICTEST kept within narrow and specific limits **STRICTLY** *adv*

STRIDE *v* STRODE or STRID, STRIDDEN, STRIDING, STRIDES to walk with long steps

STRIDENT *adj* shrill

STRIDER *n* pl. -S one that strides

STRIDING present participle of stride

STRIDOR *n* pl. -S a strident sound

STRIFE *n* pl. -S bitter conflict or dissension

STRIGIL *n* pl. -S a scraping instrument

STRIGOSE *adj* covered with short, stiff hairs

STRIKE *v* STRUCK or STROOK, STRICKEN or STRUCKEN, STRIKING, STRIKES to come or cause to come into contact with

STRIKER   *n* pl. -S one that strikes

STRING   *v* STRUNG or STRINGED, STRINGING, STRINGS to provide with strings (slender cords)

STRINGER   *n* pl. -S one that strings

STRINGY   *adj* STRINGIER, STRINGIEST resembling a string or strings

STRIP   *v* STRIPPED or STRIPT, STRIPPING, STRIPS to remove the outer covering from

STRIPE   *v* STRIPED, STRIPING, STRIPES to mark with stripes (long, distinct bands)

STRIPER   *n* pl. -S a food and game fish

STRIPIER   comparative of stripy

STRIPIEST   superlative of stripy

STRIPING   *n* pl. -S the stripes marked or painted on something

STRIPPED   a past tense of strip

STRIPPER   *n* pl. -S one that strips

STRIPPING   present participle of strip

STRIPT   a past tense of strip

STRIPY   *adj* STRIPIER, STRIPIEST marked with stripes

STRIVE   *v* STROVE or STRIVED, STRIVEN, STRIVING, STRIVES to exert much effort or energy

STRIVER   *n* pl. -S one that strives

STROBE   *n* pl. -S a device that produces brief, high-intensity flashes of light

STROBIC   *adj* spinning

STROBIL   *n* pl. -S strobile

STROBILA   *n* pl. -LAE the entire body of a tapeworm

STROBILE   *n* pl. -S the conical, multiple fruit of certain trees

STROBILI   *n/pl* strobiles

STRODE   a past tense of stride

STROKE   *v* STROKED, STROKING, STROKES to rub gently

STROKER   *n* pl. -S one that strokes

STROLL   *v* -ED, -ING, -S to walk in a leisurely manner

STROLLER   *n* pl. -S one that strolls

STROMA   *n* pl. -MATA the substance that forms the framework of an organ or cell **STROMAL** *adj*

STRONG   *adj* STRONGER, STRONGEST having great strength **STRONGLY** *adv*

STRONGYL   *n* pl. -S a parasitic worm

STRONTIA   *n* pl. -S a chemical compound **STRONTIC** *adj*

STROOK   a past tense of strike

STROP   *v* STROPPED, STROPPING, STROPS to sharpen on a strip of leather

STROPHE   *n* pl. -S a part of an ancient Greek choral ode **STROPHIC** *adj*

STROPPER   *n* pl. -S one that strops

STROPPY   *adj* -PIER, -PIEST unruly

STROUD   *n* pl. -S a coarse woolen blanket

STROVE   a past tense of strive

STROW   *v* STROWED, STROWN, STROWING, STROWS to strew

STROY   *v* -ED, -ING, -S to destroy

STROYER   *n* pl. -S one that stroys

STRUCK   a past tense of strike

STRUCKEN   a past participle of strike

STRUDEL   *n* pl. -S a type of pastry

STRUGGLE   *v* -GLED, -GLING, -GLES to make strenuous efforts against opposition

STRUM   *v* STRUMMED, STRUMMING, STRUMS to play a stringed instrument by running the fingers lightly across the strings

STRUMA   *n* pl. -MAE or -MAS scrofula

STRUMMER   *n* pl. -S one that strums

STRUMMING   present participle of strum

STRUMOSE   *adj* having a struma

STRUMOUS   *adj* having or pertaining to a struma

STRUMPET   *n* pl. -S a prostitute

STRUNG   a past tense of string

STRUNT   *v* -ED, -ING, -S to strut

STRUT   *v* STRUTTED, STRUTTING, STRUTS to walk with a pompous air

STRUTTER   *n* pl. -S one that struts

STUB   *v* STUBBED, STUBBING, STUBS to strike accidentally against a projecting object

STUBBIER   comparative of stubby

STUBBIEST   superlative of stubby

STUBBILY   *adv* in a stubby manner

STUBBING   present participle of stub

STUBBLE   *n* pl. -S a short, rough growth of beard **STUBBLED** *adj*

STUBBLY   *adj* -BLIER, -BLIEST covered with stubble

STUBBORN   *adj* unyielding

STUBBY	*adj* -BIER, -BIEST short and thick
STUCCO	*v* -ED, -ING, -ES or -S to coat with a type of plaster
STUCCOER	*n* pl. -S one that stuccoes
STUCK	past tense of stick
STUD	*v* STUDDED, STUDDING, STUDS to set thickly with small projections
STUDBOOK	*n* pl. -S a record of the pedigree of purebred animals
STUDDIE	*n* pl. -S an anvil
STUDDING	*n* pl. -S the framework of a wall
STUDENT	*n* pl. -S a person formally engaged in learning
STUDFISH	*n* pl. -ES a freshwater fish
STUDIED	past tense of study
STUDIER	*n* pl. -S one that studies
STUDIES	present 3d person sing. of study
STUDIO	*n* pl. -DIOS an artist's workroom
STUDIOUS	*adj* given to study
STUDLY	*adj* -LIER, -LIEST muscular and attractive
STUDWORK	*n* pl. -S studding
STUDY	*v* STUDIED, STUDYING, STUDIES to apply the mind to the acquisition of knowledge
STUFF	*v* -ED, -ING, -S to fill or pack tightly
STUFFER	*n* pl. -S one that stuffs
STUFFING	*n* pl. -S material with which something is stuffed
STUFFY	*adj* STUFFIER, STUFFIEST poorly ventilated **STUFFILY** *adv*
STUIVER	*n* pl. -S stiver
STULL	*n* pl. -S a supporting timber in a mine
STULTIFY	*v* -FIED, -FYING, -FIES to cause to appear absurd
STUM	*v* STUMMED, STUMMING, STUMS to increase the fermentation of by adding grape juice
STUMBLE	*v* -BLED, -BLING, -BLES to miss one's step in walking or running
STUMBLER	*n* pl. -S one that stumbles
STUMMED	past tense of stum
STUMMING	present participle of stum
STUMP	*v* -ED, -ING, -S to baffle
STUMPAGE	*n* pl. -S uncut marketable timber
STUMPER	*n* pl. -S a baffling question
STUMPY	*adj* STUMPIER, STUMPIEST short and thick
STUN	*v* STUNNED, STUNNING, STUNS to render senseless or incapable of action
STUNG	past tense of sting
STUNK	a past tense of stink
STUNNED	past tense of stun
STUNNER	*n* pl. -S one that stuns
STUNNING	*adj* strikingly beautiful or attractive
STUNSAIL	*n* pl. -S a type of sail
STUNT	*v* -ED, -ING, -S to hinder the normal growth of
STUNTMAN	*n* pl. -MEN a person who substitutes for an actor in scenes involving dangerous activities
STUPA	*n* pl. -S a Buddhist shrine
STUPE	*n* pl. -S a medicated cloth to be applied to a wound
STUPEFY	*v* -FIED, -FYING, -FIES to dull the senses of
STUPID	*adj* -PIDER, -PIDEST mentally slow **STUPIDLY** *adv*
STUPID	*n* pl. -S a stupid person
STUPOR	*n* pl. -S a state of reduced sensibility
STURDY	*adj* -DIER, -DIEST strong and durable **STURDILY** *adv*
STURDY	*n* pl. -DIES a disease of sheep **STURDIED** *adj*
STURGEON	*n* pl. -S an edible fish
STURT	*n* pl. -S contention
STUTTER	*v* -ED, -ING, -S to speak with spasmodic repetition
STY	*v* STIED or STYED, STYING, STIES to keep in a pigpen
STYE	*n* pl. -S an inflamed swelling of the eyelid
STYGIAN	*adj* gloomy
STYLAR	*adj* pertaining to a stylus
STYLATE	*adj* bearing a stylet
STYLE	*v* STYLED, STYLING, STYLES to name
STYLER	*n* pl. -S one that styles
STYLET	*n* pl. -S a small, stiff organ or appendage of certain animals
STYLI	a pl. of stylus
STYLING	*n* pl. -S the way in which something is styled
STYLISE	*v* -ISED, -ISING, -ISES to stylize
STYLISER	*n* pl. -S one that stylises
STYLISH	*adj* fashionable

STYLISING	present participle of stylise
STYLIST	*n* pl. -S one who is a master of a literary or rhetorical style
STYLITE	*n* pl. -S an early Christian ascetic **STYLITIC** *adj*
STYLIZE	*v* -IZED, -IZING, -IZES to make conventional
STYLIZER	*n* pl. -S one that stylizes
STYLOID	*adj* slender and pointed
STYLUS	*n* pl. -LI or -LUSES a pointed instrument for writing, marking, or engraving
STYMIE	*v* -MIED, -MIEING, -MIES to thwart
STYMY	*v* -MIED, -MYING, -MIES to stymie
STYPSIS	*n* pl. -SISES the use of a styptic
STYPTIC	*n* pl. -S a substance used to check bleeding
STYRAX	*n* pl. -ES storax
STYRENE	*n* pl. -S a liquid hydrocarbon
SUABLE	*adj* capable of being sued **SUABLY** *adv*
SUASION	*n* pl. -S persuasion **SUASIVE, SUASORY** *adj*
SUAVE	*adj* SUAVER, SUAVEST smoothly affable and polite **SUAVELY** *adv*
SUAVITY	*n* pl. -TIES the state of being suave
SUB	*v* SUBBED, SUBBING, SUBS to act as a substitute
SUBA	*n* pl. -S subah
SUBABBOT	*n* pl. -S a subordinate abbot
SUBACID	*adj* slightly sour
SUBACRID	*adj* somewhat acrid
SUBACUTE	*adj* somewhat acute
SUBADAR	*n* pl. -S subahdar
SUBADULT	*n* pl. -S an individual approaching adulthood
SUBAGENT	*n* pl. -S a subordinate agent
SUBAH	*n* pl. -S a province of India
SUBAHDAR	*n* pl. -S a governor of a subah
SUBALAR	*adj* somewhat alar
SUBAREA	*n* pl. -S a subdivision of an area
SUBARID	*adj* somewhat arid
SUBATOM	*n* pl. -S a component of an atom
SUBAXIAL	*adj* somewhat axial
SUBBASE	*n* pl. -S the lowest part of a base
SUBBASIN	*n* pl. -S a section of an area drained by a river
SUBBASS	*n* pl. -ES a pedal stop producing the lowest tones of an organ
SUBBED	past tense of sub
SUBBING	*n* pl. -S a thin coating on the support of a photographic film
SUBBLOCK	*n* pl. -S a subdivision of a block
SUBBREED	*n* pl. -S a distinguishable strain within a breed
SUBCASTE	*n* pl. -S a subdivision of a caste
SUBCAUSE	*n* pl. -S a subordinate cause
SUBCELL	*n* pl. -S a subdivision of a cell
SUBCHIEF	*n* pl. -S a subordinate chief
SUBCLAN	*n* pl. -S a subdivision of a clan
SUBCLASS	*v* -ED, -ING, -ES to place in a subdivision of a class
SUBCLERK	*n* pl. -S a subordinate clerk
SUBCODE	*n* pl. -S a subdivision of a code
SUBCOOL	*v* -ED, -ING, -S to cool below the freezing point without solidification
SUBCULT	*n* pl. -S a subdivision of a cult
SUBCUTIS	*n* pl. -CUTES or -CUTISES the deeper part of the dermis
SUBDEAN	*n* pl. -S a subordinate dean
SUBDEB	*n* pl. -S a girl the year before she becomes a debutante
SUBDEPOT	*n* pl. -S a military depot that operates under the jurisdiction of another depot
SUBDUAL	*n* pl. -S the act of subduing
SUBDUCE	*v* -DUCED, -DUCING, -DUCES to take away
SUBDUCT	*v* -ED, -ING, -S to subduce
SUBDUE	*v* -DUED, -DUING, -DUES to bring under control
SUBDUER	*n* pl. -S one that subdues
SUBDURAL	*adj* situated under the dura mater
SUBECHO	*n* pl. -ECHOES an inferior echo
SUBEDIT	*v* -ED, -ING, -S to act as the assistant editor of
SUBENTRY	*n* pl. -TRIES an entry made under a more general entry
SUBEPOCH	*n* pl. -S a subdivision of an epoch
SUBER	*n* pl. -S phellem
SUBERECT	*adj* nearly erect
SUBERIC	*adj* pertaining to cork
SUBERIN	*n* pl. -S a substance found in cork cells

SUBERISE   v -ISED, -ISING, -ISES to suberize

SUBERIZE   v -IZED, -IZING, -IZES to convert into cork tissue

SUBEROSE   adj corky

SUBEROUS   adj suberose

SUBFIELD   n pl. -S a subset of a mathematical field that is itself a field

SUBFILE   n pl. -S a subdivision of a file

SUBFIX   n pl. -ES a distinguishing symbol or letter written below another character

SUBFLOOR   n pl. -S a rough floor laid as a base for a finished floor

SUBFLUID   adj somewhat fluid

SUBFRAME   n pl. -S a frame for the attachment of a finish frame

SUBFUSC   adj dark in color

SUBGENRE   n pl. -S a subdivision of a genre

SUBGENUS   n pl. -GENERA or -GENUSES a subdivision of a genus

SUBGOAL   n pl. -S a subordinate goal

SUBGRADE   n pl. -S a surface on which a pavement is placed

SUBGRAPH   n pl. -S a graph contained within a larger graph

SUBGROUP   n pl. -S a distinct group within a group

SUBGUM   n pl. -S a Chinese dish of mixed vegetables

SUBHEAD   n pl. -S the heading of a subdivision

SUBHUMAN   n pl. -S one that is less than human

SUBHUMID   adj somewhat humid

SUBIDEA   n pl. -S an inferior idea

SUBINDEX   n pl. -DEXES or -DICES a subfix

SUBITEM   n pl. -S an item that forms a subdivision of a larger topic

SUBITO   adv quickly — used as a musical direction

SUBJECT   v -ED, -ING, -S to cause to experience

SUBJOIN   v -ED, -ING, -S to add at the end

SUBLATE   v -LATED, -LATING, -LATES to cancel

SUBLEASE   v -LEASED, -LEASING, -LEASES to sublet

SUBLET   v -LET, -LETTING, -LETS to rent leased property to another

SUBLEVEL   n pl. -S a lower level

SUBLIME   adj -LIMER, -LIMEST of elevated or noble quality

SUBLIME   v -LIMED, -LIMING, -LIMES to make sublime

SUBLIMER   n pl. -S one that sublimes

SUBLIMEST   superlative of sublime

SUBLIMING   present participle of sublime

SUBLINE   n pl. -S an inbred line within a strain

SUBLOT   n pl. -S a subdivision of a lot

SUBLUNAR   adj pertaining to the earth

SUBMENU   n pl. -S a secondary list of options for a computer

SUBMERGE   v -MERGED, -MERGING, -MERGES to place below the surface of a liquid

SUBMERSE   v -MERSED, -MERSING, -MERSES to submerge

SUBMISS   adj inclined to submit

SUBMIT   v -MITTED, -MITTING, -MITS to yield to the power of another

SUBNASAL   adj situated under the nose

SUBNET   n pl. -S a system of interconnections within a communications system

SUBNICHE   n pl. -S a subdivision of a habitat

SUBNODAL   adj situated under a node

SUBOPTIC   adj situated under the eyes

SUBORAL   adj situated under the mouth

SUBORDER   n pl. -S a category of related families within an order

SUBORN   v -ED, -ING, -S to induce to commit perjury

SUBORNER   n pl. -S one that suborns

SUBOVAL   adj nearly oval

SUBOVATE   adj nearly ovate

SUBOXIDE   n pl. -S an oxide containing relatively little oxygen

SUBPANEL   n pl. -S a subdivision of a panel

SUBPAR   adj below par

SUBPART   n pl. -S a subdivision of a part

SUBPENA   v -ED, -ING, -S to subpoena

SUBPHASE   n pl. -S a subdivision of a phase

SUBPHYLA   n/pl divisions within a phylum

SUBPLOT   n pl. -S a secondary literary plot

SUBPOENA   v -ED, -ING, -S to summon with a type of judicial writ

SUBPOLAR   adj situated just outside the polar circles

SUBPUBIC   adj situated under the pubis

SUBRACE   n pl. -S a subdivision of a race

SUBRENT   n pl. -S rent from a subtenant

SUBRING *n* pl. -S a subset of a mathematical ring that is itself a ring

SUBRULE *n* pl. -S a subordinate rule

SUBSALE *n* pl. -S a resale of purchased goods

SUBSCALE *n* pl. -S a subdivision of a scale

SUBSEA *adj* situated below the surface of the sea

SUBSECT *n* pl. -S a sect directly derived from another

SUBSENSE *n* pl. -S a subdivision of a sense

SUBSERE *n* pl. -S a type of ecological succession

SUBSERVE *v* -SERVED, -SERVING, -SERVES to serve to promote

SUBSET *n* pl. -S a mathematical set contained within a larger set

SUBSHAFT *n* pl. -S a shaft that is beneath another shaft

SUBSHELL *n* pl. -S one of the orbitals making up an electron shell of an atom

SUBSHRUB *n* pl. -S a low shrub

SUBSIDE *v* -SIDED, -SIDING, -SIDES to sink to a lower or normal level

SUBSIDER *n* pl. -S one that subsides

SUBSIDY *n* pl. -DIES a grant or contribution of money

SUBSIST *v* -ED, -ING, -S to continue to exist

SUBSITE *n* pl. -S a subdivision of a site

SUBSOIL *v* -ED, -ING, -S to plow so as to turn up the subsoil (the layer of earth beneath the surface soil)

SUBSOLAR *adj* situated directly beneath the sun

SUBSONIC *adj* moving at a speed less than that of sound

SUBSPACE *n* pl. -S a subset of a mathematical space

SUBSTAGE *n* pl. -S a part of a microscope for supporting accessories

SUBSTATE *n* pl. -S a subdivision of a state

SUBSUME *v* -SUMED, -SUMING, -SUMES to classify within a larger category

SUBTASK *n* pl. -S a subordinate task

SUBTAXON *n* pl. -TAXA or -TAXONS a subdivision of a taxon

SUBTEEN *n* pl. -S a person approaching the teenage years

SUBTEND *v* -ED, -ING, -S to extend under or opposite to

SUBTEST *n* pl. -S a subdivision of a test

SUBTEXT *n* pl. -S written or printed matter under a more general text

SUBTHEME *n* pl. -S a subordinate theme

SUBTILE *adj* -TILER, -TILEST subtle

SUBTILIN *n* pl. -S an antibiotic

SUBTILTY *n* pl. -TIES subtlety

SUBTITLE *v* -TLED, -TLING, -TLES to give a secondary title to

SUBTLE *adj* -TLER, -TLEST so slight as to be difficult to detect **SUBTLY** *adv*

SUBTLETY *n* pl. -TIES the state of being subtle

SUBTONE *n* pl. -S a low or subdued tone

SUBTONIC *n* pl. -S a type of musical tone

SUBTOPIA *n* pl. -S the suburbs of a city

SUBTOPIC *n* pl. -S a secondary topic

SUBTOTAL *v* -TALED, -TALING, -TALS or -TALLED, -TALLING, -TALS to total a portion of

SUBTRACT *v* -ED, -ING, -S to take away

SUBTREND *n* pl. -S a subordinate trend

SUBTRIBE *n* pl. -S a subdivision of a tribe

SUBTUNIC *n* pl. -S a tunic worn under another tunic

SUBTYPE *n* pl. -S a type that is subordinate to or included in another type

SUBULATE *adj* slender and tapering to a point

SUBUNIT *n* pl. -S a unit that is a part of a larger unit

SUBURB *n* pl. -S a residential area adjacent to a city **SUBURBED** *adj*

SUBURBAN *n* pl. -S one who lives in a suburb

SUBURBIA *n* pl. -S the suburbs of a city

SUBVENE *v* -VENED, -VENING, -VENES to arrive or occur as a support or relief

SUBVERT *v* -ED, -ING, -S to destroy completely

SUBVICAR *n* pl. -S a subordinate vicar

SUBVIRAL *adj* pertaining to a part of a virus

SUBVOCAL *adj* mentally formulated as words

SUBWAY *v* -ED, -ING, -S to travel by an underground railroad

SUBWORLD *n* pl. -S a subdivision of a sphere of interest or activity

SUBZERO *adj* registering less than zero

SUBZONE *n* pl. -S a subdivision of a zone

SUCCAH *n* pl. -CAHS or -COTH sukkah

SUCCEED *v* -ED, -ING, -S to accomplish something desired or intended

SUCCESS *n* pl. -ES the attainment of something desired or intended

SUCCINCT *adj* -CINCTER, -CINCTEST clearly expressed in few words

SUCCINIC *adj* pertaining to amber

SUCCINYL *n* pl. -S a univalent radical

SUCCOR *v* -ED, -ING, -S to go to the aid of

SUCCORER *n* pl. -S one that succors

SUCCORY *n* pl. -RIES chicory

SUCCOTH a pl. of succah

SUCCOUR *v* -ED, -ING, -S to succor

SUCCUBA *n* pl. -BAE a succubus

SUCCUBUS *n* pl. -BI or -BUSES a female demon

SUCCUMB *v* -ED, -ING, -S to yield to superior force

SUCCUSS *v* -ED, -ING, -ES to shake violently

SUCH *adj* of that kind

SUCHLIKE *adj* of a similar kind

SUCHNESS *n* pl. -ES essential or characteristic quality

SUCK *v* -ED, -ING, -S to draw in by establishing a partial vacuum

SUCKER *v* -ED, -ING, -S to strip of lower shoots or branches

SUCKFISH *n* pl. -ES a remora

SUCKLE *v* -LED, -LING, -LES to give milk to from the breast

SUCKLER *n* pl. -S one that suckles

SUCKLESS *adj* having no juice

SUCKLING *n* pl. -S a young mammal that has not been weaned

SUCRASE *n* pl. -S an enzyme

SUCRE *n* pl. -S a monetary unit of Ecuador

SUCROSE *n* pl. -S a type of sugar

SUCTION *n* pl. -S the act of sucking

SUDARIUM *n* pl. -IA a cloth for wiping the face

SUDARY *n* pl. -RIES sudarium

SUDATION *n* pl. -S excessive sweating

SUDATORY *n* pl. -RIES a hot-air bath for inducing sweating

SUDD *n* pl. -S a floating mass of vegetation

SUDDEN *adj* happening quickly and without warning **SUDDENLY** *adv*

SUDDEN *n* pl. -S a sudden occurrence

SUDOR *n* pl. -S sweat **SUDORAL** *adj*

SUDS *v* -ED, -ING, -ES to wash in soapy water

SUDSER *n* pl. -S one that sudses

SUDSLESS *adj* having no suds

SUDSY *adj* SUDSIER, SUDSIEST foamy

SUE *v* SUED, SUING, SUES to institute legal proceedings against

SUEDE *v* SUEDED, SUEDING, SUEDES to finish leather with a soft, napped surface

SUER *n* pl. -S one that sues

SUET *n* pl. -S the hard, fatty tissue around the kidneys of cattle and sheep **SUETY** *adj*

SUFFARI *n* pl. -S a safari

SUFFER *v* -ED, -ING, -S to feel pain or distress

SUFFERER *n* pl. -S one that suffers

SUFFICE *v* -FICED, -FICING, -FICES to be adequate

SUFFICER *n* pl. -S one that suffices

SUFFIX *v* -ED, -ING, -ES to add as a suffix (a form affixed to the end of a root word)

SUFFIXAL *adj* pertaining to or being a suffix

SUFFLATE *v* -FLATED, -FLATING, -FLATES to inflate

SUFFRAGE *n* pl. -S the right to vote

SUFFUSE *v* -FUSED, -FUSING, -FUSES to spread through or over

SUGAR *v* -ED, -ING, -S to cover with sugar (a sweet carbohydrate)

SUGARY *adj* -ARIER, -ARIEST containing or resembling sugar

SUGGEST *v* -ED, -ING, -S to bring or put forward for consideration

SUGH *v* -ED, -ING, -S to sough

SUICIDAL *adj* self-destructive

SUICIDE *v* -CIDED, -CIDING, -CIDES to kill oneself intentionally

SUING present participle of sue

SUINT *n* pl. -S a natural grease found in the wool of sheep

SUIT *v* -ED, -ING, -S to be appropriate to

SUITABLE *adj* appropriate **SUITABLY** *adv*

SUITCASE *n* pl. -S a flat, rectangular piece of luggage

SUITE *n* pl. -S a series of things forming a unit

SUITER   *n* pl. -S a suitcase holding a specified number of suits (sets of garments)

SUITING   *n* pl. -S fabric for making suits

SUITLIKE   *adj* resembling a suit (a set of garments)

SUITOR   *n* pl. -S one that is courting a woman

SUKIYAKI   *n* pl. -S a Japanese dish

SUKKAH   *n* pl. -KAHS or -KOTH or -KOT a temporary shelter in which meals are eaten during a Jewish festival

SULCATE   *adj* having long, narrow furrows

SULCATED   *adj* sulcate

SULCUS   *n* pl. -CI a narrow furrow **SULCAL** *adj*

SULDAN   *n* pl. -S soldan

SULFA   *n* pl. -S a bacteria-inhibiting drug

SULFATE   *v* -FATED, -FATING, -FATES to treat with sulfuric acid

SULFID   *n* pl. -S sulfide

SULFIDE   *n* pl. -S a sulfur compound

SULFINYL   *n* pl. -S a bivalent radical

SULFITE   *n* pl. -S a chemical salt **SULFITIC** *adj*

SULFO   *adj* sulfonic

SULFONE   *n* pl. -S a sulfur compound

SULFONIC   *adj* containing a certain univalent radical

SULFONYL   *n* pl. -S a bivalent radical

SULFUR   *v* -ED, -ING, -S to treat with sulfur (a nonmetallic element)

SULFURET   *v* -RETED, -RETING, -RETS or -RETTED, -RETTING, -RETS to treat with sulfur

SULFURIC   *adj* pertaining to sulfur

SULFURY   *adj* resembling sulfur

SULFURYL   *n* pl. -S sulfonyl

SULK   *v* -ED, -ING, -S to be sulky

SULKER   *n* pl. -S one that sulks

SULKY   *adj* SULKIER, SULKIEST sullenly aloof or withdrawn **SULKILY** *adv*

SULKY   *n* pl. SULKIES a light horse-drawn vehicle

SULLAGE   *n* pl. -S sewage

SULLEN   *adj* -LENER, -LENEST showing a brooding ill humor or resentment **SULLENLY** *adv*

SULLY   *v* -LIED, -LYING, -LIES to soil

SULPHA   *n* pl. -S sulfa

SULPHATE   *v* -PHATED, -PHATING, -PHATES to sulfate

SULPHID   *n* pl. -S sulfide

SULPHIDE   *n* pl. -S sulfide

SULPHITE   *n* pl. -S sulfite

SULPHONE   *n* pl. -S sulfone

SULPHUR   *v* -ED, -ING, -S to sulfur

SULPHURY   *adj* sulfury

SULTAN   *n* pl. -S the ruler of a Muslim country **SULTANIC** *adj*

SULTANA   *n* pl. -S a sultan's wife

SULTRY   *adj* -TRIER, -TRIEST very hot and humid **SULTRILY** *adv*

SULU   *n* pl. -S a Melanesian skirt

SUM   *v* SUMMED, SUMMING, SUMS to add into one total

SUMAC   *n* pl. -S a flowering tree or shrub

SUMACH   *n* pl. -S sumac

SUMLESS   *adj* too large for calculation

SUMMA   *n* pl. -MAE or -MAS a comprehensive work covering a specific subject

SUMMABLE   *adj* capable of being summed

SUMMAND   *n* pl. -S an addend

SUMMARY   *n* pl. -RIES a condensation of the substance of a larger work

SUMMATE   *v* -MATED, -MATING, -MATES to sum

SUMMED   past tense of sum

SUMMER   *v* -ED, -ING, -S to pass the summer (the warmest season of the year)

SUMMERLY   *adj* summery

SUMMERY   *adj* -MERIER, -MERIEST characteristic of summer

SUMMING   present participle of sum

SUMMIT   *n* pl. -S the highest point **SUMMITAL** *adj*

SUMMITRY   *n* pl. -RIES the use of conferences between chiefs of state for international negotiation

SUMMON   *v* -ED, -ING, -S to order to appear

SUMMONER   *n* pl. -S one that summons

SUMMONS   *v* -ED, -ING, -ES to summon with a court order

SUMO   *n* pl. -MOS a Japanese form of wrestling

SUMP   *n* pl. -S a low area serving as a drain or receptacle for liquids

SUMPTER   *n* pl. -S a pack animal

SUMPWEED   *n* pl. -S a marsh plant

SUN   *v* SUNNED, SUNNING, SUNS to expose to the sun (the star around which the earth revolves)

SUNBACK   *adj* cut low to expose the back to sunlight

SUNBAKED   *adj* baked by the sun

SUNBATH   *n* pl. -S an exposure to sunlight

SUNBATHE   *v* -BATHED, -BATHING, -BATHES to take a sunbath

SUNBEAM   *n* pl. -S a beam of sunlight **SUNBEAMY** *adj*

SUNBELT   *n* pl. -S the southern and southwestern states of the U.S.

SUNBIRD   *n* pl. -S a tropical bird

SUNBLOCK   *n* pl. -S a preparation to protect the skin from the sun's rays

SUNBOW   *n* pl. -S an arc of spectral colors formed by the sun shining through a mist

SUNBURN   *v* -BURNED or -BURNT, -BURNING, -BURNS to burn or discolor from exposure to the sun

SUNBURST   *n* pl. -S a burst of sunlight

SUNCHOKE   *n* pl. -S a type of sunflower

SUNDAE   *n* pl. -S a dish of ice cream served with a topping

SUNDECK   *n* pl. -S a deck that is exposed to the sun

SUNDER   *v* -ED, -ING, -S to break apart

SUNDERER   *n* pl. -S one that sunders

SUNDEW   *n* pl. -S a marsh plant

SUNDIAL   *n* pl. -S a type of time-telling device

SUNDOG   *n* pl. -S a small rainbow

SUNDOWN   *n* pl. -S sunset

SUNDRESS   *n* pl. -ES a dress with an abbreviated bodice

SUNDRIES   *n/pl* miscellaneous items

SUNDROPS   *n* pl. SUNDROPS a flowering plant

SUNDRY   *adj* miscellaneous

SUNFAST   *adj* resistant to fading by the sun

SUNFISH   *n* pl. -ES a marine fish

SUNG   past participle of sing

SUNGLASS   *n* pl. -ES a lens for concentrating the sun's rays in order to produce heat

SUNGLOW   *n* pl. -S a glow in the sky caused by the sun

SUNK   a past participle of sink

SUNKEN   a past participle of sink

SUNKET   *n* pl. -S a tidbit

SUNLAMP   *n* pl. -S a lamp that radiates ultraviolet rays

SUNLAND   *n* pl. -S an area marked by a great amount of sunshine

SUNLESS   *adj* having no sunlight

SUNLIGHT   *n* pl. -S the light of the sun

SUNLIKE   *adj* resembling the sun

SUNLIT   *adj* lighted by the sun

SUNN   *n* pl. -S an East Indian shrub

SUNNA   *n* pl. -S the body of traditional Muslim law

SUNNAH   *n* pl. -S sunna

SUNNED   past tense of sun

SUNNING   present participle of sun

SUNNY   *adj* -NIER, -NIEST filled with sunlight **SUNNILY** *adv*

SUNPORCH   *n* pl. -ES a porch that admits much sunlight

SUNPROOF   *adj* resistant to damage by sunlight

SUNRISE   *n* pl. -S the ascent of the sun above the horizon in the morning

SUNROOF   *n* pl. -S an automobile roof having an openable panel

SUNROOM   *n* pl. -S a room built to admit a great amount of sunlight

SUNSCALD   *n* pl. -S an injury of woody plants caused by the sun

SUNSET   *n* pl. -S the descent of the sun below the horizon in the evening

SUNSHADE   *n* pl. -S something used as a protection from the sun

SUNSHINE   *n* pl. -S the light of the sun **SUNSHINY** *adj*

SUNSPOT   *n* pl. -S a dark spot on the surface of the sun

SUNSTONE   *n* pl. -S a variety of quartz

SUNSUIT   *n* pl. -S an outfit worn for sunbathing

SUNTAN   *n* pl. -S a brown color on the skin produced by exposure to the sun

SUNUP   *n* pl. -S sunrise

SUNWARD   *adv* toward the sun

SUNWARDS   *adv* sunward

SUNWISE   *adv* from left to right

SUP   *v* SUPPED, SUPPING, SUPS to eat supper

SUPE   *n* pl. -S an actor without a speaking part

SUPER   *v* -ED, -ING, -S to reinforce with a thin cotton mesh, as a book

SUPERADD   *v* -ED, -ING, -S to add further

SUPERB adj -PERBER, -PERBEST of excellent quality **SUPERBLY** adv

SUPERBAD adj exceedingly bad

SUPERCAR n pl. -S a superior car

SUPERCOP n pl. -S a superior police officer

SUPEREGO n pl. -EGOS a part of the psyche

SUPERFAN n pl. -S an exceedingly devoted enthusiast

SUPERFIX n pl. -ES a recurrent pattern of stress in speech

SUPERHIT n pl. -S something exceedingly successful

SUPERIOR n pl. -S one of higher rank, quality, or authority than another

SUPERJET n pl. -S a type of jet airplane

SUPERLIE v -LAY, -LAIN, -LYING, -LIES to lie above

SUPERMAN n pl. -MEN a hypothetical superior man

SUPERMOM n pl. -S a superior mom

SUPERNAL adj pertaining to the sky

SUPERPRO n pl. -PROS a superior professional

SUPERSEX n pl. -ES a type of sterile organism

SUPERSPY n pl. -SPIES a superior spy

SUPERTAX n pl. -ES an additional tax

SUPINATE v -NATED, -NATING, -NATES to turn so that the palm is facing upward

SUPINE n pl. -S a Latin verbal noun

SUPINELY adv in an inactive manner

SUPPED past tense of sup

SUPPER n pl. -S an evening meal

SUPPING present participle of sup

SUPPLANT v -ED, -ING, -S to take the place of

SUPPLE adj -PLER, -PLEST pliant **SUPPLELY** adv

SUPPLE v -PLED, -PLING, -PLES to make supple

SUPPLIER n pl. -S one that supplies

SUPPLY v -PLIED, -PLYING, -PLIES to furnish with what is needed

SUPPORT v -ED, -ING, -S to hold up or add strength to

SUPPOSAL n pl. -S something supposed

SUPPOSE v -POSED, -POSING, -POSES to assume to be true

SUPPOSER n pl. -S one that supposes

SUPPRESS v -ED, -ING, -ES to put an end to forcibly

SUPRA adv above

SUPREME adj -PREMER, -PREMEST highest in power or authority

SUPREMO n pl. -MOS one who is highest in authority

SUQ n pl. -S souk

SURA n pl. -S a chapter of the Koran

SURAH n pl. -S a silk fabric

SURAL adj pertaining to the calf of the leg

SURBASE n pl. -S a molding or border above the base of a structure **SURBASED** adj

SURCEASE v -CEASED, -CEASING, -CEASES to cease

SURCOAT n pl. -S an outer coat or cloak

SURD n pl. -S a voiceless speech sound

SURE adj SURER, SUREST free from doubt

SUREFIRE adj sure to meet expectations

SURELY adv certainly

SURENESS n pl. -ES the state of being sure

SURER comparative of sure

SUREST superlative of sure

SURETY n pl. -TIES sureness

SURF v -ED, -ING, -S to ride breaking waves on a long, narrow board **SURFABLE** adj

SURFACE v -FACED, -FACING, -FACES to apply an outer layer to

SURFACER n pl. -S one that surfaces

SURFBIRD n pl. -S a shore bird

SURFBOAT n pl. -S a strong rowboat

SURFEIT v -ED, -ING, -S to supply to excess

SURFER n pl. -S one that surfs

SURFFISH n pl. -ES a marine fish

SURFIER comparative of surfy

SURFIEST superlative of surfy

SURFING n pl. -S the act or sport of riding the surf (breaking waves)

SURFLIKE adj resembling breaking waves

SURFY adj SURFIER, SURFIEST abounding in breaking waves

SURGE v SURGED, SURGING, SURGES to move in a swelling manner

SURGEON n pl. -S one who practices surgery

SURGER n pl. -S one that surges

SURGERY n pl. -GERIES the treatment of medical problems by operation

SURGICAL	*adj* pertaining to surgery
SURGING	present participle of surge
SURGY	*adj* surging
SURICATE	*n* pl. -S a burrowing mammal
SURIMI	*n* pl. SURIMI an inexpensive fish product
SURLY	*adj* -LIER, -LIEST sullenly rude **SURLILY** *adv*
SURMISE	*v* -MISED, -MISING, -MISES to infer with little evidence
SURMISER	*n* pl. -S one that surmises
SURMOUNT	*v* -ED, -ING, -S to get over or across
SURNAME	*v* -NAMED, -NAMING, -NAMES to give a family name to
SURNAMER	*n* pl. -S one that surnames
SURPASS	*v* -ED, -ING, -ES to go beyond
SURPLICE	*n* pl. -S a loose-fitting vestment
SURPLUS	*n* pl. -ES an excess
SURPRINT	*v* -ED, -ING, -S to print over something already printed
SURPRISE	*v* -PRISED, -PRISING, -PRISES to come upon unexpectedly
SURPRIZE	*v* -PRIZED, -PRIZING, -PRIZES to surprise
SURRA	*n* pl. -S a disease of domestic animals
SURREAL	*adj* having dreamlike qualities
SURREY	*n* pl. -REYS a light carriage
SURROUND	*v* -ED, -ING, -S to extend completely around
SURROYAL	*n* pl. -S the topmost prong of a stag's antler
SURTAX	*v* -ED, -ING, -ES to assess with an extra tax
SURTOUT	*n* pl. -S a close-fitting overcoat
SURVEIL	*v* -VEILLED, -VEILLING, -VEILS to watch closely
SURVEY	*v* -ED, -ING, -S to determine the boundaries, area, or elevations of by measuring angles and distances
SURVEYOR	*n* pl. -S one that surveys land
SURVIVAL	*n* pl. -S a living or continuing longer than another person or thing
SURVIVE	*v* -VIVED, -VIVING, -VIVES to remain in existence
SURVIVER	*n* pl. -S survivor
SURVIVOR	*n* pl. -S one that survives
SUSHI	*n* pl. -S a dish of cold rice cakes topped with strips of raw fish
SUSLIK	*n* pl. -S a Eurasian rodent
SUSPECT	*v* -ED, -ING, -S to think guilty on slight evidence
SUSPEND	*v* -ED, -ING, -S to cause to stop for a period
SUSPENSE	*n* pl. -S a state of mental uncertainty or excitement
SUSPIRE	*v* -PIRED, -PIRING, -PIRES to sigh
SUSS	*v* -ED, -ING, -ES to figure out
SUSTAIN	*v* -ED, -ING, -S to maintain by providing with food and drink
SUSURRUS	*n* pl. -ES a soft rustling sound
SUTLER	*n* pl. -S one that peddles goods to soldiers
SUTRA	*n* pl. -S a Hindu aphorism
SUTTA	*n* pl. -S sutra
SUTTEE	*n* pl. -S a Hindu widow cremated on her husband's funeral pile to show her devotion to him
SUTURAL	*adj* pertaining to the line of junction between two bones
SUTURE	*v* -TURED, -TURING, -TURES to unite by sewing
SUZERAIN	*n* pl. -S a feudal lord
SVARAJ	*n* pl. -ES swaraj
SVEDBERG	*n* pl. -S a unit of time
SVELTE	*adj* SVELTER, SVELTEST gracefully slender **SVELTELY** *adv*
SWAB	*v* SWABBED, SWABBING, SWABS to clean with a large mop
SWABBER	*n* pl. -S one that swabs
SWABBIE	*n* pl. -S a sailor
SWABBING	present participle of swab
SWABBY	*n* pl. -BIES swabbie
SWACKED	*adj* drunk
SWADDLE	*v* -DLED, -DLING, -DLES to wrap in bandages
SWAG	*v* SWAGGED, SWAGGING, SWAGS to sway
SWAGE	*v* SWAGED, SWAGING, SWAGES to shape with a hammering tool
SWAGER	*n* pl. -S one that swages
SWAGGED	past tense of swag
SWAGGER	*v* -ED, -ING, -S to walk with a pompous air
SWAGGIE	*n* pl. -S a swagman
SWAGGING	present participle of swag
SWAGING	present participle of swage
SWAGMAN	*n* pl. -MEN a hobo
SWAIL	*n* pl. -S swale

SWAIN	*n* pl. -S a country boy **SWAINISH** *adj*
SWALE	*n* pl. -S a tract of low, marshy ground
SWALLOW	*v* -ED, -ING, -S to take through the mouth and esophagus into the stomach
SWAM	past tense of swim
SWAMI	*n* pl. -S a Hindu religious teacher
SWAMIES	pl. of swamy
SWAMP	*v* -ED, -ING, -S to inundate
SWAMPER	*n* pl. -S one that lives in a swampy area
SWAMPISH	*adj* swampy
SWAMPY	*adj* SWAMPIER, SWAMPIEST marshy
SWAMY	*n* pl. -MIES swami
SWAN	*v* SWANNED, SWANNING, SWANS to swear
SWANG	a past tense of swing
SWANHERD	*n* pl. -S one who tends swans (large aquatic birds)
SWANK	*adj* SWANKER, SWANKEST imposingly elegant
SWANK	*v* -ED, -ING, -S to swagger
SWANKY	*adj* SWANKIER, SWANKIEST swank **SWANKILY** *adv*
SWANLIKE	*adj* resembling a swan
SWANNED	past tense of swan
SWANNERY	*n* pl. -NERIES a place where swans are raised
SWANNING	present participle of swan
SWANPAN	*n* pl. -S a Chinese abacus
SWANSKIN	*n* pl. -S the skin of a swan
SWAP	*v* SWAPPED, SWAPPING, SWAPS to trade
SWAPPER	*n* pl. -S one that swaps
SWARAJ	*n* pl. -ES self-government in British India
SWARD	*v* -ED, -ING, -S to cover with turf
SWARE	a past tense of swear
SWARF	*n* pl. -S material removed by a cutting tool
SWARM	*v* -ED, -ING, -S to move in a large group
SWARMER	*n* pl. -S one that swarms
SWART	*adj* swarthy
SWARTH	*n* pl. -S turf
SWARTHY	*adj* -THIER, -THIEST having a dark complexion
SWARTY	*adj* swarthy
SWASH	*v* -ED, -ING, -ES to swagger
SWASHER	*n* pl. -S one that swashes
SWASTICA	*n* pl. -S swastika

SWASTIKA	*n* pl. -S a geometrical figure used as a symbol or ornament
SWAT	*v* SWATTED, SWATTING, SWATS to hit sharply
SWATCH	*n* pl. -ES a sample piece of cloth
SWATH	*n* pl. -S a row of cut grass or grain
SWATHE	*v* SWATHED, SWATHING, SWATHES to wrap in bandages
SWATHER	*n* pl. -S one that swathes
SWATTED	past tense of swat
SWATTER	*n* pl. -S one that swats
SWATTING	present participle of swat
SWAY	*v* -ED, -ING, -S to move slowly back and forth **SWAYABLE** *adj*
SWAYBACK	*n* pl. -S an abnormal sagging of the back
SWAYER	*n* pl. -S one that sways
SWAYFUL	*adj* capable of influencing
SWEAR	*v* SWORE or SWARE, SWORN, SWEARING, SWEARS to utter a solemn oath
SWEARER	*n* pl. -S one that swears
SWEAT	*v* -ED, -ING, -S to perspire
SWEATBOX	*n* pl. -ES a small enclosure in which one is made to sweat
SWEATER	*n* pl. -S a knitted outer garment
SWEATY	*adj* SWEATIER, SWEATIEST covered with perspiration **SWEATILY** *adv*
SWEDE	*n* pl. -S a rutabaga
SWEENY	*n* pl. -NIES atrophy of the shoulder muscles in horses
SWEEP	*v* SWEPT, SWEEPING, SWEEPS to clear or clean with a brush or broom
SWEEPER	*n* pl. -S one that sweeps
SWEEPING	*n* pl. -S the act of one that sweeps
SWEEPY	*adj* SWEEPIER, SWEEPIEST of wide range or scope
SWEER	*adj* lazy
SWEET	*adj* SWEETER, SWEETEST pleasing to the taste
SWEET	*n* pl. -S something that is sweet
SWEETEN	*v* -ED, -ING, -S to make sweet
SWEETIE	*n* pl. -S darling
SWEETING	*n* pl. -S a sweet apple
SWEETISH	*adj* somewhat sweet
SWEETLY	*adv* in a sweet manner

SWEETSOP   *n* pl. -S a tropical tree

SWELL   *v* SWELLED, SWOLLEN, SWELLING, SWELLS to increase in size or volume

SWELL   *adj* SWELLER, SWELLEST stylish

SWELLING   *n* pl. -S something that is swollen

SWELTER   *v* -ED, -ING, -S to suffer from oppressive heat

SWELTRY   *adj* -TRIER, -TRIEST oppressively hot

SWEPT   past tense of sweep

SWERVE   *v* SWERVED, SWERVING, SWERVES to turn aside suddenly from a straight course

SWERVER   *n* pl. -S one that swerves

SWEVEN   *n* pl. -S a dream or vision

SWIDDEN   *n* pl. -S an agricultural plot produced by burning off the vegetative cover

SWIFT   *adj* SWIFTER, SWIFTEST moving with a great rate of motion

SWIFT   *n* pl. -S a fast-flying bird

SWIFTER   *n* pl. -S a rope on a ship

SWIFTLET   *n* pl. -S a cave-dwelling swift

SWIFTLY   *adv* in a swift manner

SWIG   *v* SWIGGED, SWIGGING, SWIGS to drink deeply or rapidly

SWIGGER   *n* pl. -S one that swigs

SWILL   *v* -ED, -ING, -S to swig

SWILLER   *n* pl. -S one that swills

SWIM   *v* SWAM, SWUM, SWIMMING, SWIMS to propel oneself in water by natural means

SWIMMER   *n* pl. -S one that swims

SWIMMING   *n* pl. -S the act of one that swims

SWIMMY   *adj* -MIER, -MIEST dizzy **SWIMMILY** *adv*

SWIMSUIT   *n* pl. -S a bathing suit

SWIMWEAR   *n* pl. -S garments made for swimming

SWINDLE   *v* -DLED, -DLING, -DLES to take money or property from by fraudulent means

SWINDLER   *n* pl. -S one that swindles

SWINE   *n* pl. SWINE a domestic pig

SWINEPOX   *n* pl. -ES a disease of swine

SWING   *v* SWUNG or SWANG, SWINGING, SWINGS to move freely back and forth

SWINGBY   *n* pl. -BYS a mission in which a spacecraft uses a planet's gravitational pull for making course changes

SWINGE   *v* SWINGED, SWINGEING, SWINGES to flog

SWINGER   *n* pl. -S one that swings

SWINGIER   comparative of swingy

SWINGIEST   superlative of swingy

SWINGING   *adj* -INGEST lively and hip

SWINGING   *n* pl. -S the practice of swapping sex partners

SWINGLE   *v* -GLED, -GLING, -GLES to scutch

SWINGMAN   *n* pl. -MEN a basketball player who can play guard or forward

SWINGY   *adj* SWINGIER, SWINGIEST marked by swinging

SWINISH   *adj* resembling or befitting swine

SWINK   *v* -ED, -ING, -S to toil

SWINNEY   *n* pl. -NEYS sweeny

SWIPE   *v* SWIPED, SWIPING, SWIPES to strike with a sweeping blow

SWIPLE   *n* pl. -S a part of a threshing device

SWIPPLE   *n* pl. -S swiple

SWIRL   *v* -ED, -ING, -S to move with a whirling motion

SWIRLY   *adj* SWIRLIER, SWIRLIEST swirling

SWISH   *v* -ED, -ING, -ES to move with a prolonged hissing sound

SWISHER   *n* pl. -S one that swishes

SWISHY   *adj* SWISHIER, SWISHIEST swishing

SWISS   *n* pl. -ES a cotton fabric

SWITCH   *v* -ED, -ING, -ES to beat with a flexible rod

SWITCHER   *n* pl. -S one that switches

SWITH   *adv* quickly

SWITHE   *adv* swith

SWITHER   *v* -ED, -ING, -S to doubt

SWITHLY   *adv* swith

SWIVE   *v* SWIVED, SWIVING, SWIVES to copulate with

SWIVEL   *v* -ELED, -ELING, -ELS or -ELLED, -ELLING, -ELS to turn on a pivoted support

SWIVET   *n* pl. -S a state of nervous excitement

SWIVING   present participle of swive

SWIZZLE   *v* -ZLED, -ZLING, -ZLES to drink excessively

SWIZZLER   *n* pl. -S one that swizzles

SWOB   *v* SWOBBED, SWOBBING, SWOBS to swab

SWOBBER   *n* pl. -S swabber

SWOLLEN   past participle of swell

SWOON   *v* -ED, -ING, -S to faint

SWOONER   *n* pl. -S one that swoons

SWOOP   *v* -ED, -ING, -S to make a sudden descent

SWOOPER   *n* pl. -S one that swoops

SWOOSH   *v* -ED, -ING, -ES to move with a rustling sound

SWOP   *v* SWOPPED, SWOPPING, SWOPS to swap

SWORD   *n* pl. -S a weapon having a long blade for cutting or thrusting

SWORDMAN   *n* pl. -MEN one skilled in the use of a sword

SWORE   a past tense of swear

SWORN   past participle of swear

SWOT   *v* SWOTTED, SWOTTING, SWOTS to swat

SWOTTER   *n* pl. -S one that swots

SWOUN   *v* -ED, -ING, -S to swoon

SWOUND   *v* -ED, -ING, -S to swoon

SWUM   past participle of swim

SWUNG   a past tense of swing

SYBARITE   *n* pl. -S a person devoted to pleasure and luxury

SYBO   *n* pl. -BOES the cibol

SYCAMINE   *n* pl. -S the mulberry tree

SYCAMORE   *n* pl. -S a North American tree

SYCE   *n* pl. -S a male servant in India

SYCEE   *n* pl. -S fine uncoined silver formerly used in China as money

SYCOMORE   *n* pl. -S sycamore

SYCONIUM   *n* pl. -NIA a fleshy multiple fruit

SYCOSIS   *n* pl. -COSES an inflammatory disease of the hair follicles

SYENITE   *n* pl. -S an igneous rock **SYENITIC** *adj*

SYKE   *n* pl. -S a small stream

SYLI   *n* pl. -S a former monetary unit of Guinea

SYLLABI   a pl. of syllabus

SYLLABIC   *n* pl. -S a speech sound of high sonority

SYLLABLE   *v* -BLED, -BLING, -BLES to pronounce syllables (units of spoken language)

SYLLABUB   *n* pl. -S sillabub

SYLLABUS   *n* pl. -BI or -BUSES an outline of a course of study

SYLPH   *n* pl. -S a slender, graceful girl or woman **SYLPHIC, SYLPHISH, SYLPHY** *adj*

SYLPHID   *n* pl. -S a young sylph

SYLVA   *n* pl. -VAS or -VAE the forest trees of an area

SYLVAN   *n* pl. -S one that lives in a forest

SYLVATIC   *adj* pertaining to a forest

SYLVIN   *n* pl. -S sylvite

SYLVINE   *n* pl. -S sylvite

SYLVITE   *n* pl. -S an ore of potassium

SYMBION   *n* pl. -S symbiont

SYMBIONT   *n* pl. -S an organism living in close association with another

SYMBIOT   *n* pl. -S symbiont

SYMBIOTE   *n* pl. -S symbiont

SYMBOL   *v* -BOLED, -BOLING, -BOLS or -BOLLED, -BOLLING, -BOLS to serve as a symbol (a representation) of

SYMBOLIC   *adj* pertaining to a symbol

SYMMETRY   *n* pl. -TRIES an exact correspondence between the opposite halves of a figure

SYMPATHY   *n* pl. -THIES a feeling of compassion for another's suffering

SYMPATRY   *n* pl. -RIES the state of occupying the same area without loss of identity from interbreeding

SYMPHONY   *n* pl. -NIES an orchestral composition

SYMPODIA   *n/pl* plant stems made up of a series of superposed branches

SYMPOSIA   *n/pl* conferences for the purpose of discussion

SYMPTOM   *n* pl. -S an indication of something

SYN   *adv* syne

SYNAGOG   *n* pl. -S a building for Jewish worship

SYNANON   *n* pl. -S a method of group therapy for drug addicts

SYNAPSE   *v* -APSED, -APSING, -APSES to come together in synapsis

SYNAPSID   *n* pl. -S one of a group of extinct reptiles

SYNAPSIS   *n* pl. -APSES the point at which a nervous impulse passes from one neuron to another **SYNAPTIC** *adj*

SYNC   *v* -ED, -ING, -S to cause to operate in unison

SYNCARP   *n* pl. -S a fleshy multiple fruit

SYNCARPY *n* pl. -PIES the state of being a syncarp

SYNCH *v* -ED, -ING, -S to sync

SYNCHRO *n* pl. -CHROS a selsyn

SYNCLINE *n* pl. -S a type of rock formation

SYNCOM *n* pl. -S a type of communications satellite

SYNCOPE *n* pl. -S the contraction of a word by omitting one or more sounds from the middle **SYNCOPAL, SYNCOPIC** *adj*

SYNCYTIA *n/pl* masses of protoplasm resulting from cell fusion

SYNDESIS *n* pl. -DESES or -DESISES synapsis

SYNDET *n* pl. -S a synthetic detergent

SYNDETIC *adj* serving to connect

SYNDIC *n* pl. -S a business agent **SYNDICAL** *adj*

SYNDROME *n* pl. -S a group of symptoms that characterize a particular disorder

SYNE *adv* since

SYNECTIC *adj* pertaining to a system of problem solving

SYNERGIA *n* pl. -S synergy

SYNERGID *n* pl. -S a cell found in the embryo sac of a seed plant

SYNERGY *n* pl. -GIES combined action **SYNERGIC** *adj*

SYNESIS *n* pl. -SISES a type of grammatical construction

SYNFUEL *n* pl. -S a fuel derived from fossil fuels

SYNGAMY *n* pl. -MIES the union of two gametes **SYNGAMIC** *adj*

SYNGAS *n* pl. -GASES or -GASSES a mixture of carbon monoxide and hydrogen used in chemical synthesis

SYNOD *n* pl. -S a church council **SYNODAL, SYNODIC** *adj*

SYNONYM *n* pl. -S a word having the same meaning as another

SYNONYME *n* pl. -S synonym

SYNONYMY *n* pl. -MIES equivalence of meaning

SYNOPSIS *n* pl. -OPSES a summary **SYNOPTIC** *adj*

SYNOVIA *n* pl. -S a lubricating fluid secreted by certain membranes **SYNOVIAL** *adj*

SYNTAGMA *n* pl. -MAS or -MATA a syntactic element

SYNTAX *n* pl. -ES the way in which words are put together to form phrases and sentences

SYNTH *n* pl. -S a synthesizer

SYNTONY *n* pl. -NIES the tuning of transmitters and receivers with each other **SYNTONIC** *adj*

SYNURA *n* pl. -RAE any of a genus of protozoa

SYPH *n* pl. -S syphilis

SYPHER *v* -ED, -ING, -S to overlap so as to make an even surface, as beveled plank edges

SYPHILIS *n* pl. -LISES a venereal disease

SYPHON *v* -ED, -ING, -S to siphon

SYREN *n* pl. -S siren

SYRINGA *n* pl. -S an ornamental shrub

SYRINGE *v* -RINGED, -RINGING, -RINGES to cleanse or treat with injected fluid

SYRINX *n* pl. -INGES or -INXES the vocal organ of a bird

SYRPHIAN *n* pl. -S syrphid

SYRPHID *n* pl. -S a winged insect

SYRUP *n* pl. -S a thick, sweet liquid **SYRUPY** *adj*

SYSOP *n* pl. -S the administrator of a computer bulletin board

SYSTEM *n* pl. -S a group of interacting elements forming a unified whole

SYSTEMIC *n* pl. -S a type of pesticide

SYSTOLE *n* pl. -S the normal rhythmic contraction of the heart **SYSTOLIC** *adj*

SYZYGY *n* pl. -GIES the configuration of the earth, moon, and sun lying in a straight line **SYZYGAL, SYZYGIAL** *adj*

TA *n* pl. -S an expression of gratitude

TAB *v* TABBED, TABBING, TABS to name or designate

TABANID *n* pl. -S a bloodsucking insect

TABARD *n* pl. -S a sleeveless outer garment **TABARDED** *adj*

TABARET *n* pl. -S a silk fabric

TABBED past tense of tab

TABBIED past tense of tabby

TABBIES present 3d person sing. of tabby

TABBING present participle of tab

TABBIS *n* pl. -BISES a silk fabric

TABBY *v* -BIED, -BYING, -BIES to give a wavy appearance to

TABER *v* -ED, -ING, -S to tabor

TABES *n* pl. TABES a syphilitic disease

TABETIC *n* pl. -S one affected with tabes

TABID *adj* affected with tabes

TABLA *n* pl. -S a small drum

TABLE *v* -BLED, -BLING, -BLES to place on a table (a piece of furniture having a flat upper surface)

TABLEAU *n* pl. -LEAUX or -LEAUS a picture

TABLEFUL *n* pl. TABLEFULS or TABLESFUL as much as a table can hold

TABLET *v* -LETED, -LETING, -LETS or -LETTED, -LETTING, -LETS to inscribe on a small, flat surface

TABLETOP *n* pl. -S the top of a table

TABLING present participle of table

TABLOID *n* pl. -S a small newspaper

TABOO *v* -ED, -ING, -S to exclude from use, approach, or mention

TABOOLEY *n* pl. -LEYS tabouli

TABOR *v* -ED, -ING, -S to beat on a small drum

TABORER *n* pl. -S one that tabors

TABORET *n* pl. -S a small drum

TABORIN *n* pl. -S taborine

TABORINE *n* pl. -S a taboret

TABOULI *n* pl. -S a Lebanese salad containing bulgur wheat, tomatoes, parsley, onions, and mint

TABOUR *v* -ED, -ING, -S to tabor

TABOURER *n* pl. -S taborer

TABOURET *n* pl. -S taboret

TABU *v* -ED, -ING, -S to taboo

TABULAR *adj* of or pertaining to a list

TABULATE *v* -LATED, -LATING, -LATES to arrange in a list

TABULI *n* pl. -S tabouli

TABUN *n* pl. -S a chemical compound

TACE *n* pl. -S tasse

TACET *interj* be silent — used as a musical direction

TACH *n* pl. -S a device for indicating speed of rotation

TACHE *n* pl. -S a clasp or buckle

TACHINID *n* pl. -S a grayish fly

TACHISM *n* pl. -S action painting

TACHISME *n* pl. -S tachism

TACHIST *n* pl. -S an action painter

TACHISTE *n* pl. -S tachist

TACHYON *n* pl. -S a theoretical subatomic particle

TACIT *adj* unspoken **TACITLY** *adv*

TACITURN *adj* habitually silent

TACK *v* -ED, -ING, -S to fasten with tacks (short, sharp-pointed nails)

TACKER *n* pl. -S one that tacks

TACKET *n* pl. -S a hobnail

TACKEY *adj* TACKIER, TACKIEST tacky

TACKIER comparative of tacky

TACKIEST superlative of tacky

TACKIFY *v* -FIED, -FYING, -FIES to make tacky

TACKILY *adv* in a tacky manner

TACKLE *v* -LED, -LING, -LES to seize and throw to the ground

TACKLER *n* pl. -S one that tackles

TACKLESS *adj* having no tacks

TACKLING *n* pl. -S equipment

TACKY *adj* TACKIER, TACKIEST adhesive

TACNODE *n* pl. -S a point of contact between two curves

TACO *n* pl. -COS a tortilla folded around a filling

TACONITE *n* pl. -S a low-grade iron ore

TACT *n* pl. -S skill in dealing with delicate situations

TACTFUL *adj* having tact

TACTIC *n* pl. -S a maneuver for gaining an objective
TACTICAL *adj*

TACTILE *adj* pertaining to the sense of touch

TACTION *n* pl. -S the act of touching

TACTLESS *adj* lacking tact

TACTUAL *adj* tactile

TAD *n* pl. -S a small boy

TADPOLE *n* pl. -S the aquatic larva of an amphibian

TAE *prep* to

TAEL *n* pl. -S a Chinese unit of weight

TAENIA *n* pl. -NIAE or -NIAS a headband worn in ancient Greece

TAFFAREL *n* pl. -S taffrail

TAFFEREL *n* pl. -S taffrail

TAFFETA *n* pl. -S a lustrous fabric

TAFFIA *n* pl. -S tafia

TAFFRAIL *n* pl. -S a rail around the stern of a ship

TAFFY *n* pl. -FIES a chewy candy

TAFIA *n* pl. -S an inferior rum

TAG *v* TAGGED, TAGGING, TAGS to provide with a tag (an identifying marker)

TAGALONG *n* pl. -S one that follows another

TAGBOARD *n* pl. -S a material for making shipping tags

TAGGED past tense of tag

TAGGER *n* pl. -S one that tags

TAGGING present participle of tag

TAGLIKE *adj* resembling a tag

TAGMEME *n* pl. -S the smallest unit of meaningful grammatical relation

TAGMEMIC *adj* pertaining to a grammar in which a tagmeme is the basic unit

TAGRAG *n* pl. -S riffraff

TAHINI *n* pl. -S a paste of sesame seeds

TAHR *n* pl. -S a goatlike mammal

TAHSIL *n* pl. -S a district in India

TAIGA *n* pl. -S a subarctic evergreen forest

TAIGLACH *n* pl. TAIGLACH teiglach

TAIL *v* -ED, -ING, -S to provide with a tail (a hindmost part)

TAILBACK *n* pl. -S a member of the backfield in some football formations

TAILBONE *n* pl. -S the coccyx

TAILCOAT *n* pl. -S a man's coat

TAILER *n* pl. -S one that secretly follows another

TAILFAN *n* pl. -S a fanlike swimming organ at the rear of some crustaceans

TAILGATE *v* -GATED, -GATING, -GATES to drive dangerously close behind another vehicle

TAILING *n* pl. -S the part of a projecting stone or brick that is inserted into a wall

TAILLAMP *n* pl. -S a light at the rear of a vehicle

TAILLE *n* pl. -S a former French tax

TAILLESS *adj* having no tail

TAILLEUR *n* pl. -S a woman's tailored suit

TAILLIKE *adj* resembling a tail

TAILOR *v* -ED, -ING, -S to fit with clothes

TAILPIPE *n* pl. -S an exhaust pipe

TAILRACE *n* pl. -S a part of a millrace

TAILSKID *n* pl. -S a support on which the tail of an airplane rests

TAILSPIN *n* pl. -S the spiral descent of a stalled airplane

TAILWIND	*n* pl. -S a wind coming from behind a moving vehicle	**TALION**	*n* pl. -S a retaliation for a crime
TAIN	*n* pl. -S a thin plate	**TALIPED**	*n* pl. -S a person afflicted with clubfoot
TAINT	*v* -ED, -ING, -S to touch or affect slightly with something bad	**TALIPES**	*n* pl. TALIPES clubfoot
		TALIPOT	*n* pl. -S a tall palm tree
TAIPAN	*n* pl. -S a venomous snake	**TALISMAN**	*n* pl. -S an object believed to possess magical powers
TAJ	*n* pl. -ES a tall, conical cap worn in Muslim countries	**TALK**	*v* -ED, -ING, -S to communicate by speaking
TAKA	*n* pl. TAKA a monetary unit of Bangladesh	**TALKABLE**	*adj* able to be talked about
TAKAHE	*n* pl. -S a flightless bird	**TALKER**	*n* pl. -S one that talks
TAKE	*v* TOOK, TAKEN, TAKING, TAKES to get possession of **TAKABLE, TAKEABLE** *adj*	**TALKIE**	*n* pl. -S a moving picture with synchronized sound
TAKEAWAY	*adj* designating prepared food that is sold for consumption elsewhere	**TALKING**	*n* pl. -S conversation
		TALKY	*adj* TALKIER, TALKIEST tending to talk a great deal
TAKEDOWN	*n* pl. -S an article that can be taken apart easily	**TALL**	*adj* TALLER, TALLEST having great height
TAKEOFF	*n* pl. -S the act of rising in flight	**TALLAGE**	*v* -LAGED, -LAGING, -LAGES to tax
TAKEOUT	*n* pl. -S the act of removing	**TALLAISIM**	a pl. of tallith
TAKEOVER	*n* pl. -S the act of assuming control	**TALLBOY**	*n* pl. -BOYS a highboy
		TALLIED	past tense of tally
TAKER	*n* pl. -S one that takes	**TALLIER**	*n* pl. -S one that tallies
TAKEUP	*n* pl. -S the act of taking something up	**TALLIES**	present 3d person sing. of tally
		TALLIS	*n* pl. -LISIM tallith
TAKIN	*n* pl. -S a goatlike mammal	**TALLISH**	*adj* somewhat tall
TAKING	*n* pl. -S a seizure	**TALLIT**	*n* pl. -LITIM tallith
TAKINGLY	*adv* in an attractive manner	**TALLITH**	*n* pl. TALLITHES, TALLITHIM, TALLITOTH, TALEYSIM, or TALLAISIM a Jewish prayer shawl
TALA	*n* pl. -S a traditional rhythmic pattern of music in India		
TALAPOIN	*n* pl. -S a small African monkey	**TALLNESS**	*n* pl. -ES the state of being tall
		TALLOL	*n* pl. -S a resinous liquid
TALAR	*n* pl. -S a long cloak	**TALLOW**	*v* -ED, -ING, -S to smear with tallow (a mixture of animal fats)
TALARIA	*n/pl* winged sandals worn by various figures of classical mythology		
		TALLOWY	*adj* resembling tallow
TALC	*v* TALCKED, TALCKING, TALCS or TALCED, TALCING, TALCS to treat with talc (a soft mineral with a soapy texture) **TALCKY, TALCOSE, TALCOUS** *adj*	**TALLY**	*v* -LIED, -LYING, -LIES to count
		TALLYHO	*v* -ED, -ING, -S to make an encouraging shout to hunting hounds
TALCUM	*n* pl. -S a powder made from talc	**TALLYMAN**	*n* pl. -MEN a person who tallies
TALE	*n* pl. -S a story	**TALMUDIC**	*adj* pertaining to the body of Jewish civil and religious law
TALENT	*n* pl. -S a special natural ability **TALENTED** *adj*	**TALON**	*n* pl. -S a claw of a bird of prey **TALONED** *adj*
TALER	*n* pl. -S a former German coin	**TALOOKA**	*n* pl. -S taluk
TALESMAN	*n* pl. -MEN a person summoned to fill a vacancy on a jury	**TALUK**	*n* pl. -S an estate in India
		TALUKA	*n* pl. -S taluk
		TALUS	*n* pl. -LI a bone of the foot
TALEYSIM	a pl. of tallith	**TALUS**	*n* pl. -ES a slope formed by an accumulation of rock debris
TALI	pl. of talus		

TAM	*n* pl. -S a tight-fitting Scottish cap
TAMABLE	*adj* capable of being tamed
TAMAL	*n* pl. -S tamale
TAMALE	*n* pl. -S a Mexican dish
TAMANDU	*n* pl. -S tamandua
TAMANDUA	*n* pl. -S an arboreal anteater
TAMARACK	*n* pl. -S a timber tree
TAMARAO	*n* pl. -RAOS tamarau
TAMARAU	*n* pl. -S a small buffalo of the Philippines
TAMARI	*n* pl. -S a Japanese soy sauce
TAMARIN	*n* pl. -S a South American monkey
TAMARIND	*n* pl. -S a tropical tree
TAMARISK	*n* pl. -S an evergreen shrub
TAMASHA	*n* pl. -S a public entertainment in India
TAMBAC	*n* pl. -S tombac
TAMBAK	*n* pl. -S tombac
TAMBALA	*n* pl. -S or MATAMBALA a monetary unit of Malawi
TAMBOUR	*v* -ED, -ING, -S to embroider on a round wooden frame
TAMBOURA	*n* pl. -S tambura
TAMBUR	*n* pl. -S tambura
TAMBURA	*n* pl. -S a stringed instrument
TAME	*adj* TAMER, TAMEST gentle or docile
TAME	*v* TAMED, TAMING, TAMES to make tame
TAMEABLE	*adj* tamable
TAMEIN	*n* pl. -S a garment worn by Burmese women
TAMELESS	*adj* not capable of being tamed
TAMELY	*adv* in a tame manner
TAMENESS	*n* pl. -ES the state of being tame
TAMER	*n* pl. -S one that tames
TAMEST	superlative of tame
TAMING	present participle of tame
TAMIS	*n* pl. -ISES a strainer made of cloth mesh
TAMMIE	*n* pl. -S tammy
TAMMY	*n* pl. -MIES a fabric of mixed fibers
TAMP	*v* -ED, -ING, -S to pack down by tapping
TAMPALA	*n* pl. -S an annual herb
TAMPAN	*n* pl. -S a biting insect
TAMPER	*v* -ED, -ING, -S to interfere in a harmful manner
TAMPERER	*n* pl. -S one that tampers
TAMPION	*n* pl. -S a plug for the muzzle of a cannon
TAMPON	*v* -ED, -ING, -S to plug with a cotton pad
TAN	*v* TANNED, TANNING, TANS to convert hide into leather by soaking in chemicals
TAN	*adj* TANNER, TANNEST brown from the sun's rays
TANAGER	*n* pl. -S a brightly colored bird
TANBARK	*n* pl. -S a tree bark used as a source of tannin
TANDEM	*n* pl. -S a bicycle built for two
TANDOOR	*n* pl. -DOORI a clay oven
TANG	*v* -ED, -ING, -S to provide with a pungent flavor
TANGELO	*n* pl. -LOS a citrus fruit
TANGENCE	*n* pl. -S tangency
TANGENCY	*n* pl. -CIES the state of being in immediate physical contact
TANGENT	*n* pl. -S a straight line in contact with a curve at one point
TANGIBLE	*n* pl. -S something palpable
TANGIBLY	*adv* palpably
TANGIER	comparative of tangy
TANGIEST	superlative of tangy
TANGLE	*v* -GLED, -GLING, -GLES to bring together in intricate confusion
TANGLER	*n* pl. -S one that tangles
TANGLY	*adj* -GLIER, -GLIEST tangled
TANGO	*v* -ED, -ING, -S to perform a Latin-American dance
TANGRAM	*n* pl. -S a Chinese puzzle
TANGY	*adj* TANGIER, TANGIEST pungent
TANIST	*n* pl. -S the heir apparent to a Celtic chief
TANISTRY	*n* pl. -RIES the system of electing a tanist
TANK	*v* -ED, -ING, -S to store in a tank (a container usually for liquids)
TANKA	*n* pl. -S a Japanese verse form
TANKAGE	*n* pl. -S the capacity of a tank
TANKARD	*n* pl. -S a tall drinking vessel
TANKER	*n* pl. -S a ship designed to transport liquids
TANKFUL	*n* pl. -S the amount a tank can hold
TANKLIKE	*adj* resembling a tank
TANKSHIP	*n* pl. -S a tanker
TANNABLE	*adj* capable of being tanned
TANNAGE	*n* pl. -S the process of tanning
TANNATE	*n* pl. -S a chemical salt
TANNED	past tense of tan

TANNER *n* pl. -S one that tans

TANNERY *n* pl. -NERIES a place where hides are tanned

TANNEST superlative of tan

TANNIC *adj* pertaining to tannin

TANNIN *n* pl. -S a chemical compound used in tanning

TANNING *n* pl. -S the process of converting hides into leather

TANNISH *adj* somewhat tan

TANREC *n* pl. -S tenrec

TANSY *n* pl. -SIES a perennial herb

TANTALUM *n* pl. -S a metallic element **TANTALIC** *adj*

TANTALUS *n* pl. -ES a case for wine bottles

TANTARA *n* pl. -S the sound of a trumpet or horn

TANTIVY *n* pl. -TIVIES a hunting cry

TANTO *adv* so much — used as a musical direction

TANTRA *n* pl. -S one of a class of Hindu religious writings **TANTRIC** *adj*

TANTRUM *n* pl. -S a fit of rage

TANUKI *n* pl. -S the fur of a raccoon dog

TANYARD *n* pl. -S the section of a tannery containing the vats

TAO *n* pl. -S the path of virtuous conduct according to a Chinese philosophy

TAP *v* TAPPED, TAPPING, TAPS to strike gently

TAPA *n* pl. -S a cloth made from tree bark

TAPADERA *n* pl. -S a part of a saddle

TAPADERO *n* pl. -ROS tapadera

TAPALO *n* pl. -LOS a scarf worn in Latin-American countries

TAPE *v* TAPED, TAPING, TAPES to fasten with tape (a long, narrow strip or band)

TAPELESS *adj* being without tape

TAPELIKE *adj* resembling tape

TAPELINE *n* pl. -S a tape for measuring distances

TAPER *v* -ED, -ING, -S to become gradually narrower toward one end

TAPERER *n* pl. -S one that carries a candle in a religious procession

TAPESTRY *v* -TRIED, -TRYING, -TRIES to decorate with woven wall hangings

TAPETUM *n* pl. -TA a layer of cells in some plants **TAPETAL** *adj*

TAPEWORM *n* pl. -S a parasitic worm

TAPHOLE *n* pl. -S a hole in a blast furnace

TAPHOUSE *n* pl. -S a tavern

TAPING present participle of tape

TAPIOCA *n* pl. -S a starchy food

TAPIR *n* pl. -S a hoofed mammal

TAPIS *n* pl. -PISES material used for wall hangings and floor coverings

TAPPED past tense of tap

TAPPER *n* pl. -S one that taps

TAPPET *n* pl. -S a sliding rod that causes another part of a mechanism to move

TAPPING *n* pl. -S the process or means by which something is tapped

TAPROOM *n* pl. -S a barroom

TAPROOT *n* pl. -S the main root of a plant

TAPSTER *n* pl. -S one that dispenses liquor in a barroom

TAR *v* TARRED, TARRING, TARS to cover with tar (a black viscous liquid)

TARAMA *n* pl. -S a Greek paste of fish roe, garlic, lemon juice, and olive oil

TARANTAS *n* pl. -ES a Russian carriage

TARBOOSH *n* pl. -ES a cap worn by Muslim men

TARBUSH *n* pl. -ES tarboosh

TARDIER comparative of tardy

TARDIES pl. of tardy

TARDO *adj* slow — used as a musical direction

TARDY *adj* TARDIER, TARDIEST late **TARDILY** *adv*

TARDY *n* pl. -DIES an instance of being late

TARDYON *n* pl. -S a subatomic particle that travels slower than the speed of light

TARE *v* TARED, TARING, TARES to determine the weight of a container holding goods

TARGE *n* pl. -S a small, round shield

TARGET *v* -ED, -ING, -S to make a goal of

TARIFF *v* -ED, -ING, -S to tax imported or exported goods

TARING present participle of tare

TARLATAN *n* pl. -S a cotton fabric

TARLETAN *n* pl. -S tarlatan

TARMAC   n pl. -S an asphalt road
TARN   n pl. -S a small mountain lake
TARNAL   adj damned **TARNALLY** adv
TARNISH   v -ED, -ING, -ES to dull the
               luster of
TARO   n pl. -ROS a tropical plant
TAROC   n pl. -S tarok
TAROK   n pl. -S a card game
TAROT   n pl. -S any of a set of playing
               cards used for fortune-telling
TARP   n pl. -S a protective canvas
               covering
TARPAN   n pl. -S an Asian wild horse
TARPAPER   n pl. -S a heavy paper coated
               with tar
TARPON   n pl. -S a marine game fish
TARRAGON   n pl. -S a perennial herb
TARRE   v TARRED, TARRING,
               TARRES to urge to action
TARRED   past tense of tar
TARRIED   past tense of tarry
TARRIER   n pl. -S one that tarries
TARRIES   present 3d person sing. of tarry
TARRIEST   superlative of tarry
TARRING   present participle of tar and
               tarre
TARRY   v -RIED, -RYING, -RIES to
               delay or be slow in acting or
               doing
TARRY   adj -RIER, -RIEST resembling
               tar
TARSAL   n pl. -S a bone of the foot
TARSI   pl. of tarsus
TARSIA   n pl. -S intarsia
TARSIER   n pl. -S a nocturnal primate
TARSUS   n pl. TARSI a part of the foot
TART   adj TARTER, TARTEST
               having a sharp, sour taste
TART   v -ED, -ING, -S to dress up
TARTAN   n pl. -S a patterned woolen
               fabric
TARTANA   n pl. -S a Mediterranean
               sailing vessel
TARTAR   n pl. -S a crust on the teeth
               TARTARIC adj
TARTISH   adj somewhat tart
TARTLET   n pl. -S a small pie
TARTLY   adv in a tart manner
TARTNESS   n pl. -ES the state of being tart
TARTRATE   n pl. -S a chemical salt
TARTUFE   n pl. -S tartuffe
TARTUFFE   n pl. -S a hypocrite
TARTY   adj resembling a prostitute
TARWEED   n pl. -S a flowering plant
TARZAN   n pl. -S a person of superior
               strength and agility

TASK   v -ED, -ING, -S to assign a job
               to
TASKWORK   n pl. -S hard work
TASS   n pl. -ES a drinking cup
TASSE   n pl. -S tasset
TASSEL   v -SELED, -SELING, -SELS or
               -SELLED, -SELLING, -SELS to
               adorn with dangling ornaments
TASSET   n pl. -S a piece of plate armor
               for the upper thigh
TASSIE   n pl. -S tass
TASTE   v TASTED, TASTING,
               TASTES to perceive the flavor
               of by taking into the mouth
               TASTABLE adj
TASTEFUL   adj tasty
TASTER   n pl. -S one that tastes
TASTING   present participle of taste
TASTY   adj TASTIER, TASTIEST
               pleasant to the taste **TASTILY**
               adv
TAT   v TATTED, TATTING, TATS
               to make tatting
TATAMI   n pl. -S straw matting used as
               a floor covering
TATAR   n pl. -S a ferocious person
TATE   n pl. -S a tuft of hair
TATER   n pl. -S a potato
TATOUAY   n pl. -AYS a South American
               armadillo
TATTED   past tense of tat
TATTER   v -ED, -ING, -S to become
               torn and worn
TATTIE   n pl. -S a potato
TATTIER   comparative of tatty
TATTIEST   superlative of tatty
TATTILY   adv in a tatty manner
TATTING   n pl. -S delicate handmade
               lace
TATTLE   v -TLED, -TLING, -TLES to
               reveal the activities of another
TATTLER   n pl. -S one that tattles
TATTOO   v -ED, -ING, -S to mark the
               skin with indelible pigments
TATTOOER   n pl. -S one that tattoos
TATTY   adj -TIER, -TIEST shabby
TAU   n pl. -S a Greek letter
TAUGHT   past tense of teach
TAUNT   v -ED, -ING, -S to challenge
               or reproach sarcastically
TAUNTER   n pl. -S one that taunts
TAUPE   n pl. -S a dark gray color
TAURINE   n pl. -S a chemical compound
TAUT   adj TAUTER, TAUTEST fully
               stretched, so as not to be slack

TAUT   *v* -ED, -ING, -S to tangle

TAUTAUG   *n* pl. -S tautog

TAUTEN   *v* -ED, -ING, -S to make taut

TAUTLY   *adv* in a taut manner

TAUTNESS   *n* pl. -ES the state of being taut

TAUTOG   *n* pl. -S a marine fish

TAUTOMER   *n* pl. -S a type of chemical compound

TAUTONYM   *n* pl. -S a type of taxonomic designation

TAV   *n* pl. -S a Hebrew letter

TAVERN   *n* pl. -S a place where liquor is sold to be drunk on the premises

TAVERNA   *n* pl. -S a cafe in Greece

TAVERNER   *n* pl. -S one that runs a tavern

TAW   *v* -ED, -ING, -S to convert into white leather by the application of minerals

TAWDRY   *adj* -DRIER, -DRIEST gaudy **TAWDRILY** *adv*

TAWDRY   *n* pl. -DRIES gaudy finery

TAWER   *n* pl. -S one that taws

TAWIE   *adj* docile

TAWNEY   *n* pl. -NEYS tawny

TAWNY   *adj* -NIER, -NIEST light brown **TAWNILY** *adv*

TAWNY   *n* pl. -NIES a light brown color

TAWPIE   *n* pl. -S a foolish young person

TAWSE   *v* TAWSED, TAWSING, TAWSES to flog

TAX   *v* -ED, -ING, -ES to place a tax (a charge imposed by authority for public purposes) on

TAXA   a pl. of taxon

TAXABLE   *adj* subject to tax **TAXABLY** *adv*

TAXABLE   *n* pl. -S a taxable item

TAXATION   *n* pl. -S the process of taxing

TAXEME   *n* pl. -S a minimum grammatical feature of selection **TAXEMIC** *adj*

TAXER   *n* pl. -S one that taxes

TAXI   *v* TAXIED, TAXIING or TAXYING, TAXIS or TAXIES to travel in a taxicab

TAXICAB   *n* pl. -S an automobile for hire

TAXIMAN   *n* pl. -MEN the operator of a taxicab

TAXINGLY   *adv* in an onerous manner

TAXITE   *n* pl. -S a volcanic rock **TAXITIC** *adj*

TAXIWAY   *n* pl. -WAYS a paved strip at an airport

TAXLESS   *adj* free from taxation

TAXMAN   *n* pl. -MEN one who collects taxes

TAXON   *n* pl. TAXA or TAXONS a unit of scientific classification

TAXONOMY   *n* pl. -MIES the study of scientific classification

TAXPAID   *adj* paid for by taxes

TAXPAYER   *n* pl. -S one that pays taxes

TAXUS   *n* pl. TAXUS an evergreen tree or shrub

TAXWISE   *adj* pertaining to taxes

TAXYING   a present participle of taxi

TAZZA   *n* pl. -ZAS or -ZE an ornamental bowl

TEA   *n* pl. -S a beverage made by infusing dried leaves in boiling water

TEABERRY   *n* pl. -RIES a North American shrub

TEABOARD   *n* pl. -S a tray for serving tea

TEABOWL   *n* pl. -S a teacup having no handle

TEABOX   *n* pl. -ES a box for tea leaves

TEACAKE   *n* pl. -S a small cake served with tea

TEACART   *n* pl. -S a wheeled table used in serving tea

TEACH   *v* TAUGHT, TEACHING, TEACHES to impart knowledge or skill to

TEACHER   *n* pl. -S one that teaches

TEACHING   *n* pl. -S a doctrine

TEACUP   *n* pl. -S a cup in which tea is served

TEAHOUSE   *n* pl. -S a public establishment serving tea

TEAK   *n* pl. -S an East Indian tree

TEAKWOOD   *n* pl. -S the wood of the teak

TEAL   *n* pl. -S a river duck

TEALIKE   *adj* resembling tea

TEAM   *v* -ED, -ING, -S to form a team (a group of persons associated in a joint action)

TEAMAKER   *n* pl. -S one that makes tea

TEAMMATE   *n* pl. -S a member of the same team

TEAMSTER   *n* pl. -S a truck driver

TEAMWORK   *n* pl. -S cooperative effort to achieve a common goal

TEAPOT   *n* pl. -S a vessel used in making and serving tea

TEAPOY   *n* pl. -POYS a small table used in serving tea

TEAR	*v* -ED, -ING, -S to emit tears (drops of saline liquid secreted by a gland of the eye)
TEAR	*v* TORE, TORN, TEARING, TEARS to pull apart or into pieces **TEARABLE** *adj*
TEARAWAY	*n* pl. -AWAYS a rebellious person
TEARDOWN	*n* pl. -S the process of disassembling
TEARDROP	*n* pl. -S a tear
TEARER	*n* pl. -S one that tears or rips
TEARFUL	*adj* full of tears
TEARGAS	*v* -GASSED, -GASSING, -GASES or -GASSES to subject to a gas that irritates the eyes
TEARIER	comparative of teary
TEARIEST	superlative of teary
TEARILY	*adv* in a teary manner
TEARLESS	*adj* being without tears
TEAROOM	*n* pl. -S a restaurant serving tea
TEARY	*adj* TEARIER, TEARIEST tearful
TEASE	*v* TEASED, TEASING, TEASES to make fun of
TEASEL	*v* -SELED, -SELING, -SELS or -SELLED, -SELLING, -SELS to raise a soft surface on fabric with a bristly flower head
TEASELER	*n* pl. -S one that teasels
TEASER	*n* pl. -S one that teases
TEASHOP	*n* pl. -S a tearoom
TEASING	present participle of tease
TEASPOON	*n* pl. -S a small spoon
TEAT	*n* pl. -S a mammary gland **TEATED** *adj*
TEATIME	*n* pl. -S the customary time for tea
TEAWARE	*n* pl. -S a tea service
TEAZEL	*v* -ZELED, -ZELING, -ZELS or -ZELLED, -ZELLING, -ZELS to teasel
TEAZLE	*v* -ZLED, -ZLING, -ZLES to teasel
TECHED	*adj* crazy
TECHIE	*n* pl. -S a technician
TECHNIC	*n* pl. -S technique
TECHY	*adj* TECHIER, TECHIEST tetchy **TECHILY** *adv*
TECTA	pl. of tectum
TECTAL	*adj* pertaining to a tectum
TECTITE	*n* pl. -S tektite
TECTONIC	*adj* pertaining to construction
TECTRIX	*n* pl. -TRICES a small feather of a bird's wing
TECTUM	*n* pl. -TA a bodily structure resembling or serving as a roof
TED	*v* TEDDED, TEDDING, TEDS to spread for drying
TEDDER	*n* pl. -S one that teds
TEDDY	*n* pl. -DIES a woman's undergarment
TEDIOUS	*adj* causing weariness
TEDIUM	*n* pl. -S the state of being tedious
TEE	*v* TEED, TEEING, TEES to place a golf ball on a small peg
TEEL	*n* pl. -S sesame
TEEM	*v* -ED, -ING, -S to be full to overflowing
TEEMER	*n* pl. -S one that teems
TEEN	*n* pl. -S a teenager
TEENAGE	*adj* pertaining to teenagers
TEENAGED	*adj* teenage
TEENAGER	*n* pl. -S a person between the ages of thirteen and nineteen
TEENER	*n* pl. -S a teenager
TEENFUL	*adj* filled with grief
TEENIER	comparative of teeny
TEENIEST	superlative of teeny
TEENSY	*adj* -SIER, -SIEST tiny
TEENTSY	*adj* -SIER, -SIEST tiny
TEENY	*adj* -NIER, -NIEST tiny
TEENYBOP	*adj* pertaining to a young teenager
TEEPEE	*n* pl. -S tepee
TEETER	*v* -ED, -ING, -S to move unsteadily
TEETH	pl. of tooth
TEETHE	*v* TEETHED, TEETHING, TEETHES to cut teeth
TEETHER	*n* pl. -S an object for a baby to bite on during teething
TEETHING	*n* pl. -S the first growth of teeth
TEETOTAL	*v* -TALED, -TALING, -TALS or -TALLED, -TALLING, -TALS to abstain completely from alcoholic beverages
TEETOTUM	*n* pl. -S a spinning toy
TEFF	*n* pl. -S a cereal grass
TEFILLIN	*n/pl* the phylacteries worn by Jews
TEG	*n* pl. -S a yearling sheep
TEGMEN	*n* pl. -MINA a covering
TEGMENTA	*n/pl* anatomical coverings
TEGMINAL	*adj* pertaining to a tegmen
TEGUA	*n* pl. -S a type of moccasin
TEGULAR	*adj* resembling a tile

TEGUMEN *n* pl. -MINA tegmen

TEGUMENT *n* pl. -S a covering

TEIGLACH *n* pl. TEIGLACH a confection consisting of balls of dough boiled in honey

TEIID *n* pl. -S a tropical American lizard

TEIND *n* pl. -S a tithe

TEKTITE *n* pl. -S a glassy body believed to be of meteoritic origin **TEKTITIC** *adj*

TEL *n* pl. -S an ancient mound in the Middle East

TELA *n* pl. -LAE an anatomical tissue

TELAMON *n* pl. -ES a male figure used as a supporting column

TELE *n* pl. -S a television set

TELECAST *v* -ED, -ING, -S to broadcast by television

TELEDU *n* pl. -S a carnivorous mammal

TELEFILM *n* pl. -S a motion picture made for television

TELEGA *n* pl. -S a Russian wagon

TELEGONY *n* pl. -NIES the supposed influence of a previous sire on the offspring of later matings of the mother with other males

TELEGRAM *v* -GRAMMED, -GRAMMING, -GRAMS to send a message by telegraph

TELEMAN *n* pl. -MEN a naval officer

TELEMARK *n* pl. -S a type of turn in skiing

TELEOST *n* pl. -S a bony fish

TELEPATH *n* pl. -S one who can communicate with another by some means other than the senses

TELEPLAY *n* pl. -PLAYS a play written for television

TELEPORT *v* -ED, -ING, -S to transport by a process that involves no physical means

TELERAN *n* pl. -S a system of air navigation

TELESIS *n* pl. TELESES planned progress

TELESTIC *n* pl. -S a type of acrostic

TELETEXT *n* pl. -S a communications system in which printed matter is telecast to subscribers

TELETHON *n* pl. -S a fund-raising television program

TELEVIEW *v* -ED, -ING, -S to observe by means of television

TELEVISE *v* -VISED, -VISING, -VISES to broadcast by television (an electronic system of transmitting images and sound)

TELEX *v* -ED, -ING, -ES to send a message by a type of telegraphic system

TELFER *v* -ED, -ING, -S to telpher

TELFORD *n* pl. -S a road made of stones

TELIA pl. of telium

TELIAL *adj* pertaining to a telium

TELIC *adj* directed toward a goal

TELIUM *n* pl. -LIA a sorus on the host plant of a rust fungus

TELL *v* TOLD, TELLING, TELLS to give a detailed account of **TELLABLE** *adj*

TELLER *n* pl. -S a bank employee who receives and pays out money

TELLIES pl. of telly

TELLTALE *n* pl. -S a tattler

TELLURIC *adj* pertaining to the earth

TELLY *n* pl. -LIES or -LYS a television set

TELOME *n* pl. -S a structural unit of a vascular plant **TELOMIC** *adj*

TELOMERE *n* pl. -S the natural end of a chromosome

TELOS *n* pl. TELOI an ultimate end

TELPHER *v* -ED, -ING, -S to transport by a system of aerial cable cars

TELSON *n* pl. -S the terminal segment of an arthropod **TELSONIC** *adj*

TEMBLOR *n* pl. -S or -ES an earthquake

TEMERITY *n* pl. -TIES foolish boldness

TEMP *n* pl. -S a temporary worker

TEMPEH *n* pl. -S an Asian food

TEMPER *v* -ED, -ING, -S to moderate by adding a counterbalancing agent

TEMPERA *n* pl. -S a technique of painting

TEMPERER *n* pl. -S one that tempers

TEMPEST *v* -ED, -ING, -S to agitate violently

TEMPI a pl. of tempo

TEMPLAR *n* pl. -S a lawyer or student of law in London

TEMPLATE *n* pl. -S a pattern used as a guide in making something

TEMPLE *n* pl. -S a house of worship **TEMPLED** *adj*

TEMPLET *n* pl. -S template

TEMPO *n* pl. -PI or -POS the rate of speed of a musical piece

TEMPORAL *n* pl. -S a bone of the skull

TEMPT *v* -ED, -ING, -S to entice to commit an unwise or immoral act

TEMPTER *n* pl. -S one that tempts

TEMPURA *n* pl. -S a Japanese dish

TEN *n* pl. -S a number

TENABLE *adj* capable of being held **TENABLY** *adv*

TENACE *n* pl. -S a combination of two high cards in some card games

TENACITY *n* pl. -TIES perseverance or persistence

TENACULA *n/pl* hooked surgical instruments

TENAIL *n* pl. -S tenaille

TENAILLE *n* pl. -S an outer defense

TENANCY *n* pl. -CIES the temporary occupancy of something that belongs to another

TENANT *v* -ED, -ING, -S to inhabit

TENANTRY *n* pl. -RIES tenancy

TENCH *n* pl. -ES a freshwater fish

TEND *v* -ED, -ING, -S to be disposed or inclined

TENDANCE *n* pl. -S watchful care

TENDENCE *n* pl. -S tendance

TENDENCY *n* pl. -CIES an inclination to act or think in a particular way

TENDER *adj* -DERER, -DEREST soft or delicate

TENDER *v* -ED, -ING, -S to present for acceptance

TENDERER *n* pl. -S one that tenders

TENDERLY *adv* in a tender manner

TENDON *n* pl. -S a band of tough, fibrous tissue

TENDRIL *n* pl. -S a leafless organ of climbing plants

TENEBRAE *n/pl* a religious service

TENEMENT *n* pl. -S an apartment house

TENESMUS *n* pl. -ES an urgent but ineffectual effort to defecate or urinate **TENESMIC** *adj*

TENET *n* pl. -S a principle, belief, or doctrine held to be true

TENFOLD *n* pl. -S an amount ten times as great as a given unit

TENIA *n* pl. -NIAE or -NIAS a tapeworm

TENIASIS *n* pl. -SISES infestation with tapeworms

TENNER *n* pl. -S a ten-dollar bill

TENNIES *n/pl* low-cut sneakers

TENNIS *n* pl. -NISES an outdoor ball game

TENNIST *n* pl. -S a tennis player

TENON *v* -ED, -ING, -S to unite by means of a tenon (a projection on the end of a piece of wood)

TENONER *n* pl. -S one that tenons

TENOR *n* pl. -S a high male singing voice

TENORIST *n* pl. -S one who sings tenor or plays a tenor instrument

TENORITE *n* pl. -S a mineral

TENOTOMY *n* pl. -MIES the surgical division of a tendon

TENOUR *n* pl. -S tenor

TENPENCE *n* pl. -S the sum of ten pennies

TENPENNY *adj* worth tenpence

TENPIN *n* pl. -S a bowling pin

TENREC *n* pl. -S a mammal that feeds on insects

TENSE *adj* TENSER, TENSEST taut **TENSELY** *adv*

TENSE *v* TENSED, TENSING, TENSES to make tense

TENSIBLE *adj* capable of being stretched **TENSIBLY** *adv*

TENSILE *adj* tensible

TENSING present participle of tense

TENSION *v* -ED, -ING, -S to make tense

TENSITY *n* pl. -TIES the state of being tense

TENSIVE *adj* causing tensity

TENSOR *n* pl. -S a muscle that stretches a body part

TENT *v* -ED, -ING, -S to live in a tent (a type of portable shelter)

TENTACLE *n* pl. -S an elongated, flexible appendage of some animals

TENTAGE *n* pl. -S a supply of tents

TENTER *v* -ED, -ING, -S to stretch on a type of frame

TENTH *n* pl. -S one of ten equal parts

TENTHLY *adv* in the tenth place

TENTIE *adj* TENTIER, TENTIEST tenty

TENTIER comparative of tenty

TENTIEST superlative of tenty

TENTLESS *adj* having no tent

TENTLIKE *adj* resembling a tent

TENTY *adj* TENTIER, TENTIEST watchful

TENUIS *n* pl. -UES a voiceless phonetic stop

TENUITY *n* pl. -ITIES lack of substance or strength

TENUOUS *adj* having little substance or strength

TENURE n pl. -S the holding of something **TENURED, TENURIAL** adj

TENUTO n pl. -TI or -TOS a musical note or chord held longer than its normal duration

TEOCALLI n pl. -S an Aztec temple

TEOPAN n pl. -S a teocalli

TEOSINTE n pl. -S an annual grass

TEPA n pl. -S a chemical compound

TEPAL n pl. -S a division of a perianth

TEPEE n pl. -S a conical tent of some North American Indians

TEPEFY v -FIED, -FYING, -FIES to make tepid

TEPHRA n pl. -S solid material ejected from a volcano

TEPHRITE n pl. -S a volcanic rock

TEPID adj moderately warm **TEPIDLY** adv

TEPIDITY n pl. -TIES the state of being tepid

TEPOY n pl. -POYS teapoy

TEQUILA n pl. -S a Mexican liquor

TERAI n pl. -S a sun hat with a wide brim

TERAOHM n pl. -S one trillion ohms

TERAPH n pl. -APHIM an image of a Semitic household god

TERATISM n pl. -S a malformed fetus **TERATOID** adj

TERATOMA n pl. -MAS or -MATA a type of tumor

TERAWATT n pl. -S one trillion watts

TERBIA n pl. -S an oxide of terbium

TERBIUM n pl. -S a metallic element **TERBIC** adj

TERCE n pl. -S tierce

TERCEL n pl. -S a male falcon

TERCELET n pl. -S tercel

TERCET n pl. -S a group of three lines of verse

TEREBENE n pl. -S a mixture of terpenes

TEREBIC adj pertaining to an acid derived from oil of turpentine

TEREDO n pl. -DOS or -DINES a bivalve mollusk

TEREFAH adj tref

TERETE adj cylindrical and slightly tapering

TERGA pl. of tergum

TERGAL adj pertaining to a tergum

TERGITE n pl. -S a tergum

TERGUM n pl. -GA a back part of a segment of an arthropod

TERIYAKI n pl. -S a Japanese food

TERM v -ED, -ING, -S to give a name to

TERMER n pl. -S a prisoner serving a specified sentence

TERMINAL n pl. -S an end or extremity

TERMINUS n pl. -NI or -NUSES a terminal

TERMITE n pl. -S an insect resembling an ant **TERMITIC** adj

TERMLESS adj having no limits

TERMLY adv periodically

TERMOR n pl. -S one that holds land for a certain number of years

TERMTIME n pl. -S the time when a school or court is in session

TERN n pl. -S a seabird

TERNARY n pl. -RIES a group of three

TERNATE adj arranged in groups of three

TERNE n pl. -S an alloy of lead and tin

TERNION n pl. -S a group of three

TERPENE n pl. -S a chemical compound **TERPENIC** adj

TERPINOL n pl. -S a fragrant liquid

TERRA n pl. -RAE earth; land

TERRACE v -RACED, -RACING, -RACES to provide with a terrace (a raised embankment)

TERRAIN n pl. -S a tract of land

TERRANE n pl. -S a rock formation

TERRAPIN n pl. -S a North American tortoise

TERRARIA n/pl glass enclosures for plants or small animals

TERRAS n pl. -ES trass

TERRAZZO n pl. -ZOS a mosaic flooring

TERREEN n pl. -S terrine

TERRELLA n pl. -S a spherical magnet

TERRENE n pl. -S a land area

TERRET n pl. -S a metal ring on a harness

TERRIBLE adj very bad **TERRIBLY** adv

TERRIER n pl. -S a small, active dog

TERRIES pl. of terry

TERRIFIC adj very good; fine

TERRIFY v -FIED, -FYING, -FIES to fill with terror

TERRINE n pl. -S an earthenware jar

TERRIT n pl. -S terret

TERROR n pl. -S intense fear

TERRY n pl. -RIES an absorbent fabric

TERSE adj TERSER, TERSEST succinct **TERSELY** adv

TERTIAL n pl. -S a flight feather of a bird's wing

TERTIAN n pl. -S a recurrent fever

TERTIARY   *n* pl. -ARIES a tertial

TESLA   *n* pl. -S a unit of magnetic induction

TESSERA   *n* pl. -SERAE a small square used in mosaic work

TEST   *v* -ED, -ING, -S to subject to an examination **TESTABLE** *adj*

TESTA   *n* pl. -TAE the hard outer coating of a seed

TESTACY   *n* pl. -CIES the state of being testate

TESTATE   *n* pl. -S a testator

TESTATOR   *n* pl. -S one that makes a will

TESTEE   *n* pl. -S one that is tested

TESTER   *n* pl. -S one that tests

TESTES   pl. of testis

TESTICLE   *n* pl. -S a testis

TESTIER   comparative of testy

TESTIEST   superlative of testy

TESTIFY   *v* -FIED, -FYING, -FIES to make a declaration of truth under oath

TESTILY   *adv* in a testy manner

TESTIS   *n* pl. TESTES a male reproductive gland

TESTON   *n* pl. -S a former French coin

TESTOON   *n* pl. -S teston

TESTUDO   *n* pl. -DINES or -DOS a portable screen used as a shield by the ancient Romans

TESTY   *adj* TESTIER, TESTIEST irritable

TET   *n* pl. -S teth

TETANAL   *adj* pertaining to tetanus

TETANIC   *n* pl. -S a drug capable of causing convulsions

TETANIES   pl. of tetany

TETANISE   *v* -NISED, -NISING, -NISES to tetanize

TETANIZE   *v* -NIZED, -NIZING, -NIZES to affect with convulsions

TETANUS   *n* pl. -ES an infectious disease **TETANOID** *adj*

TETANY   *n* pl. -NIES a condition marked by painful muscular spasms

TETCHED   *adj* crazy

TETCHY   *adj* TETCHIER, TETCHIEST irritable **TETCHILY** *adv*

TETH   *n* pl. -S a Hebrew letter

TETHER   *v* -ED, -ING, -S to fasten to a fixed object with a rope

TETOTUM   *n* pl. -S teetotum

TETRA   *n* pl. -S a tropical fish

TETRACID   *n* pl. -S a type of acid

TETRAD   *n* pl. -S a group of four **TETRADIC** *adj*

TETRAGON   *n* pl. -S a four-sided polygon

TETRAMER   *n* pl. -S a type of polymer

TETRAPOD   *n* pl. -S a four-footed animal

TETRARCH   *n* pl. -S one of four joint rulers

TETRODE   *n* pl. -S a type of electron tube

TETROXID   *n* pl. -S a type of oxide

TETRYL   *n* pl. -S a chemical compound

TETTER   *n* pl. -S a skin disease

TEUCH   *adj* teugh

TEUGH   *adj* tough **TEUGHLY** *adv*

TEW   *v* -ED, -ING, -S to work hard

TEXAS   *n* pl. -ES the uppermost structure on a steamboat

TEXT   *n* pl. -S the main body of a written or printed work

TEXTBOOK   *n* pl. -S a book used in the study of a subject

TEXTILE   *n* pl. -S a woven fabric

TEXTLESS   *adj* having no text

TEXTUAL   *adj* pertaining to a text

TEXTUARY   *n* pl. -ARIES a specialist in the study of the Scriptures

TEXTURAL   *adj* pertaining to the surface characteristics of something

TEXTURE   *v* -TURED, -TURING, -TURES to make by weaving

THACK   *v* -ED, -ING, -S to thatch

THAE   *adj* these; those

THAIRM   *n* pl. -S tharm

THALAMUS   *n* pl. -MI a part of the brain **THALAMIC** *adj*

THALER   *n* pl. -S taler

THALLIUM   *n* pl. -S a metallic element **THALLIC, THALLOUS** *adj*

THALLUS   *n* pl. -LI or -LUSES a plant body without true root, stem, or leaf **THALLOID** *adj*

THAN   *conj* — used to introduce the second element of a comparison

THANAGE   *n* pl. -S the land held by a thane

THANATOS   *n* pl. -ES an instinctual desire for death

THANE   *n* pl. -S a man holding land by military service in Anglo-Saxon England

THANK   *v* -ED, -ING, -S to express gratitude to

THANKER   *n* pl. -S one that thanks

THANKFUL   *adj* -FULLER, -FULLEST feeling gratitude

THARM   *n* pl. -S the belly

THAT *pron* pl. THOSE the one indicated

THATAWAY *adv* in that direction

THATCH *v* -ED, -ING, -ES to cover with thatch (plant stalks or foliage)

THATCHER *n* pl. -S one that thatches

THATCHY *adj* THATCHIER, THATCHIEST resembling thatch

THAW *v* -ED, -ING, -S to melt

THAWER *n* pl. -S one that thaws

THAWLESS *adj* never thawing

THE *definite article* — used to specify or make particular

THEARCHY *n* pl. -CHIES rule by a god

THEATER *n* pl. -S a building for dramatic presentations **THEATRIC** *adj*

THEATRE *n* pl. -S theater

THEBAINE *n* pl. -S a poisonous alkaloid

THEBE *n* pl. THEBE a monetary unit of Botswana

THECA *n* pl. -CAE a protective anatomical covering **THECAL, THECATE** *adj*

THEE *pron* the objective case of the pronoun thou

THEELIN *n* pl. -S estrone

THEELOL *n* pl. -S estriol

THEFT *n* pl. -S the act of stealing

THEGN *n* pl. -S thane **THEGNLY** *adj*

THEIN *n* pl. -S theine

THEINE *n* pl. -S caffeine

THEIR *pron* a possessive form of the pronoun they

THEIRS *pron* a possessive form of the pronoun they

THEISM *n* pl. -S belief in the existence of a god

THEIST *n* pl. -S one who belives in the existence of a god **THEISTIC** *adj*

THELITIS *n* pl. -TISES inflammation of the nipple

THEM *pron* the objective case of the pronoun they

THEMATIC *n* pl. -S a stamp collected according to its subject

THEME *v* THEMED, THEMING, THEMES to plan something according to a central subject

THEN *n* pl. -S that time

THENAGE *n* pl. -S thanage

THENAL *adj* pertaining to the palm of the hand

THENAR *n* pl. -S the palm of the hand

THENCE *adv* from that place

THEOCRAT *n* pl. -S a person who rules as a representative of a god

THEODICY *n* pl. -CIES a defense of God's goodness in respect to the existence of evil

THEOGONY *n* pl. -NIES an account of the origin of the gods

THEOLOG *n* pl. -S a student of theology

THEOLOGY *n* pl. -GIES the study of religion

THEONOMY *n* pl. -MIES rule by a god

THEORBO *n* pl. -BOS a stringed musical instrument

THEOREM *n* pl. -S a proposition that is demonstrably true or is assumed to be so

THEORIES pl. of theory

THEORISE *v* -RISED, -RISING, -RISES to theorize

THEORIST *n* pl. -S one that theorizes

THEORIZE *v* -RIZED, -RIZING, -RIZES to form theories

THEORY *n* pl. -RIES a group of propositions used to explain a class of phenomena

THERAPY *n* pl. -PIES the treatment of illness or disability

THERE *n* pl. -S that place

THEREAT *adv* at that place or time

THEREBY *adv* by that means

THEREFOR *adv* for that

THEREIN *adv* in that place

THEREMIN *n* pl. -S a musical instrument

THEREOF *adv* of that

THEREON *adv* on that

THERETO *adv* to that

THERIAC *n* pl. -S molasses

THERIACA *n* pl. -S theriac

THERM *n* pl. -S a unit of quantity of heat

THERMAE *n/pl* hot springs

THERMAL *n* pl. -S a rising mass of warm air

THERME *n* pl. -S therm

THERMEL *n* pl. -S a device for temperature measurement

THERMIC *adj* pertaining to heat

THERMION *n* pl. -S an ion emitted by a heated body

THERMITE *n* pl. -S a metallic mixture that produces intense heat when ignited

THERMOS *n* pl. -ES a container used to keep liquids either hot or cold

THEROID *adj* resembling a beast

THEROPOD *n* pl. -S a carnivorous dinosaur

THESAURI   n/pl dictionaries of synonyms and antonyms

THESE   pl. of this

THESIS   n pl. THESES a proposition put forward for discussion

THESPIAN   n pl. -S an actor or actress

THETA   n pl. -S a Greek letter

THETIC   adj arbitrary

THETICAL   adj thetic

THEURGY   n pl. -GIES divine intervention in human affairs **THEURGIC** adj

THEW   n pl. -S a well-developed muscle

THEWLESS   adj weak

THEWY   adj THEWIER, THEWIEST brawny

THEY   pron the 3d person pl. pronoun in the nominative case

THIAMIN   n pl. -S thiamine

THIAMINE   n pl. -S a B vitamin

THIAZIDE   n pl. -S a drug used to treat high blood pressure

THIAZIN   n pl. -S thiazine

THIAZINE   n pl. -S a chemical compound

THIAZOL   n pl. -S thiazole

THIAZOLE   n pl. -S a chemical compound

THICK   adj THICKER, THICKEST having relatively great extent from one surface to its opposite

THICK   n pl. -S the thickest part

THICKEN   v -ED, -ING, -S to make thick

THICKET   n pl. -S a dense growth of shrubs or small trees **THICKETY** adj

THICKISH   adj somewhat thick

THICKLY   adv in a thick manner

THICKSET   n pl. -S a thicket

THIEF   n pl. THIEVES one that steals

THIEVE   v THIEVED, THIEVING, THIEVES to steal

THIEVERY   n pl. -ERIES the act or practice of stealing

THIEVES   pl. of thief

THIEVING   present participle of thieve

THIEVISH   adj given to stealing

THIGH   n pl. -S a part of the leg **THIGHED** adj

THILL   n pl. -S a shaft of a vehicle

THIMBLE   n pl. -S a cap used to protect the fingertip during sewing

THIN   adj THINNER, THINNEST having relatively little density or thickness

THIN   v THINNED, THINNING, THINS to make thin

THINCLAD   n pl. -S a runner on a track team

THINDOWN   n pl. -S a lessening in the number of atomic particles and cosmic rays passing through the earth's atmosphere

THINE   pron a possessive form of the pronoun thou

THING   n pl. -S an inanimate object

THINK   v THOUGHT, THINKING, THINKS to formulate in the mind

THINKER   n pl. -S one that thinks

THINKING   n pl. -S an opinion or judgment

THINLY   adv in a thin manner

THINNED   past tense of thin

THINNER   n pl. -S one that thins

THINNESS   n pl. -ES the quality or state of being thin

THINNEST   superlative of thin

THINNING   present participle of thin

THINNISH   adj somewhat thin

THIO   adj containing sulfur

THIOL   n pl. -S a sulfur compound **THIOLIC** adj

THIONATE   n pl. -S a chemical salt

THIONIC   adj pertaining to sulfur

THIONIN   n pl. -S a violet dye

THIONINE   n pl. -S thionin

THIONYL   n pl. -S sulfinyl

THIOPHEN   n pl. -S a chemical compound

THIOTEPA   n pl. -S a chemical compound

THIOUREA   n pl. -S a chemical compound

THIR   pron these

THIRAM   n pl. -S a chemical compound

THIRD   n pl. -S one of three equal parts

THIRDLY   adv in the third place

THIRL   v -ED, -ING, -S to thrill

THIRLAGE   n pl. -S an obligation requiring feudal tenants to grind grain at a certain mill

THIRST   v -ED, -ING, -S to feel a desire or need to drink

THIRSTER   n pl. -S one that thirsts

THIRSTY   adj THIRSTIER, THIRSTIEST feeling a desire or need to drink

THIRTEEN   n pl. -S a number

THIRTY   n pl. -TIES a number

THIS   pron pl. THESE the person or thing just mentioned

THISTLE   n pl. -S a prickly plant

THISTLY *adj* -TLIER, -TLIEST prickly

THITHER *adv* in that direction

THO *conj* though

THOLE *v* THOLED, THOLING, THOLES to endure

THOLEPIN *n* pl. -S a pin that serves as an oarlock

THOLOS *n* pl. -LOI a circular, underground tomb

THONG *n* pl. -S a narrow strip of leather used for binding **THONGED** *adj*

THORAX *n* pl. -RACES or -RAXES the part of the body between the neck and the abdomen **THORACAL, THORACIC** *adj*

THORIA *n* pl. -S an oxide of thorium

THORIC *adj* pertaining to thorium

THORITE *n* pl. -S a thorium ore

THORIUM *n* pl. -S a metallic element

THORN *v* -ED, -ING, -S to prick with a thorn (a sharp, rigid projection on a plant)

THORNY *adj* THORNIER, THORNIEST full of thorns **THORNILY** *adv*

THORO *adj* thorough

THORON *n* pl. -S a radioactive isotope of radon

THOROUGH *adj* THOROUGHER, THOROUGHEST complete in all respects

THORP *n* pl. -S a small village

THORPE *n* pl. -S thorp

THOSE pl. of that

THOU *v* -ED, -ING, -S to address as "thou" (the 2d person sing. pronoun in the nominative case)

THOUGH *conj* despite the fact that

THOUGHT *n* pl. -S a product of thinking

THOUSAND *n* pl. -S a number

THOWLESS *adj* listless

THRALDOM *n* pl. -S servitude

THRALL *v* -ED, -ING, -S to enslave

THRASH *v* -ED, -ING, -ES to beat

THRASHER *n* pl. -S one that thrashes

THRAVE *n* pl. -S a unit of measure for grain

THRAW *v* -ED, -ING, -S to twist

THRAWART *adj* stubborn

THRAWN *adj* twisted **THRAWNLY** *adv*

THREAD *v* -ED, -ING, -S to pass a thread (a very slender cord) through

THREADER *n* pl. -S one that threads

THREADY *adj* THREADIER, THREADIEST resembling a thread

THREAP *v* -ED, -ING, -S to dispute

THREAPER *n* pl. -S one that threaps

THREAT *v* -ED, -ING, -S to threaten

THREATEN *v* -ED, -ING, -S to be a source of danger to

THREE *n* pl. -S a number

THREEP *v* -ED, -ING, -S to threap

THRENODE *n* pl. -S a threnody

THRENODY *n* pl. -DIES a song of lamentation

THRESH *v* -ED, -ING, -ES to separate the grain or seeds from a plant mechanically

THRESHER *n* pl. -S one that threshes

THREW past tense of throw

THRICE *adv* three times

THRIFT *n* pl. -S care and wisdom in the management of one's resources

THRIFTY *adj* THRIFTIER, THRIFTIEST displaying thrift

THRILL *v* -ED, -ING, -S to excite greatly

THRILLER *n* pl. -S one that thrills

THRIP *n* pl. -S a British coin

THRIVE *v* THROVE or THRIVED, THRIVEN, THRIVING, THRIVES to grow vigorously

THRIVER *n* pl. -S one that thrives

THRO *prep* through

THROAT *v* -ED, -ING, -S to utter in a hoarse voice

THROATY *adj* THROATIER, THROATIEST hoarse

THROB *v* THROBBED, THROBBING, THROBS to pulsate

THROBBER *n* pl. -S one that throbs

THROE *n* pl. -S a violent spasm of pain

THROMBIN *n* pl. -S an enzyme

THROMBUS *n* pl. -BI a clot occluding a blood vessel

THRONE *v* THRONED, THRONING, THRONES to place on a throne (a royal chair)

THRONG *v* -ED, -ING, -S to crowd into

THROSTLE *n* pl. -S a songbird

THROTTLE *v* -TLED, -TLING, -TLES to strangle

THROUGH *prep* by way of

THROVE a past tense of thrive

THROW	v THREW, THROWN, THROWING, THROWS to propel through the air with a movement of the arm	**THUYA**	n pl. -S thuja
		THWACK	v -ED, -ING, -S to strike with something flat
THROWER	n pl. -S one that throws	**THWACKER**	n pl. -S one that thwacks
THRU	prep through	**THWART**	v -ED, -ING, -S to prevent the accomplishment of
THRUM	v THRUMMED, THRUMMING, THRUMS to play a stringed instrument idly or monotonously	**THWARTER**	n pl. -S one that thwarts
		THWARTLY	adv athwart
		THY	pron a possessive form of the pronoun thou
THRUMMER	n pl. -S one that thrums	**THYME**	n pl. -S an aromatic herb
THRUMMY	adj -MIER, -MIEST shaggy	**THYMEY**	adj THYMIER, THYMIEST thymy
THRUPUT	n pl. -S the amount of raw material processed within a given time	**THYMI**	a pl. of thymus
		THYMIC	adj pertaining to thyme
THRUSH	n pl. -ES a songbird	**THYMIER**	comparative of thymey and thymy
THRUST	v -ED, -ING, -S to push forcibly	**THYMIEST**	superlative of thymey and thymy
THRUSTER	n pl. -S one that thrusts	**THYMINE**	n pl. -S a chemical compound
THRUSTOR	n pl. -S thruster	**THYMOL**	n pl. -S a chemical compound
THRUWAY	n pl. -WAYS an express highway	**THYMOSIN**	n pl. -S a hormone secreted by the thymus
THUD	v THUDDED, THUDDING, THUDS to make a dull, heavy sound	**THYMUS**	n pl. -MI or -MUSES a glandular structure in the body
THUG	n pl. -S a brutal ruffian or assassin	**THYMY**	adj THYMIER, THYMIEST abounding in thyme
THUGGEE	n pl. -S thuggery in India	**THYREOID**	adj pertaining to the thyroid
THUGGERY	n pl. -GERIES thuggish behavior	**THYROID**	n pl. -S an endocrine gland
		THYROXIN	n pl. -S an amino acid
THUGGISH	adj characteristic of a thug	**THYRSE**	n pl. -S thyrsus
THUJA	n pl. -S an evergreen tree or shrub	**THYRSUS**	n pl. -SI a type of flower cluster **THYRSOID** adj
THULIA	n pl. -S an oxide of thulium	**THYSELF**	pron yourself
THULIUM	n pl. -S a metallic element	**TI**	n pl. -S the seventh tone of the diatonic musical scale
THUMB	v -ED, -ING, -S to leaf through with the thumb (the short, thick digit of the human hand)	**TIARA**	n pl. -S a jeweled headpiece worn by women **TIARAED** adj
THUMBKIN	n pl. -S a screw that is turned by the thumb and fingers	**TIBIA**	n pl. -IAE or -IAS a bone of the leg **TIBIAL** adj
THUMBNUT	n pl. -S a nut that is turned by the thumb and fingers	**TIC**	n pl. -S an involuntary muscular contraction
THUMP	v -ED, -ING, -S to strike so as to make a dull, heavy sound	**TICAL**	n pl. -S a former Thai unit of weight
THUMPER	n pl. -S one that thumps	**TICK**	v -ED, -ING, -S to make a recurrent clicking sound
THUNDER	v -ED, -ING, -S to produce a loud, resounding sound	**TICKER**	n pl. -S one that ticks
THUNDERY	adj accompanied with thunder	**TICKET**	v -ED, -ING, -S to attach a tag to
THUNK	v -ED, -ING, -S to make a sudden, muffled sound	**TICKING**	n pl. -S a strong cotton fabric
THURIBLE	n pl. -S a censer	**TICKLE**	v -LED, -LING, -LES to touch lightly so as to produce a tingling sensation
THURIFER	n pl. -S one who carries a thurible in a religious ceremony		
THURL	n pl. -S the hip joint in cattle	**TICKLER**	n pl. -S one that tickles
THUS	adv in this manner	**TICKLISH**	adj sensitive to tickling
THUSLY	adv thus	**TICKSEED**	n pl. -S a flowering plant

TICKTACK	*v* -ED, -ING, -S to ticktock
TICKTOCK	*v* -ED, -ING, -S to make the ticking sound of a clock
TICTAC	*v* -TACKED, -TACKING, -TACS to ticktack
TICTOC	*v* -TOCKED, -TOCKING, -TOCS to ticktack
TIDAL	*adj* pertaining to the tides **TIDALLY** *adv*
TIDBIT	*n* pl. -S a choice bit of food
TIDDLER	*n* pl. -S a small fish
TIDDLY	*adj* slightly drunk
TIDE	*v* TIDED, TIDING, TIDES to flow like the tide (the rise and fall of the ocean's waters)
TIDELAND	*n* pl. -S land alternately covered and uncovered by the tide
TIDELESS	*adj* lacking a tide
TIDELIKE	*adj* resembling a tide
TIDEMARK	*n* pl. -S a mark showing the highest or lowest point of a tide
TIDERIP	*n* pl. -S a riptide
TIDEWAY	*n* pl. -WAYS a tidal channel
TIDIED	past tense of tidy
TIDIER	*n* pl. -S one that tidies
TIDIES	present 3d person sing. of tidy
TIDIEST	superlative of tidy
TIDILY	*adv* in a tidy manner
TIDINESS	*n* pl. -ES the state of being tidy
TIDING	*n* pl. -S a piece of news
TIDY	*adj* -DIER, -DIEST neat and orderly
TIDY	*v* -DIED, -DYING, -DIES to make tidy
TIDYTIPS	*n* pl. TIDYTIPS an annual herb
TIE	*v* TIED, TYING or TIEING, TIES to fasten with a cord or rope
TIEBACK	*n* pl. -S a loop for holding a curtain back to one side
TIECLASP	*n* pl. -S a clasp for securing a necktie
TIED	past tense of tie
TIELESS	*adj* having no necktie
TIEPIN	*n* pl. -S a pin for securing a necktie
TIER	*v* -ED, -ING, -S to arrange in tiers (rows placed one above another)
TIERCE	*n* pl. -S one of seven canonical daily periods for prayer and devotion
TIERCED	*adj* divided into three equal parts
TIERCEL	*n* pl. -S tercel
TIFF	*v* -ED, -ING, -S to have a petty quarrel
TIFFANY	*n* pl. -NIES a thin, mesh fabric
TIFFIN	*v* -ED, -ING, -S to lunch
TIGER	*n* pl. -S a large feline mammal
TIGEREYE	*n* pl. -S a gemstone
TIGERISH	*adj* resembling a tiger
TIGHT	*adj* TIGHTER, TIGHTEST firmly or closely fixed in place **TIGHTLY** *adv*
TIGHTEN	*v* -ED, -ING, -S to make tight
TIGHTS	*n/pl* a close-fitting garment
TIGHTWAD	*n* pl. -S a miser
TIGLON	*n* pl. -S the offspring of a male tiger and a female lion
TIGON	*n* pl. -S tiglon
TIGRESS	*n* pl. -ES a female tiger
TIGRISH	*adj* tigerish
TIKE	*n* pl. -S tyke
TIKI	*n* pl. -S a wood or stone image of a Polynesian god
TIL	*n* pl. -S the sesame plant
TILAK	*n* pl. -S a mark worn on the forehead by Hindus
TILAPIA	*n* pl. -S an African fish
TILBURY	*n* pl. -BURIES a carriage having two wheels
TILDE	*n* pl. -S a mark placed over a letter to indicate its sound
TILE	*v* TILED, TILING, TILES to cover with tiles (thin slabs of baked clay)
TILEFISH	*n* pl. -ES a marine food fish
TILELIKE	*adj* resembling a tile
TILER	*n* pl. -S one that tiles
TILING	*n* pl. -S a surface of tiles
TILL	*v* -ED, -ING, -S to prepare land for crops by plowing **TILLABLE** *adj*
TILLAGE	*n* pl. -S cultivated land
TILLER	*v* -ED, -ING, -S to put forth stems from a root
TILLITE	*n* pl. -S rock made up of consolidated clay, sand, gravel, and boulders
TILT	*v* -ED, -ING, -S to cause to slant **TILTABLE** *adj*
TILTER	*n* pl. -S one that tilts
TILTH	*n* pl. -S tillage
TILTYARD	*n* pl. -S an area for jousting contests
TIMARAU	*n* pl. -S tamarau
TIMBAL	*n* pl. -S a large drum

TIMBALE *n* pl. -S a pastry shell shaped like a drum

TIMBER *v* -ED, -ING, -S to furnish with timber (wood used as a building material)

TIMBRE *n* pl. -S the quality given to a sound by its overtones **TIMBRAL** *adj*

TIMBREL *n* pl. -S a percussion instrument

TIME *v* TIMED, TIMING, TIMES to determine the speed or duration of

TIMECARD *n* pl. -S a card for recording an employee's times of arrival and departure

TIMELESS *adj* having no beginning or end

TIMELINE *n* pl. -S a schedule of events

TIMELY *adj* -LIER, -LIEST occurring at the right moment

TIMEOUS *adj* timely

TIMEOUT *n* pl. -S a brief suspension of activity

TIMER *n* pl. -S one that times

TIMEWORK *n* pl. -S work paid for by the hour or by the day

TIMEWORN *adj* showing the effects of long use or wear

TIMID *adj* -IDER, -IDEST lacking courage or self-confidence **TIMIDLY** *adv*

TIMIDITY *n* pl. -TIES the quality of being timid

TIMING *n* pl. -S the selection of the proper moment for doing something

TIMOLOL *n* pl. -S a drug used to treat glaucoma

TIMOROUS *adj* fearful

TIMOTHY *n* pl. -THIES a European grass

TIMPANO *n* pl. -NI a kettledrum

TIMPANUM *n* pl. -NA or -NUMS tympanum

TIN *v* TINNED, TINNING, TINS to coat with tin (a metallic element)

TINAMOU *n* pl. -S a South American game bird

TINCAL *n* pl. -S crude borax

TINCT *v* -ED, -ING, -S to tinge

TINCTURE *v* -TURED, -TURING, -TURES to tinge

TINDER *n* pl. -S readily combustible material **TINDERY** *adj*

TINE *v* TINED, TINING, TINES to lose

TINEA *n* pl. -S a fungous skin disease **TINEAL** *adj*

TINEID *n* pl. -S one of a family of moths

TINFOIL *n* pl. -S a thin metal sheeting

TINFUL *n* pl. -S as much as a tin container can hold

TING *v* -ED, -ING, -S to emit a high-pitched metallic sound

TINGE *v* TINGED, TINGEING or TINGING, TINGES to apply a trace of color to

TINGLE *v* -GLED, -GLING, -GLES to cause a prickly, stinging sensation

TINGLER *n* pl. -S one that tingles

TINGLY *adj* -GLIER, -GLIEST tingling

TINHORN *n* pl. -S a showily pretentious person

TINIER comparative of tiny

TINIEST superlative of tiny

TINILY *adv* in a tiny manner

TININESS *n* pl. -ES the quality of being tiny

TINING present participle of tine

TINKER *v* -ED, -ING, -S to repair in an unskilled or experimental manner

TINKERER *n* pl. -S one that tinkers

TINKLE *v* -KLED, -KLING, -KLES to make slight, sharp, metallic sounds

TINKLER *n* pl. -S one that tinkles

TINKLING *n* pl. -S the sound made by something that tinkles

TINKLY *adj* -KLIER, -KLIEST producing a tinkling sound

TINLIKE *adj* resembling tin

TINMAN *n* pl. -MEN a tinsmith

TINNED past tense of tin

TINNER *n* pl. -S a tin miner

TINNIER comparative of tinny

TINNIEST superlative of tinny

TINNILY *adv* in a tinny manner

TINNING present participle of tin

TINNITUS *n* pl. -ES a ringing sound in the ears

TINNY *adj* -NIER, -NIEST of or resembling tin

TINPLATE *n* pl. -S thin sheet iron coated with tin

TINSEL *v* -SELED, -SELING, -SELS or -SELLED, -SELLING, -SELS to give a showy or gaudy appearance to

TINSELLY *adj* cheaply gaudy

TINSMITH *n* pl. -S one who works with tin

TINSTONE *n* pl. -S a tin ore

TINT *v* -ED, -ING, -S to color slightly or delicately

TINTER *n* pl. -S one that tints

TINTING *n* pl. -S the process of one that tints

TINTLESS *adj* lacking color

TINTYPE *n* pl. -S a kind of photograph

TINWARE *n* pl. -S articles made of tinplate

TINWORK *n* pl. -S something made of tin

TINY *adj* TINIER, TINIEST very small

TIP *v* TIPPED, TIPPING, TIPS to tilt

TIPCART *n* pl. -S a type of cart

TIPCAT *n* pl. -S a game resembling baseball

TIPI *n* pl. -S tepee

TIPLESS *adj* having no point or extremity

TIPOFF *n* pl. -S a hint or warning

TIPPABLE *adj* capable of being tipped

TIPPED past tense of tip

TIPPER *n* pl. -S one that tips

TIPPET *n* pl. -S a covering for the shoulders

TIPPIER comparative of tippy

TIPPIEST superlative of tippy

TIPPING present participle of tip

TIPPLE *v* -PLED, -PLING, -PLES to drink alcoholic beverages

TIPPLER *n* pl. -S one that tipples

TIPPY *adj* -PIER, -PIEST unsteady

TIPPYTOE *v* -TOED, -TOEING, -TOES to tiptoe

TIPSIER comparative of tipsy

TIPSIEST superlative of tipsy

TIPSILY *adv* in a tipsy manner

TIPSTAFF *n* pl. -STAFFS or -STAVES an attendant in a court of law

TIPSTER *n* pl. -S one that sells information to gamblers

TIPSTOCK *n* pl. -S a part of a gun

TIPSY *adj* -SIER, -SIEST slightly drunk

TIPTOE *v* -TOED, -TOEING, -TOES to walk on the tips of one's toes

TIPTOP *n* pl. -S the highest point

TIRADE *n* pl. -S a long, vehement speech

TIRAMISU *n* pl. -S a dessert made with ladyfingers, mascarpone, chocolate, and espresso

TIRE *v* TIRED, TIRING, TIRES to grow tired

TIRED *adj* TIREDER, TIREDEST sapped of strength **TIREDLY** *adv*

TIRELESS *adj* seemingly incapable of tiring

TIRESOME *adj* tedious

TIRING present participle of tire

TIRL *v* -ED, -ING, -S to make a vibrating sound

TIRO *n* pl. -ROS tyro

TIRRIVEE *n* pl. -S a tantrum

TISANE *n* pl. -S a ptisan

TISSUAL *adj* pertaining to tissue

TISSUE *v* -SUED, -SUING, -SUES to weave into tissue (a fine sheer fabric)

TISSUEY *adj* resembling tissue

TISSULAR *adj* affecting an organism's tissue (structural material)

TIT *n* pl. -S a small bird

TITAN *n* pl. -S a person of great size

TITANATE *n* pl. -S a chemical salt

TITANESS *n* pl. -ES a female titan

TITANIA *n* pl. -S a mineral

TITANIC *adj* of great size

TITANISM *n* pl. -S revolt against social conventions

TITANITE *n* pl. -S a mineral

TITANIUM *n* pl. -S a metallic element

TITANOUS *adj* pertaining to titanium

TITBIT *n* pl. -S tidbit

TITER *n* pl. -S the strength of a chemical solution

TITFER *n* pl. -S a hat

TITHABLE *adj* subject to the payment of tithes

TITHE *v* TITHED, TITHING, TITHES to pay a tithe (a small tax)

TITHER *n* pl. -S one that tithes

TITHING *n* pl. -S the act of levying tithes

TITHONIA *n* pl. -S a tall herb

TITI *n* pl. -S an evergreen shrub or tree

TITIAN *n* pl. -S a reddish brown color

TITIVATE *v* -VATED, -VATING, -VATES to dress smartly

TITLARK *n* pl. -S a songbird

TITLE   *v* -TLED, -TLING, -TLES to furnish with a title (a distinctive appellation)

TITLIST   *n* pl. -S a sports champion

TITMAN   *n* pl. -MEN the smallest of a litter of pigs

TITMOUSE   *n* pl. -MICE a small bird

TITRABLE   *adj* capable of being titrated

TITRANT   *n* pl. -S the reagent used in titration

TITRATE   *v* -TRATED, -TRATING, -TRATES to determine the strength of a solution by adding a reagent until a desired reaction occurs

TITRATOR   *n* pl. -S one that titrates

TITRE   *n* pl. -S titer

TITTER   *v* -ED, -ING, -S to utter a restrained, nervous laugh

TITTERER   *n* pl. -S one that titters

TITTIE   *n* pl. -S a sister

TITTIES   pl. of titty

TITTLE   *n* pl. -S a very small mark in writing or printing

TITTUP   *v* -TUPED, -TUPING, -TUPS or -TUPPED, -TUPPING, -TUPS to move in a lively manner

TITTUPPY   *adj* shaky; unsteady

TITTY   *n* pl. -TIES a teat

TITULAR   *n* pl. -S one who holds a title

TITULARY   *n* pl. -LARIES a titular

TIVY   *adv* with great speed

TIZZY   *n* pl. -ZIES a state of nervous confusion

TMESIS   *n* pl. TMESES the separation of the parts of a compound word by an intervening word or words

TO   *prep* in the direction of

TOAD   *n* pl. -S a tailless, jumping amphibian

TOADFISH   *n* pl. -ES a marine fish

TOADFLAX   *n* pl. -ES a perennial herb

TOADIED   past tense of toady

TOADIES   present 3d person sing. of toady

TOADISH   *adj* resembling a toad

TOADLESS   *adj* having no toads

TOADLIKE   *adj* resembling a toad

TOADY   *v* TOADIED, TOADYING, TOADIES to engage in servile flattering

TOADYISH   *adj* characteristic of one that toadies

TOADYISM   *n* pl. -S toadyish behavior

TOAST   *v* -ED, -ING, -S to brown by exposure to heat

TOASTER   *n* pl. -S a device for toasting

TOASTY   *adj* TOASTIER, TOASTIEST comfortably warm

TOBACCO   *n* pl. -COS or -COES an annual herb cultivated for its leaves

TOBOGGAN   *v* -ED, -ING, -S to ride on a long, narrow sled

TOBY   *n* pl. -BIES a type of drinking mug

TOCCATA   *n* pl. -TAS or -TE a musical composition usually for an organ

TOCHER   *v* -ED, -ING, -S to give a dowry to

TOCOLOGY   *n* pl. -GIES the branch of medicine dealing with childbirth

TOCSIN   *n* pl. -S an alarm sounded on a bell

TOD   *n* pl. -S a British unit of weight

TODAY   *n* pl. -DAYS the present day

TODDIES   pl. of toddy

TODDLE   *v* -DLED, -DLING, -DLES to walk unsteadily

TODDLER   *n* pl. -S one that toddles

TODDY   *n* pl. -DIES an alcoholic beverage

TODY   *n* pl. -DIES a West Indian bird

TOE   *v* TOED, TOEING, TOES to touch with the toe (one of the terminal members of the foot)

TOEA   *n* pl. TOEA a monetary unit of Papua New Guinea

TOECAP   *n* pl. -S a covering for the tip of a shoe or boot

TOEHOLD   *n* pl. -S a space that supports the toes in climbing

TOELESS   *adj* having no toes

TOELIKE   *adj* resembling a toe

TOENAIL   *v* -ED, -ING, -S to fasten with obliquely driven nails

TOEPIECE   *n* pi. -S a piece of a shoe designed to cover the toes

TOEPLATE   *n* pl. -S a metal tab attached to the tip of a shoe

TOESHOE   *n* pl. -S a dance slipper without a heel

TOFF   *n* pl. -S a dandy

TOFFEE   *n* pl. -S a chewy candy

TOFFY   *n* pl. -FIES toffee

TOFT   *n* pl. -S a hillock

TOFU   *n* pl. -S a soft Oriental cheese made from soybean milk

TOG v TOGGED, TOGGING, TOGS to clothe

TOGA n pl. -GAS or -GAE an outer garment worn in ancient Rome **TOGAED** adj

TOGATE adj pertaining to ancient Rome

TOGATED adj wearing a toga

TOGETHER adv into a union or relationship

TOGGED past tense of tog

TOGGERY n pl. -GERIES clothing

TOGGING present participle of tog

TOGGLE v -GLED, -GLING, -GLES to fasten with a type of pin or short rod

TOGGLER n pl. -S one that toggles

TOGUE n pl. -S a freshwater fish

TOIL v -ED, -ING, -S to work strenuously

TOILE n pl. -S a sheer linen fabric

TOILER n pl. -S one that toils

TOILET v -ED, -ING, -S to dress and groom oneself

TOILETRY n pl. -TRIES an article used in dressing and grooming oneself

TOILETTE n pl. -S the act of dressing and grooming oneself

TOILFUL adj toilsome

TOILSOME adj demanding much exertion

TOILWORN adj worn by toil

TOIT v -ED, -ING, -S to saunter

TOKAMAK n pl. -S a doughnut-shaped nuclear reactor

TOKAY n pl. -KAYS a Malaysian gecko

TOKE v TOKED, TOKING, TOKES to take a puff on a marijuana cigarette

TOKEN v -ED, -ING, -S to serve as a sign of

TOKENISM n pl. -S the policy of making only a superficial effort

TOKER n pl. -S one that tokes

TOKING present participle of toke

TOKOLOGY n pl. -GIES tocology

TOKOMAK n pl. -S tokamak

TOKONOMA n pl. -S a small alcove in a Japanese house

TOLA n pl. -S a unit of weight used in India

TOLAN n pl. -S a chemical compound

TOLANE n pl. -S tolan

TOLBOOTH n pl. -S a prison

TOLD past tense of tell

TOLE v TOLED, TOLING, TOLES to allure

TOLEDO n pl. -DOS a finely tempered sword

TOLERANT adj inclined to tolerate

TOLERATE v -ATED, -ATING, -ATES to allow without active opposition

TOLIDIN n pl. -S tolidine

TOLIDINE n pl. -S a chemical compound

TOLING present participle of tole

TOLL v -ED, -ING, -S to collect or impose a toll (a fixed charge for a service or privilege)

TOLLAGE n pl. -S a toll

TOLLBAR n pl. -S a tollgate

TOLLER n pl. -S a collector of tolls

TOLLGATE n pl. -S a gate where a toll is collected

TOLLMAN n pl. -MEN a toller

TOLLWAY n pl. -WAYS a road on which tolls are collected

TOLU n pl. -S a fragrant resin

TOLUATE n pl. -S a chemical salt

TOLUENE n pl. -S a flammable liquid

TOLUIC adj pertaining to any of four isomeric acids derived from toluene

TOLUID n pl. -S toluide

TOLUIDE n pl. -S an amide

TOLUIDIN n pl. -S an amine

TOLUOL n pl. -S toluene

TOLUOLE n pl. -S toluol

TOLUYL n pl. -S a univalent chemical radical

TOLYL n pl. -S a univalent chemical radical

TOM n pl. -S the male of various animals

TOMAHAWK v -ED, -ING, -S to strike with a light ax

TOMALLEY n pl. -LEYS the liver of a lobster

TOMAN n pl. -S a coin of Iran

TOMATO n pl. -TOES the fleshy, edible fruit of a perennial plant **TOMATOEY** adj

TOMB v -ED, -ING, -S to place in a tomb (a burial vault or chamber)

TOMBAC n pl. -S an alloy of copper and zinc

TOMBACK n pl. -S tombac

TOMBAK n pl. -S tombac

TOMBAL adj pertaining to a tomb

TOMBLESS adj having no tomb

TOMBLIKE adj resembling a tomb

TOMBOLA n pl. -S a gambling game

TOMBOLO *n* pl. -LOS a sandbar connecting an island to the mainland

TOMBOY *n* pl. -BOYS a girl who prefers boyish activities

TOMCAT *v* -CATTED, -CATTING, -CATS to engage in sexually promiscuous behavior — used of a male

TOMCOD *n* pl. -S a marine fish

TOME *n* pl. -S a large book

TOMENTUM *n* pl. -TA a network of small blood vessels

TOMFOOL *n* pl. -S a foolish person

TOMMED past tense of tom

TOMMING present participle of tom

TOMMY *n* pl. -MIES a loaf of bread

TOMMYROT *n* pl. -S nonsense

TOMOGRAM *n* pl. -S a photograph made with X rays

TOMORROW *n* pl. -S the day following today

TOMPION *n* pl. -S tampion

TOMTIT *n* pl. -S a small bird

TON *n* pl. -S a unit of weight

TONAL *adj* pertaining to tone **TONALLY** *adv*

TONALITY *n* pl. -TIES a system of tones

TONDO *n* pl. -DI or -DOS a circular painting

TONE *v* TONED, TONING, TONES to give a particular tone (a sound of definite pitch and vibration) to

TONEARM *n* pl. -S the pivoted part of a record player that holds the needle

TONELESS *adj* lacking in tone

TONEME *n* pl. -S a tonal unit of speech **TONEMIC** *adj*

TONER *n* pl. -S one that tones

TONETICS *n/pl* the phonetic study of tone in language **TONETIC** *adj*

TONETTE *n* pl. -S a simple flute

TONEY *adj* TONIER, TONIEST tony

TONG *v* -ED, -ING, -S to lift with a type of grasping device

TONGA *n* pl. -S a light cart used in India

TONGER *n* pl. -S one that tongs

TONGMAN *n* pl. -MEN a member of a Chinese secret society

TONGUE *v* TONGUED, TONGUING, TONGUES to touch with the tongue (an organ of the mouth)

TONGUING *n* pl. -S the use of the tongue in articulating notes on a wind instrument

TONIC *n* pl. -S something that invigorates or refreshes

TONICITY *n* pl. -TIES normal, healthy bodily condition

TONIER comparative of tony

TONIEST superlative of tony

TONIGHT *n* pl. -S the present night

TONING present participle of tone

TONISH *adj* stylish **TONISHLY** *adv*

TONLET *n* pl. -S a skirt of plate armor

TONNAGE *n* pl. -S total weight in tons

TONNE *n* pl. -S a unit of weight

TONNEAU *n* pl. -NEAUS or -NEAUX the rear seating compartment of an automobile

TONNER *n* pl. -S an object having a specified tonnage

TONNISH *adj* tonish

TONSIL *n* pl. -S a lymphoid organ **TONSILAR** *adj*

TONSURE *v* -SURED, -SURING, -SURES to shave the head of

TONTINE *n* pl. -S a form of collective life insurance

TONUS *n* pl. -ES a normal state of tension in muscle tissue

TONY *adj* TONIER, TONIEST stylish

TOO *adv* in addition

TOOK past tense of take

TOOL *v* -ED, -ING, -S to form or finish with a tool (an implement used in manual work)

TOOLBOX *n* pl. -ES a box for tools

TOOLER *n* pl. -S one that tools

TOOLHEAD *n* pl. -S a part of a machine

TOOLING *n* pl. -S ornamentation done with tools

TOOLLESS *adj* having no tools

TOOLROOM *n* pl. -S a room where tools are stored

TOOLSHED *n* pl. -S a building where tools are stored

TOOM *adj* empty

TOON *n* pl. -S an East Indian tree

TOOT *v* -ED, -ING, -S to sound a horn or whistle in short blasts

TOOTER *n* pl. -S one that toots

TOOTH *n* pl. TEETH one of the hard structures attached in a row to each jaw

TOOTH *v* -ED, -ING, -S to furnish with toothlike projections

TOOTHY *adj* TOOTHIER, TOOTHIEST having or showing prominent teeth **TOOTHILY** *adv*

TOOTLE *v* -TLED, -TLING, -TLES to toot softly or repeatedly

TOOTLER *n* pl. -S one that tootles

TOOTS *n* pl. -ES a woman or girl — usually used as a form of address

TOOTSIE *n* pl. -S tootsy

TOOTSY *n* pl. -SIES a foot

TOP *v* TOPPED, TOPPING, TOPS to cut off the top (the highest part, point, or surface) of

TOPAZ *n* pl. -ES a mineral **TOPAZINE** *adj*

TOPCOAT *n* pl. -S a lightweight overcoat

TOPCROSS *n* pl. -ES a cross between a purebred male and inferior female stock

TOPE *v* TOPED, TOPING, TOPES to drink liquor to excess

TOPEE *n* pl. -S topi

TOPER *n* pl. -S one that topes

TOPFUL *adj* topfull

TOPFULL *adj* full to the top

TOPH *n* pl. -S tufa

TOPHE *n* pl. -S tufa

TOPHUS *n* pl. -PHI a deposit of urates in the tissue around a joint

TOPI *n* pl. -S a sun helmet

TOPIARY *n* pl. -ARIES the art of trimming shrubs into shapes

TOPIC *n* pl. -S a subject of discourse **TOPICAL** *adj*

TOPING present participle of tope

TOPKICK *n* pl. -S a first sergeant

TOPKNOT *n* pl. -S an ornament for the hair

TOPLESS *adj* having no top

TOPLINE *n* pl. -S the outline of the top of an animal's body

TOPLOFTY *adj* -LOFTIER, -LOFTIEST haughty

TOPMAST *n* pl. -S a mast of a ship

TOPMOST *adj* highest

TOPNOTCH *adj* excellent

TOPOI pl. of topos

TOPOLOGY *n* pl. -GIES a branch of mathematics

TOPONYM *n* pl. -S the name of a place

TOPONYMY *n* pl. -MIES the study of toponyms

TOPOS *n* pl. -POI a stock rhetorical theme

TOPOTYPE *n* pl. -S a specimen selected from a locality typical of a species

TOPPED past tense of top

TOPPER *n* pl. -S one that tops

TOPPING *n* pl. -S something that forms a top

TOPPLE *v* -PLED, -PLING, -PLES to fall forward

TOPSAIL *n* pl. -S a sail of a ship

TOPSIDE *n* pl. -S the upper portion of a ship

TOPSIDER *n* pl. -S one who is at the highest level of authority

TOPSOIL *v* -ED, -ING, -S to remove the surface layer of soil from

TOPSPIN *n* pl. -S a forward spin imparted to a ball

TOPSTONE *n* pl. -S the stone at the top of a structure

TOPWORK *v* -ED, -ING, -S to graft scions of another variety of plant on the main branches of

TOQUE *n* pl. -S a close-fitting woman's hat

TOQUET *n* pl. -S toque

TOR *n* pl. -S a high, craggy hill

TORA *n* pl. -S torah

TORAH *n* pl. -RAHS, -ROTH, or -ROT the body of Jewish law

TORC *n* pl. -S a metal collar or necklace

TORCH *v* -ED, -ING, -ES to set on fire

TORCHERE *n* pl. -S a type of electric lamp

TORCHIER *n* pl. -S torchere

TORCHON *n* pl. -S a coarse lace

TORCHY *adj* TORCHIER, TORCHIEST characteristic of a torch song

TORE *n* pl. -S a torus

TOREADOR *n* pl. -S a bullfighter

TORERO *n* pl. -ROS a bullfighter

TOREUTIC *adj* pertaining to a type of metalwork

TORI pl. of torus

TORIC *adj* pertaining to a torus

TORIES pl. of tory

TORII *n* pl. TORII the gateway of a Japanese temple

TORMENT *v* -ED, -ING, -S to inflict with great bodily or mental suffering

TORN past participle of tear

TORNADO *n* pl. -DOES or -DOS a violent windstorm **TORNADIC** *adj*

TORNILLO *n* pl. -LOS a flowering shrub

TORO *n* pl. -ROS a bull

TOROID	*n* pl. -S a type of geometric surface **TOROIDAL** *adj*
TOROSE	*adj* cylindrical and swollen at intervals
TOROSITY	*n* pl. -TIES the quality or state of being torose
TOROT	a pl. of torah
TOROTH	a pl. of torah
TOROUS	*adj* torose
TORPEDO	*v* -ED, -ING, -ES or -S to damage or sink with an underwater missile
TORPID	*n* pl. -S a racing boat
TORPIDLY	*adv* in a sluggish manner
TORPOR	*n* pl. -S mental or physical inactivity
TORQUATE	*adj* having a torques
TORQUE	*v* TORQUED, TORQUING, TORQUES to cause to twist
TORQUER	*n* pl. -S one that torques
TORQUES	*n* pl. -QUESES a band of feathers, hair, or coloration around the neck
TORQUING	present participle of torque
TORR	*n* pl. TORR a unit of pressure
TORREFY	*v* -FIED, -FYING, -FIES to subject to intense heat
TORRENT	*n* pl. -S a rapid stream of water
TORRID	*adj* -RIDER, -RIDEST extremely hot **TORRIDLY** *adv*
TORRIFY	*v* -FIED, -FYING, -FIES to torrefy
TORSADE	*n* pl. -S a twisted cord
TORSE	*n* pl. -S a wreath of twisted silks
TORSI	a pl. of torso
TORSION	*n* pl. -S the act of twisting
TORSK	*n* pl. -S a marine food fish
TORSO	*n* pl. -SI or -SOS the trunk of the human body
TORT	*n* pl. -S a civil wrong
TORTE	*n* pl. TORTEN or TORTES a rich cake
TORTILE	*adj* twisted; coiled
TORTILLA	*n* pl. -S a round, flat cake of unleavened cornmeal
TORTIOUS	*adj* of the nature of a tort
TORTOISE	*n* pl. -S any of an order of reptiles having the body enclosed in a bony shell
TORTONI	*n* pl. -S a type of ice cream
TORTRIX	*n* pl. -ES a small moth
TORTUOUS	*adj* marked by repeated turns or bends
TORTURE	*v* -TURED, -TURING, -TURES to subject to severe physical pain
TORTURER	*n* pl. -S one that tortures
TORULA	*n* pl. -LAE or -LAS a type of fungus
TORUS	*n* pl. -RI a large convex molding
TORY	*n* pl. -RIES a political conservative
TOSH	*n* pl. -ES nonsense
TOSS	*v* TOSSED or TOST, TOSSING, TOSSES to throw lightly
TOSSER	*n* pl. -S one that tosses
TOSSPOT	*n* pl. -S a drunkard
TOSSUP	*n* pl. -S an even choice or chance
TOST	a past tense of toss
TOSTADA	*n* pl. -S a tortilla fried in deep fat
TOSTADO	*n* pl. -DOS tostada
TOT	*v* TOTTED, TOTTING, TOTS to total
TOTABLE	*adj* capable of being toted
TOTAL	*v* -TALED, -TALING, -TALS or -TALLED, -TALLING, -TALS to ascertain the entire amount of
TOTALISE	*v* -ISED, -ISING, -ISES to totalize
TOTALISM	*n* pl. -S centralized control by an autocratic authority
TOTALIST	*n* pl. -S one who tends to regard things as a unified whole
TOTALITY	*n* pl. -TIES the quality or state of being complete
TOTALIZE	*v* -IZED, -IZING, -IZES to make complete
TOTALLED	a past tense of total
TOTALLING	a present participle of total
TOTALLY	*adv* completely
TOTE	*v* TOTED, TOTING, TOTES to carry by hand
TOTEM	*n* pl. -S a natural object serving as the emblem of a family or clan **TOTEMIC** *adj*
TOTEMISM	*n* pl. -S a system of tribal division according to totems
TOTEMIST	*n* pl. -S a specialist in totemism
TOTEMITE	*n* pl. -S a totemist
TOTER	*n* pl. -S one that totes
TOTHER	*pron* the other
TOTING	present participle of tote
TOTTED	past tense of tot

TOTTER   *v* -ED, -ING, -S to walk unsteadily

TOTTERER   *n* pl. -S one that totters

TOTTERY   *adj* shaky

TOTTING   present participle of tot

TOUCAN   *n* pl. -S a tropical bird

TOUCH   *v* -ED, -ING, -ES to be in or come into contact with

TOUCHE   *interj* — used to acknowledge a hit in fencing

TOUCHER   *n* pl. -S one that touches

TOUCHUP   *n* pl. -S an act of finishing by adding minor improvements

TOUCHY   *adj* TOUCHIER, TOUCHIEST overly sensitive **TOUCHILY** *adv*

TOUGH   *adj* TOUGHER, TOUGHEST strong and resilient

TOUGH   *v* -ED, -ING, -S to endure hardship

TOUGHEN   *v* -ED, -ING, -S to make tough

TOUGHIE   *n* pl. -S a tough

TOUGHIES   pl. of toughy

TOUGHISH   *adj* somewhat tough

TOUGHLY   *adv* in a tough manner

TOUGHY   *n* pl. TOUGHIES toughie

TOUPEE   *n* pl. -S a wig worn to cover a bald spot

TOUR   *v* -ED, -ING, -S to travel from place to place

TOURACO   *n* pl. -COS an African bird

TOURER   *n* pl. -S a large, open automobile

TOURING   *n* pl. -S cross-country skiing for pleasure

TOURISM   *n* pl. -S the practice of touring for pleasure

TOURIST   *n* pl. -S one who tours for pleasure **TOURISTY** *adj*

TOURNEY   *v* -ED, -ING, -S to compete in a tournament

TOUSE   *v* TOUSED, TOUSING, TOUSES to tousle

TOUSLE   *v* -SLED, -SLING, -SLES to dishevel

TOUT   *v* -ED, -ING, -S to solicit brazenly

TOUTER   *n* pl. -S one that touts

TOUZLE   *v* -ZLED, -ZLING, -ZLES to tousle

TOVARICH   *n* pl. -ES comrade

TOVARISH   *n* pl. -ES tovarich

TOW   *v* -ED, -ING, -S to pull by means of a rope or chain

TOWAGE   *n* pl. -S the price paid for towing

TOWARD   *prep* in the direction of

TOWARDLY   *adj* favorable

TOWARDS   *prep* toward

TOWAWAY   *n* pl. -AWAYS the act of towing away a vehicle

TOWBOAT   *n* pl. -S a tugboat

TOWEL   *v* -ELED, -ELING, -ELS or -ELLED, -ELLING, -ELS to wipe with a towel (an absorbent cloth)

TOWELING   *n* pl. -S material used for towels

TOWER   *v* -ED, -ING, -S to rise to a great height

TOWERY   *adj* -ERIER, -ERIEST very tall

TOWHEAD   *n* pl. -S a head of light blond hair

TOWHEE   *n* pl. -S a common finch

TOWIE   *n* pl. -S a form of contract bridge for three players

TOWLINE   *n* pl. -S a line used in towing

TOWMOND   *n* pl. -S a year

TOWMONT   *n* pl. -S towmond

TOWN   *n* pl. -S a center of population smaller than a city

TOWNEE   *n* pl. -S a townsman

TOWNFOLK   *n/pl* the inhabitants of a town

TOWNHOME   *n* pl. -S one of a series of contiguous houses of two or three stories

TOWNIE   *n* pl. -S a nonstudent who lives in a college town

TOWNIES   pl. of towny

TOWNISH   *adj* characteristic of a town

TOWNLESS   *adj* having no towns

TOWNLET   *n* pl. -S a small town

TOWNSHIP   *n* pl. -S an administrative division of a county

TOWNSMAN   *n* pl. -MEN a resident of a town

TOWNWEAR   *n* pl. -S apparel that is suitable for wear in the city

TOWNY   *n* pl. TOWNIES townie

TOWPATH   *n* pl. -S a path along a river that is used by animals towing boats

TOWROPE   *n* pl. -S a rope used in towing

TOWY   *adj* resembling coarse hemp or flax fiber

TOXAEMIA   *n* pl. -S toxemia **TOXAEMIC** *adj*

TOXEMIA   *n* pl. -S the condition of having toxins in the blood **TOXEMIC** *adj*

TOXIC   *adj* pertaining to a toxin

TOXICAL   *adj* toxic

TOXICANT *n* pl. -S a poisonous substance

TOXICITY *n* pl. -TIES the quality of being poisonous

TOXIN *n* pl. -S a poisonous substance

TOXINE *n* pl. -S toxin

TOXOID *n* pl. -S a type of toxin

TOY *v* -ED, -ING, -S to amuse oneself as if with a toy (a child's plaything)

TOYER *n* pl. -S one that toys

TOYISH *adj* frivolous

TOYLESS *adj* having no toy

TOYLIKE *adj* resembling a toy

TOYO *n* pl. -YOS a smooth straw used in making hats

TOYON *n* pl. -S an ornamental evergreen shrub

TOYSHOP *n* pl. -S a shop where toys are sold

TRABEATE *adj* constructed with horizontal beams

TRACE *v* TRACED, TRACING, TRACES to follow the course of

TRACER *n* pl. -S one that traces

TRACERY *n* pl. -ERIES ornamental work of interlaced lines

TRACHEA *n* pl. -CHEAE or -CHEAS the passage for conveying air to the lungs **TRACHEAL** *adj*

TRACHEID *n* pl. -S a long, tubular plant cell

TRACHLE *v* -LED, -LING, -LES to draggle

TRACHOMA *n* pl. -S a disease of the eye

TRACHYTE *n* pl. -S a light-colored igneous rock

TRACING *n* pl. -S something that is traced

TRACK *v* -ED, -ING, -S to follow the marks left by an animal, a person, or a vehicle

TRACKAGE *n* pl. -S the track system of a railroad

TRACKER *n* pl. -S one that tracks

TRACKING *n* pl. -S the placement of students within a curriculum

TRACKMAN *n* pl. -MEN a railroad worker

TRACKWAY *n* pl. -WAYS a trodden path

TRACT *n* pl. -S an expanse of land

TRACTATE *n* pl. -S a treatise

TRACTILE *adj* capable of being drawn out in length

TRACTION *n* pl. -S the act of pulling or drawing over a surface **TRACTIVE** *adj*

TRACTOR *n* pl. -S a motor vehicle used in farming

TRAD *adj* traditional

TRADE *v* TRADED, TRADING, TRADES to give in exchange for another commodity **TRADABLE** *adj*

TRADEOFF *n* pl. -S a giving up of one thing in return for another

TRADER *n* pl. -S one that trades

TRADITOR *n* pl. -ES a traitor among the early Christians

TRADUCE *v* -DUCED, -DUCING, -DUCES to defame

TRADUCER *n* pl. -S one that traduces

TRAFFIC *v* -FICKED, -FICKING, -FICS to engage in buying and selling

TRAGEDY *n* pl. -DIES a disastrous event

TRAGI pl. of tragus

TRAGIC *n* pl. -S the element of a drama that produces tragedy

TRAGICAL *adj* of the nature of a tragedy

TRAGOPAN *n* pl. -S an Asian pheasant

TRAGUS *n* pl. -GI a part of the external opening of the ear

TRAIK *v* -ED, -ING, -S to trudge

TRAIL *v* -ED, -ING, -S to drag along a surface

TRAILER *v* -ED, -ING, -S to transport by means of a trailer (a vehicle drawn by another)

TRAIN *v* -ED, -ING, -S to instruct systematically

TRAINEE *n* pl. -S a person receiving training

TRAINER *n* pl. -S one that trains

TRAINFUL *n* pl. -S as much as a railroad train can hold

TRAINING *n* pl. -S systematic instruction

TRAINMAN *n* pl. -MEN a railroad employee

TRAINWAY *n* pl. -WAYS a railway

TRAIPSE *v* TRAIPSED, TRAIPSING, TRAIPSES to walk about in an idle or aimless manner

TRAIT *n* pl. -S a distinguishing characteristic

TRAITOR *n* pl. -S one who betrays another

TRAJECT *v* -ED, -ING, -S to transmit

TRAM *v* TRAMMED, TRAMMING, TRAMS to convey in a tramcar

TRAMCAR *n* pl. -S a streetcar

TRAMEL *v* -ELED, -ELING, -ELS or -ELLED, -ELLING, -ELS to trammel

TRAMELL *v* -ED, -ING, -S to trammel

TRAMLESS *adj* having no tramcar

TRAMLINE *n* pl. -S a streetcar line

TRAMMED past tense of tram

TRAMMEL *v* -MELED, -MELING, -MELS or -MELLED, -MELLING, -MELS to hinder

TRAMMING present participle of tram

TRAMP *v* -ED, -ING, -S to walk with a firm, heavy step

TRAMPER *n* pl. -S one that tramps

TRAMPISH *adj* resembling a vagabond

TRAMPLE *v* -PLED, -PLING, -PLES to tread on heavily

TRAMPLER *n* pl. -S one that tramples

TRAMROAD *n* pl. -S a railway in a mine

TRAMWAY *n* pl. -WAYS a tramline

TRANCE *v* TRANCED, TRANCING, TRANCES to put into a trance (a semiconscious state)

TRANCHE *n* pl. -S a portion

TRANGAM *n* pl. -S a gewgaw

TRANK *n* pl. -S a drug that tranquilizes

TRANQ *n* pl. -S trank

TRANQUIL *adj* -QUILER, -QUILEST or -QUILLER, -QUILLEST free from disturbance

TRANS *adj* characterized by the arrangement of different atoms on opposite sides of the molecule

TRANSACT *v* -ED, -ING, -S to carry out

TRANSECT *v* -ED, -ING, -S to cut across

TRANSEPT *n* pl. -S a major transverse part of the body of a church

TRANSFER *v* -FERRED, -FERRING, -FERS to convey from one source to another

TRANSFIX *v* -FIXED or -FIXT, -FIXING, -FIXES to impale

TRANSHIP *v* -SHIPPED, -SHIPPING, -SHIPS to transfer from one conveyance to another

TRANSIT *v* -ED, -ING, -S to pass across or through

TRANSMIT *v* -MITTED, -MITTING, -MITS to send from one place or person to another

TRANSOM *n* pl. -S a small window above a door or another window

TRANSUDE *v* -SUDED, -SUDING, -SUDES to pass through a membrane

TRAP *v* TRAPPED or TRAPT, TRAPPING, TRAPS to catch in a trap (a device for capturing and holding animals)

TRAPAN *v* -PANNED, -PANNING, -PANS to trepan

TRAPBALL *n* pl. -S a type of ball game

TRAPDOOR *n* pl. -S a lifting or sliding door covering an opening

TRAPES *v* -ED, -ING, -ES to traipse

TRAPEZE *n* pl. -S a gymnastic apparatus

TRAPEZIA *n/pl* four-sided polygons having no parallel sides

TRAPLIKE *adj* resembling a trap

TRAPLINE *n* pl. -S a series of traps

TRAPNEST *v* -ED, -ING, -S to determine the productivity of hens with a type of nest

TRAPPEAN *adj* pertaining to traprock

TRAPPED a past tense of trap

TRAPPER *n* pl. -S one that traps

TRAPPING *n* pl. -S a covering for a horse

TRAPPOSE *adj* trappean

TRAPPOUS *adj* trappean

TRAPROCK *n* pl. -S an igneous rock

TRAPT a past tense of trap

TRAPUNTO *n* pl. -TOS a decorative quilted design

TRASH *v* -ED, -ING, -ES to free from trash (worthless or waste matter)

TRASHMAN *n* pl. -MEN a person who removes trash

TRASHY *adj* TRASHIER, TRASHIEST resembling trash **TRASHILY** *adv*

TRASS *n* pl. -ES a volcanic rock

TRAUCHLE *v* -LED, -LING, -LES to trachle

TRAUMA *n* pl. -MAS or -MATA a severe emotional shock

TRAVAIL *v* -ED, -ING, -S to toil

TRAVE *n* pl. -S a frame for confining a horse

TRAVEL *v* -ELED, -ELING, -ELS or -ELLED, -ELLING, -ELS to go from one place to another

TRAVELER *n* pl. -S one that travels

TRAVELOG *n* pl. -S a lecture or film on traveling

TRAVERSE *v* -VERSED, -VERSING, -VERSES to pass across or through

TRAVESTY *v* -TIED, -TYING, -TIES to parody

TRAVOIS *n* pl. -ES a type of sled

TRAVOISE *n* pl. -S travois

TRAWL	*v* -ED, -ING, -S to fish by dragging a net along the sea bottom
TRAWLER	*n* pl. -S a boat used for trawling
TRAWLEY	*n* pl. -LEYS a small truck or car for conveying material
TRAWLNET	*n* pl. -S the large net used in trawling
TRAY	*n* pl. TRAYS a flat, shallow receptacle
TRAYFUL	*n* pl. -S as much as a tray will hold
TREACLE	*n* pl. -S molasses **TREACLY** *adj*
TREAD	*v* TROD, TRODE, or TREADED, TRODDEN, TREADING, TREADS to walk on, over, or along
TREADER	*n* pl. -S one that treads
TREADLE	*v* -LED, -LING, -LES to work a foot lever
TREADLER	*n* pl. -S one that treadles
TREASON	*n* pl. -S violation of allegiance toward one's country
TREASURE	*v* -URED, -URING, -URES to value highly
TREASURY	*n* pl. -URIES a place where funds are received, kept, and disbursed
TREAT	*v* -ED, -ING, -S to behave in a particular way toward
TREATER	*n* pl. -S one that treats
TREATISE	*n* pl. -S a formal and systematic written account of a subject
TREATY	*n* pl. -TIES a formal agreement between two or more nations
TREBLE	*v* -BLED, -BLING, -BLES to triple
TREBLY	*adv* triply
TRECENTO	*n* pl. -TOS the fourteenth century
TREDDLE	*v* -DLED, -DLING, -DLES to treadle
TREE	*v* TREED, TREEING, TREES to drive up a tree (a tall, woody plant)
TREELAWN	*n* pl. -S the strip of lawn between the street and the sidewalk
TREELESS	*adj* having no tree
TREELIKE	*adj* resembling a tree
TREEN	*n* pl. -S an article made from wood
TREENAIL	*n* pl. -S a wooden peg used for fastening timbers
TREETOP	*n* pl. -S the top of a tree
TREF	*adj* unfit for use according to Jewish law
TREFAH	*adj* tref
TREFOIL	*n* pl. -S a plant having ternate leaves
TREHALA	*n* pl. -S a sweet, edible substance forming the pupal case of certain weevils
TREK	*v* TREKKED, TREKKING, TREKS to make a slow or arduous journey
TREKKER	*n* pl. -S one that treks
TRELLIS	*v* -ED, -ING, -ES to provide with a trellis (a frame used as a support for climbing plants)
TREMBLE	*v* -BLED, -BLING, -BLES to shake involuntarily
TREMBLER	*n* pl. -S one that trembles
TREMBLY	*adj* -BLIER, -BLIEST marked by trembling
TREMOLO	*n* pl. -LOS a vibrating musical effect
TREMOR	*n* pl. -S a shaking movement
TRENAIL	*n* pl. -S treenail
TRENCH	*v* -ED, -ING, -ES to dig a long, narrow excavation in the ground
TRENCHER	*n* pl. -S a wooden platter for serving food
TREND	*v* -ED, -ING, -S to take a particular course
TRENDY	*adj* TRENDIER, TRENDIEST very fashionable **TRENDILY** *adv*
TRENDY	*n* pl. TRENDIES a trendy person
TREPAN	*v* -PANNED, -PANNING, -PANS to trephine
TREPANG	*n* pl. -S a marine animal
TREPHINE	*v* -PHINED, -PHINING, -PHINES to operate on with a surgical saw
TREPID	*adj* timorous
TRESPASS	*v* -ED, -ING, -ES to enter upon the land of another unlawfully
TRESS	*n* pl. -ES a long lock of hair **TRESSED** *adj*
TRESSEL	*n* pl. -S trestle
TRESSIER	comparative of tressy
TRESSIEST	superlative of tressy
TRESSOUR	*n* pl. -S tressure

TRESSURE *n* pl. -S a type of heraldic design

TRESSY *adj* TRESSIER, TRESSIEST abounding in tresses

TRESTLE *n* pl. -S a framework for supporting a bridge

TRET *n* pl. -S an allowance formerly paid to purchasers for waste incurred in transit

TREVET *n* pl. -S trivet

TREWS *n/pl* close-fitting tartan trousers

TREY *n* pl. TREYS a three in cards, dice, or dominoes

TRIABLE *adj* subject to judicial examination

TRIAC *n* pl. -S an electronic device used to control power

TRIACID *n* pl. -S a type of acid

TRIAD *n* pl. -S a group of three

TRIADIC *n* pl. -S a member of a triad

TRIADISM *n* pl. -S the quality or state of being a triad

TRIAGE *n* pl. -S a system of treating disaster victims

TRIAL *n* pl. -S a judicial examination

TRIANGLE *n* pl. -S a polygon having three sides

TRIARCHY *n* pl. -CHIES government by three persons

TRIAXIAL *adj* having three axes

TRIAZIN *n* pl. -S triazine

TRIAZINE *n* pl. -S a chemical compound

TRIAZOLE *n* pl. -S a chemical compound

TRIBADE *n* pl. -S a lesbian **TRIBADIC** *adj*

TRIBAL *adj* pertaining to a tribe **TRIBALLY** *adv*

TRIBASIC *adj* having three replaceable hydrogen atoms

TRIBE *n* pl. -S a group of people sharing a common ancestry, language, and culture

TRIBRACH *n* pl. -S a type of metrical foot

TRIBUNAL *n* pl. -S a court of justice

TRIBUNE *n* pl. -S a defender of the rights of the people

TRIBUTE *n* pl. -S something given to show respect, gratitude, or admiration

TRICE *v* TRICED, TRICING, TRICES to haul up with a rope

TRICEPS *n* pl. -ES an arm muscle

TRICHINA *n* pl. -NAE or -NAS a parasitic worm

TRICHITE *n* pl. -S a minute mineral body found in volcanic rocks

TRICHOID *adj* hairlike

TRICHOME *n* pl. -S a hairlike outgrowth

TRICING present participle of trice

TRICK *v* -ED, -ING, -S to deceive

TRICKER *n* pl. -S one that tricks

TRICKERY *n* pl. -ERIES deception

TRICKIE *adj* TRICKIER, TRICKIEST tricky

TRICKIER comparative of tricky

TRICKIEST superlative of tricky

TRICKILY *adv* in a tricky manner

TRICKISH *adj* tricky

TRICKLE *v* -LED, -LING, -LES to flow or fall in drops

TRICKLY *adj* -LIER, -LIEST marked by trickling

TRICKSY *adj* -SIER, -SIEST mischievous

TRICKY *adj* TRICKIER, TRICKIEST characterized by deception

TRICLAD *n* pl. -S an aquatic flatworm

TRICOLOR *n* pl. -S a flag having three colors

TRICORN *n* pl. -S a hat with the brim turned up on three sides

TRICORNE *n* pl. -S tricorn

TRICOT *n* pl. -S a knitted fabric

TRICTRAC *n* pl. -S a form of backgammon

TRICYCLE *n* pl. -S a vehicle having three wheels

TRIDENT *n* pl. -S a spear having three prongs

TRIDUUM *n* pl. -S a period of three days of prayer

TRIED past tense of try

TRIENE *n* pl. -S a type of chemical compound

TRIENNIA *n/pl* periods of three years

TRIENS *n* pl. -ENTES a coin of ancient Rome

TRIER *n* pl. -S one that tries

TRIES present 3d person sing. of try

TRIETHYL *adj* containing three ethyl groups

TRIFECTA *n* pl. -S a system of betting

TRIFID *adj* divided into three parts

TRIFLE *v* -FLED, -FLING, -FLES to waste time

TRIFLER *n* pl. -S one that trifles

TRIFLING *n* pl. -S a waste of time

TRIFOCAL *n* pl. -S a type of lens

TRIFOLD *adj* having three parts

TRIFORIA *n/pl* galleries in a church

TRIFORM	*adj* having three forms	**TRIMOTOR**	*n* pl. -S an airplane powered
TRIG	*adj* TRIGGER, TRIGGEST neat		by three engines
		TRINAL	*adj* having three parts
TRIG	*v* TRIGGED, TRIGGING, TRIGS to make trig	**TRINARY**	*adj* consisting of three parts
		TRINDLE	*v* -DLED, -DLING, -DLES to
TRIGGER	*v* -ED, -ING, -S to actuate		trundle
TRIGGEST	superlative of trig	**TRINE**	*v* TRINED, TRINING, TRINES
TRIGGING	present participle of trig		to place in a particular
TRIGLY	*adv* in a trig manner		astrological position
TRIGLYPH	*n* pl. -S an architectural ornament	**TRINITY**	*n* pl. -TIES a group of three
		TRINKET	*v* -ED, -ING, -S to deal
TRIGNESS	*n* pl. -ES the quality or state of being trig		secretly
		TRINKUMS	*n/pl* small ornaments
TRIGO	*n* pl. -GOS wheat	**TRINODAL**	*adj* having three nodes
TRIGON	*n* pl. -S an ancient stringed instrument	**TRIO**	*n* pl. TRIOS a group of three
		TRIODE	*n* pl. -S a type of electron tube
TRIGONAL	*adj* shaped like a triangle	**TRIOL**	*n* pl. -S a type of chemical
TRIGRAM	*n* pl. -S a cluster of three successive letters		compound
		TRIOLET	*n* pl. -S a short poem of fixed
TRIGRAPH	*n* pl. -S a group of three letters representing one sound		form
		TRIOSE	*n* pl. -S a simple sugar
TRIHEDRA	*n/pl* figures having three plane surfaces meeting at a point	**TRIOXID**	*n* pl. -S trioxide
		TRIOXIDE	*n* pl. -S a type of oxide
TRIJET	*n* pl. -S an airplane powered by three jet engines	**TRIP**	*v* TRIPPED, TRIPPING, TRIPS to stumble
TRIKE	*n* pl. -S a tricycle	**TRIPACK**	*n* pl. -S a type of film pack
TRILBY	*n* pl. -BIES a soft felt hat	**TRIPART**	*adj* divided into three parts
TRILL	*v* -ED, -ING, -S to sing or play with a vibrating effect	**TRIPE**	*n* pl. -S a part of the stomach of a ruminant that is used as food
TRILLER	*n* pl. -S one that trills		
TRILLION	*n* pl. -S a number	**TRIPEDAL**	*adj* having three feet
TRILLIUM	*n* pl. -S a flowering plant	**TRIPHASE**	*adj* having three phases
TRILOBAL	*adj* trilobed	**TRIPLANE**	*n* pl. -S a type of airplane
TRILOBED	*adj* having three lobes	**TRIPLE**	*v* -PLED, -PLING, -PLES to
TRILOGY	*n* pl. -GIES a group of three related literary works		make three times as great
		TRIPLET	*n* pl. -S a group of three of
TRIM	*adj* TRIMMER, TRIMMEST neat and orderly		one kind
		TRIPLEX	*n* pl. -ES an apartment having
TRIM	*v* TRIMMED, TRIMMING, TRIMS to make trim by cutting		three floors
		TRIPLING	present participle of triple
TRIMARAN	*n* pl. -S a sailing vessel	**TRIPLITE**	*n* pl. -S a mineral
TRIMER	*n* pl. -S a type of chemical compound **TRIMERIC** *adj*	**TRIPLOID**	*n* pl. -S a cell having a chromosome number that is three times the basic number
TRIMETER	*n* pl. -S a verse of three metrical feet		
		TRIPLY	*adv* in a triple degree, manner, or number
TRIMLY	*adv* in a trim manner		
TRIMMED	past tense of trim	**TRIPOD**	*n* pl. -S a stand having three
TRIMMER	*n* pl. -S one that trims		legs **TRIPODAL, TRIPODIC**
TRIMMEST	superlative of trim		*adj*
TRIMMING	*n* pl. -S something added as a decoration	**TRIPODY**	*n* pl. -DIES a verse of three metrical feet
TRIMNESS	*n* pl. -ES the state of being trim	**TRIPOLI**	*n* pl. -S a soft, friable rock
		TRIPOS	*n* pl. -ES a tripod
TRIMORPH	*n* pl. -S a substance existing in three forms	**TRIPPED**	past tense of trip
		TRIPPER	*n* pl. -S one that trips

TRIPPET   n pl. -S a part of a mechanism designed to strike another part

TRIPPING   n pl. -S the act of one that trips

TRIPPY   adj -PIER, -PIEST suggesting a trip on psychedelic drugs

TRIPTANE   n pl. -S a chemical compound

TRIPTYCA   n pl. -S a triptych

TRIPTYCH   n pl. -S an ancient writing tablet

TRIPWIRE   n pl. -S a low-placed hidden wire that sets off an alarm or a trap

TRIREME   n pl. -S an ancient Greek or Roman warship

TRISCELE   n pl. -S triskele

TRISECT   v -ED, -ING, -S to divide into three equal parts

TRISEME   n pl. -S a type of metrical foot TRISEMIC adj

TRISHAW   n pl. -S a pedicab

TRISKELE   n pl. -S a figure consisting of three branches radiating from a center

TRISMUS   n pl. -ES lockjaw TRISMIC adj

TRISOME   n pl. -S an organism having one chromosome in addition to the usual diploid number

TRISOMIC   n pl. -S a trisome

TRISOMY   n pl. -MIES the condition of being a trisome

TRISTATE   adj pertaining to an area made up of three adjoining states

TRISTE   adj sad

TRISTEZA   n pl. -S a disease of citrus trees

TRISTFUL   adj sad

TRISTICH   n pl. -S a stanza of three lines

TRITE   adj TRITER, TRITEST used so often as to be made commonplace TRITELY adv

TRITHING   n pl. -S an administrative division in England

TRITICUM   n pl. -S a cereal grass

TRITIUM   n pl. -S an isotope of hydrogen

TRITOMA   n pl. -S an African herb

TRITON   n pl. -S a marine mollusk

TRITONE   n pl. -S a musical interval of three whole tones

TRIUMPH   v -ED, -ING, -S to be victorious

TRIUMVIR   n pl. -VIRS or -VIRI one of a ruling body of three in ancient Rome.

TRIUNE   n pl. -S a trinity

TRIUNITY   n pl. -TIES a trinity

TRIVALVE   n pl. -S a type of shell

TRIVET   n pl. -S a small stand having three legs

TRIVIA   n/pl insignificant matters

TRIVIAL   adj insignificant

TRIVIUM   n pl. -IA a group of studies in medieval schools

TROAK   v -ED, -ING, -S to troke

TROCAR   n pl. -S a surgical instrument

TROCHAIC   n pl. -S a trochee

TROCHAL   adj shaped like a wheel

TROCHAR   n pl. -S trocar

TROCHE   n pl. -S a medicated lozenge

TROCHEE   n pl. -S a type of metrical foot

TROCHIL   n pl. -S an African bird

TROCHILI   n/pl trochils

TROCHLEA   n pl. -LEAE or -LEAS an anatomical structure resembling a pulley

TROCHOID   n pl. -S a type of geometric curve

TROCK   v -ED, -ING, -S to troke

TROD   a past tense of tread

TRODDEN   past participle of tread

TRODE   a past tense of tread

TROFFER   n pl. -S a fixture for fluorescent lighting

TROGON   n pl. -S a tropical bird

TROIKA   n pl. -S a Russian carriage

TROILISM   n pl. -S sexual relations involving three persons

TROILITE   n pl. -S a mineral

TROILUS   n pl. -ES a large butterfly

TROIS   n pl. TROIS the number three

TROKE   v TROKED, TROKING, TROKES to exchange

TROLAND   n pl. -S a unit of measurement of retinal response to light

TROLL   v -ED, -ING, -S to fish with a slowly trailing line

TROLLER   n pl. -S one that trolls

TROLLEY   v -ED, -ING, -S to convey by streetcar

TROLLIED   past tense of trolly

TROLLIES   present 3d person sing. of trolly

TROLLING   n pl. -S the act of one that trolls

TROLLOP   n pl. -S a prostitute TROLLOPY adj

TROLLY   v -LIED, -LYING, -LIES to trolley

TROMBONE   n pl. -S a brass wind instrument

TROMMEL *n* pl. -S a screen used for sifting rock, ore, or coal

TROMP *v* -ED, -ING, -S to tramp

TROMPE *n* pl. -S a device used for supplying air to a furnace

TRONA *n* pl. -S a mineral

TRONE *n* pl. -S a weighing device

TROOP *v* -ED, -ING, -S to move or gather in crowds

TROOPER *n* pl. -S a cavalryman

TROOPIAL *n* pl. -S troupial

TROOZ *n/pl* trews

TROP *adv* too much

TROPE *n* pl. -S the figurative use of a word

TROPHIC *adj* pertaining to nutrition

TROPHY *v* -PHIED, -PHYING, -PHIES to honor with a trophy (a symbol of victory)

TROPIC *n* pl. -S either of two circles of the celestial sphere on each side of the equator **TROPICAL** *adj*

TROPIN *n* pl. -S tropine

TROPINE *n* pl. -S a poisonous alkaloid

TROPISM *n* pl. -S the involuntary response of an organism to an external stimulus

TROPONIN *n* pl. -S a protein of muscle

TROT *v* TROTTED, TROTTING, TROTS to go at a gait between a walk and a run

TROTH *v* -ED, -ING, -S to betroth

TROTLINE *n* pl. -S a strong fishing line

TROTTED past tense of trot

TROTTER *n* pl. -S a horse that trots

TROTTING present participle of trot

TROTYL *n* pl. -S an explosive

TROUBLE *v* -BLED, -BLING, -BLES to distress

TROUBLER *n* pl. -S one that troubles

TROUGH *n* pl. -S a long, narrow receptacle

TROUNCE *v* TROUNCED, TROUNCING, TROUNCES to beat severely

TROUNCER *n* pl. -S one that trounces

TROUPE *v* TROUPED, TROUPING, TROUPES to tour with a theatrical company

TROUPER *n* pl. -S a member of a theatrical company

TROUPIAL *n* pl. -S a tropical bird

TROUPING present participle of troupe

TROUSER *adj* pertaining to trousers

TROUSERS *n/pl* a garment for the lower part of the body

TROUT *n* pl. -S a freshwater fish

TROUTY *adj* TROUTIER, TROUTIEST abounding in trout

TROUVERE *n* pl. -S a medieval poet

TROUVEUR *n* pl. -S trouvere

TROVE *n* pl. -S a valuable discovery

TROVER *n* pl. -S a type of legal action

TROW *v* -ED, -ING, -S to suppose

TROWEL *v* -ELED, -ELING, -ELS or -ELLED, -ELLING, -ELS to smooth with a trowel (a hand tool having a flat blade)

TROWELER *n* pl. -S one that trowels

TROWSERS *n/pl* trousers

TROWTH *n* pl. -S truth

TROY *n* pl. TROYS a system of weights

TRUANCY *n* pl. -CIES an act of truanting

TRUANT *v* -ED, -ING, -S to stay out of school without permission

TRUANTRY *n* pl. -RIES truancy

TRUCE *v* TRUCED, TRUCING, TRUCES to suspend hostilities by mutual agreement

TRUCK *v* -ED, -ING, -S to transport by truck (an automotive vehicle designed to carry loads)

TRUCKAGE *n* pl. -S transportation of goods by trucks

TRUCKER *n* pl. -S a truck driver

TRUCKFUL *n* pl. -S as much as a truck can hold

TRUCKING *n* pl. -S truckage

TRUCKLE *v* -LED, -LING, -LES to yield weakly

TRUCKLER *n* pl. -S one that truckles

TRUCKMAN *n* pl. -MEN a trucker

TRUDGE *v* TRUDGED, TRUDGING, TRUDGES to walk tiredly

TRUDGEN *n* pl. -S a swimming stroke

TRUDGEON *n* pl. -S trudgen

TRUDGER *n* pl. -S one that trudges

TRUDGING present participle of trudge

TRUE *adj* TRUER, TRUEST consistent with fact or reality

TRUE *v* TRUED, TRUING or TRUEING, TRUES to bring to conformity with a standard or requirement

TRUEBLUE *n* pl. -S a person of unwavering loyalty

TRUEBORN *adj* genuinely such by birth

TRUEBRED *adj* designating an animal of unmixed stock

TRUED past tense of true

TRUELOVE *n* pl. -S a sweetheart

TRUENESS *n* pl. -ES the quality or state of being true

TRUER comparative of true

TRUEST superlative of true

TRUFFE *n* pl. -S truffle

TRUFFLE *n* pl. -S an edible fungus **TRUFFLED** *adj*

TRUG *n* pl. -S a gardener's basket

TRUING a present participle of true

TRUISM *n* pl. -S an obvious truth **TRUISTIC** *adj*

TRULL *n* pl. -S a prostitute

TRULY *adv* in conformity with fact or reality

TRUMEAU *n* pl. -MEAUX a column supporting part of a doorway

TRUMP *v* -ED, -ING, -S to outdo

TRUMPERY *n* pl. -ERIES worthless finery

TRUMPET *v* -ED, -ING, -S to sound on a trumpet (a brass wind instrument)

TRUNCATE *v* -CATED, -CATING, -CATES to shorten by cutting off a part

TRUNDLE *v* -DLED, -DLING, -DLES to propel by causing to rotate

TRUNDLER *n* pl. -S one that trundles

TRUNK *n* pl. -S the main stem of a tree **TRUNKED** *adj*

TRUNKFUL *n* pl. -S as much as a trunk (a storage box) can hold

TRUNNEL *n* pl. -S treenail

TRUNNION *n* pl. -S a pin or pivot on which something can be rotated

TRUSS *v* -ED, -ING, -ES to secure tightly

TRUSSER *n* pl. -S one that trusses

TRUSSING *n* pl. -S the framework of a structure

TRUST *v* -ED, -ING, -S to place confidence in

TRUSTEE *v* -TEED, -TEEING, -TEES to commit to the care of an administrator

TRUSTER *n* pl. -S one that trusts

TRUSTFUL *adj* inclined to trust

TRUSTOR *n* pl. -S one that trustees his property

TRUSTY *adj* TRUSTIER, TRUSTIEST worthy of trust **TRUSTILY** *adv*

TRUSTY *n* pl. TRUSTIES one worthy of trust

TRUTH *n* pl. -S conformity to fact or reality

TRUTHFUL *adj* telling the truth

TRY *v* TRIED, TRYING, TRIES to attempt

TRYINGLY *adv* in a distressing manner

TRYMA *n* pl. -MATA a type of nut

TRYOUT *n* pl. -S a test of ability

TRYPSIN *n* pl. -S an enzyme **TRYPTIC** *adj*

TRYSAIL *n* pl. -S a type of sail

TRYST *v* -ED, -ING, -S to agree to meet

TRYSTE *n* pl. -S a market

TRYSTER *n* pl. -S one that trysts

TRYWORKS *n/pl* a type of furnace

TSADE *n* pl. -S sade

TSADI *n* pl. -S sade

TSAR *n* pl. -S czar

TSARDOM *n* pl. -S czardom

TSAREVNA *n* pl. -S czarevna

TSARINA *n* pl. -S czarina

TSARISM *n* pl. -S czarism

TSARIST *n* pl. -S czarist

TSARITZA *n* pl. -S czaritza

TSETSE *n* pl. -S an African fly

TSIMMES *n* pl. TSIMMES tzimmes

TSK *v* -ED, -ING, -S to utter an exclamation of annoyance

TSKTSK *v* -ED, -ING, -S to tsk

TSOORIS *n* pl. TSOORIS tsuris

TSORES *n* pl. TSORES tsuris

TSORIS *n* pl. TSORIS tsuris

TSORRISS *n* pl. TSORRISS tsuris

TSUBA *n* pl. TSUBA a part of a Japanese sword

TSUNAMI *n* pl. -S a very large ocean wave **TSUNAMIC** *adj*

TSURIS *n* pl. TSURIS a series of misfortunes

TUATARA *n* pl. -S a large reptile

TUATERA *n* pl. -S tuatara

TUB *v* TUBBED, TUBBING, TUBS to wash in a tub (a round, open vessel)

TUBA *n* pl. -BAS or -BAE a brass wind instrument

TUBAIST *n* pl. -S a tuba player

TUBAL *adj* pertaining to a tube

TUBATE *adj* tubular

TUBBABLE *adj* suitable for washing in a tub

TUBBED past tense of tub

TUBBER *n* pl. -S one that tubs

TUBBING present participle of tub

TUBBY *adj* -BIER, -BIEST short and fat

TUBE *v* TUBED, TUBING, TUBES to provide with a tube (a long, hollow cylinder)

TUBELESS *adj* having no tube

TUBELIKE	adj resembling a tube	TUGHRIK	n pl. -S tugrik
TUBENOSE	n pl. -S a bird having tubular nostrils	TUGLESS	adj being without a rope or chain with which to pull
TUBER	n pl. -S a thick underground stem	TUGRIK	n pl. -S a monetary unit of Mongolia
TUBERCLE	n pl. -S a small, rounded swelling	TUI	n pl. -S a bird of New Zealand
		TUILLE	n pl. -S a tasset
TUBEROID	adj pertaining to a tuber	TUITION	n pl. -S a fee for instruction
TUBEROSE	n pl. -S a Mexican herb	TULADI	n pl. -S a freshwater fish
TUBEROUS	adj pertaining to a tuber	TULE	n pl. -S a tall marsh plant
TUBEWORK	n pl. -S tubing	TULIP	n pl. -S a flowering plant
TUBFUL	n pl. -S as much as a tub will hold	TULLE	n pl. -S a silk material
		TULLIBEE	n pl. -S a freshwater fish
TUBIFEX	n pl. -ES an aquatic worm	TUMBLE	v -BLED, -BLING, -BLES to fall or roll end over end
TUBIFORM	adj tubular	
TUBING	n pl. -S material in the form of a tube	TUMBLER	n pl. -S one that tumbles
		TUMBLING	n pl. -S the sport of gymnastics
TUBIST	n pl. -S a tubaist	
TUBLIKE	adj resembling a tub	TUMBREL	n pl. -S a type of cart
TUBULAR	adj shaped like a tube	TUMBRIL	n pl. -S tumbrel
TUBULATE	v -LATED, -LATING, -LATES to form into a tube	TUMEFY	v -FIED, -FYING, -FIES to swell
TUBULE	n pl. -S a small tube	TUMID	adj swollen TUMIDLY adv
TUBULIN	n pl. -S a protein that polymerizes to form tiny tubules	TUMIDITY	n pl. -TIES the quality or state of being tumid
		TUMMLER	n pl. -S an entertainer who encourages audience participation
TUBULOSE	adj tubular	
TUBULOUS	adj tubular	
TUBULURE	n pl. -S a short tubular opening	TUMMY	n pl. -MIES the stomach
		TUMOR	n pl. -S an abnormal swelling TUMORAL, TUMOROUS adj
TUCHUN	n pl. -S a Chinese military governor	
		TUMOUR	n pl. -S tumor
TUCK	v -ED, -ING, -S to fold under	TUMP	n pl. -S tumpline
TUCKAHOE	n pl. -S the edible root of certain arums	TUMPLINE	n pl. -S a strap for supporting a load on the back
TUCKER	v -ED, -ING, -S to weary	TUMULAR	adj having the form of a mound
TUCKET	n pl. -S a trumpet fanfare	
TUCKSHOP	n pl. -S a confectioner's shop	TUMULI	a pl. of tumulus
TUFA	n pl. -S a porous limestone	TUMULOSE	adj full of mounds
TUFF	n pl. -S a volcanic rock	TUMULOUS	adj tumulose
TUFFET	n pl. -S a clump of grass	TUMULT	n pl. -S a great din and commotion
TUFOLI	n pl. TUFOLI a large macaroni shell	
		TUMULUS	n pl. -LI or -LUSES a mound over a grave
TUFT	v -ED, -ING, -S to form into tufts (clusters of flexible outgrowths attached at the base)	TUN	v TUNNED, TUNNING, TUNS to store in a large cask
		TUNA	n pl. -S a marine food fish
TUFTER	n pl. -S one that tufts	TUNABLE	adj capable of being tuned TUNABLY adv
TUFTY	adj TUFTIER, TUFTIEST abounding in tufts TUFTILY adv	
		TUNDISH	n pl. -ES a receptacle for molten metal
TUG	v TUGGED, TUGGING, TUGS to pull with force	TUNDRA	n pl. -S a level, treeless expanse of arctic land
		TUNE	v TUNED, TUNING, TUNES to put into the proper pitch
TUGBOAT	n pl. -S a boat built for towing	
TUGGER	n pl. -S one that tugs	
TUGGING	present participle of tug	TUNEABLE	adj tunable TUNEABLY adv

TUNEFUL	*adj* melodious
TUNELESS	*adj* not tuneful
TUNER	*n* pl. -S one that tunes
TUNEUP	*n* pl. -S an adjustment to insure efficient operation
TUNG	*n* pl. -S a Chinese tree
TUNGSTEN	*n* pl. -S a metallic element **TUNGSTIC** *adj*
TUNIC	*n* pl. -S a loose-fitting garment
TUNICA	*n* pl. -CAE an enveloping membrane or layer of body tissue
TUNICATE	*n* pl. -S a small marine animal
TUNICLE	*n* pl. -S a type of vestment
TUNING	present participle of tune
TUNNAGE	*n* pl. -S tonnage
TUNNED	past tense of tun
TUNNEL	*v* -NELED, -NELING, -NELS or -NELLED, -NELLING, -NELS to dig a tunnel (an underground passageway)
TUNNELER	*n* pl. -S one that tunnels
TUNNING	present participle of tun
TUNNY	*n* pl. -NIES a tuna
TUP	*v* TUPPED, TUPPING, TUPS to copulate with a ewe
TUPELO	*n* pl. -LOS a softwood tree
TUPIK	*n* pl. -S an Eskimo tent
TUPPED	past tense of tup
TUPPENCE	*n* pl. -S twopence
TUPPENNY	*adj* twopenny
TUPPING	present participle of tup
TUQUE	*n* pl. -S a knitted woolen cap
TURACO	*n* pl. -COS touraco
TURACOU	*n* pl. -S touraco
TURBAN	*n* pl. -S a head covering worn by Muslims **TURBANED** *adj*
TURBARY	*n* pl. -RIES a place where peat can be dug
TURBETH	*n* pl. -S turpeth
TURBID	*adj* thick or opaque with roiled sediment **TURBIDLY** *adv*
TURBINAL	*n* pl. -S a bone of the nasal passage
TURBINE	*n* pl. -S a type of engine
TURBIT	*n* pl. -S a domestic pigeon
TURBITH	*n* pl. -S turpeth
TURBO	*n* pl. -BOS a turbine
TURBOCAR	*n* pl. -S an auto powered by a gas turbine
TURBOFAN	*n* pl. -S a type of jet engine
TURBOJET	*n* pl. -S a type of jet engine
TURBOT	*n* pl. -S a European flatfish
TURDINE	*adj* belonging to a large family of singing birds
TUREEN	*n* pl. -S a large, deep bowl
TURF	*n* pl. TURFS or TURVES a surface layer of earth containing a dense growth of grass and its roots
TURF	*v* -ED, -ING, -S to cover with turf
TURFIER	comparative of turfy
TURFIEST	superlative of turfy
TURFLESS	*adj* having no turf
TURFLIKE	*adj* resembling turf
TURFMAN	*n* pl. -MEN a person who is devoted to horse racing
TURFSKI	*n* pl. -S a type of ski
TURFY	*adj* TURFIER, TURFIEST covered with turf
TURGENCY	*n* pl. -CIES turgor
TURGENT	*adj* turgid
TURGID	*adj* swollen **TURGIDLY** *adv*
TURGITE	*n* pl. -S an iron ore
TURGOR	*n* pl. -S the quality or state of being turgid
TURISTA	*n* pl. -S intestinal sickness affecting a tourist in a foreign country
TURKEY	*n* pl. -KEYS a large American bird
TURKOIS	*n* pl. -ES turquois
TURMERIC	*n* pl. -S an East Indian herb
TURMOIL	*v* -ED, -ING, -S to throw into an uproar
TURN	*v* -ED, -ING, -S to move around a central point **TURNABLE** *adj*
TURNCOAT	*n* pl. -S a traitor
TURNDOWN	*n* pl. -S a rejection
TURNER	*n* pl. -S one that turns
TURNERY	*n* pl. -ERIES the process of shaping articles on a lathe
TURNHALL	*n* pl. -S a building where gymnasts practice
TURNING	*n* pl. -S a rotation about an axis
TURNIP	*n* pl. -S an edible plant root
TURNKEY	*n* pl. -KEYS a person who has charge of a prison's keys
TURNOFF	*n* pl. -S a road that branches off from a larger one
TURNOUT	*n* pl. -S an assemblage of people
TURNOVER	*n* pl. -S an upset or overthrow
TURNPIKE	*n* pl. -S a highway on which tolls are collected
TURNSOLE	*n* pl. -S a plant that turns with the sun
TURNSPIT	*n* pl. -S one that turns a roasting spit

TURNUP *n* pl. -S a part of a garment that is turned up

TURPETH *n* pl. -S a medicinal plant root

TURPS *n* pl. TURPS turpentine

TURQUOIS *n* pl. -ES a greenish blue gem

TURRET *n* pl. -S a small tower **TURRETED** *adj*

TURRICAL *adj* resembling a turret

TURTLE *v* -TLED, -TLING, -TLES to catch turtles (tortoises)

TURTLER *n* pl. -S one that turtles

TURTLING *n* pl. -S the act of one that turtles

TURVES a pl. of turf

TUSCHE *n* pl. -S a liquid used in lithography

TUSH *v* -ED, -ING, -ES to tusk

TUSHIE *n* pl. -S the buttocks

TUSHY *n* pl. TUSHIES tushie

TUSK *v* -ED, -ING, -S to gore with a tusk (a long, pointed tooth extending outside of the mouth)

TUSKER *n* pl. -S an animal with tusks

TUSKLESS *adj* having no tusk

TUSKLIKE *adj* resembling a tusk

TUSSAH *n* pl. -S an Asian silkworm

TUSSAL *adj* pertaining to a cough

TUSSAR *n* pl. -S tussah

TUSSEH *n* pl. -S tussah

TUSSER *n* pl. -S tussah

TUSSIS *n* pl. -SISES a cough **TUSSIVE** *adj*

TUSSLE *v* -SLED, -SLING, -SLES to struggle

TUSSOCK *n* pl. -S a clump of grass **TUSSOCKY** *adj*

TUSSOR *n* pl. -S tussah

TUSSORE *n* pl. -S tussah

TUSSUCK *n* pl. -S tussock

TUSSUR *n* pl. -S tussah

TUT *v* TUTTED, TUTTING, TUTS to utter an exclamation of impatience

TUTEE *n* pl. -S one who is being tutored

TUTELAGE *n* pl. -S the act of tutoring

TUTELAR *n* pl. -S a tutelary

TUTELARY *n* pl. -LARIES one who has the power to protect

TUTOR *v* -ED, -ING, -S to instruct privately

TUTORAGE *n* pl. -S tutelage

TUTORESS *n* pl. -ES a female who tutors

TUTORIAL *n* pl. -S a session of tutoring

TUTOYER *v* -TOYERED or -TOYED, -TOYERING, -TOYERS to address familiarly

TUTTED past tense of tut

TUTTI *n* pl. -S a musical passage performed by all the performers

TUTTING present participle of tut

TUTTY *n* pl. -TIES an impure zinc oxide

TUTU *n* pl. -S a short ballet skirt

TUX *n* pl. -ES a tuxedo

TUXEDO *n* pl. -DOES or -DOS a man's semiformal dinner coat **TUXEDOED** *adj*

TUYER *n* pl. -S tuyere

TUYERE *n* pl. -S a pipe through which air is forced into a blast furnace

TWA *n* pl. -S two

TWADDLE *v* -DLED, -DLING, -DLES to talk foolishly

TWADDLER *n* pl. -S one that twaddles

TWAE *n* pl. -S two

TWAIN *n* pl. -S a set of two

TWANG *v* -ED, -ING, -S to make a sharp, vibrating sound

TWANGER *n* pl. -S one that twangs

TWANGIER comparative of twangy

TWANGIEST superlative of twangy

TWANGLE *v* -GLED, -GLING, -GLES to twang

TWANGLER *n* pl. -S one that twangles

TWANGY *adj* TWANGIER, TWANGIEST twanging

TWANKY *n* pl. -KIES a variety of green tea

TWASOME *n* pl. -S twosome

TWATTLE *v* -TLED, -TLING, -TLES to twaddle

TWEAK *v* -ED, -ING, -S to pinch and twist sharply

TWEAKY *adj* TWEAKIER, TWEAKIEST twitchy

TWEE *adj* affectedly cute or dainty

TWEED *n* pl. -S a coarse woolen fabric

TWEEDLE *v* -DLED, -DLING, -DLES to perform casually on a musical instrument

TWEEDY *adj* TWEEDIER, TWEEDIEST resembling tweed

TWEEN *prep* between

TWEENY *n* pl. TWEENIES a housemaid

TWEET *v* -ED, -ING, -S to chirp

TWEETER *n* pl. -S a loudspeaker designed to reproduce high-pitched sounds

TWEEZE *v* TWEEZED, TWEEZING, TWEEZES to pluck with a tweezer

TWEEZER *n* pl. -S a pincerlike tool

TWELFTH *n* pl. -S the number twelve in a series

TWELVE *n* pl. -S a number

TWELVEMO *n* pl. -MOS a page size

TWENTY *n* pl. -TIES a number

TWERP *n* pl. -S a small, impudent person

TWIBIL *n* pl. -S a battle-ax with two cutting edges

TWIBILL *n* pl. -S twibil

TWICE *adv* two times

TWIDDLE *v* -DLED, -DLING, -DLES to play idly with something

TWIDDLER *n* pl. -S one that twiddles

TWIDDLY *adj* -DLIER, -DLIEST having many turns

TWIER *n* pl. -S tuyere

TWIG *v* TWIGGED, TWIGGING, TWIGS to observe

TWIGGEN *adj* made of twigs (small branches)

TWIGGY *adj* -GIER, -GIEST twiglike

TWIGLESS *adj* having no twigs

TWIGLIKE *adj* resembling a twig

TWILIGHT *n* pl. -S the early evening light

TWILIT *adj* lighted by twilight

TWILL *v* -ED, -ING, -S to weave so as to produce a diagonal pattern

TWILLING *n* pl. -S a twilled fabric

TWIN *v* TWINNED, TWINNING, TWINS to bring together in close association

TWINBORN *adj* born at the same birth

TWINE *v* TWINED, TWINING, TWINES to twist together

TWINER *n* pl. -S one that twines

TWINGE *v* TWINGED, TWINGING or TWINGEING, TWINGES to affect with a sharp pain

TWINIER comparative of twiny

TWINIEST superlative of twiny

TWINIGHT *adj* pertaining to a baseball doubleheader that begins in the late afternoon

TWINING present participle of twine

TWINJET *n* pl. -S an aircraft with two jet engines

TWINKLE *v* -KLED, -KLING, -KLES to shine with a flickering or sparkling light

TWINKLER *n* pl. -S one that twinkles

TWINKLY *adj* twinkling

TWINNED past tense of twin

TWINNING *n* pl. -S the bearing of two children at the same birth

TWINSET *n* pl. -S a matching pair of sweaters to be worn together

TWINSHIP *n* pl. -S close similarity or association

TWINY *adj* TWINIER, TWINIEST resembling twine (a strong string)

TWIRL *v* -ED, -ING, -S to rotate rapidly

TWIRLER *n* pl. -S one that twirls

TWIRLY *adj* TWIRLIER, TWIRLIEST curved

TWIRP *n* pl. -S twerp

TWIST *v* -ED, -ING, -S to combine by winding together

TWISTER *n* pl. -S one that twists

TWISTING *n* pl. -S a form of trickery used in selling life insurance

TWISTY *adj* TWISTIER, TWISTIEST full of curves

TWIT *v* TWITTED, TWITTING, TWITS to ridicule

TWITCH *v* -ED, -ING, -ES to move or pull with a sudden motion

TWITCHER *n* pl. -S one that twitches

TWITCHY *adj* TWITCHIER, TWITCHIEST fidgety

TWITTED past tense of twit

TWITTER *v* -ED, -ING, -S to utter a succession of chirping sounds

TWITTERY *adj* nervously agitated

TWITTING present participle of twit

TWIXT *prep* between

TWO *n* pl. TWOS a number

TWOFER *n* pl. -S something sold at the rate of two for the price of one

TWOFOLD *n* pl. -S an amount twice as great as a given unit

TWOPENCE *n* pl. -S a British coin worth two pennies

TWOPENNY *adj* worth twopence

TWOSOME *n* pl. -S a group of two

TWYER *n* pl. -S tuyere

TYCOON *n* pl. -S a wealthy and powerful business person

TYE *n* pl. -S a chain on a ship

TYEE *n* pl. -S a food fish

TYER *n* pl. -S one that ties

TYING	a present participle of tie
TYKE	*n* pl. -S a small child
TYLOSIN	*n* pl. -S an antibiotic
TYMBAL	*n* pl. -S timbal
TYMPAN	*n* pl. -S a drum
TYMPANA	a pl. of tympanum
TYMPANAL	*adj* tympanic
TYMPANIC	*adj* pertaining to the tympanum
TYMPANO	*n* pl. -NI timpano
TYMPANUM	*n* pl. -NA or -NUMS the middle ear
TYMPANY	*n* pl. -NIES a swelling of the abdomen
TYNE	*v* TYNED, TYNING, TYNES to tine
TYPAL	*adj* typical
TYPE	*v* TYPED, TYPING, TYPES to write with a typewriter **TYPABLE, TYPEABLE** *adj*
TYPEBAR	*n* pl. -S a part of a typewriter
TYPECASE	*n* pl. -S a tray for holding printing type
TYPECAST	*v* -CAST, -CASTING, -CASTS to cast in an acting role befitting one's own nature
TYPED	past tense of type
TYPEFACE	*n* pl. -S the face of printing type
TYPESET	*v* -SET, -SETTING, -SETS to set in type
TYPEY	*adj* TYPIER, TYPIEST typy
TYPHOID	*n* pl. -S an infectious disease
TYPHON	*n* pl. -S a type of signal horn
TYPHOON	*n* pl. -S a tropical hurricane **TYPHONIC** *adj*
TYPHOSE	*adj* pertaining to typhoid
TYPHUS	*n* pl. -ES an infectious disease **TYPHOUS** *adj*
TYPIC	*adj* typical
TYPICAL	*adj* having the nature of a representative specimen
TYPIER	comparative of typey and typy
TYPIEST	superlative of typey and typy
TYPIFIER	*n* pl. -S one that typifies
TYPIFY	*v* -FIED, -FYING, -FIES to serve as a typical example of
TYPING	present participle of type
TYPIST	*n* pl. -S one who types
TYPO	*n* pl. -POS a typographical error
TYPOLOGY	*n* pl. -GIES the study of classification according to common characteristics
TYPP	*n* pl. -S a unit of yarn size
TYPY	*adj* TYPIER, TYPIEST characterized by strict conformance to the characteristics of a group
TYRAMINE	*n* pl. -S a chemical compound
TYRANNIC	*adj* characteristic of a tyrant
TYRANNY	*n* pl. -NIES the rule of a tyrant
TYRANT	*n* pl. -S an absolute ruler
TYRE	*v* TYRED, TYRING, TYRES to furnish with a covering for a wheel
TYRO	*n* pl. -ROS a beginner **TYRONIC** *adj*
TYROSINE	*n* pl. -S an amino acid
TYTHE	*v* TYTHED, TYTHING, TYTHES to tithe
TZADDIK	*n* pl. -DIKIM zaddik
TZAR	*n* pl. -S czar
TZARDOM	*n* pl. -S czardom
TZAREVNA	*n* pl. -S czarevna
TZARINA	*n* pl. -S czarina
TZARISM	*n* pl. -S czarism
TZARIST	*n* pl. -S czarist
TZARITZA	*n* pl. -S czaritza
TZETZE	*n* pl. -S tsetse
TZIGANE	*n* pl. -S a gypsy
TZIMMES	*n* pl. TZIMMES a vegetable stew
TZITZIS	*n/pl* zizith
TZITZIT	*n/pl* zizith
TZITZITH	*n/pl* zizith
TZURIS	*n* pl. TZURIS tsuris

UBIETY   *n* pl. -ETIES the state of having a definite location

UBIQUE   *adv* everywhere

UBIQUITY   *n* pl. -TIES the state of being everywhere at the same time

UDDER   *n* pl. -S a mammary gland

UDO   *n* pl. UDOS a Japanese herb

UDOMETER   *n* pl. -S a rain gauge

UDOMETRY   *n* pl. -TRIES the measurement of rain

UFOLOGY   *n* pl. -GIES the study of unidentified flying objects

UGH   *n* pl. -S the sound of a cough or grunt

UGLIER   comparative of ugly

UGLIES   pl. of ugly

UGLIEST   superlative of ugly

UGLIFIER   *n* pl. -S one that uglifies

UGLIFY   *v* -FIED, -FYING, -FIES to make ugly

UGLINESS   *n* pl. -ES the state of being ugly

UGLY   *adj* -LIER, -LIEST displeasing to the sight **UGLILY** *adv*

UGLY   *n* pl. -LIES one that is ugly

UGSOME   *adj* disgusting

UH   *interj* — used to express hesitation

UHLAN   *n* pl. -S one of a body of Prussian cavalry

UINTAITE   *n* pl. -S a variety of asphalt

UKASE   *n* pl. -S an edict

UKE   *n* pl. -S ukelele

UKELELE   *n* pl. -S ukulele

UKULELE   *n* pl. -S a small guitar-like instrument

ULAMA   *n* pl. -S ulema

ULAN   *n* pl. -S uhlan

ULCER   *v* -ED, -ING, -S to affect with an ulcer (a type of lesion)

ULCERATE   *v* -ATED, -ATING, -ATES to ulcer

ULCEROUS   *adj* being or affected with an ulcer

ULEMA   *n* pl. -S a Muslim scholar

ULEXITE   *n* pl. -S a mineral

ULLAGE   *n* pl. -S the amount that a container lacks of being full **ULLAGED** *adj*

ULNA   *n* pl. -NAE or -NAS a bone of the forearm **ULNAR** *adj*

ULNAD   *adv* toward the ulna

ULPAN   *n* pl. -PANIM a school in Israel for teaching Hebrew

ULSTER   *n* pl. -S a long, loose overcoat

ULTERIOR   *adj* more remote

ULTIMA   *n* pl. -S the last syllable of a word

ULTIMACY   *n* pl. -CIES an ultimate

ULTIMATA   *n/pl* final proposals

ULTIMATE   *v* -MATED, -MATING, -MATES to come to an end

ULTIMO   *adj* of or occurring in the preceding month

ULTRA   *n* pl. -S an ultraist

ULTRADRY   *adj* extremely dry

ULTRAHOT   *adj* extremely hot

ULTRAISM   *n* pl. -S advocacy of extreme measures

ULTRAIST   *n* pl. -S an advocate of extreme measures

ULTRALOW   *adj* extremely low

ULTRARED   *n* pl. -S infrared

ULU   *n* pl. -S an Eskimo knife

ULULANT   *adj* howling

ULULATE   *v* -LATED, -LATING, -LATES to howl

ULVA	*n* pl. -S an edible seaweed
UM	*interj* — used to indicate hesitation
UMANGITE	*n* pl. -S a mineral consisting of copper selenide
UMBEL	*n* pl. -S a type of flower cluster **UMBELED, UMBELLAR, UMBELLED** *adj*
UMBELLET	*n* pl. -S a small umbel
UMBER	*v* -ED, -ING, -S to color with a brown pigment
UMBILICI	*n/pl* navels
UMBLES	*n/pl* the entrails of a deer
UMBO	*n* pl. -BONES or -BOS the rounded elevation at the center of a shield **UMBONAL, UMBONATE, UMBONIC** *adj*
UMBRA	*n* pl. -BRAE or -BRAS a dark area **UMBRAL** *adj*
UMBRAGE	*n* pl. -S resentment
UMBRELLA	*v* -ED, -ING, -S to provide with an umbrella (a portable cover for protection from rain or sun)
UMBRETTE	*n* pl. -S a wading bird
UMIAC	*n* pl. -S umiak
UMIACK	*n* pl. -S umiak
UMIAK	*n* pl. -S an open Eskimo boat
UMIAQ	*n* pl. -S umiak
UMLAUT	*v* -ED, -ING, -S to modify a vowel sound by partial assimilation to a succeeding sound
UMM	*interj* um
UMP	*v* -ED, -ING, -S to umpire
UMPIRAGE	*n* pl. -S the function of an umpire
UMPIRE	*v* -PIRED, -PIRING, -PIRES to act as umpire (a person appointed to rule on the plays in a game)
UMPTEEN	*adj* indefinitely numerous
UMTEENTH	*adj* being the last in an indefinitely numerous series
UN	*pron* pl. -S one

U N	Following is a list of self-explanatory adjectives and adverbs containing the prefix UN- (not):

UNABATED	*adj*
UNABLE	*adj*
UNABUSED	*adj*
UNACTED	*adj*

UNADULT	*adj*
UNAFRAID	*adj*
UNAGED	*adj*
UNAGEING	*adj*
UNAGILE	*adj*
UNAGING	*adj*
UNAIDED	*adj*
UNAIMED	*adj*
UNAIRED	*adj*
UNAKIN	*adj*
UNALIKE	*adj*
UNALLIED	*adj*
UNAMUSED	*adj*
UNANELED	*adj*
UNAPT	*adj*
UNAPTLY	*adv*
UNARGUED	*adj*
UNARTFUL	*adj*
UNASKED	*adj*
UNATONED	*adj*
UNAVOWED	*adj*
UNAWAKED	*adj*
UNAWARE	*adj*
UNAWED	*adj*
UNBACKED	*adj*
UNBAKED	*adj*
UNBANNED	*adj*
UNBARBED	*adj*
UNBASED	*adj*
UNBATHED	*adj*
UNBEATEN	*adj*
UNBENIGN	*adj*
UNBIASED	*adj*
UNBILLED	*adj*
UNBITTED	*adj*
UNBITTEN	*adj*
UNBITTER	*adj*
UNBLAMED	*adj*
UNBLEST	*adj*
UNBLOODY	*adj*
UNBONED	*adj*
UNBORN	*adj*
UNBOUGHT	*adj*
UNBOUNCY	*adj*
UNBOWED	*adj*
UNBRED	*adj*
UNBRIGHT	*adj*
UNBROKE	*adj*
UNBROKEN	*adj*
UNBULKY	*adj*
UNBURIED	*adj*
UNBURNED	*adj*
UNBURNT	*adj*
UNBUSTED	*adj*
UNBUSY	*adj*

UNCALLED	adj	UNENDED	adj
UNCANDID	adj	UNENDING	adj
UNCARING	adj	UNENVIED	adj
UNCASHED	adj	UNERASED	adj
UNCASKED	adj	UNEROTIC	adj
UNCATCHY	adj	UNERRING	adj
UNCAUGHT	adj	UNEVADED	adj
UNCAUSED	adj	UNEVEN	adj -EVENER, -EVENEST
UNCHARY	adj	UNEVENLY	adv
UNCHASTE	adj	UNEXOTIC	adj
UNCHEWED	adj	UNEXPERT	adj
UNCHIC	adj	UNFADED	adj
UNCHICLY	adv	UNFADING	adj
UNCHOSEN	adj	UNFAIR	adj -FAIRER, -FAIREST
UNCIVIL	adj	UNFAIRLY	adv
UNCLEAN	adj -CLEANER, -CLEANEST	UNFAKED	adj
UNCLEAR	adj -CLEARER, -CLEAREST	UNFALLEN	adj
UNCLOYED	adj	UNFAMOUS	adj
UNCOATED	adj	UNFANCY	adj
UNCODED	adj	UNFAZED	adj
UNCOINED	adj	UNFEARED	adj
UNCOMBED	adj	UNFED	adj
UNCOMELY	adj	UNFELT	adj
UNCOMIC	adj	UNFILIAL	adj
UNCOMMON	adj -MONER, -MONEST	UNFILLED	adj
UNCOOKED	adj	UNFILMED	adj
UNCOOL	adj	UNFIRED	adj
UNCOOLED	adj	UNFISHED	adj
UNCOUTH	adj	UNFLASHY	adj
UNCOY	adj	UNFLEXED	adj
UNCRAZY	adj	UNFOILED	adj
UNCUFFED	adj	UNFOND	adj
UNCURED	adj	UNFORCED	adj
UNCURSED	adj	UNFORGED	adj
UNCUT	adj	UNFORKED	adj
UNCUTE	adj	UNFORMED	adj
UNDAMPED	adj	UNFOUGHT	adj
UNDARING	adj	UNFOUND	adj
UNDATED	adj	UNFRAMED	adj
UNDECKED	adj	UNFUNDED	adj
UNDENIED	adj	UNFUNNY	adj
UNDEVOUT	adj	UNFUSED	adj
UNDIMMED	adj	UNFUSSY	adj
UNDOABLE	adj	UNGALLED	adj
UNDOCILE	adj	UNGENIAL	adj
UNDOTTED	adj	UNGENTLE	adj
UNDREAMT	adj	UNGENTLY	adv
UNDRIED	adj	UNGIFTED	adj
UNDUBBED	adj	UNGLAZED	adj
UNDULLED	adj	UNGOWNED	adj
UNDYED	adj	UNGRACED	adj
UNEAGER	adj	UNGRADED	adj
UNEARNED	adj	UNGREEDY	adj
UNEATEN	adj	UNGROUND	adj
UNEDIBLE	adj	UNGUIDED	adj
UNEDITED	adj	UNHAILED	adj

UNHALVED	adj		UNMAPPED	adj
UNHAPPY	adj -PIER, -PIEST		UNMARKED	adj
UNHARMED	adj		UNMARRED	adj
UNHASTY	adj		UNMATED	adj
UNHEALED	adj		UNMATTED	adj
UNHEARD	adj		UNMEANT	adj
UNHEATED	adj		UNMELLOW	adj
UNHEDGED	adj		UNMELTED	adj
UNHEEDED	adj		UNMENDED	adj
UNHELPED	adj		UNMERRY	adj
UNHEROIC	adj		UNMET	adj
UNHEWN	adj		UNMILLED	adj
UNHIP	adj		UNMINED	adj
UNHIRED	adj		UNMIXED	adj
UNHOLILY	adv		UNMIXT	adj
UNHOLY	adj -LIER, -LIEST		UNMODISH	adj
UNHUMAN	adj		UNMOLTEN	adj
UNHUNG	adj		UNMOVED	adj
UNHURT	adj		UNMOVING	adj
UNIDEAL	adj		UNMOWN	adj
UNIMBUED	adj		UNNAMED	adj
UNIRONED	adj		UNNEEDED	adj
UNISSUED	adj		UNNOISY	adj
UNJADED	adj		UNNOTED	adj
UNJOINED	adj		UNOILED	adj
UNJOYFUL	adj		UNOPEN	adj
UNJUDGED	adj		UNOPENED	adj
UNJUST	adj		UNORNATE	adj
UNJUSTLY	adv		UNOWNED	adj
UNKEPT	adj		UNPAID	adj
UNKIND	adj -KINDER, -KINDEST		UNPAIRED	adj
UNKINDLY	adv -LIER, -LIEST		UNPARTED	adj
UNKINGLY	adj		UNPAVED	adj
UNKISSED	adj		UNPAYING	adj
UNKOSHER	adj		UNPEELED	adj
UNLAWFUL	adj		UNPITIED	adj
UNLEASED	adj		UNPLACED	adj
UNLED	adj		UNPLAYED	adj
UNLETHAL	adj		UNPLIANT	adj
UNLETTED	adj		UNPLOWED	adj
UNLEVIED	adj		UNPOETIC	adj
UNLICKED	adj		UNPOISED	adj
UNLIKE	adj		UNPOLITE	adj
UNLIKELY	adj -LIER, -LIEST		UNPOLLED	adj
UNLINED	adj		UNPOSED	adj
UNLISTED	adj		UNPOSTED	adj
UNLIT	adj		UNPOTTED	adj
UNLIVELY	adj		UNPRETTY	adj
UNLOBED	adj		UNPRICED	adj
UNLOVED	adj		UNPRIMED	adj
UNLOVELY	adj -LIER, -LIEST		UNPRIZED	adj
UNLOVING	adj		UNPROBED	adj
UNLUCKY	adj -LUCKIER, -LUCKIEST		UNPROVED	adj
UNMACHO	adj		UNPROVEN	adj
UNMANFUL	adj		UNPRUNED	adj
UNMANLY	adj		UNPURE	adj

UNPURGED	*adj*	
UNQUIET	*adj*	-ETER, -ETEST
UNRAISED	*adj*	
UNRAKED	*adj*	
UNRANKED	*adj*	
UNRATED	*adj*	
UNRAZED	*adj*	
UNREAD	*adj*	
UNREADY	*adj*	-READIER, -READIEST
UNREAL	*adj*	
UNREALLY	*adv*	
UNRENTED	*adj*	
UNREPAID	*adj*	
UNRESTED	*adj*	
UNRHYMED	*adj*	
UNRIFLED	*adj*	
UNRIMED	*adj*	
UNRINSED	*adj*	
UNRISEN	*adj*	
UNROPED	*adj*	
UNROUGH	*adj*	
UNRULED	*adj*	
UNRUSHED	*adj*	
UNRUSTED	*adj*	
UNSAFE	*adj*	
UNSAFELY	*adv*	
UNSALTED	*adj*	
UNSATED	*adj*	
UNSAVED	*adj*	
UNSAVORY	*adj*	
UNSAWED	*adj*	
UNSAWN	*adj*	
UNSCALED	*adj*	
UNSEARED	*adj*	
UNSEEDED	*adj*	
UNSEEING	*adj*	
UNSEEMLY	*adj*	-LIER, -LIEST
UNSEEN	*adj*	
UNSEIZED	*adj*	
UNSENT	*adj*	
UNSERVED	*adj*	
UNSEXUAL	*adj*	
UNSEXY	*adj*	
UNSHADED	*adj*	
UNSHAKEN	*adj*	
UNSHAMED	*adj*	
UNSHAPED	*adj*	
UNSHAPEN	*adj*	
UNSHARED	*adj*	
UNSHARP	*adj*	
UNSHAVED	*adj*	
UNSHAVEN	*adj*	
UNSHED	*adj*	
UNSHOD	*adj*	
UNSHORN	*adj*	
UNSHOWY	*adj*	

UNSHRUNK	*adj*	
UNSHUT	*adj*	
UNSIFTED	*adj*	
UNSIGNED	*adj*	
UNSILENT	*adj*	
UNSINFUL	*adj*	
UNSIZED	*adj*	
UNSLAKED	*adj*	
UNSLICED	*adj*	
UNSMART	*adj*	
UNSMOKED	*adj*	
UNSOAKED	*adj*	
UNSOBER	*adj*	
UNSOCIAL	*adj*	
UNSOILED	*adj*	
UNSOLD	*adj*	
UNSOLID	*adj*	
UNSOLVED	*adj*	
UNSORTED	*adj*	
UNSOUGHT	*adj*	
UNSOUND	*adj*	-SOUNDER, -SOUNDEST
UNSOURED	*adj*	
UNSOWED	*adj*	
UNSOWN	*adj*	
UNSPENT	*adj*	
UNSPILT	*adj*	
UNSPLIT	*adj*	
UNSPOILT	*adj*	
UNSPRUNG	*adj*	
UNSPUN	*adj*	
UNSTABLE	*adj*	-BLER, -BLEST
UNSTABLY	*adv*	
UNSTEADY	*adj*	-STEADIER, -STEADIEST
UNSTONED	*adj*	
UNSTUFFY	*adj*	
UNSTUNG	*adj*	
UNSUBTLE	*adj*	
UNSUBTLY	*adv*	
UNSUITED	*adj*	
UNSUNG	*adj*	
UNSUNK	*adj*	
UNSURE	*adj*	
UNSURELY	*adv*	
UNSWAYED	*adj*	
UNSWEPT	*adj*	
UNTAGGED	*adj*	
UNTAKEN	*adj*	
UNTAME	*adj*	
UNTAMED	*adj*	
UNTANNED	*adj*	
UNTAPPED	*adj*	
UNTASTED	*adj*	
UNTAXED	*adj*	
UNTENDED	*adj*	
UNTESTED	*adj*	
UNTHAWED	*adj*	

UNTIDILY	*adv*
UNTIDY	*adj* -DIER, -DIEST
UNTILLED	*adj*
UNTILTED	*adj*
UNTIMELY	*adj* -LIER, -LIEST
UNTINGED	*adj*
UNTIPPED	*adj*
UNTIRED	*adj*
UNTIRING	*adj*
UNTITLED	*adj*
UNTOLD	*adj*
UNTORN	*adj*
UNTRACED	*adj*
UNTRENDY	*adj*
UNTRIED	*adj*
UNTRUE	*adj* -TRUER, -TRUEST
UNTRULY	*adv*
UNTRUSTY	*adj*
UNTUFTED	*adj*
UNTURNED	*adj*
UNUNITED	*adj*
UNURGED	*adj*
UNUSABLE	*adj*
UNUSED	*adj*
UNUSUAL	*adj*
UNVALUED	*adj*
UNVARIED	*adj*
UNVEINED	*adj*
UNVERSED	*adj*
UNVEXED	*adj*
UNVEXT	*adj*
UNVIABLE	*adj*
UNVOCAL	*adj*
UNWALLED	*adj*
UNWANING	*adj*
UNWANTED	*adj*
UNWARIER	comparative of unwary
UNWARIEST	superlative of unwary
UNWARILY	*adv*
UNWARMED	*adj*
UNWARNED	*adj*
UNWARPED	*adj*
UNWARY	*adj* -WARIER, -WARIEST
UNWASTED	*adj*
UNWAXED	*adj*
UNWEANED	*adj*
UNWEARY	*adj*
UNWED	*adj*
UNWEDDED	*adj*
UNWEEDED	*adj*
UNWELDED	*adj*
UNWELL	*adj*
UNWEPT	*adj*
UNWETTED	*adj*
UNWHITE	*adj*
UNWIELDY	*adj* -WIELDIER, -WIELDIEST

UNWIFELY	*adj*
UNWILLED	*adj*
UNWISE	*adj* -WISER, -WISEST
UNWISELY	*adv*
UNWON	*adj*
UNWOODED	*adj*
UNWOOED	*adj*
UNWORKED	*adj*
UNWORN	*adj*
UNWORTHY	*adj* -THIER, -THIEST
UNWRUNG	*adj*
UNYOUNG	*adj*
UNZONED	*adj*

UNAI	*n* pl. -S unau
UNAKITE	*n* pl. -S an igneous rock
UNANCHOR	*v* -ED, -ING, -S to loosen from an anchor
UNARM	*v* -ED, -ING, -S to disarm
UNARY	*adj* consisting of a single element
UNAU	*n* pl. -S a two-toed sloth
UNAWARES	*adv* without warning
UNBAN	*v* -BANNED, -BANNING, -BANS to remove a prohibition against
UNBAR	*v* -BARRED, -BARRING, -BARS to remove a bar from
UNBATED	*adj* unabated
UNBE	*v* to cease to have being — UNBE is the only accepted form of this verb; it cannot be conjugated
UNBEAR	*v* -BEARED, -BEARING, -BEARS to free from the pressure of a rein
UNBELIEF	*n* pl. -S lack of belief
UNBELT	*v* -ED, -ING, -S to remove the belt of
UNBEND	*v* -BENT or -BENDED, -BENDING, -BENDS to make or allow to become straight
UNBID	*adj* unbidden
UNBIDDEN	*adj* not invited
UNBIND	*v* -BOUND, -BINDING, -BINDS to free from bindings
UNBLOCK	*v* -ED, -ING, -S to free from being blocked
UNBODIED	*adj* having no body
UNBOLT	*v* -ED, -ING, -S to open by withdrawing a bolt (a metal bar)

UNBONNET *v* -ED, -ING, -S to uncover the head

UNBOSOM *v* -ED, -ING, -S to reveal

UNBOUND past tense of unbind

UNBOX *v* -ED, -ING, -ES to remove from a box

UNBRACE *v* -BRACED, -BRACING, -BRACES to free from braces

UNBRAID *v* -ED, -ING, -S to separate the strands of

UNBRAKE *v* -BRAKED, -BRAKING, -BRAKES to release a brake

UNBREECH *v* -ED, -ING, -ES to remove the breeches of

UNBRIDLE *v* -DLED, -DLING, -DLES to set loose

UNBUCKLE *v* -LED, -LING, -LES to loosen a buckle

UNBUILD *v* -BUILT, -BUILDING, -BUILDS to demolish

UNBUNDLE *v* -DLED, -DLING, -DLES to price separately

UNBURDEN *v* -ED, -ING, -S to free from a burden

UNBUTTON *v* -ED, -ING, -S to unfasten the buttons of

UNCAGE *v* -CAGED, -CAGING, -CAGES to release from a cage

UNCAKE *v* -CAKED, -CAKING, -CAKES to break up a cake (a block of compacted matter)

UNCANNY *adj* -NIER, -NIEST strange and inexplicable

UNCAP *v* -CAPPED, -CAPPING, -CAPS to remove the cap from

UNCASE *v* -CASED, -CASING, -CASES to remove from a case

UNCHAIN *v* -ED, -ING, -S to free by removing a chain

UNCHANCY *adj* unlucky

UNCHARGE *v* -CHARGED, -CHARGING, -CHARGES to acquit

UNCHOKE *v* -CHOKED, -CHOKING, -CHOKES to free from obstruction

UNCHURCH *v* -ED, -ING, -ES to expel from a church

UNCI pl. of uncus

UNCIA *n* pl. -CIAE a coin of ancient Rome

UNCIAL *n* pl. -S a style of writing

UNCIALLY *adv* in the uncial style

UNCIFORM *n* pl. -S a bone of the wrist

UNCINAL *adj* uncinate

UNCINATE *adj* bent at the end like a hook

UNCINUS *n* pl. -NI an uncinate structure

UNCLAD a past tense of unclothe

UNCLAMP *v* -ED, -ING, -S to free from a clamp

UNCLASP *v* -ED, -ING, -S to free from a clasp

UNCLE *n* pl. -S the brother of one's father or mother

UNCLENCH *v* -ED, -ING, -ES to open from a clenched position

UNCLINCH *v* -ED, -ING, -ES to unclench

UNCLIP *v* -CLIPPED, -CLIPPING, -CLIPS to remove a clip (a fastening device) from

UNCLOAK *v* -ED, -ING, -S to remove a cloak from

UNCLOG *v* -CLOGGED, -CLOGGING, -CLOGS to free from a difficulty or obstruction

UNCLOSE *v* -CLOSED, -CLOSING, -CLOSES to open

UNCLOTHE *v* -CLOTHED or -CLAD, -CLOTHING, -CLOTHES to divest of clothing

UNCLOUD *v* -ED, -ING, -S to free from clouds

UNCO *n* pl. -COS a stranger

UNCOCK *v* -ED, -ING, -S to remove from a cocked position

UNCOFFIN *v* -ED, -ING, -S to remove from a coffin

UNCOIL *v* -ED, -ING, -S to release from a coiled position

UNCORK *v* -ED, -ING, -S to draw the cork

UNCOUPLE *v* -PLED, -PLING, -PLES to disconnect

UNCOVER *v* -ED, -ING, -S to remove the covering from

UNCRATE *v* -CRATED, -CRATING, -CRATES to remove from a crate

UNCREATE *v* -ATED, -ATING, -ATES to deprive of existence

UNCROSS *v* -ED, -ING, -ES to change from a crossed position

UNCROWN *v* -ED, -ING, -S to deprive of a crown

UNCTION *n* pl. -S the act of anointing

UNCTUOUS *adj* greasy

UNCUFF *v* -ED, -ING, -S to remove handcuffs from

UNCURB *v* -ED, -ING, -S to remove restraints from

UNCURL *v* -ED, -ING, -S to straighten the curls of

UNCUS *n* pl. -CI a hook-shaped anatomical part

UNDE *adj* wavy

UNDEAD *n* pl. UNDEAD a vampire

UNDEE *adj* unde

UNDER *prep* in a lower position than

UNDERACT *v* -ED, -ING, -S to act subtly and with restraint

UNDERAGE *n* pl. -S a shortage

UNDERARM *n* pl. -S the armpit

UNDERATE past tense of undereat

UNDERBID *v* -BID, -BIDDING, -BIDS to bid lower than

UNDERBUD *v* -BUDDED, -BUDDING, -BUDS to bud from beneath

UNDERBUY *v* -BOUGHT, -BUYING, -BUYS to buy at a lower price than

UNDERCUT *v* -CUT, -CUTTING, -CUTS to cut under

UNDERDO *v* -DID, -DONE, -DOING, -DOES to do insufficiently

UNDERDOG *n* pl. -S one who is expected to lose

UNDEREAT *v* -ATE, -EATEN, -EATING, -EATS to eat an insufficient amount

UNDERFED *adj* fed an insufficient amount

UNDERFUR *n* pl. -S the thick, soft fur beneath the outer coat of certain mammals

UNDERGO *v* -WENT, -GONE, -GOING, -GOES to be subjected to

UNDERGOD *n* pl. -S a lesser god

UNDERJAW *n* pl. -S the lower jaw

UNDERLAID past tense of underlay

UNDERLAIN past participle of underlie

UNDERLAP *v* -LAPPED, -LAPPING, -LAPS to extend partly under

UNDERLAY *v* -LAID, -LAYING, -LAYS to place under

UNDERLET *v* -LET, -LETTING, -LETS to lease at less than the usual value

UNDERLIE *v* -LAY, -LAIN, -LYING, -LIES to lie under

UNDERLIP *n* pl. -S the lower lip

UNDERLIT *adj* lacking adequate light

UNDERLYING present participle of underlie

UNDERPAY *v* -PAID, -PAYING, -PAYS to pay less than is deserved

UNDERPIN *v* -PINNED, -PINNING, -PINS to support from below

UNDERRUN *v* -RAN, -RUNNING, -RUNS to pass or extend under

UNDERSEA *adv* beneath the surface of the sea

UNDERSET *n* pl. -S a current below the surface of the ocean

UNDERTAX *v* -ED, -ING, -ES to tax less than the usual amount

UNDERTOW *n* pl. -S the seaward pull of receding waves breaking on a shore

UNDERWAY *adv* in progress

UNDERWENT past tense of undergo

UNDID past tense of undo

UNDIES *n/pl* underwear

UNDINE *n* pl. -S a female water spirit

UNDO *v* -DID, -DONE, -DOING, -DOES to bring to ruin

UNDOCK *v* -ED, -ING, -S to move away from a dock

UNDOER *n* pl. -S one that undoes

UNDOING *n* pl. -S a cause of ruin

UNDONE past participle of undo

UNDOUBLE *v* -BLED, -BLING, -BLES to unfold

UNDRAPE *v* -DRAPED, -DRAPING, -DRAPES to strip of drapery

UNDRAW *v* -DREW, -DRAWN, -DRAWING, -DRAWS to draw open

UNDRESS *v* -DRESSED or -DREST, -DRESSING, -DRESSES to remove one's clothing

UNDRUNK *adj* not swallowed

UNDUE *adj* exceeding what is appropriate or normal

UNDULANT *adj* undulating

UNDULAR *adj* undulating

UNDULATE *v* -LATED, -LATING, -LATES to move with a wavelike motion

UNDULY *adv* in an undue manner

UNDY *adj* unde

UNDYING *adj* not subject to death

UNEARTH *v* -ED, -ING, -S to dig up

UNEASE *n* pl. -S mental or physical discomfort

UNEASY *adj* -EASIER, -EASIEST marked by mental or physical discomfort **UNEASILY** *adv*

UNEQUAL *n* pl. -S one that is not equal to another

UNFAITH *n* pl. -S lack of faith

UNFASTEN *v* -ED, -ING, -S to release from fastenings

UNFENCE *v* -FENCED, -FENCING, -FENCES to remove a fence from

UNFETTER v -ED, -ING, -S to free from fetters

UNFIT v -FITTED, -FITTING, -FITS to make unsuitable

UNFITLY adv in an unsuitable manner

UNFIX v -FIXED or -FIXT, -FIXING, -FIXES to unfasten

UNFOLD v -ED, -ING, -S to open something that is folded

UNFOLDER n pl. -S one that unfolds

UNFORGOT adj not forgotten

UNFREE v -FREED, -FREEING, -FREES to deprive of freedom

UNFREEZE v -FROZE, -FROZEN, -FREEZING, -FREEZES to cause to thaw

UNFROCK v -ED, -ING, -S to divest of ecclesiastical authority

UNFURL v -ED, -ING, -S to unroll

UNGAINLY adj -LIER, -LIEST awkward

UNGIRD v -GIRDED or -GIRT, -GIRDING, -GIRDS to remove a belt from

UNGLOVE v -GLOVED, -GLOVING, -GLOVES to uncover by removing a glove

UNGLUE v -GLUED, -GLUING, -GLUES to disjoin

UNGODLY adj -LIER, -LIEST impious

UNGOT adj ungotten

UNGOTTEN adj not obtained

UNGUAL adj pertaining to an unguis

UNGUARD v -ED, -ING, -S to leave unprotected

UNGUENT n pl. -S an ointment

UNGUENTA n/pl ointments

UNGUIS n pl. -GUES a nail, claw, or hoof

UNGULA n pl. -LAE an unguis **UNGULAR** adj

UNGULATE n pl. -S a hoofed mammal

UNHAIR v -ED, -ING, -S to remove the hair from

UNHALLOW v -ED, -ING, -S to profane

UNHAND v -ED, -ING, -S to remove the hand from

UNHANDY adj -HANDIER, -HANDIEST difficult to handle

UNHANG v -HUNG or -HANGED, -HANGING, -HANGS to detach from a hanging support

UNHAT v -HATTED, -HATTING, -HATS to remove one's hat

UNHELM v -ED, -ING, -S to remove the helmet of

UNHINGE v -HINGED, -HINGING, -HINGES to remove from hinges

UNHITCH v -ED, -ING, -ES to free from being hitched

UNHOOD v -ED, -ING, -S to remove a hood from

UNHOOK v -ED, -ING, -S to remove from a hook

UNHOPED adj not hoped for or expected

UNHORSE v -HORSED, -HORSING, -HORSES to cause to fall from a horse

UNHOUSE v -HOUSED, -HOUSING, -HOUSES to deprive of a protective shelter

UNHUSK v -ED, -ING, -S to remove the husk from

UNIALGAL adj pertaining to a single algal cell

UNIAXIAL adj having one axis

UNICOLOR adj of one color

UNICORN n pl. -S a mythical horselike creature

UNICYCLE n pl. -S a one-wheeled vehicle

UNIDEAED adj lacking ideas

UNIFACE n pl. -S a coin having a design on only one side

UNIFIC adj unifying

UNIFIED past tense of unify

UNIFIER n pl. -S one that unifies

UNIFIES present 3d person sing. of unify

UNIFILAR adj having only one thread, wire, or fiber

UNIFORM adj -FORMER, -FORMEST unchanging

UNIFORM v -ED, -ING, -S to make uniform

UNIFY v -FIED, -FYING, -FIES to make into a coherent whole

UNILOBED adj having one lobe

UNION n pl. -S a number of persons, parties, or political entities united for a common purpose

UNIONISE v -ISED, -ISING, -ISES to unionize

UNIONISM n pl. -S the principle of forming a union

UNIONIST n pl. -S an advocate of unionism

UNIONIZE v -IZED, -IZING, -IZES to form into a union

UNIPOD n pl. -S a one-legged support

UNIPOLAR adj showing only one kind of polarity

UNIQUE *adj* UNIQUER, UNIQUEST existing as the only one of its kind; very unusual **UNIQUELY** *adv*

UNIQUE *n* pl. -S something that is unique

UNISEX *n* pl. -ES the condition of not being distinguishable as to sex

UNISON *n* pl. -S complete agreement **UNISONAL** *adj*

UNIT *n* pl. -S a specific quantity used as a standard of measurement

UNITAGE *n* pl. -S amount in units

UNITARD *n* pl. -S a leotard that also covers the legs

UNITARY *adj* pertaining to a unit

UNITE *v* UNITED, UNITING, UNITES to bring together so as to form a whole **UNITEDLY** *adv*

UNITER *n* pl. -S one that unites

UNITIES pl. of unity

UNITING present participle of unite

UNITIVE *adj* serving to unite

UNITIZE *v* -IZED, -IZING, -IZES to divide into units

UNITIZER *n* pl. -S one that unitizes

UNITRUST *n* pl. -S a type of annuity trust

UNITY *n* pl. -TIES the state of being one single entity

UNIVALVE *n* pl. -S a mollusk having a single shell

UNIVERSE *n* pl. -S the totality of all existing things

UNIVOCAL *n* pl. -S a word having only one meaning

UNJOINT *v* -ED, -ING, -S to separate at a juncture

UNKEMPT *adj* untidy

UNKEND *adj* unkenned

UNKENNED *adj* not known or recognized

UNKENNEL *v* -NELED, -NELING, -NELS or -NELLED, -NELLING, -NELS to release from a kennel

UNKENT *adj* unkenned

UNKINK *v* -ED, -ING, -S to remove curls from

UNKNIT *v* -KNITTED, -KNITTING, -KNITS to unravel

UNKNOT *v* -KNOTTED, -KNOTTING, -KNOTS to undo a knot in

UNKNOWN *n* pl. -S one that is not known

UNLACE *v* -LACED, -LACING, -LACES to unfasten the laces of

UNLADE *v* -LADED, -LADEN, -LADING, -LADES to unload

UNLAID past tense of unlay

UNLASH *v* -ED, -ING, -ES to untie the lashing (a type of binding) of

UNLATCH *v* -ED, -ING, -ES to open by lifting the latch (a fastening device)

UNLAY *v* -LAID, -LAYING, -LAYS to untwist

UNLEAD *v* -ED, -ING, -S to remove the lead from

UNLEARN *v* -LEARNED or -LEARNT, -LEARNING, -LEARNS to put out of one's knowledge or memory

UNLEASH *v* -ED, -ING, -ES to free from a leash

UNLESS *conj* except on the condition that

UNLET *adj* not rented

UNLEVEL *v* -ELED, -ELING, -ELS or -ELLED, -ELLING, -ELS to make uneven

UNLIMBER *v* -ED, -ING, -S to prepare for action

UNLINK *v* -ED, -ING, -S to unfasten the links (connecting devices) of

UNLIVE *v* -LIVED, -LIVING, -LIVES to live so as to make amends for

UNLOAD *v* -ED, -ING, -S to remove the load or cargo from

UNLOADER *n* pl. -S one that unloads

UNLOCK *v* -ED, -ING, -S to unfasten the lock of

UNLOOSE *v* -LOOSED, -LOOSING, -LOOSES to set free

UNLOOSEN *v* -ED, -ING, -S to unloose

UNMAKE *v* -MADE, -MAKING, -MAKES to destroy

UNMAKER *n* pl. -S one that unmakes

UNMAN *v* -MANNED, -MANNING, -MANS to deprive of courage

UNMASK *v* -ED, -ING, -S to remove a mask from

UNMASKER *n* pl. -S one that unmasks

UNMEET *adj* improper **UNMEETLY** *adv*

UNMESH *v* -ED, -ING, -ES to disentangle

UNMEW *v* -ED, -ING, -S to set free

UNMINGLE *v* -GLED, -GLING, -GLES to separate things that are mixed

UNMITER *v* -ED, -ING, -S to depose from the rank of bishop

UNMITRE *v* -TRED, -TRING, -TRES to unmiter

UNMIX *v* -MIXED or -MIXT, -MIXING, -MIXES to separate from a mixture

UNMOLD *v* -ED, -ING, -S to remove from a mold

UNMOOR *v* -ED, -ING, -S to release from moorings

UNMORAL *adj* amoral

UNMUFFLE *v* -FLED, -FLING, -FLES to free from something that muffles

UNMUZZLE *v* -ZLED, -ZLING, -ZLES to remove a muzzle from

UNNAIL *v* -ED, -ING, -S to remove the nails from

UNNERVE *v* -NERVED, -NERVING, -NERVES to deprive of courage

UNPACK *v* -ED, -ING, -S to remove the contents of

UNPACKER *n* pl. -S one that unpacks

UNPAGED *adj* having no page numbers

UNPEG *v* -PEGGED, -PEGGING, -PEGS to remove the pegs from

UNPEN *v* -PENNED or -PENT, -PENNING, -PENS to release from confinement

UNPEOPLE *v* -PLED, -PLING, -PLES to remove people from

UNPERSON *n* pl. -S one who is removed completely from recognition

UNPICK *v* -ED, -ING, -S to remove the stitches from

UNPILE *v* -PILED, -PILING, -PILES to take or disentangle from a pile

UNPIN *v* -PINNED, -PINNING, -PINS to remove the pins from

UNPLAIT *v* -ED, -ING, -S to undo the plaits of

UNPLUG *v* -PLUGGED, -PLUGGING, -PLUGS to take a plug out of

UNPUCKER *v* -ED, -ING, -S to remove the wrinkles from

UNPUZZLE *v* -ZLED, -ZLING, -ZLES to work out the obscured meaning of

UNQUIET *n* pl. -S a state of unrest

UNQUOTE *v* -QUOTED, -QUOTING, -QUOTES to close a quotation

UNRAVEL *v* -ELED, -ELING, -ELS or -ELLED, -ELLING, -ELS to separate the threads of

UNREASON *v* -ED, -ING, -S to disrupt the sanity of

UNREEL *v* -ED, -ING, -S to unwind from a reel

UNREELER *n* pl. -S one that unreels

UNREEVE *v* -REEVED or -ROVE, -ROVEN, -REEVING, -REEVES to withdraw a rope from an opening

UNRENT *adj* not torn

UNREPAIR *n* pl. -S lack of repair

UNREST *n* pl. -S a disturbed or uneasy state

UNRIDDLE *v* -DLED, -DLING, -DLES to solve

UNRIG *v* -RIGGED, -RIGGING, -RIGS to divest of rigging

UNRIP *v* -RIPPED, -RIPPING, -RIPS to rip open

UNRIPE *adj* -RIPER, -RIPEST not ripe **UNRIPELY** *adv*

UNROBE *v* -ROBED, -ROBING, -ROBES to undress

UNROLL *v* -ED, -ING, -S to open something that is rolled up

UNROOF *v* -ED, -ING, -S to strip off the roof of

UNROOT *v* -ED, -ING, -S to uproot

UNROUND *v* -ED, -ING, -S to articulate without rounding the lips

UNROVE a past tense of unreeve

UNROVEN a past participle of unreeve

UNRULY *adj* -LIER, -LIEST difficult to control

UNSADDLE *v* -DLED, -DLING, -DLES to remove the saddle from

UNSAFETY *n* pl. -TIES lack of safety

UNSAY *v* -SAID, -SAYING, -SAYS to retract something said

UNSCREW *v* -ED, -ING, -S to remove the screws from

UNSEAL *v* -ED, -ING, -S to remove the seal of

UNSEAM *v* -ED, -ING, -S to open the seams of

UNSEAT *v* -ED, -ING, -S to remove from a seat

UNSET *v* -SET, -SETTING, -SETS to unsettle

UNSETTLE *v* -TLED, -TLING, -TLES to make unstable

UNSEW *v* -SEWED, -SEWN, -SEWING, -SEWS to undo the sewing of

UNSEX *v* -ED, -ING, -ES to deprive of sexual power

UNSHELL   v -ED, -ING, -S to remove the shell from

UNSHIFT   v -ED, -ING, -S to release the shift key on a typewriter

UNSHIP   v -SHIPPED, -SHIPPING, -SHIPS to unload from a ship

UNSICKER   adj unreliable

UNSIGHT   v -ED, -ING, -S to prevent from seeing

UNSLING   v -SLUNG, -SLINGING, -SLINGS to remove from a slung position

UNSNAP   v -SNAPPED, -SNAPPING, -SNAPS to undo the snaps of

UNSNARL   v -ED, -ING, -S to untangle

UNSOLDER   v -ED, -ING, -S to separate

UNSONCY   adj unsonsie

UNSONSIE   adj unlucky

UNSONSY   adj unsonsie

UNSPEAK   v -SPOKE, -SPOKEN, -SPEAKING, -SPEAKS to unsay

UNSPHERE   v -SPHERED, -SPHERING, -SPHERES to remove from a sphere

UNSTACK   v -ED, -ING, -S to remove from a stack

UNSTATE   v -STATED, -STATING, -STATES to deprive of status

UNSTAYED   adj not secured with ropes or wires

UNSTEADY   v -STEADIED, -STEADYING, -STEADIES to make unsteady

UNSTEEL   v -ED, -ING, -S to make soft

UNSTEP   v -STEPPED, -STEPPING, -STEPS to remove from a socket

UNSTICK   v -STUCK, -STICKING, -STICKS to disjoin

UNSTITCH   v -ED, -ING, -ES to remove the stitches from

UNSTOP   v -STOPPED, -STOPPING, -STOPS to remove a stopper from

UNSTRAP   v -STRAPPED, -STRAPPING, -STRAPS to remove a strap from

UNSTRESS   n pl. -ES a syllable having relatively weak stress

UNSTRING   v -STRUNG, -STRINGING, -STRINGS to remove from a string

UNSTUCK   past tense of unstick

UNSWATHE   v -SWATHED, -SWATHING, -SWATHES to unbind

UNSWEAR   v -SWORE, -SWORN, -SWEARING, -SWEARS to retract something sworn

UNTACK   v -ED, -ING, -S to remove a tack from

UNTANGLE   v -GLED, -GLING, -GLES to free from tangles

UNTEACH   v -TAUGHT, -TEACHING, -TEACHES to cause to unlearn something

UNTENTED   adj not probed or attended to

UNTETHER   v -ED, -ING, -S to free from a tether

UNTHINK   v -THOUGHT, -THINKING, -THINKS to dismiss from the mind

UNTHREAD   v -ED, -ING, -S to remove the thread from

UNTHRONE   v -THRONED, -THRONING, -THRONES to remove from a throne

UNTIDY   v -DIED, -DYING, -DIES to make untidy

UNTIE   v -TIED, -TYING, -TIES to free from something that ties

UNTIL   prep up to the time of

UNTO   prep to

UNTOWARD   adj unruly

UNTREAD   v -TROD, -TRODDEN, -TREADING, -TREADS to retrace

UNTRIM   v -TRIMMED, -TRIMMING, -TRIMS to strip of trimming

UNTRUSS   v -ED, -ING, -ES to free from a truss

UNTRUTH   n pl. -S something that is untrue

UNTUCK   v -ED, -ING, -S to release from being tucked up

UNTUNE   v -TUNED, -TUNING, -TUNES to put out of tune

UNTWINE   v -TWINED, -TWINING, -TWINES to separate the twisted or tangled parts of

UNTWIST   v -ED, -ING, -S to untwine

UNTYING   present participle of untie

UNVEIL   v -ED, -ING, -S to remove a covering from

UNVOICE   v -VOICED, -VOICING, -VOICES to deprive of voice or vocal quality

UNWASHED   n pl. -S an ignorant or underprivileged group

UNWEAVE   v -WOVE, -WOVEN, -WEAVING, -WEAVES to undo something woven

UNWEIGHT *v* -ED, -ING, -S to reduce the weight of

UNWIND *v* -WOUND, -WINDING, -WINDS to reverse the winding of

UNWINDER *n* pl. -S one that unwinds

UNWISDOM *n* pl. -S lack of wisdom

UNWISH *v* -ED, -ING, -ES to cease to wish for

UNWIT *v* -WITTED, -WITTING, -WITS to make insane

UNWONTED *adj* unusual

UNWORTHY *n* pl. -THIES an unworthy person

UNWOUND past tense of unwind

UNWOVE past tense of unweave

UNWOVEN past participle of unweave

UNWRAP *v* -WRAPPED, -WRAPPING, -WRAPS to remove the wrapping from

UNYEANED *adj* unborn

UNYOKE *v* -YOKED, -YOKING, -YOKES to free from a yoke

UNZIP *v* -ZIPPED, -ZIPPING, -ZIPS to open the zipper of

UP *v* UPPED, UPPING, UPS to raise

UPAS *n* pl. -ES an Asian tree

UPBEAR *v* -BORE, -BORNE, -BEARING, -BEARS to raise aloft

UPBEARER *n* pl. -S one that upbears

UPBEAT *n* pl. -S an unaccented beat in a musical measure

UPBIND *v* -BOUND, -BINDING, -BINDS to bind completely

UPBOIL *v* -ED, -ING, -S to boil up

UPBORE past tense of upbear

UPBORNE past participle of upbear

UPBOUND past tense of upbind

UPBOW *n* pl. -S a type of stroke in playing a bowed instrument

UPBRAID *v* -ED, -ING, -S to reproach severely

UPBUILD *v* -BUILT, -BUILDING, -BUILDS to build up

UPBY *adv* upbye

UPBYE *adv* a little farther on

UPCAST *v* -CAST, -CASTING, -CASTS to cast up

UPCHUCK *v* -ED, -ING, -S to vomit

UPCLIMB *v* -ED, -ING, -S to climb up

UPCOAST *adv* up the coast

UPCOIL *v* -ED, -ING, -S to coil up

UPCOMING *adj* about to happen or appear

UPCURL *v* -ED, -ING, -S to curl up

UPCURVE *v* -CURVED, -CURVING, -CURVES to curve upward

UPDART *v* -ED, -ING, -S to dart up

UPDATE *v* -DATED, -DATING, -DATES to bring up to date

UPDATER *n* pl. -S one that updates

UPDIVE *v* -DIVED or -DOVE, -DIVING, -DIVES to spring upward

UPDO *n* pl. -DOS an upswept hairdo

UPDRAFT *n* pl. -S an upward movement of air

UPDRY *v* -DRIED, -DRYING, -DRIES to dry completely

UPEND *v* -ED, -ING, -S to set or stand on end

UPFIELD *adv* into the part of the field toward which the offensive team is going

UPFLING *v* -FLUNG, -FLINGING, -FLINGS to fling up

UPFLOW *v* -ED, -ING, -S to flow up

UPFOLD *v* -ED, -ING, -S to fold up

UPFRONT *adj* honest; candid

UPGATHER *v* -ED, -ING, -S to gather up

UPGAZE *v* -GAZED, -GAZING, -GAZES to gaze up

UPGIRD *v* -GIRDED or -GIRT, -GIRDING, -GIRDS to gird completely

UPGOING *adj* going up

UPGRADE *v* -GRADED, -GRADING, -GRADES to raise to a higher grade or standard

UPGROW *v* -GREW, -GROWN, -GROWING, -GROWS to grow up

UPGROWTH *n* pl. -S the process of growing up

UPHEAP *v* -ED, -ING, -S to heap up

UPHEAVAL *n* pl. -S the act of upheaving

UPHEAVE *v* -HEAVED or -HOVE, -HEAVING, -HEAVES to heave up

UPHEAVER *n* pl. -S one that upheaves

UPHELD past tense of uphold

UPHILL *n* pl. -S an upward slope

UPHOARD *v* -ED, -ING, -S to hoard up

UPHOLD *v* -HELD, -HOLDING, -HOLDS to hold aloft

UPHOLDER *n* pl. -S one that upholds

UPHOVE a past tense of upheave

UPHROE *n* pl. -S euphroe

UPKEEP *n* pl. -S the cost of maintaining something in good condition

UPLAND *n* pl. -S the higher land of a region

UPLANDER *n* pl. -S an inhabitant of an upland

UPLEAP *v* -LEAPED or -LEAPT, -LEAPING, -LEAPS to leap up

UPLIFT *v* -ED, -ING, -S to lift up

UPLIFTER *n* pl. -S one that uplifts

UPLIGHT *v* -LIGHTED or -LIT, -LIGHTING, -LIGHTS to light to a higher degree

UPLINK *n* pl. -S a communications channel to a spacecraft

UPLOAD *v* -ED, -ING, -S to transfer information from a small computer to a larger computer

UPMARKET *adj* upscale

UPMOST *adj* highest

UPO *prep* upon

UPON *prep* on

UPPED past tense of up

UPPER *n* pl. -S the part of a boot or shoe above the sole

UPPERCUT *v* -CUT, -CUTTING, -CUTS to strike an upward blow

UPPILE *v* -PILED, -PILING, -PILES to pile up

UPPING *n* pl. -S the process of marking young swans for identification purposes

UPPISH *adj* uppity **UPPISHLY** *adv*

UPPITY *adj* tending to be snobbish and arrogant

UPPROP *v* -PROPPED, -PROPPING, -PROPS to prop up

UPRAISE *v* -RAISED, -RAISING, -RAISES to raise up

UPRAISER *n* pl. -S one that upraises

UPRATE *v* -RATED, -RATING, -RATES to improve the power output of an engine

UPREACH *v* -ED, -ING, -ES to reach up

UPREAR *v* -ED, -ING, -S to upraise

UPRIGHT *v* -ED, -ING, -S to make vertical

UPRISE *v* -ROSE, -RISEN, -RISING, -RISES to rise up

UPRISER *n* pl. -S one that uprises

UPRISING *n* pl. -S a revolt

UPRIVER *n* pl. -S an area lying toward the source of a river

UPROAR *n* pl. -S a state of noisy excitement and confusion

UPROOT *v* -ED, -ING, -S to pull up by the roots

UPROOTAL *n* pl. -S the act of uprooting

UPROOTER *n* pl. -S one that uproots

UPROSE past tense of uprise

UPROUSE *v* -ROUSED, -ROUSING, -ROUSES to rouse up

UPRUSH *v* -ED, -ING, -ES to rush up

UPSCALE *adj* appealing to wealthy consumers

UPSEND *v* -SENT, -SENDING, -SENDS to send upward

UPSET *v* -SET, -SETTING, -SETS to overturn

UPSETTER *n* pl. -S one that upsets

UPSHIFT *v* -ED, -ING, -S to shift an automotive vehicle into a higher gear

UPSHOOT *v* -SHOT, -SHOOTING, -SHOOTS to shoot upward

UPSHOT *n* pl. -S the final result

UPSIDE *n* pl. -S a positive aspect

UPSILON *n* pl. -S a Greek letter

UPSOAR *v* -ED, -ING, -S to soar upward

UPSPRING *v* -SPRANG or -SPRUNG, -SPRINGING, -SPRINGS to spring up

UPSTAGE *v* -STAGED, -STAGING, -STAGES to outdo theatrically

UPSTAIR *adj* pertaining to an upper floor

UPSTAIRS *adv* up the stairs

UPSTAND *v* -STOOD, -STANDING, -STANDS to stand up on one's feet

UPSTARE *v* -STARED, -STARING, -STARES to stare upward

UPSTART *v* -ED, -ING, -S to spring up suddenly

UPSTATE *n* pl. -S the northern region of a state

UPSTATER *n* pl. -S an inhabitant of an upstate region

UPSTEP *v* -STEPPED, -STEPPING, -STEPS to step up

UPSTIR *v* -STIRRED, -STIRRING, -STIRS to stir up

UPSTOOD past tense of upstand

UPSTREAM *adv* toward the source of a stream

UPSTROKE *n* pl. -S an upward stroke

UPSURGE *v* -SURGED, -SURGING, -SURGES to surge up

UPSWEEP *v* -SWEPT, -SWEEPING, -SWEEPS to sweep upward

UPSWELL *v* -SWELLED, -SWOLLEN, -SWELLING, -SWELLS, to swell up

UPSWING *v* -SWUNG, -SWINGING, -SWINGS to swing upward

UPTAKE	*n* pl. -S an upward ventilating shaft	**URBAN**	*adj* pertaining to a city
UPTEAR	*v* -TORE, -TORN, -TEARING, -TEARS to tear out by the roots	**URBANE**	*adj* -BANER, -BANEST refined and elegant **URBANELY** *adv*
UPTHROW	*v* -THREW, -THROWN, -THROWING, -THROWS to throw upward	**URBANISE**	*v* -ISED, -ISING, -ISES to urbanize
		URBANISM	*n* pl. -S the lifestyle of city dwellers
UPTHRUST	*v* -THRUST, -THRUSTING, -THRUSTS to thrust up	**URBANIST**	*n* pl. -S a specialist in city planning
UPTICK	*n* pl. -S an increase or rise	**URBANITE**	*n* pl. -S one who lives in a city
UPTIGHT	*adj* nervous	**URBANITY**	*n* pl. -TIES the quality of being
UPTILT	*v* -ED, -ING, -S to tilt upward		urbane
UPTIME	*n* pl. -S the time during which machinery is functioning	**URBANIZE**	*v* -IZED, -IZING, -IZES to cause to take on urban characteristics
UPTORE	past tense of uptear		
UPTORN	past participle of uptear	**URBIA**	*n* pl. -S cities collectively
UPTOSS	*v* -ED, -ING, -ES to toss upward	**URCHIN**	*n* pl. -S a mischievous boy
		URD	*n* pl. -S an annual bean grown in India
UPTOWN	*n* pl. -S the upper part of a city		
UPTOWNER	*n* pl. -S one that lives uptown	**UREA**	*n* pl. -S a chemical compound
UPTREND	*n* pl. -S a tendency upward or toward growth	**UREAL** *adj*
		UREASE	*n* pl. -S an enzyme
UPTURN	*v* -ED, -ING, -S to turn up or over	**UREDIA**	pl. of uredium
		UREDIAL	*adj* pertaining to a uredium
UPWAFT	*v* -ED, -ING, -S to waft upward	**UREDINIA**	*n/pl* uredia
UPWARD	*adv* toward a higher place or position **UPWARDLY** *adv*	**UREDIUM**	*n* pl. -DIA a spore-producing organ of certain fungi
UPWARDS	*adv* upward	**UREDO**	*n* pl. -DOS a skin irritation
UPWELL	*v* -ED, -ING, -S to well up	**UREIC**	*adj* pertaining to urea
UPWIND	*n* pl. -S a wind that blows against one's course	**UREIDE**	*n* pl. -S a chemical compound
		UREMIA	*n* pl. -S an abnormal condition of the blood **UREMIC** *adj*
URACIL	*n* pl. -S a chemical compound		
URAEMIA	*n* pl. -S uremia **URAEMIC** *adj*	**URETER**	*n* pl. -S the duct that conveys urine from the kidney to the bladder **URETERAL, URETERIC** *adj*
URAEUS	*n* pl. URAEI or URAEUSES the figure of the sacred serpent on the headdress of ancient Egyptian rulers		
		URETHAN	*n* pl. -S urethane
		URETHANE	*n* pl. -S a chemical compound
URALITE	*n* pl. -S a mineral **URALITIC** *adj*	**URETHRA**	*n* pl. -THRAE or -THRAS the duct through which urine is discharged from the bladder **URETHRAL** *adj*
URANIA	*n* pl. -S uranium dioxide		
URANIC	*adj* pertaining to uranium		
URANIDE	*n* pl. -S uranium		
URANISM	*n* pl. -S homosexuality	**URETIC**	*adj* pertaining to urine
URANITE	*n* pl. -S a mineral **URANITIC** *adj*	**URGE**	*v* URGED, URGING, URGES to force forward
URANIUM	*n* pl. -S a radioactive element	**URGENCY**	*n* pl. -CIES the quality of being urgent
URANOUS	*adj* pertaining to uranium		
URANYL	*n* pl. -S a bivalent radical **URANYLIC** *adj*	**URGENT**	*adj* requiring immediate attention **URGENTLY** *adv*
URARE	*n* pl. -S curare	**URGER**	*n* pl. -S one that urges
URARI	*n* pl. -S curare	**URGING**	present participle of urge
URASE	*n* pl. -S urease	**URGINGLY**	*adv* in an urging manner
URATE	*n* pl. -S a chemical salt **URATIC** *adj*	**URIAL**	*n* pl. -S a wild Asian sheep
		URIC	*adj* pertaining to urine
URB	*n* pl. -S an urban area	**URIDINE**	*n* pl. -S a chemical compound

URINAL *n* pl. -S a fixture used for urinating

URINARY *n* pl. -NARIES a urinal

URINATE *v* -NATED, -NATING, -NATES to discharge urine

URINE *n* pl. -S a liquid containing body wastes

URINEMIA *n* pl. -S uremia **URINEMIC** *adj*

URINOSE *adj* pertaining to urine

URINOUS *adj* pertaining to urine

URN *n* pl. -S a type of vase **URNLIKE** *adj*

UROCHORD *n* pl. -S a rodlike structure in certain lower vertebrates

URODELE *n* pl. -S a type of amphibian

UROLITH *n* pl. -S a concretion in the urinary tract

UROLOGY *n* pl. -GIES the branch of medicine dealing with the urinary tract **UROLOGIC** *adj*

UROPOD *n* pl. -S an abdominal limb of an arthropod **UROPODAL** *adj*

UROPYGIA *n/pl* the humps from which birds' tail feathers grow

UROSCOPY *n* pl. -PIES analysis of the urine as a means of diagnosis

UROSTYLE *n* pl. -S a part of the vertebral column of frogs and toads

URSA *n* pl. -SAE a female bear

URSIFORM *adj* having the form of a bear

URSINE *adj* pertaining to a bear

URTEXT *n* pl. -S the original text

URTICANT *n* pl. -S an urticating substance

URTICATE *v* -CATED, -CATING, -CATES to cause itching or stinging

URUS *n* pl. -ES an extinct European ox

URUSHIOL *n* pl. -S a toxic liquid

US *pron* the objective case of the pronoun we

USABLE *adj* capable of being used **USABLY** *adv*

USAGE *n* pl. -S a firmly established and generally accepted practice or procedure

USANCE *n* pl. -S usage

USAUNCE *n* pl. -S usance

USE *v* USED, USING, USES to put into service

USEABLE *adj* usable **USEABLY** *adv*

USEFUL *adj* serving a purpose **USEFULLY** *adv*

USELESS *adj* serving no purpose

USER *n* pl. -S one that uses

USHER *v* -ED, -ING, -S to conduct to a place

USING present participle of use

USNEA *n* pl. -S any of a genus of lichens

USQUABAE *n* pl. -S usquebae

USQUE *n* pl. -S usquebae

USQUEBAE *n* pl. -S whiskey

USTULATE *adj* scorched

USUAL *n* pl. -S something that is usual (ordinary)

USUALLY *adv* ordinarily

USUFRUCT *n* pl. -S the legal right to use another's property so long as it is not damaged or altered

USURER *n* pl. -S one that practices usury

USURIES pl. of usury

USURIOUS *adj* practicing usury

USURP *v* -ED, -ING, -S to seize and hold without legal authority

USURPER *n* pl. -S one that usurps

USURY *n* pl. -RIES the lending of money at an exorbitant interest rate

UT *n* pl. -S the musical tone C in the French solmization system now replaced by do

UTA *n* pl. -S any of a genus of large lizards

UTENSIL *n* pl. -S a useful implement

UTERUS *n* pl. UTERI or UTERUSES an organ of female mammals **UTERINE** *adj*

UTILE *adj* useful

UTILIDOR *n* pl. -S an insulated system of pipes for use in arctic regions

UTILISE *v* -LISED, -LISING, -LISES to utilize

UTILISER *n* pl. -S utilizer

UTILITY *n* pl. -TIES the quality of being useful

UTILIZE *v* -LIZED, -LIZING, -LIZES to make use of

UTILIZER *n* pl. -S one that utilizes

UTMOST *n* pl. -S the greatest degree or amount

UTOPIA *n* pl. -S a place of ideal perfection

UTOPIAN *n* pl. -S one who believes in the perfectibility of human society

UTOPISM *n* pl. -S the body of ideals or principles of a utopian

UTOPIST *n* pl. -S a utopian

UTRICLE	*n* pl. -S a saclike cavity in the inner ear
UTRICULI	*n/pl* utricles
UTTER	*v* -ED, -ING, -S to give audible expression to
UTTERER	*n* pl. -S one that utters
UTTERLY	*adv* totally
UVEA	*n* pl. -S a layer of the eye **UVEAL** *adj*
UVEITIS	*n* pl. -ITISES inflammation of the uvea **UVEITIC** *adj*
UVEOUS	*adj* pertaining to the uvea
UVULA	*n* pl. -LAE or -LAS the pendent, fleshy portion of the soft palate
UVULAR	*n* pl. -S a uvularly produced sound
UVULARLY	*adv* with the use of the uvula
UVULITIS	*n* pl. -TISES inflammation of the uvula
UXORIAL	*adj* pertaining to a wife
UXORIOUS	*adj* excessively submissive or devoted to one's wife

VAC *n* pl. -S a vacuum cleaner

VACANCY *n* pl. -CIES the quality or state of being vacant

VACANT *adj* empty **VACANTLY** *adv*

VACATE *v* -CATED, -CATING, -CATES to make vacant

VACATION *v* -ED, -ING, -S to take a vacation (a period of time devoted to rest and relaxation)

VACCINA *n* pl. -S vaccinia

VACCINE *n* pl. -S a preparation given to produce immunity to a specific disease **VACCINAL** *adj*

VACCINEE *n* pl. -S one that is vaccinated

VACCINIA *n* pl. -S cowpox

VACUA a pl. of vacuum

VACUITY *n* pl. -ITIES an empty space

VACUOLE *n* pl. -S a small cavity in organic tissue **VACUOLAR** *adj*

VACUOUS *adj* empty

VACUUM *n* pl. VACUUMS or VACUA a space entirely devoid of matter

VACUUM *v* -ED -ING, -S to use a device that cleans by suction

VADOSE *adj* located above the permanent groundwater level

VAGABOND *v* -ED, -ING, -S to live like a vagabond (a vagrant)

VAGAL *adj* pertaining to the vagus nerve **VAGALLY** *adv*

VAGARY *n* pl. -RIES a whim

VAGI pl. of vagus

VAGILE *adj* free to move about

VAGILITY *n* pl. -TIES freedom of movement

VAGINA *n* pl. -NAE or -NAS the passage leading from the uterus to the vulva **VAGINAL** *adj*

VAGINATE *adj* enclosed in a sheath

VAGOTOMY *n* pl. -MIES surgical division of the vagus nerve

VAGRANCY *n* pl. -CIES the state of being a vagrant

VAGRANT *n* pl. -S a wanderer with no apparent means of support

VAGROM *adj* wandering

VAGUE *adj* VAGUER, VAGUEST not clearly expressed or understood **VAGUELY** *adv*

VAGUS *n* pl. -GI a cranial nerve

VAHINE *n* pl. -S wahine

VAIL *v* -ED, -ING, -S to lower

VAIN *adj* VAINER, VAINEST filled with undue admiration for oneself **VAINLY** *adv*

VAINNESS *n* pl. -ES the quality or state of being vain

VAIR *n* pl. -S a fur used for lining and trimming medieval garments

VAKEEL *n* pl. -S a native lawyer in India

VAKIL *n* pl. -S vakeel

VALANCE *v* -LANCED, -LANCING, -LANCES to furnish with a short drapery

VALE *n* pl. -S a valley

VALENCE *n* pl. -S the degree of combining power of an element or radical

VALENCIA *n* pl. -S a woven fabric

VALENCY *n* pl. -CIES valence

VALERATE *n* pl. -S a chemical salt

VALERIAN *n* pl. -S a perennial herb **VALERIC** *adj*

VALET *v* -ED, -ING, -S to act as a personal servant to

VALGUS *n pl.* -ES the position of a joint that is abnormally turned outward **VALGOID** *adj*

VALIANCE *n pl.* -S valor

VALIANCY *n pl.* -CIES valor

VALIANT *n pl.* -S a courageous person

VALID *adj* based on evidence that can be supported

VALIDATE *v* -DATED, -DATING, -DATES to give legal force to

VALIDITY *n pl.* -TIES the quality or state of being valid

VALIDLY *adv* in a valid manner

VALINE *n pl.* -S an amino acid

VALISE *n pl.* -S a small piece of hand luggage

VALKYR *n pl.* -S valkyrie

VALKYRIE *n pl.* -S a maiden in Norse mythology

VALLATE *adj* bordered by a raised edge

VALLEY *n pl.* -LEYS a depression of the earth's surface

VALONIA *n pl.* -S a substance obtained from dried acorn cups and used in tanning and dyeing

VALOR *n pl.* -S courage

VALORISE *v* -ISED, -ISING, -ISES to valorize

VALORIZE *v* -IZED, -IZING, -IZES to establish and maintain the price of by governmental action

VALOROUS *adj* courageous

VALOUR *n pl.* -S valor

VALSE *n pl.* -S a concert waltz

VALUABLE *n pl.* -S a possession of value

VALUABLY *adv* with value

VALUATE *v* -ATED, -ATING, -ATES to appraise

VALUATOR *n pl.* -S one that valuates

VALUE *v* -UED, -UING, -UES to estimate the value (the quality that renders a thing useful or desirable) of

VALUER *n pl.* -S one that values

VALUTA *n pl.* -S the agreed or exchange value of a currency

VALVAL *adj* resembling or pertaining to a valve

VALVAR *adj* valval

VALVATE *adj* having valves or parts resembling valves

VALVE *v* VALVED, VALVING, VALVES to provide with a valve (a device for controlling the flow of a liquid or gas)

VALVELET *n pl.* -S a small valve

VALVULA *n pl.* -LAE valvule

VALVULAR *adj* pertaining to a valve

VALVULE *n pl.* -S a small valve

VAMBRACE *n pl.* -S a piece of armor for the forearm

VAMOOSE *v* -MOOSED, -MOOSING, -MOOSES to leave quickly

VAMOSE *v* -MOSED, -MOSING, -MOSES to vamoose

VAMP *v* -ED, -ING, -S to repair or patch

VAMPER *n pl.* -S one that vamps

VAMPIRE *n pl.* -S a reanimated corpse believed to feed on sleeping persons' blood **VAMPIRIC** *adj*

VAMPISH *adj* seductive

VAN *v* VANNED, VANNING, VANS to transport in a van (a type of motor vehicle)

VANADATE *n pl.* -S a chemical salt

VANADIUM *n pl.* -S a metallic element **VANADIC, VANADOUS** *adj*

VANDA *n pl.* -S a tropical orchid

VANDAL *n pl.* -S one who willfully destroys or defaces property **VANDALIC** *adj*

VANDYKE *n pl.* -S a short, pointed beard **VANDYKED** *adj*

VANE *n pl.* -S a device for showing the direction of the wind **VANED** *adj*

VANG *n pl.* -S a rope on a ship

VANGUARD *n pl.* -S the forefront of a movement

VANILLA *n pl.* -S a flavoring extract **VANILLIC** *adj*

VANILLIN *n pl.* -S a chemical compound used in flavoring

VANISH *v* -ED, -ING, -ES to disappear

VANISHER *n pl.* -S one that vanishes

VANITORY *n pl.* -RIES a combined dressing table and basin

VANITY *n pl.* -TIES inflated pride in oneself **VANITIED** *adj*

VANMAN *n pl.* -MEN a person who drives a van

VANNED past tense of van

VANNER *n pl.* -S a person who owns a van

VANNING present participle of van

VANPOOL *n pl.* -S an arrangement whereby several commuters travel in one van

VANQUISH *v* -ED, -ING, -ES to defeat in battle

VANTAGE	*n* pl. -S superiority over a competitor
VANWARD	*adv* toward the front
VAPID	*adj* insipid **VAPIDLY** *adv*
VAPIDITY	*n* pl. -TIES the quality or state of being vapid
VAPOR	*v* -ED, -ING, -S to emit vapor (visible floating moisture)
VAPORER	*n* pl. -S one that vapors
VAPORING	*n* pl. -S boastful talk
VAPORISE	*v* -ISED, -ISING, -ISES to vaporize
VAPORISH	*adj* resembling vapor
VAPORIZE	*v* -IZED, -IZING, -IZES to convert into vapor
VAPOROUS	*adj* vaporish
VAPORY	*adj* vaporish
VAPOUR	*v* -ED, -ING, -S to vapor
VAPOURER	*n* pl. -S vaporer
VAPOURY	*adj* vapory
VAQUERO	*n* pl. -ROS a cowboy
VAR	*n* pl. -S a unit of reactive power
VARA	*n* pl. -S a Spanish unit of length
VARACTOR	*n* pl. -S a capacitor with variable capacitance
VARIA	*n/pl* a collection of various literary works
VARIABLE	*n* pl. -S something that varies
VARIABLY	*adv* in a varying manner
VARIANCE	*n* pl. -S a license to perform an act contrary to the usual rule
VARIANT	*n* pl. -S a variable
VARIATE	*v* -ATED, -ATING, -ATES to vary
VARICES	pl. of varix
VARICOSE	*adj* abnormally swollen or dilated
VARIED	past tense of vary
VARIEDLY	*adv* in a varied manner
VARIER	*n* pl. -S one that varies
VARIES	present 3d person sing. of vary
VARIETAL	*n* pl. -S a wine designated by the variety of grape
VARIETY	*n* pl. -ETIES something differing from others of the same general kind
VARIFORM	*adj* having various forms
VARIOLA	*n* pl. -S smallpox **VARIOLAR** *adj*
VARIOLE	*n* pl. -S a foveola
VARIORUM	*n* pl. -S an edition containing various versions of a text
VARIOUS	*adj* of diverse kinds
VARISTOR	*n* pl. -S a type of electrical resistor
VARIX	*n* pl. VARICES a varicose vein
VARLET	*n* pl. -S a knave
VARLETRY	*n* pl. -RIES a group of common people
VARMENT	*n* pl. -S varmint
VARMINT	*n* pl. -S an animal considered to be a pest
VARNA	*n* pl. -S any of the four main Hindu social classes
VARNISH	*v* -ED, -ING, -ES to give a glossy appearance to
VARNISHY	*adj* glossy
VAROOM	*v* -ED, -ING, -S to vroom
VARSITY	*n* pl. -TIES the principal team representing a university, college, or school in any activity
VARUS	*n* pl. -ES a malformation of a bone or joint
VARVE	*n* pl. -S a deposit of sedimentary material **VARVED** *adj*
VARY	*v* VARIED, VARYING, VARIES to become or make different
VAS	*n* pl. VASA an anatomical duct **VASAL** *adj*
VASCULAR	*adj* pertaining to ducts that convey body fluids
VASCULUM	*n* pl. -LA or -LUMS a box used to hold plant specimens
VASE	*n* pl. -S a rounded, decorative container **VASELIKE** *adj*
VASIFORM	*adj* having the form of a vase
VASOTOMY	*n* pl. -MIES a surgical cutting of the vas deferens
VASSAL	*n* pl. -S a person granted the use of land by a feudal lord in return for homage and allegiance
VAST	*adj* VASTER, VASTEST of great extent or size
VAST	*n* pl. -S a vast space
VASTIER	comparative of vasty
VASTIEST	superlative of vasty
VASTITY	*n* pl. -TIES vastness
VASTLY	*adv* to a vast extent or degree
VASTNESS	*n* pl. -ES the quality or state of being vast
VASTY	*adj* VASTIER, VASTIEST vast
VAT	*v* VATTED, VATTING, VATS to put into a vat (a large container for holding liquids)

VATFUL   *n* pl. -S as much as a vat can hold

VATIC   *adj* pertaining to a prophet

VATICAL   *adj* vatic

VATICIDE   *n* pl. -S the killing of a prophet

VATTED   past tense of vat

VATTING   present participle of vat

VATU   *n* pl. -S a monetary unit of Vanuatu

VAU   *n* pl. -S vav

VAULT   *v* -ED, -ING, -S to provide with a vault (an arched ceiling)

VAULTER   *n* pl. -S one that leaps

VAULTING   *n* pl. -S the structure forming a vault

VAULTY   *adj* VAULTIER, VAULTIEST resembling a vault

VAUNT   *v* -ED, -ING, -S to brag

VAUNTER   *n* pl. -S one that vaunts

VAUNTFUL   *adj* boastful

VAUNTIE   *adj* boastful

VAUNTY   *adj* vauntie

VAV   *n* pl. -S a Hebrew letter

VAVASOR   *n* pl. -S a high-ranking vassal

VAVASOUR   *n* pl. -S vavasor

VAVASSOR   *n* pl. -S vavasor

VAW   *n* pl. -S vav

VAWARD   *n* pl. -S the foremost part

VAWNTIE   *adj* vaunty

VEAL   *v* -ED, -ING, -S to kill and prepare a calf for food

VEALER   *n* pl. -S a calf raised for food

VEALY   *adj* VEALIER, VEALIEST immature

VECTOR   *v* -ED, -ING, -S to guide in flight by means of radioed directions

VEDALIA   *n* pl. -S an Australian ladybug

VEDETTE   *n* pl. -S a small boat used for scouting

VEE   *n* pl. -S the letter V

VEEJAY   *n* pl. -JAYS an announcer on a program of music videos

VEENA   *n* pl. -S vina

VEEP   *n* pl. -S a vice president

VEEPEE   *n* pl. -S veep

VEER   *v* -ED, -ING, -S to change direction

VEERY   *n* pl. -RIES a songbird

VEG   *n* pl. VEG a vegetable

VEGAN   *n* pl. -S one that eats only plant products

VEGANISM   *n* pl. -S the practice of eating only plant products

VEGETAL   *adj* pertaining to plants

VEGETANT   *adj* characteristic of plant life

VEGETATE   *v* -TATED, -TATING, -TATES to grow in the manner of a plant

VEGETE   *adj* healthy

VEGETIST   *n* pl. -S one that eats only plant products

VEGETIVE   *adj* growing or capable of growing

VEGGIE   *n* pl. -S a vegetable

VEGIE   *n* pl. -S veggie

VEHEMENT   *adj* ardent

VEHICLE   *n* pl. -S a device used as a means of conveyance

VEIL   *v* -ED, -ING, -S to provide with a veil (a piece of sheer fabric worn over the face)

VEILEDLY   *adv* in a disguised manner

VEILER   *n* pl. -S one that veils

VEILING   *n* pl. -S a veil

VEILLIKE   *adj* resembling a veil

VEIN   *v* -ED, -ING, -S to fill with veins (tubular blood vessels)

VEINAL   *adj* of or pertaining to the veins

VEINER   *n* pl. -S a tool used in wood carving

VEINIER   comparative of veiny

VEINIEST   superlative of veiny

VEINING   *n* pl. -S a network of veins

VEINLESS   *adj* having no veins

VEINLET   *n* pl. -S a small vein

VEINLIKE   *adj* resembling a vein

VEINULE   *n* pl. -S venule

VEINULET   *n* pl. -S venule

VEINY   *adj* VEINIER, VEINIEST full of veins

VELA   pl. of velum

VELAMEN   *n* pl. -MINA a velum

VELAR   *n* pl. -S a kind of speech sound

VELARIUM   *n* pl. -IA an awning over an ancient Roman theater

VELARIZE   *v* -IZED, -IZING, -IZES to pronounce with the back of the tongue touching the soft palate

VELATE   *adj* having a velum

VELD   *n* pl. -S veldt

VELDT   *n* pl. -S a grassland of southern Africa

VELIGER   *n* pl. -S a larval stage of certain mollusks

VELITES   *n/pl* foot soldiers of ancient Rome

VELLEITY   *n* pl. -ITIES a very low degree of desire

VELLUM   *n* pl. -S a fine parchment

VELOCE *adv* rapidly — used as a musical direction

VELOCITY *n* pl. -TIES rapidity of motion

VELOUR *n* pl. -S a fabric resembling velvet

VELOUTE *n* pl. -S a type of sauce

VELUM *n* pl. -LA a thin membranous covering or partition

VELURE *v* -LURED, -LURING, -LURES to smooth with a velvet or silk pad, as a hat

VELVERET *n* pl. -S a fabric resembling velvet

VELVET *n* pl. -S a soft, smooth fabric **VELVETED, VELVETY** *adj*

VENA *n* pl. -NAE a vein

VENAL *adj* open to bribery **VENALLY** *adv*

VENALITY *n* pl. -TIES the quality or state of being venal

VENATIC *adj* pertaining to hunting

VENATION *n* pl. -S an arrangement of veins

VEND *v* -ED, -ING, -S to sell **VENDABLE** *adj*

VENDACE *n* pl. -S a European fish

VENDEE *n* pl. -S a buyer

VENDER *n* pl. -S vendor

VENDETTA *n* pl. -S a feud between two families

VENDEUSE *n* pl. -S a saleswoman

VENDIBLE *n* pl. -S a salable article

VENDIBLY *adv* salably

VENDOR *n* pl. -S a seller

VENDUE *n* pl. -S a public sale

VENEER *v* -ED, -ING, -S to overlay with thin layers of material

VENEERER *n* pl. -S one that veneers

VENENATE *v* -NATED, -NATING, -NATES to poison

VENENOSE *adj* poisonous

VENERATE *v* -ATED, -ATING, -ATES to revere

VENEREAL *adj* involving the genital organs

VENERY *n* pl. -ERIES sexual intercourse

VENETIAN *n* pl. -S a flexible window screen

VENGE *v* VENGED, VENGING, VENGES to avenge

VENGEFUL *adj* seeking to avenge

VENIAL *adj* easily excused or forgiven **VENIALLY** *adv*

VENIN *n* pl. -S a toxin found in snake venom

VENINE *n* pl. -S venin

VENIRE *n* pl. -S a type of judicial writ

VENISON *n* pl. -S the edible flesh of a deer

VENOGRAM *n* pl. -S a roentgenogram of a vein

VENOM *v* -ED, -ING, -S to inject with venom (a poisonous secretion of certain animals)

VENOMER *n* pl. -S one that venoms

VENOMOUS *adj* poisonous

VENOSE *adj* venous

VENOSITY *n* pl. -TIES the quality or state of being venous

VENOUS *adj* full of veins **VENOUSLY** *adv*

VENT *v* -ED, -ING, -S to provide with a vent (an opening for the escape of gas or liquid)

VENTAGE *n* pl. -S a small opening

VENTAIL *n* pl. -S the adjustable front of a medieval helmet

VENTER *n* pl. -S the abdomen

VENTLESS *adj* having no vent

VENTRAL *n* pl. -S a fin located on the underside of a fish

VENTURE *v* -TURED, -TURING, -TURES to risk

VENTURER *n* pl. -S one that ventures

VENTURI *n* pl. -S a device for measuring the flow of a fluid

VENTURING present participle of venture

VENUE *n* pl. -S the locale of an event

VENULE *n* pl. -S a small vein **VENULAR, VENULOSE, VENULOUS** *adj*

VERA *adj* very

VERACITY *n* pl. -TIES conformity to truth

VERANDA *n* pl. -S a type of porch

VERANDAH *n* pl. -S veranda

VERATRIA *n* pl. -S veratrin

VERATRIN *n* pl. -S a poisonous mixture of alkaloids

VERATRUM *n* pl. -S a poisonous herb

VERB *n* pl. -S a word used to express an act, occurrence, or mode of being

VERBAL *n* pl. -S a word derived from a verb

VERBALLY *adv* in a spoken manner

VERBATIM *adv* word for word

VERBENA *n* pl. -S a flowering plant

VERBIAGE *n* pl. -S an excess of words

VERBID *n* pl. -S a verbal

VERBIFY *v* -FIED, -FYING, -FIES to use as a verb

VERBILE *n* pl. -S one whose mental imagery consists of words

VERBLESS *adj* lacking a verb

VERBOSE *adj* wordy

VERBOTEN *adj* forbidden

VERDANCY *n* pl. -CIES the quality or state of being verdant

VERDANT *adj* green with vegetation

VERDERER *n* pl. -S an officer in charge of the royal forests of England

VERDEROR *n* pl. -S verderer

VERDICT *n* pl. -S the decision of a jury at the end of a legal proceeding

VERDIN *n* pl. -S a small bird

VERDITER *n* pl. -S a blue or green pigment

VERDURE *n* pl. -S green vegetation **VERDURED** *adj*

VERECUND *adj* shy

VERGE *v* VERGED, VERGING, VERGES to come near

VERGENCE *n* pl. -S a movement of one eye in relation to the other

VERGER *n* pl. -S a church official

VERGING present participle of verge

VERGLAS *n* pl. -ES a thin coating of ice on rock

VERIDIC *adj* truthful

VERIER comparative of very

VERIEST superlative of very

VERIFIER *n* pl. -S one that verifies

VERIFY *v* -FIED, -FYING, -FIES to prove to be true

VERILY *adv* in truth

VERISM *n* pl. -S realism in art or literature

VERISMO *n* pl. -MOS verism

VERIST *n* pl. -S one who practices verism **VERISTIC** *adj*

VERITAS *n* pl. -TATES truth

VERITE *n* pl. -S the technique of filming so as to convey candid realism

VERITY *n* pl. -TIES truth

VERJUICE *n* pl. -S the juice of sour or unripe fruit

VERMEIL *n* pl. -S a red color

VERMES pl. of vermis

VERMIAN *adj* pertaining to worms

VERMIN *n* pl. VERMIN small, common, harmful, or objectionable animals

VERMIS *n* pl. -MES a part of the brain

VERMOULU *adj* eaten by worms

VERMOUTH *n* pl. -S a liqueur

VERMUTH *n* pl. -S vermouth

VERNACLE *n* pl. -S vernicle

VERNAL *adj* pertaining to spring **VERNALLY** *adv*

VERNICLE *n* pl. -S veronica

VERNIER *n* pl. -S an auxiliary scale used with a main scale to obtain fine measurements

VERNIX *n* pl. -ES a fatty substance covering the skin of a fetus

VERONICA *n* pl. -S a handkerchief bearing the image of Christ's face

VERRUCA *n* pl. -CAE a wart

VERSAL *adj* entire

VERSANT *n* pl. -S the slope of a mountain or mountain chain

VERSE *v* VERSED, VERSING, VERSES to versify

VERSEMAN *n* pl. -MEN one who versifies

VERSER *n* pl. -S a verseman

VERSET *n* pl. -S a versicle

VERSICLE *n* pl. -S a short line of metrical writing

VERSIFY *v* -FIED, -FYING, -FIES to change from prose into metrical form

VERSINE *n* pl. -S a trigonometric function of an angle

VERSING present participle of verse

VERSION *n* pl. -S an account or description from a particular point of view

VERSO *n* pl. -SOS a left-hand page of a book

VERST *n* pl. -S a Russian measure of distance

VERSTE *n* pl. -S verst

VERSUS *prep* against

VERT *n* pl. -S the heraldic color green

VERTEBRA *n* pl. -BRAE or -BRAS any of the bones or segments forming the spinal column

VERTEX *n* pl. -TEXES or -TICES the highest point of something

VERTICAL *n* pl. -S something that is vertical (extending up and down)

VERTICIL *n* pl. -S a circular arrangement, as of flowers or leaves, about a point on an axis

VERTIGO *n* pl. -GOES, -GOS, or -GINES a disordered state in which the individual or his surroundings seem to whirl dizzily

VERTU *n* pl. -S virtu

VERVAIN *n* pl. -S a flowering plant

VERVE *n* pl. -S vivacity

VERVET *n* pl. -S an African monkey

VERY *adj* VERIER, VERIEST absolute

VESICA *n* pl. -CAE a bladder **VESICAL** *adj*

VESICANT *n* pl. -S a chemical warfare agent that induces blistering

VESICATE *v* -CATED, -CATING, -CATES to blister

VESICLE *n* pl. -S a small bladder

VESICULA *n* pl. -LAE a vesicle

VESPER *n* pl. -S an evening service, prayer, or song

VESPERAL *n* pl. -S a covering for an altar cloth

VESPIARY *n* pl. -ARIES a nest of wasps

VESPID *n* pl. -S a wasp

VESPINE *adj* pertaining to wasps

VESSEL *n* pl. -S a craft for traveling on water **VESSELED** *adj*

VEST *v* -ED, -ING, -S to place in the control of

VESTA *n* pl. -S a short friction match

VESTAL *n* pl. -S a chaste woman

VESTALLY *adv* chastely

VESTEE *n* pl. -S a garment worn under a woman's jacket or blouse

VESTIARY *n* pl. -ARIES a dressing room

VESTIGE *n* pl. -S a visible sign of something that is no longer in existence

VESTIGIA *n/pl* vestiges

VESTING *n* pl. -S the right of an employee to share in and withdraw from a pension fund without penalty

VESTLESS *adj* being without a vest

VESTLIKE *adj* resembling a vest (a short, sleeveless garment)

VESTMENT *n* pl. -S one of the ceremonial garments of the clergy

VESTRY *n* pl. -TRIES a room in which vestments are kept **VESTRAL** *adj*

VESTURAL *adj* pertaining to clothing

VESTURE *v* -TURED, -TURING, -TURES to clothe

VESUVIAN *n* pl. -S a mineral

VET *v* VETTED, VETTING, VETS to treat animals medically

VETCH *n* pl. -ES a climbing plant

VETERAN *n* pl. -S a former member of the armed forces

VETIVER *n* pl. -S an Asian grass

VETIVERT *n* pl. -S the essential oil of the vetiver

VETO *v* -ED, -ING, -ES to forbid or prevent authoritatively

VETOER *n* pl. -S one that vetoes

VETTED past tense of vet

VETTING present participle of vet

VEX *v* VEXED or VEXT, VEXING, VEXES to annoy

VEXATION *n* pl. -S a cause of trouble

VEXEDLY *adv* in a vexed manner

VEXER *n* pl. -S one that vexes

VEXIL *n* pl. -S vexillum

VEXILLUM *n* pl. -LA the web or vane of a feather **VEXILLAR** *adj*

VEXINGLY *adv* in a vexing manner

VEXT a past tense of vex

VIA *prep* by way of

VIABLE *adj* capable of living **VIABLY** *adv*

VIADUCT *n* pl. -S a type of bridge

VIAL *v* VIALED, VIALING, VIALS or VIALLED, VIALLING, VIALS to put in a vial (a small container for liquids)

VIAND *n* pl. -S an article of food

VIATIC *adj* pertaining to traveling

VIATICAL *adj* viatic

VIATICUM *n* pl. -CA or -CUMS an allowance for traveling expenses

VIATOR *n* pl. -ES or -S a traveler

VIBE *n* pl. -S a vibration

VIBIST *n* pl. -S one who plays the vibraphone

VIBRANCE *n* pl. -S vibrancy

VIBRANCY *n* pl. -CIES the quality or state of being vibrant

VIBRANT *n* pl. -S a sonant

VIBRATE *v* -BRATED, -BRATING, -BRATES to move back and forth rapidly

VIBRATO *n* pl. -TOS a tremulous or pulsating musical effect

VIBRATOR *n* pl. -S something that vibrates

VIBRIO *n* pl. -RIOS any of a genus of bacteria shaped like a comma **VIBRIOID** *adj*

VIBRION *n* pl. -S vibrio

VIBRISSA n pl. -SAE one of the stiff hairs growing about the mouth of certain mammals

VIBRONIC adj pertaining to changes in molecular energy states resulting from vibrational energy

VIBURNUM n pl. -S a flowering shrub

VICAR n pl. -S a church official

VICARAGE n pl. -S the office of a vicar

VICARATE n pl. -S vicarage

VICARIAL adj pertaining to a vicar

VICARLY adj vicarial

VICE v VICED, VICING, VICES to vise

VICELESS adj having no immoral habits

VICENARY adj pertaining to the number twenty

VICEROY n pl. -ROYS one who rules as the representative of a sovereign

VICHY n pl. -CHIES a type of mineral water

VICINAGE n pl. -S vicinity

VICINAL adj nearby

VICING present participle of vice

VICINITY n pl. -TIES the region near or about a place

VICIOUS adj dangerously aggressive

VICOMTE n pl. -S a French nobleman

VICTIM n pl. -S one who suffers from a destructive or injurious action

VICTOR n pl. -S one who defeats an adversary

VICTORIA n pl. -S a light carriage

VICTORY n pl. -RIES a successful outcome in a contest or struggle

VICTRESS n pl. -ES a female victor

VICTUAL v -UALED, -UALING, -UALS or -UALLED, -UALLING, -UALS to provide with food

VICUGNA n pl. -S vicuna

VICUNA n pl. -S a ruminant mammal

VIDE v see — used to direct a reader to another item; VIDE is the only form of this verb; it cannot be conjugated

VIDEO n pl. -EOS television

VIDEOTEX n pl. -ES an electronic system for transmitting data to a subscriber's video screen

VIDETTE n pl. -S vedette

VIDICON n pl. -S a type of television camera tube

VIDUITY n pl. -ITIES the quality or state of being a widow

VIE v VIED, VYING, VIES to strive for superiority

VIER n pl. -S one that vies

VIEW v -ED, -ING, -S to look at **VIEWABLE** adj

VIEWDATA n pl. VIEWDATA a videotex

VIEWER n pl. -S one that views

VIEWIER comparative of viewy

VIEWIEST superlative of viewy

VIEWING n pl. -S an act of seeing, watching, or looking

VIEWLESS adj having no opinions

VIEWY adj VIEWIER, VIEWIEST showy

VIG n pl. -S a vigorish

VIGA n pl. -S a ceiling beam in Spanish architecture

VIGIL n pl. -S a period of watchfulness maintained during normal sleeping hours

VIGILANT adj watchful

VIGNERON n pl. -S a winegrower

VIGNETTE v -GNETTED, -GNETTING, -GNETTES to describe briefly

VIGOR n pl. -S active strength or force

VIGORISH n pl. -ES a charge paid to a bookie on a bet

VIGOROSO adv with emphasis and spirit — used as a musical direction

VIGOROUS adj full of vigor

VIGOUR n pl. -S vigor

VIKING n pl. -S a Scandinavian pirate

VILAYET n pl. -S an administrative division of Turkey

VILE adj VILER, VILEST physically repulsive **VILELY** adv

VILENESS n pl. -ES the state of being vile

VILIFIER n pl. -S one that vilifies

VILIFY v -FIED, -FYING, -FIES to defame

VILIPEND v -ED, -ING, -S to vilify

VILL n pl. -S a village

VILLA n pl. -LAE or -LAS an agricultural estate of ancient Rome

VILLADOM n pl. -S the world constituted by suburban residences and their occupants

VILLAGE n pl. -S a small community in a rural area

VILLAGER n pl. -S one who lives in a village

VILLAIN *n* pl. -S a cruelly malicious person

VILLAINY *n* pl. -LAINIES conduct characteristic of a villain

VILLATIC *adj* rural

VILLEIN *n* pl. -S a type of serf

VILLUS *n* pl. -LI one of the hairlike projections found on certain membranes **VILLOSE, VILLOUS** *adj*

VIM *n* pl. -S energy

VIMEN *n* pl. -MINA a long, flexible branch of a plant **VIMINAL** *adj*

VIN *n* pl. -S wine

VINA *n* pl. -S a stringed instrument of India

VINAL *n* pl. -S a synthetic textile fiber

VINASSE *n* pl. -S a residue left after the distillation of liquor

VINCA *n* pl. -S a flowering plant

VINCIBLE *adj* capable of being conquered **VINCIBLY** *adv*

VINCULUM *n* pl. -LA or -LUMS a unifying bond

VINDALOO *n* pl. -LOOS a curried dish made with meat, garlic, and wine

VINE *v* VINED, VINING, VINES to grow like a vine (a climbing plant)

VINEAL *adj* vinous

VINEGAR *n* pl. -S a sour liquid used as a condiment or preservative **VINEGARY** *adj*

VINERY *n* pl. -ERIES a place in which grapevines are grown

VINEYARD *n* pl. -S an area planted with grapevines

VINIC *adj* derived from wine

VINIER comparative of viny

VINIEST superlative of viny

VINIFERA *n* pl. -S a European grape

VINIFY *v* -FIED, -FYING, -FIES to convert into wine by fermentation

VINING present participle of vine

VINO *n* pl. -NOS wine

VINOSITY *n* pl. -TIES the character of a wine

VINOUS *adj* pertaining to wine **VINOUSLY** *adv*

VINTAGE *n* pl. -S a season's yield of wine from a vineyard

VINTAGER *n* pl. -S one that harvests wine grapes

VINTNER *n* pl. -S a wine merchant

VINY *adj* VINIER, VINIEST covered with vines

VINYL *n* pl. -S a type of plastic **VINYLIC** *adj*

VIOL *n* pl. -S a stringed instrument

VIOLA *n* pl. -S a stringed instrument

VIOLABLE *adj* capable of being violated **VIOLABLY** *adv*

VIOLATE *v* -LATED, -LATING, -LATES to break or disregard the terms or requirements of

VIOLATER *n* pl. -S violator

VIOLATOR *n* pl. -S one that violates

VIOLENCE *n* pl. -S violent action

VIOLENT *adj* marked by intense physical force or roughness

VIOLET *n* pl. -S a flowering plant

VIOLIN *n* pl. -S a stringed instrument

VIOLIST *n* pl. -S one who plays the viol or viola

VIOLONE *n* pl. -S a stringed instrument

VIOMYCIN *n* pl. -S an antibiotic

VIPER *n* pl. -S a venomous snake **VIPERINE, VIPERISH, VIPEROUS** *adj*

VIRAGO *n* pl. -GOES or -GOS a noisy, domineering woman

VIRAL *adj* pertaining to or caused by a virus **VIRALLY** *adv*

VIRELAI *n* pl. -S virelay

VIRELAY *n* pl. -LAYS a medieval French verse form

VIREMIA *n* pl. -S the presence of a virus in the blood **VIREMIC** *adj*

VIREO *n* pl. -EOS a small bird

VIRES pl. of vis

VIRGA *n* pl. -S wisps of precipitation evaporating before reaching ground

VIRGATE *n* pl. -S an early English measure of land area

VIRGIN *n* pl. -S a person who has never had sexual intercourse

VIRGINAL *n* pl. -S a musical instrument

VIRGULE *n* pl. -S a diagonal printing mark used to separate alternatives

VIRICIDE *n* pl. -S a substance that destroys viruses

VIRID *adj* verdant

VIRIDIAN *n* pl. -S a bluish-green pigment

VIRIDITY *n* pl. -TIES verdancy

VIRILE *adj* having masculine vigor **VIRILELY** *adv*

VIRILISM	*n* pl. -S the development of male secondary sex characteristics in a female
VIRILITY	*n* pl. -TIES the quality or state of being virile
VIRION	*n* pl. -S a virus particle
VIRL	*n* pl. -S a metal ring or cap put around a shaft to prevent splitting
VIROID	*n* pl. -S a viruslike plant pathogen
VIROLOGY	*n* pl. -GIES the study of viruses
VIROSIS	*n* pl. -ROSES infection with a virus
VIRTU	*n* pl. -S a love or taste for the fine arts
VIRTUAL	*adj* having the effect but not the actual form of what is specified
VIRTUE	*n* pl. -S moral excellence
VIRTUOSA	*n* pl. -SAS or -SE a female virtuoso
VIRTUOSO	*n* pl. -SOS or -SI a highly skilled artistic performer
VIRTUOUS	*adj* characterized by virtue
VIRUCIDE	*n* pl. -S viricide
VIRULENT	*adj* extremely poisonous
VIRUS	*n* pl. -ES any of a class of submicroscopic pathogens
VIS	*n* pl. VIRES force or power
VISA	*v* -ED, -ING, -S to put an official endorsement on, as a passport
VISAGE	*n* pl. -S the face or facial expression of a person **VISAGED** *adj*
VISARD	*n* pl. -S vizard
VISCACHA	*n* pl. -S a burrowing rodent
VISCERA	pl. of viscus
VISCERAL	*adj* pertaining to the internal organs
VISCID	*adj* thick and adhesive **VISCIDLY** *adv*
VISCOID	*adj* somewhat viscid
VISCOSE	*n* pl. -S a viscous solution
VISCOUNT	*n* pl. -S a British nobleman
VISCOUS	*adj* having relatively high resistance to flow
VISCUS	*n* pl. -CERA an internal organ
VISE	*v* VISED, VISING, VISES to hold in a vise (a clamping device)
VISE	*v* VISEED, VISEING, VISES to visa
VISELIKE	*adj* resembling a vise
VISIBLE	*adj* capable of being seen **VISIBLY** *adv*
VISING	present participle of vise
VISION	*v* -ED, -ING, -S to imagine
VISIONAL	*adj* imaginary
VISIT	*v* -ED, -ING, -S to go or come to see someone or something
VISITANT	*n* pl. -S a visitor
VISITER	*n* pl. -S visitor
VISITOR	*n* pl. -S one that visits
VISIVE	*adj* visible
VISOR	*v* -ED, -ING, -S to provide with a visor (a projecting brim)
VISTA	*n* pl. -S a distant view **VISTAED** *adj*
VISUAL	*n* pl. -S something that illustrates by pictures or diagrams
VISUALLY	*adv* with regard to the sense of sight
VITA	*n* pl. -TAE a brief, autobiographical sketch
VITAL	*adj* necessary to life
VITALISE	*v* -ISED, -ISING, -ISES to vitalize
VITALISM	*n* pl. -S a philosophical doctrine
VITALIST	*n* pl. -S an advocate of vitalism
VITALITY	*n* pl. -TIES exuberant physical strength or mental vigor
VITALIZE	*v* -IZED, -IZING, -IZES to give life to
VITALLY	*adv* in a vital manner
VITALS	*n/pl* vital organs
VITAMER	*n* pl. -S a type of chemical compound
VITAMIN	*n* pl. -S any of various organic substances essential to proper nutrition
VITAMINE	*n* pl. -S vitamin
VITELLIN	*n* pl. -S a protein found in egg yolk
VITELLUS	*n* pl. -ES the yolk of an egg
VITESSE	*n* pl. -S speed
VITIATE	*v* -ATED, -ATING, -ATES to impair the value or quality of **VITIABLE** *adj*
VITIATOR	*n* pl. -S one that vitiates
VITILIGO	*n* pl. -GOS a skin disease
VITRAIN	*n* pl. -S the material in the vitreous layers of banded bituminous coal
VITREOUS	*adj* resembling glass
VITRIC	*adj* pertaining to glass

VITRICS *n/pl* the art of making or decorating glass articles

VITRIFY *v* -FIED, -FYING, -FIES to convert into glass

VITRINE *n* pl. -S a glass showcase for art objects

VITRIOL *v* -OLED, -OLING, -OLS or -OLLED, -OLLING, -OLS to treat with sulfuric acid

VITTA *n* pl. -TAE a streak or band of color **VITTATE** *adj*

VITTLE *v* -TLED, -TLING, -TLES to victual

VITULINE *adj* pertaining to a calf

VIVA *n* pl. -S a shout or cry used to express approval

VIVACE *n* pl. -S a musical passage played in a brisk spirited manner

VIVACITY *n* pl. -TIES the quality or state of being lively

VIVARIUM *n* pl. -IA or -IUMS a place for raising and keeping live animals

VIVARY *n* pl. -RIES vivarium

VIVE *interj* — used as an exclamation of approval

VIVERRID *n* pl. -S any of a family of small carnivorous mammals

VIVERS *n/pl* food

VIVID *adj* -IDER, -IDEST strikingly bright or intense **VIVIDLY** *adv*

VIVIFIC *adj* vivifying

VIVIFIER *n* pl. -S one that vivifies

VIVIFY *v* -FIED, -FYING, -FIES to give life to

VIVIPARA *n/pl* animals that bring forth living young

VIVISECT *v* -ED, -ING, -S to dissect the living body of

VIXEN *n* pl. -S a shrewish woman **VIXENISH, VIXENLY** *adj*

VIZARD *n* pl. -S a mask **VIZARDED** *adj*

VIZCACHA *n* pl. -S viscacha

VIZIER *n* pl. -S a high official in some Muslim countries

VIZIR *n* pl. -S vizier **VIZIRIAL** *adj*

VIZIRATE *n* pl. -S the office of a vizir

VIZOR *v* -ED, -ING, -S to visor

VIZSLA *n* pl. -S a Hungarian breed of dog

VOCABLE *n* pl. -S a word

VOCABLY *adv* in a manner that may be voiced aloud

VOCAL *n* pl. -S a sound produced with the voice

VOCALIC *n* pl. -S a vowel sound

VOCALISE *v* -ISED, -ISING, -ISES to vocalize

VOCALISM *n* pl. -S the act of vocalizing

VOCALIST *n* pl. -S a singer

VOCALITY *n* pl. -TIES possession or exercise of vocal powers

VOCALIZE *v* -IZED, -IZING, -IZES to produce with the voice

VOCALLY *adv* with the voice

VOCATION *n* pl. -S the work in which a person is regularly employed

VOCATIVE *n* pl. -S a grammatical case used in some languages

VOCES pl. of vox

VOCODER *n* pl. -S an electronic device used in transmitting speech signals

VODKA *n* pl. -S a liquor

VODOUN *n* pl. -S vodun

VODUN *n* pl. -S a primitive religion of the West Indies

VOE *n* pl. -S a small bay, creek, or inlet

VOGIE *adj* vain

VOGUE *v* VOGUED, VOGUING or VOGUEING, VOGUES to imitate poses of fashion models

VOGUISH *adj* fashionable

VOICE *v* VOICED, VOICING, VOICES to express or utter

VOICEFUL *adj* sonorous

VOICER *n* pl. -S one that voices

VOICING present participle of voice

VOID *v* -ED, -ING, -S to make void (of no legal force or effect) **VOIDABLE** *adj*

VOIDANCE *n* pl. -S the act or process of voiding

VOIDER *n* pl. -S one that voids

VOIDNESS *n* pl. -ES the quality or state of being void

VOILA *interj* — used to call attention to something

VOILE *n* pl. -S a sheer fabric

VOLANT *adj* flying or capable of flying

VOLANTE *adj* moving with light rapidity — used as a musical direction

VOLAR *adj* pertaining to flight

VOLATILE *n* pl. -S a winged creature

VOLCANIC *n* pl. -S a rock produced by a volcano

VOLCANO   *n* pl. -NOES or -NOS an opening in the earth's crust through which molten rock and gases are ejected

VOLE   *v* VOLED, VOLING, VOLES to win all the tricks in a card game

VOLERY   *n* pl. -ERIES a large birdcage

VOLITANT   *adj* volant

VOLITION   *n* pl. -S the power of choosing or determining

VOLITIVE   *adj* pertaining to volition

VOLLEY   *v* -ED, -ING, -S to return a tennis ball before it touches the ground

VOLLEYER   *n* pl. -S one that volleys

VOLOST   *n* pl. -S an administrative district in Russia

VOLPLANE   *v* -PLANED, -PLANING, -PLANES to glide in an airplane

VOLT   *n* pl. -S a unit of electromotive force

VOLTA   *n* pl. -TE a turning

VOLTAGE   *n* pl. -S electromotive force expressed in volts

VOLTAISM   *n* pl. -S electricity produced by chemical action **VOLTAIC** *adj*

VOLTE   *n* pl. -S a fencing movement

VOLTI   *interj* — used to direct musicians to turn the page

VOLUBLE   *adj* talkative **VOLUBLY** *adv*

VOLUME   *v* -UMED, -UMING, -UMES to send or give out in large quantities

VOLUTE   *n* pl. -S a spiral architectural ornament **VOLUTED** *adj*

VOLUTIN   *n* pl. -S a granular substance that is common in microorganisms

VOLUTION   *n* pl. -S a spiral

VOLVA   *n* pl. -S a membranous sac that encloses certain immature mushrooms **VOLVATE** *adj*

VOLVOX   *n* pl. -ES any of a genus of freshwater protozoa

VOLVULUS   *n* pl. -LI or -LUSES a twisting of the intestine that causes obstruction

VOMER   *n* pl. -S a bone of the skull **VOMERINE** *adj*

VOMICA   *n* pl. -CAE a cavity in the body containing pus

VOMIT   *v* -ED, -ING, -S to eject the contents of the stomach through the mouth

VOMITER   *n* pl. -S one that vomits

VOMITIVE   *n* pl. -S an emetic

VOMITO   *n* pl. -TOS the black vomit of yellow fever

VOMITORY   *n* pl. -RIES an emetic

VOMITOUS   *adj* pertaining to vomiting

VOMITUS   *n* pl. -ES vomited matter

VON   *prep* of; from — used in some surnames

VOODOO   *v* -ED, -ING, -S to hex

VORACITY   *n* pl. -TIES the quality or state of being ravenous

VORLAGE   *n* pl. -S a position in skiing

VORTEX   *n* pl. -TEXES or -TICES a whirling mass of fluid **VORTICAL** *adj*

VOTABLE   *adj* capable of being voted on

VOTARESS   *n* pl. -ES a female votary

VOTARIST   *n* pl. -S a votary

VOTARY   *n* pl. -RIES a person who is bound by religious vows

VOTE   *v* VOTED, VOTING, VOTES to cast a vote (a formal expression of will or opinion)

VOTEABLE   *adj* votable

VOTELESS   *adj* having no vote

VOTER   *n* pl. -S one that votes

VOTING   present participle of vote

VOTIVE   *adj* performed in fulfillment of a vow **VOTIVELY** *adv*

VOTRESS   *n* pl. -ES votaress

VOUCH   *v* -ED, -ING, -ES to give one's personal assurance or guarantee

VOUCHEE   *n* pl. -S one for whom another vouches

VOUCHER   *v* -ED, -ING, -S to establish the authenticity of

VOUSSOIR   *n* pl. -S a wedge-shaped building stone

VOUVRAY   *n* pl. -VRAYS a French white wine

VOW   *v* -ED, -ING, -S to make a vow (a solemn promise)

VOWEL   *n* pl. -S a type of speech sound

VOWELIZE   *v* -IZED, -IZING, -IZES to provide with symbols used to indicate vowels

VOWER   *n* pl. -S one that vows

VOWLESS   *adj* having made no vow

VOX   *n* pl. VOCES voice

VOYAGE   *v* -AGED, -AGING, -AGES to travel

VOYAGER   *n* pl. -S one that voyages

VOYAGEUR *n* pl. -S a person employed by a fur company to transport goods between distant stations

VOYEUR *n* pl. -S one who is sexually gratified by looking at sexual objects or acts

VROOM *v* -ED, -ING, -S to run an engine at high speed

VROUW *n* pl. -S a Dutch woman

VROW *n* pl. -S vrouw

VUG *n* pl. -S a small cavity in a rock or lode

VUGG *n* pl. -S vug

VUGGY *adj* -GIER, -GIEST abounding in vugs

VUGH *n* pl. -S vug

VULCANIC *adj* pertaining to a volcano

VULGAR *adj* -GARER, -GAREST crude **VULGARLY** *adv*

VULGAR *n* pl. -S a common person

VULGATE *n* pl. -S the common speech of a people

VULGO *adv* commonly

VULGUS *n* pl. -ES an exercise in Latin formerly required of pupils in some English public schools

VULPINE *adj* pertaining to a fox

VULTURE *n* pl. -S a bird of prey

VULVA *n* pl. -VAE or -VAS the external genital organs of a female **VULVAL, VULVAR, VULVATE** *adj*

VULVITIS *n* pl. -TISES inflammation of the vulva

VYING present participle of vie

VYINGLY *adv* in a vying manner

W₄

WAB	*n* pl. -S a web
WABBLE	*v* -BLED, -BLING, -BLES to wobble
WABBLER	*n* pl. -S one that wabbles
WABBLY	*adj* -BLIER, -BLIEST wobbly
WACK	*n* pl. -S a wacky person
WACKE	*n* pl. -S a type of basaltic rock
WACKO	*n* pl. WACKOS a person who is wacky
WACKY	*adj* WACKIER, WACKIEST very irrational WACKILY *adv*
WAD	*v* WADDED, WADDING, WADS to form into a wad (a small mass of soft material)
WADABLE	*adj* wadeable
WADDER	*n* pl. -S one that wads
WADDIE	*n* pl. -S a cowboy
WADDIED	past tense of waddy
WADDIES	present 3d person sing. of waddy
WADDING	*n* pl. -S a wad
WADDLE	*v* -DLED, -DLING, -DLES to walk with short, swaying steps
WADDLER	*n* pl. -S one that waddles
WADDLY	*adj* having or being a waddling gait
WADDY	*v* -DIED, -DYING, -DIES to strike with a thick club
WADE	*v* WADED, WADING, WADES to walk through water
WADEABLE	*adj* capable of being passed through by wading
WADER	*n* pl. -S one that wades
WADI	*n* pl. -S the bed of a usually dry watercourse
WADIES	pl. of wady
WADING	present participle of wade
WADMAAL	*n* pl. -S wadmal
WADMAL	*n* pl. -S a thick woolen fabric

WADMEL	*n* pl. -S wadmal
WADMOL	*n* pl. -S wadmal
WADMOLL	*n* pl. -S wadmal
WADSET	*v* -SETTED, -SETTING, -SETS to mortgage
WADY	*n* pl. -DIES wadi
WAE	*n* pl. -S woe
WAEFUL	*adj* woeful
WAENESS	*n* pl. -ES woeness
WAESUCK	*interj* waesucks
WAESUCKS	*interj* — used to express pity
WAFER	*v* -ED, -ING, -S to seal with an adhesive disk
WAFERY	*adj* resembling a wafer (a thin, crisp biscuit)
WAFF	*v* -ED, -ING, -S to wave
WAFFIE	*n* pl. -S a vagabond
WAFFLE	*v* -FLED, -FLING, -FLES to talk vaguely or indecisively
WAFFLER	*n* pl. -S one that waffles
WAFFLING	*n* pl. -S an indecisive statement or position
WAFT	*v* -ED, -ING, -S to carry lightly over air or water
WAFTAGE	*n* pl. -S the act of wafting
WAFTER	*n* pl. -S one that wafts
WAFTURE	*n* pl. -S waftage
WAG	*v* WAGGED, WAGGING, WAGS to move briskly up and down or to and fro
WAGE	*v* WAGED, WAGING, WAGES to engage in or carry on
WAGELESS	*adj* unpaid
WAGER	*v* -ED, -ING, -S to risk on an uncertain outcome
WAGERER	*n* pl. -S one that wagers
WAGGED	past tense of wag
WAGGER	*n* pl. -S one that wags

WAGGERY	*n* pl. -GERIES waggish behavior	**WAKANDA**	*n* pl. -S a supernatural force in Sioux beliefs
WAGGING	present participle of wag	**WAKE**	*v* WAKED or WOKE, WOKEN, WAKING, WAKES to rouse from sleep
WAGGISH	*adj* playfully humorous		
WAGGLE	*v* -GLED, -GLING, -GLES to wag		
WAGGLY	*adj* waggling	**WAKEFUL**	*adj* not sleeping or able to sleep
WAGGON	*v* -ED, -ING, -S to wagon	**WAKELESS**	*adj* unbroken — used of sleep
WAGGONER	*n* pl. -S wagoner	**WAKEN**	*v* -ED, -ING, -S to wake
WAGING	present participle of wage	**WAKENER**	*n* pl. -S one that wakens
WAGON	*v* -ED, -ING, -S to convey by wagon (a four-wheeled, horse-drawn vehicle)	**WAKENING**	*n* pl. -S the act of one that wakens
		WAKER	*n* pl. -S one that wakes
WAGONAGE	*n* pl. -S conveyance by wagon	**WAKERIFE**	*adj* wakeful
WAGONER	*n* pl. -S one who drives a wagon	**WAKIKI**	*n* pl. -S shell money of the South Sea Islands
WAGSOME	*adj* waggish	**WAKING**	present participle of wake
WAGTAIL	*n* pl. -S a songbird	**WALE**	*v* WALED, WALING, WALES to mark with welts
WAHCONDA	*n* pl. -S wakanda		
WAHINE	*n* pl. -S a Hawaiian woman	**WALER**	*n* pl. -S an Australian-bred saddle horse
WAHOO	*n* pl. -HOOS a flowering shrub		
WAIF	*v* -ED, -ING, -S to throw away	**WALIES**	pl. of waly
WAIFLIKE	*adj* resembling a waif (a homeless child)	**WALING**	present participle of wale
		WALK	*v* -ED, -ING, -S to advance on foot **WALKABLE** *adj*
WAIL	*v* -ED, -ING, -S to utter a long, mournful cry		
		WALKAWAY	*n* pl. -AWAYS an easy victory
WAILER	*n* pl. -S one that wails	**WALKER**	*n* pl. -S one that walks
WAILFUL	*adj* mournful	**WALKING**	*n* pl. -S the act of one that walks
WAILSOME	*adj* wailful		
WAIN	*n* pl. -S a large, open wagon	**WALKOUT**	*n* pl. -S a strike by workers
WAINSCOT	*v* -SCOTED, -SCOTING, -SCOTS or -SCOTTED, -SCOTTING, -SCOTS to line the walls of with wooden paneling	**WALKOVER**	*n* pl. -S a walkaway
		WALKUP	*n* pl. -S an apartment house having no elevator
		WALKWAY	*n* pl. -WAYS a passage for walking
WAIR	*v* -ED, -ING, -S to spend	**WALKYRIE**	*n* pl. -S valkyrie
WAIST	*n* pl. -S the part of the body between the ribs and the hips **WAISTED** *adj*	**WALL**	*v* -ED, -ING, -S to provide with a wall (an upright structure built to enclose an area)
WAISTER	*n* pl. -S a seaman stationed in the middle section of a ship	**WALLA**	*n* pl. -S wallah
		WALLABY	*n* pl. -BIES a small kangaroo
WAISTING	*n* pl. -S a type of dressmaking material	**WALLAH**	*n* pl. -S a person engaged in a particular occupation or activity
WAIT	*v* -ED, -ING, -S to stay in expectation of	**WALLAROO**	*n* pl. -ROOS a large kangaroo
		WALLET	*n* pl. -S a flat folding case
WAITER	*n* pl. -S one who serves food in a restaurant	**WALLEYE**	*n* pl. -S an eye having a white cornea **WALLEYED** *adj*
WAITING	*n* pl. -S the act of one who waits	**WALLIE**	*n* pl. -S a valet
		WALLIES	pl. of wally
WAITRESS	*v* -ED, -ING, -ES to work as a female server in a restaurant	**WALLOP**	*v* -ED, -ING, -S to beat soundly
WAIVE	*v* WAIVED, WAIVING, WAIVES to give up intentionally	**WALLOPER**	*n* pl. -S one that wallops
		WALLOW	*v* -ED, -ING, -S to roll about
		WALLOWER	*n* pl. -S one that wallows
WAIVER	*n* pl. -S the act of waiving something	**WALLY**	*n* pl. -LIES waly
		WALNUT	*n* pl. -S an edible nut

WALRUS *n* pl. -ES a marine mammal

WALTZ *v* -ED, -ING, -ES to perform a ballroom dance

WALTZER *n* pl. -S one that waltzes

WALY *n* pl. WALIES something visually pleasing

WAMBLE *v* -BLED, -BLING, -BLES to move unsteadily

WAMBLY *adj* -BLIER, -BLIEST unsteady

WAME *n* pl. -S the belly

WAMEFOU *n* pl. -S a bellyful

WAMEFUL *n* pl. -S wamefou

WAMMUS *n* pl. -ES wamus

WAMPISH *v* -ED, -ING, -ES to throw about

WAMPUM *n* pl. -S a form of currency formerly used by North American Indians

WAMPUS *n* pl. -ES wamus

WAMUS *n* pl. -ES a heavy outer jacket

WAN *adj* WANNER, WANNEST unnaturally pale

WAN *v* WANNED, WANNING, WANS to become wan

WAND *n* pl. -S a slender rod

WANDER *v* -ED, -ING, -S to move about with no destination or purpose

WANDERER *n* pl. -S one that wanders

WANDEROO *n* pl. -ROOS an Asian monkey

WANDLE *adj* supple

WANE *v* WANED, WANING, WANES to decrease in size or extent

WANEY *adj* WANIER, WANIEST wany

WANGAN *n* pl. -S wanigan

WANGLE *v* -GLED, -GLING, -GLES to obtain or accomplish by contrivance

WANGLER *n* pl. -S one that wangles

WANGUN *n* pl. -S wanigan

WANIER comparative of waney and wany

WANIEST superlative of waney and wany

WANIGAN *n* pl. -S a supply chest used in a logging camp

WANING present participle of wane

WANION *n* pl. -S vengeance

WANLY *adv* in a wan manner

WANNED past tense of wan

WANNER comparative of wan

WANNESS *n* pl. -ES the quality of being wan

WANNEST superlative of wan

WANNIGAN *n* pl. -S wanigan

WANNING present participle of wan

WANT *v* -ED, -ING, -S to have a desire for

WANTAGE *n* pl. -S something that is lacking

WANTER *n* pl. -S one that wants

WANTON *v* -ED, -ING, -S to behave immorally

WANTONER *n* pl. -S one that wantons

WANTONLY *adv* immorally

WANY *adj* WANIER, WANIEST waning in some parts

WAP *v* WAPPED, WAPPING, WAPS to wrap

WAPITI *n* pl. -S a large deer

WAR *v* WARRED, WARRING, WARS to engage in war (a state of open, armed conflict)

WARBLE *v* -BLED, -BLING, -BLES to sing with melodic embellishments

WARBLER *n* pl. -S one that warbles

WARCRAFT *n* pl. -S the art of war

WARD *v* -ED, -ING, -S to turn aside

WARDEN *n* pl. -S the chief officer of a prison

WARDENRY *n* pl. -RIES the office of a warden

WARDER *n* pl. -S a person who guards something

WARDRESS *n* pl. -ES a female warden

WARDROBE *n* pl. -S a collection of garments

WARDROOM *n* pl. -S a recreation area on a warship

WARDSHIP *n* pl. -S the state of being under a guardian

WARE *v* WARED, WARING, WARES to beware of

WAREROOM *n* pl. -S a room in which goods are displayed for sale

WARFARE *n* pl. -S the act of engaging in war

WARFARIN *n* pl. -S a chemical compound

WARHEAD *n* pl. -S the front part of a missile containing the explosive

WARHORSE *n* pl. -S a musical or dramatic work that has been performed to excess

WARIER comparative of wary

WARIEST superlative of wary

WARILY *adv* in a wary manner

WARINESS *n* pl. -ES the state of being wary

WARING present participle of ware

WARISON *n* pl. -S a call to attack

WARK *v* -ED, -ING, -S to endure pain

WARLESS *adj* free from war

WARLIKE	*adj* disposed to engage in war
WARLOCK	*n* pl. -S a sorcerer
WARLORD	*n* pl. -S a military leader of a warlike nation
WARM	*adj* WARMER, WARMEST moderately hot
WARM	*v* -ED, -ING, -S to make warm
WARMAKER	*n* pl. -S one that wars
WARMER	*n* pl. -S one that warms
WARMISH	*adj* somewhat warm
WARMLY	*adv* in a warm manner
WARMNESS	*n* pl. -ES the state of being warm
WARMOUTH	*n* -S a freshwater fish
WARMTH	*n* pl. -S warmness
WARMUP	*n* pl. -S a preparatory exercise or procedure
WARN	*v* -ED, -ING, -S to make aware of impending or possible danger
WARNER	*n* pl. -S one that warns
WARNING	*n* pl. -S something that warns
WARP	*v* -ED, -ING, -S to turn or twist out of shape
WARPAGE	*n* pl. -S the act of warping
WARPATH	*n* pl. -S the route taken by attacking American Indians
WARPER	*n* pl. -S one that warps
WARPLANE	*n* pl. -S an airplane armed for combat
WARPOWER	*n* pl. -S the power to make war
WARPWISE	*adv* in a vertical direction
WARRAGAL	*n* pl. -S warrigal
WARRANT	*v* -ED, -ING, -S to give authority to
WARRANTY	*n* pl. -TIES the act of warranting
WARRED	past tense of war
WARREN	*n* pl. -S a place where rabbits live and breed
WARRENER	*n* pl. -S the keeper of a warren
WARRIGAL	*n* pl. -S a dingo
WARRING	present participle of war
WARRIOR	*n* pl. -S one engaged or experienced in warfare
WARSAW	*n* pl. -S a marine fish
WARSHIP	*n* pl. -S a ship armed for combat
WARSLE	*v* -SLED, -SLING, -SLES to wrestle
WARSLER	*n* pl. -S a wrestler
WARSTLE	*v* -TLED, -TLING, -TLES to wrestle
WARSTLER	*n* pl. -S a wrestler

WART	*n* pl. -S a protuberance on the skin WARTED *adj*
WARTHOG	*n* pl. -S an African wild hog
WARTIER	comparative of warty
WARTIEST	superlative of warty
WARTIME	*n* pl. -S a time of war
WARTLESS	*adj* having no warts
WARTLIKE	*adj* resembling a wart
WARTY	*adj* WARTIER, WARTIEST covered with warts
WARWORK	*n* pl. -S work done during a war
WARWORN	*adj* showing the effects of war
WARY	*adj* WARIER, WARIEST watchful
WAS	1st and 3d person sing. past indicative of be
WASABI	*n* pl. -S a pungent herb
WASH	*v* -ED, -ING, -ES to cleanse by immersing in or applying a liquid
WASHABLE	*n* pl. -S something that can be washed without damage
WASHBOWL	*n* pl. -S a bowl used for washing oneself
WASHDAY	*n* pl. -DAYS a day set aside for washing clothes
WASHER	*n* pl. -S one that washes
WASHIER	comparative of washy
WASHIEST	superlative of washy
WASHING	*n* pl. -S articles washed or to be washed
WASHOUT	*n* pl. -S an erosion of earth by the action of water
WASHRAG	*n* pl. -S a small cloth used for washing oneself
WASHROOM	*n* pl. -S a lavatory
WASHTUB	*n* pl. -S a tub used for washing clothes
WASHUP	*n* pl. -S the act of washing clean
WASHY	*adj* WASHIER, WASHIEST overly diluted
WASP	*n* pl. -S a stinging insect WASPISH, WASPLIKE *adj*
WASPY	*adj* WASPIER, WASPIEST resembling a wasp WASPILY *adv*
WASSAIL	*v* -ED, -ING, -S to drink to the health of
WAST	*n* pl. -S west
WASTABLE	*adj* capable of being wasted
WASTAGE	*n* pl. -S something that is wasted
WASTE	*v* WASTED, WASTING, WASTES to use thoughtlessly

WASTEFUL *adj* tending to waste

WASTELOT *n* pl. -S a vacant lot

WASTER *n* pl. -S one that wastes

WASTERIE *n* pl. -S wastry

WASTERY *n* pl. -RIES wastry

WASTEWAY *n* pl. -WAYS a channel for excess water

WASTING present participle of waste

WASTREL *n* pl. -S one that wastes

WASTRIE *n* pl. -S wastry

WASTRY *n* pl. -RIES reckless extravagance

WAT *adj* WATTER, WATTEST wet

WAT *n* pl. -S a hare

WATAP *n* pl. -S a thread made from the roots of various trees

WATAPE *n* pl. -S watap

WATCH *v* -ED, -ING, -ES to observe carefully

WATCHCRY *n* pl. -CRIES a password

WATCHDOG *v* -DOGGED, -DOGGING, -DOGS to act as a guardian for

WATCHER *n* pl. -S one that watches

WATCHEYE *n* pl. -S a walleye

WATCHFUL *adj* closely observant or alert

WATCHMAN *n* pl. -MEN a man employed to stand guard

WATCHOUT *n* pl. -S the act of looking out for something

WATER *v* -ED, -ING, -S to sprinkle with water (a transparent, odorless, tasteless liquid)

WATERAGE *n* pl. -S the conveyance of goods by water

WATERBED *n* pl. -S a bed whose mattress is a plastic bag filled with water

WATERDOG *n* pl. -S a large salamander

WATERER *n* pl. -S one that waters

WATERIER comparative of watery

WATERIEST superlative of watery

WATERILY *adv* in a watery manner

WATERING *n* pl. -S the act of one that waters

WATERISH *adj* watery

WATERLOG *v* -LOGGED, -LOGGING, -LOGS to soak with water

WATERLOO *n* pl. -LOOS a decisive defeat

WATERMAN *n* pl. -MEN a boatman

WATERWAY *n* pl. -WAYS a navigable body of water

WATERY *adj* -TERIER, -TERIEST containing water

WATT *n* pl. -S a unit of power

WATTAGE *n* pl. -S an amount of power in terms of watts

WATTAPE *n* pl. -S watap

WATTER comparative of wat

WATTEST superlative of wat

WATTHOUR *n* pl. -S a unit of energy

WATTLE *v* -TLED, -TLING, -TLES to weave into a network

WATTLESS *adj* denoting a type of electric current

WAUCHT *v* -ED, -ING, -S to waught

WAUGH *adj* damp

WAUGHT *v* -ED, -ING, -S to drink deeply

WAUK *v* -ED, -ING, -S to wake

WAUL *v* -ED, -ING, -S to cry like a cat

WAUR *adj* worse

WAVE *v* WAVED, WAVING, WAVES to move freely back and forth or up and down

WAVEBAND *n* pl. -S a range of radio frequencies

WAVEFORM *n* pl. -S a type of mathematical graph

WAVELESS *adj* having no waves (moving ridges on the surface of a liquid)

WAVELET *n* pl. -S a small wave

WAVELIKE *adj* resembling a wave

WAVEOFF *n* pl. -S the act of denying landing permission to an approaching aircraft

WAVER *v* -ED, -ING, -S to move back and forth

WAVERER *n* pl. -S one that wavers

WAVERY *adj* wavering

WAVEY *n* pl. -VEYS the snow goose

WAVIER comparative of wavy

WAVIES pl. of wavy

WAVIEST superlative of wavy

WAVILY *adv* in a wavy manner

WAVINESS *n* pl. -ES the state of being wavy

WAVING present participle of wave

WAVY *adj* WAVIER, WAVIEST having waves

WAVY *n* pl. -VIES wavey

WAW *n* pl. -S vav

WAWL *v* -ED, -ING, -S to waul

WAX *v* -ED, -ING, -ES to coat with wax (a natural, heat-sensitive substance)

WAXBERRY *n* pl. -RIES a berry with a waxy coating

WAXBILL *n* pl. -S a tropical bird

WAXEN *adj* covered with wax

WAXER *n* pl. -S one that waxes

WAXIER comparative of waxy

WAXIEST superlative of waxy

WAXILY	*adv* in a waxy manner
WAXINESS	*n* pl. -ES the quality of being waxy
WAXING	*n* pl. -S the act of one that waxes
WAXLIKE	*adj* resembling wax
WAXPLANT	*n* pl. -S a tropical plant
WAXWEED	*n* pl. -S an annual herb
WAXWING	*n* pl. -S a type of passerine bird
WAXWORK	*n* pl. -S an effigy made of wax
WAXWORM	*n* pl. -S a moth that infests beehives
WAXY	*adj* WAXIER, WAXIEST resembling wax
WAY	*n* pl. WAYS a method of doing something
WAYBILL	*n* pl. -S a list of goods relative to a shipment
WAYFARER	*n* pl. -S a traveler
WAYGOING	*n* pl. -S the act of leaving
WAYLAY	*v* -LAID, -LAYING, -LAYS to ambush
WAYLAYER	*n* pl. -S one that waylays
WAYLESS	*adj* having no road or path
WAYSIDE	*n* pl. -S the side of a road
WAYWARD	*adj* willful
WAYWORN	*adj* fatigued by travel
WE	*pron* 1st person pl. pronoun in the nominative case
WEAK	*adj* WEAKER, WEAKEST lacking strength
WEAKEN	*v* -ED, -ING, -S to make weak
WEAKENER	*n* pl. -S one that weakens
WEAKFISH	*n* pl. -ES a marine fish
WEAKISH	*adj* somewhat weak
WEAKLING	*n* pl. -S a weak person
WEAKLY	*adj* -LIER, -LIEST weak and sickly
WEAKNESS	*n* pl. -ES the state of being weak
WEAKSIDE	*n* pl. -S the side of a basketball court with fewer players
WEAL	*n* pl. -S a welt
WEALD	*n* pl. -S a woodland
WEALTH	*n* pl. -S a great quantity of valuable material
WEALTHY	*adj* WEALTHIER, WEALTHIEST having wealth
WEAN	*v* -ED, -ING, -S to withhold mother's milk from and substitute other nourishment
WEANER	*n* pl. -S one that weans
WEANLING	*n* pl. -S a recently weaned child or animal
WEAPON	*v* -ED, -ING, -S to supply with a weapon (an instrument used in combat)
WEAPONRY	*n* pl. -RIES an aggregate of weapons
WEAR	*v* WORE, WORN, WEARING, WEARS to have on one's person
WEARABLE	*n* pl. -S a garment
WEARER	*n* pl. -S one that wears something
WEARIED	past tense of weary
WEARIER	comparative of weary
WEARIES	present 3d person sing. of weary
WEARIEST	superlative of weary
WEARIFUL	*adj* tiresome
WEARISH	*adj* tasteless
WEARY	*adj* -RIER, -RIEST tired
WEARILY	*adv*
WEARY	*v* -RIED, -RYING, -RIES to make or become weary
WEASAND	*n* pl. -S the throat
WEASEL	*v* -SELED, -SELING, -SELS or -SELLED, -SELLING, -SELS to act evasively
WEASELLY	*adj* resembling a weasel (a small carnivorous mammal)
WEASELY	*adj* weaselly
WEASON	*n* pl. -S weasand
WEATHER	*v* -ED, -ING, -S to expose to atmospheric conditions
WEAVE	*v* WOVE or WEAVED, WOVEN, WEAVING, WEAVES to form by interlacing threads
WEAVER	*n* pl. -S one that weaves
WEAZAND	*n* pl. -S weasand
WEB	*v* WEBBED, WEBBING, WEBS to provide with a web (an interlaced fabric or structure)
WEBBING	*n* pl. -S a woven strip of fiber
WEBBY	*adj* -BIER, -BIEST weblike
WEBER	*n* pl. -S a unit of magnetic flux
WEBFED	*adj* designed to print a continuous roll of paper
WEBFOOT	*n* pl. -FEET a foot having the toes joined by a membrane
WEBLESS	*adj* having no webs
WEBLIKE	*adj* resembling a web
WEBSTER	*n* pl. -S a weaver
WEBWORK	*n* pl. -S a weblike pattern or structure
WEBWORM	*n* pl. -S a web-spinning caterpillar

WECHT   n pl. -S weight
WED   v WEDDED, WEDDING,
             WEDS to marry
WEDDER   n pl. -S one that weds
WEDDING   n pl. -S a marriage ceremony
WEDEL   v -ED, -ING, -S to perform a
             wedeln
WEDELN   n pl. -S a skiing technique
WEDGE   v WEDGED, WEDGING,
             WEDGES to force apart with a
             wedge (a tapering piece of
             wood or metal)
WEDGIE   n pl. -S a type of woman's
             shoe
WEDGY   adj WEDGIER, WEDGIEST
             resembling a wedge
WEDLOCK   n pl. -S the state of being
             married
WEE   adj WEER, WEEST very small
WEE   n pl. -S a short time
WEED   v -ED, -ING, -S to remove
             weeds (undesirable plants)
WEEDER   n pl. -S one that weeds
WEEDIER   comparative of weedy
WEEDIEST   superlative of weedy
WEEDILY   adv in a weedy manner
WEEDLESS   adj having no weeds
WEEDLIKE   adj resembling a weed
WEEDY   adj WEEDIER, WEEDIEST
             resembling a weed
WEEK   n pl. -S a period of seven days
WEEKDAY   n pl. -DAYS any day of the
             week except Sunday
WEEKEND   v -ED, -ING, -S to spend the
             weekend (the end of the week)
WEEKLONG   adj continuing for a week
WEEKLY   n pl. -LIES a publication
             issued once a week
WEEL   adj well
WEEN   v -ED, -ING, -S to suppose
WEENIE   n pl. -S a wiener
WEENSY   adj -SIER, -SIEST tiny
WEENY   adj -NIER, -NIEST tiny
WEEP   v WEPT, WEEPING, WEEPS
             to express sorrow by shedding
             tears
WEEPER   n pl. -S one that weeps
WEEPIE   n pl. -S a very maudlin movie
WEEPING   n pl. -S the act of one that
             weeps
WEEPY   adj WEEPIER, WEEPIEST
             tending to weep
WEER   comparative of wee
WEEST   superlative of wee
WEET   v -ED, -ING, -S to know
WEEVER   n pl. -S a marine fish

WEEVIL   n pl. -S a small beetle
             WEEVILED, WEEVILLY,
             WEEVILY adj
WEEWEE   v -WEED, -WEEING, -WEES
             to urinate
WEFT   n pl. -S a woven fabric or
             garment
WEFTWISE   adv in a horizontal direction
WEIGELA   n pl. -S a flowering shrub
WEIGELIA   n pl. -S weigela
WEIGH   v -ED, -ING, -S to determine
             the weight of
WEIGHER   n pl. -S one that weighs
WEIGHMAN   n pl. -MEN one whose
             occupation is weighing goods
WEIGHT   v -ED, -ING, -S to add weight
             (heaviness) to
WEIGHTER   n pl. -S one that weights
WEIGHTY   adj WEIGHTIER,
             WEIGHTIEST having great
             weight
WEINER   n pl. -S wiener
WEIR   n pl. -S a fence placed in a
             stream to catch fish
WEIRD   adj WEIRDER, WEIRDEST
             mysteriously strange
WEIRD   n pl. -S destiny
WEIRDIE   n pl. -S a very strange person
WEIRDIES   pl. of weirdy
WEIRDLY   adv in a weird manner
WEIRDO   n pl. WEIRDOES or
             WEIRDOS a weirdie
WEIRDY   n pl. WEIRDIES weirdie
WEKA   n pl. -S a flightless bird
WELCH   v -ED, -ING, -ES to welsh
WELCHER   n pl. -S one that welshes
WELCOME   v -COMED, -COMING,
             -COMES to greet cordially
WELCOMER   n pl. -S one that welcomes
WELD   v -ED, -ING, -S to join by
             applying heat WELDABLE adj
WELDER   n pl. -S one that welds
WELDLESS   adj having no welded joints
WELDMENT   n pl. -S a unit composed of
             welded pieces
WELDOR   n pl. -S welder
WELFARE   n pl. -S general well-being
WELKIN   n pl. -S the sky
WELL   v -ED, -ING, -S to rise to the
             surface and flow forth
WELLADAY   n pl. -DAYS wellaway
WELLAWAY   n pl. -WAYS an expression of
             sorrow
WELLBORN   adj of good birth or ancestry

WELLCURB *n* pl. -S the stone ring around a well (a hole dug in the ground to obtain water)

WELLDOER *n* pl. -S a doer of good deeds

WELLHEAD *n* pl. -S the source of a spring or stream

WELLHOLE *n* pl. -S the shaft of a well

WELLIE *n* pl. -S a Wellington boot

WELLIES pl. of welly

WELLNESS *n* pl. -ES the state of being healthy

WELLSITE *n* pl. -S a mineral

WELLY *n* pl. -LIES wellie

WELSH *v* -ED, -ING, -ES to fail to pay a debt

WELSHER *n* pl. -S one that welshes

WELT *v* -ED, -ING, -S to mark with welts (ridges or lumps raised on the skin)

WELTER *v* -ED, -ING, -S to roll about

WELTING *n* pl. -S a cord or strip used to reinforce a seam

WEN *n* pl. -S a benign tumor of the skin

WENCH *v* -ED, -ING, -ES to consort with prostitutes

WENCHER *n* pl. -S one that wenches

WEND *v* -ED, -ING, -S to proceed along

WENDIGO *n* pl. -GOS windigo

WENNISH *adj* wenny

WENNY *adj* -NIER, -NIEST resembling a wen

WENT past tense of go

WEPT past tense of weep

WERE a pl. and 2d person sing. past indicative, and past subjunctive of be

WEREGILD *n* pl. -S wergeld

WEREWOLF *n* pl. -WOLVES a person capable of assuming the form of a wolf

WERGELD *n* pl. -S a price paid for the taking of a man's life in Anglo-Saxon law

WERGELT *n* pl. -S wergeld

WERGILD *n* pl. -S wergeld

WERT a 2d person sing. past tense of be

WERWOLF *n* pl. -WOLVES werewolf

WESKIT *n* pl. -S a vest

WESSAND *n* pl. -S weasand

WEST *n* pl. -S a cardinal point of the compass

WESTER *v* -ED, -ING, -S to move toward the west

WESTERLY *n* pl. -LIES a wind from the west

WESTERN *n* pl. -S one who lives in the west

WESTING *n* pl. -S a shifting west

WESTMOST *adj* farthest west

WESTWARD *n* pl. -S a direction toward the west

WET *adj* WETTER, WETTEST covered or saturated with a liquid

WET *v* WETTED, WETTING, WETS to make wet

WETHER *n* pl. -S a gelded male sheep

WETLAND *n* pl. -S land containing much soil moisture

WETLY *adv* in a wet manner

WETNESS *n* pl. -ES the state of being wet

WETPROOF *adj* waterproof

WETTABLE *adj* capable of being wetted

WETTED past tense of wet

WETTER *n* pl. -S one that wets

WETTEST superlative of wet

WETTING *n* pl. -S a liquid used in moistening something

WETTISH *adj* somewhat wet

WHA *pron* who

WHACK *v* -ED, -ING, -S to strike sharply

WHACKER *n* pl. -S one that whacks

WHACKO *n* pl. WHACKOS wacko

WHACKY *adj* WHACKIER, WHACKIEST wacky

WHALE *v* WHALED, WHALING, WHALES to engage in the hunting of whales (large marine mammals)

WHALEMAN *n* pl. -MEN a whaler

WHALER *n* pl. -S a person engaged in whaling

WHALING *n* pl. -S the industry of hunting and processing whales

WHAM *v* WHAMMED, WHAMMING, WHAMS to hit with a loud impact

WHAMMO *interj* — used to indicate a startling event

WHAMMY *n* pl. -MIES a supernatural spell bringing bad luck

WHAMO *interj* whammo

WHANG *v* -ED, -ING, -S to beat with a whip

WHANGEE *n* pl. -S an Asian grass

WHAP *v* WHAPPED, WHAPPING, WHAPS to whop

WHAPPER   n pl. -S whopper

WHARF   v -ED, -ING, -S to moor to a wharf (a docking place for vessels)

WHARFAGE   n pl. -S the use of a wharf

WHARVE   n pl. -S a round piece of wood used in spinning thread

WHAT   n pl. -S the true nature of something

WHATEVER   adj being what or who it may be

WHATNESS   n pl. -ES the true nature of something

WHATNOT   n pl. -S an ornamental set of shelves

WHATSIS   n pl. -SISES whatsit

WHATSIT   n pl. -S something whose name is unknown or forgotten

WHAUP   n pl. -S a European bird

WHEAL   n pl. -S a welt

WHEAT   n pl. -S a cereal grass

WHEATEAR   n pl. -S a small bird of northern regions

WHEATEN   n pl. -S a pale yellowish color

WHEE   interj — used to express delight

WHEEDLE   v -DLED, -DLING, -DLES to attempt to persuade by flattery

WHEEDLER   n pl. -S one that wheedles

WHEEL   v -ED, -ING, -S to convey on wheels (circular frames designed to turn on an axis)

WHEELER   n pl. -S one that wheels

WHEELIE   n pl. -S a maneuver made on a wheeled vehicle

WHEELING   n pl. -S the condition of a road for vehicles

WHEELMAN   n pl. -MEN a helmsman

WHEEN   n pl. -S a fairly large amount

WHEEP   v -ED, -ING, -S to wheeple

WHEEPLE   v -PLED, -PLING, -PLES to give forth a prolonged whistle

WHEEZE   v WHEEZED, WHEEZING, WHEEZES to breathe with a whistling sound

WHEEZER   n pl. -S one that wheezes

WHEEZY   adj WHEEZIER, WHEEZIEST characterized by wheezing **WHEEZILY** adv

WHELK   n pl. -S a pustule

WHELKY   adj WHELKIER, WHELKIEST marked with whelks

WHELM   v -ED, -ING, -S to cover with water

WHELP   v -ED, -ING, -S to give birth to

WHEN   n pl. -S the time in which something is done or occurs

WHENAS   conj at which time

WHENCE   adv from what place

WHENEVER   adv at whatever time

WHERE   n pl. -S the place at or in which something is located or occurs

WHEREAS   n pl. -ES an introductory statement of a formal document

WHEREAT   adv at what

WHEREBY   adv by what

WHEREIN   adv in what

WHEREOF   adv of what

WHEREON   adv on what

WHERETO   adv to what

WHEREVER   adv in or to whatever place

WHERRY   v -RIED, -RYING, -RIES to transport in a light rowboat

WHERVE   n pl. -S wharve

WHET   v WHETTED, WHETTING, WHETS to sharpen by friction

WHETHER   conj if it be the case that

WHETTER   n pl. -S one that whets

WHETTING   present participle of whet

WHEW   n pl. -S a whistling sound

WHEY   n pl. WHEYS the watery part of milk **WHEYEY, WHEYISH** adj

WHEYFACE   n pl. -S a pale, sallow face

WHEYLIKE   adj resembling whey

WHICH   pron what particular one or ones

WHICKER   v -ED, -ING, -S to whinny

WHID   v WHIDDED, WHIDDING, WHIDS to move rapidly and quietly

WHIDAH   n pl. -S whydah

WHIFF   v -ED, -ING, -S to blow or convey with slight gusts of air

WHIFFER   n pl. -S one that whiffs

WHIFFET   n pl. -S an insignificant person

WHIFFLE   v -FLED, -FLING, -FLES to move or think erratically

WHIFFLER   n pl. -S one that whiffles

WHIG   n pl. -S one who interprets history as a continuing victory of progress over reactionary forces

WHILE   v WHILED, WHILING, WHILES to cause to pass pleasantly

WHILOM   adv formerly

WHILST   conj during the time that

WHIM   n pl. -S an impulsive idea

WHIMBREL	*n* pl. -S a shore bird
WHIMPER	*v* -ED, -ING, -S to cry with plaintive, broken sounds
WHIMSEY	*n* pl. -SEYS whimsy
WHIMSY	*n* pl. -SIES a whim **WHIMSIED** *adj*
WHIN	*n* pl. -S furze
WHINCHAT	*n* pl. -S a songbird
WHINE	*v* WHINED, WHINING, WHINES to utter a plaintive, high-pitched sound
WHINER	*n* pl. -S one that whines
WHINEY	*adj* WHINIER, WHINIEST whiny
WHINGE	*v* WHINGED, WHINGEING or WHINGING, WHINGES to whine
WHINIER	comparative of whiny
WHINIEST	superlative of whiny
WHINING	present participle of whine
WHINNY	*v* -NIED, -NYING, -NIES to neigh in a low or gentle manner
WHINNY	*adj* -NIER, -NIEST abounding in whin
WHINY	*adj* WHINIER, WHINIEST tending to whine
WHIP	*v* WHIPPED or WHIPT, WHIPPING, WHIPS to strike with a whip (an instrument for administering corporal punishment)
WHIPCORD	*n* pl. -S a strong, twisted cord
WHIPLASH	*n* pl. -ES the lash of a whip
WHIPLIKE	*adj* resembling a whip
WHIPPED	a past tense of whip
WHIPPER	*n* pl. -S one that whips
WHIPPET	*n* pl. -S a small, swift dog
WHIPPIER	comparative of whippy
WHIPPIEST	superlative of whippy
WHIPPING	*n* pl. -S material used to whip
WHIPPY	*adj* -PIER, -PIEST pertaining to or resembling a whip
WHIPRAY	*n* pl. -RAYS a stingray
WHIPSAW	*v* -SAWED, -SAWN, -SAWING, -SAWS to cut with a narrow, tapering saw
WHIPT	a past tense of whip
WHIPTAIL	*n* pl. -S a lizard having a long, slender tail
WHIPWORM	*n* pl. -S a parasitic worm
WHIR	*v* WHIRRED, WHIRRING, WHIRS to move with a buzzing sound
WHIRL	*v* -ED, -ING, -S to revolve rapidly
WHIRLER	*n* pl. -S one that whirls
WHIRLY	*adj* WHIRLIER, WHIRLIEST marked by a whirling motion
WHIRLY	*n* pl. WHIRLIES a small tornado
WHIRR	*v* -ED, -ING, -S to whir
WHIRRED	past tense of whir
WHIRRING	present participle of whir
WHIRRY	*v* -RIED, -RYING, -RIES to hurry
WHISH	*v* -ED, -ING, -ES to move with a hissing sound
WHISHT	*v* -ED, -ING, -S to hush
WHISK	*v* -ED, -ING, -S to move briskly
WHISKER	*n* pl. -S a hair on a man's face **WHISKERY** *adj*
WHISKEY	*n* pl. -KEYS a liquor
WHISKY	*n* pl. -KIES whiskey
WHISPER	*v* -ED, -ING, -S to speak softly
WHISPERY	*adj* resembling a whisper
WHIST	*v* -ED, -ING, -S to hush
WHISTLE	*v* -TLED, -TLING, -TLES to make a shrill, clear musical sound
WHISTLER	*n* pl. -S one that whistles
WHIT	*n* pl. -S a particle
WHITE	*adj* WHITER, WHITEST of the color of pure snow
WHITE	*v* WHITED, WHITING, WHITES to whiten
WHITECAP	*n* pl. -S a wave with a crest of foam
WHITEFLY	*n* pl. -FLIES a small whitish insect
WHITELY	*adv* in a white manner
WHITEN	*v* -ED, -ING, -S to make white
WHITENER	*n* pl. -S one that whitens
WHITEOUT	*n* pl. -S an arctic weather condition
WHITER	comparative of white
WHITEST	superlative of white
WHITEY	*adj* whity
WHITHER	*adv* to what place
WHITIER	comparative of whity
WHITIEST	superlative of whity
WHITING	*n* pl. -S a marine food fish
WHITISH	*adj* somewhat white
WHITLOW	*n* pl. -S an inflammation of the finger or toe
WHITRACK	*n* pl. -S a weasel
WHITTER	*n* pl. -S a large draft of liquor
WHITTLE	*v* -TLED, -TLING, -TLES to cut or shave bits from
WHITTLER	*n* pl. -S one that whittles
WHITTRET	*n* pl. -S a weasel

WHITY *adj* WHITIER, WHITIEST whitish

WHIZ *v* WHIZZED, WHIZZING, WHIZZES to move with a buzzing or hissing sound

WHIZBANG *n* pl. -S a type of explosive shell

WHIZZ *v* -ED, -ING, -ES to whiz

WHIZZED past tense of whiz

WHIZZER *n* pl. -S one that whizzes

WHIZZES present 3d person sing. of whiz

WHIZZING present participle of whiz

WHO *pron* what or which person or persons

WHOA *interj* — used to command an animal to stop

WHODUNIT *n* pl. -S a mystery story

WHOEVER *pron* whatever person

WHOLE *n* pl. -S all the parts or elements entering into and making up a thing

WHOLISM *n* pl. -S holism

WHOLLY *adv* totally

WHOM *pron* the objective case of who

WHOMEVER *pron* the objective case of whoever

WHOMP *v* -ED, -ING, -S to defeat decisively

WHOMSO *pron* the objective case of whoso

WHOOF *v* -ED, -ING, -S to make a deep snorting sound

WHOOP *v* -ED, -ING, -S to utter loud cries

WHOOPEE *n* pl. -S boisterous fun

WHOOPER *n* pl. -S one that whoops

WHOOPLA *n* pl. -S a noisy commotion

WHOOSH *v* -ED, -ING, -ES to move with a hissing sound

WHOOSIS *n* pl. -SISES an object or person whose name is not known

WHOP *v* WHOPPED, WHOPPING, WHOPS to strike forcibly

WHOPPER *n* pl. -S something unusually large

WHORE *v* WHORED, WHORING, WHORES to consort with prostitutes

WHOREDOM *n* pl. -S prostitution

WHORESON *n* pl. -S a bastard

WHORING present participle of whore

WHORISH *adj* lewd

WHORL *n* pl. -S a circular arrangement of similar parts **WHORLED** *adj*

WHORT *n* pl. -S an edible berry

WHORTLE *n* pl. -S whort

WHOSE *pron* the possessive case of who

WHOSEVER *pron* the possessive case of whoever

WHOSIS *n* pl. -SISES whoosis

WHOSO *pron* whoever

WHUMP *v* -ED, -ING, -S to thump

WHY *n* pl. WHYS the reason or cause of something

WHYDAH *n* pl. -S an African bird

WICH *n* pl. -ES wych

WICK *n* pl. -S a bundle of loosely twisted fibers in a candle or oil lamp

WICKAPE *n* pl. -S wicopy

WICKED *adj* -EDER, -EDEST evil **WICKEDLY** *adv*

WICKER *n* pl. -S a slender, pliant twig or branch

WICKET *n* pl. -S a small door or gate

WICKING *n* pl. -S material for wicks

WICKIUP *n* pl. -S an American Indian hut

WICKYUP *n* pl. -S wickiup

WICOPY *n* pl. -PIES a flowering shrub

WIDDER *n* pl. -S a widow

WIDDIE *n* pl. -S widdy

WIDDLE *v* -DLED, -DLING, -DLES to wriggle

WIDDY *n* pl. -DIES a hangman's noose

WIDE *adj* WIDER, WIDEST having great extent from side to side **WIDELY** *adv*

WIDE *n* pl. -S a type of bowled ball in cricket

WIDEBAND *adj* operating over a wide band of frequencies

WIDEN *v* -ED, -ING, -S to make wide or wider

WIDENER *n* pl. -S one that widens

WIDENESS *n* pl. -ES the state of being wide

WIDEOUT *n* pl. -S a receiver in football

WIDER comparative of wide

WIDEST superlative of wide

WIDGEON *n* pl. -S a river duck

WIDGET *n* pl. -S a gadget

WIDISH *adj* somewhat wide

WIDOW *v* -ED, -ING, -S to deprive of a husband

WIDOWER *n* pl. -S a man whose wife has died and who has not remarried

WIDTH *n* pl. -S extent from side to side

WIDTHWAY *adv* from side to side

WIELD *v* -ED, -ING, -S to handle or use effectively

WIELDER *n* pl. -S one that wields

WIELDY *adj* WIELDIER, WIELDIEST easily wielded

WIENER *n* pl. -S a frankfurter

WIENIE *n* pl. -S a wiener

WIFE *n* pl. WIVES a woman married to a man

WIFE *v* WIFED, WIFING, WIFES to wive

WIFEDOM *n* pl. -S the status or function of a wife

WIFEHOOD *n* pl. -S the state of being a wife

WIFELESS *adj* having no wife

WIFELIKE *adj* wifely

WIFELY *adj* -LIER, -LIEST of or befitting a wife

WIFING present participle of wife

WIFTY *adj* -TIER, -TIEST ditsy

WIG *v* WIGGED, WIGGING, WIGS to provide with a wig (an artificial covering of hair for the head)

WIGAN *n* pl. -S a stiff fabric

WIGEON *n* pl. -S widgeon

WIGGED past tense of wig

WIGGERY *n* pl. -GERIES a wig

WIGGIER comparative of wiggy

WIGGIEST superlative of wiggy

WIGGING *n* pl. -S a scolding

WIGGLE *v* -GLED, -GLING, -GLES to move with short, quick movements from side to side

WIGGLER *n* pl. -S one that wiggles

WIGGLY *adj* -GLIER, -GLIEST tending to wiggle

WIGGY *adj* -GIER, -GIEST crazy

WIGHT *n* pl. -S a living being

WIGLESS *adj* having no wig

WIGLET *n* pl. -S a small wig

WIGLIKE *adj* resembling a wig

WIGMAKER *n* pl. -S one that makes wigs

WIGWAG *v* -WAGGED, -WAGGING, -WAGS to move back and forth

WIGWAM *n* pl. -S an American Indian dwelling

WIKIUP *n* pl. -S wickiup

WILCO *interj* — used to indicate that a message received will be complied with

WILD *adj* WILDER, WILDEST living in a natural state

WILD *n* pl. -S an uninhabited or uncultivated area

WILDCAT *v* -CATTED, -CATTING, -CATS to search for oil in an area of doubtful productivity

WILDER *v* -ED, -ING, -S to bewilder

WILDFIRE *n* pl. -S a raging, destructive fire

WILDFOWL *n* pl. -S a wild game bird

WILDING *n* pl. -S a wild plant or animal

WILDISH *adj* somewhat wild

WILDLAND *n* pl. -S uncultivated land

WILDLIFE *n* pl. WILDLIFE wild animals and vegetation

WILDLING *n* pl. -S a wilding

WILDLY *adv* in a wild manner

WILDNESS *n* pl. -ES the state of being wild

WILDWOOD *n* pl. -S natural forest land

WILE *v* WILED, WILING, WILES to entice

WILFUL *adj* willful **WILFULLY** *adv*

WILIER comparative of wily

WILIEST superlative of wily

WILILY *adv* in a wily manner

WILINESS *n* pl. -ES the quality of being wily

WILING present participle of wile

WILL *v* -ED, -ING, -S to decide upon **WILLABLE** *adj*

WILL *v* past sing. 2d person WOULD, WOULDEST, or WOULDST — used as an auxiliary followed by a simple infinitive to express futurity, inclination, likelihood, or requirement

WILLER *n* pl. -S one that wills

WILLET *n* pl. -S a shore bird

WILLFUL *adj* bent on having one's own way

WILLIED past tense of willy

WILLIES present 3d person sing. of willy

WILLING *adj* -INGER, -INGEST inclined or favorably disposed in mind

WILLIWAU *n* pl. -S williwaw

WILLIWAW *n* pl. -S a violent gust of cold wind

WILLOW *v* -ED, -ING, -S to clean textile fibers with a certain machine

WILLOWER *n* pl. -S one that willows

WILLOWY *adj* -LOWIER, -LOWIEST pliant

WILLY	v -LIED, -LYING, -LIES to willow
WILLYARD	adj willful
WILLYART	adj willyard
WILLYWAW	n pl. -S williwaw
WILT	v -ED, -ING, -S to become limp
WILY	adj WILIER, WILIEST crafty
WIMBLE	v -BLED, -BLING, -BLES to bore with a hand tool
WIMP	n pl. -S a weak or ineffectual person
WIMPISH	adj wimpy
WIMPLE	v -PLED, -PLING, -PLES to pleat
WIMPY	adj WIMPIER, WIMPIEST weak, ineffectual
WIN	v WON or WAN, WINNING, WINS to be victorious
WIN	v WINNED, WINNING, WINS to winnow
WINCE	v WINCED, WINCING, WINCES to flinch
WINCER	n pl. -S one that winces
WINCEY	n pl. -CEYS a type of fabric
WINCH	v -ED, -ING, -ES to raise with a winch (a hoisting machine)
WINCHER	n pl. -S one that winches
WINCING	present participle of wince
WIND	v WOUND or WINDED, WINDING, WINDS to pass around an object or fixed center **WINDABLE** adj
WINDAGE	n pl. -S the effect of the wind (air in natural motion) on a projectile
WINDBAG	n pl. -S a talkative person
WINDBURN	v -BURNED or -BURNT, -BURNING, -BURNS to be affected with skin irritation caused by exposure to the wind
WINDER	n pl. -S one that winds
WINDFALL	n pl. -S a sudden and unexpected gain
WINDFLAW	n pl. -S a gust of wind
WINDGALL	n pl. -S a swelling on a horse's leg
WINDIER	comparative of windy
WINDIEST	superlative of windy
WINDIGO	n pl. -GOS an evil demon in Algonquian mythology
WINDILY	adv in a windy manner
WINDING	n pl. -S material wound about an object
WINDLASS	v -ED, -ING, -ES to raise with a windlass (a hoisting machine)
WINDLE	v -DLED, -DLING, -DLES to wind
WINDLESS	adj being without wind
WINDLING	n pl. -S a bundle of straw
WINDMILL	v -ED, -ING, -S to rotate solely under the force of a passing airstream
WINDOW	v -ED, -ING, -S to provide with a window (an opening in a wall to admit light and air)
WINDPIPE	n pl. -S the trachea
WINDROW	v -ED, -ING, -S to arrange in long rows, as hay or grain
WINDSOCK	n pl. -S a device used to indicate wind direction
WINDSURF	v -ED, -ING, -S to sail on a sailboard
WINDUP	n pl. -S a conclusion
WINDWARD	n pl. -S the direction from which the wind blows
WINDWAY	n pl. -WAYS a passage for air
WINDY	adj WINDIER, WINDIEST marked by strong wind
WINE	v WINED, WINING, WINES to provide with wine (the fermented juice of the grape)
WINELESS	adj having no wine
WINERY	n pl. -ERIES an establishment for making wine
WINESHOP	n pl. -S a shop where wine is sold
WINESKIN	n pl. -S a goatskin bag for holding wine
WINESOP	n pl. -S a food sopped in wine
WINEY	adj WINIER, WINIEST winy
WING	v -ED, -ING, -S to travel by means of wings (organs of flight)
WINGBACK	n pl. -S a certain player in football
WINGBOW	n pl. -S a mark on the wing of a domestic fowl
WINGDING	n pl. -S a lively party
WINGEDLY	adv swiftly
WINGER	n pl. -S a certain player in soccer
WINGIER	comparative of wingy
WINGIEST	superlative of wingy
WINGLESS	adj having no wings
WINGLET	n pl. -S a small wing
WINGLIKE	adj resembling a wing
WINGMAN	n pl. -MEN a pilot behind the leader of a flying formation

WINGOVER *n* pl. -S a flight maneuver

WINGSPAN *n* pl. -S the distance from the tip of one of a pair of wings to that of the other

WINGTIP *n* pl. -S a type of man's shoe

WINGY *adj* WINGIER, WINGIEST swift

WINIER comparative of winey and winy

WINIEST superlative of winey and winy

WINING present participle of wine

WINISH *adj* winy

WINK *v* -ED, -ING, -S to close and open one eye quickly

WINKER *n* pl. -S one that winks

WINKLE *v* -KLED, -KLING, -KLES to displace, extract, or evict from a position

WINLESS *adj* having no wins

WINNABLE *adj* able to be won

WINNED past tense of win (to winnow)

WINNER *n* pl. -S one that wins

WINNING *n* pl. -S money won in a game or competition

WINNOCK *n* pl. -S a window

WINNOW *v* -ED, -ING, -S to free grain from impurities

WINNOWER *n* pl. -S one that winnows

WINO *n* pl. WINOES or WINOS one who is habitually drunk on wine

WINSOME *adj* -SOMER, -SOMEST charming

WINTER *v* -ED, -ING, -S to pass the winter (the coldest season of the year)

WINTERER *n* pl. -S one that winters

WINTERLY *adj* wintry

WINTERY *adj* -TERIER, -TERIEST wintry

WINTLE *v* -TLED, -TLING, -TLES to stagger

WINTRY *adj* -TRIER, -TRIEST characteristic of winter **WINTRILY** *adv*

WINY *adj* WINIER, WINIEST having the taste or qualities of wine

WINZE *n* pl. -S a steeply inclined mine shaft

WIPE *v* WIPED, WIPING, WIPES to rub lightly in order to clean or dry

WIPEOUT *n* pl. -S a fall from a surfboard

WIPER *n* pl. -S one that wipes

WIPING present participle of wipe

WIRE *v* WIRED, WIRING, WIRES to fasten with wire (a slender rod, strand, or thread of ductile metal) **WIRABLE** *adj*

WIREDRAW *v* -DREW, -DRAWN, -DRAWING, -DRAWS to draw into wire

WIREHAIR *n* pl. -S a dog having a wiry coat

WIRELESS *v* -ED, -ING, -ES to radio

WIRELIKE *adj* resembling wire

WIREMAN *n* pl. -MEN one who makes or works with wire

WIRER *n* pl. -S one that wires

WIRETAP *v* -TAPPED, -TAPPING, -TAPS to intercept messages by means of a concealed monitoring device

WIREWAY *n* pl. -WAYS a tube for protecting electric wires

WIREWORK *n* pl. -S an article made of wire

WIREWORM *n* pl. -S a wirelike worm

WIRIER comparative of wiry

WIRIEST superlative of wiry

WIRILY *adv* in a wiry manner

WIRINESS *n* pl. -ES the quality of being wiry

WIRING *n* pl. -S a system of electric wires

WIRRA *interj* — used to express sorrow

WIRY *adj* WIRIER, WIRIEST resembling wire

WIS *v* past tense WIST to know — WIS and WIST are the only accepted forms of this verb; it cannot be conjugated further

WISDOM *n* pl. -S the power of true and right discernment

WISE *v* WISED, WISING, WISES to become aware or informed

WISE *adj* WISER, WISEST having wisdom

WISEACRE *n* pl. -S a pretentiously wise person

WISEASS *n* pl. -ES a wiseacre

WISED past tense of wise

WISELY *adv* -LIER, -LIEST in a wise manner

WISENESS *n* pl. -ES wisdom

WISENT *n* pl. -S a European bison

WISER comparative of wise

WISEST superlative of wise

WISH *v* -ED, -ING, -ES to feel an impulse toward attainment or possession of something

WISHA *interj* — used to express surprise

WISHBONE *n* pl. -S a forked bone in front of a bird's breastbone

WISHER *n* pl. -S one that wishes

WISHFUL *adj* desirous

WISHLESS *adj* not wishful

WISING present participle of wise

WISP *v* -ED, -ING, -S to twist into a wisp (a small bunch or bundle)

WISPIER comparative of wispy

WISPIEST superlative of wispy

WISPILY *adv* in a wispy manner

WISPISH *adj* wispy

WISPLIKE *adj* wispy

WISPY *adj* WISPIER, WISPIEST resembling a wisp

WISS *v* -ED, -ING, -ES to wish

WIST *v* -ED, -ING, -S to know

WISTARIA *n* pl. -S wisteria

WISTERIA *n* pl. -S a flowering shrub

WISTFUL *adj* yearning

WIT *n* pl. -S intelligence

WIT *v* WIST, WITING or WITTING, present sing. 1st person WOT, 2d WOST, 3d WOT, present pl. WITE to know

WITAN *n/pl* the members of a national council in Anglo-Saxon England

WITCH *v* -ED, -ING, -ES to bewitch

WITCHERY *n* pl. -ERIES sorcery

WITCHING *n* pl. -S sorcery

WITCHY *adj* WITCHIER, WITCHIEST malicious

WITE *v* WITED, WITING, WITES to blame

WITH *prep* in the company of

WITHAL *adv* in addition

WITHDRAW *v* -DREW, -DRAWN, -DRAWING, -DRAWS to move back or away

WITHE *v* WITHED, WITHING, WITHES to bind with flexible twigs

WITHER *v* -ED, -ING, -S to dry up and wilt

WITHERER *n* pl. -S one that withers

WITHHOLD *v* -HELD, -HOLDING, -HOLDS to hold back

WITHIER comparative of withy

WITHIES pl. of withy

WITHIEST superlative of withy

WITHIN *n* pl. -S an interior place or area

WITHING present participle of withe

WITHOUT *n* pl. -S an exterior place or area

WITHY *n* pl. WITHIES a flexible twig

WITHY *adj* WITHIER, WITHIEST flexible and tough

WITING present participle of wit and wite

WITLESS *adj* lacking intelligence

WITLING *n* pl. -S one who considers himself witty

WITLOOF *n* pl. -S chicory

WITNESS *v* -ED, -ING, -ES to see or know by personal experience

WITNEY *n* pl. -NEYS a heavy woolen fabric

WITTED *adj* having intelligence

WITTIER comparative of witty

WITTIEST superlative of witty

WITTILY *adv* in a witty manner

WITTING *n* pl. -S knowledge

WITTOL *n* pl. -S a man who tolerates his wife's infidelity

WITTY *adj* -TIER, -TIEST humorously clever

WIVE *v* WIVED, WIVING, WIVES to marry a woman

WIVER *n* pl. -S wivern

WIVERN *n* pl. -S a two-legged dragon

WIVES pl. of wife

WIVING present participle of wive

WIZ *n* pl. -ES a very clever or skillful person

WIZARD *n* pl. -S a sorcerer **WIZARDLY** *adj*

WIZARDRY *n* pl. -RIES sorcery

WIZEN *v* -ED, -ING, -S to shrivel

WIZZEN *n* pl. -S weasand

WO *n* pl. WOS woe

WOAD *n* pl. -S a blue dye **WOADED** *adj*

WOADWAX *n* pl. -ES an ornamental shrub

WOALD *n* pl. -S a yellow pigment

WOBBLE *v* -BLED, -BLING, -BLES to move unsteadily

WOBBLER *n* pl. -S one that wobbles

WOBBLY *adj* -BLIER, -BLIEST unsteady

WOBBLY *n* pl. -BLIES a member of the Industrial Workers of the World

WOBEGONE *adj* affected with woe

WODGE *n* pl. -S a chunk of something

WOE *n* pl. -S tremendous grief

WOEFUL *adj* -FULLER, -FULLEST full of woe **WOEFULLY** *adv*

WOENESS *n* pl. -ES sadness

WOESOME *adj* woeful

WOFUL *adj* woeful **WOFULLY** *adv*

WOK	n pl. -S a cooking utensil
WOKE	a past tense of wake
WOKEN	a past participle of wake
WOLD	n pl. -S an elevated tract of open land
WOLF	n pl. WOLVES a carnivorous mammal
WOLF	v -ED, -ING, -S to devour voraciously
WOLFER	n pl. -S one who hunts wolves
WOLFFISH	n pl. -ES a marine fish
WOLFISH	adj wolflike
WOLFLIKE	adj resembling a wolf
WOLFRAM	n pl. -S tungsten
WOLVER	n pl. -S wolfer
WOLVES	pl. of wolf
WOMAN	n pl. WOMEN an adult human female
WOMAN	v -ED, -ING, -S to play the part of a woman
WOMANISE	v -ISED, -ISING, -ISES to womanize
WOMANISH	adj characteristic of a woman
WOMANIZE	v -IZED, -IZING, -IZES to make effeminate
WOMANLY	adj -LIER, -LIEST having the qualities of a woman
WOMB	n pl. -S the uterus WOMBED adj
WOMBAT	n pl. -S a nocturnal mammal
WOMBY	adj WOMBIER, WOMBIEST hollow
WOMEN	pl. of woman
WOMERA	n pl. -S a device used to propel spears
WOMMERA	n pl. -S womera
WON	v WONNED, WONNING, WONS to dwell
WONDER	v -ED, -ING, -S to have a feeling of curiosity or doubt
WONDERER	n pl. -S one that wonders
WONDROUS	adj marvelous
WONK	n pl. -S an overly studious student
WONKY	adj -KIER, -KIEST unsteady
WONNED	past tense of won
WONNER	n pl. -S a prodigy
WONNING	present participle of won
WONT	v -ED, -ING, -S to make accustomed to
WONTEDLY	adv in a usual manner
WONTON	n pl. -S a pork-filled dumpling used in Chinese cooking
WOO	v -ED, -ING, -S to seek the affection of
WOOD	v -ED, -ING, -S to furnish with wood (the hard, fibrous substance beneath the bark of a tree or shrub)
WOODBIN	n pl. -S a bin for holding firewood
WOODBIND	n pl. -S woodbine
WOODBINE	n pl. -S a European shrub
WOODBOX	n pl. -ES a woodbin
WOODCHAT	n pl. -S a European shrike
WOODCOCK	n pl. -S a game bird
WOODCUT	n pl. -S an engraved block of wood
WOODEN	adj -ENER, -ENEST resembling wood in stiffness **WOODENLY** adv
WOODHEN	n pl. -S the weka
WOODIE	n pl. -S woody
WOODIER	comparative of woody
WOODIES	pl. of woody
WOODIEST	superlative of woody
WOODLAND	n pl. -S land covered with trees
WOODLARK	n pl. -S a songbird
WOODLESS	adj having no wood
WOODLORE	n pl. -S knowledge of the forest
WOODLOT	n pl. -S an area restricted to the growing of forest trees
WOODMAN	n pl. -MEN woodsman
WOODNOTE	n pl. -S a song or call of a forest bird
WOODPILE	n pl. -S a pile of wood
WOODRUFF	n pl. -S an aromatic herb
WOODSHED	v -SHEDDED, -SHEDDING, -SHEDS to practice on a musical instrument
WOODSIA	n pl. -S a small fern
WOODSMAN	n pl. -MEN one who works or lives in the forest
WOODSY	adj WOODSIER, WOODSIEST suggestive of a forest
WOODWAX	n pl. -ES woadwax
WOODWIND	n pl. -S a musical wind instrument
WOODWORK	n pl. -S work made of wood
WOODWORM	n pl. -S a wood-boring worm
WOODY	adj WOODIER, WOODIEST containing or resembling wood
WOODY	n pl. WOODIES a wood-paneled station wagon
WOOER	n pl. -S one that woos
WOOF	v -ED, -ING, -S to utter a gruff barking sound

WOOFER *n* pl. -S a loudspeaker designed to reproduce low-pitched sounds

WOOINGLY *adv* attractively

WOOL *n* pl. -S the dense, soft hair forming the coat of certain mammals

WOOLED *adj* having wool of a specified kind

WOOLEN *n* pl. -S a fabric made of wool

WOOLER *n* pl. -S a domestic animal raised for its wool

WOOLFELL *n* pl. -S woolskin

WOOLHAT *n* pl. -S one who works a small farm

WOOLIE *n* pl. -S a woolly

WOOLIER comparative of wooly

WOOLIES pl. of wooly

WOOLIEST superlative of wooly

WOOLLED *adj* wooled

WOOLLEN *n* pl. -S woolen

WOOLLIER comparative of woolly

WOOLLIES pl. of woolly

WOOLLIKE *adj* resembling wool

WOOLLY *adj* -LIER, -LIEST consisting of or resembling wool
WOOLLILY *adv*

WOOLLY *n* pl. -LIES a garment made of wool

WOOLMAN *n* pl. -MEN a dealer in wool

WOOLPACK *n* pl. -S a bag for packing a bale of wool

WOOLSACK *n* pl. -S a sack of wool

WOOLSHED *n* pl. -S a building in which sheep are sheared

WOOLSKIN *n* pl. -S a sheepskin with the wool still on it

WOOLWORK *n* pl. -S needlework

WOOLY *adj* WOOLIER, WOOLIEST woolly

WOOLY *n* pl. WOOLIES a woolly

WOOMERA *n* pl. -S womera

WOOPS *v* -ED, -ING, -ES to vomit

WOORALI *n* pl. -S curare

WOORARI *n* pl. -S curare

WOOSH *v* -ED, -ING, -ES to whoosh

WOOZY *adj* -ZIER, -ZIEST dazed
WOOZILY *adv*

WORD *v* -ED, -ING, -S to express in words (speech sounds that communicate meaning)

WORDAGE *n* pl. -S the number of words used

WORDBOOK *n* pl. -S a dictionary

WORDIER comparative of wordy

WORDIEST superlative of wordy

WORDILY *adv* in a wordy manner

WORDING *n* pl. -S the act or style of expressing in words

WORDLESS *adj* being without words

WORDPLAY *n* pl. -PLAYS a witty exchange of words

WORDY *adj* WORDIER, WORDIEST using many or too many words

WORE past tense of wear

WORK *v* WORKED or WROUGHT, WORKING, WORKS to exert one's powers of body or mind for some purpose

WORKABLE *adj* capable of being done

WORKADAY *adj* everyday

WORKBAG *n* pl. -S a bag for holding work instuments and materials

WORKBOAT *n* pl. -S a boat used for commercial purposes

WORKBOOK *n* pl. -S an exercise book for a student

WORKBOX *n* pl. -ES a box for holding work instruments and materials

WORKDAY *n* pl. -DAYS a day on which work is done

WORKER *n* pl. -S one that works

WORKFARE *n* pl. -S a welfare program that requires recipients to perform public-service work

WORKFOLK *n/pl* manual laborers

WORKING *n* pl. -S a mining excavation

WORKLESS *adj* unemployed

WORKLOAD *n* pl. -S the amount of work assigned to an employee

WORKMAN *n* pl. -MEN a male worker

WORKMATE *n* pl. -S a fellow worker

WORKOUT *n* pl. -S a period of physical exercise

WORKROOM *n* pl. -S a room in which work is done

WORKSHOP *n* pl. -S a workroom

WORKUP *n* pl. -S an intensive diagnostic study

WORKWEEK *n* pl. -S the number of hours worked in a week

WORLD *n* pl. -S the earth and all its inhabitants

WORLDLY *adj* -LIER, -LIEST pertaining to the world

WORM *v* -ED, -ING, -S to rid of worms (small, limbless invertebrates)

WORMER *n* pl. -S one that worms

WORMHOLE *n* pl. -S a hole made by a burrowing worm

WORMIER comparative of wormy

WORMIEST	superlative of wormy
WORMIL	n pl. -S a lump in the skin of an animal's back
WORMISH	adj wormlike
WORMLIKE	adj resembling a worm
WORMROOT	n pl. -S pinkroot
WORMSEED	n pl. -S a tropical plant
WORMWOOD	n pl. -S a European herb
WORMY	adj WORMIER, WORMIEST infested with worms
WORN	adj affected by wear or use
WORNNESS	n pl. -ES the state of being worn
WORRIED	past tense of worry
WORRIER	n pl. -S one that worries
WORRIT	v -ED, -ING, -S to worry
WORRY	v -RIED, -RYING, -RIES to feel anxious and uneasy about something
WORSE	n pl. -S something that is worse (bad in a greater degree)
WORSEN	v -ED, -ING, -S to make or become worse
WORSER	adj worse
WORSET	n pl. -S worsted
WORSHIP	v -SHIPED, -SHIPING, -SHIPS or -SHIPPED, -SHIPPING, -SHIPS to honor and love as a divine being
WORST	v -ED, -ING, -S to defeat
WORSTED	n pl. -S a woolen yarn
WORT	n pl. -S a plant, herb, or vegetable
WORTH	v -ED, -ING, -S to befall
WORTHFUL	adj worthy
WORTHY	adj -THIER, -THIEST having value or merit **WORTHILY** adv
WORTHY	n pl. -THIES a worthy person
WOST	a present 2d person sing. of wit
WOT	v WOTTED, WOTTING, WOTS to know
WOULD	past tense of will
WOULDEST	a 2d person sing. past tense of will
WOULDST	a 2d person sing. past tense of will
WOUND	v -ED, -ING, -S to inflict an injury upon
WOVE	a past tense of weave
WOVEN	n pl. -S a woven fabric
WOW	v -ED, -ING, -S to excite to enthusiastic approval
WOWSER	n pl. -S a puritanical person
WRACK	v -ED, -ING, -S to wreck
WRACKFUL	adj destructive
WRAITH	n pl. -S a ghost
WRANG	n pl. -S a wrong
WRANGLE	v -GLED, -GLING, -GLES to argue noisily
WRANGLER	n pl. -S one that wrangles
WRAP	v WRAPPED or WRAPT, WRAPPING, WRAPS to enclose in something wound or folded about
WRAPPER	n pl. -S one that wraps
WRAPPING	n pl. -S the material in which something is wrapped
WRAPT	a past tense of wrap
WRASSE	n pl. -S a marine fish
WRASSLE	v -SLED, -SLING, -SLES to wrastle
WRASTLE	v -TLED, -TLING, -TLES to wrestle
WRATH	v -ED, -ING, -S to make wrathful
WRATHFUL	adj extremely angry
WRATHY	adj WRATHIER, WRATHIEST wrathful **WRATHILY** adv
WREAK	v -ED, -ING, -S to inflict
WREAKER	n pl. -S one that wreaks
WREATH	n pl. -S a band of flowers **WREATHY** adj
WREATHE	v WREATHED, WREATHEN, WREATHING, WREATHES to shape into a wreath
WRECK	v -ED, -ING, -S to cause the ruin of
WRECKAGE	n pl. -S the act of wrecking
WRECKER	n pl. -S one that wrecks
WRECKFUL	adj destructive
WRECKING	n pl. -S the occupation of salvaging wrecked objects
WREN	n pl. -S a small songbird
WRENCH	v -ED, -ING, -ES to twist suddenly and forcibly
WREST	v -ED, -ING, -S to take away by force
WRESTER	n pl. -S one that wrests
WRESTLE	v -TLED, -TLING, -TLES to engage in a type of hand-to-hand contest
WRESTLER	n pl. -S one that wrestles
WRETCH	n pl. -ES a wretched person
WRETCHED	adj -EDER, -EDEST extremely unhappy
WRICK	v -ED, -ING, -S to wrench
WRIED	past tense of wry
WRIER	a comparative of wry
WRIES	present 3d person sing. of wry
WRIEST	a superlative of wry

WRIGGLE *v* -GLED, -GLING, -GLES to turn or twist in a sinuous manner

WRIGGLER *n* pl. -S one that wriggles

WRIGGLY *adj* -GLIER, -GLIEST wriggling

WRIGHT *n* pl. -S one who constructs or creates

WRING *v* WRUNG or WRINGED, WRINGING, WRINGS to twist so as to compress

WRINGER *n* pl. -S one that wrings

WRINKLE *v* -KLED, -KLING, -KLES to make wrinkles (small ridges or furrows) in

WRINKLY *adj* -KLIER, -KLIEST having wrinkles

WRIST *n* pl. -S the junction between the hand and forearm

WRISTLET *n* pl. -S a band worn around the wrist

WRISTY *adj* WRISTIER, WRISTIEST using much wrist action

WRIT *n* pl. -S a written legal order

WRITE *v* WROTE, WRITTEN, WRITING, WRITES to form characters or symbols on a surface with an instrument **WRITABLE** *adj*

WRITER *n* pl. -S one that writes

WRITERLY *adj* characteristic of a writer

WRITHE *v* WRITHED, WRITHING, WRITHES to squirm or twist in pain

WRITHEN *adj* twisted

WRITHER *n* pl. -S one that writhes

WRITHING present participle of writhe

WRITING *n* pl. -S a written composition

WRITTEN past participle of write

WRONG *adj* WRONGER, WRONGEST not according to what is right, proper, or correct

WRONG *v* -ED, -ING, -S to treat injuriously or unjustly

WRONGER *n* pl. -S one that wrongs

WRONGFUL *adj* wrong

WRONGLY *adv* in a wrong manner

WROTE past tense of write

WROTH *adj* very angry

WROTHFUL *adj* wroth

WROUGHT a past tense of work

WRUNG a past tense of wring

WRY *adj* WRIER, WRIEST or WRYER, WRYEST contorted **WRYLY** *adv*

WRY *v* WRIED, WRYING, WRIES to contort

WRYNECK *n* pl. -S a European bird

WRYNESS *n* pl. -ES the state of being wry

WUD *adj* insane

WURST *n* pl. -S sausage

WURZEL *n* pl. -S a variety of beet

WUSS *n* pl. -ES a wimp

WUSSY *n* pl. -SIES a wuss

WUSSY *adj* WUSSIER, WUSSIEST wimpy

WUTHER *v* -ED, -ING, -S to blow with a dull roaring sound

WYCH *n* pl. -ES a European elm

WYE *n* pl. -S the letter Y

WYLE *v* WYLED, WYLING, WYLES to beguile

WYN *n* pl. -S wynn

WYND *n* pl. -S a narrow street

WYNN *n* pl. -S the rune for W

WYTE *v* WYTED, WYTING, WYTES to wite

WYVERN *n* pl. -S wivern

XANTHAN *n* pl. -S a gum produced by bacterial fermentation

XANTHATE *n* pl. -S a chemical salt

XANTHEIN *n* pl. -S the water-soluble part of the coloring matter in yellow flowers

XANTHENE *n* pl. -S a chemical compound

XANTHIC *adj* tending to have a yellow color

XANTHIN *n* pl. -S a yellow pigment

XANTHINE *n* pl. -S a chemical compound

XANTHOMA *n* pl. -MAS or -MATA a skin disease

XANTHONE *n* pl. -S a chemical compound

XANTHOUS *adj* yellow

XEBEC *n* pl. -S a Mediterranean sailing vessel

XENIA *n* pl. -S the effect of pollen on certain plant structures **XENIAL** *adj*

XENIC *adj* pertaining to a type of culture medium

XENOGAMY *n* pl. -MIES the transfer of pollen from one plant to another

XENOGENY *n* pl. -NIES the supposed production of offspring totally different from the parent

XENOLITH *n* pl. -S a rock fragment included in another rock

XENON *n* pl. -S a gaseous element

XERARCH *adj* developing in a dry area

XERIC *adj* requiring only a small amount of moisture

XEROSERE *n* pl. -S a dry-land sere

XEROSIS *n* pl. -ROSES abnormal dryness of a body part or tissue **XEROTIC** *adj*

XEROX *v* -ED, -ING, -ES to copy on a xerographic copier

XERUS *n* pl. -ES an African ground squirrel

XI *n* pl. -S a Greek letter

XIPHOID *n* pl. -S a part of the sternum

XU *n* pl. XU a monetary unit of Vietnam

XYLAN *n* pl. -S a substance found in cell walls of plants

XYLEM *n* pl. -S a complex plant tissue

XYLENE *n* pl. -S a flammable hydrocarbon

XYLIDIN *n* pl. -S xylidine

XYLIDINE *n* pl. -S a chemical compound

XYLITOL *n* pl. -S an alcohol

XYLOCARP *n* pl. -S a hard, woody fruit

XYLOID *adj* resembling wood

XYLOL *n* pl. -S xylene

XYLOSE *n* pl. -S a type of sugar

XYLOTOMY *n* pl. -MIES the preparation of sections of wood for microscopic examination

XYLYL *n* pl. -S a univalent radical

XYST *n* pl. -S xystus

XYSTER *n* pl. -S a surgical instrument for scraping bones

XYSTOS *n* pl. -TOI xystus

XYSTUS *n* pl. -TI a roofed area where athletes trained in ancient Greece

YA *pron* you

YABBER *v* -ED, -ING, -S to jabber

YACHT *v* -ED, -ING, -S to sail in a yacht (a vessel used for pleasure cruising or racing)

YACHTER *n* pl. -S one who sails a yacht

YACHTING *n* pl. -S the sport of sailing in yachts

YACHTMAN	n pl. -MEN a yachter	**YARDBIRD**	n pl. -S an army recruit
YACK	v -ED, -ING, -S to yak	**YARDLAND**	n pl. -S an old English unit of
YAFF	v -ED, -ING, -S to bark		land measure
YAGER	n pl. -S jaeger	**YARDMAN**	n pl. -MEN a man employed to
YAGI	n pl. -S a type of shortwave		do outdoor work
	antenna	**YARDWAND**	n pl. -S a measuring stick
YAH	interj— used as an	**YARDWORK**	n pl. -S the work of caring for
	exclamation of disgust		a lawn
YAHOO	n pl. -HOOS a coarse,	**YARE**	adj YARER, YAREST nimble
	uncouth person		**YARELY** adv
YAHOOISM	n pl. -S coarse, uncouth	**YARMELKE**	n pl. -S yarmulke
	behavior	**YARMULKE**	n pl. -S a skullcap worn by
YAHRZEIT	n pl. -S an anniversary of the		Jewish males
	death of a family member	**YARN**	v -ED, -ING, -S to tell a long
	observed by Jews		story
YAIRD	n pl. -S a garden	**YARNER**	n pl. -S one that yarns
YAK	v YAKKED, YAKKING, YAKS	**YARROW**	n pl. -S a perennial herb
	to chatter	**YASHMAC**	n pl. -S yashmak
YAKITORI	n pl. -S marinated chicken	**YASHMAK**	n pl. -S a veil worn by Muslim
	pieces on skewers		women
YAKKER	n pl. -S one that yaks	**YASMAK**	n pl. -S yashmak
YALD	adj yauld	**YATAGAN**	n pl. -S yataghan
YAM	n pl. -S a plant having an	**YATAGHAN**	n pl. -S a Turkish sword
	edible root	**YATTER**	v -ED, -ING, -S to talk idly
YAMALKA	n pl. -S yarmulke	**YAUD**	n pl. -S an old mare
YAMEN	n pl. -S the residence of a	**YAULD**	adj vigorous
	Chinese public official	**YAUP**	v -ED, -ING, -S to yawp
YAMMER	v -ED, -ING, -S to whine or	**YAUPER**	n pl. -S one that yaups
	complain peevishly	**YAUPON**	n pl. -S an evergreen shrub
YAMMERER	n pl. -S one that yammers	**YAUTIA**	n pl. -S a tropical plant
YAMULKA	n pl. -S yarmulke	**YAW**	v -ED, -ING, -S to deviate
YAMUN	n pl. -S yamen		from an intended course
YANG	n pl. -S the masculine active	**YAWL**	v -ED, -ING, -S to yowl
	principle in Chinese cosmology	**YAWMETER**	n pl. -S an instrument in an
YANK	v -ED, -ING, -S to pull		aircraft
	suddenly	**YAWN**	v -ED, -ING, -S to open the
YANQUI	n pl. -S a United States citizen		mouth wide with a deep
YANTRA	n pl. -S a geometrical diagram		inhalation of air
	used in meditation	**YAWNER**	n pl. -S one that yawns
YAP	v YAPPED, YAPPING, YAPS	**YAWP**	v -ED, -ING, -S to utter a loud,
	to bark shrilly		harsh cry
YAPOCK	n pl. -S an aquatic mammal	**YAWPER**	n pl. -S one that yawps
YAPOK	n pl. -S yapock	**YAWPING**	n pl. -S a loud, harsh cry
YAPON	n pl. -S yaupon	**YAY**	n pl. YAYS yea
YAPPED	past tense of yap	**YCLEPED**	adj yclept
YAPPER	n pl. -S one that yaps	**YCLEPT**	adj called; named
YAPPING	present participle of yap	**YE**	pron you
YAR	adj yare	**YEA**	n pl. -S an affirmative vote
YARD	v -ED, -ING, -S to put in a	**YEAH**	adv yes
	yard (a tract of ground	**YEALING**	n pl. -S a person of the same
	adjacent to a building)		age
YARDAGE	n pl. -S the use of an	**YEAN**	v -ED, -ING, -S to bear young
	enclosure for livestock at a	**YEANLING**	n pl. -S the young of a sheep
	railroad station		or goat
YARDARM	n pl. -S either end of a ship's	**YEAR**	n pl. -S a period of time
	spar		consisting of 365 or 366 days

YEARBOOK *n* pl. -S a book published each year by a graduating class

YEAREND *n* pl. -S the end of a year

YEARLIES pl. of yearly

YEARLING *n* pl. -S an animal past its first year and not yet two years old

YEARLONG *adj* lasting through a year

YEARLY *n* pl. -LIES a publication appearing once a year

YEARN *v* -ED, -ING, -S to have a strong or deep desire

YEARNER *n* pl. -S one that yearns

YEARNING *n* pl. -S a strong or deep desire

YEASAYER *n* pl. -S one that affirms something

YEAST *v* -ED, -ING, -S to foam

YEASTY *adj* YEASTIER, YEASTIEST foamy **YEASTILY** *adv*

YECCH *n* pl. -S something disgusting

YECH *n* pl. -S yecch

YECHY *adj* disgusting

YEELIN *n* pl. -S yealing

YEGG *n* pl. -S a burglar

YEGGMAN *n* pl. -MEN a yegg

YEH *adv* yeah

YELD *adj* not giving milk

YELK *n* pl. -S yolk

YELL *v* -ED, -ING, -S to cry out loudly

YELLER *n* pl. -S one that yells

YELLOW *adj* -LOWER, -LOWEST of a bright color like that of ripe lemons **YELLOWLY** *adv*

YELLOW *v* -ED, -ING, -S to make or become yellow

YELLOWY *adj* somewhat yellow

YELP *v* -ED, -ING, -S to utter a sharp, shrill cry

YELPER *n* pl. -S one that yelps

YEN *v* YENNED, YENNING, YENS to yearn

YENTA *n* pl. -S a gossipy woman

YENTE *n* pl. -S yenta

YEOMAN *n* pl. -MEN an independent farmer **YEOMANLY** *adj*

YEOMANRY *n* pl. -RIES the collective body of yeomen

YEP *adv* yes

YERBA *n* pl. -S a South American beverage resembling tea

YERK *v* -ED, -ING, -S to beat vigorously

YES *v* YESSED, YESSING, YESSES or YESES to give an affirmative reply to

YESHIVA *n* pl. -VAS, -VOT, or -VOTH an orthodox Jewish school

YESHIVAH *n* pl. -S yeshiva

YESSED past tense of yes

YESSES a 3d person sing. of yes

YESSING present participle of yes

YESTER *adj* pertaining to yesterday

YESTERN *adj* yester

YESTREEN *n* pl. -S the previous evening

YET *adv* up to now

YETI *n* pl. -S the abominable snowman

YETT *n* pl. -S a gate

YEUK *v* -ED, -ING, -S to itch

YEUKY *adj* itchy

YEW *n* pl. -S an evergreen tree or shrub

YIELD *v* -ED, -ING, -S to give up

YIELDER *n* pl. -S one that yields

YIKES *interj* — used to express fear or pain

YILL *n* pl. -S ale

YIN *n* pl. -S the feminine passive principle in Chinese cosmology

YINCE *adv* once

YIP *v* YIPPED, YIPPING, YIPS to yelp

YIPE *interj* — used to express fear or surprise

YIPES *interj* yipe

YIPPED past tense of yip

YIPPEE *interj* — used to express joy

YIPPIE *n* pl. -S a politically radical hippie

YIPPING present participle of yip

YIRD *n* pl. -S earth

YIRR *v* -ED, -ING, -S to snarl

YIRTH *n* pl. -S yird

YLEM *n* pl. -S hypothetical matter from which the elements are derived

YO *interj* —used to call attention or to express affirmation

YOB *n* pl. -S a hooligan

YOBBO *n* pl. -BOS or -BOES a yob

YOCK *v* -ED, -ING, -S to laugh boisterously

YOD *n* pl. -S a Hebrew letter

YODEL *v* -DELED, -DELING, -DELS or -DELLED, -DELLING, -DELS to sing with a fluctuating voice

YODELER *n* pl. -S one that yodels

YODELLER *n* pl. -S yodeler

YODELLING a present participle of yodel

YODH   *n* pl. -S yod

YODLE   *v* -DLED, -DLING, -DLES to yodel

YODLER   *n* pl. -S yodeler

YOGA   *n* pl. -S a Hindu philosophy involving physical and mental disciplines

YOGEE   *n* pl. -S yogi

YOGH   *n* pl. -S a Middle English letter

YOGHOURT   *n* pl. -S yogurt

YOGHURT   *n* pl. -S yogurt

YOGI   *n* pl. -S a person who practices yoga

YOGIC   *adj* pertaining to yoga

YOGIN   *n* pl. -S yogi

YOGINI   *n* pl. -S a female yogi

YOGURT   *n* pl. -S a food made from milk

YOICKS   *interj* — used to encourage hunting hounds

YOK   *n* pl. -S a boisterous laugh

YOKE   *v* YOKED, YOKING, YOKES to fit with a yoke (a wooden frame for joining together draft animals)

YOKEL   *n* pl. -S a naive or gullible rustic

YOKELESS   *adj* having no yoke

YOKELISH   *adj* resembling a yokel

YOKEMATE   *n* pl. -S a companion in work

YOKING   present participle of yoke

YOKOZUNA   *n* pl. -S a champion sumo wrestler

YOLK   *n* pl. -S the yellow portion of an egg **YOLKED** *adj*

YOLKY   *adj* YOLKIER, YOLKIEST resembling a yolk

YOM   *n* pl. YOMIM day

YON   *adv* yonder

YOND   *adv* yonder

YONDER   *adv* over there

YONI   *n* pl. -S a symbol for the vulva in Hindu religion **YONIC** *adj*

YONKER   *n* pl. -S younker

YORE   *n* pl. -S time past

YOU   *pron* the 2d person sing. or pl. pronoun

YOUNG   *adj* YOUNGER, YOUNGEST being in the early period of life or growth

YOUNG   *n* pl. -S offspring

YOUNGER   *n* pl. -S an inferior in age

YOUNGISH   *adj* somewhat young

YOUNKER   *n* pl. -S a young gentleman

YOUPON   *n* pl. -S yaupon

YOUR   *adj* a possessive form of the pronoun you

YOURN   *pron* yours

YOURS   *pron* a possessive form of the pronoun you

YOURSELF   *pron* pl. -SELVES a form of the 2d person pronoun

YOUSE   *pron* you

YOUTH   *n* pl. -S a young person

YOUTHEN   *v* -ED, -ING, -S to make youthful

YOUTHFUL   *adj* young

YOW   *v* -ED, -ING, -S to yowl

YOWE   *n* pl. -S a ewe

YOWIE   *n* pl. -S a small ewe

YOWL   *v* -ED, -ING, -S to utter a loud, long, mournful cry

YOWLER   *n* pl. -S one that yowls

YPERITE   *n* pl. -S a poisonous gas

YTTERBIA   *n* pl. -S a chemical compound **YTTERBIC** *adj*

YTTRIA   *n* pl. -S a chemical compound

YTTRIUM   *n* pl. -S a metallic element **YTTRIC** *adj*

YUAN   *n* pl. -S a monetary unit of China

YUCCA   *n* pl. -S a tropical plant

YUCCH   *interj* — used to express disgust

YUCH   *interj* yucch

YUCK   *v* -ED, -ING, -S to yuk

YUCKY   *adj* YUCKIER, YUCKIEST disgusting

YUGA   *n* pl. -S an age of time in Hinduism

YUK   *v* YUKKED, YUKKING, YUKS to laugh loudly

YULAN   *n* pl. -S a Chinese tree

YULE   *n* pl. -S Christmas time

YULETIDE   *n* pl. -S yule

YUM   *interj* — used to express pleasurable satisfaction

YUMMY   *adj* -MIER, -MIEST delicious

YUMMY   *n* pl. -MIES something delicious

YUP   *adv* yep

YUPON   *n* pl. -S yaupon

YUPPIE   *n* pl. -S a young professional person working in a city

YURT   *n* pl. YURTA or YURTS a portable tent

YWIS   *adv* iwis

ZABAIONE   *n* pl. -S a dessert resembling custard

ZABAJONE   *n* pl. -S zabaione

ZACATON   *n* pl. -S a Mexican grass

ZADDICK	n pl. -DIKIM zaddik
ZADDIK	n pl. -DIKIM a virtuous person by Jewish religious standards
ZAFFAR	n pl. -S zaffer
ZAFFER	n pl. -S a blue ceramic coloring
ZAFFIR	n pl. -S zaffer
ZAFFRE	n pl. -S zaffer
ZAFTIG	adj full-bosomed
ZAG	v ZAGGED, ZAGGING, ZAGS to turn sharply
ZAIBATSU	n pl. ZAIBATSU a powerful family combine in Japan
ZAIKAI	n pl. -S the business community of Japan
ZAIRE	n pl. -S a monetary unit of Zaire
ZAMARRA	n pl. -S a sheepskin coat
ZAMARRO	n pl. -ROS zamarra
ZAMIA	n pl. -S a tropical plant
ZAMINDAR	n pl. -S a tax collector in precolonial India
ZANANA	n pl. -S zenana
ZANDER	n pl. -S a freshwater fish
ZANIER	comparative of zany
ZANIES	pl. of zany
ZANINESS	n pl. -ES the quality or state of being zany
ZANY	adj ZANIER, ZANIEST ludicrously comical **ZANILY** adv
ZANY	n pl. -NIES a zany person
ZANYISH	adj somewhat zany
ZANZA	n pl. -S an African musical instrument
ZAP	v ZAPPED, ZAPPING, ZAPS to kill or destroy instantaneously
ZAPATEO	n pl. -TEOS a Spanish dance
ZAPPER	n pl. -S a device that zaps
ZAPPY	adj -PIER, -PIEST zippy
ZAPTIAH	n pl. -S a Turkish policeman
ZAPTIEH	n pl. -S zaptiah
ZARATITE	n pl. -S a chemical compound
ZAREBA	n pl. -S an improvised stockade
ZAREEBA	n pl. -S zareba
ZARF	n pl. -S a metal holder for a coffee cup
ZARIBA	n pl. -S zareba
ZARZUELA	n pl. -S a Spanish operetta
ZASTRUGA	n pl. -GI sastruga
ZAX	n pl. -ES a tool for cutting roof slates
ZAYIN	n pl. -S a Hebrew letter
ZAZEN	n pl. -S meditation in Zen Buddhism
ZEAL	n pl. -S enthusiastic devotion
ZEALOT	n pl. -S one who is zealous
ZEALOTRY	n pl. -RIES excessive zeal
ZEALOUS	adj filled with zeal
ZEATIN	n pl. -S a chemical compound found in maize
ZEBEC	n pl. -S xebec
ZEBECK	n pl. -S xebec
ZEBRA	n pl. -S an African mammal that is related to the horse **ZEBRAIC** adj
ZEBRASS	n pl. -ES the offspring of a zebra and an ass
ZEBRINE	adj pertaining to a zebra
ZEBROID	adj zebrine
ZEBU	n pl. -S an Asian ox
ZECCHIN	n pl. -S zecchino
ZECCHINO	n pl. -NI or -NOS a former gold coin of Italy
ZECHIN	n pl. -S zecchino
ZED	n pl. -S the letter Z
ZEDOARY	n pl. -ARIES the medicinal root of a tropical plant
ZEE	n pl. -S the letter Z
ZEIN	n pl. -S a simple protein
ZEK	n pl. -S an inmate in a Soviet labor camp
ZELKOVA	n pl. -S a Japanese tree
ZEMINDAR	n pl. -S zamindar
ZEMSTVO	n pl. -VOS or -VA an elective council in czarist Russia
ZENAIDA	n pl. -S a wild dove
ZENANA	n pl. -S the section of a house in India reserved for women
ZENITH	n pl. -S the highest point **ZENITHAL** adj
ZEOLITE	n pl. -S a mineral **ZEOLITIC** adj
ZEPHYR	n pl. -S a gentle breeze
ZEPPELIN	n pl. -S a long, rigid airship
ZERK	n pl. -S a grease fitting
ZERO	v -ED, -ING, -ES or -S to aim at the exact center of a target
ZEROTH	adj being numbered zero in a series
ZEST	v -ED, -ING, -S to fill with zest (invigorating excitement)
ZESTER	n pl. -S a utensil for peeling citrus rind
ZESTFUL	adj full of zest
ZESTLESS	adj lacking zest
ZESTY	adj ZESTIER, ZESTIEST marked by zest
ZETA	n pl. -S a Greek letter

ZEUGMA   *n* pl. -S the use of a word to modify or govern two or more words, while applying to each in a different sense

ZIBELINE   *n* pl. -S a soft fabric

ZIBET   *n* pl. -S an Asian civet

ZIBETH   *n* pl. -S zibet

ZIG   *v* ZIGGED, ZIGGING, ZIGS to turn sharply

ZIGGURAT   *n* pl. -S an ancient Babylonian temple tower

ZIGZAG   *v* -ZAGGED, -ZAGGING, -ZAGS to proceed on a course marked by sharp turns

ZIKKURAT   *n* pl. -S ziggurat

ZIKURAT   *n* pl. -S ziggurat

ZILCH   *n* pl. -ES nothing

ZILL   *n* pl. -S one of a pair of finger cymbals

ZILLAH   *n* pl. -S an administrative district in India

ZILLION   *n* pl. -S an indeterminately large number

ZIN   *n* pl. -S a dry red wine

ZINC   *v* ZINCED, ZINCING, ZINCS or ZINCKED, ZINCKING, ZINCS to coat with zinc (a metallic element)

ZINCATE   *n* pl. -S a chemical salt

ZINCIC   *adj* pertaining to zinc

ZINCIFY   *v* -FIED, -FYING, -FIES to coat with zinc

ZINCITE   *n* pl. -S an ore of zinc

ZINCKED   a past tense of zinc

ZINCKING   a present participle of zinc

ZINCKY   *adj* resembling zinc

ZINCOID   *adj* zincic

ZINCOUS   *adj* zincic

ZINCY   *adj* zincky

ZINEB   *n* pl. -S an insecticide

ZING   *v* -ED, -ING, -S to move with a high-pitched humming sound

ZINGANO   *n* pl. -NI zingaro

ZINGARA   *n* pl. -RE a female gypsy

ZINGARO   *n* pl. -RI a gypsy

ZINGER   *n* pl. -S a pointed witty retort or remark

ZINGY   *adj* ZINGIER, ZINGIEST enjoyably exciting

ZINKIFY   *v* -FIED, -FYING, -FIES to zincify

ZINKY   *adj* zincky

ZINNIA   *n* pl. -S a tropical plant

ZIP   *v* ZIPPED, ZIPPING, ZIPS to move with speed and vigor

ZIPLESS   *adj* lacking vigor or energy

ZIPPER   *v* -ED, -ING, -S to fasten with a zipper (a fastener consisting of two rows of interlocking teeth)

ZIPPING   present participle of zip

ZIPPY   *adj* -PIER, -PIEST full of energy

ZIRAM   *n* pl. -S a chemical salt

ZIRCON   *n* pl. -S a mineral

ZIRCONIA   *n* pl. -S a chemical compound

ZIRCONIC   *adj* pertaining to a certain metallic element

ZIT   *n* pl. -S a pimple

ZITHER   *n* pl. -S a stringed instrument

ZITHERN   *n* pl. -S zither

ZITI   *n* pl. -S a tubular pasta

ZIZIT   *n/pl* zizith

ZIZITH   *n/pl* the tassels on the four corners of a Jewish prayer shawl

ZIZZLE   *v* -ZLED, -ZLING, -ZLES to sizzle

ZLOTY   *n* pl. ZLOTYS, ZLOTE, ZLOTIES, or ZLOTYCH a monetary unit of Poland

ZOA   a pl. of zoon

ZOARIUM   *n* pl. -IA a colony of bryozoans ZOARIAL *adj*

ZODIAC   *n* pl. -S an imaginary belt encircling the celestial sphere ZODIACAL *adj*

ZOEA   *n* pl. ZOEAE or ZOEAS a larval form of certain crustaceans ZOEAL *adj*

ZOECIUM   *n* pl. -CIA zooecium

ZOFTIG   *adj* zaftig

ZOIC   *adj* pertaining to animals or animal life

ZOISITE   *n* pl. -S a mineral

ZOMBI   *n* pl. -S zombie

ZOMBIE   *n* pl. -S a will-less human capable only of automatic movement

ZOMBIFY   *v* -FIED, -FYING, -FIES to turn into a zombie

ZOMBIISM   *n* pl. -S the system of beliefs connected with a West African snake god

ZONAL   *adj* pertaining to a zone ZONALLY *adv*

ZONARY   *adj* zonal

ZONATE   *adj* arranged in zones

ZONATED   *adj* zonate

ZONATION   *n* pl. -S arrangement in zones

ZONE *v* ZONED, ZONING, ZONES to arrange in zones (areas distinguished from other adjacent areas)

ZONELESS *adj* having no zone or belt

ZONER *n* pl. -S one that zones

ZONETIME *n* pl. -S standard time used at sea

ZONING present participle of zone

ZONK *v* -ED, -ING, -S to stupefy

ZONULA *n* pl. -LAE or -LAS zonule

ZONULE *n* pl. -S a small zone ZONULAR *adj*

ZOO *n* pl. ZOOS a place where animals are kept for public exhibition

ZOOCHORE *n* pl. -S a plant dispersed by animals

ZOOECIUM *n* pl. -CIA a sac secreted and lived in by an aquatic organism

ZOOGENIC *adj* caused by animals or their activities

ZOOGLEA *n* pl. -GLEAE or -GLEAS a jellylike mass of bacteria ZOOGLEAL *adj*

ZOOGLOEA *n* pl. -GLOEAE or -GLOEAS zooglea

ZOOID *n* pl. -S an organic cell or body capable of independent movement ZOOIDAL *adj*

ZOOKS *interj* — used as a mild oath

ZOOLATER *n* pl. -S one that worships animals

ZOOLATRY *n* pl. -TRIES the worship of animals

ZOOLOGY *n* pl. -GIES the science that deals with animals ZOOLOGIC *adj*

ZOOM *v* -ED, -ING, -S to move with a loud humming sound

ZOOMANIA *n* pl. -S an excessive interest in animals

ZOOMETRY *n* pl. -TRIES the measurement of animals or animal parts

ZOOMORPH *n* pl. -S something in the form of an animal

ZOON *n* pl. ZOA or ZOONS the whole product of one fertilized egg ZOONAL *adj*

ZOONOSIS *n* pl. -NOSES a disease that can be transmitted from animals to man ZOONOTIC *adj*

ZOOPHILE *n* pl. -S a lover of animals

ZOOPHILY *n* pl. -LIES a love of animals

ZOOPHOBE *n* pl. -S one who fears or hates animals

ZOOPHYTE *n* pl. -S an invertebrate animal

ZOOSPERM *n* pl. -S the male fertilizing element of an animal

ZOOSPORE *n* pl. -S a type of spore

ZOOTOMY *n* pl. -MIES the dissection of animals ZOOTOMIC *adj*

ZOOTY *adj* ZOOTIER, ZOOTIEST flashy in manner or style

ZORI *n* pl. ZORI or ZORIS a type of sandal

ZORIL *n* pl. -S a small African mammal

ZORILLA *n* pl. -S zoril

ZORILLE *n* pl. -S zoril

ZORILLO *n* pl. -LOS zoril

ZOSTER *n* pl. -S a virus disease

ZOUAVE *n* pl. -S a French infantryman

ZOUNDS *interj* — used as a mild oath

ZOWIE *interj* — used to express surprise or pleasure

ZOYSIA *n* pl. -S a perennial grass

ZUCCHINI *n* pl. -S a vegetable

ZWIEBACK *n* pl. -S a sweetened bread

ZYDECO *n* pl. -COS popular music of southern Louisiana

ZYGOID *adj* pertaining to a zygote

ZYGOMA *n* pl. -MAS or -MATA the cheekbone

ZYGOSIS *n* pl. -GOSES the union of two gametes ZYGOSE *adj*

ZYGOSITY *n* pl. -TIES the makeup of a particular zygote

ZYGOTE *n* pl. -S a cell formed by the union of two gametes ZYGOTIC *adj*

ZYGOTENE *n* pl. -S a stage in meiosis

ZYMASE *n* pl. -S an enzyme

ZYME *n* pl. -S an enzyme

ZYMOGEN *n* pl. -S a substance that develops into an enzyme when suitably activated

ZYMOGENE *n* pl. -S zymogen

ZYMOGRAM *n* pl. -S a record of separated proteins after electrophoresis

ZYMOLOGY *n* pl. -GIES the science of fermentation

ZYMOSAN *n* pl. -S an insoluble fraction of yeast cell walls

ZYMOSIS *n* pl. -MOSES fermentation ZYMOTIC *adj*

ZYMURGY *n* pl. -GIES a branch of chemistry dealing with fermentation

ZYZZYVA *n* pl. -S a tropical weevil